CORNERSTONE
BIBLICAL
COMMENTARY

CORNERSTONE BIBLICAL COMMENTARY

Joshua

Joseph Coleson

Judges

Lawson G. Stone

Ruth

Jason Driesbach

GENERAL EDITOR

Philip W. Comfort

featuring the text of the

NEW LIVING TRANSLATION

TYNDALE HOUSE PUBLISHERS, INC. CAROL STREAM, ILLINOIS

Cornerstone Biblical Commentary, Volume 3

Visit Tyndale online at www.tyndale.com.

Designed by Luke Daab and Timothy R. Botts.

Library of Congress Cataloging-in-Publication Data

Cornerstone biblical commentary.
p. cm.
Includes bibliographical references and index.
ISBN 978-0-8423-3429-7 (hc : alk. paper)
1. Bible—Commentaries. I. Coleson, Joseph II. Stone, Lawson G.
III. Driesbach, Jason
BS491.3.C67 2006
220.7′7—dc22 2005026928

Printed in the United States of America

29 28 27 26 25
8 7 6 5 4 3

CONTENTS

CONTRIBUTORS TO VOLUME 3

Joshua: Joseph Coleson
BA, Indiana Wesleyan University;
MS, Brandeis University;
PhD, Brandeis University;
Professor of Old Testament, Nazarene Theological Seminary.

Judges: Lawson G. Stone
BA, Asbury College;
MDiv, Asbury Theological Seminary;
PhD, Yale University;
Professor of Old Testament, Asbury Theological Seminary.

Ruth: Jason Driesbach
BA, Cedarville University
MA, Dallas Theological Seminary
Tyndale House Publishers.

GENERAL EDITOR'S PREFACE

The *Cornerstone Biblical Commentary* is based on the second edition of the New Living Translation (2007). Nearly 100 scholars from various church backgrounds and from several countries (United States, Canada, England, and Australia) participated in the creation of the NLT. Many of these same scholars are contributors to this commentary series. All the commentators, whether participants in the NLT or not, believe that the Bible is God's inspired word and have a desire to make God's word clear and accessible to his people.

This Bible commentary is the natural extension of our vision for the New Living Translation, which we believe is both exegetically accurate and idiomatically powerful. The NLT attempts to communicate God's inspired word in a lucid English translation of the original languages so that English readers can understand and appreciate the thought of the original writers. In the same way, the *Cornerstone Biblical Commentary* aims at helping teachers, pastors, students, and laypeople understand every thought contained in the Bible. As such, the commentary focuses first on the words of Scripture, then on the theological truths of Scripture—inasmuch as the words express the truths.

The commentary itself has been structured in such a way as to help readers get at the meaning of Scripture, passage by passage, through the entire Bible. Each Bible book is prefaced by a substantial book introduction that gives general historical background important for understanding. Then the reader is taken through the Bible text, passage by passage, starting with the New Living Translation text printed in full. This is followed by a section called "Notes," wherein the commentator helps the reader understand the Hebrew or Greek behind the English of the NLT, interacts with other scholars on important interpretive issues, and points the reader to significant textual and contextual matters. The "Notes" are followed by the "Commentary," wherein each scholar presents a lucid interpretation of the passage, giving special attention to context and major theological themes.

The commentators represent a wide spectrum of theological positions within the evangelical community. We believe this is good because it reflects the rich variety in Christ's church. All the commentators uphold the authority of God's word and believe it is essential to heed the old adage: "Wholly apply yourself to the Scriptures and apply them wholly to you." May this commentary help you know the truths of Scripture, and may this knowledge help you "grow in your knowledge of God and Jesus our Lord" (2 Pet 1:2, NLT).

PHILIP W. COMFORT
GENERAL EDITOR

ABBREVIATIONS

GENERAL ABBREVIATIONS

b.	Babylonian Gemara	ibid.	*ibidem*, in the same place	OL	Old Latin
bar.	baraita	i.e.	*id est*, that is	OS	Old Syriac
c.	*circa*, around, approximately	in loc.	*in loco*, in the place cited	OT	Old Testament
cf.	*confer*, compare	lit.	literally	p., pp.	page, pages
ch, chs	chapter, chapters	LXX	Septuagint	pl.	plural
contra	in contrast to	M	Majority Text	Q	Quelle ("Sayings" as Gospel source)
DSS	Dead Sea Scrolls	*m.*	Mishnah	rev.	revision
ed.	edition, editor	masc.	masculine	sg.	singular
e.g.	*exempli gratia*, for example	mg	margin	sv.	*sub verbo*, under the word
et al.	*et alii*, and others	ms	manuscript	*t.*	Tosefta
fem.	feminine	mss	manuscripts	TR	Textus Receptus
ff	following (verses, pages)	MT	Masoretic Text	v., vv.	verse, verses
fl.	flourished	n.d.	no date	vid.	*videtur*, it seems
Gr.	Greek	neut.	neuter	viz.	*videlicet*, namely
Heb.	Hebrew	no.	number	vol.	volume
		NT	New Testament	*y.*	Jerusalem Gemara

ABBREVIATIONS FOR BIBLE TRANSLATIONS

ASV	American Standard Version	NAB	New American Bible	NKJV	New King James Version
CEV	Contemporary English Version	NASB	New American Standard Bible	NRSV	New Revised Standard Version
ESV	English Standard Version	NCV	New Century Version	NLT	New Living Translation
GW	God's Word	NEB	New English Bible	REB	Revised English Bible
HCSB	Holman Christian Standard Bible	NET	The NET Bible	RSV	Revised Standard Version
JB	Jerusalem Bible	NIV	New International Version (1984)	TEV	Today's English Version
JPS	Jewish Publication Society Translation (*Tanakh*)	NIrV	New International Reader's Version	TLB	The Living Bible
KJV	King James Version	NJB	New Jerusalem Bible		
		NJPS	The New Jewish Publication Society Translation (*Tanakh*)		

ABBREVIATIONS FOR DICTIONARIES, LEXICONS, COLLECTIONS OF TEXTS, ORIGINAL LANGUAGE EDITIONS

ABD *Anchor Bible Dictionary* (6 vols., Freedman) [1992]

ANEP *The Ancient Near East in Pictures* (Pritchard) [1965]

ANET *Ancient Near Eastern Texts Relating to the Old Testament* (Pritchard) [1969]

BAGD *Greek-English Lexicon of the New Testament and Other Early Christian Literature*, 2nd ed. (Bauer, Arndt, Gingrich, Danker) [1979]

BDAG *Greek-English Lexicon of the New Testament and Other Early Christian Literature*, 3rd ed. (Bauer, Danker, Arndt, Gingrich) [2000]

BDB *A Hebrew and English Lexicon of the Old Testament* (Brown, Driver, Briggs) [1907]

BDF *A Greek Grammar of the New Testament and Other Early Christian Literature* (Blass, Debrunner, Funk) [1961]

BHS *Biblia Hebraica Stuttgartensia* (Elliger and Rudolph) [1983]

CAD *Assyrian Dictionary of the Oriental Institute of the University of Chicago* [1956]

COS *The Context of Scripture* (3 vols., Hallo and Younger) [1997–2002]

DBI *Dictionary of Biblical Imagery* (Ryken, Wilhoit, Longman) [1998]

DBT *Dictionary of Biblical Theology* (2nd ed., Leon-Dufour) [1972]

DCH *Dictionary of Classical Hebrew* (7 vols., D. Clines) [2000]

DLNTD *Dictionary of the Later New Testament and Its Development* (R. Martin, P. Davids) [1997]

DJD *Discoveries in the Judean Desert* [1955–]

DJG *Dictionary of Jesus and the Gospels* (Green, McKnight, Marshall) [1992]

DOTP *Dictionary of the Old Testament: Pentateuch* (T. Alexander, D.W. Baker) [2003]

DPL *Dictionary of Paul and His Letters* (Hawthorne, Martin, Reid) [1993]

DTIB *Dictionary for Theological Interpretation of the Bible* (Vanhoozer) [2005]

EDNT *Exegetical Dictionary of the New Testament* (3 vols., H. Balz, G. Schneider. ET) [1990–1993]

GKC *Gesenius' Hebrew Grammar* (Gesenius, Kautzsch, trans. Cowley) [1910]

HALOT *The Hebrew and Aramaic Lexicon of the Old Testament* (L. Koehler, W. Baumgartner, J. Stamm; trans. M. Richardson) [1994–1999]

IBD *Illustrated Bible Dictionary* (3 vols., Douglas, Wiseman) [1980]

IDB *The Interpreter's Dictionary of the Bible* (4 vols., Buttrick) [1962]

ISBE *International Standard Bible Encyclopedia* (4 vols., Bromiley) [1979–1988]

KBL *Lexicon in Veteris Testamenti libros* (Koehler, Baumgartner) [1958]

LCL Loeb Classical Library

L&N *Greek-English Lexicon of the New Testament: Based on Semantic Domains* (Louw and Nida) [1989]

LSJ *A Greek-English Lexicon* (9th ed., Liddell, Scott, Jones) [1996]

MM *The Vocabulary of the Greek New Testament* (Moulton and Milligan) [1930; 1997]

NA^{26} *Novum Testamentum Graece* (26th ed., Nestle-Aland) [1979]

NA^{27} *Novum Testamentum Graece* (27th ed., Nestle-Aland) [1993]

NBD *New Bible Dictionary* (2nd ed., Douglas, Hillyer) [1982]

NIDB *New International Dictionary of the Bible* (Douglas, Tenney) [1987]

NIDBA *New International Dictionary of Biblical Archaeology* (Blaiklock and Harrison) [1983]

NIDNTT *New International Dictionary of New Testament Theology* (4 vols., C. Brown) [1975–1985]

NIDOTTE *New International Dictionary of Old Testament Theology and Exegesis* (5 vols., W. A. VanGemeren) [1997]

PG *Patrologia Graecae* (J. P. Migne) [1857–1886]

PGM *Papyri graecae magicae: Die griechischen Zauberpapyri.* (Preisendanz) [1928]

TBD *Tyndale Bible Dictionary* (Elwell, Comfort) [2001]

TDNT *Theological Dictionary of the New Testament* (10 vols., Kittel, Friedrich; trans. Bromiley) [1964–1976]

TDOT *Theological Dictionary of the Old Testament* (15 vols., Botterweck, Ringgren; trans. Willis, Bromiley, Green) [1974–]

TLNT *Theological Lexicon of the New Testament* (3 vols., C. Spicq) [1994]

TLOT *Theological Lexicon of the Old Testament* (3 vols., E. Jenni) [1997]

TWOT *Theological Wordbook of the Old Testament* (2 vols., Harris, Archer) [1980]

UBS^3 *United Bible Societies' Greek New Testament* (3rd ed., Metzger et al.) [1975]

UBS^4 *United Bible Societies' Greek New Testament* (4th corrected ed., Metzger et al.) [1993]

WH *The New Testament in the Original Greek* (Westcott and Hort) [1882]

ABBREVIATIONS FOR BOOKS OF THE BIBLE

Old Testament

Gen	Genesis	Deut	Deuteronomy	1 Sam	1 Samuel
Exod	Exodus	Josh	Joshua	2 Sam	2 Samuel
Lev	Leviticus	Judg	Judges	1 Kgs	1 Kings
Num	Numbers	Ruth	Ruth	2 Kgs	2 Kings

1 Chr	1 Chronicles	Song	Song of Songs	Obad	Obadiah
2 Chr	2 Chronicles	Isa	Isaiah	Jonah	Jonah
Ezra	Ezra	Jer	Jeremiah	Mic	Micah
Neh	Nehemiah	Lam	Lamentations	Nah	Nahum
Esth	Esther	Ezek	Ezekiel	Hab	Habakkuk
Job	Job	Dan	Daniel	Zeph	Zephaniah
Ps, Pss	Psalm, Psalms	Hos	Hosea	Hag	Haggai
Prov	Proverbs	Joel	Joel	Zech	Zechariah
Eccl	Ecclesiastes	Amos	Amos	Mal	Malachi

New Testament

Matt	Matthew	Eph	Ephesians	Heb	Hebrews
Mark	Mark	Phil	Philippians	Jas	James
Luke	Luke	Col	Colossians	1 Pet	1 Peter
John	John	1 Thess	1 Thessalonians	2 Pet	2 Peter
Acts	Acts	2 Thess	2 Thessalonians	1 John	1 John
Rom	Romans	1 Tim	1 Timothy	2 John	2 John
1 Cor	1 Corinthians	2 Tim	2 Timothy	3 John	3 John
2 Cor	2 Corinthians	Titus	Titus	Jude	Jude
Gal	Galatians	Phlm	Philemon	Rev	Revelation

Deuterocanonical

Bar	Baruch	1–2 Esdr	1–2 Esdras	Ps 151	Psalm 151
Add Dan	Additions to Daniel	Add Esth	Additions to Esther	Sir	Sirach
Pr Azar	Prayer of Azariah	Ep Jer	Epistle of Jeremiah	Tob	Tobit
Bel	Bel and the Dragon	Jdt	Judith	Wis	Wisdom of Solomon
Sg Three	Song of the Three Children	1–2 Macc	1–2 Maccabees		
		3–4 Macc	3–4 Maccabees		
Sus	Susanna	Pr Man	Prayer of Manasseh		

MANUSCRIPTS AND LITERATURE FROM QUMRAN

Initial numerals followed by "Q" indicate particular caves at Qumran. For example, the notation 4Q267 indicates text 267 from cave 4 at Qumran. Further, 1QS 4:9-10 indicates column 4, lines 9-10 of the *Rule of the Community*; and 4Q166 1 ii 2 indicates fragment 1, column ii, line 2 of text 166 from cave 4. More examples of common abbreviations are listed below.

CD	Cairo Geniza copy of the *Damascus Document*	1QIsa^{b}	Isaiah copy ^{b}	4QLam^{a}	Lamentations
1QH	*Thanksgiving Hymns*	1QM	*War Scroll*	11QPs^{a}	Psalms
1QIsa^{a}	Isaiah copy ^{a}	1QpHab	*Pesher Habakkuk*	11QTemple^{a,b}	*Temple Scroll*
		1QS	*Rule of the Community*	11QtgJob	*Targum of Job*

IMPORTANT NEW TESTAMENT MANUSCRIPTS

(all dates given are AD; ordinal numbers refer to centuries)

Significant Papyri (𝔓 = Papyrus)

𝔓1 Matt 1; early 3rd
𝔓4+𝔓64+𝔓67 Matt 3, 5, 26; Luke 1–6; late 2nd
𝔓5 John 1, 16, 20; early 3rd
𝔓13 Heb 2–5, 10–12; early 3rd
𝔓15+𝔓16 (probably part of same codex) 1 Cor 7–8, Phil 3–4; late 3rd
𝔓20 Jas 2–3; 3rd
𝔓22 John 15–16; mid 3rd
𝔓23 Jas 1; c. 200
𝔓27 Rom 8–9; 3rd
𝔓30 1 Thess 4–5; 2 Thess 1; early 3rd
𝔓32 Titus 1–2; late 2nd
𝔓37 Matt 26; late 3rd
𝔓39 John 8; first half of 3rd
𝔓40 Rom 1–4, 6, 9; 3rd

𝔓45 Gospels and Acts; early 3rd
𝔓46 Paul's Major Epistles (less Pastorals); late 2nd
𝔓47 Rev 9–17; 3rd
𝔓49+𝔓65 Eph 4–5; 1 Thess 1–2; 3rd
𝔓52 John 18; c. 125
𝔓53 Matt 26, Acts 9–10; middle 3rd
𝔓66 John; late 2nd
𝔓70 Matt 2–3, 11–12, 24; 3rd
𝔓72 1–2 Peter, Jude; c. 300
𝔓74 Acts, General Epistles; 7th
𝔓75 Luke and John; c. 200
𝔓77+𝔓103 (probably part of same codex) Matt 13–14, 23; late 2nd
𝔓87 Philemon; late 2nd
𝔓90 John 18–19; late 2nd
𝔓91 Acts 2–3; 3rd
𝔓92 Eph 1, 2 Thess 1; c. 300
𝔓98 Rev 1:13-20; late 2nd
𝔓100 Jas 3–5; c. 300
𝔓101 Matt 3–4; 3rd
𝔓104 Matt 21; 2nd
𝔓106 John 1; 3rd
𝔓115 Rev 2–3, 5–6, 8–15; 3rd

Significant Uncials

א (Sinaiticus) most of NT; 4th
A (Alexandrinus) most of NT; 5th
B (Vaticanus) most of NT; 4th
C (Ephraemi Rescriptus) most of NT with many lacunae; 5th
D (Bezae) Gospels, Acts; 5th
D (Claromontanus), Paul's Epistles; 6th (different MS than Bezae)
E (Laudianus 35) Acts; 6th
F (Augensis) Paul's Epistles; 9th
G (Boernerianus) Paul's Epistles; 9th
H (Coislinianus) Paul's Epistles; 6th
I (Freerianus or Washington) Paul's Epistles; 5th
L (Regius) Gospels; 8th
P (Porphyrianus) Acts—Revelation; 9th
Q (Guelferbytanus B) Luke, John; 5th
T (Borgianus) Luke, John; 5th
W (Washingtonianus or the Freer Gospels) Gospels; 5th
Z (Dublinensis) Matthew; 6th
037 (Δ; Sangallensis) Gospels; 9th
038 (Θ; Koridethi) Gospels; 9th
040 (Ξ; Zacynthius) Luke; 6th
043 (Φ; Beratinus) Matthew, Mark; 6th
044 (Ψ; Athous Laurae) Gospels, Acts, Paul's Epistles; 9th
048 Acts, Paul's Epistles, General Epistles; 5th
0171 Matt 10, Luke 22; c. 300
0189 Acts 5; c. 200

Significant Minuscules

1 Gospels, Acts, Paul's Epistles; 12th
33 All NT except Rev; 9th
81 Acts, Paul's Epistles, General Epistles; 1044
565 Gospels; 9th
700 Gospels; 11th
1424 (or Family 1424—a group of 29 manuscripts sharing nearly the same text) most of NT; 9th-10th
1739 Acts, Paul's Epistles; 10th
2053 Rev; 13th
2344 Rev; 11th
f^1 (a family of manuscripts including 1, 118, 131, 209) Gospels; 12th-14th
f^{13} (a family of manuscripts including 13, 69, 124, 174, 230, 346, 543, 788, 826, 828, 983, 1689, 1709—known as the Ferrar group) Gospels; 11th-15th

Significant Ancient Versions

SYRIAC (SYR)

syr^c (Syriac Curetonian) Gospels; 5th
syr^s (Syriac Sinaiticus) Gospels; 4th
syr^h (Syriac Harklensis) Entire NT; 616

OLD LATIN (IT)

it^a (Vercellenis) Gospels; 4th
it^b (Veronensis) Gospels; 5th
it^d (Cantabrigiensis—the Latin text of Bezae) Gospels, Acts, 3 John; 5th
it^e (Palantinus) Gospels; 5th
it^k (Bobiensis) Matthew, Mark; c. 400

COPTIC (COP)

cop^{bo} (Boharic—north Egypt)
cop^{fay} (Fayyumic—central Egypt)
cop^{sa} (Sahidic—southern Egypt)

OTHER VERSIONS

arm (Armenian)
eth (Ethiopic)
geo (Georgian)

TRANSLITERATION AND NUMBERING SYSTEM

Note: For words and roots from nonbiblical languages (e.g., Arabic, Ugaritic), only approximate transliterations are given.

HEBREW/ARAMAIC

Consonants

א	*aleph*	= *'*	מ, ם	*mem*	= *m*
בּ, ב	*beth*	= *b*	נ, ן	*nun*	= *n*
גּ, ג	*gimel*	= *g*	ס	*samekh*	= *s*
דּ, ד	*daleth*	= *d*	ע	*ayin*	= *'*
ה	*he*	= *h*	פּ, פ, ף	*pe*	= *p*
ו	*waw*	= *w*	צ, ץ	*tsadhe*	= *ts*
ז	*zayin*	= *z*	ק	*qoph*	= *q*
ח	*heth*	= *kh*	ר	*resh*	= *r*
ט	*teth*	= *t*	שׁ	*shin*	= *sh*
י	*yodh*	= *y*	שׂ	*sin*	= *s*
כּ, כ, ך	*kaph*	= *k*	תּ, ת	*taw*	= *t, th* (spirant)
ל	*lamedh*	= *l*			

Vowels

ַ	*patakh*	= *a*	ָ	*qamets khatuf*	= *o*
חַ	*furtive patakh*	= *a*	ֹ	*holem*	= *o*
ָ	*qamets*	= *a*	וֹ	*full holem*	= *o*
ָה	*final qamets he*	= *ah*	ֻ	*short qibbuts*	= *u*
ֶ	*segol*	= *e*	ֻ	*long qibbuts*	= *u*
ֵ	*tsere*	= *e*	וּ	*shureq*	= *u*
ֵי	*tsere yod*	= *e*	ֲ	*khatef patakh*	= *a*
ִ	*short hireq*	= *i*	ֳ	*khatef qamets*	= *o*
ִ	*long hireq*	= *i*	ְ	*vocalic shewa*	= *e*
ִי	*hireq yod*	= *i*	ַי	*patakh yodh*	= *a*

GREEK

α	*alpha*	= *a*	ι	*iota*	= *i*
β	*beta*	= *b*	κ	*kappa*	= *k*
γ	*gamma*	= *g, n* (*before* γ, κ, ξ, χ)	λ	*lamda*	= *l*
			μ	*mu*	= *m*
δ	*delta*	= *d*	ν	*nu*	= *n*
ε	*epsilon*	= *e*	ξ	*ksi*	= *x*
ζ	*zeta*	= *z*	ο	*omicron*	= *o*
η	*eta*	= *ē*	π	*pi*	= *p*
θ	*theta*	= *th*	ρ	*rho*	= *r* (ῥ = *rh*)

σ, ς	*sigma*	= *s*	ψ	*psi*	= *ps*
τ	*tau*	= *t*	ω	*omega*	= *ō*
υ	*upsilon*	= *u*	ʽ	*rough breathing mark*	= *h (with vowel or diphthong)*
φ	*phi*	= *ph*			
χ	*chi*	= *ch*			

THE TYNDALE-STRONG'S NUMBERING SYSTEM

The Cornerstone Biblical Commentary series uses a word-study numbering system to give both newer and more advanced Bible students alike quicker, more convenient access to helpful original-language tools (e.g., concordances, lexicons, and theological dictionaries). Those who are unfamiliar with the ancient Hebrew, Aramaic, and Greek alphabets can quickly find information on a given word by looking up the appropriate index number. Advanced students will find the system helpful because it allows them to quickly find the lexical form of obscure conjugations and inflections.

There are two main numbering systems used for biblical words today. The one familiar to most people is the Strong's numbering system (made popular by the *Strong's Exhaustive Concordance to the Bible*). Although the original Strong's system is still quite useful, the most up-to-date research has shed new light on the biblical languages and allows for more precision than is found in the original Strong's system. The Cornerstone Biblical Commentary series, therefore, features a newly revised version of the Strong's system, the Tyndale-Strong's numbering system. The Tyndale-Strong's system brings together the familiarity of the Strong's system and the best of modern scholarship. In most cases, the original Strong's numbers are preserved. In places where new research dictates, new or related numbers have been added.[1]

The second major numbering system today is the Goodrick-Kohlenberger system used in a number of study tools published by Zondervan. In order to give students broad access to a number of helpful tools, the Commentary provides index numbers for the Zondervan system as well.

The different index systems are designated as follows:

TG	Tyndale-Strong's Greek number	ZH	Zondervan Hebrew number
ZG	Zondervan Greek number	TA/ZA	Tyndale/Zondervan Aramaic number
TH	Tyndale-Strong's Hebrew number	S	Strong's Aramaic number

So in the example, "love" *agapē* [TG26, ZG27], the first number is the one to use with Greek tools keyed to the Tyndale-Strong's system, and the second applies to tools that use the Zondervan system.

The indexing of Aramaic terms differs slightly from that of Greek and Hebrew. Strong's original system mixed the Aramaic terms in with the Hebrew, but the Tyndale-Strong's system indexes Aramaic with a new set of numbers starting at 10,000. Since Tyndale's system for Aramaic diverges completely from original Strong's, the original Strong's number is listed separately so that those using tools keyed to Strong's can locate the information. This number is designated with an S, as in the example, "son" *bar* [TA/ZA10120, S1247].

1. Generally, one may simply use the original four-digit Strong's number to identify words in tools using Strong's system. If a Tyndale-Strong's number is followed by a capital letter (e.g., TG1692A), it generally indicates an added subdivision of meaning for the given term. Whenever a Tyndale-Strong's number has a number following a decimal point (e.g., TG2013.1), it reflects an instance where new research has yielded a separate, new classification of use for a biblical word. Forthcoming tools from Tyndale House Publishers will include these entries, which were not part of the original Strong's system.

Joshua

JOSEPH COLESON

INTRODUCTION TO
Joshua

MANY CHRISTIANS first learned of Joshua when they were Sunday school children. They heard the exciting story of Jericho's falling walls and Rahab's faith. Perhaps later they learned that "Joshua" and "Jesus" are two forms of the same name in Hebrew (*yehoshua'* / *yeshua'* [TH3091/3442, ZH3397/3800]; cf. Neh 8:17), and were taught that Joshua's bringing Israel into Canaan was an Old Testament precursor of Jesus' bringing us out of our bondage to sin and into fellowship with God in the "new land" of freedom in Christ. While these things are important and true, the book of Joshua merits deeper reading on its own account.

Israel's preparations east of the Jordan, the crossing of the Jordan, and the taking of Jericho occupy fully one quarter of the book's chapters (chs 1–6). It then records Joshua's leadership in two major military campaigns, one southern and one northern, bringing Israel into position to begin settling the previously sparsely occupied Canaanite hill country west of the Jordan (chs 7–12). Some of the theological issues raised by a hurried reading of these accounts turn out to have profound significance upon closer reading. Allocation of the land, with some descriptions of boundaries and lists of towns, is the subject of most of the second half of Joshua (chs 13–21). Joshua's farewells, his death, and the burials of three leaders bring the book to its touching conclusion (chs 22–24).

Joshua 1–12 is a consciously crafted unity reporting Israel's penetration into Canaan, just as 13–24 is a consciously crafted unity reporting the beginnings of Israel's settlement in the land. Among many evidences of this crafting is the "bridge" between chapters 1–6 and 7–12, comprising chapters 6–9:

Chapter 6—Jericho: victory following obedience to God's instructions for war
Chapter 7—Ai: defeat following disobedience to God's instructions for war
(Chapter 8—Ai: victory following repentance and judgment)
Chapter 9—Gibeon: troublesome treaty following neglect of God's instructions (specifically, instruction to make oracular inquiry for war)

The book of Joshua has much to teach us and much with which to inspire the church today as we, too, follow where God would have us go. Joshua's ringing farewell affirmation, "But as for me and my family, we will serve the LORD" (24:15), is reason enough to study this important and stirring book, to discover how Joshua became a faithful follower of God.

AUTHORSHIP, DATE, AND OCCASION OF WRITING

Over the past 150 years, biblical scholars have proposed several "new" theories about the authorship, date, and occasion of the writing or compilation of Joshua. These issues are so thoroughly intertwined we cannot consider them separately.

The Talmud (early Jewish commentary on the Hebrew Bible) records the earliest tradition, which would have been held by synagogue and church alike in the early centuries AD, that Joshua himself wrote the book bearing his name, with the exception of the last few verses concerning his death (*b. Bava Batra* 15a). The book itself names no author and, for a number of reasons (see below), all scholars today agree it evidences an editorial process spanning some period of time.

First, whoever the author(s) or editor(s) of Joshua were, the book names one of its sources: *The Book of Jashar* (cited in 10:13). A second book is mentioned in 18:9, though its title is not preserved; it records descriptions of the final seven tribal territories to be allotted. Essentially early datings for Joshua accept this as evidence that Joshua's descriptions of these territories were taken from this book. Another evidence of editorial process in Joshua is the 14 occurrences of the phrase "to this day": 4:9; 5:9; 6:25; 7:26; 8:28; 9:27; 10:27; 13:13; 14:14; 15:63; 16:10; 22:3; 22:17; 23:9. Twice (22:3; 23:9) this phrase appears in a speech by Joshua, and once in a speech by Phinehas (22:17). Thus, the phrase does not require the assumption of a long period of time between the events and the writing of the book. (The assumption of some that the speeches were invented by the later author/compiler is another issue.) Still, by any accounting, this phrase comprises evidence of, at the very least, a minimal editorial process in the book of Joshua (Woudstra 1981:11).

Julius Wellhausen and others put forth the earliest of the modern, nontraditional proposals, namely, that literarily, Joshua is the final part of a Hexateuch. That is, Joshua belongs together with the traditional Pentateuch as a set of six, not five, books in the earliest section of the biblical canon. This was combined with the idea that four often parallel literary sources, commonly called J, E, P, and D, had been merged together into one larger work to form the Pentateuch. With Joshua as part of a Hexateuch, then, Joshua 2–11, the Joshua "conquest tradition," originally was (and still is by some) assigned to the "E" source, the Elohist, because it is thought to reflect an expanded version of the same events as Judges 1, which is thought to be from the "J" source, the Jahwist. Others have suggested that the Joshua material, too, is from the Jahwist, not the Elohist, or, more commonly, have assigned it to the combined "JE," which preceded the work of the Deuteronomist, without trying seriously to separate them. Whatever its origin, Joshua 2–11 was adapted and supplemented by "the Deuteronomist." The Deuteronomist (or the Deuteronomistic "school"), in this view, is thought to have worked during the reign of Josiah (640–609 BC), and to have been responsible for editing most of Joshua through Kings; in this work the Deuteronomist emphasized the covenant theology of the book of Deuteronomy (hence the name, "Deuteronomist") together with God's later covenant of a continuing Davidic kingship. The Priestly author/redactors, on this view, were responsible for most of the material in the second half of Joshua, since it comprises mostly tribal lists and other matters of priestly concern, the Levitical cities, and the cities of refuge. According to this view, then, some of the material of the first half of Joshua may be early, but the book as we have it is exilic or postexilic.

The German scholar Albrecht Alt, followed most notably by his student Martin Noth, considered all of Joshua to be the work of the Deuteronomist, who in their view used a different set of source materials than the traditional "J" and "E." Noth, particularly, described the first half of Joshua as a series of "hero stories" and etiological tales, stories told to explain place names, customs, etc. (Note that etiologies are *not*, by definition, false; some tell the true stories of how places received their names.) Since the action of Joshua 2–11 centers in the later tribal territory of Benjamin, Noth described Joshua as a local Benjaminite hero, whose exploits first were recorded at the Benjaminite sanctuary of Gilgal—also prominent in this section of Joshua. Joshua the man was transformed into a national hero when the entry and "conquest" were adopted as the epic of all Israel, beginning at the amphictyonic (Israelite tribal league) shrine and sanctuary of Shiloh (Noth 1971).

The second half of Joshua, on the view of Alt, Noth, and their followers (including, e.g., Aharoni), derives from the period of the monarchy, adopted and adapted from royal or priestly administrative lists from the reigns of Solomon and/or of Josiah. A good summary of both the Wellhausenian and the Alt/Noth theories that discusses briefly both supporting and divergent evidence is found in Harrison (1969:666-673; on Noth's view, see also Wright 1982:59-66).

Recent developments affecting the study of Joshua have not necessarily focused on the composition or redaction history of the book, whether the precritical traditional approaches, Wellhausen's conclusions, or Alt and Noth's redirection of Wellhausen and the Documentary approach. Rather, emphasis has been on the history of Israel's origins in the land of Canaan, and whether that history is reflected in, or distinct from, Israel's theologizing about its origins.

One theory, by now no longer "new," is rooted in Mendenhall's idea that at least a part of the settlement of the hill country can be attributed to breakaway elements from the various Canaanite city-states—outlaws, runaways, and others—finding refuge in the large areas of the hill country that were nearly empty of permanent settlement at the end of the Late Bronze Age. Some of Mendenhall's students, notably Gottwald (1979), have posited a "peasant revolt" that established a new social, economic, and political order. This revolt turned the tables following decades of piecemeal retreat into the hill country to escape the supposedly heavy-handed aristocracies of the Late Bronze Age system of small city-states reflected in the Amarna Letters of the fourteenth century BC. (This takes Mendenhall's thesis further than he himself is comfortable with, as I have heard him testify in a public forum.)

Another nontraditional reading of early Israel's history that now has superseded Mendenhall's approach is perhaps most popularly known as the "minimalist" view. A more descriptive label may be the "internal transformation model"; among its best-known proponents are William Dever and Israel Finkelstein. (In fairness to both, significant differences exist between their approaches, though both can be characterized as minimalist.) Rather than the peasant revolt postulated by Mendenhall's students, minimalists view the rise of Israel in Canaan as resulting from the breakdown of political, economic, and social stability in Late Bronze Age Canaan.

The internal transformation that birthed ancient Israel was driven not by outside invasion or internal class unrest, but by the necessities of survival. Numerous small communities sprang up in the previously sparsely settled central highlands, communities characterized by the need to clear forested lands, build houses and cisterns, and provide for most of their own needs through subsistence agriculture—mainly wheat and barley, olives, vineyards, and kitchen gardens, and the keeping of small numbers of cattle, sheep, and goats.

Minimalists view the accounts of Israel's exodus from Egypt and entrance into Canaan in a military conquest under Joshua as the inventions of later Israelite religion to give Israel a proper national history, an epic origin worthy of the worshipers of Yahweh. Israel and Judah as recognizable political entities date from about the mid-ninth century, perhaps with, or just before, Omri and Ahab. (Such a "minimal" sketch as this cannot be said to do justice to the internal transformation model, but we may hope at least not to have misrepresented it and its adherents.)

Anson Rainey has recently marshaled evidence from a wide variety of biblical and extrabiblical sources to suggest a similar transformation model *process*, but originating with a pastoral people who saw themselves as originally Aramean (witness Abraham, Isaac, and Jacob/Israel), and who entered Canaan from Transjordan. Thus, Rainey's view differs from the theories of peasant revolt and internal transformation (see above) in regarding the transformation from Late Bronze to Iron Age culture in the central highlands of Canaan as coming from outside, and those effecting it identifying themselves as "Israel" from the beginning. He differs from the traditional view (see below) in minimizing or discounting the numbers and effect of Israel/Israelites involved in an Egyptian sojourn and exodus, and in discounting a "conquest" under Joshua (Rainey and Notley 2006:103, 111-116).

One complicating factor in all this is a common misreading of Joshua and Judges, concluding that they relate opposing versions of Israel's early years in Canaan. (I am not charging the current scholars named above with this misreading.) On this by now almost traditional interpretation of the two books, Joshua records a quick and easy triumph for Israel, almost total annihilation of the Canaanites, and nearly total occupation of all the land by the Israelites. Judges, on the other hand, gives a more "realistic" picture, showing that Israel did not conquer all the land early and at once, did not destroy all the Canaanites, and had considerable trouble occupying the whole land once they were there. A more careful reading of the two books will show that they really do not paint such radically opposing pictures.

My view, traditionalist but updated, is that upon close reading, Joshua does *not* claim Israel conquered all the land of Canaan easily and also does *not* claim Israel annihilated all the Canaanites—or even most of them; and it does *not* claim Israel settled the land in its entirety early on. Joshua does claim much, and is saturated with an optimistic and thankful spirit because of what God did accomplish for Israel through Joshua. However, the person of faith and the skeptic should be united in one purpose, at least: not to read what is absent, and not to miss what is present, in reading the Bible or any other document.

If Joshua and Judges present a complementary, rather than a contradictory, picture, we are not obliged to explain major differences by finding evidence for the lateness of Joshua; we can notice evidences of dating that actually exist in the book. These include, among many: (1) The phrase "to this day" occurs 14 times, indicating at least minor editing some generations after Joshua's day, but not requiring either an exilic or a postexilic date for the book. (2) The importance of Sidon and the non-mention of Tyre is an argument for an early date—Tyre supplanted Sidon as the pre-eminent Phoenician city during the period of (perhaps in conjunction with) David's bringing Israel to ascendancy over the Philistines (B. Mazar 1986). (3) Archaeology does *not* prove Jericho was unoccupied when Israel entered the land; recent reexamination of the evidence shows, if anything, support for the account in Joshua (Wood 1990a). We could (and will) note other evidence, but these points already show that the book of Joshua, in substantially the form we have it today, could date from the early period of the judges, not long after Joshua's death. If substantial interest in Israel's history arose during the "Golden Age" of David and Solomon, as we have reason to believe, Joshua hardly would need to date later than that, though we need not rule out subsequent minor editorial activity, either.

We can be quite certain that at least some of the important sources of the book first were written in Joshua's own day, and many of them, if not the book itself, not long afterward (see Woudstra 1981). On the early date of the Exodus, this would be about the first half of the fourteenth century (1400–1350 BC); on the late date, about the second half of the thirteenth century (1250–1200 BC). (Of course, those unconvinced of Joshua's essential historicity will date the book much later, usually in the exilic/postexilic period, perhaps conceding the use of some earlier source material.) As implied above, the early date for Israel's exodus from Egypt is usually given as about 1440 BC, giving a date for the entrance into Canaan under Joshua of about 1400 BC. Much of the archaeological evidence, however, excepting that from Jericho,[1] seems to indicate the late date, which usually places the Exodus at about 1290 BC and the entrance into Canaan about 1250 BC. Further, the earliest nonbiblical reference to "Israel" occurs in the famous "Victory Hymn" of the Merneptah Stela. That Merneptah reigned as pharaoh from 1212 to 1202 BC (Rainey and Notley 2006:103) would seem to support the late date schema for Israel's exodus from Egypt and entry into Canaan. Therefore, most scholars who accept the historical value of the Joshua account favor the late date. I, too, tend toward the late date, hoping betimes for someone to advance a reconciliation of the Jericho data with it, if this is indeed the correct conclusion.

Since by every account several sources were available for the writing of Joshua, we can, in one sense, speak of a "compiler" of the book; Noth did use this word (German, *Sammler*). Yet a history writer, though utilizing various sources for the whole of an account, is still an author. The author decides the material to use, the emphases to give it, the arrangement of the various events (e.g., chronologically, or some other order), and the theme(s) of the work. In these and other tasks God's Spirit guided the human author(s) of the book of Joshua.

AUDIENCE

The first audience for the book of Joshua was ancient Israel. Some of its dramatic stories certainly were passed from generation to generation through oral tradition.

It is equally certain that at least some of the stories found a written form early, were preserved in priestly and/or royal archives, and thus were available for the scholarly researches of the author(s) and/or redactors of Joshua, whatever the period(s) of their activity.

Already in the first century, the church began, as it were, to add a layer of understanding—to teach Joshua, not only for its contribution to the early history of faith, but also as an important part of God's salvation plan for all the world (Heb 11:30-31). Joshua was seen as a "type" of Christ, doing for ancient Israel what Jesus did for Jews and Gentiles alike. Such an approach is not "wrong." We need to be sure, however, that we do not press the analogy too far, nor neglect Joshua's "literal" meaning in pursuit of its "spiritual" meaning. A truly Christian theology should not separate the two, and yet should always read Joshua on its own original terms.

CANONICITY AND TEXTUAL HISTORY

Canonical Placement. The Hebrew Bible arrangement of what we call the Old Testament comprises three major sections. First is the Torah, or Pentateuch: Genesis, Exodus, Leviticus, Numbers, and Deuteronomy. The second section is the Prophets; it begins with Joshua and includes eight books (21 books in English). The third section, the Writings, includes the other 11 books (13 in English). Thus, in the traditional Jewish arrangement, as in almost all Christian canonical arrangements, Joshua is the sixth book of the Bible. It follows Deuteronomy and begins the second major section of the Canon.

The placement of Joshua within the Hebrew canon is significant. First is the fact that it is a chronological placement. The events of Joshua followed the death of Moses recorded at the end of Deuteronomy. The high points and low points of the settlement process—the period of the judges—followed upon the deaths of Joshua and his younger contemporaries who outlived him. The book belongs chronologically where it is in the canonical order.

It is even more important that Joshua is the first book of the section called the Prophets in the Hebrew arrangement. This section is divided, in turn, into two subsections, the Former Prophets and the Latter Prophets. The Former Prophets are the books of Joshua, Judges, Samuel, and Kings (both originally undivided). The Latter Prophets are Isaiah, Jeremiah, Ezekiel, and The Twelve (the so-called Minor Prophets) counted together as one book.

That Joshua, Judges, Samuel, and Kings—classed in the usual English Bible arrangement as books of history—are considered prophetic books in the Hebrew arrangement is of great importance. These books are history written from a prophetic point of view. They share the theological perspective of the prophets, the men and women called by God to deliver God's oracles to Israel. This perspective teaches that Israel was God's people, brought into existence by God, blessed of God, and accountable to God. By way of illustrative example, the book of Joshua does relate a number of occasions on which Joshua and Israel consulted or worshiped God. Yet, it does not describe these occasions from the perspective of Israel's priests, nor give details of the liturgy employed. This is theological history, but it is not "cultic" or "liturgical" history.

Just as the oracles of the Latter Prophets were (and are) God's word to God's people, so the recorded history of the Former Prophets was (and is) God's word to God's people. This is history, not simply for its own sake, but to outline how God dealt with Israel in both her faithful and unfaithful times. What is important to understanding God's involvement in Israel's history is included. Many details (and even important subjects) we would like to know about are not included because they would detract from this prophetic history of Israel. Joshua is a prophetic book in that it teaches, exhorts, encourages, and warns God's people of all ages through its recounting of this period of Israel's history. Since teaching, exhorting, encouraging, and warning are the primary functions of all prophecy, rightly understood, it is fitting that Joshua stands at the head of the section titled "Prophets" in the Hebrew Bible.

Textual History. Across the last century or so, textual analysis of Hebrew and especially Greek manuscripts of the Old Testament has brought to light much in the way of textual history and relationships that previously had languished in the shadows. The best witness to the original state of the Hebrew text of Joshua remains the Hebrew Masoretic Text (MT); by comparison with some other books, it suffered relatively little in transmission. However, the Qumran discoveries (Dead Sea Scrolls) give added witness to the Hebrew text of Joshua. For Joshua so far, the fragments from Qumran Cave 4 represent passages from chapters 2–8, 10, and 17 (Boling 1982:110, reporting Greenspoon). These definitely attest a different Hebrew manuscript tradition (recension) than the Masoretic Text represents, though the differences are neither major nor extensive. We should note here, however, that some do consider 4QJosh[a] to exhibit "major" differences. It positions Joshua 8:34-35 preceding 5:2-7, with the implication that Joshua gave a full reading of the law in the presence of the people even before they had crossed the Jordan and camped at Gilgal, and well before his writing the law (or part of it) at the altar on the top of Mount Ebal. This Qumran manuscript also includes some material not present in other manuscripts or versions.

Two of the manuscripts recovered from Qumran, although in Hebrew, either are of the non-Masoretic Hebrew recension behind or, (some appear to suggest) retranslations of, the Septuagint text Codex Vaticanus (Soggin 1972:19). Besides the Qumran scrolls, important Hebrew texts include those found at other sites in the Judean Desert west of the Dead Sea, and a smaller number of manuscripts from the Geniza (storage room for worn-out, no-longer-usable Scripture and other manuscripts) of the Ezra Synagogue in Old Cairo.

The earliest translation of the Old Testament was into Greek. One tradition claims the Pentateuch was translated by Jewish scholars in Alexandria under the aegis of the Hellenistic ruler of Egypt and the Holy Land, Ptolemy Philadelphus, who ruled from 285 to 246 BC. The Prophets, including Joshua, and the Writings were translated later, by different translators. The majority of the books of the Hebrew Bible were available in Greek by the beginning of the second century BC; early on, this first translation began to be referred to as the Septuagint (LXX).

The textual history of the Septuagint is not linear; it developed from and into several recensions. The Egyptian translation and its early revisions are known as the

Old Greek. The revision(s) of the first century BC, made in conformity with the text of the Judean and Galilean rabbis (a so-called "Palestinian" text), now is called the Proto-Lucianic recension because it is the precursor of the later Lucianic recension. The Greek text revised according to the Babylonian Hebrew text is called the *kaige* recension or, sometimes, "Proto-Theodotion."

The culminating effort before the great fourth- and fifth-century manuscripts—Sinaiticus, Alexandrinus, and Vaticanus—was Origen's *Hexapla,* which he completed about AD 245. The name of this monumental work reflects its nature; it comprised six different texts arranged in six parallel columns. The first column was the Hebrew text; the second, the Hebrew text transliterated into Greek letters. Origen's third column was the Greek version of Aquila of Sinope; his fourth, the Greek version of Symmachus. Origen's own revision of the Septuagint was the fifth column, and the sixth contained the Greek translation of Theodotion.

Based perhaps on Origen's ordering of his columns, some reference works still describe Theodotion as following Aquila and Symmachus chronologically. But in an important work building especially on the work of Margolis (1931–1938), Orlinsky (1969), and Tov (1973), Greenspoon (1983) has demonstrated the true history of the Hebrew and Greek recensions of Joshua: Theodotion was the first of these. Working with both the Old Greek and the Hebrew, he produced a Greek version reflecting a Hebrew text very similar to the Masoretic Text, while still showing "great respect" for the Old Greek. Aquila followed Theodotion, and had no knowledge of the Old Greek. Symmachus used both an Old Greek text and Theodotion's version. According to Greenspoon, Theodotion also was the major source of the identifying characteristics of the *kaige* recension. Origen's *Hexapla* was the major conduit through which Theodotion's, Aquila's, Symmachus's, and the *kaige* made their way into the various recensions of the Septuagint (Greenspoon 1983:379-381).

Following Origen, Lucian (certain witnesses to the LXX) and Jerome (Latin Vulgate) are two other important witnesses to the textual history of Joshua. Aquila and Theodotion probably were Jewish; Symmachus was an Ebionite (ethnically Jewish) Christian; Origen, Lucian, and Jerome were non-Jewish Christians. Thus, both Jewish and Christian understandings and treatments of the translation of early Israel's history are reflected when we consider all their influences on the text together.

In sum, we may affirm that no lengthy or seriously important differences exist among the various Hebrew manuscripts, or between the Hebrew text and the various versions that help to substantiate or correct the Masoretic Hebrew. We are justified in placing confidence in the textual transmission of Joshua; it will not lead us astray theologically, or any other way.

LITERARY STYLE

Joshua as Epic Narrative. The first half of Joshua, chapters 1–12, consists primarily of a genre often called "narrative history" by those who take the accounts of Joshua as actual history. Some call Joshua an "epic narrative" because its major focus is the national events of Israel's early history. It is important to remember that "epic" does not mean "false." Epic literature often is historical, as can be seen from the epic narratives of other nations besides Israel.

It is reasonable to conclude that Joshua presents a true, but far from complete, account of Israel's entry into Canaan, of Joshua's victorious military campaigns that made it impossible for the two coalitions of Canaanite kings to repel the newcomers, and of arrangements for (rather than the actions of) Israel's initial settlement according to their tribal allotments. However, "far from complete" is a subjective judgment when it comes to the very beginnings of a people's existence as a nation in its homeland. Of course, we would like more detail. But Israel's entry, sufficient military success, and allotment are all we really need to know, except for one more item—namely, God's superintendence of these events. The book of Joshua was written and organized to present as vividly as possible, in every way possible, that all this was not Israel's own doing. God brought Israel into this Promised Land; God wrought victory over those who tried to prevent them; God gave Israel's tribes their allotments to settle in *shalom* [TH7965, ZH8934]. More detail in this epic narrative would not encourage, but perhaps even distract from, the reader's concurrence in this crucial perspective.

Within the epic narrative of Joshua, chapters 9–12 appear to derive from a genre of royal conquest reports, which is seen in Egyptian and Mesopotamian royal annals from both the second and the first millennia BC, and is also present in Hittite annals of the second millennium BC (Hoffmeier 1996; Niehaus 1988). Younger's (1990) research into such reports has implications for the understanding of *kherem* warfare and the conquest reports of Joshua, as will be discussed below under "Theological Concerns."

Joshua's Bifid Structure. The simplest observation, and yet an important feature of the way Joshua is organized, is that it is purposely composed as two halves, a bifid. Other Old Testament books exhibiting a bifid structure are Exodus, Isaiah, Ezekiel, Daniel, and Zechariah.

The first half of the book (chs 1–12) relates the major events of Joshua's and Israel's important early victories in Canaan. These early victories meant the Canaanites could not prevent Israel from entering the land and beginning to settle in it. Here the emphasis is on God's action on behalf of Israel that enabled them to possess the land.

The second half of the book (chs 13–24) centers on the allotment of the land among the tribes, with a view to their beginning the process of settlement. Thus, it has an aura of expectancy. This is heightened by the way the book ends, with Joshua's final words of warning and encouragement, as well as his leading the people in renewal of the covenant at Shechem.

Literary Frames in Joshua. A number of "frames" are prominent in Joshua, the most important framing the entire book. Chapter 1 records God, and then the people, exhorting Joshua in his commission to lead Israel into the land, while chapters 23–24 record Joshua's exhortation to the leaders and then all the people as he prepared to depart this life. Thus, both the beginning and the conclusion of the book highlight God's covenant faithfulness, and the necessity of faithfulness on the part of God's people.

The allotment of the land also has a frame. It begins with the apportioning of Caleb's inheritance (14:6-15) and ends with the apportioning of Joshua's inheritance (19:49-51). Caleb and Joshua were the only two of the older generation to enter the land of Canaan. They were two of the 12 men Moses had sent into Canaan (Num 13) to learn about its inhabitants and their defenses. Of the 12, only Joshua and Caleb had urged Israel to enter immediately, believing God's promise to be with Israel and make it possible for them to settle in the land. Framing the allotment of the tribal lands with the records of the inheritances of Caleb and Joshua was a powerful reminder of God's grace and faithfulness to them, in response to their faith.

The Lists of Joshua. The latter half of chapter 12 comprises a poetic listing of the Canaanite kings Joshua defeated. This list serves both to close the first half of the book and to transition to the second half, much of which is in the form of lists.

Joshua 13–24 includes the lists of cities by their districts for most of the tribes, a listing of the six cities of refuge, and a listing of the 48 Levitical cities. Connected with these lists are narrative descriptions of the borders of the various tribes; some of these descriptions are quite sketchy, while others are given in considerable detail.

We often are tempted to hurry through the lists we encounter in our reading, or to skip over them entirely because we perceive them to be uninteresting. We should resist this temptation, however, because lists always carry important information and, surprisingly often, inspirational motivation. Moreover, lists are sometimes a reminder that God works not only in dramatic and climactic moments, but also routinely—if God ever can be said to work "routinely"—in and through the mundane ordering of the affairs of daily life.

Joshua's Narrative Progression. A narrative progression of problem/resolution/peace, problem/resolution/greater peace may be discerned in the book of Joshua. The dominant narrative theme of the first half of the book (chs 1–12) is the problem of getting into the land of Canaan against the active opposition of its hostile inhabitants. The resolution of the problem was accomplished in a campaign that took approximately seven years (see commentary on 14:6-10). The peace that followed may be described as the absence of major wars until the death of Joshua and his contemporaries.

The question of how to settle into the land was the second predominant problem; it is the theme of the second half of Joshua, chapters 13–24. Joshua's allotment of the land among the tribes was the resolution. While not violent like the battles against the Canaanites, this also was a complicated and somewhat lengthy process. The "greater peace" of settlement—clearing the land, building homes, and strengthening the Israelite community—did not come to full fruition in Joshua's lifetime. But it is represented in the closing chapters of the book by the record of Joshua's farewell address, Israel's renewal of the covenant made with God at Sinai, and finally, the burials of Joshua, Joseph, and Eleazar the high priest. A land at peace is one in which a people can bury their honored dead with dignity and ceremony.

Within the broad narrative sweep of reporting the resolution of these two overarching problems, reports of many smaller problems are embedded along with their resolutions and how those resolutions furthered peace. For example, just crossing the Jordan was more than Israel could do unaided; God took a direct hand in the resolution of that problem (ch 3). The next obstacle was Jericho; God dealt with Jericho, too (ch 6). Achan's sin was a problem (ch 7); until it was resolved, Israel could move no further. Then came the battles against the Canaanites to be fought and won.

Within the second half of Joshua, a problem remained after the allotment of land to the "major" tribes: how to distribute portions to the smaller tribes. This was solved by sending out a survey party and then casting lots, tribe by tribe, for the portions the survey described. Cities of refuge and Levitical cities had to be assigned. In a covenant renewal ceremony, Joshua called on Israel to solve the problem of wavering allegiance to God by getting rid of the images they had carried with them from Egypt and by affirming for themselves the covenant their ancestors had entered into with God at Sinai a generation earlier (ch 24).

Plot patterns such as these are common in literature. But they are common precisely because they convey information and teach values in a powerful and memorable form. God invented history, if you will, and oversees its progress. We are not surprised, then, that God uses narrative history writing in the Bible to teach us how he provided for this early community of faith. We are encouraged, too, to be thankful for and to rely on God's continuing care for the community of faith through the ages.

THEOLOGICAL CONCERNS

***Kherem* in the Pentateuch and Joshua.** A theological concern connected to judgment and warfare surfaces in Joshua with the account of Jericho's destruction, namely, the nature of the *kherem* [TH2764, ZH3051], "the ban" (cf. NLT, "completely destroyed"). The noun is used in 6:17, 18; verb forms occur in 6:18, 21. On the surface, all seems clear: Jericho's inhabitants were killed, and the city was burned with all it contained, except for its precious metals, which were dedicated to the Tabernacle treasury. The same verb is used multiple times in the accounts of both of Joshua's subsequent campaigns, first in the south (10:28, 35, 37, 39, 40) and then in the north (11:11, 12, 20, 21).

Moreover, in a number of places in the Pentateuch, God seems to command such a total destruction of the population of Canaan. Deuteronomy 7:1-2 and 20:16-17 are notable examples; in both Deuteronomy 7:2 and 20:17 a very strong verbal construction occurs, using two different forms of the verb *kharam* [TH2763, ZH3049].

The traditional understanding. The basic meaning of the root *kharam* is to dedicate or reserve to God's service exclusively. Sometimes, as at Jericho, an entire city was so dedicated—including buildings with all their contents, all animals, and all humans (except for those in Rahab's house). Since it is used in many contexts (especially chs 10–11) in conjunction with statements such as, "He smote [the city] with the mouth of the sword," and "leaving/he left no survivors" (e.g., 10:28), the NLT usually translates the verb form by "he completely destroyed." Most scholars have inferred that anything designated for this total dedication was considered so sacred it had to be destroyed, rather than running the risk of its being used for nonholy purposes. Living beings (including humans) were killed, and their corpses burned, along with the material goods also included in the *kherem*.

The traditional approach has been to take these commands and the reports of their (partial) fulfillment at face value. God commanded the destruction of all Canaan's people; Israel only partially obeyed, bringing God's judgment upon themselves (cf. Judg 2:10-15). A representative example of the approaches to this issue taken by those who would defend God as just in ordering the *kherem* is found in *Show Them No Mercy: Four Views on God and Canaanite Genocide* (Cowles, et al. 2003). In this volume, C. S. Cowles ascribes both the commands and their execution to Moses and Joshua's *mistaken* belief that God had ordered them to exterminate the Canaanites. The other three authors in the volume contend that God did indeed order this, but acted justly in doing so, though this is not an action Christians (or people of any religious faith) should emulate today. Of course, many others utilizing this definition and understanding of *kharam* accuse (or wonder whether they dare accuse) God of wrongdoing in ordering this "genocide," and Joshua and Israel of wrongdoing in carrying it out. Whether inclined to accuse or excuse, most Christian believers also are troubled by these accounts.

Issues with the traditional understanding. But on closer reading, all may not be as it seems at first. An obvious issue with this traditional understanding of *kharam* as killing all living beings and burning everything is that Joshua actually burned only three towns: Jericho, Ai, and Hazor (6:24; 8:28; 11:11-13). This, despite the fact that the verb *kharam* (and/or the noun *kherem*) is used in the Pentateuchal commands regarding *all the cities* of Canaan (e.g., Deut 7:2; 20:16-17), *and* the book of Joshua in several places records Joshua's compliance—for example, "Joshua did as he was told, carefully obeying all the commands that the LORD had given to Moses" (11:15b).

A second objection to the traditional understanding of these passages in Deuteronomy and Joshua (and a few references elsewhere) is that it takes only a cursory reading of Joshua and Judges to see that Israel was a *very* long way from destroying all the people of Canaan. On the contrary, both the texts and the archaeological record of Iron Age I affirm that Israel spent their first generations in the land clearing and settling previously empty land in the central hill country. Even in the hill country, Israel did not conquer the four cities of the Gibeonite League (ch 9). Neither Judah nor Benjamin was able to dislodge the Jebusites from Jebus/Jerusalem (15:63; Judg 1:21), though Joshua killed their king (10:23-26). Israel did not conquer Shechem, though they renewed the covenant there (8:30-35). Further, Judges 1:27-36 gives a substantial list consisting primarily of towns from which Manasseh, Ephraim, Zebulun, Asher, Naphtali, and Dan could *not* dislodge their Canaanite/Amorite neighbors. Jacob's deathbed pronouncement over his son Issachar (Gen 49:14-15) usually is taken to mean that early in the settlement process Issachar even performed hard menial labor—not voluntarily, but because pressed into it by and for their Canaanite neighbors. If Israel had exterminated her neighbors by the end of Joshua's lifetime, as some passages seem to affirm, many of the events recorded in the book of Judges simply would not have happened.

We should note, too, that apart from the destructions of Jericho and Ai, the book of Joshua records Israel battling only those who came out to wage war against them, along with their supporters. The kings of Makkedah and Libnah (10:28-29), for example, appear to have supported the coalition of five kings that came out against Joshua, so Joshua engaged them after his conflict with the five kings named as the coalition leadership (10:3-5). Moreover, the author of Joshua is careful in every case to demonstrate that God fought on Israel's side (e.g., 10:42). Most casualties among Canaanite forces were the result of God's action, not Israel's (10:11b;

implicitly in 6:2, 16, 20; 11:6, 8). Of course, this point is of indirect value to our discussion here: It concerns only the deaths of actively fighting Canaanite soldiers, and affirms only that Israel's soldiers killed far fewer of those than we usually assume from a cursory reading of the text. Still, it tends to support, rather than contradict, our point that reading the text of Joshua as a report of wholesale slaughter of the Canaanite population is fraught with problems that *the text itself* raises for such a reading.

The intent of the *kherem* is also informed by phrases translated "show them no mercy" (Deut 7:2) and "without mercy" (11:20). These translations, however, are quite irregular for forms from the root *khanan* [TH2603, ZH2858], though many versions have something similar. The verb *khanan* means "be gracious/show favor"; the related noun *khen* [TH2580, ZH2834] means "grace" or "favor." The command of Deuteronomy 7:2 was that Israel was not to show favor or grace to anyone (i.e., to no city or people group over another). Israel was not to enter into treaties with cities or peoples in Canaan (Deut 20:10-18). The fact that Israel could make treaties with cities outside Canaan (Deut 20:10-14) indicates we should understand the earlier instruction of Deuteronomy 7:2, to "show no favor" to Canaanite cities, as meaning, "Do not enter into treaties of peace (even those of the suzerain/vassal type) with Canaanite cities (as you may with non-Canaanite cities)." Except in the affair of the Gibeonite cities (ch 9), Joshua acted as God had instructed (11:20); he did not act with grace or favor, that is, he did not make treaties with Canaanite cities, but fought and defeated their armies as they came out to fight against Israel.

Younger's proposal. If the text reveals in these several ways that Israel did *not* "completely destroy" all the Canaanites, what are we to make of the seemingly straightforward commands of God for Israel to do so (e.g., Deut 7:1-2; 20:15-18), and the several statements in Joshua that Joshua and Israel did kill them all (especially 10:40-42; 11:12-15)?

In a landmark study, Lawson Younger (1990) has shown that the block of narrative comprising Joshua 9–12 shares a number of features with similar records, in several genres, from Assyria, Egypt, and the Hittite Empire—records from both the second and the first millennia BC. These include commands from God (or the gods) to begin a campaign, campaign reports compiled for royal or other archives, public laudatory inscriptions, and acts of praise to God/the gods. These kinds of sources seem to be the basis of most of this block of Joshua (1990:197-237).

Key to his analysis is what Younger calls the "syntagmic valency" of the transmission code (1990:70). In nontechnical terms, this is the regular recurrence of a set of features across reports from different places, peoples, and times, and found in a variety of genres. These features include references to place and time, divine aid, gathering and movement of troops, the flight and pursuit of the enemy, combat followed by submission or pursuit, exemplary punishment and other consequences to the submissive or defeated enemy, return of the victorious army, and others. One has only to read these chapters of Joshua to see most of these elements present repeatedly in the accounts of both Joshua's southern and his northern campaigns.

For our purposes, the first feature common to all these sets of texts is the *command* of the Deity to destroy the enemy "completely," that is, to annihilate all his people and animals, and to burn all his cities. The second is the report by the victorious king (the author of Joshua, or his sources, in the biblical text) of his successful *completion* of the campaign, including the total annihilation of the enemy, just as the gods (Yahweh, in the Pentateuchal instruction) had commanded.

However, these same reports of compliance with the divine commands for total destruction contain reports of the submission or capture, and even the deportation to the conquering king's own country, of sometimes hundreds or thousands of people and livestock, with quantities of other treasures. The Assyrian king Tiglath-pileser, for example, claimed to have made two lands he conquered look like "ruin hills (created by) the Deluge," and to have "burned, razed, and destroyed their cities." Yet in the same report, he said he "made them vassals of Ashur" (Assyria's national deity), that is to say, he made them his own vassals (Younger 1990:80). The famous stela of the Egyptian pharaoh Merneptah (not cited by Younger) contains his boast that after his campaign of conquest in Canaan, "Yano'am is made non-existent; Israel is laid waste, his seed is no more" (Rainey and Notley 2006:99). Yet neither the city-state of Yano'am nor the people of Israel ceased to exist because Merneptah defeated them in battle.

This type of command and annalistic reporting has its own "transmission code" (Younger 1990:55-56), that is, its own canons of expectation in the form of the reporting, and in the understanding and interpretation of the reader. The command to destroy "totally" is an example of hyperbole in the service of vividness and emphasis. Kings went to war at the "command" of their gods and usually accompanied by their gods, convinced that the command and the presence of the god(s) guaranteed total victory. Similarly, the book of Joshua attributes Israel's victories to God's presence and God's fighting on Israel's behalf.

This total *victory* was predicted, commanded, and reported in hyperbolic terms as total *annihilation* of the enemy and all that belonged to him. What *was* totally annihilated in a genuine and complete victory was the will and the ability of the enemy Canaanites to resist the invading Israelites. If that was the intent of the command and the report from the beginning, we may not dismiss these reports of annihilation as "false" or "exaggerated" royal (or Israelite) propaganda, but should give this kind of report its rightful place as a genuine convention of ancient Near Eastern history writing, and interpret it as it was intended.

It is impossible to overstate the importance of this understanding of the pertinent biblical texts, or of its implications at a number of points. Two stand out here: (1) Joshua and Judges are not contradictory, as often claimed; rather, they are highly complementary. (2) God did not command, nor did Moses and Joshua commit, genocide upon the Canaanites or upon any group of them. If Younger is correct (and I believe he is), we must begin reading these texts for what they were intended to say, by their own literary and historical canons, and not for what our own unexamined presuppositions have imposed upon them for too long. This not only will make us better exegetes, it will have the salutary effect of freeing both God and ancient Israel from the no-longer-excusable charge of genocide against the Canaanites.

Joshua was a man of this ancient Near Eastern milieu; the book of Joshua was produced in this ancient Near Eastern milieu. We should expect that God spoke to

Joshua in terms Joshua, as Israel's military leader, could understand and comply with. It was not Joshua's place to accommodate our sensibilities. Rather, we must strive to understand and interpret Joshua accurately, with respect for what God really told him to do and for what he really did.

If Younger is correct, how *should* we understand the concept of *kherem*? First, we no longer should assume or picture the death of every enemy soldier in a battle, or of every person in a conquered city. The language of such totality is not expressed by the use of *kharam/kherem* in the text. Where the language of totality does occur, it is in phrases such as "leaving no survivors" (e.g., 10:30, 33), and "they smote [them] with the mouth of the sword" (e.g., 11:14; not translated literally by NLT). Most importantly, this language of totality represents the common literary device of hyperbole, of exaggeration for effect. It reports the total *victory* of Israel over all their Canaanite foes in Joshua's campaigns. It does not mean all Canaanites ceased to exist.

Kharam is notably present in 1 Samuel 15:3 (cf. Exod 17:14-16; Deut 25:19). Despite the vividness of the report of 1 Samuel 15, Saul's war against Amalek, we must understand it, too, as the hyperbolic tone of complete victory over Agag's clan or chieftaincy of Amalek. If not, how could Amalek attack Ziklag, and how could David pursue and vanquish Amalek in retribution, at the very time of Saul's final defeat at the hands of the Philistines (1 Sam 30)? How could David defeat Amalek yet again, once he had become king (2 Sam 8:12)?

We should return the concept of *kherem*, then, to its original, broader, and proper domain. What God commanded to be dedicated as *kherem* was off-limits to Israel, not available for private use. The case of Achan reported in chapter 7 serves as a vivid case study. Material goods were to be burned or, as in the case of the gold, silver, iron, and bronze of Jericho, devoted to the use of the cult in the Tabernacle. Animals subject to the *kherem* were killed and burned; if some were used for sacrifice, we are not told of it.

Two major reasons men have gone to war over the millennia are for the glory of victory in combat and for the riches available from conquered cities and peoples. The book of Joshua is clear and consistent in ascribing Israel's victories over their Canaanite foes to God; no individual Israelite soldier is acclaimed for his prowess in battle. The institution of the *kherem* did not eliminate the second motive, Israel's profiting from those victories, but it did cut down on it, and thus on the greed that so often fuels the desire for war. Moreover, a consistently faithful Israel, "showing no favor" toward the polytheism of their Canaanite neighbors, might have become a witness for salvation to them, even as they had been that witness to many non-Israelites of an earlier generation as God led them out of Egypt.

MAJOR THEMES

The book of Joshua is a straightforward narrative of Israel's success in gaining entry into Canaan (together with a variety of lists outlining and suggesting how their own settlement in that good land was to be accomplished). Yet, Joshua touches on or develops a surprising number of important theological themes.

God, the Center. The most important theme of Joshua is that God is the center of redemption history. God was and is beginning and end, initiator and closer, Divine

Warrior and divine peacemaker. God called Joshua to lead Israel. God brought Israel across the Jordan. God fought for Israel more than he allowed Israel to fight for itself. God fought against Canaanite kings and armies because it is his right to judge all peoples. God as owner of the Promised Land allotted land to each tribe, clan, and family as tenants. God was and is the sole proper object of human allegiance and spiritual affection. We go to our end at peace with God, or we go at peace with no one and nothing, including ourselves.

The book of Joshua recounts God's actions in fulfilling God's promise to the patriarchs: Their descendants would inherit this land, though they themselves dwelt in it as sojourners. That the initiative was God's, and not Joshua's, is abundantly clear, from God's opening charge to Joshua in chapter 1, to the notice in 24:31 that the elders with Joshua had known all the work Yahweh had done for Israel (Woudstra 1981:3-5).

Each of the other themes in Joshua is a subset of the paramount glorious theme that first, last, and always, God is, and God acts.

God's Covenant Faithfulness. In the strictest sense, a covenant is an agreement. If one party violates the terms of the agreement, the other party no longer is obligated to the covenant or to the covenant partner. But God's covenant with Abraham was much more like a promise than a bargain. Though the Sinai covenant was largely a set of agreements typical of covenant, it also featured God's promise that he never would cut off Israel completely (e.g., Lev 26:44-45), even should God be forced to execute judgment for covenant unfaithfulness.

Israel had proven unfaithful, not once, but many times during its wilderness journeys. Yet not "merely" by covenant, but by promise and oath, God had bound himself to Abraham and to Israel. So God did not walk away, but persevered, fulfilling the covenant and the promises made with and to Abraham and his descendants. Throughout the book, the narrator emphasizes that Israel's entry into Canaan was in fulfillment of God's covenant and promises.

A People Holy to God. God called Israel to be a holy people (cf., e.g., Lev 11:44; Deut 6:4-5). "Holy" means "separate." Before it is moral and ethical, holiness is first of all relational. Israel was to be holy to God, worshiping no other gods. Just as a human being can be holy (separate, dedicated) only to one spouse, so the Christian can be holy only to one God.

Joshua highlights God's call for Israel to be God's holy people throughout the book. The people of Israel purified themselves before crossing the Jordan; the men were circumcised and all Israel celebrated the Passover after crossing the Jordan; the durable spoils of Jericho were dedicated to God's Tabernacle treasury; Israel renewed the covenant at Shechem; each tribe, clan, and family received its inheritance as a gift from God; Israel renewed the covenant at Shechem a second time, and destroyed the idolatrous images some had kept all this time. If we will see it, Joshua is a book about holiness to and before God.

The Reality of Judgment upon Sin. God had given the people of Canaan every opportunity to repent of their sin (Gen 15:16), yet under Joshua's leadership, Israel became the agent of God's long-delayed judgment (cf. Deut 9:3-5). And within Israel itself, Achan stole only a modest amount of money and an imported garment, yet it cost the lives of 36 Israelite soldiers, Achan, and Achan's immediate family; an entire chapter of Joshua (ch 7) is devoted to this episode. While holiness is separation to God, sin is separation from God. As God is the only source and sustainer of life, unrepented sin can lead only to death. Joshua's farewell addresses and conversations with Israel (ch 24) also include his final reminders of the seriousness of sin.

The Land as God's Good Gift. The Bible, both Old and New Testaments, is consistent in its witness to the original goodness of God's physical, material creation, including the human race, and God's fixed purpose of restoring all creation to its original good estate as part of the total redemption wrought by Jesus Christ. Time and again throughout the Pentateuch, God reaffirms the promise to give the land of Canaan to Abraham and his descendants (e.g., Gen 15:18; Exod 6:8; Deut 6:10; 8:7-10).

The theology of the land being given according to promise finds its initial fulfillment in the pages of Joshua. Almost from first line to last, the book brims with confidence that this enterprise was God's, that its success was engineered and guaranteed by God. Repeatedly, Joshua reminded Israel they were experiencing the gift their parents had been afraid to receive. Joshua's joy, astonishment, and gratitude at God's boundless generosity underlies nearly all his utterances throughout the book, frequently bubbling to the surface in words of thanks, praise, and trust.

The extensive lists of Joshua serve a purpose in this theology of the land. Nearly half the book is a cataloging of who would settle where, comprised almost entirely of town lists and border descriptions. God, who dug his hands into the clay to create the first human, delights to give us a place where we can work the earth and guard it, growing plants, caring for animals, and enjoying family intimacy. The Gnostic doctrine that the physical, material world is an evil to be spurned and outgrown as we "mature" into spiritual beings finds no traction in Joshua.

God retained the title to the land, as it were, while allowing Israel to be tenants in perpetuity, provided they continued in a sacred relationship with God. Furthermore, being God's tenants provided far greater security for Israel than if they had claimed it as their own. When foreign armies came, as they did, to attack Israel in God's land, Israel's defense was not ultimately in their own hands, but God's. Over the centuries, when Israel remembered that and turned to God for their defense, God remembered them and delivered them because they lived in *his* land.

Though God's purposes began with ancient Israel, they did not end there. God's gift of the good earth, restored, is ultimately for all who accept the wonderful offer of membership in God's eternal family. Israel's possession of their Promised Land is an earnest of that future gift.

The Importance of Memory. God told Joshua to study Moses's instructions continually, to keep their memory fresh every day. Joshua erected a stone memorial in the Jordan River, and another near the Jordan, to commemorate Israel's crossing during the spring flood stage. The Transjordanian tribes erected a stone memorial to keep alive on both sides of the Jordan the knowledge that they, too, were part of Israel. In two covenant renewal ceremonies at Shechem, and several other times, as well, Joshua reminded Israel of the importance of keeping the memories fresh by passing them on to their children. Keeping memory alive is important.

We may take this as the author's immediate purpose in writing the book of Joshua. Joshua and the rest of the narrative portions of the Bible, altogether about half the Bible's total content, remind God's people through the ages that God is faithful.

Rest. Rest may seem a strange theme to find in Joshua, of all books, until we remember that the Hebrew concept of rest begins with "cessation." When God "rested" on the seventh day of creation (Gen 2:2), he ceased from the major creative activity outlined in Genesis 1.

The book of Joshua depicts Israel's entry into Canaan as their finally finding rest from wandering in the wilderness, from living under the sentence God pronounced after the rebellion at Kadesh (Num 14), from potential and actual harassment and confrontation with enemies along the way, and from the uncertainty always felt when people are in transition. Occupation of Canaan had been the goal for 40 years; achieving the goal brought rest from all these burdens and more, even as it also brought hard work of various kinds the people had not experienced before.

Later biblical writers (especially the writer of the book of Hebrews) emphasized the theological dimensions of this rest. Israel's physical entry into Canaan became a metaphor for, as well as an example of, the "spiritual" rest that the people of God, Jew and Gentile alike, experience when they enter into the "rest" of God's salvation and sanctification in and through Christ (Heb 3–4). God's goal for us, individually and collectively, is this salvation. When we also make that our own goal and accept as God's gift its actualization in Christ's work of redemption on our behalf, we will begin to experience the rest Joshua and the people of Israel experienced partially and proleptically as they entered upon their promised inheritance in Canaan/Israel. For them and for us, the final and complete experience of that rest remains yet future.

THE PHYSICAL GEOGRAPHY OF CANAAN

Perhaps for Joshua more than for any other biblical book, it is important that the reader understand the physical geography of Canaan, as well as its human geography at the time the events of the book occurred. Joshua is about Israel's entrance into and early stages of settlement in the land of Canaan. When we know the land, we begin to understand the events.

Canaan (which later came to be known as Israel) can be divided geographically into four major regions, running north and south through the length of the country. (The physical geography is the same today, but not all the territory is within the borders of the modern state of Israel.) Beginning in the west at the shore of the Mediterranean, these four regions are the coastal plain, the central hill country, the Jordan Rift Valley, and the Transjordanian highlands (Transjordanian plateau).

The whole of biblical Israel is approximately 150 miles long, north to south, from Dan to Beersheba, the biblical limits of normal Israelite occupation through almost all the Old Testament period (2 Sam 24:2; 1 Kgs 4:25). The width of Israel's territory east to west was about 50 miles. Thus, the total area of ancient Israel was approximately 7,500 square miles, about the size of New Jersey. Ancient Israel would have fit into modern Alaska 78 times, with a fair-sized bit of country left over. Biblical Israel was a tiny place for the large, important history experienced there.

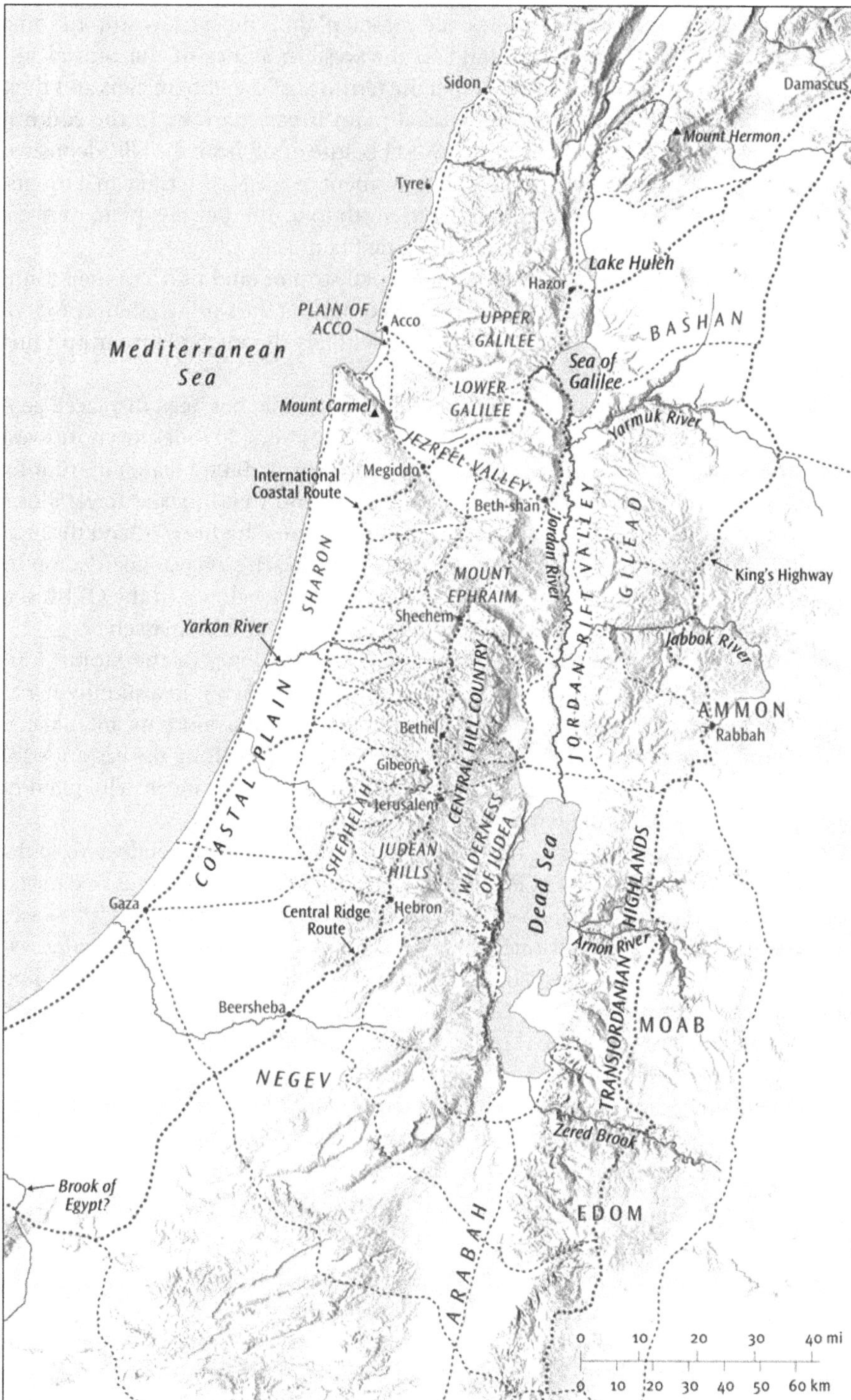

Geographical Features of Canaan

The Coastal Plain. As its name implies, the coastal plain is the narrow strip running from the Mediterranean shore inland to the western slopes of the central hill country. At its northern end, where it met the territory of the Phoenicians and their southernmost city-state of Tyre, the coastal plain is very narrow. To the south it widens as the coastline veers to the southwest because of silt from the Nile deposited along the coast over the centuries by the movement of the Mediterranean currents. The coastal plain has four subregions; from north to south they are: plain of Acco, Mount Carmel, plain of Sharon, and Philistine Plain.

The plain of Acco is the narrow crescent-shaped strip of land north of the Mount Carmel range. In the Old Testament period, it comprised the southwestern corner of the territory of the tribe of Asher. Today, it is essentially the small plain surrounding Haifa Bay, with a small extension northward.

Mount Carmel is a section of the central hill country that has been displaced geologically, so that it really is a mountain ridge running about 30 miles in a northwest to southeast direction. Mount Carmel juts out into the Mediterranean, interrupting the coastal plain and forming an impressive headland that blocked travel along the shore in antiquity. This forced the major international highway inland through one of three passes through the Mount Carmel range. Each pass was guarded on its inland end by a city at the edge of the Jezreel Valley (see below). In the Old Testament period, Mount Carmel was part of the tribal territory of Manasseh.

The plain of Sharon stretches from the southwestern slopes of the Mount Carmel range south to the Yarkon River (today, northern Tel Aviv). In antiquity it was sparsely populated because much of it was swampland, and swamps meant malaria. The international highway from Egypt to Mesopotamia ran along the eastern edge of the Sharon Plain, about 10 miles inland from the Mediterranean. The plain of Sharon was included in the territory of Manasseh.

The Philistine Plain designates the region from the Yarkon River southward, to the northeastern corner of the Sinai Peninsula, widening to the southwest as one travels south. This is a very fertile plain, well-suited to the production of grain, mostly wheat. Though very little of the Philistine Plain was ever occupied by Israel, most of it was assigned to the tribe of Judah. A northern slice was assigned to Dan, but they could not overcome Philistine pressure, and a large portion of the tribe migrated northward early on; eventually, most of the Danites who remained in the south were absorbed by Judah. At the rise of the Israelite monarchy under David and Solomon, the northern Philistine Plain became Israelite-controlled territory for the first time. A small southern inland portion was assigned to the tribe of Simeon; they, like the tribe of Dan, were essentially absorbed into Judah during the period of the monarchy.

The Central Hill Country. The central hill country is the southward continuation of the Lebanon Mountains that, farther north, hemmed in the Phoenician city-states against the Mediterranean Sea. Geologically, the range consists of three different types of limestone that weather into fertile soils, making agriculture potentially very productive. In Israel, the hill country is the widest of the four north-to-south regions, about 20 to 25 miles wide through most of its length. In biblical days, it was divided into nine subregions. Three of these are not really "hill country," but are linked with the hill country geographically, geologically, and historically. From north to south, the regions are: upper Galilee, lower Galilee, Jezreel Valley, Mount Ephraim, plateau of Benjamin, Judean hill country, Shephelah, Judean wilderness, and Negev.

Upper Galilee includes much of the most ruggedly mountainous territory in all the hill country. It stretches from the Mediterranean Sea in the west to the Huleh Valley above the Sea of Galilee in the east; it used to include a section of what is now southern Lebanon. Because of its rugged terrain, upper Galilee was more sparsely populated than lower Galilee. In the Old Testament period, the northern portions of Asher and Naphtali were in upper Galilee.

Lower Galilee lies south of upper Galilee, and also is lower in average elevation. Lower Galilee has broader valleys and gentler slopes, ideal for growing olives. In New Testament times, lower Galilee was famous for the number of its olive trees and the quality of its olive oil. Several of the valleys traversing lower Galilee were sites of locally important roads. One branch of the international highway between Egypt and Mesopotamia passed through one of these valleys, so lower Galilee regularly saw international travelers—armies, diplomats, merchants, and others.

Lower Galilee was divided among four Israelite tribes. The lower portions of Asher's territory in the west and Naphtali's territory in the east, overlooking the Sea of Galilee, were in lower Galilee. Zebulun occupied the south-central portion of lower Galilee, and Issachar its southeastern sector.

The Jezreel Valley is also known today as the Valley of Esdraelon; by later Old Testament times it could be designated "the plain of Megiddo" (cf. 2 Chr 35:22; Zech 12:11) after its largest and most important city, which guarded the central pass through the Carmel range into the valley. Revelation 16:16 refers to "the *place* called in Hebrew, 'Har-Magedon'" (Armageddon), "The Mountain of Megiddo." "The Plain/Valley of Megiddo" became (at least in John's apocalyptic vision) "the place/plain/valley of Megiddo." The Jezreel Valley separates lower Galilee to the north from Mount Ephraim to the south; it is an interruption of the north–south mountain range. The Beth-shan Valley exits the east end of the Jezreel Valley, sloping to the Jordan River. Together with the valleys running through the hills of lower Galilee, the Jezreel–Beth-shan connection provided several possibilities for the route of the international highway from Egypt to Mesopotamia as it turned inland from the coast northeast toward Damascus.

The Jezreel Valley is fertile, but in antiquity parts of it were wetlands, and thus malaria ridden and uninhabitable. For this reason, too, the road to the Jordan skirted the Jezreel Valley on its southern side. In the Old Testament period, those areas of the northern Jezreel Valley that were habitable were divided between Zebulun to the west and Issachar to the east. The valley's southern edge was the northernmost part of Manasseh's Cisjordanian allotment.

Mount Ephraim begins as the hill country resumes south of the Jezreel Valley, a bit higher in elevation and more rugged than lower Galilee, though lower in elevation and less rugged than upper Galilee. At the time of Israel's entry into Canaan, Mount Ephraim was heavily forested and sparsely settled. Israel's settlement was the first large-scale occupation of most of this region.

The center and south of Manasseh's western territory occupied the northern two-thirds of this mountain block, and the territory of Ephraim its southern third. It was because of Ephraim's prominence among the northern tribes of Israel that the entire region came to be called Mount Ephraim (e.g., 17:15, KJV; cf. Judg 2:9; 1 Sam 1:1; 1 Kgs 4:8; 1 Chr 6:67; Jer 4:15, KJV). The important city of Shechem lay at the border of Manasseh and Ephraim, guarding the pass and the road between Mount Gerizim and Mount Ebal.

The plateau of Benjamin is a small but strategic rolling plain, only about 10 miles north to south, cut off by the territory of Ephraim to the west and comprising the slopes of the northern Judean wilderness on the east. This centers northeast of Gibeon and extends towards Jerusalem and up to Bethel. Though of no external importance to trade or conquest, the plateau of Benjamin is the key to the military domination of the central hill country; whoever controls it easily controls all of Mount Ephraim to the north and the Judean hill country to the south. As its name reveals, this small strategic holding came by lot to Benjamin.

The Judean hill country, geologically and geographically, is the continuation of Mount Ephraim. The two regions are distinct only because of the relatively flatter terrain of the plateau of Benjamin between them. The central hill country continued through the tribal territory of Judah for about 30 miles south of Jerusalem, with its heights subsiding south of Hebron into the lower elevations of the Negev (see below). All the Judean hill country lay within the territorial boundaries of Judah.

Jerusalem, at the northern edge of Judah, became its most important city only when David conquered it and made it his capital. A puzzle in Joshua 15 is that the description of Judah's (northern) boundary with Benjamin clearly leaves Jerusalem in Benjamin (15:8), but then ends with the note that "Judah could not drive out the Jebusites, who lived in the city of Jerusalem" (15:63). We may wonder whether Jerusalem was assigned to Benjamin in the later allotment (18:28) because of Judah's failure; whatever the cause, Benjamin also failed to dislodge the Jebusites.

To the south of Jerusalem, Bethlehem, Beth-zur, and Hebron were other important Judean cities in the hill country.

An important aspect of the Judean hill country is its isolation. Because of its geography, central Judah was approached easily only from the north. The international highways did not cross Judea; travelers without business in Judea normally did not pass through it. This isolation gave Judea (including Jerusalem) a relatively conservative outlook that helped preserve greater faithfulness to Israel's God than in the northern kingdom of Israel. At the end of the Old Testament period, it was mainly Judean exiles who returned to reestablish faith in the Lord in its homeland, and to prepare the way for the coming of the Messiah.

The Shephelah is located between the Judean hill country and the Philistine Plain and is named from the transliteration of a Hebrew word meaning "lowland" (*shepelah* [TH8219, ZH9169]). The obvious implication is that this name was given by the Judeans in the hill country above it, rather than by the Philistines in the coastal plain below it. In the tribal allotments, the northern end (approximately one-third) of the Shephelah was assigned to the tribe of Dan. Dan was unable to hold its territory in the face of Philistine pressure, and a major portion of the tribe migrated north to the region of the city, which they renamed Dan in honor of their ancestor. Dan's portion of the Shephelah was absorbed by Judah with the rise of the monarchy under David; the southern Shephelah was assigned to Judah from the beginning.

The Shephelah rests on a foundation of limestone; in that respect it is continuous with the hill country of Judea. However, a line of north–south valleys eroded from a softer limestone separates the Shephelah from the hill country. Thus, though the Shephelah looks like foothills, it does not act like foothills. It is not just a gentle climb from the Shephelah to the hill country proper. Roads go up and then descend into the valleys, after which the traveler (or army) faces a difficult ascent back up, and higher up. For this reason the hill country of Judah is more isolated, and more easily defended from the west, than is the hill country of Mount Ephraim.

The Shephelah is fertile and well watered, sustaining a variety of agricultural pursuits. For this reason, and because of its strategic importance, Judah and Philistia fought fiercely over this small region during the early centuries of Israel's history in the land—before David's victories made it firmly Israelite and Judean.

The Judean wilderness is a steeply sloping continuation of the Judean hill country to the east. At Jerusalem and Hebron, on the watershed of the hill country, the elevation is 2,500 to 3,000 feet above sea level. But within 10 to 15 miles, the land drops away to the shores of the Dead Sea, 1,300 feet below sea level. Also, this region has worn down to a different layer of limestone, making its soils less fertile than those of the hill country proper. With poorer soil and drastically less rainfall, the wilderness of Judea has supported only sporadic settlement. Throughout history, it has been a haven for refugees, fugitives, and bandits; central governments always have held this region less firmly than any other in Israel. Ironically, it also has attracted persons in search of solitude and a place of spiritual retreat. All but a small northern segment of the Judean wilderness lay within the tribal boundaries of Judah.

The Negev is the southern down slope of the central hill country as it descends from the higher elevations south of Hebron to elevations not far above sea level. It is important to note that the biblical Negev is not congruent with the Negev of the modern state of Israel. The biblical Negev is essentially two basins stretching east and west of Beersheba. These basins narrow and meet at Beersheba, so the effect is of an hourglass or a figure eight lying on its side, with its center at Beersheba. This region normally does not receive sufficient rainfall to support cultivation of grain. However, its soil, a fine, windblown loamy soil called loess, is very fertile. With sufficient rainfall or, as in the last few decades, with irrigation water piped in from the north, the Negev produces very good yields, especially of wheat. Before the introduction of irrigation, much of the Negev was best suited to seasonal pasturing of sheep and goats.

In Joshua's allotment of tribal territories, Judah first received the entire Negev. In the survey to determine the allotments of the seven tribes who had not received land in the first round, it was noted that Judah's assigned portion was too large for it, so Simeon was given its portion within Judah, mostly in the Negev (19:1-9). Thus, Simeon occupied most of the western Negev, and Judah the eastern Negev.

The Jordan Rift Valley. The Jordan Rift Valley is the narrowest of the four major north-to-south regions. It actually is the deepest and most spectacular part of a 3,000-mile-long gash in the earth, easily visible from space; it begins in Turkey, runs south through the Red Sea, and culminates in the Great Rift Valley of east-central Africa. With respect to biblical Israel, the Jordan Rift Valley begins at the sources of the Jordan in the northern end of the Huleh Valley and stretches south of the Dead

Sea to the head of the Gulf of Elath/Aqabah, the northeastern arm of the Red Sea that borders the Sinai Peninsula on its eastern side. The Jordan Rift Valley comprises five subregions; from north to south, they are: Huleh Valley, Sea of Galilee, Jordan River, Dead Sea, and Arabah.

The Huleh Valley begins in what is today southern Lebanon. In antiquity, the territory of the tribe of Dan included essentially all the northern, habitable part of the valley. The spring in the city of Dan and two other springs comprise the three major sources of the Jordan River. Until the 1950s, these three sources flowed into Huleh Lake, then out its southern end as the Jordan River. Because an underlying layer of basalt blocked drainage, much of the valley around Huleh Lake was swampy and marshy, supporting an abundance of wildlife and waterfowl, but little human habitation. The modern state of Israel has drained most of the swamps, and most of Lake Huleh, to take advantage of the valley's fertile soil.

Hazor, at the southern end of the Huleh Valley, guarded the route of the international highway from Egypt to Mesopotamia near the point where it crossed the Jordan River. The king of Hazor headed the coalition opposing Joshua in his northern campaign; when Joshua had defeated that coalition, he captured and burned Hazor (11:1-13).

The Sea of Galilee region actually begins above the Sea of Galilee itself, at the point where the Jordan River commences its straight, precipitous plunge through the underlying layer of volcanic basalt, and through sea level, to the shores of Galilee at about 700 feet below sea level. The Sea of Galilee lies in a pronounced basin, surrounded by hills on its western, northern, and eastern sides. However, several small valleys descend from the hills, creating small plains of fertile soil bordering the shoreline. The relatively large, triangular plain at the south end of the lake is very fertile, as well.

The Sea of Galilee is shaped like a harp or lyre—thus, one of its Hebrew names, *kinnereth* [TH3672A, ZH4054], meaning "harp." Galilee is a clear, pure freshwater lake about 13 miles long, and 7 miles wide at its wider, northern section. At its narrower, southern end, the Jordan River flows on its way to the Dead Sea.

The territory of Naphtali came down to the shores of Galilee on its western side. Though Makir, half of the half-tribe of Manasseh, was assigned the territory east of the Sea of Galilee, Israel did not occupy much of that region until later. Because the international highway from Egypt to Mesopotamia offered three or four alternate routes around or near the Sea of Galilee, several important towns grew up in this region, though none of these is central to any prominent Old Testament narrative.

The Jordan River begins above the Sea of Galilee, but its greatest and most important length is between its outlet from the Sea of Galilee and its entrance into the Dead Sea about 65 miles south. Within that straight-line distance, the actual course of the Jordan is very circuitous in this segment, about 200 miles in length. Today the Jordan River is the boundary between Israel and Palestine, on its west bank, and the kingdom of Jordan, on its east bank. But the reader of the Bible must remember that in the Old Testament period, Israel was settled on both banks. (In the New Testament period, too, much of the east bank of the Jordan had Jewish inhabitants.)

In its northern half, the plain of the Jordan was and is quite fertile and well watered. Farther south, the soil becomes poorer, the rainfall becomes less, and the opportunities to draw water for irrigation lessen. Thus, the plain of the Jordan for several miles above the Dead Sea has much the character of a desert. The only major exception on the west side of the river is the large oasis of Jericho near the foot of the precipitous slopes that mark the eastern edge of the Judean wilderness. Jericho depends on its unusually large spring for its existence.

A curious characteristic of the Jordan River valley is its two-tiered landscape. The broad plain of the Jordan, as much as 12 miles wide in its lower reaches, is either level or dotted with small hillocks of marly deposits over much of its extent. Except where it is farmed, this broad plain presents a rather barren aspect. However, the Jordan has cut a deeper, winding channel through this broad plain, a channel that is a mile wide in some places. Only during flood stage does the Jordan swell to become a mile wide, so this deeper floodplain was (and is) a long, narrow, well-watered ribbon of lush growth on either side of the river's normal bed, so thick and riotous as to deserve the name "jungle." This deeper floodplain, called in the Bible "the pride of the Jordan" (Jer 49:19, ASV), was full with the spring runoff when Israel came to the point of crossing into Canaan opposite Jericho (3:15).

Few important streams descend to the Jordan from the west (the central hill country), but several do from the east (the Transjordanian highlands). The Yarmuk, entering the Jordan not far below the Sea of Galilee, doubles its volume of water. Nearly two-thirds of its way down to the Dead Sea, the Jordan is joined by the Jabbok.

The upper reaches of the Jordan River plain were occupied on both sides by the tribe of Manasseh. On its east bank, the plain of the Jordan was reckoned as part of Gilead, and northern Gilead belonged to Manasseh (specifically, the clan of Makir; 13:31; cf. Deut 3:15). The lower plain of the Jordan on the west side belonged to Ephraim, except for a small sliver (including Jericho) belonging to Benjamin. The lower portion of the plain on the east side was reckoned with that part of Gilead inhabited by Gad.

The Dead Sea shoreline is the lowest point on the surface of the earth, about 1,300 feet below the level of the Mediterranean. The waters of the Dead Sea were as much as 25 percent suspended salts in antiquity; today that figure approaches 33 percent. For this reason, the Dead Sea is called the Salt Sea in the Bible. The soil of the narrow shoreline areas can be highly saline, and much of it is of a poor marly type. Rainfall around the Dead Sea averages only two inches per year. All these factors combined to render the Dead Sea region uninhabitable throughout most of its area in antiquity.

However, a few oases occur where springs issue from the limestone strata of the mountains enclosing the Dead Sea on both its western and its eastern shores. These precious waters turn the narrow canyons through which they run into small but lush paradises of tropical growth; many plants and some animals that normally flourish only much farther south thrive in this tropical heat.

The western shores of the Dead Sea were assigned to Judah in the tribal allotments. The eastern shore in the north was the territory of Reuben, but Reuben ultimately could not hold its inheritance against Moab, and seems for the most part to have been absorbed, partly into Moab, partly into Gad, and partly into Judah. The eastern shore of the Dead Sea, south of the Arnon River that empties into it, belonged to Moab, one of the peoples descended from Lot (Gen 19:37); thus, the Moabites were related to Israel.

The Arabah is the long desert valley, about 110 miles north to south, between the mountains of Edom on the east and the complex, rugged terrain of the wilderness of Zin on the west. The Arabah is the continuation of the Jordan Rift Valley to the Red Sea at the head of the Gulf of Elath/Aqabah. It is hot and dry, possessing very few water sources.

The Arabah contains copper deposits that were worked in some periods in antiquity. It was more important as the route linking shipping on the Red Sea with overland routes to Egypt westward, to Jerusalem (in periods of Israel's and, later, of Judah's strength), and to Damascus northward via the King's Highway. The Arabah route connected, as well, with the Mediterranean trade at Gaza and/or Tyre. Control of the Arabah and the trade passing through it was the basis of much of Solomon's wealth. Insofar as the Arabah was reckoned a part of Israel, it was assigned to Judah, but it was not part of the land allotted by Joshua.

The Transjordanian Highlands. The Transjordanian highlands, or plateau, is the region rising eastward from the Jordan Rift Valley. The elevations of this plateau often are somewhat higher than those of the central hill country west of the Jordan River. On its eastern borders, the plateau blends into the northern Arabian Desert; the desert stretches about 500 miles to the east until it reaches the lower Euphrates-Tigris Valley.

In the Old Testament period, the Transjordanian plateau was home to Reuben and Gad, and to half the half-tribe of Manasseh. Israel's relatives and sometime enemies Ammon, Moab, and Edom also lived in this region. This ethnic complexity existed within the four geographic subregions of the Transjordanian highlands; from north to south, they are: Bashan/Golan, Gilead, Moab, and Edom.

Bashan/Golan, the northernmost region of the Transjordanian highlands, extends east and northeast of the Sea of Galilee. In the Bible it usually is called Bashan; today it is more often called the Golan. Bashan is protected from the desert on the east by the mountains of Hauran. Because of its elevation and its northerly latitude, Bashan usually receives adequate rainfall. Further, Bashan is a region of rich, dark, volcanic soils. With these advantages, Bashan was a desirable, productive region renowned especially for its cattle; the "cows of Bashan" were proverbial for their size and their sleek well-being (Amos 4:1 mg).

Bashan was assigned as part of the inheritance of Manasseh belonging to the descendants of Makir. But even in David's day, Geshur, in the western part of this region, was not part of Israel proper, but a dependent vassal kingdom. David's son Absalom fled to his grandfather, the king of Geshur, after killing his brother Amnon (2 Sam 13:37). Not until later did Israel control all of this region; then they had to fight the Arameans of Damascus to keep it, and often Aram took it away.

Gilead was divided from Bashan/Golan to the north by the Yarmuk River, which flows into the Jordan just below the Sea of Galilee. Gilead stretched south to a line extending eastward from the northern end of the Dead Sea, though that southern boundary was not naturally defined. The Jabbok River divided Gilead more or less in the middle.

Gilead was fertile and relatively well watered. In Old Testament times, the half of Gilead north of the Jabbok River was heavily forested, and settlement was slow. A part of the tribe of Manasseh (Makir, cf. Num 32:39) occupied Gilead in the north;

Gad was located in the middle, on either side of the Jabbok; part of the tribe of Reuben held the southern portion of Gilead.

The Ammonites, descendants of Lot (Gen 19:38) and thus related to Israel, bordered Gilead on the east. The capital of Ammon was Rabbath-Ammon, today's Amman, Jordan. Because their territory was squeezed between Israelite Gilead on their western borders and the desert on their eastern borders, the Ammonites continually tried, in their periods of strength, to wrest all or part of Gilead away from Israel (Judg 10:17ff; 1 Sam 11:1; Amos 1:13). When Israel was strong, they subjugated Ammon.

Moab proper occupied only the area east of the Dead Sea and south of the Arnon River that empties into the Dead Sea from the east. North of the Arnon lay the main part of the territory assigned to Reuben. However, Reuben seems not to have been able to hold onto its land north of the Arnon, and gradually all the territory east of the Dead Sea and west of the desert came to be regarded as Moab. Some Reubenites apparently were absorbed into Moab, some into Gad, and some into Judah.

Moab's soil generally is fertile, but its rainfall is less reliable than that of lands farther north, or of those lands west of the Jordan. Thus, Moab relied heavily on sheep for their wealth (2 Kgs 3:4). When Moab was strong, they also gained revenue from levies on travelers and goods passing along the King's Highway, which ran through Moab.

Edom is the only territory here discussed that never belonged to Israel even in part. Edom's northern border was the Zered River that flows into the Dead Sea from the southeast; thus, Edom was separated from Reuben by Moab, and from Judah by the Dead Sea. In the Arabah, during periods of Israel's or Judah's strength, Edom and Judah shared a common border. However, recent research has revealed a strong Edomite presence also west of the Arabah and south of the biblical Negev, both before and after Israel's settlement in Canaan. Edom occupied the mountains called in the Bible Mount Seir, a range that extends south nearly to Aqabah/Elath. Because these mountains reach as high as 5,600 in elevation, they can receive adequate rainfall for farming, though some years are too dry for a good yield, especially of grain. Like Moab, Edom relied, for much of its wealth, on sheep and on various revenues from travelers on the King's Highway.

God did not allow Israel to take Edomite territory because Edom was descended from Esau, Jacob's brother (Gen 36). Yet because of this close ethnic relationship, and because Edom controlled territory vital to Israel's economic and security interests, Israel always paid attention to Edom. At several points in Israel's and Judah's history—that is to say, whenever they could muster the military strength—Israel or Judah subjugated all or part of Edom. Edom took its revenge by active aid to Babylon when Babylon conquered Judah in 586 BC, putting an end to Judean independence.

THE CULTURAL GEOGRAPHY OF CANAAN AT THE TIME OF JOSHUA

The Problems of Rainfall, Forest, and Terrain. Rainfall may seem a strange place to begin a discussion of human settlement patterns in ancient Canaan/Israel. But rainfall is where we must start because human existence depends on rain. Egypt to the southwest and Mesopotamia to the northeast and east sustained their civilizations on irrigation from the great rivers, the Nile in Egypt, the Tigris and

Euphrates in Mesopotamia. But the nations of the Mediterranean coast—today's Lebanon, Syria, Israel, Jordan, and Palestine—always (until the last few decades) depended almost exclusively on rainfall for water. Their grain fields produced when the rain fell and withered when there was no rain.

Even orchards, gardens, flocks, and human beings, all of which can get water from cisterns, depend on the rain to fill those cisterns, since in this region most of the rivers and streams are only seasonal, drying up for months in summer and early autumn. The characterization of the land of Canaan as "a good land of flowing streams . . . with fountains and springs" (Deut 8:7) emphasizes this land's dependence upon God's bounty in the provision of adequate rainfall.

The normal pattern for rainfall in Canaan is that it is greater in the north and lesser in the south, as well as greater along the coast, and lesser farther inland. So, in a normal year, Galilee and Mount Carmel—in the north and along the coast—will have adequate rainfall for all agricultural purposes. The Negev (see above)—in the south and farther inland—may have adequate rainfall for a grain crop three years out of ten, on the average. The Dead Sea—south, inland, and in the rain shadow of the central hill country—receives, on average, only two inches of rain per year, insufficient for any agricultural purposes.

When Israel entered the land of Canaan, they found the Canaanite population most heavily settled in the plains and the valleys, along and near the route of the main international highway (see "Roads and Travel" below), from the southern coastal plain through the Jezreel Valley and Galilee to the edge of the Huleh Valley in the north. The Jordan Rift Valley had a number of cities, as well. The Philistines, when they entered Canaan about 50 years after Israel, settled in the southern coastal plain; that is why that region came to be known as the Philistine Plain. The Philistines, or related groups, also had a presence in other Canaanite areas.

The central hill country and the Negev, on the other hand, were sparsely settled when Israel came into the land. Canaanite cities were few and relatively far between. To this point in the history of Canaan, hill country settlement was possible only where springs of sufficient water volume and reliability occurred to support a town and all its water needs. The central hill country has no perennial streams, and if a spring did not flow year-round, permanent human habitation did not take root beside it.

A second problem for settlement was that the hill country was thickly forested over much of its area. A significant portion of this forest was virgin timber, the forest never yet having been cleared. Some areas of Canaan may have been subjected to the axes of expeditions led or sent for timber by foreign kings, expeditions that many of them boasted of in their annals. (Among the first of these was Sargon I, who campaigned as far as the Mediterranean and Asia Minor late in the third millennium BC.) Subsequently, such areas may have been covered with a second-growth forest of the type now called maquis in the Mediterranean. Up to the time Israel settled in Canaan, the clearing of either type of forest on a large scale to make room for towns and fields was well-nigh impossible.

Finally, the hill country, as is obvious from its name, has more land area in hillside slopes than in level areas of hilltop or valley. How to cultivate crops on these slopes without causing calamitous soil erosion is a problem no one solved before Israel entered Canaan.

These three problems together prevented widespread settlement of the central hill country through the nearly two thousand years of the Bronze Age. Yet, it is precisely here that Joshua, Judges, and archaeology all say Israel settled first, at the beginning of the Iron Age. Israel then spread out during the time of the judges as Israelite strength increased and Canaanite strength declined. What gave Israel the ability to do what could not be done previously?

Three technological advances, each introduced to western Asia about the beginning of the Iron Age, together made possible Israel's settlement in the central hill country and the Negev at precisely this time. Any two, without the third, would have been insufficient; all three were necessary.

Ironworking. The first technological advance was the one for which this archaeological period is named. The introduction of iron technology marked the beginning of the Iron Age. Iron is harder and holds a sharp edge longer than bronze. Iron is readily available in deposits at many points on the earth's surface. But the transformation of iron from a precious metal into the raw material of nearly all tools, implements, and weapons (a centrality of position that iron really has not given up to this day) required learning the secrets of iron smelting.

The principal problem was learning to raise the temperature of the smelting process. Bronze is smelted at about 1200° Fahrenheit, a temperature attainable with the use of bellows and small open smelting pits. Iron, however, requires temperatures in the range of 1800° Fahrenheit. To work iron, it was necessary to find a way to attain this extra 600 degrees of temperature in the smelting process, and to learn the skills of forging iron so as to introduce a small percentage of steel into the edge of tool, implement, or weapon. These skills were first learned somewhere in the Aegean region, or perhaps in the Hittite Empire of Asia Minor, which came to the end of its effective international power at about this time when it lost its monopoly on ironworking.

About the time of Israel's entrance into Canaan, the secret of ironworking came to western Asia. Iron axes made it possible to clear large tracts of forest in the central hill country, tracts that had not been settled in the Canaanite period (17:15, 18). Iron tools also made the hewing of cisterns from the limestone bedrock of the hill country more efficient, easing the intensive labor of providing water storage for the dry season.

Joshua and Judges record an irony in the uses to which Israel and their Canaanite adversaries put the new iron technology. As noted, Israel used iron axes to clear the forests of the hill country, allowing them to settle where Canaanite cities were few and far between. The Canaanites (and the Philistines), who lived mostly in the plains and the valleys, used iron, not only for these peaceful purposes, but also to build chariots (17:16, 18; Judg 1:19), the heavy weapons ("mechanized armor") of antiquity.

Chariots, like tanks later, operated very well on open, reasonably level ground. Infantry normally could not face chariots in battle on equal terms, so for some time Israel could not drive the Canaanites from the plains and valleys, nor subjugate them in those regions. However, in the hill country chariots did not operate well because of the rugged terrain. In Israel's own territory, which they had cleared for settlement with their iron axes, their infantry army had the advantage over the iron chariots of the Canaanites.

Plastered Cisterns. Recent archaeological surveys in the hill country of Galilee, Mount Ephraim, Judah, and the Negev have revealed hundreds of new small settlements attributable to the newly arriving Israelites. Most of these new settlements were at sites where no reliable water source is found. The second new technological advance that made possible these new foundations was the invention (or discovery) of a waterproof plaster with which cisterns could be coated to keep them from leaking out all the water stored in them.

The limestone bedrock underlying most of the hill country is quite easily worked when newly exposed to air. Thus, with the new iron tools, cisterns could be hewn in the bedrock, and the exposure to air would harden the new walls to minimize the danger of crumbling or collapse. However, these various limestones also are quite porous. Untreated, they never would hold water over the entire dry season, but the invention of a waterproof plaster made the cistern a realistic way of providing water once the rains had stopped. The water stored in the complex of cisterns of a whole town was sufficient for people, animals, gardens, and fruit trees, even if there was no spring, stream, or well nearby.

Israel and the rest of the nations along the Mediterranean coast still relied on the rainfall for their sustenance. Rain was necessary for the success of the grain crops that provided the staple food; grain could not be irrigated out of cisterns. And of course, the rains had to fill the cisterns year by year, or they would go dry after a few months. Thus, Israel still depended on God for survival in a way different than they had experienced in Egypt (Deut 11:10-12). The waterproof cistern allowed Israel to conserve God's gift of the rain from heaven.

Terracing of Hillsides. The third technological innovation solved the problem of conserving the soil of the hill country when farming the slopes. Much rock strewed the surface of the land in the hill country, rock that needed to be removed to make plowing, planting, cultivating, and harvesting possible. By using this rock to build terraces ringing the hillsides, the greater problem of soil erosion was solved. Building retaining walls of rock to hold the soil created, in effect, a series of long, narrow fields running around the perimeter of a hillside like a series of giant steps.

The soils of the hill country are very fertile. Retained by terraces, they could produce abundant yields for centuries. Some of the terraces built in the hill country in antiquity still are visible. They would need only to be repaired and the ground cleared for the hillsides to be productive again. In a fair number of modern villages in the hill country, terraces are still utilized in this way; it would be easy to imagine that some of these terrace-walls have been used and kept in good repair continuously over the centuries. A common practice now, and probably in antiquity as well, is to plant olives or other fruit trees on the terraced hillsides, and then to plant wheat between the trees. The soil produces two crops a year, and the grain stubble enriches the soil year by year.

Roads and Travel. Finally, as a part of the human geography of the country, we should consider roads, travel, and trade. Of course, all roads in this period were dirt tracks. Even most city streets were dirt or mud, though some were paved with flagstones or the like. Only centuries later did the Romans bring to the east their practice of surfacing roads with stone.

Two international routes were important to Israel. The most important road in the ancient Near East was the international highway from Egypt to Mesopotamia. In its western segment, it came out of Egypt and moved east across the northern Sinai. In the south of Canaan, this route passed through the Philistine Plain just inland from the Mediterranean Sea; Judah's western borders were several miles to the east of this highway. As it progressed north, the highway passed farther inland, skirting the edge of Israel's hill country (Mount Ephraim) until it reached the Carmel range.

Crossing through one of the three passes of the Carmel, usually the central pass that came out at Megiddo, the highway emerged into the plain of Jezreel. There the traveler could skirt the Jezreel Valley along either edge, going north and crossing lower Galilee in a northeasterly direction, or going on the valley's south side, descending via the Beth-shan Valley, then turning north toward Hazor, keeping the Sea of Galilee on the right. Near Hazor, the road crossed the Jordan below the swamps of the Huleh Valley near a point crossed today by the Bridge of Jacob's Daughters. Skirting Mount Hermon, the road continued on to Damascus, and from Damascus north to the Euphrates (cf. the map on p. 21).

This road often is called the Via Maris, but that is an anachronism at best and a historical error at worst. The only biblical mention of a "Way of the Sea" occurs in Isaiah 9:1; it refers to a road going to Tyre on the Mediterranean coast from the vicinity of Mount Hermon inland. The international road from Egypt to Mesopotamia, as a whole, has no name in the Bible or in the other ancient sources.

The second international highway in the area did have a name: The King's Highway ran north and south at or near the edge of the eastern desert in the Transjordanian highlands. It passed through the major cities in Edom, Moab, and Ammon (these were their major cities because they were on the King's Highway). North of Ammon and Gilead, the King's Highway passed through Bashan/Golan and joined the other international highway at Damascus.

Internally, the central ridge road, as its name implies, followed a path generally along the watershed of the hill country. Coming up from the Negev, it passed by Hebron, Bethlehem, Jerusalem, and Bethel. At Shechem, it branched east and west; both branches joined the international highway at different points.

Because humans live on the surface of the earth, geography is always important. Because every ancient Israelite, humble or great, lived in close and intimate relationship with the land, if we wish to understand ancient Israel, we need to learn ancient Israel's geography. Canaan was the Land of Promise God gave to Israel through the events recorded in Joshua; if we want to understand the message of Joshua, we need to study both the physical and the human geography of ancient Israel. God's grand plan of redemption for the human race may transcend both time and space, but God has so far worked it out in a very definite, limited place through a sequence of events in history. To understand God's plan and its fulfillment, it helps to understand the timeline and the map.

OUTLINE

The following outline, though not the only possible one, emphasizes that through Joshua, God really did bring Israel into the land and really did apportion it as their inheritance—even though by the close of the book some of the land was yet to be taken, and much of it was yet to be occupied fully in peace and security.

- I. Israel's Entrance into Canaan (1:1–6:27)
  - A. God's Commission; Joshua's Acceptance (1:1-18)
    1. God's promise to Joshua (1:1-5)
    2. God's command to Joshua to heed the Torah (1:6-9)
    3. Joshua's charge to Israel; Israel's charge to Joshua (1:10-18)
  - B. Joshua Sends Spies into Jericho (2:1-24)
    1. Rahab shelters the spies (2:1-7)
    2. Rahab's request for her family (2:8-13)
    3. The oath and the rope as signs (2:14-24)
  - C. Israel's Crossing of the Jordan (3:1–5:1)
    1. Preparations for crossing the Jordan (3:1-8)
    2. Joshua's promise of a miracle (3:9-13)
    3. Crossing on the Jordan's dry bed (3:14-17)
    4. The memorial stones (4:1-9)
    5. Resumption of the Jordan's flow (4:10-18)
    6. Israel's memorial at Gilgal (4:19–5:1)
  - D. First Circumcisions and First Passover (5:2-15)
    1. Circumcision of every male (5:2-9)
    2. First Passover in the land (5:10-12)
    3. The Divine Warrior (5:13-15)
  - E. God's Conquest of Jericho (6:1-27)
    1. God's siege instructions to Joshua (6:1-7)
    2. Circling Jericho for six days (6:8-14)
    3. Jericho's fall on the seventh day (6:15-21)
    4. The spies' faithfulness to Rahab (6:22-23)
    5. Joshua's destruction of Jericho (6:24-27)
- II. Joshua's Victories over Two Canaanite Coalitions (7:1–12:24)
  - A. Achan's Sin and Judgment (7:1-26)
    1. Israel's defeat at Ai (7:1-5)
    2. Joshua's prayer; God's response (7:6-15)
    3. Achan's conviction and execution (7:16-26)
  - B. Joshua's Conquest of Ai on the Second Try (8:1-35)
    1. Joshua's ambush strategy at Ai (8:1-13)
    2. Joshua's success at Ai (8:14-29)
    3. Covenant renewal at Mount Ebal (8:30-35)

- C. Gibeon's Successful Deception (9:1-27)
  1. Negotiation with Gibeon's envoys (9:1-15)
  2. The Gibeonites' sentence of servitude (9:16-27)
- D. Joshua's Victory at Aijalon (10:1-43)
  1. Gibeon's call for help (10:1-6)
  2. Israel's response and God's response (10:7-15)
  3. Execution of five kings (10:16-27)
  4. End of the southern campaign (10:28-43)
- E. Joshua's Victory over the Northern Coalition (11:1-23)
  1. Joshua's defeat of Jabin of Hazor (11:1-15)
  2. End of the northern campaign (11:16-23)
- F. The List of Defeated Kings (12:1-24)
  1. Moses's conquests east of the Jordan (12:1-6)
  2. Joshua's conquests west of the Jordan (12:7-24)

III. The Tribal Allotments (13:1–21:45)
- A. Allotments of the Transjordanian Tribes (13:1-33)
  1. The remaining land (13:1-7)
  2. General description of Transjordanian territories (13:8-14)
  3. Reuben's inheritance (13:15-23)
  4. Gad's inheritance (13:24-28)
  5. The inheritance of half-Manasseh (13:29-33)
- B. Caleb's Portion (14:1-15)
  1. Introduction to the western allotments (14:1-5)
  2. Caleb's witness to God's faithfulness (14:6-12)
  3. Caleb's town of Hebron (14:13-15)
- C. Judah's Portion (15:1-63)
  1. Judah's boundaries (15:1-12)
  2. Acsah's request (15:13-19)
  3. Judah's allotments: Negev, Shephelah, hill country, and wilderness (15:20-63)
- D. Joseph's Portions (16:1–17:18)
  1. Ephraim's southern border and inheritance (16:1-10)
  2. The case of Zelophehad's daughters (17:1-6)
  3. The rest of Manasseh's inheritance (17:7-13)
  4. Joseph's additional territory (17:14-18)
- E. The Allotments of the Remaining Tribes (18:1–19:48)
  1. Survey of the remaining land (18:1-10)
  2. Benjamin's borders and cities (18:11-28)
  3. Simeon's inheritance (19:1-9)
  4. The final five (19:10-48)
- F. Joshua's Portion (19:49-51)

- G. Cities of Refuge and Levitical Cities (20:1–21:45)
  1. The law of refuge (20:1-6)
  2. Cities of refuge, west and east (20:7-9)
  3. The Levitical cities (21:1-42)
  4. Benedictory summary (21:43-45)
- IV. Joshua's Farewells; Three Burials (22:1–24:33)
  - A. The Return of the Transjordanian Tribes (22:1-34)
    1. Joshua's commendation (22:1-9)
    2. Israel's confrontation of the Transjordanian tribes (22:10-20)
    3. The Transjordanian tribes' defense (22:21-34)
  - B. Joshua's Farewell to the Leaders (23:1-16)
    1. Joshua's call to faithfulness (23:1-10)
    2. Joshua's warning (23:11-16)
  - C. Covenant Renewal (24:1-28)
    1. Joshua's review of God's grace to Israel (24:1-13)
    2. Joshua's charge and the people's response (24:14-18)
    3. Joshua's rhetorical skepticism (24:19-24)
    4. Formal renewal of the covenant (24:25-28)
  - D. Burial of Joshua, Joseph, and Eleazar (24:29-33)

ENDNOTE

1. I regard the strongest evidence for the early date of the Exodus to be Bryant Wood's reevaluation of the archaeological evidence from Jericho. We must note that John Garstang excavated Jericho from 1930 to 1936, concluding that the city indeed had been destroyed as recorded in Joshua 6. Garstang's reasonable inference was that Jericho probably had been destroyed by Joshua. Acting on Garstang's request to check his results, Kathleen Kenyon renewed the excavations at Jericho, digging from 1952 to 1958. She concluded that the destruction Garstang had found was too early to be ascribed to Israel under Joshua, and that Jericho was unoccupied at the end of Late Bronze Age I (1400 BC). Bryant Wood (conveniently available in Wood 1990a) reevaluated Garstang's and Kenyon's excavation records (most of Kenyon's data was published only in the early 1980s).

   Wood's reanalysis (1990a) revealed data that Kenyon had missed in her evaluations of her findings. Wood concluded that many details of the Joshua account of Jericho's destruction in fact do have parallels in the archaeological record: (1) Jericho was strongly fortified (cf. 2:5, 7, 15; 6:5, 20); (2) the attack occurred just after the spring harvest (cf. 2:6; 3:15; 5:10); (3) Jericho's citizens could not flee with newly harvested food supplies (cf. 6:1); (4) the siege was short (cf. 6:15); (5) the city walls were leveled, possibly by an earthquake (cf. 6:20); (6) the city was not plundered for personal gain (cf. 6:17-18); (7) the city was burned (cf. 6:24).

   Some dispute Wood's evaluation (e.g., Bienkowski 1990; but cf. Wood 1990b), but I find Wood's analysis compelling, and it is difficult to avoid the conclusion that the archaeological record apparently preserves an independent witness to Joshua's capture and destruction of Jericho.

COMMENTARY ON

Joshua

◆ I. Israel's Entrance into Canaan (1:1–6:27)

A. God's Commission; Joshua's Acceptance (1:1-18)

1. God's promise to Joshua (1:1-5)

After the death of Moses the LORD's ser-
vant, the LORD spoke to Joshua son of
Nun, Moses' assistant. He said, 2"Moses
my servant is dead. Therefore, the time
has come for you to lead these people,
the Israelites, across the Jordan River
into the land I am giving them. 3I prom-
ise you what I promised Moses: 'Wher-
ever you set foot, you will be on land I
have given you—4from the Negev wilder-
ness in the south to the Lebanon moun-
tains in the north, from the Euphrates
River in the east to the Mediterranean
Sea* in the west, including all the land of
the Hittites.' 5No one will be able to stand
against you as long as you live. For I will
be with you as I was with Moses. I will
not fail you or abandon you.

1:4 Hebrew *the Great Sea.*

NOTES

1:1 ***After the death of Moses.*** The opening of the book of Joshua ties it firmly to the account of Moses's death at the end of Deuteronomy (Deut 34), which it follows. Moses, who had led Israel out of Egypt and throughout the years in the wilderness, had died on Mount Nebo east of the Jordan. Now it was time to cross the Jordan and enter Canaan. The first order of business was to confirm Joshua as Moses's successor.

1:2 ***Moses my servant is dead.*** This first short sentence is laden with finality: Moses was gone; he had fulfilled the tasks God had assigned to him; Israel had grieved for him the customary and respectful 30 days; Moses would not be back. Therefore, it was time for Joshua and Israel to rise up from their grief and enter into the land God was giving them. Even unconditional gifts must be received; Israel could receive the land only by going into it.

1:3 ***I promise you what I promised Moses.*** God took pains throughout this charge to assure Joshua that Moses's death would not end God's presence with Israel, nor God's guidance of Israel's leaders.

1:4 ***the Negev wilderness in the south.*** This is the area around Beersheba, stretching westward toward the Mediterranean and eastward toward the Dead Sea. "Negev" is not in the Hebrew text, but is a legitimate inference here, because the Negev was the southernmost region of settlement proper for ancient Israel. See also "The Negev" under "The Central Hill Country" in the Introduction.

Lebanon mountains. The northernmost of Israel's tribes settled southern portions of these mountains, becoming neighbors of the Phoenicians. Joshua did not lead Israel as far as the Euphrates River, but later David and Solomon ruled some of the kings of those regions in a suzerain-vassal relationship.

1:5 ***No one will . . . stand against you. . . . I will be with you as I was with Moses. I will not fail you or abandon you.*** This is a fantastic set of promises, and Joshua and Israel needed them. Moses, their father figure, was gone. They had very little confidence without him, either in themselves, or in God's steadfastness now that the one who had talked with God face-to-face was no longer present to talk with God for them. The modern Christian believer must understand and act on these promises in the light of the Holy Spirit's indwelling. God promises to be with us, never to fail us or abandon us.

COMMENTARY

Finally, Israel was ready for the great adventure! Through awesome deliverance from Egyptian slavery (Exod 5–14), through nation-making at Sinai, through rebellious unbelief at the edge of the Land of Promise, through the death of an entire generation, God had led and borne with Israel. Now that Moses the great leader had died, Joshua assumed leadership as the people prepared to enter the land that their parents' fears had kept them out of (Num 13–14). It was a new day with a new leader, as the new generation prepared to enter the new land. Bolstered by God's presence, Israel knew that every good thing God had promised was about to happen!

These first six chapters, the first quarter of the book of Joshua, record ancient Israel's actual setting foot into the land of Canaan for the first time and securing a foothold by the conquest of Jericho. God had promised Israel this entrance for several centuries, but the memory of the promise had grown dim in the generations of Egyptian servitude. Many of these people had come out of Egypt as children. They had waited 40 years for this entrance.

Entrances are important. The first time of doing something is an important milestone in the life of an individual or of a people. It is fitting that one-fourth of the book of Joshua is devoted to Israel's entrance into the land God had promised their ancestors so long before.

Chapter 1, God's charge to Joshua, introduces most of the themes of the book. God's sovereignty and God's initiative are highlighted. It was God who commanded Joshua to end 38 years of Israelite inactivity by leading the people across the Jordan to possess the land. The beginning of the charge to Joshua gives three promises: (1) all the land would be theirs; (2) no enemy would withstand them; (3) God would be with them and never forsake them.

We should not transfer this historical narrative in a material way when we consider whether it offers anything of promise for God's people after Joshua. We cannot conclude that, because God promised all this to Joshua, God promises a Christian today one particular house, one particular spouse, or one particular position. The transfer of a specific promise in a particular ancient context to a particular modern context is risky, because the contexts usually are not really parallel. But we can make a legitimate transfer of promise or of principle from the specific context of the ancient situation to the general human context in all ages. God gives the Christian all the "land" of his/her experience, for an eternal inheritance. Even though the Christian may suffer reverses in this life, ultimately no enemy of the soul can stand before the one whose trust is in God. No Christian ever awoke to find that God had forsaken him or her.

The land of Israel was always more than a physical entity. If we err by "spiritualizing" the material or the temporal, we equally err by "unspiritualizing" them.

God created the human race with one foot in the world of space, time, and matter, and the other foot in the eternal world. The spiritual creature is also the material creature; for this life, at least, our material destiny is an important part of our spiritual destiny. While we are here, the two really cannot be separated. The land as the promised rest for God's people is also presented in this first chapter. What Israel had held in hope for many years was soon to become a reality. This theme continues to be important, as the New Testament writer to the Hebrews picks it up again (Heb 3:18–4:11) and enlarges on it for all God's people.

Moses had been God's chosen agent to bring Israel out of Egypt to Sinai, where God made a covenant with them. Moses had been Israel's leader for 40 years, through rebellion, judgment, and repentance. Because of his own failure to give God glory for a miraculous provision of the people's need at a crucial point, Moses was forbidden entry into the Land of Promise (Num 20:2-13). As the people of Israel were poised on the east side of the Jordan River, ready to cross and enter the land God had promised them, Moses was dead.

Joshua, Moses's long-time aide, was Moses's designated successor (Num 27:18) to the leadership of Israel. But Joshua as sole leader was new, his abilities unknown and untested. How did the people, and Joshua himself, know he would be a good leader? Would God be with Joshua, as he had been with Moses? Anxiety, even fear, would be natural reactions both for Joshua and for the people at this time. Joshua may have wondered what was to come next. God had brought Israel to the plain of Moab, across the Jordan River east of Jericho. God had said he was bringing them into the land he had promised Abraham to give to his descendants. But now Moses, through whom God had worked for 40 years, was dead. What was Joshua to do now?

God reassured Joshua, first, by making himself known to him. The first verse of this narrative identifies Moses as the servant of the Lord, and Joshua as Moses's aide. Joshua had been Moses's chief aide since Israel's sojourn at Mount Sinai (Exod 24:13). The simple fact that God now spoke to Joshua as he had for years spoken to Moses was a sign that God had chosen Joshua to take Moses's place of leadership and to bring Israel into the promised land of Canaan.

Verse 2 states "Moses my servant is dead"; the last verses of Deuteronomy record Israel's 30 days of mourning for Moses. Thus, God's opening statement was not an announcement of news, but a signal that now it was time for Joshua to assume active leadership over Israel and for Israel to get moving again. God's next words emphasize the point: "the time has come." Here the command is, "Arise, cross this Jordan" (1:2, NASB). This was the goal toward which God had been leading his people for 40 years. Now it was about to happen, and God was giving Joshua his final marching orders. Israel was on the east side of the Jordan River in the plain of the Jordan Rift Valley, just north of the Dead Sea. God intended them to cross the Jordan into Canaan proper, entering opposite Jericho, and from there to proceed with the conquest of the land.

God's initiative in leading the people from Egypt to the land had been clear from the beginning, and now, as Joshua began his new role, God reminded him that this was his enterprise, not Joshua's. Joshua was to take Israel into the land, but God would give it to the Israelites. Joshua could lead Israel with confidence, knowing that God had set him to this task.

The structure of verse 3 is important because of the way it assigns emphasis. It reads literally, "Every place which the sole of your foot shall tread in it, to you I have given it, just as I spoke to Moses." The expression "every place" is first for emphasis. If Joshua walked there, it would belong to Israel. "To you" is first in its clause, again for emphasis. Finally, in case Joshua still didn't understand the force of God's declaration, God reminded Joshua that he had given Moses this same promise that Israel would enter and possess this land. God knew that Joshua needed reassurance at this time of great change. God's willingness to reassure Joshua stands as testimony to God's unfailing presence with his people always, in every situation.

God proceeded to remind Joshua of the borders of the land (1:4); God had described these borders previously to Moses (e.g., Exod 23:31). By the use of concrete geographical references, God reinforced in another way his commitment to fulfill his promise through Joshua's leadership. Joshua would remember the land as God described its borders because he had walked through it before. About 38 years earlier, Joshua had been one of the 12 men sent to scout the land, preparing for the entry, which did not happen because of Israel's unbelief (Num 13–14). Now Joshua would remember places and districts and the compass of the whole land, and his memory would help him believe that what God promised, God would deliver.

The desert refers generally to the deserts that formed the eastern and southern borders of the areas of Canaan that were already settled. This included the regions just traversed as Israel made their way from Kadesh, around Edom and Moab on the east, to their present camp east of the Jordan opposite Jericho.

Lebanon included the coastal mountain range north of upper Galilee—the land of the Phoenician cities, the inland Anti-Lebanon Mountains, and the valley between the two ranges. Since, as a geographical region, Lebanon extended in this period to the Euphrates River valley in the north, the Euphrates is mentioned here as Israel's northern boundary. Israel never actually settled most of this northern territory, but did control it for a time under David and Solomon.

As for "the Great Sea" on the west (see 1:4, NLT mg), this is the Mediterranean. The borders of Israel thus would be the deserts to the south and the east, Lebanon to the north, and the Mediterranean to the west. Throughout its history, when Israel was in right relationship with God, these were its general boundaries.

This passage is God's assurance to Joshua. In verse 5 God made a threefold, emphatic promise, with no frills, no qualifications, and no beating about the bush. Sometimes, God's people need such to-the-point reassurance. God's first promise was that Joshua did not need to fear that any enemy would be able to stand against him as he carried out the task to which God called him. Though the men of Ai did win a minor skirmish because of Achan's sin (ch 7), Joshua was victorious in every other battle throughout his life, and died having won for Israel the right to settle in the land of Canaan.

That God had been with Moses throughout his 40 years of leading the people of Israel had been evident in many ways. God's presence with Moses had encouraged, amazed, and sometimes frightened the people, but they always knew that God was with him. Joshua knew this better than any other person, for he had been with Moses on Mount Sinai when God gave him the tablets of the commandments (Exod 24:12-13). Joshua, more than any other person, had seen the effect on Moses of his close encounters with God. This second promise to Joshua, the promise of God's continued presence with him, just as God had been with Moses, certainly encouraged Joshua tremendously.

The third promise God stated in a twofold manner, again for emphasis and for Joshua's encouragement. "I will not fail you or abandon you" (1:5) was a personal restatement of a promise God had given to all Israel through Moses. On that same occasion Moses even had said the same thing to Joshua in front of all the people (Deut 31:6-8). Now God himself made the same promise to Joshua, using the personal pronoun "I." If Joshua needed reassurance, he certainly had it!

Some writers and speakers on biblical matters have pondered when it is and is not proper for God's people of today to claim promises like this for ourselves. This certainly is one promise for all God's people through all time. Though given originally to Israel, all believers since then have become part of "the Israel of God" (Gal 6:16, NLT mg). Though here given to Joshua, all God's people are invited to walk with God throughout our lives. God promises all his children that he never will leave us nor forsake us. This was Jesus' promise to his followers just before he ascended into heaven (Matt 28:20). The reality of this presence is evident in the fact that God has given his children the Holy Spirit of Jesus (John 14:15-17).

◆ 2. God's command to Joshua to heed the Torah (1:6-9)

6"Be strong and courageous, for you are the one who will lead these people to possess all the land I swore to their ancestors I would give them. 7Be strong and very courageous. Be careful to obey all the instructions Moses gave you. Do not deviate from them, turning either to the right or to the left. Then you will be successful in everything you do. 8Study this Book of Instruction continually. Meditate on it day and night so you will be sure to obey everything written in it. Only then will you prosper and succeed in all you do. 9This is my command—be strong and courageous! Do not be afraid or discouraged. For the LORD your God is with you wherever you go."

NOTES

1:6 ***Be strong and courageous.*** Three times in this short paragraph (also 1:7, 9), God repeats this specific instruction to Joshua. Joshua had been Moses's assistant for nearly 40 years, and now he was in charge. His need for encouragement is understandable.

you. This is a subject pronoun, not required in the grammar of the Hebrew text at this point; it is there for emphasis. God was saying, "You, Joshua—you, and no one else—will do this." This is both instruction and reassurance.

all the land I swore to their ancestors I would give them. This is God's reminder to Joshua of his ancient promise to Abraham, Isaac, and Jacob (Gen 17:8; 26:3; 28:13). Joshua now would become God's agent in its fulfillment. A God who remembers his promises over the centuries is a God to be trusted.

1:7 ***Be strong and very courageous.*** God's command is repeated with even greater emphasis. But now God's instruction takes an unexpected turn. God had been talking about taking possession of the land of Canaan. Strength and boldness certainly were necessary for this enterprise. The Canaanites outnumbered Israel, and Israel had relatively little experience in battle, none in conducting sieges against fortified cities.

1:8 ***Book of Instruction.*** Heb., *torah* [TH8451, ZH9368], which is better translated as "instruction" than "law" (as in many English versions). Certainly, the foundations of Israel's law codes are included, but it is much more than that. God's nature and character are revealed in God's Torah, coupled with God's unveiling of himself to those who desire to have an intimate relationship with him.

Meditate on it day and night. Joshua was to think and speak of God's instruction, discuss and ponder it, study and learn it continually. He was not to let time go by without occupying his mind and heart with the word of God as given to Moses. Such careful attention to God's written word is a good model to follow.

1:9 ***be strong and courageous!*** This is the climax of God's speech of instruction and encouragement to Joshua. Repetition in a biblical passage marks the importance of what is repeated; this is the third time in four verses God tells Joshua, "Be strong and courageous." God's people can easily allow fear and discouragement to undercut strength and courage, so God warned Joshua to keep those emotions in hand, and not let them rule him. God's continuous presence, promised here at the conclusion of God's speech, gave Joshua the confidence to follow God's instruction. The modern believer, too, has the promise of God's continuous presence, and so may go in strength and courage.

COMMENTARY

Having reassured Joshua, God now proceeded to instruct him. His first command was "Be strong and courageous" (1:6). These two imperatives are essentially synonyms in Hebrew—"be strong, stout, mighty, bold." This is so crucial that God repeated this command three times in these four verses! Then, as if to make sure that Joshua didn't miss the point, the people told him he must be strong and courageous, and they would follow him (1:18).

Israel had failed to enter the land years before because they lacked the courage to trust in God. Failure to receive the good gifts God would give his people was not only Israel's problem. God's people of today need to be alert so that we, too, do not miss out because of the failure of our courage to trust God. "Be strong and very courageous" (1:7) is God's command repeated with even greater emphasis. But now God's instruction takes an unexpected turn. God had been talking about entering and possessing the land of Canaan. Strength and boldness certainly were necessary for such an enterprise. The Canaanites outnumbered Israel, and Israel had relatively little experience in battle, none in conducting sieges against fortified cities.

But now God spoke of Joshua's being strong and bold to be careful to obey all the law Moses had given him (1:7). What had that to do with victory in battle against the Canaanites? It had everything to do with it, and with all the other ways Israel's success would be measured: settling the land, carving out productive farms, and building homes, villages, and cities. This land was (and is) God's land; God brought Israel into Canaan as tenants, not as owners. If Israel hoped for success in the Land of Promise, they would need to order their lives according to God's instruction.

Mere military prowess would not be enough for Israel to defeat the people of Canaan; mere cleverness would not be enough for them to be successful in making their homes in this new land. God had given the Torah by which they could demonstrate their faithfulness to God and order their affairs successfully in God's land. Joshua, as leader, was to set the example in careful adherence to God's instruction.

He was not to turn either to the right or to the left; by directly following God's instruction, Joshua would have success and lead Israel to success.

God did not command Joshua (and Israel) to keep the law (1:7-8) as a means of attaining righteousness through works, nor was it for the sake of the law itself. Keeping the law was not even intended as a means of gaining a desired reward—in this case, the land of God's promise—though it did (and often does) have a "reward" as a by-product. God's goal always has been a relationship of mutuality in love, intimacy, and integrity with those who respond to God's invitation of grace. The "law" God was speaking of to Joshua was instruction to him and to Israel in how they were to conduct themselves when God had brought them into the land. After all, they had "never traveled this way before" (3:4). They would *want* to know how to conduct themselves rightly in all their new relationships.

The need for constancy in Joshua's attention to the book of God's instruction is emphasized further. The expression "study this Book of Instruction continually" (1:8) suggests that Joshua was to think and talk of it, discuss and ponder it, study and learn it, continually. Joshua was not to let time go by without occupying his mind and heart with the word of God as given to Moses.

The Book of Instruction was God's covenant with Israel by which he had made Israel a nation and entered into a relationship with them as their God. It was Israel's constitution, the principles by which Israel was to govern its national life in the Promised Land. It was code—representative law in the areas of religious, civil, and criminal law—by which Israel's judges and other legal authorities could determine justice when individual cases came before them for decision. As the leader who was to bring Israel into Canaan and start them on the road to real nationhood, Joshua needed to know the Book of Instruction in all its aspects.

Since God has given so much more of his word to his people in these many centuries after Joshua, how much more should God's people today take this admonition to heart! God's word is a treasure chest, a gold mine of instruction, inspiration, and insight into God's action in this world on behalf of God's people. The best way to know the mind and heart of God, before we see God face-to-face, is to read God's revelation. What God said to Joshua, God says to each believer today: Study, ponder, assimilate the word of God! In learning of the mind of God, we become successful in following the ways of God.

Joshua was about to lead a people whose parents had refused to enter the Promised Land a generation earlier because they stood in awe of the size and might of some of the people of Canaan, regarding themselves as grasshoppers by comparison (Num 13:33; cf. Josh 11:21). The Canaanites had not changed, unless they had grown even stronger. Yet God assured Joshua that he would enable him to overcome the might of Canaan.

God concluded his talk with Joshua by repeating his promise. Again, Hebrew word order makes a point; "with you" (1:9) is up front for emphasis: "with you will be Yahweh your God everywhere you go." It is important that God used the personal name Yahweh here. As Israel went into Canaan, they would be fighting people who worshiped Baal, the Canaanite El, and other supposed deities who were expected to give their worshipers victory in battle. By reassuring Joshua that

"Yahweh your God" would be with him, God reminded Joshua that he was more powerful than any god the Canaanites might invoke against Israel, because these really were no gods at all.

◆ 3. Joshua's charge to Israel; Israel's charge to Joshua (1:10-18)

10Joshua then commanded the officers of
Israel, 11"Go through the camp and tell the
people to get their provisions ready. In
three days you will cross the Jordan River
and take possession of the land the LORD
your God is giving you."

12Then Joshua called together the tribes
of Reuben, Gad, and the half-tribe of
Manasseh. He told them, 13"Remember
what Moses, the servant of the LORD, commanded you: 'The LORD your God is giving
you a place of rest. He has given you this
land.' 14Your wives, children, and livestock
may remain here in the land Moses assigned to you on the east side of the Jordan River. But your strong warriors, fully armed, must lead the other tribes across the Jordan to help them conquer their territory. Stay
with them 15until the LORD gives them rest,
as he has given you rest, and until they, too, possess the land the LORD your God is giving them. Only then may you return and settle here on the east side of the Jordan River in the land that Moses, the servant of the LORD, assigned to you."

16They answered Joshua, "We will do
whatever you command us, and we will go
wherever you send us. 17We will obey you
just as we obeyed Moses. And may the LORD your God be with you as he was with
Moses. 18Anyone who rebels against your
orders and does not obey your words and everything you command will be put to death. So be strong and courageous!"

NOTES

1:11 ***In three days.*** God had been ready to bring the parents of these Israelites into the Promised Land from the south about 38 years earlier, but they had refused because of fear and unbelief (Num 13–14). Now, at last, their children would enter from the east, across the Jordan River.

1:12 ***Reuben, Gad, and the half-tribe of Manasseh.*** These tribes had asked and received from Moses the land on the east side of the Jordan, which Israel had taken from the two defeated Amorite kings, Sihon and Og (Num 32:33).

1:13 ***rest.*** This is not only the physical, material rest of a secure, abundant land in which to live, as important as that is; God's intended rest for the people of Israel included the spiritual, cultural, psychological, and emotional rest of a right relationship with God and with God's people. This is a significant theme in Joshua (e.g., 1:15; 21:44; 22:4; 23:1), and indeed throughout the Bible.

this land. Since Israel still was on the east side of the Jordan, all the tribes were at that time within the territory of the two and a half tribes to whom Moses had given it.

1:15 ***rest.*** See note on 1:13.

COMMENTARY

God had appointed Joshua as Moses's successor and had given him encouragement and instruction. Now Joshua began the task of leading God's people (1:10). The officers were to pass along Joshua's orders to the people (1:11). The first order was to prepare rations and other items for travel, something the people were surely experts at doing by this time!

This was the culmination of all the Israelites had hoped for, traveled toward, and even feared for four decades. Now in three days, they would cross the last barrier and enter at last the Land of Promise. To anchor the forward and encourage the backward, Joshua reminded them once again whose enterprise this was: "the LORD [Yahweh] your God" (1:11). Each Israelite individually and all the people collectively were reminded once again that God is a personal God, caring for his people, identifying with them.

Joshua told them to "take possession of the land the LORD your God is giving you" (1:11). The land was the gift of God; God would see that their entering in and taking possession were successful. There would be room neither for human pride of accomplishment nor for human doubt that it could and would be done. This was God's enterprise; this was God's time; Joshua was God's appointed leader. God would accomplish it through Joshua.

The Reubenites, the Gadites, and the half-tribe of Manasseh (1:12) already had received their land in Transjordan from Moses (Num 32:16-19). Now Joshua reminded them of their promise to help their brothers (1:14) gain their inheritance. This is a consistent theme throughout the Bible; we are our brothers' and sisters' keepers. No one is an island; when the bell tolls, it tolls for all of us (to paraphrase John Donne). All Israel together had conquered the territory the Transjordan tribes requested and received from Moses; now they in turn would help their fellow Israelites gain possession of the territory west of the Jordan River.

The Transjordan tribes answered Joshua as they had answered Moses when he gave them the responsibility; they would cross the Jordan and help the rest of Israel gain their inheritance. Their way of putting it may have given Joshua pause. Just as they fully obeyed Moses, so they would obey Joshua (1:17)—a superficial reading of Exodus and Numbers is enough to see that Israel often did not obey Moses very well. But the Transjordanian tribes did cross the Jordan with the rest of Israel, and did not return to their own land and homes until Joshua dismissed them at the end of his campaigns (22:6).

The last words of response to Joshua represent the attitude not only of the eastern tribes, but of all Israel. Just as God had told Joshua at the beginning of this chapter to be strong and very courageous, so now the people said the same thing. Also, they wanted assurance that God would be with Joshua just as he had been with Moses. The crossing of the flooded Jordan a few days later convinced the people that God was with Joshua.

The stipulation that any who disobeyed Joshua would be put to death (1:18) strikes most modern Western readers as harsh and extreme. But we must remember that Israel was entering a time of warfare. Disobedience in wartime can have serious consequences—the deaths of other people, or even, potentially, the defeat and destruction of entire nations. Furthermore, disobedience here would have been not only against Joshua, but against God, Israel's King. Finally, Joshua did not impose this upon Israel's warriors. They imposed it upon themselves, as a measure of how completely they were committing themselves to Joshua's leadership in the upcoming campaign.

B. Joshua Sends Spies into Jericho (2:1-24)

1. Rahab shelters the spies (2:1-7)

**Then Joshua secretly sent out two spies
from the Israelite camp at Acacia Grove.*
He instructed them, "Scout out the land on
the other side of the Jordan River, espe-
cially around Jericho." So the two men set
out and came to the house of a prostitute
named Rahab and stayed there that night.
2 But someone told the king of Jericho,
"Some Israelites have come here tonight
to spy out the land." 3 So the king of Jer-
icho sent orders to Rahab: "Bring out the
men who have come into your house, for
they have come here to spy out the whole
land."
4 Rahab had hidden the two men, but
she replied, "Yes, the men were here ear-
lier, but I didn't know where they were
from. 5 They left the town at dusk, as the
gates were about to close. I don't know
where they went. If you hurry, you can
probably catch up with them." 6 (Actually,
she had taken them up to the roof and
hidden them beneath bundles of flax she
had laid out.) 7 So the king's men went
looking for the spies along the road lead-
ing to the shallow crossings of the Jordan
River. And as soon as the king's men had
left, the gate of Jericho was shut.**

2:1 Hebrew *Shittim.*

NOTES

2:1 *Joshua.* Heb., *yehoshua' bin-nun* [TH5126, ZH5673] (Joshua son of Nun). Use of the longer form of Joshua's name here marks the beginning of his *action* as Israel's commander-in-chief, as its use at 1:1 marks the beginning of his *commissioning* as commander-in-chief. This longer form is not used between these two verses.

Acacia Grove. Heb., *shittim* [TH7851, ZH8850]. Numbers 22:1 says Israel "traveled to the plains of Moab and camped east of the Jordan River, across from Jericho"; Num 25:1 gives the name of the place upon Israel's first arrival there. Here we see Israel still encamped at "Shittim," probably the Abel-shittim of Num 33:49 mg. It has been identified with Tell el-Kefrein (Woudstra 1981:69), or with Tell el-Hammam (Aharoni 1979:34, 429).

especially around Jericho. Or, "even Jericho" or, "that is, Jericho." Since Jericho was to be Israel's first objective once they had crossed the Jordan, there is no reason to suppose Joshua would have sent scouts beyond Jericho until they had taken it.

Jericho. The name probably means "Moon Town," from Heb. *yareakh* [TH3394, ZH3734] (moon). Few today would doubt the identification of Jericho with Tell es-Sultan, a relatively small (about 12 acres) occupation mound, with the copious spring, Ain es-Sultan (also called Ain Elisha), just under its eastern shoulder.

the two men. The Hebrew text of 6:23 refers to them as "young men."

Rahab. The name is *rakhab* [TH7343, ZH8147] (enlarge, make wide), not *rahab* [TH7293, ZH8105] as in Isa 51:9 mg (English "h" is used to represent two different Hebrew letters). Rahab the harlot's name is a short form of a sentence name such as Rahab-el; but the divine name to complete it is absent. The full name would have meant, "Asherah [or Baal? or El?] has enlarged/caused to be wide [the womb]." The name was a prayer for the fertility of the woman bearing it.

2:2 *Some Israelites.* Hebrew was a dialect of Canaanite, a member of the Northwest Semitic cluster of the Semitic family of languages. Speaking the same language, but with small vocabulary and grammatical differences, the men probably gave themselves away by their speech.

to spy out. Here and in 2:3 the verb means to go over the land very carefully, to "dig out" the information that would help Israel succeed in the coming entry and occupation against Canaanite resistance.

2:4 *Rahab had hidden the two men.* Biblical Hebrew does not have a separate pluperfect form, but here as in many other places, the context calls for a pluperfect (past perfect) verb.

2:5 *you can probably catch up with them.* The Hebrew is a bit stronger: "Follow them quickly, for you will catch them" [or, "in order to catch them"]. Rahab's advice implied that the king's messengers did not have time to search her house, or they would miss the men they were seeking.

2:6 *flax.* This is a plant with tall, slender stems, whose fibers are processed to make linen.

2:7 *the gate . . . was shut.* Medium-sized cities like Jericho had one main gate, in which were two large wooden doors, reinforced with bronze. The planks of each door ran horizontally and were set into a vertical timber, which functioned as the door's single hinge. The gate was barred by dropping a large plank across the two doors into metal brackets on the inside. Such a gate (from Iran) has been "reset" in the British Museum.

COMMENTARY

In an approach from the east, Jericho was the key to conquering the southern hill country. It could not be bypassed. As with any good military commander, Joshua needed information about his objective. Joshua sent two men to "scout out the land . . . especially around Jericho" (2:1). They entered Jericho and came into the house of Rahab, who was a prostitute. Evidence from the ancient Near East indicates women innkeepers often were prostitutes (or "madams"). Rahab the harlot was probably also an innkeeper. What kind of house would have been better suited for young strangers to avoid unwanted attention? This does not necessarily mean that they availed themselves of all her "services," though the verb used to state that they "stayed there that night," and the Hebrew of 2:3 ("the men who came in to you") *could* indicate that. The text simply doesn't say. Josephus and the Targums also relate the tradition that Rahab was an innkeeper, as well as a prostitute.

In his message to Rahab (2:3), Jericho's king assumed her loyalty to the Canaanite cause, and assumed she was not aware of the men's mission. But Rahab believed in the divine destiny of Israel, though she knew little of Israel or of Israel's God. She realized Jericho and the rest of the Canaanites were doomed, and she wanted to become a believer in Israel's God. Jericho was a small enough town, and Rahab was knowledgeable and astute enough to know that it was only a matter of time before the king's agents came around to her place, frequented as it was by townsmen and strangers alike. Preparing for that moment, Rahab already had hidden the spies on the flat roof of her house, under the flax stalks she had laid out there to dry.

Rahab's deception leaps out at the modern Western reader. In her own culture, however—and in Israel's, also—"truth" was more importantly defined, not as "agreement with fact," but as "loyalty toward the neighbor and the Lord" (Woudstra 1981:71). Similar examples of such loyalty that involved deceptive speech toward others who intended harm are the Hebrew midwives' reports to Pharaoh that the Hebrew women delivered too quickly for them to carry out his orders (Exod 1:19), and Moses's request of Pharaoh to allow Israel to "take a three-day journey into the wilderness" (Exod 5:3).

City gates were shut for the night and opened again in the morning. By shutting the gates immediately after the pursuers had departed, the authorities were taking a sensible precaution. If the two Israelite scouts had not left the city as Rahab implied, perhaps they would be discovered in Jericho during the night. And wherever the two spies were, there was no need to leave the city open to any other dangers.

◆ 2. Rahab's request for her family (2:8-13)

8Before the spies went to sleep that night, Rahab went up on the roof to talk with them. 9"I know the LORD has given you this land," she told them. "We are all afraid of you. Everyone in the land is living in terror. 10For we have heard how the LORD made a dry path for you through the Red Sea* when you left Egypt. And we know what you did to Sihon and Og, the two Amorite kings east of the Jordan River, whose people you completely destroyed.* 11No wonder our hearts have melted in fear! No one has the courage to fight after hearing such things. For the LORD your God is the supreme God of the heavens above and the earth below.

12"Now swear to me by the LORD that you will be kind to me and my family since I have helped you. Give me some guarantee that 13when Jericho is conquered, you will let me live, along with my father and mother, my brothers and sisters, and all their families."

2:10a Hebrew *sea of reeds.* 2:10b The Hebrew term used here refers to the complete consecration of things or people to the LORD, either by destroying them or by giving them as an offering.

NOTES

2:9 ***the LORD.*** Heb., *yhwh* [TH3068, ZH3378] (Yahweh), the personal name by which God revealed himself to Moses at the burning bush (Exod 3:14-15). This is the beginning of Rahab's declaration of her faith in Yahweh.

living in terror. Lit., "are melting."

2:10 ***Sihon and Og, the two Amorite kings east of the Jordan River.*** Their kingdoms had been conquered earlier under Moses's leadership, as related in Num 21:21-35.

you completely destroyed. This is the first use in Joshua of the Hebrew term *kharam* [TH2763, ZH3049]; see NLT mg on 2:10b, and commentary on 6:24-27.

2:11 ***melted in fear!*** Though a different verb, it is a synonym of the one in 2:9.

the LORD your God. Lit., "Yahweh your God." As in 2:9, Rahab again used the divine name in her declaration of faith in Israel's God.

2:12 ***you will be kind . . . I have helped.*** Lit., "I have done *khesed* . . . you will do *khesed*." *Khesed* [TH2617, ZH2876] includes "loyalty" (a common translation), to be sure, but *khesed* is much more than "mere" loyalty (see commentary on 2:14).

some guarantee. Lit., "a sign of faithfulness," i.e., "a sure (or faithful) sign."

2:13 ***and all their families.*** Lit., "and all that belongs to them." This would have included all their relatives, as well as servants, employees, and even others—potentially, many more persons.

COMMENTARY

Rahab's statements to the spies indicate how much God's acts on Israel's behalf, even a generation earlier, had inspired fear in Canaan's inhabitants. Forty years previously, God had parted the waters of the Red Sea when Israel seemed trapped by Pharaoh and his chariots. The Egyptians, attempting to follow, had been drowned when the walls of water collapsed upon them and the sea returned to normal (Exod 14:21-31). Israel's defeat of the armies of Sihon and Og only months previously (Num 21:21-35) was recognized by Rahab and the other citizens of Jericho as the work of a God much greater than their own.

Rahab's statement was her personal confession of faith in Yahweh. It may be translated in full, "Yahweh your God, He is God in the heavens above and upon the earth beneath" (2:11). Her faith declaration, proven genuine by her aid to Joshua's scouts, brought Rahab into the people of God, despite her Canaanite birth and her occupation. Throughout the Torah, references to the *ger* [TH1616, ZH1731] ("resident alien," "sojourner," "foreigner"; cf. Exod 12:38; Lev 17:8; Deut 1:16; 16:11, 14), which deal with their rights or responsibilities in Israel, show an expectation that many of them were proselytes or that their descendants would become so. One implication of Deuteronomy 23:3 is that people other than Ammonites and Moabites could and did "convert" to Israel's God and worship more readily than descendants of those two peoples. From Israel's entrance into Canaan, Rahab and her family were just the first of many who would join Israel. Though Canaan as a whole was under judgment (cf. Gen 15:16), some were delivered by their faith in Israel's God.

Rahab's faith was memorialized centuries later in the New Testament tradition. In Jesus' genealogy (Matt 1:5-6) Matthew celebrated Rahab as the wife of Salmon, mother of Boaz, and great-great-grandmother of David, ancient Israel's greatest king. Together with Sarah, Rahab was one of only two women mentioned by name in the great faith "hall of fame" recital (Heb 11:31). Perhaps most amazingly, James held Rahab up together with Abraham as an example of living faith demonstrated by works (Jas 2:25-26).

Rahab's report of Jericho's terror at Israel's coming (2:9-11) reminds us of the dismay of the 10 Israelite spies and the people who heard their report about the people of Canaan. The spies had said, "Next to them we felt like grasshoppers, and that's what they thought, too" (Num 13:33). Most of Israel's men had responded in fear: "Our wives and our little ones will be carried off as plunder" (Num 14:3). All the while, the Canaanites had been trembling at this people whom God was bringing to judge them (2:9).

We also are God's people, called to journey with God by faith, called to assail the strongholds of the enemy with the liberating Good News of redemption in Jesus Christ. How often have we trembled in fear, not realizing or not remembering that our adversaries quake before the mighty deeds and the amazing grace of "the supreme God of the heavens above and the earth below" (2:11).

◆ 3. The oath and the rope as signs (2:14-24)

14"We offer our own lives as a guarantee for your safety," the men agreed. "If you don't betray us, we will keep our promise and be kind to you when the LORD gives us the land."

15Then, since Rahab's house was built into the town wall, she let them down by a rope through the window. 16"Escape to the hill country," she told them. "Hide there for three days from the men

searching for you. Then, when they have
returned, you can go on your way."
17 Before they left, the men told her,
"We will be bound by the oath we have
taken only if you follow these instruc-
tions. 18 When we come into the land, you
must leave this scarlet rope hanging from
the window through which you let us
down. And all your family members—your
father, mother, brothers, and all your
relatives—must be here inside the house.
19 If they go out into the street and are
killed, it will not be our fault. But if any-
one lays a hand on people inside this
house, we will accept the responsibility
for their death. 20 If you betray us, how-
ever, we are not bound by this oath in
any way."
21 "I accept your terms," she replied. And
she sent them on their way, leaving the
scarlet rope hanging from the window.
22 The spies went up into the hill coun-
try and stayed there three days. The men
who were chasing them searched every-
where along the road, but they finally re-
turned without success.
23 Then the two spies came down from
the hill country, crossed the Jordan River,
and reported to Joshua all that had hap-
pened to them. 24 "The LORD has given us
the whole land," they said, "for all the
people in the land are terrified of us."

NOTES

2:14 ***we will . . . be kind to you.*** Lit., "we will do to you loving-kindness and faithfulness," i.e., "we will deal with you in faithful loving-kindness."

2:15 ***built into the town wall.*** City walls were expensive to build and to maintain. Thus, ancient walled cities were compact and crowded; it was relatively common to build private houses utilizing the city wall as part of their own architecture. The archaeological excavations of Jericho show it had an inner and an outer defensive wall on different levels of the slope on which the city wall was built. Rahab's house was inside the lower (revetment) wall, but outside the upper (parapet) wall. Thus, she could hide the men on the flat roof of her house (2:6) and also let them down through her window, down the outer side of the city wall (Wood 1990a:56). (Earlier suggestions that Jericho's walls at this time were of the common casemate construction do not seem to be borne out by Wood's reassessment of the evidence on the ground.)

2:16 ***Escape to the hill country.*** Westward to the edge of the hills of central Canaan (which begin their steep rise just west of Jericho) was the last direction the king's agents would have expected the two scouts to go because Israel's camp lay eastward across the Jordan.

for three days. This time frame is not necessarily in conflict with Joshua's instructions of 1:11 that Israel would cross the Jordan River in three days. It is possible Joshua had "sent out [the] two spies" (2:1) *before* that announcement to the camp of Israel. Alternatively, Joshua's plan to cross the Jordan in three days may have been delayed by a day or more. "Three days" may even have been an idiomatic way of saying "soon" (or "recently," when referring to the recent past), as it often is elsewhere.

2:17 ***Before they left.*** This is implied, rather than stated, in the Hebrew text (see commentary).

2:18 ***you must leave.*** Lit., "you must tie."

this scarlet rope. This is the first mention of the color of the rope. Woudstra (1981:75) suggests the scouts may have brought the rope with them.

2:19 ***If they go . . . their death.*** The formulaic statement is literally, "His blood [will be] on his own head," and "His blood [will be] on our head." This is a standard biblical way of stating responsibility for someone's safety or, alternatively, for that person's death. The spies accepted responsibility for any and all of Rahab's family who remained with her in her house. However, if anyone were to leave her house before Jericho was taken, that one would be responsible for his or her own death.

2:21 ***leaving the scarlet rope.*** Lit., "She tied the scarlet rope in the window."

2:22 ***three days.*** See note on 2:16.

everywhere along the road. This implies the king's agents looked mostly or exclusively in the direction of the Jordan, as Rahab had suggested they should.

2:24 ***all the people in the land are terrified of us.*** The scouts reported to Joshua exactly what Rahab had told them, using the verb Rahab had used, *mug* [TH4127, ZH4570] (to melt).

COMMENTARY

More than a third of this chapter details the provisions of the scouts' oath to spare the lives of Rahab and her family. This demonstrates Rahab's faith in Israel and in Israel's God. It also shows the seriousness of an oath taken in God's name. The author reported in his account of the conquest of Jericho that Joshua did take his men's oath seriously, and dispatched these two to see that Rahab and her family were spared (6:22).

The text implies that only Rahab knew of the scout's mission; as long as she kept their secret, they were bound by their oath to her, sworn in Yahweh's name at her request. Then, when the Israelite forces actually entered Jericho, safety for Rahab's family lay in their staying inside her house. Any who wandered outside, or who came out prematurely, thinking the fighting was over when it wasn't, had no one to blame but themselves if they died.

This may serve us as a timely reminder. In many life situations, we are afforded a refuge, a safe house, by God's grace. But just as Rahab's family found refuge only as they actually made their way to her house and entered it, so we must accept the gift of God's grace. A gift accepted is no less a gift, but a gift unaccepted is not ours.

Rahab had used the Hebrew words *khesed* [TH2617, ZH2876] and *'emet* [TH571, ZH622] in her request (2:12, see notes). In their reply, the young men responded accordingly, using these same two words (2:14). *Khesed* is best translated "loving-kindness," that is, love and kindness going beyond obligation or duty. *'Emet* is "faithfulness, truth." These are the most important characteristics of God, if we reckon by the number of times they are used of God in the Hebrew Scriptures. God's people should reflect God's character. In Joshua 2 we see two of God's people promising to act in character with God—that is, in "faithful loving-kindness"—in their dealings with Rahab.

The timing and sequence of some of the dialogue and some of the action of this chapter can be confused if we are not careful. Rahab hid Joshua's scouts under bundles of flax on her roof before the king's agents appeared at her door. After they left, but before the scouts had gone to sleep, she went back up to the roof to talk with them, and make their arrangements for the future. We may assume they slept a few hours, then Rahab let them down the wall outside her window in the dead of night, by the scarlet rope either she or they had provided. This scenario avoids the precarious assumption that all the arrangements were made while the two scouts dangled on the rope, below the window but several feet (at least) above the ground below them. The tenses of the Hebrew verbs in the narrative give us perfect freedom to picture the scenes this way.

As for the rope, Rahab may have left it tied to the window frame from that night on. No one could have seen it from inside the city. Alternatively, the grammar of the narrative does not require that Rahab left the rope tied in her window that night. She could have removed it then, and replaced it later, at any time during the first six days of Israel's march around Jericho. The text of 2:18 says simply, "she tied" it.

The scarlet rope (2:18, 21) often has been interpreted as a type of redemption in Christ, of our escape from the doom of sin's judgment through his blood, shed on Calvary's cross. There is nothing wrong with this symbolic understanding if we don't press it to make the text say more than it intends to say and if we don't allow the metaphorical understanding to obscure the very real deliverance Rahab found in God's grace mediated through the two young Israelite spies.

Joshua sent the spies to gather military intelligence of strategic and/or tactical importance. They brought him more. Their report of the fear possessing the people of Jericho surely raised the spirits and morale of the Israelites, about to cross the Jordan and engage the Canaanites in the battles their parents had died in the wilderness to avoid.

◆ C. Israel's Crossing of the Jordan (3:1–5:1)

1. Preparations for crossing the Jordan (3:1-8)

Early the next morning Joshua and all the
Israelites left Acacia Grove* and arrived at
the banks of the Jordan River, where they
camped before crossing. [2]Three days later
the Israelite officers went through the
camp, [3]giving these instructions to the
people: "When you see the Levitical
priests carrying the Ark of the Covenant
of the LORD your God, move out from your
positions and follow them. [4]Since you
have never traveled this way before, they
will guide you. Stay about a half mile*
behind them, keeping a clear distance be-
tween you and the Ark. Make sure you
don't come any closer."
[5]Then Joshua told the people, "Purify
yourselves, for tomorrow the LORD will do
great wonders among you."
[6]In the morning Joshua said to the
priests, "Lift up the Ark of the Covenant
and lead the people across the river." And
so they started out and went ahead of
the people.
[7]The LORD told Joshua, "Today I will
begin to make you a great leader in the
eyes of all the Israelites. They will know
that I am with you, just as I was with
Moses. [8]Give this command to the priests
who carry the Ark of the Covenant:
'When you reach the banks of the Jordan
River, take a few steps into the river and
stop there.' "

3:1 Hebrew *Shittim.* 3:4 Hebrew *about 2,000 cubits* [920 meters].

NOTES

3:1 ***Acacia Grove.*** See note on 2:1.

arrived at the banks of the Jordan. If the identification of Acacia Grove (*shittim* [TH7851, ZH8850]) as the modern Tel el-Hammam in Jordan is correct, it was about 8 miles east of the Jordan River, an easy day's journey.

3:2 ***Three days later.*** This period is not the three-day period of 1:11, nor that of 2:16, 22 (see note on 2:16).

3:3 ***the Ark of the Covenant of the Lord.*** This was a chest of acacia wood, nearly four feet long by just over two feet wide and two feet high, overlaid inside and out with gold. The Ark was the only furnishing of the Holy of Holies, the Tabernacle's most sacred room and God's dwelling place among Israel. God was said to occupy the mercy seat (covering) between the two cherubim of gold surmounting the Ark; thus, it was the most holy of the Tabernacle's furnishings. Whenever Israel moved, a contingent of priests led them, carrying the Ark (Exod 25:13-15; Num 10:33-36).

3:4 ***about a half mile.*** Lit., "about two thousand cubits." A cubit was about 18 inches; two thousand cubits, then, was about 3,000 feet, not quite six-tenths of a mile, not quite one kilometer.

3:5 ***Purify yourselves.*** Lit., "Make yourselves holy," or "Separate yourselves."

3:8 ***Give.*** The first Hebrew word in this verse is actually "you." It should therefore be translated: "*Now as for you*, give this command." God had just reassured Joshua of God's presence with him. Now as for *Joshua*, he was to *respond* in faith to God's firm reassurance.

COMMENTARY

The account of Israel's crossing of the Jordan occupies two chapters, in keeping with the prominence of God's actions on Israel's behalf throughout the narrative. The length and detail of this account also is important evidence that the author's primary interest in the book of Joshua is not the military history of the conquest, but its theological or faith history.

As we have seen in the story of Rahab and the two scouts, the narrative does not proceed in smooth chronological order. The narrator hints at events early on that he only unfolds later; he fills in details later that could have come earlier, but which, by their postponed entry into the story heighten its dramatic effect; he delays reporting a climactic event, heightening the reader's anticipation; he repeats details and even refers again to events already reported. All these, far from being "disjointed" (Pressler 2002:28-30), or being evidence for clashing story lines, are the artistic touches of the master narrator.

The crossing of the Jordan is emphasized because of its nature as a turning point in the life of Israel. The crossing meant this generation would not turn back, as their parents had. Under Joshua, and by the power of God, Israel really would occupy the land promised for so long. This crossing became a spiritual and psychological entrance as well as a physical one. Central to the account is the role of the priests bearing the Ark of the Covenant as they led the people in entering the Jordan and then standing in the river bed as the people crossed. The Ark, a visible symbol of God's presence, was a further reminder this was a divine, not a human, enterprise.

God had appointed Joshua leader of Israel following the death of Moses; the people had accepted Joshua's leadership. His first task was to get them across the Jordan River. Joshua now knew the conditions in Jericho and, thanks to the good work of his two scouts, he also knew the state of mind of Jericho's citizens. It was time for Israel to move.

Joshua had Israel camp at the bank of the Jordan for three days, yet not until 3:15 is the reader told the Jordan was in flood this time of year; for dramatic effect, that information was not revealed earlier in the story. But already it occurs to the reader to wonder why Joshua did not have Israel cross the day after they reached the Jordan. Part of the answer, mundane but realistic, is that last-minute repairs, inventories, repacking, and other physical preparations were necessary. The wanderings were over; this was a new enterprise.

A more important reason for the pause was to let Israel experience close-up the impossibility of crossing the Jordan. For three days and nights they camped beside the swollen river, knowing they were to cross it soon, but knowing, too, that crossing it while it was at flood stage was humanly impossible. God had led Israel to this point. Israel needed a dramatic reminder that they could go further only if and as God led them on.

"You have never traveled this way before" (3:4) was true of most journeys in Israel's 40 years in the Sinai. But it was of immeasurably greater significance now that the way referred to was the way across the Jordan into the Promised Land. The truth of this statement helps explain the power of the metaphor of pilgrimage in the life and thinking of God's people from that time until today. On one level, the life of every believer is a series of familiar journeys: to church, to work, to market, etc. But at a deeper level we, like ancient Israel, travel every day a way we have not been before. Though our physical surroundings usually are familiar, our real "journey" is not. We, too, are following God with each step.

The Ark of the Covenant symbolized God's throne. Thus, Israel knew God led them because they saw the Ark going before them. The leading groups in Israel's march were to leave a gap of more than half a mile between themselves and the Ark. Though God is present among his people in grace and mercy, God's people are not to take his presence for granted. God is holy, and God's people acknowledge his holiness with reverence, respect, and awe; the old terminology for this is the "fear" of God.

The officers had given the people their instructions for the next day's crossing of the Jordan. But Joshua himself gave the most important directive: "Purify yourselves" (3:5). God intended to bring across the Jordan a holy people, who had separated themselves *to* Yahweh, the God of Israel, and *from* all the gods of their neighbors. This involved ritual acts of purification from all that was unclean, all that would bar an Israelite from coming into the presence of God in the Tabernacle. For this crossing of the Jordan, Israel was to be pure before God, as when they came into his sanctuary. In one sense, only God can sanctify. But to be holy is to be separate to God, and God will not sanctify us (i.e., separate us to himself) against our will. Only as we separate ourselves *to* God, and *from* everything else that would be god in our lives—responding to God's initiative, and in God's strength, to be sure—will God sanctify us, filling us with his Spirit.

With his command to the priests (3:6), Joshua launched the enterprise. Everything to this point had been preparatory. Now God would begin to fulfill his promises to the patriarchs and bring their descendants to possess the land in which they themselves had been resident aliens.

One of God's purposes was to lift up Joshua (3:7)—not to heighten his ego, but to reassure the people. Moses was the only leader Israel had known; now they had lost him just as they were embarking on the most difficult, dangerous, and important part of this enterprise. They needed reassurance that God had not brought them this far to abandon them on the doorstep of success. God's words reassured Joshua personally, too, for they repeated the promise God already had given him (1:5).

For this crossing of the Jordan, the Ark was to lead the way until the feet of the priests were actually in the water. The priests were not to stop on the dry bank, but in the river itself. Israel had no way to cross the Jordan in flood, yet God commanded them to cross. By carrying the Ark into the water first, the priests would show their faith, or at least their obedience. We may go further and say that when God clearly directs his people to act, obedience *is* faith.

2. Joshua's promise of a miracle (3:9-13)

**9 So Joshua told the Israelites, "Come and
listen to what the LORD your God says.
10 Today you will know that the living God
is among you. He will surely drive out the
Canaanites, Hittites, Hivites, Perizzites,
Girgashites, Amorites, and Jebusites
ahead of you. 11 Look, the Ark of the Cov-
enant, which belongs to the Lord of the
whole earth, will lead you across the Jor-
dan River! 12 Now choose twelve men from
the tribes of Israel, one from each tribe.
13 The priests will carry the Ark of the
LORD, the Lord of all the earth. As soon as
their feet touch the water, the flow of wa-
ter will be cut off upstream, and the river
will stand up like a wall."**

NOTES

3:10 ***Canaanites.*** These were the people living in the coastal areas and in some of the valleys and plains. Sometimes this term includes all the ethnic groups that were living in the land when Israel entered.

Hivites, Perizzites, Girgashites. Many suggestions have been made, but in the larger picture we can be certain only that these ethnic groups were in some parts of the hill country, probably from before Abraham's time (cf. Gen 15:20-21), until their absorption as Israel became established in the land.

Amorites. In this context these were primarily the other pre-Israelite peoples of the hill country; in other contexts, "Amorite," with or without "Canaanite," can be a more comprehensive term.

Jebusites. These were the people who lived in (or near) the city-state of Jerusalem; Israel did not conquer them permanently until David's time (2 Sam 5).

3:11 ***will lead you across the Jordan River!*** Lit., "will pass before you *into* the Jordan." The emphasis is not yet upon getting *across* the river, but on encouraging the priest's faith to step *into* the flood-swollen stream. Their faith-action of stepping in would precede their witnessing of the miraculous stopping of the waters.

3:13 ***As soon as their feet touch the water.*** Lit., "As soon as the soles of [their] feet rest upon the waters of the Jordan." Joshua's phrasing emphasized the abruptness with which the waters would be stopped, even though the Jordan was in its spring flood stage. It would be obvious to all that God's act here was dramatic and miraculous.

COMMENTARY

Joshua summoned Israel to hear his final instructions, referring to God as "your God," another small way to encourage the faith of the anxious or the fearful. All who had been adults when Moses led Israel out of Egypt had died. Those who now entered Canaan with Joshua remembered those events dimly, if at all. The people needed to know that the events of this day would be a sign of God's presence with them, and of God's intention to fulfill his promises to their ancestors and to them.

In Canaan, Israel would live among pagan polytheistic neighbors. They would be tempted to join them in worship of their gods and goddesses. The phrase "the living God" (3:10) reminded them that only Yahweh lives, that this living God was among them, not far off or inaccessible. By contrast, all other gods are dead or inanimate objects, created beings, or abstractions of created beings—none is worthy of worship. The phrase "the Lord of the whole earth" (3:11), is another reminder that God is no local, limited deity, as most of the gods of the ancient world were conceived by their worshipers. Since the Ark of the Covenant would be going ahead of Israel, they would know that their God, the God of all the earth, was leading them into Canaan.

But there is more here. The full statement, "the Ark of the Covenant, which belongs to the Lord of the whole earth, will lead you across the Jordan" (see note on 3:11), was to be the sign by which Israel would know the living God was among them and that he would "surely drive out" the inhabitants of Canaan before them (3:10). The question for the modern reader is: How could the entry of the Ark into the Jordan ahead of Israel signify all that?

We must remember two things: (1) the Canaanites worshiped Baal as their principal god; (2) the Ark of the Covenant was the physical symbol of Yahweh's (God's) real presence with Israel. Thus, in the eyes of the Canaanites and perhaps, too, in the eyes of many in Israel, Israel's God Yahweh was challenging Canaan's god Baal to prove rightful ownership of the land.

In popular Canaanite belief and practice, Baal was the most powerful of the gods and ruled Canaan itself because he had defeated in battle Yam, the god of the sea. Dealing with Canaan on their own terms, Yahweh was about to show—by entering the flooded Jordan, stopping its waters, and allowing his people Israel to cross—that he is the true God with power over mighty waters. Canaan already had heard a report of such an event at the Red Sea (2:10), and that report still melted their hearts with fear a generation after God's mighty act. In ancient polytheistic thinking, nations won battles on the earth because their patron gods won battles in the cosmos. If Yahweh, God of Israel, could defeat and bend so easily to his purposes the power of the river-god in full flood, what would he do to Baal? What, then, would Yahweh's people do to Canaan?

A further aspect of this demonstration on Canaan's own theological terms revolves around the belief that rivers were deities eminently suited to render judgment. Trial by water sometimes was practiced in capital cases. A person accused of a crime was ordered to be thrown into the river. If the person drowned, she or he was guilty; if the accused were innocent, she or he would survive the river ordeal unharmed (cf. *Code of Hammurabi* 2.132). The gods, too, were thought to act in judgment on one another. By surviving the crossing of the river when it was at its strongest, Yahweh demonstrated the rightness of his cause and of his claim to the land of Canaan over the claims of Baal or of any other Canaanite "deity."

The people of Canaan could not be convinced of Yahweh's preeminence on monotheistic grounds because they worshiped many gods. (Monotheism is the belief there is one God only, such as is held in Judaism and Christianity.) However, a successful crossing of the flooded Jordan by Yahweh and his people would be a convincing demonstration of Yahweh's power, according to Canaan's own polytheistic way of understanding. By that same thinking, the crossing of the Jordan would establish the justice of Yahweh's claim to the land of Canaan.

Joshua repeated "the Lord of all the earth" because repetition means emphasis; it was crucial that Israel learn that God is the universal, transcendent God. Just as important, this means God is Lord, not only over humans, but over nature, including the Jordan at flood stage. As Israel entered a land where the dominant culture regarded the river as a god barring Israel's entrance, God showed himself to be Lord over the river at its strongest, cutting off its waters and letting his people in.

◆ 3. Crossing on the Jordan's dry bed (3:14-17)

**14So the people left their camp to cross
the Jordan, and the priests who were carrying the Ark of the Covenant went ahead
of them. 15It was the harvest season, and
the Jordan was overflowing its banks. But as soon as the feet of the priests who were carrying the Ark touched the water
at the river's edge, 16the water above that
point began backing up a great distance away at a town called Adam, which is near Zarethan. And the water below that point flowed on to the Dead Sea* until the riverbed was dry. Then all the people crossed over near the town of Jericho.**

17Meanwhile, the priests who were carrying the Ark of the LORD's Covenant stood on dry ground in the middle of the riverbed as the people passed by. They waited there until the whole nation of Israel had crossed the Jordan on dry ground.

3:16 Hebrew *the sea of the Arabah, the Salt Sea.*

NOTES

3:15 ***the harvest season.*** At Jericho, the barley and wheat harvest usually stretched from early March to late May (Hareuveni 1980:52-53).

the Jordan was overflowing its banks. In the lower Jordan, this resulted from the spring runoff of the winter's rainfall and snowfall (the latter especially from Mount Hermon) in the valleys of the Jordan, the Yarmuk, and the Jabbok rivers.

3:16 ***Adam . . . near Zarethan.*** Adam, modern Damiya, is about 19 miles upstream from Jericho. Zarethan has not been positively identified.

the Dead Sea. The Hebrew text has "the Sea of the Arabah," followed by a scribal note incorporated into the text, "[that is,] the Salt Sea," the normal biblical Hebrew name for this body of water. The name "Dead Sea" is not used in the OT.

near the town of Jericho. Lit., "facing Jericho," i.e., in full view of anyone on the watch atop Jericho's east-facing defensive wall. God's people did not sneak into the land God had promised them.

3:17 ***the whole nation.*** Heb., *kol-haggoy;* here and again in 4:1, *goy* [TH1471, ZH1580] is used of Israel, which is rare. Usually, *goy* designates foreign nations or peoples. Here, the emphasis is on Israel as an ethnic and political entity, rather than as the chosen people of God in a religious sense.

COMMENTARY

Ancient Near Eastern annalists and historians often employed a narrative sequence of command, performance, and (sometimes) report. Following this pattern, the writer of Joshua related God's commands to Joshua, and Joshua's to the people, about crossing the Jordan. He then immediately recorded that Joshua and the people had done as instructed; the command must be seen to have its fulfillment. This technique, combined with the nonchronological sequencing of significant narrative elements discussed above, is not always easy for modern readers to understand.

Furthermore, in the Hebrew text, 3:14-16 is one sentence, and its main verbs come only in 3:16. Though many words and phrases are repetitions from the previous paragraph's command, it would be a mistake to hurry over this paragraph. The author also included new information, both because it is important, and to avoid monotony in the story. This long sentence tells us that the water stopped flowing from upstream as soon as the feet of the priests who were carrying the Ark of the Covenant touched the edge of the Jordan's overflowing waters (3:15-16). Yet the priests themselves continued to move forward until they were standing in the middle of the Jordan's normal bed (3:17). Then all the people crossed, passing by the priests who stood still once they had reached the middle.

The long sentence also reveals the water stopped flowing "a great distance away at a town called Adam, which is near Zarethan" (3:16). The usual naturalistic explanation is that the Jordan's flow was blocked by an earth dam. The earth dam was created by a landslide from the Jordan's banks, probably triggered by an earthquake. Historically, the banks of the Jordan at Adam/Damiyeh have been liable to being undercut by the current more than at many other places. Earth dams created by landslides (some triggered by earthquakes) have occurred in AD 1160, 1267, 1546, 1834, 1906, and 1927; they have stopped the Jordan's flow from 16 hours up to two days (Wood 1990a:54; quoting Nur, referencing Garstang). Did God stop the Jordan's waters on Israel's behalf in the same way? Since we cannot verify a natural cause for that stoppage, there is no historical certainty that there was one. God can and sometimes does act without utilizing natural means. That natural earth dams have stopped the Jordan's flow six times in the last 900 years, however, would suggest that perhaps Joshua's stoppage, too, resulted from an earthquake triggering a landslide at Adam, since this is precisely the location mentioned in the account.

If this explanation is accepted, was the stopping of the Jordan still a miracle? If we define a miracle as God's unusual (though not always supernatural) intervention in earthly events for God's glory and the benefit of God's people, then it was. With the Jordan in flood, Israel could not have crossed by any human means available to them. Just as God has the right to choose whether or not to intervene, so God has the right to choose whether to intervene by natural or by supernatural means. Either way, it was a miracle in the biblical sense, for the modern distinction between God's supernatural acts and those involving his extraordinary providence was not known to the biblical writers.

However we may explain it, two wonders occurred; first, the water began backing up at Adam. Whatever the cause, the effect was that the waters of the Jordan were dammed up at this spot. The second wonder, caused by the first, occurred downstream. The Jordan had been well over its normal banks; then the entire course of the river, including its normal bed, which carries water year-round, became dry! That, too, would have been a most unusual sight. The phrase "on dry ground," repeated twice in 3:17, emphasizes once again the extraordinary nature of this event.

This emphasizes, too, the *effectiveness* of God's intervention. The bed of the Jordan was so dry and firm that the priests could stand in the middle of it without slipping or falling, and all the people, even the elderly, the infirm, and parents carrying infants, could cross safely. *When God acts, God acts effectively.*

◆ 4. The memorial stones (4:1-9)

**When all the people had crossed the Jor-
dan, the LORD said to Joshua, 2"Now
choose twelve men, one from each tribe.
3Tell them, 'Take twelve stones from the
very place where the priests are standing
in the middle of the Jordan. Carry them
out and pile them up at the place where
you will camp tonight.' "**

**4So Joshua called together the twelve
men he had chosen—one from each of the
tribes of Israel. 5He told them, "Go into
the middle of the Jordan, in front of the
Ark of the LORD your God. Each of you
must pick up one stone and carry it out on
your shoulder—twelve stones in all, one
for each of the twelve tribes of Israel. 6We
will use these stones to build a memorial.
In the future your children will ask you,
'What do these stones mean?' 7Then you
can tell them, 'They remind us that the
Jordan River stopped flowing when the
Ark of the LORD's Covenant went across.'
These stones will stand as a memorial
among the people of Israel forever."**

**8So the men did as Joshua had com-
manded them. They took twelve stones
from the middle of the Jordan River, one
for each tribe, just as the LORD had told
Joshua. They carried them to the place
where they camped for the night and con-
structed the memorial there.**

**9Joshua also set up another pile of
twelve stones in the middle of the Jordan,
at the place where the priests who carried
the Ark of the Covenant were standing.
And they are there to this day.**

NOTES

4:1 ***all the people.*** See note on 3:17.

4:2 ***Now choose.*** Lit., "Take"; Joshua was to "take" the 12 men previously chosen (3:12), and give them the task for which they had been chosen.

twelve men. Jacob's 12 sons were the ancestors of the 12 tribes of Israel. However, the tribe of Levi was consecrated to the priesthood and the service of the Tabernacle; its families were to be settled in designated cities throughout the territories of the other tribes to be teachers of the Torah (ch 21). To complete the number of 12 tribes for the settlement of the land, Joseph was divided into two (half-)tribes, Ephraim and Manasseh, named after Joseph's two sons.

4:5 ***on your shoulder.*** The men were to choose stones large enough to require the strength of their legs and backs to carry them. Each stone could have weighed 100 pounds or more. When I first lived in the Middle East as a student in the 1960s and 1970s (Turkey, Egypt, Israel), I often used to see a variety of such large and heavy items carried this way, on the porter's upper back and/or shoulder.

4:6 ***a memorial.*** Lit., "a sign in your midst." The heap of stones would be a sign, a reminder, a memorial, of what God had done for Israel that day.

What do these stones mean? Lit., "What are these stones *to you?*" The pronoun is plural; every Israelite that day participated personally in this great event. In years to come, each would have opportunities in many different settings to relate their memories personally, besides the regular occasions of community and national remembrance.

4:7 ***as a memorial.*** Or, "as a remembrance."

4:9 ***another pile of twelve stones.*** "Another" is a translation that resembles those of the LXX and Vulgate. The Hebrew text does not say "another," though the straightforward meaning of this verse is that this is another memorial—in addition to the one already mentioned in 4:8 (see commentary).

COMMENTARY

Many commentators have struggled with this chapter, as well as the chapter's relationship with chapter 3, thinking perhaps too much in Western narrative categories and customs, and making the whole account more complicated than necessary. Woudstra's advice (1981:90) is excellent: "if the chief purpose of ch 4, the erection of the memorial stones, is kept in mind, the apparent lack of order and of composition, which many have thought to characterize the account at this point, ceases to be a pressing problem."

In the Hebrew text, the first clause of this passage repeats the last clause of the preceding passage, "[When] the whole nation had completed the crossing of the Jordan," a literary technique tying the two narratives together, to show that the second is intended to follow the first. But chapter 4 is not a sequel. The first section (4:1-9) brings the reader back to the 12 tribal representatives of 3:12 and their task of gathering stones. Likewise, 4:10-18 reports the movements of the priests who carried the Ark. Both paragraphs fill in details that would have distracted from the straightforward narrative of chapter 3. Only in 4:19-24, then, does the author recount Israel's arrival at Gilgal and the setting up of the 12 stones as a teaching memorial.

Moreover, chapter 4 contains a classic example of the literary pattern (already noted) of command, execution, and report. God told Joshua what to do (4:1-3); Joshua relayed the command to the stone bearers representing the 12 tribes, amplifying it to reveal to them its purpose (4:4-7); then, by way of a satisfying climax for the ancient reader/hearer, the author reports: "the men did as Joshua had commanded them" (4:8).

The modern reader who is tempted to find the account too repetitious is nevertheless invited to reflect on the faithfulness both of God and of God's ancient people. God was, is, and always will be faithful; God's people were, are, and always will be invited to respond in trust and obedience. This report of Israel's faithful response encourages our own faithful response to God. We are reminded by the repetitions in the account that many of life's most important lessons—this surely is one—we begin to learn early, and we continue to learn often. As is also common when repetition occurs in ancient narrative literature, new elements are added. From Joshua's instructions to the stone bearers, they (and we) learned the stones were "to build a memorial" (4:6), a teaching device to instruct their children in the great things God had done for Israel.

It cost the 12 unnamed Israelite men who carried the stones from the bed of the Jordan a good deal of effort, and most probably some pain, to bring those stones to the site where the memorial would be erected. But their memorial would be worth its cost. So shall we find our memorials to be worth their cost as they help our children to make the faith their own.

If 4:9 reports *another* memorial of 12 stones in the middle of the Jordan itself, as it seems to, then that memorial was submerged beneath the waters of the Jordan as soon as they resumed their flow, only becoming partially visible again in the dry summer season, when the volume of the Jordan's flow decreased. One reason to think Joshua really did build a memorial *in* the Jordan, in addition to the one at Gilgal, is the prominence of the Ark in this account. One could summarize the point of view in both chapters 3 and 4 as follows: This is the account of the Ark of God crossing the Jordan—oh, and by the way, God brought Israel across with him. It would have been only natural for Joshua to mark the exact spot all Israel had seen and passed the Ark as they crossed this second "uncrossable" body of water by God's gracious power exercised on their behalf.

5. Resumption of the Jordan's flow (4:10-18)

[10]The priests who were carrying the Ark
stood in the middle of the river until all
of the LORD's commands that Moses had
given to Joshua were carried out. Mean-
while, the people hurried across the river-
bed. [11]And when everyone was safely on
the other side, the priests crossed over
with the Ark of the LORD as the people
watched.

[12]The armed warriors from the tribes
of Reuben, Gad, and the half-tribe of
Manasseh led the Israelites across the
Jordan, just as Moses had directed. [13]These
armed men—about 40,000 strong—were
ready for battle, and the LORD was with
them as they crossed over to the plains of
Jericho.

[14]That day the LORD made Joshua a
great leader in the eyes of all the Israelites,
and for the rest of his life they revered him
as much as they had revered Moses.

[15]The LORD had said to Joshua, [16]"Com-
mand the priests carrying the Ark of the
Covenant* to come up out of the river-
bed." [17]So Joshua gave the command. [18]As
soon as the priests carrying the Ark of the
LORD's Covenant came up out of the river-
bed and their feet were on high ground,
the water of the Jordan returned and
overflowed its banks as before.

4:16 Hebrew *Ark of the Testimony.*

NOTES

4:10 ***commands that Moses had given.*** This is the first intimation that some of Joshua's instruction for this day's events had come from Moses, rather than directly to Joshua from God.

4:12 ***Reuben, Gad, and . . . Manasseh.*** Israel had conquered the territories of Sihon and Og east of the Jordan (Num 21:21-35). Moses had given these tribes permission to settle those eastern territories if they would help the rest of Israel on the west of the Jordan when the time came (Num 32:20-33). Now they began to keep their promise to Moses.

4:13 ***about 40,000 strong.*** According to the tribal tallies of the second census (Num 26), as they stand now in the Hebrew text, the total number of warriors for Reuben, Gad, and the half of Manasseh settled east of the Jordan was about 110,000. For a variety of weighty reasons, most scholars view these numbers, as they stand, as too large (see Mendenhall 1958 and J. Wenham 1973 for two different solutions). Whatever the numbers, these tribes committed a strong contingent to the task of occupying the land west of the Jordan, though many men remained at home to defend their own families and lands.

the plains of Jericho. This relatively level and open ground between Jericho and the point where Israel crossed the Jordan River extended about six miles west of the Jordan, approaching the beginning of the slopes of the Benjaminite (Judean) hill country. As noted, Israel did nothing to hide their crossing and their approach from the view of Jericho's defenders. Quite the opposite; intimidation was part of Joshua's preparation for battle.

4:14 ***they revered him.*** This is the typical Hebrew verb often translated "fear," "feared," when used of human attitude toward God. Here it applies to attitudes toward Joshua. Today, "revere" is the better choice for translation, even if the object of our reverence is God. "Fear" usually connotes an inchoate anxiety inimical to faith, or even craven, abject terror, whereas God invites us to revere him as our loving Father. Using "revere" and "reverence" is better (and easier!) than continually explaining the "real" meaning of "fear."

COMMENTARY

This paragraph is the summarizing report (with an added detail or two) that the ancient listener or reader would have expected following chapter 3. Verses 10 and 11 bring closure to the gathering of the stones for the memorial from the bed of the Jordan ("until all of the LORD's commands . . . were carried out") and to the people's crossing ("the people hurried across").

The author's emphasis is on Joshua's and Israel's detailed obedience to God's instructions. In crossing the Jordan River when it was in flood, Israel undertook a dangerous endeavor on faith. They could not see the stoppage of the Jordan's floodwaters before the priests actually stepped into the water, but the priests did step into the water, the waters stopped, and Israel crossed. Israel did all this on the strength of their faith in God, and their willingness to obey God's instruction in all details. Israel's crossing of the Jordan has stood as an example to people of faith ever since.

The expression "hurried across" is the only note of urgency in the entire account. It is enough to remind us that while God's timing is perfect, we are to act on the opportunities God provides while they remain available. Just as the bed of the Jordan was not dry forever, the various doors of opportunity that stand before us will not remain open indefinitely. If and when God's direction is clear, the time to move is now.

Verses 12 and 13 provide the "added detail" to this account of the crossing. In 1:12-18, Joshua had reminded the leaders of Reuben, Gad, and half-Manasseh of their pledge to Moses to aid in the conquest of the land west of the Jordan. Here, they are recorded, not just "present," but leading the people across the first great obstacle, ready for battle "before Yahweh" and in full view of confident Israel and cowering Jericho alike.

The day before, Joshua had announced God's intended "wonders" for this day (3:13). Now that God had brought the people across the Jordan in the face of human impossibility, Israel "revered [Joshua] as much as they had revered Moses" (4:14). In the years ahead, Israel's confidence in Joshua would be crucial. God's confidence in Joshua made Israel's confidence in him possible. God's glory is not diminished when God works in and through a faithful believer in ways that bring greatness, honor, and human renown to that believer. In a faithful believer, all those things are reflective of God's own glory, and are reflected back to God's own glory and praise. So it was with Joshua, and so it is with any believer today who follows God with faithfulness and integrity.

This scene had opened dramatically; it was only as the feet of the priests carrying the Ark of the Covenant actually touched the water that the Jordan's flow was stopped (3:15-16). Now that all the people had crossed, the scene closed with equal drama. Using parallel language, the author carefully pointed out again that all still proceeded according to God's direction. God gave the word and Joshua relayed it to the priests; it was time for them to come up from the riverbed (4:15-17).

Twenty times in Joshua 3:1–4:18 (about 60 lines of Hebrew text), the author referenced the Ark of the Covenant and the priests carrying the Ark. In the earlier crossing of the Red Sea, God's presence was manifested by a pillar of fire and cloud (Exod 14:19-24). Here, in the crossing of the Jordan, it was manifested in the Ark's opening of the way through the Jordan. Yet neither the pillar nor the Ark was magic. It is not that they "were" God, or even "contained" God. They symbolized and manifested God's presence, an accommodation in the very first steps of God's people learning to walk by faith with the unseen God. We ought not judge young Israel, for although we have less reason than they to need such accommodation, we often seek it. God sometimes grants it to us, but with the caution that we must not treat objects or "signs" as having magical powers. The real point of mentioning the Ark 20 times in this narrative is to report *God's* crossing of the Jordan, both to fulfill God's ancient promise to Abraham, and to render upon Canaan the justice long delayed in mercy (Gen 15:16). God brought Israel along as his people in whom he delighted, and as his agents in fulfilling these two purposes, but the crossing of the Jordan was *God's* crossing.

When the priests stepped foot on the ground the floodwaters had not reached, the Jordan reverted to its harvesttime, flood-stage level (4:18). The author stressed this so as to form a climactic conclusion to the entire episode. The problem had been for Israel to cross the Jordan in flood, and God had solved the problem. By noting that the Jordan overflowed its banks as before, the author reminds the reader of the magnitude of the problem, which in turn highlights the miraculous nature of God's provision. Extraordinary problems do not stop the extraordinary demonstrations of the grace of "the Lord of all the earth" (3:13).

◆ 6. Israel's memorial at Gilgal (4:19–5:1)

19The people crossed the Jordan on the
tenth day of the first month.* Then they
camped at Gilgal, just east of Jericho. 20It
was there at Gilgal that Joshua piled up the
twelve stones taken from the Jordan River.

21Then Joshua said to the Israelites, "In
the future your children will ask, 'What do
these stones mean?' 22Then you can tell
them, 'This is where the Israelites crossed
the Jordan on dry ground.' 23For the LORD
your God dried up the river right before
your eyes, and he kept it dry until you
were all across, just as he did at the Red
Sea* when he dried it up until we had all
crossed over. 24He did this so all the na-
tions of the earth might know that the
LORD's hand is powerful, and so you might
fear the LORD your God forever."

CHAPTER 5

When all the Amorite kings west of the Jordan and all the Canaanite kings who lived along the Mediterranean coast* heard how the LORD had dried up the Jordan River so the people of Israel could cross, they lost heart and were paralyzed with fear because of them.

4:19 This day in the ancient Hebrew lunar calendar occurred in late March, April, or early May. 4:23 Hebrew *sea of reeds.* 5:1 Hebrew *along the sea.*

NOTES

4:19 ***tenth day of the first month.*** This is the day for selecting the Passover lamb (Exod 12:3) to be sacrificed the evening of the 14th. Nisan, the first month of Israel's agricultural calendar, usually begins in the latter half of March and ends in the first half of April on our calendar.

Gilgal, just east of Jericho. Gilgal has not been certainly identified, though several locations have been suggested (cf. Boling 1982:191-192).

4:22 ***Then you can tell them.*** The Hebrew grammatical form is stronger: "Then you shall cause them to know."

4:24 ***the LORD's hand . . . the LORD your God.*** Lit., "Yahweh's hand . . . Yahweh your God." God's *name* is important especially in contexts referring to other nations (their gods had *other* names), as well as to contexts regarding the temptation to turn from the reverence and worship of Yahweh.

5:1 ***Amorite kings.*** These were kings of the Amorite city-states in the central hill country.

Canaanite kings. These were kings of the Canaanite city-states along and near the Mediterranean coastline, and of some of the valleys and plains inland. As noted above, "Amorite" and "Canaanite" can (and here they do) include all the peoples listed in greater detail elsewhere (see note on 3:10).

so the people . . . could cross. Lit., "from before the people of Israel until *we* had crossed over" (my italics). The first person pronoun is evidence of a first person source for this account; at least some of the book of Joshua is based on personal recollections, oral or written, of Joshua or of one (or some) of those under his command.

they lost heart and were paralyzed with fear because of them. Lit., "their hearts melted and they no longer had any spirit at the prospect of facing Israel."

COMMENTARY

The timing of the crossing was not coincidental. Israel had celebrated their first Passover just before crossing the Red Sea; they would celebrate this one just after crossing the Jordan River. For a time, Gilgal became a worship center of early Israel because of this memorial Joshua set up there. It was a reminder and a teaching aid for Israel's subsequent generations of God's goodness to Israel at the banks of the Jordan (see note on 5:9).

Most people eventually want to know something of the past. When Israel's children were prompted by the sight of Gilgal's stone monument to ask about their past, it served its purpose. Gilgal was in the Jordan Valley on the easiest route to Jerusalem from the north and from across the Jordan. After David established Jerusalem as the center of Israel's worship, many young pilgrims passed by this monument, asked their parents about it, and received vivid instruction in the gracious care of Israel's God.

Joshua's concern to preserve and nurture succeeding generations' interest in God's work at the Jordan was so great that he posed the expected question, and the answer Israel's people were to give, not once, but twice (4:6-7, 21-24). This second time, the question and Joshua's expanded answer suggest Joshua made this catechism a part of the dedication ceremony for the stone memorial.

This is a vivid reminder of the value of "memorial stones" all along the journey of faith. The biblical stories, including all the book of Joshua, are the primary "memorial stones" of the Christian faith, teaching us to trust that God *has* provided for our redemption, teaching us *how* to walk as children of God and heirs of God's promises. But if all the "memorial stones" were 2,000 or more years old, today's children would be likely to ask, not, "What do these stones mean?" but "How can these stones mean anything?" The church since New Testament times has continued to erect "memorial stones" telling of God's wonderful works on behalf of his people. Works of art in architecture, sculpture, painting, music, and literature, and our own personal stories passed on to our children are only a few examples of what a "memorial stone" may look like today. To prompt their active inquiry into our faith is to help our children make the faith their own.

Joshua's reference in 4:24 to "all the nations of the earth" is a timely reminder that teaching about God's power is not just for the children of the faithful, but for everyone. When the stories of God's care for his people are told in ways they can relate to and understand, at least some persons in every people group respond to the God who cares for all. Joshua's instructions include the mandate to tell this story as an invitation to everyone to trust in Israel's God, who had shown himself all-powerful at the Jordan.

The first verse of chapter 5 is the real conclusion to the story of Israel's crossing the Jordan; it shows Joshua's expectations were not just so much wishful thinking. All of southern Canaan, at least, was in a state of alert awaiting Israel's expected invasion. It is not surprising that word of their crossing the Jordan soon spread throughout the land. With Israel's "impossible" crossing, the Canaanites knew they faced the people of a God more powerful than any they had until now recognized, more powerful than any they worshiped.

◆ D. First Circumcisions and First Passover (5:2-15)

1. Circumcision of every male (5:2-9)

2At that time the LORD told Joshua, "Make flint knives and circumcise this second generation of Israelites.*" 3So Joshua made flint knives and circumcised the entire male population of Israel at Gibeath-haaraloth.*

4Joshua had to circumcise them because all the men who were old enough to fight in battle when they left Egypt had died in the wilderness. 5Those who left Egypt had all been circumcised, but none of those born after the Exodus, during the years in the wilderness, had been circumcised. 6The Israelites had traveled in the wilderness for forty years until all the men who were old enough to fight in battle when they left Egypt had died. For they had disobeyed the LORD, and the LORD vowed he would not let them enter the land he had sworn to give us—a land flowing with milk and honey. 7So Joshua circumcised their sons—those who had grown up to take their fathers'

places—for they had not been circumcised on the way to the Promised Land. [8]After all the males had been circumcised, they rested in the camp until they were healed.

[9]Then the LORD said to Joshua, "Today I have rolled away the shame of your slavery in Egypt." So that place has been called Gilgal* to this day.

5:2 Or *circumcise the Israelites a second time.* 5:3 *Gibeath-haaraloth* means "hill of foreskins." 5:9 *Gilgal* sounds like the Hebrew word *galal,* meaning "to roll."

NOTES

5:2 ***circumcise this second generation.*** Lit., "circumcise a second time" (see NLT mg and commentary).

5:3 ***Gibeath-haaraloth.*** This means "the Hill of the Foreskins" (cf. NLT mg). The name suggests Joshua circumcised the men on a hill or hillock near Israel's camp at Gilgal. The foreskin (*'arelah* [TH6190, ZH6889]) is the skin covering the glans; in circumcision, it is surgically cut away.

5:6 ***the LORD vowed . . . he had sworn.*** The Hebrew phrasing is the same in both places: "which Yahweh had sworn."

flowing with milk and honey. This means it had especially good pastureland for the flocks of sheep and goats, which produced the milk, and abundant flowering plants for the bees, which made the honey. "Date honey" was not a product of the hill country of Canaan/Israel; moreover, jellied grape and other fruit juices hardly qualify as "honey," in light of the numerous Egyptian (south), Hittite (north), and other references to bee honey throughout the eastern Mediterranean and western Asia from many periods. We now have also the evidence of the large apiary from the tenth to ninth centuries BC at Rehov in the upper Jordan Valley, just below Beth-shan (Mazar and Panitz-Cohen 2007:202-219).

5:7 ***those who had grown up to take their fathers' places.*** Lit., "so their children [Yahweh] established [in the fulfillment of God's covenant promises] instead of them." The emphasis is not on the children's growing up, but on their receiving from God what their parents had refused.

5:9 ***Gilgal.*** See NLT mg. The name has been associated with the root *galal* [TH1556, ZH1670] (to roll), the noun *gilgal* [TH1536, ZH1651] meaning "wheel" and referring to the stone monument Joshua set up there (4:20). Given the forms involved (*gilgal, galal,* and possibly others), Gilgal may refer *both* to the presumed circular shape of the stone memorial *and* to the rolling away of "the shame . . . of Egypt."

COMMENTARY

First actions in new circumstances often are of great symbolic value. Before Israel turned their attention to Jericho, the first military objective, God directed Joshua to perform a covenant renewal ceremony, circumcising all the males born in the 40 years since their exodus from Egypt. For males, circumcision was the sign of participation in the covenant, the sign instituted already when God established the covenant relationship with Abraham (Gen 17:9-14).

"Circumcise this second generation of Israelites" (5:2) is the correct understanding of the Hebrew here (lit., "and return again [to] circumcise the sons of Israel a second [time]") as the following verses make clear. All who had left Egypt in the Exodus had been circumcised before they left, but no circumcisions had been performed during the wilderness sojourn. With Israel about to begin taking possession of the land, a central aspect of God's covenant with them, now was the time to circumcise the men under 40 years of age. They and all Israel needed this physical sign of their inclusion within the covenant people.

The explanation of 5:4-7 is an unexpected detour from the straight line of the narrative events. Its length indicates its importance as a reminder of Israel's unfaithfulness at Kadesh-barnea, where they had refused to believe God would bring them safely into the land of Canaan (Num 14). This summary of God's judgment upon their fathers reminded the present generation that trust in God still was necessary if they were to occupy the land their fathers had forfeited. It also served the purpose of announcing the completion of that judgment God had pronounced upon the earlier generation. The sentence God had previously pronounced was now fully carried out.

The author's admonitory discourse functions also as a reminder that God's promises are sure and unchangeable, but our individual participation in them depends on our response (keeping always in mind that our response, too, is rooted in God's initiating grace). God was about to fulfill his sworn promise to Israel's ancestors that he would bring their descendants back to the land of their own sojourn and give it to them as a perpetual inheritance. At the same time, those who had refused to believe God's word (or God's ability to perform his word, which amounts to the same thing) all had died, never accepting their share in God's bountiful promises.

The phrase "the shame of your slavery in Egypt" (5:9) is literally "the reproach of Egypt." This phrase may have recalled to the older Israelites their enslavement in Egypt when they were very young, but "slavery" is not actually present in the Hebrew phrase. Moreover, the reproach of slavery had been done away with long before this time, when God liberated Israel, administering disastrous justice upon Egypt in the process. There was no reproach left to Israel (if ever there had been any) because of her slavery in Egypt. More probably, "the reproach of Egypt" refers to a scenario Moses had raised with God in his several intercessory prayers (Exod 32:12; Num 14:13-16; Deut 9:28). If Israel perished in the wilderness, Moses had argued, the Egyptians would hear about it. They would reason that though God had delivered Israel out of Egypt, he had not been powerful enough to bring them safely through the wilderness. This would bring reproach not only upon Israel, but also upon God. With Israel now safely in the land of Canaan, their disappearance in the wilderness no longer was a possibility; God had "rolled away the [potential] reproach of Egypt."

◆ 2. First Passover in the land (5:10-12)

**10While the Israelites were camped at Gilgal
on the plains of Jericho, they celebrated
Passover on the evening of the fourteenth
day of the first month.* 11The very next day
they began to eat unleavened bread and
roasted grain harvested from the land. 12No
manna appeared on the day they first ate
from the crops of the land, and it was never seen again. So from that time on the
Israelites ate from the crops of Canaan.**

5:10 This day in the ancient Hebrew lunar calendar occurred in late March, April, or early May.

NOTES

5:10 ***on the plains of Jericho.*** See note on 4:13.

celebrated Passover. See Exod 12–13 and commentary below.

5:11 ***unleavened bread.*** Passover inaugurates the Festival of Unleavened Bread, observed for the next seven days (Lev 23:6). Thus, the notice about eating "unleavened bread and roasted grain" confirms that Israel observed the Festival of Unleavened Bread that year.

roasted grain. This was a favorite food of the harvest season, because it is quick, easily made, and tasty (cf. Ruth 2:14). As the name indicates, heads of ripe barley or wheat are placed in the fire until the kernels are roasted.

5:12 ***manna.*** These were the small, sweet, round grains or flakes with which God fed Israel during the wilderness sojourn. Manna appeared every morning with the dew (except on Sabbath days), until this day (cf. Exod 16:13-36).

from that time on. Lit., "in that [very] year." In the Hebrew text the word is "year" rather than "day" or "time" because crops grow year to year, rather than day to day. This phrase is a small indication of the editorial process by which the text reached its present form. (Neither a text frozen early, nor wholesale late invention, accounts for the evidence of the biblical text as it stands.)

COMMENTARY

Joshua and Israel's second significant action, before turning their attention to Jericho, was the celebration of the first Passover in the land. As the inaugural Passover in Egypt had marked the exodus from slavery, so this first Passover in Canaan marked attainment of the goal toward which God had been leading them ever since. The Passover has always commemorated God's ancient act of deliverance from Egypt. This one also anticipated God's new act of giving his people the promised rest in the new land.

Apparently, this was the first Passover Israel had celebrated since the encampment at Sinai (Num 9:1-5). For the younger ones, then, this was their first Passover; for the older, their first since childhood (or early adulthood). For all, celebrating the Passover after such a long lapse, and celebrating it on the eve of the campaign to take the Promised Land, heightened both the joy and the solemnity of the occasion.

This Passover was connected also with cessation of the daily provision of manna (5:12). Miraculous provision, by definition, is not the norm. Now that the produce of the land was available, the manna no longer was needed. Even in this detail, the completeness and graciousness of God's provision is evident. The people of Jericho had not had time to harvest all their grain before Israel crossed the Jordan, forcing Jericho's citizens to seek the protection of the city walls. Israel was thus able to harvest the grain planted by the people of Jericho. Living off the land was standard practice for invading forces until quite recently; we ought not pass moral judgment on Israel for doing so at Jericho. The Joshua narrative and the archaeological data from Jericho agree that Israel took the city during the harvest season, after some of the early harvest, at least, had been completed (Wood 1990a:51, 56-57). As Jericho is in the Jordan Valley, below sea level, its harvest is earlier than that of the hill country.

God had brought Israel across the uncrossable Jordan. The generation born in the wilderness had been circumcised. Israel had observed its first Passover in the land.

The provision of manna had ceased. The sense of turning a corner, of opening a new chapter, is climaxed by the matter-of-fact, understated tone of 5:12 (lit.), "Now the manna ceased on the morrow, after they had eaten of the produce of the land, and manna did not come again to the people of Israel." The wilderness experience was behind them; the Land of Promise lay ahead. It was time to move.

3. The Divine Warrior (5:13-15)

[13]When Joshua was near the town of Jericho, he looked up and saw a man standing in front of him with sword in hand. Joshua went up to him and demanded, "Are you friend or foe?"

[14]"Neither one," he replied. "I am the commander of the LORD's army."

At this, Joshua fell with his face to the ground in reverence. "I am at your command," Joshua said. "What do you want your servant to do?"

[15]The commander of the LORD's army replied, "Take off your sandals, for the place where you are standing is holy." And Joshua did as he was told.

NOTES

5:13 ***near the town of Jericho.*** Joshua was scouting the lay of the land and the defenses of Jericho, following up on the report of the two young men he had sent into the city (ch 2). Joshua's personal courage is shown by his approach to the unknown figure, who was standing with his sword already drawn.

5:14 ***fell . . . in reverence.*** Though this verb often is used of worshipers prostrating themselves before God, prostration was customary also in the presence of humans who occupied a clearly superior social position. It is not necessarily proof Joshua regarded this unknown one as God.

5:15 ***Take off your sandals, for the place where you are standing is holy.*** Yahweh said nearly the same thing to Moses when he revealed himself to him in the burning bush (Exod 3:5). This seems to imply (though it is not absolute proof) that the unknown hero confronting Joshua was God.

COMMENTARY

The first five chapters of Joshua lead up to the siege of Jericho, Israel's first engagement with the Canaanites. These chapters are framed at the beginning by God's encounter with Joshua in a strong, lengthy speech of encouragement, and here at the end by a short encounter with the "commander of the LORD's army." This, too, was for Joshua's encouragement, on the eve of real action against the enemy. This was the person who would give Joshua his instructions about the conduct of the siege of Jericho, instructions recorded in 6:2-5. Thus, 5:13-15 serves a twofold function. Not only is this paragraph the end piece of the frame for the narrative of the first five chapters, it also introduces the siege and conquest of Jericho that follows.

Joshua challenged the unknown figure with the question "Are you friend or foe?" but the response was not a direct answer. The stranger did not indicate support for either side; rather, his response showed Joshua that he had not yet grasped the significance of this one's appearance to him. The issue was not whether this one would fight on Israel's or on Jericho's side. The real question was which of those two peoples would fight on Yahweh's side. To bring that central question into focus, this one went on to identify himself. We may translate 5:14 a little more literally, "No [or, "Neither"], for I am the commander of Yahweh's army; now I have come." Once Joshua understood, this statement was a tremendous encouragement to him.

To put the matter in biblical terms, we do not ask God to be on our side. Rather, we declare our commitment to God's side and make ourselves available to God's service, wholeheartedly, without reservation. This is what Joshua did when he realized who stood before him; he "fell with his face to the ground in reverence" (5:14). This we too will do, if our commitment to God is as it should be. At its heart, this is what holiness, or sanctification, is all about.

Scenes such as these in the Old Testament are called "theophanies," appearances of God to human beings, often in human form. Debate continues whether God himself or perhaps the preincarnate Christ appeared in human form, or whether these personages were angels, in which case they are not in fact instances of theophany after all. In considering Joshua's encounter, this one's self-reference, "commander," could imply he was an angel. However, he did not prevent Joshua from prostrating himself, as angels did in later accounts (Dan 8:18; Rev 19:10).

One could argue that the command, "Take off your sandals, for the place . . . is holy," proves this was God, because this is what God told Moses when he encountered God at the burning bush (Exod 3:5). That may be evidence, but it is not quite proof. However, we may infer that Joshua recognized the similarity of his present situation with Moses's earlier one, and the author of Joshua intended the reader to recognize it, also. That would have been a final encouragement to Joshua on the eve of Israel's first action against Canaan. Just as God had appeared to Moses to commission him to liberate Israel from Egypt's pharaoh, now God, or God's commander, appeared to Joshua to commission him to engage the armies of Canaan and bring Israel into their promised inheritance. We may ask, with Woudstra (1981:106), "What more [was] there to know before the Conquest [began] in earnest?"

◆ E. God's Conquest of Jericho (6:1-27)

1. God's siege instructions to Joshua (6:1-7)

Now the gates of Jericho were tightly shut because the people were afraid of the Israelites. No one was allowed to go out or in. 2But the LORD said to Joshua, "I have given you Jericho, its king, and all its strong warriors. 3You and your fighting men should march around the town once a day for six days. 4Seven priests will walk ahead of the Ark, each carrying a ram's horn. On the seventh day you are to march around the town seven times, with the priests blowing the horns. 5When you hear the priests give one long blast on the rams' horns, have all the people shout as loud as they can. Then the walls of the town will collapse, and the people can charge straight into the town."

6So Joshua called together the priests and said, "Take up the Ark of the LORD's Covenant, and assign seven priests to walk in front of it, each carrying a ram's horn." 7Then he gave orders to the people: "March around the town, and the armed men will lead the way in front of the Ark of the LORD."

NOTES

6:1 ***Now the gates of Jericho were tightly shut.*** Lit., "Now Jericho was closed up and tightly closed up"—a very strong and somewhat unusual verbal construction.

6:3 ***march around the town.*** Jericho's walls were about three-fifths of a mile in circumference. Staying out of reach of the arrows and sling stones of Jericho's defenders on the walls would have meant a route of about 1.25 miles for each circuit.

6:4 ***Seven priests.*** Seven is a biblical number of perfection; "seven" or "seventh" occur 14 times (twice seven, or double perfection/completeness) in the Hebrew text of 6:4-16, leading up to the actual charge of Israel's warriors into the city after its walls fell.

ram's horn. Two different Hebrew terms occur in this account; both refer to the signal horn used in worship and in battle contexts. Israel's part in the fall of Jericho was primarily the worship of God, who "gave" Jericho into their hand (6:2).

6:5 ***will collapse.*** Lit., "will fall down in its place." Woudstra says, "the wall will fall flat, not outward or inward, but downward" (1981:111). See commentary on 6:20 below.

6:7 ***the armed men.*** Not all of Israel's warriors, as 6:9 makes clear. Those in front of the Ark were the vanguard; those behind, the rear guard. They marched ahead and behind, not to protect, but to honor it, as the Ark represented the presence of God with Israel's army.

COMMENTARY

Jericho lies at the western edge of the plain of the Jordan, just beside the first outcroppings of the central hill country. One well might ask, Why not just bypass Jericho, since Israel's objective was the hill country itself? The answer lies in Jericho's strategic position. Jericho guarded the lower entrances to two important passes into the very heart of the hill country. Bypassing it would have left a well-armed enemy at Israel's back; Jericho had to be conquered.

Joshua 6:1 is a parenthesis in the story of Joshua's encounter with the commander of the Lord's army (5:15). For God's instructions to Joshua to make sense, the reader must be confirmed in what he or she already suspects; Jericho was "tightly shut" (6:1, see note). All of Jericho's defenses were in place to withstand a lengthy siege. Several factors combined to ensure that, speaking in human terms, Israel could not expect to conquer Jericho.

First, Jericho was well defended, with two strong walls, one partway down the slope of the mound on which the city sat, and one at the crest of the mound. Between the two walls was a sloping rampart with various buildings whose walls added to the city's defensive strength. Both walls would have been strengthened with towers, strong gate complexes, and other defensive works. If the Israelites managed to penetrate the outer, lower wall, they would have to attack the upper wall, too, from much more cramped, exposed, and dangerous positions (Wood 1990a:54-56). Second, Israel possessed none of the sophisticated equipment required for a siege: battering rams, fire arrows, scaling ladders, etc. Without these, a successful assault on any city was virtually impossible. Third, Jericho's soldiers could man their walls adequately, and everyone inside, soldier and civilian alike, was well supplied—excavations at Jericho have revealed ample food in the city when Israel captured it (Wood 1990a:56). Fourth, Jericho was well watered. It sits beside one of the most abundant springs in the land (later called Elisha's Spring; cf. 2 Kgs 2:19-22). Jericho's preparations certainly included provision for protecting the spring during a time of siege.

Jericho's king had every reason to believe his city was secure; he merely had to sit tight and wait Israel out. But God gave Joshua a unique siege plan, beginning with the reassurance that God indeed had delivered this strongly fortified city into his hands (6:2). Joshua knew what he faced; God's words must have boosted his confidence enormously. All Joshua had to do was obey God, and he had a lifetime of practice at that.

God told Joshua to "march around the town" (6:3). The plan was straightforward and easily carried out, at least for the first six days. Readers long have puzzled over what such a strategy could have accomplished. But framing the question this way assumes Israel's marching caused the destruction of the walls, while God's instructions are clear that this was to be God's battle and God's victory. Some have suggested Israel's marching set vibrations going in the earth, weakening the walls, so the shouting of the seventh day caused them to fall. That is doubtful. If God used any natural force to bring down Jericho's walls, it most likely was an earthquake, as the archaeological evidence suggests.

Seven priests with seven rams' horns were to precede the Ark of the Covenant; the Ark always signaled God's presence. Thus, Israel knew (and Jericho came to know) that God was leading this military action against Jericho. God himself was fighting against the city. This, then, was the beginning of God's judgment on the iniquity of the Amorites, a judgment God had promised Abraham centuries before (Gen 15:16). Israel had only to march and observe, then shout and observe, and finally to mop up after God had delivered the city into their hands. In their march, Israel would have Jericho surrounded. When the walls fell, no warrior would have to run to some other place to find an entrance into the city. Each man simply would "charge straight into the town" (6:5).

◆ 2. Circling Jericho for six days (6:8-14)

8After Joshua spoke to the people, the seven priests with the rams' horns started marching in the presence of the LORD, blowing the horns as they marched. And the Ark of the LORD's Covenant followed behind them. 9Some of the armed men marched in front of the priests with the horns and some behind the Ark, with the priests continually blowing the horns. 10"Do not shout; do not even talk," Joshua commanded. "Not a single word from any of you until I tell you to shout. Then shout!" 11So the Ark of the LORD was carried around the town once that day, and then everyone returned to spend the night in the camp.

12Joshua got up early the next morning, and the priests again carried the Ark of the LORD. 13The seven priests with the rams' horns marched in front of the Ark of the LORD, blowing their horns. Again the armed men marched both in front of the priests with the horns and behind the Ark of the LORD. All this time the priests were blowing their horns. 14On the second day they again marched around the town once and returned to the camp. They followed this pattern for six days.

NOTES

6:8-9 *blowing the horns . . . continually blowing the horns.* In the Hebrew text this is repeated three times in these verses to indicate its importance.

horns. The word for horn is *shopar* [TH7782, ZH8795], a trumpet made from a ram's horn.

COMMENTARY

In the common pattern of biblical narrative we have seen before, the author now reports that what God and Joshua had ordered was carried out. Not only did an armed guard precede the seven priests with horns, as Joshua had specified (6:7); a rear guard also came "behind the Ark" (6:9). Thus the Ark and its priests had a military honor guard before and behind, and the Ark was preceded by the honor guard of the *shopar*-carrying priests. These priests were heralds, announcing the progress of the Ark—in reality, the progress of God—around the city.

The absolute silence God required during this time, except for the rams' horns, is emphasized in Joshua's command (6:10), repeated three times with increasing emphasis. The first, literally, "Do not give a war cry," is startling enough. Normally shouts and war cries were employed in battle to intimidate the enemy and to lift morale on one's own side. The second, literally, "Do not cause your voices to be heard," is stricter; even normal talking was not allowed. The third is, literally, "Do not cause [or allow] a word to go out of your mouths." Had anyone not yet understood Joshua, surely with this command he realized he was to march, but not to talk!

Joshua conveyed the starkness of the contrast God intended between the seven days of marching around Jericho and the final climactic moments on the seventh day. For six days the inhabitants of Jericho heard the trumpets while Israel marched once around the city. The seventh day they heard trumpets while Israel marched around the city seven times. But in all that time they heard no word from the marchers, only the blowing of the horns. As long as several horns were sounding (while others were temporarily silent for their bearers to catch their breath), the daunting sound of the *shopar* continually reached Jericho's walls. The words "until I tell you" let the Israelite soldiers (and the reader) know there would come a day for shouting. When that day came, after 13 circuits of Jericho by Israel's army, in which trumpets but not voices were heard, the psychological shock to Jericho's defenders would be devastating.

From verses 11 to 14, the emphasis is on the Ark of the Lord circling Jericho. This was God's battle, not Israel's. For six days, the procedure was the same. The Ark with its honor guard of priests and Israel's soldiers circled once around the city with trumpets blowing and voices silent. Then they returned to camp. The lack of new information in this part of the narrative (6:12-14) emphasizes that just as God's command was consistent for the first six days of the siege, so was Israel's obedience.

◆ 3. Jericho's fall on the seventh day (6:15-21)

15On the seventh day the Israelites got up at dawn and marched around the town as they had done before. But this time they went around the town seven times.
16The seventh time around, as the priests sounded the long blast on their horns, Joshua commanded the people, "Shout! For the LORD has given you the town!
17Jericho and everything in it must be completely destroyed* as an offering to the LORD. Only Rahab the prostitute and the others in her house will be spared, for she protected our spies.

18"Do not take any of the things set

apart for destruction, or you yourselves will be completely destroyed, and you will bring trouble on the camp of Israel. [19]Everything made from silver, gold, bronze, or iron is sacred to the LORD and must be brought into his treasury."

[20]When the people heard the sound of the rams' horns, they shouted as loud as they could. Suddenly, the walls of Jericho collapsed, and the Israelites charged straight into the town and captured it. [21]They completely destroyed everything in it with their swords—men and women, young and old, cattle, sheep, goats, and donkeys.

6:17 The Hebrew term used here refers to the complete consecration of things or people to the LORD, either by destroying them or by giving them as an offering; similarly in 6:18, 21.

NOTES

6:15 ***this time.*** Lit., "only on *that* day," i.e., not on any of the first six days.

6:17 ***must be completely destroyed.*** See NLT mg and Introduction under "Theological Concerns." Cf. 6:21.

Only Rahab. See the promise of the two young scouts in 2:14, 17-21.

6:18 ***set apart for destruction.*** See NLT mg on 6:17 and commentary below. The root *kharam* [TH2764, ZH3051] (dedicate for destruction or offering) occurs four times in this verse, once as a verb, and thrice as a noun.

6:19 ***silver, gold, bronze, or iron.*** In Joshua's day, these were all precious metals (cf. 6:24).

6:20 ***collapsed.*** Lit., "fell down in its place." See note on 6:5.

6:21 ***completely destroyed.*** See NLT mg on 6:17, commentary on 6:24-27, and "Theological Concerns" in the Introduction.

COMMENTARY

On the *seventh* day Israel did as they had done the previous six, but circled Jericho *seven* times. This number of perfection, used twice, doubly stresses that this was God's battle. Some have suggested this was a Sabbath. If so, that was another means of emphasizing God's sovereignty and complete control in this battle.

Joshua's last-minute reminder to his troops is fewer than 60 words in Hebrew; Joshua could have spoken them in less than 20 seconds. Still, they do serve an important literary function here. As this passage moves along, the action slows, stopping altogether at this point, just as—with Joshua's command to *shout!* (6:16)—the reader expects it to speed up furiously. Instead, the reader, too, is brought up short by the astonishing necessity to think theologically even as one sets off at a run toward battle. But with 6:20, the action resumes again, full speed, and Israel's active part in Jericho's capture is told in less than two verses. This is still another way of putting the reader on notice that this was God's battle. A final trumpet blast, and seven days of silence ended in thunder; the people shouted, and "the wall fell down in its place"—in other words, it collapsed upon itself, rather than toppling either inward or outward.

Still, since both Jericho's upper and lower walls were of brick, the collapsing brickwork had to go somewhere. The archaeology of this level of Jericho shows that much of it tumbled or slid down the slope, forming a natural (if rough) causeway up the slope, such that Israel's warriors could "charge straight into the town" (6:5). The walls built to keep enemies out helped God's people come in.

4. The spies' faithfulness to Rahab (6:22-23)

[22]Meanwhile, Joshua said to the two spies, "Keep your promise. Go to the prostitute's house and bring her out, along with all her family."

[23]The men who had been spies went in and brought out Rahab, her father, mother, brothers, and all the other relatives who were with her. They moved her whole family to a safe place near the camp of Israel.

NOTES

6:22 ***the prostitute's house.*** See note on 2:1 and commentary on 2:1-3.

6:23 ***Rahab . . . with her.*** See notes and commentary on 2:12-21.

moved . . . to a safe place. Lit., "caused them to rest." The text uses a verb rich in positive theological content and associations (Heb., *wayyannikhum*, Hiphil imperfect of *nuakh* [TH5117, ZH5663]). Joshua summed up Israel's situation at the end of his life as God's having brought them into their promised "rest" (22:4; 23:1). Jesus promised rest for those who come to him (Matt 11:28). The author of Hebrews interpreted the "rest" of the people of God, through Christ, in terms of Israel's entering into the promised "rest" of Canaan (Heb 3:18–4:11), even mentioning Joshua by name (Heb 4:8). Rahab's faith made it possible for her and her family to share in this rich and permanent (cf. Heb 11:31) blessing of rest.

COMMENTARY

The attentive and interested reader wants to know what happened to Rahab. The reader still deciding whether the people of God can and ought to be trustworthy wants to know, too. Could the faith of a pagan non-Israelite really be rewarded? Does God care for "outsiders"?

Joshua sent the young men who had gone into Jericho earlier to fetch Rahab. They knew Rahab and where she lived; she would recognize and trust them. The long sentence of 6:23 records their exemplary actions. It is important for the reader to know not only that they fulfilled Joshua's command to them, but also that they fulfilled their oath to Rahab. God's people, and through them God himself, are seen to be trustworthy. A pagan may believe in Israel's God and find deliverance from certain death.

Rahab's house certainly was full to bursting; "other relatives" would have included aunts, uncles, and cousins several times removed, as well as in-laws. All who accepted Rahab's whispered invitation would have been present, together with their children, servants, and even guests, if any. Since Rahab's house was a place of business, probably an inn (see commentary on 2:1), it is not impossible that 20 percent (300–400) of Jericho's estimated 1,500–2,000 people took refuge with Rahab. (The population estimate is based on our knowledge that 150–200 people per acre was the average within walled towns, and Jericho's area was about 10 acres.) Of course, it may have been a significantly smaller number; we cannot know for sure. But when death is the alternative, a lot of people can squeeze into a small space! Whatever the number, any of Rahab's relatives who perished did so because of their unbelief in Israel's God, or even because of their unbelief in Rahab, on this occasion God's agent of grace to them.

The two young men brought these people outside Jericho because it was to be burned (6:24). They put them "outside the camp of Israel" (6:23, lit.) because they were not yet part of Israel. Yet "a safe place near the camp of Israel" expresses perfectly these two men's attitude toward Rahab and her family. That Rahab and, by inference, her family did find acceptance into Israel, and not merely deliverance from Jericho, we know from the further note in 6:25.

◆ 5. Joshua's destruction of Jericho (6:24-27)

24Then the Israelites burned the town and everything in it. Only the things made from silver, gold, bronze, or iron were kept for the treasury of the LORD's house. 25So Joshua spared Rahab the prostitute and her relatives who were with her in the house, because she had hidden the spies Joshua sent to Jericho. And she lives among the Israelites to this day.

26At that time Joshua invoked this curse:

"May the curse of the LORD fall on
anyone
who tries to rebuild the town of
Jericho.
At the cost of his firstborn son,
he will lay its foundation.
At the cost of his youngest son,
he will set up its gates."

27So the LORD was with Joshua, and his reputation spread throughout the land.

NOTES

6:25 ***Rahab.*** Tradition accepts the Rahab mentioned in Matt 1:5 as the woman of this account. Comparison of the relevant genealogies tends to confirm she is the same woman. Ruth 4:21 lists Salmon as the father of Boaz, while Matt 1:5 adds that Rahab was Salmon's wife and Boaz's mother (1 Chr 2:11-12 agrees with this listing, but does not mention Rahab).

6:26 ***its gates.*** Lit., "its doors," i.e., in the fortified gate room built into the city wall, the two swinging wooden doors sheathed in bronze that could be closed and barred from within to deny entrance into the city.

6:27 ***his reputation.*** Lit., "his name."

COMMENTARY

This final paragraph concludes the account, recording Joshua's disposition of the city and its contents; Jericho's burning fulfilled God's sentence. Moreover, by that act Israel acknowledged that in the disposition of the spoils of war, as in all else, the firstfruits of material possessions belong to God. Not incidentally, the way Jericho was taken and its devotion to destruction together undercut the two primary human motivations for war: the lust for glory in battle, and the lust for wealth in the spoils of conquest.

Fire does not destroy silver, gold, bronze, or iron; it melts them if temperatures are high enough. Thus, the tendency of fire is to purify metal. When passed through the fire that destroyed every impure thing in Jericho, these metals were melted down and purified. Some of them, no doubt, had existed as the outer sheathing (or even the entire cast figure) of the images of pagan gods and goddesses. These, too, melted and became merely metal, purified and fit for dedication into the treasury of Israel's God, whom even Jericho's citizens knew (without being told by the Israelites) to be "God of the heavens above and the earth below" (2:11).

Jericho's destruction was an act of judgment, and in its light, faith and mercy shine all the more brightly. Thus, another repetition is welcome here, the reminder that Joshua spared Rahab and her family. The new word, that Rahab "lives among the Israelites to this day" (6:25), is further affirmation of the breadth and depth of God's grace and mercy. This statement can be taken either of two ways. If we assume this to be an ancient record incorporated into the text of Joshua, it was first written when Rahab still lived as the wife (or widow) of Salmon (Matt 1:5). If Rahab had passed on before this was written, it would mean she still lived through her descendants, who included her son Boaz, her great-great-grandson David, and notable offspring all the way down the line to that greatest scion of David's line, Jesus of Nazareth (Matt 1:5). Such "living in Israel" would be living indeed. Not only was Rahab accepted into Israel, she became a mother in Israel and, ultimately, an ancestress in the line of the Messiah himself!

After this powerful reminder of mercy in the midst of judgment, the narrative returns to Joshua's final statement: a curse upon the site of the ruined city (6:26). After Israel's crossing of the Jordan, Jericho was the first of the cities of Canaan to resist God's purposes in bringing Israel into the land. Jericho was first to undergo God's judgment upon Canaan's great wickedness. Jericho was the firstfruits of Israel's conquest of Canaan; as firstfruits, the city belonged to God. For all these reasons, Jericho was to be left as a sign and a reminder, both of God's judgment upon sin, and of God's grace toward Israel.

Joshua's curse took the form of a prediction of tragedy in the family of the person who first rebuilt Jericho. First Kings 16:34 records that Hiel of Bethel did rebuild the walls of Jericho in the days of Israel's King Ahab, bringing Joshua's curse of death upon his eldest and youngest sons.

God had promised to be with Joshua (1:5, 9). Now at the successful end of the first action against a real human enemy, God's presence was obvious to all. Though hardly necessary (see 4:14), this of course enhanced Joshua's standing in Israel. Of great importance for what lay ahead, though, was the ease with which well-prepared Jericho fell into Joshua's hands. This caused his reputation (and his terror) to spread "throughout the land" (6:27), upon all the Canaanites.

The first phase in Israel's conquest of Canaan has ended. The importance of these first events is established by the fact that they take up a full quarter of the book of Joshua. Crossing the Jordan and taking Jericho had established Israel's presence in the land. It must have seemed to Joshua and to all Israel that not much could go wrong after that. But calamity often strikes when we least expect it. In the very moment of completion of this great victory for Israel, one Israelite sowed the seeds of a disaster that would overtake them in their next military encounter.

◆ II. Joshua's Victories over Two Canaanite Coalitions (7:1–12:24)

A. Achan's Sin and Judgment (7:1-26)

1. Israel's defeat at Ai (7:1-5)

But Israel violated the instructions about the things set apart for the LORD.* A man named Achan had stolen some of these dedicated things, so the LORD was very angry with the Israelites. Achan was the son of Carmi, a descendant of Zimri* son of Zerah, of the tribe of Judah.

2Joshua sent some of his men from

Jericho to spy out the town of Ai, east of
Bethel, near Beth-aven. 3 When they re-
turned, they told Joshua, "There's no need
for all of us to go up there; it won't take
more than two or three thousand men to
attack Ai. Since there are so few of them,
don't make all our people struggle to go
up there."

4 So approximately 3,000 warriors were
sent, but they were soundly defeated. The
men of Ai 5 chased the Israelites from the
town gate as far as the quarries,* and they
killed about thirty-six who were retreat-
ing down the slope. The Israelites were
paralyzed with fear at this turn of events,
and their courage melted away.

7:1a The Hebrew term used here refers to the complete consecration of things or people to the LORD, either by destroying them or by giving them as an offering; similarly in 7:11, 12, 13, 15. **7:1b** As in parallel text at 1 Chr 2:6; Hebrew reads *Zabdi.* Also in 7:17, 18. **7:5** Or *as far as Shebarim.*

NOTES

7:1 ***things set apart.*** Heb., *kherem* [TH2764, ZH3051] (see NLT mg). This noun occurs eight times in 7:1-15, out of a total of 29 occurrences in the entire OT. Though Younger's work (1990) requires reassessing the concept as a whole, in this context we still may say that *kherem* signifies Israel's destruction by fire of all the goods of Jericho (except, of course, the four metals dedicated to service of the Tabernacle—gold, silver, iron, and bronze) as an offering to Yahweh, the real conqueror of the city.

Zimri. This follows LXX (see NLT mg). That four of Achan's ancestors are named here, at the beginning of the narrative and well before the scene of discovery in which Achan was revealed as the culprit, suggests that Achan was a prominent, or at least a promising, member of his clan and tribe.

7:2 ***Ai.*** Usually identified with et-Tell; both names usually are understood as "ruin mound."

Bethel. This means "house [temple] of God"; it is modern Beitin (Rainey and Notley 2006:116-118).

Beth-aven. Lit., "house of iniquity." Usually the name is taken as an intentional, derogatory, and sarcastic play on the name Bethel, because Bethel was the site of a pagan shrine later in Israel's history (1 Kgs 12:28-33). However, here the MT mentions both names as though they were two different towns, and Aharoni (1979:431) tentatively identifies Beth-aven with Tell Maryam. LXX does not mention Beth-aven here.

7:5 ***from the town gate.*** This suggests, as 8:5 confirms, that Ai's defenders left the city through the main gate and attacked the Israelite force directly. This was a common tactic in ancient warfare when defenders thought they could rout an attacking force.

the quarries. Heb., *shebarim* [TH7671, ZH8696]. This could be a place name (see NLT mg). Alternatively, the grammar allows for translating it as either "the breaks" or "the canyons." Translating it as "canyons" makes good sense (see commentary), but this would be the only such usage of this noun. The more common (and expected) word would be *nakhal* [TH5158, ZH5707] (meaning "wadi, streambed"). The NLT's "the quarries" is a fitting understanding based on the Hebrew word, but the apparent distance of this location from the town of Ai makes it unlikely.

thirty-six. This is the only number recorded in this section. Probably Ai's soldiers killed a total of 36 Israelites, from their initial charge from the city gate until they stopped pursuing them.

their courage melted away. Lit., "the hearts of the people melted and became like water," just as the hearts of the Canaanites had melted at the approach of Israel (2:11; 5:1).

COMMENTARY

This second major section of the book of Joshua records, in broad outline only, Joshua's southern and northern campaigns against two different coalitions of Canaanite kings. These two major campaigns followed the taking of Jericho. Joshua's victories in these campaigns assured that the Canaanites would not be able to deny Israel access to the Negev, the hill country of Judah, Mount Ephraim, and Galilee.

Joshua's first military concern, now that Jericho belonged to Israel, was to secure a foothold in the hill country itself. The conquest of Jericho had roused Israel to inspired confidence and consigned the people of Canaan to discouragement and despair. But in the aftermath of Jericho's fall, unknown to Joshua and the rest of Israel, one man had created a far greater problem for the nation than the military one.

The skill of the biblical narrator again is highlighted in his revealing this crucial information to the reader before most of the characters in the narrative can know about it. This allows the reader to realize from the start the significance of the narrative action as it unfolds. However, the narrator gives no details, relating only that Achan "had stolen some of these dedicated things." This statement is only a transition into the new episode. The reader, too, will endure the suspense of waiting to know all that happened.

The importance of this occasion lay in the fact that Jericho was Israel's first victory and first conquest in the land God was giving them. As such, Jericho was a kind of firstfruits of the land and belonged to God. This was symbolized and carried out in the institution of the *kherem* [TH2764, ZH3051]. Of all Jericho's wealth, Achan took only a little gold and silver, and one imported garment (7:21). But most human actions are more than they seem on the surface, and sin is never as limited in its consequences as we think when we decide to do it; it spreads its disastrous effects beyond our wildest imaginings.

Achan's sin, with its terrible consequences for all Israel, is an early example of a principle embedded in the way God has designed this world and the working out of its affairs. The more important the occasion and the more prominent the person, the more significant and influential are his or her actions, for good or for evil. God holds leaders (and Achan was a potential leader) to a higher standard of accountability.

As he had done before the battle for Jericho, Joshua sent men to assess the situation of Ai, about 10 miles west of Jericho, in the heart of the hill country. Ai lies on the plateau of Benjamin, a saddle connecting Judah to the south with Mount Ephraim to the north; it was the military key to both those sections of the hill country. As Jericho guarded the two passes into Benjamin from the bottom (east), Ai and Bethel guarded them from the top (west). If Israel meant to gain access to the hill country, Ai could not be bypassed; it had to be taken.

The reader suspects, from the report of these spies and Joshua's uncritical acceptance, that God's victory for Israel at Jericho had bred complacency and overconfidence, as though Israel had accomplished the victory on their own (7:3). Joshua did not bother consulting with God before sending his small contingent of troops to Ai.

If complacency indeed was the attitude of the few men ascending the pass to Ai, it was shattered abruptly by the beating they took from Ai's stout defenders. Again, the narrator shows exceptional skill; every word portrays Israelite confidence in an easy victory until suddenly, in just four Hebrew words, a disaster is reported (7:4), which in English is "but they fled before the men of Ai," who pursued them as far as "the breaks" or "the canyons" (see note on 7:5).

"The breaks," understood as "[the place of] the breakings," would be an appropriate name for a stone quarry. However, Ai's stone quarries would have been near the city—the ancients did not transport building stones farther than they had to! Ai's men would not have stopped pursuing the fleeing enemy as close to Ai as we may assume the stone quarries to have been. If the reference is to "the canyons," it would mean the ravines that cut from the hill country eastward down through the slopes to the Jordan Valley. This would make excellent sense. When the fleeing Israelites reached the ravines, it would have been risky for the men of Ai to continue the pursuit. They would have been exposed in difficult terrain by ones and twos, or in very small groups, not knowing whether some of the Israelites might have seen them and hidden behind rocky outcrops to ambush them as they came.

With the vivid metaphor, "the hearts of the people melted and became like water" (7:5, NIV), the narrator expressed in five short Hebrew words the psychological condition of Israel's men, who quickly went from overconfidence to abject terror. Such often happens when God's people rely on their own strength or their own resources. Given the physical advantages of the adversaries they faced, Israel needed God's intervention to prevail. However, having seen the overwhelming way God helped them prevail at Jericho, Israel forgot the victory really was God's. In the warfare God's people wage today against the forces of evil (cf. 2 Cor 10:3-5; Eph 6:12), we dare not forget as Israel did, or we, too, will meet defeat at our "Ai."

◆ 2. Joshua's prayer; God's response (7:6-15)

6Joshua and the elders of Israel tore their clothing in dismay, threw dust on their heads, and bowed face down to the ground before the Ark of the LORD until evening. 7Then Joshua cried out, "Oh, Sovereign LORD, why did you bring us across the Jordan River if you are going to let the Amorites kill us? If only we had been content to stay on the other side! 8Lord, what can I say now that Israel has fled from its enemies? 9For when the Canaanites and all the other people living in the land hear about it, they will surround us and wipe our name off the face of the earth. And then what will happen to the honor of your great name?"

10But the LORD said to Joshua, "Get up! Why are you lying on your face like this? 11Israel has sinned and broken my covenant! They have stolen some of the things that I commanded must be set apart for me. And they have not only stolen them but have lied about it and hidden the things among their own belongings. 12That is why the Israelites are running from their enemies in defeat. For now Israel itself has been set apart for destruction. I will not remain with you any longer unless you destroy the things among you that were set apart for destruction.

13"Get up! Command the people to purify themselves in preparation for tomorrow. For this is what the LORD, the God of Israel, says: Hidden among you, O Israel, are things set apart for the LORD. You will never defeat your enemies until you remove these things from among you.

14"In the morning you must present

yourselves by tribes, and the LORD will point out the tribe to which the guilty man belongs. That tribe must come forward with its clans, and the LORD will point out the guilty clan. That clan will then come forward, and the LORD will point out the guilty family. Finally, each member of the guilty family must come forward one by one. 15The one who has stolen what was set apart for destruction will himself be burned with fire, along with everything he has, for he has broken the covenant of the LORD and has done a horrible thing in Israel."

NOTES

7:6 ***tore their clothing . . . threw dust on their heads.*** These were customary, public gestures of grief and despair in the ancient Near East.

7:7 ***the Amorites.*** These were the inhabitants of Canaan; "Amorite" and "Canaanite" sometimes stand for the whole population of the land.

7:9 ***what will happen to the honor of your great name?*** Lit., "what will *you* do for your great name?" (See Moses's similar prayers in Exod 32:11-12; Num 14:13-19.)

7:11 ***have lied.*** The verb (*kikhashu,* Piel perfect of *kakhash* [TH3584, ZH3950]) is, more precisely, "they have acted deceitfully," though by this time Achan's deception may have included lies.

7:12-13 ***destruction . . . destruction . . . things set apart . . . these things.*** All four are translations of the word *kherem* [TH2764, ZH3051] (see note on 7:1).

7:14 ***present yourselves by tribes.*** This refers to each of the tribes descended from Jacob's 12 sons (Gen 35:23-26).

will point out. This reflects the Hebrew root *lakad* [TH3920, ZH4334] (to catch), a word that also appears in 7:15, 16, 17 (2x), 18.

clans. These are smaller units within the tribes; as tribal allotments in the land were assigned, often a clan was given possession of a town and its surrounding fields, forest, and pastureland.

family. Lit., "house." This denotes related males (with their dependents) who could be counted as *go'el* [TH1350B, ZH1457], kinsman-redeemer, to each other, i.e., brothers, uncles, and cousins.

each member. Lit., "by the men [of fighting age]." This denotes the individual males of a family—normally, all who were old enough to be called "men" would have been married.

7:15 ***a horrible thing.*** Heb., *nebalah* [TH5039, ZH5576] (foolishness, folly). This root designates the kind of folly that in Hebrew wisdom theology is regarded as impiety, or even rebellion, not "merely" ignorance or simplemindedness (cf., e.g., Prov 17:7; 30:22).

COMMENTARY

Joshua's prostrating himself on the ground before the Ark of the Lord was his belated admission that Israel did need God's direction in the matter of Ai. But in his first question ("Why did you bring us across the Jordan River if you are going to let the Amorites kill us?" 7:7), the reader may sense an accusatory tone toward God. This tone comes across even more strongly in the Hebrew text. Joshua's irritability here, given his utter neglect in seeking God's guidance concerning their next step after Jericho, helps the reader understand the sharp tone of God's reply, beginning in 7:10.

Joshua's prayer is filled with hyperbole, as biblical prayers of lament sometimes are. Joshua can hardly have thought that Israel really should have stayed on the other side, east of the Jordan, but he was at a loss over what to do next. Though he ought not to have blamed God (even indirectly), Joshua's fears for Israel were entirely realistic. All Canaan had been in terror, thinking Israel invincible. Now that tiny Ai had defeated Israel, Canaan would be encouraged to fight Israel. In fact, the forces of southern Canaan soon did join together to fight against Israel (ch 10).

It is a striking witness to Joshua's character and faithfulness to God that only here and in the matter of the Gibeonites (ch 9) is there even a hint of censure regarding his judgment or his conduct. Otherwise, throughout his long career, first as Moses's aide, then as leader of Israel himself, Joshua's actions, words, and attitudes were above reproach.

God's response to Joshua's lament confirms the reader in the knowledge that Israel's defeat would have been avoided had Joshua consulted God before sending the small force to attack Ai. God had no sympathy for Joshua's exaggerated rhetorical questioning of God's motives. One of Israel's own had brought this trouble upon them, and the sin had to be discovered and dealt with before God could act again for Israel. God's command was abrupt and stern. Sorrow and grief, however sincere, could not help in this instance. Joshua must act swiftly and decisively if Israel were to regain God's favor.

God's words, "Get up! Why are you lying on your face like this?" (7:10) are important for another reason. A regular biblical witness is that God prefers engaging humans in face-to-face conversation over talking to the backs of heads. Appropriate fear of God—honor, awe, respect, reverence—is a matter of heart and mind more than of posture, and false reverence cannot be concealed from God by hiding one's face in the dirt. The God who made us for relationship favors relational encounter, even when correcting those he loves.

Six of the seven verbs in 7:11 accuse Israel of serious sin: "Israel has sinned . . . broken . . . stolen . . . stolen . . . lied . . . hidden." Few more powerful examples exist of how one individual's sin, though carefully rationalized and hidden, can rip the fabric of an entire community. One man had acted alone, secretly, but all Israel stood indicted as rebellious against God until they remedied his sin. There really is no such thing as "harmless" sin. The word *kherem* [TH2764, ZH3051] occurs four times in 7:12-13. In taking items designated for *kherem* (destruction), Achan had made all Israel *kherem* (liable to destruction), by the principle of contagion. Contagion is not limited to physical disease; in the moral realm it can also operate either for good or for ill.

God's command (7:13) is literally: "Sanctify the people. Tell them, 'Sanctify yourselves for tomorrow.'" There is a sense, of course, in which only God can sanctify. But sometimes God's people are called to sanctify themselves. This was one such occasion in the life of Israel. Since Achan's desecration had made all Israel unholy, their actions on the morrow would sanctify them anew.

God, who created the human mind, may have had a reason for delaying the investigation until the following day. Achan had thought no one would know what he had done, but Israel's disaster at Ai destroyed that illusion. All night long, Achan feared the coming dawn, the secret knowledge of his bloodguilt fanning his readiness to confess. Secret sin is an almost impossible burden for humans to bear. It is doubtful Achan slept much that night. God's chosen method of revealing the guilty party only would have added to Achan's dread and apprehension throughout the process. God instructed Joshua to do it through a process of elimination, to *point out* the guilty, first tribe by tribe, then clan by clan, then family by family, then finally man by man. Even the numerous times when the answer was "no," served to build the suspense for all, especially for Achan. (See further comments on 7:16-18 below.)

The Hebrew root *lakad* [TH3920, ZH4334] (point out, catch), the first verb of 7:15, is in a passive (Niphal) form. This verse should begin, "And the one who is pointed out [*not* "the one who has stolen"] with the items destined for destruction (*kherem* [TH2764, ZH3051]) will be burned in the fire." The pointing out ("catching") was to end only when it revealed the guilty individual. The stolen goods were to have been destroyed, or purified, by fire. They would be burned, just as Achan himself, along with everything he owned, was burned with fire. Achan's *horrible* deed was not merely "foolishness" (*nebalah* [TH5039, ZH5576]), it was rebellion against God (see note on 7:15).

◆ 3. Achan's conviction and execution (7:16-26)

16 Early the next morning Joshua brought
the tribes of Israel before the LORD, and the
tribe of Judah was singled out. 17 Then the
clans of Judah came forward, and the clan
of Zerah was singled out. Then the families
of Zerah came forward, and the family of
Zimri was singled out. 18 Every member of
Zimri's family was brought forward person
by person, and Achan was singled out.

19 Then Joshua said to Achan, "My son,
give glory to the LORD, the God of Israel,
by telling the truth. Make your confession
and tell me what you have done. Don't
hide it from me."

20 Achan replied, "It is true! I have
sinned against the LORD, the God of Israel.
21 Among the plunder I saw a beautiful
robe from Babylon,* 200 silver coins,* and
a bar of gold weighing more than a
pound.* I wanted them so much that I
took them. They are hidden in the ground
beneath my tent, with the silver buried
deeper than the rest."

22 So Joshua sent some men to make a
search. They ran to the tent and found the
stolen goods hidden there, just as Achan
had said, with the silver buried beneath
the rest. 23 They took the things from the
tent and brought them to Joshua and all
the Israelites. Then they laid them on the
ground in the presence of the LORD.

24 Then Joshua and all the Israelites
took Achan, the silver, the robe, the bar
of gold, his sons, daughters, cattle, don-
keys, sheep, goats, tent, and everything
he had, and they brought them to the
valley of Achor. 25 Then Joshua said to
Achan, "Why have you brought trouble
on us? The LORD will now bring trouble on
you." And all the Israelites stoned Achan
and his family and burned their bodies.
26 They piled a great heap of stones over
Achan, which remains to this day. That is
why the place has been called the Valley
of Trouble* ever since. So the LORD was no
longer angry.

7:21a Hebrew *Shinar.* **7:21**b Hebrew *200 shekels of silver,* about 5 pounds or 2.3 kilograms in weight. **7:21**c Hebrew *50 shekels,* about 20 ounces or 570 grams in weight. **7:26** Hebrew *valley of Achor.*

NOTES

7:21 ***beautiful robe.*** Heb. *'adereth* [TH155, ZH168] denotes a very high quality garment, perhaps even a royal robe (Jonah 3:6). Possibly, Achan's plunder came from the king's palace.

200 silver coins. These 200 pieces are called shekels in the Hebrew, a reference to their weight; see NLT mg. The NLT introduces "coins," which, strictly speaking, is anachronistic; coinage was invented in the Lydian kingdom of Asia Minor in the seventh century BC, and did not come into use in this part of western Asia until the Persian period, probably with the first Judean return, about 536 BC.

a bar of gold. Lit., a "tongue," or wedge, of gold (see NLT mg). Though the gold weighed one-fourth as much as the silver, it was by far the most valuable of the three items Achan stole.

7:24 ***Achan.*** Lit., "Achan, the descendant of Zerah."

cattle, donkeys. In the Hebrew, both terms are singular, "his ox, his donkey." Biblical Hebrew attests plurals for these nouns elsewhere. The present text is noting that Achan had one ox and one donkey (cf. NET).

the valley of Achor. The name *'akor* [TH5911, ZH6574] means "trouble." This valley, still named Achor/Trouble, is located southwest of Jericho in the Judean wilderness west of the Dead Sea.

COMMENTARY

To discover the culprit, it is possible (though not provable) that Joshua used the Urim and Thummim, a God-given system of lots. The high priest (Eleazar at this time) wore them on his person, probably contained in a bag or a pouch (Exod 28:30; Num 27:21). They may have been two objects, perhaps gemstones, differing only in their coloring, one darker and one lighter. Inquiries were phrased as "yes" or "no" questions. We must stress that this description is conjectural, but if this was the system, then for each tribe, clan, family, and man, the question would have been, "Is this the one?" until the priest drew out the object (probably the Urim) signaling "yes." In Joshua's day, God's revelation was far from complete; Israel was a brand-new people of faith with little experience in walking with God. The Urim and Thummim were a necessary means of ensuring that God's will could be known and acted on. For the Christian today, use of such methods (technically called "divination"), including reading palms, tea leaves, or tarot cards, or even randomly opening one's Bible and pointing at a verse for guidance, would represent, not mature and knowledgeable faith, but a retreat from faith.

Moving through the clans of Judah, then the families of Zerah's clan, the choice came down to Achan (7:18). No one (including the reader) knew precisely what he had done, but now all knew the responsibility for Israel's defeat at Ai lay with him. Joshua's gentle, compassionate form of address, "my son," reveals him as a caring leader, sorry for this young man trapped by his impulsive greed.

Joshua's advice to Achan is literally, "I pray you, render glory to Yahweh, the God of Israel, and give him thanks/confession" (7:19). This was a plea for him to repent and cast himself upon God's mercy for the salvation of his soul (as we would say today), though both knew Achan would die for his crime. Achan's response was a full confession (7:20-21); it may have also been a genuine repentance.

The beautiful robe should have been burned with the rest of Jericho's perishable goods. That it was from Babylon is just one among a great many pieces of evidence that long-distance trade was a significant factor in the life of the Near East at this time. The Hebrew term *Shinar* (cf. 7:21a, NLT mg) indicates lower Mesopotamia around and above the head of the Persian Gulf. The silver and the bar of gold belonged to the treasury of the Lord's house (6:24). In a real, not just a metaphorical sense, Achan had stolen from God. The progression of his sin is, almost without exception, the progression of all sin. Achan *saw;* the appeal also may be to the hearing, or to some other of the senses. He *coveted* (Heb., *khamad* [TH2530, ZH2773])—Achan used the same verb employed in the Tenth Commandment (Exod 20:17; Deut 5:21). And he *took;* the last step, the inevitable fruit when covetousness is not nipped in the bud, is the overt act, the punishable offense.

The author continued to remind the reader of the seriousness and the urgency of this matter: Joshua's messengers did not walk; "They ran to the tent" (7:22) to confirm Achan's confession. They laid out the stolen items as evidence, not only for Joshua and all Israel, but also before "the presence of the LORD" (7:23). The careful listing (7:24) of persons, animals, and all Achan's possessions, including the stolen items, has the tone of a legal statement setting forth the final disposition of a case. Achan and all that pertained to him had been compromised by their contact with the stolen items that were supposed to be devoted to God. To avert judgment from Israel, all had to be included in Achan's judgment. This record showed that all had been done properly.

But why were Achan's sons and daughters executed with him? The easy answer is, they knew what he had done, they were old enough to understand it was a terrible sin against God and against Israel, and they had failed to inform Joshua or anyone else, thereby becoming, in legal terms, accomplices after the fact. If some of Achan's children were too young to know or to understand, the answer becomes more difficult. Then, we simply must recognize that, just as Achan's sin earlier had cost the lives of (at least) 36 adult Israelite warriors (7:5), now it cost the lives of his own children.

Joshua's final words to Achan reflect this legal aspect, but they also are liturgical in nature. Achan had troubled Israel; now his sin had brought the ultimate trouble upon himself and his family. By his death, Israel's destruction (*kherem* [TH2764, ZH3051]) was averted. God's anger (7:26) was neither capricious nor baseless. Achan's sin had brought disaster upon Israel; his severe punishment was just. Moreover, it underscores in a somber way that God's people must be holy. To trifle with things belonging to God is dangerous because it really is rebellion against God. Such sin always "brings trouble" (*'akor* [TH5916, ZH6579]; 7:25) upon God's people.

◆ B. Joshua's Conquest of Ai on the Second Try (8:1-35)

1. Joshua's ambush strategy at Ai (8:1-13)

Then the LORD said to Joshua, "Do not be afraid or discouraged. Take all your fighting men and attack Ai, for I have given you the king of Ai, his people, his town, and his land.
2You will destroy them as you destroyed Jericho and its king. But this time you may keep the plunder and the livestock for yourselves. Set an ambush behind the town."

3So Joshua and all the fighting men set

out to attack Ai. Joshua chose 30,000 of
his best warriors and sent them out at
night [4]with these orders: "Hide in ambush
close behind the town and be ready for
action. [5]When our main army attacks, the
men of Ai will come out to fight as they did
before, and we will run away from them.
[6]We will let them chase us until we have
drawn them away from the town. For they
will say, 'The Israelites are running away
from us as they did before.' Then, while we
are running from them, [7]you will jump up
from your ambush and take possession of
the town, for the LORD your God will give it
to you. [8]Set the town on fire, as the LORD
has commanded. You have your orders."

[9]So they left and went to the place of
ambush between Bethel and the west side
of Ai. But Joshua remained among the
people in the camp that night. [10]Early the
next morning Joshua roused his men and
started toward Ai, accompanied by the
elders of Israel. [11]All the fighting men who
were with Joshua marched in front of the
town and camped on the north side of Ai,
with a valley between them and the town.
[12]That night Joshua sent 5,000 men to lie
in ambush between Bethel and Ai, on the
west side of the town. [13]So they stationed
the main army north of the town and the
ambush west of the town. Joshua himself
spent that night in the valley.

NOTES

8:1 *Ai.* See note on 7:2.

8:2 ***You will destroy them as you destroyed Jericho and its king.*** Lit., "You will do to Ai and to its king just as you did to Jericho and to its king." Specific mention of both kings, when not strictly necessary to the narrative, is a reminder that the kings of Canaan (with their advisors) were directly responsible for the decisions of their cities to oppose Israel's entrance into the land.

behind the town. This location was between Bethel and the west side of Ai (cf. 8:9, 12).

8:3 ***30,000 of his best warriors.*** J. Wenham (1973:191-192) has shown that most of the large numbers of the OT were misunderstood early on in the scribal process of transmitting the texts by means of hand copying. Reducing these numbers eliminates distortion in the record, and brings them into harmony with many other points of biblical data. Here we should read "30," the original number according to Wenham's solution, and a reasonable number to take up an ambush position undetected.

8:4 ***close behind the town and be ready for action.*** Lit., "Do not stray far from the town at all, and be ready, all of you." See note on 8:2.

8:9 ***the camp.*** Apparently, Israel was still encamped at Gilgal (9:6); thus, the men setting the ambush moved up the eastern slopes and some distance into the plateau of Benjamin to arrive and conceal themselves in their position west of Ai before daybreak—a rugged trek of about 12 miles, mostly uphill, and all in the dark of night.

8:12 ***sent 5,000 men.*** This should read "five men" (see note on 8:3). This was not a second ambush, but a small detachment to check on the success and readiness of the unit Joshua had sent earlier, which they would join when Joshua signaled them into action.

8:13 ***in the valley.*** We may assume this was the valley of 8:11; thus, Joshua spent the night with his forward observers, ready to lead, not send, his men into battle in the morning.

COMMENTARY

Before the second attempt at conquering Ai, God spoke to Joshua again and gave him a strategy. More importantly, in light of Israel's recent disaster, God gave Joshua a word of encouragement and a promise. Some details of Joshua's arrangements for the battle present difficulties, and scholars have proposed various solutions. The main lines of Joshua's strategy, however, and the progress and outcome of the battle are clear.

The centerpiece of the strategy for the capture of Ai was the laying of an ambush. God's instructions were simple, and Joshua executed them well. The point of the biblical narrator, with his emphasis on God's speech to Joshua in the first two verses of the chapter, is the contrast between the disaster of the first attempt on Ai and the success of this second attempt. The first was done without consulting God; the second was carried out at God's command and according to God's direction.

Knowing Joshua's confidence had been shaken, God began with a word of encouragement: "Do not be afraid or discouraged" (8:1). This is similar in tone and content to the encouragement God had given Joshua before sending him against Jericho (6:2). As a military strategist, Joshua knew full well that Israel's taking of any one of the four elements mentioned—the king of Ai, his people, his city, or his land—would mean that all would be taken. The separate listing of all four elements was God's assurance that this time Israel would not fail. Ai, with everyone and everything in it and belonging to it, would fall to Israel.

At Jericho, everything had belonged to God, because Jericho was the firstfruits of the conquest of Canaan. Now, at Ai, all the plunder and livestock (8:2) would go to Israel, a beginning of the possessions they would need to live successfully in the land. The taking of anything of value from a conquered enemy was an accepted and normal part of ancient warfare. The chance to enrich oneself and one's kingdom with captives, with animals, and with any other form of portable wealth was almost the only incentive for offensive warfare in the ancient world. But it was different for Israel because God intended Israel to be different from the world around her. Israel did not conquer Ai and Canaan to gain material wealth. Rather, Israel was God's agent of judgment upon Canaan (Gen 15:16), and the spoils of war were incidental. But since the spoils would be useful, Israel would be allowed to keep them.

As often occurs in biblical narrative, the first sentence is a summary statement. In this narrative, the details of the action are filled in over the next seven paragraphs. Joshua began by giving his squad of night rangers explicit instructions (8:4-8), since they would be separated from his command for nearly 48 hours. Joshua needed to know they understood their mission exactly. From a human standpoint, Israel's success in this second attempt on Ai depended on the precise timing of their rush into the city. Joshua's final words, "You have your orders," reflect the pivotal nature of their role in the looming battle.

Joshua then waited until the next morning to march the main army up from Gilgal to Ai. Until recently in the history of warfare, it was difficult to move large bodies of troops at night, except with adequate moonlight, and then any hoped-for element of surprise was likely lost. The 10 miles or so of this march, mostly uphill, to arrive at a position on the north of Ai, would have taken most of the daylight hours.

In this passage, directions and topography are reported very carefully. We may understand "in front of the town" to mean to the east of the town. Also, this phrase means Joshua did not try to hide his main army from the defenders in Ai. Circling to the north, Joshua and the main army ended the day "camped on the north side of Ai" (8:11). The men in ambush were west of Ai, between Ai and Bethel. Joshua's preparations were complete. He was ready for round two of the battle of Ai.

◆ 2. Joshua's success at Ai (8:14-29)

[14]When the king of Ai saw the Israelites
across the valley, he and all his army hur-
ried out early in the morning and attacked
the Israelites at a place overlooking the
Jordan Valley.* But he didn't realize there
was an ambush behind the town. [15]Joshua
and the Israelite army fled toward the wil-
derness as though they were badly beat-
en. [16]Then all the men in the town were
called out to chase after them. In this way,
they were lured away from the town.
[17]There was not a man left in Ai or Bethel*
who did not chase after the Israelites, and
the town was left wide open.

[18]Then the LORD said to Joshua, "Point
the spear in your hand toward Ai, for I will
hand the town over to you." Joshua did as
he was commanded. [19]As soon as Joshua
gave this signal, all the men in ambush
jumped up from their position and poured
into the town. They quickly captured it
and set it on fire.

[20]When the men of Ai looked behind
them, smoke from the town was filling
the sky, and they had nowhere to go. For
the Israelites who had fled in the direction
of the wilderness now turned on their
pursuers. [21]When Joshua and all the oth-
er Israelites saw that the ambush had suc-
ceeded and that smoke was rising from
the town, they turned and attacked the
men of Ai. [22]Meanwhile, the Israelites who
were inside the town came out and at-
tacked the enemy from the rear. So the
men of Ai were caught in the middle, with
Israelite fighters on both sides. Israel at-
tacked them, and not a single person sur-
vived or escaped. [23]Only the king of Ai
was taken alive and brought to Joshua.

[24]When the Israelite army finished
chasing and killing all the men of Ai in the
open fields, they went back and finished
off everyone inside. [25]So the entire popu-
lation of Ai, including men and women,
was wiped out that day—12,000 in all.
[26]For Joshua kept holding out his spear
until everyone who had lived in Ai was
completely destroyed.* [27]Only the live-
stock and the treasures of the town were
not destroyed, for the Israelites kept these
as plunder for themselves, as the LORD
had commanded Joshua. [28]So Joshua
burned the town of Ai,* and it became a
permanent mound of ruins, desolate to
this very day.

[29]Joshua impaled the king of Ai on a
sharpened pole and left him there until
evening. At sunset the Israelites took
down the body, as Joshua commanded,
and threw it in front of the town gate.
They piled a great heap of stones over him
that can still be seen today.

8:14 Hebrew *the Arabah.* **8:17** Some manuscripts lack *or Bethel.* **8:26** The Hebrew term used here refers to the complete consecration of things or people to the LORD, either by destroying them or by giving them as an offering. **8:28** *Ai* means "ruin."

NOTES

8:14 ***overlooking the Jordan Valley.*** Lit., "before the Arabah," the desert plain north of the Dead Sea.

8:15 ***toward the wilderness.*** This was eastward, back the way they had come just the day before, and the same direction they had fled the first time they had attacked Ai.

8:17 ***or Bethel.*** LXX omits "or Bethel" (see NLT mg). Boling (1982:240) suggests that *beth 'el* here may refer, not to the nearby city of Bethel, but to the *beth 'el* [TH410A/1004, ZH446/1074] (sanctuary, house of [the] god) in Ai itself. The suggestion is plausible, inasmuch as a sanctuary usually would have been defended, and the more difficult reading is preserved and explained. If Bethel is not mentioned in this account, except as a directional referent (8:9, 12), it could mean Bethel did not challenge Israel, so Israel left Bethel alone (but cf. also 12:16). Some have suggested Ai in this period was essentially a small fortified outpost of Bethel; the two were, in effect, one town. Yet, the movements of the two opposing forces fit the topography of Ai well. Therefore, there is every reason to suppose this is a real account of a real ambush used to dislodge a strong enemy, a tactic also used later in the civil war between Benjamin and the rest of Israel (Judg 20:29-48).

8:20 ***the wilderness.*** See note on 8:15.

8:24 ***in the open fields.*** Lit., "in the fields, in the wilderness."

8:25 ***12,000 in all.*** If Ai's population was 12,000 men and women, it was one of the largest cities of Canaan at this time—its conquest a topic worthy of record. Yet Joshua's scouts had reported Ai as small and insignificant (7:3); if this number should be reduced, it is unclear by what principle that should be done.

8:26 ***completely destroyed.*** See NLT mg and the discussion "Theological Concerns" in the Introduction.

8:27 ***were not destroyed.*** This is added for clarity. The Hebrew text reads, "Only the livestock and [other] treasure of this town Israel took as a spoil for themselves, according to the word of Yahweh which he had instructed Joshua."

8:28 ***burned . . . ruins.*** "Ai" means "ruin." Such a story regarding the naming of a place is termed etiological. That one of the functions of a given story is to explain a place name does not mean, however, that the story must be regarded as fictional, as some have maintained.

to this very day. This is one of many indicators in Joshua that the final editing of the book occurred at least several generations after the events recorded.

8:29 ***impaled.*** The verb (*talah* [TH8518, ZH9434]) allows for, but does not require, impalement as the means of execution of Ai's king. Joshua 10:26 suggests Joshua may have killed him by the sword, hanged him on a tree until evening, and then buried him in accordance with Moses's instructions (Deut 21:22-23).

heap of stones. This is a second memorial to Ai's destruction, the first being the ruin of the city itself.

today. See note on 8:28.

COMMENTARY

Early the following morning, the army of Ai stormed out of the city gate to engage Israel in battle, just as they had done the first time (7:5). The Hebrew of 8:14 depicts the men of Ai as recklessly eager to repeat the heroics of the previous battle. Before identifying "the men of the city" as the subject, the narrator used three vivid and forceful verbs in succession, literally, "Then they hurried, and rose early in the morning, and went out."

We can learn from all the characters in a biblical story, God's people or not. The king of Ai and his people reinforce for us a lesson that Joshua and Israel learned in their first attack on Ai: *Reckless overconfidence is dangerous*. What we don't know can kill. Joshua and Israel did not know Achan had sinned; 36 Israelite soldiers died. The king of Ai and his people did not know Joshua had set an ambush; all of them died. Through the word of God and other means of grace, God makes available the knowledge to keep his people from being ambushed by the enemy of our souls. But we must take the time and effort to learn and assimilate this knowledge for it to be an effective safeguard for us.

Joshua and Israel fell back before the onslaught, as the small army Joshua had sent the first time had done. The king of Ai pursued the "fleeing" Israelites, as before, and left the city open (8:17). One reason the king gave little thought to leaving the city open while pursuing the Israelites was likely his overconfidence at seeing Israel flee as they had fled before. But another important factor was Ai's soldiers' desire for booty. Much of the gain the individual soldier received from ancient warfare was his share of the spoils of battle taken from a defeated enemy. Often, too, a king would reward his soldiers for each enemy killed in battle.

The narrator's notice (8:18) that God told Joshua to "point the spear in your hand toward Ai" is another reminder that Israel succeeded in this second attack because God directed the battle this time. Because of the recklessness and greed of Ai's king and his men, the Israelite men in ambush west of the city faced no opposition as they rose from their hiding place, rushed into the city, and set it on fire (8:19). In an account notable for vivid detail, this description of Joshua closing the trap on Ai's fighters stands out. The narrator's double mention of the smoke of the burning town (8:20-21) is a large part of that. So much smoke lingers over the whole scene, the reader can almost smell it.

Ai's king was taken alive (8:23). As leaders of their individual city-states, he and the other Canaanite kings ought to have led their people in righteousness. Instead, they led them in continuing wickedness so that now the sin of the Amorites had reached its full measure (Gen 15:16). The execution of the king (8:29) showed that Israel was God's agent in the judgment of the people of Canaan for their wickedness.

◆ 3. Covenant renewal at Mount Ebal (8:30-35)

30 Then Joshua built an altar to the LORD, the God of Israel, on Mount Ebal. 31 He followed the commands that Moses the LORD's servant had written in the Book of Instruction: "Make me an altar from stones that are uncut and have not been shaped with iron tools."* Then on the altar they presented burnt offerings and peace offerings to the LORD. 32 And as the Israelites watched, Joshua copied onto the stones of the altar* the instructions Moses had given them.

33 Then all the Israelites—foreigners and native-born alike—along with the elders, officers, and judges, were divided into two groups. One group stood in front of Mount Gerizim, the other in front of Mount Ebal. Each group faced the other, and between them stood the Levitical priests carrying the Ark of the LORD's Covenant. This was all done according to the commands that Moses, the servant of the LORD, had previously given for blessing the people of Israel.

34 Joshua then read to them all the blessings and curses Moses had written in the Book of Instruction. 35 Every word of every command that Moses had ever given was read to the entire assembly of Israel, including the women and children and the foreigners who lived among them.

8:31 Exod 20:25; Deut 27:5-6. **8:32** Hebrew *onto the stones.*

NOTES

8:30 ***Mount Ebal.*** This mountain defined the north side of the pass of Shechem, about 20 miles north of Bethel and Ai.

8:32 ***onto the stones of the altar.*** Lit., "onto stones." The object is presumed to be a stone altar.

8:33 ***Mount Gerizim.*** This mountain defined the south side of the pass of Shechem, about 20 miles north of Bethel and Ai (see note on 8:30). The pass carried the most important interior road in the central hill country, making it of great symbolic and theological, as well as strategic, importance.

the commands that Moses . . . had previously given. See Deut 11:29; 27:11-13.

COMMENTARY

The ceremony of covenant renewal recounted in this passage began with the building of "an altar to the LORD" on Mount Ebal (8:30). Recently, an altar of uncut stones, on which no iron tool had been used (8:31), was discovered on the ridge of Mount Ebal. No inscription was found with it, but some think it may be the altar built by Joshua (Zertal 1985).

The "burnt offerings and peace offerings" (8:31) were two of the sacrifices prescribed (Lev 1 and 3, respectively) in the laws of sacrifice God gave Moses while Israel still was at Mount Sinai. We probably should assume that the prescribed daily sacrifices (Num 28:3-8) were already being carried out regularly, but this is the first time sacrifices are mentioned in Joshua, except for the Passover (5:10).

The text then tells us that "Joshua copied . . . the instructions Moses had given" (8:32), to fulfill the command recorded in Deuteronomy 27:2-8. There Moses had told some Israelites to set up stones and coat them with plaster. Woudstra calls them "whitewashed stones" and notes this is an Egyptian technique (Woudstra 1981:147, citing Craigie). This would suggest that the lettering of the laws on the stones was done in a colored ink or paint. (The colored monumental and tomb paintings of Egypt are famous down to the present.) Thus the laws, or a representative sampling, were placed permanently on display in a public place revered as the first location of Israel's formal worship of Yahweh after entering the land God had given them. Such a public display of laws was done in other places by other rulers; the best-known example is the famous Code of Hammurabi, which is preserved for us on an inscribed stela that Hammurabi set up in Babylon, his capital.

Still carrying out Moses's instructions, recorded first in Deuteronomy 11:26-32, and then in more detail in Deuteronomy 27–28, Joshua read "all the blessings and curses" (8:34). Half of Israel stood on the lower slopes of the north side of Mount Gerizim; the other half stood on the lower slopes of the south side of Mount Ebal, with Shechem guarding the mouth of the pass between them. Deuteronomy 27:12-13 even lists the tribes that were to comprise the two groups for Gerizim and Ebal, respectively.

With every person in Israel involved, and the Ark positioned in the valley between the two groups standing "in front of" the two mountains, this ceremony was a physical enactment of Israel's promise to keep the covenant God had made with them at Sinai. The blessings enumerated all the good things God would do for them as they remained faithful to him. The curses described the disasters that would befall them if they forsook the covenant and rebelled against God.

It is important to note that "the entire assembly of Israel, including the women and children and the foreigners who lived among them," were present (8:35). The casual reader sometimes infers that religious participation was reserved for men in ancient Israel. This reference, together with many others, corrects that mistaken notion. Women were active participants in Israel's worship, and even children were allowed to be present on many occasions. The "foreigners" were all those people, not Israelite by birth, who had accepted Yahweh as their God and had joined Israel when they saw the great things God had done for Israel. These included those who had come out of Egypt with Israel in the Exodus (Exod 12:38, 48-49), and probably now included Rahab and her family, as well (6:25).

This occasion marked a sense of taking possession of the land, though the campaigns against the Canaanite coalitions were still to come. By a ritual of sacrifice and reading of the law, the event brought to Israel's memory, individually and collectively, the promises and obligations of the covenant that had been mediated to them through Moses. As a ritual of anticipated possession, it demonstrated their faith in God's promise, whose fulfillment was beginning to unfold before them. The solemnity and inclusiveness of the occasion is emphasized throughout this short account.

◆ C. Gibeon's Successful Deception (9:1-27)

1. Negotiation with Gibeon's envoys (9:1-15)

Now all the kings west of the Jordan River heard about what had happened. These were the kings of the Hittites, Amorites, Canaanites, Perizzites, Hivites, and Jebusites, who lived in the hill country, in the western foothills,* and along the coast of the Mediterranean Sea* as far north as the Lebanon mountains. 2These kings combined their armies to fight as one against Joshua and the Israelites.

3But when the people of Gibeon heard what Joshua had done to Jericho and Ai, 4they resorted to deception to save themselves. They sent ambassadors to Joshua, loading their donkeys with weathered saddlebags and old, patched wineskins. 5They put on worn-out, patched sandals and ragged clothes. And the bread they took with them was dry and moldy. 6When they arrived at the camp of Israel at Gilgal, they told Joshua and the men of Israel, "We have come from a distant land to ask you to make a peace treaty with us."

7The Israelites replied to these Hivites, "How do we know you don't live nearby? For if you do, we cannot make a treaty with you."

8They replied, "We are your servants."

"But who are you?" Joshua demanded. "Where do you come from?"

9They answered, "Your servants have come from a very distant country. We have heard of the might of the LORD your God and of all he did in Egypt. 10We have also heard what he did to the two Amorite kings east of the Jordan River—King Sihon of Heshbon and King Og of Bashan (who lived in Ashtaroth). 11So our elders and all our people instructed us, 'Take supplies for a long journey. Go meet with the people of Israel and tell them, "We are your servants; please make a treaty with us."'

12"This bread was hot from the ovens when we left our homes. But now, as you can see, it is dry and moldy. 13These wineskins were new when we filled them, but now they are old and split open. And our clothing and sandals are worn out from our very long journey."

14So the Israelites examined their food, but they did not consult the LORD. 15Then Joshua made a peace treaty with them and guaranteed their safety, and the leaders of the community ratified their agreement with a binding oath.

9:1a Hebrew *the Shephelah*. 9:1b Hebrew *the Great Sea*.

NOTES

9:1 ***Hittites . . . Jebusites.*** See notes on 3:10.

9:2 ***combined . . . as one.*** This reflects the Hebrew, "gathered together as one . . . [with] one mouth," i.e., in one unanimously expressed intention to fight against Israel.

9:3 ***Gibeon.*** This is probably modern el-Jib, about seven miles (11 km) southwest of Ai, though not all agree that this identification is certain (cf. Woudstra 1981:154-155).

9:5 ***moldy.*** Or, "nothing but crumbs" (Woudstra 1981:151; cf. NASB).

9:7 ***these Hivites.*** By using this, the narrator heightened the irony of Israel's developing mistake. To date, this name occurs only in the Bible, and refers only to a non-Semitic ethnic group that lived in various parts of Canaan. Joshua and the elders should have recognized these visitors for who they really were.

How do we know you don't live nearby? For if you do, we cannot make a treaty with you. Lit., "Perhaps you [sg.] dwell near me; then how can I cut [make] a treaty with you [sg.]?" The language indicates that Joshua, as Israel's leader, was speaking to the leader of the Gibeonite delegation. The prohibition against making treaties with near neighbors is found in Deut 20:15.

9:9 ***of all he did in Egypt.*** This refers to God's actions in bringing Israel out of Egypt in the Exodus (Exod 7–14).

9:10 ***We have also heard what he did to the two Amorite kings.*** This is recorded in Num 21:21-35 and celebrated again (in greater detail) in Deut 2:24–3:11.

Heshbon. This was a city east of the northern end of the Dead Sea, on the Transjordanian plateau and the King's Highway. Sihon's kingdom extended south from his capital city to the gorge of the Arnon, which flows into the Dead Sea about midway along its eastern shore.

Ashtaroth. This was a city east of the Sea of Galilee, also on the King's Highway, in the region known throughout the OT period as Bashan.

9:12 ***moldy.*** See note on 9:5.

9:14 ***examined.*** Lit., "took." This means either that Israel's leaders actually tasted the bread, or only handled and looked at it. Either way, they were convinced.

did not consult the LORD. Lit., "did not consult the LORD's mouth." See note on 9:2 and commentary below.

9:15 ***guaranteed their safety.*** Lit., "cut [made] with them a covenant for their lives."

COMMENTARY

This section recounts the making of a treaty between the Israelites and the Gibeonites, though God had forbidden Israel to enter into treaties with near neighbors as they occupied the land of Canaan (Deut 20:15). This second mistake in Israel's occupation of the land was brought on by Joshua's failure to consult God when an unexpected situation arose. Narration of these less-than-flattering events demonstrates that the author's intent was not to portray heroic leaders, as many other ancient Near Eastern accounts aimed to do. Joshua and the elders are shown in their shortcomings as well as in their triumphs. God is the real hero whose exploits the author wished to recount.

As always, the narrator of Joshua was careful to note the pertinent geography in his record. "The hill country" (9:1) here includes the Negev in the south and the highlands of the territories later assigned to Judah, Ephraim, and Manasseh. "The western foothills" is the Shephelah, the fertile region of lower hills between the highlands of Judah and the southern coastal plain. The coast of the Mediterranean Sea was not occupied along its entire length, but several important cities did exist there during this period. The kings of these small city-states, as far north as Mount Carmel, could have been expected to join this southern coalition against Joshua and Israel.

Chapter 9 records two different Canaanite responses to the news that Israel was coming into the hill country. Chapter 10 is a fuller recital of these kings and their determination to fight against Israel. They may have taken heart from Israel's initial defeat at Ai, thinking that by fighting together they could defeat them again. Even if Ai's destruction had dimmed their hopes, apparently they felt it was better to die fighting than not to fight at all. Thus, this short notice contrasts vividly the unheroic and deceptive response of the Gibeonites with that of the other southern cities. After the treaty was concluded, the Gibeonites told Joshua why they thought deceiving Israel was their only hope (9:24).

The Gibeonite cities occupied what would come to be called the plateau of Benjamin, the strategic slice of the hill country, about 10 miles north to south, lying between Judah and Ephraim. They chose a different approach to Israel. Gibeon is only about seven miles from Ai, and not more than 15 miles from Gilgal, where Israel continued to maintain their camp. But to carry out their deception, the Gibeonite "ambassadors" had to arrive at Gilgal looking travel worn and ill-used; long-distance travel in those days was hard, dirty, and dangerous.

Upon encountering these "weary travelers," Joshua began well. His reasonable supposition, "perhaps you live among us," (9:7) means, "in the land we are coming to possess and live in." Following the ambassadors' short, evasive reply, Joshua even asked two pertinent, direct questions, point-blank, as a responsible leader charged with his people's welfare should do. The Gibeonite reply, "from a very distant country," was not only another vague answer, but this time also an insulting one, if Joshua had taken the time to think about it—because he should have known the name of *any* country they could have come from. These "ambassadors" could not have come from beyond present-day Turkey to the north, or Iran to the east, and any kingdom or people from within that range, Joshua should/would have known about or heard of. For them to insinuate otherwise was a verbal slap to a knowledgeable and capable leader. Joshua should have continued to vigorously insist on a name!

Joshua's and Israel's skepticism was short-lived. Distracted by the deception, by the Gibeonites' seemingly reverent words about Israel's God, and by the flattering notion that a faraway people wanted to make a treaty with them and become their vassals, no one among the Israelite leaders noticed they had failed to answer Joshua's questions. Israel still did not know who these people were or where they had come from.

Joshua had neglected once more to seek God's guidance, forgetting the recent lesson of Ai. Even on merely human terms, Joshua should have been suspicious at this point. If the travelers' wineskins were worn out and cracked, then their bread taken "hot from the ovens" (9:12) should have been gone long ago. If some of their bread really had lasted the whole journey, it could not have been so great a distance as to wear out their wineskins. The narrator's chiding of Israel's leadership for this foolish decision at first seems very gentle. He notes only "they did not consult the LORD" (9:14). But in light of all that had just happened, this is not such a gentle chiding after all. Not asking God's counsel had cost lives at Ai. The victories at Jericho and Ai both had been won when Israel followed God's instructions precisely. How could they so soon forget?

Another issue also should have occurred to Joshua. The Gibeonite envoys were asking Israel to enter with them into what is called today a vassal-suzerain treaty (but cf. Woudstra 1981:160-161). They were willing to swear a binding covenant with Israel and become a vassal state if only their lives were spared (9:11); this seems enough to conclude that the treaty was granted by a stronger power (Israel) to a weaker power (the Gibeonite cities). The request alone, though, ought to have raised suspicions; why would a faraway people be concerned with a treaty of protection with Israel?

There was even more, had Joshua thought of it. Israel, too, were vassals, the vassals of God. They had entered into just such a treaty with God at Sinai. Israel did not have authority to enter into treaties on her own, without the approval of her own suzerain. The narrator subtly contrasted the fierce determination of the Canaanite coalition's decision "with one mouth" to fight against Israel (9:2, see note), with Israel's failure to inquire of "the mouth of Yahweh" (9:14, see note), their divine suzerain, whom they always should have sought "with one mouth."

The important points for the succeeding action of this episode are that this covenant allowed the Gibeonites to live, and "the leaders of the community" ratified it "with a binding oath" (9:15). Covenants in this period were ratified by a ceremony involving cutting several animals in half lengthwise. It was as though the participants were saying, "Just as we have cut these animals in two, so may we be cut in two if we break this treaty" (cf. Gen 15:7-21). In Israel, moreover, binding oaths were sworn in the name of Yahweh. To violate the oath was to invite Yahweh's judgment for false swearing (Exod 20:7).

◆ 2. The Gibeonites' sentence of servitude (9:16-27)

16Three days after making the treaty, they
learned that these people actually lived
nearby! 17The Israelites set out at once to
investigate and reached their towns in
three days. The names of these towns
were Gibeon, Kephirah, Beeroth, and
Kiriath-jearim. 18But the Israelites did not
attack the towns, for the Israelite leaders
had made a vow to them in the name of
the LORD, the God of Israel.

The people of Israel grumbled against
their leaders because of the treaty. 19But
the leaders replied, "Since we have sworn
an oath in the presence of the LORD, the
God of Israel, we cannot touch them.
20This is what we must do. We must let
them live, for divine anger would come
upon us if we broke our oath. 21Let them
live." So they made them woodcutters and
water carriers for the entire community,
as the Israelite leaders directed.

22Joshua called together the Gibeonites
and said, "Why did you lie to us? Why did
you say that you live in a distant land
when you live right here among us? 23May
you be cursed! From now on you will

always be servants who cut wood and
carry water for the house of my God."
24 They replied, "We did it because we—
your servants—were clearly told that the
LORD your God commanded his servant
Moses to give you this entire land and to
destroy all the people living in it. So we
feared greatly for our lives because of
you. That is why we have done this. 25 Now
we are at your mercy—do to us whatever
you think is right."
26 So Joshua did not allow the people of
Israel to kill them. 27 But that day he made
the Gibeonites the woodcutters and water
carriers for the community of Israel and
for the altar of the LORD—wherever the
LORD would choose to build it. And that is
what they do to this day.

NOTES

9:17 ***three days.*** Gibeon is only about 15 miles from Gilgal, albeit mostly by an uphill route. A first day of travel *not* begun early, a full second day, and arrival well before evening on the third day, easily could be represented by the phrase "three days." Alternatively, "three days" here may be an idiomatic way of saying "a few days later," as it is in some other narratives. Moreover, in view of 10:6, it is not necessary to suppose all Israel made this journey; it was enough that Joshua sent or, perhaps, led a company of soldiers to investigate.

Gibeon. See note on 9:3.

Kephirah. Khirbet el-Kifirah is five miles west-southwest of el-Jib, the site of Gibeon (see note on 9:3).

Beeroth. This is probably Khirbet el-Burj, two miles south-southeast of el-Jib (Gibeon). Though this identification is not certain, Rainey (Rainey and Notley 2006:126) considers it the best candidate.

Kiriath-jearim. This is Tell Deir el-'Azhar (Abu Ghosh), two miles south of Kephirah, and six miles southwest of Gibeon (el-Jib).

9:20 ***divine anger.*** Heb., *qetsep* [TH7110, ZH7912], often translated "wrath" (e.g., NRSV, NASB); this response of God is never capricious, but always "morally conditioned" (Woudstra 1981:163).

9:21 ***for the entire community.*** This is defined more precisely in 9:23, 27.

9:23 ***May you be cursed!*** This is a theological and judicial sentence of misfortune or punishment, never uttered in a private capacity, or for private purposes, such as revenge. It corresponds to a judge's declaration, "You have been found guilty, and are hereby sentenced to . . . ," that one may hear in a modern courtroom.

9:24 ***were clearly told.*** Heb., *huged hugad* [TH5046, ZH5583], a very strong verbal construction, both in the verb forms and in the syntax employed. The NLT provides an appropriate rendering.

9:25 ***at your mercy.*** Lit., "in your hand."

think is right. This translates two Hebrew nouns, with their prepositions. The clause may be translated, "as [is] the good, and as [is] the right in your eyes to do to us, do [it]." Acknowledging Joshua's absolute power over them, the Gibeonites nevertheless emphasized his responsibility to do the right thing by them, in light of Israel's oath.

9:27 ***to this day.*** See note on 8:28.

COMMENTARY

Israel discovered the Gibeonites' deception too late. In reporting Israel's discovery, the author twice used the same word Joshua had used in voicing his suspicion; literally, "They were *near* to them; even in their *midst* they lived" (9:16). Joshua ought to have followed his instincts, to say nothing of asking God for guidance on the matter.

The note (9:17) that it took the Israelite investigating party "three days" to reach the Gibeonite towns is another example of the narrator's skill in commenting by the barest reporting. Three days is hardly a "very long journey" (9:13) "from a very distant country" (9:9)! On the contrary, these four towns were clustered strategically in the center of what would come to be known as the plateau of Benjamin. Benjamin, scarcely more than 10 miles long by 10 miles wide, is the military key to the highlands. The force that controls Benjamin effectively controls all the southern hill country.

The four Gibeonite towns were northwest of Jerusalem, all within 10 miles of it. No king of Gibeon is mentioned in the text. Adoni-zedek, king of Jerusalem, called on four allied kings to help him recapture the Gibeonite towns to the Canaanite cause (10:3-5). Taking these data together, it is reasonable to surmise that the Gibeonite towns were part of Adoni-zedek's kingdom of Jerusalem. If so, they took this extraordinary step, which amounted to rebellion against their overlord, in a desperate attempt to save themselves, just as they said.

We may wonder what the people of the four towns thought when they saw Israelite soldiers approaching. They surely hoped Israel had spoken with greater integrity than they themselves had, but until the Israelites actually arrived, and then refrained from killing, they had no way of knowing.

The modern reader may assume Israel was entitled to declare this covenant null and void, since they had entered into it only because of Gibeonite fraud. But Israel's leaders understood, correctly, that to break a covenant sworn by "an oath in the presence of the LORD" (9:19) would have been to treat lightly God's name and God's honor. Moreover, the deceit of the Gibeonites was probably not as great a moral issue for people of the ancient world as it is to moderns.

Since the Israelite community was angry with the Gibeonites over their own gullibility, Israel's leaders may have suggested in self-defense that Israel make "woodcutters and water carriers" of the Gibeonites (9:21). Joshua accepted and followed through on their proposal. Verse 21 is a proleptic summary; the rest of the chapter is a more detailed report.

As their new overlord, Joshua had the right to summon the Gibeonites before him for an accounting. If Joshua led the investigating company, this may have occurred in or in front of Gibeon, the principal city of the four. If Joshua remained in Israel's camp at Gilgal, then the Gibeonite leaders were escorted to him there. Joshua's question acknowledged that he ought to have known better than to accept the Gibeonites' word that they lived far away. He repeated as a statement—literally, "since you live right here among us" (9:22)—what he earlier had asked as a question, "perhaps you live among us?" (9:7). But Joshua had not followed up when the Gibeonites avoided giving a clear answer. Now Joshua knew; now he knew also that he should have known earlier.

Their deception of Israel made the Gibeonites morally accountable, so Joshua placed them under a curse, even before hearing their explanation for their action (9:23). As always with this verb, the curse took the form of punishment for a moral violation. There was nothing capricious nor vindictive about it. This was an appropriate judicial sentence for serious wrongdoing. Joshua's curse took the form of a decree of perpetual service to "the house of my God" (9:23). The verb used in covenant-making was to *cut* a covenant. Using the same verb, Joshua decreed that the service of hewing wood and drawing water never would *be cut* from them.

The expression "the house of my God" may refer to the Tabernacle God had instructed Moses to make at Sinai (cf. Exod 34:26; Deut 23:18), and later to the Temple of Solomon at Jerusalem. The Levitical sacrifices required a great deal of wood for burning. To be holy, the Tabernacle had to be clean. To maintain the cleanliness of a large slaughtering operation (Israel's sacrificial system, from a strictly physical point of view) required much water. The Gibeonites, Joshua ordained, would hew the wood and draw the water, and carry them to the Tabernacle. In this way, they would serve the entire community, as Israel's leaders had proposed. An alternate possibility for understanding this service is that Joshua charged the Gibeonites with the upkeep of a sanctuary in Gibeon itself. That Gibeon was an important worship center is clear from an episode early in Solomon's reign (1 Kgs 3:4-5; 2 Chr 1). Given that even the worship of Yahweh was not fully centralized in Jerusalem until the reign of Josiah (2 Kgs 23:8-9), it is possible that a pagan sanctuary in Gibeon was rededicated to the worship of Yahweh.

The Gibeonite response amounts to a statement of faith in Israel's God. They believed that what God had instructed Moses, God would enable Israel to do, so they acted deceptively to save their lives.

The author closed his account of this episode with a brief summarizing statement (9:26-27) of a kind seen before (cf. 8:28); it suggests that the book of Joshua received its final form some generations after the events it records. This summary closes the account of Joshua's second, and last, major recorded leadership mistake.

◆ D. Joshua's Victory at Aijalon (10:1-43)

1. Gibeon's call for help (10:1-6)

**Adoni-zedek, king of Jerusalem, heard
that Joshua had captured and completely
destroyed* Ai and killed its king, just as he
had destroyed the town of Jericho and
killed its king. He also learned that the
Gibeonites had made peace with Israel
and were now their allies. [2]He and his
people became very afraid when they
heard all this because Gibeon was a large
town—as large as the royal cities and
larger than Ai. And the Gibeonite men
were strong warriors.**

**[3]So King Adoni-zedek of Jerusalem sent
messengers to several other kings: Hoham
of Hebron, Piram of Jarmuth, Japhia of
Lachish, and Debir of Eglon. [4]"Come and
help me destroy Gibeon," he urged them,
"for they have made peace with Joshua
and the people of Israel." [5]So these five
Amorite kings combined their armies for
a united attack. They moved all their
troops into place and attacked Gibeon.**

**[6]The men of Gibeon quickly sent mes-
sengers to Joshua at his camp in Gilgal.
"Don't abandon your servants now!" they
pleaded. "Come at once! Save us! Help us!
For all the Amorite kings who live in the hill
country have joined forces to attack us."**

10:1 The Hebrew term used here refers to the complete consecration of things or people to the LORD, either by destroying them or by giving them as an offering; also in 10:28, 35, 37, 39, 40.

NOTES

10:1 ***Adoni-zedek.*** The name means "Lord of righteousness" or "my Lord is righteous"; it is similar to the name of an earlier king of Jerusalem, Melchizedek, meaning "king of righteousness" or "my King is righteous." Melchizedek had been a friend of Abraham (Gen 14:18-20), but Adoni-zedek was no friend to Joshua.

Jerusalem . . . Ai . . . Gibeonites. Ai was about 10 miles north of Jerusalem; Gibeon was only six miles north-northwest of Jerusalem. From Adoni-zedek's point of view, these new allies of the encroaching Israelites were dangerously close.

completely destroyed. The Hebrew root is *kharam* [TH2763, ZH3049]. See NLT mg, and see also discussion under "Theological Concerns" in the Introduction (p. 13). So also in 10:28, 35, 37, 39, 40.

10:2 ***very afraid.*** This is the seventh and last report that Canaan was afraid of Israel (cf. 2:9-11; 2:24; 5:1; 6:1; 9:9-11; 9:24). Their "perfect" fear (represented by the number seven) led the Gibeonites to submit to Israel, but led most of the Canaanite kings to choose war.

10:3 ***Hebron.*** This was about 20 miles south-southwest of Jerusalem, in the hill country.

Jarmuth. This was about 15 miles west-southwest of Jerusalem, in the northern Shephelah, the lower "foothills" region lying west of the Judean hill country proper.

Lachish. This was an important city about 30 miles southwest of Jerusalem, near the southwestern edge of the Shephelah.

Debir. This is possibly an error in transmission, or a mispointing of the vowels because Debir is the name of a town in the hill country south of Hebron. LXX Vaticanus has "Dabein"; as both consonants are liquids, "r" and "n" sometimes were confused.

Eglon. This was about seven miles southeast of Lachish, in the southern Shephelah.

10:5 ***five Amorite kings.*** The Hebrew text lists them again, though not by name: "the king of Jerusalem, the king of Hebron, the king of Jarmuth, the king of Lachish, the king of Eglon." When a distinction was made, the Amorites were located in the hill country, and the Canaanites in the larger valleys and the coastal plain. Three of these five cities were in the Shephelah, not geographically part of the hill country, and carefully distinguished from it throughout the Bible. We may excuse the Gibeonites, however, for not naming the Shephelah separately in their desperate message to Joshua (10:6).

COMMENTARY

In chapter 10, we see that the treaty with the Gibeonites precipitated events that led to the breaking of Canaanite resistance in the south. Gibeon was only six miles from Jerusalem, and it guarded the approach to a major route ascending from the coastal plain into the hill country. Gibeon and its neighboring cities occupied the plateau of Benjamin (as it came to be called), a relatively level rectangle immediately to the north of Jerusalem, about 100 square miles in area. Control of this plateau was essential to control of the entire hill country. Throughout history, with few exceptions, whoever controlled Benjamin controlled the hill country. With Gibeon now allied to Israel, control of the plateau, and thus of the hill country, belonged to Israel. The Canaanite kings had to conquer Gibeon before Joshua could come to its rescue, or their cause was lost.

The Amorite coalition reached Gibeon, but the Gibeonites sent a message (probably via a runner) to Joshua, on a crescendo of urgency. Beginning with a relatively restrained, "Don't abandon your servants now!" (10:6), it moved to the more urgent, "Come at once!"—climaxing with the almost-panicked, "Save us! Help us!" The Gibeonites knew they had brought upon themselves a life-or-death crisis from which only Joshua could save them. "Don't abandon" in Hebrew is "don't slacken your hand from," an idiomatic way of asking Joshua's help, but also a tacit recognition that Joshua could have been tempted to drag his heels (to use a modern English idiom). He easily could have delayed to "equip the men" (or something else), and Israel would have arrived too late.

Instead, Joshua responded quickly and in good faith. To come to the rescue of a vassal threatened by outside enemies was practically the only obligation a suzerain pledged himself to in the kind of treaty Israel had entered into with Gibeon. Having sworn by Yahweh to rescue Gibeon when they were threatened, Joshua and Israel undertook now to do it. However, this initiative was in Joshua's interests, too. If he could rout the combined Canaanite forces by this lightning strike, it would give Israel a tremendous advantage, both in position and in momentum.

◆ 2. Israel's response and God's response (10:7-15)

7So Joshua and his entire army, including his best warriors, left Gilgal and set out for Gibeon. 8"Do not be afraid of them," the LORD said to Joshua, "for I have given you victory over them. Not a single one of them will be able to stand up to you."

9Joshua traveled all night from Gilgal and took the Amorite armies by surprise. 10The LORD threw them into a panic, and the Israelites slaughtered great numbers of them at Gibeon. Then the Israelites chased the enemy along the road to Beth-horon, killing them all along the way to Azekah and Makkedah. 11As the Amorites retreated down the road from Beth-horon, the LORD destroyed them with a terrible hailstorm from heaven that continued until they reached Azekah. The hail killed more of the enemy than the Israelites killed with the sword.

12On the day the LORD gave the Israelites victory over the Amorites, Joshua prayed to the LORD in front of all the people of Israel. He said,

> "Let the sun stand still over Gibeon,
> and the moon over the valley of
> Aijalon."

13So the sun stood still and the moon stayed in place until the nation of Israel had defeated its enemies.

Is this event not recorded in *The Book of Jashar**? The sun stayed in the middle of the sky, and it did not set as on a normal day.* 14There has never been a day like this one before or since, when the LORD answered such a prayer. Surely the LORD fought for Israel that day!

15Then Joshua and the Israelite army returned to their camp at Gilgal.

10:13a Or *The Book of the Upright.* 10:13b Or *did not set for about a whole day.*

NOTES

10:9 *Joshua traveled all night from Gilgal.* Lit., "All night he ascended from Gilgal."

10:10 *slaughtered . . . chased . . . killing.* The Hebrew forms allow for either God (Yahweh) or Israel as subject of all three verbs. KJV and NASB make the subject of all three "God"; LXX has "the Lord" (*kurios* [TG2962, ZG3261]) as subject of the first. Most versions, ancient and modern, agree on Israel as the subject of all three. The grammatical and syntactical ambiguity may be deliberate; this narrative clearly is intended to stress that God defeated this Amorite coalition, using Joshua and his men only in a relatively minor way as his agents on the ground.

along the road to Beth-horon. Lit., "the Way [Road] of the Ascent of Beth-horon." This is the proper name of a specific road, the easiest and best road to Jerusalem, in this period, from the Mediterranean and the northern coastal plain. The two towns of Upper Beth-horon and Lower Beth-horon marked the path of its main ascent into the hill country. This road branches off from the main interior north–south road near Gibeon—one reason for Gibeon's importance to Jerusalem as reflected in this narrative.

Azekah and Makkedah. These were two towns in the Shephelah southwest of Gibeon; by the route described here, Azekah lay about 25 miles southwest of Gibeon, Makkedah another 10 miles south of Azekah.

10:11 *terrible hailstorm from heaven.* Lit., "great stones from the heavens."

The hail. Lit., "The stones of the hail."

10:12 *the valley of Aijalon.* From Lower Beth-horon (descending), the Beth-horon road veered left (southward) into the valley of Aijalon, named for a town partway along its course toward Gezer.

10:13 *The Book of Jashar.* Or, "The Book of the Upright" (cf. NLT mg); the presence of the Hebrew definite article supports the rendering "upright." Traditionally, it is taken as the work of a man named (or titled) Jashar. This book, or scroll, mentioned also in 2 Sam 1:18, no longer exists; it was one of a number of written sources Israel's early historians had available to them.

it did not set as on a normal day. Grammar and syntax allow for both the NLT reading in the text and the NLT mg note: "did not set for about a whole day." The vocabulary here and in 10:12 also can support either reading, but the NLT text reading seems better, for reasons discussed in the commentary.

COMMENTARY

To rescue Gibeon, Joshua undertook an all-night march of about 20 miles, the first part of it up the rugged passes and steep slopes from the Jordan Rift Valley to gain the plateau of Benjamin. Then he crossed the plateau from east to west, moving quickly but inconspicuously, still under cover of darkness, to take the Amorite army besieging Gibeon by surprise (lit., "suddenly") at first light (10:9). Attacking at sunrise, just as the camp was beginning to stir, Joshua's army would have seemed to come out of the sun, blinding the Amorites as they turned eastward to fight a foe they could not see.

As at Jericho, here also God took a hand, and what began as a battle turned into a rout. From Gibeon down the Beth-horon road, then south through the Shephelah to Azekah, is about 25 miles. This was in a homeward direction for many or most of the fleeing men, but few reached home, on this or any other day. God's intervention in this battle is another reminder of the nature of miracles. Some construe this "terrible hailstorm" as a fortunate coincidence for Israel, who then interpreted it as God's intervention. But those who take seriously God's sovereignty over all creation and God's interest in the affairs of individuals and of nations usually do not interpret it so. God, who reserves the storehouses of the hail for the day of battle and war (Job 38:22-23), opened them that day. Modern meteorological knowledge requires God neither to abdicate his freedom to act, nor to relinquish his choice of instruments.

This account also is the clearest notice in the book of Joshua that the judgment upon Canaan was God's doing, and no one else's. God did use Israel as God's agent of judgment, and Israel's soldiers killed many who came against them in battle, hoping to destroy all God's people if they could. But even more, God judged directly. Israel did not cause Jericho's walls to collapse. Israel did not propose the successful strategy against Ai. And now God's hail killed more Amorite soldiers than did Israel's swords (10:11). God's people may trust God to judge justly, mercifully, and at the proper time.

The record of the sun and the moon standing still (10:12-13) raises unanswerable questions. The traditional understanding is reflected in the common title, "Joshua's Long Day": This day had about twice the number of hours (at least, of daylight hours) as any other day in history. Certainly, the omnipotent God could do such a thing, and could suppress or correct the effects of inertia, such as tidal waves and earthquakes, that would be expected to follow a sudden stoppage of the earth's rotation. The usual meanings of "stood still" and "the middle of the sky," the facts that both pursued and pursuers seem to have covered 40 miles before the pursuit was ended, and that many more Amorite warriors probably would have escaped had this normally two-day journey required two (or more) days of pursuit, as well as Israel's amazement at this singular event—all seem to argue for the traditional understanding.

But equally devout believers may look for another way to understand this event, asking why such a cataclysmic event would be necessary after God already had flung hail on the fleeing enemy. Is there another way to understand this event, since it seems out of proportion to Israel's need?

The verb *damam* [TH1826, ZH1957], used twice here ("stand/stood"; 10:12-13), means basically "to be silent." In effect, Joshua commanded the sun, "Stand still where you are, and be quiet until your Master (and mine) releases you." (Of course, this was a prayer to Yahweh, but the grammar, by a rhetorical figure, addresses it to the sun and moon directly.) Alfrink (1952:66ff) connects this verb to a Babylonian-Assyrian usage of *nabu*, referring to the darkening of the sun and the moon. The other verb, *'amad* [TH5975, ZH6641], ("the moon stayed in place"; 10:13) occurs in Habakkuk 3:11 with the same meaning (i.e., that it was darkened). Alfrink understands the sun and moon to have been darkened by the hailstorm, while the sun still stood "in the middle of the sky." The perfectly plausible NLT, "it did not set as on a normal day" (10:13), can support this understanding, as well as the traditional one. In this case the sun's not setting is taken as a clarification that although it was dark, it was not because the sun had set.

Scholars and lay students alike have proposed many other solutions, but it can be conceded that not all miracles are understandable (especially this one), whether in purpose, scope, or mechanism. What is clear is the tremendous impression this event made on Israel, that "the LORD answered such a prayer" (10:14). Since the sun and the moon were Canaanite deities, it would have made a great impression upon the Canaanites, too. Not only was Israel's God dominant over two of Canaan's most powerful gods, but Israel's God even listened to Israel's commander-in-chief, and did this great thing in response to Joshua's request. (In addition, it should be remarked that no agency of any government has "found" this "lost day." That rumor remains entirely baseless.)

It may be best to regard 10:12-15, together, as a quotation from the ancient source, *The Book of Jashar*—except for the parenthetical attribution in the middle, "Is this event not recorded in *The Book of Jashar*?" Verse 15 then would make sense as the conclusion of the quotation, which recorded only the stopping of the sun and the moon. Alternatively, 10:15 is another of the author's many summary episodic conclusions, followed by more details once the "main" events had been recounted. Whichever its origin, as used here it is an effective narrative technique.

3. Execution of five kings (10:16-27)

16 During the battle the five kings escaped and hid in a cave at Makkedah. 17 When Joshua heard that they had been found, 18 he issued this command: "Cover the opening of the cave with large rocks, and place guards at the entrance to keep the kings inside. 19 The rest of you continue chasing the enemy and cut them down from the rear. Don't give them a chance to get back to their towns, for the LORD your God has given you victory over them."

20 So Joshua and the Israelite army continued the slaughter and completely crushed the enemy. They totally wiped out the five armies except for a tiny remnant that managed to reach their fortified towns. 21 Then the Israelites returned safely to Joshua in the camp at Makkedah. After that, no one dared to speak even a word against Israel.

22 Then Joshua said, "Remove the rocks covering the opening of the cave, and bring the five kings to me." 23 So they brought the five kings out of the cave—the kings of Jerusalem, Hebron, Jarmuth, Lachish, and Eglon. 24 When they brought them out, Joshua told the commanders of his army, "Come and put your feet on the kings' necks." And they did as they were told.

25 "Don't ever be afraid or discouraged," Joshua told his men. "Be strong and courageous, for the LORD is going to do this to all of your enemies." 26 Then Joshua killed each of the five kings and impaled them on five sharpened poles, where they hung until evening.

27 As the sun was going down, Joshua gave instructions for the bodies of the kings to be taken down from the poles and thrown into the cave where they had been hiding. Then they covered the opening of the cave with a pile of large rocks, which remains to this very day.

NOTES

10:16 *Makkedah.* This is now conclusively identified with Khirbet el-Qom, about 10 miles south of Azekah, seven miles east-southeast of Lachish (Rainey and Notley 2006:127). Limestone caves are numerous in the region.

10:17 *When Joshua heard that they had been found.* Lit., "Then it was reported to Joshua, saying, 'The five kings have been found, hiding in the cave at Makkedah.' "

10:18 *Cover the opening of the cave with large rocks.* Lit., "Roll large stones to the mouth of the cave."

10:21 *no one dared to speak even a word against Israel.* NLT captures the sense; the Hebrew verb is "point," meaning either, "no one moved his tongue [pointed his tongue to speak] against" or "no one sharpened his tongue [to speak] against the people of Israel."

10:23 *Jerusalem . . . Eglon.* See notes on 10:1, 3.

10:27 *covered the opening of the cave with a pile of large rocks.* Both the Hebrew verb and the Hebrew preposition here are different from 10:18, probably to signify the permanence of this "covering," compared with the temporary nature of the first, which was only to prevent the five kings from escaping.

COMMENTARY

The narrator now completes the account of the mopping-up operations at the end of that amazing day when the sun and the moon stood still. It was a common practice in Semitic narrative to tell a story in its main outlines with all the important and stirring highlights and then come back and fill in details that would have bogged down the account if told with the main events and themes. (An even more important example is Gen 2:5-25, the more detailed account of the forming of the first humans, which would grossly misshape the climax of Gen 1 if placed there after verse 27, where it "belongs," sequentially.)

The five kings had led the southern coalition against God's people at Gibeon. Now in defeat they led their people also in retreat, for Makkedah is the farthest point mentioned by name on the retreat route that day (10:10).

Joshua's orders show him as a military commander who was always thinking. To "cover the opening of the cave" (10:18) not only reduced the number of guards needed to keep the kings from escaping, it also eliminated the danger to the guards that the kings might try to fight their way out. Warriors in flight for their lives often throw away their weapons, so that danger may have been slight, but a good commander does not allow soldiers to take even small risks when they are avoidable.

That Israel "returned safely" indicates they suffered few casualties and perhaps no deaths in this battle. A low number of Israelite casualties was always a sign of God's favor toward Israel in battle. The reference to "the camp at Makkedah" confirms that Israel took several days to complete the mopping up after their rout of the Amorite forces, and that 10:15 probably is the conclusion of the quote from *The Book of Jashar*. Abhorrent as it is to many in our age, Joshua's public humiliation of the five kings (10:24) represents common practice in the ancient Near East. We are not required to condone Joshua's action.

In any event, Joshua spoke (10:25) the same words God had used when encouraging him before the crossing of the Jordan (1:9), and again before the battle of Ai (8:1). This was, after all, only the third battle in Israel's campaign to take the land. From a human point of view the outcome of their campaign still may have looked uncertain to those of a timid spirit. Joshua's strong words—two vigorous prohibitions against fear, two vigorous exhortations to courage—were spoken while their defeated enemies lay prostrate under their feet. This served as a powerful visual aid to Israel's troops, giving them hope and incentive for the daunting tasks that still lay before them.

Joshua's execution of the five kings followed the pattern established by the execution of the king of Ai (see note on 8:29). We should note that Joshua killed each one before impaling him. Israel did not practice the cruelty of the Assyrians, who later impaled captured Judean soldiers alive at Lachish, not far from Makkedah. The cave where the five kings had taken refuge, which had become their prison, Joshua now made their tomb. The "large rocks" (10:27) covering the mouth of the cave became for Israel another stone memorial in the land. As always, "to this very day" means until the time of the narrator, or even of a later scribal editor or copyist.

4. End of the southern campaign (10:28-43)

[28]That same day Joshua captured and destroyed the town of Makkedah. He killed everyone in it, including the king, leaving no survivors. He destroyed them all, and he killed the king of Makkedah as he had killed the king of Jericho. [29]Then Joshua and the Israelites went to Libnah and attacked it. [30]There, too, the LORD gave them the town and its king. He killed everyone in it, leaving no survivors. Then Joshua killed the king of Libnah as he had killed the king of Jericho.

[31]From Libnah, Joshua and the Israelites went to Lachish and attacked it. [32]Here again, the LORD gave them Lachish. Joshua took it on the second day and killed everyone in it, just as he had done at Libnah. [33]During the attack on Lachish, King Horam of Gezer arrived with his army to help defend the town. But Joshua's men killed him and his army, leaving no survivors.

[34]Then Joshua and the Israelite army went on to Eglon and attacked it. [35]They captured it that day and killed everyone in it. He completely destroyed everyone, just as he had done at Lachish. [36]From Eglon, Joshua and the Israelite army went up to Hebron and attacked it. [37]They captured the town and killed everyone in it, including its king, leaving no survivors. They did the same thing to all of its surrounding villages. And just as he had done at Eglon, he completely destroyed the entire population.

[38]Then Joshua and the Israelites turned back and attacked Debir. [39]He captured the town, its king, and all of its surrounding villages. He completely destroyed everyone in it, leaving no survivors. He did to Debir and its king just what he had done to Hebron and to Libnah and its king.

[40]So Joshua conquered the whole region—the kings and people of the hill country, the Negev, the western foothills,* and the mountain slopes. He completely destroyed everyone in the land, leaving no survivors, just as the LORD, the God of Israel, had commanded. [41]Joshua slaughtered them from Kadesh-barnea to Gaza and from the region around the town of Goshen up to Gibeon. [42]Joshua conquered all these kings and their land in a single campaign, for the LORD, the God of Israel, was fighting for his people.

[43]Then Joshua and the Israelite army returned to their camp at Gilgal.

10:40 Hebrew *the Shephelah.*

NOTES

10:28 ***That same day.*** This is one of the phrases that mark this as a battle report of the type common throughout the Near East of this time. This and the Hebrew phrasing do not require us to understand that this was the same day noted in 10:27, as often inferred from translation; the Hebrew phrases are different in the two verses.

Makkedah. See note on 10:16.

no survivors. Cf. 10:30, 32, 33, 35, 37, 39, 40. These phrasings are intended to convey the completeness of Israel's victories; see "Theological Concerns" in the Introduction.

10:29 ***Libnah.*** Rainey identifies Libnah with Tell Bornat, about nine miles northwest of Makkedah, and about six miles north of Lachish (Rainey and Notley 2006:127).

10:31 ***Lachish.*** See note on 10:3.

10:33 ***Gezer.*** This was a very important city near the northwest corner of the Shephelah, about 20 miles north of Lachish.

10:34 ***Eglon.*** See note on 10:3.

10:36 ***Hebron.*** See note on 10:3.

10:38 ***Debir.*** This has been identified as Khirbet Rabud, located in the hill country about six miles south of Hebron (see also commentary on 15:13-19).

10:40 ***the hill country . . . the mountain slopes.*** This encompasses the entire south of Canaan (see Introduction, "The Physical Geography of Canaan"). The success of Joshua's southern campaign made it impossible for the Canaanites to prevent Judah and the other southern tribes from settling in the land.

10:41 ***Kadesh-barnea.*** Located in the wilderness of Zin, this was at the southwestern boundary of the area of influence of this southern campaign. From there, the western boundary of this campaign's effectiveness ran due north to Gaza, on the southern Mediterranean coast.

Goshen. This is not the region of the same name in Egypt's eastern Nile Delta. This Goshen was in the same hill country district as Debir (15:51), south of Hebron.

COMMENTARY

With the rout of the five kings and their coalition, southern Canaan lay open before Joshua and Israel's army. None of the city-states mentioned could mount serious opposition, as their best warriors lay dead along the road from Gibeon to Aijalon to Azekah to Makkedah, and five of their principal kings were buried in Makkedah's cave. The account from here on is clearly a series of summary statements, with no detail provided. None was needed; after the execution of the five kings, the rest of the southern campaign was only finishing touches. But this took time. Joshua 11:18 refers to Joshua "waging war for a long time," first in the south and then the north. Armies usually move quite slowly, and fighting so as to minimize Israelite casualties would have added to Joshua's planning time on each occasion. The note in 10:42 that Joshua did this "in a single campaign" is true, but says nothing about the duration of that campaign.

The geographical progression of Joshua and his army makes sense, both from place to place, and from region to region: west into the Shephelah, then back east into the hill country. Six cities were taken; between the first three and the second three, the only real army Joshua faced came from Gezer to Lachish, but too late to rescue Lachish, whose king already lay dead. The phrase "as [Joshua] had done to X" is repeated a perfect seven times in this summary report (10:28, 30, 32, 35, 37, 39 [2x]). In the end, Israel could not be kept out of southern Canaan.

Having buried the five kings in a cave, Joshua took Makkedah (10:28). Next came Libnah (10:29), about nine miles northwest, then Lachish, about six miles south of Libnah. The notice that Joshua took Lachish "on the second day" (10:32) may be connected with the arrival of Horam of Gezer from the north (10:33). From Lachish, Joshua and Israel moved to Eglon (10:34), about seven miles southeast of Lachish; Eglon's king also lay buried at Makkedah. After capturing Eglon, Israel ascended east into the hill country about 12 miles and took Hebron. The final city subdued in this campaign was Debir, about six miles south of Hebron, and still in the hill country. Only for Hebron and Debir are dependent towns mentioned. This may be because settlement in the hill country was sparse, so the kingdoms of the few dominant cities spread more widely. Smaller towns could not maintain their independence. The Hebrew word used of these outlying cities in 10:37 and 39 refers to walled towns (*'ir* [TH5892, ZH6551]), not to unwalled settlements.

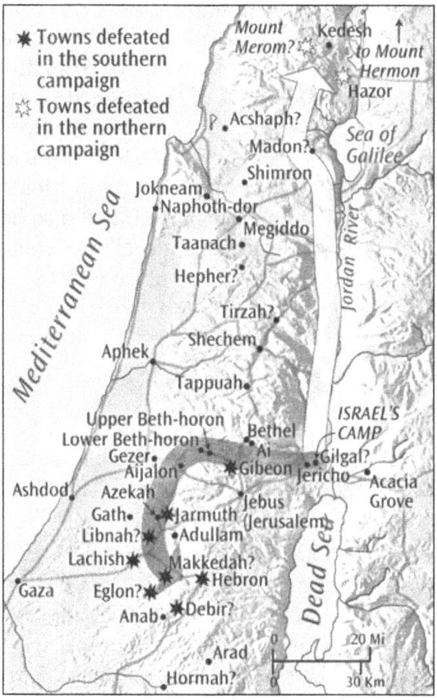

Israel's Conquest of Canaan

Joshua's successes from Jericho until this point are summarized in 10:40-42. The four regions named include the whole of the south of Canaan. "Kadesh-barnea to Gaza" denotes, in general, the western section, and "Goshen up to Gibeon," in general, the eastern section. This span shows the effectiveness of this southern campaign. Gibeon, northwest of Jerusalem, was the city whose actions had triggered this whole campaign. In another example of the narrator's skill, the relating of this episode now has come full circle, from Gibeon back to Gibeon.

In view of the notices concerning the land that remained to be taken, we must remember this was a military campaign and not yet the settlement of the tribes. Some of these cities apparently had to be retaken later. But this campaign did make it impossible for the surviving Canaanites to prevent Judah and the other southern tribes from settling, when the time came. Joshua's southern campaign had cleared the way.

◆ E. Joshua's Victory over the Northern Coalition (11:1-23)

1. Joshua's defeat of Jabin of Hazor (11:1-15)

When King Jabin of Hazor heard what had
happened, he sent messages to the fol-
lowing kings: King Jobab of Madon; the
king of Shimron; the king of Acshaph; 2all
the kings of the northern hill country; the
kings in the Jordan Valley south of Gali-
lee*; the kings in the Galilean foothills*;
the kings of Naphoth-dor on the west;
3the kings of Canaan, both east and west;
the kings of the Amorites, the Hittites, the
Perizzites, the Jebusites in the hill country,
and the Hivites in the towns on the slopes
of Mount Hermon in the land of Mizpah.
4All these kings came out to fight. Their
combined armies formed a vast horde.
And with all their horses and chariots,
they covered the landscape like the sand
on the seashore. 5The kings joined forces
and established their camp around the
water near Merom to fight against Israel.
6Then the LORD said to Joshua, "Do not
be afraid of them. By this time tomorrow
I will hand all of them over to Israel as
dead men. Then you must cripple their
horses and burn their chariots."
7So Joshua and all his fighting men
traveled to the water near Merom and at-
tacked suddenly. 8And the LORD gave them
victory over their enemies. The Israelites
chased them as far as Greater Sidon and
Misrephoth-maim, and eastward into the
valley of Mizpah, until not one enemy
warrior was left alive. 9Then Joshua crip-
pled the horses and burned all the chari-
ots, as the LORD had instructed.
10Joshua then turned back and captured

Hazor and killed its king. (Hazor had at
one time been the capital of all these
kingdoms.) 11 The Israelites completely de-
stroyed* every living thing in the city, leav-
ing no survivors. Not a single person was
spared. And then Joshua burned the city.
12 Joshua slaughtered all the other kings
and their people, completely destroying
them, just as Moses, the servant of the
LORD, had commanded. 13 But the Israelites
did not burn any of the towns built on
mounds except Hazor, which Joshua
burned. 14 And the Israelites took all the
plunder and livestock of the ravaged towns
for themselves. But they killed all the peo-
ple, leaving no survivors. 15 As the LORD had
commanded his servant Moses, so Moses
commanded Joshua. And Joshua did as he
was told, carefully obeying all the com-
mands that the LORD had given to Moses.

11:2a Hebrew *in the Arabah south of Kinnereth.* **11:2b** Hebrew *the Shephelah;* also in 11:16. **11:11** The Hebrew term used here refers to the complete consecration of things or people to the LORD, either by destroying them or by giving them as an offering; also in 11:12, 20, 21.

NOTES

11:1 *Hazor.* This was the largest and most important city of inland Canaan at that time, because it was on the international trade route between Egypt and Mesopotamia. Hazor lay 10 miles north of the Sea of Galilee, and overlooked the Huleh Valley to the north.

Madon. LXX reads *Marrōn*. Rainey (2006:129) follows LXX and identifies this site with the Merom of 11:5, locating it "at a well-known water source near Marun er-Ras, a centrally located mountain in Upper Galilee." Woudstra (1981:188) follows MT and locates Madon at the Horns of Hattin, in lower Galilee west of Tiberias. Because the Hebrew letters Daleth and Resh are easily confused and Madon is unattested except here and 12:19, Rainey's seems the better conclusion.

Shimron. LXX reads *Sumoōn*, reflecting Heb. *shim'on* [TH8095, ZH9058], today's Tel Shimron on the northern edge of the Jezreel Valley and southern edge of lower Galilee (Rainey and Notley 2006:129).

Acshaph. This is at the foot of the Carmel range, on the southern edge of the plain of Acco.

11:2 *the northern hill country.* I.e., upper and lower Galilee. This reflects the usual biblical identification of the hill country as stretching from the Negev of Judah in the south through all of upper Galilee in the north (including today's southernmost part of Lebanon).

the Jordan Valley south of Galilee. Heb. *'arabah* [TH6160A, ZH6858] (see NLT mg) is a geographical descriptor, applied to several regions in the Jordan Valley and south of the Dead Sea. *Kinnereth* (see NLT mg) is the OT name for the Sea of Galilee, though it is used only a handful of times. The Hebrew noun here actually is *kinaroth* [TH3672A, ZH4054], possibly denoting a location near the Sea of Galilee, named for this proximity.

the Galilean foothills. Heb., *shepelah* [TH8219, ZH9169] (see NLT mg); these northern "foothills" between the Mediterranean Sea and the Lebanon Mountains proper resemble in their appearance and their geology the southern Shephelah of Judah. Woudstra (1981:189) suggests the Judean Shephelah, but that is impossible here, both geographically and literarily.

Naphoth-dor. I.e., the "districts of Dor," on the coast, south of the cape of Mount Carmel.

11:3 *Canaan . . . the Hivites.* See notes on 3:10.

the Jebusites. This is the only reference we have to Jebusites outside the region of Jerusalem.

Mount Hermon. The southern anchor of the Anti-Lebanon Range, about 9,200 feet above sea level at its summit. Hermon was the northern limit of Israelite conquest and settlement.

Mizpah. This means "Point Lookout"; several locations named Mizpah are recorded in Scripture.

11:5 *Merom.* See note on Madon in 11:1.

11:8 ***The Israelites chased them.*** Lit., "and [Israel] smote them and they chased them."

Greater Sidon. Or, "Great Sidon." At this time, this was the most important southern Phoenician city and port, as evidenced by the nonmention of Tyre in early biblical texts—though Sidon is nearly 40 miles north of Tyre, and much farther from this battle site and from Dan (Judg 18). (See B. Mazar 1986:63ff.)

Misrephoth-maim. This is Khirbet Musheirefeh, at the northern end of the plain of Acco—i.e., as far west as the defeated Canaanite warriors could flee, to the coast of the Mediterranean.

the valley of Mizpah. This is the same Mizpah mentioned in 11:3.

11:10 ***at one time.*** I.e., at the time Joshua captured and burned it. This clause explains why Joshua burned Hazor and no other cities in the north. Whether written by the author/editor or a later scribe, it is an explanatory note by a hand later than the source document from Joshua's time that "at one time" (sometimes translated "formerly"; cf. NASB), Hazor headed those kingdoms.

capital. Lit., "head"; Jabin was suzerain, the kings of the surrounding cities his vassals. Even if some (e.g., Jobab, 11:1) were allies rather than vassals, Jabin was *primus inter pares* ("first among equals").

11:11 ***completely destroyed.*** See NLT mg and also the discussion in the Introduction, under "Theological Concerns." So also 11:12, 20, 21.

11:13 ***any of the towns built on mounds.*** Lit., "all the cities which stood upon their tells." All the elements making a city site advantageous (e.g., proximity to water and roadways) still were present even after its destruction (by fire, earthquake, or warfare). Most cities were rebuilt numerous times, rising to become the flat-topped mounds, or tells, now seen commonly throughout the Middle East.

COMMENTARY

For the fourth time in three chapters, the narrator begins a section with "when *X* heard." This time *X* was Jabin of Hazor, who marshaled his forces at the waters of Merom in the hills of upper Galilee, a few miles west of Hazor itself. From the Mediterranean in the west to the desert in the east, from the borders of Phoenicia in the north to Beth-shan and northern Mount Ephraim, virtually all the kings and their armies in the north of Canaan responded to Jabin's summons, as they were bound to do, whether they were his vassals or his allies.

Jabin's horses (11:4) were chariot horses; cavalry and mounted bowmen did not appear in western Asia until centuries later. Chariots are most effective on relatively level terrain, so the Amorites of the southern hill country almost certainly did not use chariots against Israel; if they had, the author of Joshua would have mentioned it. Israel's warriors now faced horses and chariots for the first time; they knew only of their reputation as a terrifying force on an open battlefield. God's words to Joshua (11:6) were intended to calm Israel's anxiety over this new face of the enemy, as well as over the greater numbers of Canaanites. As in the south, so now in the north against an enemy even more heavily armed, God would give Israel the victory.

Chariots were the heavy mechanized weapons of the battlefield, functioning against infantry much as tanks have done in modern warfare. Most ancient Near Eastern kings thought no weapon better, but Israel was different. Putting down the horses and burning the chariots would be a sign of God's trustworthiness and of Israel's trust in God (11:6, 9).

The accounts of the battles of Joshua's southern campaign are usually filled with interesting and marvelous details of how God gave Israel victory and of how Israel cooperated with (or delayed) God's conduct of the campaign. By contrast, no details are given for this campaign, except the bare notice that Joshua "attacked suddenly" near Merom (11:7). The vicinity of Merom is relatively level, so it was a suitable staging area for the Canaanite chariots. It may be that Jabin intended to move out of upper Galilee and meet Israel on a more advantageous battlefield when his forces were assembled. If so, Joshua beat him to the punch, attacking Jabin in his camp at Merom. Whether capitalizing only on surprise, or also on the more limited mobility afforded Jabin's chariots, Joshua's bold decision here, as at Gibeon against the southern coalition, was a decisive factor in Israel's smashing victory over a larger force.

The panic of the beaten and demoralized Canaanite army is evident in the short notice of their flight (11:8). They scattered in opposite directions, fleeing to the west all the way to the Mediterranean coast ("Greater Sidon"), and to the east as far as the lower slopes of Mount Hermon ("the valley of Mizpah"). Panicked, without direction or purpose, they became easy targets for the Israelites.

The paragraph of 11:12-15 is a summary statement of Israel's military ascendancy over the north of Canaan following this decisive battle. Because this was the second campaign, and the first had been described already in much greater detail, this second account is abbreviated.

Archaeological excavation has affirmed and illuminated the size and importance of Hazor. Joshua's destruction of the city appears to be confirmed by the pottery and architectural evidence from this period. But Joshua burned only Hazor in this northern campaign because its king had initiated and led the move against Israel, because it was the leading city of the north, and because it was the first city taken after the battle.

◆ 2. End of the northern campaign (11:16-23)

16 So Joshua conquered the entire region—the hill country, the entire Negev, the whole area around the town of Goshen, the western foothills, the Jordan Valley,* the mountains of Israel, and the Galilean foothills. 17 The Israelite territory now extended all the way from Mount Halak, which leads up to Seir in the south, as far north as Baal-gad at the foot of Mount Hermon in the valley of Lebanon. Joshua killed all the kings of those territories, 18 waging war for a long time to accomplish this. 19 No one in this region made peace with the Israelites except the Hivites of Gibeon. All the others were defeated. 20 For the LORD hardened their hearts and caused them to fight the Israelites. So they were completely destroyed without mercy, as the LORD had commanded Moses.

21 During this period Joshua destroyed all the descendants of Anak, who lived in the hill country of Hebron, Debir, Anab, and the entire hill country of Judah and Israel. He killed them all and completely destroyed their towns. 22 None of the descendants of Anak were left in all the land of Israel, though some still remained in Gaza, Gath, and Ashdod.

23 So Joshua took control of the entire land, just as the LORD had instructed Moses. He gave it to the people of Israel as their special possession, dividing the land among the tribes. So the land finally had rest from war.

11:16 Hebrew *the Shephelah, the Arabah.*

NOTES

11:16 ***the hill country.*** This is the southern hill country of Judah.

the entire Negev. See Introduction, "The Physical Geography of Canaan."

Goshen. See note on 10:41.

the western foothills, the Jordan Valley. See Introduction, "The Physical Geography of Canaan."

the mountains of Israel. Lit., "the hill country of Israel," here, the hill country of what would be known as Ephraim and Manasseh (later, Samaria), and of lower and upper Galilee—i.e., the hill country that was *not* Judah.

the Galilean foothills. Heb., *shepelah* [TH8219, ZH9169]. The western foothills of Ephraim and Manasseh south of Mount Carmel sometimes are referred to as a *shepelah,* as are the western foothills of lower Galilee (see note on 11:2), though neither region is identical in its geomorphology to the Judean Shephelah. Either, or both, may be intended here.

11:17 ***Mount Halak . . . Seir.*** This is a mountain northeast of Kadesh-barnea, toward the Dead Sea and Seir, which is in Edom east of the Arabah trough that runs south from the Dead Sea.

Baal-gad . . . Lebanon. This location is low on the western slopes of Mount Hermon in the north.

11:21 ***the descendants of Anak.*** This was a people whom Israel had feared because of their greater-than-normal height; see the fearful report of the 10 spies in Num 13:22, 28, 33.

11:22 ***Gaza, Gath, and Ashdod.*** These were three of the five major Philistine cities.

COMMENTARY

This pericope is the second of three successive summaries, the second of three concentric circles. The first partial summary, 11:12-15, is but a bare outline of the northern campaign. This one (11:16-23), following immediately, is a larger circle. Longer and a bit more comprehensive (though not much) in its details, it offers intriguing conclusions about the scope and larger meanings of Joshua's conquests. The third summary comprises all of chapter 12.

In 11:16, seven regions are listed. This cannot be accidental; the author was making a statement. Joshua's role as a conqueror was finished—successfully, triumphantly, perfectly. Joshua had cleared four regions in the south, most of the southern half of the Land of Promise and nearly all the hill country and adjacent areas. In three regions representing most of the northern hill country, and even in some of the valley areas, he had done the same. None of the Canaanite peoples, living mostly on the periphery of the hill country, were able to prevent Israel from undertaking the long and arduous process of settling what had been, heretofore, largely empty country.

The short, almost offhand notice of Joshua's "waging war for a long time to accomplish this" (11:18) provides a needed balance. Though the initial victories in both campaigns were quick and decisive, dealing with desperate local resistance in place after place was a longer process. Even advancing without opposition took time; armies almost never sustain significant movement over a long period. The total campaign for Canaan may have lasted about seven years (cf. commentary on 14:6-10) after Israel crossed the Jordan River. Not only faith, but also perseverance, was needed.

It is fitting that the descriptions of Joshua's campaigns for the land should end with the notice that "the descendants of Anak" were vanquished in the territory

Israel would settle (11:21-22). The 10 spies (Num 13:28, 33) had discouraged Israel from entering the land in the previous generation with their report of the Anakites and their great size. What must Joshua's victorious soldiers have thought of their fathers' lack of faith, which had cost them entry into the Land of Promise?

In 15:13-14, Caleb is named as the one taking Kiriath-arba (or, Hebron); in Judges 1:10, it is the tribe of Judah. The simplest explanation may be that Caleb was a Kenizzite, a member of a non-Israelite clan that had allied itself with Judah. It is proper, in one account, to attribute an action or accomplishment to the overall commander (Joshua); in another, to name the tribe (Judah); and in still another, to name the person who apparently took the leading role in the action, and who received the place as his inheritance (Caleb).

God had appeared to Joshua at the beginning of this enterprise, and told him, "Be careful to obey all the instructions Moses gave you" (1:7). With respect to the entrance into the land, the author could now report that Joshua had done "just as the LORD had instructed Moses" (11:23). "Dividing the land among the tribes" (11:23) is the major theme of the second half of Joshua; this notice is proleptic. The reader is invited to anticipate the good things to come for Israel.

The last statement of the chapter, "so the land finally had rest from war" (11:23) is literally, "the land was quiet from war." Here already, this statement has a theological and metaphorical dimension. God's faithful people receive God's gifts as a "special possession"; rest is one of God's best gifts. Rest is more than the cessation of active warfare; rest includes life in harmonious relationship with God, with God's people, and with God's land. This simple, delightful declaration, too, anticipates the second half of the book.

◆ F. The List of Defeated Kings (12:1-24)

1. Moses's conquests east of the Jordan (12:1-6)

These are the kings east of the Jordan River who had been killed by the Israelites and whose land was taken. Their territory extended from the Arnon Gorge to Mount Hermon and included all the land east of the Jordan Valley.*

2King Sihon of the Amorites, who lived in Heshbon, was defeated. His kingdom included Aroer, on the edge of the Arnon Gorge, and extended from the middle of the Arnon Gorge to the Jabbok River, which serves as a border for the Ammonites. This territory included the southern
half of the territory of Gilead. 3Sihon also
controlled the Jordan Valley and regions to the east—from as far north as the Sea of Galilee to as far south as the Dead Sea,* including the road to Beth-jeshimoth and southward to the slopes of Pisgah.

4King Og of Bashan, the last of the
Rephaites, lived at Ashtaroth and Edrei.
5He ruled a territory stretching from Mount Hermon to Salecah in the north and to all of Bashan in the east, and westward to the borders of the kingdoms of Geshur and Maacah. This territory included the northern half of Gilead, as far as the boundary of King Sihon of Heshbon.

6Moses, the servant of the LORD, and the Israelites had destroyed the people of King Sihon and King Og. And Moses gave their land as a possession to the tribes of Reuben, Gad, and the half-tribe of Manasseh.

12:1 Hebrew *the Arabah;* also in 12:3, 8. **12:3** Hebrew *from the Sea of Kinnereth to the Sea of the Arabah, which is the Salt Sea.*

NOTES

12:1 ***the Arnon Gorge.*** The Arnon flows into the Dead Sea, about midway down its eastern side.

Mount Hermon. This is about 25 miles north-northeast of the Sea of Galilee; one of the Jordan's sources is the large spring of Banias in its lower elevations. From the Arnon in the south to the lower slopes of Mount Hermon in the north is about 130 miles.

the Jordan Valley. This is as extensive a use of the designation "the Arabah" (see NLT mg), as can be found in Scripture; usually it denotes one of several much smaller areas. See note on 11:2.

12:2 ***Sihon.*** The brief record of his defeat by Moses occurs in Num 21:21-26.

Heshbon. The modern Tell Hisban, about 15 miles east-northeast of the northern end of the Dead Sea, on the King's Highway in the fertile Transjordanian plateau.

the Jabbok River. This is an eastern tributary of the Jordan, entering it about two-thirds of its course down from the Sea of Galilee to the Dead Sea. On the western side of the Transjordanian plateau just above the Jordan Valley, the Jabbok was Sihon's northern boundary. But farther east, the Jabbok's upper reaches were in Ammonite territory.

Gilead. These are the eastern slopes of the Jordan Valley, and the Transjordanian plateau above it to the east, from the Yarmuk River in the north, just below the Sea of Galilee, to Heshbon in the south. Gilead is about 50 miles north to south; about 20 miles east to west.

12:3 ***from as far north as the Sea of Galilee.*** This description may seem to place the northern half of Gilead, too, within Sihon's kingdom. But 12:5 indicates that Gilead's northern half belonged to Og, king of Bashan. Sihon, then, controlled the northern Jordan Valley as far as the Sea of Galilee, but not the northern part of Gilead on the Transjordanian plateau above.

Beth-jeshimoth. This was Israel's camp in the plains of Moab (Num 33:49)—probably Tell 'Azeimeh, about four miles east of where the Jordan empties into the Dead Sea.

Pisgah. Probably the highest of Mount Nebo's peaks. Moses had viewed the Promised Land from here (Deut 34:1).

12:4 ***Bashan.*** Og's kingdom (see description in commentary below) overlapped, but was not coextensive with, the region later designated "Bashan" (for which, see Introduction, "The Physical Geography of Canaan").

Ashtaroth. This is modern Tell 'Ashtarah, on the northern slope of the Yarmuk Valley, about 25 miles east of the Sea of Galilee.

Edrei. This is modern Der'a, on the edge of the plateau above the southern slope of the Yarmuk, about 17 miles south-southeast of Ashtaroth.

12:5 ***Salecah.*** This was a town on the eastern border of Bashan, near the desert. Salecah was near the northeastern border of Og's kingdom, but about 80 miles southeast of Mount Hermon.

Geshur and Maacah. These were two small kingdoms. Geshur lay east and northeast of the Sea of Galilee; Maacah was north of Geshur, south of Mount Hermon.

Gilead. See note on 12:2.

COMMENTARY

We may think of the three successive summaries in chapters 11–12 as concentric circles. The first partial summary (11:12-15) is but a bare outline of the northern campaign. The next (11:16-23) is a larger circle; longer, and just a bit more comprehensive, it offers intriguing conclusions about the scope and larger meanings of Joshua's conquests. Chapter 12 is the third and largest circle; it begins by summarizing Moses's conquests east of the Jordan (12:1-6), with territorial limits outlined, and concludes with a reprise of Joshua's successes west of the Jordan (12:7-24). As always, though, the biblical author is not merely repetitive. A quick reminder of the geography of Joshua's campaigns leads up to a most striking and poignant listing of the kings whom he defeated.

Israel's brief, decisive encounters with Sihon and Og are related first in Numbers 21:21-35. Moses had asked Sihon's permission to pass through his lands, promising not to stray off the King's Highway while within his borders, even offering to pay for food and drink (Deut 2:27-28). Sihon not only refused; he fought Israel, and lost. Not taking the lesson, Og tried his hand against Israel; he, too, lost both the battle and his life.

Both these kingdoms lay east of the Jordan River. Sihon's kingdom extended from about the middle of the Dead Sea, where the Arnon River empties into it, northward to the Jabbok River. Sihon's northern border probably followed the southern tributaries of the Jabbok, as most of the upper Jabbok basin was Ammonite territory. In the valley of the Jordan itself, though, Sihon's kingdom apparently continued to the southern shore of the Sea of Galilee.

Og's kingdom of Bashan bordered Sihon's kingdom along the lower reaches of the Jabbok, where it descended the eastern slopes of the Transjordanian highlands. It blended into the desert on its eastern borders, farther east in the north than in the south. Its northern border ran northwest from Salecah near the edge of the desert to Mount Hermon north of the Sea of Galilee. Og's kingdom did not, however, reach that sea, as the small kingdoms of Geshur and Maacah lay between the Sea of Galilee and Og's northern territories.

The Rephaites, or Rephaim, were an indigenous people who lived on both sides of the Jordan. Since other Rephaites are mentioned later (2 Sam 21:15-22 mg; 1 Chr 20:4-8 mg), the phrase "the last of the Rephaites" should be translated "from the remnant of the Rephaites," indicating not that they were extinct but that their numbers had been greatly reduced. From those later references, and from Moses's description of Og himself (Deut 3:11), many have concluded that the Rephaim as a people were unusually tall. Most rulers of larger kingdoms had palaces in more than one of their cities. That only Og is credited in Joshua with as many as two palaces indicates that his kingdom was much larger than any of the others Israel encountered, except for Sihon's.

The author of Joshua was always concerned that Israel not forget their kin on the east side of the Jordan; they too belonged to Israel. Their strongest claim lay in the fact that Moses himself had led Israel in conquering the lands east of the Jordan (12:6), and Moses himself had given them to these tribes. Thus, this short summary ends by once again reminding all Israel of that history.

◆ 2. Joshua's conquests west of the Jordan (12:7-24)

7The following is a list of the kings that
Joshua and the Israelite armies defeated
on the west side of the Jordan, from Baal-
gad in the valley of Lebanon to Mount
Halak, which leads up to Seir. (Joshua
gave this land to the tribes of Israel as
their possession, 8including the hill coun-
try, the western foothills,* the Jordan

Valley, the mountain slopes, the Judean wilderness, and the Negev. The people who lived in this region were the Hittites, the Amorites, the Canaanites, the Perizzites, the Hivites, and the Jebusites.) These are the kings Israel defeated:

9 The king of Jericho
The king of Ai, near Bethel
10 The king of Jerusalem
The king of Hebron
11 The king of Jarmuth
The king of Lachish
12 The king of Eglon
The king of Gezer
13 The king of Debir
The king of Geder
14 The king of Hormah
The king of Arad
15 The king of Libnah
The king of Adullam
16 The king of Makkedah
The king of Bethel
17 The king of Tappuah
The king of Hepher
18 The king of Aphek
The king of Lasharon
19 The king of Madon
The king of Hazor
20 The king of Shimron-meron
The king of Acshaph
21 The king of Taanach
The king of Megiddo
22 The king of Kedesh
The king of Jokneam in Carmel
23 The king of Dor in the town of Naphoth-dor*
The king of Goyim in Gilgal*
24 The king of Tirzah.

In all, thirty-one kings were defeated.

12:8 Hebrew *the Shephelah.* 12:23a Hebrew *Naphath-dor,* a variant spelling of Naphoth-dor. 12:23b Greek version reads *Goyim in Galilee.*

NOTES

12:7 ***Baal-gad . . . Seir.*** See note on 11:17.

the valley of Lebanon. This is modern Lebanon's *Beqaa* ("valley" in Arabic); it separates the coastal Lebanon range from the inland Anti-Lebanon range.

12:8 ***the hill country . . . the Negev.*** See respective sections under "The Physical Geography of Canaan" in the Introduction.

Hittites . . . Jebusites. See note on 3:10; only the Girgashites are missing from this list.

These are the kings Israel defeated. This statement is not in the Hebrew but is supplied from the context for clarity.

12:9-24 Following each city name, the Hebrew text has the ordinal, *'ekhad* [TH259, ZH285] (one). The reader should experience the somber gravity of the text by reading aloud and reading "one" following each place name: "the king of Jericho, one; the king of Ai, near Bethel, one; the king of Jerusalem, one"; etc.

12:24 ***were defeated.*** The verbal phrase is not in the Hebrew but is supplied by the NLT for clarity.

COMMENTARY

In this first half of Joshua, the author takes great care at every opportunity to emphasize that the conquest of Canaan was for God's purposes. For Israel, God's purpose was to give them their promised inheritance. For Canaan, God's purpose was to bring the long-delayed judgment. In view of this, the roster of defeated kings should be read as a litany of the accomplishment of God's purposes. It is a solemn yet joyful recital for Israel, summarizing and symbolizing God's mighty acts on behalf of his people, for the exaltation of his own great name.

As the name of Moses, Israel's leader to the Promised Land, climaxes the first section of this chapter (12:6), so the name of Joshua, Israel's leader in the conquest of the Promised Land, leads off the second section (12:7). Moses and Joshua had faithfully carried out the tasks God had given them. In this summarizing list that showcases their successes, they receive proper recognition for their faithfulness.

Again, the careful use of names for the geographical divisions of the land is evident. Only those regions are included that Joshua had conquered and that Israel would receive in the allotment to be described in the following chapters. Of course, this allotment is referred to here as in the past, "Joshua gave," because it was past at the time of the writing of the chapter. The six ethnic names concluding verse 8 match the six geographical names of the first part of the verse. In fact, no verb or adjective occurs in 12:8; it is a list of six nouns (regions), followed by a list of six nouns (peoples).

The first half of this list of 31 kings and their towns (i.e., the first 16) refers to locations in the south of Canaan, from Ai and Bethel southward. The second half of the list (i.e., the final 15 names), are in the north and the north-central part of Canaan. It is important to note that this list is not a claim to have conquered these towns, though some were conquered. The list claims Joshua defeated the kings of 31 towns who brought their forces to fight against Israel—most of them in the two campaigns summarized in chapters 10 and 11.

The list of the 31 defeated kings is at once solemn and moving; the Hebrew is achingly beautiful in its measured cadences. This is a surprisingly poetic passage in the stark, spare simplicity of its presentation. All these kings died fighting Israel and Israel's God, whom they neither knew nor understood. Each king is presented as an unknown soldier, his city named, but not he himself. These men, renowned in their own place and time, could not have imagined a more grievous fate than to be referred to but left unnamed, as they are here. Most of them (but cf. 10:3) rest somewhere in Canaan until the end of time, unknown and unremarked, except in this somber litany affirming the righteousness of God's judgments upon all the earth.

Joshua's conquering work was done. The remaining inhabitants of the hill country, the Shephelah, the Arabah, the slopes, the wilderness, and the Negev (12:8) would not be able to prevent Israel from settling into their inheritance. God had brought Israel into the land as he had promised Abraham so long ago (Gen 22:15-18). To the allotment of the land, then, Joshua would turn his attention next.

◆ III. The Tribal Allotments (13:1–21:45)

A. Allotments of the Transjordanian Tribes (13:1-33)

1. The remaining land (13:1-7)

When Joshua was an old man, the LORD said to him, "You are growing old, and much land remains to be conquered. 2This is the territory that remains: all the regions of the Philistines and the Geshurites, 3and the larger territory of the Canaanites, extending from the stream of Shihor on the border of Egypt, northward to the boundary of Ekron. It includes the territory of the five Philistine rulers of Gaza, Ashdod, Ashkelon, Gath, and Ekron. The land of the Avvites 4in the south also remains to be

**conquered. In the north, the following area
has not yet been conquered: all the land of
the Canaanites, including Mearah (which
belongs to the Sidonians), stretching
northward to Aphek on the border of the
Amorites; 5the land of the Gebalites and all
of the Lebanon mountain area to the east,
from Baal-gad below Mount Hermon to
Lebo-hamath; 6and all the hill country
from Lebanon to Misrephoth-maim, in-
cluding all the land of the Sidonians.**

**"I myself will drive these people out of
the land ahead of the Israelites. So be sure
to give this land to Israel as a special pos-
session, just as I have commanded you.
7Include all this territory as Israel's posses-
sion when you divide this land among the
nine tribes and the half-tribe of Manasseh."**

NOTES

13:2 ***the Philistines.*** They were one of several groups in the great migration of the Sea Peoples from the Aegean region, about 75–100 years after Israel's entry into Canaan.

the Geshurites. This was a southern territory and people, probably bordering Philistia; see also 1 Sam 27:8. These were not the northern Geshurites of 12:5; 13:11, 13.

13:3 ***Shihor.*** This Egyptian loanword meaning "river" or "stream" probably indicates the traditional boundary between Canaan/Israel and Egypt, Wadi el-'Arish in the northern Sinai.

Ekron. This was the northernmost of the five major Philistine cities. Thus, the northern limit of Ekron's control would have been Israel's southern boundary on the Mediterranean and inland for about 10 miles or a little more.

the five Philistine rulers of Gaza, Ashdod, Ashkelon, Gath, and Ekron. These five cities formed the Philistine Pentapolis. Gaza, Ashdod, and Ashkelon were on the Mediterranean coast, Gath and Ekron a few miles inland. The biblical writers normally do not refer to their leaders as kings. The Hebrew word is *seren* [TH5633A, ZH6249], probably a loanword from (or related to) Greek *turannos* [TG5180.1, ZG5599] (tyrant).

the Avvites. These were the people the Philistines displaced (Deut 2:23).

13:4 ***in the south.*** This is correctly included with the end of 13:3 as the concluding phrase.

also remains to be conquered. Although not in the Hebrew, this clause is supplied from context (13:1-2).

including Mearah. No town of this name is known. An alternative reading, with LXX and requiring only the reasonable emendation of Resh to Zayin, is "from Gaza." Resh and Zayin are orthographically similar enough during several periods that such a confusion is conceivable and, as importantly, it is difficult to imagine how else LXX would have arrived at "Gaza."

Sidonians. See note on 11:8.

Aphek. This was northern Aphek, about 40 miles north of Sidon, about 10 miles southeast (inland) from Gebal/Byblos (13:5).

13:5 ***Gebalites.*** Ancient Gebal/Byblos is modern Jubayl, about 45 miles north of Sidon, 20 miles north of Beirut.

Baal-gad. See note on 11:17.

Lebo-hamath. This is the Lebo belonging to the kingdom of Hamath, indentified as modern Lebweh, at the eastern edge of the northern Beqaa (Valley of Lebanon), just on the Orontes (north) side of the Orontes/Litani watershed, and on the southern border of the ancient kingdom of Hamath (B. Mazar 1986:189).

13:6 ***Misrephoth-maim . . . Sidonians.*** See notes on 11:8.

COMMENTARY

With the Canaanites unable to prevent Israelite settlement, it was time to apportion the land to the tribes. At first glance, most of the second half of Joshua is only dry lists of territorial borders and cities. Yet these lists are actually of great importance, and their inclusion defines the literary structure of the book as a whole.

First, these border descriptions and city lists give concrete expression to the fulfillment of God's promise to Abraham, Isaac, and Jacob. They represent a kind of title deed to the land—under God, of course. Secondly, the people of God in the Old Testament period were a people of the land. The land of Canaan/Israel was a major part of God's covenant with Israel. The lists of tribal allotments in this second half of Joshua give geographical reality to the importance of the land for the people of Israel in covenant with God, who owns the land. Thirdly, because God does own the land, this apportionment to the tribes is spoken of consistently as a gift (cf., e.g., 1:3; 2:9; 9:24; 18:3; 23:15-16; 24:13; Gen 12:7; 28:4, 13; Exod 6:4; Deut 6:10). God gave them the land to dwell in, but its distribution was at God's direction. In the same way, God's presence and all God's good provision down through the ages have been God's gift, and gifts, to those who walk with God by faith.

Finally, in the discussion of the tribal allotments, it is important to remember that each of Israel's tribes was named for the son of Jacob from whom they were descended—except, of course, for Ephraim and Manasseh, named for their ancestors, the sons of Joseph, grandsons of Jacob. In considering the land as both a part of and a shaper of the several tribes of Israel, their characters, and their histories, the distinction between tribe and ancestor is not always a wide distinction. The characters and the destinies of Jacob's sons, as found in the narratives of Genesis and in Jacob's blessing of Genesis 49, are reflected in the character and the situations—geographic, political, economic, etc.—of the tribes, their descendants.

Within the lists of tribal allotments, the reader will find that some borders are described in sufficient detail to plot them on a map and some are not. Also, though many cities' locations are known today, some have been lost to us. Rightly understood, the book of Joshua never claims Israel conquered all the land of Canaan under Joshua. Thus, this second section begins with a notice about the land yet remaining. The areas least populated by Canaanites were the areas opened up by Joshua's campaigns and were the first to be settled by Israel. The areas listed as remaining were the most populous Canaanite regions; Israel did not conquer them in Joshua's day.

The summary of the land not yet taken is presented in two sections, southern regions followed by northern regions, the same order in which Joshua had taken land in his two campaigns. The northern border of the lands not yet taken in the south was the northern boundary of Ekron and its hinterlands. This probably included Tel Qasile on the Yarkon River (in the northern suburbs of modern Tel Aviv). The Sharon Plain north of the Yarkon was largely uninhabited swampland in antiquity; for this reason, the summary of the northern areas not yet taken begins about the plain of Acco north of Carmel, with Misrephoth-maim (13:6).

The Philistines settled along the southwestern Mediterranean coast, west and southwest of Judah, 75 to 100 years after Israel arrived in Canaan (following Rainey's date [Rainey and Notley 2006:109] of about 1140 BC for the Philistine arrival). Deuteronomy 2:23 and Amos 9:7 note they came from Caphtor (Crete), which explains the emphasis here that the Philistine cities were part of "Canaan" (13:3—lit., "to the Canaanite it is reckoned"). If the Philistines had not yet arrived in Canaan by Joshua's time, the narrator or a later scribe identified this territory and the Pentapolis as Philistine because that is how they came to be known shortly thereafter. Certainly, the Philistines are not mentioned as adversaries of Joshua in his southern campaign.

Geographically, these unconquered areas lay mostly in the plains and the valleys, in areas that later became part of Israel, proper. The Philistines, Canaanites, and others who lived there had iron chariots (17:16); Israel did not. Thus, it was several generations before Israel became strong enough to absorb (or in a few cases, conquer) these regions and their peoples. Most of the Philistines, and most of the people of Lebanon, never were absorbed into Israel, though many came into a vassal relationship with Israel during David's reign. Following Solomon's death, when Israel strayed from God, that control was lost, and regained only intermittently by later Judean or Israelite kings.

This entire section is presented as God's speech to Joshua. Just as God had taken the initiative and directed the two campaigns of conquest, now God prompted Joshua to begin distribution of the land. Joshua's moral authority forestalled complaints about the portions the individual tribes received—were there any who were disposed to complain. It would seem, however, that the people had faith in the lots (14:2; 18:10) as revealing God's will. The land just listed had not yet been conquered, but Joshua was to show his faith in God's promises by allotting it to the tribes against the future, when it was to be taken.

◆ 2. General description of Transjordanian territories (13:8-14)

8 Half the tribe of Manasseh and the tribes of Reuben and Gad had already received their grants of land on the east side of the Jordan, for Moses, the servant of the LORD, had previously assigned this land to them.

> 9 Their territory extended from Aroer on the edge of the Arnon Gorge (including the town in the middle of the gorge) to the plain beyond Medeba, as far as Dibon. 10 It also included all the towns of King Sihon of the Amorites, who had reigned in Heshbon, and extended as far as the borders of Ammon. 11 It included Gilead, the territory of the kingdoms of Geshur and Maacah, all of Mount Hermon, all of Bashan as far as Salecah, 12 and all the territory of King Og of Bashan, who had reigned in Ashtaroth and Edrei. King Og was the last of the Rephaites, for Moses had attacked them and driven them out. 13 But the Israelites failed to drive out the people of Geshur and Maacah, so they continue to live among the Israelites to this day.

14 Moses did not assign any allotment of land to the tribe of Levi. Instead, as the LORD had promised them, their allotment came from the offerings burned on the altar to the LORD, the God of Israel.

NOTES

13:9 ***Aroer . . . Arnon Gorge.*** Aroer is a city on the north side of the Arnon Gorge, about 15 miles upstream (east) of where the Arnon empties into the Dead Sea, about midway down its eastern shore.

the town. This possibly refers to an expansion of Aroer's population outside its walls, into the wadi; if not, this town is no longer identifiable.

the plain beyond Medeba. Lit., "and all the plain (*mishor* [TH4334, ZH4793]) of Medeba." We should understand this as a proper name, the Plain of Medeba. It stretches from the vicinity of Medeba southward to the vicinity of Dibon. Otherwise, Dibon should occur first in this south-to-north summary.

Dibon. This was a city about five miles northwest of Aroer, on the major northern tributary of the Arnon. Dibon later became the capital of Moab for a time.

13:10 ***Sihon . . . Heshbon.*** See note on 12:2.

Ammon. This was a city-state centered on Rabbath-bene-ammon, modern Amman, Jordan, on the upper reaches of the Jabbok River, on the Transjordanian plateau, and a stop along the King's Highway. The Ammonites were descendants of Abraham's nephew Lot, so God did not allow Israel to take their territory.

13:11 ***Gilead.*** See note on 12:2.

Geshur and Maacah. See note on 12:5.

Bashan . . . Salecah. See notes on 12:4 and 12:5.

13:12 ***Ashtaroth and Edrei.*** See notes on 12:4.

13:14 ***offerings burned on the altar to the LORD, the God of Israel.*** "Burned on the altar" does not appear in the Hebrew but is part of the NLT's description of what is most likely a scribal gloss—the insertion of *'ishe* [TH801, ZH852] (to be read as "[offerings by] fire"), which does not appear in the LXX and results in a strange construction to describe the sacrifices upon the altar of the Tabernacle. Without this gloss, the verse reads, "Only to the tribe of Levi, he did not give a possession [a tribal land allotment]; Yahweh, the God of Israel, he was his [Levi's] possession, just as he [Yahweh] had promised him [Levi]." This makes excellent sense, and recalls vividly the promises of Num 18:20 and Deut 18:1-2. With the addition of "Moses" as the subject, 13:33 records what this verse should report (and would without the scribal gloss). It is likely that a scribe uncomfortable with the text as it stood—possibly implying Yahweh as a human "possession" held by Levi—has inserted the minimum possible gloss (*'ishe*), hoping for the effect he achieved, "[offerings by] fire."

COMMENTARY

Moses himself had assigned the two and a half tribes of Transjordan their allotments several years before the conquest of Canaan west of the Jordan (Num 32). This was so important in reminding all Israel that the Transjordanian tribes were part of the nation that the narrator repeated this information five times in this chapter (13:8, 15, 24, 29, 32). In return for receiving their lands east of the Jordan, Reuben, Gad, and half-Manasseh had promised to help the rest of Israel take possession of their inheritance west of the Jordan. This they had done (1:12-18; 4:12-13). Now it was time to confirm them in their own lands by including them in the descriptions of the lands of all Israel's tribes. Given their faithfulness, and the fact that their lands were assigned first, it was fitting that their portion should be described first.

The first paragraph is a general description of the three tribes' territories together. It corresponds generally to the descriptions of the kingdoms of Sihon and Og (12:1-5) because those were the two kingdoms these tribes had received from Moses. The double mention of Geshur and Maacah (13:11, 13) reinforces the fact that Israel did not conquer and dispossess them, despite taking all of Og's territories to the south, the east, and the north of them, and Jabin's kingdom of Hazor to their west. These two small kingdoms (east and northeast of the Sea of Galilee, respectively) remained distinct; Geshur appears to have been an ally, and Maacah, a vassal, of David and Solomon. One of David's wives was named Maacah—same spelling as the neighboring country, but a daughter of the king of Geshur, Talmai (2 Sam 3:3). Both kingdoms, apparently, were swallowed by the larger Aramaean kingdom of Damascus in the ninth century BC (B. Mazar 1986:113-125).

The short notice that Levi received no inheritance of tribal land (13:14) anticipates the description of the system of Levitical cities among the lands of the other tribes, as set forth in chapter 21—though this notice does not yet mention the cities. In addition, the mention of the offering by fire seems to be a scribal addition (see note on 13:14). The end of the verse should be read "Yahweh, the God of Israel, he is Levi's allotment, just as he promised him." In practice, this was the presence of God among them, experienced primarily in their continual service in the Tabernacle (and, later, in the Temple).

◆ 3. Reuben's inheritance (13:15-23)

[15]Moses had assigned the following area to the clans of the tribe of Reuben.

[16]Their territory extended from Aroer on the edge of the Arnon Gorge (including the town in the middle of the gorge) to the plain beyond Medeba. [17]It included Heshbon and the other towns on the plain—Dibon, Bamoth-baal, Beth-baal-meon, [18]Jahaz, Kedemoth, Mephaath, [19]Kiriathaim, Sibmah, Zereth-shahar on the hill above the valley, [20]Beth-peor, the slopes of Pisgah, and Beth-jeshimoth.

[21]The land of Reuben also included all the towns of the plain and the entire kingdom of Sihon. Sihon was the Amorite king who had reigned in Heshbon and was killed by Moses along with the leaders of Midian—Evi, Rekem, Zur, Hur, and Reba—princes living in the region who were allied with Sihon. [22]The Israelites had also killed Balaam son of Beor, who used magic to tell the future. [23]The Jordan River marked the western boundary for the tribe of Reuben. The towns and their surrounding villages in this area were given as a homeland to the clans of the tribe of Reuben.

NOTES

13:16 ***Aroer . . . Medeba.*** See note on 13:9.

13:17 ***Heshbon.*** See note on 12:2.

Dibon. See note on 13:9.

13:20 ***Pisgah, and Beth-jeshimoth.*** See note on 12:3.

COMMENTARY

The tribal inheritance of Reuben was not central and important, as would have been expected for the descendants of Jacob's firstborn (Gen 29:32). The beginning of the explanation arises in Jacob's life as he was building his family. First, we must note that Rachel—Jacob's favorite wife and Reuben's aunt—had given Bilhah, her handmaid (Gen 29:29), to Jacob as a concubine, when Rachel concluded she would be unable to bear children herself (Gen 30:3-8). Years later, Reuben slept with Bilhah; this may have been an attempt by Reuben to begin to establish himself as head of the family, as he fancied he saw his father beginning to decline. Jacob heard about Reuben's act, but did not do or say anything at the time (Gen 35:22). Jacob's response came many years later, upon his deathbed in Egypt. Acknowledging Reuben in glowing terms as his firstborn (Gen 49:3), Jacob nevertheless finally broke his silence over Reuben's transgression, and demoted him from the firstborn's place of honor and preeminence among his brothers (Gen 49:4) and, hence, that of his descendants among the tribes of Israel.

Reuben's territory extended from the Arnon in the south to a small slice of southern Gilead in the north, to the desert in the east, and to the extreme southern end of the Jordan River on the west. It was fertile and potentially a very good inheritance, but early on, the tribe of Reuben experienced difficulty defending their inheritance from Moab, and eventually lost all the southern part. Other biblical references indicate close relationships with Judah and Benjamin, with some clan names overlapping. As a distinct geographical and tribal entity, Reuben eventually just faded away. Already in the Song of Deborah, Reuben is mentioned only to chide him for not heeding the call to arms (Judg 5:15-16). After Deborah's war, Reuben is scarcely mentioned again, and then usually in perfunctory acknowledgment that Reuben was (or had been) a tribe within Israel (e.g., Ezek 48:6-7; Rev 7:5).

The five "leaders" of Midian (13:21) are called "kings" in Numbers 31:8. These five were clan or tribal leaders; in this pre-monarchial period (Iron Age I) the titles "leader" and "king" were interchanged more than in later times. These men probably were vassals of Sihon, but this verse is not intended to imply they died fighting by his side. In Numbers 31:8, their deaths are recorded some time after that of Sihon (Num 21:24).

Israel's grievance against Balaam (13:22; cf. 24:9-10) was his successful plan to seduce Israel into sexually expressed idolatry, even after God had forbidden him to prophesy against Israel (Num 22–25; 31:8, 16). This specific treachery on the part of a prophet of God (albeit, not an Israelite) probably was fresh enough in Israel's memory that it did not require mention here.

The phrase "the towns and their surrounding villages" in 13:23 expresses a typical settlement pattern throughout much of Israel's history in the land. Many towns large enough to need and to build a defensive wall had a number of unwalled villages nearby. When danger threatened, the villagers sought refuge inside the town. In peaceful times, the picture was more idyllic. As 13:23 portrays, town and village alike were "a homeland to the clans of the tribe of Reuben."

4. Gad's inheritance (13:24-28)

[24]Moses had assigned the following area to the clans of the tribe of Gad.

[25]Their territory included Jazer, all the towns of Gilead, and half of the land of Ammon, as far as the town of Aroer just west of* Rabbah. [26]It extended from Heshbon to Ramath-mizpeh and Betonim, and from Mahanaim to the territory of Lo-debar.* [27]In the valley were Beth-haram, Beth-nimrah, Succoth, Zaphon, and the rest of the kingdom of King Sihon of Heshbon. The western boundary ran along the Jordan River, extended as far north as the tip of the Sea of Galilee,* and then turned eastward. [28]The towns and their surrounding villages in this area were given as a homeland to the clans of the tribe of Gad.

13:25 Hebrew *in front of.* **13:26** Hebrew *Li-debir,* apparently a variant spelling of Lo-debar (compare 2 Sam 9:4; 17:27; Amos 6:13). **13:27** Hebrew *Sea of Kinnereth.*

NOTES

13:25 *Gilead.* See note on 12:2.

Aroer . . . Rabbah. This description indicates another Aroer than that of 13:9, 16. Rabbah is present-day Amman, Jordan; it was the capital and only large city of the Ammonites, descendants of Lot (Gen 19:38), Abraham's nephew.

13:26 *Heshbon.* See note on 12:2.

Mahanaim. The name means "two camps"; it is on the bank of the Jabbok in its lower course, about seven miles from its confluence with the Jordan.

Lo-debar. Or, Debir; the reading is uncertain (see NLT mg). MT reads *Lidbir,* from which it is difficult to derive Lo-debar. Still, Lo-debar in Transjordan is mentioned elsewhere (2 Sam 9:4; 17:27), and neither a Debir nor a Lidbir is known east of the Jordan. The location of Lo-debar also is uncertain.

13:27 *In the valley.* I.e., the Jordan Valley.

Succoth. This was at the edge of the Jabbok Valley about where it comes into the eastern edge of the Jordan Valley, and about four miles west of Mahanaim.

13:28 *The towns . . . Gad.* The language is identical to that regarding Reuben (13:23).

COMMENTARY

Gad was Jacob's seventh son, born to Zilpah, Leah's handmaid whom she gave to Jacob as a concubine (Gen 30:9) in the competition between sisters for their husband's favor. The family position of Gad, the son, was peripheral. Likewise, the position of Gad, the tribe, was peripheral through most of Israel's history as a nation, with only brief periods of national importance.

Gad's southern boundary ran from just north of Heshbon, which belonged to Reuben, westward toward the Jordan. On the plateau and the slopes of Gilead toward the Jordan, Gad occupied territory described here as "half of the land of Ammon" (13:25), though there is no record of Israel fighting the Ammonites to acquire this land. Geographically, this part of Gilead belongs with Rabbah; but if the Ammonites occupied it when Israel arrived, it was only very sparsely.

In the Jordan River valley itself, on the east bank of the river, Gad's territory "extended as far north as the [southern] tip of the Sea of Galilee" (13:27). On the plateau, apparently beginning at the slopes just above the Jordan, Gad bordered Manasseh at the Jabbok (13:30), dividing Gilead about evenly north to south. Through Israel's early history, Gad sometimes came under pressure from the Ammonites to the east. For much of the ninth century BC, as part of the northern kingdom of Israel, Gad (included within the region often called Gilead in the prophets; cf., e.g., Amos 1:3, 13) came under even heavier pressure from the Arameans of Damascus to the north.

◆ 5. The inheritance of half-Manasseh (13:29-33)

29Moses had assigned the following area to the clans of the half-tribe of Manasseh.

30Their territory extended from Mahanaim, including all of Bashan, all the former kingdom of King Og, and the sixty towns of Jair in Bashan.
31It also included half of Gilead and King Og's royal cities of Ashtaroth and Edrei. All this was given to the clans of the descendants of Makir, who was Manasseh's son.

32 These are the allotments Moses had made while he was on the plains of Moab, across the Jordan River, east of Jericho.
33But Moses gave no allotment of land to the tribe of Levi, for the LORD, the God of Israel, had promised that he himself would be their allotment.

NOTES

13:30 ***Mahanaim.*** See note on 13:26.

Jair. He was a great-grandson of Manasseh (1 Chr 2:21-22).

13:31 ***Gilead.*** See note on 12:2.

Ashtaroth and Edrei. See note on 12:4.

COMMENTARY

Manasseh was Joseph's elder son. Joseph was the elder son of Rachel, Jacob's favorite (and chosen) wife; he also saved Jacob's family by bringing them to Egypt to escape the famine (Gen 47:11-12). Perhaps for both these reasons, Jacob gave both of Joseph's sons an inheritance with their uncles, giving Joseph the double portion of the birthright.

Jacob did, however, give preeminence in his blessing to Manasseh's younger brother Ephraim. This is reflected in the tribal allotments: Although Manasseh had the larger territory, including these lands east of the Jordan and a central portion just north of Ephraim, west of the Jordan, Ephraim's importance west of the Jordan, because of its position in the center-north of the hill country, and its proximity to Judah, outweighed Manasseh's territorial advantage.

Makir was "Manasseh's son" (13:31); his territory and descendants are noted also on the west side of the Jordan, in ways that are not always clear. But on the east side, Moses assigned "half of Gilead" and all of Bashan to these clans. This is the briefest and least detailed of all the tribal land descriptions, probably because the author already had discussed Og's kingdom more than once, and it basically became Manasseh/Makir's inheritance. Similarly, because he had said it for Reuben and again for Gad, the author did not repeat the summarizing statement of 13:23, 28.

Verse 32 is the fifth time in this chapter that the author affirmed Moses as the authority for these tribes' possession of their territory east of the Jordan. Israel west of the Jordan was constrained not to forget or deny their brethren east of the Jordan River. That this emphasis was needed would become all too clear before the author finished his reporting.

Mention of Levi for a second time in this chapter builds the reader's anticipation of the time when Levi's apportionment of cities among the other tribes will be discussed (ch 21). But as before, no cities are mentioned. And this time, the textual issue that clouds the first statement is not present (see note on 13:14). Levi could take comfort and courage in the repeated affirmation (lit.) "Yahweh, the God of Israel, he is Levi's portion, just as he promised him" (13:33).

◆ B. Caleb's Portion (14:1-15)

1. Introduction to the western allotments (14:1-5)

The remaining tribes of Israel received land in Canaan as allotted by Eleazar the priest, Joshua son of Nun, and the tribal leaders.
[2] These nine and a half tribes received their grants of land by means of sacred lots, in accordance with the LORD's command through Moses. [3]Moses had already given a grant of land to the two and a half tribes on the east side of the Jordan River, but he had given the Levites no such allotment.
[4]The descendants of Joseph had become two separate tribes—Manasseh and Ephraim. And the Levites were given no land at all, only towns to live in with surrounding pasturelands for their livestock and all their possessions. [5]So the land was distributed in strict accordance with the LORD's commands to Moses.

NOTES

14:1 ***Eleazar.*** Eleazar had succeeded to the high priesthood at the death of his father Aaron (Num 20:28).

14:3 ***he had given the Levites no such allotment.*** See 13:14, 33.

14:4 ***Manasseh and Ephraim.*** See commentary on 13:29-33.

COMMENTARY

The allotment of land to the tribes on the west side of the Jordan begins with chapter 14 and ends with chapter 21, the assignment of the Levitical cities. The early reference, "in Canaan" (14:1), emphasizes that Israel now had come to the land of God's promise to the fathers and mothers. Abraham and Sarah, Isaac and Rebekah, Jacob, Leah, and Rachel had all sojourned in this land in the assurance that God would give it to their offspring. Now that promise stood to be fulfilled.

Eleazar represented the institution and the authority of the Tabernacle. Given the people's confidence in him, and God's demonstration of confidence in him with the command that he was to succeed his father as high priest (Num 20:25-26), Eleazar assured the integrity of the process, and God's blessing upon it. For convenience, we may say Joshua's and the tribal leaders' participation in and oversight of the process represented the "civil" authority in Israel, though a separation between "civil" and "religious" would have seemed strange; indeed, the concept would not have occurred to anyone in that era. In any case, the participation of all recognized leadership, including at least one elder from each tribe, prevented dissatisfaction from arising later; all Israel witnessed that the distribution had been honest and just.

In Israel's antiquity, in the absence of a substantial canon of written Scripture, the casting of lots was permitted by God and was viewed as a legitimate means of discerning God's will. In that time, God spoke in a number of ways; one was by causing the lots to come up as he willed. The New Testament witness seems clear that this method no longer is countenanced by God, because it no longer is needed. We have the revelation of God in Jesus Christ, the witness of the Holy Spirit, and the direction of the completed canon of Scripture. In situations requiring random choices for fairness, such means still can be appropriate. They ought not to be called "discerning the will of God," however, except as an affirmation that God mandates justice and equity in all things, even in our small choices.

Joseph was the elder son of Jacob's first-chosen wife, Rachel. Thus Joseph, through Ephraim and Manasseh, received the double portion of the inheritance, sometimes called the birthright (cf. 1 Chr 5:1). This is mentioned here, together with the repeated notice that Levi did not receive a separate tribal territory, to explain how the total number of landed tribes still could be counted at 12. The Levitical towns are mentioned here for the first time in Joshua, anticipating the record of their distribution in chapter 21.

◆ 2. Caleb's witness to God's faithfulness (14:6-12)

**[6]A delegation from the tribe of Judah, led
by Caleb son of Jephunneh the Kenizzite,
came to Joshua at Gilgal. Caleb said to
Joshua, "Remember what the LORD said to
Moses, the man of God, about you and me
when we were at Kadesh-barnea. [7]I was
forty years old when Moses, the servant
of the LORD, sent me from Kadesh-barnea
to explore the land of Canaan. I returned
and gave an honest report, [8]but my broth-
ers who went with me frightened the
people from entering the Promised Land.
For my part, I wholeheartedly followed
the LORD my God. [9]So that day Moses sol-
emnly promised me, 'The land of Canaan
on which you were just walking will be
your grant of land and that of your de-
scendants forever, because you whole-
heartedly followed the LORD my God.'**

**[10]"Now, as you can see, the LORD has
kept me alive and well as he promised for
all these forty-five years since Moses
made this promise—even while Israel
wandered in the wilderness. Today I am
eighty-five years old. [11]I am as strong now
as I was when Moses sent me on that
journey, and I can still travel and fight as
well as I could then. [12]So give me the hill
country that the LORD promised me. You
will remember that as scouts we found
the descendants of Anak living there in
great, walled towns. But if the LORD is
with me, I will drive them out of the land,
just as the LORD said."**

NOTES

14:6 ***Caleb . . . Kenizzite.*** The Kenizzites were not Israelites originally (Gen 15:19); Gen 36:11 records a Kenaz, grandson of Esau. With only a handful of references, it is not possible to say with certainty whether Caleb was descended from Esau, and if so, how the Kenizzites became attached to Judah. (Did Caleb's father Jephunneh marry a Judean woman?) This makes it all the more remarkable that Caleb represented Judah in the mission to spy out the land (Num 13:6).

Gilgal. Apparently, Israel's main camp remained at Gilgal through the end of the allotment of the tribal territories. Gilgal has not been certainly identified, though several locations have been suggested (cf. Boling 1982:191-192).

Kadesh-barnea. This was Israel's encampment through most of the 38 years between their leaving Sinai and their entrance into Canaan. It is located at 'Ain el-Qudeirat, near the border between Canaan and the northeastern Sinai; the name is preserved at nearby 'Ain Qedeis (Rainey and Notley 2006:121).

14:7 ***an honest report.*** Lit., "a word just as was with [in] my heart."

14:8 ***frightened the people.*** Lit., "melted the heart of the people [with fear]."

14:11 ***travel and fight.*** Lit., "for war, and for going out, and for coming in,"—i.e., for the ordinary and extraordinary pursuits of life.

14:12 ***the descendants of Anak.*** See note on 11:21.

COMMENTARY

Following the short introduction, this long section describing the allotment of tribal lands west of the Jordan is framed by the assignment of land to Caleb at the beginning, and to Joshua at the end. Of the 12 men, one from each tribe, whom Moses had sent to scout the land of Canaan, only Caleb and Joshua had been confident Israel could take it (Num 13:30; 14:6-9). The rest of their generation died in the wilderness as God had decreed (Num 14:20-23), but Joshua and Caleb entered Canaan, took part in its conquest, and were rewarded for their faithfulness and trust in God by receiving their own portions of land.

It is possible that Caleb's ancestry was within the tribe of Judah (Woudstra 1981:227). However, he is referred to as "the Kenizzite" (14:6) here and elsewhere, and the Kenizzites usually are regarded as a clan that attached itself to Judah, rather than being ethnically Judahite from the beginning. If that is the case, Caleb's faith as an "outsider" should have been an example to his fellow spies, but in their own lack of faith and vision they did not respond positively to his faith. But Caleb expressed no lingering rancor toward the other, now deceased, spies whose fearful report had kept him from his inheritance for 40 years, but called them "my brothers."

Joshua 11:18 reported simply that Joshua's campaigns took "a long time." Caleb revealed his age as 40 when chosen for scout duty (14:7). From then until the crossing of the Jordan was about 38 years. Now, Caleb was 85, suggesting seven years in all for the decisive southern and northern victories, together with a considerable number of largely unreported movements and smaller battles. Given that years, but not months, are part of Caleb's declaration, we cannot be positive, but seven years is both a reasonable deduction and a reasonable approximation. Most importantly for Caleb at 85, he judged himself to be as fit as he had been at 40.

The descendants of Anak (14:12), were a tall, strong people who lived in the hill country of Judah. The first reference to them is Numbers 13:22, in the report of the scouts' itinerary through the land. Israel had stayed out of Canaan for almost 40 years because they feared these people. Now Caleb asked Joshua to fulfill God's promise to him (Num 14:24), and give him the ground his feet had trod, the territory of Anak at Hebron. The life of faith is filled with delicious ironies. Faith calls for giving up everything to walk with God, and then God gives it all back, or better.

Jesus himself issued this challenge and promise to those who would follow him (Mark 10:29-30). Faith is agreeing to walk blind, if necessary, and then seeing more than one ever knew there was to see.

Here again, the literary artistry is outstanding. The final report of actual conflict in the author's campaign accounts was of Joshua's defeat of these people in and around Hebron and Debir (11:21-22). In 14:6-12, as the first of the reports of the allotment of the land, Caleb asked for and received this very district. (As noted in the commentary on 11:21, the conflict in the texts over whether Joshua or Caleb took Hebron is more apparent than real; see also commentary on 14:13-15.)

Caleb, too, was a rhetorical master. At the conclusion of this excellently crafted request, he expressed faith that God would give him success in this endeavor. The expression "if the LORD is with me" begins with the Hebrew word *'ulay* [TH194, ZH218] (perhaps). The phrase would usually mean "perhaps Yahweh will be with me." But here (and other places), *'ulay* expresses confidence through a figure of speech called litotes (or meiosis), understatement through use of the uncertain "perhaps" to emphasize the intended affirmative. Caleb was declaring his strong faith that God would help him acquire the land he was asking for.

◆ 3. Caleb's town of Hebron (14:13-15)

[13]So Joshua blessed Caleb son of Jephunneh and gave Hebron to him as his portion of land. [14]Hebron still belongs to the descendants of Caleb son of Jephunneh the Kenizzite because he wholeheartedly followed the LORD, the God of Israel. [15](Previously Hebron had been called Kiriath-arba. It had been named after Arba, a great hero of the descendants of Anak.)

And the land had rest from war.

NOTES

14:13 ***Hebron.*** This was about 20 miles south-southwest of Jerusalem in the hill country.

14:14 ***the Kenizzite.*** See note on 14:6.

14:15 ***the descendants of Anak.*** See note on 11:21.

COMMENTARY

The biblical authors did not always arrange their narratives chronologically, nor did they always present the details of narrative events as fully as we might wish. The initial notice of Hebron's conquest is in 10:36-37. There it is presented as the conquest of all Israel acting together under Joshua's leadership. Did Caleb make his initial request for Hebron as his allotment at that time? It is possible, but we simply have no way of knowing.

In 11:21-22, the author included the conquest of Hebron, Debir, and Anab, and the routing of the Anakites, within his summary statement of all of Joshua's military victories in Canaan. This notice does not contradict Caleb's taking of Hebron, because in summary statements the actions of individuals often are included under the more broadly stated achievements of the leader. We would like more details of Hebron's conquest, but we must be content, unless and until more information comes to light, with the knowledge that Caleb was involved in some significant manner in the permanent conquest of Hebron for Israel. That happened because of Caleb's faith, and he received Hebron for his inheritance as God's reward for his long life of faithfulness, as this short account reminds us three times (14:8, 9, 14). The summary statement, "And the land had rest from war" (14:15), is repeated from 11:23. The allotment of the land west of the Jordan was well begun with Joshua's assignment of Hebron to Caleb. Now it could proceed for all the tribes, without the disruption of military action (offensive *or* defensive) during this important interlude. (See also the end of the commentary on 11:16-23.)

◆ C. Judah's Portion (15:1-63)

1. Judah's boundaries (15:1-12)

The allotment for the clans of the tribe of Judah reached southward to the border of Edom, as far south as the wilderness of Zin.

2The southern boundary began at the south bay of the Dead Sea,* 3ran south of Scorpion Pass* into the wilderness of Zin, and then went south of Kadesh-barnea to Hezron. Then it went up to Addar, where it turned toward Karka. 4From there it passed to Azmon until it finally reached the Brook of Egypt, which it followed to the Mediterranean Sea.* This was their* southern boundary.

5The eastern boundary extended along the Dead Sea to the mouth of the Jordan River.

The northern boundary began at the bay where the Jordan River empties into the Dead Sea, 6went up from there to Beth-hoglah, then proceeded north of Beth-arabah to the Stone of Bohan. (Bohan was Reuben's son.) 7From that point it went through the valley of Achor to Debir, turning north toward Gilgal, which is across from the slopes of Adummim on the south side of the valley. From there the boundary extended to the springs at En-shemesh and on to En-rogel. 8The boundary then passed through the valley of Ben-Hinnom, along the southern slopes of the Jebusites, where the city of Jerusalem is located. Then it went west to the top of the mountain above the valley of Hinnom, and on up to the northern end of the valley of Rephaim. 9From there the boundary extended from the top of the mountain to the spring at the waters of Nephtoah,* and from there to the towns on Mount Ephron. Then it turned toward Baalah (that is, Kiriath-jearim). 10The boundary circled west of Baalah to Mount Seir, passed along to the town of Kesalon on the northern slope of Mount Jearim, and went down to Beth-shemesh and on to Timnah. 11The boundary then proceeded to the slope of the hill north of Ekron, where it turned toward Shikkeron and Mount Baalah. It passed Jabneel and ended at the Mediterranean Sea.

12The western boundary was the shoreline of the Mediterranean Sea.*

These are the boundaries for the clans of the tribe of Judah.

15:2 Hebrew *the Salt Sea;* also in 15:5. **15:3** Hebrew *Akrabbim.* **15:4a** Hebrew *the sea;* also in 15:11. **15:4b** Hebrew *your.* **15:9** Or *the spring at Me-nephtoah.* **15:12** Hebrew *the Great Sea;* also in 15:47.

NOTES

15:1 ***Edom.*** An Edomite presence existed south of the biblical Negev (west of the southern Arabah) earlier than is generally recognized (cf. Rainey and Notley 2006:120).

the wilderness of Zin. The biblical extent of this region is unknown, but it probably included much of the higher elevation immediately south of the biblical Negev.

15:2 ***the south bay.*** This refers to the southern third of the Dead Sea, from the Lisan Peninsula ("the tongue") that extends into the Dead Sea from its eastern shore.

15:3 ***Scorpion Pass.*** Lit., "the Ascent of Akrabbim"; the precise identification of this pass is debated.

Kadesh-barnea. See note on 10:41.

Hezron . . . Addar . . . Karka. Together with Azmon (15:4), these are locations near Kadesh-barnea, though none is identified with certainty. These names may reflect the grouping of three proximate springs, and "Kadesh-barnea" the whole vicinity (Boling 1982:365).

15:4 ***Brook of Egypt.*** Modern Wadi el-'Arish, the traditional boundary between Egypt and Canaan throughout the OT period.

their southern boundary. See NLT mg, which points out that the Hebrew pronoun is *your*, reflecting an oral expression, originally, perhaps, even Joshua's direct address to Judah's leaders.

15:6 ***Beth-hoglah.*** Lit., "Partridge House," at or near Ain-Hajlah, which preserves the name.

Beth-arabah. Lit., "the House of the Arabah," probably north-northwest of Beth-hoglah, at el-Gharabeh, which preserves the name. Both these locations are southeast of Jericho.

15:7 ***valley of Achor.*** See note on 7:24.

Debir. This is not the same town as Debir/Kiriath-sepher of 15:15. Boling (1982:367) proposes the site of the modern Inn of the Good Samaritan, on the Jerusalem-Jericho Road.

Gilgal. This is not the same as Israel's camp (4:19). We should read "Geliloth" with 18:17; both names mean "circle." Boling (1982:367) proposes a site just over a mile west of a Byzantine ruin, Khan el-Ahmar, which is "across from the slopes of Adummim."

the valley. Wadi Qelt is "the valley" of this area, because of its impressive gorge.

En-shemesh. This means "Spring of the Sun(-god)," and is identified as Ain el-Hod, just east of Bethany.

En-rogel. Also known as Bir Ayyub (Job's Well), located in the Kidron Valley just below where the Hinnom Valley enters the Kidron on its west side.

15:8 ***the valley of Ben-Hinnom.*** At this point, this was the northern border of Judah, but Jerusalem occupied a ridge rising northward from the lower end of this valley. It was thus on Judah's border but within Benjamin's territory. The valley floor rises as it goes westward from the Kidron, and continues rising as it curves north around today's Old City.

the mountain above the valley of Hinnom. The crest of the ridge that forms the west side ("shoulder") of the Hinnom Valley, a bit north of the Scottish Church in Jerusalem today. Looking southwest from there, one can see a ridge standing at the head of the valley of Rephaim.

15:9 ***Nephtoah.*** There was (and is) a spring at Nephtoah, modern Lifta, at the northwest edge of modern Jerusalem, before the immense expansion of the last decades. Since that expansion, one would say Nephtoah/Lifta is on the slope of the valley just north of the Givat Shaul neighborhood.

Mount Ephron. Possibly the group of hills including modern Har Adar (also called Radar Hill; Rainey and Notley 2006:181), northeast of Abu Ghosh; these hills extend southwest toward Mevaseret Tsiyon.

Baalah (that is, Kiriath-jearim). The old name means "Lady" and refers to the goddess (Anath, Asherah); Kiriath-jearim means "city of forests." This is Deir el-'Azar in Abu Ghosh, west of Jerusalem, and a little west of Mount Ephron.

15:10 ***Mount Seir.*** This is not the Mount Seir of the Edomites, southeast of Judah, but a hill southwest of Kiriath-jearim, modern Shoresh (Rainey and Notley 2006:181).

Kesalon. Kesla, about nine miles west of Jerusalem.

Beth-shemesh. Lit., "House (Temple) of the Sun(-god)," Tell er-Rumeilah, about 16 miles west of Jerusalem.

Timnah. Tell el-Batashi, about five miles northwest of Beth-shemesh, down the Sorek Valley.

15:11 ***Ekron.*** Khirbet el-Muqanna, about five miles west-southwest of Timnah.

Shikkeron. Perhaps this is the Tell el-Ful about four miles northwest of Ekron (Aharoni 1979).

Mount Baalah. Either a peak or a range of hills west-northwest of Shikkeron. A second place name "Baalah" is not surprising; the goddess was worshiped at many places.

Jabneel. Or, Yibna. All these locations, from Beth-shemesh to the Mediterranean, are in or near the Sorek Valley; thus, the Sorek forms the border here in Judah's northwest corner.

COMMENTARY

Judah's tribal allotment is described in much more detail than are those of the rest of the tribes, one of the many testimonies to Judah's prominence throughout Israel's history. Judah was Jacob and Leah's fourth son. Reuben, Judah's oldest brother, had forfeited his birthright and place of leadership among Jacob's sons (Gen 35:22). Simeon and Levi had lost their chances at family leadership by their treachery against Shechem (Gen 34:25-31; 49:5-7). His brothers' failures put Judah in line to receive Jacob's blessing.

One way Jacob's blessing of Judah (Gen 49:8-12) was brought to reality was in the tribal allotments. The descriptions of Judah's borders are the most detailed, and the list of Judah's cities the most complete, of any tribe. Judah's geographical position among the tribes was central, guaranteeing Judah leadership in the affairs of the nation. Reuben, Simeon, and Levi, whose transgressions had caused Jacob to pass them over, each became, as tribes in the land, dependent upon Judah. The geography of the tribal allotments both reflected and helped to shape the fulfillment of each tribe's spiritual inheritance as given by Jacob, and confirmed, in general, by Moses (Deut 33).

The description of Judah's southern boundary here is the same (but with a bit more detail) as Moses had given for the southern boundary of Canaan (Num 34:1-5). This border is a large southward-looping arc, from the southern end of the Dead Sea in a southwesterly line toward the region of Kadesh-barnea, then turning northwesterly toward the Mediterranean Sea along the line of the Brook of Egypt, today's Wadi el-'Arish. This boundary line is well south of the main territory of the biblical Negev, which is centered on Beersheba. Judah's southern border ran well into the desert and had little settled population throughout most of the Old Testament period.

Judah's eastern border coincided with the western shoreline of the Dead Sea along its entire length. The western border was the Mediterranean Sea to the mouth of the Sorek, about midway between Ashdod and Joppa. The northern boundary of Judah, from the northern end of the Dead Sea to the Mediterranean Sea, is the most detailed of all the boundary descriptions in this section of Joshua. Even so, a few segments of this border are not certain in their identification.

As with several of the tribes, we must remember that Joshua was allotting to Judah land they should have been able to occupy and settle, then or later (13:1-7). But later in the course of allotment, occupation, and settlement, Simeon's entire allotment would come from some of Judah's southern territory (19:1-9). Also, about 75–100 years later, the Philistines, coming from the eastern Mediterranean Greek islands, settled all the southern coastal plain allotted to Judah, and began to press on Judah's territory in the Shephelah. Judah never occupied all the territory described here, though late in the Second Temple period, one almost could say the Jewish people did.

◆ 2. Acsah's request (15:13-19)

[13]The LORD commanded Joshua to assign some of Judah's territory to Caleb son of Jephunneh. So Caleb was given the town of Kiriath-arba (that is, Hebron), which had been named after Anak's ancestor. [14]Caleb drove out the three groups of Anakites—the descendants of Sheshai, Ahiman, and Talmai, the sons of Anak.

[15]From there he went to fight against the people living in the town of Debir (formerly called Kiriath-sepher). [16]Caleb said, "I will give my daughter Acsah in marriage to the one who attacks and captures Kiriath-sepher." [17]Othniel, the son of Caleb's brother Kenaz, was the one who conquered it, so Acsah became Othniel's wife.

[18]When Acsah married Othniel, she urged him* to ask her father for a field. As she got down off her donkey, Caleb asked her, "What's the matter?"

[19]She said, "Give me another gift. You have already given me land in the Negev; now please give me springs of water, too." So Caleb gave her the upper and lower springs.

15:18 Some Greek manuscripts read *he urged her.*

NOTES

15:13 ***Hebron.*** See note on 14:13.

15:14 ***Anakites.*** See note on 11:21.

15:15 ***Debir.*** About six miles south of Hebron; the modern village on this site is Rabud.

Kiriath-sepher. The name means "town of the book" (or scroll).

COMMENTARY

This is now the fourth brief account of the taking of Hebron; the previous three occur in 10:36-37; 11:21-22; 14:12-15. A fifth notice occurs in Judges 1:10. The implication of Caleb's speech to Joshua (in which he asked, "Give me the hill country," and referenced the descendants of Anak as though they still dwelt in Hebron) is that Caleb would lead the battle against them, then occupy Hebron as his inheritance (14:12). It may be that we should see 15:13-14 as simply a summary reminder, and translate the verbs as past perfects: "The Lord had commanded . . . Caleb had been given . . . Caleb had driven out." The main narrative, then, the account of Othniel and Acsah, has its necessary prologue freshly in the mind of the hearer or reader.

By the canons of military reporting virtually through the ages, Joshua as commander could be given credit in the first two (summary) reports (10:36; 11:21-22), without discrediting Caleb. Caleb's clan, the Kennizites, had attached itself to Judah (see note and commentary on 14:6); by the same token, then, the tribe of Judah could be named (Judg 1:10) as taking Hebron, though Caleb led the action. A solution along these lines seems to take seriously the circumstances and details of Caleb's request of Joshua (14:12). Two references (14:12-14; 15:13-14) clearly name Caleb as the conqueror of Hebron.

Turning his attention to Debir, Caleb offered an opportunity to a younger man. We cannot know whether his nephew Othniel was the only one or the expected man to take up Caleb's challenge. We do know that first-cousin marriages have been desirable matches through much of the history of the Middle East (cf. de Vaux 1965:29-32).

Giving a daughter's hand in marriage as reward for a great exploit is not an invention of medieval fairy stories; now and again, it really happened in the ancient world. This is not to say Caleb had the absolute moral right to give Acsah in marriage this way; he did not. But in the world of ancient Israel it would not have occurred to anyone, including Acsah, to think Caleb in the wrong in making this offer. From the brief episode that follows, we may surmise that Acsah did not object to her new husband. In any case, Othniel became Israel's first judge (Judg 3:9-11), so from a historical perspective, Acsah married well. From the evidence of these few verses, so did Othniel.

The Septuagint reading in 15:18 is: "He [Othniel] urged her [Acsah] to ask her father for a field [as a wedding present]." The rendering is easy to explain because the ensuing conversation was between Caleb and Acsah, not between Caleb and Othniel. However, "urged" is a very forceful verb; some have translated it "nagged," then conjectured whether the editors of the Hebrew text changed it to protect the first of Israel's judges from the charge of "nagging" (Boling 1982:373-374). Given several plausible scenarios, with little knowledge of their personalities, we cannot be sure which of the newlyweds urged the other to ask for the field. We do know Acsah was the one who spoke to her father.

Caleb spoke first. The NLT's "What's the matter?" (15:18) may be a bit too strong. The Hebrew phrase is a normal greeting or initial inquiry, "How are you?" or, "What's going on?" Caleb was not inviting Acsah to ask him for something. But since she was *not* doing well without a water source for the town her husband had conquered, her father's greeting, "How are you?" gave Acsah the opening she needed. Acsah's response was, literally, "Please give me a blessing"; in this context, though, "Give me another gift" (15:19) is not a distortion. "In the Negev" (15:19) is misleading, however. The Negev is the semi-arid and southernmost of Judah's districts, but in the ensuing list, Debir clearly is located in the hill country (15:49). Here, we should understand *negeb* [TH8486, ZH9402] as "the [dry] southland" of Hebron, the district Caleb possessed. Acsah called her new home of Debir, "the Negev" ("dry"), because it had no water source of its own. "The upper and lower springs" are two water sources close together, but too far from Debir to belong to it naturally, hence Acsah's need to ask her father for the blessing of water. The Hebrew word *gulloth* [TH1543, ZH1657] is not "springs"; these are more like wells, and Acsah was asking for them specifically.

These wells are about one-and-a-half miles north of the modern village of Khirbet Rabud. Their modern Arabic names translate as "The Upper Well of the Leech" and "The Lower Well of the Leech." Rabud, like Debir of old, has no natural water source of its own; these wells still provide water for the vicinity. Given their presence just where they should be, and given that the archaeology and geography of Rabud fit the requirements for Debir perfectly, there no longer can be the slightest doubt that Rabud is Debir and that these two wells are the "springs" Acsah asked her father to give her as a wedding gift. Looking into them and drinking from them is a most moving experience.

◆ 3. Judah's allotments: Negev, Shephelah, hill country, and wilderness (15:20-63)

20 This was the homeland allocated to the
clans of the tribe of Judah.

21 The towns of Judah situated along
the borders of Edom in the extreme
south were Kabzeel, Eder, Jagur,
22 Kinah, Dimonah, Adadah, 23 Kedesh,
Hazor, Ithnan, 24 Ziph, Telem, Bealoth,
25 Hazor-hadattah, Kerioth-hezron (that
is, Hazor), 26 Amam, Shema, Moladah,
27 Hazar-gaddah, Heshmon, Beth-pelet,
28 Hazar-shual, Beersheba, Biziothiah,
29 Baalah, Iim, Ezem, 30 Eltolad, Kesil,
Hormah, 31 Ziklag, Madmannah,
Sansannah, 32 Lebaoth, Shilhim, Ain,
and Rimmon—twenty-nine towns
with their surrounding villages.

33 The following towns situated in
the western foothills* were also given
to Judah: Eshtaol, Zorah, Ashnah,
34 Zanoah, En-gannim, Tappuah, Enam,
35 Jarmuth, Adullam, Socoh, Azekah,
36 Shaaraim, Adithaim, Gederah, and
Gederothaim—fourteen towns with
their surrounding villages.

37 Also included were Zenan,
Hadashah, Migdal-gad, 38 Dilean,
Mizpeh, Joktheel, 39 Lachish, Bozkath,
Eglon, 40 Cabbon, Lahmam, Kitlish,
41 Gederoth, Beth-dagon, Naamah,
and Makkedah—sixteen towns with
their surrounding villages.

42 Besides these, there were Libnah,
Ether, Ashan, 43 Iphtah, Ashnah, Nezib,
44 Keilah, Aczib, and Mareshah—nine
towns with their surrounding villages.

45 The territory of the tribe of
Judah also included Ekron and its
surrounding settlements and villages.
46 From Ekron the boundary extended
west and included the towns near
Ashdod with their surrounding
villages. 47 It also included Ashdod
with its surrounding settlements and
villages and Gaza with its settlements
and villages, as far as the Brook of
Egypt and along the coast of the
Mediterranean Sea.

48 Judah also received the following
towns in the hill country: Shamir,
Jattir, Socoh, 49 Dannah, Kiriath-
sannah (that is, Debir), 50 Anab,
Eshtemoh, Anim, 51 Goshen, Holon,
and Giloh—eleven towns with their
surrounding villages.

52 Also included were the towns of
Arab, Dumah, Eshan, 53 Janim, Beth-
tappuah, Aphekah, 54 Humtah, Kiriath-
arba (that is, Hebron), and Zior—nine
towns with their surrounding villages.

55 Besides these, there were Maon,
Carmel, Ziph, Juttah, 56 Jezreel,
Jokdeam, Zanoah, 57 Kain, Gibeah, and

Timnah—ten towns with their
surrounding villages.
[58]In addition, there were Halhul,
Beth-zur, Gedor, [59]Maarath, Beth-
anoth, and Eltekon—six towns with
their surrounding villages.
[60]There were also Kiriath-baal (that
is, Kiriath-jearim) and Rabbah—two
towns with their surrounding villages.
[61]In the wilderness there were the
towns of Beth-arabah, Middin,
Secacah, [62]Nibshan, the City of Salt,
and En-gedi—six towns with their
surrounding villages.
[63]But the tribe of Judah could not drive
out the Jebusites, who lived in the city of
Jerusalem, so the Jebusites live there
among the people of Judah to this day.

15:33 Hebrew *the Shephelah.*

NOTES

15:21 ***extreme south.*** Lit., "the Negev." The biblical Negev was a figure-eight-shaped region centered on Beersheba. (See Introduction, "The Physical Geography of Canaan.")

Eder. One recension of the LXX reads "Arad," which should be about here in the list, and was too important a town to be left out. The two Hebrew words differ only in the order of the very similar looking letters Resh and Daleth. We probably should read "Arad" here.

15:28 ***Beersheba.*** Tell es-Seba' (Tel Sheva), three miles east of modern Beersheba.

Biziothiah. This is not a recognizable place name; we should read, with LXX, "Beersheba and its surrounding villages."

15:31 ***Ziklag.*** This was an important town in David's early career. Rainey locates it at Tell esh-Shari'ah, about 15 miles east-southeast of Gaza (Rainey and Notley 2006:149).

15:33 ***western foothills.*** Heb., *shepelah* [TH8219, ZH9169]. (See Introduction, "The Physical Geography of Canaan.")

15:35 ***Jarmuth.*** This was one of the five towns of the southern coalition against Joshua (10:3).

15:36 ***and Gederothaim.*** This word should be read "and its sheepfolds," as in LXX.

15:39 ***Lachish . . . Eglon.*** These are two of the five towns of the southern coalition (10:3).

15:48 ***hill country.*** This refers to the central highlands of Judah, from Jerusalem in the north to just past Debir in the south. (See Introduction, "The Physical Geography of Canaan.")

15:49 ***Kiriath-sannah.*** If correct, this would be yet a third name for Debir; however, we should probably follow the LXX, which reads "Kiriath-sepher."

15:55 ***Carmel.*** This is not the Mount Carmel in the north of the country.

15:56 ***Jezreel.*** This is not the northern Jezreel. This Judean Jezreel was the hometown of Ahinoam, David's wife and the mother of his eldest son, Amnon (2 Sam 3:2).

15:59 Following this verse, a district is missing in the Hebrew text (see commentary below).

15:61 ***wilderness.*** This designates the arid region west of the Dead Sea. (See Introduction, "The Physical Geography of Canaan.")

COMMENTARY

Even specialists cannot identify many of the locations in this passage with certainty. Many are unknown except for their occurrence in this and other lists; some receive passing mention in other texts. But their inclusion here is a concrete reminder that God has acted and continues to act in real time, in the real space of this real world. Salvation history is history, it is not "merely" moral and theological systems; it is real redemption into the real presence of the personal God.

Thirty-six names occur in the Negev list, though 29 is the total given in 15:32. Possible factors in reconciling the discrepancy: Some names occur also in Simeon's list (19:1-9); the Septuagint and the Masoretic Text differ at some points in the list, as well as at some points in their word divisions—perhaps we should understand some names as compounds, rather than as two names. Similar issues occur in some district lists further along in the chapter, as well.

In this list, the Shephelah is divided into four districts. Through most of the Old Testament periods, Lachish (15:39), near the southwest border and facing Egypt, was the most important city of the 39 listed for the Shephelah. During the Judean monarchy, Lachish was second only to Jerusalem in the entire kingdom. Altogether, the Shephelah was extremely important to Judah, not only for economic and military reasons, but for theological and spiritual reasons as well (e.g., the prophet Micah was from this region).

The fourth district list (15:45-47) functions as an appendix, or a parenthesis. Most of the area mentioned is coastal, and not part of the Shephelah. Ekron, Ashdod, and Gaza soon became three of the five cities of the Philistine Pentapolis. If Judah occupied these territories at all early on, their hold was tenuous and short. This coastal region became at least partly (and perhaps mostly) Jewish only late in the Hellenistic period.

In the Hebrew text, the hill country is divided into five districts. However, following 15:59, the Septuagint preserves another district of 11 cities, including Bethlehem, whose absence from any list of Judean towns would be surprising. This also brings the number of districts to 12, which makes more sense than a total of 11 districts, given the prominence of the number 12 in the Bible, generally, and its importance to the political organization of Israel, specifically. The fact that this last district is lacking in the Masoretic Text is due to scribal error: A copyist's eye passed over this district in the Hebrew text because the district lists all end with the same word, an error called haplography. Reinserted, the list would read here: "Tekoa, Ephrathah (that is, Bethlehem), Peor, Etam, Koloun, Tatam, Sores, Karem, Gallim, Bether, Manahath—eleven towns with their surrounding villages."

The eastern slopes comprised the wilderness district, which was sparsely settled; because of the rain-shadow effect, it receives much less rainfall than the western Shephelah and the central hill country. The wilderness district extended to the western shore of the Dead Sea; two of its six towns were on that shoreline, the others, not far away.

The concluding note about the Jebusites reflects the strong Judean presence following David's conquest of the city, and therefore must have been penned some hundred years or so after Joshua's time. Jerusalem itself was assigned to Benjamin (18:28). The note is also a reminder that not all the Promised Land was conquered in Joshua's day.

◆ D. Joseph's Portions (16:1–17:18)

1. Ephraim's southern border and inheritance (16:1-10)

The allotment for the descendants of Joseph extended from the Jordan River near Jericho, east of the springs of Jericho, through the wilderness and into the hill country of Bethel. 2From Bethel (that is, Luz)* it ran over to

Ataroth in the territory of the Arkites.
3Then it descended westward to the
territory of the Japhletites as far as
Lower Beth-horon, then to Gezer and
over to the Mediterranean Sea.*

4This was the homeland allocated to the
families of Joseph's sons, Manasseh and
Ephraim.

5The following territory was given to
the clans of the tribe of Ephraim.

The boundary of their homeland
began at Ataroth-addar in the east.
From there it ran to Upper Beth-
horon, 6then on to the Mediterranean
Sea. From Micmethath on the north,
the boundary curved eastward past
Taanath-shiloh to the east of Janoah.
7From Janoah it turned southward to
Ataroth and Naarah, touched Jericho,
and ended at the Jordan River. 8From
Tappuah the boundary extended
westward, following the Kanah Ravine
to the Mediterranean Sea. This is the
homeland allocated to the clans of the
tribe of Ephraim.

9In addition, some towns with their
surrounding villages in the territory
allocated to the half-tribe of Manasseh
were set aside for the tribe of Ephraim.
10They did not drive the Canaanites out
of Gezer, however, so the people of
Gezer live as slaves among the people
of Ephraim to this day.

16:2 As in Greek version (also see 18:13); Hebrew reads *From Bethel to Luz.* **16:3** Hebrew *the sea;* also in 16:6, 8.

NOTES

16:1 ***east of the springs of Jericho.*** The spring of Jericho is the copious 'Ain es-Sultan, adjacent to the Tell es-Sultan, the site of OT Jericho. Since Jericho was to be allotted to Benjamin (18:12), Ephraim's border passed to the north of the city.

16:2 ***Ataroth . . . Arkites.*** This Ataroth would seem to be southwest of Bethel/Luz toward Upper Beth-horon (16:5), but the name is mentioned two other times in this chapter (once compounded, 16:5). The Arkites are mentioned as an ethnic group in Gen 10:17, but are otherwise unknown in southern Canaan (but see 2 Sam 15:32).

16:3 ***Japhletites.*** An otherwise unknown town or ethnic group.

Lower Beth-horon. See note on 10:10.

Gezer. See note on 10:33.

16:5 ***Ataroth-addar.*** Geographically, this could be the Ataroth mentioned in 16:2.

Upper Beth-horon. See note on 10:10.

16:6 ***Micmethath.*** Probably Khirbet Makhneh el-Foqa, about three miles south of Shechem (Rainey and Notley 2006:182).

Taanath-shiloh. Khirbet Ta'na el-Foqa, about seven miles southeast of Shechem.

Janoah. Khirbet el-Yanun, about two miles south-southeast of Taanath-shiloh. Ephraim's border ran between these two towns.

16:7 ***Ataroth.*** This is not the same location(s) mentioned in 16:2 and 16:5. Boling (1982:403) locates it at Tell el-Mazar, about eight miles east-southeast of Janoah, in Wadi Far'ah, but Rainey considers this location too far to the east (Rainey and Notley 2006:182).

Naarah. Rainey identifies this site with Tell el-Jisr, just west of Jericho at the foot of the Judean hills, beside 'Ain Duq (Rainey and Notley 2006:182).

16:8 ***Tappuah.*** Sheikh Abu Zarad, about 10 miles south-southwest of Shechem.

Kanah Ravine. This is a small river with one source near Shechem; by the time it joins the Yarkon near the latter's outlet to the Mediterranean, it is about as large as the Yarkon.

The Hebrew name, *nakhal qanah,* suggests that in its upper reaches at least, the Kanah is a seasonal stream. Hebrew *nakhal* [TH5158, ZH5707], Arabic *wadi,* and Spanish *arroyo* all usually designate a ravine or valley riverbed with intermittent (seasonal), rather than perennial (year-round), flow.

16:10 ***slaves.*** Heb., *mas-'obed* [TH4522/5647, ZH4989/6268], not slaves to be bought and sold, but corvée workers, impressed into service for a set number of days of labor per year, or for the duration of a specific building project (to fulfill, in effect, a labor tax).

COMMENTARY

Joseph was the firstborn of Rachel, the only wife Jacob really desired. Joseph had two sons, Manasseh and Ephraim, by his Egyptian wife Asenath (Gen 41:50-52). Half of Manasseh had their inheritance across the Jordan. Ephraim and the rest of Manasseh now received their allotments, mostly in the north-central part of the hill country.

Both Ephraim and Manasseh received land, bringing the total number of allotments to 12. (Levi did not receive an inheritance of land.) The double allotment to the Joseph tribes also fulfilled the bountiful blessing Jacob had pronounced upon Joseph (Gen 49:22-26). Like Judah in the south, Joseph (especially Ephraim) exercised leadership from its central position in the north. That Judah's and Joseph's inheritances are listed and described first is further evidence of their preeminence in Israel.

The first paragraph (16:1-4) is a general description of Joseph's descendants' southern boundary. Jericho was assigned to Benjamin (18:21). Ephraim's border with Benjamin ran a bit north of Jericho, through the northern portion of the wilderness of Judea, and up into the hill country at Bethel. From Bethel, Ephraim's border ran generally southwest toward Gezer, then west and northwest until it reached the Mediterranean.

Verse 5 is but a brief summary of the southern border as Ephraim's, since it already had been outlined (16:1-3) as belonging to "the descendants of Joseph," Mannaseh and Ephraim. The description of Ephraim's northern border with Manasseh actually begins in the middle, south of Shechem at Micmethath. On one view, it went eastward to Wadi Far'ah, then followed it down to the Jordan. On another view, Ephraim was confined to the hill country on its eastern borders, with the Jordan Valley belonging to Manasseh as far down as just north of Jericho. Given Ephraim's later war with Jephthah across the Jordan (Judg 12:1-7), the former seems more likely.

The description comes back to Tappuah, southwest of Micmethath (16:8), and says only that the border then followed the Kanah Ravine to the Mediterranean. This is a very general and incomplete description of Ephraim's northern boundary with Manasseh; many questions are unanswerable. Ephraim's western border was the Mediterranean; its eastern border was either the foot of the hill country at the western edge of the Jordan Valley, or the Jordan River itself, the latter being more likely.

The statement in 16:9 that some towns within the territory of Manasseh belonged to Ephraim is mirrored and slightly expanded in a corresponding statement concerning Manasseh (17:8-10). Though the text is not entirely clear, we may say that together the two notices show that tribal boundaries were not always rigid and impermeable. Neighboring tribes could be neighborly.

Gezer was a large, important Canaanite city at the juncture of the coastal plain with the hill country (16:10). As with some other regions and cities, this description of Ephraim's borders included what God intended Ephraim to possess ultimately. Gezer came into Israel's possession only in the time of Solomon (1 Kgs 9:16).

◆ 2. The case of Zelophehad's daughters (17:1-6)

The next allotment of land was given to the half-tribe of Manasseh, the descendants of Joseph's older son. Makir, the firstborn son of Manasseh, was the father of Gilead. Because his descendants were experienced soldiers, the regions of Gilead and Bashan on the east side of the Jordan had already been given to them. [2]So the allotment on the west side of the Jordan was for the remaining families within the clans of the tribe of Manasseh: Abiezer, Helek, Asriel, Shechem, Hepher, and Shemida. These clans represent the male descendants of Manasseh son of Joseph.

[3]However, Zelophehad, a descendant of Hepher son of Gilead, son of Makir, son of Manasseh, had no sons. He had only daughters, whose names were Mahlah, Noah, Hoglah, Milcah, and Tirzah. [4]These women came to Eleazar the priest, Joshua son of Nun, and the Israelite leaders and said, "The LORD commanded Moses to give us a grant of land along with the men of our tribe."

So Joshua gave them a grant of land along with their uncles, as the LORD had commanded. [5]As a result, Manasseh's total allocation came to ten parcels of land, in addition to the land of Gilead and Bashan across the Jordan River, [6]because the female descendants of Manasseh received a grant of land along with the male descendants. (The land of Gilead was given to the rest of the male descendants of Manasseh.)

NOTES

17:1 ***Manasseh . . . Bashan.*** See commentary on 13:29-31.

17:2 ***Abiezer.*** This clan's territory lay west of Shechem.

Helek. Helek's district was north-northwest of Shechem.

Asriel. The clan of Asriel was allotted territory south of Abiezer, on the border with Ephraim.

Shechem. This area was centered on the city of Shechem, which antedated Israel's entry into the land (cf. Gen 34); the early relationship between Shechem and Israel remains a puzzle.

Hepher. Hepher's only son, apparently, was Zelophehad (17:3), who in turn sired no sons but had five daughters who inherited allotments with their uncles west of the Jordan (cf. Num 27 and 36).

Shemida. This clan's territory lay northwest of Abiezer.

17:3 ***Gilead . . . Makir.*** The presence of these names on both sides of the Jordan is another indication of mobility within (and between) the tribes of Israel in this period.

Mahlah . . . Milcah. The locations of the clans descended from these women are unknown.

Noah, Hoglah . . . Tirzah. The clans descended from these three of the sisters lay north of the districts allotted to their uncles, from west to east, respectively. (Noah is not the same name as the Genesis hero of the Deluge; the names are spelled differently in Hebrew.) In addition to this district, Tirzah also lent her name to a principal city of the district, which became the capital of northern Israel early in the divided monarchy (1 Kgs 14:17–16:23);

Tirzah is identified with Tell el-Far'ah (north), at the head of Wadi Far'ah (cf. Aharoni 1979:368-369).

17:4 ***The Lord commanded Moses.*** See Num 27:1-8; 36:1-12.

17:5 ***ten parcels.*** There were five for Manasseh's male descendants (17:2), and five for Zelophehad's daughters.

COMMENTARY

The allotments to Zelophehad's daughters fulfilled God's command to Moses (Num 27:1-8), when they had come to Moses to present their case. Ordinarily, daughters joined the families of their husbands when they married; sons inherited the family land and preserved and passed on the family name.

But in making their request of Moses, the five daughters of Zelophehad initiated a precedent in Israel. God instructed Moses that daughters without brothers were to receive an inheritance. This and many other episodes and regulations in Scripture demonstrate that God did not intend Israel's society to be totally patriarchal. Women were people; women were citizens; women could usually participate in worship (except on conditions of ceremonial uncleanness, which also barred men, Lev 11–15); women could fill leadership positions, except within the priesthood; women sometimes could inherit real property.

The daughters of Zelophehad received their inheritance with the rest of western Manasseh in the hill country. Two of their names, Noah and Hoglah, show up centuries later as names of clans in the time of Jehu, king of Israel in the ninth century BC, on some of the Samaria ostraca (inscriptions in ink on potsherds; Aharoni 1979:361-362, 368-369). Tirzah, the second capital of the northern kingdom of Israel (1 Kgs 15:21, 33), was named for another daughter. Zelophehad's daughters made their mark in Israel.

◆ 3. The rest of Manasseh's inheritance (17:7-13)

7The boundary of the tribe of Manasseh extended from the border of Asher to Micmethath, near Shechem. Then the boundary went south from Micmethath to the settlement near the spring of Tappuah. 8The land surrounding Tappuah belonged to Manasseh, but the town of Tappuah itself, on the border of Manasseh's territory, belonged to the tribe of Ephraim. 9From the spring of Tappuah, the boundary of Manasseh followed the Kanah Ravine to the Mediterranean Sea.* Several towns south of the ravine were inside Manasseh's territory, but they actually belonged to the tribe of Ephraim. 10In general, however, the land south of the ravine belonged to Ephraim, and the land north of the ravine belonged to Manasseh. Manasseh's boundary ran along the northern side of the ravine and ended at the Mediterranean Sea. North of Manasseh was the territory of Asher, and to the east was the territory of Issachar.

11The following towns within the territory of Issachar and Asher, however, were given to Manasseh: Beth-shan,* Ibleam, Dor (that is, Naphoth-dor),* Endor, Taanach, and Megiddo, each with their surrounding settlements.

[12]But the descendants of Manasseh were unable to occupy these towns. They could not drive out the Canaanites who continued to live there. [13]Later, however, when the Israelites became strong enough, they forced the Canaanites to work as slaves. But they did not drive them out of the land.

17:9 Hebrew *the sea;* also in 17:10. 17:11a Hebrew *Beth-shean,* a variant spelling of Beth-shan; also in 17:16. 17:11b The meaning of the Hebrew here is uncertain.

NOTES

17:7 *Asher.* Asher's southern border reached to the plain of Acco, at the foot of Mount Carmel on its northern slope.

Micmethath . . . Tappuah. See notes on 16:6 and 16:8.

17:9 *Kanah Ravine.* See note on 16:8.

Several towns . . . Ephraim. The text presents difficulties here. BHS suggests deleting the two Hebrew words behind "several towns." Boling (1982:406-407, 412-413), in an attempt to retain them and make sense of the text as it stands, reads the second sentence of 17:9 as a parenthetic scribal query, later incorporated as an integral part of the text: "(In the southern corridor of the Gorge [the Kanah Ravine] are terebinths. Do these belong to Ephraim, amidst towns of Manasseh?)." Boling's proposal seems better than the suggestion in BHS, but the text remains difficult.

17:11 *Beth-shan.* Tell el-Husn, at the mouth of the Beth-shan Valley as it enters the Jordan Valley.

Ibleam. Tell Bel'ameh, near modern Jenin.

Dor . . . Endor. As the NLT mg note indicates, the Hebrew is obscure. Dor is on the coast of the Mediterranean south of Mount Carmel. Endor is on the slope of the Hill Moreh. "Naphoth-dor" is an attempt to clarify the difficult Hebrew phrase ending the verse.

Taanach. Tell Ta'annek is near the southeastern corner of the Jezreel Valley; Taanach guarded the southernmost of the three passes through the Carmel range from the coast to the Jezreel Valley.

Megiddo. After Hazor, this was the largest city in northern Canaan and was at least as important as Hazor. Megiddo guarded the middle and most heavily traveled of the three passes through Carmel to the Jezreel Valley.

17:13 *slaves.* See note on 16:10. Here the term is *mas* [TH4522, ZH4989], which denotes conscription into a corvée labor force.

COMMENTARY

As with Ephraim, Manasseh's territory is defined by a general description of its borders, with few details. Asher and Manasseh shared a common border only at the northern foot of Mount Carmel on Manasseh's northwestern corner. Only in the northeast did Manasseh border Issachar. Southeast of Issachar, Manasseh's eastern border was the Jordan River.

The inclusion of Micmethath in 17:7 following Asher was probably intended to reference Manasseh's northern- and southernmost points in the hill country proper. What follows (17:8-10) is a general description of Manasseh's southern border with Ephraim, longer, but with hardly more detail than is found in the description of Ephraim's northern border (16:8). Verses 8-9, together with 16:9, indicate less rigidity about the border than we might expect (see commentary on 16:9).

As indicated in the note on 17:11 (*Dor . . . Endor*), the text has suffered in transmission. Still, most of the towns listed are identifiable and, except for Endor, all were important towns. But as with other cities located where Canaanite superiority in chariots could be brought to bear on the battlefield, they did not fall to Manasseh in the beginning of the settlement process. The statement in 17:12, "the Canaanites who continued to live there," translates a Hebrew clause that could be rendered, "for the Canaanites were determined to keep on living in this land." The natural desire to continue living where they had lived for generations was not the Canaanites' sin. Their sin was the immoral and violent idolatry by which they had polluted God's land. Influenced by the Canaanites whom they gradually absorbed, Israel succumbed to the worship of Canaan's gods and goddesses. Ultimately, this cost Israel their privileged tenancy of God's land.

◆ 4. Joseph's additional territory (17:14-18)

14The descendants of Joseph came to Joshua and asked, "Why have you given us only one portion of land as our homeland when the LORD has blessed us with so many people?"

15Joshua replied, "If there are so many of you, and if the hill country of Ephraim is not large enough for you, clear out land for yourselves in the forest where the Perizzites and Rephaites live."

16The descendants of Joseph responded, "It's true that the hill country is not large enough for us. But all the Canaanites in the lowlands have iron chariots, both those in Beth-shan and its surrounding settlements and those in the valley of Jezreel. They are too strong for us."

17Then Joshua said to the tribes of Ephraim and Manasseh, the descendants of Joseph, "Since you are so large and strong, you will be given more than one portion.
18The forests of the hill country will be yours as well. Clear as much of the land as you wish, and take possession of its farthest corners. And you will drive out the Canaanites from the valleys, too, even though they are strong and have iron chariots."

NOTES

17:15 *Perizzites.* See note on 3:10. We do not know how far their territory extended, nor do we know how numerous a people they were.

Rephaites. Or, "Rephaim"; often understood as one of the groups of giants in the land, but not always regarded as a separate ethnic group. See commentary on 12:1-6.

17:16 *Beth-shan . . . Jezreel.* The valley of Jezreel is a geological "interruption" of the hill country, separating lower Galilee to the north from the hill country of Manasseh to the south. The valley of Beth-shan connects the valley of Jezreel and the Jordan Valley; the city of Beth-shan guards the junction of its valley with the Jordan.

COMMENTARY

Ephraim and Manasseh's "one portion" (17:14) was much larger than any other in Cisjordan, except Judah's. The request of the Joseph tribes in 17:14-18 seems to focus on the smallness of the territory already cleared and occupied. The potential of the forested hill country, the larger part of the land they already had been assigned, had not occurred to them, or they regarded it as impossible to clear for farming.

Joshua's solution to their dilemma was to encourage them to move out from those parts of the hill country they already occupied, and clear the forested areas beyond. The response of the tribal leaders shows they did not take Joshua's suggestion as a serious possibility. In effect, they ignored it, and stated their real anxiety, the continuing presence of Canaanite chariotry in the two valleys bordering Manasseh to the north.

Chariots plated with iron were the heavy weapons of the day. They operated well in the plains and the valleys, but less effectively in the hill country. As a result, Ephraim and Manasseh were restricted to the hill country in the early part of the settlement period and on into the period of the judges. Most of the cities already named in 17:11 were on the edges of the Beth-shan and Jezreel Valleys; the notice of 17:12 that they could not drive the Canaanites out of these towns is here explained. Rather than rebuke the tribal leaders for their fear, Joshua repeated his instructions to clear forest land for settlement. Hard work would enlarge their inheritance. Joshua's statement in 17:17 is negative in form in the Hebrew, "You will not have [only] one portion." In effect, Joshua was saying, "What you are thinking of now as 'only one portion,' will become more than one portion, if only you will take the initiative to clear the forests in the hill country." His promise that eventually they would drive out the Canaanites (17:18) gave them a hope by which they could enlarge their faith and conquer their fear. And so it transpired. Ephraim and Manasseh became two large and influential tribes ("portions") in Israel, just as the allotment descriptions of these two chapters (chs 16–17) had indicated.

Much of the hill country was forested, and Canaanite settlement was sparse there. If Ephraim and Manasseh had contented themselves with land already cleared, they would have had little room for settlement. But with the introduction of iron technology at about this time, including the iron axe head, they could clear the virgin forests and open up new land for settlement. Joshua himself may have set the example. His allotment was at Timnath-serah (19:50) in the Ephraimite hill country, in a region that has been forested at times even since Joshua's day. Joshua may have been the first to clear his own homestead.

E. The Allotments of the Remaining Tribes (18:1–19:48)

1. Survey of the remaining land (18:1-10)

**Now that the land was under Israelite
control, the entire community of Israel
gathered at Shiloh and set up the Taber-
nacle.* 2But there remained seven tribes
who had not yet been allotted their grants
of land.**

**3Then Joshua asked them, "How long
are you going to wait before taking pos-
session of the remaining land the LORD,
the God of your ancestors, has given to
you? 4Select three men from each tribe,
and I will send them out to explore the
land and map it out. They will then return
to me with a written report of their pro-
posed divisions of their new homeland.
5Let them divide the land into seven sec-
tions, excluding Judah's territory in the
south and Joseph's territory in the north.
6And when you record the seven divisions
of the land and bring them to me, I will
cast sacred lots in the presence of the
LORD our God to assign land to each tribe.**

**7"The Levites, however, will not receive
any allotment of land. Their role as priests**

of the LORD is their allotment. And the tribes of Gad, Reuben, and the half-tribe of Manasseh won't receive any more land, for they have already received their grant of land, which Moses, the servant of the LORD, gave them on the east side of the Jordan River."

[8]As the men started on their way to map out the land, Joshua commanded them, "Go and explore the land and write a description of it. Then return to me, and I will assign the land to the tribes by casting sacred lots here in the presence of the LORD at Shiloh." [9]The men did as they were told and mapped the entire territory into seven sections, listing the towns in each section. They made a written record and then returned to Joshua in the camp at Shiloh. [10]And there at Shiloh, Joshua cast sacred lots in the presence of the LORD to determine which tribe should have each section.

18:1 Hebrew *Tent of Meeting.*

NOTES

18:1 ***Shiloh.*** This was about 20 miles north of Jerusalem, in the hill country of Ephraim.

18:4 ***from each tribe.*** These came from each of the seven tribes that had not yet received their allotments.

18:5 ***Judah's territory.*** This was already assigned (see ch 15).

Joseph's territory. This was already assigned (see chs 16–17).

18:7 ***The Levites.*** See also 13:14, 33; 14:3b; 21:1-42.

Gad, Reuben, . . . Manasseh. Their territory was already assigned (see ch 13).

COMMENTARY

When Caleb had first asked Joshua for the inheritance Moses promised him, Israel's camp was at Gilgal in the Jordan Valley (14:6). Now it was time to move to a more central location. The Tabernacle was Israel's meeting place for worship. By setting it up at Shiloh, Joshua made Shiloh Israel's religious and political center. Shiloh's new status is emphasized in this segment by mention of its name in each of the last three verses.

Without allegorizing the details, we are justified in thinking of Israel's journey from bondage in Egypt to freedom in Canaan as a metaphor for the life and journey of faith in all ages. The seven yet-to-be-settled tribes of Israel should have been clamoring for their inheritance in the land. Instead, Joshua had to prompt them to get moving. Sometimes we, too, need to hear Joshua's question: "How long are you going to wait before taking possession of the remaining land the LORD . . . has given to you?" (18:3). It is yours; no enemy can stand in your way or hinder you. Take it. Enjoy it. Grow closer to God in it. Pass it on to your children. Of course, for believers in every age (even in ancient Israel), God's promises are not limited to "land"; they may not even include a physical location. Yet, God's promises are real and eternal, and ought to prompt a response of vigorous faith in all, as Joshua's encouragements did in the men of Ephraim and Manasseh who came to him.

Joshua's instruction to the surveying party that they should return to him with "a written report" (18:4) is one of numerous indications in the Old Testament that early Israel was not entirely an oral society, as is so often asserted. If something was important enough to remember over time, they wrote it down.

Joshua's instructions were succinct, emphatic, and vigorous. The verbs (18:8) are *go, walk to and fro, write,* and *return*. The 21 men of the survey party obeyed Joshua's four strong imperatives, which are then reported in four corresponding verbs: They *went, passed through, wrote [mapped],* and *returned* (18:9). Joshua's challenge was beginning to call forth the right response. This survey mission also demonstrated that the fear of Israel had overcome the hill country Canaanites; 21 men could walk through all these territories and return unharmed.

The "written record" (18:9) the men returned with is called specifically a *seper* [TH5612, ZH6219], a scroll. The descriptions of the tribal allotments that follow in these two chapters have their ultimate source in that scroll. These portions, too, were assigned by Joshua's use of "sacred lots" (18:10). All the tribal allotments were God's gifts, leaving no room for envy or suspicion.

◆ 2. Benjamin's borders and cities (18:11-28)

11The first allotment of land went to the clans of the tribe of Benjamin. It lay between the territory assigned to the tribes of Judah and Joseph.

12The northern boundary of Benjamin's land began at the Jordan River, went north of the slope of Jericho, then west through the hill country and the wilderness of Beth-aven.
13From there the boundary went south to Luz (that is, Bethel) and proceeded down to Ataroth-addar on the hill that lies south of Lower Beth-horon.

14The boundary then made a turn and swung south along the western edge of the hill facing Beth-horon, ending at the village of Kiriath-baal (that is, Kiriath-jearim), a town belonging to the tribe of Judah. This was the western boundary.

15The southern boundary began at the outskirts of Kiriath-jearim. From that western point it ran* to the spring at the waters of Nephtoah,*
16and down to the base of the mountain beside the valley of Ben-Hinnom, at the northern end of the valley of Rephaim. From there it went down the valley of Hinnom, crossing south of the slope where the Jebusites lived, and continued down to En-rogel.
17From En-rogel the boundary proceeded in a northerly direction and came to En-shemesh and on to Geliloth (which is across from the slopes of Adummim). Then it went down to the Stone of Bohan. (Bohan was Reuben's son.)
18From there it passed along the north side of the slope overlooking the Jordan Valley.* The border then went down into the valley,
19ran past the north slope of Beth-hoglah, and ended at the north bay of the Dead Sea,* which is the southern end of the Jordan River. This was the southern boundary.

20The eastern boundary was the Jordan River.

These were the boundaries of the homeland allocated to the clans of the tribe of Benjamin.

21 These were the towns given to the clans of the tribe of Benjamin.

Jericho, Beth-hoglah, Emek-keziz,
22Beth-arabah, Zemaraim, Bethel,
23Avvim, Parah, Ophrah,
24Kephar-ammoni, Ophni, and Geba—twelve towns with their surrounding villages.
25Also Gibeon, Ramah, Beeroth,
26Mizpah, Kephirah, Mozah,
27Rekem, Irpeel, Taralah,
28Zela, Haeleph, Jebus (that is, Jerusalem), Gibeah, and

Kiriath*—fourteen towns with their surrounding villages.

This was the homeland allocated to the clans of the tribe of Benjamin.

18:15a Or *From there it went to Mozah.* The meaning of the Hebrew is uncertain. **18:15b** Or *the spring at Me-nephtoah.* **18:18** Hebrew *overlooking the Arabah,* or *overlooking Beth-arabah.* **18:19** Hebrew *Salt Sea.* **18:28** Some Greek manuscripts read *Kiriath-jearim.*

NOTES

18:17 *proceeded in a northerly direction.* This rendering (cf. ASV, NRSV, NIV, NASB, ESV) is problematic because En-shemesh is east-southeast of En-rogel, and it also would disagree with the parallel description for Judah (15:7). Given the Hebrew verb used, it would make sense to read something like, "then it [the boundary] turned [away] from a northerly direction and proceeded to En-shemesh" (cf. KJV, NKJV).

18:28 *Kiriath.* Since 15:60 and 18:14 specify Kiriath-jearim as belonging to Judah, it may be better to read (with MT), "Kiriath," even though some Greek mss have Kiriath-jearim (cf. NLT mg). This is especially the case since the previous two names, Jebus/Jerusalem and Gibeah, are not close to Kiriath-jearim.

COMMENTARY

Benjamin was the second son of Rachel, Jacob's favorite wife, who died giving him birth (Gen 35:16-18). He was Jacob's twelfth and last son. His descendants reflected this favored position, receiving a small but central portion "between . . . Judah and Joseph" (18:11). Benjamin's northern boundary was the same as Ephraim's southern boundary, as far as Lower Beth-horon. Then Ephraim's boundary continued westward to the Mediterranean Sea (16:3), while Benjamin's boundary turned south at that point. Thus, Benjamin's western border ran from Lower Beth-horon in the north to Kiriath-jearim in the south, a town assigned to Judah, Benjamin's southern neighbor (18:14-15). From Kiriath-jearim east to the Jordan River was Benjamin's southern boundary, coinciding here with Judah's northern boundary, described already in 15:5b-9. Some details differ in the two descriptions, but the major difference is that Benjamin's border is described from west to east, while Judah's is from east to west.

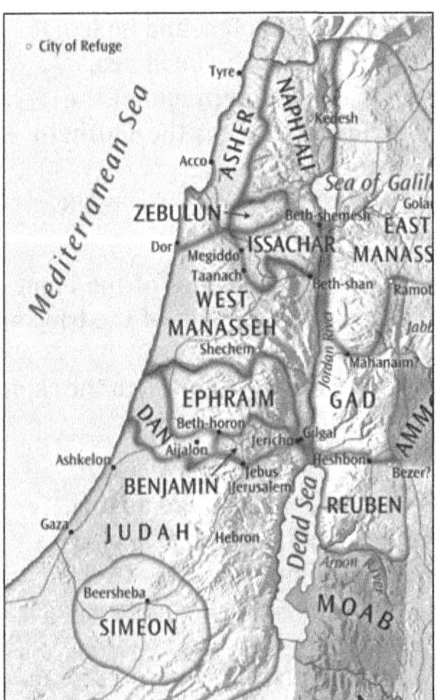

Tribal Allotments

While Judah comprised 12 districts (see note and commentary on 15:59), Benjamin had only two, totaling 26 towns. However, its location between Judah and Joseph gave Benjamin much greater economic and military importance than its small size would warrant. Benjamin received Jerusalem in its assignment of cities, but could not take it (see note on 15:8); only in David's reign did Jerusalem become Israelite.

◆ 3. Simeon's inheritance (19:1-9)

The second allotment of land went to the clans of the tribe of Simeon. Their homeland was surrounded by Judah's territory.

[2]Simeon's homeland included
Beersheba, Sheba, Moladah, [3]Hazar-
shual, Balah, Ezem, [4]Eltolad, Bethul,
Hormah, [5]Ziklag, Beth-marcaboth,
Hazar-susah, [6]Beth-lebaoth, and
Sharuhen—thirteen towns with their
surrounding villages. [7]It also included
Ain, Rimmon, Ether, and Ashan—four
towns with their villages, [8]including
all the surrounding villages as far
south as Baalath-beer (also known as
Ramah of the Negev).

This was the homeland allocated to the clans of the tribe of Simeon. [9]Their allocation of land came from part of what had been given to Judah because Judah's territory was too large for them. So the tribe of Simeon received an allocation within the territory of Judah.

NOTES

19:2-8 Most of the towns in Simeon's list already had been included in Judah's Negev district (15:21-32); the author explains this in 19:9. The NLT's translation in 18:5, "excluding Judah's . . . and Joseph's territory," introduces a problem where there is none in the Hebrew text. Joshua was not commanding the surveying party to stay out of Judah and Joseph (Ephraim and Manasseh). Rather, his instruction, "Judah shall continue in its territory from the south, and the house of Joseph shall continue in their territory from the north," indicates that neither Judah, nor Ephraim and Manasseh, needed to be involved in this venture. Their allotments already were set.

19:2 ***Sheba.*** This should probably read "Shema," as in 15:26.

19:6 ***Sharuhen.*** Probably the Egyptian spelling of Shilhim of Judah's list (15:32). Sharuhen had been an Egyptian administrative center and the staging point of several pharaohs for military campaigns farther north. Most place it at Tell el-Far'ah (south).

thirteen towns. The list has 14 names to this point. Boling (1982:438) suggests the two chariot towns listed consecutively, Beth-marcaboth (meaning "house of the chariots") and Hazar-susah (meaning "corral of the mare"), were counted mistakenly "as one and the same" town (perhaps by a later copyist, who then "corrected" the total).

COMMENTARY

Simeon was Jacob and Leah's second son and thus was older than Judah. But Simeon (with his brother Levi) had forfeited his right to a central role by his violence against Shechem (Gen 34:25-31). The tribal inheritance of his descendants reflects this, since it was carved out of the inheritance of Judah, on Judah's southern periphery in the Negev, far from any permanent centers of influence and power. Simeon's most important town was Beersheba, which became the center of the Negev during the monarchical period. As the monarchy progressed, Simeon (as did most of the tribes) ceased to function effectively *as a tribal polity*. However, individuals and families still could trace their Simeonite lineage, probably until after the fall of Jerusalem to the Romans in AD 70 (as Rev 7:7 would imply). By the time of the Judean return from the Babylonian exile, though, most of Simeon's tribal territory had become occupied by the Idumeans, Edomites displaced from their Edomite homeland by the Nabateans.

The notice that "Judah's territory was too large for them" is quite a contrast with the protest of the Joseph tribes that their inheritance was too small (17:14-18)! It is another early bit of evidence, however, for the comprehensive picture, from Exodus through 1 Samuel, of Judah as, at best, an equal to Ephraim (among the central tribes), until the rise of David as king.

◆ 4. The final five (19:10-48)

[10]The third allotment of land went to the clans of the tribe of Zebulun.

The boundary of Zebulun's homeland started at Sarid. [11]From there it went west, going past Maralah, touching Dabbesheth, and proceeding to the brook east of Jokneam. [12]In the other direction, the boundary went east from Sarid to the border of Kisloth-tabor, and from there to Daberath and up to Japhia. [13]Then it continued east to Gath-hepher, Eth-kazin, and Rimmon and turned toward Neah. [14]The northern boundary of Zebulun passed Hannathon and ended at the valley of Iphtah-el. [15]The towns in these areas included Kattath, Nahalal, Shimron, Idalah, and Bethlehem—twelve towns with their surrounding villages.

[16]The homeland allocated to the clans of the tribe of Zebulun included these towns and their surrounding villages.

[17]The fourth allotment of land went to the clans of the tribe of Issachar.

[18]Its boundaries included the following towns: Jezreel, Kesulloth, Shunem, [19]Hapharaim, Shion, Anaharath, [20]Rabbith, Kishion, Ebez, [21]Remeth, En-gannim, En-haddah, and Beth-pazzez. [22]The boundary also touched Tabor, Shahazumah, and Beth-shemesh, ending at the Jordan River—sixteen towns with their surrounding villages.

[23]The homeland allocated to the clans of the tribe of Issachar included these towns and their surrounding villages.

[24]The fifth allotment of land went to the clans of the tribe of Asher.

[25]Its boundaries included these towns: Helkath, Hali, Beten, Acshaph, [26]Allammelech, Amad, and Mishal. The boundary on the west touched Carmel and Shihor-libnath, [27]then it turned east toward Beth-dagon, and ran as far as Zebulun in the valley of Iphtah-el, going north to Beth-emek and Neiel. It then continued north to Cabul, [28]Abdon,* Rehob, Hammon, Kanah, and as far as Greater Sidon. [29]Then the boundary turned toward Ramah and the fortress of Tyre, where it turned toward Hosah and came to the Mediterranean Sea.* The territory also included Mehebel, Aczib, [30]Ummah, Aphek, and Rehob—twenty-two towns with their surrounding villages.

[31]The homeland allocated to the clans of the tribe of Asher included these towns and their surrounding villages.

[32]The sixth allotment of land went to the clans of the tribe of Naphtali.

[33]Its boundary ran from Heleph, from the oak at Zaanannim, and extended across to Adami-nekeb, Jabneel, and as far as Lakkum, ending at the Jordan River. [34]The western boundary ran past Aznoth-tabor, then to Hukkok, and touched the border of Zebulun in the south, the border of Asher on the west, and the Jordan River* on the east. [35]The fortified towns included in this territory were Ziddim, Zer, Hammath, Rakkath, Kinnereth, [36]Adamah, Ramah, Hazor, [37]Kedesh, Edrei, En-hazor, [38]Yiron, Migdal-el,

Horem, Beth-anath, and Beth-
shemesh—nineteen towns with their
surrounding villages.

[39]The homeland allocated to the clans of
the tribe of Naphtali included these towns
and their surrounding villages.

[40]The seventh allotment of land went to
the clans of the tribe of Dan.

[41]The land allocated as their homeland
included the following towns: Zorah,
Eshtaol, Ir-shemesh, [42]Shaalabbin,
Aijalon, Ithlah, [43]Elon, Timnah, Ekron,
[44]Eltekeh, Gibbethon, Baalath,
[45]Jehud, Bene-berak, Gath-rimmon,
[46]Me-jarkon, Rakkon, and the territory
across from Joppa.

[47]But the tribe of Dan had trouble
taking possession of their land,* so
they attacked the town of Laish.* They
captured it, slaughtered its people,
and settled there. They renamed the
town Dan after their ancestor.

[48]The homeland allocated to the clans of
the tribe of Dan included these towns and
their surrounding villages.

19:28 As in some Hebrew manuscripts (see also 21:30); most Hebrew manuscripts read *Ebron.* **19:29** Hebrew *the sea.* **19:34** Hebrew *and Judah at the Jordan River.* **19:47a** Or *had trouble holding on to their land.* **19:47b** Hebrew *Leshem,* a variant spelling of Laish.

NOTES

19:13 ***Gath-hepher.*** This was the hometown of the prophet Jonah (2 Kgs 14:25).

19:15 ***Bethlehem.*** Not to be confused with the birthplace of David and of Jesus, which was Bethlehem of Judah, five miles south of Jerusalem.

twelve towns. The number of towns named is more than 12; some apparently did not belong to Zebulun, but were on its borders.

19:25 ***Acshaph.*** This was at the south edge of the plain of Acco, near the foot of Mount Carmel. Acshaph was one of the leading cities in the northern coalition against Israel (11:1).

19:30 ***Ummah.*** This should read "Acco," reflecting LXX (Vaticanus), and with Judg 1:31. Otherwise, Acco is missing from this list, and it was too important a city to be left out (cf. Boling 1982:453, 455).

twenty-two towns. Not counting Tyre and Sidon, which Israel never controlled. The grammar of this list is not intended to claim Israelite control over them. Boling (1982:455) and others, however, propose different solutions.

19:36 ***Hazor.*** This was 10 miles north of the Sea of Galilee at the southwestern edge of the Huleh Valley. King Jabin of Hazor led the northern coalition against Israel (11:1, 10).

19:38 ***nineteen towns.*** With present knowledge, there is no sure way of reconciling this total with the 22 names in the text as it stands. As with several other lists, some border towns may not have belonged to the tribe whose borders are here described.

19:46 ***Me-jarkon.*** The Hebrew makes little sense as it stands: "and the waters of the Yarkon." If we restore a missing final Mem, following LXX, it reads, "And on the west (lit., "from the sea"), the Jarkon, as far as the border facing Joppa." This would designate the Mediterranean shoreline, from the Jarkon in the north, and southward to the northern edge of Joppa's lands.

19:47-48 The text of these two verses varies greatly between MT and LXX, with each leaving out major elements, and a considerable difference in arrangement.

Dan had trouble taking possession of their land. See NLT mg, which is closer to the idea of the Hebrew: "but the borders of the Danites went out from them"— i.e., escaped their possession, were taken from them.

Laish. The Hebrew spelling *Leshem* [TH3959, ZH4386] probably includes enclitic Mem, a suffixed feature that must be discounted for purposes of recognition of the proper name of the city. Laish/Dan is at the northern end of the Huleh Valley, near the spring that is the middle one of the three major sources of the Jordan River.

COMMENTARY

The five final tribes were the descendants of five of the six sons born in the contest between Rachel and Leah for their husband Jacob's affection (Gen 30:1-24). The sixth, Gad, already had received its inheritance across the Jordan (Num 32). All six of these tribal allotments were on the periphery of the national territory; these were small tribes, with lesser influence in Israel's affairs.

Zebulun was Leah's sixth son, Jacob's tenth. Leah bore first Issachar, then Zebulun, when she "hired" Jacob for the mandrakes her son Reuben had found (Gen 30:14-17). Zebulun's territory lay partly in the valley of Jezreel, partly in the hills of lower Galilee. Its southern border ran mostly along the Kishon and its tributaries along the foot of Mount Carmel in the southwest. Northward, Zebulun reached to the Beth Netophah Valley; its east-central border reached to Mount Tabor. Zebulun was bordered to the south by Manasseh, to the east by Issachar, to the north and northeast by Naphtali, and to the west and northwest by Asher. Both by the number of towns and by the size of its tribal territory, Zebulun was smallest among the tribes. However, the New Testament village of Nazareth, where Jesus grew up (Matt 2:19-23), was in the former tribal territory of Zebulun. We ought not despise either the day or the place of small things!

Issachar was Leah's fifth son, and Jacob's ninth (Gen 30:18). Issachar's tribal lands bordered Zebulun to the west and northwest, Naphtali to the north, and Manasseh to the south; on the east, Issachar extended to the Jordan River. Issachar's allotment included the eastern portions of the fertile Jezreel Valley. In antiquity, this valley was ill-drained and swampy; therefore, it was mosquito- and malaria-ridden. Around its perimeter, however, a number of prosperous and important cities flourished. Early on, Issachar's allotment was a center of Canaanite strength, so this small tribe had trouble gaining a foothold. This is the backdrop to Jacob's deathbed prophecy that Issachar would be a strong donkey, willing to shoulder the burden of hard labor because he was content in his good land (Gen 49:14-15). Not to sugarcoat Issachar's situation, Jacob's last words concerning him were *mas 'obed* [TH4522/5647, ZH4989/6268], which we have seen earlier means "corvée laborer" (see note on 16:10). Early on, it would appear, when the Canaanites still overmatched Issachar in their allotted territory, Issachar's labor profited Canaanite overlords as much as it did Issachar.

Both Zebulun and Issachar were strategically located because branches of the major international highway from Egypt to Mesopotamia ran through their territories. When Israel was strong, this brought prosperity. But whenever Israel was weak, these two tribes found their territory was the battleground for the armies of Egypt and the successive eastern powers Assyria, Babylonia, and Persia as they fought for control of western Asia.

Asher was Jacob's eighth son and the second son of Zilpah, Leah's maid (Gen 30:12-13). Asher's tribal allotment included the plain of Acco on the Mediterranean coast, and the western portions of lower and of upper Galilee. On its southern border, Asher "touched Carmel" and shared a short common border with Manasseh. On the southeast, Asher bordered Zebulun; on the west, the Mediterranean Sea. To the north, Asher occupied territory inland from the Phoenician cities of Tyre and Sidon. Most of Asher's eastern border was shared with Naphtali. Asher's significance in Israel diminished considerably when Solomon transferred 20 of its cities to pay Hiram, king of Tyre, for his crucial help in building the Temple and Solomon's palace in Jerusalem (1 Kgs 9:10-11).

Naphtali was Jacob's sixth son, and the second son of Bilhah, Rachel's maid (Gen 30:8). The tribe of Naphtali occupied the eastern portions of lower and upper Galilee. Its northern border is not defined here, but certainly Naphtali extended farther north than does the Huleh Valley. Naphtali's western neighbor was Asher. On the south, Naphtali bordered Zebulun (west) and Issachar (east). Naphtali's eastern boundary was the Jordan River and the Sea of Galilee. Two of the three major alternative routes of the international highway from Egypt to Mesopotamia ran through the territory of Naphtali. Because of this, Naphtali enjoyed periods of prosperity, first under David and Solomon, then at times in the divided monarchy when various Israelite kings were strong.

Dan was Jacob's fifth son, the first born in the contest between Leah and Rachel (Gen 30:6). The first son of Rachel's maid Bilhah, Dan was Naphtali's older brother. Dan's original tribal allotment lay west of Judah's, and southwest of Ephraim's main territory, between Judah and Philistia. Several of the towns listed here also occur in the list of Judah's towns in chapter 15. The Philistines moved into the southern coastal plain 75 to 100 years after Israel came into Canaan under Joshua. Over the course of several generations, they proved too much for Dan in this originally assigned territory. The Israelite hero and judge, Samson, was a Danite, but his exploits did not relieve Philistine pressure for very long. The move northward to Laish of a group of Danites, only briefly mentioned here, is recorded in greater detail in Judges 18. The remaining Danites seem to have been absorbed into Judah and (perhaps) Ephraim.

◆ F. Joshua's Portion (19:49-51)

[49]After all the land was divided among the tribes, the Israelites gave a piece of land to Joshua as his allocation. [50]For the LORD had said he could have any town he wanted. He chose Timnath-serah in the hill country of Ephraim. He rebuilt the town and lived there.

[51] These are the territories that Eleazar the priest, Joshua son of Nun, and the tribal leaders allocated as grants of land to the tribes of Israel by casting sacred lots in the presence of the LORD at the entrance of the Tabernacle* at Shiloh. So the division of the land was completed.

19:51 Hebrew *Tent of Meeting.*

NOTES

19:49 ***After all the land was divided among the tribes.*** Lit., "So they completed the distribution of the land according to its boundaries." The verb is both active and intensive, making the sentence an emphatic closing affirmation. See the note on 19:51, where this statement is repeated in synonymous, but not identical, language.

19:50 ***Timnath-serah.*** This site is identified with modern Khirbet Tibnah and was 15 miles west of Shiloh in the western Ephraimite hill country. In Judg 2:9 (NLT mg), Joshua's town is called Timnath-heres.

rebuilt. The archaeology of Timnath-serah shows an occupational gap from Middle Bronze Age II to Iron Age I; Joshua built on a site that had been long abandoned.

19:51 ***So the division of the land was completed.*** Lit., "So they completed the division of the land." The verb is both active and intensive, making the sentence an emphatic closing affirmation. The double affirmation beginning and ending this short section (19:49, 51) redoubles the narrator's insistence that the process of apportionment, ordained by God, now was complete in every way, though the process of settlement still lay before them.

COMMENTARY

As Caleb's allotment opened the apportioning of land to the tribes, so Joshua's closed it, another example of the author's literary framing of his material. Because Joshua was an Ephraimite, his request for "Timnath-serah in the hill country of Ephraim" was natural. The simple, elegant understatement of this final paragraph in the record of the tribal allotments bears emphatic and powerful testimony to Joshua's years of faithful service to God and to his leadership of Israel. Just as eloquently, it reminds the reader of God's faithfulness and grace to Joshua. Though a strong and courageous military leader, Joshua was not a dictator or a tyrant. He was a servant of God and of God's people. Because he delighted himself in the Lord, the Lord gave him the desire of his heart, simply his own place in the land of God's promise.

◆ G. Cities of Refuge and Levitical Cities (20:1–21:45)

1. The law of refuge (20:1-6)

The LORD said to Joshua, [2]"Now tell the Israelites to designate the cities of refuge, as I instructed Moses. [3]Anyone who kills another person accidentally and unintentionally can run to one of these cities; they will be places of refuge from relatives seeking revenge for the person who was killed.

[4]"Upon reaching one of these cities, the one who caused the death will appear before the elders at the city gate and present his case. They must allow him to enter the city and give him a place to live among them. [5]If the relatives of the victim come to avenge the killing, the leaders must not release the slayer to them, for he killed the other person unintentionally and without previous hostility. [6]But the slayer must stay in that city and be tried by the local assembly, which will render a judgment. And he must continue to live in that city until the death of the high priest who was in office at the time of the accident. After that, he is free to return to his own home in the town from which he fled."

NOTES

20:2 ***as I instructed Moses.*** See Num 35:9-34.

20:3 ***relatives seeking revenge.*** Heb., *go'el haddam* [TH1350B/1818, ZH1457/1947], meaning "the blood redeemer."

COMMENTARY

Two tasks remained in the allotment of the land. First, God commanded Joshua to designate six cities (three on each side of the Jordan) as cities of refuge as he had previously instructed Moses (Num 35; Deut 4:41; 19:1-12). Secondly, Joshua needed to designate cities for the Levites to live in, the so-called "Levitical cities." The first of these issues is dealt with in Joshua 20 and the second in chapter 21. Though the cities of refuge are presented here first, God already had instructed Moses they would be six of the cities that would be given to the Levites (Num 35:6).

The background of the cities of refuge lies in one element of retributive justice in ancient Israel: A relative of the victim, usually his closest male kin, was charged with seeing murder avenged. If this relative, the *go'el* [TH1350B, ZH1457], found the killer outside the city of refuge, before or after the trial, he could kill him (Num 35:26-28). It was a matter of life or death, then, for the accidental killer to flee quickly to the nearest city of refuge and stay there.

The elders of each city were the normal court both for civil and criminal cases; they usually conducted legal business at the city gate. Having entered a plea of "innocent," the accused was to receive a place to live with them until his trial. The purpose of the trial was to determine whether the killing truly was accidental, or had been intentional. This had the effect of removing the "preliminary hearing," at least, from the scene of the incident to a location where impartial judgment, based only on the facts of the case, could reasonably be expected. This concept and practice continues in Western law when deemed necessary; at trial it is called a change of venue.

However, Numbers 35:25, from the passage detailing the handling of homicide cases, suggests the trial was not necessarily held in the city of refuge. In some cases, at least, the accused may have been taken back to his own city in protective custody for the trial. The *go'el* had the right to present evidence, if he had it, to persuade the court the death had been murder, and not an accident. If the court decided it was not murder, the *go'el* and the rest of the deceased's family were to abide by that finding.

If the trial found a death to be by murder, the murderer was bound for execution, even if he had made it to a city of refuge. The cities of refuge were not intended to protect an intentional murderer. In the extreme case of Joab's flight, not to a city of refuge, but to the altar in the Tabernacle itself, even the holiness of the shrine did not prevent him from being executed on the spot when he refused to come out (1 Kgs 2:28-35).

Even if the trial determined that the death was caused unintentionally, bloodshed still requires accountability in biblical law (Num 35:31-34). Thus, the mandated residence in the city of refuge was a kind of "city arrest." Enforcement lay in the provision that the *go'el* still had the right to execute him, if he found him outside the city of refuge before the death of the current high priest (Num 35:26-28).

The institution of the city of refuge was designed to limit the scope and destructive power of personal vengeance, which could escalate into blood feuds lasting generations. Putting responsibility for justice in the hands of the assembly, rather than solely in the hands of the victim's relatives, took passion, grief, and revenge out of reckoning when determining guilt or innocence. If the accused were found guilty and executed, it did not stir his relatives to revenge. All interested parties could be satisfied that justice had been served.

◆ 2. Cities of refuge, west and east (20:7-9)

[7]The following cities were designated as cities of refuge: Kedesh of Galilee, in the hill country of Naphtali; Shechem, in the hill country of Ephraim; and Kiriath-arba (that is, Hebron), in the hill country of Judah. [8]On the east side of the Jordan River, across from Jericho, the following cities were designated: Bezer, in the wilderness plain of the tribe of Reuben; Ramoth in Gilead, in the territory of the tribe of Gad; and Golan in Bashan, in the land of the tribe of Manasseh. [9]These cities were set apart for all the Israelites as well as the foreigners living among them. Anyone who accidentally killed another person could take refuge in one of these cities. In this way, they could escape being killed in revenge prior to standing trial before the local assembly.

NOTES

20:7 ***were designated.*** Lit., "they sanctified," a play on words (the verb is *yaqdishu* [TH6942, ZH7727]) with the name of the first city, Kedesh. We could translate, "they sanctified [the town named] Sanctification."

Kedesh . . . Shechem . . . Hebron. The cities west of the Jordan are named from north to south.

Kedesh of Galilee. Rainey's identification of this Kedesh with Khirbet Qedish (Rainey and Notley 2006:138) makes sense both for the distances between cities of refuge, and for the story of Deborah (Judg 4–5). Kedesh lay in the mountains of Naphtali above the Sea of Galilee, about three miles northwest of its southern tip, and about 40 miles north of Shechem.

Shechem. This was about 30 miles north of Jerusalem.

Hebron. This was about 20 miles south-southwest of Jerusalem.

20:8 ***Bezer . . . Ramoth . . . Golan.*** The cities east of the Jordan are named from south to north.

Bezer. Probably Tell el-Jalul, about five miles east of Medeba (Rainey and Notley 2006:204).

Ramoth in Gilead. Tell er-Rumeith, about 25 miles east of the Jordan, near the edge of the desert, and about 55 miles north of Bezer.

Golan. Probably Sahem el-Jolan, in the Golan region about 15 miles east of the Sea of Galilee, and about 20 miles northwest of Ramoth-gilead.

COMMENTARY

Most of the cities of refuge were already well-known to everyone in Israel; all six were also Levitical cities (21:13, 21, 27, 32, 36, 38). No one fleeing a pursuing blood redeemer would have wondered where to go to find safety. Moreover, for the vast majority of Israelites, the nearest city of refuge was not more than one long day's journey distant.

The instruction to include "the foreigners living among them" (20:9) in this legislation is yet another reminder (e.g., Lev 17:8; Deut 1:16; 16:11, 14) that the mandate in ancient Israel for just treatment of noncitizens is one of the great advances in the history of human relations. God ordained justice for resident aliens, intending that outsiders attracted to the worship of Israel's God would find acceptance in the community of faith, in its legal and economic systems, as well as in its faith and worship.

◆ 3. The Levitical cities (21:1-42)

Then the leaders of the tribe of Levi came to consult with Eleazar the priest, Joshua son of Nun, and the leaders of the other tribes of Israel. [2]They came to them at Shiloh in the land of Canaan and said, "The LORD commanded Moses to give us towns to live in and pasturelands for our livestock." [3]So by the command of the LORD the people of Israel gave the Levites the following towns and pasturelands out of their own grants of land.

[4]The descendants of Aaron, who were members of the Kohathite clan within the tribe of Levi, were allotted thirteen towns that were originally assigned to the tribes of Judah, Simeon, and Benjamin. [5]The other families of the Kohathite clan were allotted ten towns from the tribes of Ephraim, Dan, and the half-tribe of Manasseh.

[6]The clan of Gershon was allotted thirteen towns from the tribes of Issachar, Asher, Naphtali, and the half-tribe of Manasseh in Bashan.

[7]The clan of Merari was allotted twelve towns from the tribes of Reuben, Gad, and Zebulun.

[8]So the Israelites obeyed the LORD's command to Moses and assigned these towns and pasturelands to the Levites by casting sacred lots.

[9]The Israelites gave the following towns from the tribes of Judah and Simeon [10]to the descendants of Aaron, who were members of the Kohathite clan within the tribe of Levi, since the sacred lot fell to them first: [11]Kiriath-arba (that is, Hebron), in the hill country of Judah, along with its surrounding pasturelands. (Arba was an ancestor of Anak.) [12]But the open fields beyond the town and the surrounding villages were given to Caleb son of Jephunneh as his possession.

[13]The following towns with their pasturelands were given to the descendants of Aaron the priest: Hebron (a city of refuge for those who accidentally killed someone), Libnah, [14]Jattir, Eshtemoa, [15]Holon, Debir, [16]Ain, Juttah, and Beth-shemesh—nine towns from these two tribes.

[17]From the tribe of Benjamin the priests were given the following towns with their pasturelands: Gibeon, Geba, [18]Anathoth, and Almon—four towns. [19]So in all, thirteen towns with their pasturelands were given to the priests, the descendants of Aaron.

[20]The rest of the Kohathite clan from the tribe of Levi was allotted the following towns and pasturelands from the tribe of Ephraim: [21]Shechem in the hill country of Ephraim (a city of refuge for those who accidentally killed someone), Gezer, [22]Kibzaim, and Beth-horon—four towns.

[23]The following towns and pasturelands were allotted to the priests from the tribe of Dan: Eltekeh, Gibbethon, [24]Aijalon, and Gath-rimmon—four towns.

[25]The half-tribe of Manasseh allotted the following towns with their pasturelands to the priests: Taanach and Gath-rimmon—two towns. [26]So in all, ten towns with their pasturelands were given to the rest of the Kohathite clan.

[27]The descendants of Gershon, another clan within the tribe of Levi, received the following towns with their pasturelands from the half-tribe of Manasseh: Golan in Bashan (a city of refuge for those who accidentally killed someone) and Be-eshterah—two towns.

[28]From the tribe of Issachar they received the following towns with their pasturelands: Kishion, Daberath, [29]Jarmuth, and En-gannim—four towns.

[30]From the tribe of Asher they received the following towns with their pasturelands: Mishal, Abdon, [31]Helkath, and Rehob—four towns.

[32]From the tribe of Naphtali they received the following towns with their pasturelands: Kedesh in Galilee (a city of refuge for those who accidentally killed someone), Hammoth-dor, and Kartan—three towns. [33]So in all, thirteen towns with their pasturelands were allotted to the clan of Gershon.

34The rest of the Levites—the Merari
clan—were given the following towns
with their pasturelands from the tribe of
Zebulun: Jokneam, Kartah, 35Dimnah, and
Nahalal—four towns.

36From the tribe of Reuben they re-
ceived the following towns with their pas-
turelands: Bezer, Jahaz,* 37Kedemoth, and
Mephaath—four towns.

38From the tribe of Gad they received
the following towns with their pasture-
lands: Ramoth in Gilead (a city of refuge
for those who accidentally killed some-
one), Mahanaim, 39Heshbon, and Jazer—
four towns. 40So in all, twelve towns were
allotted to the clan of Merari.

41The total number of towns and pas-
turelands within Israelite territory given
to the Levites came to forty-eight. 42Every
one of these towns had pasturelands sur-
rounding it.

21:36 Hebrew *Jahzah*, a variant spelling of Jahaz.

NOTES

21:2 ***Shiloh.*** See note and comments on 18:1.

The Lord commanded Moses. See Num 35:1-8.

21:13, 21, 27, 32, 38 ***city of refuge.*** On the locations of the cities of refuge, see the notes and commentary on 20:7-9.

21:18 ***Anathoth.*** Also called Anata', about three miles northeast of Jerusalem. It later became famous as the hometown of Jeremiah, the priest called to become a prophet (Jer 1:1).

21:36 ***Bezer.*** The Hebrew text has dropped the comment on Bezer's status as a city of refuge, but the LXX preserves it; see 20:8, with note, and commentary on ch 20. (Since the MT notes the "city of refuge" status of each of the other five, as they are named in this chapter, we safely can conclude this is an omission in the MT, rather than an addition in the LXX.)

COMMENTARY

Eleazar, Joshua, and the tribal elders had been in charge of the distribution of the tribal allotments (14:1). Now the Levitical leaders approached, reminding them of Moses's instructions while they were camped across the Jordan (Num 35:1-8). One of the priestly and Levitical duties was to teach Israel God's Torah. They could accomplish this better if they lived spread among the tribal territories. That, at least, was the ideal.

The descendants of Aaron constituted Israel's priests, so it should not be surprising that the lot fell to them first. Within Judah, the Aaronides received eight cities, within Simeon one, and within Benjamin four. Solomon eventually built the Temple in Jerusalem; thus, the priestly towns were in the tribal territories closest to Jerusalem.

Ephraim bordered Dan to the southwest and Manasseh to the north. Thus, the remaining Kohathite families were assigned cities in the central portion of the hill country, mostly north of Jerusalem. The Gershonite families also were allotted cities in contiguous tribes, the northernmost four in Israel. Reuben and Gad bordered each other east of the Jordan, but Zebulun was west across the Jordan, separated from Gad by Issachar. Thus, Merari was not quite kept "together," as the other Levitical clans were.

The total of 48 Levitical cities included four received from each tribe. The exceptions were that in Judah, they received eight; in Simeon, one; and in Naphtali, three.

Six of these were the cities of refuge previously designated (20:7-8); these six were both Levitical cities and cities of refuge.

We should not assume that only Levites lived in the cities included in this apportionment to Levi. The presence of Shechem, Gibeon, Hebron, Gezer, and others in this list already demonstrates a different reality from that. Israel's subsequent history also makes it clear that these cities had non-Levites among their inhabitants. Some were important cities throughout Israel's history, but seldom for their status as Levitical cities.

Exactly how this Levitical apportionment functioned, then, we do not know. The author's concern here was to emphasize God's gracious provision for those not given a tribal territory because of their service to him (cf. 13:33). God was their portion and provider. Part of God's provision for them was this designation of cities for them to live in, together with guaranteed access to grazing lands surrounding those cities.

The Hebrew noun *migrash* [TH4054, ZH4494], translated "pasturelands" by the NLT, usually is understood as "common grazing ground." It occurs 57 times in this chapter, with each of the 48 cities named, as well as prominently in both the opening and the closing paragraphs. This impressive repetition gives the list the character of a legal record and guarantee of the Levites' access to lands immediately surrounding each of the Levitical cities (Num 35:4-5).

◆ 4. Benedictory summary (21:43-45)

43So the LORD gave to Israel all the land he had sworn to give their ancestors, and they took possession of it and settled there.
44And the LORD gave them rest on every side, just as he had solemnly promised their ancestors. None of their enemies could stand against them, for the LORD helped them conquer all their enemies.
45Not a single one of all the good promises the LORD had given to the family of Israel was left unfulfilled; everything he had spoken came true.

NOTES

21:43 ***all the land he had sworn to give.*** See Gen 12:7; 15:18; 26:3-5; 28:13-15.

21:45 ***everything . . . came true.*** Heb., *hakkol ba'* [TH935, ZH995] (only five Hebrew letters, meaning "the whole came to be" or "everything came to pass"), a beautiful, stunning, perfect finish to this entire report of God's amazing faithfulness.

COMMENTARY

With all distributions completed, the author reminds the reader that God had kept his promises (e.g., Gen 12:7; 28:4, 13; Exod 6:4; Deut 6:10). The fulfillment of God's promises is the central element in each of the three statements of this short evaluative summary, the unifying theme of the paragraph. Each statement begins with a general affirmation that God had done something, followed by a reminder that God had promised to do this.

The reader of Joshua will remember God had made three promises to Joshua himself (1:3-5). These now had been fulfilled. God's promises of land and of rest, made to Israel's ancestors generations ago, as the author noted here, had been renewed to Joshua personally. God's third promise to Joshua had been that no one would be able to stand before him in battle. This promise, too, God had kept.

Everything pulls together in 21:45, the author's finale to the enterprise of taking possession of the land. That task was now finished, in the sense that Joshua's victories over the Canaanites gave Israel's tribes the freedom to disperse and settle into their allotments (cf. 23:1-5). But the emphasis in this benedictory statement of completion is not on Joshua, nor on Israel. It is on God, who had made Israel many "good promises"; not one had failed. The reader is not mistaken in concluding that the God of Israel, the God of the church, is the God who keeps promises.

◆ IV. Joshua's Farewells; Three Burials (22:1–24:33)

A. The Return of the Transjordanian Tribes (22:1-34)

1. Joshua's commendation (22:1-9)

Then Joshua called together the tribes of Reuben, Gad, and the half-tribe of
Manasseh. [2]He told them, "You have done as Moses, the servant of the LORD, commanded you, and you have obeyed every
order I have given you. [3]During all this time you have not deserted the other tribes. You have been careful to obey the commands of the LORD your God right up
to the present day. [4]And now the LORD your God has given the other tribes rest, as he promised them. So go back home to the land that Moses, the servant of the LORD, gave you as your possession on the
east side of the Jordan River. [5]But be very careful to obey all the commands and the instructions that Moses gave to you. Love the LORD your God, walk in all his ways, obey his commands, hold firmly to him, and serve him with all your heart and all
your soul." [6]So Joshua blessed them and sent them away, and they went home.

[7]Moses had given the land of Bashan, east of the Jordan River, to the half-tribe of Manasseh. (The other half of the tribe was given land west of the Jordan.) As Joshua sent them away and blessed them,
[8]he said to them, "Go back to your homes with the great wealth you have taken from your enemies—the vast herds of livestock, the silver, gold, bronze, and iron, and the large supply of clothing. Share the plunder with your relatives."

[9]So the men of Reuben, Gad, and the half-tribe of Manasseh left the rest of Israel at Shiloh in the land of Canaan. They started the journey back to their own land of Gilead, the territory that belonged to them according to the LORD's command through Moses.

NOTES

22:2 *as Moses . . . commanded . . . every order I have given you.* See 1:12-18; Num 32:20-32.

22:4 *home.* Lit., "to your tents"; so also in 22:6-8. The Transjordanian tribes had not as yet built homes in their land, but were still living in tents. Home building was a large part of the task to which they were returning.

22:5 *all your heart and all your soul.* See Deut 6:5.

22:7 *west of the Jordan.* Lit., "across the Jordan, westward." Almost always "across the Jordan" means east of the Jordan. When, as here, it is said from the perspective of the east side of the Jordan, "westward" or some other indicator is used to avoid confusion.

22:9 *the rest of Israel.* Lit., "the Israelites"; "rest of" is added based on the context. It is reasonable to see the term here as denoting "Israel assembled as a nation"; they were assembled at Shiloh. Equally reasonably, this usage presages the split between the eastern and the western tribes, threatened and only narrowly averted as the events of this chapter played out and, late in Israel's history, a tragic reality. It may be that both nuances are intended.

Shiloh. See note and comments on 18:1.

Gilead. See note on 12:2.

COMMENTARY

The conquest and allotment of the land were accomplished. Much of the hard work of actually settling it—building houses; clearing, plowing, and planting new ground; hewing out cisterns; and a myriad of other tasks—still lay ahead. For Joshua, though, in his role as leader of Israel, all that remained was to say farewell.

Joshua's first farewell was to the Transjordanian tribes as he sent them home (22:1-9). His exhortation that they remain faithful is characteristic of Joshua the man, and of the themes of the book. Joshua's words to his departing fellow Israelites recall God's words to Joshua himself as this whole enterprise was beginning (1:1-9). The heart of the matter would be faithfulness to God. Israel's guide to faithful living *in the land* was God's instructions given through Moses. Joshua stressed this vividly by using six infinitives in 22:5: "be very careful *to obey* all the commands and the instructions that Moses gave to you." What does this mean? "*To love* Yahweh your God, and *to walk* in all his ways, and *to keep* his commandments, and *to cleave* to him, and *to serve* him (be his agent) with all your heart and with all your being" (my translation).

Israel was now a nation, living in its own God-given land. God was their suzerain, and his ordinances were to ensure good relationships and good practice in the land, just as every land must have civil order if its citizens are to be safe and to prosper. If the tribes across the Jordan wished to continue as part of Israel, their religious and civil affairs must be in harmony with the rest of Israel.

Reminders such as "Moses had given" (22:7, and elsewhere through much of Joshua) may seem redundant to the modern reader. But they indicate the great care the writer took to emphasize the Transjordanian tribes' identity as part of Israel, in hopes that they and the western tribes would never forget it. That these reminders were warranted is demonstrated emphatically by the report of the confrontation at the end of this very chapter. Even the sharp contrast, just two verses later (22:9), between "Shiloh in the land of Canaan" and "back to their own land of Gilead" is a sobering hint of the ever-lurking potential for trouble between the eastern and the western tribes.

In 22:8, Joshua mentions the plunder that belonged to these tribes. From the perspective of absolute ethical integrity, plundering a vanquished foe cannot be condoned; it must be labeled as theft. But this connection would not yet have occurred either to Israel or to any of the armies they defeated in Joshua's campaigns. Israel reckoned all plunder as the gift of God (cf. 24:13; Deut 20:14), just as their Canaanite foes would have reckoned their plunder as the gift of their gods, had they defeated Israel. Those whose goods were taken mourned their losses, of course. But they did not, and could not have, charged Israel with moral failure. That concept lay still in the future, in the fullness of God's revelation in Jesus Christ, thence through the rest of the New Testament record, and into the (often imperfect) practice of the people of God.

The plunder Joshua listed was the most common taken by victorious armies and peoples, partly because these things constituted most of the easily portable human possessions at the end of the Late Bronze Age. Sheep, goats, cattle, and perhaps donkeys would have been the greater part of the "livestock" (22:8). The four metals listed were by far the most important metals known and used at this time. Silver was the usual medium of exchange, though gold was more precious because it was rarer. Bronze, an alloy of copper and tin, was still the common material for tools, implements, and weapons. Iron was beginning to come into use for these, though iron technology was still quite new and limited in Canaan.

◆ 2. Israel's confrontation of the Transjordanian tribes (22:10-20)

[10]But while they were still in Canaan, and when they came to a place called Geliloth* near the Jordan River, the men of Reuben, Gad, and the half-tribe of Manasseh stopped to build a large and imposing altar.

[11]The rest of Israel heard that the people of Reuben, Gad, and the half-tribe of Manasseh had built an altar at Geliloth at the edge of the land of Canaan, on the west side of the Jordan River. [12]So the whole community of Israel gathered at Shiloh and prepared to go to war against them. [13]First, however, they sent a delegation led by Phinehas son of Eleazar, the priest, to talk with the tribes of Reuben, Gad, and the half-tribe of Manasseh. [14]In this delegation were ten leaders of Israel, one from each of the ten tribes, and each the head of his family within the clans of Israel.

[15]When they arrived in the land of Gilead, they said to the tribes of Reuben, Gad, and the half-tribe of Manasseh, [16]"The whole community of the LORD demands to know why you are betraying the God of Israel. How could you turn away from the LORD and build an altar for yourselves in rebellion against him? [17]Was our sin at Peor not enough? To this day we are not fully cleansed of it, even after the plague that struck the entire community of the LORD. [18]And yet today you are turning away from following the LORD. If you rebel against the LORD today, he will be angry with all of us tomorrow.

[19]"If you need the altar because the land you possess is defiled, then join us in the LORD's land, where the Tabernacle of the LORD is situated, and share our land with us. But do not rebel against the LORD or against us by building an altar other than the one true altar of the LORD our God. [20]Didn't divine anger fall on the entire community of Israel when Achan, a member of the clan of Zerah, sinned by stealing the things set apart for the LORD*? He was not the only one who died because of his sin."

22:10 Or *to the circle of stones;* similarly in 22:11. **22:20** The Hebrew term used here refers to the complete consecration of things or people to the LORD, either by destroying them or by giving them as an offering.

NOTES

22:10 ***Geliloth near the Jordan River.*** Lit., "the circles of the Jordan" (cf. NLT mg); so also in 22:11.

22:11 ***on the west side.*** This phrase does not occur in the Hebrew text. See commentary below.

22:13 ***sent a delegation.*** This was in accordance with Moses's instruction (Deut 13:12-15).

22:14 ***the ten tribes.*** These were the tribes west of the Jordan, not counting Levi, but counting both Ephraim and western Manasseh as separate tribes.

22:16 ***The whole community of the LORD demands to know.*** Lit., "Thus says all the congregation of Yahweh." This is a typical introduction to a messenger report in the ancient Near East throughout much of the biblical record. The delegation brought the message the 10 tribes had agreed on when they met at Shiloh upon hearing of the altar at the Jordan.

22:17 ***Peor.*** See Num 25.

22:20 ***Achan.*** See ch 7.

COMMENTARY

Given its syntax, and the context of this entire episode, we are justified in translating 22:10: "And they came to the districts [circles] of the Jordan that [still] are in the land of Canaan, and there the Reubenites, and the Gadites, and those of the half-tribe of Manasseh built an altar upon [the bank of] the Jordan, a large, impressive-looking altar [lit., an altar large for seeing]." Geliloth is not the place name of 18:17, nor is it Gilgal (4:19); neither was on the bank of the Jordan as this altar was. We should understand "circles" here in the sense of "districts" of the Jordan, i.e., the area bounded on the east by the Jordan River. Given that these districts are noted emphatically as being "in the land of Canaan" (22:10), we hardly can conclude, from verse 10 alone, anything other than that the altar upon the Jordan also was on its west bank.

The ambiguous language of 22:11, though, allows Boling (1982:511-512) and others to conclude differently. One may reasonably translate verse 11, "Then the Israelites heard that the Reubenites, the Gadites, and the people of the half-tribe of Manasseh had built the altar towards the land of Canaan, at the circles of the Jordan, over against [i.e., across from] the Israelites." Boling makes several excellent observations on 22:10-11. He suggests the Transjordanian tribes may have built their altar at Shittim, Israel's original encampment in the plains of Moab east of the Jordan, as in 2:1.

Thus, verse 10 indicates the Transjordanian tribes built the offending altar on the west side of the Jordan, "in the land of Canaan." Verse 11 places it (though with a bit less certainty) on the east side of the Jordan "towards the land of Canaan," and "over against the [other] Israelites." Which was it? We cannot be sure, but the reasoning of the Transjordanian tribes for their building this altar in the first place may favor a location on the east side of the Jordan. They wanted a conspicuous memorial, visible from both sides (v. 10). They also wanted a teaching aid for both sides of the Jordan, so their descendants could not be prevented from coming across the Jordan to worship with (and as part of) Israel (vv. 24-28).

The easterners' fears were not unfounded. This is conveyed subtly but clearly in the author's use of "the Israelites" six times in 22:9-13 to refer to the westerners only, excluding the easterners even in the way this narrative was reported and passed down. This may not have been the author/compiler's own attitude, but the westerners already, at least by implication, were excluding their eastern kin from identity with "Israel." This attitude usually was not expressed openly, but neither was it far below the surface through much of Israel's subsequent history.

When they heard of the newly built altar, the western tribes interpreted it as a violation of commands such as those found in Leviticus 17:8-9 and Deuteronomy 13:12-15. Their war preparations were consonant with God's instructions for such cases as they thought they faced now. God's instructions included investigation, however, so sending a delegation (22:13) came first. Arrows shot from a bow cannot be summoned back.

The questions and accusations of the delegation were direct and hard-hitting. The modern reader may be startled at the nondiplomatic language. But these leaders of Israel had good reason to be forceful in making sure nothing happened to bring God's wrath upon the nation again. Two such episodes had happened already, too recently for them to be calm about this new altar. It certainly looked like the beginning of another rebellion. The Hebrew of the first accusatory question is, "What is this trespass you have trespassed against the God of Israel?" The noun and the verb are from the same root, and both are also used in introducing the episode of Achan's trespass (7:1). The delegation went on to make their fear of a repeat of Achan's sin explicit (22:20). "Our sin at Peor" (22:17) refers to the idolatrous rebellion in Moab, just as Israel was about to enter Canaan (Num 25). Phinehas, the leader of this delegation, had acted to save Israel from complete destruction at that time. He did not want to see any part of Israel turn away from God again.

Again, the subtle division between the two groups shows up in the phrase, "the LORD's land," applied to the land west of the Jordan (22:19). Strictly in terms of promise, there is justification for that phrasing in the consistent wording of God's promises of the land to include Canaan west of the Jordan, but without reference to Transjordan. But it is important to note, further, that the delegation from the western tribes also made a very generous offer, demonstrating their commitment to national unity in faithfulness to God. The well-being of their eastern kin was more important to them than the size of their own portions in the Land of Promise. This would have been a difficult arrangement to carry out, so it is a mark of the seriousness of the situation, in the eyes of the westerners, that they made the offer.

◆ 3. The Transjordanian tribes' defense (22:21-34)

21Then the people of Reuben, Gad, and the half-tribe of Manasseh answered the heads of the clans of Israel: 22"The LORD, the Mighty One, is God! The LORD, the Mighty One, is God! He knows the truth, and may Israel know it, too! We have not built the altar in treacherous rebellion against the LORD. If we have done so, do not spare our lives this day. 23If we have built an altar for ourselves to turn away from the LORD or to offer burnt offerings or grain offerings or peace offerings, may the LORD himself punish us.

24"The truth is, we have built this altar because we fear that in the future your descendants will say to ours, 'What right do you have to worship the LORD, the God of Israel? 25The LORD has placed the Jordan River as a barrier between our people and you people of Reuben and Gad. You have no claim to the LORD.' So your descendants may prevent our descendants from worshiping the LORD.

26"So we decided to build the altar, not for burnt offerings or sacrifices, 27but as a memorial. It will remind our descendants and your descendants that we, too, have the right to worship the LORD at his sanctuary with our burnt offerings, sacrifices, and peace offerings. Then your descendants will not be able to say to ours, 'You have no claim to the LORD.'

[28]"If they say this, our descendants can reply, 'Look at this copy of the LORD's altar that our ancestors made. It is not for burnt offerings or sacrifices; it is a reminder of the relationship both of us have with the LORD.' [29]Far be it from us to rebel against the LORD or turn away from him by building our own altar for burnt offerings, grain offerings, or sacrifices. Only the altar of the LORD our God that stands in front of the Tabernacle may be used for that purpose."

[30]When Phinehas the priest and the leaders of the community—the heads of the clans of Israel—heard this from the tribes of Reuben, Gad, and the half-tribe of Manasseh, they were satisfied. [31]Phinehas son of Eleazar, the priest, replied to them, "Today we know the LORD is among us because you have not committed this treachery against the LORD as we thought. Instead, you have rescued Israel from being destroyed by the hand of the LORD."

[32]Then Phinehas son of Eleazar, the priest, and the other leaders left the tribes of Reuben and Gad in Gilead and returned to the land of Canaan to tell the Israelites what had happened. [33]And all the Israelites were satisfied and praised God and spoke no more of war against Reuben and Gad.

[34]The people of Reuben and Gad named the altar "Witness,"* for they said, "It is a witness between us and them that the LORD is our God, too."

22:34 Some manuscripts lack this word.

NOTES

22:22 ***The LORD, the Mighty One, is God! The LORD, the Mighty One, is God!*** Heb., *'el 'elohim yhwh 'el 'elohim yhwh* [TH410A/430/3068, ZH446/466/3378]. Another possible translation is, "The God of gods is Yahweh! The God of gods is Yahweh!"

22:23 ***burnt offerings or grain offerings or peace offerings.*** These were three important offerings prescribed in the instructions for sacrifices (Lev 1–3).

22:27 ***memorial.*** Lit., "witness."

COMMENTARY

The dramatic formula, "The LORD, the Mighty One, is God!" and its twofold repetition indicate the Transjordanians' shock at being accused of rebellion. In effect, they were swearing by God's name that they were not guilty. It is not unreasonable to infer that it had not occurred to them their action would be so radically misinterpreted.

At this time, Israel's worship was centered in the Tabernacle at Shiloh. Another altar, if used for sacrifice, would have spread out worship, and tended toward dilution of Israel's belief in and faithfulness to God. That was the fear of the western tribes. The eastern tribes' fear was the opposite; they feared exclusion from Israel at some later time, because of the geographical divide—the Jordan River and its deep valley (22:25)—between them and the western tribes, a fear justified by the tendencies already evident in the western tribes referring to themselves as Israel.

This altar near the bank of the Jordan would stand as a silent witness through the generations, testifying by its presence, and the memory of its construction by the eastern tribes, that they, too, were part of Israel, though they lived across the

Jordan from the major center of Israelite worship. That this was its only intended purpose is stressed by the easterners' use of the term "copy" (22:28). A copy, or model, reminds those who see it of the real thing by its form, not its function. This altar was to be seen, not used.

Phinehas and the delegation were both satisfied and relieved with this explanation, as evidenced by Phinehas's words, "We know the LORD is among us," and "you have rescued Israel" (22:31). At Peor, Phinehas's actions had turned God's anger from Israel. Now, in his reply to the Transjordanian tribes, Phinehas used language very similar to what God had said about Phinehas himself at Peor (Num 25:11). More importantly, in dismissing the charge, Phinehas used the same verb and noun the delegation had used (22:16) in bringing the accusation against the eastern tribes, "You have not committed this treachery" (22:31). ("You have not betrayed [with] this betrayal" would reflect the Hebrew usage of related noun and verb.)

Most Hebrew manuscripts, and the Septuagint, lack the name of the altar, "Witness," in 22:34 (see NLT mg). In Hebrew, this word is only two letters, and another very similar word ("Gad") occurs only two words earlier. It was not uncommon for a copyist's eye to skip a word in a context like this, in the eras before exacting safeguards were instituted to ensure almost perfect transmission of the text. If we restore the name (with NLT and other English versions), the last two short dependent clauses explain the significance the Transjordanian tribes attached to the altar of witness they had built on their way home from helping their western relatives take possession of their promised inheritance.

◆ B. Joshua's Farewell to the Leaders (23:1-16)

1. Joshua's call to faithfulness (23:1-10)

**The years passed, and the LORD had given
the people of Israel rest from all their
enemies. Joshua, who was now very old,
2called together all the elders, leaders,
judges, and officers of Israel. He said to
them, "I am now a very old man. 3You
have seen everything the LORD your God
has done for you during my lifetime. The
LORD your God has fought for you against
your enemies. 4I have allotted to you as
your homeland all the land of the nations yet unconquered, as well as the
land of those we have already conquered—from the Jordan River to the
Mediterranean Sea* in the west. 5This
land will be yours, for the LORD your God
will himself drive out all the people living there now. You will take possession
of their land, just as the LORD your God
promised you.**

**6"So be very careful to follow everything
Moses wrote in the Book of Instruction. Do
not deviate from it, turning either to the
right or to the left. 7Make sure you do not
associate with the other people still remaining in the land. Do not even mention
the names of their gods, much less swear
by them or serve them or worship them.
8Rather, cling tightly to the LORD your God
as you have done until now.**

**9"For the LORD has driven out great and
powerful nations for you, and no one has
yet been able to defeat you. 10Each one of
you will put to flight a thousand of the
enemy, for the LORD your God fights for
you, just as he has promised.**

23:4 Hebrew *the Great Sea.*

NOTES

23:3 ***The*** **LORD** ***your God has fought for you against your enemies.*** See 6:20; 10:11; 11:8.

23:5 ***This land will be yours.*** This phrase is not in Hebrew text, though the emphasis certainly is there.

23:6 ***So be very careful to follow.*** Lit., "So be very strong to keep and to do."

everything Moses wrote in the Book of Instruction. Lit., "the scroll of the torah of Moses." The NLT is correct; "instruction" is a more accurate translation of *torah* [TH8451, ZH9368] than is "law."

23:7 ***Do not even mention.*** Lit., "Do not cause [anyone/yourselves] to remember," i.e., do not bring them to remembrance even by mentioning their names.

23:9 ***great and powerful nations.*** E.g., the Anakites (11:21-22) and the city of Hazor (11:10).

23:10 ***put to flight a thousand of the enemy.*** See Lev 26:8; Deut 28:7.

COMMENTARY

This chapter is the second of Joshua's final three exhortations. It sounds as though Joshua was already on his deathbed because of the close repetition of these two statements: "was now very old" (23:1), and "I am now a very old man" (23:2). However, chapter 24 records that all Israel met with Joshua at Shechem in a ceremony of covenant renewal. Thus, we are justified in thinking of this as a preliminary meeting with Israel's leadership, preparing them for the covenant ceremony soon to follow, and for the responsibilities they would assume at Joshua's death, whenever it would come.

The direction of any nation's leadership largely determines the direction of the nation. These Israelite leaders (23:2) had experienced, along with Joshua, what God had done for them in defeating their enemies. Throughout the lifetimes of the leaders who outlived Joshua, Israel continued to be faithful to God, because they kept before Israel their witness to God's faithfulness to them (Judg 2:7). Again, Joshua reminded these leaders (23:4-5) that Israel did not yet occupy all the land he had assigned the various tribes. As the book of Judges relates, rather than driving out the remaining Canaanites, Israel absorbed most of them. Worshiping the gods of their new neighbors, Israel became unfaithful to Yahweh, delaying their secure possession of the land by generations (cf. Judg 2:20–3:4). That Joshua knew this was a real danger is clear from the rest of this chapter.

Since before crossing the Jordan, Joshua's guiding principle had been to follow "the Book of Instruction" (1:7-8). Now he passed it on as his commission to those who would succeed him in the leadership of Israel. Verse 7 ends with a series of four prohibitions. Doing these things would (and eventually did, for Israel) constitute a progression of involvement in idolatry; thus, Joshua's counsel was sound. If Israel had been careful not even to "mention the names" of Canaan's gods and goddesses, they would not have been tempted to "swear by them," then to "serve them," and, finally, to "worship them" wholeheartedly (lit., "Do not prostrate yourselves before them"). This remains a sound principle for avoiding evil, especially that which sorely tempts us. If we stay far from the beginnings of iniquity, we are less likely to be attracted to it, because its true character will be more obvious. Also, if we do begin to be attracted, we will notice it more readily, and can invoke God's help to resist.

"Cling tightly" (23:8) is the same verb used in Genesis 2:24 of a man clinging to his wife, and in Ruth 1:14 of Ruth clinging to Naomi. To cling tightly, passionately, to God is to render impotent the temptation to stray off toward other gods, whatever the form or abstraction in which they may appear.

The end of 23:10 features a participial construction expressing God's continuing action and character, without regard for time: literally, "for Yahweh your God, he is the one who fights for you, just as he promised you." God had fought for Israel in the past (e.g., 10:11-14), and would continue to fight for them in the future.

◆ 2. Joshua's warning (23:11-16)

**11 So be very careful to love the LORD your
God.
12 "But if you turn away from him and
cling to the customs of the survivors of
these nations remaining among you, and if
you intermarry with them, 13 then know for
certain that the LORD your God will no longer drive them out of your land. Instead,
they will be a snare and a trap to you, a
whip for your backs and thorny brambles in
your eyes, and you will vanish from this
good land the LORD your God has given you.
14 "Soon I will die, going the way of
everything on earth. Deep in your hearts
you know that every promise of the LORD
your God has come true. Not a single one
has failed! 15 But as surely as the LORD
your God has given you the good things
he promised, he will also bring disaster on
you if you disobey him. He will completely destroy you from this good land he has
given you. 16 If you break the covenant of
the LORD your God by worshiping and
serving other gods, his anger will burn
against you, and you will quickly vanish
from the good land he has given you."**

NOTES

23:11 This verse may also conclude the preceding paragraph (as in NLT's paragraph divisions). I have placed it leading off this paragraph primarily because of the opening particles of 23:12, *ki 'im* [TH3588A, ZH3955] (but if). This phrase usually connects what follows with what precedes it.

23:12 ***if you intermarry with them.*** The Hebrew follows with, "and if you associate with [go into] them, and they with you."

23:14 The full Hebrew text, with its repetitions for emphasis, can be rendered, "Now, behold, I am going today the way of all the earth. And you know in all your heart[s] and in all your being[s] that there has not fallen one word of all the good promises that Yahweh your God promised you. Everything has come to you. There has not fallen of them one word."

COMMENTARY

The section begins with an admonition: "So be very careful to love the LORD your God" (23:11, see note). A literal rendering is "Strongly keep yourselves by your very lives to love Yahweh your God." The Hebrew word *'ahab* [TH157, ZH170] (love) is a function of will and intention (as is Gr., *agapaō* [TG25, ZG26]). Emotion and attraction can precede love, or result from it, but they are not the essence of love. Because love must be willed, we are instructed to love (though love cannot be coerced).

Joshua's farewell exhortation is very solemn, carrying both hope and warning. God is holy, so Joshua could speak (as above) with optimism and hope of God's good words and of the good land into which God had brought them. God is holy, so he cannot change his character even if his people change. If Israel (or anyone) rebels against God, it cannot damage God's being or dominion, but rebellion can destroy the rebel.

The expression "cling to" (23:12) is the same strong Hebrew verb used in 23:8 (see commentary above). Intermarriage with the Canaanites definitely would be "clinging to" them, but so would any other intimate dealings, if the Canaanites were hostile to Yahweh—or even if they were willing to add Yahweh as just one more god to their already well-stocked cupboard of gods and goddesses. This prohibition is a reminder of Deuteronomy 7:3-4. Intermarriage between God's people and their polytheistic neighbors would lead many Israelites astray. If, however, a Canaanite or other non-Israelite wished to worship Yahweh and join God's people, he or she was welcomed in most situations. Rahab and Ruth are well-known examples. Race, language, and ethnicity had no bearing on God's prohibition of intermarriage. It was solely a matter of faith in Yahweh.

In the end, God usually gives us (or allows us to have) what we think we desire, whether we seek it in God or in rebellion against God. If Israel were to cling to the Canaanite remnant (23:12), God would oblige them by not driving out that remnant (23:13). The dire promise of the Canaanites becoming "a snare," "a trap," "a whip," and "thorny brambles" is a sober reminder that what we seek in opposition to God never turns out to be as attractive in the end as it seems in the beginning.

In concluding this charge, Joshua invoked God's reliability just as in the conclusion of the report of the apportionment of the land (21:45; 23:14). The same phrasings and the same emphasis on God's promise keeping occur in both passages. Joshua, however, went one step further here (23:15-16), invoking the sureness of God's promises as a warning against apostasy. The certainty of fulfillment they had seen working for their good would also guarantee God's judgment upon Israel if they turned away from God. A warning against apostasy is a solemn and unpleasant message, but a necessary one. Apostasy is the deliberate breaking of a good relationship, treachery against God, who is our friend as well as our provider and protector. Israel needed that solemn warning. In an age much more self-centered than Israel's, God's people today need to hear and heed it, as well. We, too, could turn from God to serve other gods, if we neglect our relationship with the one who gave himself for us.

In simplest terms, holiness is being so in love with God that other "gods" hold no real attraction for us. We have eyes and ears, heart and mind, body and soul, only for God. If the things of this world help to sustain us and guide us to God, they are wholesome and may be enjoyed. If not, they surely will cloud our vision of God and should be avoided. Such evaluation of the many things that could become other gods for us is not legalism. It is love for God. Sadly, Joshua's warning went unheeded. Israel did turn away from God; to test them, then, God ceased to drive out the remaining Canaanites (Judg 2:20-23).

◆ C. Covenant Renewal (24:1-28)

1. Joshua's review of God's grace to Israel (24:1-13)

Then Joshua summoned all the tribes of Israel to Shechem, including their elders, leaders, judges, and officers. So they came and presented themselves to God.

[2]Joshua said to the people, "This is what the LORD, the God of Israel, says: Long ago your ancestors, including Terah, the father of Abraham and Nahor, lived beyond the Euphrates River,* and they worshiped other gods. [3]But I took your ancestor Abraham from the land beyond the Euphrates and led him into the land of Canaan. I gave him many descendants through his son Isaac. [4]To Isaac I gave Jacob and Esau. To Esau I gave the mountains of Seir, while Jacob and his children went down into Egypt.

[5]"Then I sent Moses and Aaron, and I brought terrible plagues on Egypt; and afterward I brought you out as a free people. [6]But when your ancestors arrived at the Red Sea,* the Egyptians chased after you with chariots and charioteers. [7]When your ancestors cried out to the LORD, I put darkness between you and the Egyptians. I brought the sea crashing down on the Egyptians, drowning them. With your very own eyes you saw what I did. Then you lived in the wilderness for many years.

[8]"Finally, I brought you into the land of the Amorites on the east side of the Jordan. They fought against you, but I destroyed them before you. I gave you victory over them, and you took possession of their land. [9]Then Balak son of Zippor, king of Moab, started a war against Israel. He summoned Balaam son of Beor to curse you, [10]but I would not listen to him. Instead, I made Balaam bless you, and so I rescued you from Balak.

[11]"When you crossed the Jordan River and came to Jericho, the men of Jericho fought against you, as did the Amorites, the Perizzites, the Canaanites, the Hittites, the Girgashites, the Hivites, and the Jebusites. But I gave you victory over them. [12]And I sent terror* ahead of you to drive out the two kings of the Amorites. It was not your swords or bows that brought you victory. [13]I gave you land you had not worked on, and I gave you towns you did not build—the towns where you are now living. I gave you vineyards and olive groves for food, though you did not plant them.

24:2 Hebrew *the river;* also in 24:3, 14, 15. **24:6** Hebrew *sea of reeds.* **24:12** Often rendered *the hornet.* The meaning of the Hebrew is uncertain.

NOTES

24:2 *Euphrates.* Until his father Terah died, Abram/Abraham lived at Haran in Mesopotamia beyond the Euphrates (Gen 11:31-32). The site of Haran is in south-central Turkey, just north of the Syrian border.

24:3 *led him into the land of Canaan.* More precisely, "through all the land of Canaan." Abraham's travels through Canaan foreshadowed Israel's entry and settlement begun under Joshua. See Gen 12.

24:4 *Jacob and Esau.* See Gen 25:19-26.

Seir. See Gen 36:8-9. Mount Seir is the heart of Edom, the homeland of the Edomites, Esau's descendants.

24:6 *the Red Sea.* Lit., "sea of reeds" (see NLT mg); cf. Exod 13:18; 14:9. Hoffmeier (1996:212) considers Lake Timsah ("Crocodile Lake") a strong candidate for the Red Sea (or, Reed Sea).

24:8 *Amorites . . . their land.* See Num 21:21-35.

24:9 *Balak . . . Balaam.* See Num 22–25.

24:10 ***I made Balaam bless you.*** The Hebrew syntax is more emphatic and ironic: "caused him to bless you repeatedly," recalling Balak's mounting frustrations with Balaam's four successive oracles of blessing upon Israel.

24:11 See notes on 3:10.

24:12 ***terror.*** This word (*tsir'ah* [TH6880, ZH7667]) is usually rendered "the hornet" (see NLT mg), though hornets are not mentioned elsewhere in Joshua. The discouragement and terror of the Canaanites has been referred to by the author, but using other nouns (cf. 2:9, 11, 24). The meaning here remains uncertain.

the two kings of the Amorites. These kings were Sihon and Og, who lived east of the Jordan (cf., e.g., 2:10), though the immediate context here is west of the Jordan. With this reference, Joshua brought his recital of Israel's God-given victories full circle to their beginnings under Moses.

24:13 ***I gave you vineyards and olive groves.*** See Deut 6:10-11.

COMMENTARY

If this covenant renewal ceremony occurred after Joshua's farewell to Israel's leaders recorded in the previous chapter, it constituted Joshua's last public act. In form and content, this ceremony is patterned after ancient Near Eastern suzerain-vassal treaties, known from both the second and the first millennia BC. These include a number of treaties imposed upon their vassals by Hittite emperors of the fourteenth and thirteenth centuries, and a few imposed on their vassals by Assyrian emperors from about 850–650 BC. While the pattern is not rigidly applied, these treaties usually included most of the features noted here. Joshua's renewal of Israel's covenant (treaty) with God begins with a preamble (24:2), and continues with a historical prologue relating the suzerain's (God's) gracious acts on behalf of the people (24:3-13); abbreviated stipulations (24:14-15); abbreviated curses and blessings (24:19-20); deposit of the text with arrangement for periodic reading and renewal (here only implied, 24:26); and witness (24:22, 27).

Shechem had been the location of the first ceremony of covenant affirmation after Israel had entered the land (8:30-35; Shechem lies in the valley between Mount Gerizim and Mount Ebal). That first ceremony had been an act of faith, for it occurred even before Israel's victories over the two Canaanite coalition armies. This covenant renewal, too, was an act of faith, though under different circumstances.

Joshua acted as God's agent in this covenant renewal ceremony, reciting aloud the mighty and gracious acts of Israel's great King. The recital of Israel's faith journey (the historical prologue) from earliest times to that very day stressed God's initiative throughout. God drew Abraham out of the worship of many gods to worship the one true God, and brought him to Canaan. God gave Abraham, Isaac, and Jacob offspring, each under exceptional circumstances. The Exodus and the entrance into Canaan were God's initiative.

Joshua intended this familiar summary to remind Israel why they should continue to choose loyalty to God, their great King. For that purpose, he cast his summary exclusively in terms of God's intentions, initiatives, and actions, even to the point that Joshua put some of the action verbs in the first person, "I," meaning God. But whether first person ("I") or third person ("he") in the Hebrew text, all but a handful of the verbs in this section have God as their subject. In short, all Israel's blessings were of God's grace.

This passage illustrates an important point with regard to human faith in and response to God. It would be possible to explain almost everything Joshua recounted in 24:1-13 in natural and human terms and to reckon the rest as the product of overactive human spiritual fervor or imagination; many have explained these accounts just that way. But if God does exist and continues to act in the world he created, attributing these great events to God's initiative is eminently reasonable. God initiated in grace; Israel responded in faith. Looking back, the skeptical reader will attribute all to human decision, chance, and mischance. But the reader of faith will see God at work here, as Joshua insisted, and as inviting human response to, in, and for his great enterprise of redemption.

Joshua's last statements here (24:13) do not imply that Israel did no work at all once they entered the land. The tribe of Joseph already had been assigned by Joshua a forested region above and beyond their first allotment, a region they had to clear in order to settle it (17:14-18). What this statement does mean is that Israel received Canaanite wealth as the spoils of war, wealth Israel themselves had not created.

◆ 2. Joshua's charge and the people's response (24:14-18)

14"So fear the LORD and serve him wholeheartedly. Put away forever the idols your ancestors worshiped when they lived beyond the Euphrates River and in Egypt. Serve the LORD alone. 15But if you refuse to serve the LORD, then choose today whom you will serve. Would you prefer the gods your ancestors served beyond the Euphrates? Or will it be the gods of the Amorites in whose land you now live? But as for me and my family, we will serve the LORD."

16The people replied, "We would never abandon the LORD and serve other gods. 17For the LORD our God is the one who rescued us and our ancestors from slavery in the land of Egypt. He performed mighty miracles before our very eyes. As we traveled through the wilderness among our enemies, he preserved us. 18It was the LORD who drove out the Amorites and the other nations living here in the land. So we, too, will serve the LORD, for he alone is our God."

NOTES

24:14 ***wholeheartedly.*** Heb., *bethamim ube'emeth* [TH8549/571, ZH9459/622], meaning "with integrity and with faithfulness."

24:15 ***if you refuse.*** Lit., "if it is evil in your eyes."

beyond the Euphrates. This was in Ur, where Terah had lived, or in Haran, where he had brought his family before his own death (Gen 11:31-32).

the Amorites. See note on 3:10.

24:17 ***For the LORD our God is the one who rescued us.*** This could be rendered: "For Yahweh is our God. He is the one who rescued us."

mighty miracles. Lit., "these great signs."

24:18 ***It was the LORD who drove out the Amorites and the other nations living here in the land.*** Perhaps a bit more precisely, avoiding potential ambiguity, this could be rendered:

"Moreover, Yahweh drove out from before us all the peoples, even the Amorite [used here collectively and representatively for all Canaan's inhabitants], dwelling in the land."

COMMENTARY

The first two verses constitute Joshua's charge to Israel to choose their overlord. God did not create humans to be autonomous with respect to God. "Fear of the Lord is the attitude of awe and of filial reverence, which befits the child of God over against his Maker and Redeemer" (Woudstra 1981:351). To "serve" Yahweh is to act as his loyal agent. "Wholeheartedly" combines two Hebrew nouns. "With integrity" means wholly, fully, without division among one's attitude, intention, action, and desire of outcome—without hypocrisy. "With faithfulness" means to act loyally, truthfully, or faithfully over the long haul, without wavering or changing sides. As one reasonably expects this of a human companion, such as a spouse or a business partner, so it is reasonable that God expects this of those he calls and redeems. It is, in one sense, a high compliment that God deems anyone capable (though, of course, only by God's gracious enabling) of rendering this kind of fear and service with integrity and faithfulness.

"Put away forever the idols" (24:14) may be a surprising admonition, but Israel had not yet broken completely with the polytheistic traditions of Mesopotamia. Moreover, some had added to their supply of gods while living in Egypt, and Joshua knew "the gods of the Amorites" (24:15) would become a temptation to many. Now was the day to choose. The rich irony of the "choice" Joshua laid before Israel that day builds to its climax in the second clause that the NLT renders as a question, "Or will it be the gods of the Amorites in whose land you now live?" (24:15). These "gods" had not been able to save the Amorites from the judgment of Israel's God. Why would Israel *ever* be interested in serving them? Yet, once a person or a people take their eyes off the only one who truly *is* God, even ridiculous choices can seem plausible, because we *will* worship something or somebody. Fearing and serving God with integrity and faithfulness is the only antidote to such folly.

Of the three choices he laid before Israel, and acting as agent for his family, Joshua chose Yahweh (24:15). His declaration threw the influence of his leadership and his many accomplishments on the side of the choice for Yahweh. In contrast to individual choice, such total patriarchal agency is ultimately not God's perfect will, but it would not have been questioned in ancient Israel—nor in many cultures today, for that matter. Moreover, individual members of Joshua's family still had to ratify his choice for themselves, just as the individual members of Achan's family had somehow ratified his sin (7:24-25).

The people affirmed Joshua's choice because they recognized that God had been with them. Their short recital of God's intervention highlighted the three movements of their journey (24:17-18), "God . . . rescued us . . . preserved us . . . drove out the Amorites." They, too, recognized God's initiative and power at each stage of their odyssey. Unlike English, Hebrew does not require the phrase "we, too" (24:18). The fact that the Hebrew does use this pronoun and particle here adds emphasis, reflecting the people's determination and their following of Joshua's lead in declaring for Yahweh.

◆ 3. Joshua's rhetorical skepticism (24:19-24)

19 Then Joshua warned the people, "You
are not able to serve the LORD, for he is a
holy and jealous God. He will not forgive
your rebellion and your sins. 20 If you
abandon the LORD and serve other gods,
he will turn against you and destroy you,
even though he has been so good to you."
21 But the people answered Joshua, "No,
we will serve the LORD!"
22 "You are a witness to your own deci-
sion," Joshua said. "You have chosen to
serve the LORD."
"Yes," they replied, "we are witnesses to
what we have said."
23 "All right then," Joshua said, "destroy
the idols among you, and turn your hearts
to the LORD, the God of Israel."
24 The people said to Joshua, "We will
serve the LORD our God. We will obey him
alone."

NOTES

24:20 ***other gods.*** Lit., "strange gods."

24:22 ***You are a witness to your own decision.*** Lit., "You are witnesses against yourselves."

24:23 ***Joshua said.*** Not in the Hebrew text, but necessarily inferred.

destroy the idols. Lit., "put away the strange gods"; the phrase uses the same verb as in 24:14 and the same adjective as in 24:20.

24:24 ***We will obey him alone.*** Lit., "And to his voice we will listen."

COMMENTARY

To underscore the seriousness of this commitment, and to make sure the decision to serve Yahweh was genuine and not merely a result of the enthusiasm of the moment, Joshua approached the matter from a different perspective. He challenged the peoples' ability to keep this commitment, should they make it. Would they be able to serve a holy and jealous God (24:19)? Presented with a second emphatic declaration by the people (24:21; cf. 24:16), Joshua pressed them to repeat it as a legal affirmation (24:22). If Israel later turned away from God, they would be perjuring themselves.

With respect to God, "holy" means transcendent. God is separate from all creation, over and above all he has created. God has no beginning and is noncontingent, needing nothing outside himself for continued existence. Every pagan god, by contrast, is a humanly deified manifestation, representation, aspect, or abstraction of some created entity. In pagan thought, even the gods are finite, and everything in nature is, or will become, a god.

The Godhead revealed in Scripture—God the Father, God the Son, and God the Holy Spirit—exist and live in relationship, in community. Life in community gives holiness its moral and ethical aspects. God's character is righteousness, always doing what is right, and doing so in and for relationships of integrity. What is right originates from God's character. God created humans for relationship with himself. That is God's desire and every human's need. Without relationship with God, humans ultimately do not survive. God desires every human not only to survive, but to *thrive* in relationship with God and in community with each other.

Divided or misguided allegiances provoke God's jealousy because God knows they destroy his precious creatures. The Hebrew term may be translated either "jealous" or "zealous." God is zealous for the good of human beings, whom he created in his own image. God is zealous for the relationship with us for which he created us and jealous (for us) over anything that corrupts that relationship.

Of course, this is not to say God is not grieved by human rejection; God is. God feels grief, hurt, and even anger, as we do. In fact, we feel these and other emotions *because* we are created in God's image. In our fallen state, however, humans often (usually?) experience hurt, grief, and jealousy as personal or corporate diminishment and/or dishonor, so we try to "get even" with those who have wronged us. This can be no part of God's grief, hurt, or anger, though, because, objectively, God cannot *be* diminished or dishonored. Objectively, God's "jealousy" cannot be hurt at human turning away to other "gods," because no human action can injure or diminish God's nature, character, or glory. Our unfaithfulness, however, can and does injure or end our relationships with God and with each other. God passionately desires relationship with us (Isn't that amazing!), so our unfaithfulness *does* grieve and even anger God—for God's own sake, as well as for ours.

Some Israelites had carried "gods" with them since they left Egypt, "gods" inherited from parents or grandparents who died in the wilderness before God allowed Israel to enter Canaan. It may be difficult to understand how they could continue to worship images made by human hands. Hadn't they experienced, over 40 years, God's love and power exercised for them? But if we remember that we too sometimes create or embrace entities that challenge God for our loyalties, we will be more charitable toward ancient Israel. Further, we will ask God to help us identify the idols we have been carrying, throw them away, and set ourselves with renewed purpose to serve God alone.

◆ 4. Formal renewal of the covenant (24:25-28)

25 So Joshua made a covenant with the people that day at Shechem, committing them to follow the decrees and regulations of the LORD. 26 Joshua recorded these things in the Book of God's Instructions. As a reminder of their agreement, he took a huge stone and rolled it beneath the terebinth tree beside the Tabernacle of the LORD.

27 Joshua said to all the people, "This stone has heard everything the LORD said to us. It will be a witness to testify against you if you go back on your word to God."

28 Then Joshua sent all the people away to their own homelands.

NOTES

24:26 ***rolled it.*** Lit., "set it up" or "erected it," implying a stone sculpted into the shape of a stela, a standing stone monument, such as have been recovered in many places in the Near East. Though the text does not say so, Joshua also may have had a memorial inscription chiseled into this stone monument (cf. the inscription at the altar on Mount Ebal, 8:30-32).

beside the Tabernacle of the LORD. Lit., "at the sanctuary of Yahweh." The Tabernacle was at Shiloh, not Shechem (18:1). See commentary.

24:28 ***to their own homelands.*** Lit., "each man to his own inheritance."

COMMENTARY

After the people's second affirmation (24:19-24), Joshua led them in a covenant renewal ceremony (24:25); literally, Joshua "cut (*karath* [TH3772, ZH4162]) a covenant with/for the people that day." The verbal root *karath* occurs in most of the ancient Semitic languages. "To cut a covenant" became the technical term for entering into a covenant treaty, and was used regularly to record the making and ratifying of covenant treaties in the ancient Near East. As a technical term, "to cut a covenant" arose in the practice of dividing (one, or each of several) sacrificial animal(s) lengthwise into two pieces. The covenant parties then walked between the two halves as they lay on the ground (e.g., Gen 15:9-10, 17, but note here that only *God* passed between the halves of the sacrificial animals—God visible to Abram as a "smoking firepot and a flaming torch" [v. 17]). This action symbolized the intention of each covenant partner to be hewn in two like the sacrifice if he violated the terms of the covenant. Though our passage does not record it, Joshua probably did perform this sacrifice as part of this covenant renewal ceremony. In any case, the term "cut a covenant" continued as a reminder of the seriousness of entering into a covenant.

"The Book of God's Instructions" (24:26) is, literally, "the scroll of the Torah of God." Whether this particular scroll contained anything from Moses's time, or from earlier in Joshua's life, or only what Joshua recorded in writing from this covenant renewal ceremony, we cannot say. If any of its content survives in the scriptural record, beyond the events recorded in this chapter of Joshua, it no longer is identifiable as having its source in this scroll.

Joshua probably carried the scroll to Shiloh following this ceremony, and deposited it with the priests there, for safekeeping with other items of national importance. The Tabernacle was at Shiloh, not Shechem (18:1). However, Shechem had been a sacred location for Israel, with a holy place, since the time of Abraham (Gen 12:6), when a venerable oak, or "terebinth," also stood there, perhaps even the same tree mentioned in 24:26. Down to the present day, ancient trees in western Asia usually have been preserved as sacred or venerable, rather than being cut down. Joshua knew what he was doing; a memorial stone (not an altar) set up under *this* tree indeed would be a powerful "witness" to Israel's faithfulness—or, as it turned out, to their unfaithfulness toward God.

Whether Joshua had an inscription placed upon the stone or not, he was saying that everyone who had been there would remember the stone was there, too. What they had done was real; the necessity of remaining faithful to God was real. Every Israelite who saw the stone would remember that day and the ceremony of covenant renewal, either because of being there or because of being told about it. As Joshua intended, this ceremony at Shechem had a lasting effect on its participants. The author recorded (24:31) that Israel served God faithfully as long as that generation lived.

◆ D. Burial of Joshua, Joseph, and Eleazar (24:29-33)

29 After this, Joshua son of Nun, the servant of the LORD, died at the age of 110.
30 They buried him in the land he had been allocated, at Timnath-serah in the hill country of Ephraim, north of Mount Gaash.

31 The people of Israel served the LORD throughout the lifetime of Joshua and of

the elders who outlived him—those who had personally experienced all that the LORD had done for Israel.

32The bones of Joseph, which the Israelites had brought along with them when they left Egypt, were buried at Shechem, in the parcel of ground Jacob had bought from the sons of Hamor for 100 pieces of silver.* This land was located in the territory allotted to the descendants of Joseph.

33Eleazar son of Aaron also died. He was buried in the hill country of Ephraim, in the town of Gibeah, which had been given to his son Phinehas.

24:32 Hebrew *100 kesitahs;* the value or weight of the kesitah is no longer known.

NOTES

24:29 ***servant of the LORD.*** This designation was accorded to Moses at the beginning of the book (1:1, 13, 15). Now Joshua had also "earned" it.

the age of 110. Joshua's ancestor Joseph also had lived 110 years (Gen 50:22). This was the ideal life span in ancient Egypt (Speiser 1964:376, note 22), where Joseph served as prime minister to a pharaoh, and where Joshua had been born.

24:30 ***Timnath-serah.*** See 19:49-51 and notes.

24:32 ***the parcel of ground Jacob had bought from the sons of Hamor.*** See Gen 33:18-20.

24:33 ***in the hill country of Ephraim, in the town of Gibeah.*** Unless "the hill country of Ephraim" carries here a uniquely broad significance, the Gibeah mentioned is not Gibeah in Benjamin (e.g., Judg 19:14; 20:21).

COMMENTARY

These three burials are the final notice in the book of Joshua that Canaan was now Israel's land, however much work, vigilance, and even fighting still lay ahead. If Israel could bury a venerated ancestor and two revered leaders in this soil, they truly had come into their inheritance. When Sarah died, Abraham had to purchase a field with its cave to bury her (Gen 23:17-20); except for Rachel, all the first-generation matriarchs and patriarchs had been buried at that cave. Now Joshua, the patriarch of his generation, could be buried "in the land he had been allocated," his own inheritance, which he already had received and lived upon. God had kept his promise.

The book of Joshua is not intended to be the biography of Joshua, the man, nor an apology for his leadership. The author recorded his shortcomings as well as his strengths. But the final assessment is positive. Joshua's legacy was so strong that Israel remained faithful to God throughout the lifetime "of the elders who outlived him" (24:31).

Joseph had died in Egypt as second in command to Pharaoh. He was embalmed, probably mummified after the Egyptian fashion, and placed in a coffin (Gen 50:26). Israel had carried Joseph's corpse out of Egypt and into Canaan to honor Joseph's last request that he be buried in the land God had promised Israel (Gen 50:25; Exod 13:19). He, like Joshua, was buried "in the territory allotted to" his descendants (24:32), near the border between Ephraim and Manasseh. This particular plot had been Israelite for centuries, by right of Jacob's purchase (Gen 33:18-20).

Eleazar the high priest had stood beside Joshua in the process of dividing the land and allotting portions to the tribes of Israel. All three men, Joshua, Joseph, and Eleazar, were buried in Mount Ephraim, in the central part of the newly conquered land. The burial of these three was a final, important signal of God's fulfillment of his promise to give Israel the land. Where a people can bury their honored dead with dignity, there is a sense of peace and security.

Joshua's major themes of God's faithfulness, God's fulfillment of his promises, God's gift of the land, and the spiritual importance of the land are carried down to the very last verse of the book. Thus, the book of Joshua from the first verse to the last encourages God's people in every age to trust God even when the forces against us seem larger than life. God has promised many "good things" to his people. More important by far, God has promised always to be with us. In that assurance, we can enter with confidence into the inheritance and the rest God has promised (cf. Heb 4:1-10). May God make it so for all God's people.

BIBLIOGRAPHY

Aharoni, Yohanan

1976 Nothing Early and Nothing Late. *Biblical Archaeologist* 39:55-76.

1979 *The Land of the Bible: A Historical Geography.* Translator, Anson F. Rainey. Philadelphia: Westminster.

Albright, William F.

1926 The Topography of the Tribe of Issachar. *Zeitschrift für die alttestamentliche Wissenschaft* 44:225-236.

1939 The Israelite Conquest of Canaan in the Light of Archaeology. *Bulletin of the American Schools of Oriental Research* 74:11-23.

Alfrink, B. J.

1952 *Josué. uit de grondtekst vertaald en uitgelegd.* De Boeken van het Oude Testament 3. Roermond.

Alt, Albrecht

1959 Das System der Stammesgrenzen im Buche Josua. Pp. 193-202 in *Kleine Schriften I.* Munich: C. H. Beck.

1967 *Essays on Old Testament History and Religion.* Translator, R. A. Wilson. Garden City, NY: Doubleday & Co.

Anderson, George W.

1970 Israel: Amphictyony; 'Am; Kahal; 'Edah. Pp. 135-151 in *Translating and Understanding the Old Testament.* Editors, H. T. Frank and W. L. Reed. Nashville: Abingdon.

Auld, A. Graeme

1975 Judges 1 and History: A Reconsideration. *Vetus Testamentum* 25:261-285.

1984 *Joshua, Judges, and Ruth.* Philadelphia: Westminster.

Baly, A. Denis

1974 *The Geography of the Bible.* New York: Harper & Row.

Bartlett, John R.

1978 The Conquest of Sihon's Kingdom: A Literary Re-examination. *Journal of Biblical Literature* 97:347-351.

Bienkowski, Piotr

1990 Jericho Was Destroyed in the Middle Bronze Age, Not the Late Bronze Age. *Biblical Archaeology Review* 16/5:45-46, 69.

Biran, Avraham

1976 Tell Dan, 1976. *Israel Exploration Journal* 26:202-206.

Blenkinsopp, Joseph

1972 *Gibeon and Israel.* Cambridge: Cambridge University Press.

Block-Smith, Elizabeth

2003 Israelite Ethnicity in Iron I: Archaeology Preserves What Is Remembered and What Is Forgotten in Israel's History. *Journal of Biblical Literature* 122:401-425.

Boling, Robert G.

1975 *Judges.* Anchor Bible 6A. Garden City, NY: Doubleday & Co.

1982 *Joshua.* Anchor Bible 6. Introduction by G. E. Wright. Garden City, NY: Doubleday & Co.

Bright, John

1981 *A History of Israel.* 3rd ed. Philadelphia: Westminster.

Butler, Trent C.

1983 *Joshua.* Word Biblical Commentary 7. Waco: Word.

Callaway, Joseph A.

1968 New Evidence on the Conquest of 'Ai. *Journal of Biblical Literature* 87:312-320.

1976 Excavating Ai (Et Tell): 1964–1972. *Biblical Archaeologist* 39:18-30.

Calvin, John

1949 *Commentaries on the Book of Joshua.* Grand Rapids: Eerdmans.

Childs, Brevard S.
1963 A Study of the Formula "Until This Day." *Journal of Biblical Literature* 82:279-292.
1974 The Etiological Tale Re-examined. *Vetus Testamentum* 24:385-397.

Coleson, Joseph E.
2003 William G. Dever's *Who Were the Early Israelites and Where Did They Come From?* A Review Article. *The Tower: The Journal of Nazarene Theological Seminary* 7:51-57.

Collins, John J.
2003 The Zeal of Phinehas: The Bible and the Legitimization of Violence. *Journal of Biblical Literature* 122:3-21.

Cowles, C. S., Eugene H. Merrill, Daniel L. Gard, and Tremper Longman III
2003 *Show Them No Mercy: Four Views on God and Canaanite Genocide.* Counterpoints. Editor, Stanley N. Gundry. Grand Rapids: Zondervan.

Crisler, B. Cobbey
1976 The Acoustics and Crowd Capacity of Natural Theaters in Palestine. *Biblical Archaeologist* 39:128-141.

Cross, Frank M., and G. Ernest Wright
1956 The Boundary and Province Lists of the Kingdom of Judah. *Journal of Biblical Literature* 75:202-226.

Cundall, Arthur E., and Leon Morris
1968 *Judges and Ruth.* Tyndale Old Testament Commentaries. Downers Grove, IL: InterVarsity.

Demsky, Aharon
1973 Geba, Gibeah, and Gibeon: An Historic-Geographic Riddle. *Bulletin of the American Schools of Oriental Research* 212:26-31.

Dever, William G.
1995 Ceramics, Ethnicity, and the Question of Israel's Origins. *Biblical Archaeologist* 58:200-213.
2003 *Who Were the Early Israelites and Where Did They Come From?* Grand Rapids: Eerdmans.

Dorsey, David A.
1980–1981 The Location of Biblical Makkedah. *Tel Aviv* 7-8:185-193.
1991 *The Roads and Highways of Ancient Israel.* Baltimore: The ASOR Library of Biblical and Near Eastern Archaeology.
1999 *The Literary Structure of the Old Testament.* Grand Rapids: Baker.

Fensham, F. C.
1964 The Treaty between Israel and the Gibeonites. *Biblical Archaeologist* 27:96-100.

Finkelstein, Israel
1981 The Shephelah of Israel. *Tel Aviv* 8:84-94.
1984–1985 The Iron Age Fortresses of the Negev Highlands: Sedentarization of the Nomads. *Tel Aviv* 11-12:189-205.

Finkelstein, Israel, and N. Na'aman, editors
1994 *From Nomadism to Monarchy: Archaeological and Historical Aspects of Early Israel.* Jerusalem: Israel Exploration Society.

Franken, H. J.
1976 The Problem of Identification in Biblical Archaeology. *Palestine Exploration Quarterly* 108:3-11.

Friedman, Richard Elliott
1987 *Who Wrote the Bible?* New York: Simon & Schuster.

Fritz, Volkmar
1981 The Israelite "Conquest" in the Light of Recent Excavations at Khirbet el-Meshash. *Bulletin of the American Schools of Oriental Research* 241:61-73.
1987 Conquest or Settlement? *Biblical Archaeologist* 50:84-100.
1995 *The City in Ancient Israel.* Translator, Jill Pittinger. Sheffield: Sheffield Academic.

Gal, Zvi
1982 The Settlement of Issachar: Some New Observations. *Tel Aviv* 9:79-96.

Giblin, C. H.
1964 Structural Patterns in Jos 24, 1-25. *Catholic Biblical Quarterly* 26:50-69.

Goslinga, C. J.
1986 *Joshua, Judges, Ruth.* Bible Student's Commentary. Translator, Ray Togtman. Grand Rapids: Zondervan.

Gottwald, Norman K.
1979 *The Tribes of Yahweh.* Maryknoll, NY: Orbis.

Gray, John
1966 Hazor. *Vetus Testamentum* 16:26-52.

1986 *Joshua, Judges, Ruth.* New Century Bible Commentary. Grand Rapids: Eerdmans.

Greenberg, Moshe
1959 The Biblical Conception of Asylum. *Journal of Biblical Literature* 78:125-132.

Greenspoon, Leonard J.
1983 *Textual Studies in the Book of Joshua.* Harvard Semitic Monographs 28. Chico, CA: Scholars.

Grintz, J. M.
1961 Ai Which Is beside Beth-Aven. *Biblica* 42:201-216.

1966 The Treaty of Joshua with the Gibeonites. *Journal of the American Oriental Society* 86:113-126.

Halbe, J.
1975 Gibeon and Israel. *Vetus Testamentum* 25:613-641.

Haldar, Alfred
1971 *Who Were the Amorites?* Monographs on the Ancient Near East 1. Leiden: Brill.

Halpern, Baruch
1975 Gibeon: Israelite Diplomacy in the Conquest Era. *Catholic Biblical Quarterly* 37:303-316.

Har-El, Menashe
1978 The Pride of the Jordan—The Jungle of the Jordan. *Biblical Archaeologist* 41:65-75.

Haran, Menahem
1961 Studies in the Account of the Levitical Cities. *Journal of Biblical Literature* 80:45-54, 156-165.

Hareuveni, Nogah
1980 *Nature in Our Biblical Heritage.* Kiryat Ono: Neot Kedumim, Ltd.

Harrison, Roland K.
1969 *Introduction to the Old Testament.* Grand Rapids: Eerdmans.

Hawk, L. Daniel
2000 *Joshua.* Berit Olam. Collegeville, MN: Liturgical.

Hendel, Ronald
2001 The Exodus in Biblical Memory. *Journal of Biblical Literature* 120:601-622.

Herzog, Ze'ev
1983 Enclosed Settlements in the Negeb and the Wilderness of Beer-sheba. *Bulletin of the American Schools of Oriental Research* 250:41-49.

Hess, Richard S.
1996 *Joshua: An Introduction and Commentary.* Tyndale Old Testament Commentaries 6. Downers Grove, IL: InterVarsity.

Hillers, Delbert R.
1969 *Covenant: The History of a Biblical Idea.* Baltimore: Johns Hopkins University Press.

Hoffmeier, James K.
1996 *Israel in Egypt: The Evidence for the Authenticity of the Exodus Tradition.* New York: Oxford University Press.

Holladay, J. S.
1968 The Days the Moon Stood Still. *Journal of Biblical Literature* 87:166-178.

Japhet, Sara
1979 Conquest and Settlement in Chronicles. *Journal of Biblical Literature* 98:205-218.

Jones, Gwilym H.
1975 "Holy War" or "Yahweh War"? *Vetus Testamentum* 25:642-658.

Kallai (Kleinmann), Zecharia
1958 The Town Lists of Judah, Simeon, Benjamin and Dan. *Vetus Testamentum* 8:134-160.

2003 Simeon's Town List: Scribal Rules and Geographical Patterns. *Vetus Testamentum* 53:8-96.

Kaufmann, Yehezkel
1985 *The Biblical Account of the Conquest of Canaan.* Translator, M. Dagut. Jerusalem: Magnes.

Keil, Karl F.
1857 *Commentary on the Book of Joshua.* Translator, James Martin. Edinburgh: T&T Clark.

Kempinski, Aharon
1974 Tell el-'Ajjul—Beth-Eglayim or Sharuhen? *Israel Exploration Journal* 24:145-152.

Kenyon, Kathleen
1957 *Digging Up Jericho.* New York: Praeger.

King, Philip J., and Lawrence E. Stager
2001 *Life in Biblical Israel.* Louisville: Westminster John Knox.

Kitchen, Kenneth A.
1966a *Ancient Orient and Old Testament.* Downers Grove, IL: InterVarsity.

1966b Historical Method and Early Hebrew Tradition. *Tyndale Bulletin* 17:63-97.

Kitz, Anne M.
2000 Undivided Inheritance and Lot Casting in the Book of Joshua. *Journal of Biblical Literature* 119:601-618.

Knauf, Ernst A.
2000 Jerusalem in the Late Bronze and Early Iron Ages: A Proposal. *Tel Aviv* 27:75-90.

Kochavi, Moshe, editor
1972 *Judaea, Samaria and the Golan, Archaeological Survey 1967–1968.* Jerusalem: Carta.

1974 Khirbet Rabud = Debir. *Tel Aviv* 1:1-33.

Lapp, Paul
1967 The Conquest of Palestine in the Light of Archaeology. *Concordia Theological Monthly* 38:283-300.

Lemche, Nels P.
1991 *The Canaanites and Their Land.* Journal for the Study of the Old Testament Supplement 110. Sheffield: Sheffield Academic.

Liver, Jacob
1963 The Literary History of Joshua IX. *Journal of Semitic Studies* 8:227-243.

Long, Burke O.
1968 *The Problem of Etiological Narrative in the Old Testament.* Beihefte zur Zeitschrift für die alttestamentliche Wissenschaft 108. Berlin: Toppelmann.

Malamat, Abraham
1960 Hazor "the Head of All Those Kingdoms." *Journal of Biblical Literature* 79:12-19.

1962 Mari and the Bible: Some Patterns of Tribal Organization and Institutions. *Journal of the American Oriental Society* 82:143-150.

1989 Hazor and Mari. *Eretz Israel* 20:68-71.

Margolis, Max L.
1931–1938 *The Book of Joshua in Greek.* 4 vols. Paris: Librairie Orientaliste Paul Geuthner.

Martin, W. J.
1969 "Dischronologized" Narrative in the Old Testament. *Supplements to Vetus Testamentum* 17:179-186.

Mazar, Amihai, editor
2001 *Studies in the Archaeology of the Iron Age in Israel and Jordan.* Journal for the Study of the Old Testament Supplement 331. Sheffield: Sheffield Academic.

Mazar, Amihai, and Nava Panitz-Cohen
2007 It Is the Land of Honey: Beekeeping at Tel Rehov. *Near Eastern Archaeology* 70/4:202-219.

Mazar, Benjamin
1960a The Cities of the Priests and the Levites. *Supplements to Vetus Testamentum* 7:193-205.

1960b The Cities of the Territory of Dan. *Israel Exploration Journal* 10:65-77.

1971 *Judges. The World History of the Jewish People, First Series: Ancient Times,* vol. 3. New Brunswick: Rutgers University Press.

1986 *The Early Biblical Period: Historical Essays.* Jerusalem: Israel Exploration Society.

McCarthy, Dennis J.
1971a Some Holy War Vocabulary in Joshua 2. *Catholic Biblical Quarterly* 33:228-230.

1971b The Theology of Leadership in Joshua 1–9. *Biblica* 52:165-175.

Mendenhall, George E.

1958 The Census Lists of Numbers 1 and 26. *Journal of Biblical Literature* 77:52-66.

1962 The Hebrew Conquest of Palestine. *Biblical Archaeologist* 25:66-87.

1973 *The Tenth Generation: The Origins of the Biblical Tradition.* Baltimore: The Johns Hopkins University Press.

Miller, J. Maxwell

1975 Geba/Gibeah of Benjamin. *Vetus Testamentum* 25:145-166.

1977 Archaeology and the Israelite Conquest of Palestine: Some Methodological Observations. *Palestine Exploration Quarterly* 109:87-93.

Miller, J. Maxwell, and John H. Hayes

1986 *A History of Ancient Israel and Judah.* Philadelphia: Westminster.

Miller, J. Maxwell, and Gene Tucker

1974 *The Book of Joshua.* The Cambridge Bible Commentary. London: Cambridge University Press.

Moran, William L.

1963 The Ancient Near Eastern Background of the Love of God in Deuteronomy. *Catholic Biblical Quarterly* 25:77-87.

Muilenburg, James

1955 The Site of Ancient Gilgal. *Bulletin of the American Schools of Oriental Research* 140:11-27.

1959 The Form and Structure of the Covenantal Formulations. *Vetus Testamentum* 9:347-365.

Na'aman, N.

1999 Four Notes on the Size of Late Bronze Age Canaan. *Bulletin of the American Schools of Oriental Research* 313:31-37.

Naveh, Joseph

1958 Khirbat al-Muqannah'—Ekron: An Archaeological Survey. *Israel Exploration Journal* 8:87-100, 165-170.

Neufeld, Edward

1980 Insects as Warfare Agents in the Ancient Near East (Ex. 23:28; Deut. 7:20; Josh. 24:12; Isa. 7:18-20). *Orientalia* 49:30-57.

Niehaus, Jeffrey J.

1988 Joshua and Ancient Near Eastern Warfare. *Journal of the Evangelical Theological Society* 31:45-50.

Noth, Martin

1937 Die funf Konige in der Hohle von Makkeda. *Palestinajahrbuch* 33:22-36.

1960 Der Beitrag der Archaologie zur Geschichte Israels. *Supplements to Vetus Testamentum* 7:262-282.

1971 *Das Buch Josua.* 3rd ed. Tubingen: J. C. B. Mohr.

Oren, Eliezer D.

1982 Ziklag—A Biblical City on the Edge of the Negev. *Biblical Archaeologist* 45:155-166.

Orlinsky, Harry M.

1939 The Supposed Qiryat-Sannah of Joshua 15:49. *Journal of Biblical Literature* 58:225-261.

1969 The Hebrew Vorlage of the Septuagint of the Book of Joshua. *Supplements to Vetus Testamentum* 17:187-195.

Orni, Efraim, and Elisha Efrat

1971 *Geography of Israel.* 3rd ed. Jerusalem: Israel Universities Press.

Pressler, Carolyn

2002 *Joshua, Judges, and Ruth.* Westminster Bible Companion. Louisville: Westminster John Knox.

Pritchard, James B.

1962 *Gibeon, Where the Sun Stood Still.* Princeton: Princeton University Press.

Rainey, Anson F.

1970-1971 Bethel Is Still Beitin. *Westminster Theological Journal* 33:175-188.

1975 The Identification of Philistine Gath. *Eretz Israel* 12:63-76.

1983 The Biblical Shephelah of Judah. *Bulletin of the American Schools of Oriental Research* 251:1-10.

1987 Review of Gottwald, N. H., *The Tribes of Yahweh. Journal of the American Oriental Society* 101:541-543.

1996 Who Is a Canaanite? A Review of the Textual Evidence. *Bulletin of the American Schools of Oriental Research* 304:1-15.

Rainey, Anson F., and R. Stephen Notley

2006 *The Sacred Bridge: Carta's Atlas of the Biblical World.* Jerusalem: Carta.

Rowlett, Lori L.

1996 *Joshua and the Rhetoric of Violence: A New Historicist Analysis.* Journal for the Study of the Old Testament Supplement 226. Sheffield: Sheffield Academic.

Smith, George Adam

1931 *The Historical Geography of the Holy Land.* 25th ed. London: Hodder & Stoughton. Repr., New York: Harper & Row / Torchbooks, 1966.

Soggin, J. Alberto

1972 *Joshua: A Commentary.* The Old Testament Library. Philadelphia: Westminster.

Speiser, Ephraim A.

1960 People and Nation in the Old Testament. *Journal of Biblical Literature* 79:157-163.

1964 *Genesis.* Anchor Bible 1. Garden City, NY: Doubleday.

Stackert, Jeffrey

2006 Why Does Deuteronomy Legislate Cities of Refuge? Asylum in the Covenant Collection (Exod 21:12-14) and Deuteronomy (19:1-13). *Journal of Biblical Literature* 125:23-49.

Strange, J. F.

1966 The Inheritance of Dan. Studia Theologica. *Nordic Journal of Theology* 20:120-139.

Talmon, Shemaryahu

1963 The Gezer Calendar and the Seasonal Cycles of Ancient Canaan. *Journal of the American Oriental Society* 83:177-187.

1965 The Town Lists of Simeon. *Israel Exploration Journal* 15:235-241.

Tov, Emanuel

1973 Transliterations of Hebrew Words in the Greek Versions of the Old Testament. Pp. 78-92 in *Textus 8: Annual of the Hebrew University Bible Project.* Editor, Shemaryahu Talmon. Jerusalem: Magnes.

Van Seters, John

1972 The Conquest of Sihon's Kingdom: A Literary Examination. *Journal of Biblical Literature* 91:182-197.

Vaux, Roland de

1965 *Ancient Israel. Volume I: Social Institutions.* New York: McGraw-Hill Book Company.

1970 The Settlement of the Israelites in Southern Palestine and the Origins of the Tribe of Judah. Pp. 108-134 in *Translating and Understanding the Old Testament.* Editors, H. T. Frank and W. L. Reed. Nashville: Abingdon.

1971 Le These de l'amphictyonie israelite. *Harvard Theological Review* 64:415-436.

Vries, Simon J., de

1975 Temporal Terms as Structural Elements in the Holy-War Tradition. *Vetus Testamentum* 25:80-105.

Wellhausen, Julius

1876 *Die Komposition des Hexateuchs und der historischen Bucher des Alten Testaments.* Berlin: Walter de Gruyter.

Wenham, Gordon J.

1971 The Deuteronomic Theology of the Book of Joshua. *Journal of Biblical Literature* 90:140-148.

Wenham, John

1973 The Large Numbers of the Old Testament. Pp. 191-192 in *Eerdmans' Handbook to the Bible.* Editors, David Alexander and Pat Alexander. Grand Rapids: Eerdmans.

Wiseman, Donald J., editor

1973 *Peoples of Old Testament Times.* Oxford: Oxford University Press.

Wood, Bryant G.

1990a Did the Israelites Conquer Jericho? A New Look at the Archaeological Evidence. *Biblical Archaeology Review* 16/2:44-58.

1990b Dating Jericho's Destruction: Bienkowski Is Wrong on All Counts. *Biblical Archaeology Review* 16/5:45, 47-49, 68-69.

Woudstra, Marten H.

1981 *The Book of Joshua.* New International Commentary on the Old Testament. Grand Rapids: Eerdmans.

Wright, George Ernest

1946 The Literary and Historical Problem of Joshua 10 and Judges 1. *Journal of Near Eastern Studies* 5:105-114.

1971 A Problem of Ancient Topography: Lachish and Eglon. *Biblical Archaeologist* 34:76-86.

1982 Introduction to *Joshua*, by Robert G. Boling. Anchor Bible 6. Garden City, NY: Doubleday & Co.

Yadin, Yigael

1958-1961 *Hazor I-IV.* Jerusalem: Magnes.

Yeivin, S.

1971a The Benjaminite Settlement in the Western Part of Their Territory. *Israel Exploration Journal* 21:141-154.

1971b *The Israelite Conquest of Canaan.* Istanbul: Netherlands Institute for the Near East.

Younger, K. Lawson

1990 *Ancient Conquest Accounts: A Study in Ancient Near Eastern and Biblical History Writing.* Journal for the Study of the Old Testament Supplement 98. Sheffield: Sheffield Academic.

Zertal, Adam

1985 Has Joshua's Altar Been Found on Mount Ebal? *Biblical Archaeology Review* 11:26-43.

Zevit, Ziony

1983 Archaeological and Literary Stratigraphy in Joshua 7-8. *Bulletin of the American Schools of Oriental Research* 251:23-35.

Judges

LAWSON G. STONE

INTRODUCTION TO

Judges

THE BOOK OF JUDGES provides some of the most memorable stories in the Bible. The stories of Gideon and Samson have entertained and inspired generations. Paradoxically, the very qualities that give the book its appeal also make it one of the most troubling in all of Scripture. Gideon's heroics are accompanied by a darker, vengeful side. Samson's victories against the Philistines never fully distract the reader from his personal foibles and ultimate tragedy. Ehud seems a tricky assassin, not a divinely empowered "savior," and the story of Jephthah encloses an obscenity within a horror. The gruesome narrative with which the book ends seems to offer little opening for an edifying theological or spiritual interpretation. More than any other book of the Bible, the book of Judges puts before the reader the issue of violence. Its major characters are all persons who perform acts of violence, sometimes heroic, other times horrific. A *Dodge City* feeling pervades the book, and one almost expects Clint Eastwood to be among its characters. Most notably the violence is visited upon women, such as Jephthah's daughter, Samson's first wife, the Levite's concubine, and the virgins of Shiloh. Violence is also wrought *by* women such as Jael and Delilah, and even celebrated by women like Deborah and, in her own blind way, Sisera's mother. And yet, somehow the book's presentation of violence, even at times with approval, does not finally encourage the reader to perpetrate violence. The book's celebration of heroic individuals who tower over ordinary Israelites, the victims, does not point toward an unbridled individualistic ethos for the community. Rather, the prowess of individuals is celebrated as an expression of Yahweh's faithfulness to his people. Indeed, Judges seems concerned to harness the energies of its restless subject matter—oppressors, liberators, villains and heroes, assassins, gangsters, whores, and tricksters—to point the reader to a larger vision of the community and kingdom toward which Yahweh is leading his people.[1]

The English book of Judges derives its name from the Latin Vulgate title, *Iudices*, translating the Greek *kritai*, which, in turn, renders the Hebrew *shopetim* [TH8199A, ZH9149] (judges). These terms reflect the terminology denoting the individuals who dominate the book's central chapters, *shopetim*. The title derives mainly from Judges 2:16-19. Rarely do the narratives refer to their protagonists by this title. Indeed, only Deborah (4:4) and Yahweh (11:27) bear the participial label *shopet* [TH8199A, ZH9149]. The other occurrences of the root appear in verbal forms (3:10; 10:2, 3; 11:27; 12:7, 11, 13, 14; 15:20; 16:31).

The title's significance goes far beyond its mere origin. For most readers, "judge" seems an odd title for the characters immortalized in these pages. The force of the traditional translation is felt even in the NLT, which translates the root "judge" every time it occurs except once (11:27, "decide"). A brief summary of the range of usage of the Hebrew term *shapat* reveals much more than its English counterpart implies. With its noun derivatives, the word-family derived from *shapat* [TH8199, ZH9149] encloses four functions that, far from being distinct "meanings," constitute instead four overlapping circles. First, the term denotes judicial functions in which cases are heard and their merits weighed with a view to determining the best outcome. The noun *mishpat* [TH4941, ZH5477] (judgment, justice) can denote a scene or tribunal of judgment (cf. Ps 1:5). But in the social structure of ancient Israel, which was grounded in tribal and clan processes of conflict resolution, the term refers to the restoration of the community's equilibrium, its well-being, denoted by the term *shalom* [TH7965, ZH8934] (peace). While this responsibility normally fell to the elders, at the higher social levels such as the clan and tribe, the term *shapat* designated this restoration of community rhythm.

The restoration of *shalom* also denotes, secondly, an executive function, to intervene directly to effect justice. In this sense, the verb can point to a discrete action or to a sustained process. This sense dominates in the occurrences of *shapat* (or its cognates) in ancient texts outside the Old Testament, where it generally designates a governor or other royally appointed official (Soggin 1981:1-4). Yahweh is the quintessential judge in his active intervention and constant rule in history as expressed in Jephthah's appeal, climaxing his negotiations with the king of Ammon (11:27). For the ideal portrait in 2:16-19, the judges personified Yahweh's government by embodying his will and saving action. This point emerges clearly in the phrase that often concludes the early judges' careers—"and the land was quiet"—that is, the serenity of the community was restored. Perhaps the full significance of this restoration of quiet derives from the use of *shaqat* for the conclusion of the military phase of the conquest in Joshua 11:23, literally, "the land was quiet from war" (cf. Josh 14:15). The successful judge restored the community to the situation immediately following Joshua's successful campaign. Perhaps it is not entirely coincidental that *shaqat* [TH8252, ZH9200] (be quiet) shares some sounds and spelling with *shapat* [TH8199, ZH9149] (judge). Full appreciation of this nuance of *shapat* also exposes how the distinction between "major" judges (military deliverers) and "minor" judges, who are merely listed with no exploits (10:1-5; 12:8-15), is artificial from a cultural-linguistic standpoint, since the "minor judges" maintained the order effected by the "major judges." Moreover, the parallel between Yahweh as the Judge (11:27) and the prominence of human judges exposes the contradiction in rejecting human kingship based on claims of Yahweh's kingship. That Yahweh occupies a role need not preclude an analogous, derivative human role. Ironically, although some passages in Judges advocate human kingship (17:6; 18:1; 19:1; 21:25), Judges never calls God king.

The third and fourth nuances of *shapat* function as connotations of the term, but their presence is so strongly felt that they constitute an integral part of the word's function. The third emerges in the noun form, *mishpat* [TH4941, ZH5477] (justice, judgment). The act of restoring the community's balance became part of the shared heritage of the community leading to the affirmation of a code or standard of individual and communal behavior considered to support maintenance of the community's equilibrium. Thus, *mishpat* can denote a legal claim, a right, and metaphorically a pattern, plan, or habit. To "do *mishpat*" is to conduct oneself in accordance with the traditions of the community that support its peace and welfare. This third, traditional sense of the term emerges in passages expressing ethical concerns. Thus, the translation "justice" with its frequent assumption of an abstract standard of right, or an ideological demand for egalitarian uniformity, fails utterly to grasp the term's ethical or traditional sense of living in harmony with the community's remembered heritage, defining the behavior that ensures community well-being. The casuistically formulated laws of the Covenant Code in Exodus 21–23 and the hortatory proclamation of the law seen in Deuteronomy 12–26 express the kinds of customary standards that emerged in Israel as *mishpat*.

Israel understood Yahweh to be the author of its life in the land, and so grounded all actions of governing in him. Therefore a fourth, theological nuance functions in the semantics of *shapat*. The remembered traditional standards of behavior, especially as codified in the legal corpora noted above, appear not as human reflection, though the signs of human deliberation and traditional legal formulation are unmistakably evident, but as revelation from Yahweh. The trajectory of *shapat* ultimately arrives at the emergence of documents regarded not as fossilized ideological abstractions or "laws" in the modern sense, but as standards or authoritative examples of faithful behavior seamlessly integrating the wisdom of the community with the revelation of Yahweh through the mediator Moses. Indeed, ultimately, to live in *mishpat* could well mean, in a larger, canonical sense, to live according to Scripture. The persons found in the book of Judges do reflect much of the Hebrew term's meaning, and indeed the book, as sacred canonical Scripture, might itself be a powerful embodiment of *mishpat*. Whether or not the unknown scribe who assigned the name "Judges" to this book realized its full implications, the term well articulates the book's many facets.

AUTHOR

We do not know who wrote the book of Judges. Neither the New Testament nor ancient tradition nominates a compelling name. Indeed, Judges does not seem to have resulted from a single authorial act. The book contains material of great age, and from several ages, that unknown persons compiled and organized, with unknown others supplementing the collection further at a later period. The process of composition will be discussed under "Canonicity and Textual History" but for now, I will assign the title of "author" to whoever undertook the final, substantial formation of the book, which is composed of the "deliverer narratives" of 2:6–16:31 and the framing material of 1:1–2:4; 17:1–21:25.

Though the author is unknown, a descriptive profile does emerge. First, this writer appears likely to have been a Judean. The introduction to the book (1:1–2:5) commends the Judeans for successfully conquering their territories, but exposes the failure of the northern tribes in a sweeping south-to-north movement. The ideal judge, Othniel, stands out as the only southern judge. The Ephraimites often receive negative portrayal, as do the Danites, including the sanctuary at Dan. The final chapters present a heinous crime that took place because the Levite in the story passed up a chance to stay in Jerusalem (Jebus) and stayed instead in a town of Benjamin (Saul's home). Second, the author expresses support for the monarchy in 17:6; 18:1; 19:1-2; and 21:25, likely the Davidic monarchy, given the Judean orientation noted above. That the support comes with little reservation implies the author had not witnessed the catastrophic apostasies of kings like Manasseh. Indeed, the point of the recurring comment "Israel had no king" seems to be that the aberrations and scandals of chapters 17–21 would not have occurred had there been a king. These statements suggest a view of the kingship that advocated, first and foremost, religious leadership that restrained the selfish and centrifugal tendencies of the Israelites. So the author appears to have been a Judean supporter of the Davidic monarchy who saw this institution primarily in terms of a guardianship of the religious standard of Israel's covenant with Yahweh, but who was not yet explicitly a passionate advocate of the ideology that many scholars have termed the "Zion Theology," as articulated in passages like Psalms 48, 78, 79, 87, 89, 102, 110, 120–134, and Isaiah 2:1-4. Lastly, the substantive author needed access to oral traditions, written documents, and the time and materials to produce this book. Such a person might have been found in the court of any of the faithful Judean kings such as Hezekiah or Josiah.

DATE AND OCCASION OF WRITING

The reflections above, and those offered below under "Canonicity and Textual History," provide a framework for hazarding a date for the final composition of Judges. The final writer's Judean identity and view of the kingship as a morally restraining force would be at home in a period of the Judean monarchy prior to the radicalization of the "Zion Theology," which led to the royal complacency criticized by Jeremiah (627–585 BC). This dating of the final compilation also comports well with the absence of any strong ideology of centralization of worship and the absence of claims for the sacred status of Jerusalem. Indeed, the book locates the "house of God" in Shiloh (18:31), a place which would clash with the pejorative reference to Shiloh found in Jeremiah and the public outrage it caused (Jer 7:12-15; 26:6, 9; cf. also Ps 78:60). Then again, the story in chapters 19–21 could point to the kinds of developments at Shiloh that could have led to Jeremiah's use of it as an example of divine destruction of a sanctuary. These considerations might suggest a date prior to the time of Jeremiah. The latest event to which Judges alludes (18:30) is a deportation. The Babylonian exile seems unlikely since no other allusion to that catastrophe appears in Judges. Since the geographic context of 18:30 is the extreme north of Israel, commentators suggest that the Assyrian depredations in northern Galilee following the Syro-Ephraimite war (734–732 BC) might be in view. Since that story also satirizes an official northern sanctuary (Dan; cf. Judg 17–18), the writer could have been speaking of the deportation of the whole northern kingdom in 721 BC. In any event, either of these dates would place the book's final edition in the late eighth century at the earliest, perhaps in Hezekiah's time (715–640 BC). Hezekiah would also embody the royal religious fidelity that the author of Judges envisions.

Composition of the book in Hezekiah's reign could also suggest an occasion for writing. According to 2 Kings, Hezekiah instituted a range of reforms and political expansions based on a reassertion of the covenant between Yahweh and his people. By presenting the monarchy as a moral force necessitated by the collapse of leadership on the tribal level and the moral bankruptcy of the northern kingdom—poignant in the era of 732–721 BC—the book would have provided the aspirations of Hezekiah with a strong historical and theological rationale, especially as Judah faced the same Assyrian army that had annexed northern Galilee just a few years earlier (cf. 2 Kgs 18:13). The book would provide the ideal opening unit of a history of the monarchy that began with a demonstration of the need for kingship (Judges), proceeding through the story of kingship and climaxing with Hezekiah, the author's ideal king. This view of Judges would mesh well with suggestions that 2 Kings, at an early stage of its development, ended at 2 Kings 19 with the vindication of Hezekiah in Jerusalem's deliverance from Sennacherib, a stage in the development of the Deuteronomistic History preceding the commonly accepted Josianic and exilic editions (Stone 1988:478-481; Richter 2005:225).

AUDIENCE

A vexing question in Old Testament studies is that of the audience of the biblical material. Little is known of how widely the biblical materials were distributed, who read them, and what functions they served for the audience. If we assume a "fit" between the book's content, structure, and themes, and the audience it served, several inferences about the audience may be drawn. First, for the traditions in Judges to have a claim on ancient readers or hearers, the audience would likely have held in high regard the great heroes of Israel's past, the "judges." Indeed, if the near-universal form-critical suggestion that the main stories in Judges are popular oral tales is accurate, their very preservation points to an appreciative audience. The author showed how the monarchy was superior to these charismatic leaders, but he did so without directly attacking the validity of the earlier institution. Rather, the book allows the weaknesses of charismatic leadership to emerge naturally in the way the stories are arranged. Second, the writer focuses strongly on the northern tribes, suggesting that the audience might have held reservations about the claims of Judah to be the tribe from whom the legitimate king was to come. Addressing such a group, the story of Abimelech demonstrates the bankruptcy of Shechem, a one-time capital of the northern kingdom, as a possible home of the Israelite monarchy. Third, the exposure of the deficits of charismatic rule that emerges in chapters 3–16 could have been seen during the divided kingdom era as a critique of the northern pattern of monarchic succession, which was not dynastic, as in Judah, but resembled more the charismatic pattern. Thus, it would appear that the book was written to those who would have questions about whether Judean monarchic and dynastic claims genuinely met the true need of Israel for leadership and legitimately fulfilled the will of Yahweh. Since the final years and ultimate collapse of the northern Israelite kingdom occurred in Hezekiah's reign, we might even suggest the audience included members of the northern population and leadership who now looked to Judah, the sole surviving heir to the covenant promises, with a poignant mixture of hope and doubt. The fall of the northern kingdom in 721 BC produced a flood of new arrivals swelling the population of Jerusalem, especially on the western hill. Hezekiah was sufficiently concerned about them to enclose part of the western hill in a new "broad wall," so it is not hard to imagine he might also be interested in presenting to them a historical apology for the Judean monarchy, of which he was the culmination. As part of a larger literary demonstration of the legitimacy of the Davidic, Judean monarchy, Judges would have addressed the concerns of this northern refugee community.

CANONICITY AND TEXTUAL HISTORY

Place in the Canon. The place of Judges in the Canon has never been disputed. A consideration of its role and function in the canons of Judaism and Christianity reveals a range of theological functions. Unlike the tradition represented in English Bibles, which groups the books of Joshua—2 Kings together with Ezra, Nehemiah, Esther, and Chronicles as "historical books," the Hebrew Bible classifies Joshua, Judges, Samuel, and Kings as the "Former Prophets" and follows them immediately with Isaiah, Jeremiah, Ezekiel, and "The Twelve" (i.e., the Minor Prophets) designating these the "Latter Prophets." This canonical categorization intimates a function transcending merely antiquarian or historiographic reportage. Prophecy in ancient Israel entailed a divine revelation that concretely addressed the historical and social particulars of a concrete circumstance in the life of Israel. These highly particular words generated a tradition of response and interpretation around the memory of their speakers, bearing fruit ultimately in the large compilations found in the Old Testament prophetic books. On first sight, discerning a prophetic function in Joshua—Kings, and especially in Judges, seems difficult. But the messages found in the classical prophetic books hardly make sense outside the framework established in the Former Prophets, which pursue relentlessly the theme of Israel as a nation whose fate is determined at every point by its response to the divine word. The Former Prophets supply the dimension of "situation" to which the Latter Prophets provide the divine revelation. The dialectical relationships between these two portions of the Canon open up a rich understanding of divine speech that is historically particular, and yet also universally applicable. It is not timeless in the sense of being abstract, but it is ever timely. The Former Prophets constitute a unified historical narrative striving not simply to inform, but to confront the reader with a proclamation of the ways, truth, and judgment of God.

The explicitly theological dimension of Joshua—Kings in general, and Judges in particular, arises directly from the compositional dynamics behind the books. Contemporary scholarship has almost uniformly seen Joshua—Kings as the work of writers with both historical and theological purposes inspired by the book of Deuteronomy. Noth (1958) suggested that a single historian, writing after the destruction of Jerusalem (587 BC), composed the core material of Joshua—Kings and included the Deuteronomic law code as a preface to present a cogent explanation for that destruction. Noth's work popularized the term "Deuteronomistic History" for the Former Prophets. Subsequent scholarship nuanced Noth's theory considerably, with North American scholarship generally moving first to a theory of two editions of the Deuteronomistic history, the main work (Dtr^1) appearing during the reign of Josiah, and then an expanded exilic edition (Dtr^2) reframed in the light of the destruction of the Temple in 587 (Cross; Nelson; J. D. Levenson). More recent research has also suggested an edition of the history predating Josiah, probably produced in the time of Hezekiah (Provan 1988; Stone 1988). For a number of reasons, this model is preferable to that of scholars on the European continent, who have tended to retain the Exile as the setting of the history's entire editorial development, positing a series of revisions, necessarily in rapid succession, emphasizing legal or prophetic themes (Richter 2002). Then again, a number of scholars (e.g., P. R. Davies) have gone further, arguing that the whole historical narrative of the Old Testament, including the Deuteronomistic History and all its editions, resulted from Persian era scribes writing to produce propaganda to undergird the claims of a recent immigrant population in the province of Yehud. This latter view requires a skepticism that, in my view, is not warranted by the evidence.

The most impressive consideration in favor of the view of Cross and his followers seems to be its recognition of the need for considerable social and institutional support for the production of major works of political, historical, and religious literature, especially literature drawing upon such a wide range of source materials as is found in Joshua—Kings. By locating the substantive composition of these books during the Judean State period, the Cross-Nelson-Provan axis of thought supplies a plausible series of contexts for both the resources and the purposes behind these books. It therefore serves as the general backdrop for this commentary.

If the sketch offered above approximates reality, all or at least part of the material in Judges functioned in at least three different contexts. (1) In the "Hezekian" corpus, Judges provided the introduction to the story of Israel in the land by highlighting how, after an incomplete conquest, Israel soon fell into religious, military, and social crisis. The resultant social implosion of Israel, seen most clearly in chapters 17–21, provided a basis for arguing the need for a new social and political order, namely, the monarchy (cf. 17:6; 18:1; 19:1; 21:25). This apologia for monarchy appropriately introduced a narrative that moved from the failure of Saul through the successes and redemption of David to the vindication of Hezekiah. (2) With the Josianic reforms came important contextual shifts in the material. The placement of all or a significant portion of the present book of Deuteronomy as the introduction to the Josianic edition of the history created a new set of resonances with material in Judges. The moral causality highlighted in Judges could serve the more defined theological conception of retribution expressed in Deuteronomy and Kings. Likewise, the emphasis on the paradigmatic status of Joshua throws the struggles depicted in the book of Judges into even sharper relief. The opening phrase "after the death of Joshua" (1:1) makes explicit the book's concern with succession. Joshua was the appropriate successor to Moses and the paradigm for all subsequent successors. Who is the one who will be the proper successor to Joshua? The answer, for the Josianic stage of the Deuteronomistic History, is not merely "the Davidic king in Jerusalem" but Josiah, the reformer. In both of these contexts, Judges does much more than merely introduce kingship by documenting the need for a new communal structure in Israel. The book's stress on charismatic leaders, presented with increasing complexity and decreasing effectiveness (note the absence of *wattishqot ha'arets* [the land had rest] in the stories coming after Gideon), and its analysis of the chaos described in chapters 17–21 (17:6; 21:25) also provide a kind of inverse job description for the king. By detailing Israel's problem, the writer establishes an agenda for the solution, a prescriptive pattern for kingship. (3) The exilic edition of the book imposed yet another lens for viewing the book of Judges. Rather than ending on the note of vindication, the debacle of 2 Kings 24–25 causes the stress on Israel's intransigent evil to stand unchanged by the monarchy. Judges' affirmation of the crown can no longer apply directly to any king that Israel and Judah have known. Either the affirmation must be repudiated as false, raising the question why the Judeans preserved the book at all after the Exile, or the ancient readers projected the hope for a king expressed in Judges, still in search of the king implicitly called for by the dark portrayal of the book of Judges.

The compositional history and changing historical and literary contexts of the book of Judges have enriched its potential canonical functions. As part of an ongoing corpus of theological historiography, Judges functions as a chapter in a larger story, portraying the abyss of sin and confusion, portending Israel's subsequent violations of the covenant. However, its compositional development has given it literary autonomy as well. The witness of Judges can stand on its own, offering directly its own analysis of Israel's spiritual, social, and political confusion for readers of all subsequent generations. True to the prophetic tradition's integration of eternal divine revelation addressing particular life settings, Judges both analyzes Israel's need and projects the future solution to that need. Only the passing of the centuries would reveal just how prophetic that projection would be.

The Text. In general, the Hebrew text of Judges appears to have been transmitted "better . . . than any other of the historical books" (Moore 1895:xliii) and is "particularly pure" (Soggin 1981:12). The Qumran materials include fragments of Judges, and will be discussed in connection with the passages they represent. Here I note only the most significant Qumran fragment, 4QJudges[a], which contains a portion of chapter 6 that omits several phrases from 6:1-13, and all of 6:7-10. The Septuagintal tradition features two parallel, apparently independent Greek translations. The majority of Septuagint manuscripts represent the text type found in codex Alexandrinus, but codex Vaticanus displays dramatic deviations from the Alexandrian translation. Scholars have debated whether we should think of a revision of the Alexandrinus, or two independent translations of Judges into Greek, Alexandrinus being the older and Vaticanus being the more recent. Alexandrinus seems to be the better translation, and the differences between the two seem to point to contrasting translation strategies rather than to different *Vorlagen* (Butler 2009:xxxlix-xliii). So while these two Septuagint traditions might point to developments in the history of interpretation, they do not provide much light on the scribal transmission of the Hebrew text. The Syriac and Targum versions of Judges provide intriguing hints about how the book was interpreted in late antiquity, but generally seem dependent on the Masoretic textual tradition.

Textual History. The discussion of authorship above located the final edition of the book of Judges at the end of a process of compilation and structuring. The book does offer the reader many clues about the process by which it came to its present shape, clues that have attracted the attention of interpreters of every persuasion. The book possesses a diversity of voices, and yet we can also discern a coherent message.

The book of Judges speaks with several voices. Scholars of the nineteenth century analyzed this diversity of voice thoroughly, suggesting various passages could be attributed to writers of different eras. Moore and Burney expressed the consensus that found frequent restatement in the decades to follow, with little change for almost a century despite vigorous debate and a multitude of attempted alternatives. The consensus identified at least three types of material in the book, or three "voices."

First, all identified the critical mass of Judges in the individual narratives featuring the actions of the so-called "major" judges, as single, dynamic individuals who either deliver Israel from enemies or harass and decimate the enemy. Alert readers noticed early the diversity among these stories. Each reflects a distinct regional orientation. They also display linguistic and stylistic differences indicating regional variations in Hebrew dialects, a feature of Judges not given sufficient attention until after the turn of the century (Burney 1920:171-176). Scholars began envisioning these stories as originally independent, the properties of the respective tribes and clans whose heroes they celebrate, but they thought mainly in terms of written materials, not oral tradition. Early modern interpreters also noticed that a few of these stories also display an internal complexity and diversity that seemed best explained in terms of materials written by different persons.

The second kind of material noted by early source critics was a set of introductory and concluding formulas employing expressions and ideas also found in 2:11-23.

PROLOGUE	STORY	EPILOGUE
3:7-9a	Othniel 3:10*	3:11
3:12-14	Ehud 3:15-30a	3:30b
4:1-2	Deborah 4:3–5:31a	4:23-24/5:31b
6:1-10	Gideon 6:11–8:27	8:28-32
10:6-18	Jephthah 11:1–12:6	12:7
13:1	Samson 13:1–16:30*	15:20/16:31

These prologues and epilogues create a framework for the narratives in which the crisis of the story is the result of God's "selling" or "giving" Israel over to an enemy because "the Israelites did what was evil in Yahweh's eyes." The oppression drives Israel to "cry out to Yahweh," who then prompts a leader to arise and defeat the enemy. At the end of the story, the epilogues indicate the defeat of the enemy, the duration of the hero's career, and the hero's death in most cases. Together with the ideological introduction in 2:6–3:6 (though this unit is by no means ideologically consistent, as later scholars noted), the frameworks summarized the entire era depicted in the tradition. Interpreters agree that a compiler gathered these diverse hero stories, composed the introduction, and created the prologues and epilogues to mesh the stories with the conception of the introduction, within which the stories functioned like slides in a slide show. Most importantly, scholars almost universally characterize the language of the introduction and of the frameworks as derived from and imitative of Deuteronomy. Thus was born the notion of a Deuteronomistic redaction of the Judges tradition.

The third voice might simply be called "the rest" or "miscellaneous additions" that do not fit into the framed deliverer story pattern. Thus, chapter 1 provides a report of the efforts of individual tribes to gain control over their territories. Chapters 17–18 depict a Yahwistic but idolatrous shrine, the migration of the Danites, and their subsequent slaughter of the inhabitants of Laish culminating in the establishment of a sanctuary in Dan. Chapters 19–21 depict the brutal rape of a Levite's concubine followed by a war of tribal retribution. Critics see these last five chapters as "appendices" with no organic connection to the book's "main body." In addition, several other passages appear to be later supplements. First, the Abimelech story (8:33–9:57) involves no story of deliverance from a foreign foe by a charismatic hero. Second, the so-called minor judge lists in 10:1-5 and 12:8-15 do not present spontaneously arising leaders, but a more orderly succession of clan leaders. Third, chapter 16 presents data indicating it was presented as a balance to chapters 14–15 (for which see the commentary). Fourth, three passages (2:1-5; 6:7-10; 10:10-16) offer theological commentary that seems simultaneously to diverge from both the frameworks and the narratives. Indeed, 6:7-10 is lacking in a Qumran fragment of Judges. All these "miscellaneous" passages interrupted the series of framed Deuteronomistic hero stories. Moreover, 1:1–2:5 appears between two literarily interdependent accounts of the death of Joshua (Josh 24:29-33 and Judg 2:6-10), suggesting the material was carefully inserted into the book as part of its final composition.

Running parallel to studies of the book's diversity has always been a steady voice arguing for unified authorship based on claims for unitary structure. This approach links unity of theme and plot to singularity of authorship. Gooding (1982) argues for an intricate, 14-part chiastic ring-structure uniting the book so deeply as to preclude source separation, but his analysis falls under the same weaknesses as those of Keil a century before. The critique of Halpern (1988:126), who asked, "is the book to be read with the aid of a pogo stick?" suffices. Still, Gooding certainly demonstrates a level of cohesion in Judges that requires notice. The book stands out as a "book" (Cf. Block 1999:49, contra Frolov 2009).

Some interpreters reject any attempt to discern the activities of authors in Judges but attribute its unity entirely to the reader. Gros-Louis's essay (1974) offers a "new critical" reading, and as new literary methods have emerged, new literary readings have appeared. Webb's (1987) "integrated reading" probably fits the new-critical approach as well. Polzin (1980) provides a structuralist analysis, while Klein (1989) employs irony to the point of crushing the book's plain sense. Increasingly, rhetorical criticism and its attendant interest in ideological perspectives have influenced literary reading. Concern for women in the book dominates recent literary analysis, seen in the work of Trible (1984), Bal (1988), and the essays compiled in the volumes edited by Yee (1995) and Brenner (1993), respectively. Exum's wide-ranging publications on Judges provide a thorough orientation to this mode of interpretation by a reader of formidable insight. The fruit of this whole tradition of reading appears in the commentary of Schneider (2000). Few dispute that many penetrating insights into the text have accompanied these analyses, though few readers would concede that historical and authorial questions can simply be ignored.

The present commentary will take an integrated approach in which the diverse voices of the book, so clearly identified by historical criticism, are seen to have been orchestrated into a coherent composition not unlike a symphony that incorporates traditional motifs and other well-known compositions into a new work.

LITERARY STYLE AND CONCERNS

All questions of literary style or genre in Judges focus on the deliverer stories. Whatever drove the development of the book of Judges into its final form crystalized around the role of these remarkable, irascible individuals designated "judges." It was von Rad (1966) who provided the best lead when he compared the Gideon story with the Succession Narrative and characterized the former as "hero saga." Heroic literature is well known from the ancient world and has been studied extensively for over a century.

Heroic literature is a recognized type of ancient literature from the Bible to Homer to the Beowulf poet and beyond (Armerding 1968; Chadwick 1926; Gordon 1965; Kramer 1959; Lord 1960, 1991, and 1995; D. Miller 2002; Steiner 1962; Whitman 1958). Representative of an integrated approach, Steiner (1962) grasped the heroic in ancient literature as a dynamically emerging sensibility, a vision of existence, and one that was viewed differently at different times in history. His analysis provides vital insights to guide our understanding of the book of Judges.

Research on heroic literature reveals a clear, but flexible set of characteristics that allow us generally to define the material and its popular appeal as "heroic." More importantly, all of these studies point out that despite their popular appeal, the era of the heroes passed, typically with the end of the liminal era in which they lived and the emergence of a more complex social hierarchy, such as the monarchy in Israel. Heroic literature thus began to become problematic for later, more restrained eras, precipitating a crisis of preservation and interpretation. In short, heroic literature forced later readers to reposition these traditions in order to retain and continue using them. This dialectic of veneration and reservation seems also to have driven the process by which Judges was composed. Each of the successive voices shaping this book received the heroic tradition in some form, and in turn had to echo and reshape that tradition to allow it to be accessible to later generations possessed of vastly changed sensibilities.

The Storyteller. The first voice in the compositional development that culminated in the canonical book of Judges was a voice that simply told the stories of the deliverers, the heroes. Like all heroic literature, these stories celebrate the exploits of an outstanding individual. No eulogizing of the ordinary here, no democracy of the mediocre. Physicality becomes the idiom of excellence. Whether handsome or ugly, heroes are never common. Saul was the tallest of his peer group, David was "ruddy." Ehud's left-handedness is expressed in terms suggesting he was a warrior trained in two-handed fighting (Halpern 1988). Samson's wild hair also comes to mind. The storyteller relates the deeds of the heroes, invariably violent encounters, with delicious detail. Such gusto, such exaltation of the violent, scandalizes the domestic sensibility of later readers, ancient and modern. The tale master recounts the murder of Eglon by Ehud and of Sisera by Jael with gleeful energy, celebrating the heroes' craftiness with humor, sometimes scatological or sexual. Likewise, his interest in the weaponry or implements of the heroes—Ehud's dagger, Jael's tent-peg, Gideon's torches—is an element of this savoring of every violent detail. In that context, Deborah's song takes on new clarity:

> Most blessed of women be Jael,
> the wife of Heber the Kenite,
> most blessed of tent-dwelling women.
> He asked for water and she gave him milk;
> in lordly bowl she brought him curds.
> Her hand reached for the tent peg,
> her right hand for the workman's hammer.
> She smashed Sisera, she cracked his head,
> she shattered and pierced his temple.
> Between her knees he collapsed, he fell, he lay.
> Between her knees he collapsed, he fell;
> where he collapsed, there he fell — dead (Judg 5:24-27, author's translation)

The sheer brutal joy of such passages confronts the reader sharply with a vision of life in which honor, valor, and a good death count for more than mere comfort or longevity. The hero functions not from some external "law" but rather from an internalized "code," more expressive of the clan and its right to vengeance than "the law" and its claims to justice. The hero accepts the wager of battle with grim joy. Indeed, somehow the carnage of battle and the fury of the spirit-endowed berserker serve to establish, not destroy, the rule of Yahweh. The heroic narrator does not flinch from the violence but "looks on life with those blank, unswerving eyes which stare out of the helmet slits on early Greek vases. His vision is terrifying in its sobriety, cold as the winter sun" (Steiner 1962:8). Deborah would agree that those who love Yahweh will "rise like the sun in all its power" (5:31).

The Moralist. "Heroic Ages" typically occur in liminal periods when one social model has collapsed and another is emerging, such as we see precisely in the book of Judges (Whitman 1958; Steiner 1962; Armerding 1968). The heroic individual cannot "work and play well with others," and societies must decide what to do with their triumphant warriors and the value system they embody. And yet, notwithstanding their restless, decentering energy, can a society simply dispose of its heroes? Can a society long endure without inspiring models of courage and valor? Judges laments the rise of a generation of Israelites who did not know war, and as a result, did not know how Yahweh could act on their behalf (2:10; 3:1-2).

So the voice of remembrance and celebration could not speak definitively for Israel, but clearly Israel felt the need to preserve the memory of these persons and their achievements. The second voice in Judges speaks for a higher level of social organization, a morally reflective writer who appreciates the dynamism of the heroes but hopes to channel and direct it. First, the "moralist" voice identifies an underlying regularity in an otherwise diverse, even motley assemblage of leaders. The unruliness of the individual is subordinated to a pattern, an "office." Second, this voice speaks with a theological inflection, stating Israel's need for the heroes. Third, the moralist voice expects the heroes to exercise a religious influence. The description in 2:16-19 is ambivalent since several of the leaders in Judges exercised poor religious leadership or none at all. Fourth, their chronological notices serialize the hero stories, placing events that likely transpired contemporaneously into a linear series. The effect here is to dole out the heroes one at a time, one per generation, rather than characterize the era as one dominated by randomly appearing berserkers or Nazirite wild-men.

Contrary to most interpretations, Judges does not present the reader with an unaltering "cycle" or pattern. First of all, elements appear in the stories that do not appear in the introduction, and vice versa. Thus, the introduction tells us that Yahweh "raised up" deliverers, but only Othniel and Ehud are explicitly said to be "raised up" by Yahweh. Other means of manifestation appear for subsequent judges, raising the intriguing question of their status. Likewise, the semantics of the verb *za'aq* [TH2199, ZH2410] (to cry) orient more toward an intense, emotion-laden cry of anguish or even accusation, but with no inherent connotations of repentance (Greenspahn 1986:391-396; Stone 1988:311-326; O'Connell 1996:39-41; TDOT 4:112-122; NIDOTTE 1:1131-1132), a point increasingly recognized by commentators (Block 1999:148; Younger 2002:102; Butler 2009:65). Greenspahn rightly notes that the pattern in Judges is not "reward-punishment/repentance-deliverance" but simply punishment followed by grace. Yahweh, it seems, delivers his people out of his compassion and mercy, to show his power and to claim Israel's allegiance. Only in 10:6-16 does the outcry find expression in confession and remorse, and that passage is fraught with conflict and ambivalence. The omission of the outcry from the programmatic introduction of 2:6–3:6 and from the Samson story reinforces the fact that Yahweh's action derives not from Israel's meeting some condition (repentance), but from Yahweh's simple compassion for them. Additionally, the Spirit of Yahweh—and, less frequently, the angel of Yahweh—plays a role in the stories that has no place in the introduction or the frameworks, and ironically, the Spirit plays no role in the Ehud story or the Deborah story, the two judges with the most unreserved praise from the author. By contrast, the Spirit's involvement with Gideon, Jephthah, and Samson raises more questions than it answers (see the commentary). So we do not have a pattern that is mechanically repeated but rather a collection of features and formulas that are deployed variously to direct our attention to other factors in the stories.

Was the moralist a "Deuteronomist"? Other than Burney (1920), and in our day, Greenspahn (1986), Stone (1988), and Brettler (1989), most say yes. But serious problems attend this identification: We don't find the classic markers of Deuteronomistic theology. We find no urge toward the centralization of worship as the result of the land "resting," a central theme of Deuteronomistic theology. The Deuteronomic distinctive in which Yahweh, like a conqueror of old, sets up his memorial "name" in the form of a monument erected in a specific, elect place within the conquered territory (Richter 2002) is starkly absent from Judges, which expresses little theological interest in the name Yahweh. Nor do we find in Judges much concern for the "book of the Law." Similarly, the term "covenant" appears only seven times in the book. Three appear in proper names (8:33; 9:4, 46), once the "Ark of the Covenant" is mentioned (20:27), and once covenants with non-Israelites are noted (2:2). Only twice (2:1, 20) does the word appear denoting Yahweh's bond with Israel, and these are not *distinctively* Deuteronomistic uses unless one restricts all religious covenantal language to Deuteronomistic rhetoric. And Judges displays no sustained interest in prophecy on the model of Deuteronomy. An unknown prophet speaks in 6:7-10, and Deborah is said simply to be a prophet, but otherwise we miss the prophetism so evident in Samuel—Kings. Furthermore, Deuteronomy strongly identifies Levites with priests. While 17:13 reports an assumed advantage in having a Levite as a priest, Judges as a whole shows no interest in the exclusive legitimacy of the Levite in the priestly service, and chapters 19–21 feature a Levite without once implying any cultic functions for him. Again, we find no talk of that supremely distinctive demand of Deuteronomy and its derivatives, to "love" Yahweh. Lastly, while 18:30 possibly hints at the destruction of the north in 721 BC or even the earlier depredations of 732, we find no sign in Judges of the Babylonian exile, the body blow to Hebrew faith around which Deuteronomy-derived theological "schools" are thought to have crystallized. Alien to Deuteronomy, but prominent in Judges, is the role of possession by the Spirit of Yahweh. Deuteronomy has all the appearances of a constitutional document (McBride 1987). It envisions an ordered community in which leaders occupy "offices" as extensions of the authority of Moses and signs of the moral government of Yahweh. One would expect that if the author of Judges sought to match the narrative to Deuteronomy, some connection between the heroes and Deuteronomy would appear. But nothing in Deuteronomy prepares the reader for the charismatic heroes of Judges.

That said, some features of Judges do prompt an over-the-shoulder look at Deuteronomy. The notion of moral causality found in the frameworks is not exclusive Deuteronomic property, but it is certainly comfortably so. Again, the militant hostility of Deuteronomy toward non-Israelite culture and religion is clearly expressed in the frameworks and introduction. In contrast to Judges, however, Deuteronomy envisions Israel not as one nation of twelve tribes, but more as one large tribe. All Israelites are "kinsmen," and Deuteronomy ignores the tribal divisions except for its provisions concerning the Levites and the blessing of Moses. Here, we note that one of the primary emphases of the moralist voice in Judges is its desire to recontextualize the local heroes so that each now serves the whole nation for a generation. Lastly, both Deuteronomy and Judges have a programmatic concern for leadership. The opening question of Judges "Which tribe should go first to attack the Canaanites?" (1:1) and its echo in the book's final story (20:18) clearly express concern for leadership.

So what may we say about the voice responsible for the introduction and frameworks? His seems to be the voice of the clan or tribal order. Somewhat like the conquest or *kherem* [TH2764, ZH3051] traditions in Joshua, the heroic tradition was becoming an unusable past that had to somehow be modulated into another key in order to serve the community. This is the task of the "moralist" voice. The hero is acknowledged, but within boundaries. The energies of the heroic are channeled and directed into the values of the religious and social order.

The Monarchist: The Voice of Nostalgic Doubt. The final stage of the growth of the book of Judges pertains to that "fragmentary preface," those vexing "miscellaneous additions," and the "appendices." These last included materials established the present flow of the book and reshaped yet again the heroic tradition. First, the addition of 1:1–2:5 provides the book with a new introduction. This passage starts with the death of Joshua and then lists the tribes from Judah in the south to Dan (ultimately) in the far north, and the order of presentation is from success through qualified success through substantial failure to abject failure, culminating in Yahweh's word of judgment, essentially canceling the conquest (2:1-5). This parallels the "moralist" introduction (2:6–3:6), which also displays a parallel movement, starting with Joshua's death, noting the faithfulness and success of one group, then passing to a series of failures culminating in Yahweh's cancellation of the conquest. Thus, the book now has a dual preface: one military, the other theological in emphasis, depicting the dialectical relationship between failure and faithlessness.

Next, the Othniel story (3:7-11) contains elements from the stories, from the frameworks, and from the introduction, suggesting it was composed by the last editor to serve as an exemplary passage, a kind of scorecard for assessing the rest of the narratives featuring the only southern judge (Stone 1988). With the Othniel story as the "scorecard," comparison of each successive story with it provides a text-immanent standard for mapping precisely the evaluation of each judge.

Such a comparison demonstrates a trend of decline. First, the expression (lit.,) "doing evil in Yahweh's eyes" (e.g., 3:7) becomes steadily more detailed as the book progresses. Likewise, the oppressions become more severe, as witnessed either in more circumstantial descriptions (Deborah, Gideon) or in historical severity (Philistines). Third, the outcry becomes problematic. In the Othniel and Ehud stories, the outcry of Israel immediately brings the reader to the appearance of a savior. With Gideon, however, the outcry leads not to the rise of a savior, but to a prophetic rebuke, upon which the narrative of Gideon's call follows directly. The call of Gideon thus stands under a question mark. Turning to the Jephthah story, Israel's outcry leads to Yahweh's refusal to deliver them and his referral of them to the gods they had chosen. The career of Jephthah thus might not reflect Yahweh's direct provision of a savior at all. In the Samson story, we find no outcry at all: Israel falls silent before its offended Lord. Fourth, the hero stories grow in biographical complexity through the book. Little is said of Ehud or Deborah, but with Gideon a call narrative and a series of preparatory episodes precede the deliverance story. The Jephthah narrative features a biography of Jephthah and a report not of his divine election, but rather a hard-nosed negotiation with his tribesmen. With Samson we encounter a full birth narrative. This increasing biographical complexity correlates with the decline through the series of heroes, generating a subtle critique of the underlying individualism of the heroic tradition. The more we hear, the less we like. More disturbingly, the Spirit of Yahweh becomes more prominent toward the end of the series, suggesting reservations about this particular manifestation of divine power. Fifth, the outcome of the heroes' activity is less obviously positive. The text notes that (lit.,) "the land had rest" after Othniel, Ehud, Deborah, and Gideon (3:11, 30; 5:31; 8:28). But with Jephthah and Samson a change appears: the text only reports "[he] judged . . ." (12:7; 16:31). Taking the Othniel account as the standard, the absence of the land's resting constitutes a negative judgment on Jephthah and Samson. In addition, the chronological material reinforces this impression. Othniel nets Israel 40 years of rest. Ehud's murder of Eglon is followed by 80 years of rest, and the narrator almost neglects to state that Ehud died—an important point since the death of the hero is supposed to trigger a fresh outbreak of evil. The Deborah and Gideon narrative likewise note 40 years. In all these cases, the time of rest is at least a multiple of the years of oppression. Jephthah's career of six years is but a third of the length of the time of oppression, and Samson's 20 years of "judging" do not end the Philistine oppression, since Samson will only "begin" to save Israel (13:5). The chronological material clearly reinforces the sense of deterioration as one moves through the series of heroes. The effect of these literary moves is to segment the hero stories into three units: "Triumphant" Leaders (Ehud and Deborah), Transitional Leaders (Gideon and Abimelech), and Tragic Leaders (Jephthah and Samson). The latter two are also linked in that the destiny of each is shaped by a vow, one tragically kept, the other tragically ignored.

The sense of decline is confirmed also by comparing the end of the dual introduction, 3:5-6, with the end of the series of heroes. Judges 3:5-6 states that as a result of Israel's apostasy and decline, they intermarried with non-Israelites and served their gods. This is precisely what the reader encounters in the story of Samson, who lived for his liaisons with non-Israelite women and who died in a pagan festival.

Finally, the "appendices" present the ultimate outcome of rule by judges. Far from being a mere appendix, the writer has joined these admittedly distinct materials to the rest of the book by means of several important literary features. First, the formula, to "do X in the eyes of Y," juxtaposes the central section's (lit.) "did evil in the eyes of Yahweh" (e.g., 3:7) with the darker anarchy of "a man did what was right in his own eyes" (e.g., 17:6). The construal of this idiom as anarchic, arrogant self-will is shaped by the final hero story, in which Samson rebuffs parental objections to his Philistine fiancée by demanding (lit.), "get her for me; she is right (*yashar* [TH3474, ZH3837]) in my eyes." In chapters 17–21, all Israel has become Samson. Secondly, against the central section of the book's presentation of the heroes, chapters 17–21 juxtaposes its own statement about leadership, "Israel had no *king*." Thirdly, the editor employs the connective "in those days" (*bayyamim hahem* [TH3117, ZH3427]). This formula was a compositional device by which a writer presents two blocks of chronologically unlinked material in order to compare or contrast them. The comparable Assyrian term *inumeshu* was used by the editors of Neo-Assyrian royal annals when they inserted sections out of chronological sequence in order to secure a thematic point (Stone 1988). By including chapters 17–21 the writer achieves a deeper analysis of the period. Finally, the general chronological notice "in those days" contrasts with the rigorously serial chronology of the central section, suggesting a terminal position, a negative climax.

These passages nuance and refocus the heroic elements of Judges. As noted above, heroic tales often clashed with the more domestic sensibilities of later readers. Thus, within the heroic tradition, one often finds poignant portrayals of the hero no longer fitting into his culture. For example, after his distinguished valor at Troy, Odysseus finds he cannot simply go home, and the reader learns that in Odysseus's absence, "home" has become a place of crisis. Even the great Achilles laments to Odysseus that, despite all the rewards of having been a great hero, he simply longs to see his son grow into manhood. Steiner (1997:17) observes in later heroic literature that, "We hear . . . a skepticism, sometimes playful, sometimes tragic . . . as to the unexamined exaltation of murderous heroism . . . a searching, in some sense domestic, sensibility looks back on the earlier epic." The later heroic narrator looks upon the older narratives "across a wide distance of the soul—with a nostalgia of smiling doubt" (Steiner 1962:14).

The ultimate human author of Judges stands for orderly government and domestic tranquility, and advocates the monarchy. Such a vision cannot tolerate "everyone doing what is right in their own eyes." But this advocate of monarchy realizes that his readers venerate the heroic tradition, necessitating a demonstration of the ultimate inadequacy of this ideal. The editor achieves this decentering of the heroic ideal by framing it as something that worked in its era, but ultimately failed and had to be replaced by something else, that something else being the Judean, Davidic monarchy. The effect is best seen by juxtaposing the two basic movements of the "main body" of Judges and the "appendices." For the moralist voice, the "problem" in Israel is that people "did what was evil in the eyes of Yahweh." For the monarchist, the problem is "every man did what was right in his own eyes." For this last editor, there lay beneath Israel's propensity to sin against Yahweh something even deeper, an arrogant anarchism that sets itself up as its own standard for what is right. Although for the moralist voice, the consequences of Israel's evil against Yahweh is oppression by foreign power, the final editor asserts that arrogant self-will is capable of destroying Israel just as thoroughly. Indeed, Israel emerges in these last chapters as its own worst enemy. Finally, for the earlier tradition, the heroes appeared as "the solution" to Israel's leadership need. But the final editor has structured the material to point out how the heroes ultimately failed to enable an orderly community, and now the absence of a king is noted. Perhaps the editor, pondering the moral anarchy of self-will, calls the reader to ask, who indeed will deliver Israel from that? In so doing, the writer implicitly states the role of the king. Where is the King who will save Israel from itself?

GENERAL HISTORICAL CONTEXT

The book of Judges, on first sight, seems to organize its materials chronologically, at least for the central section (3:7–16:31). Information appears for the duration of Israel's suffering under each enemy and then the tenure of the judge. The data from the text may be summarized:

PERSON OR GROUP	YEARS OF OPPRESSION	JUDGE'S CAREER	BIBLICAL REFERENCE
Cushan-rishathaim	8		3:8
Peace under Othniel		40	3:11
Oppression under Eglon	18		3:14
Peace with Ehud		80	3:30
Oppression under Jabin	20		4:3
Peace after Deborah		40	5:31
Oppression under Midianites	7		6:1
Peace with Gideon		40	8:28
Rule of Abimelech		3	9:22
Judgeship of Tola		23	10:2
Judgeship of Jair		22	10:3
Oppression under Ammonites	18		10:8
Judgeship of Jephthah		6	12:7
Judgeship of Ibzan		7	12:9
Judgeship of Elon		10	12:11
Judgeship of Abdon		8	12:14
Oppression under Philistines	40		13:1
Judgeship of Samson		20	15:20/16:31
Total Years			410
Years of Oppression	111		
Years of Judges		299	

Most scholars, however, agree that the events do not appear in strict chronological order, though they nevertheless offer a riveting portrait of Israel in the premonarchic era. Rather, the events recorded in the book of Judges appear in a sequence that advances a thematic, theological argument. Since this commentary will set each of the stories in its concrete historical framework, a word about that time frame is in order.

The historical framework of the book begins "after the death of Joshua" (1:1), which connects it with the larger chronology of the Exodus and conquest. Space precludes full discussion of this very complex historical problem, so the position taken in this commentary will simply be stated. Rather than dating the Exodus by reference to the suspiciously round and typologically pregnant "480 years" of 1 Kings 6:1, this commentary adopts a slightly later chronology based on the note in Exodus 12:40-41 that the Exodus took place 430 years after Jacob entered Egypt. If Jacob migrated into Egypt under the Hyksos, a reasonable assumption, that would date his entry to the late 1700s BC yielding an Exodus in the early thirteenth century BC. The terrific destruction of Hazor by fire, a point emphasized in Joshua 11, may be dated by an Egyptian inscription from Hazor to about 1235 BC (Kitchen 2003). Joshua 14:6-12 indicates that the military phase of the conquest occupied five years, placing entry into the land around 1240 BC. If we take the 40 years of wilderness wandering literally, the Exodus would then be datable to about 1280 BC, in fact, the early years of Ramses II, the last truly great pharaoh of New Kingdom Egypt.

The successor to Ramses II, Merneptah, campaigned in Canaan and, in an inscription datable to 1209 BC, he claims to have annihilated Israel (COS 2:40-41). Following Merneptah, Egyptian control over Canaan deteriorated rapidly as Egypt came into increasing conflict with the "Sea Peoples," among whom were the Philistines, who settled the southern coast of Canaan around 1170 BC (Singer 1994; Stager 2006). The atrophy of Egyptian power in the last decade of the 1200s BC occurred alongside a general collapse of the urban centers and palace cultures that defined the eastern Mediterranean in the Late Bronze Age (1550–1200 BC). The demise of the Late Bronze Age culture was sudden, traumatic, and despite some continuities, marked a permanent shift in the history of the ancient Near East (Stone 2009:656-657 and works cited there). Indeed, some have called it "The Catastrophe," characterizing it as comparable to the fall of the western Roman Empire (Drews 1993). The end of the Bronze Age gave way to a liminal era of uncertainty and change, a "dusky" age if not a dark one (Muhly 2003:26), in which many cultures of the ancient Near East sought to redefine themselves and their institutions. During this era, Canaan became the point of encounter among Israelites, Canaanites, Philistines, and even Egyptians, who made a final attempt to regain control of their dissolving empire (Singer 1994; Killebrew 2005).

The era covered in Judges—1 Samuel thus corresponds to Iron Age I (c. 1200–1000 BC). In Canaan, Iron I opens with Egypt losing its grip on its holdings, producing a power vacuum into which the Israelites could expand. The stories of Othniel and Ehud could fit within this period. Around 1170 BC, the Philistines begin settling the coastal cities, but they do not begin aggressively expanding into the hills and highlands until 1100–1075 BC. Shamgar's encounter with a group of Philistines could reflect an early encounter with them shortly after their arrival (3:31). The Philistine expansion was delayed by an attempt by Egypt about 1160 BC to regain control of their empire in Canaan by a series of military thrusts into the highlands and up toward the Jezreel valley. The story of Deborah and Barak describes a massive mobilization of the Israelites to face a grave threat in the Jezreel valley, which well could have been instigated by the Egyptians, working through mercenaries and Canaanite surrogates in their renewed efforts at imperial domination. This effort collapsed abruptly, resulting in Egypt's abandonment of Canaan around 1150 BC (Singer 1994). It was still several decades before the Philistines became a serious threat, but in the meantime, the opening of the Jezreel valley allowed Israelites to move in to grow wheat and cultivate the vineyards in that fine agricultural land. Unfortunately, that same opening allowed groups from east of Jordan to raid and pillage, as attested in the Gideon story. The Abimelech narrative (8:33–9:57) portrays a local chieftain's power-grab characteristic of the power vacuum between the times of Egyptian and Philistine domination. Within a few decades, the Philistines began their aggressive expansion, precipitating a crisis for the very survival of Israel, seen initially in the Samson story.

The events reported in chapters 17–21 are hard to pin down historically, but all are events characteristic of an era in which no centralized authority exists to secure cultic and social order. Iron Age I was indeed just such an era. Scholars often characterize Israel in this period as an unstable, complex chiefdom, a kind of middle stage between a completely decentralized coalition of tribes on the one hand, and a centralized monarchic state on the other (R. Miller 2005). Applied with due caution, the model of chiefdom is indeed helpful. Just as the liminal era of Iron I yielded newly organized states all over the eastern Mediterranean, so also the book of Judges ends by scanning the disorder and amorality of Israel and pointing the reader to the absence of—and thus the need for—a monarchy. More details on this historical and cultural setting and its pertinence to the stories in Judges appear in the commentary.

THEOLOGICAL THEMES

Judges concerns itself with the most momentous issue faced by early Israel: the character and structure of the community before Yahweh. In order to be faithful as Yahweh's people, must Israel remain a confederation of tribes led by charismatic leaders, without adaptation or change? Should the people take the bold step toward national statehood and kingship, or would such a move involve a reversion to paganism? The book presumes a negative answer to the first question and a positive answer to the second. Readers of the eighth century BC also debated whether the southern monarchy of a single (Davidic) dynasty was superior to the charismatic approach to kingship taken in the northern kingdom. Was the northern way closer to Israel's ancient ideal, and more faithful to Yahweh? Moreover, how might a community coordinate the demand for rigorous obedience to Yahweh, which is unchanging, with its emerging political structures, which necessarily change to address new problems and possibilities?

The author addresses the issues of community structure and leadership by exploring Israel's spiritual fortunes during the period of the tribal confederacy, analyzing Israel's evil and noting two solutions: charismatic leadership and kingship. The book views the time of the tribal confederacy as spiritually disastrous. Judges asserts from its opening chapters the failure of the Hebrews to build faithfully on the achievements of Joshua and the faithful conquest generation. The central section (3:7–16:31) then depicts their faithlessness as inexorably increasing apostasy: Israel does what is evil in the eyes of the Lord. Then the final section (17:1–21:25) probes deeper, finding the roots of apostasy in an intransigent, imploded self-will by which "all the people did whatever seemed right in their own eyes" (17:6; 21:25). Thus, chapters 17–21 climax the process of deterioration narrated in 3:7–16:31. But they also provide the demonstrable proof for the thesis advanced in 1:1–3:6. Chapters 17–18 resume the narrative that broke off in 1:34-35 and depict the only "conquest" of which the Danites were capable, while chapters 19–21 depict an outrageous breach in the covenant community matching the covenant-breaking of 2:6–3:6.

The book also traces the consequences of Israel's sinfulness. Apostasy brings ever more grave foreign oppressions, but more pervasive as the story unfolds is the collapse of the covenant community and the metamorphosis of its sacred traditions from blessings into curses. Tribal discord increases, political crises grow in gravity, and Israel's "saviors" become increasingly monstrous (Jephthah) or tragic (Samson). The divine voice becomes increasingly strident in its condemnation (6:7-10; 10:11-14). Ultimately, even the wind of the Spirit seems transformed into a destructive force, driving self-willed Samson over the precipice. In chapters 17–21 Israel's inner collapse comes to the center. The Danites despoil their brethren (chs 17–18) before massacring Laish, and united Israel, exercising "covenant community justice," slaughters more of its own than any foreign foe ever did in ancient times (chs 19–21). The external oppressors of chapters 3–16 vanish in chapters 17–21 before an Israel fully capable of destroying itself.

Finally, Judges explores solutions to Israel's woes. In chapters 3–16 the Spirit-driven "charismatic" appears ultimately impotent to save Israel. The judges come to represent the very forces threatening Israel. Occasional onrushes of the Spirit's power have no impact on the downward spiral, and, in the cases of Jephthah and Samson, even appear to accelerate it. Israel's faithlessness arises from a madness deep in the nation's heart and cannot be dislodged by a tour de force of the Spirit. In contrast to the ecstatic-charismatic "power" approach to leadership embodied by the judges, chapters 17–21 insinuate an alternative: kingship. "In those days Israel had no king; all the people did whatever seemed right in their own eyes." The writer envisions not simply a perpetual, inherited "office" of judge as hoped for by the elders of Israel (8:21-22), still less a usurper-tyrant like Abimelech (ch 9). This king must confront Israel's relentless idolatry, its penchant for self-destruction, and most of all, its case-hardened, arrogant self-will. The true task of the king is to save Israel from its most dangerous foe: itself. Israel's destiny does not depend on power, but on character. The advocacy of kingship in chapters 17–21 reinforces the primacy of Judah and David, conceived of specifically as the solution to Israel's moral and spiritual dilemma, pointing to those righteous sons of David who "did right in the eyes of the Lord"—kings such as Asa, Jehoshaphat, Uzziah, Hezekiah, and Josiah. Judges offers a fundamental witness to the primacy of the spiritual and moral dimensions of kingship—messiahship—in Israel.

Christian interpretation of Judges of necessity pushes past the Old Testament context of the book and seeks a responsible correlation of the book's themes with the realities proclaimed by the New Testament. The presentation of Israel's evil in Judges complements that offered in the New Testament, which often probes beneath sin as a disobedient act to the underlying sin of willful human arrogance. The New Testament also depicts sin's consequences both objectively, as bondage to oppressive principalities and powers beyond the person, and subjectively, as moral impotence and disintegration "in the flesh," emphasizing the self-destructive propensity of sinful, godless, self-imploded humanity. Judges portrays a community embodiment of the anguished, frustrated impotence of one in bondage to sin, as Paul describes in Romans 7 (where the first-person pronoun appears over 35 times). Christian theology has classically understood sin as far more than mere juridical or forensic guilt before

God, but has also stressed the human predicament of imprisonment in self-will, broken only by the hallowing grace of God. To the extent that Judges depicts the ravages of self-will gone amok in the community of faith, it portrays that carnality that threatens the very fulfillment of the divine promises.

Unexpectedly, the solution to human depravity proffered in Judges is not the Spirit of God. In Judges, the occasional outpouring of the Spirit is, itself, diverted and perverted as Israel falls under the weight of its own corruption. Instead, the writer calls for an authority to resist each person's doing "what is right in their own eyes." A Spirit-impelled Samson is a disaster, not for lacking propulsion, but direction—hence the call for a king and the essential Old Testament linkage of kingship with national religious fidelity. Likewise in the New Testament, the emphasis on the moral and spiritual dimensions of the Kingdom of God and its demand that the disciple of Christ deny self and take up the cross always informs and fully controls its statements about the believer and the Holy Spirit. Thus, the unknown author of Judges would affirm with the New Testament that charisma corrupts when devoid of character.

OUTLINE

Despite its diverse contents, the book possesses a coherent structure moving the reader from the beginnings of trouble after Joshua's death to the full collapse of the Israelite community and the need for kingship. The book's structure orchestrates diverse material into a coherent literary and theological witness in the final form of the text without flattening the differences among the stories. The following outline summarizes the major movement.

- I. Introductory Overview: The End from the Beginning (1:1–3:6)
  - A. Faltering Conquest: The View from the Outside (1:1–2:5)
  - B. Fractured Covenant (2:6–3:6)
- II. The Succession of the Judges: Dissolution (3:7–16:31)
  - A. Othniel: The Exemplary Judge (3:7-11)
  - B. Stage One: Triumph (3:12–5:31)
    1. Ehud the assassin (3:12-30)
    2. Shamgar: Minor judge, major achiever (3:31)
    3. Deborah the prophet (4:1–5:31)
  - C. Stage Two: Transition (6:1–10:5)
    1. Gideon: Ambiguity embodied (6:1–8:32)
    2. Abimelech the usurper (8:33–9:57)
    3. Minor judges: Order restored (10:1-5)
  - D. Stage Three: Tragedy (10:6–16:31)
    1. Jephthah: A vow tragically kept (10:6–12:7)
    2. Minor judges: Measure of mediocrity (12:8-15)
    3. Samson: A vow tragically broken (13:1–16:31)
- III. The Finale: A Decadent Community (17:1–21:25)
  - A. Inverted War of Conquest (17:1–18:31)
  - B. Inverted War of Covenant Justice (19:1–21:25)

The complete outline of Judges for this commentary is as follows:

I. Introductory Overview: The End from the Beginning (1:1–3:6)
   A. Faltering Conquest: The View from the Outside (1:1–2:5)
   B. Fractured Covenant (2:6–3:6)
II. The Succession of the Judges: Dissolution (3:7–16:31)
   A. Othniel: The Exemplary Judge (3:7-11)
   B. Stage One: Triumph (3:12–5:31)
      1. Ehud: The assassin deliverer (3:12-30)
      2. Shamgar: Minor judge, major deliverer (3:31)
      3. Deborah and Barak: The unidentified deliverer (4:1-24)
      4. The Song of Deliverance (5:1-31)
   C. Stage Two: Transition (6:1–10:5)
      1. Gideon: Authority and ambivalence (6:1–8:32)
         a. Ambivalence before the call (6:1-40)
         b. Authority accepted (7:1–8:3)
         c. Authority exercised (8:4-21)
         d. Authority abdicated (8:22-27)
         e. Epilogue: Retirement and reversion (8:28-32)
      2. Abimelech: Authority usurped (8:33–9:57)
      3. Tola and Jair: Authority restored (10:1-5)
   D. Stage Three: Tragedy (10:6–16:31)
      1. Jephthah: A vow tragically kept (10:6–12:7)
         a. The prologue (10:6-18)
         b. The victory in battle (11:1-40)
         c. Slaughter of kinsmen (12:1-7)
      2. The Quiet Alternatives: Ibzan, Elon, and Abdon (12:8-15)
      3. Samson: A vow tragically ignored (13:1–16:31)
         a. Samson's birth: Word, vow, and spirit (13:1-25)
         b. The riddle of Samson: Marriage (14:1-4)
         c. The riddle of Samson: Mayhem (14:5-20)
         d. The revenge of Samson: Vengeance, victory, and vindication (15:1-20)
         e. The reversion and redemption of Samson (16:1-31)
III. The Finale: A Decadent Community (17:1–21:25)
   A. The Failed Mission (17:1–18:31)
      1. Substitute worship and priesthood (17:1-13)
      2. Substitute conquest (18:1-31)
   B. The Fractured Vision (19:1–21:25)
      1. The Levite and his concubine (19:1-30)
      2. Israel's war with Benjamin (20:1-48)
      3. Israel provides wives for Benjamin (21:1-25)

ENDNOTE

1. This commentary crystallizes over 30 years lived, almost daily, with the book of Judges. What began as a sermon series grew into a seminar paper and then a doctoral dissertation at Yale University in 1986–1987. For decades, studying Judges has been my passion—one drawing in my family and closest friends. Indeed, my children's honest questions about Judges shaped this commentary at many points, and my wife and life partner, Angie, who has endured my obsession with Judges for our entire marriage, read this whole commentary in draft form. I am therefore hopelessly and gratefully indebted to my family, as well as to friends, colleagues, and teachers, such as Victor P. Hamilton, David L. Thompson, Sandra L. Richter, Paul H. Wright, and Carl G. Rasmussen, whose contribution to specific aspects of this project have been crucial to its completion. Series editor Phillip Comfort displayed astounding patience with a manuscript very slow in the making that seemed to increase in size faster than it progressed to a conclusion. Jason Driesbach offered scores of insightful comments, queries, criticisms, and learned conference on this manuscript and on the book of Judges. Despite such outstanding help, many shortcomings will still be found here and, of course, they remain my own peculiar property.

COMMENTARY ON

Judges

◆ I. Introductory Overview: The End from the Beginning (1:1–3:6)

A. Faltering Conquest: The View from the Outside (1:1–2:5)

After the death of Joshua, the Israelites asked the LORD, "Which tribe should go first to attack the Canaanites?"

2 The LORD answered, "Judah, for I have given them victory over the land."

3 The men of Judah said to their relatives from the tribe of Simeon, "Join with us to fight against the Canaanites living in the territory allotted to us. Then we will help you conquer your territory." So the men of Simeon went with Judah.

4 When the men of Judah attacked, the LORD gave them victory over the Canaanites and Perizzites, and they killed 10,000 enemy warriors at the town of Bezek. 5 While at Bezek they encountered King Adoni-bezek and fought against him, and the Canaanites and Perizzites were defeated. 6 Adoni-bezek escaped, but the Israelites soon captured him and cut off his thumbs and big toes.

7 Adoni-bezek said, "I once had seventy kings with their thumbs and big toes cut off, eating scraps from under my table. Now God has paid me back for what I did to them." They took him to Jerusalem, and he died there.

8 The men of Judah attacked Jerusalem and captured it, killing all its people and setting the city on fire. 9 Then they went down to fight the Canaanites living in the hill country, the Negev, and the western foothills.* 10 Judah marched against the Canaanites in Hebron (formerly called Kiriath-arba), defeating the forces of Sheshai, Ahiman, and Talmai.

11 From there they went to fight against the people living in the town of Debir (formerly called Kiriath-sepher). 12 Caleb said, "I will give my daughter Acsah in marriage to the one who attacks and captures Kiriath-sepher." 13 Othniel, the son of Caleb's younger brother, Kenaz, was the one who conquered it, so Acsah became Othniel's wife.

14 When Acsah married Othniel, she urged him* to ask her father for a field. As she got down off her donkey, Caleb asked her, "What's the matter?"

15 She said, "Let me have another gift. You have already given me land in the Negev; now please give me springs of water, too." So Caleb gave her the upper and lower springs.

16 When the tribe of Judah left Jericho—the city of palms—the Kenites, who were descendants of Moses' father-in-law, traveled with them into the wilderness of Judah. They settled among the people there, near the town of Arad in the Negev.

17 Then Judah joined with Simeon to fight against the Canaanites living in Zephath, and they completely destroyed* the town. So the town was named Hormah.* 18 In addition, Judah captured the towns of Gaza, Ashkelon, and Ekron, along with their surrounding territories.

19 The LORD was with the people of Judah, and they took possession of the hill country. But they failed to drive out the people living in the plains, who had iron chariots. 20 The town of Hebron was given to Caleb as Moses had promised. And Caleb drove out the people living there, who were descendants of the three sons of Anak.

21 The tribe of Benjamin, however, failed to drive out the Jebusites, who were living in Jerusalem. So to this day the Jebusites live in Jerusalem among the people of Benjamin.

22 The descendants of Joseph attacked the town of Bethel, and the LORD was with them. 23 They sent men to scout out Bethel (formerly known as Luz). 24 They confronted a man coming out of the town and said to him, "Show us a way into the town, and we will have mercy on you." 25 So he showed them a way in, and they killed everyone in the town except that man and his family. 26 Later the man moved to the land of the Hittites, where he built a town. He named it Luz, which is its name to this day.

27 The tribe of Manasseh failed to drive out the people living in Beth-shan,* Taanach, Dor, Ibleam, Megiddo, and all their surrounding settlements, because the Canaanites were determined to stay in that region. 28 When the Israelites grew stronger, they forced the Canaanites to work as slaves, but they never did drive them completely out of the land.

29 The tribe of Ephraim failed to drive out the Canaanites living in Gezer, so the Canaanites continued to live there among them.

30 The tribe of Zebulun failed to drive out the residents of Kitron and Nahalol, so the Canaanites continued to live among them. But the Canaanites were forced to work as slaves for the people of Zebulun.

31 The tribe of Asher failed to drive out the residents of Acco, Sidon, Ahlab, Aczib, Helbah, Aphik, and Rehob. 32 Instead, the people of Asher moved in among the Canaanites, who controlled the land, for they failed to drive them out.

33 Likewise, the tribe of Naphtali failed to drive out the residents of Beth-shemesh and Beth-anath. Instead, they moved in among the Canaanites, who controlled the land. Nevertheless, the people of Beth-shemesh and Beth-anath were forced to work as slaves for the people of Naphtali.

34 As for the tribe of Dan, the Amorites forced them back into the hill country and would not let them come down into the plains. 35 The Amorites were determined to stay in Mount Heres, Aijalon, and Shaalbim, but when the descendants of Joseph became stronger, they forced the Amorites to work as slaves. 36 The boundary of the Amorites ran from Scorpion Pass* to Sela and continued upward from there.

CHAPTER 2

The angel of the LORD went up from Gilgal to Bokim and said to the Israelites, "I brought you out of Egypt into this land that I swore to give your ancestors, and I said I would never break my covenant with you. 2 For your part, you were not to make any covenants with the people living in this land; instead, you were to destroy their altars. But you disobeyed my command. Why did you do this? 3 So now I declare that I will no longer drive out the people living in your land. They will be thorns in your sides,* and their gods will be a constant temptation to you."

4 When the angel of the LORD finished speaking to all the Israelites, the people wept loudly. 5 So they called the place Bokim (which means "weeping"), and they offered sacrifices there to the LORD.

1:9 Hebrew *the Shephelah.* **1:14** Greek version and Latin Vulgate read *he urged her.* **1:17a** The Hebrew term used here refers to the complete consecration of things or people to the LORD, either by destroying them or by giving them as an offering. **1:17b** *Hormah* means "destruction." **1:27** Hebrew *Beth-shean,* a variant spelling of Beth-shan. **1:36** Hebrew *Akrabbim.* **2:3** Hebrew *They will be in your sides;* compare Num 33:55.

NOTES

1:1 ***After the death of Joshua.*** This chapter weaves blocks of material adapted from the book of Joshua into a syntactical network shaped by Hebrew consecutive and disjunctive clauses (Stone 1988:190-259). The opening temporal clause *wayhi 'akhare moth yehoshua'* [TH3091, ZH3397] begins a chain of Hebrew Waw-consecutive clauses continuing through the end of 1:8, with 1:9 beginning a new syntactical segment of the narrative. That segment, adapted from materials in the book of Joshua (see commentary below) runs through 1:15. At 1:16 a pair of Hebrew disjunctive clauses starts a new subsection running through 1:21. Starting in 1:21, the writer relies almost completely on material adapted from the book of Joshua to make the major points (cf. Stone 1988; O'Connell 1996; Brensinger 1999; Olson 1998). The critical note in BHS suggests the word "Joshua" here is a textual error for "Moses," since the events following are directly derived from Josh 13–24, which occur during Joshua's lifetime. Plus, Joshua's death appears again in Judg 2:6-10 adapted directly from Josh 24:29-31. No manuscript evidence supports the change, however, and the author of Judg 1 seems to be adapting material with a specific purpose, so "Joshua" should be retained.

the Israelites asked the LORD. The reference here, and in most other passages in which persons "inquire" of Yahweh, is to structured inquiry employing a set ritual, probably involving the Urim and Thummim. The Urim and Thummim are associated in the Pentateuch with the ephod, which was apparently used for inquiring of Yahweh, particularly in battle (cf. 1 Sam 23:9-11; 30:7-9).

Which tribe should go first to attack the Canaanites? This chapter frequently uses the Hebrew verb "go up" (*'alah* [TH5927, ZH6590]) in the sense of "move out on the attack" (cf. 1:2-4, 16, 22). The use of "go up" in the original is obscured in NLT for stylistic reasons.

1:2 ***The LORD answered, "Judah, for I have given them victory over the land."*** Normally the reference to victory specifies a foe or territory, but here Judah is given victory over "the land," suggesting a more extensive divine commission.

1:3 ***Join with us. . . . Then we will help you.*** The Hebrew construction behind "then we will help you" is emphatic, stressing Judah's promise of mutuality.

1:4 ***When the men of Judah attacked.*** Again, the verb "go up" (*'alah* [TH5927, ZH6590]) is used for a military assault. This verse looks like a generalization concerning the whole of 1:4-21, with "Canaanites and Perizzites" possibly denoting city dwellers and village dwellers, or urban and rural population. It would serve as a merism for "everyone" (ABD 5.231).

Bezek. This seems not to be Khirbet Ibzik, but Salhab, a site near Jerusalem that matches the details of this passage as well as 1 Sam 11:8-11 (ABD 1.717-718). The name "Bezek" seems to have passed from Salhab to Khirbet Ibzik by the middle of the Iron Age, suggesting the reference in Judges derives from the early part of the Iron Age.

1:5 ***Adoni-bezek.*** This looks like a typical northwest Semitic personal name in which a divine name is associated with the word "my lord," such as Adonijah, meaning "my Lord is Yah(weh)." But no deity named "Bezek" has been documented. G. E. Wright (1946) suggested the name is a corruption of "Adoni Zedeq" and should be identified with the king of Jerusalem captured and killed by Joshua in Josh 10.

Some see here the intentional change of a name to an "alias" with pejorative nuance, citing the similarity of "Bezek" to a term meaning "potsherd," thereby making "lord of the potsherd" a demeaning alias for this Canaanite king. The use of apparent "aliases" elsewhere in Judges might support this interpretation of the name. Most likely the name is simply a title: "Master of [the town] Bezek" (ABD 1.174). Since 1:1-21 stresses how Judah continued the faithful victories begun by Joshua, even replicating Joshua's achievements, some resonance with Adoni Zedeq could still be present.

1:6 ***cut off his thumbs and big toes.*** Compare the ordination of Aaron in Lev 8:23, where the sacrificial blood is dabbed on Aaron's earlobe, his right thumb, and his right big toe. There it is a symbolic enabling. The mutilation described in Judges likely served not only as a literal disabling of the king, but as a ritual humiliation or shaming. That a shaming figures in the event seems clear from 1:7, where the vanquished, mutilated king confesses the justice of what the Judeans have done.

1:7 ***paid me back.*** The text employs the verbal root *shalem* [TH7999, ZH8966] in the Piel. The popular association of this root (*sh-l-m*) with "peace" obscures its strict sense. The root denotes the equilibrium of the community resulting from every member fulfilling their obligations, and the community itself maintaining its equilibrium with its social and natural environment. Thus *sh-l-m* (often, "peace") can denote just retribution per the lex talionis (i.e., "payback"), reminding the reader that "peace" in the OT was not seen merely as the end of conflict, or an abstract serenity, but rather the restoration of the community's equilibrium, often by actions of punishment or restitution—this is the case in the present passage. That the Judeans could take Adoni-bezek to Jerusalem, where he died, suggests a modicum of control over the area around Jerusalem. That Josh 12:10 also records a vanquished "king of Jerusalem" suggests some basis for the writer in Judges asserting a victory over Jerusalem.

1:8 ***The men of Judah attacked Jerusalem and captured it, killing all its people and setting the city on fire.*** The capture of Jerusalem by the Judeans stands in tension with the report in Josh 15:63 and later tradition of an unvanquished city of Jerusalem (cf. 2 Sam 5:6-10). But no report of Judean glories could possibly be convincing without a report of Jerusalem's capture. The idiom employed for the burning of the city, lit. "to send (off) the city to the fire" is not common, appearing in the form used in 1:8 only in 20:48; 2 Kgs 8:12; and Ps 74:7. Most translations render it "set on fire," suggesting only the torching of the city, not its permanent or even complete destruction, though the usage in Ps 74:7 could suggest total destruction. Had the author wanted to stress the total destruction of the city, stronger expressions existed.

1:9 ***Then they went down.*** The NLT registers a major geographical transition here, signaled syntactically in the Hebrew by a disjunctive temporal clause *we'akhar yaredu* [TH3381, ZH3718] (go down). The Judeans turned from a successful campaign in the center of the country to the south, just as Joshua and the original conquest army turned south (Josh 10:29-43) following the successful penetration of the central highlands (Josh 6–10:28).

the western foothills. Heb., *shepelah* [TH8219, ZH9169] (Shephelah, foothills); these hills formed the critical transitional zone from the "hill country"—the high watershed ridge and the highway running atop it, to the coastal plain with its urban centers, international highways, and resources. Land forces moving between the hill country and the coast, whether the Israelites and the Philistines, the Maccabees and the Syrians, or Saladin and the Crusaders, are funneled down one of six wadis, making control of these seasonal streambeds and the valleys they have carved out a tactical necessity (Smith 1931:201). Early in the era of the judges, by 1165 BC, the Philistines had established themselves on the Coastal Plain and would eventually start pushing up through the Shephelah via these valleys, making immediate control of the Shephelah critical not just to Israel's full possession of Canaan, but to its very survival.

1:10 ***Judah marched . . . defeating the forces of Sheshai, Ahiman, and Talmai.*** In Judg 1:10 and 20 the author splices material from Josh 14:6, 13, 15 and 15:13-14 to create a frame for Judg 1:11-19, which in turn includes a block adapted from Josh 15:15-19 (Judg 1:11-15). The editor of BHS suggests replacing "Judah" with "Caleb" here, citing the parallel with Josh 15, ignoring the apparent intentions of the author to adapt the Joshua material toward a different purpose. The LXX here also adds "and Hebron came out against them," which conceivably could have dropped out of the Hebrew via haplography, though no other manuscript evidence supports the reading. Also, LXX conflates the names "Kiriath Arba" and "Kiryath Sepher" (cf. 1:11) and reads "Kiriath Arbaksepher," suggesting the LXX is expansionistic here. The three commanders noted are named as "sons of Anak," and characterized by the Israelite spies as "nephilim" in Num 13:33. So daunting in appearance, their very presence unhinged 10 of the spies and caused them to despair of victory. Caleb's victory over these Anakites (cf. Josh 15:13-14) in the book of Joshua vindicated his confidence in divine power. But in Judges, these persons lack any such luster of legendary battle prowess. A number of etymological parallels might be proposed between these foes and a range of other persons, but none seems relevant to this passage (Boling 1975:374). The passage directly resonates Josh 15:13-14, which attributes the capture of Hebron and the defeat of Sheshai, Ahiman, and Talmai directly to Caleb. Since Josh 15 locates his inheritance lit., "in the midst of the Judahites," the writer in Judg 1 could link Caleb's victory explicitly to the Judeans. Caleb was one of only two heroes of the Exodus generation to survive into the conquest generation. Associating his victory with Judah highlights Judah's faithfulness and success.

1:11 *From there they went to fight against the people living in the town of Debir (formerly called Kiriath-sepher).* The narrative makes perfect topographic sense. The National Highway or Watershed Ridge route ran past Jerusalem at about 2,400 feet elevation, then climbed about 600 feet in 20 miles to Hebron before descending 840 feet over 7 miles to the "huge, impressive Bronze and Iron Age site" (Stern 1993–2008.4:1252) of Khirbet Rabud, the likely site of Debir (ABD 2:112), and then on to Beer Sheba, the southwestern gateway to Judah. Often this route runs on the narrow spine of the ridge between deep ravines, following the watershed. Clearly the Israelites understood the importance of controlling this vital thoroughfare. Still quoting Josh 15, the Judges author changes the geographically logical verb in Josh 15:15, "and he went up" (*'alah* [TH5927, ZH6590]) to the more generic "and he went." This preserves the "downward" movement of the Judeans started in 1:9, maintaining the analogy with Joshua's geographical movement in Josh 6–11. Additionally, the antecedent of the pronoun subject "he went" was "Caleb" in the Joshua passage, but with "Judah" as the named subject in 1:10, the reader must see Judah as the agent in 1:11 as well. What Caleb accomplished as an individual is assimilated into Judah's achievement.

The former name of Debir, Kiriath-sepher, is traditionally taken as "town of (the) book" or, with a repointing of the text, "Scribe Town." While the Targum envisions a city functioning as an archive, Boling (1975:56) rightly suggests reference to a monumental inscription or stele. A victory stele inscribed with the name of a conquering king and his god would constitute a religious challenge to the Israelites, as well as an appealing military objective. The obliteration of previous conqueror's names from monuments and the inscription of the new conqueror's name figure prominently in ancient Near Eastern monumental tradition (Richter 2002:153-184).

1:13 *Othniel, the son of Caleb's younger brother, Kenaz.* The story in 1:11-15 reproduces the account from Josh 15:15-19, but with strategic changes to highlight the writer's point. Most important is the simple addition of the phrase *haqqaton* [TH6996A, ZH7785] *mimmennu* (lit., "the one smaller than him"). Why would Judges add this phrase? Grammatically, the "younger brother of Caleb" could be either Othniel or Kenaz. The most common interpretation sees Othniel as Caleb's brother, with the author of Judges adding "the one younger than him" adjusting his age to allow marriage to Caleb's daughter. The NLT rightly parts company with this view, regarding Kenaz as the younger brother, making Othniel Caleb's nephew. This position was most cogently argued by Bachmann (1868:114-116) and is argued in detail by Stone (1988:202-207).

The book of Judges extends the generational structure of the Pentateuch in which one generation, the Exodus generation, failed and experienced divine judgment. Within that generation, though, were two faithful men, Joshua and Caleb, who alone survived to serve as a witness to the next generation. That next generation was the faithful conquest generation, for whom Joshua and Caleb provided leadership. The third generation, according to 2:10, apostatized. To interpret Othniel as Caleb's brother violates the claim that only Joshua and Caleb survived from the conquest generation (Num 14:26-38; 32:10-12; Deut 1:34-40). However, to see Othniel as Caleb's nephew (i.e., seeing Kenaz as Caleb's younger brother) construes Othniel as a member of the faithful conquest generation. Since the third generation will be apostate, seeing Othniel as a member of the conquest generation aligns his function with that of Caleb. Each man was a faithful survivor of the preceding generation whose function was to bear witness and provide leadership for his contemporaries, the "next" generation. Since the writer of Judges works so carefully with this generational pattern, it seems likely that the addition of "the one younger than him" to the Joshua story serves this theme. The full importance of this addition only emerges in connection with the story found in 3:7-11.

1:16 ***Jericho—the city of palms.*** Here the NLT makes explicit what is not explicit in the original: the identity of the "city of palms" as Jericho. The writer anticipates the reoccupation of Jericho by Eglon in 3:13, where the same title appears; and by alluding to Jericho, the writer also evokes a connection with the conquest. To settle in the south locates the Kenites with the Judeans, reinforcing the impression of Judah as a tribe that brings the Israelites, including client groups such as the Kenites, together, in contrast to the isolation of the northern tribes seen in 1:22-36. The decision by these descendants of Moses's father-in-law to affiliate with the southern tribes contrasts directly with the choice of another Kenite named "Partner" (NLT, "Heber") to move north and ally (lit., to have *shalom* [TH7965, ZH8934]) with Israel's enemy Jabin of Hazor (4:11-12, 17).

1:17 ***they completely destroyed the town. So the town was named Hormah.*** Ironically, despite the war and destruction in Judges, the preeminent Hebrew root denoting holy war, *kharam* [TH2763, ZH3049] (to devote to destruction), appears only twice in the book (1:17; 21:11), and the derived noun *kherem* [TH2764, ZH3051] (that which is devoted) does not appear at all, probably because the enemies against which Israel typically fights in Judges are outside intruders, not the original inhabitants of the land. In contrast, the two terms occur some 27 times in Joshua and 11 times in Deuteronomy. Either the wars in Judges were not construed as classic "Yahweh war" or the writer was not influenced by the Deuteronomistic terminology. Since Judges makes direct use of the Joshua material, the latter seems more likely, especially since Judges repeatedly describes the kind of behavior that, according to Joshua, should have made Israel subject to *kherem*.

1:18 ***In addition, Judah captured the towns of Gaza, Ashkelon, and Ekron, along with their surrounding territories.*** The towns of Gaza, Ashkelon, and Ekron fell in the territory allotted to Judah (Josh 15:45-47, no mention of Ashkelon though), but they remained unpossessed in Joshua's lifetime. Gaza remained one of the last refuges of the Anakim, archetypical foes of the Israelites (Josh 11:22), and Ekron is explicitly reckoned Canaanite in Josh 13:3. It is noteworthy that Judah is not here said to destroy these towns, only to have seized them. These towns did not become Philistine territory until Ramses III settled them there around 1175 BC. Israel likely had been in Canaan since the 1240s BC, so the towns would not have been in Philistine hands when Judah seized them. In fact, Ashkelon had been conquered by Merneptah at the close of the thirteenth century BC (ABD 1:488-490) making it possible that the Israelites' capture of the sites would not entail a massive operation. By taking these strongholds, the Judahites exceeded the achievements of Joshua. The later association of these towns with the Philistines suggests an anticipation of the victories of David.

1:19 ***The LORD was with the people of Judah, and they took possession of the hill country. But they failed to drive out the people living in the plains, who had iron chariots.*** This verse poses a conundrum. On one hand, "[Yahweh] was with . . . Judah" expresses full divine support and approval, but on the other hand, the expression "failed to drive out the people" suggests failure. That the affirmation of Yahweh's favor should be stressed seems clear from the triple reference in 1:2-19. Yahweh's own promise "I have given . . ." in 1:2 flows into "[Yahweh] gave" in 1:4, culminating in the summary "[Yahweh] was with the people of Judah" in 1:19. This theme of uniform approval hardly leaves room for a failure report, necessitating a closer look at the problematic final clause. Literally translated, 1:19b reads "because (*ki* [TH3588, ZH3954]) not to drive out the people living in the valley." The term translated "plains" in NLT is actually the term *'emeq* [TH6010, ZH6677], typically indicating a flat-bottomed valley, such as the Soreq or Elah valleys or, more directly, the Jezreel valley. The associated reference to iron chariotry is one of only four in the OT. The other three are all situated in the Galilee, and Josh 17:16-18, the closest parallel to the Judges text, refers explicitly to Beth-shan and "the valley of Jezreel." The negation and the infinitive are an open-ended construction permitting the translation "[it was/they were] not to drive out the people" and taking the *ki* adversatively would reasonably allow "The Lord was with Judah . . . but it was not (for them) to drive out the people of the valley." If the writer in ch 1 is alluding to Josh 17, and if "the valley" refers to the Jezreel valley, then the Judean failure is mitigated by placing the locale of their failure far beyond their own allotted responsibility. Indeed, for Judah to have reached so far attests a zeal and determination not seen among the northern tribes.

1:20 ***The town of Hebron was given to Caleb as Moses had promised. And Caleb drove out the people living there, who were descendants of the three sons of Anak.*** The NLT's passive "was given" represents the Hebrew "they gave." But is this impersonal passive the best rendering? Since this section subordinates Caleb's deeds to the larger Judean campaign, the text likely wants to suggest "they [the Judeans] gave Hebron to Caleb."

1:21 ***The tribe of Benjamin, however, failed to drive out the Jebusites, who were living in Jerusalem. So to this day the Jebusites live in Jerusalem among the people of Benjamin.*** A clear failure notice, this verse reports that despite the capture of Jerusalem by the Judeans reported in 1:8, the Benjaminites failed to retain it. The verse quotes directly from Josh 15:63, except that in Joshua the Judeans, not the Benjaminites, fail to expel the Jebusites from Jerusalem. The tension between the two passages is resolved if we grant that the writer of Judges recognized that Jerusalem, though on the border between Judah and Benjamin, was included within the Benjaminite inheritance and was thus Benjamin's responsibility. By the author's time, Jerusalem was a Judean city. Thus, consistent with the positive portrayal of Judah in ch 1, the author clarifies that Jerusalem's persistence as a Jebusite stronghold was not the fault of Judah during the premonarchic period, but Benjamin (the tribe of Saul).

1:22 ***The descendants of Joseph attacked the town of Bethel, and the LORD was with them.*** "Descendants of Joseph" translates the literal "house of Joseph," a curious reference that appears as a descriptor of Israel only 10 times. In Josh 17:17 it clearly denotes Ephraim and Manasseh, but then in Josh 18:5 the "house of Joseph" is admonished to stay in its portion in the north, just as Judah should stay in its portion in the south. Thus, "house of Joseph" identifies the north programmatically contrasted with the south, a usage compatible with 1:22-36, where the phrase brackets the whole account of all the northern tribes (cf. 1:35). Subsequently, the expression continues to define the northern tribes as a whole and could allude to the later northern kingdom (2 Sam 19:20; 1 Kgs 11:28). Amos also addressed the northern state as "house of Joseph" (Amos 5:6). While Obad 1:18 seems not to draw the contrast as sharply, as late as Zech 10:6, the "house of Judah" is the natural counterpoint to the "house of Joseph." The expression, used of the premonarchic community, already addresses the nation as two separate communities.

the LORD was with them. This is the last statement of divine approval in 1:1–2:5. Yahweh was "with" the house of Joseph as they attacked Bethel, but the condemnation issued in 2:1-5 suggests that somewhere between 1:22 and 1:36, the divine favor was lost.

1:23 *They sent men to scout out Bethel.* The Hebrew term *tur* [TH8446, ZH9365], translated "scout out," finds its most frequent usage (11 occurrences out of 24) in characterizing the mission of the spies in Num 13–14, infamous for having miscarried and become a paradigmatic rebellion. Here it appears rather than the equally common *ragal* [TH7270, ZH8078] (e.g., 18:2, 14, 17; Gen 42:9, 11, 14; Num 21:32; Deut 1:24; Josh 6:22-23, 25). Perhaps in using *tur* the writer wanted to associate the "scouting" of the house of Joseph with the abortive mission of the spies. That the word cannot be entirely or inherently pejorative appears from its use to describe Yahweh's seeking of a place for his people (cf. Deut 1:33; Num 10:33; Ezek 20:6), but the simple literary association still might suggest that the house of Joseph was duplicating an unhappy precedent.

1:23-26 *(formerly known as Luz). . . . Later the man moved to the land of the Hittites, where he built a town. He named it Luz, which is its name to this day.* The notation about Bethel being formerly Luz seems odd, since the name change would have been centuries old, being noted in Gen 28:19. Yet the OT notes the continued use of the older name (cf. Gen 35:6; 48:3; Josh 16:2; 18:13). Perhaps 1:23-26 provides an answer. Rather than exterminate the occupants of Canaanite Bethel, as the conquest mandate required, the house of Joseph allowed the betrayer of Luz/Bethel to escape, and he ultimately founded another city by the same name, which the writer notes existed "to this day." Here is the first departure from Israel's mandate in Canaan. Rather than destroy the Canaanite culture, the house of Joseph allowed it to exist, though at a distance—and perhaps not a great distance, since "the land of the Hittites" could refer to close-by Syria, or even the hill country near Bethel (ABD 4.420). Perhaps also the writer hoped to contrast the bold assault of the Judeans (1:1-21) with the conniving of the northerners. This possibility is suggested by the similarity of language between 1:8 and 1:25, both of which speak of striking the city with "the mouth of the sword" and of "dismissing/consigning." In 1:8, Judah is said to consign Jerusalem to the fire; in 1:25, the house of Joseph "consigns" the betrayer to banishment.

1:27 *Beth-shan, Taanach, Dor, Ibleam, Megiddo, and all their surrounding settlements.* The cities mentioned here constitute a strategic chain of centers defining the Carmel ridge and the barrier it casts across the land, forcing north–south traffic through a limited number of routes. A high, imposing mound at the intersection of the Jordan and Jezreel valleys, Beth-shan served as an Egyptian garrison and home to some high officials, though the principle city in the vicinity during Iron Age I stood a few miles south, on Tel Rehov. An Egyptian inscription of Seti I and a set of anthropoid coffins confirm the Egyptian-Philistine identity of the town. From Beth-shan, the narrow Harod valley moves northwest bounded by Mount Gilboa on the left and Moreh on the right, like the shaft of an arrowhead whose tip rests on the narrow pass above Yokneam. At Jezreel, the valley suddenly broadens out joining the Carmel ridge on the south at Ibleam and the Nazareth ridge to the north at Mount Tabor. These two edges of the arrowhead converge as the valley moves. Ibleam, Taanach, and Megiddo define this left "edge," and all guard strategic entries from the hills to the southwest into the valley proper. From the time of Thutmose III, Taanach and Megiddo controlled the vast bottomlands of the valley as Pharaonic estates, and they remained in non-Israelite hands until Iron Age II. Roads crossing southwest over the Carmel ridge wound their way to the major coastal highway first at the town of Dor. Thus, vital, strategic sites controlling the flow of all traffic through the Jezreel valley and, therefore, all north–south traffic, lay firmly in non-Israelite hands, separating the Israelite tribes south of the valley from those in the Galilee.

because the Canaanites were determined to stay in that region. The will of the Canaanites stressed here transcended mere stubbornness. Egypt, having momentarily been distracted by the Sea Peoples around 1200 BC, renewed its interest in controlling Canaan in the early twelfth century. In keeping with New Kingdom policy, Egypt controlled Canaan via local rulers whom Egypt either dominated or bought. The Canaanites sought to hold these cities to ensure Egypt an uninterrupted flow of trade and luxury goods through the Jezreel valley and out to the International Coastal Highway, thus also ensuring their own wealth and power under Egyptian sponsorship.

1:28 *When the Israelites grew stronger, they forced the Canaanites to work as slaves, but they never did drive them completely out of the land.* In ironic contrast to the dismal failure recorded in 1:27, this verse reports the Israelites reducing some Canaanites to forced labor. Here Israel actually participates in the very social evils from which they themselves were delivered by Yahweh. Moreover, as the Amarna correspondence graphically documents, forced labor characterized the Egyptian-Canaanite management style. It directly contradicted the central ethos of the covenant; the Israelites had begun to operate like their former oppressors and their current enemies.

1:29-30 *The tribe of Ephraim failed to drive out the Canaanites living in Gezer, so the Canaanites continued to live there among them.* Gezer occupied a strategic position on the main road running from Jerusalem and towns in the Benjaminite area westward through Upper and Lower Beth Horon, through Gezer, and out toward the coastal highway. This axial crossroad in southern Canaan is mentioned in both Egyptian and Mesopotamian documents. Destroyed, or at least damaged, by Thutmose III, Gezer revived somewhat later and served Egyptian administrative purposes, attested by the Amarna letters. In the same inscription where he claims to have annihilated Israel, Pharaoh Merneptah also boasts of capturing Gezer, which indeed remained non-Israelite until Solomon received it as a wedding present from his Egyptian father-in-law (1 Kgs 9:15-17). So not only was Gezer a point of Israelite failure, it potentially served Egyptian imperial interests through most of the period of the Judges.

1:30 *The tribe of Zebulun failed to drive out the residents of Kitron and Nahalol.* These two sites have not been located for certain. Nahalol is likely the same as Nahalal in Josh 19:15, thus equating Kitron with Kattath in that passage. Rainey and Notley (2006:135), following a rabbinic association of Nahalol with later Mahalul, plausibly suggest Nahalal/Nahalol should be equated with modern Tell el-Beida, which, unlike other candidates, is located in the northwest portion of the Jezreel valley where Zebulun's assigned territory lay.

1:31-32 *The tribe of Asher failed to drive out the residents of Acco, Sidon, Ahlab, Aczib, Helbah, Aphik, and Rehob. Instead, the people of Asher moved in among the Canaanites, who controlled the land, for they failed to drive them out.* The cities noted here lie on the plain of Acco, which extends northwest of the valley of Jezreel, opening up toward the sea from the narrow, pinched pass above Yokneam. The tribe of Asher's assigned location here along the sea likely contributed to their failure to fulfill their commission. The urban rulers of Canaan, some of whom were involved in seafaring, fretted over their sagging agricultural production due to the heavy demands of pharaoh for tribute and gifts (Na'aman 2005:216-241). Possibly the Asherites found a niche as farmers. Moreover, Stager (1988:233-234) has argued that the Asherites entered into client relationships with Canaanites and their shipping interests (cf. 5:17b). Having become economically enmeshed, even dependent, on the Canaanites, the Asherites were hardly in a position to expel them since in doing so they would be burning their meal ticket! The subordination of Asher emerges from a startling change in phrasing: Rather than the Canaanites remaining as enclaves among the Israelites (cf. 1:21, 29), both Asher and Naphtali moved in among the Canaanites as minority enclaves.

1:33 ***Likewise, the tribe of Naphtali failed to drive out the residents of Beth-shemesh and Beth-anath.*** Each of these towns commemorates a Canaanite deity. Beth-shemesh honors the sun-god; Beth-anath extols the Canaanite goddess of war and the hunt, who was also Baal's paramour. The Beth-shemesh noted here is not the town in the southern Shephelah overlooking the Wadi Sorek, but rather sits, with Beth-anath, high up in the remote hills of the upper Galilee, which apparently began to be settled at the onset of Iron Age I. A steep ridge running west from near the northern tip of the Sea of Galilee almost to the coast rises abruptly over 3,000 feet and defines the starting point of these rugged, but beautiful, "heights of Naphtali." For Naphtali to "live among" Canaanites implies cultural submission. That the Canaanites periodically managed to enslave the locals only reinforces the loss of their distinct Israelite ethos. Despite this discouraging report, the city of Kadesh in Naphtali, located northwest of Hazor, became the home of an Israelite hero, Barak, who figures in chs 4–5.

1:34 ***As for the tribe of Dan, the Amorites forced them back into the hill country and would not let them come down into the plains.*** Dan's inheritance fell in the Shephelah, in the vicinity of the Sorek valley. Vigorous resistance forced them to stay in the hills in Zorah and Eshtaol overlooking the rich, red agricultural soil of the valley with its vineyards, famed for their dark red grapes. The Philistines made the Sorek valley an early staging ground for attempting to move into the hill country in their quest to control trade over both the coastal highway and the watershed ridge highway, a quest ultimately bringing them directly into conflict with Israel. Their presence and the contrast between them and the Danites is a theme in the Samson story in chs 13–16. Even (especially?) with a hero like Samson, the Danites ultimately abandoned their divinely appointed territory and moved far north in search of an easier inheritance. Once again, the "house of Joseph" being able to subject the locals to forced labor hardly counts as success by the standards of the conquest.

1:36 ***The boundary of the Amorites ran from Scorpion Pass to Sela and continued upward from there.*** Sadly, this notes the boundary of the Amorites, not the Danites! Moreover, the traditional locations of the places mentioned are southwest of the Dead Sea (cf. Num 34:4; Josh 15:3) and do not fit the locale of 1:34-35 and the vicinity of the Sorek valley. However, the reference to "rock" (*sela'* [TH5554, ZH6153]) in connection with the Danites echoes with the Samson narrative (15:8, 11) in which Samson hides out in "the cleft of the rock (*sela'*) of Etam," in Judean territory. One wonders if "Ascent of Akrabbim" is not a textual corruption for some other expression, now lost to us.

2:1 ***The angel of the LORD.*** This first appearance of the "angel of Yahweh" (2:1, 4) foreshadows his appearance commissioning Gideon (6:11, 12, 21, 22) and announcing

Samson's birth (13:3, 13, 15-18, 20-21). His role cursing those who declined to report for battle (5:23) suggests a role leading the armies of Yahweh.

went up. Heb., *'alah* [TH5927, ZH6590]; it appears in the preceding material solely in the sense of "move out against" militarily. If the sense holds, there is a hostile intent implicit as the angel of Yahweh figuratively "moves out against" the Israelites!

from Gilgal. Gilgal, just a mile northeast of Jericho, served as the base camp of the conquest and the first sanctuary of the Ark in Joshua, marked by a cairn of 12 stones commemorating the crossing of the Jordan (Josh 3–4). Here Joshua encountered the angel of Yahweh and received assurance of victory after he had circumcised the new, wilderness-bred conquest generation on the eve of the attack on Jericho (Josh 5). The victorious Israelites returned to Gilgal after the southern campaign (Josh 10:43) and from here Joshua began the apportionment of the land to the tribes (Josh 14–20) until the sanctuary moved to Shiloh (Josh 21:1-4). Gilgal remained an important religious center on Samuel's "circuit" (1 Sam 7:16), and Saul was named king there (1 Sam 11:14-15). Saul's impatient and presumptuous offering occurred at Gilgal (cf. 1 Sam 10:8; 13:8-15). Gilgal also provided the scene for Saul's rejection as king. A later religious pilgrimage to Gilgal was censured by Amos and Hosea (Hos 4:15; 12:11; Amos 5:5). In Israelite memory, Gilgal remained part of the conquest, summarized by Micah as (lit.) "what happened between Shittim and Gilgal" (Mic 6:5). The name (normally with the definite article) the Gilgal, likely refers to a circle of stones and likely designates a fortified camp. Thus, it would be fitting for Yahweh's angel to launch a sort of military attack for religious failure against the Israelites from this location.

Bokim. See note on 2:5.

said to the Israelites. This is one of three speeches in Judges in which Yahweh or a mediator, as opposed to the narrator, indicts Israel for apostasy.

my covenant with you. Explicit reference to Yahweh's covenant (*berith* [TH1285, ZH1382]) with Israel is rare in Judges, as is much of the semantic field associated with it.

2:2 ***you were not to make any covenants with the people living in this land.*** Covenant-making produced a bond or union between the covenanters. This charge calls for no bonds of cooperation or union of any kind with the inhabitants of the land.

But you disobeyed my command. Why did you do this? The narrative in 1:1-36 makes no reference to any command, nor does it ever censure the tribes who failed to drive out the inhabitants of the land as having done evil, just as the material in Josh 13–22 (from which much of ch 1 derives) refrains from criticism for this lack. But 2:1-5 looks over this process and renders a judgment: The failure of ch 1 is now to be seen as the sin of making a covenant, a bond, with the Canaanites.

2:5 ***So they called the place Bokim (which means "weeping"), and they offered sacrifices there to the Lord.*** Bokim simply means "weepers" and reflects 2:4. The location remains unknown, but the mention of sacrifices implies some connection with the sanctuary, implying the passage notes the transfer of the sanctuary from Gilgal to Bokim. Scholars typically assume this is a site near Bethel, but a transfer of the sanctuary in this context would more likely have been to Shiloh or Shechem. Ironically, the OT speaks of another "Gilgal," a site known in Arabic as *El 'Unuq* near Shechem, Ebal, and Gerizim (Deut 11:26-30). Archaeological survey reveals a hilltop stone circle, a "gilgal," in the vicinity with pottery dating from the 1200s BC and a peculiar cairn of stones at one end, on the long axis (Zertal 1991). Perhaps Bokim refers to this "second" Gilgal. The implications of this identification are noted in the commentary.

COMMENTARY

Judges 1:1–3:6 forms a long, internally diverse introduction that provides both a summary and an analysis of the dynamics at work overall during the period covered by the book. Marshaling divergent materials, the prologue asserts twice unequivocally that after Joshua and the conquest generation died, Israel steadily deteriorated. The introduction tracks the decline in two roughly parallel sections, each devoted to a distinct perspective. First, 1:1–2:5 traces the stalling of the military conquest of the land from south to north, saving any theological critique for the very end. Then 2:6–3:3 returns to the death of Joshua and retraces the same period emphasizing spiritual deterioration. Instead of proceeding geographically, as 1:1–2:5 does, 2:6–3:3 proceeds genealogically, from one generation to the next. Judges 3:5-6 then integrates the two perspectives in a terse summary.

Parallel Structure of Judges 1:1–3:6

	MILITARY AND GEOGRAPHICAL	THEOLOGICAL AND GENERATIONAL
Joshua's Death	Noted in 1:1a	Narrated in 2:6-9
Early Successes	Southern Tribes Canaan Occupied 1:1b-21	Generation I: Covenant Honored 2:7, 10a
Steady Decline	Northern Tribes Canaan Increasingly Resistant 1:22-36	Generation II Covenant Broken 2:10-19
Yahweh's Denunciation	For Compromising the Conquest 2:1-5	For Compromising the Covenant 2:20–3:4
Summary of Consequences	An Unfulfilled Destiny 3:5-6	

This unit also acts as an "overture" to the whole book, articulating emphases that are spelled out in detail in the rest of the book. This prologue or overture also removes any suspense about the book's main point: With Israel militarily impotent and spiritually bankrupt, the story is virtually finished before it begins.

Theologically, 1:1–2:5 explores an explosive and vital question. How could the nation squander its inheritance? How could it be that, having received from Joshua the possession of the Promised Land as the historical realization of the promise and oath of God, Israel would allow that gift to slip through its fingers? How could the successors of Joshua, the heirs of the divine promise, lose their grip on that gift that stood as the goal and apex of the entire work of God narrated from the Creation through the Exodus experience to the conquest? The answer given in this carefully constructed and complex chapter is chilling: Israel frittered away its inheritance a little bit at a time. Before any claims of overt apostasy appear, the text impresses on the reader a process in which the nation simply compromised the divine purpose. Before settling for something *other than* Yahweh's covenant promises, Israel settled for something *less than* Yahweh's covenant promises.

In certain ways 1:1-36 sets up a series of expectations fulfilled in the following stories:

1. Judges 1 asserts Judean/Southern superiority, illustrated preeminently by Othniel. Othniel is the first judge, and fully exemplifies the ideal of the judge.
2. Judges 1:3, 16-20 underscores cooperation, while from 3:12 through the rest of the book, the vision of cooperation will collapse.
3. Judges 1:16 identifies the Kenites as being in league with the Israelites. The note prepares the reader to understand the later actions of Jael, the wife of a Kenite, who killed Sisera (4:21), even though her husband had established a formal relationship with Israel's enemies (cf. 4:11,17b). She thus exemplified the former Kenite loyalty to Israel.
4. The reference to the "city of palms" in 1:16 possibly resonates with the reference to Eglon's oppressing Israel from the "city of palms" in 3:13.
5. The slur on Benjamin (1:21) possibly sets up a return to the questionable status of Benjamin in chapters 19–21.
6. The south-north movement in 1:1-36 generally corresponds to the course of the narrative in 3:7–16:31.
7. The pattern of deterioration set out in 1:1-36 is duplicated in 3:7–16:31.
8. Both 1:1-36 and 3:7–16:31 conclude with the tribe of Dan as the topic.
9. The narrative about Dan in chapter 18 appears to resume about where 1:34-35 leaves off: Dan is expelled from its inheritance in 1:34-35. In 18:1-2, Dan is in search of an inheritance.
10. The description of the "weepers" in 2:1-5 possibly matches the repeated weeping at Bethel in chapters 19–21 (especially 20:18-26). Proposals to relate 2:1-5 to Bethel would, if correct, strengthen this linkage. Judges 2:1-5 concludes a unit beginning with an inquiry (1:1-2) that is distinctively matched in 20:18-26.

Prologue (1:1-3). In addition to introducing the book as a whole, this section serves as the prologue to 1:4-21. The temporal formula *after the death of* also appears in Joshua 1:1 and 2 Samuel 1:1, which begin their narratives with reference to the death of Moses and Saul, respectively. The formulas demarcate a period from the death of Joshua to the death of Saul, consigning Saul to the premonarchic era. These references likely identify the eras of the premonarchic period for one of the earlier strata of the Deuteronomistic History since the formula is not similarly used again to begin a narrative block in the Deuteronomistic History. The only other similar usage is Genesis 25:11, in which the notation of Abraham's death provides a comparable transition to the next block of that book. The campaign divinely initiated in 1:1-3 unfolds in 1:4-8.

Judges 1:1-3 strikes three keynotes that resonate through the entire book of Judges. First, it dates the narrative "after the death of Joshua." More than a mere chronological notice, this reference establishes an intertextuality with the book of Joshua that pervasively shapes 1:1–2:5. Placing the events of chapter 1 after Joshua's death generates strong tensions because much of the material in chapter 1 derives directly from Joshua 13–24 and actually occurred during Joshua's lifetime. However the historical issue is resolved, this tension establishes a canonical linkage to Joshua and reveals the writer's main theological evaluation of the era from Joshua's death to that of Saul. By making this explicit tie back to Joshua's lifetime, the writer holds up a standard. Joshua affirms the complete victory of Israel (e.g., Josh 11:23; 13:1, 14; 21:43-45), in which context Joshua 13–21 summarizes Israel's successful taking of the land, despite some territories identified as not fully under Israelite control. Other than the Othniel passage, chapter 1 excerpts only the incomplete possession reports and sets Israel's actions *after* the fulfillment of that promise. This shift in the context of the material generates the question of how faithfully Israel built on that sound beginning. The failure passages in Joshua 13–21 constitute a portrayal of the remaining task: "Yet more land" remained to be taken. In Joshua, these passages are marginalia to the overarching fact of Israel's triumph in Canaan. But in chapter 1, the accumulation of all the failure reports dramatically shifts the perception of their importance. Thus chapter 1, for the reader familiar with Joshua, has framed the time after Joshua's death as probationary, and sets out the failure reports as a scorecard.

Another function served by the death formula is to define an era from the death of Moses to the death of Joshua. That era was characterized by faithful fulfillment of the covenant requirements and promises. The death of Joshua now inaugurates another period that will run to the death of Saul. That era's crises of character and leadership contrast sharply with the time of Joshua. Already, the writer sets the stage for a clue to his assessment of the period covered by Judges: The oracular inquiry of 1:1, "which tribe should go first to attack the Canaanites?" resonates with the inquiry near the end of the book when, once again, the Israelites inquire who should go up against the enemy (20:18), where once again, the answer is "Judah is to go first." The measure of the historical process between the two passages may be seen by the enemies named: In 1:1, the enemy is the Canaanite, but in 20:18, the enemy is a fellow Israelite tribe. Again, the inquiry in 1:1 leads to success, but in 20:18 the victory over Benjamin only produces a more painful and complex circumstance.

The second note struck by 1:1-3 is the primacy of Judah, enunciated by none other than Yahweh himself, who declares Judah the custodian of the promise and offers victory as confirmation. The book's paucity of references to Judah throws this surprising claim into sharp relief. The writer will go on to expose the failures and sins of the northern tribes as a prelude to advocating monarchy, with strong hints at a Judean center of gravity for that institution. Emphasis on Judean primacy includes the third note, the stress on intertribal cooperation. Judah asks Simeon's assistance, offering to reciprocate. The rest of 1:1–2:5 unfolds these two themes in two contrasting sections. Judges 1:4-21 narrates a victorious Judean campaign and emphasizes tribal cooperation, but in 1:22-36 the separate northern tribes encounter only increasing failure and frustration as they lose their grip on the Promised Land.

Victory for Judah (1:4-21). This section glorifies Judah by relating an attack climaxing in the burning of Jerusalem. The defeated enemy, Adoni-bezek (1:7), identifies Judah as the arm of divine justice and characterizes his own defeat and dismemberment as just retribution for his own cruelty. The burning of Jerusalem (1:8) confirms Yahweh's promise of Judean victory, but contrasts with Joshua 15:63 where Judah fails to control Jerusalem. Judges 1:21 quotes Joshua 15:63 but substitutes Benjamin for Judah, suggesting a Judean capture of the city (1:8) followed by Benjaminite forfeiture (1:21). David later recaptured the city as his capital (2 Sam 6). (See notes on 1:8 and 1:21.)

Verses 9-15 follow the victorious Judeans down to the foothills and Negev. Othniel personifies victorious Judah. His genealogy (1:13) epitomizes his exemplary role. A three-generation pattern spans the period from the Exodus to the judges. The exodus generation rebelled and died in the wilderness, leaving only Caleb and Joshua to see the Promised Land. The second generation, bred in the wilderness, was faithful and inherited the land. Judges 2:10 brands the third apostate. Othniel, as Caleb's young nephew, represents the faithful conquest generation in the unfaithful postconquest period (see note on 1:13). Rising to Caleb's challenge, he shows he has the "righteous stuff." The story about Acsah (1:14-15) further stresses the role of Othniel, linking him with the courage and determination of Caleb.

Verses 16-21 list further triumphs bracketed by references to cooperation among the tribes—the realization of the theme announced in 1:3. Cooperation entailed no loss of independence, and Judah kept faith with those who assisted: The Kenites (1:16) cooperate with Judah, yet retain their autonomy; Judah keeps its promise and assists Simeon in conquering its own inheritance (1:17; cf. 1:3) and keeps faith with Moses's command, awarding Hebron to Caleb (1:20). Judean victories (1:18-19) extend even to Philistine cities. This success is remarkable, since the rest of the Old Testament shows a Philistine monopoly on power broken only by David. Judah's activity thus foreshadows David's triumphs.

Only two failures appear. First, failure to capture the plains (1:19) possibly involves an area beyond Judah's allotment, since the only "valley" mentioned elsewhere in the Old Testament in connection with "iron chariots" is Jezreel in the north. Joshua 17:16-18 treats "iron chariots" as a licit explanation for failing to defeat the Canaanites. The Hebrew text of 1:19 is better translated "they were not to drive the people from the plains" (see note). Where the Judeans were not successful, they were exonerated. The second failure involves Jerusalem, which was captured by Judah in 1:8, but forfeited by Benjamin in 1:21.

Four literary features embody the section's emphasis. (1) Judah's victories evoke comparison with Joshua's exploits, and follow a geographical pattern comparable to Joshua's: Victories in central Canaan lead to a southern campaign and possibly to northern efforts. Judah is Joshua *redivivus*! (2) Two references to Moses (1:16, 20) assert Judah's continuity with the founder of the Hebrew faith. (3) The focus on Hebron (1:9-10, 20) and Jerusalem (1:7-8, 21), key cities in David's reign, and the Judean foreshadowing of David's achievements, link a pro-Davidic orientation to the pro-Judean tone noted above. (4) Benjamin's forfeiture of Jerusalem (1:21) could censure Saul's tribe, also a pro-Davidic sentiment. Thus, 1:1-21 identifies Judah with Joshua, Moses, and David. Judah and David's line are the true heirs of the Promised Land.

Achievements of the House of Joseph (1:22-36). The next section narrates the achievements of the "descendants [lit., house] of Joseph" (1:22, 35), a general expression here embracing the non-Judean tribes. The section begins with Bethel (1:22-26) and ends with Dan (1:34), the two sacred cities of the northern kingdom (cf. 1 Kgs

12:25-33), in contrast to the focus on Hebron and Jerusalem in 1:1-21. Verses 22-36 display progressive military failure. Victory at Bethel (1:22-26) gives way to a victory qualified by the continuing presence of Canaanites (1:27-28). Quoting Joshua 17:11-13, Judges 1:27-28 emphasizes Manasseh's failure by rearranging the Joshua passages to place failure notices at the beginning and end of the report, and suggest the blameworthiness of that failure by removing the "could not" of Joshua 17:12. With Ephraim and Zebulun (1:29-30, with 1:29 quoting Josh 16:10), the Canaanites remain in enclaves among the Hebrews. Asher and Naphtali, however, live in enclaves surrounded by the Canaanites (1:31-33). The tide had clearly turned against the northern tribes. Finally, the Danites (1:34-35) are forced out of most of the land assigned to them, their destiny left hanging until chapter 18. This progressive failure corresponds to a geographical movement; the gradually deepening failure plots a steady northern movement, associating northern tribes with failure. Additionally, in contrast to the cooperation evident in 1:1b-21, the staccato catalogue of isolated northern tribes gives no hint of cooperation. Judges 1:22-36, therefore, contrasts starkly with 1:4-21, reinforcing the claim that Judah was the rightful bearer of the divine promise.

It should be noted that 1:27-36 continues the pattern of quoting from Joshua, with less restructuring. In Joshua, these cities constitute a residuum, a margin that establishes the task and challenge of the next generation (cf. Josh 23:5-13). Judges 1, by identifying the events as "after the death of Joshua" and by citing these passages, serves as a report card, documenting the degree to which the post-Joshua generation fulfilled its mission. Thus Judges 1:27-28 cites Joshua 17:11-13, and Judges 1:29 adapts Joshua 16:10. Judges 1:30-35 does not directly quote Joshua, but the order of the tribes—Zebulun, Asher, Naphtali, and Dan—is found in no list of the tribes except that found in Joshua 19:10-51. Even there, Issachar intervenes between the first two tribes. Judges 1:34-36 also bears close comparison with Joshua 19:40-48. The second half of chapter 1 thus extends in detail the chapter's geographical orientation, moving steadily north. Intentional geographical ordering of material is well known from Assyrian display inscriptions.[1]

This northward movement embraces the entire chapter. It begins with Judah and Simeon. Simeon, according to Joshua 19:9, had its territory within Judah. Judges 1:21 then moves to Benjamin, who occupied the diamond-shaped plateau immediately north of Judah. Next the writer speaks in 1:22-26 of the "descendants of Joseph," which traditionally refers to Ephraim and Manasseh. He appears here, however, to consider all the northern tribes as the "descendants of Joseph," judging from the framing reference in 1:35b. Manasseh's mention before Ephraim in 1:27-29 is the only point in the sequence that does not strictly move northward, since Ephraim was south of Manasseh. Although Dan had been assigned land in the south, they migrated to the far north (ch 18), thus appearing last in the list. In a skilled literary move, 1:34-35a leaves Dan's fate uncertain as the tribe is still without an inheritance, creating an arc of tension resolved only by the resumption of this issue in chapter 18. Throughout, the passages cited from Joshua are altered, sometimes slightly, other times significantly, to focus the success or failure of the tribes, stressing the specifics of the failure of the tribe noted, followed by a statement of the results.

The Lord's Messenger Comes to Bokim (2:1-5). This section brings the first part of the prologue to a conclusion by depicting the angel of the Lord moving against Israel. The term "went up" (Heb., *'alah* [TH5927, ZH6590]) appears repeatedly in 1:1-36 denoting military assault; here, it also implies hostile intent. The angel's speech in 2:1b-3 bristles with hostility, branding the failures of 1:1-36 as breaches of the covenant. This condemnation comes as a surprise, since neither idolatry nor any clear charge of sin appear in 1:1-36. Judges 2:1-5 unmasks the "failure" of chapter 1 as sin by omission. If the identification of Bokim with the "other" Gilgal near Shechem is correct (see note on 2:1), then the angel's path from Gilgal to Bokim embraces the full movement of the sanctuary in Joshua from Gilgal (Josh 4:18-19) to Shechem (Josh 24), adding to the poignancy of this unit's main point: The era of Joshua is long gone. The despair and weeping with which the first section of the prologue concludes augurs ill for the story to come. The sacrifices closing the paragraph are thus vacant gestures.

This chapter provides a paradigm of compromise and failure. It explores the degrees by which Israel's mission was eroded and the inexorable process inaugurated by compromise. Most chilling is the fact that, though no explicit intention to compromise the covenant is ever expressed by Israel in chapter 1, the angelic indictment of 2:1-5 clearly brands their failure as grievous sin. Compromise, by its very nature, never announces itself as sin; but in its subtle degrees and shades, it undercuts the entire mission and life of the community of faith.

ENDNOTE

1. For specific information, see A. K. Grayson, "Histories and Historians of the Ancient Near East: Assyria and Babylonia," *Orientale* 49 (1980):152; H. Tadmor, "The Historical Inscriptions of Adad-Nirari III," *Iraq* 35 (1973):141.

B. Fractured Covenant (2:6–3:6)

[6]After Joshua sent the people away, each
of the tribes left to take possession of the
land allotted to them. [7]And the Israelites
served the LORD throughout the lifetime
of Joshua and the leaders who outlived
him—those who had seen all the great
things the LORD had done for Israel.

[8]Joshua son of Nun, the servant of the
LORD, died at the age of 110. [9]They buried
him in the land he had been allocated, at
Timnath-serah* in the hill country of
Ephraim, north of Mount Gaash.

[10]After that generation died, another generation grew up who did not acknowledge
the LORD or remember the mighty things
he had done for Israel.

[11]The Israelites did evil in the LORD's
sight and served the images of Baal.
[12]They abandoned the LORD, the God of
their ancestors, who had brought them
out of Egypt. They went after other gods,
worshiping the gods of the people around
them. And they angered the LORD. [13]They
abandoned the LORD to serve Baal and the
images of Ashtoreth. [14]This made the LORD
burn with anger against Israel, so he
handed them over to raiders who stole
their possessions. He turned them over to
their enemies all around, and they were
no longer able to resist them. [15]Every time
Israel went out to battle, the LORD fought
against them, causing them to be defeated, just as he had warned. And the people
were in great distress.

16Then the LORD raised up judges to res-
cue the Israelites from their attackers.
17Yet Israel did not listen to the judges
but prostituted themselves by worshiping
other gods. How quickly they turned
away from the path of their ancestors,
who had walked in obedience to the
LORD's commands.
18Whenever the LORD raised up a judge
over Israel, he was with that judge and
rescued the people from their enemies
throughout the judge's lifetime. For the
LORD took pity on his people, who were
burdened by oppression and suffering.
19But when the judge died, the people re-
turned to their corrupt ways, behaving
worse than those who had lived before
them. They went after other gods, serving
and worshiping them. And they refused to
give up their evil practices and stubborn
ways.
20So the LORD burned with anger
against Israel. He said, "Because these
people have violated my covenant, which
I made with their ancestors, and have ig-
nored my commands, 21I will no longer
drive out the nations that Joshua left un-
conquered when he died. 22I did this to
test Israel—to see whether or not they
would follow the ways of the LORD as their
ancestors did." 23That is why the LORD left
those nations in place. He did not quickly
drive them out or allow Joshua to conquer
them all.

CHAPTER 3

These are the nations that the LORD left
in the land to test those Israelites who
had not experienced the wars of Canaan.
2He did this to teach warfare to genera-
tions of Israelites who had no experience
in battle. 3These are the nations: the Phi-
listines (those living under the five Phi-
listine rulers), all the Canaanites, the
Sidonians, and the Hivites living in the
mountains of Lebanon from Mount Baal-
hermon to Lebo-hamath. 4These people
were left to test the Israelites—to see
whether they would obey the commands
the LORD had given to their ancestors
through Moses.
5So the people of Israel lived among the
Canaanites, Hittites, Amorites, Perizzites,
Hivites, and Jebusites, 6and they inter-
married with them. Israelite sons married
their daughters, and Israelite daughters
were given in marriage to their sons. And
the Israelites served their gods.

2:9 As in parallel text at Josh 24:30; Hebrew reads *Timnath-heres,* a variant spelling of Timnath-serah.

NOTES

2:6 *After Joshua sent the people away, each of the tribes left to take possession of the land allotted to them.* In 2:6-9 the writer quotes Josh 24:28-31 with a change in order. In Joshua, the dismissal of the people (Josh 24:28) is followed by Joshua's death and burial (Josh 24:29-30) and then by a notation that the people served Yahweh all the days of Joshua and the elders who outlived him (Josh 24:31). The author of Judges repeats the passage, but places the statement about the faithfulness of Israel directly after the dismissal. The shift creates a caesura that heightens the contrast between the era of faithfulness and the rise of the new, faithless generation.

2:7 *those who had seen all the great things the LORD had done for Israel.* In speaking of the previous generation's experience of Yahweh's mighty acts, the Joshua author used the term "knew" ("experienced" in NLT, Josh 24:31). The Judges author changed this to "had seen" to highlight the direct experience of the previous generation as witnesses. (On Judges' literary dependence on Joshua, see references in note on 1:1.)

2:9 *Timnath-serah.* Lit., "Timnath-Heres" or "portion of the sun," entailing a possible allusion to a solar deity. This is probably the correct place name, but the NLT alters it to match Josh 19:50 and Josh 24:30, which have "Timnath-serah," which, if not a misspelling, might mean "portion of excess" (ABD 6.557-558).

2:10 ***another generation grew up.*** The Hebrew construction emphasizes "other"; the new generation was not merely subsequent, but different in character.

did not acknowledge the LORD. The NLT renders an important nuance of "know" (*yada'* [TH3045, ZH3359]). The term can denote mere cognition, but typically implies a deeper engagement of the knower with the known, as in recognizing a friend or relative, or coming to care deeply about something. It also has a political nuance derived from treaties and oaths, suggesting acknowledgment of the claims and authority of one's superior to the exclusion of others.

2:11 ***The Israelites did evil in the LORD's sight.*** This expression becomes fundamental for a large section of the book, with variants ("again/still did evil" in 3:7, 11-12; 4:1; 6:1; 10:6; 13:1). Israel's evildoing forms the most consistent element of the so-called cyclical pattern of the book. Though specified as violating the first commandment in 3:7, this specification does not appear again until 10:6-18, leaving the reader to imagine what forms this evil took in the meantime. A review of the occurrences of "evil in Yahweh's eyes" in the OT reveals numerous possibilities! The delaying of specific claims to idolatry (after the Othniel account) until 10:6-18 contributes to the sense that the later narratives paint a darker portrait of the nation than the earlier ones.

served the images of Baal. Lit., "served the Baals." "Baal" can denote a plurality of gods, including a range of local variants on the Canaanite storm and fertility deity. While the Decalogue distinguishes between worshiping other gods and worshiping images, in the Canaanite context the distinction is moot.

2:13 ***Baal and . . . Ashtoreth.*** Baal is the storm god and the god of fertility in northwest Semitic religion. In the Ugaritic texts his consort is normally Anat, but Ashtoreth also appears as a consort of Baal, though less frequently. She is associated with Ishtar and the planet Venus, and in the OT with Sidon. A temple to Ashtoreth apparently stood in Beth-shan, where the Philistines exhibited Saul's weapons after hanging his corpse on the city wall (1 Sam 31:8-13).

2:14 ***raiders.*** Heb., *shosim* [TH8154A, ZH9115] (also in 2:16); it could possibly refer to a category of groups in ancient Canaan, mentioned in Egyptian texts. The "Shasu" of the Egyptian texts were tribally organized "enclosed" nomadic pastoralists. They were fierce in battle, wielding axes and spears, and wore clothing resembling berets and kilts (Yadin 1963:1.230-233; Redford 1992:271-280; Drews 1993:183; R. Miller 2005:95-96; Rainey 2008). Egyptian texts portray them as rebellious, quarrelsome highwaymen, mercenaries, and brigands. Documentation places them throughout Palestine and on both sides of the Jordan. Interestingly, three Egyptian texts associate the Shasu with the name Yahweh (Redford 1992:271-272). Their presence typifies the chaos that reigned not just in Palestine, but throughout the whole eastern Mediterranean following the cultural meltdown accompanying the transition between the Late Bronze Age and the first Iron Age.

2:16 ***the LORD raised up judges.*** The expression "raised up," asserting the divine origin of the judges, appears subsequently in Judges only in connection with Othniel and Ehud (3:9, 15). This clearly connotes the author's approval of these two judges, and leaves some question about the others. The sense of "judge" for the actions and actors in these stories is discussed in the Introduction. In comparison with the stories that follow, the absence from this passage of any reference to Israel's outcry or repentance, or to the Spirit of Yahweh, is striking.

2:17 ***Yet Israel did not listen to the judges.*** Note the friction between this claim and 2:18-19, which seems to imply that Israel did serve Yahweh during the judges' lifetimes. This passage, however, makes no statement about the judges' impact on the obedience of the people. Ambivalence about the actual religious effectiveness of these figures marks the book as a whole.

prostituted themselves. This expression uses the term *zanah* [TH2181, ZH2388], typically denoting adultery or prostitution, as an image for Israel's apostasy. This idiom, rather common in the OT and so critical in this passage, ironically appears only seldom in the rest of the book to denote apostasy (cf. 8:27, 33) though the noun form "prostitute" appears (11:1; 16:1) along with a related verbal form denoting marital abandonment (19:2, but cf. note there).

by worshiping other gods. How quickly they turned away from the path of their ancestors, who had walked in obedience to the LORD's commands.

2:18 ***the LORD took pity on his people.*** The writer predicates deliverance not on the outcry or repentance of the people, but appeals solely to Yahweh's pity.

2:20 ***the LORD burned with anger against Israel.*** This outbreak of divine wrath is the second reported in this passage, suggesting a structure of two "sin-wrath" sequences, structuring the unit not as a "cycle" but as a linear slope from apostasy to wrath, leading to deliverance by judges, to which the Israelites responded with even worse rebellion, leading to a renewed divine wrath, issuing in the statements of 2:20b-23 and the state of affairs summarized in 3:1-4.

these people have violated my covenant. Explicit references to the Lord's "covenant" (*berith* [TH1285, ZH1382]) with his people are rare in Judges (cf. 2:1-5). Direct divine speech to Israel as a whole, as opposed to speech mediated by an oracle (cf. 1:2-3; 20:18, 23, 27-28), angel (2:1-5), or prophet (6:7-10), appears only in 2:20-23 and 10:10-14, though it is not clear how these messages were conveyed to the Israelites. Both instances of direct divine speech are condemnations.

2:21 ***I will no longer drive out the nations that Joshua left unconquered when he died.*** The exact reasons given for nations remaining in the land after Joshua vary (cf. 3:1-5) and reflect the complexity of the process of the settlement and of Israel's emerging national and religious awareness. A range of theological perceptions arose as Israel pondered the problem of its national and religious identity and boundaries.

2:22 ***to test Israel.*** The verb used here is identical to that in Gen 22:1, used of God's testing Abraham by commanding the sacrifice of Isaac. These verses state that Yahweh chose to allow some of the nations to remain by design, specifically to see if Israel would be obedient. This stands in some tension with the idea that the nations remained solely because of Israel's failure to drive them all out (cf. 1:19, 27, 31; 2:2-3). The text goes on to state that Yahweh intentionally limited Joshua's success in order to test the next generation's obedience. This theme returns in 3:4 after a digression in 3:1-3 that modifies this theme significantly.

3:1 ***to test those Israelites who had not experienced the wars of Canaan.*** Here the term "test" connotes something different from 2:22 and carries a more pedagogical nuance. The present Israelites lacked the knowledge (NLT "experience") of the "wars of Canaan" (by which the writer might be referring to the conquest but possibly also the ongoing wars of settlement).

3:2 ***He did this to teach warfare to generations of Israelites who had no experience in battle.*** The syntax of the sentence in this passage is difficult for translators attempting to link its phrases together into a coherent whole. The Hebrew reads "only in order that the generations of the Israelites might know, to teach them war, only those who had not formerly known them." Note this statement softens the punitive note of the previous words about the remaining nations.

3:3 ***the nations.*** The nations that follow largely resided outside the original area of Israelite settlement. The list loosely mirrors the list of lands yet to be taken in Josh 13:1-7. The

Philistines settled in Gaza on the southern coast, which marked the southern boundary of Canaan in most Egyptian texts (ABD 6.17-18). Sidon was a port city of ancient Phoenicia on the northern coast that lay in the region assigned to the tribe of Asher (Josh 19:28), noted as unconquered in 1:31. Later, the Sidonians are said to have oppressed Israel (10:12), and Israel served the gods of Sidon, among others (10:6). The Sidonians typified peaceful, secure isolation to the Danite spies (18:7, 28). Lebo-hamath, Mount Lebanon, seems to denote the region between Mount Baal-hermon, the tallest peak in the region at over 10,000 feet (ABD 4:269-270) and Lebo-hamath. The latter literally means "the entrance of Hamath" and in several passages marks the upper limit of the Promised Land (Num 34:7-9; Josh 13:5; Ezek 47:16; ABD 3:36-37). Thus the author's noting the presence of these people, particularly in the north, is somewhat puzzling, since these regions did not form the objective of the conquest. These northern points previously demarcated the boundary between the Egyptian and Hittite spheres of influence.

3:4 ***to test the Israelites.*** The author turns back to the theme noted in 3:1, that the remaining nations serve as a test of obedience, a function not identical to serving simply as punishment for failure.

3:5 ***lived among.*** The use of the phrase "lived among" harks back to 1:29-30, near the end of that chapter's step-wise decline. Israel, intended to be triumphant, is reduced to an enclave among the nations over which they were to be victorious.

3:6 ***and they intermarried . . . and . . . served their gods.*** The writer in 3:5-6 summarizes the whole failure of Israel. They lived among the enemies, they intermarried among the enemies, and they capitulated and served their enemies' gods.

COMMENTARY

As with 1:1, so also the second part of the prologue links back to the book of Joshua, recapitulating and reframing the report of Joshua's death. This section also presents what is commonly taken to be the "Deuteronomistic" prologue to the hero narratives. Noth (1991:69-76) argued that the original form of the Deuteronomic History passed from the end of Joshua 23 directly to Judges 2:6, with Joshua 24 and Judges 1:1–2:5 being later interpolations, though not necessarily from the same hand. His literary analysis coheres whether or not 2:6–3:6 is considered "Deuteronomistic" in perspective. Joshua 24—Judges 3:6 greatly enlarges on and interprets the historical transition between Joshua and the era of apostasy between Joshua's death and the rise of the monarchy. That 2:6–3:6 is Deuteronomistic seems doubtful, though it certainly does not contradict Deuteronomy's perspective (see Introduction).

This section views Israel's experience after Joshua's death from the angle of religious faithfulness rather than from a military perspective. As in the preceding unit, Joshua's death is made the turning point (2:6-9) at which Israel turns away from Yahweh, despite the efforts of the judges (2:10-19). The section then moves to a speech of divine anger in which Yahweh's promises to drive out the nations are rescinded as Joshua had threatened (Josh 23:13) per the warnings of Moses (cf. Exod 34:12; Num 33:55; Deut 7:16), and the settlement as a victorious military operation is terminated (2:20–3:4). A summary of the entire opening section closes the first major unit of Judges (3:5-6).

Judges 2:6-9 quotes Joshua 24:28-31, but rearranges the sentences to identify

Joshua's death with Israel's spiritual transition. The description asserts the effectiveness of Joshua and the "leaders [lit., elders] who outlived him" (the conquest generation) in eliciting Israel's fidelity, a task at which later leaders failed. A standard is set by which later generations will be judged. By declaring that Joshua dismissed them "to take possession of the land" (2:6), the writer frankly accepts that the conquest did not complete this task. The conquest was about defeating the foe, breaking the back of the Late Bronze Age imperium, shattering the hegemony of Egypt exercised via its oppressive surrogates (the Canaanite city-state kings), ending the chaotic warring and looting of plunderers and pillagers, and creating an environment in which a new community could be formed. The book of Judges should have been the story of how Israel constructed that community as an alternative to both the preceding imperium and the barbarism that had blanketed Canaan in the form of the Sea Peoples, Apiru, Shasu, bedouin, and bandits. But such was not to be. Judges 2:10-13 declares the faithlessness of the generation after Joshua and the elders, which knew neither Yahweh nor his acts. This language, reminiscent of Pharaoh's in Exodus 5, denotes not innocent ignorance, but intentional ignorance of Yahweh's gracious salvation and self-disclosure.

Judges 2:11-19 is often understood as introducing the "cyclical" stories in 3:7–16:31, since many of the introductory and concluding phrases are brought together here. This, however, is not strictly accurate. A simple overview of 3:7–16:31 would need to emphasize the *repeated* character of the apostasies, oppressions, etc., as 2:18-19 does. Judges 2:11-13, on the other hand, speaks of a single doing evil in Yahweh's eyes. The entire period is thus branded as a single, gigantic falling away. The "cycles" are part of one cycle. The sequence of verbs in 2:11b-13 identifies the violation of the first commandment as the essence of Israel's evil. A chiastic bracket formed by the words "served (2:11b) . . . abandoned . . . abandoned . . . serve[d] (2:13)" encloses three verbs: "went after . . . worship[ed] . . . angered." Though there are many ways that an Israelite might do evil in Yahweh's eyes, all other evils descend from this first, fatal confusion.

Judges 2:14-15 describes the outworking of Yahweh's wrath—his personal opposition to his people's infidelity. Yahweh acted indirectly through historical forces to hand Israel over to its enemies. He left Israel impotent in defense (2:14b) and offense (2:15a). It could neither hold on to the land already taken, nor expand its possession. The fulfillment of the promise of the land was thus in immediate jeopardy. Apostate Israel could now count Yahweh himself among its foes.

Judges 2:16-19 describes the judges as God's overture to unfaithful Israel. In contrast to the stories in 3:7–16:31, the judges are not said to be raised up in response to Israel's cry, but are sent on divine initiative, an expression of divine compassion (2:16, 18). Verses 17-19 identify two problems with the judges: Verses 18-19 show a judge's impact was limited to that judge's lifetime. Moreover, 2:17 emphatically states—in tension with 2:18-19—that Israel did not even heed the judges during their lives, but "prostituted themselves." This unusual term appears elsewhere in Judges only in 8:27-35, where it describes the Hebrews' infatuation with the image made by Gideon. Verses 16-19 also fail to state explicitly that the judges actually elicited faithful service to Yahweh. Thus, 2:19b notes the judges had no effect on

Israel's penchant for treachery (a point emphasized by 2:17-19's use of several terms found in 2:11-13).

In 2:20-23, Yahweh's wrath breaks out afresh. This unit describes not a recurring cycle, but a process of decline: Apostasy led to oppression (2:11-15), and when Israel persisted in betrayal despite the judges (2:16-19), divine wrath reasserted itself. Here at last, Yahweh's wrath finds expression not in inarticulate historical forces, but in a rare divine speech (see note on 2:20). In this indictment, as in 2:1-3, God accuses Israel of breaking covenant, which causes him to withdraw support in the conquest. This speech also makes explicit what 1:1–2:5 only implied: The nations remaining after Joshua would be a test for Israel.

Judges 3:1-4 concludes the second unit of the introduction, listing the nations Yahweh allowed to remain, and taking up the concept, implicit in 1:1–2:5 and explicit in 2:20-23, of Yahweh intentionally leaving some of Joshua's enemies undefeated as a trial for Israel's fidelity. The Hebrew *nasah* [TH5254, ZH5814], usually translated "tempt," is better rendered "test" (NLT, NIV) or "try." It connotes not so much incitement to evil as the attempt to discern the quality or suitability of something, as when David "tries" Saul's armor (1 Sam 17:39). The list of remaining nations (3:3) is bracketed by statements specifying the nature of the test. Judges 3:1b-2 emphasizes the test's beneficent, pedagogical intent. The nations remained so that a new generation might learn directly of Yahweh's action for Israel in the "wars of Canaan." In the context of the conquest, learning warfare meant instruction in total fidelity to Yahweh, total obedience to his instructions, and total confidence in his power. Verse 4 makes this explicit: The remaining enemies would challenge Israel to an obedience comparable to that of their faithful fathers. The new generation would have the chance to be like their faithful forebears, to experience God's direct saving action in their own lifetime.

Verses 5-6 note three specific failures of Israel after the death of Joshua that summarize the sad outcome of Israel's testing and give the essence of both major sections of the introduction (1:10–2:5 and 2:6–3:4). First, "lived among the Canaanites" (3:5; cf. 1:31-33) epitomizes Israel's military failure, as 1:1–2:5 depicts. They failed the challenge of 3:1b-2. Second, intermarriage with the Canaanites (3:6) constitutes a cultural surrender that, though not specifically mentioned in 1:1–3:4, seems the logical outcome of the military failure and the making of covenants with the Canaanites (2:1-5). This is a clear expression of compromise and a failure of the test of 3:4. The element of intermarriage also probably foreshadows the career of Samson. Third, "served their gods" (3:6) well captures the invective of 2:6–3:4.

As a whole, 1:1–3:6 characterizes the entire period "after the death of Joshua" as one of increasing faithlessness and frustration. Judges 1:1–2:5 explores the tacit apostasy of compromise, while 2:6-23 delineates explicit apostasy and its debilitating impact on Israel's mission. No easy relationship between sinfulness and failure, or faithfulness and success is presented. In 1:1–2:5 failure *is* sin; in 2:6-23 failure *results* from sin. In 3:1-6, the failures of a past generation provide a challenge and opportunity to the next. Both introductory units emphasize in advance that Israel will not stop sinning. The judges, even when successful in deliverance, still ultimately fail in eliciting covenant fidelity. This introduction (1:1–3:6) reveals that

Israel's problem is not inadequate power but vacillating character. The report of the ultimate failure of the judges (2:16-19; 3:5-6) and its acclaim of Judah (1:1-18) hint at Judah, and possibly its most famous tribesman, David, as the true channel for realizing God's promise. More importantly, the introduction teaches that even while living in the land, Israel could abort its mission. To live in Canaan, without serving Yahweh, was to cease to be truly "Israel." Holding God's gift (the land) without faithfully holding to God himself is a doomed travesty. Centuries later, the exiled Judeans who preserved the book of Judges discovered the crucial converse of this principle: A community keeping faith with Yahweh, even outside the land, constitutes the true Israel.

◆ II. The Succession of the Judges: Dissolution (3:7–16:31)

A. Othniel: The Exemplary Judge (3:7-11)

7 The Israelites did evil in the LORD's sight.
They forgot about the LORD their God, and
they served the images of Baal and the
Asherah poles. 8 Then the LORD burned
with anger against Israel, and he turned
them over to King Cushan-rishathaim of
Aram-naharaim.* And the Israelites served
Cushan-rishathaim for eight years.
9 But when the people of Israel cried out
to the LORD for help, the LORD raised up a
rescuer to save them. His name was Othniel,
the son of Caleb's younger brother, Kenaz.
10 The Spirit of the LORD came upon him, and
he became Israel's judge. He went to war
against King Cushan-rishathaim of Aram,
and the LORD gave Othniel victory over him.
11 So there was peace in the land for forty
years. Then Othniel son of Kenaz died.

3:8 *Aram-naharaim* means "Aram of the two rivers," thought to have been located between the Euphrates and Balih Rivers in northwestern Mesopotamia.

NOTES

3:7 ***The Israelites did evil in the LORD's sight.*** In subsequent episodes (e.g., 3:12; 4:1), except for 6:1, the form of this introductory statement will be akin to "Once again [or better, "still"] the Israelites did evil."

They forgot about the LORD. The specific nature of Israel's evil will not be specified so directly as a violation of the first and second commandments again until 10:6-16.

3:8 ***King Cushan-rishathaim of Aram-naharaim.*** The name means "the Ethiopian King of Double-Wickedness from Mesopotamia." Scholars sometimes propose changing "Aram" to "Edom" under the impression that a minor south-Judean figure could not have defeated a Syrian king. Others emend *rish'athaim* [TH3573, ZH3937] to *rosh hattamani* [TH7218/8489, ZH8031/9404] (chief of the Temanites). Still others try to equate this figure with a Syrian ruler who seized the throne of Egypt around 1200 BC (ABD 1.1220), hence explaining the tie both to Cush and Mesopotamia. Clearly not the name his mother gave him, the title is an alias serving the literary function of the story.

3:9 ***But.*** Cf. NIV, RSV, ESV. No contrast is implied in the Hebrew. The verbs move relentlessly in a series of consecutive forms for the entire narrative without a single disjunctive clause. Only the introduction of the deliverer's name and title break the flow of the verbs.

when the people of Israel cried out to the LORD for help. The verb "cry" carries no inherent nuance of repentance or even appeal, but simply denotes the cry of one in agony. Sometimes it characterizes the "sound track" of sin as it comes to Yahweh's ears (cf. Gen 18:20-21; 19:13; Isa 5:7).

the* LORD *raised up a rescuer to save them. The verb "save" and the title "savior" have a peculiar usage in Judges (see commentary).

His name was Othniel, the son of Caleb's younger brother, Kenaz. The name and patronymic of the hero intrude awkwardly into the flow of verbs. Lit., "Yahweh raised up a savior, and he saved them, Othniel the son of Kenaz, the youngest brother of Caleb, and the Spirit of Yahweh came upon him, and he judged Israel."

3:10 *The Spirit of the* LORD *came upon him.* Lit., "the Spirit of the Lord *was* (*hayah* [TH1961, ZH2118]) upon him" (cf. 11:29). This grammatical construction normally connotes an event transpiring and also appears in the receipt of prophetic revelation, lit., "the word of Yahweh was (or, happened) to me" (Jer 1:4). The sense is, "the Spirit of Yahweh happened to Othniel," captured in the NLT as "came upon."

he became Israel's judge. Despite the book title and the statements of 2:16-19, the heroes rarely receive the title of "judge" in the narratives. Of the major judges, Deborah alone performs the functions of a judge (4:4-5). The schematic notes on the minor judges, Jephthah, and Samson employ the verb "to judge."

He went to war . . . and the* LORD *gave Othniel victory. The account strikingly lacks the vivid narration characteristic of the subsequent stories. The presence of all the framing formulas both from 2:11–3:6 and from the narratives themselves, combined with the absence of any real "story" lends it a "fill in the blanks" quality.

3:11 *So there was peace in the land for forty years. Then Othniel son of Kenaz died.* The writer uses the concluding summaries to render a judgment on the heroes. Up through the Gideon story, the land "rests" for a period that is a multiple of the time of oppression. After Gideon, not only does the time of oppression exceed the period of the hero's career, the term "rest" drops out of the conclusions in silent censure.

COMMENTARY

Having presented a summary and analysis of the historical and theological dynamics of the era, the narrative now shifts to the demonstration of the writer's thesis that both the settlement and Israel's fidelity to Yahweh collapsed during the premonarchic era. Following the presentation of Othniel as the exemplary deliverer, the central section of the book divides into three segments, each featuring two major figures with a strong literary link: Ehud and Deborah (3:12–5:31), Gideon and Abimelech (6:1–10:5), and Jephthah and Samson (10:6–16:31). The first pair receives uncompromisingly positive treatment and may be termed "triumphant" judges. Both stories climax with the private, devastating murder of the principle villain. The curious shifting of Ehud's death notice from the concluding rubrics of his own story to a mere parenthetical clause in the introduction to the Deborah story (4:1) "hook-and-eye" these two major blocks of material together. The second major section explicitly links Gideon and Abimelech both by genealogy and by direct causation: Gideon's decline of inherited rule creates a power vacuum cited by Abimelech in 9:1-2 as the basis for his own elevation to power. Israel's lapse into chaos under Abimelech, preceded by the thoroughly ambivalent portrayal of Gideon/Jerub-baal, merits labeling this unit as "transitional judges." The Jephthah and Samson stories articulate with one another around the theme of a vow and carry strong signs of the author's disapproval—hence, the characterization "tragic judges." Indeed, the Samson narrative provides an extended illustration of the threefold critique of 3:5-6—in the person of Samson, Israel lives among their enemies, intermarries with them, and serves their gods.

In chapter 3 the story of Othniel has four distinct features. First, the narrative consists almost entirely of skeleton expressions, with little actual narrative. It looks like a preliminary report form for the narratives in Judges in which the blanks were simply filled in with the names of the oppressor and judge. Second, it contains the most complete and representative set of framework expressions in the book. The narrator includes all the elements of the pattern found in 2:11-19, as well as elements found in the later narratives but *not* found in the preface, such as reference to Israel's outcry and the coming of the Spirit of Yahweh upon the judge. Third, the enemy's name, Cushan-rishathaim, draws attention. As it stands, the name means "The Ethiopian King of Compound-Criminality (or Double-Dastardliness) from Mesopotamia." All attempts to emend the text flounder on their speculative character and failure to fit the narrative. Characteristic of the heroic tradition, the villain's name was likely an alias or nickname for a now unknown person. As a caricature, the name emphasizes Othniel's foe as the quintessential enemy. The regional sweep implied by "Cushite . . . Syria" also suggests "baddest man in the country." Fourth, Othniel is probably the only southern judge, and is the only judge representing the faithful conquest generation (see note on 1:13). The narrative thus pits an ideal hero against an archetypical foe in a regionally comprehensive context. Furthermore, the Othniel story contains elements from all aspects of the Judges material: the stories, the frameworks, and even the introduction. The author intended it to serve as an exemplar passage, highlighting all the characteristics by which the reader can evaluate a judge.

Because this is a story of an exemplary judge, every feature of this narrative constitutes a standard. The sin of Israel finds explicit identification as forgetting Yahweh and serving Baal and Asherah. As a result, the wrath of Yahweh consigns them to "serve" Cushan for eight years. Upon their cry (not necessarily their repentance, see note on 3:9), Yahweh brings deliverance by raising up Othniel, who is explicitly named a "savior," a title used sparingly in the book (see below). Empowered by the Spirit of Yahweh, Othniel "judges" Israel (3:10)—the only time these two elements appear together in the book. Following the victory, the land rests for 40 years (five times the length of the period of oppression) until Othniel's death.

Forms of the word *yasha'* [TH3467, ZH3828] (to save, rescue) figure prominently in the preface (2:11-19) but display an unusual distribution in the rest of the book. The word, in various forms, appears just 22 times in Judges. After the moral-historical prologue (2:16, 18) only Othniel (3:9) and Ehud (3:15) of the "major" judges and Shamgar (3:31) and Tola (10:1) of the "minor" judges are said to "rescue" Israel, and only Othniel and Ehud receive the title "savior." Gideon, though called to save Israel "with the strength you have," denied his ability to do so (6:14-15). Yahweh thinned out Gideon's army due to confusion that might result as to who really saved Israel (7:2, 7). Despite these precautions, the Israelites came to believe Gideon saved them and subsequently offered him hereditary rule (8:22). In the prologue to the Jephthah story the verb stresses the impotence of Israel's chosen gods and the importunity of the remorseful (but not repentant) nation (10:12-14). Jephthah ultimately declares his need to save himself when abandoned by the Ephraimites, declaring (lit.) "there was no savior" (12:2-3). The angel of Yahweh says only that Samson will "begin to save" Israel (13:5). The last occurrence of the term appears in Samson's desperate cry of thirst in which he declares his own death would somehow negate the salvation wrought by God through him (15:18).

As the "total judge," Othniel became the standard by which to measure subsequent judges and, by extension, anyone claiming a charismatic anointing and the right to leadership. Later Jewish legends accentuate this exemplary portrayal, seeing "Othniel" as another name for Judah, said to be the direct successor of Joshua. Legend also claimed he was a scholar of the Torah, reproducing Moses's teachings from sheer "dialectic reasoning"; it even claimed he did not die, but was taken to paradise alive (Ginsberg 1913:4.29-30). It is hard to imagine how subsequent figures could even match, much less exceed, this standard. Thus, he provides, on one hand, a pattern for effective leadership, but on the other hand, a reminder of how rare that is! So rare, in fact, that the writer likely expects the reader to look for leadership outside the charismatic tradition.

B. Stage One: Triumph (3:12–5:31)

1. Ehud: The assassin deliverer (3:12–30)

[12]Once again the Israelites did evil in the LORD's sight, and the LORD gave King Eglon of Moab control over Israel because of their evil. [13]Eglon enlisted the Ammonites and Amalekites as allies, and then he went out and defeated Israel, taking possession of Jericho, the city of palms. [14]And the Israelites served Eglon of Moab for eighteen years.

[15]But when the people of Israel cried out to the LORD for help, the LORD again raised up a rescuer to save them. His name was Ehud son of Gera, a left-handed man of the tribe of Benjamin. The Israelites sent Ehud to deliver their tribute money to King Eglon of Moab. [16]So Ehud made a double-edged dagger that was about a foot* long, and he strapped it to his right thigh, keeping it hidden under his clothing. [17]He brought the tribute money to Eglon, who was very fat.

[18]After delivering the payment, Ehud started home with those who had helped carry the tribute. [19]But when Ehud reached the stone idols near Gilgal, he turned back. He came to Eglon and said, "I have a secret message for you."

So the king commanded his servants, "Be quiet!" and he sent them all out of the room.

[20]Ehud walked over to Eglon, who was sitting alone in a cool upstairs room. And Ehud said, "I have a message from God for you!" As King Eglon rose from his seat, [21]Ehud reached with his left hand, pulled out the dagger strapped to his right thigh, and plunged it into the king's belly. [22]The dagger went so deep that the handle disappeared beneath the king's fat. So Ehud did not pull out the dagger, and the king's bowels emptied.* [23]Then Ehud closed and locked the doors of the room and escaped down the latrine.*

[24]After Ehud was gone, the king's servants returned and found the doors to the upstairs room locked. They thought he might be using the latrine in the room, [25]so they waited. But when the king didn't come out after a long delay, they became concerned and got a key. And when they opened the doors, they found their master dead on the floor.

[26]While the servants were waiting, Ehud escaped, passing the stone idols on

his way to Seirah. 27When he arrived in the hill country of Ephraim, Ehud sounded a call to arms. Then he led a band of Israelites down from the hills.

28"Follow me," he said, "for the LORD has given you victory over Moab your enemy." So they followed him. And the Israelites took control of the shallow crossings of the Jordan River across from Moab, preventing anyone from crossing.

29They attacked the Moabites and killed about 10,000 of their strongest and most able-bodied warriors. Not one of them escaped. 30So Moab was conquered by Israel that day, and there was peace in the land for eighty years.

3:16 Hebrew *gomed,* the length of which is uncertain. **3:22** Or *and it came out behind.* **3:23** Or *and went out through the porch;* the meaning of the Hebrew is uncertain.

NOTES

3:12 ***Once again the Israelites did evil.*** The Hebrew idiom translated "once again" could just as easily be rendered "continued" [to do evil]. Though periods of rest are noted in the text, explicit references to repentance or righteousness are rare. Since 2:17-18 emphasizes that the Israelites did not in fact listen to their judges, but "played the harlot" more and more, perhaps "continued to do evil" resonates deeper than "once again."

the LORD gave King Eglon of Moab control over Israel. The name "Eglon" combines a word for "calf" (*'egel* [TH5695, ZH6319]) with a suffix (*-on*) common in Hebrew for forming adjectives, abstract nouns, or diminutives (Waltke and O'Connor 1990:92). It likely derived from an Akkadian noun formation designating a particular member of a larger class. Hence, the name Eglon likely means "little calf" or "the calflike one." Given Eglon's description in 3:17b, most readers cannot resist observing that the "calf" was fatted, though the language for Eglon's size does not support that view! Attempts to construe the name "Eglon" as demeaning or satiric appeal to English connotations of bovine nomenclature, but ancient Near Eastern usage identifies bulls and calves with deity, so that no such connotation attaches to the name in Hebrew.

because of their evil. The NLT compresses the Hebrew, which uses the full statement "because they did that which was evil in the eyes of Yahweh." The repetition in Hebrew strongly emphasizes this aspect of the introductory form. Only in this story does this formula appear twice.

3:13 ***Jericho, the city of palms.*** The Hebrew does not contain the word "Jericho," but the NLT rightly infers it from "city of palms" (cf. Deut 34:3). Perhaps the author wanted to put the connection between the headquarters of Israel's oppressor and the scene of Joshua's greatest triumph between the lines. Jericho, modern Tel Es-Sultan, possesses a fine spring that supports a date-palm grove. The town was allotted to Ehud's tribe, Benjamin (Josh 16:1, 7; 18:21). Strategically positioned near the northern tip of the Dead Sea, Jericho controlled the three roads leading up through the Judean desert to the strategic plateau that formed the Benjaminite heartland. By holding Jericho, Eglon cut off Benjamin from any contact to the east and gained three invasion routes. With the Philistines present in the western lowlands (cf. 3:31), the Benjaminites were confined to the little plateau between Jerusalem and Bethel, an area not much larger than 10 square miles. Jericho also provided Eglon with the best possible access back to his homeland in Moab.

3:15 ***But when the people of Israel cried out to the LORD for help.*** The NLT addition of "for help," though not explicit in the Hebrew, captures the idea that the verb employed does not imply repentance, but desperation.

the LORD again raised up a rescuer to save them. Only Othniel and Ehud receive the sobriquet "rescuer" (*moshia'* [TH3467B, ZH4635]), and they alone are said to be "raised up"

(Hiphil of *qum* [TH6965, ZH7756]) by Yahweh. The words "again" and "to save them," however, are lacking in the Hebrew. Their inclusion by the NLT harmonizes this passage with its counterpart in the Othniel story (3:9) but has no textual basis and is unnecessary.

His name was Ehud son of Gera, a left-handed man of the tribe of Benjamin. Since "Benjaminite" means "son of the right hand," Ehud's left-handedness strikes an ironic chord: A left-handed right-hander is one tricky guy! But "left-handed" scarcely captures the Heb., *'itter yad-yemino* [TH334, ZH360] (bound on/by his right hand), which suggests more a disabling of the right hand than a preference for the left. But it hardly denotes injury or defect, since 20:16 notes 700 more Benjaminite crack slingers and archers of the same condition. First Chronicles 12:1-2 identifies David's Benjaminite allies who could wield the bow or sling with either hand. Halpern (1988:40-43) comments on the peculiar advantage that a left-handed swordsman would have against right-handers in battle, reversing the normal sword-on-shield orientation, and rightly proposes Ehud belonged to a Benjaminite warrior elite whose training began early with boys having their right hands tied to promote facility with the left.

The Israelites sent Ehud to deliver their tribute money to King Eglon of Moab. It appears that Ehud is actually part of a group (cf. 3:18), but he clearly is the leader of the group. Indeed, Ehud's specialized combat skills made him the logical person to ride shotgun on the tribute run, ensuring the tribute arrived safely. Did his kinsmen know of his plan to assassinate Eglon? Their immediate response to his call to arms in 3:27-28 suggests readiness, so perhaps they intentionally dispatched Ehud with his hidden agenda.

3:16 ***So Ehud made a double-edged dagger.*** For Ehud to craft his own sword, likely from bronze, contrasts with the OT observation of a general lack of metallurgy and weapons among the Israelites (cf. 5:8b; 1 Sam 13:19-22) and comports well with his membership in an elite class with special abilities and resources. Bronze remained the dominant material in arms and armor throughout the first Iron Age (cf. 1 Sam 17:1-7).

about a foot long. The word *gomed* [TH1574, ZH1688] (about a foot) appears only here in the OT. Translators and commentators assume the word denotes a relatively short unit of measure since it governs *'orkah* [TH753, ZH802] (its length) and since the entire weapon seems to vanish into Eglon's belly. The LXX guesses "span" while the Targumists and rabbinic interpreters suggest "[short] cubit," i.e., the distance from the elbow to the knuckles, but with no valid philological basis. But must the word denote a unit of length? Since no ancient lexical sources identify this term as a unit of measure, and common terms for length were at hand, perhaps the author stresses not the sword's length, but its construction. Along with being double-edged, it possessed another feature characteristic of its entire length. The only cognate for *gomed* is Arabic *gamada,* which inscribes ideas such as rigidity or stiffness. Perhaps the author, who displays a strong interest in heroes' weapons, calls attention to the sword as "rigid or stiff" over its length.

he strapped it to his right thigh, keeping it hidden under his clothing. Although the text says nothing directly about the length of the sword (see note above "about a foot long"), the need for concealment implies a sword short enough to conceal while long enough to do the job (see below). The traditional Canaanite *khopesh* or sickle-sword could not be sheathed due to its shape and was ineffective at thrusting. These hindrances were overcome by straight blades (cf. Stone 2009:657-663; Yadin 1963:1.172-173, 206-207), which arrived in the Levant with the Sea Peoples during the transition between the Late Bronze Age and the Iron Age and are known to scholars as the Naue Type II. The functional (as opposed to decorative or ritual) Naue Type II swords found so far range from 19.5 to just over 33 inches. Ehud's sword would fall on the shorter end of that spectrum. In the end it is best to see this weapon as being a "double-edged combat sword." The sword would be long enough that its thrust would strike deeply and damage enough tissue to cause instantaneous, or at least very rapid, death.

Judging from reliefs from the ancient Near East, warriors typically slung their swords across their backs, or even across their chests, sometimes in scabbards, often not. Swords worn on the waist typically rode on the hip opposite the fighting hand, the "cross-draw" (cf. Yadin 1963: 1.222-223, 2.334-337). Ehud's left-handedness shifted his sword to an atypical position on the right thigh, increasing the likelihood that his weapon would go unnoticed until the moment of attack. A perusal of combat scenes from the ancient Near East reveals comparatively few left-handed swordsmen.

3:17 ***fat.*** Heb., *bari'* [TH1277, ZH1374] typically denotes the fatness of health and prosperity. Obesity does not seem to inhere in the word. Daniel and his friends, after some time on a diet of vegetables and water, are observed to be *bari'* (Dan 1:15; "better nourished," NLT). However, only here in the OT is *bari'* modified by "very," and 3:22 notes that Eglon's fat closed over the blade. But popular portrayals that make Eglon as a pile of blubber like "Jabba the Hutt" are misplaced. Rather, Eglon is better understood as a very prosperous, healthy, robust guy. Consider Eglon's era: The collapse of the Late Bronze Age imperial cultures ca. 1200 BC witnessed the emergence of new territorial states whose kings rose up through tribal cultures of chieftains and warlords. Such men were not ineffectual tubs of jello, but tough, resourceful men, always alert to potential threats to their power. Eglon likely was just such a man: powerful, resourceful, imposing, and dangerous.

3:18 ***with those who had helped.*** Lit., "and he dismissed the people who bore the tribute." It becomes clear at this point that Ehud is accompanied by a party of tribute bearers, whose dismissal allows him to return alone to complete his more pressing errand of assassinating Eglon.

3:19 ***the stone idols.*** Heb., *pesilim* [TH6456, ZH7178] (carved stones), typically used to denote idols that fit the traditional translation "graven image" (e.g., Deut 7:5, 25; 12:3); the term can also denote cast images. They need not be stone. The word, with its cognate *pesel* [TH6459, ZH7181], appears 54 times in the OT. Though Deuteronomy condemns *pesilim*, the Deuteronomistic History seldom utters the word with the same explicit revulsion found in the book of Deuteronomy. The word does not seem to be a distinctive Deuteronomistic term, but is more characteristic of prophetic texts. Second Chronicles 33–34 also uses the term in its distinctive supplements to the Deuteronomistic narratives of Amon and Josiah.

Gilgal. The name *gilgal* [TH1537, ZH1652] appears 40 times in the OT, only twice without the definite article. Possibly not a true proper name, it can denote any stone-encircled encampment (cf. Zertal 1991:28-49). Several sites in Israel could be in view in the several OT references to Gilgal (ABD 2.1022-1024). Located within sight of Jericho, Gilgal was the base camp of the conquest, first home of the Ark, and the scene of the circumcision of the wilderness-born conquest generation of Israelites and the first Passover in Canaan (Josh 5). It later became a pilgrimage destination (Hos 4:15; Amos 4:4; 5:5). There also, Joshua erected stone monuments when the Israelites crossed the Jordan (Josh 4). Might the "carved stones" mentioned here be those monuments? Joshua 4 did not use *pesel* or *pesilim* (see note above) and did not refer to the stones as carved or inscribed. Moreover, these terms never denote a legitimate monument to Yahweh. Still, the presence of idols at Gilgal, the very place where stone monuments from Joshua's time stood, would underscore the depths to which Israel had sunk.

he turned back. This rendering obscures a potentially important theological point. The Hebrew more literally reads "but he (emphatic) turned from the stone idols that were at

Gilgal." The images (*pesilim*; see note above) form a bracket around this section of the narrative. The murder of Eglon begins when Ehud "turns from the idols." (Notably, the LXX explicitly says Eglon returned from the idols.) Ehud's getaway is complete in 3:26b: "now he (emphatic) had crossed over the carved stones." Again, in 3:26, a word with dual use occurs; "cross over" in theological contexts means "transgress." While the author used these words in their normal senses of turning and crossing, the association with idols might also function ironically to connote repentance and violation of idols, as a framework for deliverance.

He came to Eglon and said. The Hebrew is quite abrupt, omitting the words "he came to Eglon" but moving from Ehud's about-face at the idols directly to his address to Eglon.

I have a secret message for you. "Secret message" (*debar-sether* [TH1697/5643, ZH1821/6260]) seems to be a double entendre, given the range of meaning for *dabar* [TH1697, ZH1821] (word, thing). On one hand, Ehud claimed to have a secret message for Eglon, on the other, he had a secret agenda for Eglon's demise. At this point, Eglon likely viewed Ehud as a collaborator; he had delivered the tribute and now returned without his countrymen present, claiming a secret message.

the king commanded his servants, "Be quiet!" and he sent them all out of the room. Ehud's plan required that the servants be outside and unsuspecting. What would have been so important about Ehud's announcement as to require total privacy? The delivery of tribute implied Ehud's loyalty as a vassal. Perhaps the king hoped for news of even more Israelite leaders submitting to his rule.

3:20 ***Ehud walked over to Eglon, who was sitting alone in a cool upstairs room.*** Halpern (1988:43-58) notes that the palace would have been two-stories high, with the throne at one end on the second level (*'aliyyah* [TH5944, ZH6608]), with a maintenance and storage area on the ground level. The audience chamber would be on the ground level, with the second story open above. Petitioners entered through a front door and stood below the king, who sat at the far end of the house in the upper chamber, which could be closed and locked. Windows on the second story of the house provided ventilation, hence the designation "cool upstairs room." While correct, the architectural features are somewhat muddled in the translation. Ehud did not "walk over" to Eglon so much as he "went up" into the king's physical presence. If Eglon assumed Ehud was a collaborator with a secret message, this face-to-face proximity would not disquiet him.

Ehud said, "I have a message from God for you!" The phrase *debar-sether* [TH1697/5643, ZH1821/6260] (a secret thing; 3:19) now becomes *debar-'elohim* [TH1697/430, ZH1821/466] (thing of/from God). The choice of *'elohim* rather than the Israelite national name for God, Yahweh (*yhwh* [TH3068, ZH3378]), perhaps served to further reduce the king's suspicions and reinforce his sense of Ehud's complicity.

3:21 ***plunged it into the king's belly.*** The Hebrew verb *taqa'* [TH8628, ZH9546] emphasizes the violence of the thrust that would have been necessary to damage enough tissue to cause what appears to be instantaneous incapacitation. When describing penetration, the verb can denote pounding a peg into the ground for a firm hold (Isa 22:23, 25) or through Sisera's temple (4:21) or even through Samson's braids (16:13-14). In the latter two, the text specifies not merely piercing, but piercing through: Jael's peg strikes the ground under Sisera's head, Delilah's peg fastens Samson's locks to the wall. The verb also describes Joab's ramming of three spears into (through?) the heart of Absalom (2 Sam 18:14) and also the fastening of the body of Saul to the wall of the temple in Beth-shan (1 Sam 31:10, MT). Clearly the writer describes a fierce, devastating, and deep thrust: Ehud "ran him right through." See further 3:22.

3:22 *The dagger went so deep that the handle disappeared beneath the king's fat. So Ehud did not pull out the dagger.* The NLT and a majority of interpreters assume Eglon was obese and that the text emphasizes this feature here. But Eglon's "fat" is better understood as thriving health (see note on 3:17), and the text suggests instead the violence of Ehud's thrust, such that the tip of the sword broke out through Eglon's back. This is seen in the use of *taqa'*[TH8628, ZH9546] ("thrust"; see note on 3:21). The thrust was so deep that the hilt entered the king's body and the fat of his abdomen enclosed around the grip. The writer's use of a hapax legomenon, *hannitsab* [TH5325, ZH5896], to describe the grip, points to the uniqueness of the sword's construction in this regard: Examples of the Naue II sword all lack a cross guard, making entry of the hilt after the blade possible. Most also featured a rounded pommel to facilitate a complete final thrust driven by the palm. The pommel would remain visible, but the grip could be thrust deeper. Ehud may well have left the sword in Eglon as a gruesome calling card.

the king's bowels emptied. A minority of scholars (so NIV translators) think this phrase, though present in Hebrew, is a scribal error. The clause visually and aurally resembles the next clause, leading some to suspect a miscopied text (dittography). On the other hand, medical professionals report that evacuation of the bowels often follows immediately upon massive trauma or death, so this event is not out of place and suggests the king was instantly killed or at least incapacitated. No short knife or dagger could have the effect of immediate incapacitation or death on a sizeable man. I received the following communication from Dr. Joseph W. Richardson, MD, an emergency medicine physician at St. Joseph's Hospital in Lexington, Kentucky, in response to a query about whether and how a single blade to the abdomen might have the effects noted in this story (emphasis added):

> There are two possible causes for immediate (or almost immediate) loss of consciousness with a belly wound. The first would result in a very rapid death. The aorta is large in the upper abdomen. If it were transected at a level above the navel, a human's entire blood volume would/could be spilled in less than 45 seconds. No blood flow to the brain and a person loses consciousness in about 5 seconds. This injury could produce almost immediate incapacitation. It would probably require a sword being thrust completely through the abdomen and exiting to the left of the spine, as the aorta is somewhat protected by the boney spine at that level. The second phenomenon would produce an immediate loss of consciousness, but would not necessarily be followed by death. The tenth cranial nerve controls both heart rate and bowel motility. When this nerve is stimulated in the abdomen, a decrease in heart rate rapidly ensues. A decrease in heart rate translates as a decrease in cardiac output which translates as decreased blood flow to the brain. This again results in a loss of consciousness within 5 seconds. I strongly suspect that this poor king experienced both of these phenomena. Vagal stimulation producing a rapid loss of consciousness from which he never awakened as his blood volume was probably either spilled on the floor or lost within his abdominal cavity. I wish I could say that I've never seen this scenario, but I have. A few years ago a local businessman committed suicide by the Japanese traditional hara-kiri. In this ritual, a sword is thrust through the abdomen just left of the naval and pulled upwards with a violent thrust/pull. Again, a rapid loss of consciousness with rapidly following death. (Richardson 2008)

Incidentally, Dr. Richardson had, only a short time prior to this communication, treated a man who had attempted hara-kiri, so he had become intimately familiar with traumatic abdominal sword wounds. Likewise, ancient heroic literature provides vivid descriptions of these wounds and their effects (Stone 2009:658-660).

3:23 ***Then Ehud closed and locked the doors of the room and escaped down the latrine.*** King and Stager (2001:30-33) have a helpful description of ancient locks and keys. Though lacking a key, Ehud had to have a way of locking the door, likely from the inside, which left him in the room. How did he escape the scene of his deed? Halpern (1988:59-60) has shown how an upper throne chamber toilet emptied into a chamber below, on the ground level of the building. Iron Age toilets often had a removable seat over a larger opening. Ehud could have removed the toilet seat, dropped (carefully) through the opening into the area below and then walked out into the audience chamber. From there, he exited the palace normally, whereupon the guards returned to their normal posts inside. All seemed perfectly normal, as 3:24 notes.

3:24 ***After Ehud was gone, the king's servants returned and found the doors to the upstairs room locked.*** Clearly to the servants, nothing seemed amiss, suggesting their presumption that Ehud was not particularly dangerous. Ehud's exit must have appeared to them perfectly innocuous. This rules out a leap or descent from an upper window, suggested by some commentators.

They thought he might be using the latrine. The Hebrew idiom "covering the feet" lies behind the NLT's "using the latrine." Since this toilet was a permanent architectural feature of the building, and private, the term "latrine" with its communal and even improvised connotations might not be the best representation of the Hebrew. Since the Hebrew idiom names an activity, not a place, "relieving himself" might be the best expression. More notable is the implication of the grammatical construction of the clause, which begins with the restrictive particle *'ak* [TH389, ZH421], followed by the participle "covering" with the independent pronoun, then the object "feet." It can be graphically translated, "he must be the one relieving himself in the cooling chamber." The text suggests the servants already knew someone was in the process of using the toilet. The locked doors of the upper chamber confirmed who it was.

3:25 ***so they waited. But when the king didn't come out after a long delay.*** One did not simply walk in on a king in the ancient world. Entering a king's private chambers uninvited risked death (Esth 4:11).

they became concerned. Lit., "until they were ashamed." Shame in the ancient world was not mere embarrassment, but a sense of social paralysis, of not knowing what to do, because, for whatever reason, no correct or socially appropriate action presented itself. Intruding on the king was potentially fatal, but the king's silence and inaccessibility also posed problems.

got a key. Getting a key was more trouble than modern readers might think. Keys to Iron Age locks were "large enough to be slung over the shoulder" (King and Stager 2001:33).

they found their master dead on the floor. The Hebrew is more abrupt in presenting the humiliating scene, using *hinneh* [TH2009, ZH2180] to stress immediacy: "[Right] there was their master, fallen down dead." The phrase is similar to that of the discovery of Sisera dead on the tent floor (4:22).

3:26 ***While the servants were waiting, Ehud escaped, passing the stone idols.*** The Hebrew uses disjunctive clauses to frame the narrative of 3:24b-25 with a series of stops and starts, sending some sequences of action to the background while pulling another set of actions to the foreground. Verse 26 resumes Ehud's escape from 3:24a.

Seirah. The identity of Seirah remains obscure. The term does not refer to the Edomite territory of "Seir" since flight there could not have facilitated Ehud's sounding the trumpet in Mount Ephraim (3:27). Etymologically, the word might imply a forested place.

Fleeing from the barren flats around Jericho and Gilgal up toward the Benjaminite heartland below Mount Ephraim would have entailed moving toward more forested regions. Perhaps a stand of trees marked a rendezvous point for Ehud's compatriots, who then could muster their comrades for battle.

3:27 ***When he arrived in the hill country of Ephraim, Ehud sounded a call to arms.*** Rainey (Rainey and Notley 2006:39) notes that Mount Ephraim designated a zone that included the northern Benjaminite region; thus, we need not suggest that the reference to Ephraimite involvement in the battle is a secondary expansion of the story's interests. The slope of Mount Ephraim descended into the Benjaminite territory, which formed a "saddle" of land before the road sloped upward toward the Judean highlands. Ehud had quite a hike! From Jericho at 722 feet below sea level, he would have traveled 13 miles, and climbed over 3,500 feet in elevation, to reach the vicinity of Bethel, the southernmost reach of Mount Ephraim, traveling over some of the most formidable terrain imaginable, only to turn right around and rush back at the head of the Israelite forces to engage the enemy on the floodplain of the Jordan.

3:28 ***the Israelites took control of the shallow crossings of the Jordan River across from Moab, preventing anyone from crossing.*** This ford, ironically, would have been the one used by Joshua (Josh 3) just a few generations earlier. The grim aim of the Israelite strategy is clear. More than liberation from a tyrant, they seek to destroy him. Rather than just expelling the Moabites, the Israelites seized the crossing and prevented the Moabites from escaping, slaughtering them all. One of the hardest features of the biblical message to absorb is Israel's hatred of tyranny. Israel does not simply represent liberation from oppression, it embodies the destruction of tyranny itself.

3:29 ***They attacked the Moabites and killed.*** The Hebrew simply says "struck," but the term virtually always describes a fatal blow. Omitted in the NLT here is the temporal expression "at that time." That, combined with the expression "that day" in 3:30, seems to stress the past aspect of Israel's stunning victory, similar to the slang expression in English "back in the day." From the perspective of the final author, those days were long gone.

about 10,000 of their strongest and most able-bodied warriors. The writer expresses the number in approximate terms, and "thousand" can refer to a fighting unit, not a literal number of men. The author uses two Hebrew phrases to describe the enemy. The second uses the term *khayil* [TH2428, ZH2657], the normal term for denoting a man of substance and standing, a hero. The first, however, uses the term *shamen* [TH8082, ZH9045], "oil/fat." Like the term used for Eglon's "fatness," this word seldom involves obesity but designates prosperous, well-nourished, well-supplied persons or places. Hence, the NLT rightly translates "strongest and most able-bodied warriors." These fighters, like their slain leader, were substantial, well-provisioned men of war. The narrator did not celebrate the slaughter of incompetent buffoons, nor engage in dark humor with an ethnic edge. He identified Eglon and his men as splendid and formidable fighters in their prime, cut down by Yahweh through Israel's valor, inspired by Ehud's blade.

Not one of them escaped. The Hebrew text repeats the word "man" (*'ish* [TH376, ZH408]) three times in a half-verse to stress the totality of Israel's victory. Lit., "every robust man, every man of valor, not a man escaped."

3:30 ***So Moab was conquered by Israel that day.*** The verb "was conquered" rather blandly renders a more graphic term typically translated "was humbled, subdued, brought low," which stresses the totality of Israel's victory over the Moabites.

there was peace in the land for eighty years. This remarkable statement records the longest period of rest in the entire book, over five times the length of the period of oppression, and twice the length of its nearest competitors (Othniel, Deborah, Gideon). Just enough wordplay operates between 3:14's "eighteen" (*shemoneh 'esreh* [TH8083/6240A, ZH9046/6926]) and "eighty" (*shemonim* [TH8083, ZH9046]) here to provide a satisfying aural closure to the story.

COMMENTARY

The stories of Ehud, Shamgar, and Deborah (3:12–5:31) present Israel successfully overcoming its oppressors under divinely prompted and enabled leadership. The stories of Ehud and Deborah are vigorous; they fully embody the "heroic" qualities noted in the introduction. Both distill the threat represented by an army into a single oppressive figure: Eglon and Sisera. Both concentrate the heroic saving action of God into an act by a single individual, Ehud and Jael. Both culminate in an assassination and the dramatic discovery of the slain oppressor's sprawled corpse. Even Shamgar, who gets only one verse, performs a remarkable and classically heroic deed with an improvised weapon and "saves Israel." On first blush, it appears that these stories exult in the rule of charismatic heroes, and indeed, they do. A closer inspection, though, reveals a surprising undertow drawing the reader in another direction.

Two tendencies mark commentary on the Ehud story (3:12-30). Scholars universally see the story as satirizing Eglon, leaving the reader with the impression that almost anyone could have killed the hulking, slow-witted, Moabite monarch. This view typically also suggests an ethnic edge to the humor. The other tendency is to see in Ehud a "decline" in the quality and character of the judges, citing the alleged silence or absence of Yahweh, and even the silence of the narrator, who they claim reports the story with no added comment (cf. Younger 2002:122-125). These claims impose on the text a standard external to the stories themselves and foreign to the culture in which the events occurred. In fact, the description of Eglon is anything but satiric, emphasizing he was an imposing, dangerous man, as were all his fighters (see note on 3:17; cf. Stone 2009). More importantly, the narrator gives Ehud highest accolades: Ehud alone, after Othniel, is said to be "raised up" by Yahweh. Ehud alone after Othniel is labeled "savior/rescuer." Ehud also procures for Israel 80 years of peace, and his death notice is omitted from the narrative proper and relegated to a circumstantial or concessive clause at the start of the Deborah story (4:1). Ehud also bears immediate testimony to Yahweh's power when he calls his countrymen to battle, seizing none of the glory for himself.

Perhaps the original storyteller shared the historical sophistication marking the Succession Narrative (2 Sam 9–20; 1 Kgs 1–2), which also displays reservation in referring to God's actions in the story. The "absence" of Yahweh, in fact, creates a space in which human actions on Yahweh's behalf become meaningful. If the book's overall structure offers a steadily developing critique of the charismatic office, then the omission of the *ruakh yhwh* [TH7307/3068, ZH8120/3378] (Spirit of Yahweh) from this story, just as it is omitted from the Deborah story, should not be seen as a criticism of these characters. Unless we resort to an extreme hermeneutic of irony, we must assume that the framework's straightforward approval of Ehud is expounded by the narrative itself. Ehud is not presented as deficient in character or skill; rather, the story affirms that his background, training, skill, daring, initiative, and willingness to risk everything provided Yahweh with precisely the moment he needed to elicit heroism from his people and draw the whole community from oppression to victory.

As noted in the introduction, the "decline" of the judges is not a story-by-story affair, but is organized into three stages. Thus, Othniel, Ehud, Shamgar, and Deborah all stand on the level of "triumphant" judges, revealing how the theocratic community could function effectively, even in the context of the people's periodic sin and failure.

The dark tone created by the introduction's twofold statement that Israel did evil in the Lord's sight (3:12) becomes deeper with the note that the oppressor, Eglon, has been directly strengthened by Yahweh for his role. Though Israel's evil is not specified as the fatal sin of idolatry, the reference later in the story to stone images at Gilgal at least raises the specter of other gods. The tide turns when Israel "cries to Yahweh" (3:15), though the text says nothing of repentance. Yahweh raises up Ehud as Israel's savior. He is a "Benjaminite," a name meaning "son of the right hand." Immediately, however, the text notes that Ehud is left-handed. A "left-handed right-hander" suggests a wily hero. The wordplay also possibly offsets the assignment of a positive role to a Benjaminite, a tribe often censured in Judges, by implying he is not a real "son of the right hand."

The story vividly unfolds Ehud's daring deed. Verses 15-17 set the stage by noting the occasion for Ehud's action: an audience with Eglon for presenting tribute (3:15c). It then shifts to the implement to be employed: the double-edged sword; then the stratagem: concealing it on his right thigh, to be drawn with the left hand (3:16). Despite attempts to construe this killing as the sacrifice of a "fatted calf," the term *minkhah* [TH4503, ZH4966] (tribute) derives its cultic use from the more common sense of a simple offering or gift. The cultic usage, moreover, typically denotes a nonbloody offering of cereals and grains (cf. Lev 2). The sense of "tribute" or "gift, present" is common (e.g., Gen 32:13; 43:11; 1 Sam 10:27; 2 Sam 8:2; 2 Kgs 20:12), so no cultic nuance need be ascribed here. Indeed, the political situation is obvious; subordinated peoples are bringing tribute to their overlord. Each prop and setting noted in 3:15c-17 figures in Eglon's assassination (3:18-26). The unit is bracketed by references to Ehud's turning back from the idols (3:19) and crossing/passing by the idols (3:26), thus creating a spatial, and perhaps implicit theological framework for his action, since the terms "turn" and "cross" connote repentance and transgression respectively in religious contexts (Polzin 1980:158-161).

The opportunity presented by the tribute offering (3:15c) is seized in 3:18b-20. Ehud returns alone (3:18a), probably creating the impression of being a collaborator, and cleverly secures privacy with Eglon (3:19) by announcing a "secret message." Ehud's secret "divine message" (3:20) turns out to be double-edged, with a fatally secular point. The sword, so carefully described by the narrator (3:16), fulfills its destiny in a single thrust (3:21) clear through the king's imposing frame (3:21-22), probably causing immediate incapacitation followed by a swift death. The king's evacuated bowels figure centrally in the next stage of the story.

The narrator often brackets events inside of other events. Verses 23 and 26 bracket the discovery of Eglon's body (3:24-25) with the escape of Ehud. Scholars almost universally accept the explanation of Halpern (1988:43-60) regarding the palace's structure, and most accept his reconstruction of Ehud's escape: After stabbing Eglon, Ehud locked the doors from the inside, passed through the latrine passage from the upper to the lower floors and back into the audience room, and exited the palace normally. The attendants returned and discovered the doors to the upper chamber locked (3:24). They assumed the king was relieving himself, no doubt smelling the matter released from the king's bowels. They waited, but the king never came out (3:25). Finally, they opened the door, and discovered their assassinated sovereign. Meanwhile, Ehud was long gone.

In 3:27-30 Ehud's lone achievement adorns the glory of Yahweh and becomes the property of Israel as he proclaims to Israel that (lit.) "Yahweh has given your enemy, Moab, into your hands!" He musters the people, who employ a clever stratagem, capturing the fords of the Jordan against the Moabites, who, like their king, are substantial, well-provisioned men of war. The generalization of Ehud's victory to all Israel links the true hero to the community. Great and daring deeds alone do not suffice; the hero must also lead his people to great exploits of their own. Ehud, like Othniel, fills the role admirably, and the result is an astounding 80 years of rest for the land.

This story is as double-edged as the sword that lies at its center. This celebrated "judge" is never said to judge Israel and is no Spirit-anointed, miraculous deliverer. His divine enablement resides in his wits, his status, and ability as an elite warrior. The story thus holds before the reader the mystery of God's ways. He works in the "secular" cleverness of an Ehud even as he does in the Spirit-inflamed charismatic. That which seems "religious" may not be; that which comes with no theological calling card may yet be the ever-hidden, always double-edged, Word of God that still finds its mark and cannot be withdrawn.

◆ 2. Shamgar: Minor judge, major deliverer (3:31)

31 After Ehud, Shamgar son of Anath rescued Israel. He once killed 600 Philistines with an ox goad.

NOTES

3:31 ***After Ehud.*** Lit., "And after him"; this formula occurs in the so-called minor judge lists (cf. 10:1-5; 12:8-15). No death notice has appeared for Ehud, nor does the text speak of Israel doing evil, leading to oppression, necessitating salvation. The introduction to the Deborah story links directly to the Ehud account, without reference to Shamgar. Perhaps the Ehud-Deborah sequence existed already in the inherited source material, and our final author inserted the Shamgar note because the reference to him in 5:6 positions him as a contemporary to Deborah and Jael. This suggests that, whatever rearrangements of the chronology the author might have made, he did at times group persons roughly in their correct periods. Literary artifice does not entirely preclude antiquarian seriousness.

Shamgar. The name is not Hebrew, some think not even Semitic, but possibly of Hurrian or Anatolian origin. He likely was among the "Sea Peoples" who settled the coast of Canaan in the early twelfth century BC, but earlier groups had also migrated into Canaan from the north. While the suggestion that Shamgar was a "legendary bandit" who preyed on caravans (cf. 5:6), thus harming the Israelites and bringing down the wrath of the Canaanite kings (Lindars 1995:236) seems unlikely and unnecessary, the possibility of his role as a brigand who sided with the Israelites against the urban Philistines deserves consideration. Coote and Whitelam (1987:88-116) note the complex interactions in Iron I Canaan among urban elites, peasant farmers, bedouin, and bandits. Banditry at times could serve the urban elites, but could also undercut attempts by those elites to control the countryside. Shamgar could possibly represent such a person.

Although Shamgar was not a descendant of Israel, saying he "was not an Israelite" fails to grasp the nature of the Israelite community as primarily unified by an oath to serve Yahweh that created a bond that took the form of a lineage society. As such, Rahab or Ruth, Jael or Shamgar, could be considered "Israelites" regardless of their lack of an "Israelite" pedigree.

son of Anath. The puzzle with Shamgar's patronymic is that Anath was the name of the Canaanite warrior goddess, hardly fitting for an Israelite hero. Perhaps the name points to the village of Beth Anath in Galilee, but that would place Shamgar far from any early Philistine presence. Others suggest that "son of Anath" referred to a specific warrior class or guild. A number of early Iron Age bronze projectile points bear the inscription *bn 'nt* (son of Anath), and others *'bdlb't* (servant of the Lion Lady), the latter being an epithet of the ancient Near Eastern war goddess, Ishtar in Babylon or Anat in the west (Mobley 2005:27-31). An elite fighter would display facility with any weapon, real or improvised.

rescued. This is also the term, *yasha'* [TH3467, ZH3828], used of the action of Othniel, Ehud, and Tola (10:1)—all of whom are said by the narrator to have "saved" Israel. Missing from the NLT is the unusual emphasis on Shamgar in the final clause of the Hebrew text, which includes the independent pronoun and the emphatic particle *gam* [TH1571, ZH1685]: "Even he saved Israel" could express the meaning.

600 Philistines. The number "600" appears frequently in descriptions of fighting forces (cf. 18:11; 1 Sam 13:15; 14:2; 27:2; 2 Sam 15:18). It likely denotes a particular type of fighting unit rather than a literal number. Reference to the Philistines, one of the "Sea Peoples," whose arrival in Canaan may be dated to about 1175, would seem to date this story accordingly. Since Shamgar is said to be a contemporary of Deborah, Barak, and Jael (5:6), this also implies the chronological context of chs 4–5 (see note on 4:2). It was not until 1070 BC that the Philistines began pressing effectively into Canaan's interior, but Shamgar engaged them prior to that time. The Philistines do not figure as characters again in the narrative until the Samson story (10:6 anticipates Israel's worship of Philistine gods). Apparently, the author wanted to place the southernmost stories earlier in the narratives. When we meet the Philistines again in the Samson story, the context is the tribe of Dan, ultimately (18:28-29) identified with the far northern extent of Israel.

with an ox goad. Ever interested in the heroes' weaponry, the author notes the hero's ability to improvise a weapon. The use of improvised weapons is the hallmark of great heroes. The ox goad (*malmad habbaqar* [TH4451/1241, ZH4913/1330]) was likely the handle of the plow, used as a prod for oxen, usually with a nail or other sharp point on the tip. The very shape of the Hebrew letter Lamedh, which provides the root for our word, looks like a prod or plough handle. The word also denoted teaching and learning (HALOT 2.594). The ox goad is likely associated with the *dorban* [TH1861, ZH1995] or plow-tip, mentioned in 1 Sam 13:21, which underscores a link between metallurgy and the Philistines. Considering what Shamgar could do with a stick sporting a metal point, the Philistines were wise to guard their metallurgical monopoly against the Israelites for as long as possible!

COMMENTARY

Shamgar, like his predecessor, is famous for his choice of weaponry: the ox goad. This notice adds to the atmosphere of triumph pervading 3:12–5:31 in three ways: (1) Shamgar comes "after" Ehud, but no apostasy intervenes, implying Ehud somehow acted to restrain the cycle of apostasy. (2) Shamgar "saves Israel." (3) Shamgar defeats the Philistines, an enemy that Samson only managed to harass, and that was not overcome until David's time. This is the only exploit attributed to a so-called "minor judge," although Tola, following the catastrophic career of Abimelech, is said to have rescued Israel (10:1).

Why did the author present this notice between Ehud and Deborah? In addition to the southern focus of these initial stories and the need to prepare for the reference to Shamgar in 5:6, perhaps the author wanted to stress the remarkable variety in God's choices of deliverers in these early stories in order to show that no single model of leadership does justice to the creativity of Yahweh. From a judge with explicit religious authentication (Othniel and the spirit's empowerings), followed by the elite warrior (Ehud), and then the improvisational deliverer (Shamgar), the reader's attention will be drawn subsequently in chapters 4–5 to a communal victory enacted through an established religious leader (Deborah), a warrior leader (Barak), and another unexpected improviser (Jael).

◆ 3. Deborah and Barak: The unidentified deliverer (4:1-24)

After Ehud's death, the Israelites again did
evil in the LORD's sight. 2So the LORD turned
them over to King Jabin of Hazor, a
Canaanite king. The commander of his
army was Sisera, who lived in Harosheth-
haggoyim. 3Sisera, who had 900 iron
chariots, ruthlessly oppressed the Israelites
for twenty years. Then the people of Israel
cried out to the LORD for help.

4Deborah, the wife of Lappidoth, was a
prophet who was judging Israel at that
time. 5She would sit under the Palm of
Deborah, between Ramah and Bethel in
the hill country of Ephraim, and the
Israelites would go to her for judgment.
6One day she sent for Barak son of Abin-
oam, who lived in Kedesh in the land of
Naphtali. She said to him, "This is what
the LORD, the God of Israel, commands
you: Call out 10,000 warriors from the
tribes of Naphtali and Zebulun at Mount
Tabor. 7And I will call out Sisera, com-
mander of Jabin's army, along with his
chariots and warriors, to the Kishon River.
There I will give you victory over him."

8Barak told her, "I will go, but only if
you go with me."

9"Very well," she replied, "I will go with
you. But you will receive no honor in this
venture, for the LORD's victory over Sisera
will be at the hands of a woman." So
Deborah went with Barak to Kedesh. 10At
Kedesh, Barak called together the tribes
of Zebulun and Naphtali, and 10,000
warriors went up with him. Deborah also
went with him.

11Now Heber the Kenite, a descendant
of Moses' brother-in-law* Hobab, had
moved away from the other members of
his tribe and pitched his tent by the oak
of Zaanannim near Kedesh.

12When Sisera was told that Barak son
of Abinoam had gone up to Mount Tabor,
13he called for all 900 of his iron chariots
and all of his warriors, and they marched
from Harosheth-haggoyim to the Kishon
River.

14Then Deborah said to Barak, "Get
ready! This is the day the LORD will give
you victory over Sisera, for the LORD is

marching ahead of you." So Barak led his 10,000 warriors down the slopes of Mount Tabor into battle. [15]When Barak attacked, the LORD threw Sisera and all his chariots and warriors into a panic. Sisera leaped down from his chariot and escaped on foot. [16]Then Barak chased the chariots and the enemy army all the way to Harosheth-haggoyim, killing all of Sisera's warriors. Not a single one was left alive.

[17]Meanwhile, Sisera ran to the tent of Jael, the wife of Heber the Kenite, because Heber's family was on friendly terms with King Jabin of Hazor. [18]Jael went out to meet Sisera and said to him, "Come into my tent, sir. Come in. Don't be afraid." So he went into her tent, and she covered him with a blanket.

[19]"Please give me some water," he said. "I'm thirsty." So she gave him some milk from a leather bag and covered him again.

[20]"Stand at the door of the tent," he told her. "If anybody comes and asks you if there is anyone here, say no."

[21]But when Sisera fell asleep from exhaustion, Jael quietly crept up to him with a hammer and tent peg in her hand. Then she drove the tent peg through his temple and into the ground, and so he died.

[22]When Barak came looking for Sisera, Jael went out to meet him. She said, "Come, and I will show you the man you are looking for." So he followed her into the tent and found Sisera lying there dead, with the tent peg through his temple.

[23]So on that day Israel saw God defeat Jabin, the Canaanite king. [24]And from that time on Israel became stronger and stronger against King Jabin until they finally destroyed him.

4:11 Or *father-in-law.*

NOTES

4:1 ***After Ehud's death.*** The Hebrew text places this as a parenthetical notice at the end of the verse: "meanwhile, Ehud had died." His death opened the door for Israel's reversion to apostasy (2:19). Ehud's death notice does not appear in his story, but in the introduction of the Deborah story (4:1), with the Shamgar notice in between (3:31). In separating the account of Ehud's career from the notice of his death, perhaps the author is further emphasizing his positive view of Ehud.

the Israelites again did evil in the LORD's sight. As in 3:7, the evil Israel commits is not specified. The reference to "new gods" being chosen (5:8) might imply defection from Yahweh, but readers do well to avoid narrowing the scope of "evil in Yahweh's eyes" to violations of the first two commandments. All the covenant's stipulations must stay in view, as must the main sin of the Israelites (stressed in ch 1) of failing to fulfill the conquest mandate.

4:2 ***the LORD turned them over to King Jabin of Hazor, a Canaanite king.*** The previous oppressors came from outside the land (Mesopotamia, Moab), reflecting the limited areas of Israel's settlement in the early Iron Age. The Philistines settled the coastal plain in the mid-twelfth century (cf. 3:31), and the failure of the Israelites to gain control of the lowland urban centers (cf. 1:22-36) appears in the Deborah story with its attention to the Jezreel valley and the urban sites of Hazor, Megiddo, and Taanach. The consequences of incomplete obedience, noted in the preface, came home to roost in the form of a persistent Canaanite power armed with chariots. Jabin is noted six times in this chapter, and his status as "king of Canaan" (rendered variously in the NLT, and inaccurately in 4:2 as "*a* Canaanite king") finds notice three times (4:2, 23, 24). The name "Jabin" appears for the king of Hazor in Josh 11, and the presence of the name in its Akkadian form (Ibni) in a cuneiform text found there from an even earlier era suggests it was a recurring royal name; so it is not necessary or possible to combine or even reverse the stories in Judg 4–5 and Josh 11. Nor need we posit (with Wood 2007) a rebuilding of Hazor after Joshua, followed by a catastrophic destruction by Deborah.

Hazor. Hazor is mentioned twice (4:2, 17) but plays no role in the story line. Reference to it poses a historical problem: Deborah is presented as contemporary with Shamgar (see 5:6 and note) who fought the Philistines, thus dating the narrative to around the mid-twelfth century BC or later; but Hazor was destroyed in the Late Bronze Age in a terrific, fiery destruction, now well-dated by an inscription to the 1230s BC (Kitchen 2003:20-28) with no signs of rebuilding afterwards. Thus, it appears to have been unoccupied, or occupied only by villagers living in huts or tents. Some claim this destruction resulted from the Deborah-Barak campaign, suggesting an earlier destruction in the 1400s for Joshua (Wood 2007:26, 78), but no evidence for this proposed destruction has been found (Ben-Tor 2007). Further, the thirteenth-century destruction evidence, including a massive conflagration, matches the emphases of the account in Josh 11 too well to be shifted to Deborah's time, especially since Judges reports no Israelite action against the city of Hazor.

But if Hazor lay in ruins in early Iron Age I, why is Jabin twice associated with the city? The reason likely resides in the prestigious history of the site, and possibly testifies to Jabin's aspirations to restore the citadel to its former glory. The 200-acre mound of Hazor loomed for centuries as the principal city in the region, the "capital of all these kingdoms" (Josh 11:10b). No ruler could claim to be "king of Canaan" without claiming rule over Hazor. Indeed, the ruler of Hazor alone refers to himself as "king" in the Amarna letters, indicating the city's high status (ABD 5.578-581). Hazor was also strategically located to exercise control over the entire trade route connecting the Sharon plain with the gateways to Syria. Finally, Hazor serves the writer's theme because it resonates with the book of Joshua, where victory at Hazor is paired with the victory at Jericho to reveal Yahweh's power and faithfulness. Both sites appear in Judges in Canaanite hands to underscore the depth of Israel's failure after Joshua. The center of gravity for this story, however, remains the Jezreel valley around Megiddo and Taanach, not the vicinity of Hazor and the Huleh basin.

The commander of his army was Sisera. The text shows ambivalence about the relationship between Sisera and Jabin. The Song of Deborah (ch 5) makes no mention of Jabin, who remains in the background of ch 4 until the conclusion. The name "Sisera" is not Northwest Semitic and might be of Anatolian origin, possibly identifying him as a member of one of the many Aegean groups that scoured the eastern Mediterranean from around 1200 BC. Egypt hired members of these various groups as mercenaries, and Jabin, a nominal servant of Egypt, perhaps did the same.

A larger issue is also in play, however. In the middle of the twelfth century, the time of our story, Egypt was striving aggressively to maintain its imperial grip on Canaan, specifically to control "all the lowlands of Canaan, through which the important trade routes passed" (Singer 1994:293). The routes ran from the Sharon plain over the Carmel ridge, past Megiddo, across the Jezreel valley, past Hazor, to Syria and beyond. Egypt also had been gaining valuable produce from agricultural plantations in the Jezreel valley, managed by their surrogates, the "kinglets" of Canaan. The oppressive practices of Jabin and Sisera, therefore, would have been aimed at protecting Egyptian interests, including the practice of conscripting labor and produce from the peasant population.

Moreover, in the final years of Rameses III, the whole region from the central hill country of Ephraim all the way to Dan became the scene of a desperate, last-ditch Egyptian effort to keep extracting wealth from Canaan, with Egypt aggressively probing the hill country south of the Jezreel valley in search of alternate access points to the lucrative trade routes to Asia. These desperate moves cut off Israelites in the Galilee from those in Manasseh and Ephraim, creating a crisis in the entire northern portion of the land—and this situation was exacerbated by a period of drought and, in many places, famine.

who lived in Harosheth-haggoyim. Rainey (Rainey and Notley 2006:150-151) has plausibly related the name Harosheth-haggoyim to the Semitic root *kharash* [TH2790, ZH3086] (to plough, cultivate), with the Akkadian cognate *erishtu* (cultivated land). The word denotes farms or plantations owned by "the nations." The pharaohs, starting with Thutmose III, established royal estates in the portion of the Jezreel valley east of the highway running between Megiddo and Taanach, managed by local city-state rulers. One Amarna letter identifies an Egyptian agricultural estate near Shunem in the east end of the Jezreel valley, and Thutmose III's estimate of the wheat yield from the Megiddo plantation to the west implies an estate of over 12,000 acres—this plantation country at least covered the entire south end of the Jezreel plain! If Harosheth-haggoyim can refer to any location in the whole southern end of the valley, then none of the distances mentioned in the story are problematic. This same region also regularly served as an assembly point for military forces throughout the Late Bronze Age, which meshes well with the story.

4:3 ***Sisera, who had 900 iron chariots.*** Reference to 900 chariots in the Jezreel valley calls to mind the daring attack of Thutmose III against Megiddo in the fifteenth century, in which he claims to have captured 924 Canaanite chariots after defeating them in a surprise march through the Aruna Pass. The biblical story will also describe the overwhelming defeat of a Canaanite chariot force on the plain of Jezreel. "Iron chariots" might refer to iron reinforcement of critical joints, but more likely denotes the chariots' axles being forged from iron (King and Stager 2001:189), which made for a much sturdier vehicle.

ruthlessly oppressed the Israelites for twenty years. As noted earlier, Pharaoh expected the Canaanite kinglets to supply forced labor for the plantations. The Amarna letters repeatedly indicate the constant efforts of the local rulers to conscript peasant labor.

4:4 ***Deborah, the wife of Lappidoth.*** Deborah's name means "honeybee," a name referring to only one other person in the Bible, Rebekah's nurse (Gen 35:8). The nurse's burial near a tree called the "Oak of Weeping" in the vicinity of Bethel suggests some connection with our story (4:5, "Bethel"), and sparks association with the place-name Bokim ("weeping"), mentioned in 2:1-5. Lappidoth's name means "torches."

who was judging Israel. The text's use of the participle (*shopetah* [TH8199A, ZH9149]) suggests that Deborah's role as judge was a customary or continuing one, even a title. Deborah's dual role as both prophet and judge, seen as separate theocratic offices in Deuteronomy (Deut 16:18-19; 17:8-12; 18:9-22), underlines her unique identity. As prophet, she spoke concrete, divine words regarding the specific situations in which her people lived. As judge, she functioned principally to restore the community to *shalom* [TH7965, ZH8934] by adjudicating conflicts. As noted in the introduction, the role of judge seems also to suggest a range of influence beyond the kinship system's genealogically defined roles.

4:5 ***She would sit under the Palm of Deborah.*** In Hebrew, the participial construction continues from 4:4, describing the typical practice of Deborah's administration. The term "palm" shares a common root with the term used to denote Jericho in 1:16 and 3:13. This allusion possibly links this story to the Ehud story (3:13) and anticipates the Kenite reference of 4:11 (1:16).

between Ramah and Bethel in the hill country of Ephraim. Deborah's "court" in the area of Bethel places her about 50 miles from the scene of the battle. This distance does not compromise the topographic and historical accuracy of the account. Ancient records confirm that movement around Canaan over such distances was not unusual. Also, the widespread implications of the crisis (see note on 4:2) linked problems in Jezreel and the Huleh basin to a growing pressure on the central hill country. In addition, a hallmark of the "judges" was that their influence reached beyond the constraints of their location (i.e., the tribal network's kinship system) and thus beyond their natural base of authority, necessitating some further form of authentication, as witnessed by Barak's question in reply to her summons. In Deborah's case, this additional authorization derived from her prophetic office. Thus, the story makes good geographic, historical, and political sense.

and the Israelites would go to her for judgment. The text here shifts to the Waw-consecutive construction. The NLT (cf. NET) does not register this syntactic and stylistic shift. The approach of the Israelites here is the first event of the story proper. Deborah's exercise of authority made her not just a spiritual leader (prophet) but also a political leader. Combined with her role in creating the liturgical poetry found in ch 5 and leading Israel in the liturgical celebration of Yahweh's mighty victory, Deborah adumbrates the three principle theocratic offices of prophet, king, and priest.

4:6 ***One day she sent for Barak son of Abinoam.*** The NLT implies a break in the text, but syntactically Deborah's dispatch to Barak flows with the preceding clause. The effect of the Hebrew is to make her summons to Barak, far away in Kedesh-Naphtali, a direct consequence of the Israelites approaching her for judgment. Perhaps the "coming up for judgment" involved a plea to Deborah to intervene in the growing crisis ignited by Sisera and Jabin.

who lived in Kedesh in the land of Naphtali. The references to Kedesh in this story have vexed interpreters. Most deny that "Kedesh of Naphtali" could plausibly be Tell Kedesh, the large mound six miles northwest of Hazor, and opt for a site on the southwest corner of the Sea of Galilee. While that location might fit the location of Jael's tent, nothing in the text demands that Barak and Jael come from the same town. The proximity of the northern site to Hazor fits the otherwise tangential references to Hazor in the story. If our story reflects the Egyptian reassertion of control over the main trade routes, or if Jabin aspired to renew a centralized regime at Hazor, then someone living near Hazor would naturally be concerned. Deborah at the south end, and Barak at the north, together confront the regional crisis brewing in the Jezreel valley.

the tribes of Naphtali and Zebulun at Mount Tabor. The southern slopes of the hilly regions of Naphtali and Zebulun formed the northern boundary of the very valley whose plantations and trade routes formed the strategic crux of the challenge that faced Israel. The Jezreel valley is often compared to an arrowhead pointing northwest. Mount Tabor, where the Israelites positioned themselves (4:12), stands at the northern shoulder of the arrowhead, near where the narrow shaft of the arrow, the Harod valley, leads southeast to Beth-shan and the Jordan River. With Beth Haggen forming the southern shoulder of the arrowhead, a routed chariot force would find its only practical escape route to the same road by which they entered the battlefield. Zebulun's location along the flank of the retreating Canaanite force provided them with a tactical opportunity noted in 5:13a.

4:7 ***I will call out Sisera, commander of Jabin's army, along with his chariots and warriors.*** This was a ludicrous strategy: Barak would position a militia of farmers and pastoralists armed with improvised weaponry and no armor in a virtual cul-de-sac, with Tabor forcing the Israelite retreat away from the homes of most of the warriors. They would then face a crack force of iron chariots and trained infantry. No wonder Barak sought reassurance!

Kishon River. The Kishon is a seasonal stream flowing northeast from the area of Mount Tabor toward Jokneam and out to the plain of Acco. A modest stream in the dry season, a sudden rain can cause it to burst its banks, turning the deep, dark red soil of the valley floor into a pasty muck.

4:8 ***Barak told her, "I will go, but only if you go with me."*** The LXX includes an additional line: "because I do not know the day that the Lord will prosper his angel to go with me." The line is likely original, since this fits wells with Deborah's call to attack in 4:14, "This is the day!" Barak expresses no unbelief here. Instead, considering the dangerous nature of the "plan" Deborah describes, and her prophetic role, Barak realized this battle was a matter not of tactics but of divine timing and direction. Thus, he wanted the prophet present with him.

4:9a ***"Very well," she replied, "I will go with you. But you will receive no honor in this venture, for the LORD's victory over Sisera will be at the hands of a woman."*** The NLT makes Deborah's words sound like a rebuke. But literally, the text reads, "But your honor will not be on the way you are going." Deborah does not deny Barak honor in battle. Indeed, under Barak's command, Israel's army triumphs, and Deborah lauds him in liturgical poetry in 5:12 as one of the leaders who acted valiantly. Nevertheless, she identifies that his honor will not come in the manner he expects, i.e., in the slaying of the enemy commander. In warrior cultures, special honor derives from striking the killing blow against the opposing leader. This honor will fall to a woman. The text to this point creates the expectation that this woman will be Deborah, but in fact the honored woman will be someone else who has been moved into position to strike that blow by an ironic circumstance (see below on 4:11).

4:9b-10 ***Kedesh.*** The Kedesh in view here need not be the same as Barak's home, and likely is Khirbet Qadish on the southwest shore of the Sea of Galilee. Despite the appeal of Tell Abu Qudeis, a small shrine site along the Kishon in the Jezreel valley near Taanach and Megiddo that features mid-twelfth century destruction levels, the association in 4:11 of this Kedesh with the "oak of Zaanannim" (cf. Josh 19:33) compels locating it at Khirbet Qadish. As an assembly point, "Kedesh by the Sea" cloaked the ultimate destination of the various tribal militias as they moved into position, since they would not appear to be headed into the Jezreel valley. This location also allowed a less easily observed approach to Mount Tabor, potentially hiding Barak's movement of forces.

4:11 ***Now Heber the Kenite, a descendant of Moses' brother-in-law Hobab, had moved away from the other members of his tribe and pitched his tent by the oak of Zaanannim near Kedesh.*** This important note puts another piece of the story in place. In the OT Kenites are associated with metalworking and likely served as itinerant tinkers and craftsmen. That such traveling tradesmen existed in the first Iron Age in Canaan is supported by Killebrew's argument for itinerant potters (2005:177-181). The full identification and association with Moses calls attention to 1:16, which indicates the Kenites' solidarity with Israel. Heber, however, "split off" from the Kenites. This separation will emerge in the narrative as more than a mere relocation.

4:12-13 ***When Sisera was told that Barak son of Abinoam had gone up to Mount Tabor, he called for all 900 of his iron chariots and all of his warriors.*** In Hebrew this is an impersonal construction: "(someone) told Sisera . . . ." Coming on the heels of the otherwise odd notation of Heber's change of address, this strongly implies that Heber betrayed the Israelite presence to the Canaanite commander, a suggestion supported by the later note in 4:17 that Heber had been in league with Jabin, whom Sisera served (Block 1999:203). A metalworker might indeed find lucrative employment in the service of a force employing over 900 chariots that used iron in their construction (Olson 1998:780-781).

4:14 ***Deborah said to Barak, "Get ready! This is the day the LORD will give you victory over Sisera."*** Deborah fulfills the role Barak requested of her by identifying the precise moment to launch the attack. Deborah disappears from the story until 5:1. Her activities serve as prologue and epilogue to the victory; she was catalyst and celebrant.

4:15 ***When Barak attacked, the LORD threw Sisera and all his chariots and warriors into a panic.*** The expression "threw . . . into a panic" translates the verb *hamam* [TH2000, ZH2169]. Used in Exod 14:24, where the verb also describes Yahweh's overturning of enemy chariots, the verb universally denotes the routing of his foes (Exod 14:24; 23:27; Josh 10:10; 1 Sam 7:10; 2 Chr 15:6; Pss 18:14; 144:6). Very often, phenomena such as rain, thunder, and lightning appear as Yahweh gains his victory. It seems that a sudden thunderstorm caused the Kishon to overflow its banks, dousing the dense, deep, red soil with enough water to turn the valley floor into a gooey mess. Nineteenth-century travelers report donkeys sinking up to their bridles in this dense, viscous mud. The mud would immobilize and neutralize Sisera's chariots. The typical armor worn by chariot crews—a mail coat reaching to the ankles—limited motion, hindering them from fighting on the ground. Without the decimation of the foe via deluges of arrows, Sisera's infantry would lack its normal tactical advantage. In the confusion, the Israelite militia had a chance to gain the upper hand. Ironically, thunderstorms featured strongly in the iconography of Baal, the deity to whom Sisera likely prayed on the eve of this battle. Yahweh prevailed over Baal's servants, using Baal's weapons.

Sisera leaped down from his chariot and escaped on foot. This was the only recourse for a man whose mobile firing platform was immobilized.

4:16 ***Barak chased the chariots and the enemy army all the way to Harosheth-haggoyim, killing all of Sisera's warriors.*** Between Mount Tabor and Megiddo runs a geologic feature, an uplifted vein of basalt extending like an elevated roadway over 100 feet higher than the surrounding plain. When the valley is flooded, this "central rise" constitutes the only pathway. Sisera's troops sought to escape down this narrow path, which dips down to the valley level where the Kishon crosses. As the note on 5:13a suggests, at this point the tribe of Zebulun swept down from the hill country above the town of Sarid, attacking the flank of the retreating Canaanites, closing off the causeway, and driving them into the worst of the muddy plain.

4:17 ***Heber's family was on friendly terms with King Jabin of Hazor.*** The expression "friendly terms" translates *shalom* [TH7965, ZH8934]. The term denotes not merely amicable relations, but often occurs in covenantal contexts to denote the good relations formalized by the treaty (Wiseman 1982). In Josh 9:15, the phrases "make peace" and "make covenant" appear synonymous; thus some suggest a formal treaty between Heber and Jabin here (Butler 2009:99-101). While we need not think in terms of a written treaty or an oath between Heber and Jabin—though Heber's name is formed from a root connoting association and alliance (TDOT 4:193-197)—we must certainly understand a commitment, clearly recognized, to cooperation, mutual benefit, and good relations between them. Given the oppression the Israelites suffered at the hands of Jabin and Sisera and the state of war between Jabin's forces and Israel, for an Israelite to be "at peace" with Jabin would necessarily entail a betrayal of Israel and Yahweh. No faithful Israelite family compound could possibly provide sanctuary for the commander of Jabin's chariots apart from a breach of covenant with Israel's God. Heber's name derives from a term meaning "to associate, become a partner." As is often the case in Judges, names point to important themes. Sisera might be at peace with Heber, but perhaps he presumed in thinking that peace extended to Jael. Likewise, acting as she does, Jael shatters the good relations established with Jabin by her husband.

4:18 ***Jael went out to meet Sisera and said to him, "Come into my tent, sir."*** Claims that Sisera violated the mores of hospitality by imposing himself on Jael collapse in the face of the obvious initiative taken by Jael. Interpreters have been too prone to rigidly apply concepts or "rules" of hospitality that are themselves only scholarly constructions. In the midst of the slaughter and pursuit of open warfare, Sisera, Jael, and the Israelite forces were not going to say "please" and "thank you" and scrupulously observe some formal code of hospitality, especially given that Heber had already betrayed the Israelites in the first place and was an accomplice to Sisera. One suspects these characters were acting much more on impulse under duress.

4:21 ***fell asleep from exhaustion.*** The text takes special note of Sisera's exhausted sleep as an additional parenthetical remark at the end of the verse in Hebrew. Sisera's sudden slumber may have been accelerated by the beverage served him by Jael (see note on 5:25).

tent peg. The tent peg (*yathed* [TH3489, ZH3845]) proved to be a more formidable implement than typically imagined. Though the pegs for the Tabernacle were bronze (Exod 27:19), wood was likely more common, though it had to be strong (cf. Ezek 15:3). The word *yathed* also denotes the implement (trowel?) used to cover excrement outside the camp (Deut 23:13), so perhaps the stake was bladed. To anchor a large bedouin-style tent to the ground—not to mention an enemy's head—required more than the stubby "tent peg" moderns might envision. This long, heavy stake required a steady hand and a stout blow with a substantial mallet. (Jael was not named "mountain goat"—*ya'el* [TH3277/3278, ZH3604/3605]—for nothing!) Outside this story (4:21-22; 5:26), Judges contains *yathed* only in 16:14, as the means by which Delilah bound Samson's hair. In Judges, women wielding pointy objects pose a positive danger to carelessly sleeping males.

through his temple and into the ground. Traditionally interpreted as "temple," the Hebrew term employed has been plausibly argued to mean "(open) mouth" (NIDOTTE 2.921-922). The stake thus would be driven into and through Sisera's mouth and throat, possibly piercing the cervical vertebrae, and thence into the ground.

4:22 ***found Sisera lying there dead.*** The wording for the discovery of the demolished Sisera (*wehinneh sisera' nopel meth* [TH5307/4191, ZH5877/4637], "and there was Sisera, fallen dead") corresponds closely to that used of Eglon's servants encountering his remains (*wehinneh 'adonehem nopel 'artsah meth*, "and there was their lord, [fallen] dead on the floor," 3:25). Similar stress on Sisera's "falling" appears in 5:27, followed by *shadud* [TH7703, ZH8720] (devastated).

4:23 ***Israel saw God defeat Jabin.*** Lit., "God subdued Jabin . . . before Israel." The text contains a wry wordplay. The term translated "defeat" renders the somewhat rare Hebrew verb *kana'* [TH3665, ZH4044], which in the Qal stem denotes being bent over, passive, or humiliated. In the Hiphil, it denotes both a decisive victory that effectively ends the capacity of a given foe to do harm and the shattering of arrogant pride. The same root consonants also form the ethnic label "Canaanite" (*kena'ani* [TH3669, ZH4050]), likely related to the original Canaanite homeland on the lowlands of the Levant. The NLT's "Israel saw . . ." translates the Hebrew idiom *lipne bene yisra'el* [TH3807.1/6440, ZH4200/7156] (before the sons of Israel). The other two occurrences of *kana'* with *lipne* suggest instrumentality: God subdued Jabin by means of Israel, or through Israel (Deut 9:3; Neh 9:24), not "in front of" or "in view of." Though mentioned six times in the chapter, Jabin seems strangely distant from the actual events narrated. His defeat likely is seen as mediated through the defeat of his subordinate, Sisera.

4:24 ***from that time on Israel became stronger and stronger against King Jabin.*** The skeletal conclusion conceals a political bombshell. The claim of a steadily growing dominance over Jabin suggests Israelites gained control at least over the lower portion of the Jezreel valley. If we have located these events in the correct historical setting, by breaking the power of Jabin and Sisera, Israel had simultaneously frustrated the Egyptian move to lock up Canaan for itself and neutralized, at least for the moment, the local Canaanite threat. In fact, by the time Rameses III died (c. 1151 BC), Egyptian artifacts largely disappear from Canaan, indicating Egypt's rapid withdrawal from Canaan (Singer 1994:284-295). Israel could begin cultivating the fields of the Jezreel valley, and traffic between the central and northern tribes became possible. Unfortunately, the withdrawal of Egypt and the discomfiting of the Canaanites left the field open to opportunistic exploitation from the East (chs 6–8; 10:6–11:7), from within (ch 9), and ultimately, from the Philistines (chs 13–16). Moreover, the battle itself, despite the victory, disclosed fault lines in the community whose effects are felt in the stories of Abimelech (ch 9) and in the book's concluding section (chs 17–21).

until they finally destroyed him. Some erroneously take this phrase to imply that the Israelites attacked and destroyed Hazor. The text says absolutely nothing about military action beyond the Jezreel valley. The Hebrew, "they cut off Jabin," denotes the personal destruction of the man and his power, not the destruction of the city, which likely had not been significantly restored since its destruction around 1230 BC. See note on 4:2.

COMMENTARY

The dense interplay of language, land, and history makes this narrative especially compelling to readers. A historical and military crisis provides the setting in which the tide is turned decisively by Israel's obedient response to the word of Yahweh given through the prophet and judge, Deborah. Her role in the prose account of chapter 4 is that of catalyst: She stirs Barak to action, and the Israelites go to war against Sisera. Obedience to the divine word then triggers a completely unpredictable chain of events culminating in an act of betrayal that sets the stage for the victory of God's people over Jabin. The literary flow of the story accentuates both the certainty of Yahweh's word being fulfilled and the utter unpredictability of the instruments through which it was fulfilled.

The introduction (4:1-3), though noting Israel again did evil in Yahweh's eyes, still does not identify the evil as idolatry, though 5:8 hints at idolatry by noting that "new gods" had been chosen. The death of Ehud, which did not appear in 3:12-30, is noted in 4:1. The death of the judge typically implied a reversion to evil, but the delayed report of Ehud's death and its relegation to a parenthetical remark, combined with the 80 years of peace following Ehud (3:30), suggests Israel did not revert to evil as quickly or egregiously as 2:11-23 suggests. Thus, the generally positive tone of the first section (3:12–5:31) is retained. However, the oppression described in 4:2 is more grave than in previous stories. Now the enemy is not from beyond Israel, as was Cushan (Mesopotamia) or Eglon (Moab); the enemy is a Canaanite based in Hazor, a city that had been destroyed by Joshua (Josh 11). Another token of the growing gravity of the situation is Israel's cry for help (4:3), which did not lead immediately to the divine elevation of a leader, as with Othniel and Ehud. Instead, the cry is followed by details identifying Deborah before there is any rescue. In other words—unlike the preceding two stories—we are not ushered immediately into the hero's actions.

In 4:4-10, Deborah is seen issuing judgments as a prophet. She is a judge, but will not end up being the deliverer. In fact, this story keeps the reader guessing as to who will finally take the credit for delivering Israel. Deborah's prophetic message summoned Barak to be the deliverer, promising divine support (4:6-7), but Barak refused unless Deborah would join him (4:8). Deborah's compliance came with a cost: The "honor" would not be Barak's, but would belong to an unspecified woman

(4:9). Barak, accompanied by Deborah *per* his request, then mustered the armies (4:10) in the fashion typical of the judges (3:27; 6:34-35; 11:29).

Judges 4:11-24 narrates a stupendous victory for Barak and his army. Probably his advance was made known to Sisera (4:12) by Heber, who is said to have split off from the other Kenites (4:11, see note); if true, this implies he has betrayed the former Kenite alliance with God's people. Typical terminology of a divinely wrought victory appears in 4:13-16; prophetic encouragement (4:14) is followed by Yahweh's fouling of Sisera's chariot wheels (4:15), reminiscent of the Exodus (Exod 14:24-25). The ensuing rout forced Sisera to abandon his chariotry and flee on foot, while all of his soldiers were destroyed (4:15). Contrary to Deborah's words, it appeared as if Barak would get all the glory for the victory.

Judges 4:17-22 switches the focus from the battle to Sisera's flight to the tent of Jael, wife of Heber. Sisera naturally expected refuge because Jabin had a covenant with Heber, pointing again to Heber the Kenite's abandonment of Israel to serve Jabin. Jael's double-crossing of Sisera thus abrogated an unfaithful alliance, undoing a compromise. Ehud-like, Jael maneuvered Sisera into a vulnerable position; she snuck in, tent peg and mallet in hand, and spiked Sisera's head to the ground (4:21). The "honor" indeed bypassed Barak (4:9) and went to a woman. But the "woman" was not Deborah, who dropped out of the story after 4:14. Jael's intrepid defiance of her husband's illegitimate treaty with a Canaanite king won her a permanent place in the lore of Israel. The very triumphant tone of this story ironically undercuts the ideal of the single hero who wins deliverance for Israel. The prophetic word, not the Spirit of Yahweh (which does not appear in the story), instigates and sustains the victorious military leader, who plays a secondary role. The real honor goes to an obscure woman who rejected her husband's compromise with Canaan. Far from extolling the "hero-judge," the story extols the heroics of an ordinary person choosing the Lord's side and dramatizes the catalytic power of the prophetic word to elicit daring faithfulness. The Christian reader recalls Jesus' words in Luke 14:25-26, in which devotion to following Christ so exceeds earthly ties that disciples appear to be "hating" their relatives.

The prose story concludes in 4:23-24 by affirming that the victory recounted here eliminated the threat posed by Jabin and Sisera, leading to the destruction of Jabin "the king of Canaan" (lit.). While the Israelites probably did not attack Hazor, which was far to the north of the action, they might well have attacked Megiddo and Taanach, both of which suffered significant (though not final) damage in the mid-1100s BC, about the time of our story (Stern 1993–2008:3.1013, 4.1432). This could have included the destruction of the residence of Sisera's mother and her own death, fulfilling the grim words concluding Deborah's song (cf. 5:28-30).

The defeat of the Egyptian-Canaanite alliance freed the Jezreel valley for Israelite use. Though the tribe of Manasseh is not mentioned in chapter 5, the opening up of the Jezreel valley and lower Galilee to Israelite settlement meant that this area of Manasseh could be settled and become the setting of the Gideon story. After this victory, Judges reports no further oppression by alliances of Canaanite city-state rulers common in the Late Bronze Age, but accurately portrays the political realities of Canaan in the late twelfth and early eleventh centuries. The withdrawal of Egypt and the defeat of its Canaanite surrogates created a power vacuum, into which came the Midianites and Ammonites from Trans-Jordan, setting the stage for the Gideon and

Jephthah stories. The power struggle in Canaan came to a head with the Philistine threat in the late twelfth century BC, creating the foil for Samson's career and leading ultimately to the rise of the Hebrew monarchy. But for the time being, Israel exulted in a decisive divine victory that not only ended their suffering, but also opened up fertile lands for cultivation. They had every reason to celebrate, and they did!

4. The Song of Deliverance (5:1-31)

On that day Deborah and Barak son of Abinoam sang this song:

2 "Israel's leaders took charge,
and the people gladly followed.
Praise the LORD!

3 "Listen, you kings!
Pay attention, you mighty rulers!
For I will sing to the LORD.
I will make music to the LORD, the God of Israel.

4 "LORD, when you set out from Seir
and marched across the fields of Edom,
the earth trembled,
and the cloudy skies poured down rain.
5 The mountains quaked in the presence of the LORD,
the God of Mount Sinai—
in the presence of the LORD,
the God of Israel.

6 "In the days of Shamgar son of Anath,
and in the days of Jael,
people avoided the main roads,
and travelers stayed on winding pathways.
7 There were few people left in the villages of Israel*—
until Deborah arose as a mother for Israel.
8 When Israel chose new gods,
war erupted at the city gates.
Yet not a shield or spear could be seen
among forty thousand warriors in Israel!
9 My heart is with the commanders of Israel,
with those who volunteered for war.
Praise the LORD!

10 "Consider this, you who ride on fine donkeys,
you who sit on fancy saddle blankets,
and you who walk along the road.
11 Listen to the village musicians*
gathered at the watering holes.
They recount the righteous victories of the LORD
and the victories of his villagers in Israel.
Then the people of the LORD
marched down to the city gates.

12 "Wake up, Deborah, wake up!
Wake up, wake up, and sing a song!
Arise, Barak!
Lead your captives away, son of Abinoam!

13 "Down from Tabor marched the few
against the nobles.
The people of the LORD marched
down against mighty warriors.
14 They came down from Ephraim—
a land that once belonged to the Amalekites;
they followed you, Benjamin, with your troops.
From Makir the commanders marched down;
from Zebulun came those who carry a commander's staff.
15 The princes of Issachar were with Deborah and Barak.
They followed Barak, rushing into the valley.
But in the tribe of Reuben
there was great indecision.
16 Why did you sit at home among the sheepfolds—

to hear the shepherds whistle for
their flocks?
Yes, in the tribe of Reuben
there was great indecision.
17 Gilead remained east of the Jordan.
And why did Dan stay home?
Asher sat unmoved at the seashore,
remaining in his harbors.
18 But Zebulun risked his life,
as did Naphtali, on the heights of
the battlefield.

19 "The kings of Canaan came and
fought,
at Taanach near Megiddo's springs,
but they carried off no silver
treasures.
20 The stars fought from heaven.
The stars in their orbits fought
against Sisera.
21 The Kishon River swept them away—
that ancient torrent, the Kishon.
March on with courage, my soul!
22 Then the horses' hooves hammered
the ground,
the galloping, galloping of Sisera's
mighty steeds.
23 'Let the people of Meroz be cursed,'
said the angel of the LORD.
'Let them be utterly cursed,
because they did not come to help
the LORD—
to help the LORD against the mighty
warriors.'

24 "Most blessed among women is Jael,
the wife of Heber the Kenite.
May she be blessed above all
women who live in tents.
25 Sisera asked for water,
and she gave him milk.
In a bowl fit for nobles,
she brought him yogurt.
26 Then with her left hand she reached
for a tent peg,
and with her right hand for the
workman's hammer.
She struck Sisera with the hammer,
crushing his head.
With a shattering blow, she pierced
his temples.
27 He sank, he fell,
he lay still at her feet.
And where he sank,
there he died.

28 "From the window Sisera's mother
looked out.
Through the window she watched
for his return, saying,
'Why is his chariot so long
in coming?
Why don't we hear the sound of
chariot wheels?'

29 "Her wise women answer,
and she repeats these words to
herself:
30 'They must be dividing the captured
plunder—
with a woman or two for every
man.
There will be colorful robes for
Sisera,
and colorful, embroidered robes
for me.
Yes, the plunder will include
colorful robes embroidered on
both sides.'

31 "LORD, may all your enemies die like
Sisera!
But may those who love you rise
like the sun in all its power!"

Then there was peace in the land for forty years.

5:7 The meaning of the Hebrew is uncertain. **5:11** The meaning of the Hebrew is uncertain.

NOTES

5:1 ***Deborah and Barak son of Abinoam sang this song.*** The text's inclusion of Barak in the song of victory alongside Deborah reinforces the observation (see note on 4:9a) that neither the author nor Deborah censured Barak. The song begins by praising the kinds of leaders of which Barak was the most conspicuous representative, which also accentuates his heroic place in the narrative, even if he was not ultimately the center of attention.

5:2 ***Israel's leaders took charge.*** "Took charge" (*para'* [TH6544, ZH7276]) can be translated variously (Lindars 1995:225-227). Its usages, such as "release from restraints," "releasing hair (in a disheveled manner)," or "taking the lead," likely all participate in a common set of ideas rooted in either charismatic leadership or a battle-worthy "berserker" spirit. Thus, the NLT's rendering is tame; it misses the sense of something being turned loose, of hair let down, of restraints thrown off as leaders passionately embraced their task.

gladly followed. The verbal root here (*nadab* [TH5068, ZH5605]) connotes a free choice, whether describing "freewill" offerings or responding to the call to battle. The unleashed passion of the leaders was met by a ready response from the warriors among the people.

5:4 ***LORD, when you set out from Seir . . . Edom.*** Several allusions in the OT depict Yahweh coming in power from Edom/Seir and the south in general (cf. Exod 15:1-18; Deut 33:1-3; Hab 3:3). This movement of Yahweh from the south, accompanied by torrential rains, forms an important element in the motif of Yahweh as the Divine Warrior (Cross 1971:86, 100-103). These hymns of divine triumph formed a vital part in the earliest Israelite worship in Canaan (Cross 1971:91-111). These motifs indicate that the song is not merely a song of victory, but liturgical poetry by which all Israel celebrated Yahweh's power.

5:5 ***mountains quaked in the presence of the LORD, the God of Mount Sinai.*** The theophanic themes (cf. Ps 68:7-8) of Yahweh marching out to war and the outbreak of a thunderstorm and earthquake resonate both with Canaanite religious imagery—Baal being the god of the thunderstorm—and with the narrative itself in which the storm-swelled Kishon served Yahweh's purpose in overturning his enemy. The whole cosmos participating in the divine victory also features in the motif of the Divine Warrior (cf. note on 5:4). God's appearance at Sinai (Exod 19:9-25; 20:18-21) was the theophany par excellence, hence God is identified as *zeh sinay* [TH2088/5514, ZH2296/6099], meaning "this One of Sinai" (NLT, "God of Mount Sinai").

5:6 ***In the days of Shamgar . . . in the days of Jael.*** The implication that Shamgar (3:31) was a contemporary of Jael suggests the time period of the Deborah story. Regarding this, see the note on 4:2. The logic of the poem does not require that the first named person (Shamgar) be an oppressor; Shamgar might have been a brigand or bandit who did Israel a good turn (see note on 3:31). Mentioning Jael in the context of travelers comports with the note in 4:11 that Heber had moved his household north to the Beth-shan valley area, likely from the area around Arad (cf. 1:16).

people avoided the main roads, and travelers stayed on winding pathways. The economy of Canaan depended on the trade routes. With the coastal routes open, trade flowed easily, but as the urban centers of the eastern Mediterranean began to fall in the decades surrounding 1200 BC to a variety of forces, such as the Sea Peoples, trade was interrupted and forced up to the watershed ridge routes. These were less secure and were exploited by bandits as they wound through the hill country. The confusion intervening between the withdrawal of Egypt from Canaan (c. 1150 BC) and the rise of Philistia (1070 BC) and then Israel (c. 1010 BC) would have made any movement on the ridge road precarious. With traffic shunted off to secondary roads exposed to looting, the aspect of the economy dependent on trade was shut down.

5:7 ***There were few people left in the villages of Israel.*** The NLT suggests depopulation of the hill country villages, and commentators since Rashi have suggested the villagers abandoned their homes and fled to cities. Many proposals for *perazon* [TH6520, ZH7251] (villages) exist in the literature, ranging from "peasantry," "leaders," and even "iron" (reading *parzon*, a dialectal variant on *barzel* [TH1270, ZH1366], and linking the line to the note that Israel lacked weapons in 5:8). The reference to occupants of unwalled villages seems most likely.

Archaeological findings indicate, however, a burgeoning of the village population of the Israelite hill country throughout Iron Age I, so how did the "villager cease?" The key must be the verb, *khadelu* [TH2308, ZH2532]. Traditionally translated "cease," the verb embraces a wider range of meanings, including restraint of various kinds. In 5:6, the caravans *khadelu*—they do not "cease" but are diverted to circuitous paths—i.e., they are restrained. Perhaps here the idea is that the economic crisis cramped the growing population of the Israelite villages that were dotting the hill country with increasing density.

until Deborah arose as a mother for Israel. The NLT follows the LXX and Vulgate in abandoning the first-person reference, lit., "until I, Deborah, arose, I arose, a mother in Israel." Thinking of Deborah as mother "of/for" Israel might imply more than the text's "in Israel" (*beyisra'el* [TH871.2, ZH928]) says. Is Deborah metaphorically the mother of the nation, or was she identifying herself simply as one of the people? Nothing else in the text suggests the former, but the volunteer spirit celebrated throughout this song might favor the latter. Emphasizing Deborah as a mother generates a powerful contrast with Sisera's mother at the end of the poem (Lindars 1995:238).

5:8 *When Israel chose new gods.* The NLT makes explicit what is implicit in the Hebrew, which only says "(one/he) chose new gods," implying "Israel" as the subject. Since Israel had been named immediately prior to this verse, the poet perhaps felt no need to repeat the name. The clause might also be interpreted idiomatically as an impersonal passive "new gods were chosen." Another suggested translation "God chose new (men)" (Lindars 1995:239-241; followed by Block 1999) fits the text but not the larger context, even granting elements of his construal of the next line.

war erupted at the city gates. The NLT seems more dramatic than the Hebrew, which reads "then war (was in the) gates." The particle *'az* [TH227, ZH255] (then) sometimes introduces the apodosis of a conditional clause. The difficulty of the line has led to suggestions involving different word divisions and vocalizations, the most convincing being Lindars's re-reading *'az lakhem she'arim* (then war [was in the] gates) as *'az ['az]elu khamushe 'arim*, "then the armed men of the cities came forth" (Lindars 1995:240), which would follow well on his suggestion for the preceding line. The main problem lies in the use of *'azal* [TH235, ZH261] in biblical Hebrew meaning not "come forth" but rather "disappear, pass away" (cf. Deut 32:36; 1 Sam 9:7; Job 14:11). If the sense is "then the armed men of the cities vanished," we might see a reason why God had to choose "new (men)" (see note on 5:8a), or, declining Lindars's suggestion for 5:8a, we could see malaise among leaders as part of the larger reality of economic depression and religious defection.

Yet not a shield or spear could be seen among forty thousand warriors in Israel! The lack of arms and armor could point to the lack of metallurgy in twelfth-century BC Israel, noted by the oft-cited (and misunderstood) 1 Sam 13:19-22. Certainly if my suggestion has merit that Heber the Kenite was an itinerant metalworker who put his skills at the disposal of Jabin and Sisera rather than Israel (see note on 4:11), then the claim of unarmed Israelites gains poignancy. Claims of deficient military resources might actually have been a part of ancient Israel's ideology of self-identification that shifted the emphasis to Yahweh's power rather than human prowess. Ironically, archaeological evidence currently does not suggest Israel was less well-armed than its nearest neighbors, though obviously the evidence is incomplete (Bloch-Smith 2003:416-420). The "forty thousand" likely refers to "40 militia companies" and not a literal 40,000. Before we feel too bad for the underarmed Israelites, we do well to remember that an earlier pharaoh, Merneptah, even in claiming to have defeated "Israel," still named Israel in company with Ashkelon, Gezer, and Yanoam—no mean ranking (Stager 1988:223).

5:9 ***commanders.*** The NLT's "commanders," though accurate and in accord with most translations, might miss an important nuance of the term *khoqeqe* [TH2710A, ZH2980], a participle based on a verb meaning to hollow out, inscribe, or engrave. The Qal participle in Isa 22:16 referring to one hewing out a tomb testifies to the active persistence of this nuance. The derived noun is traditionally translated "statutes" in reference to specific prescribed obligations. Influenced by the Polel participle appearing in 5:14 ("commanders"), some would emend this reference, but it is not necessary. While it is not fashionable to claim literacy for premonarchic Israel, the term *khoqeq* could imply an official whose duties involved the writing of specific orders or instructions, or even one who records the name of those who report for battle (Block 1999:228). Certainly the author speaks of writing elsewhere in the book (cf. 8:14). The Targum follows this lead and develops a whole interpretation of this phrase based on Israel's adherence to the written Torah.

those who volunteered for war. The NLT here expands slightly on the Hebrew text, which reads "those volunteering among the people." While war is clearly in the context, it is not in this clause, which instead repeats the complementary mention of both leaders and volunteers found in 5:2.

5:10 ***ride on fine donkeys, you who sit on fancy saddle blankets.*** The term "fine" actually denotes a preferred color of donkey, but the suggestion that these are rich merchants showing off their finery (Block 1999:228) conflicts with empirical evidence. Israelite material culture in Iron I is conspicuous for its lack of luxury items such as imported or painted pottery and the broad repertoire of pottery forms found in Canaanite and Philistine sites. This seems to have been a choice based on a commitment to simplicity (Faust 2009). Traders, they likely were, but mainly in necessary goods the Israelites could not make themselves. Likewise, the translation of *middin* [TH4055, ZH4496] as "fancy saddle blankets," though traditional, imports the term "saddle" to a term that actually only refers to garments in general, following the tradition of LXX Alexandrinus, which translates with *lampēnē* (covered chariot or wagon). Less likely, some suggest "sit in judgment" by deriving *middin* from the root *d-y-n* [TH1777, ZH1906], a tradition reflected by LXX Vaticanus, the Vulgate, and Targums. As a point of cultural and historical authenticity, the text notes donkeys in caravan, not camels (see note on 6:5). The reference to caravans and traders fits well with the fact that while early Israel was largely a subsistence economy, exchange and contact among the tribes and even peoples outside of Israel remained a necessity. Indeed, in a complex chiefdom (likely early Israel's social structure), the elite families maintained their influence largely by facilitating the exchange of selected prestige goods among the various satellite villages in their domains (R. Miller 2005:6-14). If the donkeys and blankets mentioned are in fact signs of wealth, such as that might have been in Iron I agrarian villages, the reference could be to the relatively more affluent members of the community. A breakdown in exchange among the regions of Canaan directly threatened Israel's unity and coherence. Some find in the three clauses of this verse three different social classes, but this is unlikely.

5:11 ***Listen to the village musicians gathered at the watering holes.*** This line in the Hebrew compounds obscurities: "from the sound of the ones dividing between the drinking troughs." Numerous alternatives exist (Lindars 1995:245-247); the NLT captures the most likely understanding.

righteous victories of the LORD and . . . of his villagers. The word *tsidqoth* [TH6666, ZH7407] expresses the concept of vindication, thus "Yahweh's acts of vindication." This line articulates the essential theme of the song: Yahweh acts mightily to demonstrate his supremacy simultaneously with his people stepping forward to venture mighty acts in his name. He vindicates both his own character and their trust in him.

the people of the LORD marched down to the city gates. Here the song turns definitively to the responses of the people to the challenge as they gather at the gates, where they seek a word from Deborah and urge Barak to battle. Here the roles are (at last) reversed. Instead of a demoralized and suppressed populace that needs urging from its leaders, now the people come down and ask the leaders to take action. Again, we hear no hint of shame associated with Barak, nor any hint of tension between Deborah and Barak.

5:13 ***Down from Tabor marched the few against the nobles.*** Lit., "then a survivor went down to/ruled the nobles." The NLT makes a bold stab at this difficult line, construing the word *sarid* [TH8300, ZH8586] (survivor) as "few," and adding a reference to Mount Tabor. A much simpler proposal comes from Na'aman (2005:303-305), who points out the village of Sarid (Tell Shadud) located on the southernmost spur of the Nazareth ridge, at the southern border of Naphtali, and just north of the main path of the Canaanite retreat. Israelites from the tribe of Naphtali, sweeping over from Sarid against the retreating Canaanites would constitute a flanking movement to push the Canaanites off the higher ground into the slush and mud created by sudden storm. The translation, "Then Sarid came down to/against the mighty ones" easily fits the text, illuminates the narrative, and requires no emendation.

The people of the LORD marched down against mighty warriors. Lit., "Yahweh's people came down to me against the mighty ones." The NLT omits "to me" but if we retain the first-person character of the poem in which Deborah is both poet and participant in the action, the line can be rendered more literally with the MT.

5:14 ***They came down from Ephraim—a land that once belonged to the Amalekites.*** A notoriously vexing line, only four words in Hebrew! *Minni 'eprayim shorsham ba'amaleq*: "From Ephraim, their root (is) in Amalek." The NLT takes "root" (*shoresh* [TH8328, ZH9247]) to refer to previous occupancy, but Amalek is characteristically associated with the southern desert and is not noted as originating in the hill country of Ephraim. Judges 12:15 does refer to Ephraim as "the hill country of the Amalekites," while 7:12 links the Amalekites to the Midianites who ravaged the lower Jezreel valley in the Gideon story. These links, however, do not allow for Amalek as the erstwhile claimants of Mount Ephraim, as "their root" would require. Most scholars think the text has suffered in the copying process, with two changes suggested (Lindars 1995:252-253): First, *ba'amaleq* [TH6002, ZH6667] (in Amalek) is a scribal error for *be'emeq* [TH6010, ZH6677] ("in the valley"—the Jezreel valley). This reading is reflected in LXX Alexandrinus and Theodotian, and is followed by many contemporary translations. Second, "their root" is taken as a loan word from Egyptian denoting a high officer (cf. Gen 37:36). These two suggestions yield this sense: "from Ephraim, officers [went down] to the valley."

they followed you, Benjamin, with your troops. The NLT paraphrases what seems to be a battle cry: "After you, O Benjamin, with your peoples!" The plural of "people" often denotes fellow kinsmen of tribe or clan (Lindars 1995:253-254; Burney 1920:134).

Makir. Makir (e.g., Gen 50:23; Num 26:29; 27:1), along with Ephraim and Benjamin, constitute the inhabitants of the central hill country north of Jerusalem and south of the Jezreel valley.

those who carry a commander's staff. The stress on the leaders of the tribes, as well as on the warriors themselves, drives the poet to employ a wide range of terms. The NLT follows most modern translations, but *beshebet soper* [TH5608A, ZH6221] is literally "a scribe's staff." Most commentators and translators presuppose that pre-monarchial Israel had little or no writing, certainly no scribes. Recent discoveries, such as the Khirbet Qeiyafa ostracon (Garfinkel and Ganor 2009:243-272) possibly allow us to move writing in Israel back at least to c. 1000 BC. The biblical author was thinking of scribes, contra modern versions. The reference might well be to leaders capable of writing.

5:15 ***The princes of Issachar were with Deborah and Barak. They followed Barak.*** To the extent that "prince" implies a royal culture, it misses the sense of *sar* [TH8269, ZH8569]. In a tribal culture, "sheikh" or "chief" better expresses the social reality. The Hebrew for this line is awkward, reading "Issachar's chiefs (were) with Deborah, and Issachar likewise (was with) Barak." "Likewise" (*ken* [TH3651A, ZH4027]) might also be translated "was true." The sense of the verse, though, seems to be that Issachar followed Barak and Deborah with equal alacrity.

in the tribe of Reuben there was great indecision. "Tribe" here is better rendered "divisions," referring to the clans and families of Reuben. Tribal cultures at times cannot respond decisively to a crisis, but bog down in debates and discussions among elders as competing interests of different branches of the community come to the fore. This inability contributed to Israel morphing into a dynastic, monarchic state. Since Reuben deliberated to the point of paralysis, even dereliction, perhaps "factions" best renders the term: "in the factions of Reuben, there was great indecision." The use of the root *kh-q-q* [TH2710, ZH2980] to denote indecision puns wickedly on the occurrence of this root elsewhere in the song to denote the courageous initiative of Israel's leaders (cf. 5:9, 14). The Reubenites might be castigated as "armchair warriors" (Lindars 1995:260).

5:16 ***Why did you sit at home among the sheepfolds?*** "At home" is not literally in the Hebrew text, but since the same image appears in Gen 49:14 (cf. NLT mg), where it is applied to Issachar, Lindars suggests this is an idiom for "stay at home." Stager (1989) notes that Reuben and Gilead/Gad were principally pastoralist tribes, and points out the deep enmeshment between pastoralist groups and fixed settlements. Had these tribes struck out against the Canaanites, they would have jeopardized their own way of life. By contrast, the tribes who came to the battle all lived in areas characterized by self-sufficient farming villages; they had nothing to lose and much to gain from the destruction of Canaanite urban centers.

5:17 ***And why did Dan stay home?*** The traditional translation "why did he abide with the ships?" encounters problems. Dan originally settled in the Shephelah region near Zorah and Eshtaol, and later migrated to the far north (cf. ch 18). Craigie (1983:84-86), based on a Ugaritic parallel, renders *'oniyyoth* [TH591, ZH641] (ships) as "at ease," making the reference one of complacency. The idea is similar to the NLT's "stay home." Stager (1988, 1989) revived the proposal of Moore (1895:155-156) that the verse asserts Dan's status as a dependent or client of the seafaring coastal communities, implying Dan had reached an economic impasse. Being economically entangled with non-Israelites, the Danites could not bite the hand that fed them. Interestingly, in 18:7, 28 the town Laish/Dan is compared to Sidon, a coastal shipping center.

Asher sat unmoved at the seashore. Asher settled in the coastal plain of Acco but lived "among the Canaanites," implying subjection to them (1:31-32). Since the coastal Levantine economy benefited from a revived Egyptian-Canaanite imperial cooperation, it is likely the Asherites saw that military action against them would risk their own meal ticket.

5:18 ***Zebulun risked his life.*** Lit., "Zebulun was a people [who] scorned their [own] lives to the point of death!" The very strong wording is reminiscent of the commendation of the holy martyrs in Rev 12:11.

as did Naphtali. Here finally the tribe of Barak finds mention.

on the heights of the battlefield. For infantry to present themselves to chariot forces in the open field constituted an extreme military risk. Such unconventional tactics account for Barak's caution when first urged by Deborah to lead the battle. Once the Israelite foot soldiers took the open field before the chariotry of Sisera, something extraordinary needed to happen or the Israelites would be butchered. Such is the boldness celebrated in this song.

5:19 ***at Taanach near Megiddo's springs.*** This location fits the suggestion that Harosheth-haggoyim was the southern end of the valley of Jezreel. Both of these cities saw destruction in the late 1100s BC, though the text does not claim that Israel destroyed them. Whether they were standing at the time of the battle, or fell later with the collapse of Egyptian imperial aspirations, is not clear. These conspicuous sites, however, would have been well known.

no silver treasures. "Treasures" translates *betsa'* [TH1215, ZH1299], derived from a word meaning "cut," which denotes a range of gain from interest on a loan to any kind of advantage or profit. Sisera got no "cut" from this battle. This note of his failure foreshadows the poem's final section in which Sisera's mother harbors vain fantasies of material gain from the battle.

5:20 ***The stars fought from heaven . . . against Sisera.*** The name "Sisera" was delayed for the entire poem until this moment, where its entry has dramatic impact. The reference to stars is typically taken to suggest a divine cause for the thunderstorm and swollen waters of the Kishon. But the appearance of a star or other heavenly body as a sign of divine power for Israel may also be in view (cf. e.g., Num 24:17). In the first Asiatic campaign of Thutmose III (1479 BC), in which his victory against Megiddo figures conspicuously, a shooting star apparently convinced both Thutmose and his enemies that divine power was on the pharaoh's side (COS 2:17). More importantly, a common element in the OT Divine Warrior motif is the involvement of the cosmos in the victory of Yahweh (Cross 1971).

5:21 ***The Kishon River swept them away.*** The Kishon, normally a modest stream, becomes treacherous when flooded, as the waters drench the red soil of the valley, turning it into mire. Ironically, in dry weather, the same soil is ideal ground for chariot maneuver, as Thutmose III found in 1479 BC when he surprised the Canaanites on this battleground near Megiddo.

5:22 ***horses' hooves hammered . . . galloping, galloping.*** The introduction of the verb "hammer" (*halam* [TH1986, ZH2150]) prepares for the striking irony of Jael "hammering" Sisera's head (5:26). The NLT's alliteration, along with "galloping, galloping" captures exactly the sonic impact of the Hebrew verbs: *halemu . . . middaharoth dahroth.*

5:23 ***Let the people of Meroz be cursed.*** The identity of Meroz remains contested. That it is a place name is implied by the following line in Hebrew: "cursed . . . be its inhabitants." Conjectures abound, but since this is the only reference to Meroz in the OT, they remain guesswork. More interesting is the fact that aside from shaming and cursing, Deborah had no other means of securing the cooperation of the reluctant tribes. Shaming and cursing had sociological consequences, and in all probability, the shamed and cursed noncombatants later found themselves isolated from the assistance offered by their highland brothers.

said the angel of the LORD. Already in 2:15, the angel or messenger of Yahweh (*mal'ak yhwh* [TH4397/3068, ZH4855/3378]) had delivered a stinging rebuke, near Bethel, on the derelict northern tribes, who failed to remove Canaanite religion and culture completely from Israel's territory.

because they did not come to help the LORD. The term translated "help" (*'ezrah* [TH5833, ZH6476]) denotes not mere assistance, but a vital support and cooperation. The Hebrew reads "the help of Yahweh"; while "to help the LORD" is correct, interpreters should take care not to conclude from the text that Yahweh needs assistance! The line might have the sense, "they did not enter into the help [provided by] Yahweh." The text has emphasized Yahweh's power in the battle, but also celebrates the willing and valiant response of the people. Though Yahweh is the supreme God, needing no assistance, he does call his people to participate in his work.

5:24 ***Most blessed among women is Jael.*** The blessing pronounced here reminds the Christian reader of the cry of Elizabeth upon seeing the pregnant Mary (Luke 1:42).

5:25 ***yogurt.*** Pastoralist cultures develop forms of milk beverages based on the controlled curdling and, often, fermentation of milk to prevent spoiling, such as Indian ghee or Kenyan *mursik*. To serve a fermented beverage to one who has only asked for water suggests that Jael intended to dull the awareness of the already-exhausted Sisera (cf. note on 4:21). Maybe Sisera was hammered before he got hammered!

5:26 ***She struck Sisera with the hammer.*** The NLT's "struck . . . with the hammer" translates the verb *halam* [TH1986, ZH2150], used in 5:22 to convey the hammering of the hooves of Sisera's steeds. The derivative noun (*halmuth* [TH1989, ZH2153], "hammer") appears in the previous line, producing alliteration. "Struck . . . with the hammer" could well be rendered "hammered" here, yielding a line reproducing the abruptness of the original (cf. NET).

crushing. The verb *makhaq* [TH4277, ZH4735] appears only here in the OT. Cognates in other Semitic languages suggest "exterminate, obliterate," underscoring along with the next verb the terrific destructive force of the blow.

With a shattering blow, she pierced. This represents two verbs, "and she smashed and she pierced," which underline the brutality of the attack, especially if "his temples" (*raqqatho* [TH7541, ZH8377]) refers to Sisera's "(open) mouth" (see note on 4:21).

5:27 ***He sank, he fell, he lay still.*** These three staccato verbs provide a stop-action, almost cinematic image of Sisera's collapse. The first verb, *kara'* [TH3766, ZH4156], resonates somewhat with the root *kana'* [TH3665, ZH4044], "to be low," that occurs four times in 4:23-24.

at her feet. The description in 5:26 poses a few issues, but is notable for its devastating dramatic force. The differences between poetry and prose readily account for the differences in detail between the poem and the prose of ch 4. "At her feet" carries a satiric sexual connotation, being more directly translated as "between her feet," a rare combination of "between" with "feet" (cf. Deut 28:57, KJV). Rather than sexually exploiting a woman after a victorious battle, Sisera had been dominated by a woman. Assertions of any actual sexual event in the story, however, miss the thrust of the imagery.

there he died. See the note on 4:22. The Heb., *sham napal shadud* [TH7703, ZH8720] (there he fell, devastated), resonates with the prose account's conclusion in 4:22, (lit.) "and there was Sisera, fallen down dead," and with the discovery of Eglon's death (3:25). This record of the sight of each great enemy destroyed seems a literary way of celebrating the enemy's demise.

5:28 ***Sisera's mother looked out.*** We now encounter the third woman of the story. First, Deborah arose as a "mother in Israel." Then the scene shifts to Jael, "most blessed among women." Now Sisera's mother provides the foil against which the victory of Israel is seen. If her residence was in Harosheth-haggoyim, in the vicinity of Megiddo or Taanach, she might well have been able to hear the sounds of battle. The complete ruination of Jabin and Sisera (see note on 4:23-24) could imply the destruction of Canaanite residences in the Jezreel valley, including the capture and death of Sisera's mother, throwing this scene into grim relief.

5:30 ***with a woman or two for every man.*** The crass brutality of the language does not immediately appear in English. Rape and pillage are in view. For "woman" the text uses a word coined from "womb," naming captive females by reference to their sexual organs. HALOT (2.1218; s.v. *rakhamah* [TH7361, ZH8169]) grimly identifies this as "a euphemism for vaginas, meaning one or two women as spoils of war, bed-mates, in vulgar conversation of soldiers." Thus, Lindars (1995:285) suggests "wenches." That such vulgarity toward captive girls finds expression on the lips not of a rough soldier, but of high-born women at court, reveals the callous heart of an oppressor.

5:31 *LORD, may all your enemies die like Sisera!* Lit., "thus will all your enemies perish, O Yahweh." Limiting the analogy to Sisera blunts the edge of this verse. Coming on the heels of the portrait of Sisera's mother, who possibly faced her own demise that day, this declaration by a woman lends poignancy to the poem's climactic ultimatum. On the other hand, the killing of women does not feature prominently in Israelite heroism, so it is possible the poet leaves her fate unresolved. As the poem "fades to black," it leaves the reader imagining her awestruck grief when she learns the truth.

may those who love you rise like the sun. "Love" is known to be a covenant term, denoting the full loyalty and devotion of the vassal to the king (Moran 1963:77-85). The rising sun figures in ancient Near Eastern lore as a hero going forth in triumph (cf. Ps 19:5). This line could therefore portray the lovers of Yahweh as the genuinely valiant heroes. The kinglets of Canaan in their correspondence regularly address the pharaoh of Egypt as "my sun god." How right that those who have defeated the petty potentates of Canaan, Yahweh's own loyal covenant vassals, are now compared to the morning sun, while for Canaan, pharaoh's sun has set.

Then there was peace in the land for forty years. The standard framework formula concludes the story and brings the reader back to the linear historical pattern shaping 3:7–16:31.

COMMENTARY

The Song of Deborah (5:1-31a) intervenes between the prose conclusion (4:23-24) and the final author's epilogue (5:31b). This song originated in the twelfth century BC and often manifests archaic vocabulary, grammar, and stylistic features. It likely began as an oral song and found constant reuse in Israel's celebrations and remembrance. Oral material adapts over time; thus, the song does not appear in Judges in its original form. The language was updated periodically to reflect the usage of subsequent generations much as we today freshen up the English style and diction of texts written in earlier centuries, such as is done in modern renderings of Beowulf or Chaucer. Thus, the responsive echo of later generations who affirmed their own faith through this song finds a voice in the text. Attempts to reconstruct the original twelfth-century poem, though insightful, can obscure the integrated historical and spiritual dynamics of the canonical text.

The song's archaic language and poetic style confused ancient scribes and translators, and continues to challenge modern scholars. Lindars (1995:212-222) provides an assessment of scholarly approaches to the song's interpretive issues. Rather than attempt a reconstruction of the original poem, the NLT and this commentary generally follow the canonical text (MT), though some emendation remains necessary to allow the poem's voice to emerge clearly.

Issues of genre, date, and purpose engage much scholarly attention (Block 1999:211-219; Butler 2009:110-135). Most refer to the song as a "hymn," reflecting the consensus that it is very likely liturgical poetry, seen in its communal, public performance, its celebration and bold proclamation of the mighty acts of Yahweh, its use of the Divine Warrior motif, its appeal to the hearer to join in the spirit of the song, and in its pronouncement of blessings and curses on tribes who fought and those who did not. The singer praises Yahweh and urges the hearer to join in the praises of Yahweh for a mighty victory against the foe. More importantly, in the Old Testament, liturgical song preserves and proclaims the historical memory of Yahweh's mighty acts in a manner that makes that same power available to the contemporary worshipers. Von Rad (1966:166-204) aptly terms this *Vergegenwärtigung*, meaning "actualization." The song re-presents the historical acts of Yahweh to enable the later hearer to appropriate Yahweh's promise for the present. The very real past meets the very needy present in the worshiping congregation. When this oral poetry is committed to writing, its *content* is enabled to transcend its "live" social-liturgical function as an object of reflection beyond the ethnic boundaries of the communal worship experience. By embedding the song in the total literary context of the book, the author allowed the process of re-actualization to occur as the poem interacts thematically and theologically with its surrounding literary context. Thus, the text is neither exclusively antiquarian nor entirely abstract; it is not "timeless" but ever-timely.

The song evinces a clear structure. It proclaims its thesis in 5:2, then moves to an epiphany of Yahweh (5:3-5). The description of the crisis in 5:6-8 slips over into the defining moment presented by the call to arms (5:9-11a), followed by the praise of those who dared to join the battle (5:11b-15, 18), and enclosing a bitter shaming of those who chose not to heed the call (5:16-17). The battle description proper moves in a series of images, but does not necessarily offer a rigidly consecutive narrative (5:19-23). The closing scenes dramatically portray Jael's murder of Sisera (5:24-27) and the repulsive picture of Sisera's mother awaiting his arrival with captives and spoil (5:28-30). The song's ending (5:31) confronts the reader with the defining significance of one's relationship with Yahweh as either a foe or a friend.

Judges 5 is distinctive in that alongside its praise of the Divine Warrior, it ascribes mighty deeds also to the people of Israel, who do not simply stand silent and behold the victory won by Yahweh. Yahweh fights, but Israel must "come to help the LORD" (5:23). Just as Deborah had challenged Barak to lead the army, now she celebrates the volunteers and chides those who sat the battle out. The tribal militia of Israel fighting for their lives against the Egyptian-Canaanite allied forces is reminiscent of William Wallace and his fellow kinsmen as portrayed in *Braveheart*. Far from merely informing the people, the prophet stirred the people with Yahweh's word to rise to the challenge of battle. Deborah is both catalyst in her word of commission to Barak, and celebrant of the victory in the song (5:1).

Deborah's praise of Israel's leaders and the volunteers (5:2) lauds their unbridled battle-passion and willing embrace of the call to arms as human instruments for Yahweh's power. Turning to address pagan rulers, the song emphasizes that the coming of Yahweh, not military might, procures Israel's victory (5:3-5), just as the prose battle narrative (4:11-16) emphasized the primacy of divine intervention. Judges 5:6-9 then turns back to the human dimension and accentuates the resurgence of the volunteer spirit by stressing the paralysis and powerlessness brought on by oppression and, possibly, apostasy. As in 4:6-10, Deborah shook her people out of their lethargy (5:7); the princes and volunteers are praised again (5:9). Judges 5:10-12 emphasizes the power of reciting Yahweh's righteous acts in provoking the Hebrews to mobilize, concurring with the stress of chapter 4 on the prophetic word as the key to victory. The roll call of the tribes (5:13-18) praises initiative and daring (5:13-15a), including the action of a single village, Sarid, in attacking the flank of the Canaanites (see note on 5:13). The song then castigates Reuben's indecisiveness (15b-16), Gilead's isolation, Dan's cooptation, and Asher's unwillingness to risk its security (5:17). Praise for Zebulun and Naphtali's bold embrace of mortal risk climaxes the list (cf. 4:6, 10). The saving action of Yahweh is celebrated in 5:19-23, but the primary vehicles of his power are not the judges, as one might expect, but the forces of nature: the stars and the torrents of the river Kishon. That Yahweh alone is the main protagonist in the battle throws the decision to join or avoid battle into a new light. Those who stayed away did not betray humans, but Yahweh himself. Thus Meroz is cursed emphatically (5:23), while the wife of a Kenite traitor, by throwing in her lot with Israel, becomes "most blessed among women" and the real hero of the story. Her actions are immortalized in 5:24-27. In contrast to the gutsy faith of Jael stands the mother of Sisera and her attendants, who callously fantasize that Sisera is slow to return because he's busy despoiling the Hebrews and molesting their maidens; they thought he would soon be back—with presents! The brutal irony is that Israel's women would stand over the bodies of slain Canaanites while she and her wealthy attendants would likely face imminent capture or death as the victorious Israelites completed the task of humbling Canaan and completely cutting off Jabin and his lackeys like Sisera.

Judges 5:31a declares the point of the entire story and song: To oppose Yahweh is to perish; to love him is to know ever-growing strength. The sun metaphor and reference to loving Yahweh employs the same rhetoric that Canaan's kinglets used in addressing pharaoh (see note on 5:31). One can, in love and loyalty to Yahweh, face the sunrise, or one can defy Yahweh and walk into the darkness of death with Jabin, Sisera, and all their camp (4:16). The love of Yahweh is embodied in the faithful and risky choices made by Barak, the volunteers of Israel, and Jael. Most of all, the stimulus, sustenance, and celebration of that love is embodied by Deborah, mother in Israel (5:7), the bearer of the divine word. She and the word she represents are the true heroes of the story. Naturally, no death notice appears at the story's end. The deeds of charismatic individuals fade with their death, flashes in the pan. But the action of God, the passionate commitment of his people, and the all-embracing and empowering word are not confined by a single human lifetime.

◆ C. Stage Two: Transition (6:1–10:5)

1. Gideon: Authority and ambivalence (6:1–8:32)

a. Ambivalence before the call (6:1-40)

The Israelites did evil in the LORD's sight. So the LORD handed them over to the Midianites for seven years. [2]The Midianites were so cruel that the Israelites made hiding places for themselves in the mountains, caves, and strongholds. [3]Whenever the Israelites planted their crops, marauders from Midian, Amalek, and the people of the east would attack Israel, [4]camping in the land and destroying crops as far away as Gaza. They left the Israelites with nothing to eat, taking all the sheep, goats, cattle, and donkeys. [5]These enemy hordes, coming with their livestock and tents, were as thick as locusts; they arrived on droves of camels too numerous to count. And they stayed until the land was stripped bare. [6]So Israel was reduced to starvation by the Midianites. Then the Israelites cried out to the LORD for help.

7When they cried out to the LORD because of Midian, 8the LORD sent a prophet to the Israelites. He said, "This is what the LORD, the God of Israel, says: I brought you up out of slavery in Egypt. 9I rescued you from the Egyptians and from all who oppressed you. I drove out your enemies and gave you their land. 10I told you, 'I am the LORD your God. You must not worship the gods of the Amorites, in whose land you now live.' But you have not listened to me."

11Then the angel of the LORD came and sat beneath the great tree at Ophrah, which belonged to Joash of the clan of Abiezer. Gideon son of Joash was threshing wheat at the bottom of a winepress to hide the grain from the Midianites. 12The angel of the LORD appeared to him and said, "Mighty hero, the LORD is with you!"

13"Sir," Gideon replied, "if the LORD is with us, why has all this happened to us? And where are all the miracles our ancestors told us about? Didn't they say, 'The LORD brought us up out of Egypt'? But now the LORD has abandoned us and handed us over to the Midianites."

14Then the LORD turned to him and said, "Go with the strength you have, and rescue Israel from the Midianites. I am sending you!"

15"But Lord," Gideon replied, "how can I rescue Israel? My clan is the weakest in the whole tribe of Manasseh, and I am the least in my entire family!"

16The LORD said to him, "I will be with you. And you will destroy the Midianites as if you were fighting against one man."

17Gideon replied, "If you are truly going to help me, show me a sign to prove that it is really the LORD speaking to me. 18Don't go away until I come back and bring my offering to you."

He answered, "I will stay here until you return."

19Gideon hurried home. He cooked a young goat, and with a basket* of flour he baked some bread without yeast. Then, carrying the meat in a basket and the broth in a pot, he brought them out and presented them to the angel, who was under the great tree.

20The angel of God said to him, "Place the meat and the unleavened bread on this rock, and pour the broth over it." And Gideon did as he was told. 21Then the angel of the LORD touched the meat and bread with the tip of the staff in his hand, and fire flamed up from the rock and consumed all he had brought. And the angel of the LORD disappeared.

22When Gideon realized that it was the angel of the LORD, he cried out, "Oh, Sovereign LORD, I'm doomed! I have seen the angel of the LORD face to face!"

23"It is all right," the LORD replied. "Do not be afraid. You will not die." 24And Gideon built an altar to the LORD there and named it Yahweh-Shalom (which means "the LORD is peace"). The altar remains in Ophrah in the land of the clan of Abiezer to this day.

25That night the LORD said to Gideon, "Take the second bull from your father's herd, the one that is seven years old. Pull down your father's altar to Baal, and cut down the Asherah pole standing beside it. 26Then build an altar to the LORD your God here on this hilltop sanctuary, laying the stones carefully. Sacrifice the bull as a burnt offering on the altar, using as fuel the wood of the Asherah pole you cut down."

27So Gideon took ten of his servants and did as the LORD had commanded. But he did it at night because he was afraid of the other members of his father's household and the people of the town.

28Early the next morning, as the people of the town began to stir, someone discovered that the altar of Baal had been broken down and that the Asherah pole beside it had been cut down. In their place a new altar had been built, and on it were the remains of the bull that had been sacrificed. 29The people said to each other, "Who did this?" And after asking around and making a careful search, they learned that it was Gideon, the son of Joash.

30"Bring out your son," the men of the

town demanded of Joash. "He must die for
destroying the altar of Baal and for cut-
ting down the Asherah pole."
31But Joash shouted to the mob that
confronted him, "Why are you defending
Baal? Will you argue his case? Whoever
pleads his case will be put to death by
morning! If Baal truly is a god, let him
defend himself and destroy the one who
broke down his altar!" 32From then on
Gideon was called Jerub-baal, which
means "Let Baal defend himself," because
he broke down Baal's altar.

33Soon afterward the armies of Midian,
Amalek, and the people of the east formed
an alliance against Israel and crossed the
Jordan, camping in the valley of Jezreel.
34Then the Spirit of the LORD took posses-
sion of Gideon. He blew a ram's horn as a
call to arms, and the men of the clan of
Abiezer came to him. 35He also sent mes-
sengers throughout Manasseh, Asher,
Zebulun, and Naphtali, summoning their
warriors, and all of them responded.
36Then Gideon said to God, "If you are
truly going to use me to rescue Israel as
you promised, 37prove it to me in this way.
I will put a wool fleece on the threshing
floor tonight. If the fleece is wet with dew
in the morning but the ground is dry, then
I will know that you are going to help me
rescue Israel as you promised." 38And that
is just what happened. When Gideon got
up early the next morning, he squeezed
the fleece and wrung out a whole bowlful
of water.
39Then Gideon said to God, "Please
don't be angry with me, but let me make
one more request. Let me use the fleece
for one more test. This time let the fleece
remain dry while the ground around it is
wet with dew." 40So that night God did as
Gideon asked. The fleece was dry in the
morning, but the ground was covered
with dew.

6:19 Hebrew *an ephah* [20 quarts or 22 liters].

NOTES

6:1-10 The NLT does a good job of untangling the irregular Hebrew syntax of the opening 10 verses, especially 6:1-7. The difficulty of the Hebrew text is noted by all commentators, some going so far as to call it "ungrammatical" (Moore 1895:178-180). A small Qumran fragment (4QJudg^a [4Q49]) seems to represent an earlier literary edition of the text that lacked some phrases from 6:1-6 and all of 6:7-10 (Ulrich and Cross 1995:161-164, pl. 49; Abegg, Flint, and Ulrich 1999:208-209). The other deliverance narratives in Judges begin with "the Israelites again did evil," translating a distinct idiom (e.g., 3:12; 4:1; 10:6; 13:1). The formula here lacks the idea "again" that appears in the other formula, and it mirrors the report of the first occurrence of "evil" in the book (2:11; 3:7). The variation seems intentional, indicating that, following Deborah, Israel's pause in sinning was of such a kind that the sin in 6:1 is not a resumption of an old evil, but the emergence of a new one. While idolatry is cited in the Othniel story (3:7), it seems to recede into the background in the Ehud-Deborah complex, not featuring in the programmatic introductory passages. In the Gideon story an altar to Baal stands in the center of Gideon's hometown, sponsored by his father.

6:1 ***Midianites.*** The settling Israelites, previously migratory pastoralists like the Midianites and Amalekites, came under pressure from these seminomadic groups as all sought more secure holdings. The Midianites had a long history with Israel: Gen 25:1-6 asserts a genealogical connection between Midian and Israel, reinforced by Moses's sojourn in Midian and marriage to the daughter of Jethro (or Hobab), priest of Midian (Exod 3:1), who also guided the Israelites through the wilderness (Num 10:29; Judg 4:11). The Midianites, however, conspired with Moab to curse and corrupt Israel (Num 22–25), resulting in a command to destroy them (Num 25:16-18; 31:1-20) and the perennial hostility evident in Judges.

Though scholars normally associate the Midianites with the Arabian desert, the stories in Numbers join Josh 13:21 in locating them east of the Jordan River. This location fits the narrative and the topography (see note on 6:2).

6:2 *hiding places.* The term *minharoth* [TH4492, ZH4953] derives from *nahar* [TH5104, ZH5643] (river); it parallels an Arabic word *manhar,* meaning "stream bed, rocky gorge" (Boling 1975:122). The Israelites were driven out of the Jezreel valley back into the hills and their labyrinthine ravines, which they knew well from generations of living in the high country. The LXX Vaticanus tradition translates the word as *trumalia* [TG5168, ZG5584], which is used for the "eye" of a needle (cf. Mark 10:25), capturing the narrow, almost impassible character of these places.

in the mountains, caves, and strongholds. The retreat back to the hill country indicates the Israelites had earlier moved down into the plain of the Esdraelon valley, as the later reference to Ophrah and the Harod stream also imply. Following the breaking of the Egyptian-Canaanite alliance in the valley (ch 4) and the withdrawal of Egypt, Israelites felt free to move into the rich agricultural land of the valley to cultivate crops, thereby abandoning their highland villages. But the Egyptian withdrawal created a vacuum, drawing in other smaller, predatory powers, as various groups vied for control of Canaan. The vicinity of Beth-shan and Rehov, where the Esdraelon valley intersects the Jordan valley, provided a swinging door for groups east of Jordan to flood in and wreak havoc over the very same trade routes running up the valley, across the Carmel ridge, and down the coast to Gaza. The Israelite newcomers found themselves forced to return to their earlier hill-country haunts.

6:3 *Amalek.* Amalek has a distinct place in the OT narrative: their unprovoked, vicious attacks on Israel after the Exodus earned them the permanent antipathy of Israel and Yahweh (Exod 17:8-13; Deut 25:17-19). Saul's failure to subject them to the *kherem* [TH2764, ZH3051] (destruction) triggered his rejection as king by Yahweh (1 Sam 15). Except for their attacks after the Exodus and at Ziklag (1 Sam 30), the Amalekites appear in league with other groups such as the Moabites (3:13) and here, the Midianites. A puzzling reference in the Song of Deborah (unless the text is damaged) associates them with the territory of Ephraim (5:14), as does 12:15, but the Amalekites normally appear in the Negeb and have been associated, archaeologically, along with the Midianites, with the complex of Iron Age I sites at Tel Masos, just east of Beer Sheba, considered by some to be Hormah (Stern 1993–2008:3.986-989). Their presence in ch 6 opposite Beth-shan possibly reflects the highly mobile manner of life of a seminomadic people. Their role as Israel's archenemy appears as late as the book of Esther, where the evil Haman is an "Agagite," a descendant of Agag, king of the Amalekites (1 Sam 15).

6:4 *camping in the land and destroying crops . . . taking all the sheep, goats, cattle, and donkeys.* The list of depredations here well summarizes the mixed agro-pastoralist economy of the Israelite villages. Gideon's tribe and clan apparently had a reputation for viticulture (cf. 8:2), which also could provide one of their few crops for exchange or export. But viticulture demands stability (King and Stager 2001:98). Given the five to seven years needed for vineyards to mature, their wanton destruction by raiders would undo the efforts of many years. Ancient Near Eastern law makes the trampling of fields with one's livestock a grave offense. The Midianites not only raided, but actually set up camp and rustled Israelite cattle, leaving the relatively new Israelite farmsteads wrecked. The story evokes the image of the "Wild West" in which hostile ranchers ran settlers off the range by stampeding cattle over the new homesteads, trampling newly planted crops, wrecking corrals, burning barns, and scattering livestock.

6:5 ***droves of camels too numerous to count.*** While the camel might well have been domesticated around 2000 BC in southern Arabia, large numbers of them used for caravans do not appear in the textual or archaeological record of the Levant until the twelfth century (ABD 1.824-826). The shock and awe conveyed here reflects Israel's—and apparently the narrator's—limited prior exposure to camels, especially in such overwhelming numbers. Camels allowed an enemy to hide deep in the desert, strike quickly, and retire without requiring a pause to refresh the animals (NIDB 1.530-531). Their use clearly added to the terror of the Midianite depredations; so much livestock undoubtedly trampled and ruined the fields and vineyards of the Israelites.

6:6 ***reduced to starvation.*** The words "to starvation" do not appear in the Hebrew text, which simply reads "were brought low." But the inference seems sound, since the entire agricultural production of the newly settled bottomland was shut down.

6:7 ***When they cried out to the LORD because of Midian.*** It is striking that the reference to Israel's cry is repeated, since this formula is not repeated elsewhere. The Qumran fragment 4QJudg[a] (4Q49) omits 6:7-10, and thus the repeated reference to Israel's cry. For that pre-canonical form of the book, the description of the crisis moved directly to the account of the deliverer's appearance.

6:8 ***the LORD sent a prophet.*** The following prophetic invective stands alone in Judges as an example of a classic prophetic "messenger speech" and seems to represent an intentional ancient literary enrichment of the text.

6:9 ***I rescued you from the Egyptians and from all who oppressed you. I drove out your enemies and gave you their land.*** The Egyptians cannot be the same as "all who oppressed you" since the latter, whom Yahweh "drove out," previously claimed the land as their own ("I gave you their land"). The verse hints that some members of Israel originated from within the land and suffered under oppressive rule. For such, the arrival of the Israelites constituted a deliverance. Since the oppressive Canaanite kings ruled under the authority of Egypt, these "Canaanite converts" (cf. Josh 2) could also claim deliverance from Egypt. In concert with Gideon's skepticism about the mighty acts of Yahweh in the past, perhaps the story in part concerns a segment of Israel that originated in the land and became a part of the Israelite community in the covenant ceremony reported in Josh 24.

6:10 ***But you have not listened to me.*** Normally prophetic invective, such as 6:8-10 presents, shifts to a judgment speech. This final note of invective, however, leaves the outcome of Yahweh's rebuke hanging. This raises a question: Is the following story one of salvation or of judgment?

6:11 ***beneath the great tree at Ophrah.*** Rainey locates Ophrah in the heartland of Manasseh, near Shechem (Rainey and Notley 2006:139-140). But all the other locales in the story derive from the Jezreel valley and its openings into the Jordan valley. In addition, part of the story's force is the new opening into the Jezreel valley made possible by the victory of Deborah and Barak. More likely is Aharoni's location of Ophrah near the current site of the city of Afula, in the center of the Jezreel valley at the junction of the traffic arteries (Aharoni and Avi-Yonah 1979:263). This location would be quite close to the area where the chariot force of Sisera became mired in the mud and slaughtered by Barak's forces. Trees (NLT, "great tree") often identify places of divine disclosure such as the "Oak of Deborah" (ABD 5:27-28; Boling 1975:130). Ophrah later hosts Gideon's divinatory ephod (8:27). Perhaps the ominous note that Abimelech murdered all the sons of Gideon/Jerub-baal at Ophrah "on one stone" (9:5) also hints at a religious significance to the place.

Gideon. The root of the name means "hack, cut" while the ending, *-on,* generally means the person so named is characterized by the word to which it is attached. Thus, Samson means

"Sun man," and Eglon (3:12-30) means "Bullock Man." Gideon's name possibly foreshadows his role cutting down the Asherah pole and wrecking Baal's altar.

threshing wheat at the bottom of a winepress. Threshing floors were typically open, high areas where the wheat could be separated from the chaff in the wind. By contrast, a winepress is a depression or basin in which grapes are crushed and their juice collected. No more unsuitable place for threshing wheat could be found than a winepress. Such was the fear inspired by the Midianite marauders.

6:12 ***The angel of the LORD appeared to him and said, "Mighty hero."*** The address is a rebuke because a "mighty hero" (*gibbor khayil* [TH1368/2428, ZH1475/2657]) should not be hiding from the enemy but seeking a means to strike him. The contrast with Othniel and Ehud, who saw the need and took decisive action, or Deborah and Barak, for whom the prophetic word inspired confrontation with the enemy, could not be greater.

6:13 ***why has all this happened to us?*** Lit., "why has all this found us?" The passivity in Gideon's statement matches his resignation. Curiously, the messenger of Yahweh did not answer Gideon's question by referring to the sin noted in 6:1 or the prophetic reproof of 6:8-10, which should have been more than an adequate answer to the hiding hero's complaint. Some commentators see here evidence that the story was compiled from separate episodes without the writer harmonizing them closely (Burney 1920:176-177).

6:14 ***Then the LORD turned to him.*** The identity of Yahweh with his messenger becomes apparent to the reader (though not to Gideon) with this switch of the verbal subject.

Go with the strength you have. Unless these words are ironic or mocking, the divine call is understood to be sufficient empowerment for the task; Gideon's pedigree (6:15) was irrelevant. Similarly, Jeremiah's call was sufficient empowerment (cf. Jer 1:4-10).

6:15 ***Lord.*** "Lord" here is not the divine name, but the word often translated simply "sir." Gideon did not yet recognize with whom he spoke.

My clan. The term used, *'elep* [TH504A, ZH548], typically is translated "thousand" and normally denotes the number of men available for battle from a "clan," which is the association of extended families that could also encompass a small village. Often, in military contexts, the term should not be translated "thousand" but something like "militia units." For Gideon to use this term instead of the more typical *mishpakhah* [TH4940, ZH5476] shows that he was already thinking in military terms.

the weakest in the whole tribe of Manasseh, and I am the least in my entire family! Accusing Gideon of an "attempt to evade personal responsibility" (Younger 2002:175) anachronistically imposes modern sentiments on an ancient person. Ancient tribal cultures authorized roles according to location and seniority in the family structure, expressed in the genealogy. Only the heads of father's houses, typically the grandfathers and elders of a town, had the authority to make decisions for the community. In actual combat, the eldest son of the ruling clan in the dominant tribe would possess intrinsic authority to lead. Stepping out to lead his people, Gideon would appear to sidestep the entire structure of authority in his community. Such presumption would require extraordinary authentication to mark him as God's choice to lead his people. Gideon was not hiding behind his family, but expressing his hesitancy to overthrow the entire family structure of his people.

6:16 ***The LORD said to him, "I will be with you."*** The divine presence was the only authorization Gideon needed. His authentication would indeed be that God would use him to bring victory over the Midianites. As with the call of Moses (Exod 3–4), the "proof" of the call's validity can only come in the future as God works.

6:17 ***show me a sign.*** Here begins the first of a series of signs by which Gideon sought evidence that his leadership, though irregular in terms of the tribal structure of Israel, was nevertheless legitimate and under divine blessing. The object of this first "test" was to prove that the message truly came from Yahweh.

that it is. Hebrew readers note the rather unusual use of the relative particle *sha-* [TH7578.7, ZH8611] (that, who, which) here. The particle is used here and elsewhere in this story (7:12; 8:26), but otherwise in Judges, only in 5:7, which is centered in the same region as the Gideon story. It might be a vestige of a regional, north-central dialect.

6:18 ***Don't go away until I come back and bring my offering.*** Gideon still did not seem to grasp that Yahweh was before him, but the proposed offering raised no objection. The offering given resembles nothing found in the Pentateuchal sacrificial regulations. Either the laws were not intended to be exhaustive, or Gideon was innocently unaware of both the proper sacrificial ritual and the need for priestly mediation.

6:22 ***I'm doomed! I have seen the angel of the LORD face to face!*** The OT often expresses the fear that to see God directly is certain death (13:22; Gen 32:30; Exod 33:20; Deut 5:26; Isa 6:5). Indeed, some who did intrude presumptuously into Yahweh's presence perished (2 Sam 6:1-7). Still, none who reverently and obediently witness a divine epiphany find the encounter fatal (Exod 24:11).

6:24 ***And Gideon built an altar to the LORD.*** Noteworthy is Gideon's (and Yahweh's!) apparent indifference to the strict limits placed on the location of the sacrificial altar in Deut 12, as well as the requirement for priestly mediation characteristic of the Mosaic law. The Mosaic law stresses a strongly regulated altar and sacrificial praxis, not the spontaneity expressed in this narrative. If Judges were indeed written by a Deuteronomistic editor, surely this deviation would have called forth comment or even censure.

The altar remains . . . to this day. The continuing presence of the altar at Ophrah, its enduring significance to the narrator, combined with the tradition about the ephod (8:27), not to mention the Baal altar (6:25), strongly suggests Ophrah was a sacred location of long standing.

6:25 ***bull from your father's herd.*** Israelites seem to have been primarily herders of sheep and goats, not cattle. Oxen were used mainly for agricultural work, and few would own an ox. Yahweh thus called on Gideon to strike a hard economic blow to his own extended family.

second bull . . . seven years old. Lit., "take the bull of the ox that belongs to your father, *and* the second bull, seven years." The NLT follows the KJV and NIV suggesting Gideon is to take the "second" bull. The particle translated "and" may also be rendered explicatively: "*that is,* the second bull." Only one bull is in view for the sacrifice, and Yahweh specified it exactly. Perhaps Yahweh sought to link the crisis to the Baal altar: The bull sacrificed by Gideon would have been born the year that the Midianite oppression began (Keil 1863:335-336; cf. 6:1). And yet, reference to a "second" bull suggests Gideon's father owned two, which would mark him as a wealthy man.

Pull down your father's altar to Baal. Gideon's action also defies the religious authority of his father, who was the principal patron of the Baal altar. Gideon's deference to the tribal hierarchy formed part of his objection to Yahweh's call (cf. 6:15). Challenging that hierarchy became Gideon's first act of obedience.

cut down the Asherah pole standing beside it. Asherah, in Canaanite mythology, was the wife of the high god El and the mother of the gods, who are known in the Ugaritic texts as her "70 sons." Her name also denoted a cult object, a wooden pole that was paired with the image of Baal (cf. 3:7). Certain syncretistic Israelites also paired her with Yahweh, as seen in the inscriptions found in the far south, at Kuntillet Ajrud, which name "Yahweh of Samaria and his Asherah," and those from Khirbet el-Qom (also in the south), which speak of Yahweh and "his Asherah" (ABD 1:483-487). The obvious threat to Israel's distinctive faith required that pagan images be eliminated. Ironically, the very fertility deities whom the Israelites sought to provide their crops were impotent to protect those crops from Midianite raiders.

6:26 ***Then build an altar to the LORD.*** The location, construction, and absence of a Levitical priest at this altar are without precedent in the liturgical legislation of the Pentateuch, especially Deuteronomy. Even though Gideon reasserted Israel's true worship, modern readers should not underestimate the rebellion against his family and community that Gideon's action embodied. Before confronting the pagan hordes oppressing Israel, Gideon must confront the pagan tendencies of his family and town.

6:27 ***he did it at night because he was afraid.*** Gideon's fear, born of his low position in the clan, transformed what should have been a radical act of evangelism into simple vandalism in the eyes of the community. Though he did what the Lord commanded, he merely complied, not truly obeying.

6:31 ***let him defend himself.*** The text plays on the Hebrew verb *rib* [TH7378, ZH8189] (to contend), which typically expresses formal litigation. Ironically, the man most singled out by Gideon's action, his father, expresses most forcibly what Gideon's action was supposed to mean.

6:32 ***From then on Gideon was called Jerub-baal.*** For the rest of the story, the name Jerub-baal will alternate with "Gideon." This duality pairs with a repetitive tendency in the story, and even with an ambivalence about the character of Gideon himself.

6:33 ***Soon afterward.*** The scenario sketched in 6:1-6 begins to unfold again. The Midianites and their allies prepare once again for a raiding foray into Israel.

6:34 ***Spirit . . . took possession of Gideon.*** The expression used is often mistranslated as "the spirit . . . clothed Gideon." The verb used (*labash* [TH3847, ZH4252], "to put on, to wear"), takes a single direct object, which is always the item put on or worn (HALOT 1.519, s.v. *labash*). Thus in Isa 51:9 we read "wake up, wake up. . . . Clothe yourself (*labash*) with strength!" Gideon thus metaphorically becomes the garment of the Spirit, an idiom with an Akkadian parallel. Akkadian texts speak of the gods as possessing a fearsome radiance, denoted by the term *pulkhu* (or the fem. *pulukhtu*). The gods "wear" (Akkadian *labashu*) this radiance as they manifest themselves, typically through a king or warrior (CAD 12.503-504, 505-509). Thus, we might read 6:34 as the Spirit of Yahweh putting on Gideon as a radiant garment of awe-inspiring glory. This glory would have been visible, observably manifesting Yahweh's power and thus authenticating Gideon as the divinely appointed leader to his people. Since Gideon was least in his family (6:15), extraordinary authentication in this form became necessary. Gideon's immediate success in raising an army from his previously demoralized and apostate kinsmen testifies to the effectiveness of the confirmation. In addition, Baal had failed to bring any consequences to bear on Gideon, in spite of the destruction of his altar and the taunt inherent in Gideon's new name, Jerub-baal (6:32). The Abiezrites consequently rallied to him (Keil 1863:338).

6:35 ***He also sent messengers throughout Manasseh, Asher, Zebulun, and Naphtali.*** One who lacked authority in his own tribe certainly could not claim the allegiance of other tribes. The Spirit's authenticating presence also certified Gideon to the surrounding tribes. The tribes that are named all border on the complex lowland system that constitutes the Jezreel valley. Asher lies westernmost, on the coast, with Zebulun just to the east. Naphtali's territory ran from the area at the southwest tip of the Sea of Galilee northward. Issachar, resting southeast of Zebulun, is unmentioned.

6:36 ***If you are truly going to use me to rescue Israel as you promised.*** So jolting is this expression of doubt coming on the heels of so many tokens of divine favor, that some scholars believe the Gideon story existed originally as two separate narratives, with different but related episodes, which were combined in the present text without any effort at smoothing out the kinks (cf. Soggin 1981:102-109). It certainly is striking that the only person apparently remaining in doubt about Yahweh's choice is the chosen one. Gideon first sought a sign that it was truly Yahweh speaking to him (6:17). Now his uncertainty seems directed to the truthfulness of Yahweh's word. Though Yahweh complied with both requests, Gideon's uncertainty remains until 7:15.

COMMENTARY

The stories of Gideon and Abimelech mark a decided turn in Israel's history. The exuberance and clarity of 3:12–5:31 now give way to uncertainty and ambivalence. At this crucial juncture a question of enormous importance emerges: What form of leadership is best for Israel?

Like the preceding stories, the Gideon episode begins with a crisis. Judges 6:1-10 signals a new stage in the history, however. In 6:1, the sin-cycle does not resume, but has a fresh start (see note on 6:1-10). In addition, the defection from Yahweh seems more severe. Whereas after the Othniel story, idolatry had not been explicitly identified in the introductions as the evil done by Israel, Yahweh charges Israel (6:1-10) with worshiping the gods of the Amorites. The military crisis resulting from Israel's evil is presented in much more detail and gravity than in the previous episodes. And more than a political attack, the Midianite crisis threatened the very physical survival of Israel, whose economic basis consisted in a mix of subsistence agriculture (some crops raised for exchange; i.e., grapes) and herding. The Midianites forced the Israelites out of the newly settled Jezreel valley back into their hill-country haunts. Large hosts of raiders could travel far and fast to terrorize the Hebrews due to increased numbers of camels. The resultant destitution—and not repentance—drove Israel to cry to Yahweh (6:6), revealing another omen of this new, more grave stage in Israel's history. The Othniel and Ehud stories portrayed Yahweh leaping to Israel's defense in raising up a savior, in accordance with the common religious convictions of the ancient world that any deity worthy of the name would fly to the help of desperate worshipers who cried out to him or her. The Deborah story introduced a slight break between Israel's cry and salvation. Here, however (6:7-10), Israel's cry is answered with a prophetic denunciation similar to 2:1-5 and 2:20-23, emphasizing that they had not listened to Yahweh's voice. The invective is left hanging, with neither threat nor promise of redemption following. This unresolved tension places the career of Gideon under the sign of Yahweh's growing disaffection with Israel. He does not unambiguously become "Yahweh to the rescue." Indeed, ambiguity is the undercurrent of the whole Gideon story.

This introduction can leave us uncomfortable. We prefer a clear, black-and-white context for understanding Gideon. We want heroes or villains. Unfortunately, the narratives of the Old Testament do not provide much help in sorting out the world so tidily. Accordingly, there is a limit on what we can say about Gideon's career and how we can see him as a model. God was clearly present, and we who have read the story repeatedly know that deliverance is coming from Yahweh through Gideon. But this deliverance will be fraught with ambivalence.

This story also emphasizes the obvious but eternal fact that our God is merciful! Israel cried out not in repentance, but simply in anguish before the threat of starvation. Yahweh did not wait for their response to be perfect. Indeed, as we read the Gospels we conclude that if Jesus only helped people who came to him the "right" way, he wouldn't be helping very many people. People came to Jesus out of the daily pain of their lives, often with little thought of repenting and being spiritually transformed. Desperation drove them, as it drove Gideon's countrymen. Still, the fact of Israel's unresolved sin places the story of Gideon under a question mark. Divine mercy is not denied, but the presence of that mercy should not lead us to think God has no interest in his people discovering the real reasons why they should cry out to him.

The battle narrative falls into two large sections: a preparatory unit (6:11–7:14), and the battle itself (7:15-21), culminating in the offer of permanent rule to Gideon and his descendants, which he refuses (8:22-27). The standard conclusion (8:28, 32) is expanded by the inclusion of the background for the Abimelech story (8:29-31). A thematic pattern weaving through the entire account is the contrast between the human and divine perspectives, reflected also in the portrayal of Gideon as, on the one hand, a champion of God, and, on the other hand, an all-too-human and vengeful leader.

The preparation section (6:11–7:14) begins with an angelic visitation summoning Gideon to save Israel. The call itself (6:11-24) contrasts Gideon and the angel of Yahweh repeatedly. Gideon was fearful (6:11) and therefore got down in a winepress to thresh his wheat. He was resentful (6:13) regarding the oppression as utterly unmerited; he even questioned God's character, apparently unaware of the apostasy and rebuke of 6:1-10. For Gideon, the "mighty acts of God" constituted a dead past, even though the very ground of the Jezreel valley had been won for him by an open display of divine might (ch 4). Pleading his low position in the tribal hierarchy, Gideon questioned his own capacity to save Israel (6:15). By contrast, the angel greeted him as "mighty hero" (6:12), answered his challenge by calling him to "go with the strength you have, and rescue Israel" (6:14), promising the divine presence (6:16). As is so often the case, God's method in accomplishing his will in history is to choose a human instrument. The answer to Gideon's questions (6:13) was Gideon himself! Unconvinced of his visitor's divine identity, Gideon tested him with an offering (6:17-19) that was consumed in flames at the touch of a staff (6:20-22). Gideon's terror at having encountered Yahweh directly was allayed by a divine promise (6:22b-23; cf. note on 6:14). An altar, "[Yahweh] is peace," commemorated the encounter (6:24). Gideon serves here as an example of human frailty upheld by the confidence, patience, and power of God. Far from *embodying* Yahweh's saving government, Gideon personifies the *need* for it.

The contrast between the human and divine perspective appears in Gideon's first task (6:25-32)—a small, local act of resistance. Replacing the Baal altar with one to Yahweh would at first seem easier than confronting the hostile Midianite hordes. Yet in this act, Gideon must assert publicly Yahweh's claim on Israel's loyalty, thus revealing the depth of Israel's sinfulness, since the Baal altar was patronized by the entire town under the sponsorship of Gideon's own father. This action would also carry a cost, a precious bull, in a time of economic crisis. Gideon, in this act, must transcend the paralyzed hopelessness in which God's actions are just a dead past, and become the occasion for God to begin a fresh work. Gideon's nocturnal compliance, compromised by fear, muddled the revolutionary character of the action and failed to send the very message Yahweh intended. Gideon's second name, Jerub-baal (lit., "let Baal make his case"), should have been a sign of Gideon's bold confrontation of false gods, revealing their emptiness before Yahweh's reality. Now, however, it can only speak of Gideon's halfhearted fear. Gideon's second name captures his essential ambiguity.

In 6:33–7:14 the duality of Gideon's character and his contrast with God becomes sharper. In 6:33-35, Gideon experiences dramatic authentication in which he becomes the very clothing, the armor, of the Spirit of Yahweh (see note on 6:34). Divine power and human receptivity could not be more forcibly depicted. Thus empowered, he called his kinsmen to arms. And they came! He raised a militia of 32,000 (cf. 7:3), not merely from his own tribesmen, but also from tribes ringing the Jezreel valley. But the pendulum swings back to uncertainty. Neither the Spirit's authentication nor the great army raised reassured Gideon, who demanded two signs from Yahweh (6:36-40).

Gideon in these passages might seem reminiscent of many believers who, uncertain of God's will, have sought a "sign" by "laying out a fleece" (6:37). But Gideon's desire for a sign marked his lack of faith (cf. Matt 16:4). Gideon had encountered the very messenger of Yahweh. He had heard Yahweh's word of promise, seen a miraculous flaming sacrifice, been radically anointed by Yahweh's Spirit, and had around him hearty companions ready to do battle at his lead. And yet he still did not act on God's command. The fleece is not a means of finding God's will, but possibly a maneuver by one who knew God's will but simply did not want to do it. Though Gideon's experience of the Spirit's anointing authenticated him, it did not seem to shift him from doubt to faith.

By the end of chapter 6, the reader fully expects that Gideon, equipped with a divine call, authenticated by the Spirit of Yahweh, accompanied by an intertribal militia, his mission confirmed by two divinely wrought miracles, will now follow in the footsteps of Othniel, Ehud, and Barak, leading his people victoriously against the foe. Such, however, did not occur. Not only did Gideon still doubt the outcome of his mission, it appears that Yahweh had a few doubts of his own.

◆ b. Authority accepted (7:1–8:3)

So Jerub-baal (that is, Gideon) and his army got up early and went as far as the spring of Harod. The armies of Midian were camped north of them in the valley near the hill of Moreh.
2The LORD said to Gideon, "You have too many warriors with you. If I let all of you fight the Midianites, the Israelites will boast to me that they saved themselves by their own strength.
3Therefore, tell the people, 'Whoever is timid or afraid may leave this mountain* and go home.' " So 22,000 of them went home, leaving only 10,000 who were willing to fight.
4But the LORD told Gideon, "There are still too many! Bring them down to the spring, and I will test them to determine who will go with you and who will not."
5When Gideon took his warriors down to the water, the LORD told him, "Divide the men into two

groups. In one group put all those who cup water in their hands and lap it up with their tongues like dogs. In the other group put all those who kneel down and drink with their mouths in the stream." [6]Only 300 of the men drank from their hands. All the others got down on their knees and drank with their mouths in the stream.

[7]The LORD told Gideon, "With these 300 men I will rescue you and give you victory over the Midianites. Send all the others home." [8]So Gideon collected the provisions and rams' horns of the other warriors and sent them home. But he kept the 300 men with him.

The Midianite camp was in the valley just below Gideon. [9]That night the LORD said, "Get up! Go down into the Midianite camp, for I have given you victory over them! [10]But if you are afraid to attack, go down to the camp with your servant Purah. [11]Listen to what the Midianites are saying, and you will be greatly encouraged. Then you will be eager to attack."

So Gideon took Purah and went down to the edge of the enemy camp. [12]The armies of Midian, Amalek, and the people of the east had settled in the valley like a swarm of locusts. Their camels were like grains of sand on the seashore—too many to count! [13]Gideon crept up just as a man was telling his companion about a dream. The man said, "I had this dream, and in my dream a loaf of barley bread came tumbling down into the Midianite camp. It hit a tent, turned it over, and knocked it flat!"

[14]His companion answered, "Your dream can mean only one thing—God has given Gideon son of Joash, the Israelite, victory over Midian and all its allies!"

[15]When Gideon heard the dream and its interpretation, he bowed in worship before the LORD.* Then he returned to the Israelite camp and shouted, "Get up! For the LORD has given you victory over the Midianite hordes!" [16]He divided the 300 men into three groups and gave each man a ram's horn and a clay jar with a torch in it.

[17]Then he said to them, "Keep your eyes on me. When I come to the edge of the camp, do just as I do. [18]As soon as I and those with me blow the rams' horns, blow your horns, too, all around the entire camp, and shout, 'For the LORD and for Gideon!' "

[19]It was just after midnight,* after the changing of the guard, when Gideon and the 100 men with him reached the edge of the Midianite camp. Suddenly, they blew the rams' horns and broke their clay jars. [20]Then all three groups blew their horns and broke their jars. They held the blazing torches in their left hands and the horns in their right hands, and they all shouted, "A sword for the LORD and for Gideon!"

[21]Each man stood at his position around the camp and watched as all the Midianites rushed around in a panic, shouting as they ran to escape. [22]When the 300 Israelites blew their rams' horns, the LORD caused the warriors in the camp to fight against each other with their swords. Those who were not killed fled to places as far away as Beth-shittah near Zererah and to the border of Abel-meholah near Tabbath.

[23]Then Gideon sent for the warriors of Naphtali, Asher, and Manasseh, who joined in chasing the army of Midian. [24]Gideon also sent messengers throughout the hill country of Ephraim, saying, "Come down to attack the Midianites. Cut them off at the shallow crossings of the Jordan River at Beth-barah."

So all the men of Ephraim did as they were told. [25]They captured Oreb and Zeeb, the two Midianite commanders, killing Oreb at the rock of Oreb, and Zeeb at the winepress of Zeeb. And they continued to chase the Midianites. Afterward the Israelites brought the heads of Oreb and Zeeb to Gideon, who was by the Jordan River.

CHAPTER 8

Then the people of Ephraim asked Gideon, "Why have you treated us this way? Why didn't you send for us when you first went out to fight the Midianites?" And they argued heatedly with Gideon.

2But Gideon replied, "What have I ac-
complished compared to you? Aren't even
the leftover grapes of Ephraim's harvest
better than the entire crop of my little
clan of Abiezer? 3God gave you victory
over Oreb and Zeeb, the commanders of
the Midianite army. What have I accom-
plished compared to that?" When the men
of Ephraim heard Gideon's answer, their
anger subsided.

7:3 Hebrew *may leave Mount Gilead.* The identity of Mount Gilead is uncertain in this context. It is perhaps used here as another name for Mount Gilboa. 7:15 As in Greek version; Hebrew reads *he bowed.* 7:19 Hebrew *at the beginning of the second watch.*

NOTES

7:1 ***his army.*** Lit., "the people who were with him." The term "army" should not evoke images of consistently armed, well-trained, cohesive fighting units, but rather the muster of males from each clan capable of bearing arms.

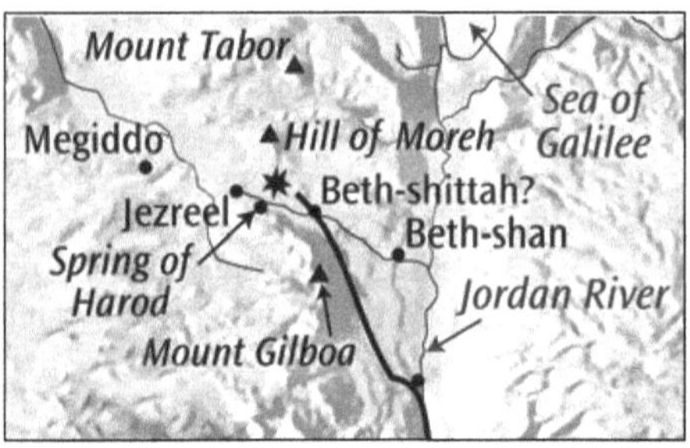

Jezreel Valley, Spring of Harod, and Hill of Moreh

the spring of Harod. En-Harod flows southeast down the valley, connecting Afula/Ophrah to the Jordan valley and running past the north base of the mound of Beth-shan. The site is identified with the contemporary spring En-Jalud, where there is now a modern swimming complex (Soggin 1981:135). The name Harod (*kharod* [TH5878, ZH3008]) means "trembling," in reference to the bubbling up of the natural spring water in the cave where the spring originates (Smith 1931:396-399). "Trembling" also resonates with the process of weeding out those men who were "afraid" to go to war (see note on 7:3). With Mount Gilboa forming its southern flank and the formation that climaxes in the hill of Moreh forming its northern wall, the valley appears to have concealed the Israelites from the Midianite encampment.

The armies of Midian were camped north of them in the valley near the hill of Moreh. The Midianites appear to have camped on the north side of the ridge forming the northern wall of the Harod valley, near Endor (cf. Ps 83:10-11; Aharoni and Avi-Yonah 1977:54; Rainey and Notley 2006:139), though it is also possible they stayed on the south side of Moreh in the valley, right under the noses of Gideon and his 300 men (Cundall 1968:109). The location name, "Moreh," probably means "oracle giver," (HALOT 560-561) suggesting a place of spiritual inquiry. At the foot of this hill is Endor, where Saul sought out the medium on the night before he met his death in this same area (1 Sam 28).

7:2 ***too many.*** The paring down of the force need not appear as a surprise. The thinning down of the force via a series of exemptions constitutes the normal pattern according to Deut 20:1-10. According to the census lists in Num 1:34-35, Manasseh would be responsible for 32 "thousands" or, better, "squads" (cf. notes on 3:29; 5:8; 6:15), comparable to the number 32,000 used in this narrative (Boling 1975:144). Just a few miles separated the 32 "squads" of Israelites from the massive Midianite force of 135 fighting units (135,000). Still, severely outnumbered, hiding so close to the enemy, Israel needed every man. Again, "warriors" might evoke too ambitious an image of the Israelite force.

warriors. The Hebrew simply reads "people." Just a few days prior, these were all farmers, herdsmen, and vintners. This day, they carried whatever weapons they could find, trusting in the extraordinary divine authentication of their leader, Gideon.

the Israelites will boast to me that they saved themselves. Yahweh's concern is not to have sole "credit" for the battle, but to prevent Israel from boasting "to me,"—that is, claiming their victory proved they had no need for Yahweh's power. The statement does not negate humans a role in winning battles, or deny them potential accolades for faithful obedience. When Yahweh's people are faithful, they share in his glory, as in the time of Deborah (cf. 4:9; 5:2, 7, 9, 11-12). But a prideful claim of autonomy over against the need for grace is in view here. The issue of who actually is credited with the victory recurs in 8:22 when the people credit Gideon with saving them. The critical point of this battle is not the outcome, but whether it glorifies Yahweh or his human servants. The theme of who receives the glory runs through this whole section of the narrative.

7:3 ***afraid.*** This translates *khared* [TH2730, ZH3007] (trembling), a word based on the same root as the name of the spring Harod (see note on 7:1). Gideon's release of fearful recruits mirrors the exemption expressed in Deut 20:8.

leave this mountain. The Hebrew reads, "Mount Gilead" (cf. NLT mg). Mount Gilead is located east of the Jordan River, and its mention here seems to result from a misspelling in the text. Some suggest "Gilboa," which would fit the context (Keil 1863:341). Another suggestion pursues the similarity between "Gilead" and another name for the Harod spring, Galud, noting that the word means "fear" and suggests "let him depart from Mt. Galud = 'Mt. Fear' " (Burney 1920:207-209; Boling 1975:145). In addition, however, there is uncertainty about the meaning of the verb translated "leave." The JPS translation thus notes the similarity of this verb with the term for "bird" and translates "depart as a bird flies from Mount Gilead." Many scholars, as reflected in the RSV and NRSV, make a conjectural correction of the spelling of the verb and of "Gilead" to "Gideon" to translate "so Gideon sifted them out," which reflects the use of *tsarap* [TH6884, ZH7671] in 7:4 (cf. Moore 1895:203; Soggin 1981:136).

22,000 of them went home, leaving only 10,000. Note the instantaneous loss of two-thirds of Gideon's force, whose hearts were not in the battle. For a leader lacking inherent tribal authority and depending only on divine charisma, this had to be disheartening. As a result, the Israelites were outnumbered 13.5 to 1.

7:4 ***I will test them to determine.*** This conveys accurately the import of the Hebrew verb *tsarap* [TH6884, ZH7671], but at the cost of the underlying image. The verb refers to smelting and refining of precious metal by heating it and skimming off the slurry of waste material that comes to the surface. It is also used of sifting the character of persons, often by traumatic experiences of judgment such as the Babylonian exile. Boling (1975:145) sees here a more formal ceremony in which the citizenry are reorganized into Yahweh's militia, but this perhaps reads too much into the text.

7:5 ***all those who cup water in their hands and lap it up with their tongues like dogs.*** The exact significance of this test remains a matter of speculation. Vivid descriptions of the various drinking methods appear in the travel literature of the late-nineteenth century (Burney 1920:210-212). Some suggest the one group drank so as never to take their eyes off the enemy, while the other allowed their physical thirst to dominate their attention, disqualifying themselves (Smith 1931:397). Josephus argued the opposite, that the cowardly 300 in fact were Yahweh's choice to show his glory (Soggin 1981:137; Matthews 2004:92)! All the biblical writer tells us is that Yahweh set this criterion. Whether or not it involved some intrinsic rationale remains unresolved (Cundall 1968:110; Schneider 2000:111-112; Block 1999:277; Younger 2002:189).

7:6 ***Only 300 of the men drank from their hands.*** The narrative unfolds so as to build suspense, repeating the characterization "drank from their hands" three times, in 7:6-7, and often noting the number 300 through the passage. Gideon perhaps expected the 300 to be dismissed. Actually, 300 soldiers would be a significant force. For example, the Moabite Stone, composed about 300 years later, records a Moabite king attacking an Israelite-held city with a force of "200 men, all first-class warriors" (ANET 320).

7:8 ***Gideon collected the provisions and rams' horns of the other warriors.*** Collecting the rams' horns suggests Gideon already had an idea of the tactic he would later employ; otherwise, how could he find horns for all 300 of his men? (Moore 1895:202-203).

sent them home. Lit., "sent them to their tents." Some commentators infer that Gideon only dismissed them back to "base" rather than "home" since he called up soldiers again once the attack started (Schneider 2000:111-112; Block 1999:277 n. 597). And the expression could be an idiom for releasing obligated persons from service (NIDOTTE 1.301; von Rad 1991:50-51). However, tents in the OT often serve as a metaphor for "home." When the northern tribes say, "To your tents, O Israel, Now look after your own house, David," (1 Kgs 12:16b, cf. KJV), the contrast is not between the suburban Judeans and the nomadic northerners. Here, "tents" most likely stands for "home."

The Midianite camp was in the valley just below Gideon. The valley floor between Endor and the foot of Mount Tabor, where the Midianites encamped, is at about 325 feet above sea level. For the Midianites to be "below" Gideon, he must have moved north from the Harod spring to a position somewhere on the hill of Moreh, which rose some 1,200 feet higher, between the Harod valley and the Midianite camp.

7:10 ***But if you are afraid to attack.*** By acting on this divine offer, Gideon demonstrated he was in fact afraid! Being fearful also identifies him with those whom Yahweh dismissed from battle earlier in the story.

7:12 ***swarm of locusts. Their camels were . . . too many to count!*** The phrasing is identical to parts of 6:5 (see note). The one-humped Arabian camel could facilitate raids across hundreds of miles of desert. Neo-Assyrian reliefs depict Arabian tribesmen using camels as mobile archery platforms. While the Assyrians were able to defeat these "camel-tanks" rather easily, they would have been terrifying to ground-bound farmer-militiamen (Anglim, Jestice et al. 2002:132-133; Aharoni and Avi-Yonah 1977:54).

7:13 ***a loaf of barley bread came tumbling.*** The image of a large loaf of bread careening through the Midianite camp and smashing a tent has a comic appearance. Because of its hardiness, quick-growing season, and ability to thrive in limestone soils where few other cereals grow, barley became a staple cereal for the Israelite hill country farmers—hence the linkage of the loaf with the Israelites. Carbonized barley has been excavated in the Iron Age I (1200–1000 BC) levels at Afula, the likely location of Gideon's home town, Ophrah (Borowski 2002:91-92). Some in antiquity regarded barley as fit mainly for animals, which underscores the poverty of the Israelites (Moore 1895:205-206). This dream, featuring the most humble of cereals, could point to the larger theme of the story: Yahweh uses the lowly and unlikely to achieve his purposes. Ironically, the dream could well have been interpreted to warn the Midianites to watch for a surprise attack from the Israelites, but they drew a different meaning. The exact type of loaf that was seen in the dream is unclear since the word appears only here. The Arabic cognate means hard, stale, or dry (HALOT 2.1025, s.v. *tsalul* [TH6742, ZH7501]) but can also connote "putrid, moldy," a suggestion that, if correct, would certainly add an odd nuance to an already strange dream (Cundall 1968:111-112; Boling 1975:146).

7:14 ***God has given Gideon son of Joash, the Israelite, victory.*** Apparently, Gideon was known to the Midianites as the leader of the Israelite forces, so perhaps he was not as insignificant as he thought. Later we learn the Midianite kings (not the chiefs captured by the Ephraimites, 7:25) murdered Gideon's brothers (cf. 8:18-19). Perhaps he was known already to them. The NLT's idiomatic rendering "given Gideon . . . victory" obscures the Hebrew's literal "this is . . . the sword of Gideon," later a part of the Israelite battle cry (cf. 7:20).

7:15 ***he bowed in worship before the LORD.*** Gideon's immediate, spontaneous worship of Yahweh sounds the story's theme that Yahweh, and no other, should receive glory from this victory, despite the fact that the Israelites will ascribe the victory to him (8:22). Gideon also seems fully assured in his faith, issuing the jump-off order for the attack. Not until 8:22-27 will Gideon again hesitate to take his responsibilities as a leader.

7:16 ***He divided the 300 men into three groups and gave each man a ram's horn and a clay jar with a torch in it.*** Commentators tend to think that Gideon's men, here and in the next several verses, had their hands full—too full, in fact (Soggin 1981:145-146). They infer that the story's details became confused when different versions of the same account were combined. These claims seem exaggerated, however. A ram's horn could be slung over the shoulder, and at the decisive moment, one shatters the pot, holding the torch aloft, and then with the other hand holds the ram's horn (Cundall 1968:112-113). Smith (1931:398) notes the habit, in his day, of Syrian peasants carrying their torches in earthen pitchers on windy nights. The torch might simply smolder in the confines of the jar, but burst into flames when waved in the open air.

7:20 ***A sword for the LORD and for Gideon!*** Commentators often cite "for Gideon" as proof that Gideon violated Yahweh's purpose by claiming "billing" for the victory (see Schneider 2000:115). But this charge fails on two counts. First, Yahweh expressed concern that Israel would claim to have gained the victory in its own strength, not that Israel's faithful heroes and leaders would be unsung. Second, shouting the phrase "a sword for Gideon" resonated with the interpretation of the Midianite soldier's dream (7:13; cf. Matthews 2004:93). This shout thus reinforced the terror of the moment, as though to say, "Here comes your nightmare!" Swords and other weapons seem to have been comparatively rare in Israel. Material remains from Iron Age I Israelite sites show no true swords, a few knives, but a surprisingly high count of arrow points (Bloch-Smith 2003:416-420). The Israelites apparently fought mainly with bows, short daggers, and slings. Block (1999:282) suggests that Israel had no swords, but this seems unlikely, especially in light of 8:20.

7:21 ***Each man stood at his position around the camp and watched as all the Midianites rushed around in a panic, shouting as they ran to escape.*** The narrative of Gideon's battle strategy thus has points of contact with other descriptions of divinely effected victory in ancient Near Eastern literature, which is filled with references to the terror that the gods pour out on an enemy (see note on 6:34). When ancient kings went to battle, they celebrated how the splendor of their god and of their own royal presence inflicted paralyzing terror on their foes, causing panic and flight. The splendor of the deity and his chosen ruler was typically represented in a standard featuring a winged solar disk, something also readily portrayed by a torch (Mendenhall 1973:32-66). Akkadian literature employed technical terms for the god's garment (*pulkhu*/*pulukhtu*) and his radiant headgear or mask, *melammu*; this was the majestic divine splendor that routed the foe. One Assyrian king boasted, "The fear of the splendor of Asshur my lord overwhelmed them. In order to save their lives they went up [stream]. I razed, destroyed and burned the city" (Kurkh Monolith, COS 1.29b). Another typical Assyrian inscription reads, "I caused the awe-inspiring splendor of Asûsûur, my lord, to overwhelm the people of the land of Egypt and the Arabians; and at the mention of my name their hearts palpitated, (and) their arms collapsed" (COS Nimrud Prisms D & E, lines 42-49).

7:22 ***as far away as Beth-shittah near Zererah and to the border of Abel-meholah.*** The Midianites fled south, along the eastern slope of the hill of Moreh, towards Beth-shan, down the Harod valley. The sites of Beth-shittah and Zererah have not been located with certainty, but all proposed locations lie southeast of the main site of the battle. The debate centers on whether the sites are west or east of the Jordan (ABD 1.698; 6.1082-1083). Abel-Meholah was on the west bank of the Jordan valley where it joins the Harod valley, and was the home of the prophet Elisha. Located at the ford of Jordan, it was a strategic point; so Gideon sent word ahead to have the crossing captured and cut off the Midianite retreat (ABD 1.11-12).

7:23 ***Then Gideon sent for the warriors.*** Possibly these warriors included the ones who had been dismissed earlier. If so, their status as previously disqualified from battle could explain the offense taken by the Ephraimites (8:1), whom Gideon also called to the battle late. The Ephraimites probably did not like being associated with the "rejects," an impression Gideon will be careful to alleviate. Ehud had similarly summoned the Ephraimites to intercept a fleeing foe, and they did so quickly and effectively (3:27-28). Later, Jephthah will face complaints from the Ephraimites, also about being called up late, and another river-crossing incident will prove catastrophic (12:1-6). The claim, however, that Gideon disobeyed divine instructions by summoning his countrymen (Klein 1989:57-58; Block 1999:284-285) is not supported in the text, which never stresses Gideon's need to act without assistance from the other tribes. Indeed, these narratives celebrate the involvement of Israelites in the struggles of their kinsmen and have harsh words for those who hang back (cf. ch 5). Likewise, nothing in the context expresses or implies divine disfavor. God granted victory to the 300 at the Midianite camp; and like Ehud and Deborah before him, Gideon offered his fellow Israelites the chance to be part of Yahweh's mighty act of salvation in the "mopping up" stage. Klein (1989:58) says that "the spirit of the LORD . . . seems to slip from Gideon's shoulders." It simply is not clear how Klein discerns this. Commentators show a strange interest in claiming as many errors and flaws as possible for Gideon, who seems already to have enough clearly identified for him in the text!

7:24 ***the hill country of Ephraim.*** The Ephraimites occupied the central hill country between Shechem and Bethel, and were well-placed to move quickly east to cut off the retreat of the Midianites.

crossings of the Jordan River at Beth-barah. The site is unknown, and the meaning of the name unclear, leading scholars to suspect that spelling errors have crept into our existing manuscripts. The original text probably mentioned the crossings of the Jordan, but not a specific place (Burney 1920:225; Soggin 1981:147).

7:25 ***They captured Oreb and Zeeb, the two Midianite commanders, killing Oreb at the rock of Oreb, and Zeeb at the winepress of Zeeb.*** "Commanders" seems a bit too official for the leaders of nomadic tribesmen. The term employed, *sar* [TH8269, ZH8569], does, however, convey status and dignity. In the east-Semitic languages it regularly signifies "king," but in west-Semitic tongues it denotes a variety of high authorities. "Commander" would suffice for a high officer in a professional or mercenary army, like Sisera (cf. 4:2), but in denoting the comparable role in a tribal militia, perhaps "chief" better conveys the sociological reality. Using the same English term in every occurrence can obscure the context (contra Schneider 2000:118-119). The names of these chieftains colorfully evoke animals, as do other names in Judges. "Oreb" means "raven" and "Zeeb" means "wolf" or sometimes, "jackal." Given the place names that follow using both these names, many form-critical scholars, assuming the priority of toponyms, suggest the chiefs were named for their place of execution, though the reverse is just as possible. The significance of this capture appears in Isaiah's allusion to it as a paradigm of Yahweh's judgment and liberation (cf. Ps 83:9-12; Isa 10:26).

brought the heads of Oreb and Zeeb to Gideon. The gruesome Ephraimite trophies would be complimented by Gideon, to their credit, as "the leftover grapes of Ephraim's harvest" (8:2). But however symbolically potent the beheading of a couple of chiefs might have been, "Gideon was put in a most curious position; for the Ephraimites had brought him the wrong heads" (Boling 1975:152). Indeed, the two senior chiefs ("kings") of the Midianites, Zebah and Zalmunna (8:5), slipped through the Ephraimite blockade.

8:1 *Then the people of Ephraim . . . argued heatedly with Gideon.* "Argued" translates the verb *rib* [TH7378, ZH8189], which denotes formal censure or complaint, evoking Gideon's contention with Baal that prompted his second name, Jerub-baal, "Let Baal Contend." Heroic literature often portrays, paradoxically, rapport between enemies and friction among allies, with disputes over glory and spoils forming a standard trope (Niditch 2008:103). Whether or not this episode reflects fragmentation of Israelite unity depends on larger contextual observations. The Ephraimites apparently prided themselves on battle prowess. Their reputation accounts for the three times in Judges that they are associated with the capture of the Jordan River crossings. In 3:27-29 Ehud calls up the Ephraimites who hold the Jordan crossing against the Moabites, preventing anyone from crossing so that ultimately not one of them escaped. In 7:24–8:3, the Ephraimites fail to stop the Midianites from crossing the Jordan and protest their late summons, possibly because it associated them with the other rejected warriors. In the Jephthah story, the crossings will be held against the Ephraimites, who will die for their criticism of Jephthah for calling them late to battle (12:1-6). These three vignettes, conspicuously connected to the same tactical setting, open a window into the vanity of the Ephraimites and the deterioration of Israel's unity. The story also underlines the fragility of Gideon's authority. Lacking the inherent authority of a high position in the tribal structure, his power derives solely from his divine anointing manifested in continuing victory in battle.

8:2 *Aren't even the leftover grapes of Ephraim's harvest better than the entire crop of my little clan of Abiezer?* "Leftover grapes" translates a term never used of cereals, but only of grapes and olives (HALOT 1.834, s.v. *'oleloth* [TH5955, ZH6622]). The verb from the same root appears in 20:45, speaking of capturing stragglers tangential to the main body of the army. The Ephraimites got the message: "Your leftovers are better than my whole crop." They missed Gideon's insinuation that they had only a couple of chieftains rather than taking in the whole crop.

COMMENTARY

Though Gideon's uncertainty has dominated the story line, the episode in 7:1-8 reveals that Yahweh lacked confidence in the battle prospects. Just when Gideon seemed reassured, Yahweh undercut any human confidence Gideon and his compatriots might still possess. Yahweh rejected 94 percent of the soldiers responding to the draft call that was inspired by his own Spirit's presence with Gideon. Yahweh made it clear that Israel is his servant, through whom he works, not an autonomous power capable of saving itself. While dismissal from battle because of fear could easily amount to shaming those who departed, Yahweh's aim was not to separate effective warriors from ineffective ones, as some have suggested. While Gideon doubted victory, Yahweh doubted a victorious Israel would do anything other than credit its salvation to its own capabilities. This captures the essence of the tension between Gideon's perspective and God's. What matters most about the upcoming battle is not its military outcome, however vital that might be, but the *meaning* of that outcome. A defeated foe and puffed-up Israelites would constitute a catastrophe. Just as the plagues in Exodus mainly served not to liberate Israel but to make clear the identity and supremacy of Yahweh, so this battle's real purpose was to display the character and power of Israel's God. Any outcome leaving that point in doubt would be failure worse than defeat.

Yahweh's supreme power in giving deliverance does not render human obedience or participation moot. Yahweh's power not only summons human participation, it makes that participation meaningful and effective—the point celebrated in the Song of Deborah (ch 5).

Yahweh offered his encouragement in 7:9-14. Ironically, it is a matter of simple intelligence-gathering that reveals a vital fact. While Gideon had been asking why Yahweh no longer seemed to be working (6:13), Yahweh in fact had already been at work in the enemy camp. As part of the theme of Yahweh as the sole author of deliverance, Gideon and the reader alike learn that God worked in advance of his servants, preparing the way so that their faithful service could be effective. The dream recounted in 7:13, which might be entitled "Attack of the Killer Dinner Roll," revealed the erosion of Midianite morale, and possibly gave Gideon a crucial element of his strategy, the cry, "A sword for Yahweh and for Gideon," echoing the Midianite soldiers' interpretation of the dream in the phrase, "This is nothing but the sword of Gideon!"

Because the divine encouragement included a reference to Gideon, Yahweh showed he was not indifferent to Gideon's ever-fragile status as a charismatic leader. In the Old Testament, God regularly displays a concern to authenticate his servants. The plagues, which revealed the supremacy of Yahweh, also exalted Moses in Egypt (Exod 11:3). Moreover, the Exodus narrative culminates not merely in the Israelites fearing Yahweh, but also in their believing in his servant, Moses (Exod 14:31). Likewise, Yahweh repeatedly and openly validated Joshua's leadership (Josh 3:7; 4:14; 6:27). Thus commentators (e.g., Schneider 2000:115) are mistaken to draw too brute a contrast between Yahweh's glory and human glory. Indeed, when Yahweh is truly exalted, his servants are exalted with him. The real sin against Yahweh's glory is the arrogant claim of self-sufficiency that demands credit and recognition, as though God had no other choice of servants for his work.

The battle itself (7:15–8:21) is narrated in two roughly parallel sections that develop contrasting perspectives on the character and motivations of Gideon himself. On the one hand, Gideon is the tribal hero and man of God (7:15–8:3), and on the other, he is the hard-driving leader avenging his family and punishing any defiance of his authority (8:4-21). Scholars often attribute these two portrayals to different literary sources depicting the same battle, but the present text places the conflict with Ephraim between them and draws distinctions in detail. As observed above, the Ephraimite failure to seal the Jordan crossings cost Gideon and his men a long pursuit east of Jordan, deep into the arid country. We might well expect the weary, frustrated leader to reveal a different side.

Judges 7:15–8:3 describes the tactic of a night-ruse with pitchers, torches, trumpets, and war-whoops, which caused the Midianites to panic and turn on one another before taking flight. The narrative employs physical implements to portray elements of classic ancient Near Eastern victory descriptions in which the deity throws the enemy into stark terror and headlong flight. Indeed, the combination at midnight of 300 simultaneous blasts on ram's horns, 300 bursts of blazing torchlight, and 300 voices shouting a war-cry echoing the enemy's ominous dream would be a potent mixture to produce the panic and chaos described in these verses.

Gideon pursued the enemy and, at the critical moment, summoned both his kinsmen—presumably the warriors who had previously gone home—and the fighters of Ephraim. Gideon directed the Ephraimites to capture the crossing points of the Jordan River (7:24, see notes) to prevent the Midianites from escaping. Instead, they capture and behead two Midianite chieftains who, though important, were not the top leadership. In addition, while the Ephraimites were preoccupied with "Raven Man" and "Wolf Man" (see note on 7:25), the Midianites slipped over Jordan and went eastward across the Transjordanian plateau. This arid countryside was their native habitat and presumably they knew every trick. Gideon and his men, however, would have to continue the pursuit on unfamiliar ground. Even this pursuit was delayed, however, by the protest of the Ephraimites. Despite their inadequate performance, they resented being included with the "second round" draft choices, the rejects of the previous lottery. Gideon's reply can be read at two levels: By referring to their execution of the two Midianite commanders as "gleanings," he could well have been noting the secondary priority represented by their capture. The same could be said of his comment that he had not done anything like what they did—in fact, he could not because the enemy got away! All the same, Gideon framed his statement so that the Ephraimites heard it as a high compliment for their valiant effort and sterling achievement. Meanwhile, having completed his "pastoral care," Gideon had a war to finish, with or without Ephraimite assistance.

This phase of the battle account accentuates the importance of who ultimately should have received the glory and credit for what was accomplished, though the Israelites ultimately fail to get the point. Yahweh winnowed the army down to an impossibly small size precisely to make it clear that the victory belonged to him—yet he still left a significant role for his human servants. The Ephraimites seem to miss the point of Yahweh's larger aims in their desire to play a more prominent role. Gideon's behavior and speech reinforce this point. Centuries later, the prophet Isaiah would remind the king of Assyria of the same point, asking "Is the axe to boast itself over the one who chops with it?" (Isa 10:13-15). Likewise, Deuteronomy 8:11-20 sternly warns the Israelites against forgetting their debt to Yahweh's power and grace. Reassured by the dream report, Gideon acted decisively, and Yahweh granted a stunning rout. By contrast, the Ephraimites displayed precisely that concern for glory and credit that Yahweh sought to undercut at the story's outset. That Gideon responded diplomatically, not debating the point with the Ephraimites, coheres well with the realization that those who serve Yahweh and fight his battles need invest no effort worrying about who gets the credit, since Yahweh can save by many or by few, shaming the mighty and exalting the weak and insignificant (1 Cor 1:25-27). The suggestion that Gideon's approach was "psychological" rather than "theological" (Younger 2002:197) misses the integrated nature of true obedience enacted on the plane of human relationships.

c. Authority exercised (8:4-21)

4 Gideon then crossed the Jordan River with his 300 men, and though exhausted, they continued to chase the enemy. 5 When they reached Succoth, Gideon asked the leaders of the town, "Please give my warriors some food. They are very tired. I am chasing Zebah and Zalmunna, the kings of Midian."

6 But the officials of Succoth replied, "Catch Zebah and Zalmunna first, and then we will feed your army."

7 So Gideon said, "After the LORD gives me victory over Zebah and Zalmunna, I will return and tear your flesh with the thorns and briers from the wilderness."

8 From there Gideon went up to Peniel* and again asked for food, but he got the same answer. 9 So he said to the people of Peniel, "After I return in victory, I will tear down this tower."

10 By this time Zebah and Zalmunna were in Karkor with 15,000 warriors—all that remained of the allied armies of the east, for 120,000 had already been killed. 11 Gideon circled around by the caravan route east of Nobah and Jogbehah, taking the Midianite army by surprise. 12 Zebah and Zalmunna, the two Midianite kings, fled, but Gideon chased them down and captured all their warriors.

13 After this, Gideon returned from the battle by way of Heres Pass. 14 There he captured a young man from Succoth and demanded that he write down the names of all the seventy-seven officials and elders in the town. 15 Gideon then returned to Succoth and said to the leaders, "Here are Zebah and Zalmunna. When we were here before, you taunted me, saying, 'Catch Zebah and Zalmunna first, and then we will feed your exhausted army.' " 16 Then Gideon took the elders of the town and taught them a lesson, punishing them with thorns and briers from the wilderness. 17 He also tore down the tower of Peniel and killed all the men in the town.

18 Then Gideon asked Zebah and Zalmunna, "The men you killed at Tabor—what were they like?"

"Like you," they replied. "They all had the look of a king's son."

19 "They were my brothers, the sons of my own mother!" Gideon exclaimed. "As surely as the LORD lives, I wouldn't kill you if you hadn't killed them."

20 Turning to Jether, his oldest son, he said, "Kill them!" But Jether did not draw his sword, for he was only a boy and was afraid.

21 Then Zebah and Zalmunna said to Gideon, "Be a man! Kill us yourself!" So Gideon killed them both and took the royal ornaments from the necks of their camels.

8:8 Hebrew *Penuel,* a variant spelling of Peniel; also in 8:9, 17.

NOTES

8:4 ***Gideon then crossed the Jordan River with his 300 men.*** The Jordan forms a boundary in the story. West of Jordan, Gideon has, despite his uncertainty, been brilliantly successful both militarily and diplomatically. East of Jordan, the portrayal changes: Gideon appears sure of himself and not inclined to trifle.

exhausted. The term is used of Esau as he approached Jacob and his infamous pot of soup (Gen 25:29); it is also used of the Israelites who followed Saul under a compulsory fast (1 Sam 14:28, 31). In 4:21, weary Sisera falls deep asleep as soon as he enters Jael's tent (cf. 2 Sam 21:15; Jer 4:31; NIDOTTE s.v. *'ayep* [TH5889, ZH6546]). The term denotes a combination of exhaustion and hunger that puts a person at the edge of their capacity to continue. Perhaps we who have known little of oppression, battle, exhaustion, or hunger should beware of judging Iron Age fighting men by modern standards. Then again, even by modern standards Gideon's 300 measures up quite well. By the time they reach Succoth they've traveled 26–30 miles, and that after a vigorous engagement with the enemy. Both ancient and modern armies consider 15–20 miles to be a day's march on foot—and that's not counting effort and time exerted in contact with the enemy.

chase the enemy. "The enemy" is not in the Hebrew, which reads simply "pursuing." Many translators and commentators see a spelling problem and want to translate "hungry," noting the request for food. But the term used for "exhausted" already carries a nuance of hunger, so the change is unnecessary.

8:5 ***Succoth.*** This lies where the Jabbok River empties into the Jordan from the east. Since the town lay in the inheritance of Gad (Josh 13:27), it should have been nominally Israelite and loyal to Gideon. An Egyptian stele mentions several sites in the "Valley of Succoth," including both Succoth and Penuel/Peniel. The modern site Tell Deir 'Alla remains the best candidate for Succoth. In the Late Bronze Age, it featured a sanctuary that served as an area shrine; its religious significance seems to have continued up through the 800s BC. The site's destructions in the early 1100s BC and again a century later have each been credited by some to Gideon's vengeance, though the excavators think otherwise (ABD 6.217-218). If Gideon lived between the withdrawal of Egypt from Canaan (c. 1150 BC) and the rise of Philistine dominance in the interior of Canaan (c. 1100), neither destruction at Tell Deir 'Alla would fit the story. But the text never credits Gideon with any damage to this city, though his damage to Succoth's elders and to Peniel was considerable.

Gideon asked the leaders of the town. Most war leaders would simply "requisition" what they needed at force of arms. Gideon's respectful request, not a demand (contra Younger 2002:198), and his decision not to resort initially to force, demonstrates a restraint that recognized the boundaries of his authority.

Please give my warriors some food. "Warriors" is simply "the people who are at my feet," i.e., the people following me. The request for "round (loaves) of bread" recalls the dream about a loaf of bread (7:13). That Succoth and Peniel were nominally Israelite cities obligated them to assist Gideon and his men, a point often missed (Schneider 2000:121).

Zebah and Zalmunna. The two names as written in the MT mean "Sacrificial Victim" and "Protection Refused" respectively (Burney 1920:228). The author probably derisively changed the names to reflect the men's destiny, as occurred also with Adoni-bezek (1:5) and Cushan-rishathaim (3:8) (Burney 1920:229).

kings of Midian. The term "kings" need not imply absolute monarchs. The term could be used also of rulers over cities or particular domains who might owe allegiance to a higher ruler, but who exercised sovereignty within their own sphere (Hess 2008:39-40). An enemy composed of several groups and subgroups might reasonably have more than one king in their midst.

8:6 ***the officials of Succoth replied.*** The versatile term *sar* [TH8269, ZH8569] appears here, having previously denoted Jabin's professional commander, Sisera (4:2), and the sheikhs leading part of the Midianite force (7:25). Later, in 8:14, these officials will be distinguished from the "elders" (*zeqenim* [TH2205, ZH2418]), who would represent the senior members of the community. Possibly, *sar* denotes a military function. These different social contexts clearly require different translation equivalents in order for readers to grasp the concrete social realities of the text, thus illustrating the weakness of a mechanically formal-equivalent approach to translation (Schneider 2000:118-119).

Catch Zebah and Zalmunna first. Lit., "Are the palm of Zeba and Zalmunna in your hands?" Ancient Near Eastern texts and art abundantly document that the question was literal. Victorious commanders typically appear in reliefs posing among their enemies' cut-off hands, heads, and other body parts. The city leaders talked tough in taunting Gideon.

Living on the east side of Jordan, the residents of Succoth had to decide whose enmity they could most tolerate—aiding Gideon would bring disaster if the Midianites defeated him. From their attitude, they appear to have bet on the Midianites.

8:7 *After.* Gideon begins his answer with the word "therefore" (*laken* [TH3807.1/3651A, ZH4200/4027]), which is unusual at the beginning of a statement. Normally it follows as the conclusion of what has been said. Gideon took the statements of the men of Succoth as the cause statement to which he supplied the consequence. Burney (1920:229) finely suggests "Well, then . . . ."

the LORD gives me victory. The claim by some commentators that Gideon is "glib" (Block 1999:290; Younger 2002:198) lacks any textual basis. Gideon's certainty of victory over the Midianite kings contrasts with the uncertainty with which he began the campaign, suggesting a solidified faith.

tear your flesh. Gideon here does not "take the law into his own hands" (contra Block 1999:290). What should he have done? Dial 9-1-1? In "wild and wooly" Iron Age I Israel, there was no effective law enforcement, and societies such as Gideon's had little or no structure above the tribal level. Gideon, as Yahweh's called and authenticated servant, was the law. In defying Gideon's authority, the men of Succoth defied Yahweh's choice. So Gideon accepted their challenge, but reminded them that they had taken cards in a grim game. The verb *dush* [TH1758, ZH1889] conveys trampling or threshing, as with wheat, suggesting an image of dragging the men of Succoth over thorns on a threshing floor, or dragging a thorny threshing sledge over them (Moore 1895:219; Burney 1920:229-230; Soggin 1981:149-150). Gideon's fulfillment of his threat in 8:16, however, suggests carding (see note on 8:16). The NLT's "tear your flesh" fits both contexts.

thorns and briers from the wilderness. Moore (1895:219) aptly notes, "Palestine has a great variety of thorny plants and shrubs, many of which are formidably armed."

8:8 *Peniel.* Peniel (or Penuel) was probably located about five miles up the Jabbok River valley from Succoth, if the identification with the modern unexcavated site Tell ed-Dahab esh-Sherqiyeh (the Hill of Gold) is correct (ABD 5.223). Like Succoth, it is also mentioned in Shishak's list of conquered cities from the late 900s BC. The story of Jacob's wrestling match with a mysterious "man" there provides the inner-biblical explanation of the place-name, which means "face of God" (Gen 32:24-32).

8:9 *After I return in victory.* "Victory" renders *shalom* [TH7965, ZH8934]. Far from meaning "peace" in the conventional sense of the word, *shalom* is the restored healthy function of the community by means of violated or neglected obligations being made right. The verbal form often denotes retribution, revenge, and restitution. In this context it carries a dual implication. Completion of the defeat of the Midianites certainly would seal *shalom* for Israel. But by refusing support, both Succoth and Penuel violated their obligation of solidarity with their fellow Israelites; so a "payback" would be due these traitors, as well.

I will tear down this tower. Gideon did not threaten to harm the citizens of Penuel, though he did so in the end. Still, destruction of the tower might imply a traditional destruction of the city, which would certainly include casualties.

8:10 *Zebah and Zalmunna were in Karkor.* The name "Karkor" means "ground" and could refer to an open area suitable for a caravan to encamp and graze. Scholars suggest a well-watered site lying over 120 miles southeast of Peniel (Soggin 1981:151), but this seems too distant for the story line since Gideon's posse seems ill-prepared for a long desert trek. The precise location thus remains uncertain, but probably lies on the King's Highway (see note on 8:11).

15,000 warriors . . . 120,000. "Thousand" here again (see notes on 3:29; 5:8; 7:2) could refer to squads or other battle units, not lit. a thousand, or 15,000 actual fighters. From these numbers, we calculate the original strength of the Midianite force. The numbers involved, if literal, far exceed what would be expected of a nomadic, Iron Age, tribal nation. But reading "squad" or the like for *'elep* [TH505, ZH547] (thousand) makes easy sense.

8:11 ***circled around by the caravan route east of Nobah and Jogbehah.*** The location of Nobah remains uncertain, but is associated with Manasseh (Num 32:40-42). The location would fit the region where Gideon pursued the Midianites (ABD 4.1133). Jogbehah is probably Rugm 'al-Gubekhah, an Ammonite fortress. Numbers 32:35 attributes the building of Jogbehah to the Gadites (ABD 3.880). The "caravan route" (lit., "the way of those who dwell in tents") that ran east of these towns was probably the King's Highway, the main trunk route running north-south between the Red Sea and Damascus, east of and parallel to the Jordan River but up on the high plateau (Soggin 1981:151; ABD 5.776-782). The Midianites probably took the highway running southeast from Penuel, which intersected the King's Highway near Jogbehah. Once the Midianites struck that highway, their getaway would be complete, so Gideon needed to intercept them. Gideon took the more direct route 12 miles straight east from Peniel, up the Jabbok gorge, climbing about 2,000 feet to the King's Highway, where they turned south, thus passing, as the text says, east of the two towns noted, climbing an additional 2,000 feet over about 13 more miles to the intersection of the King's Highway and the east-west caravan route. The NLT's "circled around" for the lit., "and he went up," captures the movement well, though Gideon also did a lot of ascending in this pursuit.

taking the Midianite army by surprise. Reaching the King's Highway and seeing no sign of pursuit along the road they took, the Midianites assumed they escaped successfully, not expecting Gideon's circling maneuver. Gideon caught them napping. The NLT's translation is correct, but obscures the term *betakh* [TH983, ZH1055], which describes the Midianite camp as "trusting, feeling secure." The term often denotes false feelings of trust or security.

8:12 ***but Gideon chased them down and captured all their warriors.*** The NLT's rendering has no counterpart to the last verb of Hebrew verse (*hekherid* [TH2729, ZH3006], "cause to fear or panic"), instead connecting "their warriors" (lit., the camp) to the verb "captured" used earlier in the verse. The final clause of the MT reads "now the whole camp went into a panic." This verbal root of *hekherid* is familiar from the first sifting of Gideon's troops at the Harod (*kharod* [TH5878, ZH3008]) spring when any who feared (*khared* [TH2730, ZH3007]) could depart (7:3). Some suggest reading *hekherim* [TH2763, ZH3049] (he totally annihilated) instead of *hekherid*, but the suggested word and its particular nuance are virtually absent from Judges, appearing only in 1:17; 21:11. The wars in the main body of the book are not wars of "conquest" like those in Joshua (Boling 1975:156) and so do not fall under its strictures.

8:13 ***Heres Pass.*** Burney (1920:232) cleverly proposes deleting this puzzling place-name as a scribal error duplicating the end of 8:12, but the suggestion itself requires a change also in 8:12. The site, which might have been known as the "Ascent of Horus," has been identified with the steep ravine dropping sharply down to Succoth. This also would not be the route Gideon took initially, and so he might have created an element of surprise in his return to Succoth (Soggin 1981:153-155).

8:14 ***a young man . . . write down the names.*** The text assumes at least functional literacy on the part of Gideon and a "young man" from the city apprehended at random (Burney 1920:253-263; contra Moore 1895:225). Interestingly, Tell Deir Alla (cf. note above) features textual discoveries, including clay tablets inscribed in an unknown script from the Iron Age I levels (Gideon's time) and a set of intriguing Aramaic texts from the Iron Age II period, referring to Balaam the Seer.

8:15 ***you taunted me.*** More than mere rude talk, this strong verb denotes demeaning something or someone by complete devaluation, defiance, or despising (cf. HALOT 1.355, s.v. *kharap* II [TH2778, ZH3070]). In an "honor-shame" culture such as that of ancient Israel, to leave such a taunt unanswered amounts to an abdication of leadership, surrendering the community's order to defiant covenant breakers. Gideon's actions are not a "high-handed" reprisal (contra Block 1999:292), but an admittedly stern upholding of a wartime social order.

8:16 ***taught them a lesson, punishing them with thorns and briers from the wilderness.*** The torture in view is known as "carding," and involves ripping the victims' flesh with a sharp instrument, in this case, thorns of the wilderness. Traditional carding was performed with the combs used for preparing wool for spinning, which had rows of metal teeth several inches long (Oxford English Dictionary, s.v. "card"; Moore 1895:224-226). That Gideon used thorns, not metal combs, suggests he intended reproof, not execution, and befits the verb rendered by the NLT's "taught them a lesson," which could be translated lit. "made them know." The LXX has the excruciating *katexanen autous* (he shredded them). The NLT adds "punishing them" for clarity. The citizens of Succoth and Peniel, as Israelites, had an obligation of solidarity with Gideon and his band in resisting the Midianites (contra Soggin 1981:156). As a responsible wartime leader, Gideon could not allow Israelite towns to break covenant with impunity and stand with Israel's enemies.

8:17 ***He also tore down the tower of Peniel and killed all the men in the town.*** The Hebrew clause structure here is contrastive: "but he tore down the tower of Peniel. . . ." The syntax would thus emphasize the contrast between the two towns. Instead of "all the men in the town," the Hebrew expression used likely means the leading men, or elders of the city. The more extreme punishment of Peniel suggests their offense exceeded that of Succoth. But was death so extreme? Succoth and Penuel appear to have permitted the unmolested passage of the murderous, pillaging Midianites whose violence and atrocities had driven their fellow Israelites into the hills. How many Israelites starved or died because Succoth and Penuel looked the other way when camel-mounted raiders crossed the Jordan? Attributing Gideon's actions to "rage" (Block 1999:293) does not take seven years of suffering abetted by treason quite seriously enough.

8:18 ***The men you killed at Tabor— what were they like?*** The question is lit., "Where are the men you killed at Tabor?" Commentators have no idea how to render the "where." Boling (1975:157) suggests, "how about the men . . . . ?" Tabor identifies the murders taking place less than 10 miles from Ophrah, Gideon's home. If this happened prior to the account of Gideon's call, he likely would have known of the murders. Possibly he had been hiding precisely because, with his brothers murdered, he was next.

Like you . . . the look of a king's son. Despite biblical avowals that God remains unimpressed with appearances, the biblical stories often note royal mien (1 Sam 9:2; 16:7, 18; 1 Kgs 1:6). The introduction of explicitly royal language here comes as a surprise, especially since Gideon at first appeared such an unlikely, hesitant leader.

8:19 ***They were my brothers, the sons of my own mother!*** In polygamous societies, a brother might often be the son of one's father, but not of one's mother. Sons of the same mother might share a special loyalty, hence Gideon's ardor. This vital bit of "back story" illuminates Gideon's actions: First, the murder of his brothers could explain Gideon's protest that his family was the least in Manasseh (6:15). Second, it underscores Gideon's solemn obligation to fight the Midianites to avenge the murder of a relative. Since the murderers were non-Israelite oppressors, none of the strictures limiting inner-Israelite blood-vengeance, such as flight to a city of refuge (cf. Josh 20), could be meaningful. The charge that here Gideon violates Yahweh's prerogatives and acts wrongly (Boling 1975:157; Block 1999:293-294), or is on a personal vendetta (Schneider 2000:123), ignores these social realities. The text expresses no negative judgments on Gideon, and Yahweh's "silence" (Schneider 2000:121-122) proves nothing, since the narrator or Yahweh could have as easily expressed disapproval as approval. The characters adhere to classic heroic expectations (Soggin 1981:156-157). In fact, the report of his brothers' murders shows that Gideon was not boiling over with rage for revenge. He did not take action without divine prodding, investiture with the Spirit, and repeated signs. Moreover, he waited until after ensuring his people's victory before leading his loyal posse to fulfill his obligation as the "avenger/ redeemer of blood" (Num 35:9-34). Far from taking Yahweh's name in vain in his oath (Boling 1975:157; Block 1999:295), Gideon's vengeance obligation served both the need of his people and the purpose of Yahweh.

8:20 ***Turning to Jether, his oldest son, he said, "Kill them!" But Jether did not draw his sword, for he was only a boy and was afraid.*** The use of young men to kill captives might have been a tradition of early nomadic tribes (Robertson-Smith 1892:417; Burney 1920:234). Jether need not have been a "boy" since the term *na'ar* [TH5288, ZH5853] often denotes a young man, often unmarried, of warrior age. The execution of prisoners figured routinely in military practice, as graphically portrayed on the bronze gates from the Assyrian city of Balawat (Parrot 1961:122-123). However much we moderns squirm before such scenes, in many cultures through history, young men have worn the sword as Jether did. We cannot demand that Gideon act like a modern youth pastor rather than a war leader.

8:21 ***Be a man! Kill us yourself!*** The Midianite warlords wanted, at least, the honor of being killed by a peer. Recall the umbrage taken by Goliath at having a mere boy sent out to fight him (1 Sam 17:41-43). Recall also how well that boy acquitted himself, in contrast to Gideon's son. The kings, taking a page out of Homer, embrace their fate "with the true savage instinct" (Burney 1920:234; Moore 1895:226).

the royal ornaments from the necks of their camels. Since this was not *kherem* [TH2764, ZH3051] warfare, the taking of spoils was permitted (contra Schneider 2000:126). The term "royal" (8:21, 26) does not appear in the text, and the same term appears in Isa 3:18 ("crescent necklaces"). The ornaments were golden crescents, here adorning the necks of the camels, and not necessarily belonging to royalty. For samples of ancient gold jewelry, including crescent-shaped items, see King and Stager (2001:276-280).

COMMENTARY

If the question of who received the glory for the victory dominated 7:1–8:3, the related but contrasting theme of recompense and honor controls 8:4-21. The narrative explores how each of the characters participates in a network of retribution—people getting "what's coming to them"—based on the issue of honor. Just as the glory issue revealed more complexity than simply "Yahweh *versus* Israel," so the honor issue involves more than the facile contrast of "self *versus* spirit" that controls so much of the interpretive literature on this passage.

Commentators have a field day excoriating Gideon in 8:4-21, psychoanalyzing his every move and employing pejorative language ("glib," "rage") with scant textual basis to impugn Gideon's motives (Block, Schneider, Younger). Such eisegesis typically betrays the middle-class western perspective of the interpreters rather than illuminating the Iron Age culture and behavior of Gideon. Interpreters have all noted that 8:4-21 reflects a different style of narration. Some (Moore, Burney) have argued that the author, as a historian using various documents and sources, had simply switched here to a different source document that had a different focus and style. Whether or not a different document is in view, 8:4-21 exhibits a shift in literary genre from one that highlights divine activity to one that focuses on human actions, allowing the divine to slip into the background (von Rad 1966). The shift in genre does not imply a judgment on the characters but reflects the author's purpose, which is to present God's deliverance in all its dimensions, both wondrous divine deeds and acts of human valor. Likewise, the author presents the actions of Gideon in their full dimensions both as prompted and empowered by God and, at the same time, as implemented through very human qualities of courage, valor, and perseverance.

Some interpreters accuse Gideon in this episode of abandoning his trust in Yahweh and succumbing to base motives of vengeance. Was Gideon, like his son Abimelech, a vengeful warlord ruthlessly exercising his power? Unlike Abimelech, Gideon acted under a divine call to arms, a call neither sought nor eagerly embraced. Authenticated by the presence of the divine Spirit, confirmed by divinely given signs, Gideon knew he must remain within a boundary set by God in his dealings with his countrymen. He was able and willing to give up his claim of honor to reconcile with the Ephraimites (contrast Jephthah, 12:1-7). Thus the narrative of 6:11–8:3, rather than contrasting with 8:4-21, sets a positive framework for reading it. We know our man. By contrast, Abimelech will seek only to establish his own power, by any means he chooses, and will know neither limit nor boundary. Gideon kills because he *must*, both to save his people and to punish betrayal (cf. 8:17). Abimelech will kill because he *can*.

The narrative in 8:18-21 presents two surprises. First, though the story has stressed how unlikely Gideon seemed as a leader, here the marks of royalty seem obvious to vanquished pagan enemies. In fact, 6:11–8:3 presents a gradual emergence of Gideon's qualities as a leader, and now the Midianite kings affirm this explicitly. Second, we have heard nothing of atrocities perpetrated by the Midianites, much less that the victims were Gideon's brothers. As noted earlier, to characterize Gideon's action merely as personal revenge ignores his cultural context in a tribal society and judges him by the standards of modern pious expectations. What we would call vengeance, Gideon and his fellow Israelites would call justice, or better, *shalom* [TH7965, ZH8934] (see note on 8:9). Gideon's avenging his brothers serves a larger concern for right. Those could have been *any* Israelite's brothers, mothers, or children. In the classic western movie *Tombstone*, Wyatt Earp brutally and dramatically kills the man who murdered his brother, while a corrupt sheriff looks the other way. One of Earp's companions remarks, "If it were my brothers, I'd want revenge too." But the notorious Doc Holiday somberly replies, "Oh, make no mistake; it's not *revenge* he's after; *it's the reckoning.*" Gideon indeed wanted not simple revenge; he wanted to make the world right, *the reckoning*.

Too easily modern readers, with our comfortable lives protected by police, ambulance, and civil legal structures, instructed by a whole Bible and 2,000 years of Christian tradition, pass judgment on Gideon. But Gideon's historical and literary world more resembled that of Achilles or Beowulf. Canaan in the midst of Iron

Age I remained dark and bloody ground. A civilization of 2,000 years standing, the Bronze Age culture of the eastern Mediterranean had collapsed in flames in a generation, accompanied by invasions, wars, earthquakes, famine, and epidemic. Men like Gideon, called and empowered by Yahweh, provided the only "law" there was. If individuals and communities could not be held accountable to the commitments that defined their community identities, then what little social order remained would fall apart. Under depredations by the Midianites, Gideon sought to lead his community to reassert its true identity. With no human authority above his own charisma, Gideon's honor and standing embodied in time and space the thin red line between savagery and *shalom* under Yahweh's covenant. We may debate whether that context justifies Gideon's actions, but the wise interpreter will not lightly charge Gideon with pursuing merely personal vendettas, or following "self *versus* the Spirit" as though he had not had devotions that morning. Where the text does not condemn him, neither should we, unless the context provides clear markers.

The question remains, however, what this story could say to contemporary believers. First, the features of this narrative ought to warn against an easy devotional free association between Gideon and ourselves. Some have found here scriptural warrant for not fuming in anger in traffic while driving to work (Younger 2002:202). But did God inspire this narrative of a desperate pursuit of justice by an exhausted band of heroes merely to check our impatience during the morning commute? Interpreters making a facile connection between Gideon "in the Spirit" (7:1–8:3) and Gideon "motivated by self" (8:4-21) perpetrate anachronistic eisegesis. The narrator offers no critique of Gideon in 8:4-21. This episode of the story presents as exemplary a portrayal as the earlier portion.

Second, the story unmasks the parochial, privatized character of our notions of spirituality. The text features a man radically inhabited and animated by the Spirit of Yahweh who does not conform to any norms of religious service familiar to us. Gideon hesitated, but once emboldened, he was tough, persistent, and zealous. Gideon's very human character and qualities were put in the service of Yahweh and his purposes. Perhaps contemporary readers could broaden their understanding of the temperaments, personalities, and skills that God can use. God does not annihilate the "self" but energizes and animates it. A "sword for Yahweh" need not rule out "a sword for Gideon."

Third, Gideon's story *as a whole* discloses a commendable distaste for power as the prerequisite for its use. Gideon, like the quiet man of the B-western, does not want to take those holstered guns off the peg where they hang; but once he straps them on, he will not hang them up again until the job is done. Those who do not seek power and take no pleasure in its exercise might just be the ones to whom God can most safely entrust his power. Gideon repeatedly subjected his impressions of God's will to testing and confirmation. He prioritized the divine victory and affirmative relationships with other faithful and obedient, even if vain, servants, as opposed to the defiant men of Succoth. He pursued the mission to its end.

Finally, Gideon's obedience, though energized by the divine charisma, led him to assert and enforce the God-ordained order of his community. Whether it be worship of Yahweh alone, liberation from plunderers, or avenging atrocity, Gideon's call and charisma had driven him to serve Yahweh's purpose. Yahweh had constituted Israel as an oath-bound tribal confederation in covenant with him and one another. We see in Gideon the "conservative charismatic" described by sociologist Philip Rieff in his landmark study *Charisma: The Gift of Grace and How It Has Been Taken Away From Us*. Unlike the stereotypical "charismatic rebel" who honors no authority and would shatter any claims of absolute truth, subjecting the community ultimately to himself, the true charismatic first submits to transcendent moral truth, then attacks the community's bondage to bogus truth-claims in order to bring it under true moral authority. Gideon thus had no final interest in subordinating Israel to himself (as 8:22-27 shows) but reasserted Yahweh's absolute authority over his people. Unfortunately, though Gideon succeeded brilliantly at shattering those powers that blocked Israel's ability to obey Yahweh, he would ultimately fail at fully implementing Yahweh's order in Israel, as the next and final episode reveals.

◆ d. Authority abdicated (8:22-27)

**22 Then the Israelites said to Gideon, "Be
our ruler! You and your son and your
grandson will be our rulers, for you have
rescued us from Midian."**

**23 But Gideon replied, "I will not rule
over you, nor will my son. The LORD will
rule over you! 24 However, I do have one
request—that each of you give me an ear-
ring from the plunder you collected from
your fallen enemies." (The enemies, being
Ishmaelites, all wore gold earrings.)**

**25 "Gladly!" they replied. They spread out
a cloak, and each one threw in a gold ear-
ring he had gathered from the plunder.
26 The weight of the gold earrings was
forty-three pounds,* not including the royal
ornaments and pendants, the purple cloth-
ing worn by the kings of Midian, or the
chains around the necks of their camels.**

**27 Gideon made a sacred ephod from the
gold and put it in Ophrah, his hometown.
But soon all the Israelites prostituted
themselves by worshiping it, and it be-
came a trap for Gideon and his family.**

8:26 Hebrew *1,700 shekels* [19.4 kilograms].

NOTES

8:22 *Then the Israelites said to Gideon.* This takes place in Ophrah (8:27). If Zeba and Zalmunna were executed in Ophrah, rather than in Transjordan, the saga of oppression and liberation would have come full circle. Ophrah stood in the heart of the area oppressed by Midian, threatened by the swarms of nomadic raiders, and intimidated by the murder of Gideon's brothers. In addition, Gideon apparently unified the nation, since the offer came from the "Israelites."

Be our ruler! What a change from the defiance of 8:4-9 and friction of 8:1-3. Gideon's execution of the kings of Midian and presentation of the spoils to his ravaged and impoverished countrymen sealed his reputation. The text is widely read as a summons to kingship. The standard Hebrew root expressing kingship, *malak* [TH4427, ZH4887] (reign), does not appear, but some commentators simply force the translation "reign over us" on the text (Boling 1975:159; Block 1999:297). Instead, the writer uses *mashal* [TH4910, ZH5440], a word covering a semantic range far broader than the reigning of kings, and not especially characteristic of royal rule (HALOT 1.647, s.v. *mashal* II; NIDOTTE 1.1136-1138, s.v. *mashal* II). If the writer wanted to zero in on kingship as his main interest, he chose the wrong word.

You and your son and your grandson will be our rulers. Inherited rule does not imply monarchy. Many leadership roles are inherited (such as that of chief), and kingship itself need not be dynastic. Historians and sociologists of ancient societies recognize a form of social organization intermediate in complexity (though not necessarily in historical development) between a decentralized confederation and a centralized monarchic state. The term "chiefdom" designates this intermediate type of social organization and has been analyzed in an enormous body of literature (Kletter 2004:15-29; R. Miller 2005:6-14). Kingship involves state formation, which for Iron Age cultures included, among other things: centralization of administration, urbanization, a complex social stratification, centralized management of agricultural surpluses, control of commerce outside the community, monumental architecture, a system of taxation, a standing army, and a defined territory. At the other extreme, decentralized tribal societies feature leadership via "achieved status," a polite term for achieving a monopoly of force, even if temporary. The chiefdom involves stable, inherited leadership vested in a family, or "ascribed status." Other than certain limited functions involving management of surpluses, a chiefdom would not present the features noted above for a monarchy. Chiefdoms can be simple or complex, with two to three levels of social stratification. Archaeologists have noted a network of town centers and satellite villages in the hill country of Israel, suggesting a complex chiefdom (R. Miller 2005:15-90). Thus, the men of Israel were not offering Gideon a kingship. They were simply offering him and his family senior rank as "chief" over the region.

for you have rescued us from Midian. These words likely triggered Gideon's refusal. The battle had been premised on Yahweh being credited with the victory. The wording of the request contradicts Yahweh's concern (7:2). Faulting Gideon for not lecturing the Israelites on their error (Younger 2002:204) presumes to read into the text's omissions rather than simply expound what is actually said. If Gideon indeed lacked the genealogical rank to be a regular leader (cf. 6:15), we might see here the beginning of a shift from leadership by achieved status to leadership by ascribed status. Gideon's achievements, not his familial rank, earned him this offer. But the offer of a patrimonial office constituted Gideon as the head of a new senior-ranked family in Israel.

8:23 ***I will not rule. . . . The LORD will rule over you!*** Some argue that Gideon's refusal is a "sham" (Block 1999:296), but accepting the text's witness about these events seems best. Gideon wrongly thought that human rule and divine rule were incompatible, rejected the people's reasoning, and asserted divine rule over Israel. The serious question is whether his rightly motivated abdication was the right choice. The answer cannot derive from modern piety or guesswork about Gideon's motives. In the remainder of the story, the author casts Gideon's refusal in a catastrophically negative light (see notes on 8:27).

8:24 ***give me an earring from the plunder.*** The text does not specify "ear" rings. The term *nezem* [TH5141, ZH5690] can just as easily denote nose rings! Piercings were as popular in the twelfth century BC as they are in the twenty-first century AD. Since plunder was permitted, Gideon's battle should not be seen as a classic "holy war" or "Yahweh war" in which the plunder must all be donated to Yahweh's sanctuary. Still, Gideon was within his rights to levy a sort of sanctuary tax on the plunder. We have no sign that Gideon took any plunder of his own.

Ishmaelites. This is the first mention of Ishmaelites in the story, though Ishmaelites and Midianites are interchanged elsewhere in the OT (Gen 37:25-28).

8:26 ***royal ornaments and pendants.*** Again (cf. 8:21), "royal" seems an unwarranted addition in the translation. The "pendants" (*netipoth* [TH5188, ZH5755]) mentioned were drop-shaped, from the term *natap* [TH5197, ZH5752], "to drop" (King and Stager 2001:279). The weight of these items is excluded to make clear how much the people gave from their own shares. The items noted in this "exception" clause were assumed from the beginning to be donated to the service of Yahweh's sanctuary. The clothing items likely served as the raiment of the image. Decorated with royal purple garments, the ephod might indeed seem to represent, however wrongly, Yahweh's rule over his people.

8:27 ***a sacred ephod from the gold.*** The ephod was an important piece of liturgical gear with a complex portrayal in the OT. Documented also in ancient Near Eastern texts outside Israel, the ephod apparently was a golden cuirass thought of as the deity's clothing or armor; it represented the splendor of the deity. From OT descriptions, it resembled a "tank top" over the priestly garments. As a freestanding religious object in the premonarchic sanctuaries of Israel, an ephod was carried into battle for making inquiries of Yahweh. Judges 17–18 includes an ephod with household spirit images (*terapim* [TH8655, ZH9572]) and an image of Yahweh in Micah's sanctuary—items later permanently borrowed by the migrating Danites (NIDOTTE 1.476-477; ABD 2.550; NIDB 2.278-279). The high priest's ephod contained a pouch for the Urim and Thummim, used for making inquiries of Yahweh. The Urim and Thummim employed a complex numerical system matching a binary instrument to 12 jewels, offering a vast range of possible divinatory combinations (Douglas 1999:119-124). Even ephods such as Gideon's seem to fulfill the function of inquiring of Yahweh (Moore 1895:232-333; Burney 1920:236-243). Crüsemann (1978:47-50), after summarizing the arguments for seeing the ephod as a ritual apparatus for inquiring of God, links that process to the concrete exercise of divine government, a point made by Gideon. Thus Gideon asserts that for God to rule, humans must not rule. Then, as an alternative to his own leadership, he constructs a piece of cultic equipment that was to provide a means of divine rule. The failure of this plan becomes evident below.

and put it in Ophrah, his hometown. The story that began with a divine revelation and the destruction of idols in the Ophrah sanctuary culminates sadly in the erection of a new cultic image in that very place. Gideon's image might not violate the first commandment, since presumably this ephod was dedicated to Yahweh. It did put the second commandment at risk: the worship of the right God in the wrong manner, rejecting divinely revealed truth for images of God of one's own manufacture. The motivation for Yahweh's prohibition of images flows from the biblical vision of men and women as the only true "image of God" (Richter 2008:107-108). Gideon as a human ruler would have more closely represented the divine dominion over Israel than any golden image.

the Israelites prostituted themselves by worshiping it. "Worshiping it" does not appear in the original, but certainly is implied. Judges only three times speaks of apostasy or idolatry under the image of prostitution. When it does, it signals the failure of the judge as a covenant leader. The first reference comes in 2:17, where Israel's "playing the harlot" is presented paradigmatically as proof of Israel's defiance of their judges. The image does not appear again until this verse, which links Gideon's ephod to the programmatic statement of Israelite apostasy! The last reference appears in 8:33 denoting Israel's apostasy following Gideon's death. The term thus serves as a giant arrow pointing to Gideon's ephod. This image was a seismic shift downward in Israel's relationship with Yahweh.

it became a trap for Gideon and his family. The intentional resonance between this passage and the prologue to the book continues with the term "trap" (*moqesh* [TH4170, ZH4613]), which appears in Judges only here and in 2:3. Linking these two verses ties pagan idols to Gideon's ephod. Since the story also reflects on Gideon's family connections, both as inadequate to support him as a leader, and then nominated as his perpetual successors, the fact that the ephod ensnares his family reinforces the failure. Had Gideon accepted and faithfully discharged the office that he was offered by his countrymen, however misguided their motives, one suspects this horrible episode could have been averted, as well as the one that follows.

COMMENTARY

No discussion of the theme of leadership in Judges can ignore 8:22-27. The traditional exposition sees in 8:22-23 a stout rejection of kingship in Israel on the principle that a nation with God as its king can tolerate no human king (Mendenhall 1975). This view finds expression also in 1 Samuel 12:8-12 in the context of Israel's desire for a king in clear rejection of divine rule. Yet this position is not as evident in the narrative as the traditional view supposes. First, as seen in the note on 8:22, the key word *malak* [TH4427, ZH4887] is missing from the text. Indeed, the very logic that divine kingship excludes human kingship is absent from Judges. Jephthah, for example, clearly states that Yahweh is "the judge" (11:27); yet this seems to have led no one to suggest that, with a heavenly judge, Israel had no need of earthly judges. Moreover, nowhere in Judges is the claim of Yahweh's kingship actually asserted explicitly. Yahweh not only allowed Israel to have a king "like the other nations," he provided for the role in Deuteronomy 17:14-20, even giving the people the right to choose the king themselves, within a few parameters. That Yahweh intended Israel to have an "anointed" king appears programmatically in 1 Samuel 2:10. The king, with the prophet and priest, occupies one of the three classic Old Testament theocratic offices. The central issue in Samuel's interaction with Yahweh in 1 Samuel 8:7 is not the incompatibility of human and divine kingship, but rather a choice of human kingship as a rejection of God's rule (Barth 1961:II.2.366-393)—desiring what God has willed in a manner contrary to God's purpose in willing it. Thus, the popular interpretation of 8:22-23 does not appear warranted in the text itself and is theologically superficial.

Judges 8:22-23 reports that Gideon refused to accept a position of permanent, patrimonial rule over Israel. Rather than opposing kingship, Gideon's statement repudiates any permanent human institution of government (Buber 1932:59-65). The position is radical: Israel needs no human government, no structures of power, and no institutions to secure continuity. Israel can survive simply by being governed by Yahweh. The passage that follows (8:24-27) suggests that Gideon expected this to happen with the construction of an ephod.

Intended for obtaining oracles (see note on 8:27), this ephod represented the alternative to human government since through it Yahweh could govern Israel by direct revelation. Gideon, who exhibited such a preoccupation at the beginning of his career with finding and confirming Yahweh's will, climaxed his career by creating a cult object he (mistakenly) hoped would provide enhanced access to the divine will (Moore 1895:232-233; Crüsemann 1978:47-50). He likely did not consider it an actual idol or image (Burney 1920:236-243), but clearly the people soon treated it so. In contrast to this ephod, Gideon had begun his career by *himself* becoming the glorious garment of the Spirit of Yahweh and the living proof of Yahweh's will to save his people (see note on 6:34). Gideon's rejection of the offer of permanent rule and establishment of the ephod exchanged a living "garment" of Yahweh for a dead one made of gold.

The result of Gideon's rejection of human government and erection of a symbol of purely divine government is that Israel, in the memorable rhetoric of the KJV, "went thither a whoring" after the ephod (8:27). Israel not only betrayed Yahweh, but the text also states that the ephod ensnared Gideon and his family. The author wove a web linking together (1) Gideon's rejection of his people's consensus in favor of patrimonial rule, (2) the resulting national apostasy, and (3) their betrayal of the family of the human leader. Then the author introduced the theme of succession, which will unfold in the Abimelech story (8:33–9:57).

In depicting the folly of Gideon's rejection of human government, with the consequences of apostasy following, the narrator criticized the premonarchic community structure and began making the case for a polity characterized by regular patrimonial succession. Seen sociologically, the writer gave a strong nod toward Israel progressing to the next level of complexity as a nation; as the tribal confederation and its judges crumble, the author was preparing the way to assert the legitimacy and the necessity of Israel's transition to permanent, inherited rule that ultimately took the form of kingship.

God's people, whether in the Old Testament or the New Testament, and especially afterward, often struggle with the human, historical form of the community. In the midst of that struggle, voices always cry out for wiping the slate clean and simply being a community with no traditions, no structures, and no institutions. The quest for purity and simplicity often becomes a mistaken drive toward pious primitivity. A docetic tendency (the tendency to deprecate the human) lurks within the Christian heart. We cannot believe that the human can actually be taken up into the divine, redeemed, transformed, *and released* to function in the world. Gideon's sin was not vengeance, but that he abdicated his responsibility to lead the people he had so effectively and faithfully served by fighting Yahweh's battles. In shirking that responsibility, he attempted to connect Israel directly to God and put before them a substitute that destroyed their faith and wrecked his own legacy.

For Christians, the notion of incarnation, of the divine becoming human, the Word becoming flesh, places before us the challenge to embrace not only Jesus' humanity, but also our own. Indeed, biblical "spirituality" is nothing other than redeemed flesh-and-blood humanity! Instead of abandoning, Gideon-like, the responsibilities of institutions, positions, and roles, and reverting to safe but ultimately false claims of direct divine leadership, we—flawed, fallible people and institutions that we are—should embrace the challenges God has given us.

◆ e. Epilogue: Retirement and reversion (8:28-32)

**28 That is the story of how the people of
Israel defeated Midian, which never recovered. Throughout the rest of Gideon's
lifetime—about forty years—there was
peace in the land.
29 Then Gideon* son of Joash returned
home. 30 He had seventy sons born to him,
for he had many wives. 31 He also had a
concubine in Shechem, who gave birth to
a son, whom he named Abimelech.
32 Gideon died when he was very old, and
he was buried in the grave of his father,
Joash, at Ophrah in the land of the clan of
Abiezer.**

8:29 Hebrew *Jerub-baal;* see 6:32.

NOTES

8:28 ***the people of Israel defeated Midian.*** Something of the flavor of the original, which reads "so Midian was brought low before the Israelites," vanishes from the NLT rendering. The use of language for bringing low or humbling also resonates with the beginning of the crisis (6:6), which also speaks of Israel being reduced or "brought low" (*dalal* [TH1809, ZH1937]). The NLT may also obscure the idea that it was Yahweh who had defeated Midian.

which never recovered. That Midian never again threatened Israel is apparent from the remainder of the OT narrative. Though his final abdication connects Gideon with the decline of Israel, his effective elimination of the Midianite threat associates him with the previous, effective judges, underscoring the tragedy of his abdication of responsibility at the very end.

Throughout the rest of Gideon's lifetime—about forty years. The NLT might not be precisely correct here. The text says "and the land rested forty years in the days of Gideon." Normally these epilogues state simply, "and the land rested X years, and X died." The plain wording here, however, suggests that the land's 40-year rest is included in Gideon's lifetime, but does not demand that he died immediately after the 40 years. The possibility exists that Gideon lived to see some of the unraveling of the peace he won for Israel, particularly Israel's "prostituting" themselves with the ephod.

there was peace in the land. This is the final occurrence of the standard formula for rest. Its absence from the remainder of the stories registers a critique of those leaders.

8:29 ***Then Gideon son of Joash returned home.*** That Gideon's death is not immediately reported suggests perhaps his life extended beyond the 40 years of peace. Gideon is the only judge whose retirement is reported. It is very unlikely that the verb in this passage is to be read "mansively" to mean that Gideon "sits [on a throne]" = "reign as kin in his house" (Block 1999:300-301). Gideon was indeed a prominent chief or *sheikh* who exerted great influence, possibly dominating affairs in the region. This does not imply the institution of monarchy.

8:30 ***He had seventy sons born to him, for he had many wives.*** The Hebrew syntax makes this verse something of a footnote or aside, as if to say "By the way, Gideon had 70 sons." Prodigious reproduction featuring the number 70 also appears with the "minor" judge Abdon (12:14). King Ahab had 70 sons who, like Gideon's, were murdered in a coup (9:5; 2 Kgs 10:1). This notation links Gideon with the so-called minor judges, several of whom are noted for their many children. A leader who did not occupy a position of leadership by virtue of his genealogy often could claim respect and authentication other ways. To be anointed by the Spirit of Yahweh was one way, but a prosperity and power extending beyond one's own immediate clan would be another. Through his 70 sons and their marriages, Gideon occupied the center of a network of marriage alliances that would have generated vast influence in a tribal society. Even though Gideon declined hereditary rule, he clearly remained a highly influential leader by virtue of his achievements and his extended family. Likewise, his sons collectively would wield great influence.

8:31 ***He also had a concubine.*** The Hebrew text suggests a contrast with the preceding verse, as if to say "but his concubine who was in Shechem." Since the concubine features in the next story, the writer highlights her. Far more than mere sex slaves, concubines functioned as subordinate wives. Subordination resulted from diverse causes, such as lack of a dowry or possibly non-Israelite status (NIDOTTE 3.618-619; NIDB 1.713-714). See note on 19:1.

Shechem. The concubine's home, Shechem, stood as the most important town in the area of Israelite settlement, the de facto capital of the region (Richter 2007:361-362). The fourteenth-century-BC Amarna letters record the actions of a chief named Labayu who used Shechem as the center of a mini-empire based on deception, betrayal, and sharp dealing. Shechem appears not to have been a uniformly or distinctively Israelite town, so a full marriage to a Shechemite woman probably violated Israelite intermarriage taboos. Taking a concubine might have allowed a marriage alliance in Shechem that extended Gideon's influence via family ties into that important town. He seems to have had some influence there (cf. 9:2). Such an arrangement, however, certainly violated the spirit of OT marriage law, if not also the letter (cf. Deut 7:1-3), and directly triggered the betrayal of his house about which the author warned.

Abimelech. The name means "my father (is) king." Typically Northwest Semitic names were statements about deities, hence the meaning is likely "my [divine] father is king" or "my father is the [divine] king." Therefore this name does not imply Gideon himself had claimed kingship, however regally he may have comported himself. The text also uses an unusual phrase for Gideon's naming of Abimelech. The normal construction is "and he called (*qara'* [TH7121, ZH7924]) his name (*shem* [TH8034, ZH9005]) X." The author here uses a phrase that appears only three other times in the OT for the naming of persons, literally, "he set (*sim* [TH7760, ZH8492]) his name (*shem*) [as] Abimelech." The verb *sim* with *shem* as the direct object has four uses in the OT: (1) Most often, the expression is a calque of the idiom *leshakken shem* [TH7931, ZH8905] (to place the name), which is an inscriptional formula denoting placement of a monument bearing the speaker's name, employed to signify Yahweh's claim on the sanctuary and land (Deut 12:5, 21; 14:24; 1 Kgs 9:3; 11:36; 14:21; 2 Kgs 21:7; 2 Chr 6:20; 12:13; 33:7; cf. Richter 2002:127-205; 2007:343-344). (2) It expresses the establishment of a reputation or legacy (2 Sam 7:23; 14:7; 2 Kgs 21:4; 1 Chr 17:21). (3) A single reference denotes a liturgical blessing (Num 6:27). (4) It four times signifies the naming of a person (8:31; 2 Kgs 17:34; Neh 9:7; Dan 1:7). These latter passages(except 8:31) explicitly entail bestowing new names on adults (Boling 1975:162). Thus, Abimelech was not the man's "birth" name, but one bestowed on him by Gideon, possibly either to claim him as a legitimate son or to confer on him some special status. The uncertain status of children of concubines or other women would necessitate such an action. That Abimelech considered himself his father's proper successor certainly seems clear in the story to follow.

8:32 ***Gideon died when he was very old.*** The author does not note the age, great or otherwise, of any other judge.

the grave of his father, Joash. While several burials are noted in Judges, in most cases the author only notes the town, without referencing a tomb (2:9; 10:2, 5; 12:7, 10, 12, 15). Only the tombs of Gideon and Samson (16:31) are specified, and they are family tombs. Burial practices in Canaan prior to the era of Israel's settlement are well documented. The typical burial prior to 1200 BC involved placing the body on a shelf in a cave-tomb. After the body had desiccated, the bones were separated and pushed to the end of the chamber to make room for the next body. Thus, the dead were literally "gathered to their people" in the accumulation of bones in the tomb. Burial practice in Canaan seems to change with the end of the Late Bronze Age. Extensive survey and excavation have failed to locate highland burials from the Iron I era, leading to the conclusion that burial in this period was by simple inhumation, thus leaving no trace. This practice expressed Israel's egalitarian ethos, since a permanent tomb would suggest high social status (Gonen 1992; Kletter 2002; Bloch-Smith 2004; Faust 2004; 2006:92-107). Judges reflects this in the vagueness of its references to burials. The writer singles out the burials of Gideon and Samson, which deviated from normal practice. Perhaps these families were held in unusually high esteem.

Ophrah. Scholars debate the precise location of Ophrah. Indications in the narrative suggest it to be the mound located in Afula, in the center of the Jezreel valley (cf. note on 6:11). If this association is correct, Gideon's hometown was a fairly significant site, one of the "daughter" towns of Megiddo (Josh 17:11). The site is noted in the list of place names recorded by Pharaoh Thutmose III (Rainey and Notley 2006:72-73). The site had a long, if sporadic history of settlement, but solid remains from early Iron Age I (1200–1150 BC) exist, despite serious damage to the site by modern development. The Iron IA remains include a brick-walled building with side rooms and a courtyard, granaries, and other artifacts including a board game! The mid-eleventh century BC saw the destruction of the site (Stern 1993–2008:1.37-38).

COMMENTARY

Commentators often glide over these final verses as the "standard conclusion" that recurs in the book (e.g., in 10:1-5). But the author actually tailors these conclusions to leave a precise impression on the mind of the reader and to prepare for the next account, often by introducing material distinctive to a particular judge. The standard elements appear in 8:28, 32, sandwiching 8:29-30, which report additional information. In the more standard elements, Gideon is credited with decisively and permanently ending the Midianite threat. The claim that the land rested 40 years is no mere convention: No subsequent judge will receive this commendation. Thus, Gideon is associated with Othniel, Ehud, and Deborah-Barak over against Jephthah and Samson. Moreover, Gideon's 40 years of rest following seven years of oppression is the last time in the book that the period of a judge's influence will be longer than the period of oppression that preceded his career. From now on, oppression will dominate over leadership, and the land will have no rest. The author thus used the standard elements to characterize Gideon as the last of the "good" judges.

However, the additional material in 8:29-30 introduces information that, in the context of the whole story, suggests, for the first time in the book, criticisms of a judge in the framework material. Gideon's many marriages and 70 sons need not be taken negatively, since similar observations appear without criticism in the notes about the so-called minor judges (10:1-5; 12:8-15). Gideon's continued dominance in the community, and the impression that all 70 of his sons somehow tyrannized the region (cf. 9:2), appear negatively in the context of his refusal to accept permanent, inherited responsibility. Instead of one successor, Gideon had 70! In this context, his siring of a son from a Shechemite secondary wife, whom he apparently claimed by renaming him Abimelech, created even more confusion and sowed the seeds of devastating conflict.

Gideon presents a mixed legacy. None of this should surprise the reader. The history of the Christian church includes many "great servants of God" who accomplished fine things for the Kingdom, but whose legacy was tarnished or corrupted by their refusal to accept responsibility for their achievements and for the next generation. One could name founders of worldwide mission organizations, great evangelists and pastors, prolific and profound authors, who all did powerful work for the gospel in the world. But the tales told by wives, children, friends, and colleagues often reveal a tarnished legacy. Gideon stands as a reminder that not only must we answer the call and fight the battles, winning the war; we must also win the peace. The responsibility of leadership, continuity, and wholeness in our relationships is as much a part of our legacy as souls won, books written, or kingdoms built.

◆ 2. Abimelech: Authority usurped (8:33–9:57)

33As soon as Gideon died, the Israelites
prostituted themselves by worshiping the
images of Baal, making Baal-berith their
god. 34They forgot the LORD their God,
who had rescued them from all their en-
emies surrounding them. 35Nor did they
show any loyalty to the family of Jerub-
baal (that is, Gideon), despite all the good
he had done for Israel.

CHAPTER 9

One day Gideon's* son Abimelech went to
Shechem to visit his uncles—his mother's
brothers. He said to them and to the rest
of his mother's family, 2"Ask the leading
citizens of Shechem whether they want to
be ruled by all seventy of Gideon's sons or
by one man. And remember that I am your
own flesh and blood!"

3So Abimelech's uncles gave his mes-
sage to all the citizens of Shechem on his
behalf. And after listening to this pro-
posal, the people of Shechem decided in
favor of Abimelech because he was their
relative. 4They gave him seventy silver
coins from the temple of Baal-berith,
which he used to hire some reckless trou-
blemakers who agreed to follow him. 5He
went to his father's home at Ophrah, and
there, on one stone, they killed all sev-
enty of his half brothers, the sons of Gid-
eon.* But the youngest brother, Jotham,
escaped and hid.

6Then all the leading citizens of She-
chem and Beth-millo called a meeting
under the oak beside the pillar* at She-
chem and made Abimelech their king.

7When Jotham heard about this, he
climbed to the top of Mount Gerizim and
shouted,

"Listen to me, citizens of Shechem!
Listen to me if you want God to
listen to you!
8 Once upon a time the trees decided
to choose a king.
First they said to the olive tree,
'Be our king!'
9 But the olive tree refused, saying,
'Should I quit producing the olive oil
that blesses both God and people,
just to wave back and forth over the
trees?'

10 "Then they said to the fig tree,
'You be our king!'
11 But the fig tree also refused, saying,
'Should I quit producing my sweet
fruit
just to wave back and forth over
the trees?'

12 "Then they said to the grapevine,
'You be our king!'
13 But the grapevine also refused, saying,
'Should I quit producing the wine
that cheers both God and people,
just to wave back and forth over
the trees?'

14 "Then all the trees finally turned to
the thornbush and said,
'Come, you be our king!'
15 And the thornbush replied to the
trees,
'If you truly want to make me your
king,
come and take shelter in my shade.
If not, let fire come out from me
and devour the cedars of Lebanon.' "

16Jotham continued, "Now make sure
you have acted honorably and in good
faith by making Abimelech your king, and
that you have done right by Gideon and
all of his descendants. Have you treated
him with the honor he deserves for all he
accomplished? 17For he fought for you
and risked his life when he rescued you
from the Midianites. 18But today you have
revolted against my father and his de-
scendants, killing his seventy sons on one
stone. And you have chosen his slave
woman's son, Abimelech, to be your king
just because he is your relative.

19"If you have acted honorably and in
good faith toward Gideon and his descen-
dants today, then may you find joy in

Abimelech, and may he find joy in you. 20But if you have not acted in good faith, then may fire come out from Abimelech and devour the leading citizens of Shechem and Beth-millo; and may fire come out from the citizens of Shechem and Beth-millo and devour Abimelech!"

21Then Jotham escaped and lived in Beer because he was afraid of his brother Abimelech.

22After Abimelech had ruled over Israel for three years, 23God sent a spirit that stirred up trouble between Abimelech and the leading citizens of Shechem, and they revolted. 24God was punishing Abimelech for murdering Gideon's seventy sons, and the citizens of Shechem for supporting him in this treachery of murdering his brothers. 25The citizens of Shechem set an ambush for Abimelech on the hilltops and robbed everyone who passed that way. But someone warned Abimelech about their plot.

26One day Gaal son of Ebed moved to Shechem with his brothers and gained the confidence of the leading citizens of Shechem. 27During the annual harvest festival at Shechem, held in the temple of the local god, the wine flowed freely, and everyone began cursing Abimelech. 28"Who is Abimelech?" Gaal shouted. "He's not a true son of Shechem,* so why should we be his servants? He's merely the son of Gideon, and this Zebul is merely his deputy. Serve the true sons of Hamor, the founder of Shechem. Why should we serve Abimelech? 29If I were in charge here, I would get rid of Abimelech. I would say* to him, 'Get some soldiers, and come out and fight!' "

30But when Zebul, the leader of the city, heard what Gaal was saying, he was furious. 31He sent messengers to Abimelech in Arumah,* telling him, "Gaal son of Ebed and his brothers have come to live in Shechem, and now they are inciting the city to rebel against you. 32Come by night with an army and hide out in the fields. 33In the morning, as soon as it is daylight, attack the city. When Gaal and those who are with him come out against you, you can do with them as you wish."

34So Abimelech and all his men went by night and split into four groups, stationing themselves around Shechem. 35Gaal was standing at the city gates when Abimelech and his army came out of hiding. 36When Gaal saw them, he said to Zebul, "Look, there are people coming down from the hilltops!"

Zebul replied, "It's just the shadows on the hills that look like men."

37But again Gaal said, "No, people are coming down from the hills.* And another group is coming down the road past the Diviners' Oak.*"

38Then Zebul turned on him and asked, "Now where is that big mouth of yours? Wasn't it you that said, 'Who is Abimelech, and why should we be his servants?' The men you mocked are right outside the city! Go out and fight them!"

39So Gaal led the leading citizens of Shechem into battle against Abimelech. 40But Abimelech chased him, and many of Shechem's men were wounded and fell along the road as they retreated to the city gate. 41Abimelech returned to Arumah, and Zebul drove Gaal and his brothers out of Shechem.

42The next day the people of Shechem went out into the fields to battle. When Abimelech heard about it, 43he divided his men into three groups and set an ambush in the fields. When Abimelech saw the people coming out of the city, he and his men jumped up from their hiding places and attacked them. 44Abimelech and his group stormed the city gate to keep the men of Shechem from getting back in, while Abimelech's other two groups cut them down in the fields. 45The battle went on all day before Abimelech finally captured the city. He killed the people, leveled the city, and scattered salt all over the ground.

46When the leading citizens who lived in the tower of Shechem heard what had happened, they ran and hid in the temple

of Baal-berith.* 47 Someone reported to
Abimelech that the citizens had gathered
in the temple, 48 so he led his forces to
Mount Zalmon. He took an ax and
chopped some branches from a tree, then
put them on his shoulder. "Quick, do as I
have done!" he told his men. 49 So each of
them cut down some branches, following
Abimelech's example. They piled the
branches against the walls of the temple
and set them on fire. So all the people
who had lived in the tower of Shechem
died—about 1,000 men and women.
50 Then Abimelech attacked the town of
Thebez and captured it. 51 But there was a
strong tower inside the town, and all the
men and women—the entire population—
fled to it. They barricaded themselves in
and climbed up to the roof of the tower.
52 Abimelech followed them to attack the
tower. But as he prepared to set fire to the
entrance, 53 a woman on the roof dropped
a millstone that landed on Abimelech's
head and crushed his skull.
54 He quickly said to his young armor
bearer, "Draw your sword and kill me!
Don't let it be said that a woman killed
Abimelech!" So the young man ran him
through with his sword, and he died.
55 When Abimelech's men saw that he was
dead, they disbanded and returned to
their homes.
56 In this way, God punished Abimelech
for the evil he had done against his father
by murdering his seventy brothers. 57 God
also punished the men of Shechem for all
their evil. So the curse of Jotham son of
Gideon was fulfilled.

9:1 Hebrew *Jerub-baal's* (see 6:32); also in 9:2, 24. **9:5** Hebrew *Jerub-baal* (see 6:32); also in 9:16, 19, 28, 57. **9:6** The meaning of the Hebrew is uncertain. **9:28** Hebrew *Who is Shechem?* **9:29** As in Greek version; Hebrew reads *And he said.* **9:31** Or *in secret;* Hebrew reads *in Tormah;* compare 9:41. **9:37a** Or *the center of the land.* **9:37b** Hebrew *Elon-meonenim.* **9:46** Hebrew *El-berith,* another name for Baal-berith; compare 9:4.

NOTES

8:33 *As soon as Gideon died.* The Hebrew implies an immediate, even concurrent, event. The death of a judge is stated in 2:16-19 to signal a new plunge into apostasy. Othniel's (3:11-12) and Gideon's (8:33-35) deaths follow this pattern. There is no such pattern for the intervening judges.

prostituted themselves by worshiping. "By worshiping" is an accurate expansion on the Hebrew. This is the third and final use of the verb *zanah* [TH2181, ZH2388] (meaning "play the harlot, prostitute oneself"), which refers to apostasy in Judges (see note on 19:2). In the prologue (2:17), the verb marks the fact that Israel did not listen to their judges and fell into worse depravity than their forefathers—it is an explicit statement of downward decline. Then in 8:27 the author uses the term to describe Israel's idolatrous veneration of Gideon's ephod, again uniting the idea of apostasy to disobedience to a judge. The final use (8:33), in which Israel worships the Baals, also explicitly includes a betrayal of the judge (cf. 8:35; 9:16).

the images of Baal. Lit., "the Baals," but the author means multiple images, not various kinds of Baals, though that is not impossible. The plural of Baal in reference to deities appears only four times in Judges, and each time it appears in the author's commentary on events, rather than in the events themselves. It figures prominently in the preface to the book (2:11), reappearing in the Othniel account (3:7), which serves as the scorecard for the whole series of judges. It then appears here, where the prologue's claim of an incremental decline into idolatry is explicitly fulfilled. Lastly in 10:6, 10 the "Baals" find mention in the Jephthah account, where Yahweh finally seems to run out of patience with his people.

making Baal-berith their god. "Baal-berith" means "Baal of the Treaty/Covenant." Israel's harlotry with Baal reverses the first act Gideon performed: the destruction of the Baal altar and renewal of offerings to Yahweh at Ophrah. Shechem seems to have been a diplomatic and political center for the region, thus worship of a "Treaty God" seems fitting. Later in the story, though, Shechem's deity is named "El Berith." The language here is quite strong. Israel did not simply worship Baal, but actually made Baal-berith their national god, in essence abrogating the covenant (*berith* [TH1285, ZH1382]) made with Yahweh in Josh 24, a covenant that actually constituted them as Yahweh's people in the land. Ironically, that very covenant likely incorporated Shechem into the Israelite community of Yahweh. Israel "converted" in the other direction, adopting Shechem's old Canaanite god. In the story to follow, Shechem will abrogate its covenant, as well. The seriousness of this apostasy cannot be overstated: It is a blade to the heart of Israel's identity.

8:34 ***They forgot the LORD their God.*** Lit., "the children of Israel did not remember (*welo' zakeru* [TH2142, ZH2349]) Yahweh . . . ." Remembrance in the OT goes far beyond the mere retention of facts or persons in one's mind (NIDOTTE s.v. *zakar*). The activities described by the word in OT usage include the active maintenance of the ongoing effects of an event or relationship, typically by public, communal commemoration such as we see in ch 5. Failing to remember Yahweh goes together with not "knowing" Yahweh (see note on 2:10). To forget Yahweh is to live so that Yahweh's deeds, and Israel's relationship with him, have no effect, no visible sign or trace. Yahweh and his actions have become a dead past.

who had rescued them from all their enemies surrounding them. Typically, Israel is said to have forgotten, or is commanded to remember, Yahweh's deliverance of his people from Egypt (Exod 13:3; Deut 5:15; 6:12; 7:18; 15:15; 16:12; 24:22). Here, however, Israel's amnesia was concerning the acts of deliverance performed since entering the land. Victory over the remaining nations in the land constituted Yahweh's education plan for Israel (cf. 3:1-4) as well as his means of demonstrating openly, via testing, the faithfulness of Israel. Israel flunked.

8:35 ***Nor did they show any loyalty.*** "Loyalty" translates the term *khesed* [TH2617, ZH2876], one of the richest theological terms in the entire OT. This intensely relational term assumes a structured relationship between two parties, and it designates the behavior that maintains and nurtures the relationship. It classically, though not exclusively, denotes the obligation of care that a superior shows to a subordinate, such as a host to guest, or patron to client, and quintessentially, Yahweh to Israel. Dereliction at doing *khesed* fundamentally undermined relationships. Thus, *khesed* simultaneously names the fundamental core value of ancient Israelite tribal society and the essential bond of fidelity between Yahweh and Israel. The present context lacks the superior-inferior aspect, but envisions Israel as bearing a strong obligation to Gideon and his family; it asserts (in almost the strongest possible terms) Israel's betrayal of their deliverer. The author directly links apostasy from Yahweh with the betrayal of Yahweh's human servant. It is therefore astounding to hear Gideon characterized as "one of these faithless persons" constituting "the greatest obstacle to the work of God" (Block 1999:307). Far from condemning Gideon's faithlessness, the text condemns Israel for not showing good faith to Gideon and his family. Indeed, Gideon did fail at the end of his career, but our author does not charge him with unbelief and credits him with 40 years of "rest" in line with Othniel, Ehud, and Deborah.

Jerub-baal (that is, Gideon). The narrator in fact juxtaposes the two names directly, as if hyphenating them: "Jerub-baal-Gideon," using no parenthetical construction as he did in 7:1, "Jerub-baal (that is, Gideon)." The two names function thematically in the story. Gideon's name predominates, appearing 40 times in 6:1–9:57, though never in 9:1-57, where he is only called Jerub-baal. Despite the nickname "Jerub-baal," bestowed by his father in 6:32 and used 13 times in 6:1–9:57, this name is used of Gideon only once in the battle narrative (7:1). The name is applied to him in the epilogue once without the additional "Gideon" (8:29) and then here, where the names fall side-by-side. All nine mentions of Gideon in ch 9 will employ Jerub-baal, though the NLT changes them to "Gideon" for clarity. The author introduced the name Jerub-baal to stress Gideon's role as a combatant against Baal (6:32), but returns to it to stress the miscarriage of Gideon's legacy (8:29-30) and Israel's reversion to the worship of Baal (8:33-35). By contrast, the author saves the name "Gideon" for what he affirms: rest (8:28) and death at a ripe old age (8:32). "Jerub-baal" bespeaks a mission aborted, a legacy repudiated. Gideon's name is a taunt: "Let Baal Contend!" In the end, Baal did, and apparently won.

despite all the good he had done for Israel. This statement is not an attempt to "salvage" Gideon (contra Block 1999:306). Despite the toxic legacy created by Gideon's abandonment of his leadership obligation and erection of the ephod, the text never undermines the worth of his achievement as a deliverer, however much his latter-day interpreters try to force that impression on the text. The author does, however, maintain an unrelenting dialectic between Gideon's stunning achievement and the sad consequences of his final hesitation.

9:1 ***One day.*** The Hebrew text has no time indicator. The text could suggest that as soon as Gideon died, Abimelech put his plan into action. Such would fit the power-hungry cynicism evinced by Abimelech.

Gideon's son Abimelech. Lit., "Jerub-baal's son" (cf. NLT mg). The presence of both names, Gideon and Jerub-baal, in 8:35 obviates the need to change the text. See note on 8:35 regarding its significance. The name "Abimelech" was not unique to our despot. The Amarna Letters of the 1300s BC attest it for pharaoh's appointed ruler in Tyre (Moran 1992:232-242), and the name *abmlk* appears in two Ugaritic texts, not to mention its presence in Gen 20–21 and 26.

went to Shechem. Shechem features in treaty-making in the OT: Jacob and his sons entered into an agreement with the inhabitants of Shechem (Gen 34); Israel, upon entering the land, renewed the covenant at Ebal and Gerizim, the two mountains overlooking Shechem (Deut 27, Josh 8:30-35); and the book of Joshua ends at Shechem (Josh 24:1, 25) with Joshua making a covenant. This covenant united Yahweh, the Israelites, and apparently others who had joined with them. A stone and an oak figure in Joshua's covenant, as they do in the crowning of Abimelech (cf. 9:6). Shechem certainly has the stone, but the tree, naturally, is long-gone, though numerous archaeological indications at other sanctuaries all but ensure that one was indeed present at Shechem (Stager 1999:241-243). The Hebrew word for treaty or covenant, *berith* [TH1285, ZH1382], appears in the name of the deity "whored after" by Israel, Baal-berith (8:33). Later referred to in the narrative as El-berith (9:46, NLT mg), his temple treasury in Shechem funded Abimelech's adventures (9:4). Shechem emerges one last time as a town for deal-making in 1 Kings 12, where Rehoboam seeks the rubber-stamp approval of the northern tribes for his kingship (ABD 5.1174–1186; Stager 1999:2003).

Additional information about Shechem appears as relevant in the notes below, but a basic introduction is pertinent here. No other town in the central highlands of Israel equaled Shechem in importance (Smith 1931:117-118; ABD 5.1174-1186; Richter 2007:361-362). It easily paralleled Jerusalem in influence. A low 15-acre mound situated now in the modern town of Balata, beside modern Nablus, ancient Shechem stood at the intersection of the major north–south highway along the watershed ridge and a vital east–west route linking the Jordan valley to the coast (Moore 1895:240). The north–south road connected Jerusalem and Bethel to Shechem, and then turned northeast to Tirzah (or slightly southeast of it) to join Wadi Far'a. From there, the Far'a highway drops southeast for 1,700 feet traversing 17 miles to the Jordan valley (Dorsey 1991:174-175). The east–west route passes between mounts Ebal (2,600 feet) and Gerizim (2,800 feet), with Shechem situated strategically along the pass (Dorsey 1991:164-165). Shechem thus provided a perfect perch for traffic, trade, and trouble in the central highlands. The well-watered soil, eroded from hard limestone, offered excellent prospects for farming and herding.

The city emerged about 1900 BC, peaked around 1600 BC, and was destroyed around 1540 BC by the Egyptians in their pursuit of the Hyksos who had dominated Egypt for a hundred years. Shechem lay abandoned but was revived around 1450 BC when Pharaoh Thutmose III decided to exploit Canaan and appointed local lackeys as rulers in Canaanite towns. Shechem blossomed into a splendid Late Bronze Age city ruled by a thuggish scoundrel named Laba'yu, the incarnation of Late Bronze Age realpolitik. We know this gangster's Machiavellian machinations from his correspondence with the pharaoh. Pledging loyalty and charging his colleagues with treason, he laid siege to Megiddo and attacked Gezer. After his murder, his sons continued fleecing caravans and raking in riches until around 1300 BC when unknown persons burned Shechem to the ground. Clearly Shechem knew well the shenanigans of strongmen grasping for power, men like Abimelech.

the rest of his mother's family. This smooths out an awkward Hebrew phrase: *mishpakhath beth 'abi 'immo* (lit., "the clan of the father's-house of his mother"). "Father's house" normally denotes the basic localized family in the OT. This could refer to the mother's father and extended family. Ironically, just as the present story's troubles start with a liaison between an Israelite and a Shechemite, so the first significant engagement between God's people and Shechem began with the rape of Jacob's daughter Dinah by "Shechem son of Hamor" (Gen 34). This story also turns on a covenant between "Israel" and Shechem that led to violence (Schneider 2000:134).

9:2 ***Ask the leading citizens of Shechem.*** Repeatedly, the Hebrew text refers to the *ba'ale shekem* [TH1167, ZH1251], the "lords [lit., 'baals'] of Shechem." Our modern notion of "leading citizens" does not convey the authority and responsibility for a community that the town elders bore in the ancient world.

all seventy of Gideon's sons. The NLT renders Jerub-baal as "Gideon" throughout ch 9, as noted in its mg notes to 9:1, 5. This replacement obscures the contrasting perspective of 9:1-57 over against 6:1–8:35. Far from indicating that Gideon actually did accept kingship, the fact that all 70 of his sons dominated Shechem, rather than one select heir, underscores that in the wake of Gideon's abdication of his responsibility, his very influential family dominated local affairs the way any large, wealthy family might. Such behavior typifies a complex chiefdom (R. Miller 2005), for which Iron Age I Shechem provides an excellent example.

or by one man. Indeed, rule by one, one who has proven his worth serving under Yahweh's call, one who was bred to that responsibility by a father who cared about the future, certainly would be better than being suffocated by 70. Abimelech also could be hearkening back to earlier, better days in Shechem under Laba'yu and other kinglets, who maintained a steady stream of income for the city.

And remember that I am your own flesh and blood! Abimelech's appeal to "flesh and blood" raises the question of Shechem's ethnicity and affiliations. Shechem does not appear in Josh 12 in the list of cities whose kings Joshua killed, nor does it feature in any conquest narratives. Its absence from the list of cities still to be conquered, and its presence in the list of cities of refuge (Josh 20:7; 21:21), as well as the access Israel had to a sanctuary there for covenant making (Josh 24:25-26) and for the burial of Joseph (Josh 24:32) suggest its incorporation into Israel. The region just north of Shechem, known as the Shechem Syncline, was the traditional territory of Manasseh and scene of the heaviest new village settlements in Iron Age I, settlements thought to be Israelite (Zertal 1994, 2004). Closer analysis by R. Miller (2005:34-36, 99-101, 119-121) reveals Shechem's actual sphere of influence to be to its south, in the Ephraimite region, also densely settled very early by Israelites (Finkelstein 1988:119-204). Shechem controlled nine smaller towns and their dependent villages—a solidly Israelite affiliation. However, the facts that Gideon's Shechemite wife held lower status (8:29-30) and that Abimelech appealed to blood ties to Shechem that his 70 half brothers apparently lacked, indicate a perceived ethnic difference between Israel and Shechem. Might the Shechemites have been among the "foreigners" (or, "sojourners/strangers") of Josh 8:33, and among those still worshiping false gods in Josh 24:23-24, who were incorporated into Israel via treaty? Lacking more data, definitive conclusions remain out of reach. But if Shechem was party to the covenant with Yahweh reported in Josh 24, Abimelech here virtually dissolves that covenant—all in the name of Baal-berith, "Baal of the Covenant."

Abimelech asserts blood ties as a basis for loyalty, apart from any appeal to fidelity to Yahweh, his covenant, or the obligations binding the Israelites to one another. Even though descended from Jacob, Israel existed in Canaan essentially as an oath-bound community, devoted by treaty to Yahweh, to the land he granted them, and to each other as joint holders of his promise. This community certainly contained many who were not literal blood kin to the Israelites, such as Rahab and her household, the Gibeonites, Ruth, and others like them. Kinship in Israel was fictive, a social bond resulting from an allegiance to Yahweh that bound them all together, regardless of their pedigree. Allegiance to Yahweh came first, and that in turn created the kinship that bound Israel into a great family. In grounding his bid for power on the divisive wedge of blood ties, Abimelech reversed this principle, making mere blood ties the basis for political allegiance. Incidentally, interpreters placing too much emphasis on "racial" ethnicity could distort the viewpoint of the author who stresses covenant bonds and a shared culture of faith as the true basis of Israelite identity.

9:4 ***They gave him seventy silver coins.*** The Hebrew omits any unit of measure, so attempts to calculate the weight of the payment are irrelevant (Younger 2002:221). The "seventy [in] silver" could suggest that each brother was only worth one piece of silver, or it could suggest a price—like a "hit contract"—for each brother.

from the temple of Baal-berith. Archaeological excavations at Shechem have unearthed several sanctuaries, including one massive temple, dubbed the Migdal Temple. Until recently, archaeologists thought this massive temple, built around 1650 BC, had been destroyed about 1540 BC, only to be replaced by one that was one-third its size, which stood in Abimelech's day. Stager's (1999:228-249) reassessment of the data demonstrates that the massive temple in fact endured right up until the destruction of Shechem around 1125 BC. The temple was 86 feet long by 70 feet wide, with stone foundations 17 feet thick that supported walls of mud-brick and timber. Such massive foundations imply a multistory structure. A pair of towers with staircases stood forth 16 feet on either side of the entrance. Just outside the temple entrance stood a large altar of earth and stone, and two stone slabs 4–5 feet wide, judging from the notches into which they fit, and possibly standing twice that height. (Such standing stones are called *matseboth* [TH4676, ZH5167] in the OT; e.g., Gen 28:18.) Further out, conspicuously placed on a promontory jutting out from the main structure, stands yet another base with a notch for a stele 5 feet wide and 16 inches thick. Nearby was found a slab of superbly polished fine limestone that fit the notch perfectly. The broken slab still stands about 5 feet high but was likely 10 feet tall. If numerous other ancient parallels are valid, the surface of this slab seems to have been prepared for an ink inscription, now long eroded (Richter 2007:358-361; cf. Deut 27:1-8). Interestingly, both narratives of Joshua writing the terms of Yahweh's covenant on a stone monument appear at Shechem (Josh 24:25-28; the inscription in Josh 8:30-35 is near Shechem). Whether or not the monuments are the same, Abimelech's political pact, formed in a sanctuary in Shechem, stands exactly opposite the moment in Josh 24 when, in Shechem, the people of God were constituted in the land of Canaan. The Shechemites' crowning of Abimelech may thus amount to an abrogation of the covenant.

reckless troublemakers. This represents two phrases. The first, *'anashim reqim* [TH7386, ZH8199], "empty men," does not by itself imply anything about the men's character, but identifies them as disenfranchised, "portionless men deprived of their land in a culture in which social identity was rooted in kinship networks and inherited land. Second sons of secondary wives, misfits and mercenaries, outlaws and outlanders are just some of those who fell between the kinship cracks . . . forming pseudofamilies under the patronage of warlords, trading their services for portions of martial harvests and brigandage" (Moore 1895:244). These men with nothing at stake had only their loyalty and their sword to offer, not unlike the men who gathered around David (1 Sam 22:2; cf. 11:3). Of course, men with no investment in a community might well be unprincipled, and the second term, "troublemakers" (*pokhazim* [TH6348, ZH7069]), has the idea of bubbling over, being undisciplined or boisterous. The idea is more hotheadedness than evil.

9:5 *his father's home at Ophrah.* This employs the term *beth-'ab* [TH1004, ZH1074] to denote the actual family farm plot. In the case of a very substantial citizen with a large family, such as Jerub-baal's, the family farm would include several houses with a range of domestic installations such as grinding stones and vegetable plots encircled by a low partition wall (cf. King and Stager 2001:18 for an illustration). This farm might have earlier included the altars mentioned in 6:25-26. That these murders occurred in the very homestead of Jerub-baal, makes them that much more heinous.

on one stone. The phrase could be rendered "at one stone." This very peculiar and ominous note suggests a ritual character to the killing. Three alternatives exist. (1) The stone could have been an altar, which would have made it essentially a slaughter block, such as in 1 Sam 14:33-35, where Saul calls for a "large stone" for a mass sacrifice (Moore 1895:242-243; Soggin 1981:68). The text has clearly identified Ophrah as a sacred site with an altar belonging to Gideon's father (6:25). Archaeologists have excavated a sacred site just 12 miles to the south, still within the boundaries of Manasseh, known as the Bull Site. In addition to a bronze bull figurine, the site features a flat stone slab at one end of a round enclosure (R. Miller 1999:161). The slab might well be a simple stone altar, but as easily could have been a *matsebah* [TH4676, ZH5167], a sacred standing stone. While some doubt if the Bull Site was a true public worship site (Coogan 1987), it might well have been a private or family shrine not unlike the one associated with Gideon's family at Ophrah. Against this view, the Hebrew word *'eben* [TH68, ZH74], in reference to a single stone, seldom denotes an altar, and even then, only one improvised on the spot (1 Sam 6:14-15; 14:33-35).

(2) The stone could be a grave marker. Ancient Near Eastern texts associate stones with graves. In the Egyptian tale of the refugee courtier, Sinuhe, the pharaoh's invitation for the hero to return home reminds him that "your tomb-pillars . . . are among those of the royal children" (COS 1.38:80). Gideon's grave gets conspicuous notice (8:32) and would make the atrocity a brazen betrayal of his legacy. Again, nowhere in the OT does a single stone (*'eben*) serve as a grave monument, though a heap of stones does.

(3) The stone could be a monument associated with Gideon's authority, intentionally desecrated by Abimelech. The Panamuwa Inscription (COS 2.37.2-11a) tells of a curse on the royal house of the land of Y'dy in Syria: The ruler Bartzur and his 70 sons are murdered by

a usurper, but Panamuwa, like Jotham, escapes. The usurper's oppressive reign persists until Panamuwa allies with the king of Assyria, who restores Panamuwa to his place. The Assyrian king then "killed the stone of destruction from his father's house" (COS 2.37.2-11a, pp. 158-159). The identity of this "stone of destruction" remains unclear. Superficially, the Aramaic phrase, *'bn shkht*, resembles the Hebrew phrase, "one stone" (*'eben 'ekhath*). The Aramaic text might refer metaphorically to the usurper (Gibson 1975:83). The murder of 70 sons in a coup, reference to the "father's house," prominent reference to a stone, and the theme of a curse and its outworking, resonate strongly with ch 9. Commemoration or desecration of the legacy of a ruler (or usurper) involved setting up, destroying, or restoring (as appropriate) a monument, often, as with the Panamuwa story, an image of the ruler himself, carrying his inscription (Richter 2002:127-205). The stone in the Panamuwa story could be a monument representing the usurper, "killed," i.e., demolished, by Tiglath-pileser III.

Single stones appear in the OT often as monuments: Joshua's monument to the covenant in Josh 24:26-27; the "one stone" (*'eben 'ekhath* [TH68/259, ZH74/285], as here) set up by Samuel (1 Sam 7:12); and likely also the "great stone" at Gibeon (2 Sam 20:8). The "Stone of Zoheleth/Serpent's Stone" (1 Kgs 1:9) could also be an altar or a sacred pillar. The "Stone of Bohan" (Josh 15:6; 18:17) is probably just a topographical feature. While our biblical story does not specify a monument, the "one stone" could easily be a monument associated with Gideon in Ophrah that Abimelech desecrated by the atrocity he perpetrated. This is the most likely of the three options.

Like other usurpers, Abimelech clearly intended not just to kill his rivals, but to send a message. To slay Jerub-baal's sons in Jerub-baal's home, in the very shrine where Jerub-baal got his name, clearly announced not merely a seizure of power, but the repudiation of Jerub-baal (Gideon), his family, and all that he stood for. When Abimelech terminated the rest of Gideon's lineage and abrogated his legacy, he threw down a gauntlet before the God who had called and empowered Gideon. In essence, he shook his fist at Gideon's God and said, "Let Yahweh contend for himself, if he is a God!" God took that challenge up with a vengeance, as the story shows.

they killed all seventy of his half brothers. Abimelech actually only got 69, or one less than all, since the number itself might be idiomatic, not literal (Fensham 1977:113-115). The 70 murdered by Abimelech calls to mind the many uses of the number in the OT. The mutilated Adoni-bezek, before his death, spoke of 70 kings, maimed in like manner, who had been subservient to him (1:5-7). Ahab's 70 sons fell to Jehu's sword in a coup (2 Kgs 10:1-11).

But the youngest brother, Jotham, escaped and hid. The scenario of all the royal sons being executed with a single survivor is a common trope. Normally the survivor ultimately replaces the usurper. The most striking biblical example remains Athaliah's murder of the royal family and the escape of Joash (2 Kgs 11). Unlike Joash, Jotham would not replace Abimelech; after issuing his stinging, parabolic condemnation of Abimelech, he disappears (9:21).

9:6 *Beth-millo.* Lit., "the house of the filling." Ancient engineers typically constructed temples and palaces either on a high site, or on one artificially raised by building a retaining wall and then filling it with rubble. The "city of David" in Jerusalem has a massive stepped stone structure that functioned as a retaining wall for the fill supporting the Jebusite citadel that David ultimately controlled. The Bible calls this filled-in platform "the Millo" (e.g., 2 Sam 5:9 mg). Likewise, at Shechem, the massive temple was constructed on almost 15 feet of rubble and fill. So the term "Beth-millo" serves here simply as another term for the temple at Shechem.

under the oak beside the pillar at Shechem. On the stone pillar, cf. note on 9:4. Stager has collected examples of temples similar and contemporary with the Shechem temple, noting that altars and stelae were also typically accompanied by sacred trees. A Canaanite temple in Egypt, for example, had a courtyard in front where excavators found pits that had been occupied by trees, now long dead. Caches of acorns on the altars suggest the trees were a species of oak. At a sacred oak in Shechem, named Moreh, Abram built his first altar to Yahweh (Gen 12:6-7). There also Jacob buried his household idols (Gen 35:4), and Joshua made the covenant constituting Israel as Yahweh's people in Canaan (Josh 24:26).

made Abimelech their king. This short statement employs the words *malak* [TH4427, ZH4887] (make king) and *melek* [TH4428, ZH4889] (king) affirming Abimelech as the king, and made king by the leaders of Shechem. Noteworthy is the fact that in the Amarna Texts, in letters exchanged between Canaan and Egypt in the 1300s BC (just prior to the arrival of the Israelites), no ruler in Canaan refers to himself as a "king" except for the king of Hazor. By contrast, Joshua 12 lists 31 cities, each tagged with "one king," suggesting that what these leaders called themselves among their subjects and colleagues differed sharply from how they represented themselves to higher authority.

9:7 *the top of Mount Gerizim.* The top of Mount Gerizim would be a half-mile from Shechem and a thousand feet higher. Jotham probably stood on one of the rises on Gerizim's lower slopes. Boling (1975:plate 4) suggests this is the site where he excavated the Middle Bronze age "Tananir Sanctuary" on the lower slope of Gerizim. In the canonical ordering of the OT, Gerizim hearkens back to Joshua's fulfillment of Moses's instructions (Deut 11, 27) to confirm the covenant on Gerizim and Ebal (Josh 8:30-35). Though Jotham stood on the "blessing" mountain, he uttered a stinging condemnation.

9:8-15 *the trees decided to choose a king.* Since the truly productive members of the forest society decline the role of king and only the worthless member, the briar, accepts it, many interpreters see this parable as an attack on kingship. Jotham, however, gives this parable a major twist, using it to condemn usurpers and their coconspirators and implicitly defending legitimate rule.

the olive tree . . . the fig tree . . . the grapevine. These plants are among the seven crops cited as typifying Yahweh's blessing on the land (Deut 8:7-8). All represent domesticated agricultural species, requiring long-term cultivation. They reflect a vision of life that embraces continuity and stability to flourish. These crops were also the prime export products for which the land was famous. The chief of each area controlled trade with outsiders, negotiating trade on behalf of his community. These three agricultural products appear quite appropriately on the lips of an heir of the great chief, Jerub-baal. Each plant spurns the offer of kingship, claiming they are already too important to bother with being king. The outcome reveals this claim as a sham.

9:14 *the thornbush.* The thornbush produces nothing of value. In contrast to the three cultivated, domesticated plants, the thornbush grows wild and interferes with the orderly work of agriculture. Thorns also burn voraciously once ignited.

9:16 *honorably and in good faith.* The terms here are "in truth" (*'emeth* [TH571, ZH622]) and "in wholeheartedness" (*tamim* [TH8549, ZH9459]). The first term has to do with something having such a stable character that it will not change. To be "true" in this sense means to be reliable and unwavering. The second word relates more to unmixed motives and undivided allegiances. Noah was *tamim*, wholehearted or blameless, before God (Gen 6:9), and Abraham was called by God to "be *tamim*" traditionally translated, "perfect" or "wholehearted" (Gen 17:1). These words describe everything that the citizens of Shechem were not.

9:17 ***risked his life.*** The Hebrew is impossible to translate exactly, but too good to ignore, reading along the lines of "he dumped his life/soul out there."

9:20 ***may fire . . . devour.*** Jotham identified two consequences: Fire from Abimelech would consume his coconspirators, but they would also destroy him. The story's structure will follow up both elements of Jotham's pronouncement.

9:21 ***Beer.*** The location of Beer (meaning "a well") is unknown.

9:22 ***After Abimelech had ruled over Israel for three years.*** Though Abimelech was a king, (*melek* [TH4428, ZH4889]), the verb used here (*sarar* [TH8323, ZH8606]) connotes a lesser function often associated with military command. Perhaps the writer wanted to avoid attributing actual kingly office to Abimelech. That the rebellion occurs after three years, i.e., in his fourth year, ironically connects with the vintage festival—see note on 9:27.

9:23 ***God sent a spirit that stirred up trouble.*** In contrast to the legitimate saviors of Israel, who were possessed by the Spirit of Yahweh, Abimelech the usurper received a kind of charisma of his own, lit. "God sent an evil spirit between Abimelech and the lords of Shechem." The term "evil" (*ra'* [TH7451, ZH8273]) embraces the entire semantic domain of trouble, calamity, mischief, and moral evil from the point of view of the person involved. It does not denote objective evil. For example, Joshua challenged his people, "If it is *ra'* in your eyes to serve Yahweh" (Josh 24:15). Clearly serving Yahweh is not a bad thing, but someone conceivably could perceive it as such. Thus God put a spirit between Abimelech and the Shechemites that caused bad feelings. The authenticating, loyalty-inspiring charisma of the divinely chosen leader had its dark counterpart. God had taken up the challenge implicit in Abimelech's repudiation of Gideon.

9:24 ***God was punishing Abimelech.*** With this verse and 9:56-57 the narrator frames the story that follows as the fulfillment of Jotham's fable-curse. By specifying the fulfillment, the author also specifies the meaning of Jotham's fable for this specific context. In some other context, the fable might yield to a variety of interpretations, but for the biblical narrative, the author clearly delineates a single meaning: the divine condemnation and punishment of Abimelech as a fratricidal usurper who seized power by brute force rather than being chosen and empowered by God. The parable also censures Abimelech's coconspirators, the leaders of Shechem, who repudiated their ties with Gideon and his God.

9:25 ***The citizens of Shechem set an ambush.*** The judgment of God unfolds not in a direct, miraculous intervention, but in the ripening fruit of Abimelech's own treachery, energized by the divinely sown spirit of hostility. The very men he had won now turn against him.

on the hilltops. The text probably refers to the heights of Gerizim and Ebal. Ebal in particular offers a commanding view in all directions. A vast portion of the land of Israel becomes visible in a dramatic panorama from its peak (Smith 1931:115-121).

robbed everyone who passed that way. Since the ruler of Shechem profited from intercepting and "facilitating" caravan trade over the main routes passing by the town, Shechemite brigands robbing the caravans before they arrived deprived Abimelech of his income, but still provided wealth for the town (Burney 1920:277; Matthews 2004:109). Abimelech's actual residence in Arumah (9:31) prevented his direct management of affairs in Shechem, which he appears to have delegated to Zebul.

9:26 ***Gaal son of Ebed.*** It is hard to imagine a name in Hebrew that could carry a more loathsome connotation than that of Abimelech's nemesis. The verbal form of this name means, in varying contexts, "to loathe, feel disgust" (HALOT 1.199, s.v. *ga'al* [TH1603, ZH1720]). The noun based on it might mean "dung beetle." In short, nothing can be found in this word that one would relish as a name. His patronymic,"son of Ebed" means "son of a slave," and does not add much to the man's character or status. Nor does the following narrative help the reader gain a higher estimate of the man. The scene almost smacks of a B-western movie in which a gang of low-life rustlers and rabble-rousers move into town—except, of course, Shechem was already such a town! Only a century or so earlier, the gangster-king Lab'ayu and his *'apiru* consorts provided an exact historical prototype for Abimelech and his coconspirators.

9:27 ***During the annual harvest festival . . . the wine flowed freely, and everyone began cursing Abimelech.*** The festival was a celebration of the Canaanite deity Baal-berith. The NLT smooths out the details of the verse, which literally reads, "they went out to the field, they gathered their vineyards, they trod, and they performed praises, and they entered the house of their god and they ate, and they drank, and they cursed Abimelech." Thus the original conveys a process that is glossed over in many modern translations. Ironically, the only other OT occurrence of the word for "festival" (*hillulim* [TH1974, ZH2136]) is in Lev 19:23-24, which requires that fruit trees be left alone for three years, with the fourth-year fruit reserved as holy. Abimelech had ruled Shechem for three years, and with this fourth-year festival offering of the fruit harvest, his own fate had ripened.

9:28 ***"Who is Abimelech?" Gaal shouted. "He's not a true son of Shechem."*** The NLT captures the gist of Gaal's drunken reviling, though the original is more choppy and reflects the presumably inebriated condition of the speaker rather well. The symmetry of divine judgment emerges here. Not only do the Shechemites turn on the king they elected, the interloper Gaal now seduces them, just as Abimelech had done (9:2), by appealing to blood ties. Ironically, Gaal's lineage is not known.

He's merely the son of Gideon. Where Abimelech had emphasized his blood ties to Shechem, Gaal reminds everyone that Abimelech was still the son of the foreigner Gideon (Jerub-baal).

the true sons of Hamor, the founder of Shechem. Hamor, the name of the clan associated with Shechem in the OT (Gen 34), is the Hebrew word for "donkey." Presumably such a name carried no pejorative connotations, or perhaps was a nickname bestowed on him by the narrator. Ancient treaty making in the Levant often featured the sacrifice of a donkey. Archaeologists excavated a donkey's skeleton, minus its head, formally buried by Shechem's ancient citizens, apparently as a sacrifice for a foundation deposit (ABD 5.1182). Given the Shechemites' appreciation for jackasses, it's no wonder they followed the likes of Abimelech and Gaal!

9:31 ***in Arumah.*** The Hebrew text reads *betormah*, meaning "in *tormah*." The meaning of *tormah* [TH8649, ZH9564] remains obscure, and many rightly discern here a spelling error. The original phrase was *be'arumah* [TH725, ZH777], "in Arumah." Even though the leaders of Shechem elected Abimelech king, he actually seems to have resided in the town of Arumah, now identified with Khirbet El-Urmah, five miles south of Shechem. This fortified and well-watered site served as a satellite administrative center for Shechem (R. Miller 1999:195; 2005:34-35). It also lay along an alternative route linking Shechem to the Jordan valley should Abimelech require an escape route (Dorsey 1991:178). If Abimelech suspected ill will from the men of Shechem, Arumah provided a secure headquarters. Having founded his rule on betrayal, Abimelech, like usurpers before and after him, had to maintain constant awareness of flight routes and fallback positions.

9:35 ***Gaal was standing at the city gates.*** From excavations, two gates are known at the site. Both originated in the Middle Bronze era (2000–1550 BC), were damaged or destroyed, and rebuilt at least partially in the Late Bronze Age (1550–1200 BC), lasting until around 1150 BC. The eastern gate originally featured impressive single blocks of stone, called orthostats, and a series of steps leading from the gate-level down to the roadway (E. Campbell 2002:131-143; 169-174). If this was Gaal's point of observation, then the hillside where he saw troops descending would have been the eastern slope of Mount Ebal or the lower hillocks directly outside the gate. He might have referred to the lower hills in the plain east of Shechem. The northwest gate, for which the site is famous, also featured what appear to have been administrative residences, a shrine, and possibly a barracks, and would have afforded a clear view of Gerizim and Ebal. Zebul's suggestion that he was seeing shadows (9:36) might suggest it was morning, as the eastern sun would throw shadows on the mountains to the west, visible from the northwest gate.

9:37 ***the hills.*** Heb., *tabbur ha'arets* [TH2872, ZH3179], or "navel of the earth/land," a term of uncertain meaning. The NLT passes over the difficulty in its main text but notes in the margin "center of the land." The expression "navel of the earth" is often taken to have cosmological implications derived from the notion of a place being the point of junction between the realms of the gods and humans. Such lofty cosmological nuances seem unlikely in the speech of the thug Gaal. The notion of nexus or connection, however, fits the location topographically. The hill country of Ephraim and Manasseh posed obstacles to travel. Shechem lay at the junction of several crucial valleys. From its northwest gate, the Shechem valley led to the coastal plain. From before the east gate, the Mukhna Plain stretched south, facilitating travel toward Jerusalem. Likewise, a valley led north with branches to Wadi Far'ah, which descends east to the Jordan valley and north to the Jezreel valley (cf. note on 6:1; Rainey and Notley 2006:39; ABD 5.1175). The region of Shechem was indeed, not metaphorically or cosmologically, but quite physically and literally, "the junction of the land."

another group is coming down the road past the Diviners' Oak. Many trees in the OT are named for various types of religious functions conducted there. Diviners and divination were prohibited in the OT (Lev 19:26; Deut 18:10-14), though prophetic denunciations make it clear that divination was practiced (cf. Isa 2:6; Mic 5:12).

9:38 ***Now where is that big mouth of yours?*** More than just mockery, Zebul shamed Gaal. They were in the city gate, where the town elders gathered for legal and civil business. In the presence of the same men to whom Gaal had boasted the night before, Zebul threw his boast back in his face. In an ancient society where honor and shame exerted a powerful force on behavior, Gaal had no choice, if he wanted to retain his standing before the men of Shechem, but to gather his men and engage Abimelech's force.

9:41 ***Abimelech returned to Arumah, and Zebul drove Gaal and his brothers out of Shechem.*** The expulsion of Gaal and his gang from town and Abimelech's return to Arumah likely persuaded the Shechemites that this unhappy little episode was past. They could return either to their harvest or to their looting of caravans.

9:42 ***the people of Shechem went out into the fields to battle.*** The words "to battle" do not appear in the original. The Shechemites might simply be resuming their grape harvest, the onset of which they celebrated earlier, since the crisis appeared to have passed (Boling 1975:179; Soggin 1981:191-192). Or they could have resumed their armed interdiction of traffic. Whatever their errand, they were caught off guard and massacred. Abimelech—and God—had plans for the residents of Shechem as well as for Gaal.

9:45 ***The battle went on all day before Abimelech finally captured the city.*** The NLT creates the impression of a daylong battle culminating in the capture of the city, though the actual engagement hardly seems one that would take an entire day. The text simply says that there was fighting "in the city" all that day. The battle in the fields could have been quite swift, but the conflict in the confines of the city might have been long and tedious, moving from house to house before reaching its grisly climax.

He killed the people, leveled the city, and scattered salt all over the ground. "The city" likely refers to the lower city, since the assault on the acropolis follows next. Archaeologists confirm that the city of Shechem, including its palatial temple, was destroyed c. 1125–1100 BC, in line with the chronology suggested in this commentary. This places Gideon around 1150 BC. Commentators tend to attribute uncontrollable rage to Abimelech (e.g., Matthews 2004:110-111), but in fact, Abimelech's actions constitute the norm for conquering an ancient city. Sowing with salt appears as a curse form in the Aramaic treaty of Sefire (COS 2.82.35b-42). The Assyrian king Tiglath-pileser I (1114–1076 BC) describes his destruction of the city of Khunusu: "I burnt the city. The three walls . . . I razed, destroyed, turned into a ruin hill and strewed *sipu*-stones over it" (Grayson 1991:24). The identity of the *sipu*-stones is unclear, but the verb employed is the exact cognate to the one found in the Abimelech story, translated "scattered" (lit., "sowed"). The reference appears to have been a mineral strewn over a conquered site to dramatize its total annihilation (CAD 16.205). Much later, the Assyrian king Ashurbanipal boasts of strewing the ruins of conquered cities with salt and a peculiar thorny plant. Both salt and the plant also feature in an obscure reference to an oath (CAD 15.64). Perhaps the destruction of cities that had profaned a sacred oath involved scattering these substances on the ruins. At any rate, Shechem remained abandoned until the early tenth century BC, only to meet destruction again in 918 BC by Pharaoh Shishak.

9:46 ***the leading citizens who lived in the tower of Shechem.*** Heb., *ba'ale migdal-shekem* [TH4026, ZH4463], meaning "the lords/ of the tower/citadel of Shechem." This tower should be understood as a reference to the massive temple in Shechem (see note on 9:4), and the passage is not describing where these people lived in the city (contra NLT's "who lived in"). Temples had civic as well as religious functions, so leading citizens might well be associated with the temple.

hid in the temple of Baal-berith. The NLT offers no equivalent to the term *tseriakh* [TH6877, ZH7663], which names the part of the temple that people fled to. Comparative studies all point to a trench or narrow cave excavated into rock, but no such structure exists, or was possible at the Shechem temple, which was founded on fill, not bedrock (Boling 1975:181). The space referred to may be another part of the Shechem temple: Walls as wide as those found at Shechem were not solid. An inner and outer wall created chambers around the perimeter of the temple, partitioned by stone and timber, accessible via the stairwells found in the two towers at the temple entrance. Thus, the Shechemite worthies packed into the temple, but rather than go into the open worship space, they crammed into the side chambers (Stager 1999, 2003).

9:48 ***Mount Zalmon.*** This location is not known with certainty, but must have been nearby. Probably it was one of the lower, bench-like projections from Mount Ebal or Mount Gerizim.

9:49 ***cut down some branches.*** The cutting of trees, indeed, of whole forests and orchards, figures prominently in ancient Near East warfare accounts (Hasel 1998, 2005). The text, in stressing "branches" being cut rather than whole trees, might bear witness to the early Israelite taboo against destroying trees in warfare (contra Matthews 2004:107; cf. Deut 20:19-20).

They piled the branches against the walls of the temple and set them on fire. As Stager (1999, 2003) notes, the smoke from the fires would be suffocating in the narrow, cramped space in which Shechem's upper crust had hidden. In addition, the temple's construction would be both brick and timber; ultimately, the entire structure would collapse.

about 1,000 men and women. This number should be taken literally and would require that the tower or temple in the text be the massive fortress temple (see note on 9:4). No other structure excavated at Shechem could accommodate so many persons for this fiery demise.

9:50 *Thebez.* The town is one of two sites close together near the modern village of Tubas, 13 miles northeast of Shechem (Zertal 2008:107-108, 204-205, 210-212, 219-223). In early Iron Age I, Thebez actually lay outside the administrative sphere of Shechem, being attached to the chiefdom at Tirzah (R. Miller 2005:29-90). Abimelech's reasons for attacking Thebez remain obscure. Since he had just destroyed Shechem, perhaps he intended to annex the nearby Thebez as the beginning of a move on Tirzah itself. The site also provided strategic access to Dothan, another center of influence in the highlands. Unlike Shechem, Thebez does not seem targeted for destruction by Abimelech. Perhaps he intended to use it as an interim headquarters.

9:51 *there was a strong tower inside the town.* Both possible sites for Thebez, Khirbet Fuqahah and Khirbet 'Eynun, feature signs of fortification. The latter features an eight-acre tell sporting a surrounding fortification wall enclosing much pottery, including types distinctive to this site, and crowded with building remains. In addition, six curious circles of standing stones 65–130 feet in diameter were along the bottom of the tell. Zertal (2008:220) notes Khirbet 'Eynun was "undoubtedly a central site during Iron Age I (Early Israelite Settlement period)." Abimelech might indeed find such a site appealing for his next move.

9:53 *a woman on the roof dropped a millstone.* The phrase *pelakh rekeb* [TH6400/7393, ZH7115/8207], "riding millstone," specifies this is the upper millstone. Women typically milled grain in a handmill featuring a *pelakh takhtiyt* [TH6400/8482, ZH7115/9397] (cf. Job 41:24), the lower grinder, which was larger, flat, and slightly concave, and the *pelakh rekeb*, or "riding grinder." The miller knelt, crushing the grain by rolling the oblong, almost football-shaped "rider" over the kernels. Made from black basalt, upper millstones possessed sufficient value to rate a taboo against use as collateral for debt (Deut 24:6). The cessation of the sound of grinding offered Jeremiah a symbol for the end of life as Judah knew it during the Exile (Jer 25:10). Such a stone, weighing 4–9 pounds, would constitute a formidable projectile shaped perfectly for throwing (King and Stager 2001:94). It is impressive that the Thebezite woman, in the pandemonium of flight, had the foresight to take her upper millstone. Some scholars claim this mention of "stone" is a kind of bookend to the "one stone" on which Abimelech executed his 70 half brothers. In English, this works—the word "stone" is repeated, but in Hebrew it does not. Nothing about "one stone" (*'eben 'ekhath* [TH68/259, ZH74/285]) resonates with "upper millstone" (*pelakh rekeb*).

that landed on Abimelech's head and crushed his skull. Though the wording is different, one cannot avoid comparison with the crushed skull of Sisera, also at the hands of a strong, stout-hearted woman (4:21-22; 5:26).

9:54 *Draw your sword and kill me! Don't let it be said that a woman killed Abimelech!* Abimelech here anticipates Saul's similar plea, as he also was dying in shame, far from God (1 Sam 31:1-6). The heroic tradition's concern for honor finds sad expression in the plea of the fratricidal usurper not to die at the hands of a woman. The woman, however, remains immortalized, though nameless, in the annals of killers of tyrants, whom the Bible uniformly celebrates. That Abimelech's request failed to secure his honor appears in the later citation of this event as proof of his careless battle tactics, where the woman is credited with killing him after all (2 Sam 11:21).

ran him through. The verb used here, *daqar* [TH1856, ZH1991] (to pierce through), is rare (elsewhere only in Num 25:8; 1 Sam 31:4; 1 Chr 10:4; Isa 13:15; Jer 37:10; 51:4; Lam 4:9; Zech 12:10; 13:3). Additionally, swords in this era rarely exceeded 24 inches in length, and none have been found from Iron Age I sites; to "run someone through" might have been harder than it seems. Along with the dialogue, this verb links the account to that of Saul's death (HALOT 1.230, s.v. *daqar*).

9:55 ***When Abimelech's men saw.*** Lit., "when the men of Israel saw," identifying those who fought alongside Abimelech as Israelites, further puzzling readers about exactly what connections existed between Israel and Shechem. It is possible, though, that the reference is not to soldiers. Possibly "men of Israel" had gathered to observe the outcome of the battle, and when they saw Abimelech was dead, they went home.

saw that he was dead, they disbanded and returned to their homes. The NLT uses terms connoting the breakup of a militia, a legitimate possibility, but not the only one.

9:56 ***In this way, God punished Abimelech.*** The writer here makes the theological point explicit. God's wrath was expressed in the alienation of the Shechemites against Abimelech, the arrival of a seducer, the rebellion, the siege, the destruction of Shechem, and Abimelech's ultimate death at the hands of the woman. The only real deed performed by God in this story is the insinuation of a spirit of hostility amongst Abimelech and his coconspirators. For the rest, human arrogance and aggression served well enough.

for the evil he had done against his father by murdering his seventy brothers. Claims that Gideon had actually turned against God fail because of this clear statement that God avenged the evil done against him, destroying the man who repudiated Jerub-baal, his family, and his God.

9:57 ***God also punished the men of Shechem for all their evil.*** If the suggestions above about Shechem's covenant with Yahweh dating back to Josh 24 (see note on 9:2) serving to constitute them as members of Israel despite their indigenous Canaanite ethnicity are accepted, then the decision to affiliate along bloodlines with Abimelech and join him in the repudiation of their heritage in Jerub-baal/Gideon did constitute the abrogation of their covenant with Yahweh, which he here punishes.

So the curse . . . was fulfilled. The book of Judges repeatedly locates the divine purpose in the activities of a fallible, often flawed human being. Jotham served no role in the story other than the pronouncement of the word of God unmasking the treachery of Abimelech and Shechem. He does not return for vindication, and no claim is made that he should rule. Gideon had, after all, rejected inherited rule. But Jotham's curse clearly condemned usurpers and asserted the principle of legitimate inheritance. For God to fulfill the curse of Jotham amounts (in the logic of the narrative) to a divine condemnation on usurpers and endorsement of legitimate succession.

COMMENTARY

Few statements epitomize the story of Abimelech's father, Gideon, better than that associated with the founder of the modern missionary movement, William Carey, who said, "Expect great things from God; attempt great things for God." Such should have been Gideon's legacy. But just as the church founded to honor Carey's legacy in Lester, England, has become a Hindu temple, so the legacy of Gideon dissolved in the events that followed his death.

The story of Abimelech illustrates how meaning, in the Bible, resides at the intersection of past events, geography, culture, other ancient texts, literary features, and the readers. The meaning of this text remains obscure unless we also know the context, concerns, and aims of the characters—a point totally lost in a superficial reading. By the same token, merely reconstructing the historical events fails to place the story in its theological context. All Scripture seeks to reveal the ways and character of God and the nature of the human response. This story brings to the forefront the particular issue of leadership in Israel, which it treats with much more nuance and complexity than mere contrasts between "pro" and "anti" kingship positions can hope to capture.

Gideon's refusal of a position of leadership and the construction of the ephod (8:22-27) dramatized an important principle: When legitimate human leadership abdicates, effectual divine leadership evaporates. Thinking he was assuring God's continued rule over Israel, Gideon actually ensured that the people would "play the harlot" and abandon Yahweh. With Yahweh abandoned, the legacy and family of his servant Gideon was doomed. Not only had Gideon's repudiation of human rule ended up perverting divine rule, it had actually recoiled on his own career, spoiling his legacy. The prologue to the Abimelech story (8:33-35), coming on the heels of the ephod debacle, shows that when divine rule is rejected, as in Israel's apostasy, human rule is threatened as well. So divine rule and human rule, far from being antagonists, would stand as joint victims of spiritual harlotry.

The structure of the Abimelech story works out clearly as a cause-effect or crime-punishment movement accompanied by a theological explanation. The result is the pattern shown below:

THE CRIME (8:1-21)	THE PUNISHMENT (8:22-57)
The Cause (8:1-6) The Crime Perpetrated: Abimelech's Fratricidal Usurpation of Power	*The Effect* (8:25-55) Punishment Effected: Abimelech Meets His End in Avenging Himself against Usurpation
Explanation: The Crime Decried Its Character (8:7-15) Its Consequences (8:16-21)	*Explanation: The Punishment Interpreted* Its Divine Source Indicated (8:22-24) Its Divine Source Confirmed (8:56-57)

The speech of Jotham has been typically construed as critical of kingship, but this interpretation runs into difficulties in this context. The fable does not actually criticize kingship, but attacks those who refused the responsibility of ruling, leaving the nation to worthless scoundrels. The thornbush actually articulates the point of the parable (9:15). It is not hungry for power but shrewdly unmasks the folly of the trees in offering the thorn a task it patently cannot fulfill. All commentators note that "shade" (*tsel* [TH6738, ZH7498]) appears in the ancient Near East as a common term for the protection extended by a king over his domain. Rather than attacking the institution of kingship (Block 1999:320-321), the fable exposes the danger created when worthy candidates, preoccupied with their own admittedly productive lives, decline leadership, thereby abandoning the field to unworthy pretenders, with catastrophic consequences. Its vindication in the story that follows demonstrates the wrath of God on those who wrest power from its rightful possessors. Applied to the story, the three productive plants that declined compare with Gideon, who was offered permanent, patrimonial rule, but who refused and instead retired as a prosperous and influential *sheikh*. His refusal created a vacuum filled by the useless, fruitless, uncultivated Abimelech (Moore 1895:244-248). The moral of the story is that when fit persons refuse to lead, unfit persons will seize power.

In Jotham's speech, awareness of this issue is profoundly magnified as the speaker is none other than the sole surviving legitimate heir of Gideon/Jerub-baal, criticizing one who has just seized power by slaughtering his 70—or 69—rivals. The context unmistakably assumes legitimate rule is inherited, and the speech as a whole attacks not kingship, but usurpers and their coconspirators. Moreover, this betrayal of Gideon is linked back verbally to 8:33-35 and becomes part of Israel's betrayal of its God. Thus, the speech uttered is a dynast's protest against usurpation.

The punishment (9:22-57) unfolds as the inexorable outworking of the action of God, who intervened to exact vengeance on behalf of Gideon in fulfillment to Jotham's message. Abimelech's struggle against outside agitators (9:26-41) is framed by reference to conniving insider insurrectionists (9:25, 42-50), and the whole is bracketed with claims that God personally worked to sow discord and bring vengeance (9:22-24, 56-57) all in fulfillment of Jotham's word. This literary arrangement transposes a typical story of Late Bronze/Iron Age I city-state insurrection into a paradigm of divine judgment on a usurper in vindication of the sole surviving legitimate dynast. That judgment did not work through miracles or charismatic heroes, but through the relentless unfolding of the moral and social consequences of the choices made by the characters. In the end, the thornbush had it right (9:15). Far from being a critique of kingship, the Abimelech story stands as an affirmation that when legitimate human rule is usurped, divine rule asserts itself in defense of human rule—and (dare I say) dynastic, human rule at that.

The inspired author organized this material to move the reader away from the position articulated by Gideon. Gideon had proposed that permanent, dynastically self-perpetuating rule was incompatible with divine rule, and set up the ephod to make divine rule complete. But 8:27 demonstrates that when human rule is declined, divine rule is perverted. Judges 8:28-35 takes another step away from Gideon by correlating and coordinating the rejection of divine rule and human rule: Both fall together. The way was then open for the Abimelech story to function as a prodynastic narrative in which God is depicted as vindicating the speech of the sole surviving son of Gideon: Divine rule asserts itself against fratricidal usurpation. Far from advocating a charismatic model of leadership, the writer expressed a commitment to political institutions, specifically the institution of dynastic rule. Behind the whole process, for this writer, stands the view that God is best honored by a community with regular structures of human rule and succession, and who sets in place forces of judgment when those structures are violated.

Do issues like inheritance and succession matter to the church of the twenty-first century? Perhaps they do. The Christian church in its early centuries faced a problem: Once the apostles had died, how were believers to ensure the purity of their doctrine, worship, and practice? The earliest church fathers spoke of succession: If the teaching came from one who had sat at the feet of the apostles, then the teaching was considered true. Over time, this principle of trusting the authorized, human channel of revelation traced back to the apostles solidified into two forms. On the one hand, the canon of the New Testament took shape primarily around debates about what actually constituted the true apostolic witness. The New Testament documents represented a universally accepted standard of apostolic preaching and teaching. On the other hand, the early church continued to treasure the chain of teaching from leader to leader in the great urban churches of the Mediterranean world, a chain extending back to the apostles. This view ultimately crystallized in the view represented in the Roman Catholic and Eastern Orthodox traditions. Even Protestants, who reject the claims of the centrality of any one human leader, still esteem highly the witness of past believers and teachers, as they affirm *sola scriptura*. While Christians for centuries have debated these two sets of claims, a third approach has always haunted the church. The church has always had those who claimed to need no ties to the past, no standards of teaching, no rule of faith. Such believers claim they need only the Spirit of God to inspire them and guide their reading of the Bible (if they are bound to the Bible!). Proudly declaring their independence from any tradition or precedent, spurning the wisdom of others, past and present, they set out to establish their faith and life *de novo*. Such need no leadership except that of the Spirit, and they become a law unto themselves. The history of Christianity is replete with examples of how such leadership solely by the Spirit, or solely by Scripture, eventually becomes the chaotic, tyrannical rule of one person. In many ways, these believers bear a strong resemblance to Abimelech and his comrades. Authority emerging from illegitimate origins ends in the abuse of power. As noted earlier, the great divide between Gideon and Abimelech is that Gideon embraced power only after a long process of testing and clarification. Even though his abdication in the end was wrong, it still revealed how little Gideon actually loved power. Abimelech, however, and those like him, live only for power, worshiping the god of raw force. Abimelech blindly repudiated any authority beyond himself, an error brought forcibly to mind by the Thebezite woman's millstone.

The church must always recognize that however new and fresh our experience of God's grace in Christ might be, we also receive that faith as a legacy from those who have gone before us. When we read the Scriptures as our sole authority, we dare not read them alone, arrogantly ignoring the wisdom, experience, and insight of our forebears. We have been preceded, and to those who have paid the ultimate price for their faith, we owe a debt of covenantal loyalty and faithfulness, both to them and to Christ.

◆ 3. Tola and Jair: Authority restored (10:1-5)

**After Abimelech died, Tola son of Puah,
son of Dodo, was the next person to rescue Israel. He was from the tribe of Issachar but lived in the town of Shamir in
the hill country of Ephraim. [2]He judged
Israel for twenty-three years. When he
died, he was buried in Shamir.
[3]After Tola died, Jair from Gilead judged
Israel for twenty-two years. [4]His thirty
sons rode around on thirty donkeys, and they owned thirty towns in the land of Gilead, which are still called the Towns of
Jair.* [5]When Jair died, he was buried in
Kamon.**

10:4 Hebrew *Havvoth-jair.*

NOTES

10:1 *After Abimelech died.* The so-called minor judges represent an orderly succession that is not dynastic. Each arises "after" the other, made explicit in Hebrew by the preposition *'akhare* [TH310, ZH339]. But they do not seem to succeed each other directly in the same office. The Hebrew writers normally express direct succession in one office by means of the preposition *takhath* [TH8478A, ZH9393], meaning "below" or "in place of."

Tola son of Puah, son of Dodo. Tola's name means "red worm." Some parents, upon looking at their newborn, might think the name appropriate. He is the only judge whose ancestral information extends three generations, possibly accentuating his high status (Younger 2002:238). The name "Dodo" derives from the same root as the name of David, and resembles it in the consonantal text. No intentional association is likely, however.

to rescue Israel. The use of the expression "rescue [save] Israel" for a so-called minor judge is unusual, especially since no narrative details appear to flesh out the claim. Boling (1975:187) wisely notes, "in contrast with Abimelech's effort and short-lived success as king, what Israel needed was good administration, which Tola provided."

the tribe of Issachar but lived in the town of Shamir in the hill country of Ephraim. A mark of the "judge" seems to be that he functioned with a wider portfolio than might be expected from his position in the clan or tribe. Those in the book who are called judges (*shopet* [TH8199A, ZH9149] cf. 4:4) or who are said to "judge [*shapat*] Israel" (cf. 3:10; 10:2, 3; 12:7, 11, 13, 14; 15:20; 16:31) can all be shown to be persons operating in some way beyond their expected scope. So here, though Tola is of the tribe of Issachar, we find him active and residing in Shamir in Ephraim, possibly the site of later Samaria, about seven miles northwest of the salted ruins of Shechem.

10:2 ***He judged Israel for twenty-three years.*** The so-called minor judges seem to be chiefs or paramounts. Such persons acquired property, offspring, or wealth beyond the norm, and as a result, exercised influence wider than would be expected of a mere town elder.

10:3 ***After Tola died, Jair from Gilead.*** Gilead lies on the east side of the Jordan River, an unusual home for a man who governed "Israel." This region also would be the next to suffer oppression when Israel fell back into apostasy.

judged Israel for twenty-two years. Notably, no apostasy intervenes between the death of Tola and the rise of Jair. By blatantly diverging from the paradigm stated in 2:15-19, the writer as much as indicates the superiority of the "minor" judges over the major judges on the point of continuity. A total of 55 years of orderly and uneventful governance with no apostasy intervening exceeds the times of peace procured by all the "major" judges except Ehud.

10:4 ***thirty sons . . . thirty donkeys.*** Here the judge's scope of influence seems extreme: 30 sons on 30 donkeys. The term for donkey here, *'ayir* [TH5895A, ZH6555], refers to prime riding stock that was "the mount of the noble rather than the lowly" (Soggin 1981:196; cf. Moore 1895:274; NIDB 2.158). Passages traditionally taken to be messianic promises (Gen 49:11; Zech 9:9) portray the Messiah riding a donkey, an image taken up in the NT by all four Gospel writers (Matt 21:2; Mark 11:1-3; Luke 19:29-31; John 12:14-15).

thirty towns . . . the Towns of Jair. "Towns" is *'arim* [TH5892, ZH6551] (cities), and the word closely resembles the term used for "donkeys," causing some ancient scribal confusion in copying this text. The JPS translation adroitly captures the pun with "burros" and "boroughs." The term, *khawwoth ya'ir* [TH2334, ZH2596], appears altogether in six OT passages. Numbers 32:41 and Deut 3:14 credit "Jair the son of Manasseh" (KJV) with conquering villages in Transjordan during the Mosaic era and naming them *khawwoth ya'ir* [TH2333/2971A, ZH2557/3281] (the Towns of Jair). Joshua 13:30 refers to these events, adding the detail that the towns of Jair were in fact "sixty towns," a point enlarged upon in 1 Kgs 4:13 where these 60 cities are reported to be walled with bronze bars. The texts also locate the towns in either Gilead or Bashan, to the north. Judges alone attributes the naming of this region to the post-Mosaic era, fixing the number of towns at 30. The similarities tempt us to equate the Mosaic-era Jair with his post-Mosaic counterpart, but that in turn raises chronological conflicts. These dots will probably not be connected without more topographical and historical information.

10:5 ***When Jair died, he was buried in Kamon.*** The town where Jair was buried remains unknown, with several possible sites east and west of the Jordan.

COMMENTARY

The author Ernest Hemingway is reported to have been challenged to write a complete story in only six words. Hemingway rose to the challenge: "For Sale: Baby Shoes, Never Worn." A story need not be long to convey a vital slice of life to the reader. Although the so-called minor judges come to us only in very brief vignettes, they open revealing windows into the experience of early Israel. Commentators insisting that every single judge in the book represents a step downward morally and spiritually tend to fault these figures for not doing anything to reverse the evils of their predecessors. To force every story somehow to display yet more decline seems heavy-handed. In fact, hints appear in these records that the author assessed the minor judges positively.

Students of social organization point out that Israel, up to the time of Abimelech, had become a "complex chiefdom" (R. Miller 2005:6-14, 97-103, 112-124). A complex chiefdom vests authority in a single family head, the chief or paramount, who passes that authority down as an inheritance. A complex chiefdom involves a central site, such as Shechem or Shiloh, each with its series of satellite towns and their dependent villages, which all form a network of communication, trade, intermarriage, and common defense. Chiefdoms lack "state" features like professional administrators, standing armies, and standardized monumental architecture. Hints at this social structure appear in the Gideon-Abimelech material. Social historians also note that complex chiefdoms break down. The central town or family can lose power, resulting in the former satellite towns achieving independence, becoming a series of "simple chiefdoms" until a new network forms, possibly around another center. Archaeological data suggests that about 1100 BC the complex chiefdom that centered on Shechem collapsed with the destruction of the city, which was not reoccupied for over a century. The extermination of Gideon's family ended the influence of his family in the region, thus demolishing completely the social structure that had emerged. To the south, several towns, including Gibeah, had already fallen about 1150 (throwing the Benjaminite hill country into confusion); this is possibly reflected in chapters 19–21. Shiloh would meet with a fiery fate around 1050, probably at the hands of the Philistines (cf. 1 Sam 4). The stories of Tola and Jair in 10:1-5 could mirror the new situation resulting from the collapse of these complex chiefdoms—the rise of new networks of power, centered at other sites.

These little vignettes allow the author to point to certain core values about leadership that will be sorely lacking in the stories of the major judges. First, the minor judges show us just what a "judge" (*shopet* [TH8199A, ZH9149]) was. A judge was a leader whose influence reached beyond the range defined by his genealogical position. For each minor judge, the author will identify some unusual characteristic that will point to this broader scope of influence. Jair, for example, lives in Transjordan, but judges "Israel." Second, the minor judges show us intrinsic leadership. The judges do indeed exercise power in a manner not precisely grounded in the family system of ancient Israel, but their rule emerges from their rootedness in their own clan or tribe. Their many sons and daughters identify them as families who soon morphed into virtual clans. In each case, some outstanding point of competence or achievement will be noted, upon which their rule is grounded. It will never be coercion or violence, but likely prestige and respect well-earned. Third, they succeed one another without any intervening sin or oppression. The uneventful transfer of power might be taken for granted in Western democracies, but in most of the world throughout most of history, transfers of power come with violence and trauma. Fourth, these two judges show us something about salvation. The narrator notes that Tola arose to save Israel, but does not tell of any battles or murders. Perhaps salvation can take the form not just of dramatic displays of power, divine or human, but also the quiet, steady presence of competent leadership.

These little notes all point to an underlying theme in Judges that will become more obvious with the stories of Jephthah, Samson, and the outrages of chapters 17–21. The desire for overt displays of dramatic divine power that overwhelm the human element and shove aside human institutions and traditions in fact do not constitute Yahweh's way for his people. Yahweh's plan was for Israel to construct a community in which his will was done on earth as it is in heaven, with traditions and institutions in which his order, his *shalom* [TH7965, ZH8934], prevails, and in which, to borrow Jotham's words, people live in integrity, honor, and faithfulness (8:35; 9:16; Heb., *'emeth* [TH571, ZH622], *tamim* [TH8549, ZH9459] and *khesed* [TH2617, ZH2876]). Though this community would be grounded in Yahweh's gracious promise, living each moment solely by his presence, it was nevertheless a thoroughly human community in which human memory, aspirations, and achievements pointed to the glory of God. The minor judges remind us of the book of Ruth, which transpires in "the days when the judges ruled" (Ruth 1:1). In that book, each character behaves with dignity, honor, and integrity. In the human network of faithfulness, every person in the story finds redemption, and that without a single miracle. Perhaps the salvation of God is after all most evident in the quiet succession of good men who direct their growing families and thriving peoples in peace.

◆ D. Stage Three: Tragedy (10:6–16:31)

1. Jephthah: A vow tragically kept (10:6–12:7)

a. The prologue (10:6-18)

**6Again the Israelites did evil in the LORD's
sight. They served the images of Baal and
Ashtoreth, and the gods of Aram, Sidon,
Moab, Ammon, and Philistia. They aban-
doned the LORD and no longer served him
at all. 7So the LORD burned with anger
against Israel, and he turned them over to
the Philistines and the Ammonites, 8who
began to oppress them that year. For
eighteen years they oppressed all the
Israelites east of the Jordan River in the
land of the Amorites (that is, in Gilead).
9The Ammonites also crossed to the west
side of the Jordan and attacked Judah,
Benjamin, and Ephraim.**

**The Israelites were in great distress.
10Finally, they cried out to the LORD for
help, saying, "We have sinned against you
because we have abandoned you as our
God and have served the images of Baal."**

**11The LORD replied, "Did I not rescue you
from the Egyptians, the Amorites, the
Ammonites, the Philistines, 12the
Sidonians, the Amalekites, and the Maon-
ites? When they oppressed you, you cried
out to me for help, and I rescued you.
13Yet you have abandoned me and served
other gods. So I will not rescue you any-
more. 14Go and cry out to the gods you
have chosen! Let them rescue you in your
hour of distress!"**

15But the Israelites pleaded with the

LORD and said, "We have sinned. Punish us as you see fit, only rescue us today from our enemies." 16Then the Israelites put aside their foreign gods and served the LORD. And he was grieved by their misery.

17At that time the armies of Ammon had gathered for war and were camped in Gilead, and the people of Israel assembled and camped at Mizpah. 18The leaders of Gilead said to each other, "Whoever attacks the Ammonites first will become ruler over all the people of Gilead."

NOTES

10:6 ***Again the Israelites did evil in the LORD's sight.*** This unit demolishes any conception of a standardized recurring "cyclical" pattern in the narratives. Here the Hebrew resumes the idiom employed in the stories of Ehud and Deborah (3:12; 4:1) that stresses the continuous nature of Israel's evildoing. This comes after having used the more direct, nonrepeating idiom for the Gideon account (6:1) that also appeared in the Othniel story at the beginning the series (3:7) (Stone 1988:301-305). The result is not a steady downward slope but of a decline in three distinct steps. The Gideon-Abimelech unit formed a lower step, now the Jephthah-Samson unit steps down again.

They served the images of Baal. Commentators often wrongly conclude from the summary in 2:11-16 every instance of Israel's evil is idolatry, but twice no reference to idolatry occurs (3:12; 4:1), and twice the connection to idolatry is indirect, via a reference elsewhere in the narrative (6:10; 13:1). Twice the link to idolatry is explicit, in the Othniel story (3:7) and here. The author's linking of (lit.) "did evil in Yahweh's eyes" to idolatry accentuates the "step-down" quality of Israel's deteriorating bond with Yahweh. Unspecified evildoing in the "triumphant" block of text (Ehud-Deborah) yields to evil with idolatrous associations in the context that gradually become explicit in the "transitional" block (Gideon-Abimelech). With the Jephthah-Samson section, idolatry is stated explicitly from the start, signaling the "tragic" block of text, the last stage before chaos is unleashed in chs 17–21 (Stone 1988:296-299, 464-471). That Israel worshiped the gods of seven nations corresponds to seven nations from whom Yahweh delivered Israel in 10:11-12, as well as to the seven judges preceding this account (Younger 2002:242-243). The symmetry suggests that Israel's apostasy exactly negates the past saving actions of God (Keil 1863:374-375).

Ashtoreth. Heb., *'ashtaroth* [TH6253, ZH6956]; it refers to the goddess Astarte (or images of her), strongly associated with the port city of Sidon (cf. 1 Kgs 11:5). Astarte's devotees celebrated her embodiment of sexual love and fertility; they celebrated her as a great goddess "who conceives but does not bear." Astarte also figured prominently in war, being depicted armed with shield and spear or bow, astride a horse. When Saul died, the Philistines displayed his armor in the temple of Astarte in Beth-shan while his body hung on the city wall (1 Sam 31:10). Our author would have known of the prominence of Astarte in the public shaming of defeated Israel. Egypt, in the era leading up to the Exodus, experienced a surge in the popularity of Astarte worship; she was the patron deity of the city of Pi-Rameses, constructed by Rameses II with the forced labor of Hebrew slaves (Exod 1:11). This was an ironically evil choice for Yahweh's replacement (ABD 1.491-494; NIDB 1.337-338).

the gods of Aram. These foreign gods all derive from outside the Promised Land, even the "gods of . . . Philistia" who probably originated from the Aegean region. Some scholars suggest that this passage is a very late fictional creation, claiming that the nations noted are historically better documented for later periods of Israel's history than for the premonarchic era (Niditch 2008:122-123). The references in Judges, however, do not imply full statehood, even when kings are mentioned. Disputes over territorial claims occur among chiefdoms as easily as among states, and references to kings can either be harmless anachronisms or reflect greater diversity in the meaning of *melek* [TH4428, ZH4889] than interpreters typically assume (Hess 2008:39-40). Again, that fully organized states such as Aram might not have existed in early Iron Age I does not mean the peoples who eventually formed that state did not exist. For example, Aram was a coalition of tribes centered on Damascus, but this state did not emerge clearly until about a century later than our story. Surely the Arameans predated their state so that the term could designate people groups occupying the northern bend of the Fertile Crescent, known to later writers as Aram. Aram worshiped Hadad, the storm god, who shared most of his attributes with Baal. Aram was the home of Cushan-Rishathaim, the enemy defeated by Othniel, the very first judge (3:7-11). Israel now worshiped the god of a formerly defeated foe.

Sidon. This major port on the coast of Lebanon represented the farthest northern extent of the Israelite conquest (Josh 11:8; 19:28), though the Hebrews never controlled it. In the OT and extrabiblical texts, Sidon defines the boundary of Canaanite territory. Well-documented in the Late Bronze and Iron Age I periods, the name became synonymous with "Phoenicia" both in the Bible and in Homer (ABD 6.17-18). Sidon might have exercised nominal control over the northern portion of Israel (cf. 18:7). The chief deity of Sidon was the goddess of sexual love and war, Astarte (cf. note on Ashtoreth, above). Being in the vicinity of Ugarit, we may also suppose that Sidon venerated the whole crew of Canaanite deities.

Moab. Moab is the strip of land 15 miles east/west and 60 miles north/south running along the east side of the Dead Sea, extending from its shore eastward up the steep escarpment some 3,000 feet to the desert (ABD 4.882-893). The OT identifies the Moabites as descendants of Lot's incest (Gen 19:37). Their corruption of the Israelites in the wilderness through fornication and idolatry won them perennial banishment from Yahweh's sanctuary (Deut 23:3). The claim that Moabite statehood comes later than the Judges is answerable along the same lines as those noted for Aram above. Chemosh, Moab's deity, was associated with the realm of the dead. Texts like the ninth-century-BC Moabite Stone show how the Moabites attributed invasions and defeats to the anger of Chemosh. They expressed their divinely enabled victories in battle with the term *kharam* [TH2763, ZH3049], just as Israel did. In 2 Kgs 3:27 the king of Moab is said to offer his oldest son as a burnt offering, but this desperate move does not imply that human sacrifice figured normally in the worship of Chemosh (ABD 1.895-897). Ehud delivered Israel from the Moabites (3:12-30), so Israel's worship of Moabite deity involved embracing the very power that Yahweh had previously broken on their behalf.

Ammon. This region likewise lies east of the Jordan, north of the Dead Sea. Like Moab, the OT identifies Ammon as the fruit of Lot's incest (Gen 19:36-38) and in the Mosaic era, Israel was not to take either of their lands (Deut 2:9, 19). The tribes of Gad, Reuben, and half-Manasseh settled on the borders of Ammonite territory. Ammon joined Moab in the oppression of Israel ended by Ehud (3:13). Perhaps the hands-off policy of Israel and Ammon's being surrounded on three sides by Israelite territory, explain the king of Ammon's aggravation regarding Israel's occupation of Gilead (11:13). The god of Ammon was Milcom, about whom we know only that the author of 1–2 Kings condemns him as "the abomination of the Ammonites" (1 Kgs 11:5 KJV; ABD 4.895-898).

Philistia. The Philistines, as one of several tribes constituting the "Sea Peoples," first became a factor in Israel's territory c. 1175 BC when they settled the coastal plain near Gaza, noted in Josh 13:2-3 and 3:3 as still unconquered by the Israelites. Of Greek/Aegean origins, various tribes of the Sea Peoples settled the coast and lower reaches of the valleys, ultimately penetrating as far as Beth-shan near the Jordan. The biblical authors tend to label all these diverse peoples as "Philistines." Though not a clear and present danger until after c. 1100, the Philistine presence did cause concern earlier. Interaction between Israelites and Philistines occurred in the hill country fringe between them, allowing for mutual influences. This passage is the first we learn of Israel worshiping the gods of the Philistines, and later Samson will entertain the Philistines in a feast to their god Dagon (16:23-27; see note on 16:23).

They abandoned the LORD and no longer served him at all. The terminology here hearkens back to the programmatic preface of Judges, which, like an overture sounding all the themes to be heard in the musical drama, accents how Israel would "abandon" Yahweh and "serve" other gods (2:11-13). These words end the verse with a twist—Israel served every god but their own.

10:7 ***So the LORD burned with anger against Israel.*** The Hebrew idiom, "the nose of Yahweh grew hot," is normally considered part of the standard, cyclical pattern of the book. But it actually appears only in the preface (2:14, 20), in the Othniel story (3:8), and here. In the preface, two cycles of sin and divine wrath appear: the first leading to oppression and deliverance by judges (2:11-19) and the second triggered by Israel's refusal to listen to its judges (2:17-19), which leads to Yahweh's withdrawal of his power, the cancellation of the conquest (2:20–3:4), shifting the role of the remaining nations from education—teaching the Israelites war—to probation—revealing openly the unfaithfulness of Israel.

turned them over. The Hebrew idiom is derived from the world of commerce: "he sold them into the hands of," and appears elsewhere in Judges only in the preface (2:14b) and in the Deborah story (4:2). Elsewhere Yahweh is said to "give" them into the hands of enemies (6:1; 13:1) or to "strengthen" the enemy (3:12). The writer seems to select which term to use, since rarely does more than one of these appear in the same place (Stone 1988:307-310). Perhaps the use of the term is tied to the intensity of the oppression. The Deborah and Jephthah accounts recount a menace to all, or almost all, of Israel, conceivably threatening the nation's continued existence.

to the Philistines. The Philistines never constituted a threat to Gilead, east of Jordan, the scene of most of our story. This reference to the Philistines anticipates 13:1, so that 10:6-16 serves as a prologue to the entire unit including Jephthah, the second minor judge list, and Samson. The Philistine oppression also appears to have been simultaneous with the Ammonite crisis, so that the careers of Samson and Jephthah might well have overlapped. In the narrative, the Philistine oppression emerges ultimately as the dagger pointed at the very heart of Israel's survival, a threat the judges and Israel failed to meet, even with Samuel's victory over them in 1 Sam 7. Though Samuel could summon Yahweh's power over the Philistines, his ministry faltered at the Achilles' heel of tribal confederations, the gap Gideon had earlier refused to fill in his abdication: continuity of leadership. Samuel's victory did not survive his unworthy sons, and the Philistine crisis resumed with a vengeance. That distant threat now appears as a cloud on the reader's horizon.

10:8 ***who began to oppress them that year. For eighteen years they oppressed all the Israelites east of the Jordan River in the land of the Amorites (that is, in Gilead).*** The NLT's "began to" and "they oppressed" ease the difficult construction of the Hebrew, which reads: "and they shattered and smashed the Israelites in that year, eighteen years all the Israelites who were beyond the Jordan in the land of the Amorites, which is Gilead." A translator puzzles over "in that year" and "eighteen years." The LXX Vaticanus family has "at that time," which, though easier, is suspect just for that reason. Others identify "that year" as the year of Jair's death (10:5). In any event, the writer stresses that oppression began with a bang, then lasted for 18 years. The writer viewed the Ammonite and Philistine crises as unfolding concurrently. Thus this 18 years, Jephthah's 6 years, and the 25 years of the three minor judges (12:8-15)—a total of 49 years—could roughly enclose the 40 years attributed to the Philistine oppression (13:1), which in turn also incorporated the 20 years of Samson's career, since he did not end the Philistine threat.

Schneider (2000:160) rightly notes, "For the first time both sides of the Jordan and most of the tribes of Israel were explicitly involved." Gilead lies in the region east of the Jordan roughly between the northern tip of the Dead Sea and the southern tip of the Sea of Galilee. The term sometimes loosely designates the whole region east of the Jordan.

10:9 *The Ammonites also crossed to the west side of the Jordan.* The chaotic period between the withdrawal of Egypt (c. 1150 BC) and the dominance of the Philistines (after c. 1075 BC) featured competition among various smaller ethnic groups for control of Canaan, or at least of certain resources such as trade routes. The Midianites had crossed the Jordan to raid the highways crossing the Jezreel valley and extending south to Gaza (chs 6–7) but were eliminated by Gideon. With the failure of Israel (and specifically Gideon) to put in place a polity that could maintain the peace and the consequent implosion of Shechem (the main city-state in the central highlands), a power vacuum developed that provided Ammon a chance to address Israel's encroachment on their territory and to advance their own influence west of the Jordan.

attacked Judah, Benjamin, and Ephraim. These attacks make the Ammonite threat the most comprehensive crisis in the book so far. For these three areas to come under simultaneous threat was remarkable, but Ammon's location, significantly overlapping Gilead, made it feasible. The Ammonites had no access to trade routes or the resources of the larger region: They were bordered by desert to the east and otherwise hemmed in by Israelite tribes, which minimized the benefit of the King's Highway passing through Ammon's land. Their need for Lebensraum prompted a campaign that probably sought first to open up the King's Highway more fully. To further capitalize on that route, there followed attacks west of the Jordan, aimed at controlling the north–south highway running atop the watershed ridge, known to biblical geographers as the "National Highway" (Dorsey 1991:118-146). This route, like the King's Highway, was one of three lucrative north–south trade routes in the area. It ran north from Beersheba to Hebron, passed just west of Jerusalem, through Bethel, past Shiloh, and through Shechem to connect with the east-west routes running up the Wadi Far'a and Jezreel valley before passing along the west side of the Sea of Galilee to all points north. Once Ammon seized critical points in the south, middle, and north of this road—in Judah, Benjamin, and Ephraim—they would have strategic control over two of the three major trade routes and a choke hold over the competing Israelite highland economy that produced the same olives and grapes—major cash crops—that grew in Ammonite territory.

The Israelites were in great distress. Between the Ammonites shutting down the main traffic artery in the heartland of the Israelite settlements and the Philistine pressure from the west, the Hebrew's literal "it got very tight for Israel" is quite appropriate.

10:10 *We have sinned against you.* For the first time in the book, Israel's outcry finds articulation, even confession. This is the first occurrence in the book of the word *khata'*, meaning "miss the mark, sin." It appears with the meaning "sin" only in the Jephthah story (cf. 10:15; 11:27). Its use as a marksmanship term appears in 20:16, where the Benjaminite 700-man brigade can "sling a rock and hit a target . . . without missing" (*khata'* [TH2398, ZH2627]).

because we have abandoned you as our God and have served the images of Baal. The confession mirrors the words—"abandon, serve"—of the narrator (10:6) and of Yahweh's reply (10:13).

10:11-12 ***The LORD replied, "Did I not rescue you?"*** This speech, the only unmediated divine speech to all Israel in the book, should be compared to the word of the angel at Bokim (2:1-5) and to the word of the prophet prior to Gideon's call (6:7-10). The three passages accentuate the step-wise deterioration of Israel's relationship with Yahweh (Stone 1988:358-364). The sentence structure of 10:11-12 in Hebrew is convoluted, with a rhetorical question beginning in 10:11, lit., "was it not from . . ." but with no verb following in the Hebrew ("rescue you" is added for clarity). Verse 12 abruptly begins a new sentence. The Hebrew text is almost untranslatable, resulting in many hypotheses based on reasonable conjectures of possible scribal misspellings. Faced with an insoluble problem, the best suggestion seems to be to follow the LXX Alexandrinus and Vulgate traditions in deleting the repeated (and atypical, for Judges) "and from" (*umin* [TH2050.1/4480, ZH2256/4946]) as a scribal duplication (Burney 1920:296-297; Soggin 1981:202). The text then reads smoothly with 10:11-12a serving as a compound, sevenfold subject leading up to the verb in 10:12b: "Did not the Egyptians and the Amorites . . . oppress you?"

10:11 ***from the Egyptians.*** This could refer to the Exodus, of course, but could also allude to the Egyptian control over Canaan up until c. 1150 BC. The Deborah story represents Egypt's last push to retain its hold on Canaan. The crushing defeat dealt to Sisera and his company not only liberated Israel, but contributed to the abrupt withdrawal of Egypt from Canaan.

the Amorites. The Amorites appear in early extrabiblical texts as the inhabitants of the northern Fertile Crescent. An Amorite kingdom arose in the north Levant along the Orontes River during the Late Bronze Age (1550–1200 BC) and collapsed along with the other Late Bronze Age cultures around 1200 BC. Amorite presence and influence is evident throughout the Levant in this period. The pre-Israelite dynasty of Jerusalem appears to have been Amorite, and was a vassal of the Egyptian pharaohs. The collapse of the Late Bronze Age cultures resulted in widespread population shifts (though not necessarily tidal waves of migration), and by 1200 BC, the land that Israel settled was far more diverse ethnically than most Bible readers recognize (ABD 1.199-202; NIDB 1.134). A number of OT passages identify a group in the region east of Jordan as Amorites (Num 21:13, 21-25; 32:39; Deut 2:24–3:8), and the term sometimes appears as a general term for the occupants of Canaan. Still, commentators puzzle over this reference and can find no oppression of the Israelites by the Amorites in the OT. In keeping with the tendency of this passage to allude to earlier portions of Judges, perhaps the text evokes 1:34-36, which states that the Amorites oppressed the Danites and drove them out of their inheritance into the hills. As a mark of the Israelites' utter failure to fulfill their conquest commission, ch 1 closes by describing the border of the Amorites, not that of Israel. The resulting position of the Danites and its consequences will occupy an inordinate amount of space: chs 13–18.

10:12 ***the Sidonians.*** No oppression by the Sidonians appears in the OT narrative up to this point, though the Sidonians are noted as one of the nations left behind by Yahweh to test Israel and contribute to Israel's education in warfare (3:3). Sidon possibly exercised some control over the northern portion of the land and might have been part of the Canaanite coalition emerging around Hazor, against which Deborah mobilized Barak (4:1-7). Younger (2002:242) correctly cautions that the author could easily allude to oppressions and deliverances not recorded in Judges.

Amalekites. This ancient nemesis of Israel (Exod 17) joined with the Moabites (3:13) and with the Midianites (7:12).

Maonites. Two places named Maon appear in the OT, but both are part of Israelite territory and hardly provide candidates for oppressors (ABD 4.512-513). The LXX has "Midian," whose Hebrew consonants resemble "Maon," possibly generating a scribal misspelling. The omission of the stunning and permanent victory over Midian seems strange, so the LXX reading "Midian" is preferable to "Maon." Another suggestion reads "Meun" instead, referring to a group possibly allied with the Midianites.

When they oppressed you. If the suggestion noted above for 10:11 is accepted, this line could simply read "oppressed you" without requiring the temporal clause.

you cried out to me for help, and I rescued you. The divine retrospective over the whole story thus far reinforces the impression that with the Jephthah-Samson block, the story enters a distinctly new stage.

10:13 ***Yet you have abandoned me and served other gods.*** The "you" in Hebrew is emphatic. Yahweh here uses the original words found both in the narrator's speech (10:6) and in Israel's plea.

I will not rescue you anymore. This is startling. Claims that Yahweh essentially was saying "you made your bed, so sleep in it" (Block 1999:347), however homiletically appealing, fail to grasp the deeper nature of the exchange.

10:14 ***Go and cry out to the gods you have chosen!*** This complaint rarely appears on the lips of Israel's God. In Jer 2:28 we read the climactic taunt, "But why not call on these gods you have made? When trouble comes, let them save you if they can! For you have as many gods as there are towns in Judah." In Deut 32:39, Yahweh, employing the covenant lawsuit form in anticipation of Israel's faithlessness, chides his people for the worthlessness of the gods they have chosen in a manner that approaches this, but he does not use this statement. This reproof signals the point of no return for that audience, which will slip away if they fail to repent.

10:15 ***Punish us as you see fit.*** Lit., "you (emphasizing the pronoun) do to us what is good in your eyes." The Israelites likely envision a range of divine responses other than mere punishment. The line conveys the idea of being reconciled to any action Yahweh might take, which sounds like complete surrender to his will, except for the next petition.

only rescue us today. The word "only" (*'ak* [TH389, ZH421]) translates a particle that, while sometimes emphatic, typically functions restrictively. Thus, "whatever else happens, this has to happen: Rescue us today." The inner contradiction of Israel surfaces: They prayed, in essence, "Thy will be done—as long as it includes you saving us today!" The time reference, "today," reinforces the note of demand. Far from sincere confession and repentance, their words express precisely the duplicity that has characterized them all along (Stone 1992:339-340).

10:16 ***Then the Israelites put aside their foreign gods and served the LORD.*** Though these acts, in isolation, might express repentance, the whole discourse preceding has generated a conflict and tension that is hardly resolved by such a hasty rearrangement of the deck chairs on their spiritual Titanic.

grieved by their misery. This line is the crux of the passage. The Hebrew reads graphically: "and his soul became short at their misery/toil"—their toil being their desperate play at religious reform. The word *nephesh* [TH5315, ZH5883], traditionally translated "soul," often appears in idioms with the verbs "be long" or "be short" to express patience and exasperation. When the "soul is short," the person has reached a limit of endurance resulting in bitter complaint and capitulation (Num 21:4), the death penalty (Zech 11:8), or a very unwise yielding to badgering (16:16) (cf. Stone 1988:319-325). Nowhere in the OT does a "shortened" soul or spirit express rekindled compassion, or that "his soul was cut to the quick" (Niditch 2008:124); rather, it expresses "complete discouragement, when endurance itself is exhausted" (Moore 1895:282). In the other instances of this idiom, a caving in, a yielding to an unwise or undesirable impulse, accompanies the exasperation. In possibly the boldest anthropomorphism in the entire OT, Yahweh is said to give up and yield to Israel's plea for relief; he gives up against his better judgment, wearily caving in like Samson to Delilah. Yahweh's reaction (even if he gives military relief) cannot be viewed positively, and forgiveness certainly is not in view. He yields, and will release them from the foe; but he will not save them or restore them to *shalom* [TH7965, ZH8934], to the wholeness of a right relationship with him.

10:17 ***At that time.*** The phrase does not appear in the Hebrew and interrupts the flow of the text, which moves from the desperate "fox-hole" prayer of the Israelites directly to the account of the Ammonites' muster for war.

gathered for war. The term for "gathered" is, pregnantly, "they were called up," using the same verb family (*tsa'aq* [TH6817, ZH7590] / *za'aq* [TH2199, ZH2410]) employed in the standardized introductions to the accounts to denote Israel's cry of desperation to Yahweh. The answer to their cry is the Ammonite call to arms.

camped in Gilead. An important thread connecting this account of a so-called major judge to the minor judges appears in the setting. This narrative concerns Gilead, the northern half of the region east of Jordan. Jair, the minor judge immediately preceding the Jephthah account, resided in this region, bestowing his name on 30 towns (cf. 10:3-5). Locating the next oppression in the territory of this positively portrayed judge serves the author's thematic movement from judges who meet the criteria exemplified by Othniel to those who increasingly do not, of which the Jephthah-Samson block is the third stage.

Mizpah. Several sites carry the name Mizpah or Mizpeh, which loosely means "lookout." A frequently noted place of sacred and military assembly in the Bible, scholars consider most of these references to "Benjaminite Mizpah," identified as Tell en-Nasbeh (see note on 20:1). Though west of Jordan, Tell en-Nasbeh does lie directly across from Gilead on the highway the Ammonites sought to control. Since every event occurring in Mizpah in this story is a communal-ritual act, the site is fitting (ABD 4.879-881). We need not look for another Mizpah except in 11:29, which refers to Mizpah of Gilead, suggesting a distinct place in that reference.

10:18 ***The leaders of Gilead.*** The Hebrew text says, literally, "The people the princes of Gilead said," placing the people in apposition with their leaders, lest the reader think the leaders do not actually speak for the people. The term *sar* [TH8269, ZH8569] appears here. It has designated Sisera, the commander of Jabin's troops (4:2, 7); the militia leaders of Issachar (5:15); the two Midianite leaders Oreb and Zeeb (7:25; 8:3); the leaders of the city of Succoth, somehow distinguished from the "elders" (8:6, 14); and Zebul, Abimelech's appointed administrator in Shechem (9:30). On the surface, the noun *sar* appears to denote a subordinate official who has been delegated military responsibilities but is answerable to others. Since "Gilead" is not a tribe in Israel but a region, all these leaders planning the resistance against Ammon would represent different kin-groups and likely answered to tribal and clan-level elders in their own communities.

Whoever attacks the Ammonites first. The wording is different, but 1:1 opens the book with a similar inquiry to Yahweh, "Which tribe should go first to attack the Canaanites?" Likewise, at the book's end (20:18), the tribes inquire regarding who should lead against the Benjaminites. The Jephthah account thus resonates with the book's beginning and end. The question, "Who will go first?" captures the essence of battle leadership in this period. These leaders were not distant bureaucrats or disengaged administrators casually ordering other men to be heroes while they attended to other matters. The leader stepped out in front of his men, first in the fray, taking the greatest risks, and reaping the greatest rewards.

He might be a brutal warlord or a noble freedom fighter, but he was a man of war, first and foremost. The text tacitly but tellingly underscores that the "princes of Gilead" were not made of that stuff—whoever would "go first" would not come from among their number! It is this, not their consultation among themselves, that demeans their deliberations.

ruler over all the people of Gilead. "Ruler" translates *ro'sh* [TH7218, ZH8031] (head). Unlike *sar*, which implies delegated authority, "head" names the person at the top of a social unit, whether the "head" of a father's house (i.e., extended family), or of a clan, or of the nation—i.e., a king (Boling 1975:195). Within the social unit and community ethos, the *ro'sh* exercised autonomous authority.

COMMENTARY

The introduction to the Jephthah story (10:6-18) marks a palpable step-down from the preceding stories (Stone 1988:469-471). The writer expanded the customary notation of Israel's evil (10:6a) by explicitly charging the nation with idolatry, listing seven deities served by Israel (10:6b). Israel actually worshiped the gods of its oppressors, omitting only Yahweh from their promiscuous devotion. With the expanded account of Israel's evil comes an ominous reference to God's anger. Yahweh's wrath burns (10:7a) for the second time in the history of the judges. Judges 2:6–3:6 had projected two kindlings of divine wrath. The first initiated Yahweh's attempt to chasten Israel with oppression and deliverance by judges. When Israel's faithlessness only deepened, a second outbreak signaled a fatal alienation of Yahweh from his people and the end of his saving victories. Likewise, in the history of the judges the first reference to divine wrath comes in the first account (3:8); the second inaugurates the final stage. Yahweh says explicitly that he will not save them.

To these two outbursts of divine wrath, two outbursts in the book itself correspond. The Othniel story reports Yahweh's wrath burning (3:8), thereby opening a series of deliverance stories. But with the Gideon story, the narrator reports that the Israelites specifically repudiated the legacy of Gideon by following the Baals and by following Abimelech (8:33-35). This refusal to heed the judge (2:17-19) has shifted the story to a deeper level of alienation from Yahweh expressed in the second outburst of divine wrath (10:7). Just as in the preface that second outburst signaled a deeper alienation from Yahweh, so in the present unit, things will take a dark turn (Stone 1988:305-307).

The gravity of the oppression Israel suffered appears in the reference to the Ammonites and the Philistines. Judges 10:6-16 introduces both the oppression by the Ammonites that occupies 10:17–12:7, and that of the Philistines who do not appear until 13:1. The loose tribal organization of Israel could not effectually resist the better organized and equipped Philistines, who became the external stimulus leading to the transformation of Israel from a tribal confederation into a monarchic state. Thus, the reference to the Philistines foreshadows the end of Israel as a kingless tribal league. Israel's outcry also betokens a darkening of the situation. The cry brought instant divine succor in the form of the divinely raised-up hero in 3:9 and 3:15 (Othniel, Ehud). In the Deborah story, a slight pause separates the emergence of salvation from Israel's plea (4:3-4), which encounters sharp prophetic rebuke in the transitional Gideon story (6:7-10). With 10:10-16, the cry contains a confession of sin (10:10b) and meets a flat divine refusal: "I will not rescue you anymore. Go and cry out to the gods you have chosen!" Israel's response exposes its duplicitous desperation: "Punish us as you see fit, only rescue us today from our enemies."

In the religious culture of the ancient Near East, any cry of desperation from someone with no remaining hope or resort, such as the orphan, the widow, the laborer denied his wage, or the debtor whose cloak was seized, was believed virtually to compel a response from any deity worth their salt. Human desperation triggered divine action. Thus, for Israel to shriek in terror, only for Yahweh to say a flat "No!," dissolved the very fabric of the ancient human conception of religion, namely, that the gods existed to secure the happiness of humanity (Stone 1988:311-318). But refuse he does, and mere religion shatters into shrapnel before the sovereign freedom of a God who will not be compelled or blackmailed. This grave statement ("I will not rescue you anymore," 10:13) corresponds to the divine decision to suspend the fulfillment of the promised settlement in the preface to the book (2:20-23) and should not be taken as a passing mood that Yahweh reverses in 10:16b. Whatever happens next, even if it be relief from the Ammonite oppression, Yahweh has clearly declared that it will not be their salvation.

In such a context, the people's actions in 10:16a can only describe a fleeting fit of foxhole fidelity, not true repentance (see note on 10:16). As noted above, the divine response in 10:16b ("he was grieved by their misery") does not portray divine compassion overruling wrath, but a shocking collapse of divine resolve. The text speaks of divine exasperation, not compassion. The Old Testament often depicts God as weary or even worn-out with his people's sin and hypocrisy (e.g., Isa 1:14; 43:24; Mal 2:17). This, like the last utterance of Yahweh in 10:13, bristles with hostility.

The episode epitomizes the impasse between Israel and Yahweh. Though Israel's previous outcries led to the emergence of a divinely sent hero, the stalemate of 10:10-16 leads to a human canvas for a leader that only exposes the unworthiness of the so-called leaders of Gilead (10:17-18), none of whom will take the lead against the foe. The career of Jephthah, even though he will be victorious, unfolds under a cloud of apostasy, alienation, and aggravation.

It should be said that some commentators castigate the leaders of Gilead for a "secular" or human approach to their search for a leader, as though it was a sign of how "Canaanized" Israel had become (Block 1999:350-351). Such accusations miss the social setting in which these events transpired. The offer of position hardly constitutes a sign of divine absence: Saul's offers of reward brought forward the young David, and Caleb's offer of his daughter flushed out the heroism of Othniel, the ideal judge. The minor judges also reflect no signs of supernatural selection, yet the text voices no criticism of them. Deborah praised the "volunteers" of Israel and the tribal leaders who took up the challenge of battle. A Canaanized Israel would have sought Baal or Asherah for salvation, as Yahweh had suggested earlier. By the same token, explicit notes that Israel "asked Yahweh" (or their omission) are not clear indicators of spiritual states. The Israelites inquire of Yahweh in 20:18, but in that context, the inquiry and even Yahweh's answer are enmeshed in a skein of amoral anarchy. So we must guard against attributing modern sins such as "secularism" (which did not even exist in Iron Age I!) to the characters. There was plenty of guilt to go around, as we shall see, but this specific action *per se* does not contribute to it.

All in all, this story bristles with theological questions. Central to them all, however, is the recognition that divine grace and love cannot be presumed upon. Israel's profligate idolatry and faithlessness had reached a point where the only deity that they did not worship was their own. Only under the pressure of oppression, with the Ammonite fist locked around their throats and the Philistine dragon about to leap from its lair, did they cry out to Yahweh. Even then, they proved arch hypocrites. The cry, "We have sinned" (10:15) resonates with Saul's repeated, but ultimately inconsequential protestations of "I have sinned" (1 Sam 15:24, 30; 26:21). In both cases, the phony penitent's hypocrisy is revealed by asking for a continuance of things as usual: Saul wants David to rejoin his entourage, begs Samuel to accompany him before the people, and Israel wants Yahweh to do whatever he wishes, as long as he saves them. Even their hysterical disposal of their foreign gods rings hollow. Yahweh yields, and will release them from the foe, but he will not save them or restore them to *shalom* [TH7965, ZH8934], to the wholeness of a right relationship with him. The story of the Gileadite so-called leaders looking for a champion, though legitimate in itself (10:17-18), stands in eerie isolation from the intense exchange between Yahweh and Israel narrated in 10:6-16—as though nothing had happened.

A delicate issue broached by this account has to do with the bold portrayal of God acting, but not in accord with his best will for his people. They hypocritically begged for relief. Yahweh refused to "save" them, but in the story to come, he will empower Jephthah, who will bring victory. This victory, however, comes at an enormous cost, and the land will not rest. One dead daughter and 42,000 dead Ephraimites will utterly negate Jephthah's accomplishment. Are there times when God gives his people what they ask for in selfishness, and that answer to prayer (however expedient in the short-term) expresses his wrath and judgment, not his compassion and salvation? When God's people fail to come to terms with the dark depths of their sin, but proceed instead to work out a "practical" solution through otherwise legitimate channels, when they seek relief instead of true integration into his purposes, where does that leave them? The text makes it clear that however responsive God is to his people, they do not control or manipulate him. God cannot be held hostage to his own promises or even to his mercy. The psalmist, writing of Israel craving meat in the wilderness, said that God "gave them their request; but sent leanness into their soul" (Ps 106:15, KJV). Instead of praying, as they did, "Punish us as you see fit, only rescue us today from our enemies," the Israelites needed to express the faith proclaimed by the three friends of Daniel before Nebuchadnezzar when faced with his fiery furnace:

> *O Nebuchadnezzar, we do not need to defend ourselves before you. If we are thrown into the blazing furnace, the God whom we serve is able to save us. He will rescue us from your power, Your Majesty.* But even if he doesn't, *we want to make it clear to you, Your Majesty, that* we will never serve your gods *or worship the gold statue you have set up (Dan 3:16-18; emphasis added).*

An Israel that turned from its lies and apostasies and cast itself on divine mercy, surrendering any hope of deliverance or relief into the hands of Yahweh, an Israel that truly repented, even without the promise of salvation before them, might have found grace that is beyond all mercy, even beyond all comprehension.

b. The victory in battle (11:1-40)

Now Jephthah of Gilead was a great warrior. He was the son of Gilead, but his mother was a prostitute. 2Gilead's wife also had several sons, and when these half brothers grew up, they chased Jephthah off the land. "You will not get any of our father's inheritance," they said, "for you are the son of a prostitute." 3So Jephthah fled from his brothers and lived in the land of Tob. Soon he had a band of worthless rebels following him.

4At about this time, the Ammonites began their war against Israel. 5When the Ammonites attacked, the elders of Gilead sent for Jephthah in the land of Tob. The elders said, 6"Come and be our commander! Help us fight the Ammonites!"

7But Jephthah said to them, "Aren't you the ones who hated me and drove me from my father's house? Why do you come to me now when you're in trouble?"

8"Because we need you," the elders replied. "If you lead us in battle against the Ammonites, we will make you ruler over all the people of Gilead."

9Jephthah said to the elders, "Let me get this straight. If I come with you and if the LORD gives me victory over the Ammonites, will you really make me ruler over all the people?"

10"The LORD is our witness," the elders replied. "We promise to do whatever you say."

11So Jephthah went with the elders of Gilead, and the people made him their ruler and commander of the army. At Mizpah, in the presence of the LORD, Jephthah repeated what he had said to the elders.

12Then Jephthah sent messengers to the king of Ammon, asking, "Why have you come out to fight against my land?"

13The king of Ammon answered Jephthah's messengers, "When the Israelites came out of Egypt, they stole my land from the Arnon River to the Jabbok River and all the way to the Jordan. Now then, give back the land peaceably."

14Jephthah sent this message back to the Ammonite king:

> 15"This is what Jephthah says: Israel did not steal any land from Moab or Ammon. 16When the people of Israel arrived at Kadesh on their journey from Egypt after crossing the Red Sea,* 17they sent messengers to the king of Edom asking for permission to pass through his land. But their request was denied. Then they asked the king of Moab for similar permission, but he wouldn't let them pass through either. So the people of Israel stayed in Kadesh.
>
> 18"Finally, they went around Edom and Moab through the wilderness. They traveled along Moab's eastern border and camped on the other side of the Arnon River. But they never once crossed the Arnon River into Moab, for the Arnon was the border of Moab.
>
> 19"Then Israel sent messengers to King Sihon of the Amorites, who ruled from Heshbon, asking for permission to cross through his land to get to their destination. 20But King Sihon didn't trust Israel to pass through his land. Instead, he mobilized his army at Jahaz and attacked them. 21But the LORD, the God of Israel, gave his people victory over King Sihon. So Israel took control of all the land of the Amorites, who lived in that region, 22from the Arnon River to the Jabbok River, and from the eastern wilderness to the Jordan.
>
> 23"So you see, it was the LORD, the God of Israel, who took away the land from the Amorites and gave it to Israel. Why, then, should we give it back to you? 24You keep whatever your god Chemosh gives you, and we will keep whatever the LORD our God gives us. 25Are you any better than Balak son of Zippor, king of Moab? Did he try to make a case against Is-

rael for disputed land? Did he go to
war against them?
[26]"Israel has been living here for
300 years, inhabiting Heshbon and its
surrounding settlements, all the way
to Aroer and its settlements, and in all
the towns along the Arnon River. Why
have you made no effort to recover it
before now? [27]Therefore, I have not
sinned against you. Rather, you have
wronged me by attacking me. Let the
LORD, who is judge, decide today which
of us is right—Israel or Ammon."

[28]But the king of Ammon paid no atten-
tion to Jephthah's message.

[29]At that time the Spirit of the LORD came
upon Jephthah, and he went throughout
the land of Gilead and Manasseh, includ-
ing Mizpah in Gilead, and from there he
led an army against the Ammonites. [30]And
Jephthah made a vow to the LORD. He
said, "If you give me victory over the
Ammonites, [31]I will give to the LORD what-
ever comes out of my house to meet me
when I return in triumph. I will sacrifice it
as a burnt offering."
[32]So Jephthah led his army against the
Ammonites, and the LORD gave him vic-
tory. [33]He crushed the Ammonites, devas-
tating about twenty towns from Aroer to
an area near Minnith and as far away as
Abel-keramim. In this way Israel defeated
the Ammonites.
[34]When Jephthah returned home to
Mizpah, his daughter came out to meet
him, playing on a tambourine and danc-
ing for joy. She was his one and only child;
he had no other sons or daughters.
[35]When he saw her, he tore his clothes in
anguish. "Oh, my daughter!" he cried out.
"You have completely destroyed me!
You've brought disaster on me! For I have
made a vow to the LORD, and I cannot take
it back."
[36]And she said, "Father, if you have
made a vow to the LORD, you must do to
me what you have vowed, for the LORD has
given you a great victory over your ene-
mies, the Ammonites. [37]But first let me do
this one thing: Let me go up and roam in
the hills and weep with my friends for two
months, because I will die a virgin."
[38]"You may go," Jephthah said. And he
sent her away for two months. She and
her friends went into the hills and wept
because she would never have children.
[39]When she returned home, her father
kept the vow he had made, and she died
a virgin.
So it has become a custom in Israel
[40]for young Israelite women to go away
for four days each year to lament the fate
of Jephthah's daughter.

11:16 Hebrew *sea of reeds.*

NOTES

11:1 *Jephthah.* The name Jephthah is probably the short form for Jephthah-El, "God opens [the womb]," not a surprising name for a firstborn son, but an extremely ironic name for a man repudiated by his people and deprived of any descendants. The short form of the name does not imply uncertainty about the deity whom Jephthah served any more than it would with Caleb, Ehud, Deborah, Barak, Jael, or Gideon.

of Gilead. The term "Gilead" in the OT carries various usages. Most frequently it names the region east of the Jordan between the north end of the Dead Sea and the south end of the Sea of Galilee, from the Jordan and east about 40 miles to the high plateau country of the Bashan (Smith 1931:603-620). Scholars suggest an etymology meaning "curly (hair), difficult (terrain)," apt for the hills and forests of Gilead. The term also denotes the occupants of the region collectively (cf. 5:17). Gilead held strategic importance both for its control of the north-south trade route known as the King's Highway and for its produce of grapes, olives, and a precious balm. The OT stresses the integration of Gilead and the Bashan into greater Israel, also testifying to the fragility of the tie (cf. Josh 22:19). The region's obvious importance to ancient Israel is often missed by modern readers (ABD 2.1020-1022). Despite the focus on Gilead, the battle itself seems to occur in the region allotted to the tribe of Reuben (cf. 11:33). Reuben seems very early in Israelite history to have exercised great influence, but soon faded (Cross 1998). Our story's failure to mention Reuben (or Gad, for that matter), though significant action occurs in those regions, suggests Reuben had fallen from its early preeminence by the time of the book's composition.

great warrior. Heb., *gibbor khayil* [TH1368/2428, ZH1475/2657], traditionally translated "mighty man of valor," designates a substantial, influential member of the community, typically a person skilled and bloodied in battle, but often also a respected person of wealth and standing. Possibly their military valor gained them a grant of land, thus connecting valor and wealth, making them warrior aristocracy (Gordon 1965:195-298; Armerding 1968:239-253). Not one of the 40 other occurrences of the phrase in the OT refers to an unworthy person. To suggest that the narrator's characterization "hardly commends him spiritually for the role of savior of Israel" (Block 1988:50) misses the sociological import of this term and assumes a dichotomy between the "spiritual" and practical worlds that the OT does not share. Sometimes status as *gibbor khayil* is contrasted with some unfortunate circumstance, such as Naaman's leprosy, but the term itself unreservedly connotes dignity and honor. The narrator presents Jephthah "as a person who inspires sympathy" (Soggin 1981:208), hardly the "bramble in the tradition of Abimelech" (Block 1999:351).

son of Gilead. The author, before identifying Jephthah's mother, identifies Jephthah clearly as Gilead's son, preparing the reader to see the actions of the other sons of Gilead in disinheriting Jephthah in a negative light. The sudden use of Gilead as the proper name of an individual is disconcerting since it typically denotes a region or its inhabitants, though the OT genealogies name a Gilead (e.g., Num 26:29; 36:1; 1 Chr 2:21-23; cf. ABD 2.1019-1020). Perhaps by naming him Gilead the author suggests Jephthah's father was an eminent leader in the region. For the era of the judges, and for this kind of literature, such naming practices would not be surprising.

prostitute. Though *zonah* [TH2181B, ZH2390] can denote a prostitute, it also signifies any woman having sex outside of marriage (ABD 5.505-510). The later reference to Jephthah as the "son of another woman" suggests his origin in an irregular union, not prostitution. By naming Jephthah the "son of Gilead," the author signals that Gilead had in fact claimed Jephthah as his son (Younger 2002:248-249). The author contrasts Jephthah's inherent quality as a leader with the unfortunate circumstances of his parentage. He also contrasts Jephthah with the "legitimate" but unheroic tribal militia leaders in 10:17-18 who cannot gather the courage to lead the charge against the Ammonites. Those of social legitimacy lack the caliber to lead; the man with no status is the "great warrior." Such is the egalitarianism and elitism of valor in a dark age of social collapse and reorganization.

11:2 *half brothers.* Though evident from the context, the Hebrew does not make the distinction "half brothers" in the text. They are simply called Jephthah's brothers.

they chased Jephthah off the land. The biblical author describes not a violent act, but a judicial stripping of Jephthah's status as the firstborn son of Gilead, resulting in his banishment. In a tribal society, such "shunning" deprives a person of every possible support the community can offer, forcing on him the life of an outlaw (Moore 1895:287).

You will not get any of our father's inheritance. The point is sharper than the NLT suggests. Rather than using a construction parallel to "any of," the Hebrew directly identifies the "father's house" as the object of inheritance. In the OT, "father's house" embraces the extended family in conjunction with its inherited property. As the eldest, Jephthah was to become the head of the family estate; this was something the "legitimate" sons would not tolerate because they would have to continue living on the same compound while having to defer to Jephthah as the *ro'sh beth-'ab* [TH7218, ZH8031], the head of the "father's house."

you are the son of a prostitute. The term "prostitute" does not occur in this verse (see note on 11:1), only "another woman." The expression, *'ishah 'akhereth* [TH802/312, ZH851/337], simply indicates an additional wife (cf. Exod 21:10; 1 Chr 2:26). Perhaps Gilead's first wife bore no children, so he sired a son with "another woman" (cf. Abraham, Sarah, and Hagar) and acknowledged his offside offspring. Subsequently his legal wife bore sons who later successfully challenged Jephthah's inheritance right. Wrangling over inheritance is well known in the literature of the ancient Near East. The outlines of this story are familiar and perennial: Shunning deprived Jephthah of the survival resources of the clan, leaving him landless and without legal protection. Thus, he had to flee, seeking his fortune wherever he could find it; he was a leader in exile (Matthews 2004:117). Readers familiar with ancient literature recall stories such as the biography of Idri-mi (fifteenth century BC), ruler of Alalakh in Syria, who was expelled from his home and had to live in the cracks and shadows among tribes of nomadic warriors until he was finally reinstated (COS 1.148). Similarly, the Egyptian tale of Sinuhe (COS 1.38), though not about inheritance, depicts a fine warrior who flees his homeland, lives among nomadic peoples where he distinguishes himself as a warrior, and finally returns home with honor.

11:3 *the land of Tob.* The word "Tob" means "good" in Hebrew. This place is possibly documented by Pharaoh Thutmose III in the mid-1400s BC as *t-b*. Archaeologists have tentatively identified Tob as Et-Tayibeh, located about 40 miles east of the Jordan River in modern Syria. Gilead rises from the Jordan valley to 2,500–3,000 feet above sea level and descends eastward until the rolling hill country intersects a wide lava flow running from Mount Hermon southeast for about 80 miles. This basalt plateau called "the Bashan" features rich volcanic soil ideally suited for cattle. Flat, rugged volcanic outcroppings break up the terrain, making for challenging travel. Some places feature ground so harsh not even camels travel there. "Tob" sat right on the seam between the hills of Gilead and this basaltic plateau and, more importantly, on the boundary of Ammonite territory. Thus, assuming an outlaw style of life, Jephthah could "operate" and reside in the nicer clime of Gilead, but hightail it east to the badlands when the Ammonite posse came hunting.

band of worthless rebels. Heb., *'anashim reqim* [TH7386, ZH8199] (empty men) denotes essentially disinherited or disenfranchised men (cf. note on 9:4), not necessarily immoral or criminal (Block 1999:352; Younger 2002:249). Such might be good men thrown into hard times, or evil men; but "empty" denotes their social standing, not their character (Burney 1920:308-309). Finding in Jephthah a man they could admire and follow as a "mighty man of valor," they joined him.

following him. Lit., "and they went out with him." The reference likely is to foraging and raiding along the Ammonite and Aramean border country, much like David in exile pillaged the Philistines.

11:4 *At about this time, the Ammonites began their war against Israel.* The author here catches the reader up to the point of action (10:17) that was temporarily set aside in order to provide the flashback on Jephthah's background.

11:5 *the elders of Gilead.* The elders constitute a different group than the "leaders of Gilead" in 10:17-18. Those men bore the delegated responsibility of organizing and leading the tribal militia but decided that rather than lead, they would canvas for someone else to do the job. The "elders" would be the senior heads of households and clan leaders, likely beyond fighting age, who provided wisdom and moral leadership. With their militia leaders no better than tin soldiers, they had to find a leader of proven martial valor (Boling 1975:199; Matthews 2004:119-120). Perhaps this sort of internal wrangling and paralysis lies behind Deborah's twice-repeated complaint about the indecision of the Reubenites, who like Jephthah's kinsmen, were occupants of Transjordan, and whose internal divisions prevented them from joining the battle against Sisera (5:15-16).

sent for Jephthah. Though he was banished, apparently his kin had remained aware of his location and maintained some form of contact. The text does not portray a "live" conversation between the elders and Jephthah. The verb "sent" implies the dispatch of messengers.

11:6 *commander.* Heb., *qatsin* [TH7101, ZH7903], a word appearing only 12 times in the OT, most often designating a subordinate level leader. The elders took an opening bargaining position, offering less than "head of all the inhabitants of Gilead" (HALOT 2.1122, s.v. *qatsin*; TDOT 13.86-88).

11:7 *Aren't you the ones who hated me and drove me from my father's house?* Since the "father's house" was the ancestral heritage or inheritance, Jephthah was saying, "You disinherited me!" In a tribal society, leadership and authority derive from one's location in the genealogical structure, as seen in Gideon's protest that his family was the least in his tribe. Jephthah was not merely expressing resentment at having been rejected, but stated the plain fact that the very people seeking his aid had denied him the very position and stature needed to provide it.

Why do you come to me now when you're in trouble? Recall Yahweh's reply to the importunate Israelites (10:13), when he directed them to appeal to the gods they had chosen instead of him. The people's rejection of Yahweh followed by their desperate and groundless appeal to him for aid parallels their interaction with Jephthah.

11:8 *ruler over all the people of Gilead.* With Jephthah's rejection of their offer, the elders offered the full extent of the pact of 10:17-18, agreeing he would become "head" or chief ruler over all the occupants of the region of Gilead (Boling 1975:198; Soggin 1981:208; Matthews 2004:118-120).

11:9 *If I come with you.* The NLT here glosses over an important nuance. Jephthah literally says, "if you are causing me to return," meaning restoration to his former status. Thus, Jephthah might indeed have been the legitimate heir of one of the paramount chiefs, if not the paramount, in the region, and his return to lead in battle would necessarily entail a restoration of his status.

will you really make me ruler over all the people? Jephthah ensures that the role being offered is indeed that of chief over the whole region. Was Jephthah being arrogant or power-hungry, exploiting the desperation of his people? Jephthah probably only asked for what was rightfully his by birth in a lineage-based society. In addition, these Israelites were the same idolatrous, fickle, shallow people portrayed in 10:10-16, with whom Yahweh himself lost patience. Jephthah, like Yahweh, and even Jesus, "didn't trust them, because he knew human nature. No one needed to tell him what mankind is really like" (John 2:24-25). If these leaders represent the duplicity and hypocrisy expressed by "Israel" in 10:6-16 (cf. note on 10:18), it is puzzling that some commentators (Block; Younger) still seem more sympathetic with the elders and censure Jephthah as one driven only by self-interest.

11:10 *The LORD is our witness.* Lit., "Yahweh will be listening between us, if we do not act according to your words." This is the language of sacred oath-taking. The elders here again evoke the memory of Israel's desperate promises and penitent behavior (10:15-16) after Yahweh's refusal of salvation. Appealing to Yahweh in an oath formula is not manipulation (Block 1999:356) but rather exposure of oneself to his retribution if the oath is violated.

11:11 ***the people made him their ruler and commander of the army.*** "The people" confer both titles on Jephthah, marking the broadest possible recognition in a pattern that began with the promise of the commanders (10:18), moving to the offer made by the elders (11:5-6), to appointment by the people. Jephthah next turns to the sacred domain, not moving forward without divine confirmation.

At Mizpah, in the presence of the LORD, Jephthah repeated what he had said to the elders. The phrase "in the presence of the LORD" indicates a solemn, sacred setting for the pact. Whether the phrase implies the presence of the ark, an altar, or a sanctuary remains uncertain. Much depends on how consistently Israel enforced the demand for a single valid sanctuary (cf. Josh 22), which the writer of Judges believes was in Shiloh (18:31). At least it was a place of solemn, sacred assembly, though possibly not a full cult site.

11:12 ***Jephthah sent messengers to the king of Ammon.*** The narrative of Jephthah's negotiations with Ammon reflects serious political awareness (Boling 1975:202-205; Block 1999:359-363). Far from being extraneous, this exchange sets the conflict in a historical and legal context, demonstrating the application of an earlier biblical tradition (Num 20–24) to a subsequent situation and revealing Israel's thought about its territorial claims and rights. This passage also sets the context for Jephthah's character. Far from being rash, hotheaded, or impulsive, Jephthah proved to be a tough, but patient negotiator. Rather than charge off to war, Jephthah sought first to avoid bloodshed and establish the legitimacy of his actions in the region by negotiation.

11:13 ***they stole my land from the Arnon River to the Jabbok River and all the way to the Jordan.*** The king of Ammon rightly described his territory from north to south, but he could not rightly claim the territory all the way west to the Jordan, since that had been controlled by the Amorites, and before them, apparently the Moabites. In fact, a complex history of conquest had made this territory contested (cf. Num 21:26; Josh 13:15-28). The king of Ammon was apparently asserting an earlier claim based on a merging of Ammonite ambitions and earlier Moabite claims (Keil 1863:380-381; Boling 1975:203-204).

11:15 ***This is what Jephthah says: Israel did not steal any land from Moab or Ammon.*** Jephthah switches between Moab and Ammon throughout this exchange. Some suggest Jephthah was offering nothing but propaganda quilted together from half-truths, even compromising Israel's beliefs (Block 1999:362). Others accuse him of theological deviation (Younger 2002:256-259). The text recognizes what scholars often forget: the tangled skein of territorial claims and counterclaims—and the long memories—of tribal societies. By introducing Moab into the discussion, Jephthah put the king of Ammon on notice that he was aware of the larger regional conflicts and would not confine the discussion to Ammon and Israel.

11:16 ***When the people of Israel arrived at Kadesh on their journey from Egypt after crossing the Red Sea.*** In rebutting the Ammonite king's description of Israel's actions (11:13), Jephthah displays detailed knowledge of Israel's history and traditions, which is rare in the book of Judges (Schneider 2000:172). However his actions might be interpreted later in the story, they cannot be ascribed to ignorance.

11:17 ***they sent messengers to the king of Edom.*** Jephthah created a set of parallels between the nations defeated by Israel and the Ammonites. Reference to Israelite messengers, for example, could not have been missed by the king of Ammon, who had an Israelite messenger reciting the story to him. The story will echo crucial phrases and terms from Num 20–21, as seen in the following: 11:17 // Num 20:14-21, 27; 11:18 // Num 21:4, 10-13; 11:19 // Num 21:21-32; 11:20 // Num 21:23; 11:21 // Num 21:24; 11:24 // Num 21:29; 11:25 // Num 22:2; 11:26 // Num 21:25-26; 11:30 // Num 21:1-3. A parallel emerges between Jephthah and Moses as leaders of the Israelites during their respective eras. Also, these passages report victories that, in the book of Numbers, signal the end of the era of judgment and curse on the "old" generation and the dawning of the era of blessing and victory for the "new" generation. Such parallels reflect positively on Jephthah. Such a series of resonances also call attention to the last note of the series, namely the vow (11:30-31).

11:19 ***Then Israel sent messengers to King Sihon of the Amorites, who ruled from Heshbon.*** In this verse and through 11:23, Jephthah's message summarizes a narrative found in Num 21:21-32. Heshbon lies 15 miles east of the Jordan, in line with the northern tip of the Dead Sea, in the region claimed by the king of Ammon. Jephthah clarifies how that region had been held previously by the Amorites, in the person of Sihon. In this statement, Jephthah neatly undercuts the "legal" basis of the Ammonite claim.

Arnon River gorge—site of conflict between King Sihon and Israel

11:20 ***But King Sihon didn't trust Israel.*** This is a somewhat unusual use of the verb "trust" (*he'emin* [TH539, ZH586]). The parallel passages (Num 21:23; Deut 2:30) have, respectively, "Sihon would not permit (*natan* [TH5414, ZH5989])" and "Sihon was not willing (*'abah* [TH14, ZH14])." In this verse, Codex Vaticanus reflects the MT, but Codex Alexandrinus, taken by most scholars as the most reliable Greek witness to the text of Judges, has *ouk ēthelēsen* "he was not willing," possibly representing the Hebrew verb *ma'en* [TH3985, ZH4412], "to refuse," easily confused with the root for "trust" (*'mn*), though the negative particle *lo'* would remain unexplained. The translation "Sihon refused to allow Israel to pass" might be preferable (Burney 1920:312). However, Soggin (1981:210) makes the intriguing suggestion that the verb translated "trust" can also mean "give assurance, safe passage," which fits this context.

he mobilized his army at Jahaz and attacked. Jephthah related Israel's "conquest" of Transjordan as a defensive action.

11:21 ***But the LORD, the God of Israel, gave his people victory over King Sihon.*** Jephthah consistently relates the past to Yahweh's actions. His argument with the king of Ammon centers not on Israel's rights, achievements, or prerogatives, but on Yahweh, the God of Israel.

Israel took control of all the land of the Amorites. By calling this region "the land of the Amorites," Jephthah reverses the Ammonite king's claim.

11:22 ***from the Arnon River to the Jabbok River, and from the eastern wilderness to the Jordan.*** Jephthah here accurately describes the extent of Israel's territorial claims. "The eastern wilderness" would be a point somewhat east of the King's Highway, 25–30 miles east of the Jordan. He accepted the Ammonites' claims to the territory east of the highway between the two rivers noted.

11:24 ***You keep whatever your god Chemosh gives you, and we will keep whatever the LORD our God gives us.*** Jephthah did not take the opportunity to debate the philosophical fine points of abstract monotheism versus polytheism. He speaks of Chemosh on the same level as he does Yahweh, rhetorically accepting the other party's gods, just as the first commandment tacitly accepts the existence of other gods when prohibiting Israel from having any other gods before Yahweh. Jephthah clearly asserts the supremacy of Yahweh.

Accusing Jephthah of syncretism or "contempt for his own theological traditions" (Block 1999:362) reads too much into the text. Jephthah's words dug deep into the ego of the Ammonite king.

your god Chemosh. First Kings 11:5 suggests the Ammonites served "Milcom," (cf. KJV) not "Chemosh," who was actually the god of the neighboring Moabites. Some suggest Jephthah made a blunder here (Younger 2002:255-259), but he probably did not. (1) Jephthah could have been insinuating that whatever the Ammonites had, they had it only by the permission of the god worshiped by their more powerful neighbor, Moab. (2) The Ammonites might well have venerated Chemosh as a war-god. Despite having national gods, these nations were not monotheistic like Israel. Ammon might well have honored Chemosh in certain situations. The ninth-century-BC Moabite Stone shows clearly that Chemosh was celebrated as a god who gave victory in warfare (Arnold and Beyer 2002:160-162; ANET 320-321). (3) A pact between Ammon and Moab, who are often paired, could have made their respective gods party to their mutual territorial claims. As the last of the early Iron Age tribal states to emerge, Ammon had to carve out its niche over against well-established competitors on every side. Ironically, Ehud's defeat of Moab (ch 3) and Gideon's trouncing of Midian (chs 7–8) opened the door for the emergence of the Ammonite state.

11:25 ***Are you any better than Balak son of Zippor, king of Moab?*** Here Jephthah's message alludes to events reported in Num 22–24.

Did he try to make a case against Israel for disputed land? The Hebrew verb *rib* [TH7378, ZH8189] is used here, which often denotes a formal legal complaint or charge.

Did he go to war against them? Having ended his previous argument by speaking of what Yahweh and Chemosh had done, Jephthah aptly now turns to Israel's spiritual triumph over the Moabites, who, rather than persisting in fruitless military action (cf. Josh 24:9), hired a famous shaman, Balaam, to curse them (Num 22–24). Balaam's attempts to curse Israel, however, produced only blessing (Num 24:10-13). Jephthah stressed not Israel's territorial prerogatives, but the action of Yahweh on Israel's behalf. If the great king of Moab respected Yahweh, then how much more the upstart Ammonite sheikh?

11:26 ***Israel has been living here for 300 years.*** In a fascinating later parallel recorded on the Moabite Stone, King Mesha of Moab notes that the "men of Gad" (often another name for Gilead) had "settled the land of Atharot from of old" (ANET 320-321). Their long tenure in the land, however, did not stop Mesha from slaughtering them and seizing their territory (Arnold and Beyer 2002:162). The 300-year figure has stirred debate because the current evidence for Ammon's emergence as a nation and the surrounding historical context place Jephthah around 1075 BC. Those who place the Exodus in 1446 BC and take this number to precisely date Jephthah to 1146 BC encounter problems because the date is too early for this narrative. Advocates of a 1280 BC date for the Exodus can make sense of the archaeological and historical context, but cannot fit 300 years into the chronology of the period. Readers affirming the veracity of the biblical record cannot dismiss the question. Christian belief in the reliability of Scripture, however, extends only to the affirmations intended by the inspired authors themselves, not necessarily to the statements made by characters in the narratives. The biblical narrator truthfully reports what Jephthah said without endorsing Jephthah's chronology, which could well have been exaggerated. Coincidentally, adding up all the years of oppression and years of the judges' rule up to the Ammonite oppression yields 301 years (Moore 1895:296-297). This coincidence is not relevant to Jephthah's statement, however, which claims 300 years for the time from Moses to his own day.

inhabiting Heshbon . . . to Aroer . . . the Arnon River. Jephthah describes accurately the territory occupied after the victories over Sihon and Og. The settlement, or more likely, fortress, of Aroer lay on the north bank of the Arnon River, which flows into the Dead Sea from the east halfway down its length (ABD 1.399-400). The line from Heshbon to Aroer follows exactly the King's Highway, linking Damascus in the north to ports in the south. Moab claimed territory south of the Arnon, claims Israel honored.

Why have you made no effort to recover it before now? Jephthah exposed the reality that this newly emerging state faced almost no open doors for claiming territory, trade routes, and territory for expansion, and thus must trump up a casus belli with Israel as the easiest target. That plan was working until Jephthah took the reins.

11:27 ***I have not sinned against you. Rather, you have wronged me.*** The analogy between Yahweh and Jephthah increases in this verse. The word *khata'* [TH2398, ZH2627], translated "sin," appears only four times in Judges, and only in the Jephthah story with the meaning "sin" (the literal, marksmanship-oriented meaning of "missing the target" appears in 20:16). Israel confessed twice to Yahweh "we have sinned against you" in 10:10, 15, and here Jephthah declares he has not sinned against Ammon. Jephthah associates Ammon with Sihon and Og, who rebuffed Israel's diplomatic efforts and attacked, only to be defeated and forfeit their territory.

Let the LORD, who is judge, decide today which of us is right. This is the only time in the book of Judges that Yahweh is declared to be "the judge" (*hashopet* [TH8199A, ZH9149]). By putting matters into the hands of Israel's God, Yahweh, Jephthah unambiguously stated that, short of the Ammonites desisting from their attacks on Israel, war was inevitable. Here also Jephthah stated his own theological view: Yahweh alone is the judge who disposes the affairs and conflicts of nations.

11:28 ***But the king of Ammon paid no attention to Jephthah's message.*** The Ammonite king's refusal to heed makes war inevitable (Keil 1863:384). In none of this has Jephthah behaved rashly or harshly, though he has proven a formidable negotiator.

11:29 ***At that time the Spirit of the LORD came upon Jephthah.*** God's Spirit "happens to" Jephthah (cf. note on 3:10), validating his leadership, since he, like Gideon, had a vulnerable position in the normal hierarchy of authority in the community. This idiom expressing the Spirit's possession of Jephthah appears elsewhere in the book only with Othniel (Matthews 2004:123-124). This resonance with the standard-bearer of the book accentuates the narrative's positive portrayal of Jephthah up to his vow (Boling 1975:207).

he went throughout the land. "Went throughout" (*'abar* [TH5674, ZH6296]) appears three times in the Hebrew of this verse, where it appears to possess a specialized function signifying a "muster tour," in which a leader combs the land, building up popular support and gathering a militia.

Gilead and Manasseh. Half of the tribe of Manasseh had settled east of Jordan in Gilead (Num 32). Apparently, the similarity of territory between Gilead on the east and Ephraim-Manasseh on the west engendered a commonality of outlook and interest. At one point in David's battle against Absalom, Gilead is called "the forest of Ephraim" (2 Sam 18:6-8), again showing the sense of community across the river. Perhaps this explains the Ephraimite annoyance at not having been called up to battle (12:1-6).

including Mizpah in Gilead. The location of Mizpah in Gilead remains uncertain. The context clearly demands a location east of the Jordan. The story of Josh 22 so stresses the prohibition of sacrifice east of the Jordan, the biblical author could hardly pass over reference to a ritual or cultic site functioning east of the Jordan without some word of criticism or context. Mizpah in Gilead could have been a place of sacred assembly, but not sacrifice.

11:30 ***And Jephthah made a vow to the LORD.*** Block (1999:365) notes this is the only time Jephthah actually speaks to Yahweh, and argues that he is attempting to manipulate God. But is the frequency of a character's speech to God a sign of the author's religious endorsement? Neither Othniel, the ideal judge, nor Ehud, the judge procuring the longest period of peace, is depicted addressing Yahweh, yet they receive the full approval of the author. Nor does the author depict Deborah or Barak praying prior to the battle against Sisera (ch 4). Jael, the heroine of ch 4, slays Sisera without any prompting from or interaction with God, but receives Deborah's praise in ch 5 as fulfilling the divine plan. Thus, the presence or absence of converse with God in a narrative cannot be adduced in isolation to determine the author's religious evaluation of a character. Such emphases likely derive from whether the literary genre employed by the author emphasizes the overt role of the divine (e.g., Exod 2–16) or, though equally theological, stresses the role of human actions, behind and through which God works in a hidden manner (von Rad 1980:139-159). To evaluate these ancient characters by a modern standard of piety risks misunderstanding them and missing the points being made by the author. Still, readers rightly pause here, wondering just why Jephthah made this vow (see commentary below).

If you give me victory over the Ammonites. The story in this chapter echoes many passages from the account in Num 20–21 (see note on 11:17), which also includes Transjordan victories. The wording of the vow echoes the words of Israel's vow in Num 21:1-3 as they went to battle the king of Arad. The "then" clause of the vow in Numbers was a promise to utterly annihilate the enemy and his cities, whereas the "then" clause of Jephthah's is to give to the Lord whatever comes out of his house.

11:31 ***I will give to the LORD.*** Lit., "it will belong to Yahweh." The NLT's dynamic equivalence rendering here rearranges the order of the statements in Jephthah's vow, which confuses the interpretation on a critical point. The exact sequence of his statements, so vital to understanding the vow, is given here in a woodenly literal translation to clarify the statements: "If you indeed put the sons of Ammon in my hand, and/then it shall be, the one coming out, that comes out of the doors of my house to meet me upon my return in peace from the sons of Ammon, and he/it shall become Yahweh's, and/or I will offer up him/it as a burnt offering."

The phrase "he/it shall become Yahweh's" (NLT, "I will give to the LORD") comes immediately before the statement about presenting a burnt offering. The connection between these two clauses controls how the vow is understood, making their separation in the translation a barrier to comprehension. Short of a burnt offering, what might "it shall become Yahweh's" signify? One answer comes from another biblical story of a vow, 1 Sam 1, where Hannah vows that if Yahweh gives her a son, "I will give him back to you. He will be yours for his entire lifetime" (1 Sam 1:11). In this case, a human being belonging to Yahweh due to a vow becomes a permanent servant of Yahweh, subject to whatever limitations that vocation might impose.

whatever comes. Jephthah does not say "whatever comes first" but simply "that which comes." Since the Latin Vulgate translation in the fourth century AD, which added *primus* in the translation, readers assume "first," probably rightly. We do well, though, to monitor how deeply our prejudices mask the text. The Hebrew has a repetition, with a participle "the one coming out" followed by a relative clause with the identical sense, "that which will come out." Either a scribe has combined two slightly different, but equivalent readings, or the statement is emphatic. The NLT's "whatever" (rather than "whoever" since the Hebrew makes no distinction between the terms) suggests that Jephthah did not consciously anticipate a human as the object of the vow.

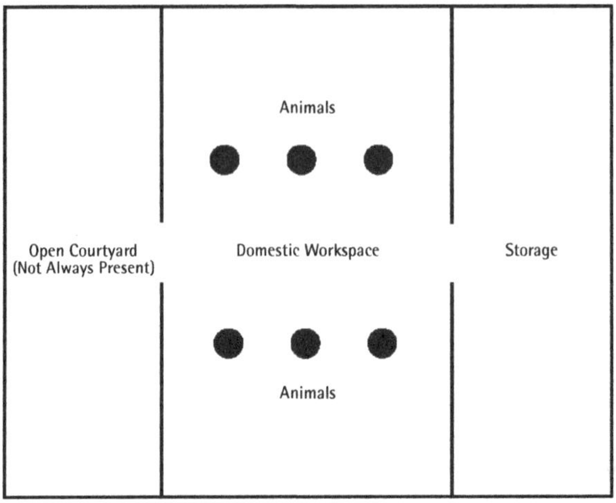

out of my house. Jephthah could not have long occupied this house, having only recently moved to Mizpah. Probably he had reclaimed his familial farm, denied him when his kinsmen drove him out. Under that scenario, the "house" could have been a compound with two or more "pillared houses" and other typical Iron Age installations such as a baking oven, handmills, water cistern, etc., surrounded by a low wall (King and Stager 2001:18). On this compound would have lived Jephthah's unmarried siblings, his married brothers, their wives, and children along with their animals and possessions. Jephthah says lit. "the doors of my house," meaning the doors on Jephthah's personal house or, more likely, the entrance into the compound itself. Some think he could only have imagined a human, since moderns can hardly imagine a sheep or goat meandering out of a house (cf. Moore 1895:300). But if "house" denotes the compound as a whole, this problem disappears. Also, the typical Israelite pillared (or "four-room") house featured a back room with three long parallel rooms at right angles. Two rows of pillars divided these three longer rooms. The side rooms stabled animals, which were brought in at night or during times of danger such as warfare. Jephthah could have anticipated that his animals would be kept in the house until the outcome of the battle was known. The verbal forms used here are all masculine singulars, but Hebrew has no fixed form for undetermined gender, using either masculine or feminine forms, so this point should not be pressed.

to meet me. Since the complete idiom "go out . . . to meet" is used only of humans, some claim Jephthah here betrays his intention to sacrifice a human. But the two verbs each can be used of nonhumans, and "meet" (*qara'* [TH7122, ZH7925]) is used also of a lion (14:5), a horse (Job 39:21), and Sheol (Isa 14:9).

when I return in triumph. The NLT's "in triumph" translates well *beshalom*, "in peace." The term *shalom* [TH7965, ZH8934] does not equate with the modern English "peace," but rather denotes the restoration of the health and balance of the community. This can occur through reconciliation, of course, but also through restitution or retribution. Clearly the latter is what Jephthah had in mind, as did Gideon in his retort to the men of Succoth (cf. note on 8:9).

I will sacrifice it as a burnt offering. The "burnt offering" (*'olah* [TH5930, ZH6592]) had strict requirements. The sacrificial animal was killed, bled, skinned, cut up in a specific way, and then the parts were arranged on a legitimate altar in prescribed order. The animal was then burned entirely, with the worshiper receiving nothing back. Leviticus 1 specifies that only perfect male animals may be offered as burnt offerings, and they must be free of imperfections. Yahweh would hardly have been honored by violating the standards of the offering. In Hebrew this sentence follows "it shall belong to Yahweh" with only the conjunction *we-* [TH2050.1, ZH2256] linking the two clauses. The usage could be consequential or explicative ("and/thus I will offer") or alternative ("or I will offer"). Jephthah might be saying he will dedicate who/what meets him to Yahweh, or, if it meets the standards of the *'olah*, offer it up as a burnt offering. It is easy to imagine other things meeting him not suitable for offerings: A donkey or dog, for example, or anything that had a blemish or imperfection, would fail to qualify for this offering; nor, incidentally, would any female creature! Some scholars link the sacrifice with the "ban" (*kherem* [TH2764, ZH3051]), the extermination of all the occupants of a city, but they fail to note the absence of the *kherem* in chs 3–16. Additionally, the ranges of signification of *kherem* and *'olah* (whole-burnt offering) do not overlap. Something "banned" is not the same as something "sent up" (*'olah*). Those determined to see Jephthah's daughter burn typically dismiss these considerations as attempts to sanitize the text; but needlessly attempting to criminalize a character is equally poor interpretation.

11:32 ***the LORD gave him victory.*** In one of the shortest battle accounts in the entire book, the author unreservedly affirms Jephthah's divinely granted victory. Schneider (2000:176) rightly notes that the vastly disproportionate space given to the battle versus the processes surrounding Jephthah's rise points to leadership dynamics as a primary theme of the story. This line uses the terminology from the condition of Jephthah's original agreement with the elders in 11:9: Yahweh "gives" (*natan* [TH5414, ZH5989]) the enemy into Jepthah's hand. The idiom "give . . . into the hand of" is also used in Jephthah's summary of Israel's victory over Sihon (11:21), and in his vow (11:30). The author aligned Yahweh's actions both with the promises made by the elders, the precedent cited by Jephthah, and his vow.

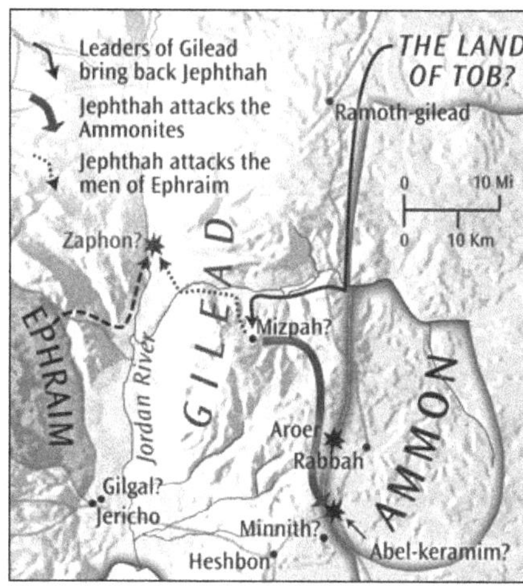

Jephthah's Travels

11:33 ***twenty towns from Aroer to an area near Minnith and as far away as Abel-keramim.*** Aroer, noted above, lies on the Arnon River, the traditional northern boundary of Moab (ABD 1.10-11). Minnith and Abel-keramim remain uncertain (ABD 4.482). Despite these uncertain identifications, archaeologists working in the region have excavated several sites that could well be representative of the "twenty cites" noted in the text. Tel El Umeiri, located about 25 miles east of the Jordan, near modern Amman in Jordan (ancient Rabbah), is one of the largest and best preserved Judges era (Iron Age I) town sites in the lands of the Bible. It also features one of the finest examples of the pillared house known to historians. The site clearly demonstrates the existence of well-constructed walled towns in Iron Age I Transjordan inhabited either by Israelites or their culture-twins (ABD 6.722-724; Herr and Clark 2001). The author's brief summary of Jephthah's achievement comports with what is known of the region's history.

defeated the Ammonites. The Hebrew conveys a somewhat sharper sentiment, seen earlier with the defeat of the Moabites (3:30), of Sisera (4:23), and the Midianites (8:28). In each case the victory was so decisive that the threat was effectively eliminated. The term used (*kana'* [TH3665, ZH4044]) means "to be depressed, low, humiliated." It carries a strong emotional tone (Lev 26:41; Deut 9:3) probably associated with the shaming of a person or people who have been decisively beaten in battle (HALOT 1.484; NIDOTTE 2.668-669). The three cases prior to Jephthah all climax in very pointed descriptions of the killing of the enemy king. Perhaps the appearance of the term here indicates that Jephthah also captured and executed the Ammonite king.

11:34 ***his daughter came out to meet him.*** The Hebrew uses the particle *hinneh* [TH2009, ZH2180], often mistranslated as "behold." It denotes immediacy, suggesting a translation like, "Jephthah entered Mizpah, to his house, and there was his daughter coming out." The construction suggests that she emerged virtually the moment he approached the compound. The Hebrew has a wordplay: Jephthah approaches "his house" (*betho* [TH1004, ZH1074]) only to meet "his daughter" (*bitto* [TH1323, ZH1426]).

playing on a tambourine and dancing for joy. The scene evokes the singing of Miriam and all the women who celebrated Yahweh's victory at the sea with tambourines and dancing (Exod 15:20). Though the story mentions only the daughter, normally a whole procession would be expected (cf. 1 Sam 18:6-7).

She was his one and only child. The compactness of the Hebrew behind the sentence here defies fluent translation: "Now [there was] only she, all by herself, he had nobody besides her, [neither] son nor daughter." Most poignant is the term "one and only" (*yekhidah* [TH3173, ZH3495]), which occurs only 12 times in the OT. In its masculine form, it is used three times of Isaac by God when he asks Abraham to sacrifice Isaac: "Take your son, your only son—yes, Isaac, whom you love so much—and go to the land of Moriah. Go and sacrifice him as a burnt offering" (Gen 22:2). Three other times it refers to the way one grieves an only child (Jer 6:26; Amos 8:10; Zech 12:10) and four times it stresses the vulnerability and distress of being alone (Pss 22:20; 25:16; 35:17; 68:6). Only once does it appear free of shadow or danger, expressing the delightfulness of being the sole object of a parent's pleasure (Prov 4:3). The text leaves the reader to ponder whether Jephthah, who began deprived of his ancestry, will end his deprived of progeny in some form.

he had no other sons or daughters. The term *yakhid* [TH3173, ZH3495] can be used even when other children are in the family, as with Isaac who is *yakhid* despite Ishmael's presence. Thus, the author stresses that Jephthah's daughter is a literal "only child." That the household might have other dependents, such as servants, remains a possibility.

11:35 ***When he saw her, he tore his clothes in anguish.*** Tearing the garments served as a traditional expression of anguish in the ancient world.

Oh, my daughter! . . . You have completely destroyed me! Most interpreters see in this passage Jephthah crassly blaming his daughter, resulting in a "tragic figure, presenting a pathetic picture of stupidity, brutality, ambition, and self-centeredness" (Block 1999:372). Such severe judgment presumes to know Jephthah's motives and cannot see that his grief for her and for his own loss and undoing were intertwined. His lament underscores the hope a parent would have pinned to his daughter, he to whom lineage would have meant so much. Since this is a historical account of a genuine grief, we should provide a shocked, grieving father latitude in the words he speaks.

The verb translated "destroy" has a similar sound to the word used in 11:33b when Ammon was "humbled": there, *kana'*[TH3665, ZH4044], here, *kara'* [TH3766, ZH4156], another verb meaning "to be low." The word carries a strong "charge," the idea of being struck down or driven to one's knees (Boling 1975:208).

You've brought disaster on me! The "you" in the Hebrew is emphatic. The writer also uses the verb "to be, to happen," which is not needed in a normal Hebrew sentence, thus characterizing his daughter's unexpected role more actively, perhaps "You are the very one who has become X." The description of what his daughter has become is often rendered "among those who trouble me" (*be'okeray* [TH5916, ZH6579]), but the preposition translated "among" can also stress the essence of a person or situation (Keil 1863:387; Arnold and Choi 2003:106), which would fit the hyperemphatic quality of the sentence: "Oh my daughter . . . you are the very one who has become [precisely what] troubles me!"

One curious observation deserves notice, even if offered cautiously. The two verbal roots involved, *kara'* and *'akar*, use the same consonants: *Kaph, Resh*, and *Ayin*. Only one other root in biblical Hebrew uses these consonants: *'arak* [TH6186, ZH6885]. This verb has two specialized uses in liturgical contexts. One relates to the arranging of the pieces of a sacrificial animal on the altar, and the other appears in Leviticus denoting the assessed price for redeeming an extraordinary (*pala'* [TH6381, ZH7098]; cf. Lev 27:2) vow to Yahweh that cannot be fulfilled. Specifically, Lev 27:1-8 describes the redemption of persons, male or female, vowed to Yahweh, according to their "assessment" (*'erek* [TH6187, ZH6886]). The occurrence of the two other roots so similar in Jephthah's complaint could have triggered in the reader's mind the only other word in biblical Hebrew to use those consonants, which ironically signifies the two possible resolutions of the story. But the wise interpreter remains suspicious of such fanciful speculation.

For I have made a vow to the LORD, and I cannot take it back. Interestingly, the NLT uses the language of vows here, but the Hebrew does not, reading lit. "I have opened my mouth to Yahweh, and I am not able to turn back." The expression "open the mouth" (*patsah peh* [TH6475/6310, ZH7198/7023]) does not seem to carry a nuance peculiar to vows or oaths. The verb *patsah* (to open) appears only 15 times in the OT and all but four have "mouth" as the object, one has "lips" (HALOT 2.953, s.v. *patsah*; NIDOTTE 3.653). If any nuance is peculiar to it, perhaps the idea is simply of intentional utterance or pronouncement. Perhaps in this passage, the sense is "I have made an unusual and solemn pronouncement to Yahweh, and I cannot turn back."

11:36 ***Father, if you have made a vow to the LORD.*** Lit., "My father, you have opened your mouth to Yahweh"; "if" and "vow" are not in the original.

you must do to me what you have vowed. Again, the Hebrew does not reuse the vow language but stresses rather Jephthah's words requiring exact fulfillment: "do to me exactly according to what went out of your mouth." Her utterance in this verse lacks the conjunctions the Hebrew uses to string clauses together smoothly. Each sentence stands on its own, imparting to her statement a very deliberative tone.

for the LORD has given you a great victory over your enemies, the Ammonites. The original uses an arresting term instead of "victory" that means "vengeance, vindication." She actually says, "Yahweh has effected your vindication." The word-family used for "vengeance" here (*naqam* [TH5359/5360, ZH5934/5935]) is not simple revenge and never denotes the custom of sanctioned blood-vengeance, i.e., the killing of one who has taken the life of a family member. It refers rather to the divinely sanctioned vindication of legitimate rule (Mendenhall 1973:69-104; NIDOTTE 3.154-157). Indeed, the term appears very prominently in passages where the vengeance spoken of falls on those who defy Yahweh's appointed servant. The word seldom signifies personal revenge but points to the observable vindication of Yahweh's rule, particularly through his chosen servant. This legitimacy is what the Gileadites had denied Jephthah, and what the elders restored and God confirmed through the Spirit's anointing. That this word of vindication appears on the lips of the daughter upon whom he must perform his vow stuns the reader. Whatever we might feel for this woman, it cannot be pity. She faces her future affirming her father's divinely validated legitimacy as Israel's leader.

11:37 ***But first let me do this one thing: Let me go up and roam in the hills.*** The NLT accepts a commonly suggested change in the Hebrew, which actually says "Let me go down on the hills." The Heb., *yaradti* [TH3381, ZH3718] (let me go down), can, with modification to the spelling, be translated "let me wander." The reason for the change is that going down to hills seems odd. Iron Age I villages, however, tended to be on the high ridges, which in Gilead top out around 3,000 feet. From these ridges, one might indeed descend to other lower hills.

and weep with my friends for two months. The tendency of interpreters to see the daughter as a mere child, presumably because of her virginity, is shown false by the fact that she can plan, with her friends, two months of wandering in the hills. Her speech is not the naïve words of a child, but the courageous utterance of a young woman confronting her destiny and speaking to her father virtually as an equal.

because I will die a virgin. The NLT leaves open whether Jephthah actually slaughtered his daughter for Yahweh or consigned her to the social sacrifice of perpetual virginity. Though the Hebrew text does not mention her death, saying only, "that I may weep over my virginity," the NLT's rendering expresses the practical fact that whether she dies as a sacrifice after 60 days, or of natural causes after 60 years, she will die a virgin.

11:38 ***because she would never have children.*** The NLT adds this, while the Hebrew text nowhere says a word about childbearing being the point of Jephthah's daughter's grief. Schneider (2000:179-182) rightly points out that the text reads that they wept for her "virginity," defined later as "she had not known a man." The point of virginity is not a failure to bear children, but a lack of sexual experience (contra Block 1999:374). The text reflects the robust affirmation of sexual experience that characterizes the Bible as a whole. The biblical authors view it as wrong to deny a young person sexual fulfillment within God's law. To be sure, motherhood forms a part of that experience. But this text laments her lack of intimacy with a man, not her failure to bear children.

11:39 ***When she returned home.*** The dynamic equivalent translation loses the poignancy of the original. The text says, "She returned to her father." For all the sorrow expressed over Jephthah's vow, the text never allows father and daughter to stand in opposition one to the other. In fact, we cannot speak meaningfully of this woman merely submitting to her fate. In an eerie manner, she seems fully in control of events, a strong character.

her father kept the vow he had made. Here also the original is more direct: "and he did to her what he had vowed." Commentators all note the surprising failure of the narrator to say, "And he offered her as a burnt offering." Rather, the clause following stresses her lack of sexual intimacy with a man. From this omission and unexpected conclusion arose the view that rather than being sacrificed literally, Jephthah's daughter was consigned to some sacred service requiring perpetual virginity (Marcus 1986).

she died. The NLT adds this phrase, introducing death where the original text creates doubt; cf. note on 11:37.

a virgin. Lit., "she had not known a man." In the Hebrew text this clause follows the first clause, "so Jephthah did with her what he had vowed" using a disjunctive construction that some interpreters construe as a parenthetical or circumstantial clause. This view sees the text noting that when Jephthah sacrificed her, she had not known a man sexually. Her virginity, however, has been noted twice before and if a human sacrifice is in view, this third note that she was a virgin would skirt the larger theological scandal of an act viewed with revulsion in the OT. Other interpreters suggest the clause is consequential, indicating her virginity results from the vow (Marcus 1986:33-34). A stronger argument would note that in Hebrew syntax a disjunctive clause that refers to a different participant from the preceding clause is often explanatory in nature (Waltke and O'Connor 1990:651-652). The second clause thus would stand as a parallel, a counterpart, to the first, specifying its meaning. The sense then would be, "Her father kept the vow he had made, that is, she never knew a man sexually." On this interpretation, Jephthah's daughter faced a life of consecrated celibacy, abandoning the hope of marriage, not bloody death and consignment to flames on the altar. While the OT says little of the role of women in the service of Yahweh in ancient Israel, it does note women serving at the door of the sanctuary and the crime of their sexual purity being violated by the sons of Eli (1 Sam 2:22; cf. Exod 38:8). Either reading is plausible grammatically. The reader must examine the larger story in the context of the book to adjudicate between them (see commentary below).

So it has become a custom in Israel. The Hebrew text also allows the translation, "so she became a custom in Israel" (Trible 1984:106). Ritual remembrance of a person in antiquity crystallizes around the commemoration of their name (Radner 2005:70-73). That this nameless woman would be perennially remembered "in Israel" draws attention to her tragedy and her nobility. Jephthah has no progeny, hence no legacy, but his name endures through the story. His daughter's name remains unknown, but her character and courage constitute an enduring exemplar in Israel. Targum Jonathan, a paraphrase of the text into Aramaic that became popular in the centuries after Christ, added a note to this verse: "And it was for a decree in Israel that a man should not offer up his daughter as a burnt offering as Jephthah the Gileadite had done, who had not enquired of Phinehas the priest. But if he had asked of Phinehas the priest, he would have redeemed her with a price." (The price is mentioned in Lev 27:1-8.) That this ancient interpreter needed to account (in his view) for the presence of the scandal—human sacrifice—underscores the absence of any such explanation by the biblical author. But the author's silence actually suggests there was no scandal, no human sacrifice, that required explanation.

11:40 *young Israelite women to go away for four days each year.* Viewed from the perspective of the whole Bible's ethos, if Jephthah sacrificed his daughter, nothing can excuse or redeem the deed. Thus, it is hard to imagine our author routinely noting an annual festival in remembrance of the atrocity of a human sacrifice. From the perspective of the culture of the early Iron Age, however, the perpetual recollection and grieving for Jephthah's daughter by girls like her in succeeding generations would actually have been perceived as saving her from the tragedy, wresting some shard of meaning out of what, to us, is a meaningless action, and possibly even securing a measure of redemption for Jephthah himself.

to lament. The NLT here follows ancient Greek and Latin translations, which assume an expression of grief, again based on the assumption of the daughter's premature and abominable death. But the Hebrew verb employed, *tanah* [TH8567, ZH9480], as used here with the Piel stem, means "to narrate, recount, commemorate" (HALOT 2.1759, s.v. *tanah*). Again, either the author has chosen not to make the sacrifice explicit, or the sacrifice did not occur.

the fate of Jephthah's daughter. The NLT here introduces an unfortunate nuance, "fate," which is lacking in the original. It also omits the concluding identification of Jephthah "the Gileadite," which recapitulates the introduction of Jephthah in 11:1 with the same words. A lasting mystery in this story is the absence of any overt word from the author about the moral value of Jephthah's deed. The actual sacrifice finds no mention: Jephthah performed his vow, but we must continue pondering the content of the vow. Human sacrifice remains for the OT the most heinous and abominable act imaginable. The narrator(s) in Judges always notes the particulars of liturgical actions. Altars of sacrifice tend to be named, sanctuaries noted, and irregularities often find condemnation, such as Gideon's ephod. That a human sacrifice could occur, perpetrated by a man who had been empowered by the Spirit of Yahweh, to whom Yahweh had granted victory and vindication, and for the author to say absolutely nothing against it, seems strange indeed.

COMMENTARY

Few biblical stories have provoked readers as deeply as the story of Jephthah and his daughter, and few biblical stories have inspired the quantity and intensity of interpretive literature (cf. especially Gunn 2005:133-169; Block 1999; Younger

2002). The notes and commentary presented here have minimized citations of secondary sources, but the major commentaries cited will refer the reader to hundreds of relevant books and articles.

The story opens with Israel in a double-crisis, seen in 10:6-18. First, they face a determined and dangerous foe, the Ammonites, with the Philistines flexing their muscles as well. Second, they have played out all their cards with Yahweh, whose alienation from his people has apparently reached a point of no return. Will he save his people? In this context, the military leaders of Gilead decide to hunt for someone else to take on their dangerous responsibilities. The murkiness of this situation places the narrative to follow under a question mark. Jephthah's career, therefore, partakes of an ambivalence that can entrap the interpreter. That Yahweh does in fact save the people points not to the authenticity of their response, but to Yahweh's overwhelming grace and indomitable will to save, a point painfully missed by Jephthah himself in the end.

Too easily commentators have made of Jephthah an embittered, power-hungry, vengeful gangster who stops at nothing. This portrayal usually reveals more of the interpreter's sedentary, middle-class "niceness" than it does of the Iron Age leader and his struggle for legitimacy. Indeed, if Jephthah had been met by anything other than a human being when he returned, he would be remembered as a man of great character, faith, ability, and even goodness. God, in his Word, never gives us cartoons or crude stereotypes. The judges are real persons, who lived in real times and places. Their characters, struggles, and faith, like ours, possess a multilayered complexity that defies the simple categories of white-hat and black-hat. As with many other individuals, the biblical author presents Jephthah on a model of rise and fall, triumph and tragedy.

Jephthah's Triumph. Jephthah appears with a complex identity. First identified as "Jephthah the Gileadite" (11:1 KJV), the writer next identifies the quality of the man by designating him a *gibbor khayil* [TH1368/2428, ZH1475/2657], a mighty man of valor, a man of distinction and worth. If the *gibbor khayil* indeed was a man who held land as a result of military service, the author is also signaling that Jephthah belonged in the aristocracy, his subsequent exile notwithstanding. Although Jephthah descended from an irregular union, his father seems to have claimed him as his heir, hence the statement that Gilead "begat" Jephthah, the verb most closely associated with genealogy. Ironically, Jephthah's brothers were born of Gilead's legal wife, but the text does not say he "begat" them. The brothers conspired successfully to deny Jephthah his inheritance. With no family, home, or stake, he can only be known as "the Gildeadite" as he sought his fortune on the fringes of his community.

Meanwhile, Israel fell under the heel of the Ammonites, suffering for 18 long years until the militia leaders of Israel, probably at the behest of the village and clan elders, met to organize resistance. But these men who ought to have led the resistance were unequal to the challenge and offered paramount status over all Gilead to anyone who would answer the call. When nothing happened, it fell back on the elders to adopt a new plan. Surely it came as a hard decision to bring back one whom they had stripped of his position, family, land, and standing. But just as Israel finally had to cry out to Yahweh in their pain (despite their running after other gods), so the elders finally appealed to the one man with the quality and courage to lead their fight, the man they had repudiated and shunned. Even then, their offer to him was only that of commander of the militia, *qatsin* [TH7101, ZH7903]. Jephthah's response reflects the pain and bitterness of his experience, but more so his wrath at the double-dealing and contempt of these elders. His refusal forces them to offer the pact originally stated (10:17-18): The successful leader of the resistance against Ammon would be *head* over all Gilead, a proper role for a man ultimately known only as "the Gileadite."

In its ancient context of tribal societies and their allegiances of blood and kinship, the story sounds the note of true nobility, which resides in character and action, not blood. The theme is common, finding expression much later in the Anglo-Saxon *Beowulf*. Facing his last battle, Beowulf turned to his select band of soldiers, all of high birth, but with disappointment, and then a surprise:

> No help or backing was to be had then
> from [Beowulf's] high-born comrades; that hand-picked troop
> broke ranks and ran for their lives
> to the safety of the wood. But within one heart
> sorrow welled up: in a man of worth
> the claims of kinship cannot be denied.
> (*Beowulf*, 2596-2601 [Heaney translation])

Ironically, Wiglaf, the "one heart" who could not deny the claims of kinship, was no kin of Beowulf, nor even a Geat! He descended from ancient enemies fought by the ancestors of the men surrounding him. His grandfather had battled against Beowulf's forebears, but somewhere, valor had embraced valor, and Wiglaf's grandfather had been given a place among the Geats. Now, with Beowulf abandoned by his "high-born comrades," it is the heart of kinship birthed in battle valor that beats most truly. Indeed, it is a truth known to the Wiglafs and Jephthahs of this world, and with them the multitude of young men and women, mostly of only modest family, heritage, and standing, who, as I write these words, hold guns, standing in dark places of danger so that I can finish this book. Such heroes without portfolio understand the kinship of valor, service, and sacrifice more clearly than those whose birth certificates are as unsullied as their trust funds. If Jephthah fails—and he ultimately will—neither his parentage nor his associations bear the fault. The Israelite tribal chiefs, all too ready to ask bastards and bad boys to face the blade on their behalf, must have known that while Jephthah failed for his own sins, he also fought, won, and failed, for their sins as well.

Interpreters since the late 1980s rightly discern that the sequence of judges presents a decline through the book (Stone 1988; 1992; 2005; O'Connell 1996; Olson 1998; Brensinger 1999; Schneider 2000; Block 1988; 1999; Younger 2002). This observation, however, should not obscure the fact that no judge appears *unambiguously* evil or inept. "Decline" takes many forms. Nor does the theme of decline demand that each judge *necessarily* be worse in every way than the previous one. The so-called minor judge stories, for example, function in several ways unrelated to the "decline" motif. Often they contrast with the charismatic model presented by the major judges. I have argued that the decline is more of a three-tiered "step-down" process, with variation within each era or stage, and I have located the dynamic of decline mainly in the theme of the judge's legacy, typically flowing from an action at the end of his career that shapes the framework for the next story. The caution against seeing the judges as flat characters applies with special urgency to Jephthah.

Throughout the narrative, Jephthah acts with patience and care. Confronted with rejection by his brothers, he fled to the wilderness rather than fight for his inheritance rights. Aware that his ejection had destroyed his authority within the tribal system, Jephthah carefully sought the public, sacred oath of the elders of Gilead for legitimacy before assuming command (11:9-11). Unlike the leaders and elders, Jephthah persistently spoke of Yahweh as the power and authority behind his actions. He then sought to persuade the Ammonites to avoid bloodshed, appealing to history and even local precedent, showing an awareness of the complex interaction of the various tribal communities in the region, as well as knowledge of Israelite sacred traditions (11:12-28).

Jephthah's anointing by the Spirit (11:29) likewise signals at least divine presence and power, if not endorsement. The Spirit does not appear in the stories where the deliverers already possess legitimacy within the tribal structure (Ehud, Deborah, Barak, minor judges). Those lacking such legitimacy, or who propose to exercise authority beyond their familial sphere of influence instead, gained authentication by the Spirit. In Jephthah's case, the terminology matches that used of the paradigm judge, Othniel, again accentuating the positive view of Jephthah's leadership. His victory emerges as a Spirit-anointed, divinely empowered, saving triumph over the enemy. Unlike Gideon's force, Jephthah's army raises no questions in Yahweh's mind as to who will receive the glory. In fact, the fielding of this force climaxes the theme of Jephthah's rehabilitation and validation as a leader. Jephthah secured legitimate affirmation from the elders (11:11), made efforts at negotiation (11:12-28), and finally was anointed by the Spirit (11:29)—a sequence of events that paid off as he raised an effective force that engaged the Ammonites with brilliant success. His fulfillment of his disastrous vow, and later, his extreme vengeance on the Ephraimites, does not eclipse the fact that, like Gideon, he decisively ended the threat confronting him. The land would not "rest" in the aftermath, but his victory stands. Thus, Samuel invoked the memory of Jephthah along with Jerub-baal and himself as deliverers of Israel (1 Sam 12:9-11). Likewise, the author of the letter to the Hebrews cites Jephthah as a model of faith in company with Gideon, Barak, Samson, David, and Samuel (Heb 11:32). While remaining aware of his considerable failings, readers should not turn a blind eye to Jephthah's divinely empowered achievement, and must let it inform how they assess his subsequent actions. Indeed, the height of his rise underscores the heartbreak of his fall. So where exactly must we look to account for Jephthah's tragedy?

Jephthah's Tragedy. Every indication has pointed to Jephthah's popular rehabilitation and recognition by his people and Yahweh, culminating in his victory over the Ammonites. All locate the beginning of Jephthah's tragedy in his vow (11:30-31), made amidst the preparations for battle. Most interpreters assume that Jephthah knowingly committed himself to a human sacrifice, and consider the vow either a rash or crass attempt to manipulate God. These assumptions find no support in the narrative. The character of Jephthah so far militates against seeing him as one who would knowingly offer a sacrifice detestable to Yahweh, even as an attempt at manipulation. Jephthah quite plausibly could have envisioned an animal as the object, and the wording of the vow seems to allow for alternative fulfillments should the object of the meeting not fit the requirements of the burnt offering (see notes on 11:31). Moreover, nothing about Jephthah suggests he was rash or impulsive (Keil 1863:389-390; Soggin 1981:215-216). Claims that he attempted to manipulate God also presume to read his mind and intentions from a remove of 3,000 years. Rather, we face an intentional, deliberate action, which forces the question, "why?" Jephthah, like Gideon, was possibly ensnared by one of his virtues. Both men acted deliberately to build a base of legitimacy for their actions, Gideon through a succession of verifying signs that amounted to hesitation, Jephthah through a process of deliberation, clarification, and sacred confirmation. Perhaps Jephthah, having been denied due process, sought to employ every due process in pursuit of his people's freedom, hence his vow to Yahweh.

The best answer for why Jephthah made his vow lies in the role of equivalent gift-giving in tribal societies, especially complex chiefdoms (Matthews 2004:124). In communities where identity, relationship, and even power flows over channels of gifting and obligation, parties seek to avoid excessive imbalance in the exchange. The chief or paramount consistently displays the capacity to "bankrupt" others in his ability to out-give them. Inability to reciprocate identifies one as a subordinate, while matching a gift establishes peer status. While exchange can take the form of hostility or manipulation, it more often reflects a due respect for one's obligations in the community. Jephthah's vow, seen almost universally as an attempt to manipulate Yahweh, was probably a tragically misguided, but well-intentioned, attempt to honor Yahweh. First, note the magnitude of the gift Jephthah envisions receiving. The condition, "if you give me victory over the Ammonites" (11:30) mirrors the promise made by the elders to restore him fully to the community (11:8-10; cf. 10:17-18). More than victory or mere power, Jephthah, the exiled chief of Gilead, would receive full reinstatement and recognition if Yahweh delivered the Ammonites into his hands. If Yahweh did this, he was giving Jephthah back his life as a respected man in his community, something for which Jephthah surely hungered. As a conscientious member of a tribal community whose peace and health flowed from reciprocity and balanced obligations, Jephthah stood to receive an inconceivably large gift—one that would create an imbalance between the two parties. How does one respond to the total restoration of family, property, and dignity?

Jephthah's response, his vow, expresses his profound sense of indebtedness to Yahweh. Jephthah's flaw is not that he was selfish, power-hungry, conniving, or "Canaanized," nor that he had offended modern commentators' standards of piety. At least three fatal confusions seem apparent in Jephthah's vow. First, Jephthah failed to understand the vastness of Yahweh's abounding grace and generosity. As a man scrupulously attentive to reciprocal obligations, paying his dues and expecting the same from others, Jephthah imagined that Yahweh expects repayment. That Yahweh's deliverance flows from sheer, selfless bounty did not seem to occur to Jephthah. Second, Jephthah, apparently thinking he must match Yahweh's gift, operated as though Yahweh was a *peer*. Inability to repay a gift places one in a vastly subordinate position, which shames one before an equal, but is completely appropriate for a vassal toward his suzerain who has proven a generous benefactor, especially a *divine* suzerain-benefactor. Realizing Yahweh had "broken the bank" with his gift,

Jephthah's best response would be stunned, humble submission before his sovereign, whom he could never out-give—a response modeled by David's thanksgiving for Yahweh's promise of an eternal house (2 Sam 7:18-29). Thirdly, Jephthah's behavior seems to assume that some cultic action is required to compel God, when what God calls for is simple obedience. Samuel's later word to Saul applies: "What is more pleasing to the LORD: your burnt offerings and sacrifices or your obedience to his voice? Listen! Obedience is better than sacrifice, and submission is better than offering the fat of rams" (1 Sam 15:22). While proper cultic actions and obedience to the Lord certainly are not mutually exclusive, the Bible often notes humans have a propensity to emphasize the one while neglecting the other.

Centuries later, the prophet Micah answered the hysterical questions of his hearers who felt Yahweh demanded too much:

What can we bring to the LORD?
  What kind of offerings should we give him?
Should we bow before God
  with offerings of yearling calves?
Should we offer him thousands of rams
  and ten thousand rivers of olive oil?
Should we sacrifice our firstborn children
  to pay for our sins?

No, O people, the LORD has told you what is good,
  and this is what he requires of you:
to do what is right, to love mercy,
  and to walk humbly with your God. (Micah 6:6-8)

In the end, however, we can only guess what went on in the mind of this ancient leader. But his behavior speaks not of one trying to manipulate God, but one who feared simply to throw his life down before the mercy of a God whose gifts can never be repaid.

But did Jephthah actually offer his daughter as a burnt offering? The majority view for centuries has been that he did. Marcus (1986) reviewed many arguments on either side of the issue, with no firm resolution. In my judgment, seven considerations make the narration of a human sacrifice unlikely: (1) The offering itself constituted no simple procedure, and surely would have left a mark on the text and subsequent Old Testament tradition. Indeed, Jephthah's daughter asked for the chance to bewail her virginity, not her death by knife and flames. No sign of such an atrocity appears. (2) As the paradigmatic first offering in Leviticus (Lev 1), the burnt offering is an entire sacrifice of the most valuable thing the worshiper owns. For stockmen, that is the male with no flaws—the choice breeding animal, prized and jealously protected. Offering such an animal meant great loss affecting the future productivity of the herd. To offer anything imperfect, unclean, or of the wrong gender, violated the strictures of this offering. In this context, the offering of a female failed to meet the criteria for the *'olah* [TH5930, ZH6592]. (3) The magnitude of the abomination represented by human sacrifice must be faced. The Old Testament makes it clear that Yahweh despises human sacrifice (Lev 18:21; Deut 18:10-14;

2 Kgs 16:3; 17:17; 21:6) and provides for the redemption of the firstborn in commemoration of the Passover plague that killed the firstborn of Egypt. The portrayal of Jephthah in 11:12-28 presents a character well-versed in the history and ethos of his people. Whatever views one might hold of Israelite religious practice in the early Iron Age, the Jephthah of our story knew his people's religious traditions. (4) The author of Judges attends closely to deviations from correct worship and certainly would not give a human sacrificer a "pass." (5) It is hard to imagine that an annual festival celebrated by virgin girls, originating from an abomination perpetrated by a "Canaanized" judge, would become a recognized custom in Israel without the narrator or redactor breathing the slightest reservation. (6) The earliest history of interpretation on this story is 1 Samuel 12:11, a programmatic speech for the entire Joshua—Kings history in which Samuel includes Jephthah with Gideon *and himself* as proof of Yahweh's saving power. Would Samuel, or the theologically strict "Deuteronomistic historian" responsible for placing this speech in the final account, include in that company one who had committed the most heinous abomination possible? (7) Hebrews 11 also reflects an extremely ancient interpretation that groups Jephthah with Gideon, Barak, Samson, and David—all imperfect, but all heroes of faith commended as examples by the author to Christian readers (Heb 11:32). The inclusion of one believed to have committed the ultimate abomination among those who were "too good for this world" (Heb 11:38) seems unlikely. These arguments are circumstantial, but in my judgment, where there is no smoke, there was no fire.

So what did Jephthah do with his daughter? As discussed in the notes on 11:31, his vow may be analyzed as a general promise ("it shall belong to Yahweh") followed by a more specific possibility ("I will even offer it as a burnt offering"). But, assuming an animal sacrifice, would a burnt offering be sufficiently extraordinary to match Yahweh's "gift" to Jephthah? Because of the extreme loss involved, the burnt offering by its very nature, was an extraordinary offering. In fact, it was a freewill offering, not obligatory or dictated by the liturgical calendar for the individual Israelite. Thus, an *'olah* of the appropriate animal would constitute an extraordinary response to Yahweh's gift of victory.

Jephthah's daughter, however, did not qualify as a burnt offering (see two paragraphs above and notes on 11:31). Thus, to fulfill his vow Jephthah had to, in some way, give his daughter to Yahweh. From the following narrative, her virginity, noted three times in three verses, stood at the center of this dedication. Indeed, the author states, literally, "And he did with her what he vowed, and she did not know [sexually] a man." The Old Testament notes that women served at the doorway of the sanctuary in the wilderness (Exod 38:8) and at Shiloh (1 Sam 2:22). Judges 21 also describes a festival at Shiloh in which virgin women played a prominent role. This admittedly slender evidence suggests that possibly Jephthah's daughter was consigned to a lifetime of service at the sanctuary and required to remain a virgin until her death.

But would her dedication to the sanctuary merit Jephthah's outburst of grief? Here the text's emphasis on her being his one, only, sole child becomes vital. As one who was denied his ancestry and patrimony, Jephthah's restoration opened the door for him to become a true and noble sheikh, with many descendants, since Old Testament law permits a daughter to inherit her father's full estate (Num 36). In company with Jair the Gileadite before him, who had 30 sons (10:3-5), and Ibzan after him with 30 sons *and* 30 daughters (12:8-10), Jephthah could envision a life he thought had eluded him. His entire hope of progeny and remembrance resided in his daughter, a hope she would have shared as well, until the moment she picked up her tambourine. Interpreters puzzle over whether she knew what she was doing. Did she determine that her father would receive a celebration, whatever the cost? If so, Jephthah's words to her take on added poignancy.

From our modern perspective, the event has a tragic dimension—by the fiat of her father a girl of marriageable age is suddenly deprived of the God-given privileges of marriage, sex, and parenthood. But from the perspective of their time and culture, despite their grief, the actions of Jephthah and his daughter are not evil in themselves. Many men and women alike have dedicated their lives to perpetual virginity in the service of God, some willingly, others through the harsh fortunes of life, which they have turned to the divine purpose. Their legacy of service endures. But as a symptom of Jephthah's failure to grasp the all-surpassing generosity of Yahweh, as a sign that he possibly sought a kind of parity with Yahweh, and as a substitute for that obedience that goes beyond sacrifices and vows, Jephthah's actions point to a distorted vision of Yahweh's character. Whether Jephthah sinned or not, his vow and his daughter's zeal together shattered all their hopes.

Legacies, however, can assume many forms. The honorable and courageous demeanor of Jephthah's daughter has endeared her to readers for centuries, and indeed, remembrance of her steadfastness before shattered hopes became a part of Israel's cultural memory. Though nameless, she could never be forgotten. Indeed, as the prologue to her story, Jephthah's own story now would be told as well, securing him the legacy in Israel's tradition and Scripture that he never found in the hills of Gilead.

◆ c. Slaughter of kinsmen (12:1-7)

Then the people of Ephraim mobilized an
army and crossed over the Jordan River to
Zaphon. They sent this message to Jeph-
thah: "Why didn't you call for us to help
you fight against the Ammonites? We are
going to burn down your house with you
in it!"
2Jephthah replied, "I summoned you at
the beginning of the dispute, but you re-
fused to come! You failed to help us in our
struggle against Ammon. 3So when I real-
ized you weren't coming, I risked my life
and went to battle without you, and the
LORD gave me victory over the Ammonites.
So why have you now come to fight me?"
4The people of Ephraim responded, "You
men of Gilead are nothing more than fu-
gitives from Ephraim and Manasseh." So
Jephthah gathered all the men of Gilead
and attacked the men of Ephraim and de-
feated them.
5Jephthah captured the shallow cross-
ings of the Jordan River, and whenever a
fugitive from Ephraim tried to go back
across, the men of Gilead would challenge
him. "Are you a member of the tribe of
Ephraim?" they would ask. If the man
said, "No, I'm not," 6they would tell him to
say "Shibboleth." If he was from Ephraim,
he would say "Sibboleth," because people
from Ephraim cannot pronounce the word
correctly. Then they would take him and
kill him at the shallow crossings of the
Jordan. In all, 42,000 Ephraimites were
killed at that time.
7Jephthah judged Israel for six years.
When he died, he was buried in one of the
towns of Gilead.

NOTES

12:1 *Then the people of Ephraim mobilized an army and crossed over the Jordan River.* This captures the intentional, hostile nature of Ephraim's actions, which are expressed more compactly in the Hebrew. This was not just a controversy, but a military attack by Ephraim on the Gileadites.

Zaphon. A town near Succoth in the Jordan valley is likely in view, though the Hebrew text could simply be translated "northward."

They sent this message to Jephthah. This rightly unpacks the very terse Hebrew. The author uses the sending of messengers and messages throughout the whole Jephthah story to carry the action. Messages between Jephthah and the elders result in his restoration; messages between Jephthah and the Ammonite king shape the conflict with Ammon, and now messages between Ephraim and Jephthah articulate the terms of the next episode.

Why didn't you call for us to help you fight against the Ammonites? This encounter completes a series of three stories involving the Ephraimites' participation in battle. In 3:27-29 the Ephraimites close the trap at the precise moment, shutting off the fords of Jordan against the fleeing Moabites, resulting in 10,000 slain. Then in 7:24–8:3, Gideon, in pursuit of the Midianites, summons the Ephraimites, who again seize the fords of Jordan, capturing two leaders of Midian (7:24-25), though their preoccupation with gloating over the decapitation of Oreb and Zeeb and their complaints about their place in the order of battle threatened insurrection and delayed the pursuit, necessitating a grueling chase by Gideon and his 300 men (8:4-21). Ephraim's preoccupation with the glory of the chase and dividing the spoils likely motivated their aggravation. Gideon's ability to avert dangerous internal conflict contrasts sharply with Jephthah's "bring it on" attitude in this story.

We are going to burn down your house with you in it! Reference to Jephthah's house, the focal point of his disinheritance, his return, and the tragedy of his vow makes these words especially poignant. Destruction by burning also figures in Jotham's fable of divine vengeance (9:15, 20) and in Abimelech's behavior (9:46-49). In addition, this anticipates somewhat the Philistines burning Samson's Timnite father-in-law and bride (14:15; 15:6). Ephraim's rejection of Jephthah's leadership is not a sign of his failure. Anointing by the Spirit served to authenticate leaders to Israel as a whole when their scope would extend beyond their normal tribal sphere of influence. By defying Jephthah, the Ephraimites also defied the anointing of Yahweh's Spirit. Thus, to claim that Jephthah's defense of his leadership "lacks any moral interest, not to mention any concern for the solidarity of Israel" (Block 1999:383) violates the context of this conflict.

12:2 *I summoned you.* The term used is the same one that appears in 12:1, to "call up," and serves as a technical term for the militia summons to arms. While no direct reference to Jephthah's summons of Ephraim appears, Ammon had threatened Ephraim directly (10:9), and Jephthah, during his Spirit-anointed tour to raise a militia, did tour Manasseh, half of which settled east of Jordan (11:29). Manasseh appears alongside Ephraim in the tribal insult reported in 12:4, and an area east of Jordan is also referred to as the "forest of Ephraim" (2 Sam 18:6-8), again showing connections across the river. With this reasonable basis for Jephthah's statement in the text, presuming that Jephthah simply lied for a psychological advantage seems extreme (Block 1999:382; Younger 2002:272).

at the beginning of the dispute. Lit., "I indeed was a man of contention, and my people, with the sons of Ammon exceedingly." This rather awkward sentence strongly emphasizes Jephthah's own sense of being embattled and alone. Since the word translated "dispute" is *rib* [TH7379, ZH8190], meaning a lawsuit or formal controversy, Jephthah possibly indicated that the Ephraimites had been called while Jephthah was attempting to negotiate with the Ammonites as a "man of diplomacy" (Boling 1975:212).

12:2-3 ***but you refused to come! You failed to help us. . . . So when I realized you weren't coming.*** "Refused" and "failed" are not direct translations of the text; Jephthah twice, using the same verb in two different constructions, simply says "you did not save/help us." What seemed, between the lines, evident in the Gideon story, namely that the Ephraimites had more of an eye for glory than for actually getting the job done, emerges here as a bitter fact for Jephthah: When the crisis came, the Ephraimites did not show.

12:3 ***I risked my life and went to battle without you.*** Lit., "I put my soul in my hand and crossed over to the Ammonites." The language resonates with Jotham's claim about his father, Gideon, who "flung down his soul" (NLT, "risked his life," 9:17) to deliver Israel. Likewise, Deborah celebrated the tribe of Zebulun for (lit.) "despising its soul/life" (5:18). These affirmations of the human cost and risk in deliverance in no way detract from the role played by Yahweh, but are in fact the human response to Yahweh's actions, though no less frightening and dangerous, nor less heroic and praiseworthy (contra Schneider 2000:184).

and the LORD gave me victory over the Ammonites. Once again, the idiom "to put . . . in the hand" for military victory appears in the story (11:21, 30, 32; cf. 11:9). Here it serves virtually as a threat: Yahweh put Ammon in my hand; are you now going to fight me?

So why have you now come to fight me? While commentators normally contrast Gideon's successful pacifying of the Ephraimites with Jephthah's failure, his attempt to talk the controversy out, even when facing a massed Ephraimite force, shows the same deliberate approach seen earlier. He has eliminated their grievance as a legitimate casus belli before the other tribes and surrounding peoples.

12:4 ***The people of Ephraim responded.*** Appealing to some ancient translations, some commentators suggest the words from "The people" to "Manasseh" were added to this verse inadvertently by a scribe whose eyes wandered to the next verse, where the terms "fugitive" and "Ephraim" appear again (Moore 1895:307-308; Burney 1920:327). The contrast, however, between the Ephraimites' slur on the Gileadites in 12:4 and the annihilation of the ones who uttered that slur in 12:5 argues for the originality of the line. The Ephraimite "reply," in fact, is no answer, but simply an insult leaving no doubt about their intentions. Contrast the story in Josh 22, when the east-bank tribes set up an altar and the west-bank tribes mustered for battle. In that case, the explanation offered by the east-bankers, however far-fetched it seemed, was accepted by their west-bank kinsmen, who stood down and went home. Ephraim would not allow this slight to their tribal honor to go unpunished.

You men of Gilead are nothing more than fugitives from Ephraim and Manasseh. The contrast between the regional name, "men of Gilead," and the tribal names of Ephraim and Manasseh—two very distinguished tribes—expresses a strong prejudice against Israelites living east of the Jordan River, also discernible in the altar conflict story of Josh 22 (Younger 2002:273).

So Jephthah gathered all the men of Gilead and attacked the men of Ephraim and defeated them. In the Hebrew, this sentence actually appears before the preceding statement about the Ephraimites' abusive insult. The NLT makes it appear that Jephthah's attack was motivated by the insult. But the Hebrew order of clauses links the attack to the end of his speech in 12:2-3, which was not an attempt to talk his way out of the crisis, but rather to establish the public legitimacy of his action against Ephraim. The tribal slur then becomes a circumstantial observation on the Ephraimite attitude. That Jephthah "gathered" (lit., "called," using the same verb, in the military sense, as in 12:1) indicates the Gileadite fighters had dispersed following the battle. Possibly the two months referred to in 11:37-38 had passed, as well. While the Ephraimite grievance falls far short of a justification for war,

Jephthah's response here appears extreme as he subjected his fellow Israelites to virtual annihilation (Schneider 2000:185).

12:5 ***Jephthah captured the shallow crossings of the Jordan River.*** This had been the objective achieved by the Ephraimites in 3:27-29 and for which they were called by Gideon in 7:24–8:3. Now Jephthah uses it against them.

a fugitive from Ephraim. The Ephraimites had insulted Jephthah and his force by pinning this phrase on them. The reversal of the Ephraimites' proud taunt matches the use of the favored Ephraimite tactic at the river ford against them, reinforcing the theme of Jephthah as a man driven by perfect, symmetrical reciprocity. While one might think this story ridicules the Ephraimites, few readers, ancient or modern, would chuckle over frightened, exhausted refugees, one's own countrymen, being struck down one by one as they attempted to escape.

12:6 ***"Shibboleth" . . . "Sibboleth," because people from Ephraim cannot pronounce the word correctly.*** Since the Israelite tribes had no other easily observed distinctions, this dialect feature served to sift them out. Again, the Ephraimites' pride seems undercut by the use of their inability to pronounce a sound correctly. In stories about mispronunciations, typically the outsider or foreigner, often seen as a boor, is incapable of speaking correctly (Niditch 2008:138). Here, the prestigious Ephraimites, who have branded the men of Gilead half-breeds, become the unsophisticated outsiders whose flawed accent betrays them to the Gileadite blades. The word itself might mean "ear of corn" or "current," the latter allowing the word to come up naturally while questioning those crossing the Jordan. This passing comment about dialects has spawned an enormous body of scholarly literature dealing with the dialect geography of Transjordan (Boling 1975:212-213; Soggin 1981:220-222; Block 1999:384; Younger 2002:273-274).

they would take him and kill him. The scene's emphasis on the individual "slaughter" (*shakhat* [TH7819, ZH8821]) of each refugee from the battle drives home the exacting precision exercised by Jephthah—every "fugitive of Ephraim" will be killed by the "fugitive of Ephraim." The cost of Jephthah's drive for reciprocal exchange, which cost him his own future through his tragic vow, now makes him not just victor, but executioner.

42,000 Ephraimites. This is more Ephraimites than appear in any OT census list. Comparison with the census lists in Num 1:32-33 (40,500) and Num 26:35-37 (32,500) underscores the magnitude of the Ephraimite losses. Jephthah has done more harm to Israel than Ammon—or any other enemy in Judges!

12:7 ***Jephthah judged Israel for six years.*** For the first time, the author omits from the conclusion of a major judge episode the observation that the land rested (Stone 1988:341-343; 1992:341). But with the note of sadness surrounding Jephthah's vow, and the atrocity he perpetrated on his countrymen, how could the land rest? His tenure is the shortest career of any of the judges for whom we have chronological data.

When he died. The author once again, in Hebrew, identifies Jephthah as "the Gileadite," resonating with the story's outset (11:1), the conclusion of the central episode (11:40), and now the final summation. Deprived of his patrimony, bereft by his own actions of any posterity, he dies alone simply as "the Gileadite."

one of the towns of Gilead. The Hebrew reads only, "he was buried in the cities of Gilead." Rabbinic interpreters, disturbed that Jephthah received no punishment for his vow, claimed that, in fact, Jephthah was punished, and this verse explains how. They claimed Jephthah died one body part at a time. As each body part fell off, it was buried; thus Jephthah was literally buried "in the cities of Gilead" (Moore 1895:310). Different interpretive assumptions really do produce different results! Several scholars suggest that a minor scribal misspelling has obscured the original wording, which was, "in his city in Gilead" (Boling 1975:213).

COMMENTARY

This episode serves a crucial thematic role in the Jephthah story and for the book as a whole. It brings the story of Jephthah to a sad end. Jephthah's defeat of Ephraim inflicted multiple wounds. Ephraim prided itself, however vacuously, on battle prowess, judging from the Ehud and Gideon stories and Deborah's accolades (5:13-14). A defeat at the hands of Gilead shamed them beyond words. In honor-shame societies, shaming a kinsman never builds up the community. Second, not satisfied with victory, Jephthah and the Gileadites pursued the defeated fighters, trapping them at the Jordan River by the very tactic associated with the Ephraimites in Judges—shame again—and massacring the now unresisting refugees, with a body count of 42,000 Ephraimites. On any interpretation of "thousand," this is more Ephraimites than are listed in any Old Testament census and constitutes the most devastating loss of Israelite lives in the book so far. However justified Jephthah's complaint with Ephraim, his treatment of them as a common enemy rather than errant kin marks Jephthah for vindictive cruelty.

Despite the obnoxious pugnacity of the Ephraimites, readers rightly wonder how this man who saved his people could now become their most prodigious slaughterer. How could this man who rose from rejection to reclaim his patrimony, who distinguished himself in negotiating with an enemy so that all the peoples around would know Israel's war had been just, who was anointed by the Spirit of Yahweh to raise a militia and win an overwhelming victory—how could this man become the slaughterer of his own countrymen? Whence this dark transformation? Simply chalking it up to "a willingness to sacrifice anything and anyone to satisfy his own ambition, which knew no bounds" (Block 1999:386), reduces a complex human being to a simplistic cartoon.

Between Jephthah "the deliverer from Ammon" and Jephthah "the bane of Ephraim" stands the vow and what it represented. We cannot enter his mind, nor dare we psychoanalyze this Iron Age hero by reducing his vastly different, culturally alien outlook to mere neurosis, claiming he "compensates for his . . . sense of inferiority" through violence (Younger 2002:275). As noted in the discussion of chapter 11, the story raises the question whether this man who shaped his entire life around reciprocal exchange and who apparently could not receive restoration and victory from Yahweh as a simple gift, was unable to resolve a conflict with Ephraim. Jephthah, so skilled and careful at diplomacy, adopted an approach alien to grace and magnanimity toward the blind pettiness of his own people. But such will always happen when the gifts of God appear as loans to be repaid in a culture of rigid, reciprocal gift-exchange. A great gulf separates the conscientious steward who knows that from one to whom much is given, much is expected, and a craven servant who constantly hears the meter running and must always "pay back."

Jesus' parable of the talents ended with a man who declared his master a hard man and feared anything other than strict repayment (Matt 25:24-25). This man, like Jephthah, failed utterly to see the generosity of the master and the very different quality of obligation that is engendered by gratitude rather than driven by reciprocity. In another parable, Jesus told of a great king who forgave his servant an incalculable debt. That servant, oblivious to the gift he had received, harshly sought to extract every penny owed him by others (Matt 18:21-35). When grace is not seen as grace, it becomes a crushing burden of obligation expressed in harsh, inflexible demands on others. Not inferiority, but an inferior vision of divine grace, accounts for Jephthah's tragedy.

Again, aware of the fallacy in substituting popular psychology for exegesis, we note Jephthah's sense of abandonment articulated in 12:2-3. Jephthah asserted that he did summon the Ephraimites, stating twice that their inaction forced him to act on his own. The Ephraimites then uttered abusive "insider-outsider" slurs about the Gileadites, again potentially aggravating the shame implicit in Jephthah "the Gileadite's" own mixed parentage and expulsion from his social position. At the Jordan, Jephthah turned the tables, making the former arrogant "insiders" into rejected, refugee "outsiders," inept at their own language (Block 1999:386-387). The narrative bleeds abandonment and toxic alienation, both of which also are foreign to the magnanimity and generosity of Yahweh.

This episode also serves vital functions in the book as a whole. First, it reinforces the three-step downward movement of Israel through the book of Judges (Stone 1988:366-369; 1992:341; Matthews 2004:129). As noted above, the Ephraimite episode resonates with the Ehud and Gideon stories as a recurring measure of community integration or alienation. Also, the narrator failed to state that the land rested for the first time in the book following a major judge. Again, as Israel declined into chaos, and the judges' legacies become increasingly toxic, the narrative takes more space than ever with the judge's biography. Biographical complexity becomes the literary marker of moral decline and leadership failure. Jephthah is not so much evil, as tragic. Lastly, the book's larger concern is with the nature of the Israelite community and its leadership. Niditch (2008:137) rightly observes that the story "highlights the weaknesses of epic models of leadership and polity." The style of leadership reflected by the judges can neither hold the nation together nor secure the future.

◆ 2. The Quiet Alternatives: Ibzan, Elon, and Abdon (12:8-15)

8After Jephthah died, Ibzan from Bethlehem judged Israel. 9He had thirty sons and thirty daughters. He sent his daughters to marry men outside his clan, and he brought in thirty young women from outside his clan to marry his sons. Ibzan judged Israel for seven years. 10When he died, he was buried at Bethlehem.

11After Ibzan died, Elon from the tribe of Zebulun judged Israel for ten years. 12When he died, he was buried at Aijalon in Zebulun.

13After Elon died, Abdon son of Hillel, from Pirathon, judged Israel. 14He had forty sons and thirty grandsons, who rode on seventy donkeys. He judged Israel for eight years. 15When he died, he was buried at Pirathon in Ephraim, in the hill country of the Amalekites.

NOTES

12:8 ***After Jephthah died.*** The Hebrew text only says "after him," with no reference to Jephthah. The similarities between this list and the one found in 10:1-5, combined with the total of the years being 70, leads most scholars to hypothesize one list of five minor judges. The author inserted the story of Jephthah immediately after Jair because of the connection with Gilead. While some of the major judges might be contemporaries, the minor judges appear in an explicit chronological sequence. Per the notes on 10:6-16, it is possible that the 49 years of the Ammonite oppression, Jephthah's career, and the three minor judges noted here were roughly simultaneous with the 60-plus years occupied with the Philistine oppression and Samson's career, though Samson's 20 years might well be included within the 40 years of Philistine rule since he never delivered Israel from them.

Ibzan from Bethlehem. Though some locate this Bethlehem in Judah (Block 1999:388-389), most suggest this is Bethlehem in the territory of Zebulun about seven miles west of Nazareth (ABD 1.712-715). In favor of the southern location is the absence of any regional specification. Probably Bethlehem in Judah was better known; a lesser-known town would be more specifically distinguished. Also, the minor judge lists play a role in linking the stories: Tola links specifically to Abimelech, Jair to Jephthah (10:1-5). A reference to Bethlehem in Judah would turn the reader's attention south, where the Samson story transpires. Based on the belief that this was Bethlehem of Judah, rabbinic interpreters suggested Ibzan was Boaz, who married Ruth, thus integrating the story of Ruth into the history of the judges (cf. Ruth 1:1). However, the Zebulunite Bethlehem links two judges in the sequence to the same region, just as Jair and Jephthah both came from Gilead (cf. below). Without more information, the matter cannot be resolved definitively, though the Zebulunite locale seems preferable.

12:9 *He had thirty sons and thirty daughters.* The minor judges represent intrinsic authentication as leaders. In a tribal society, such a large family commended a man to his community as a sheikh. This commentary has suggested that "judge" was a role that extended authority beyond the expected sphere of influence created by familial ties, thus requiring extraordinary authentication. That might be intrinsic, such as conspicuous networks of relationships via marriages (minor judges), or extrinsic, such as an exhibition of divine call or possession by the Spirit of Yahweh (major judges). We should sit lightly on the terms "sons" and "daughters." These could well identify not literal offspring, but subordinate covenant or treaty partners, i.e., subchiefs or allies, for whom the paramount chief could arrange marriages (Boling 1975:187-188, 216; Matthews 2004:131). These large numbers of children are often taken to suggest harems (Younger 2002:276-277), else one must imagine some very resilient Israelite mothers.

He sent his daughters to marry men outside his clan, and he brought in thirty young women from outside his clan to marry his sons. In seeing the marriage of all 60 of his children, Ibzan stands in agonizing contrast to Jephthah, who by his own doing denied marriage to his only daughter, thus denying himself of the honors enjoyed by his immediate successor (Block 1999:388-389). The Hebrew only says "outside"; the NLT adds "his clan." Lacking specification, the text could be saying Ibzan violated Israelite marriage rules and intermarried with non-Israelites (Schneider 2000:188). But of the 164 occurrences of the specific term translated "outside" (*khutsah* [TH2351, ZH2575]) only three appear in marriage contexts: the two in this verse, and Deut 25:5. The latter passage is the "levirate" law prescribing that, when two brothers live on the same compound and one dies without children, the other brother will marry the widow rather than marrying her to someone "outside." Clearly here "outside" relates to preserving the immediate family circle, and the issue is preserving land tenure (Nelson 2002:297-300). Thus the NLT is probably correct in rendering "outside the clan" with no implication of intermarriage with non-Israelites. By contracting 60 marriages, all outside the clan, Ibzan established ties of obligation, gift exchange, trade and inheritance, including land tenure, to 60 other families in the region (Younger 2002:276-277). By doing this, he achieved extraordinary influence, making him, in effect, a one-man tribe. This was not, however, an attempt merely to build a power base purely from self-interest; rather, this extraordinary sphere of influence captures the social function of "judging" in pre-state Israel.

Ibzan judged Israel for seven years. Given the interpretation we have suggested for judges and their roles, this (and 12:11, 13) might well be translated, "was paramount chief in Israel for seven years."

12:10 ***When he died, he was buried at Bethlehem.*** That the minor judges succeed one another without intervening declensions into sin, resulting in oppression, contrasts deeply, even if quietly, with the "cyclical" pattern represented by the major judges. While the book as a whole shows Israel in decline, the minor judges probably signal an alternative to the charismatic military leader. Niditch (2008:138) notes, "the peaceful patrilocal burial betokens the end of a respected career."

12:11 ***After Ibzan died, Elon from the tribe of Zebulun.*** One of the clans of Zebulun was "Elon" (Gen 46:14; Num 26:26). The text possibly indicates continuity of place alongside the undisturbed succession of judges. If Ibzan ruled from Zebulunite Bethlehem, then we have two judges from the same tribal district, and Elon might continue the career of Ibzan, possibly as one of 30 sons or sons-in-law. Just as the narrative showed continuity of location from Jair the Gileadite to Jephthah the Gileadite, so here we see continuity between judges from Zebulun.

12:12 ***When he died, he was buried at Aijalon in Zebulun.*** The writer specifies Zebulun because of the prominence of the town of Aijalon in the southern Shephelah. The location of Zebulunite Aijalon remains unknown (ABD 1.131). Interestingly, the Hebrew consonants for spelling the name of Elon are identical to those used to spell Aijalon. They differ only in the vowels. Block's suggestion (1999:389-390) that we should read the place name as "Elon," i.e., bestowed for the man who ruled and was buried there, has merit. No place named Elon in Zebulun, however, is known.

12:13 ***After Elon died, Abdon son of Hillel.*** Of the minor judges, only Tola (10:1) and Abdon appear with their fathers' names mentioned. Abdon's grandchildren also receive notice.

from Pirathon. The scene here shifts south to the central hill country. Pirathon is located about eight miles west of Shechem. One of David's mighty men, Benaiah the Pirathonite, claimed Pirathon as his home (2 Sam 23:30; 1 Chr 11:31; 27:14).

12:14 ***He had forty sons and thirty grandsons.*** As with Jair (10:3-5) and Ibzan (above), prodigious reproduction marks this man as a paramount among his people. His 70 offspring stir memories of Gideon's 70 less-fortunate sons. Unique among the minor judges is reference to his grandsons, particularly in light of how both Gideon and Jephthah were conspicuously deprived of posterity. The troubles in Judges began, however, with the failure of one generation to transmit the faith effectively to the next (cf. 2:10). In that context, lack of progeny (Gideon, Jephthah) contrasts negatively with multigenerational progeny. Scholars note a number of connections between these minor judges and the names of clans, sometimes suggesting these figures stand for clans. Whether that is the case, they probably hint at a social structure such as a chiefdom; reference to children and grandchildren might also suggest a complex chiefdom (cf. R. Miller 2005).

who rode on seventy donkeys. On the prestige of donkeys as riding stock, and the concomitant status implied, see note on 10:4. Possibly this donkey-powered mobility signals a period of security. The claim that the author's depiction ridicules Abdon's descendants as "royal wannabes" and "parodies of kingship" (Younger 2002:278) misses the point both of the role of chiefs and of the importance of transgenerational influence, the problem with which the book began (cf. 2:10).

12:15 ***When he died, he was buried at Pirathon in Ephraim.*** Pirathon actually lies in an area traditionally assigned to Manasseh. R. Miller (2005:32-36) identifies a number of sites surrounding Pirathon as part of Shechem's sphere of influence, suggesting also social linkages to Manasseh. Block (1999:390) observes that the brook Kanah divided Manasseh from Ephraim (Josh 17:7-9), and Pirathon is north of the Kanah. Nevertheless, Pirathon is associated with Ephraim here and in 1 Chr 27:14. This association probably reflects Solomon's administrative districts, which greatly enlarged the region associated with Ephraim and all but eliminated Manasseh.

in the hill country of the Amalekites. The reference to the Amalekites remains a conundrum, but we are not likely to read this as reference to Israel's fragile hold on the land. The central hill country of Ephraim and Manasseh was the heartland of the Israelite settlement, as evidenced in the Bible and by archaeology.

COMMENTARY

Far from being merely a chance for readers to catch their breath (Schneider 2000:1189-1190), the two lists of minor judges provide commentary on the so-called major judges. As a transition from the Gideon-Abimelech complex to the Jephthah-Samson complex, 10:1-5 offered a judgment on Abimelech and introduced Jair the Gileadite. Jephthah the Gileadite both connects and contrasts with Jair, as the second Gileadite fought to save the legacy of the first. The present list (12:8-15) also provides a basis for evaluating the Gideon-Abimelech and Jephthah-Samson material.

The minor judge lists, by their very form and structure, stand outside the major pattern for which Othniel is the exemplar. Judging them by that standard mangles the text. Taken at face value, the minor judges, whatever else they might represent, occupy periods of normalcy in which Israel functioned as a reasonably healthy lineage based upon complex chiefdom. They succeeded each other with no fanfare, no plunge into idolatry, no suffering under oppressors, and no divinely raised-up saviors with all their drama. The concern that the text does not mention "how or why Israel needed a judge" or that these judges were "deity-appointed" (Schneider 2000:188-189) wrongly assumes that judges only represented divine intervention during emergencies. This view fails to understand the social structure of ancient Israel as a coalition of tribal chiefdoms. Several linkages between the minor and major judge narratives, seen in the context of Iron Age I culture, highlight the role of these brief vignettes.

First, the judges' many children, representing marriage alliances with other Israelite clans and tribes, point to far-flung influence. Bound together by ties of marriage and family, the areas presided over by these paramounts had a natural basis for unity and mutual care, in contrast with the fractiousness and bickering so characteristic of the Gideon, Abimelech, and Jephthah stories. To accuse the minor judges of aping the ways of kings by having so many wives puts the reader not only in the position of similarly accusing other biblical worthies, but also of possibly missing the writer's main emphasis, which was not to comment on polygamy. That institution, though contrary to the biblical ethos on marriage, seems to have been tolerated for a time and was not the writer's main concern.

Second, Gideon, Abimelech, and Jephthah all encountered obstacles related to authentication and respect as leaders. The minor judges, by contrast, seem wholly integrated with their communities; they were the very image of prosperous, powerful, and well-respected chiefs. The process of rising as a young father to a position of respect in one's village, of presiding over an orderly and productive family, to becoming a village or town elder, would be extended by the natural prosperity resulting from a wholesome, hardworking family. Such a person would be appealing as an in-law so that marriages with other similar families would naturally follow. The result? Not a bogus parody of monarchy, but a whole region knit together by multiple levels of solid familial and economic ties. The resistance of many commentators on the book toward this simple concept is impressive, but when we consider the state of the family in modern life, perhaps it is not surprising. The author uses the minor judges to register a protest against the "myth of theocracy," the distorted notion that divine rule over his people contradicts and precludes all normal human structures of leadership. Infatuation with this myth appears when interpreters read any absence of divine intervention as a sign of trouble, and constantly want to play the human element against the divine. But if a healthy, family-based community in which power flowed through familial relationships formed part of Yahweh's plan for his people, then the major judges represent the wrong road! The minor judges would actually point toward Yahweh's goals more directly.

Moreover, the stories of Gideon, Abimelech, and Jephthah draw their greatest pathos from the leaders' ultimate failure to leave a human legacy. Abimelech murdered Gideon's 70 sons only to perish himself. Jephthah's lack of descendants deepened the sadness already inhering in his daughter being deprived of marriage. Following the Jephthah story, the emphasis on daughters and weddings in 12:8-15 throws the fate of Jephthah's own daughter into sharp relief. Again, the ready ease with which Ibzan of Bethlehem could find mates for his children contrasts with the agonized question of Samson's parents: "Isn't there even one woman in our tribe or among all the Israelites you could marry?" (14:3). It also contrasts with the marital strife and in-law issues that trigger the horrific climax to the whole book (ch 19).

Thus, the presentation of minor judges, rooted in communities held together by ties of family and faith, surrounded by sons and daughters traveling freely, points to the central problem of the so-called charismatic or extraordinary leader, the problem with which Judges began: the nurture and continuity of Israel's faith, unity, identity, and covenant order over successive generations. While the dynastic principle is not explicitly stated here, the regular succession of these leaders, combined with a strong emphasis on their familial ties, links progeny and posterity with leadership.

◆ 3. Samson: A vow tragically ignored (13:1–16:31)

a. Samson's birth: Word, vow, and spirit (13:1-25)

**Again the Israelites did evil in the LORD's
sight, so the LORD handed them over to
the Philistines, who oppressed them for
forty years.**

**2 In those days a man named Manoah
from the tribe of Dan lived in the town of
Zorah. His wife was unable to become
pregnant, and they had no children. 3 The
angel of the LORD appeared to Manoah's
wife and said, "Even though you have
been unable to have children, you will
soon become pregnant and give birth to a
son. 4 So be careful; you must not drink
wine or any other alcoholic drink nor eat
any forbidden food.* 5 You will become
pregnant and give birth to a son, and his
hair must never be cut. For he will be
dedicated to God as a Nazirite from birth.
He will begin to rescue Israel from the
Philistines."**

[6]The woman ran and told her husband, "A man of God appeared to me! He looked like one of God's angels, terrifying to see. I didn't ask where he was from, and he didn't tell me his name. [7]But he told me, 'You will become pregnant and give birth to a son. You must not drink wine or any other alcoholic drink nor eat any forbidden food. For your son will be dedicated to God as a Nazirite from the moment of his birth until the day of his death.' "

[8]Then Manoah prayed to the LORD, saying, "Lord, please let the man of God come back to us again and give us more instructions about this son who is to be born."

[9]God answered Manoah's prayer, and the angel of God appeared once again to his wife as she was sitting in the field. But her husband, Manoah, was not with her. [10]So she quickly ran and told her husband, "The man who appeared to me the other day is here again!"

[11]Manoah ran back with his wife and asked, "Are you the man who spoke to my wife the other day?"

"Yes," he replied, "I am."

[12]So Manoah asked him, "When your words come true, what kind of rules should govern the boy's life and work?"

[13]The angel of the LORD replied, "Be sure your wife follows the instructions I gave her. [14]She must not eat grapes or raisins, drink wine or any other alcoholic drink, or eat any forbidden food."

[15]Then Manoah said to the angel of the LORD, "Please stay here until we can prepare a young goat for you to eat."

[16]"I will stay," the angel of the LORD replied, "but I will not eat anything. However, you may prepare a burnt offering as a sacrifice to the LORD." (Manoah didn't realize it was the angel of the LORD.)

[17]Then Manoah asked the angel of the LORD, "What is your name? For when all this comes true, we want to honor you."

[18]"Why do you ask my name?" the angel of the LORD replied. "It is too wonderful for you to understand."

[19]Then Manoah took a young goat and a grain offering and offered it on a rock as a sacrifice to the LORD. And as Manoah and his wife watched, the LORD did an amazing thing. [20]As the flames from the altar shot up toward the sky, the angel of the LORD ascended in the fire. When Manoah and his wife saw this, they fell with their faces to the ground.

[21]The angel did not appear again to Manoah and his wife. Manoah finally realized it was the angel of the LORD, [22]and he said to his wife, "We will certainly die, for we have seen God!"

[23]But his wife said, "If the LORD were going to kill us, he wouldn't have accepted our burnt offering and grain offering. He wouldn't have appeared to us and told us this wonderful thing and done these miracles."

[24]When her son was born, she named him Samson. And the LORD blessed him as he grew up. [25]And the Spirit of the LORD began to stir him while he lived in Mahaneh-dan, which is located between the towns of Zorah and Eshtaol.

13:4 Hebrew *any unclean thing;* also in 13:7, 14.

NOTES

13:1 ***Again the Israelites did evil in the LORD's sight.*** This is the last occurrence of this formulaic statement, the most frequently repeated element of the repeated framework (cf. 2:11; 3:7, 12; 4:1; 6:1 [differently constructed]; 10:6; note also the apostasy formula used to introduce Abimelech, 8:33-35). The author did not name the specific evil, but linked the Philistine oppression to the apostasy described in 10:6-16.

the LORD handed them over to the Philistines, who oppressed them for forty years. The phrase "who oppressed them" does not appear in the Hebrew, though it fits the negative connotation of being "handed over." Forty years is by far the longest period of oppression in the book of Judges. It is also the only period that did not definitively end with a deliverance, since the Philistine threat increased until the time of David. This 40-year period probably includes the 20 years of Samson's activity as well as at least part of the era of Samuel. If the Philistine threat as portrayed in the Samson story can be dated to around 1100–1075 BC, the 40 years would carry the story up to the time of Saul and conceivably could include the events of chs 17–21 as well. No outcry to Yahweh appears in this narrative. Possibly the sectional introduction in 10:6-16, which references the Philistine oppression as well as that of the Ammonites, applies to this story. However, the author often controls the reader's perceptions of the narrative by manipulating the repeated introductory and concluding elements. Omitting the outcry might suggest that Israel, insensible to its suffering as divine judgment, cannot even come to cry out in anguish (Block 1999:395). This suggestion comports well with the apparent acquiescence to Philistine domination that appears in the Samson story (cf. 14:4; 15:11). Perhaps the writer is suggesting Israel, after the catastrophic interaction in 10:10-16, has given up on crying out to Yahweh.

13:2 *In those days a man named Manoah.* Lit., "there was a man." This expression in Judges—2 Samuel often prepares the reader to meet a "key player" in the larger narrative (Niditch 2008:141). The author ironically introduced Manoah by name, even though his own role in the narrative to follow is only a foil against which his (unnamed) wife's experiences will be projected.

the tribe. Lit., "clan" or "family" (*mishpakhah* [TH4940, ZH5476]) rather than one of the words that usually denote "tribe" (*shebet* [TH7626, ZH8657], *matteh* [TH4294, ZH4751]). Dan in Judges is twice referred to as "the clan [*mishpakhah*] of the Danites" (13:2; 18:11) and twice as "the tribe of the Danites" (18:1, 30), and once as both (18:19). No other Israelite tribe is referred to in the OT as "the clan of the X-ites," so some Danite distinctive must be in view. Indeed, Dan is listed in the genealogy of Num 26:42-43 as having only one son, or "clan," but the count—64,400—is the second largest in the census! Yet they only muster 600 men to attack Laish in 18:11.

Dan. This is one of the most marginal of Israelite tribes in the overall biblical narrative. After Judges, the Danites as a tribe do not appear in the narrative of Samuel—Kings, and have little or no role anywhere else in the biblical narrative. They are even absent from the book of Revelation's listing of the Israelite tribes (Rev 7:5-8), suggesting perhaps the Danites represent a kind of biblical-theological "dead end." In addition to the Bible's ambivalence about Dan, scholars puzzle over the ethnicity of the Danites, who do not seem to have meshed with Israel. Jacob's "blessing" hints that they were not fully accepted among the Israelites (Gen 49:16-18).

The Danites are associated with ships (5:17) and metallurgy (Exod 31:6; 35:34; 38:23; cf. 2 Chr 2:13), both of which are connected more with the Sea Peoples than Israel—especially with the Philistines. Arrestingly, one of the Sea Peoples mentioned in ancient texts bears a name parallel to Dan, allowing for grammatical endings: *danuna/denyen* (Egyptian), *dnym* (Phoenician), and *danaoi* (Greek). If the Philistines settled the southern coast, and (as scholars suggest) other groups of Sea Peoples settled farther north, *perhaps* the Danuna occupied the area around Joppa. This region would coincide with the territory allotted to Dan in Josh 19:40-46. In short, then, the possibility exists that a segment of the tribe of Dan did not enter Canaan with the rest of the Israelites, but originally belonged to the Danuna/Denyen, a group among the Sea Peoples that was absorbed into Israelite Dan. The Sea Peoples groups were not homogeneous nor fully unified. Some of the groups included among the Sea Peoples groups practiced circumcision since the Egyptian pharaoh Mernepta records that to count the enemies slain in battle he collected the penises of the circumcised and the hands of the uncircumcised (King 2006:334), a practice that the Philistines even adopted in the period of the Israelite monarchy (Faust 2006:88-89). But whether the

Danuna practiced circumcision remains unknown. The Philistines, on the other hand, during Iron I are the quintessential "uncircumcised" peoples of the OT, with the overwhelming preponderance of pejorative references to "uncircumcision" or to circumcision as a major cultural marker for Israel occurring in reference to the Philistines (Bloch-Smith 2003:415). Perhaps the Danuna felt a cultural distance from their Sea Peoples confederates, the Philistines, and found Israelite affiliation more congenial, much as the Canaanite inhabitants of Shechem did. The pressure of Judah and Ephraim on the east and north, and the Philistines on the south, combined with the solid Canaanite enclave at Gezer (Singer 1994:307-309) to cramp the Danites (possibly including their Danuna population) to the point that they sought fresh territory in the far north about 1175 BC. Perhaps they were never a large or vigorous group, since they are referred to in the OT as the "camp of Dan" or the "clan of Dan." This sense of confinement to the hill villages of Zorah and Eshtaol features strongly in the Samson stories. (For more on the Danites, see ABD 2.10-12; NIDB 2.7-10; Spina 1977; Machinist 2000; but cf. arguments against the identification of Danuna and Danites in Rainey and Notley 2006:110.)

lived in the town of Zorah. The geographical situation defined for the Samson story meshes exactly with the nature of the regional conflict triggered by the Philistines settling the coast just as the Israelites had become established in the hills. (See the geographical discussion in the commentary below.)

and they had no children. Lit., "she had not born." Unlike all the other women in the Samson story, his mother "lacks any hint of overt sexuality" (Matthews 2004:140). While barrenness could be a covenant curse, and while Israel in its sin certainly stood under the curse, the suggestion (Block 1999:401) that this specific woman's barrenness resulted from the divine curse finds no support in the text. In fact, no individual barren woman figuring in the redemptive story line of the OT is ever said to be cursed. Barren Israelite women in the OT, far from standing under divine wrath, uniformly stand as illustrations of God's gracious intervention and life-giving power, which is exactly what happens in this story.

13:3 ***The angel of the LORD.*** The reader knows the identity of the messenger, but the characters explicitly do not and discern it only gradually. The term "angel" translates *mal'ak* [TH4397, ZH4855], which as easily denotes a human messenger as a divine one. Messengers in antiquity represented their senders, their masters; for the practical purpose of conveying the message, they rhetorically stood as substitutes for the sender, delivering the message in the first person as though they themselves were the sender. Commonly, more than one messenger was sent to ensure delivery of the message. A single messenger often implied a highly sensitive message, and only the most reliable agent would be dispatched alone. Thus, when David gave Uriah the orders that would result in Uriah's own death, he knew Uriah's integrity well enough to trust Uriah would not violate the privacy of the message (2 Sam 11:14). Thus, the prophet as messenger embodies both the closeness of the prophet's relationship with Yahweh and the high level of integrity needed for Yahweh to entrust his word to the prophet. The recipient's treatment of the messenger signaled the recipient's respect or disdain for the sender, such that to harm or abuse a messenger was a casus belli (cf. 2 Sam 10:1-8). The term "messenger/angel of the LORD" (*mal'ak yhwh* [TH3068, ZH3378]) often in the OT denotes a figure who stands in for Yahweh much more closely and directly than even the standard sender-messenger relationship would suggest. The *mal'ak yhwh* is often a preliminary or preparatory manifestation of Yahweh who, by the end of the encounter, discloses himself more directly and intensely. Thus, it is imprecise to say the messenger of Yahweh is Yahweh himself, but correct still to stress the unique function of the messenger as a preparatory manifestation of Yahweh (TDOT 8.308-325; NIDOTTE s.v. *mal'ak*). Judges 13 clearly shows the movement from a preliminary encounter to the full realization that, in fact, they have met God himself.

appeared to Manoah's wife. Like so many other women playing significant roles in the Judges narrative, Manoah's wife goes unnamed. By contrast, the naming of Sarah in her annunciation story is central to that narrative, though Sarah herself stands in the background, only overhearing (Schneider 2000:195-197).

13:4 ***So be careful.*** Except for the prohibition of cutting hair, the angel curiously binds the woman to the terms of the Nazirite vow that in fact regulates the life of her future son.

you must not drink wine. The terms of the Nazirite vow, articulated in Num 6, banned the consumption not only of alcohol but of any grape product, including the seeds and skins (cf. Num 6:3-4; cf. 13:14 below). The ancients typically drank wine mixed with water, reducing its alcoholic content.

or any other alcoholic drink. While most consider the Hebrew term used here, *shekar* [TH7941, ZH8911], a reference to some form of strong wine, Boling (1975:219) claims that it refers to brewed alcoholic drinks, i.e., beer, which had a higher alcohol content than typical wine. Recent research confirms the prevalence of barley beer in Israel. Since the Hebrew term denotes both the drink and the state of drunkenness, it seems likely that this beer had higher alcohol content than most wines (Homan 2010). The Philistines seem to have been noteworthy drinkers, judging from the frequency of carafes with integral strainers in the Philistine pottery inventory (King and Stager 2001:101-103).

nor eat any forbidden food. Heb., *tame'* [TH2931, ZH3238], here translated "forbidden," traditionally means "unclean." The conundrum with this text is that the dietary laws normally applied to all Israelites, not just Nazirites. No Israelite was to eat unclean food. The text might imply that most Israelites did in fact violate the clean-unclean laws, sometimes unwittingly, sometimes out of necessity, but that such violations were not considered grave sins. Minor defilement possibly was accepted as a fact of daily life. Indeed, some forms of uncleanness are inevitable and unavoidable. The Nazirite, however, lived in an intensified state of devotion that excluded even unwitting or necessary contact with uncleanness. Without the provision regarding cutting the hair, it is not clear whether Samson's mother was freed from these strictures upon the birth of Samson, or whether she too was bound to them for life.

13:5 ***You will become pregnant and give birth to a son.*** The verbal forms used here, participles, combined with the opening particle *hinnak* [TH2009, ZH2180], suggest the angel is declaring an immediate fact: "For you are now/already pregnant and about to bear a son" (Boling 1975:220).

his hair must never be cut. In this word of instruction about the boy, the only Nazirite proscription mentioned is the cutting of the hair, which in turn is the only aspect of the Nazirite that Samson ever acknowledges (Matthews 2004:141). Hairstyle served as one important cultural feature distinguishing the Israelites from the Philistines. The clean-shaven and barbered Philistines contrasted with the Israelite practice, which discouraged excessive trimming of the hair and beard (Bloch-Smith 2003). The Nazirite's long hair thus intensified an already obvious contrast between the Israelites and Philistines, accentuating the identity boundary so vital to this story (Niditch 2008:145).

he will be dedicated to God as a Nazirite. Lit., "a Nazirite of God he will be." The verb, *nazar* [TH5144, ZH5692], comports a dedication to and a separation from. A revealing window, however, for understanding the term "nazirite" (*nazir* [TH5139A, ZH5687]), is its agricultural usage in Lev 25:5, 11, where it refers to unhindered, free-growing crops sprouting during sabbatical years. The idea of unrestrained, unhindered growth appears in the ban on cutting the hair of Nazirites. While natural baldness constituted no uncleanness (Lev 13:40-41), the OT forbids the shaving of the head, normally an expression of extreme grief (Isa 3:24; Ezek 7:18; Amos 8:10), except in cases of cleansing from leprosy (Lev 14:8-9) and the termination of the Nazirite vow, either successfully or due to defilement (Num 6:5, 9, 18). Priests, as special servants of God, were not permitted to shave their heads (Lev 21:5), suggesting that uncut hair in some way symbolized unhindered service to Yahweh. Thus, the Nazirites left their hair uncut to identify themselves as persons undergoing a time of extreme, extraordinary devotion to Yahweh. The other restrictions, prohibiting any contact with the dead and any consumption of the fruit of the vine, point to extraordinary purity that excluded even involuntary or "unavoidable" uncleanness. The prohibition against the Nazirite's contact with the dead is matched only by those bearing on the high priest (TDOT 9.306-311; Matthews 2004:134-136). The Nazirite vow possibly originated in Israelite holy war traditions where the vow's abstinences expressed the warrior's dedication to battle (cf. Deut 29:6 [5]; Boling 1975:220). The long locks of the Nazirite are sometimes seen as the referent in Deborah's praise of the volunteers in Israel, "when the locks are long in Israel" (5:2a, NRSV; see note on 5:2)—in that context, symbolic of unbridled battle passion.

begin to rescue Israel from the Philistines. The interpretation that Samson will not actually effect deliverance, but will only begin to do so, though common, might be incorrect, as the Hebrew could also be rendered, "he will be the first to rescue" (Moore). The verb translated "begin" normally denotes not the initiation of a process (in contrast to its completion) but the first in a series. Though the construction is different, Samson's mission statement here is reminiscent of the question with which the book of Judges opens: "Which tribe should go first to attack?" (1:1) and with which it begins reaching its tragic climax, "Which tribe should go first to attack?" (20:18) (Schneider 2000:195). Of course, in the former instance, the enemy was the Canaanites, in the latter, the Benjaminites.

13:6 *The woman ran and told her husband.* Lit., "the woman came and said to her husband." While commentators often dismiss or malign Manoah, his wife in the narrative emphasizes her eagerness to include him in the encounter with the messenger.

A man of God appeared to me! Here begins a gradual process by which Manoah and his wife discern whom they are dealing with. "Man of God" implies more than simply a person close to God. Prior to this story, nobody in the OT is called a "man of God" except Moses (Deut 33:1; Josh 14:6). The next person so termed is the unnamed prophet of 1 Sam 2:27, followed by Samuel (cf. 1 Sam 9:6). The term mainly designates prophets. "Man of God" appears, therefore, to imply "the man who mediates God's presence and will." The Hebrew construction can also be descriptive, meaning "a godlike man"—i.e., an angelic being. This suggestion seems likely from the next line.

He looked like one of God's angels, terrifying to see. This explanation hints at the possibly supernatural origin of the figure, unless she simply meant to say the man looked incredibly scary! "Angels" translates the word routinely referring to both angels and human messengers.

I didn't ask where he was from, and he didn't tell me his name. Her comment about the messenger not telling his name anticipates Manoah's question in 13:17-18. The important point here is (1) her immediate recognition that the man was an authentic messenger of God and (2) her focus completely on the message brought, not the secondary aspects of the encounter. Manoah, by contrast, will grope after the secondary features and fumble over the message.

13:7 *For your son will be dedicated to God as a Nazirite from the moment of his birth.* The Nazirite status normally was temporary, and voluntary, with the shaving of the head signaling the end of the period of the vow and return to ordinary life. If the Nazirite status originated in the consecration of holy warriors, the cutting of the hair amounted to an honorable discharge from service (Boling 1975:221). Samson's vow, however, was involuntary and permanent. Yahweh's word of devotion enclosed his entire existence and defined his destiny. This prophecy could also imply that even a failed Samson shorn of his hair still lived under the claims of the Nazirite.

until the day of his death. Interpreters sometimes seize on the fact that the phrase "until the day of his death" did not appear in the messenger's original speech. But the term "from [the] womb" appears often in the OT as an idiom for one's entire life, especially seen explicitly in terms of a divine vocation (cf. Pss 22:9, 10; 71:6; Isa 44:2, 24; 46:3; 48:8; 49:1, 5). Callings effective from birth have no expiration date (cf. Jer 1:5). Similarly, John the Baptist in the NT is filled with the Holy Spirit while still in his mother's womb (Luke 1:15). Again, the clear implication is an entire lifetime infused by the Holy Spirit. Thus, Manoah's wife actually adds nothing substantive to the message but actually clarifies its implications and even foreshadows both Samson's downfall (cf. 16:17) and his death.

13:8 ***Then Manoah prayed to the LORD, saying, "Lord, please let the man of God."*** The text uses all three means by which God is designated. Manoah prays to "the LORD" (*yhwh* [TH3068, ZH3378]), but addresses him as *'adonay* [TH136, ZH151] (lord, master) and then asks for the return of the "man of *God*" (*'elohim* [TH430, ZH466]).

more instructions. The Hebrew lacks "more." Manoah did not pray for additional instruction. Rather than respond directly to his wife's report, he asked God for confirmatory revelation. Similarly, Joseph (Matt 1:18-25) needed reassurance regarding his unexpected "fatherhood." To egalitarian modern readers devoid of historical and cultural sensitivities and preoccupied with gender questions, Manoah's request might appear that of a "restless and insecure individual" attempting to "take control" or "assert his superiority," as a male, perhaps even "resentful" (Block 1999:397, 406). An Iron Age "head of the father's house," however, would feel not arrogant superiority, but a sober obligation to discern responsibly the exact nature of the religious experience and message being conveyed by his wife. Manoah does not disrespect his wife; nor is he seen as unspiritual. However, the story persistently presents his wife as more directly responsive to Yahweh's word. As the story unfolds, Manoah will be painfully slow to discern that Yahweh is indeed "coloring outside the lines."

13:9 ***the angel of God appeared once again to his wife. . . . Manoah, was not with her.*** The messenger appeared to Manoah's wife, even though his appearance was in answer to Manoah's prayer. God graciously combined an answer to Manoah's prayer with a clear sign that his wife would be the primary witness to the divine plan (Schneider 2000:198-199).

13:10 ***she quickly ran and told her husband.*** As in 13:6, Manoah's wife betrays no desire to marginalize him or subvert his role. Her eager interest in including him gives the narrative a tender note.

13:12 ***When your words come true.*** "When" represents the particle *'attah* [TH6258, ZH6964], normally translated "now," but often carrying the force of "therefore." Claims that Manoah actually doubted the message fail before his very clear assumption, expressed here, that the words will, in fact, come to pass.

what . . . rules should govern? Manoah asked what the boy's *mishpat* [TH4941, ZH5477] would be. The term derives from the verbal root *shapat* [TH8199, ZH9149], normally translated "judge." But as noted in the commentary introduction, the term covers a wide range of functions. *Mishpat* can refer to a legal decision or the action enforcing such a decision, even a decision viewed as divine revelation. Some suggest the term refers to the oracle given by the messenger, so that Manoah simply asked, "What was the content of the oracle?" (Block 1999:408-409). The term can also denote more abstractly the patterns or principles of life that result from such decisions over time, i.e., a kind of tradition, custom, or rule of life. In the case of an individual such as Samson, perhaps "rule of life" would also translate well here.

13:14 ***She must not eat grapes or raisins, drink wine or any other alcoholic drink, or eat any forbidden food.*** Other than the general statement that the boy will be a Nazirite, the Hebrew text does not expressly impose the dietary restrictions on the boy, but only on his mother. The messenger does not repeat the full instructions originally given to the woman, but repeats the exhortation of 13:13, she must follow "the instructions I gave her," which is omitted from the NLT in 13:14. The two exhortations that she is to obey the instructions originally given to her (13:13-14) form an inclusio around the central instructions, strongly locating the authoritative memory of the message with the woman, not Manoah. His words to Manoah are only a secondary confirmation.

13:15 ***Then Manoah said to the angel of the LORD, "Please stay here until we can prepare a young goat for you to eat."*** Again, Manoah attempted to assume the responsibilities of the head of household, offering hospitality to his guest, the messenger. Far from being an attempt to assert his superiority over the messenger (Block 1999:406), Manoah attempted to reframe the encounter in comprehensible cultural terms. Block's suggestion that this meal is "secular" rather than religious is also puzzling, since it occurs as his response to a revelation from God which has been confirmed for Manoah.

13:16 ***you may prepare a burnt offering as a sacrifice to the LORD.*** The angel's reply gently provided Manoah another clue to his true identity. By suggesting sacrifice instead of a meal, the angel shifts the encounter away from peripheral matters to the central, divine reality.

Manoah didn't realize it was the angel of the LORD. Though as a head of household Manoah surely needed assurance about Yahweh's will, the author consistently stresses Manoah's failure to perceive, contrasted with the natural and spontaneous responses of his wife.

13:17 ***Then Manoah asked the angel of the LORD, "What is your name? For when all this comes true, we want to honor you."*** Encounters with God in the OT at times include this request, always with a less than definitive answer affirming God's freedom and mystery. Jacob's query resulted in a rebuke followed by a blessing (Gen 32:29). Moses asked God his name, and the answer spawned millennia of speculation about the mystery of God's name (Exod 3:13-22). Gideon, whose encounter with Yahweh's messenger bears many similarities to ch 13, did not pose the question, but did ask for a sign to authenticate the messenger's word.

13:18 ***too wonderful for you to understand.*** The Hebrew does not have "for you to understand" but simply follows the angel's question with *wehu' pel'i* (lit., "and it is marvelous"). Probably the clause is circumstantial, "Why do you ask my name, when it is incomprehensible [to you]?" Manoah, in a word, was way over his head. The NLT's "wonderful" translates *pel'i* [TH6383, ZH7100], from the root *pala'*. The term vexes translators since it captures a range of perception and sensibility, not just a simple idea. The idea seems to be something different, extraordinary, or unusual. It can denote the miraculous, the portentous, or sometimes that which is extremely difficult or impossible either literally or conceptually, i.e., incomprehensible. The idea is of a boundary: On one side is utter inconceivability, on the other is the ability to do the inconceivable (HALOT 2.927; NIDOTTE s.v. *pala'*; TDOT 11:533-546). Often expressions of mystification or resistance to understanding are linked to the word, so that the NLT reasonably adds "too . . . for you to understand."

13:19 *offered it on a rock.* The Hebrew has "the rock" as though it was a specific rock known to the reader and recognized as a place of offering.

And as Manoah and his wife watched, the LORD did an amazing thing. This line is a famous crux interpretatum. The sentence can hardly be translated: "and a marvelous one . . . to do, and Manoah and his wife were seeing." The opening participle, *mapli'*, is a causal form of the verb *pala'* [TH6381, ZH7098]. The NLT has done about as well as can be expected with such a difficult line, rendering the sense while working freely with the wording.

13:20 *the altar.* The suspicion that "the rock" referred to in 13:19 denotes a permanent or regular place of sacrifice is confirmed here by the author calling it "the altar."

13:22 *for we have seen God!* It is possible the translation of *'elohim* [TH430, ZH466] could be indefinite, "for we have seen a god" or "divine being" (JPS) or even "gods," rather than as a proper name. But as Manoah and his wife emerge in the story as faithful Israelites, the NLT's treatment is contextually appropriate. The construction is also emphatic, suggesting "for [it is a] god [that] we have seen!" The gradual realization of the messenger's nature reaches its climax.

13:24 *she named him.* The messenger had given no instructions regarding the child's name. While the naming of Samson by his mother certainly reinforces her centrality in the purposes of God in this account, in no way does this marginalize Manoah. In fact, the majority of actual accounts of naming in the OT feature the mother bestowing the name, not the father (Block 1999:416).

Samson. Interpreters have made much of Samson's name, based as it is upon the word for "sun" followed by a characterizing (not diminutive) suffix (Burney 1920:352; see note on 3:12). Some suggest the name points to the origins of the story as one of solar mythology that has assumed a nonmythic form in the Hebrew Scriptures, a view reinforced by the proximity of the town Beth-Shemesh, "Temple of the Sun [god]," to Samson's home (Burney 1920:391-408). But the name could well be shortened from a form that included the name Yahweh or El, yielding "Yahweh is (my) Sun" or the like. Claims linking the name to pagan mythology fail to grasp that solar imagery and rhetoric figures prominently in almost any religion's views of deity for self-evident reasons. The OT frequently and closely associates Yahweh with the sun, as Ps 19 shows. OT authors also freely employed solar imagery, rhetoric, and even phraseology found in other ancient religions, even characterizing Yahweh with solar iconography (Taylor 1993). Doubtless, apostate or deviant Israelites might falsely worship the sun, or falsely identify Yahweh as the sun-god. The word "sun" can be used in personal names a variety of ways, as ancient Near Eastern literature shows. In Akkadian, "sun" can be an expression of devotion or affection. One woman is named Tulid Shamshi, "She [who] bore my Sun," showing "sun" as an affectionate name for the child. Subordinates often expressed their devotion and affection for their superiors by addressing them as "my sun [god]" (CAD 17/1:335-338; 17/2:173-174). More importantly, the winged solar disc, without device, seems to have served as the "coat of arms" for the Davidic dynasty, appearing on jar handles manufactured by the Judean state (Mendenhall 1973:32-68; Taylor 1993:24-91). Malachi expressed the hope of Yahweh's future sudden return to his Temple and a resurgent Davidic monarchy by declaring, "The Sun of Righteousness will rise with healing in his wings" (Mal 4:2). Thus, Samson's name probably does not point to mythology. Contextually, his parents have had an encounter with God's messenger, intend to comply with the Nazirite strictures, and will be horrified later when their son wants to marry a Philistine. It seems unlikely they would name this promised child after a figure in pagan mythology. The name could express the love of parents for a much-longed-for son, or the naming could intimate the author's endorsement of the Judean (Davidic) monarchy. Finally, in ancient literature, the sun bears close associations with overt manifestations of divine and royal glory and power, denoted, for example, in Akkadian by the terms *melammu* and *pulkhu* (see note on 6:34). Assyrian royal reliefs portray the king in his chariot, with the winged solar disc hovering over him. Importantly, the posture and weapons of the king always match that of the solar-divine emblem, indicating the perfect identity of the divine and the human (Mendenhall 1973:45-48). Samson experienced the onrush of the Spirit of Yahweh more frequently, and with more intensity, than any other character in the OT. In Samson's solar title we see glimmers of his intended role as the mirror image of divine power and as the bearer of the manifested divine splendor, the Spirit of Yahweh. Such high hopes only throw the subsequent behavior of Samson into dark relief.

And the LORD blessed him as he grew up. The NT evokes this passage in describing the maturation of Jesus (cf. Luke 2:52). This very positive note encounters a darker counterpoint in the next verse, establishing the ambiguity and tension that marks the Samson narrative.

13:25 ***began to stir him.*** Most translations, using "stir him," conceal an important feature of Samson's experience of the Spirit. The Hebrew term used (*pa'am* [TH6470, ZH7192]) covers actions like "strike, pound, harass, plague, afflict." In the Joseph story, when Pharaoh has his dream, it troubles him—the same word used here of the Spirit's relationship with Samson (HALOT 2.952; TDOT 12.44-49; NIDOTTE s.v. *pa'am*; Burney 1920:353; Stone 1988:336-339). The combination of such a troubling term with the blessing of Yahweh (13:24) adumbrates the tension animating the story. Samson was Yahweh's chosen servant, hallowed by a special, sacred vocation, marked out by unshorn hair, and propelled by the Spirit of Yahweh, but at the same time, the Spirit was an unsettling force prodding and driving him.

while he lived in Mahaneh-dan, which is located between the towns of Zorah and Eshtaol. Mahaneh-dan literally identifies Dan as a "camp" (*makhaneh* [TH4264, ZH4722]), pointing to the diminished nature of the Danites (cf. 1:34), who seem wholly confined to the region around these two villages. The pair of villages, Zorah and Eshtaol, appears three times in the stories dealing with Dan, forming a trajectory. First, they provide the scene for Samson's initial prodding by the Spirit. Second, they locate Samson's burial place (16:31). Third, they locate the point from which the Danites, having failed to possess their inheritance among the Israelite tribes, launched out on their own to find an inheritance more suited to their limited abilities (18:1-2). From the high hopes created by the Spirit's moving, we move to the ignominious death of Samson, then to the Danites' final abandonment of their divinely decreed inheritance.

COMMENTARY

General Orientation to the Samson Story. The Samson story offers a compelling narrative about the encounter of a minor tribe of Israel (the Danites) with an archenemy of Israel (the Philistines) on some of the most strategic ground in the entire country (the Shephelah). Four major points of background inform the entire account.

First, the Samson story concentrates on the tribe of Dan. Indeed, in the book of Judges, this tribe occupies a disproportionate amount of space (see the note on 13:2). Judges 1 concludes by noting how the Amorites had prevented the Danites from possessing the territory Yahweh had allotted to them. The Samson story now depicts the Danites in the villages of Zorah and Eshtaol, calling the region "the camp of Dan" (13:25; 18:12). Following Samson, chapter 17 provides a prologue to the story of the Danite migration to the far north (ch 18). Thus, six chapters of the book treat the fortunes of the Danites, always negatively. It is unclear whether the entire tribe migrated north, or only part, but the chapters concerning Dan, particularly their establishment of a sanctuary in opposition to the "house of God" at Shiloh (18:31), bring the narrative of failure in chapter 1 to a crescendo and provide the book with its final and least exemplary judge.

Second, the story foregrounds the emergence of the Philistines as Israel's most formidable foe to that point. The Philistines were one among several Aegean peoples collectively labeled "Peoples of the Sea" in Rameses III's mortuary temple inscription at Medinet Habu, and in another document known as Papyrus Harris I (ANET 260-263). A tide of urban destructions that began around 1250 BC and brought the Bronze Age to an end ebbed approximately 1175 BC, when Rameses III defeated these "Sea Peoples" in land and sea battles. Various groups of Sea Peoples then settled along the coast of Canaan over the next generation. The most enduring settlement occurred in the south in Gaza, Ashkelon, Ashdod, and inland, in Ekron and Gath, by a group known as the *pelishtim* [TH6430, ZH7149]—Philistines (Singer 1994:299-309). Thus, Judah's capture of Gaza, Ekron, and Ashkelon (1:18) probably preceded the Philistine arrival. The Egyptians increased efforts to secure their control of Canaan, but by 1150 BC, they had all but abandoned the country. The Philistines did not effectively project their power inland for a century, apparently blocked by a Canaanite enclave centered on Gezer that also obstructed Danite expansion from the east. In this period an encounter such as Shamgar's (3:31) could well have occurred. The next 75 years saw rival groups struggling to dominate the hill country and watershed ridge trade route (cf. Gideon and Jephthah stories). The Abimelech story captures the inner conflicts characteristic of this "in between" era, just as the "minor judge list" points out times of relative security.

Unlike the Egyptian imperialists, who occupied Canaan militarily to secure its produce for Egypt, or opportunistic raiders such as the Midianites, the Philistines were colonists, seeking to make the land their own. The Philistines were thus establishing themselves on the coast about the same time that the Israelites were occupying the central hill country. Far from being unsophisticated boors, the Philistines lived in cities ruled by "lords" (*seren* [TH5633A, ZH6249]) and excelled over the Israelites in weapons technology and military organization. They rapidly absorbed Canaanite culture, including its deities, and dined on pork and fine wines while apparently celebrating a vigorous Aegean style of eroticism. The Israelites in the hills, by contrast, lived on family farms, raised no pigs despite ideal conditions, had deficiencies in weapons and metal technology, and observed more narrow sexual boundaries. Both groups sought expansion. The Israelites, believing God had given them the whole land, eyed the rich agricultural land in the valleys, while the Philistines, a trading people, sought control of major trade routes. These two peoples were destined to collide. That collision happened in the rolling hills and flat-bottomed valleys that form the transition from the central highlands to the coastal plain, the Shephelah (*shepelah* [TH8219, ZH9169]; see note on 1:9). Not a dramatic crash, the collision happened more like a traffic pileup as the Philistine cities one at a time attempted, *ad hoc*, to move up the valleys of the Shephelah, beginning with the Sorek valley in our story. Readers should remember the enormous imbalance of power in the Samson story. The Philistines represent an urbanized, militarized, highly organized political force that ravaged the eastern Mediterranean, brought down the Hittite empire, and fought Egypt to a draw. Skilled and well-armed, in their ambition to seize the highlands of Canaan, the Philistines posed a mortal threat to the very survival of the unfortified and unarmed Israelite farming villages situated there. Against this foe, Samson alone stood up on behalf of Israel. However sharply we end up judging Samson's behavior, these facts cannot be forgotten. Though he did not eliminate the Philistine threat, Samson frustrated their attempt to use the Sorek as an invasion route into the Israelite heartland. Later Philistine forays would probe other valley routes until they grasped the need for a coordinated campaign against a determined foe.

The Samson story as a "border epic" (Stager 2006) captures the early era of Philistine expansion. The almost comic stories reveal how badly the Philistines underestimated the tenacity of their hill-country opponents, who in turn grasped only slowly the colonial ambitions of the Philistines. Hence, the biblical author notes that Samson only "begins" to save Israel from the Philistines. Interpreters who see in Samson's hit-and-run tactics mere self-interest fail to grasp the difficulty Israel had in discerning the danger posed by this new and intriguing enemy (Singer 1994:297-298; Killebrew 2005:197-245; Rainey and Notley 2006:104-110).

Third, the geographical setting clarifies the characters' actions and relationships in the story. The village of Zorah was perched on a hilltop overlooking a major valley intersection at a strategic point in the land. The central "Judean highlands" (see map) do not gradually transition west to the rolling hills of the Shephelah and

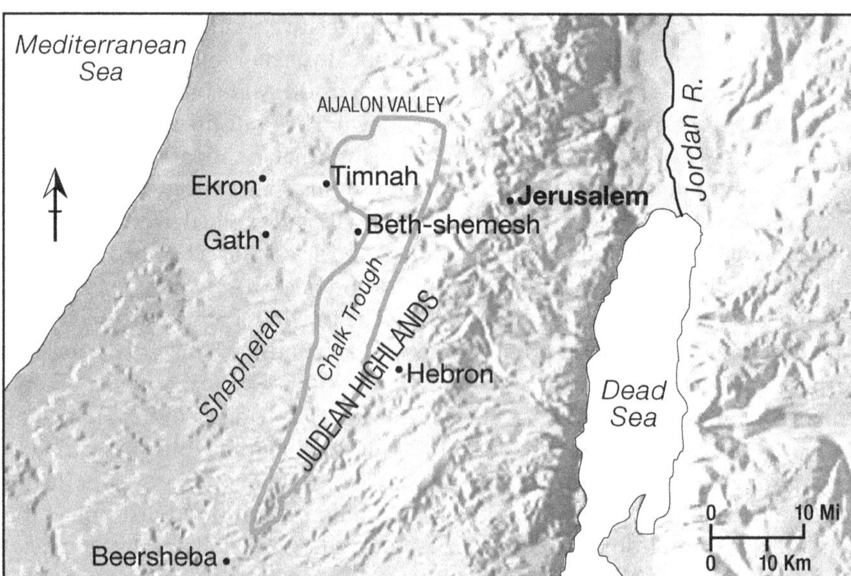

Chalk Trough running south from the Aijalon Valley, adjacent the Shephelah

then the coast. Instead, an abrupt gash into the chalky rock starts near Aijalon and runs south to a point south of Tel Bet Mirsim, a distance of over 30 miles, forming a distinctive topographic boundary separating the hard limestone hill country on the east from the softer limestone hills on the west. This "chalk trough" had a double strategic value: It provided a north–south thoroughfare defining the western physical boundary of the Judean hill country, and it formed a formidable "dry moat" or "great fosse" beyond which enemies would face narrow ravines (wadis), and a steep ascent topping out over 3,000 feet (Smith 1931:201-205; Baly 1974:142-147; Rainey 1983; Brodsky 1987; Rainey and Notley 2006:39; Chesnut 2006). But just west of this trough lies the "Shephelah" (see map), a lower, rolling, rocky plateau, cut by broad east–west valleys that provide fertile agricultural land and the only decent means of east–west traverse. Many of the main cities of the Shephelah stand where these valleys join the coastal plain, or where they connect to the chalk trough. One of the fourteenth-century-BC Amarna letters (Knudtzon 1978:273), in noting towns that had fallen from Egyptian control, lists Aijalon and Zorah—two strategic points along the moat (Moran 1992:318).

A prominent east–west valley crossing the Shephelah is the Sorek valley, which joins the trough at a point where several ravines descend westward to meet it from the Judean hills. This intersection, like the one at the Elah valley, six miles south (where David met Goliath, 1 Sam 17:2), forms a flat, fertile park desirable for cultivation and perfect as a base camp for staging military resources. The Sorek was famous for its red soil, used for cosmetics, and its fine grapes. The town of Beth-shemesh loomed over this valley-park from its southern rim, while two miles north on the opposite rim sat the village of Zorah with its companion town of Eshtaol on an adjacent hilltop two miles northeast. These two towns define the "camp of Dan" in the Samson story, while also underlining the perpetual appeal and frustration posed by the Danite tribal allotment (Josh 19:40-46). Though the two principal Danite villages looked down on verdant farmland all around, the Danites could not take advantage of it because of competition first from the "Amorites" who harassed them into the hills (1:34-35), and later from the Philistines, who quickly dominated the valleys, at least on their lower reaches. Eventually the Danites decided they had no future in their divinely granted allotment (cf. 18:1-2) and sent a survey team to the far north seeking some easier challenge.

The writer of Judges structured the book so that the dark events of chapters 17–21 appear as the consequence of the events of 3:7–16:31, so that the migration of Dan naturally seems to follow the career of Samson, implicitly reinforcing the author's negative judgment of him. Historians still struggle to clarify the chronology of Judges overall, wondering if the book's sequence is more thematic than chronological. But the causal relationship between the recurring apostasy and lack of continuity leadership represented in 3:7–16:31 and the spiritual and social meltdown of chapters 17–21 still stands, even if the chronological connection is not exact at every point.

Fourth, the Samson story, the longest single account in the book, evinces a definite literary structure that scholars have examined extensively (see Block 1999:398, n. 206 for literature). Judges 13 establishes expectations surrounding Samson, namely, his lifelong extreme devotion to Yahweh expressed in his Nazirite status and his being the first to deliver Israel from the Philistines. Alongside this criterion of the divine word is the power of the divine Spirit that prods and drives him. The vow defines a set of boundaries or constraints, while the Spirit "driving" him (13:25) seems to imply a tendency to push beyond boundaries. The repeated summary of Samson's 20-year rule found in 15:20 and 16:31 partitions the remainder of the account into two sections easily characterized as Samson's Triumphs (chs 14–15) and Samson's Tragedy (ch 16).

Chapters 14–15 present a unified story of Samson's defiance of his parents and violation of elements of his Nazirite vow as he pursued an ill-fated marriage to a Philistine woman, which triggered a chain reaction of revenge, climaxing after Samson's slaying of 1,000 Philistines with the jawbone of an ass (15:15). This Samson appears untouchable. Not even violation of the Nazirite prohibition against wine or contact with the dead stops him! At the same time, Samson also partly personifies failed Israel as described in 3:5-6, by his fraternizing and intermarrying with pagans. The final act, serving their gods, comes in chapter 16 (see note on 16:24). Judges 16 narrates Samson's "fall" by returning to the theme of his relationships with women, except that now rather than marry Philistines, he fornicates. Ultimately, he betrays the secret of his strength to Delilah, leading to his downfall. Just as chapters 14–15 end with an answered prayer for vengeance, so also chapter 16 concludes with such a prayer.

The Prologue. The Samson story brings to a climax the book's progressive exposé of the evils and troubles that Israel brought on itself after Joshua's death. First, Israel's apostasy came to a climax in 10:6-9 triggering *both* the Ammonite *and* the Philistine oppressions, with signs only of a kind of pause or truce (10:14-16), not a genuine repentance (Stone 1988:291-326). Second, like Goliath stepping out from the ranks of the enemy, the Philistines top off the series of oppressors who afflicted the Israelites, posing the most serious threat yet to Israel's existence in the Promised Land. They succeeded in breaking down Israel's unity as a decentralized tribal confederacy and so deeply threatened Israel's grasp on the land that they ultimately made Israel take the next step in its political life—the step of national statehood, including a king. More importantly, the Philistines become for the biblical authors the standard of what Israel is *not,* the quintessential "other" over against which Israel persistently defined itself. Samson's fraternization with the Philistines occurred at a genuine topographical border defined by the "chalk trough" between the hills and the Shephelah, but also violated the boundary between Israelite and non-Israelite identity, Yahweh's people and "not" Yahweh's people. Samson's story constitutes both a border epic and a narrative of identity definition, even if by identity violation (Machinist 2000:67-69; Bloch-Smith 2003). Third, in addition to apostasy and oppression, the theme of Israel's outcry comes to a climax here—by its *absence.* The progression is one of the clearest in the book: At first the cry leads to immediate divine aid (3:8, 15; 4:3), then we read of a prophetic rebuke in response to Israel's cry (6:7-10), and then an outright divine refusal (10:11-14). Here we find no outcry at all: Apostate Israel stands speechless under Yahweh's wrath (Stone 1988:311-325). It is a time of crisis in every conceivable way—spiritual, social, political. If ever Israel needed a Spirit-empowered savior, this was the time.

The Potential of the Promise through the Word and Spirit. No judge after Ehud is said explicitly to have been "raised up" by Yahweh in keeping with the paradigm articulated in 2:15-17 and illustrated in the Othniel story (3:7-11). Subsequent judges either worked in the context of an office they held already, or received extraordinary authentication. In keeping with the climactic position of the Samson story, his birth narrative (13:2-25) climaxes the book's increasingly detailed description of each judge's background. Othniel and Ehud appear with only the slightest background. Deborah's role is sketched only a bit more fully. With Gideon we encounter a long narrative of call and assurance. Abimelech's parentage and rise to power are narrated in detail. With Jephthah, the judge's own personal history becomes a central issue in the story. Samson's narrative begins even further back, prior to his conception (Stone 1988:327-332). His origin is the result of a divine promise. This chapter, in fact, identifies two powerful forces that shape Samson's destiny. One is God's word of promise, embodied by Samson's womb-to-tomb vow as a Nazirite. The other is the Spirit of Yahweh, sporadic, bruising, and overwhelming in its driving power. In setting out this tension, the text actually points to the complex and mysterious nature of human freedom. No human is unconditionally free in the sense of all moral options standing equally open at all times. God directly and through providence indirectly hedges humans about with a range of boundaries, challenges, resources, and tasks, waiting to see how we will use these resources. Human capacity itself is subject to change. While persons can choose good or evil, the goods and evils from which they can choose can become limited. In the end, the only good remaining for blind, bound Samson, who had presumed on his freedom precisely when he "didn't realize the LORD had left him" (16:20), was to choose death with the Philistines. Life is like a loom, opening and closing, the shuttle flying back and forth with each cycle. God tosses the shuttle through the loom to his servants, and their destiny is shaped by how and when they toss it back.

Samson's life is quite literally defined and determined by the word of God, spoken concerning his life before his conception. His anonymous mother received God's promise of a child, a promise that also decreed the child to be a lifelong Nazirite. The author accentuated the importance of this vow by repeating the requirements three times (13:2-5, 7, 14). This ancient status, described in Numbers 6, involved a voluntary period of temporary, radical devotion to God and uncompromising separation from any uncleanness. This state required abstinence from alcohol and from any grape product, strict avoidance of the dead, and leaving the hair uncut. These behaviors apparently pointed to absolute freedom from any corruption and an uncontrolled, unhindered freedom for God. According to Numbers 6, Nazirites undertook these obligations voluntarily for a limited period of time, cutting their hair when their time of dedication ended. Not so, however, with Samson. He did not choose his vow, but prenatal divine election imposed it on him. Nor is Samson's vow temporary: He was to be a lifelong Nazirite. His life unfolds strictly in interaction with the word of divine demand, a word that he only once confesses as binding on his life (16:17).

The story's central enigma arises from the convergence of Samson's Nazirite status, his experience of possession by the Spirit of Yahweh, and his great strength. Nothing in the traditions governing the Nazirite speaks of the Spirit of Yahweh or of supernatural strength, though many scholars associate it with the holy war traditions. Again, if the Nazirite vow is the source of his strength, this status certainly was no secret. Nazirites stood as highly visible and public signs of radical devotion to Yahweh, not as possessors of secrets. Moreover, Samson's violations of Nazirite prohibitions in chapters 14–15 have no debilitating consequences either regarding his strength or his access to God. But not all of Samson's feats of strength are empowered by the Spirit, and no connection between the Spirit and Samson's Nazirite status is noted in the text dealing with the vow. Samson stands, therefore, at a rather untidy intersection of three forces in Israelite faith: the liturgical (the vow), the charismatic (the Spirit), and the martial (his strength). All these forces are released and governed by the divine word spoken at Samson's conception.

Stories in which childless women are promised children typically mark turning points in the biblical narrative. These stories all highlight the mother, climaxing in the annunciation to Mary in the New Testament. Every such birth announces the arrival of a strategic moment in God's redemptive plan, the entry of Yahweh to confirm his promise and liberate his people (Matthews 2004:139-140). This is the word of promise that balances the word of demand under which Samson is born. We get the first intimations, however, that Samson might not fulfill this promise, when the messenger states that he will "*begin* to rescue Israel" or will "be the first to rescue Israel" (13:5b). With Jephthah, the deliverance morphed into tragedy; with Samson, deliverance itself slips away. The divine word of promise finds only sketchy fulfillment in Samson.

Far from being deliberately minimized as a "complication" to the plot (Block 1999:397, 406), Manoah, Samson's father, unwittingly poses the central issue of the story. Branding Manoah as dim-witted, "a restless and insecure individual . . . a comical figure bound by ignorance and obtuseness" (Block 1999:397) or a "dolt of a husband" (Niditch 2008:143) ignores a common feature of this type of story. Birth announcements to the childless, from Abraham and Sarah all the way to Zechariah in the New Testament, typically provoke a confused and *superficially* unbelieving response. The parents of Jesus alone seem able to embrace the amazing word of a miraculous conception. Readers should therefore handle these moments gently, recognizing the tortured mix of emotions that childlessness creates. Caricaturing Manoah also ignores the cultural setting of the story. In the family structure of Iron Age Israel as portrayed both in the Old Testament and evidenced in the archaeological record (cf. Stager 1985), the *paterfamilias* bore spiritual responsibility for the entire household. Manoah could not simply abandon that obligation (see note on 13:8). Manoah's wife's eagerness to communicate with Manoah (13:6, 10) shows she also had no interest in minimizing his role, however much modern exegetes would like to. Yahweh, however, chose to transcend cultural conventions, not to marginalize Manoah, but to accentuate the primacy of his word whose reality does not depend on the recipient's gender or social location. Manoah is likely a representation of the typical reader: not an evil person, just one so settled in their familiar expectations and cultural paradigm that they discern Yahweh's fresh work only with difficulty. The narrator portrays Manoah as consistently missing this point. His failure to align with the way Yahweh was working contrasts with his wife, who accepted God's word of demand and promise joyfully. Enthralled with the message itself and possibly aware of the stirrings of her newly conceived child, Mrs. Manoah did not need to see an ID, but Manoah became obsessed with the messenger and his identity (13:8). Manoah's prayer for "more instructions about this son who is to be born" had already been answered if he could only overcome his uncertainty. Manoah's attempts to fit Yahweh's word into a set of religious and traditional expectations are evident in his offer of a ceremonial meal (13:15-16) and probing of the messenger's identity (13:17-18). In the presence of the naked word of Yahweh, rituals and names become secondary and subservient, not central. The urge to add to the simple act of listening to God's word in the testimony of a human witness dies hard. When the messenger did confirm his divine identity, Manoah switched from assertiveness to terror upon realizing his impertinence (13:19-23). How different was his wife's response. Rather than fall back on custom and superstition—the spiritual dimension—she used simple reason based on God's expressed purpose. He would not reveal himself to them, accept their offering, and give them his word if all he had in mind was killing them (13:23). Her response is simultaneously "unspiritual" and profoundly faithful. Before we castigate Manoah as the poster boy for spiritual cluelessness or male domination, perhaps we should all take a look in the mirror and assess how much our own cultural baggage prevents us from simply believing the word of the living God. Compared to us, Manoah might not seem so clueless after all.

Samson's birth and blessing (13:24-25) fulfill God's promise and sound a warning. The affirmation of Yahweh's blessing makes it impossible for the reader to write Samson off as a buffoon or sensualist. Though not the flannel-graph hero of Vacation Bible School, Samson is not to be caricatured as a clown with a weakness for exotic women. The word of blessing (13:24) completes the introduction's emphasis on the divine word of promise and demand that encompasses Samson's life. The spirit also intervened in Samson's life (13:25). The Spirit of Yahweh always points to the freedom of Yahweh to act decisively, even intrusively. Here the role of the Spirit of Yahweh emerges as a troubling presence. The author's word choice—"drive, prod, provoke" (see note on 13:25)—insinuates a note of tension. To be sure, the Spirit of Yahweh will empower Samson and accentuate divine freedom. Samson will experience intense and frequent visitations by the Spirit of Yahweh, but the Spirit's presence will not be unambiguously beneficent, but will disturb Samson—a haunting as much as an anointing. Just as Samson in birth was subject to a vow over whose making he had no control, so in adult life he was subject to a troubling by the Spirit over which he had no control. In the accounts that follow, the Spirit's role will be prominent, but it will ultimately be the *word* that silently shapes Samson's destiny. The Spirit as a source of imbalance is a theme that will unfold through the next two chapters, bringing to a climax the book's careful but somewhat critical treatment of the charisma of the Spirit. One thing is clear: The onrush of the Spirit of Yahweh alone, without faithful obedience to the word of Yahweh, cannot guarantee salvation, and can even drive the disobedient servant to destruction (Stone 1988:332-338). As will be discussed in the commentary on 14:5-20, one should not easily equate the Spirit of Yahweh of the Old Testament with the Holy Spirit, the third person of the Trinity of the New Testament and Christian theology.

Word, Spirit, and Freedom. As one born under a previously spoken word of God, Samson stands potentially analogous to every person born into the world after Christ's resurrection. The Christ event inaugurated a new era. God spoke a word that decisively circumscribed the fate of every person born thereafter. Each human being is born confronting the divine promise and demand of the gospel, as well as the living, illuminating, convicting presence of the Spirit in the world. Some theological traditions speak of "prevenient grace" to define the distinctively post-Easter quality of God's outreach of grace to every person on planet Earth springing from Christ's unconditional death for all without regard to merit or even response. Far from simply the restraint of evil recognized under the concept of "common grace," the prevenient grace of God flows from Christ's death for Adam, for all, and the gift of life bestowed upon all (cf. Rom 5:12-21), even though some will disregard and forfeit this gift of life. Based on the divine word spoken in Christ, God's word to the whole world can be one of love, grace, and invitation. This very gift underscores darkly the heinousness of turning away from God's word in Christ. Those who are not saved will have perished not merely for their inborn depravity, but more for having resisted the prior word of grace spoken over them before they were even born. None is born into a neutral world. All, like Samson, are born confronted by, and to confront, the word of the living God that is always prior to us. The prologue to the Samson story broaches the question of freedom—how would Samson act in response to the word and Spirit? In the same way, God's word of promise and command spoken in Christ calls every human being to answer first, before any other question, the one posed ironically by Pontius Pilate: "What should I do with Jesus who is called the Messiah?" (Matt 27:22).

◆ b. The riddle of Samson: Marriage (14:1-4)

One day when Samson was in Timnah, one of the Philistine women caught his eye. [2]When he returned home, he told his father and mother, "A young Philistine woman in Timnah caught my eye. I want to marry her. Get her for me."

[3]His father and mother objected. "Isn't there even one woman in our tribe or among all the Israelites you could marry?" they asked. "Why must you go to the pagan Philistines to find a wife?"

But Samson told his father, "Get her for me! She looks good to me." [4]His father and mother didn't realize the LORD was at work in this, creating an opportunity to work against the Philistines, who ruled over Israel at that time.

NOTES

14:1 *One day when Samson was in Timnah.* Lit., "And Samson *went down* to Timnah." The author threads the action seamlessly with the end of ch 13, as the direct sequel to the spirit's prodding of Samson. Timnah's elevation is about 600 feet below that of Zorah, and Samson would likely have descended even further to travel along the wadi Sorek before going up again to enter the city of Timnah (a total walk of about 6 miles). Thus, Samson "went down" quite literally from the Danite villages to Timnah, where he saw the Philistine woman. But, one could be forgiven for suspecting the writer might be thinking of descending in a religious or ethical sense as well—consider the following: Archaeologists identify Timnah as Tel Batash, where finds evince Philistine presence and advanced material culture around this time (ABD 1.625-626; 6.556-557). This is a marked difference from finds at nearby Beth-shemesh, which was then a small, probably Israelite squatter village that sat atop an earlier, Israelite unwalled city (Stern 1993–2008:1.249-254; 5.1644-1645). It appears the functional boundary between Israelite and Philistine influence lay between these two sites. To travel to Timnah thus was to step definitively outside the sphere of the Hebrew ethos. Additionally, Timnah, on the northern frontier of Judah (Josh 15:10), had been assigned to the Danites (Josh 19:43), so its Philistine identity points to the Danites' failure to possess it. Timnah was sophisticated—the "big city" in the eyes of Samson's subsistence-farming kinsmen. And Samson likely appeared to them as the country boy who considered himself too smart and sophisticated for his backward relatives.

one of the Philistine women caught his eye. The idiom employed here, literally, "Samson saw a woman," is not common in the OT. In each case, it narrates a man's random sighting of a woman followed by illicit or irregular sexual congress (cf. 16:1; Deut 21:11; 2 Sam 11:2). The NLT's rendering captures this nuance. Reference to a "woman" (*'ishah* [TH802, ZH851]) rather than "girl" (*na'arah* [TH5291, ZH5855]) or "maiden" (*betulah* [TH1330, ZH1435]) could imply a mature woman, but her residence with her father would require her to be a widow or divorced woman. Burney (1920:356) suggests the word carries a "shade of contempt."

The text does not disclose Samson's motivations, though commentators suggest blind sensual lust or the lure of an exotic, foreign woman (Younger 2002:299-300). But a good many OT characters consort with prostitutes, take concubines, and so forth without receiving censure or labels from commentators. Without approving of Samson's actions, we must let the text tell us about his character—and on his psychology, the text here is silent.

14:2 *he told.* The Samson story (chs 13–16) is dominated by "telling." The verb *nagad* [TH5046, ZH5583], meaning to narrate or tell in detail, appears 23 times in the Samson story, but only three other times in the whole book of Judges. Pronouncing and announcing loom large in this tale.

his father and mother. Some ancient mss do not include "and mother," but the prominence of Samson's mother in the narrative weighs in favor of including the reference.

A young Philistine woman. "Young" is not in the Hebrew, which reads "a woman . . . among the daughters of the Philistines." The formula "daughters of the Philistines" simply refers to Philistine women, not specifically to an age group.

Get her for me. The grammar of Samson's words to his parents is abrupt, conveying a peremptory demand. The introduction to the book flagged three indices of Israel's failure in the land: fraternizing with pagans, intermarrying with pagans, and serving pagan gods (3:5-6). Samson moves from participation in the first of these to involvement in the second.

14:3 *His father and mother objected.* "Objected" expands on the Hebrew, which simply says "his father and mother said to him."

Why must you go . . . to find a wife? The conversation of 14:2-3 employs many independent pronouns, not strictly necessary in Hebrew and typically emphatic. The "you" in "you go" is such a case. The Hebrew participle of "go" in this context suggests the imminent future, "about to go" or "intend to go."

pagan Philistines. The NLT "pagan" translates "uncircumcised." This word climaxes Manoah's protest, and one can almost hear him spit the word out. Since the Egyptians and most west-Semitic peoples practiced circumcision, including, according to Jer 9:25-26 the Ammonites, Moabites, and Edomites, most references to the "uncircumcised" in the OT apply to the Philistines (Boling 1975:229; King and Stager 2001:43-45). Despite the high concern in the Samson story (and in this pericope) for the Philistine presence, the term *'arel* [TH6189, ZH6888] foreskinned/uncircumcised appears only at 14:3 and 15:18. Of the three women involved with Samson, only this one is explicitly designated a Philistine. The term *'arel* has a broad range of uses, from denoting fruit trees that have not yet borne (Lev 19:23-25), to metaphorical descriptions of poor speech and hearing (cf. Exod 6:12, 30; Jer 6:10), to ethnic boundaries (ABD 1.1025-1031).

Get her for me! The Hebrew is very emphatic with the object first and the abrupt command: "Her—get for me!" These words to his father highlight how impertinent and out of order Samson is in this patriarchal society.

She looks good to me. The author uses the identical idiom, "she is right (*yasherah* [TH3474, ZH3837]) in my eyes," that appears in 17:6 and 21:25, where everyone did "whatever seemed right (*yashar*) in their own eyes." The parallel is deliberate: Samson parallels and personifies the nation in its willful determination to do what it pleases and define its own standards of conduct. This statement might well foreshadow the ultimate result of Samson doing what is right in his own eyes—he will lose them and live in permanent darkness (Schneider 2000:204).

14:4 ***His father and mother didn't realize.*** The Hebrew construction here is disjunctive, marking a break in the flow of the narrative as the author turns to the reader. The expression "did not know" recurs through the Samson story (13:16; 16:20) as part of a larger theme of secrets and ignorance.

the LORD was at work in this. Lit., "From Yahweh (was) she/it." Hebrew grammar does not have a neuter gender and must use either masculine or feminine. The sentence could well suggest "she" (i.e., the Philistine woman) was from Yahweh, or that "it" (the whole circumstance) was from Yahweh. The observation articulates a theme that recurs through the story, that Yahweh's actions contradict what the characters expect.

creating . . . against the Philistines. Lit., "he was seeking an opportunity from the Philistines." The identity of the "he" remains unclear. "He" could be Yahweh, or "he" could be Samson, who would have then contracted the marriage precisely to gain a pretext for harassing the Philistines. The closest grammatical reference for the "he" is Yahweh, suggesting the latter is more likely.

an opportunity. LXX Alexandrinus translates with *antapodoma* [TG468, ZG501] "repayment, recompense," while LXX Vaticanus offers *ekdikēsis* [TG1557, ZG1689], "revenge." Clearly the ancient versions saw here a note of hostility and aggression.

who ruled over Israel at that time. This clause is a parenthetical observation to the reader. "Ruled" translates the verbal root *mashal* [TH4910, ZH5440], which refers to the actual exercise of dominance or power without implying an official, political relationship of subordination. This note anticipates the Judeans' complaint to Samson in 15:11, "Don't you realize the Philistines rule over us?" The assertion that the Philistines dominated Israel during a time shortly to be characterized as ". . . those days [when] Israel had no king" (17:6; 18:1; 19:1; 21:25) gives the lie to any claim that kinglessness somehow implies liberty.

COMMENTARY

The story of Samson's exploits (chs 14–15) divides into two parts, with a cause-effect connection linking them as the narrative rises to its climax at the end of chapter 15. Judges 14 centers on Samson's riddle, which is framed within the account of his marriage to the woman of Timnah. Posed during his wedding feast, the riddle shatters Samson's trust in his bride and ultimately prevents their union altogether. The soured marriage in turn provides the opening scenario in chapter 15, where the theme shifts dramatically to Samson's revenge against his rivals, which triggers ever-widening conflicts with the Philistines and even other Israelites. The narrative reaches its high point when Samson, victorious over the Philistines with the jawbone of a donkey, cries out to Yahweh for water and receives a lifesaving answer (15:16-19). From that high point the story will turn downhill until Samson's death. Judges 14:1-4 introduces the story of Samson's triumphant harassment of the Philistines while also sounding all the notes that will resonate through the rest of the story, including the vital theological theme of the hiddenness of Yahweh's purpose. This short passage follows directly, without a grammatical break, on the heels of 13:25 with its claim that the Spirit of Yahweh "began to [prod]" Samson in the camp of Dan. Since the verb there connotes disturbance, annoyance, anxiety, and not empowerment or motivation, it could portend dark things for Samson. We must consider the possibility of an agonistic relationship between Samson and the Spirit as the underlying driving force in the stories to follow.

Judges 14:1-4 also parallels 16:1-3 where Samson has yet another Philistine liaison, this time in Gaza, which will start a process bringing Samson back to Gaza, minus his hair . . . and eyes. This passage sets the stage, depicting Samson's determined insistence on marrying a Philistine woman despite parental protest, but also characterizing it as Yahweh's opportunity to confront the Philistines. The text boldly inhabits a rending tension: Samson's actions defy his parents and disregard the boundaries placed on Israelite marriages to non-Israelites, yet at the same time, they are from Yahweh and constitute a direct confrontation of the Philistines who are mentioned five times in four verses, at a town occupying a salient into Israelite territory, Timnah, mentioned three times in 14:1-2a. Against the backdrop of Philistine intimidation Samson's repeated "Get her for me" (14:2, 3) also sounds a note of determination: Not cowed by the Philistine dominance, Samson makes love with the result that he will make war.

Several important themes for the whole story find mention here. First, the author presents the conflict between Samson's vocation as a deliverer, his identity as the "ultimate Israelite" (Nazirite), and his choices to affiliate with Israel's oppressors (cf. 3:5-6). Again, the author draws an intriguing contrast between Samson's clear violation of the boundaries of Israelite identity and Yahweh's larger purposes, which somehow his choices will serve. Moreover, the writer then underscores how little the characters, both the apparent bad guy (Samson) and the apparent good guys (Samson's parents) actually know of Yahweh's actions and plans. Though Samson will play too close to the edge and presume on God's power with him, the Lord is at work in this. Despite the secret purposes of Yahweh served by Samson's wrong choices, they remain wrong choices and ultimately bring catastrophe upon him. Theologically, the story raises the possibility that God's ability to work through the sins we commit still does not suggest that our actions will have no consequences. Even when God weaves our sin into the fabric of his purpose, the threads of our own lives remain broken unless we allow his grace to transform our character—something to which Samson seems utterly oblivious.

c. The riddle of Samson: Mayhem (14:5-20)

5 As Samson and his parents were going down to Timnah, a young lion suddenly attacked Samson near the vineyards of Timnah. 6 At that moment the Spirit of the LORD came powerfully upon him, and he ripped the lion's jaws apart with his bare hands. He did it as easily as if it were a young goat. But he didn't tell his father or mother about it. 7 When Samson arrived in Timnah, he talked with the woman and was very pleased with her.

8 Later, when he returned to Timnah for the wedding, he turned off the path to look at the carcass of the lion. And he found that a swarm of bees had made some honey in the carcass. 9 He scooped some of the honey into his hands and ate it along the way. He also gave some to his father and mother, and they ate it. But he didn't tell them he had taken the honey from the carcass of the lion.

10 As his father was making final arrangements for the marriage, Samson threw a party at Timnah, as was the custom for elite young men. 11 When the bride's parents* saw him, they selected thirty young men from the town to be his companions.

12 Samson said to them, "Let me tell you a riddle. If you solve my riddle during these seven days of the celebration, I will give you thirty fine linen robes and thirty sets of festive clothing. 13 But if you can't solve it, then you must give me thirty fine linen robes and thirty sets of festive clothing."

"All right," they agreed, "let's hear your riddle."

14 So he said:

"Out of the one who eats came
something to eat;
out of the strong came something
sweet."

Three days later they were still trying to figure it out. 15 On the fourth* day they said to Samson's wife, "Entice your husband to explain the riddle for us, or we will burn down your father's house with you in it. Did you invite us to this party just to make us poor?"

16 So Samson's wife came to him in tears and said, "You don't love me; you hate me! You have given my people a riddle, but you haven't told me the answer."

"I haven't even given the answer to my father or mother," he replied. "Why should I tell you?" 17 So she cried whenever she was with him and kept it up for the rest of the celebration. At last, on the seventh day he told her the answer because she was tormenting him with her nagging. Then she explained the riddle to the young men.

18 So before sunset of the seventh day, the men of the town came to Samson with their answer:

"What is sweeter than honey?
What is stronger than a lion?"

Samson replied, "If you hadn't plowed with my heifer, you wouldn't have solved my riddle!"

19 Then the Spirit of the LORD came powerfully upon him. He went down to the town of Ashkelon, killed thirty men, took their belongings, and gave their clothing to the men who had solved his riddle. But Samson was furious about what had happened, and he went back home to live with his father and mother. 20 So his wife was given in marriage to the man who had been Samson's best man at the wedding.

14:11 Hebrew *they.* **14:15** As in Greek version; Hebrew reads *seventh.*

NOTES

14:5 ***As Samson and his parents were going down to Timnah.*** The NLT's rendering obscures the fact that the wording of this verse is identical to the opening words of 14:1, except for the addition of "and his father and his mother."

a young lion. The Asian lion (*panthera leo persica*) is apparently extinct in the Levant today but once thrived all over the ancient Near East. Assyrian kings prided themselves on maintaining lions and delighted in depicting themselves engaged in hunting lions (Strawn 2005). One hesitates to call imprisoning lions in cages and releasing them just in time for the king to ride by in his chariot and kill them with his bow a "sport"; perhaps "game" is apropos. But the killing of a large beast of prey is an emblematic heroic deed, and the killing of a lion bespeaks royal status. David also slew a lion empty-handed (1 Sam 17:34-37) and gave glory to Yahweh for delivering him.

suddenly attacked Samson. Lit., "was roaring to meet him." The term for "roaring" always expresses strong emotion, whether the literal angry roar of a lion in midpounce or the metaphorical roaring of a distraught supplicant bewailing his sins (HALOT 2.1367, s.v. *sha'ag*).

near the vineyards of Timnah. Located in the Sorek valley, Timnah sat in the heart of wine country. Indeed, the Levant is one of the earliest sites for viticulture. The prized Soreq grape, for which the valley was named, was dark red and famous for its excellent wine. The Egyptian pharaoh Thutmose III brought grapevines from Canaan to Egypt in the hope of improving Egyptian stocks. Typically vineyards were surrounded by walls, with narrow passages weaving between sections of the vineyard (King and Stager 2001:98-103; Borowski 2002:102-114). Possibly a blind corner between two vineyard walls provided the lion with a cover for an ambush. Ironically, the scene of Samson's first triumph, and the source of his riddle with its subsequent vendetta, was associated with a product prohibited to Samson as a Nazirite.

14:6 *Spirit . . . came powerfully upon him.* This renders the strong words *wattitslakh 'alayw ruakh* [TH5921, ZH6584]. The verb employed, *tsalakh* [TH6743, ZH7502], denotes violent seizure, with contextualized meanings such as "to split, set on fire, be successful, intrude, succeed, advance" (TDOT 12.382). The LXX typically translates the verb with *ephallomai* (to spring upon, to jump). Up until now in the book of Judges, the coming of the Spirit of Yahweh has served to authenticate the leadership of a judge. No other overt manifestations of the Spirit have been emphasized except that immediately the judge has a following of Israelites ready for battle. Here, though, the emphasis falls on superhuman acts, thus the different term is employed. In contexts involving the Spirit of Yahweh or of God, the sense of overwhelming, even violent domination appears strongly. In 1 Sam 18:10 a "tormenting spirit from God" seizes (*tsalakh*) Saul, and he raves like a madman. The frenzy of the Spirit impels Samson to rip apart a lion with his bare hands, to kill 30 men in Ashkelon, and to use the jawbone of an ass to slaughter a Philistine attacking force (14:6, 19; 15:14). Such a fierce and agonistic experience of the Spirit befits the note in 13:25 that the Spirit began to prod or drive Samson.

he ripped the lion's jaws apart. The NLT's "jaws" is not found in the Hebrew, likely reflecting common misconceptions about how the lion was slain. Josephus interpreted Samson as strangling the lion (*Antiquities* 5.8.5). But depictions of heroic figures grappling barehanded with lions portray a variety of ways in which the deed might be done, including the hero holding the animal by the hind legs about to rip the hip joint apart (Burney 1920:Plate vi; Parrot 1961:201). The Qal form of the verb *shasa'* [TH8156, ZH9117] means to be divided or separated. The form used here (Piel) is factitive, meaning "to divide up, to tear up." The closest biblical parallel is Lev 1:17, which speaks of tearing up a bird to be offered as a sacrifice, though the text there explicitly says the bird is not "severed." Samson did not fully dismember the lion, but frightfully wrenched it open, possibly in the pubic area. In the latter case, the honey would have been made not in the lion's chest as most commentators assume (Moore 1895:331; Burney 1920:358), but at the other end, adding a wry scatological irony to Samson's riddle, "Out of the eater came something to eat, out of the strong came something sweet!"

with his bare hands. David also claimed the unarmed killing of wild predators (1 Sam 17:34-36; cf. also 2 Sam 23:20). Commentators have assembled examples of ancient texts narrating the bare-handed slaying of a predatory beast (Moore 1895:331; Burney 1920:358). Most portrayals of heroes slaying lions involve weapons, so the empty-handed confrontation is unusual (Strawn 2005:243 n. 43). Samson's slaying the lion likely did not violate his vow, even though he "produced a corpse" (Younger 2002:302). The law in Num 6 about someone dying suddenly and touching a Nazirite hardly compares with Samson's behavior here. Indeed, the lion might not have been dead when Samson left it behind. Also, if the Nazirite vow originated in holy war customs, the killing of enemies might not have been considered the same as defilement of a corpse.

He did it as easily as if it were a young goat. The NLT expands on the Hebrew, which simply reads "and he tore it like [one] tears a young goat, without anything in his hands." Moore (1895:331) wryly observes, "to dismember a living animal in this way, even a kid, is not very easy." The author's assumption that the reader knows well the minimal effort required to rip apart a young goat suggests the readership is less than genteel, upper-class Judean elites! In the Ugaritic myth of Baal and Mot, the god of death, Mot boasts to have devoured the god Baal as easily as he might gulp down a lamb or kid (Arnold and Beyer 2002:61). The Hebrew, however, does not require the idea of "ease." The comparison with tearing a kid might suggest a distinctive manner of mangling the animal.

But he didn't tell his father or mother about it. Since his parents accompanied him on this journey, and since presumably the ripping up of a live lion with one's bare hands would be a messy business, the reader is left to puzzle just what explanation Samson offered upon returning from the vineyard with blood on him. His parent's ignorance of the deed figures later in their enjoyment of the honey.

14:7 *When Samson arrived in Timnah.* The Hebrew repeats "and he went down" a third time, as though the author wanted to emphasize descent. Cf. note on 14:1.

was very pleased with her. This expression is the verbal equivalent of the phrase Samson uses in 14:3b "right in my eyes," which also echoes the summary of Israel's behavior in 17:6 and 21:25—"all the people did whatever seemed right in their own eyes."

14:8 *carcass of the lion. . . . honey in the carcass.* The text uses two different words for "carcass." The first, *mappeleth* [TH4658, ZH5147], most properly means "downfall, fallen one" so the phrase most likely means "the fall (site) of the lion," i.e., the place where the lion fell. The second instance of "carcass," like that in 14:9, translates *gewiyyah* [TH1472, ZH1581], which typically denotes the body of a living person or animal (e.g., Gen 47:18). Its use to denote a corpse or carcass is rare (NIDOTTE 1.834-835). Some suggest that bees avoid carcasses, hence the unusual nature of the beehive in the lion's body. Keil notes how rapidly the dry heat can desiccate a corpse, but the time required for the body to dry and the bees to form their comb and produce the honey would still be considerable. If honey in a lion's carcass had been common or predictable, the story would not have been worth telling!

bees had made some honey. Most scholars suggest that "honey" (*debash* [TH1706, ZH1831]) in the OT, including references to the "land of milk and honey," mainly refers to fruit-extracted syrups, typically date and fig syrup, since the essential sense of the term is merely "sweet stuff." Only twice do bees appear in the OT in connection with honey, here and in 1 Sam 14:27. References to the "comb" (e.g., Ps 19:10; Prov 16:24) might imply bee honey. Egyptian texts also refer to honey from bees imported from Canaan, but no apiaries for honey production had been excavated until Amihai Mazar's team unearthed an industrial complex featuring scores of beehives at Tel Rehov, just south of the Sea of Galilee, in Iron IIA levels (1000–840 BC; cf. Mazar and Panitz-Cohen 2007). Thus, bee honey might have been more prevalent in Israel than has been thought. Still, in the OT, the discovery of bee honey in the wild typically occurs as a stroke of good luck (NIDOTTE 1.916-917; TDOT 3.128-131). The honey might have actually seemed to be a sign to Samson.

14:9 ***He scooped . . . ate.*** The use of the verb "scoop" (*radah* [TH7287A, ZH8098]) here, and later in the verse (NLT, "taken") resonates with the repeated verb "to go down" (*yarad* [TH3381, ZH3718], cf. 14:10) since the two, when inflected in context, sound very similar (Boling 1975:230-231). Samson's eating the honey from the carcass of the lion violated his Nazirite vow to avoid any contact with the dead. Indeed, eating anything from a dead body would violate any Israelite's commitment to avoid uncleanness. In the ancient Near East, honey figured prominently in religious rituals (Boling 1975:230), but the OT excludes honey from offerings (Lev 2:11), though it was legitimate as a tithe of produce. The prohibition possibly derived from honey's prominence in pagan sacrificial rituals, or from its tendency to enhance fermentation.

he didn't tell them. This is the second time Samson's secrecy about the lion finds mention, reinforcing the theme of secrecy in general, but also secrecy toward his parents, which finds note also at the climactic moment of the riddle narrative (14:16). Samson not only violated his vow and general Israelite laws of defilement, he also deceived his parents into unknowingly defiling themselves.

14:10 ***As his father was making final arrangements for the marriage.*** The verse again begins with "went down" (see note on 14:7), lit., "And his father went down to the woman." Since the very next clause reports Samson throwing the wedding feast, the NLT correctly interprets this visit as wedding arrangements. But, that Manoah consulted with the woman, rather than with her parents, whom we know are alive from later references, does not fit the normal practice in antiquity. For this reason, some scholars suggest changing "his father" to "Samson," but the change has no manuscript support. Probably the alien nature of the marriage customs involved in the events is reflected in the confusing structure of the narrative, which in turn generated a variety of misspellings and mistranslations in ancient versions.

at Timnah, as was the custom. The narrator here positions himself at a time sufficiently later than the events reported as to require an annotation about a wedding practice unknown to his readers. This has led to suggestions that the book was written in the time of David (Davis 1990:200 note 5). See the Introduction: "Author," "Date and Occasion of Writing," "Canonicity and Textual History."

elite young men. Heb., *bakhur* [TH970, ZH1033], refers to a young, single man in all his youthful vigor. Based on the verb "to choose," the term and its cognates in neighbor languages often denote the "choice" young men, even elite troops in the army. In the OT, it seems to refer to grown young men who are not yet married and thus still living in the household of their fathers, the male equivalent of *bethulah* [TH1330, ZH1435] (NIDOTTE 1.634-635).

14:11 ***When the bride's parents saw him.*** The Hebrew does not indicate who saw Samson. Presumably most of those at the wedding knew what Samson looked like, so the reference is puzzling. The Greek, Latin, and Syriac translations as well as Josephus imply the very similarly spelled verb "to fear," which in the Hebrew Bible is sometimes confused with "to see" (Burney 1920:361; Boling 1975:231). The translation "for fear of him" makes excellent sense.

they selected thirty young men from the town to be his companions. Again, the Hebrew is quite terse: "they took thirty friends and they were with him." No reference to "young men" appears here. The lack of any representation from Samson's extended family other than his parents seems odd, and perhaps reflects the rejection of this match by his relatives, accompanied by a shunning of Samson and his family. In fact, *mere'im* [TH4828, ZH5335] (NLT, "young men") often refers to persons of official capacity such as attendants at court (NIDOTTE 3.1144-1149, especially 1147). These 30 were clearly much more than "party animals" bussed in to fill seats, but came to keep Samson under control.

14:12 ***Samson said to them, "Let me tell you a riddle."*** Soggin (1981:243) points out that the riddle (*khidah* [TH2420, ZH2648]) typically united a thorny question of fact with clever wording, relying on obscure or ironic double meanings of words. Posing such a conundrum required intelligence, wit, and readiness with words. Samson had his flaws, but low intelligence was not one of them. Scholars often use the term "trickster," but the trickster typically has no other resource for power and must rely on wit. Samson is more analogous to Homer's Odysseus *polumēchanos*—the one of many schemes, resources, and tactics. The story refutes the image of Samson as a dumb country bumpkin with a weakness for sophisticated city ladies. Confronted with force in the form of the 30 "friends," Samson decided to defeat them with his wits, propounding a riddle that would vex and shame the Philistines, proving his worthiness to take one of their daughters as a wife.

fine linen robes. Heb., *sedinim* [TH5466, ZH6041], rendered in the LXX as *sindonas* [TG4616, ZG4984], could indicate the tunic worn next to the skin (Keil 1863:411). Alternatively, the term could denote any fine linen wrapper (Moore 1895:335).

thirty sets of festive clothing. Lit., "thirty changes of clothing," referring to the outer garments to go with the 30 tunics (NLT, "robes") just mentioned. The NLT's "festive" elaborates on the term traditionally translated "changes," which sometimes denotes the changes of seasons and thus, by extension, festivals (HALOT 319, s.v. *khalipah*). Though possible, the text certainly does not require this sense.

14:13 ***But if you can't solve it, then you must give me thirty fine linen robes and thirty sets of festive clothing.*** The nature of the riddle is that if Samson loses, presumably he is so impoverished by having to obtain 30 complete outfits that he likely cannot meet the bride-wealth to complete the marriage. If he wins, he is greatly enriched, but his companions suffer little, giving only one outfit apiece. Despite their protest at risking impoverishment (14:15b), the loss they would incur involved more of a loss of face, a public shaming, rather than economic loss.

14:14 ***Out of the one who eats came something to eat.*** The possible location of the honey in the lion's body (see note on 14:6) could impart a scatological edge to both lines of Samson's riddle.

out of the strong came something sweet. Just as "eater" and "eaten" pose opposites, so also "sweet" opposes "strong," taken as a reference to a biting or strong taste (Burney 1920:362-363; Soggin 1981:241).

Three days later. The number problems in this story (14:14, 15, 17, 18) vex interpreters. Judges 14:15 (see note) speaks of the seventh day, but the NLT, NIV, and others (following LXX) emend the text to "fourth" day. Alternatively, "three" (*shelosheth* [TH7969, ZH8993]) might be a misspelling for "six" (*shesheth* [TH8337, ZH9252]) in Hebrew (Burney 1920:363-364). On any explanation, the exact chronology of this week of partying, drinking, riddling, and crying remains unclear—perhaps it was to the participants as well.

they were still trying to figure it out. Riddling was the intellectual blood sport of antiquity, the sign of a man's intelligence, wit, and sophistication—in this case Samson's sophistication. In Proverbs, the mastery of riddles marks the wise man (Prov 1:6), and Solomon demonstrated his sagacity by unraveling the riddles posed by the Queen of Sheba (1 Kgs 10:1).

14:15 ***On the fourth day.*** Lit., "on the seventh day." The LXX reads "fourth," but no Hebrew authority exists for the change. The ancient Latin translation of Jerome from the 400s has *septimus*, "seventh" indicating that his Hebrew text agreed with ours. The difference between "seventh" and "fourth" in Hebrew consonants is only a single letter, so a spelling error could have occurred. Reading "fourth" comports better with the reference in 14:17 to the seventh day, with the passing of some time presumed. Despite the lack of textual support, the logic of the story itself and the slight difference in spelling between the words weighs in favor of the NLT's reading.

they said to Samson's wife. The narrator here either anticipates the consummation of the marriage, or the very feast itself, which legally united the bride and groom. Betrothal in antiquity normally had almost the same binding authority as marriage (King and Stager 2001:54-56). Boling (1975:231) argues that the marriage was actually consummated on the first day of the feast, appealing to Gen 29:23, 27, so that she was his wife in every sense. The text does not provide enough information to resolve this matter.

Entice your husband. Again, the narrator speaks as though the marital relationship is sealed. "Entice" translates a curious verb (*pathah* [TH6601, ZH7331]). The base form of the verb has the idea of being "wide open" to ideas or suggestions, usually suggesting ideas like "naive, simple, inexpert, gullible," or easy to seduce. The form used here, the Piel, is factitive, which would convey "make someone gullible, naive." In short, the idea would be "make a fool out of your husband," which naturally is translated by terms suggesting insincere or manipulative persuasion: seduce, entice, beguile (NIDOTTE 3.714-716). The term is used in Exod 22:16 [15] for the seduction of a virgin and in 16:5 for Delilah's seduction of Samson. The Philistine men were asking her to employ her sexual charms to do something manipulative, dishonorable, and demeaning to her husband.

we will burn down your father's house with you in it. The death threat perhaps indicates how extreme the shame would be if they were to lose this wager.

make us poor. Lit., "to possess us." Perhaps the idea is more than simple impoverishment, which would not result from each Philistine giving Samson a nice change of clothing. Idioms of possession can connote domination (see *Merriam-Webster's Collegiate Dictionary*, 11th ed., s.v. "own," 1b), such as the slang idiom "got owned," which implies being dominated and humiliated. The 30 young men feared public shaming and loss of face more than any loss of property. Block (1999:434) notes also that the term could allude ironically to the Danites' failure to possess this Philistine territory that Yahweh had assigned them through Joshua.

14:18 ***So before sunset.*** Lit., "before he entered sunward." The term used for "sun" (*hakharsah* [TH2775A, ZH3064]) is unusual, and does not stand as the subject of the verb as would be expected here. Some scholars (Moore 1895:339; Burney 1920:365) and contemporary translations (NJB) suggest the word is a very slight misspelling of a word appearing in 15:1, *hekhadrah* [TH2315, ZH2540], meaning "to the [bridal] chamber." On this view, the men of the city confronted Samson at the door of the bridal chamber at the very moment he was about to enter to consummate his marriage.

What is sweeter than honey? What is stronger than a lion? As noted earlier, riddles integrated a problem of life or logic with a play on words and were a kind of guessed poem. The form of the answer was as important as its content. As in the game show, *Jeopardy!*, the solution is stated as a question.

Samson replied. Samson's retort possesses poetic cadence and even rhyme, as though he had given the Philistines the first two lines of a poem, they responded with the third, and he capped it with the fourth, in essence winning the riddle by creating a devastating rejoinder, which Samson will then underscore with force and violence. Samson clearly was a person of intellect and wit.

If you hadn't plowed with my heifer. Most commentators see a sexual innuendo in Samson's line here. At least figuratively, they guessed the riddle because they were in league with—"in bed with," as it were—Samson's wife. However insulting "heifer" might sound to modern ears, bovine comparisons are not necessarily derogatory (cf. Jer 46:20).

14:19 ***Then the Spirit of the LORD came powerfully upon him.*** See note on 14:6. Previous judges experienced the onrush of the Spirit of Yahweh in preparation for battle against oppressive enemies. With Samson, possession by the Spirit has all the appearances of a kind of berserker Spirit devoid of purpose or moral direction.

Ashkelon. The famous Philistine port city of Ashkelon lies about 30 miles from Timnah by the main roads, raising the question how such a long trip squares with the rage of the moment in this narrative. Attempts by earlier interpreters to locate another site named Ashkelon have not persuaded most (Moore 1895:338).

killed thirty men, took their belongings. "Belongings" translates *khalitsah* [TH2488, ZH2723]. This infrequently occurring word can denote the equipment of a solder taken as plunder on the battlefield, leading Schneider (2000:211) to suggest these were soldiers Samson slaughtered, inciting a military conflict. Claims that Samson here commits "murder and larceny" (Younger 2002:304) seem to ignore Samson's role, which is to do as much harm on the Philistines as he can. Samson was a Spirit-impelled warrior of the late Iron I era.

Samson was furious about what had happened. Commentators are prone to psychologize, speaking of Samson "sulking" (e.g., Younger 2002:305). But this culture was one of warriors, to whom honor and shame meant everything. For Samson to be deceived by his wife, humiliated before the wedding party, and deprived of his bride constituted a great offense. Whether or not moderns approve, Samson could not immediately return to the arms of a woman and family who had betrayed and shamed him. Having paid his wager and done harm to the Philistines, Samson would wait an interval before returning to his wife and her family.

14:20 ***his wife was given in marriage to the . . . best man at the wedding.*** To abandon his bride and storm home shamed her and her family. Whether they were considered legally married is unclear, since it is not stated whether Samson consummated the union. The story's reference to her as "Samson's woman/wife," and Samson's resolve to go to her in 15:1, suggest the narrator considered them married. Samson's angry refusal to consummate the union apparently was viewed as a breach of the contract.

COMMENTARY

The story in chapters 14–15 moves in a loose parallel to the narrative of chapter 16. Samson determines to seek a sexual liaison with a Philistine woman (14:1-4 // 16:1-3). A secret becomes a point of contention between Samson and his paramour (14:12-18 // 16:5-17), resulting in violence with the Philistines climaxing in a prayer for vengeance and the catastrophic death of many Philistines (14:19–15:19 // 16:23-30). But the first story presents Samson's rollicking adventures of vengeance, while the second narrates his humiliating defeat and possible redemption. Within the first story, chapter 14 focuses on Samson's marriage, while chapter 15 moves to the broadening circle of mayhem that resulted. Niditch (2008:154) well cautions interpreters against reading these stories stereotypically, seeing Samson as a bumpkin, a sensualist, a trickster, and so forth. All such readings fail to do justice to the multiple dimensions of the man as a genuine figure of the late Iron Age I era who is portrayed in all his complexity.

Samson's secret, Spirit-driven slaying of a lion inspires the riddle at the heart of the story, thereby integrating the idea of cunning into the larger marriage narrative (Block 1999:428). By presenting a classic heroic deed like that portrayed in many examples of ancient art, namely the bare-handed slaying of the lion (probably by rending it open by the hind legs; see note on 14:6), the author ranks Samson among some of the great heroes and kings of antiquity. The discovery of the honey in a most unlikely and unclean location might have appeared as a sign, but Samson chose to eat the defiling honey in direct violation of Israel's purity laws, as well as his Nazirite status; he then shared the honey with his parents, making them impure as well. Samson's concealment of the honey's origin, implicating them unknowingly in his impurity, parallels his dragging them into his breach of the purity boundary in his marriage to a Philistine.

The wedding banquet, which would have featured wines and strong drink, also points to Samson's possibly violating another term of his Nazirite vow. "Party" (*mishteh* [TH4960, ZH5492], 14:10), is actually derived from the Hebrew verb meaning "to drink." Drinking wine at a wedding would not be noteworthy for an ordinary Israelite, but for a Nazirite, it would violate the vow. The text does not say Samson drank, but at his own wedding, at a party he himself staged and where he was clearly the center of attention, it seems likely. If he did not violate his vow, it is hard to imagine him coming any closer to it than to throw a wedding feast among a people distinguished by their sumptuous dining. Samson seems to have separated himself from every possible support of his own people, and even seems to have dared Yahweh, playing fast and loose with his spiritual identity. The riddle wager reveals Samson's rarely noted intelligence as he frustrated his Philistine companions with an impossible, profoundly obscene riddle whose solution would also humiliate and discomfit his own parents, who would suddenly learn to their dismay what they had eaten (14:10-14). Only threats to burn Samson's fiancée and her family alive persuaded her to nag him into telling his secret (14:15-17)—an episode that parallels the nagging of Delilah in chapter 16. Confronted with humiliation and betrayal, possibly in the moments prior to consummating his marriage, Samson exploded and, energized by the Spirit of Yahweh, stormed away in a rage, murdering 30 Philistines and stripping them of their gear to pay off his wager. Abandoning his new bride subjected her and her family to open, public humiliation (14:18-20). The Philistines won their bet, but at a frightening cost.

Samson's character is not the only one about which the story raises a question. The story underscores the ambivalent role of the Spirit of Yahweh and should caution the reader against too easily equating the *ruakh yhwh* [TH7307/3068, ZH8120/3378] of the Old Testament with the Holy Spirit, the third person of the Trinity of the New Testament and Christian theology. The phrase has a wide range of possible meanings since the term *ruakh* covers ideas such as air, breath, wind, sense, mind, frame of mind, spirit, force, emotion, mood, and mental state (TDOT 13.357-365; 365-402; NIDOTTE 3.1070-1078). In the Old Testament, the Spirit of Yahweh authenticates leaders, enables striking deeds, and provides dramatic manifestation of Yahweh's presence. Once Samson's impulsive self-will launched this Philistine adventure (14:1-4), the Spirit of Yahweh accelerated the action but did not alter its moral quality.

Perhaps here we see something of how the gifts of God work. We all know of persons who clearly have divine gifts of intelligence, talent, or other abilities, but whose use of those gifts fails to serve the Kingdom. While it is disturbing that divine gifting does not ensure a righteous outcome, this reality nevertheless underscores the fact that God's gifts in our lives constitute a challenge to stewardship. The gifts of God exert their influence, but the character of the outcome derives from the moral quality of choices made by those who possess and use the gifts. Though all might serve the ultimate purpose of God (14:4), few could question that righteous choices would always serve that purpose *better*, and with less human cost and muddying of the meaning of that giftedness.

This story also accentuates Israel's concerns for the boundaries distinguishing Yahweh's people from those not in covenant with him. This is not racism, or mere distrust of "the other." Yahweh's gift of the land was transmitted in Israel through the human institution of patrilineal inheritance. For Samson to marry outside Israel risked passing on his familial inheritance, his portion of the Promised Land, to the Philistines, abetting their ambitions to conquer the country and displace the Israelites. By flirting and philandering among the Philistines, Samson jeopardized the very promise of the land that stood at the center of Israel's faith. Also, the concern in the text for fraternizing and intermarrying with pagans underscores an essential reality of biblical faith: the enormous power of direct personal relationships. Biblical faith is not merely a set of propositions, an ideology or ethical code, though it certainly contains such. Biblical faith lives in an embodied, integrated reality of human interaction with others, with the land, with neighbors, and through all these, with God. Just as Paul charged Timothy to impart the faith face-to-face to "trustworthy people" who in turn would teach others (2 Tim 2:2), so Old Testament faith stressed intimate human relationships, defined in familial terms, as the vital conduit through which the faith flowed. Godly character and spiritual depth cannot simply be downloaded, but can be "caught" by association with others traveling the path of discipleship. More than a brain-to-brain transmission of propositions, Old Testament faith entailed life-to-life transmission of personal realities. In such a context, careless choices about one's most intimate relationships clearly put the transmission of the faith and continued fulfillment of Yahweh's promise at risk. The boundary between "Israel" and "not Israel" is not a boundary of mere race or culture, but one of vitally energized, relationship-grounded faith.

This story also raises the perennial issue of violence. Classical clan vengeance sought to equalize a community thrown out of balance by some injustice or negligence, restoring *shalom* [TH7965, ZH8934] to the community. But with Samson, we observe how one power play simply throws the balance off in the other direction, resulting in countervengeance, which accelerates the cycle of violence even more. The very intimacy Samson sought, he lost by the end of the story precisely because of his exercise of his power. Killing the lion provided the riddle, whose solution led to his vendetta against the Philistines, which in turn caused his father-in-law to give his bride to another. Moreover, Samson's actions could never restore *shalom* to the community because, by seeking a Philistine wife, and by seeking his own will over that of his own family and of Yahweh, he destabilized the community. An unrighteous, self-centered choice lies at the center of his life. This self-centered bent of life is not altered by the legitimacy of his vengeance, nor the power of the Spirit, nor even the ultimate outworking of Yahweh's secret purpose.

Finally, this story illustrates the importance of context for interpreting biblical stories. In the events of chapters 14–15, Samson not only violates his Nazirite vow, but also displays supreme disregard for almost every boundary defining Israel as God's people. In the larger context of the whole narrative, though, we can see in these early stories the explosive truth that even when the consequences of disobedience fail to appear, even when someone seems to "get away with" an utter disregard for God's will, that appearance is illusory and short-lived. Samson exercised his freedom in defiance of Yahweh's stated will for his life. The final and climactic violation of his vow, however, would not occur as his free action, but came in the night as he slumbered, unaware that Yahweh had left him. Samson, grinding in the prison in Gaza, would learn this. But for now, he was "on a roll" and believed himself invincible, the most dangerous consequence of sin.

◆ d. The revenge of Samson: Vengeance, victory, and vindication (15:1-20)

Later on, during the wheat harvest, Samson took a young goat as a present to his wife. He said, "I'm going into my wife's room to sleep with her," but her father wouldn't let him in.

2"I truly thought you must hate her," her father explained, "so I gave her in marriage to your best man. But look, her younger sister is even more beautiful than she is. Marry her instead."

3Samson said, "This time I cannot be blamed for everything I am going to do to you Philistines." 4Then he went out and caught 300 foxes. He tied their tails together in pairs, and he fastened a torch to each pair of tails. 5Then he lit the torches and let the foxes run through the grain fields of the Philistines. He burned all their grain to the ground, including the sheaves and the uncut grain. He also destroyed their vineyards and olive groves.

6"Who did this?" the Philistines demanded.

"Samson," was the reply, "because his father-in-law from Timnah gave Samson's wife to be married to his best man." So the Philistines went and got the woman and her father and burned them to death.

7"Because you did this," Samson vowed, "I won't rest until I take my revenge on you!" 8So he attacked the Philistines with great fury and killed many of them. Then he went to live in a cave in the rock of Etam.

9The Philistines retaliated by setting up camp in Judah and spreading out near the town of Lehi. 10The men of Judah asked the Philistines, "Why are you attacking us?"

The Philistines replied, "We've come to capture Samson. We've come to pay him back for what he did to us."

11So 3,000 men of Judah went down to get Samson at the cave in the rock of Etam. They said to Samson, "Don't you realize the Philistines rule over us? What are you doing to us?"

But Samson replied, "I only did to them what they did to me."

12But the men of Judah told him, "We have come to tie you up and hand you over to the Philistines."

"All right," Samson said. "But promise
that you won't kill me yourselves."
13"We will only tie you up and hand you
over to the Philistines," they replied. "We
won't kill you." So they tied him up with
two new ropes and brought him up from
the rock.
14As Samson arrived at Lehi, the Philis-
tines came shouting in triumph. But the
Spirit of the LORD came powerfully upon
Samson, and he snapped the ropes on his
arms as if they were burnt strands of flax,
and they fell from his wrists. 15Then he
found the jawbone of a recently killed
donkey. He picked it up and killed 1,000
Philistines with it. 16Then Samson said,

"With the jawbone of a donkey,
I've piled them in heaps!
With the jawbone of a donkey,
I've killed a thousand men!"

17When he finished his boasting, he threw
away the jawbone; and the place was
named Jawbone Hill.*
18Samson was now very thirsty, and he
cried out to the LORD, "You have accom-
plished this great victory by the strength of
your servant. Must I now die of thirst and
fall into the hands of these pagans?" 19So
God caused water to gush out of a hollow
in the ground at Lehi, and Samson was re-
vived as he drank. Then he named that
place "The Spring of the One Who Cried
Out,"* and it is still in Lehi to this day.
20Samson judged Israel for twenty years
during the period when the Philistines
dominated the land.

15:17 Hebrew *Ramath-lehi.* 15:19 Hebrew *En-hakkore.*

NOTES

15:1 ***Later on.*** The impression created here is of an appreciable interval. To characterize Samson as "sulking" during this period (Younger 2002:305) ignores the culture in which Samson lived and superimposes modern psychological categories on the text. Samson had lost face before his in-laws, had countered in a move to recover face and pay the lost bet without bankrupting himself, and then publicly humiliated his wife and her family in reprisal for their betrayal. In an honor-shame culture, Samson had taken the superior position. He rightly waited a significant interval before returning in order to offer a restoration on his own terms. His Philistine father-in-law, however, would turn the tables on him and prove dishonorable in every way.

wheat harvest. The Sorek valley, along which Timnah stood, is prime agricultural land. The hard limestone of the highlands washes down the creek beds and accumulates on the winding, flat valley floors in the Shephelah to form a deep layer of fertile soil. The wheat harvest varied in Israel according to the altitude, but for the Sorek valley it normally came in May-June.

Samson took a young goat. A young goat figured previously in the author's description of Samson's rending of the lion. Far from the ridiculous suggestion that the kid was the ancient equivalent to a "box of chocolates" (Boling 1975:234) or even a "peace offering" (Matthews 2004:151), Samson's gift was a signal that his anger had subsided. Until this moment, Samson believed he had the upper hand. He bested the Philistines even after they broke his riddle, and he properly shamed his new wife and her family for betraying him. Having waited a reasonable interval, Samson now graciously (in his mind) came to make the first move toward reconciliation, removing their shame by ending his rejection of them.

took a young goat as a present to his wife. Lit., Samson "attended to his wife with a goat-kid." The verb "attended to" (*paqad* [TH6485, ZH7212]) is often undertranslated "visit." The idea is a visit that entails the exercise of a right or responsibility.

I'm going into my wife's room to sleep with her. Samson seemed to regard it as normal that he reside with his family, and his wife with hers, and that he periodically visited her. The

Hebrew text uses the idiom "to go in to my wife (into) the inner room." The idiom "go into" is used for sexual congress, but not exclusively. The NLT thus elaborates, probably rightly.

15:2 ***I truly thought you must hate her.*** The Hebrew emphasizes both the father's speaking and his reference to Samson's hatred. The term "hate" (*sane'* [TH8130, ZH8533]) connotes not merely malice and hostility, but rejection. This word figures in divorce proceedings, so that the father-in-law actually was implying that he interpreted Samson's behavior as divorce.

her father explained, "so I gave her in marriage to your best man." Commentators often claim that the father was stuck: He'd given the woman to another man, and according to Deut 24:1-4 could not give her back to her original husband (Boling 1975:235; Soggin 1981:245). But the man was a Philistine and utterly indifferent to Israelite marriage law (Schneider 2000:213). Moreover, Samson's marriage to a Philistine already violated biblical boundaries. If anything, the text underscores the murky mix of expectations created by violating the exogamy/endogamy boundaries established by Yahweh for Israel and highlighted by the author of Judges (cf. 3:5-6).

But look, her younger sister is even more beautiful than she is. Marry her instead. That Samson refused the offer of the more beautiful, younger sister might suggest he was more devoted to his chosen bride than claims of his being a sensualist or womanizer might suggest. Or perhaps he was more focused on justice and honor, and how he was being wronged. More importantly, the author portrays the Philistine father treating his daughters like mere property to be disposed of, whereas Samson remained devoted to the woman he loved. These women were interchangeable in Philistine eyes, but not in Samson's eyes. Moreover, Samson realizes what was at stake was not his conjugal rights, but his own honor and the honor of his people, which resided in him as their champion.

15:3 ***This time.*** Heb., *happa'am* [TH6471, ZH7193]. The verbal form of this word appears in Samson's first encounters with the Spirit of Yahweh (13:25) in which the Spirit impels or drives him. It suggests an acute occurrence of some kind. Used temporally, it denotes a discrete moment or distinct event. It appears only 14 times with the definite article, and in all these cases it has the sense either of "at last" or "just this once."

I cannot be blamed for everything I am going to do to you Philistines. The core idiom in this sentence involves more than mere blame. The verb *naqah* [TH5352, ZH5927] (to be innocent, unpunished) when followed by the preposition *min* [TH4480, ZH4946] (from) always denotes a direct or literal freedom from something such as an obligation or a consequence, even a kind of immunity. Samson was not talking so much of blame as actual obligation or punishment. The line is best rendered, "As of now I am free of any Philistine obligation," or even, "I will be free of the Philistines." Previously, Samson was obligated by his wager and marriage. With Samson's wager paid and his marital obligation terminated, the Philistines had no claim on him, nothing to expect from him but retribution. Ironically, Samson articulated the boundary between Israel and the Philistines, a boundary he seems unable to observe regularly. For the moment, though, Samson seems to envisage himself "divorced" from the Philistines altogether, free from his enmeshment with them. He had no idea how wrong he was!

15:4 ***Then he went out and caught 300 foxes.*** "Foxes" probably refers to an animal usually called a "jackal" (Boling 1975:235).

He tied their tails together in pairs, and he fastened a torch to each pair of tails. Commentators often note the similarity of this story to a Roman festival in which foxes, with torches tied to their tails, ran through the circus (Burney 1920:369, 393-395; Soggin 1981:248-249). The ancient world was probably full of stories of such exploits, so that no direct connection need be claimed.

15:5 ***Then he lit the torches and let the foxes run through the grain fields of the Philistines. He burned all their grain to the ground.*** Younger (2002:306) brands Samson's action as "wrong," claiming Samson's motives were purely personal; he cites the law in Exod 22:6, making one who burns a field of standing grain liable to replace it, observing that such destruction implied "the potential for famine and death." But are we to apply to Philistine oppressors a civil liability law governing relationships among Israelites? Moreover, Samson was, for all practical purposes, at war with the Philistines who sought ultimately to dominate Israel completely. His actions, though personal, were not merely personal, and concerns about the personal element of his vengeance anachronistically impose the politically correct standards of our age on Iron Age antagonists. All conflicts of force feature a motley mix of motives and methods.

He also destroyed their vineyards and olive groves. Burning the grain destroyed a year's worth of crops. But vineyards and olive orchards require years of growth and cultivation before they yield. Contrary to the claim that this "ancient dry farming society that lived on the edge of hunger" (Younger 2002:306), the Sorek valley was rich agricultural land producing surpluses of grain, wine, and olive oil, much for export (Matthews 2004:151). Egyptian pharaohs prized the produce of the Sorek, Aijalon, and Jezreel valleys. Samson set back the economy of the Philistine invaders in Timnah by a generation. In fact, never again in the OT do the Philistines attempt a move up the Sorek valley. While the destruction in war of enemy trees bearing any kind of food or fruit was prohibited by Mosaic law (Deut 20:19-20), it is not clear whether this law applied only to cities "far away" or to those in Israel's land. Recent commentators often charge Samson with an excessively violent response, destroying a whole town's economy. They forget, however, that the Philistines invaded land that Yahweh had promised to Israel, and thus were oppressors of Israel (13:1). This was land under the conquest mandate. Samson's vengeance, though far from the dispassionate dispensing of justice admired by moderns, nevertheless embodied Yahweh's quest for an opportunity against the Philistines as a whole (cf. 14:4).

15:6 ***"Who did this?" the Philistines demanded. "Samson," was the reply, "because his father-in-law from Timnah gave Samson's wife to be married to his best man."*** Referring to the woman's father as Samson's "father-in-law" and assuming that punishing him was appropriate suggests the Philistines regarded Samson and his Philistine lover as married. Schneider (2000:214-215) rightly comments that on any view of Samson's ties to the woman, the Philistines committed a heinous act. If they were truly married, then they had given his wife to another man. If they were not truly married, then these men, in blaming the woman and her father, lied about the relationship as a pretext.

So the Philistines went and got the woman and her father and burned them to death. The very threat Samson's wife hoped to avoid in betraying him (14:15) was visited on her anyhow. Like the Judeans in 15:9-19, who hoped that by betraying Samson they could avoid aggravating the Philistines, Samson's Philistine in-laws discovered that betraying him did not avert the retribution they feared.

15:7 ***"Because you did this," Samson vowed.*** The NLT interprets certain particles in the sentence as indicating a vow. Samson was to avenge a deed done against his own wife and father-in-law. To reduce this to a petty, personal vendetta is to deny the historical, human ties depicted in the story. Standing before the smoking ruins of the home of his brutally murdered wife, living in a culture whose fundamental notion of justice was rooted in reciprocal actions of honoring and shaming, who would not have vowed to even the score? To walk away would also have left the Philistines confident that they could defy Israel with impunity. Samson's vengeance is therefore much more than a personal grudge.

I won't rest until I take my revenge on you! Lit., "I will take my revenge on you, and afterwards, I will cease." The overall construction of the sentence in most translations, as in the NLT, makes the second clause "afterwards I will cease" a statement of Samson's determination. Instead, given his claim earlier that he was terminating his entanglement with the Philistines (see note on 15:3), Samson more likely meant to declare this as his final act of vengeance. However much moderns disapprove of Samson's penchant for revenge, we must recall that Israel in Iron Age I had no central government. The family and clan bore the obligation to uphold what was right, and vengeance was much more than a mere feud: It was a passionate belief that every wrong must be balanced out by a reciprocal act. Samson's honor was not simply the machismo of an egomaniac. He, and others in such cultural settings, believed they were derelict of their duty to their family if they did not pursue proper vengeance. In addition, Samson was the divinely empowered and called judge of Israel, and if any vengeance was to be taken, he would be the one authorized to do so. Properly translated, Samson's statement also indicates he hoped to set a boundary on his quest for vengeance: "I will cease." Nevertheless, the context of Samson's liaison with the Philistines, his violation of the basic identity boundaries of his people, and his failure to honor his Nazirite status complicate his otherwise culturally appropriate concern for vengeance within proper limits. Samson had in fact become enmeshed with the Philistines, and his expectation of legitimate vengeance undermined his efforts to be free of them. His cry, "Just one more time and I'm finished," is ever the mantra of the addict. God will use Samson's entanglement to harm the Philistines, but that very power only accelerates the cycle of revenge.

15:8 ***So he attacked the Philistines with great fury.*** The NLT renders Heb. *shoq 'al yarek* [TH7785/3409, ZH8797/3751] (hip on thigh) safely enough: Clearly Samson did wallop them thoroughly. Burney (1920:370) suggests the expression is a wrestling term and notes Mesopotamian art depicting Gilgamesh throwing his antagonist over his own thigh. The author thus perhaps presents imagery from hand-to-hand grappling.

killed many of them. No onrush of the Spirit of Yahweh occurs here. Samson's strength is never inextricably tied to the Spirit, but only to his vow. The Spirit's coming provoked him in the use of his strength.

the rock of Etam. Many proposals for this location exist, but none is definitive.

15:9 ***The Philistines retaliated by setting up camp in Judah.*** With this verse, for the first time, the reader sees Samson's feuds with the Philistines in a context larger than his own personal vendetta, but the image of "larger Israel" is not positive. Judah's territory lay just south of the Danite inheritance. The Philistines attempted to move up to the Israelite heartlands up on the watershed ridge by means of the valleys through the Shephelah. This would bring them into direct contact with Judah, as occurred later when their thrust up the Elah valley brought David to confront Goliath (1 Sam 17).

15:10 ***We've come to capture Samson.*** The word "capture" translates *'asar* [TH631, ZH673] (to bind), foreshadowing both the fateful pillow talk of Delilah who asked how Samson might be "bound" (9 occurrences in 16:4-20) and his incarceration (3 occurrences in 16:21-25).

We've come to pay him back. The Philistines ignored the fact that Samson's actions were provoked by Philistine duplicity and betrayal.

15:11 ***So 3,000 men of Judah went down to get Samson.*** Whether "thousand" (*'elep* [TH505, ZH547]) denotes the number or a clan-muster (i.e., "contingent") of the militia (see note on 8:10), it reflects a remarkable concern about Samson's ability to resist. Also, the Judeans here outnumber the Philistines three to one (cf. 15:15), but still whined in anxiety about them. That the Judeans served the purposes of the Philistines suggests at best that they were poorly integrated into the needs and concerns of the rest of the Israelite tribes. Conversely, their attitude could also reflect a sense that the Danites were second-class members of the Israelite coalition, and the Judeans felt no particular loyalty to a Danite hero.

Don't you realize the Philistines rule over us? This interaction underscores how little kinship the Judeans felt with the Danites. No appeal to Israelite unity appears, nor is there any sense that they faced a common foe. If the Danites, or a segment of them, were originally from among the Sea Peoples (see note on 13:2), the Judeans might well see them as more closely tied to the Philistines. At any rate, the Judeans express no sense that Samson was the ordained deliverer of the nation. He only upset the equilibrium of compromise and acquiescence the Judeans had struck with the Philistines. The "rule" of the Philistines likely took the form of practical domination, not colonial administration. Judah, at least in the Shephelah, lived under the shadow of Philistine power.

"What are you doing to us?" But Samson replied, "I only did to them what they did to me." The Judeans were clearly trapped between two parties, each of which claimed only to be repaying a wrong done by the other. The reader knows the balance of justification probably lies with Samson, and that the Philistines were probably using Samson as a pretext to extend their power over more Israelite territory. Samson's reply, however, cannot have sounded very hopeful to the Judeans. Whether the reader should see Samson here as failing to serve as the deliverer, only complicating further the oppression, or whether the Judeans emerge as singularly reluctant to deal with deliverance, remains unclear. But one thing is so obvious it is often missed: Samson, who would "judge Israel for twenty years" (15:20; 16:31b), displayed a very keen, perhaps extreme, sense of reciprocity and justice. The narrative's emphasis on "reprisals and counterreprisals" (Younger 2002:310) does not imply that the characters cared only for vengeance. Rather, in the absence of any overarching authority, they were thrown back on their ability to assert justice themselves. This reality, however unpalatable to more civilized readers, predominates any frontier region and characterized Iron Age I generally. To criticize the characters for talking about vengeance provokes the question of what else they should be discussing under the circumstances.

15:12 ***We have come to tie you up.*** As in 15:10 and in 15:13, the term is "bound" (*'asar* [TH631, ZH673]), foreshadowing Samson's final binding in ch 16.

15:13 ***two new ropes.*** "New ropes" anticipates 16:11, where Samson baits Delilah with the claim that new ropes will bind him.

15:14 ***As Samson arrived at Lehi, the Philistines came shouting in triumph.*** As with the lion (14:6), a sudden, loud, hostile sound immediately preceded the onrush of the Spirit of Yahweh.

But the Spirit of the LORD came powerfully upon Samson. The expression in Hebrew is the same as found in 14:6 and 19 and is the last time the Spirit is said to possess Samson in the narrative. Ironically, the impulse of the Spirit results in Samson violating his vow. In 14:6 the slaying of the lion led to Samson's eating honey from the corpse; the slaughter of the Philistines in 14:19 was followed by his stripping of the bodies and transport of the contaminated clothing all the way back to Timnah. Here, the Spirit-empowered hero wielded an unclean weapon (see note on 15:15).

15:15 ***jawbone of a recently killed donkey.*** The term "jawbone" is *lekhi* [TH3895, ZH4305], the ultimate name of the location where the encounter occurs. "Recently killed" translates a term that seems to mean "fresh," and is used of open wounds in Isa 1:6. Moore (1895:346) cites an Arabic cognate meaning "fresh, moist, juicy." Touching a dead animal, especially with blood and putrefaction present, violated once again Samson's Nazirite vow.

He picked it up and killed 1,000 Philistines with it. Ironically, the Judeans had sent three times as many men to talk to Samson as the Philistines sent to capture him. Single combat against the Philistines forms an important theme in the OT traditions associated with Iron Age I. Shamgar (3:31) had killed 600 with an ox goad. David's mighty men (2 Sam 23:8-23) included several who defeated large groups of Philistines alone, as had Jonathan (1 Sam 14:1-15). Many of these stories, like Samson's battle here, call attention to some distinctive feature of the weaponry or of the ground on which the fight occurred, in keeping with Iron Age I heroic tradition. Even Samson's thirsty cry for water finds a reverberation in David's longing for the water of Bethlehem's spring (2 Sam 23:13-17).

15:16 ***Then Samson said.*** Just as ch 14 ended on a poetic note (as Samson dueled with the Philistines via his riddles), here Samson erupts in poetry to celebrate his victory. The portrayal of Samson as a witty wordsmith is in accord with the high value ancients placed on speaking well. Israel's greatest hero, David, was "articulate" (1 Sam 16:18, NET) and a poet of great renown.

With the jawbone of a donkey, I've piled them in heaps! In Hebrew the term for donkey (*khamor* [TH2543/2543A, ZH2789/2790]) is identical to the word translated "heaps." The line is literally "with the jawbone of a donkey, heap and double-heap." Burney (1920:373) also suggests that the pun might imply something more rude, "with the jawbone of an ass, I have made asses out of them" (cf. NIV's rendering: "with a donkey's jawbone I have made donkeys of them").

15:17 ***he threw away the jawbone . . . Jawbone Hill.*** A double pun appears. In addition to the repetition of "jawbone," the term for "hill" or (better) "height," (*ramath* [TH7413, ZH8229]) bears a superficial similarity to a verb meaning to throw or hurl (Moore 1895:345).

15:18 ***Samson was now very thirsty, and he cried out to the LORD.*** Though Samson's strength gave him victory over the Philistines, his thirst presents a crisis for which strength cannot provide the answer. The term for "cry" is not that used in the introductions to the stories in which oppressed Israel "cries out" to Yahweh (omitted in the introduction to the Samson story). Rather, the idiom employed connotes the invocation of the deity by name. This was not a cry of desperation, but a summons he believed would be answered. The sensible appeal of his prayer evokes the memory of his mother's reassurance in 13:23.

You have accomplished this great victory by the strength of your servant. Far from haranguing God (Boling 1975:239), Samson here expresses clearly a proper interpretation of the event: Yahweh gave the victory through the strength of his servant. This theocentric cry stands alone as Samson's only affirmation of the essence of his strength until his revelation to Delilah in ch 16.

pagans. Lit., "the uncircumcised." Here Samson, for the first time, articulates the boundary separating himself as an Israelite from the Philistines, namely, their uncircumcision. Upon his declaration of Yahweh as the author of the victory and his affirmation of the basic boundary between Israel and the Philistines, Yahweh answered by miraculously providing water.

15:19 ***So God caused water to gush out of a hollow in the ground at Lehi, and Samson was revived as he drank.*** The cleaving of the rock to produce water to refresh Samson ends a narrative sequence that began with Samson's ripping of the lion and finding honey for his refreshment. The term "hollow" (*maktesh* [TH4388, ZH4847]) also has the meaning "tooth socket."

The Spring of the One Who Cried Out. The expression, "the one who cried out," is also the typical Hebrew term for "partridge." Many scholars suggest the spring's actual name was "Partridge Spring," a name assigned a new meaning by Samson's actions.

15:20 ***Samson judged Israel for twenty years.*** This statement does more than merely summarize. In fact, Samson did not "judge Israel" in any meaningful way in chs 14–15. The events of these two chapters occupy only a few months in Samson's early life. Boling (1974:240) suggests they record Yahweh's efforts to "enlist" Samson as a judge, culminating in the prayer in 15:18-19 where Samson finally accepted his calling. This seems overclever. So to what does the author refer? Chapters 14–15 could well record the wild doings of the young Samson who then led Israel without incident for the next 20 years until his debacle in ch 16.

during the period when the Philistines dominated the land. Unlike the other judges, Samson's activity parallels the presence of a foreign oppressor that does not flee or leave in defeat at the end of the story as the prior enemies of Israel did. The NLT's "dominated the land" is not in the Hebrew. The text simply reads "in the days of the Philistines." Although the Philistines arrived about 1175 BC, they did not achieve real dominance until a century later, about the time of Samson.

COMMENTARY

This chapter unfolds the consequences of Samson's enmeshment with the Philistines, narrated in chapter 14. At the end of chapter 14, the balance of offense and retribution lay in Samson's favor—his victory and prayer climax the chain of events inaugurating a 20-year period of service. However wrong the choice of a Philistine bride had been, he had sought her in good faith and did in fact pay off his lost wager. Moreover, he lost the wager through the dishonorable conduct of the Philistines and the coerced duplicity of his wife. Judges 14 ends with Samson as the party who has defended his honor most successfully, and that against a vastly superior, more militarized, and better-equipped foe. Since he had been treated dishonorably, Samson had a right of further revenge but chose to return home, rather than take out his anger in further violence against the Timnites. As chapter 15 opens, far from being driven by sensuality or anger, Samson took what seems to be a somewhat conciliatory approach. Having waited an interval appropriate to his sense of injury, he traveled to Timnah with a gift for his wife and her household, only to meet deeper betrayal as his wife had been given to another man. Despite the wrongness of Samson's marriage to a Philistine, this was still a betrayal. Interpreters who use this chapter as a paradigm for the pathology of violence or the endless cycle of revenge, or who wish to portray Samson as driven solely by a personal vendetta, fail to note these important points. This was war; if the Philistines weren't prepared to have their crops burned, they should have not oppressed Israel. But the author's principle point does not seem to be to approve or defend the character of Samson as much as to stress the deceitful character of the Philistines. In that light, Samson's overtures to the Philistines take on a different function. Rather than emphasizing Samson's betrayal of Israelite law, the stories illustrate that even someone who tried to affiliate with the Philistines discovered them to be utterly ruthless and dishonorable, meriting whatever vengeance they received.

Samson's months of waiting to visit his wife were months of delusion in that she had, the whole time, lived with another husband. This must not only have shocked him, but would have underscored more starkly the utterly unprincipled character of the Philistines. The rest of the chapter unfolds in a series of reprisals, analyzed very well by Matthews and Younger (Matthews 2004:152; Younger 2002:304-305). The interchange between Samson and the Philistines shifts scenes ranging from Timna to an unknown place in the Judean Shephelah.

PHILISTINE INJURY	SAMSON'S REPRISAL
Refusing Samson's Conjugal Rights (15:1-2)	Samson Burns Timnite Produce (15:3-5)
Samson's Wife and Her Father Burned (15:6)	Samson Slaughters the Philistines (15:7-8)
Samson Captured (15:9-13)	Samson's Defeat of Philistines (15:14-17)

The important features of this section actually come at the beginning and the end. At the beginning, Samson is at peace, evidencing no remaining animosity against the Philistines. After the series of engagements in 15:3-17 in which Samson wrought enormous damage on the Philistines, he cried out to God, acknowledging God's power in the victory, acknowledging the boundary between Israel and the Philistines, refusing to be identified with them, and crying for relief. God miraculously answered Samson's prayer. This conclusion places the narrative under divine approval. Not only had Samson magnificently fulfilled Yahweh's desire for an occasion against the Philistines (14:4), Samson himself confessed the divide separating himself from Israel's enemies. He was fully avenged, he had harmed the Philistines deeply, he had been sustained and vindicated by God, and he knew who he was: a servant of God who refused to be aligned with the uncircumcised. Thus, Samson could now lead his people as chief, or paramount (judge), and did so for 20 uneventful years.

With the completion of Samson's vengeance in 15:14-19, his marital entanglement with the Philistines ended, and he assumed his role as judge, a period that the author passes over in silence (15:20). The statement in 15:20 ("Samson judged Israel for twenty years") begins the concluding formula of the story, forming an *inclusio* with the retrospective note at the very end of the story in 16:31b. The concluding formulas noted, where pertinent, the land resting (omitted from the judges after Gideon), the duration of the judge's influence, and a notation of the judge's death. Previously in Judges, the concluding materials have been expanded. The concluding notes of the Deborah story begin in 4:23-24, but the long poem of 5:1-31a intervenes before the final concluding notation in 5:31b. Similarly, the conclusion of the Gideon story begins in 8:28, with the notes about Gideon's retirement and large family intervening before the notation of his death in 8:32. In the same way, the note that Samson ruled 20 years (15:20) prepares the reader to see the next unit (ch 16) as part of the conclusion of the story whose final rubrics appear in 16:31. Indeed, the death of the judge, which figures prominently in these concluding formulas, is the central theme of chapter 16. Thus, the reader understands chapters 14–15 to record Samson's earliest deeds, followed by two decades of what must have been uneventful leadership, followed by the very dramatic narrative of the events leading up to Samson's death. As one whose early deeds circled around retribution and revenge, perhaps Samson was in a place to understand justice, and judging; likewise, that his end would follow from the violation and renewal of the very vow he had ignored in the early stories, rings true with the theme of retribution. Not even the judge was immune.

Recent evangelical commentators typically depict Samson as devoid of all positive character, being only ruthless and self-centered. One hears criticisms of the "tone" of Samson's prayer in 15:18-19, as though 3,000 years later we can assess such things in the absence of clear linguistic markers. These charges reveal more about the interpreter's pious, anachronistic perspective than about the Samson of real history. Like his Iron Age I peers, Achilles and Odysseus, Samson realized he had a divine gift that made him a distinctive and unique person. He lived in a culture devoid of overarching structures of unity and order. He and his struggling people confronted in the Philistines a new, formidable, determined enemy. In such an era, the honor and dignity of a people often rested in the honor and dignity of their paramount chief. If Samson did not demonstrate a strong response to the Philistines, then he exposed his people to worse indignities, especially given the vastly superior position of the Philistines as an urbanized, politically organized force with greater military resources and discipline. The Philistines, as part of the Sea Peoples, had raided, looted, and burned throughout the entire eastern Mediterranean. Egypt only barely repulsed them, resulting in the Philistine settlement on the south coast of Canaan about 70 years after the Israelites had arrived. Samson had to confront them alone. Nothing in the story evidences any willingness on the part of the Israelites to join him in resisting the Philistine oppression; in fact, the Judeans collaborate with the Philistines. In actual fact, Samson's actions appear to have stymied the Philistine attempt to expand up the Sorek valley.

Lastly, this story illustrates the importance of the boundary between God's people and their enemies. The initial protest of Manoah that Samson sought a wife from among the uncircumcised marks the story as one concerned with this distinction. Readers often puzzle over the author's failure to criticize Samson himself both for the Philistine marriage and for his apparent violation of the Nazirite vow. The author paradoxically shows Samson going from victory to victory, killing thousands of Philistines and destroying the economy of the Philistine town of Timnah, the very heart of the Sorek valley. God, whose secret purpose is conveyed in 14:4, answers Samson's prayer at the end of the story—a prayer that, tellingly, asserts a repugnance for the uncircumcised. Samson's border adventures have vindicated the necessity of the boundary. Moreover, the story shows that even when an Israelite does his very best to cooperate with the Philistines, they prove treacherous, dishonorable, and amoral. No Israelite, after reading this story, could believe it worthwhile to compromise on the distinctives of Israelite faith and culture for the sake of an easy truce with the enemies of God. Samson maps that territory for the reader, going there so that readers need not do so themselves.

Does the positive framework of the story created by Yahweh's secret intention (14:4) and ultimate vindication (15:18-19) justify Samson's violation of his ethnic identity and his Nazirite vow? Though the author expresses no criticisms in chapters 14–15, the larger framework of the story answers this question negatively, and we will see Samson stumble in chapter 16 precisely at the points where he triumphed before. The author has told the reader back in 3:5-6 that the key to Israel's downfall is to mingle among the pagans, intermarry with the pagans, and ultimately serve the gods of the pagans. Though Samson emerged from his border adventures victorious, the boundaries remained vital and would determine Samson's destiny after all. But what of Yahweh's purpose? This story, perhaps more than any other in the book of Judges, shows that God chooses to work through human beings. He chooses to descend into the fragility, and at times, unbelief and disobedience of his servants in order to bring forth his purposes. From the moment in creation that God vested his honor, dignity, and very image in human beings, he committed himself to manifesting his power, glory, and character through people. So the mystery is not how God could fulfill his purposes through Samson, but why he would ever choose to work through sinful human beings at all.

e. The reversion and redemption of Samson (16:1-31)

One day Samson went to the Philistine town of Gaza and spent the night with a prostitute. 2Word soon spread* that Samson was there, so the men of Gaza gathered together and waited all night at the town gates. They kept quiet during the night, saying to themselves, "When the light of morning comes, we will kill him."

3But Samson stayed in bed only until midnight. Then he got up, took hold of the doors of the town gate, including the two posts, and lifted them up, bar and all. He put them on his shoulders and carried them all the way to the top of the hill across from Hebron.

4Some time later Samson fell in love with a woman named Delilah, who lived in the valley of Sorek. 5The rulers of the Philistines went to her and said, "Entice Samson to tell you what makes him so strong and how he can be overpowered and tied up securely. Then each of us will give you 1,100 pieces* of silver."

6So Delilah said to Samson, "Please tell me what makes you so strong and what it would take to tie you up securely."

7Samson replied, "If I were tied up with seven new bowstrings that have not yet been dried, I would become as weak as anyone else."

8So the Philistine rulers brought Delilah seven new bowstrings, and she tied Samson up with them. 9She had hidden some men in one of the inner rooms of her house, and she cried out, "Samson! The Philistines have come to capture you!" But Samson snapped the bowstrings as a piece of string snaps when it is burned by a fire. So the secret of his strength was not discovered.

10Afterward Delilah said to him, "You've been making fun of me and telling me lies! Now please tell me how you can be tied up securely."

11Samson replied, "If I were tied up with brand-new ropes that had never been used, I would become as weak as anyone else."

12So Delilah took new ropes and tied him up with them. The men were hiding in the inner room as before, and again Delilah cried out, "Samson! The Philistines have come to capture you!" But again Samson snapped the ropes from his arms as if they were thread.

13Then Delilah said, "You've been making fun of me and telling me lies! Now tell me how you can be tied up securely."

Samson replied, "If you were to weave the seven braids of my hair into the fabric on your loom and tighten it with the loom shuttle, I would become as weak as anyone else."

So while he slept, Delilah wove the seven braids of his hair into the fabric. 14Then she tightened it with the loom shuttle.* Again she cried out, "Samson! The Philistines have come to capture you!" But Samson woke up, pulled back the loom shuttle, and yanked his hair away from the loom and the fabric.

15 Then Delilah pouted, "How can you tell me, 'I love you,' when you don't share your secrets with me? You've made fun of me three times now, and you still haven't told me what makes you so strong!" 16 She tormented him with her nagging day after day until he was sick to death of it.

17 Finally, Samson shared his secret with her. "My hair has never been cut," he confessed, "for I was dedicated to God as a Nazirite from birth. If my head were shaved, my strength would leave me, and I would become as weak as anyone else."

18 Delilah realized he had finally told her the truth, so she sent for the Philistine rulers. "Come back one more time," she said, "for he has finally told me his secret." So the Philistine rulers returned with the money in their hands. 19 Delilah lulled Samson to sleep with his head in her lap, and then she called in a man to shave off the seven locks of his hair. In this way she began to bring him down,* and his strength left him.

20 Then she cried out, "Samson! The Philistines have come to capture you!"

When he woke up, he thought, "I will do as before and shake myself free." But he didn't realize the LORD had left him.

21 So the Philistines captured him and gouged out his eyes. They took him to Gaza, where he was bound with bronze chains and forced to grind grain in the prison.

22 But before long, his hair began to grow back.

23 The Philistine rulers held a great festival, offering sacrifices and praising their god, Dagon. They said, "Our god has given us victory over our enemy Samson!"

24 When the people saw him, they praised their god, saying, "Our god has delivered our enemy to us! The one who killed so many of us is now in our power!"

25 Half drunk by now, the people demanded, "Bring out Samson so he can amuse us!" So he was brought from the prison to amuse them, and they had him stand between the pillars supporting the roof.

26 Samson said to the young servant who was leading him by the hand, "Place my hands against the pillars that hold up the temple. I want to rest against them." 27 Now the temple was completely filled with people. All the Philistine rulers were there, and there were about 3,000 men and women on the roof who were watching as Samson amused them.

28 Then Samson prayed to the LORD, "Sovereign LORD, remember me again. O God, please strengthen me just one more time. With one blow let me pay back the Philistines for the loss of my two eyes." 29 Then Samson put his hands on the two center pillars that held up the temple. Pushing against them with both hands, 30 he prayed, "Let me die with the Philistines." And the temple crashed down on the Philistine rulers and all the people. So he killed more people when he died than he had during his entire lifetime.

31 Later his brothers and other relatives went down to get his body. They took him back home and buried him between Zorah and Eshtaol, where his father, Manoah, was buried. Samson had judged Israel for twenty years.

16:2 As in Greek and Syriac versions and Latin Vulgate; Hebrew lacks *Word soon spread.* **16:5** Hebrew *1,100 shekels*, about 28 pounds or 12.5 kilograms in weight. **16:13-14** As in Greek version and Latin Vulgate; Hebrew lacks *I would become as weak as anyone else. / So while he slept, Delilah wove the seven braids of his hair into the fabric.* [14]*Then she tightened it with the loom shuttle.* **16:19** Or *she began to torment him.* Greek version reads *He began to grow weak.*

NOTES

16:1 ***One day.*** This story (16:1-3) seems to float in time. The chronological note in 15:20 marks the end of that narrative. The Delilah story, beginning in 16:4, is introduced with a chronological break as well. In between comes this curious little story of Samson in Gaza. The author introduces Gaza, where the story will finally end. The move to Gaza also presents, rather abruptly, a reminder of Samson's tendency to violate the sacred boundaries marking off God's people from pagans. Twenty years had elapsed since Samson's triumph of the Philistines at Lehi, during which time he apparently presided as chief over his people without incident, though the Philistines were still present. The story now moves to the end of Samson's career, revisiting the issues treated in chs 14–15, namely, the cultural and religious boundaries between Israel and the Philistines, the pivotal role of Samson's love for women, and the place of vengeance. Like the beginning of Samson's exploits, the Philistines would seek to discover a secret by conniving with the object of Samson's affections. In the early story, the secret had to do with a feat of strength, but now the heart of Samson's very identity will be at stake.

the Philistine town. "Philistine town" is lacking in Hebrew, but is supplied to give the reader essential context that would be self-evident to the ancient reader. As noted below, Gaza not only was Philistine, but would have been perhaps the major city of the Philistines. Claims that the Philistine identity of Gaza or the prostitute are uncertain (Schneider 2000:217-218) seem unfounded.

Gaza. The mound that covers ancient Gaza stands in the northeast corner of the modern city of Gaza. The sea on the west and the desert on the east force all traffic moving between Egypt in the south and Canaan, Syria, and Mesopotamia in the north into a narrow strip that provided the perfect strategic location for a fortified town, which was blessed as well with fertile soil and copious freshwater wells. The Egyptian pharaoh Thutmose III reports possessing Gaza c. 1468 BC. Gaza marked the south boundary of Canaan and served its capital under the Egyptians until c. 1200–1150 BC. Gaza is mentioned in the Amarna correspondence of the mid-1300s BC, as Jerusalem's city ruler complained that the pharaoh had not cared for Jerusalem's defense as attentively as he had Gaza's (Moran 1992:332-333; 338-339). When the Sea Peoples, among whom were the Philistines and possibly the Danites (see note on 13:2), settled the coast, Gaza became a major city in the five-city Philistine coalition (ABD 2.912-915; NIDB 2.527-529). Gaza might have slipped out of Egyptian control before their arrival. Ancient art depicts Gaza with towers and fortified gates. Following typical routes, the trip from Zorah to Gaza was about 45 miles, making it the farthest major Philistine city from Samson's home.

spent the night with a prostitute. The NLT's rendering obscures the similarity between 16:1 and 14:1. In both cases, the text says Samson traveled to a city and "saw a woman," typically linked in the OT to irregular sexual unions (see note on 14:1). But in ch 14, Samson pursued marriage in a neighboring town within the Danite inheritance; here Samson merely fornicates far afield. The narrative of Samson's debacle thus begins with a similar episode as the story of his triumph: He sees a Philistine woman. The construction here is literally "a woman, a prostitute," (*'ishah zonah* [TH2181B, ZH2390]). Hebrew often places "man" or "woman" or other very general words before terms denoting more specific roles (Waltke and O'Connor 1990:226-230). Thus, Deborah (4:4) is a "woman, prophet" (*'ishah nebi'ah* [TH5031, ZH5567]) and in response to Israel's cry in 6:7-8 is to send a "man-prophet" (*'ish nabi'* [TH5030, ZH5566]). Jephthah's mother, like the woman of Gaza, was *'ishah zonah*, "a woman, prostitute." This normal, appositional function of the words "man" and "woman" should not be stressed unduly, as though the author intended to emphasize gender (cf. Schneider 2000:217).

16:2 ***Word soon spread.*** The NLT follows the LXX here. The phrase, one word in Hebrew, is lacking in the MT, likely due to a copyist's error.

gathered together. The term *'arab* [TH693, ZH741] explicitly refers to waiting in ambush.

the town gates. Modern scholars rightly note the complex structure of city gates, which were more than just big doors (Block 1999:450). But the Israelite/Canaanite gate might not be the best parallel. If the gate of nearby Philistine Ashdod offers an analogy, the Gaza gate featured a roadway about 45 feet long and 14 feet wide, with a turn at the end and chambers on either side, like the Canaanite gates. In Ashdod, however, one end of the gate passage constricted to a narrow opening set at a sharp angle (Stern 1993–2008:1.98-99). City gates served as places of business, legal disputation, and even religious observance. The chambers also served for defense. An invader would be exposed to flanking fire from the side-chambers. Thus, the gate offered a natural point of ambush for assassins.

They kept quiet. Lit., "they were silent," a comical image of enough men of Gaza to take on Samson skulking in the city gate, shushing one another to silence as they await the strongman's groggy emergence from taking his sensual pleasure all night. Alternatively, perhaps they watched all day and, assuming the gate was closed, slept at night, giving Samson his chance (Burney 1920:376).

during the night. In these three short verses, the Hebrew word "night" appears four times. Tellingly, the term in Hebrew, *laylah* [TH3915A, ZH4326], resonates with the name of Samson's ultimate femme fatale, *Delilah*, which could be construed to mean "the one of the night."

16:3 ***But Samson stayed in bed.*** The NLT correctly translates, but misses the innuendo in the Hebrew, which says Samson "lay until midnight." The verb *shakab* [TH7901, ZH8886] (to lie) appears in euphemisms for sexual intercourse.

midnight. No reason for Samson's midnight departure appears, but his enemies certainly counted on him enjoying his full night of pleasure and being complacent and slow as he departed, easy bait for an ambush.

Then he got up, took hold of the doors of the town gate, including the two posts, and lifted them up, bar and all. The actual doorways of the gate would be heavy wooden doors, often plated with metal, that turned on pivots seated in sockets in the roadway (Soggin 1981:253). Thus, they could be "popped" out with sufficient force. A crossbar secured the double doors. Samson apparently unseated the large pivots and lifted the whole doorway out of its assembly with the crossbar. The gates of the city embodied the entire civic and cultural life of the town, as well as providing security. The gate was the opening in the boundary between the safety of civilization inside, and the threats of disorder on the outside. In desecrating the gates, Samson violated the city's vision of itself as a place of security and order.

the top of the hill across from Hebron. We need not imagine Samson carrying the gates all the way to Hebron itself: No point between Gaza and Hebron stands higher than Hebron itself, so any hilltop between Gaza and Hebron could be identified as a hilltop "facing Hebron." Keil (1863:418-419) notes a site near Gaza traditionally considered the hilltop in question, though later commentators scoff at the identification (e.g., Moore 1895:349-350). Hebron sits 38 miles east of Gaza and over 3,000 feet above it, high atop a geological uplift known as the "Judean Arch," which runs from Bethlehem south for about 25 miles. This ridge dominates the view westward from any point in the Shephelah. Perhaps it was no accident that Samson took the gates into the territory of his Judean brethren who had earlier betrayed him to the Philistines.

16:4 ***Some time later.*** Heb., *wayehi 'akhare ken* [TH310/3651A, ZH339/4027] (and it was, afterwards), which marks a notable pause in time, and often marks major episode divisions, such as in the latter part of the story of David (cf. 2 Sam 2:1; 8:1; 10:1; 13:1; 15:1; Matthews 2004:158).

Samson fell in love. Lit., "he loved a woman." Contrary to claims that "love" was Samson's weakness, it is not stated that Samson loved any woman prior to Delilah. The text is also silent about whether Samson married in the 20 years he led Israel. Assuming he did not, the book of Judges remarkably presents a series of heroes: Gideon, Jephthah, and Samson, who ultimately have no offspring to continue their line. In the ancient society, to die with no offspring was a horrible fate.

a woman named Delilah. Scholars debate the meaning of her name. Some suggest a tie to a word meaning "a thin thread," which makes little sense, except that Delilah did possess a loom. Another suggestion links the word to dangling curls or loose hair, a plausible connection to the story. Yet another possibility, the most popular one, is a word meaning "flirtation" (HALOT 1.222, s.v. *delilah* [TH1807, ZH1935]). No reader of the Hebrew, however, could miss the aural resonance between Delilah's name and the Hebrew word for "night" (*laylah* [TH3915A, ZH4326]), which appears four times in 16:1-3. Though most interpreters presume Delilah was a Philistine, the narrator never names her as such, and does not even name her town. Her name has a Northwest Semitic form, so she might well have been a Canaanite—or perhaps even an Israelite. What if Samson was ultimately betrayed by an Israelite woman who, like Samson, had engaged in Philistine liaisons?

the valley of Sorek. The Sorek valley brings the story back to Samson's home area, near Timnah, Zorah, and Beth-shemesh. Due to several phonetic shifts among the Semitic languages, several variant meanings attach to the Hebrew root, *s-r-q* (cf. *soreq* [TH7796, ZH8604]), which can be difficult to sort out. The various uses of the word also seem to function ironically in this account. The term can denote a foxy-red or sorrel color; it comes from the color of the red soil washed into the valley from the hard limestone hills. "Sorek" is also the name of a very fine and famous strain of dark red grapes used for wine making, potentially ironizing on a wine-refusing Nazirite meeting his match in the Sorek. Again, the connection with Samson's fate provokes a rueful smile from the alert reader of the Hebrew text. "Sorek" also denotes women's cosmetics, also resonating with our story featuring a woman who captures Samson's affection (HALOT 2.1314, 1361-1362; NIDOTTE 3.1293-1294; Matthews 2004:159). Although the valley is named, Delilah's town is not named. Timnah remains a possibility, of course, but Ekron or even Beth-shemesh would also serve the story's purpose. Although the central narrative occurs in the Sorek valley, it is framed by events in Gaza (16:1-3, 23-30; cf. "General Orientation to the Samson Story" in commentary on ch 13, and note on 14:1).

16:5 *rulers of the Philistines.* "Rulers" translates the plural of *seren* [TH5633A, ZH6249], which seems to be a loan word from the Philistine language. Only Philistine city rulers receive this title in the OT. The term derives either from the Greek *turannos* or the Hittite *sarawanas,* both denoting a ruler. Scholars incline toward one or the other depending on their views of the origin of the Philistines, either Greece or Anatolia. Both have a military connotation befitting the appearance in the OT that the Philistine cities were ruled by a military aristocracy (NIDOTTE 3.295-298). That now the Philistine city elites, rather than mere disgruntled town elders, sought Samson's destruction signals the higher stakes of this game. Moreover, the only previous reference in Judges to the "rulers of the Philistines" specifically names them as functioning to test Israel's faithfulness to Yahweh (3:3). Their appearance here likely implies the testing of Samson, a test he will fail miserably.

Entice Samson. See note on 14:15, and note the parallel with that story: Powerful men came to Samson's beloved with an appeal to seduce him into betraying an important secret.

to tell you what makes him so strong. The parallel with chs 14–15 here presents a contrast. Before, the Philistines simply sought to embarrass Samson as he tried to marry one of their women. Here, the goal was Samson's destruction. The Philistines thought some amulet, object, or "trick" lay behind Samson's strength (Keil 1863:419). Samson might not have appeared muscular, the way artists often portray him, otherwise "working out every day" would have been a sufficient answer to the secret of his strength! But his strength seemed incongruous somehow, demanding a "secret" or magical cause. This story brings the larger theme of knowing and not knowing to a climax.

how he can be overpowered. The NLT presents no equivalent for a word in this verse that also appears in 16:6 and 19. The rulers' request includes three verbs: to overpower, to bind, and to "afflict." This last word (*'anah* [TH6031, ZH6700]) goes beyond mere physical defeat. In the Qal stem, the verb denotes cringing humiliation and wretchedness. Twice it describes women who have been raped and thus humiliated before their community: Dinah (Gen 34:2) and Tamar (2 Sam 13:22, 32; NIDOTTE 3.449-452; Niditch 2008:165). In the honor-shame-oriented culture of the ancient Near East (especially in the chaotic, liminal era of Iron Age I), the Philistines' desire not simply to defeat, but to humiliate and shame Samson assumes paramount importance. Samson had shamed the Philistines when he paid off his wager despite their guessing his riddle. He shamed them again by winning the vendetta feud of ch 15. His 20 years of leadership, apparently unimpeded by the Philistines, would have shamed their military elites by frustrating their ambitions to expand from the coastal plain into the Israelite heartland. Being held at bay by someone they viewed as a backwards, hill-country strongman rankled their honor, so they sought to even the score.

tied up securely. The repeated reference to "binding" in this exchange (*'asar* [TH631, ZH673]) resonates with the promise of the Judeans only to bind Samson (cf. 15:10-13). This root is a leitmotif in this story, appearing in 16:5, 6, 7, 8, 10, 11, 12, 13, 21, 25, ranging in use from references to tying up Samson, to fetters of bronze, to the prison where he was confined.

then each of us will give you 1,100 pieces of silver. Previously, the men intimidated Samson's wife with threats of violence; the Philistine lords here appeal to Delilah's greed. Boling (1975:248-249) suggests scribes and translators misrendered the phrase, which originally read "[from] each unit, one hundred." Here the Hebrew term "thousand" bears its other sense, namely a unit of military command tied to a town, region, or clan (see note on 8:10). The resultant 500 shekels would still be rich payment for her betrayal of Samson.

16:6 ***what it would take to tie you up securely.*** Again, the expression, "to humiliate you" (cf. note on 16:5), is omitted from the NLT's rendering. Delilah clearly states her game: What is required to defeat Samson? The interpretation of the story must account for the fact that Samson cannot have been deceived about what Delilah sought: his utter defeat and open humiliation. The two subsequent episodes also show her utter ruthlessness in acting on the information Samson gave her. Samson could not have doubted her intent.

16:7 ***Samson replied, "If I were tied up with seven."*** Samson, in each of his teasing replies, betrays a clue to the truth. This first ruse actually contains more than one. Here the number seven matches the number of braids of his hair.

new bowstrings that have not yet been dried. "New" (*lakhim* [TH3892, ZH4300], "fresh, moist") aurally evokes the word for "jawbone" (*lekhi* [TH3895, ZH4305]), yet another link between the narrative in chs 14–15 and 16. Samson's use of the "fresh" jawbone violated his vow, as would his contact with "moist" bowstrings, which were typically made from the intestines or tendons of animals. Contact with them would violate the Nazirite prohibition on contact with dead bodies. Especially strings that had "not yet been dried" might retain a stronger association with the dead body of the animal (Soggin 1981:254). Thus, Samson hints already at his devoted condition and how violation of it would compromise his strength (Block 1999:457-458). Since no previous contact with the dead—eating from the lion or handling the donkey's jawbone—had diminished his strength, Samson presumed himself safe.

I would become as weak as anyone else. This expression (*ke'akhad ha'adam* [TH120, ZH132], meaning "like one of humanity" or "like anyone else," recurs three more times (16:11, 13, 17). The underlying question is not simply Samson's strength. The issue resides in what makes Samson different from every other person, i.e., it is a question of boundaries. His strength derives from his distinctive identity, not from any magical properties or mana that might be staunched by some special technique or maneuver. Only the destruction of Samson's unique relationship with Yahweh would make him "like other men" and allow him to be humiliated.

16:9 ***She had hidden some men in one of the inner rooms of her house.*** "Some men" is lit., "the ambush"; it could refer to several persons. Like Rahab in Josh 2, Delilah maintained her own house independently, a house large enough to conceal Samson's would-be captors in another room during the proceedings of the entire evening. In a patriarchal society, a woman presiding over such a house would be wealthy and influential (Matthews 2004:159). She certainly had an easy rapport with the Philistine military urban elites.

the secret of his strength was not discovered. Lit., "his strength was not known." More importantly, Samson had once again violated his Nazirite vow with no ill effects, reinforcing his apparent belief that nothing could rob him of his strength.

16:10 ***You've been making fun of me.*** The charge appears also in 16:13, 15, Delilah's principle complaint against Samson. The verb employed (*talal* [TH2048A, ZH9438]) has close affinities with a root attested in Arabic, *dalla,* which has the same consonants as "Delilah" and means "to flirt." While the verb can mean "to mock, to trifle," the overarching sense conveyed is one of deception or cheating, even reneging on a promise. A power or status differential also figures in the word's usage, in which one gains superiority over another by cunning and deception (NIDOTTE 4.298-299; TDOT 15.672-681). For Delilah to speak this way rhetorically puts her in the weaker position: "you are gaining superiority over me by deceit," when in fact, she was the one who would bring down Samson through deceit (cf. 16:19b). "Making fun of me" thus seems to miss the sinister connotations of the term.

16:11 ***If I were tied up with brand-new ropes.*** Note the echo with 15:13. The ruse shares with the bowstrings the idea of something that is utterly unused, as though such an item possessed a unique power. Rope seems to have been a weave of plant fibers. Flax, acacia fibers, and those from the date-palm were used to make rope (ABD 2.804, 807). In connection with Samson's name, some interpreters note the Babylonian custom where the "rope of Shamash" was draped over the naditu priestess's arm when she entered into the temple service of the sun god as his daughter-in-law or bride (ABD 6.949-950). This Mesopotamian ceremony likely was far from our author's mind. Niditch (2008:165) notes that the "braids" of Samson might well have looked like woven ropes or "dreadlocks," and thus this ruse could gesture indirectly to his hair. Most importantly, the reader already knows, of course, that new ropes could not bind Samson since Samson's great victory with the jawbone began with his being bound in "new ropes." So this ruse points to its own falsehood by repeating a strategy known to be ineffective.

16:13 ***If you were to weave the seven braids of my hair.*** Here Samson betrays part of the truth about his strength. Only here does the reader learn that Samson's hair formed seven braids. Whether Delilah had to unbraid or unbind Samson's seven locks in order to weave them into her fabric remains unclear, but seems likely. Burney (1920:379-380) notes how ancient art portrays the Mesopotamian hero Gilgamesh, like most Mesopotamian heroes, with curled locks of hair.

into the fabric on your loom. The text in 16:13-14 has been disrupted. The Hebrew of 16:13 closes 16:13 with this clause and resumes in 16:14 with Delilah already fastening Samson's hair with a peg (NLT, "shuttle"). A fuller text appears in the ancient Greek translations. While some think the shorter Hebrew simply has an ellipsis (Keil 1863:421), it seems more likely that the longer text in the LXX (followed by NLT, NIV, NASB, et al.) is original and was omitted by a Hebrew copyist due to repetition.

16:14 ***she tightened it with the loom shuttle.*** If Delilah was a Philistine, the reference to her loom evokes one of the most distinctive aspects of Philistine material culture. In the Sorek valley, the excavation of the site of Timnah (Tel Batash) revealed many household looms, particularly the type featuring two upright pieces and a crossbar from which the vertical strands, the warp, hung, steadied by loom weights tied to the ends of the threads. The cross-strands, the woof/weft, were pushed through the warp repeatedly to create the fabric. Periodically the cross-woven strands were packed together by a batten inserted into the warp and used to ram the woven threads tightly together. This flat piece of wood was not the "shuttle" the NLT mentions, which was the leader for the cross-woven threads. So Samson noted that his hair must be woven into the fabric and rammed tight with the batten (Moore 1895:353). The text, in using the noun *yathed* [TH3489, ZH3845] (peg, stick) and the verb *taqa'*[TH8628, ZH9546] (thrust, ram), also evokes Jael's murder of Sisera (4:21) and possibly Ehud's murder of Eglon (3:21). Several different types of loom weights, often of a distinctively Philistine type, have been excavated, often deposited on the floors of houses in a tidy row right where they fell from the threads when the house was burned. Egyptian art portrays this sort of loom and allows us rather easily to imagine the scene (Barber 1991:79-125; King and Stager 2001:152-158).

Samson woke up, pulled back the loom shuttle, and yanked his hair away from the loom. If Delilah in fact wove Samson's hair into the fabric on the loom and compacted it, he probably did not simply "yank" his hair free. His rising probably destroyed the loom, pieces of which would be in his hair, still woven into the cloth, dragging along behind him. The image is quite dramatic and even comical.

16:15 ***Delilah pouted.*** The NLT expands on the Hebrew, which simply reads "and she said." Translators often inject a color or tone into the text's often bland wording to make explicit something they think is implicit in the text, based on their larger impression of the narrative. "Pouted" suggests one possible demeanor of Delilah; she might also have "cooed" or spoken angrily, protested, or even used a calm tone that threatened perhaps the end of the relationship.

How can you tell me, "I love you." Delilah's appeal echoes that of Samson's Timnite wife, except that the narrator has made a point of telling us that Samson, in fact, loved Delilah (16:4).

16:16 ***until he was sick to death of it.*** Lit., "his soul (*nepesh* [TH5315, ZH5883]) became short unto death." The idiom of exasperation, "the *nepesh* was/is short," appeared in 10:16 (see note).

16:17 ***Finally, Samson shared his secret with her.*** Samson's strength would have been rather obviously associated with his Nazirite status, whose most obvious feature was unshorn hair. The text rather emphasizes "he declared to her his whole heart." In what follows, Samson does not merely note that a haircut will drain his potency. He explicitly unfolds the full connection between his hair, his vow, and his devotion to Yahweh. He thus makes clear that his hair functions sacramentally via his vow as a marker of his relationship with Yahweh, showing in fact it is not a "secret" such as a magical trick. Rather, his devotion with Yahweh, signaled by the hair, is the key. The link between a hero's powers and hair appears frequently in popular traditions (Soggin 1981:257-259).

My hair has never been cut . . . I was dedicated to God as a Nazirite from birth. For the very first time the story ties Samson's great strength to his Nazirite status and his uncut hair. In chs 14–15, his Nazirite status and hair go without notice as his strength derives from Yahweh's enabling. This statement arcs back to ch 13 and the vow over Samson's life, though even there, supernatural strength is not stated to result from Samson's vow. Samson clearly states the connection between his devotion and his strength. Even here, though, Samson does not name Yahweh as his God, but describes himself as "dedicated [a Nazirite] to God," using the term *'elohim* [TH430, ZH466]. Did Samson discern in the name of Israel's God at least one boundary he dare not desecrate? The irony of Samson's "testimony" in this setting should not be missed.

16:18 ***his secret.*** Lit., "his heart," as also in 16:15. The NLT shifts the emphasis to the content of the betrayal, but the Hebrew focuses on its character. A man had given his heart to the wrong person, and would pay the price.

16:19 ***Delilah lulled Samson to sleep with his head in her lap.*** Lit., "on her knees," but ancient Greek versions also read *ana meson* [TG3319, ZG3545] (between) her knees, which would render Heb. *bayin* [TH996, ZH1068], a sexual reference. Indeed, from a comparative literature standpoint, all of the "recurring acts of tying" appear to be "subversive play in an erotic context" (Niditch 2008:166-169). Samson, after making love, promptly dropped into a deep sleep. This was especially unwise when his lover was in possession of a razor.

she called in a man to shave off. The Hebrew text is confusing. It reads lit., "she called a man, and she shaved off." The fem. verbal form is indisputable; it was Delilah who did the shaving. She also performed the previous actions intended to debilitate Samson, so suddenly expecting someone else to do the deed violates the context. Most translations fix this by interpreting the Piel *wattegallakh* [TH1548, ZH1662] (she shaved) as though it were a Hiphil: "she called a man and [made him] shave." The causal sense of the Piel, however, is not agental, but factitive; the subject causes a condition, not an event, thus the Piel often sounds resultative or intensive, e.g., "shaved off." Moreover, the verb never appears in the OT in the Qal, and in all its other occurrences simply means "shaved," not "caused [someone] to shave [someone else]." Short of speculation, we can only assume she wanted the man present while she shaved Samson's head.

the seven locks of his hair. Since the OT sets certain limits on the cutting of the hair (e.g., Lev 19:27; 21:5 [priests]; Deut 14:1), any shaving of the head indicated a noteworthy change in a person's status. Whether signifying separation or reintegration, shaving the head betokened the crossing of a vital boundary and was surrounded by taboo and ritual (Olyan 1998). The shaving of a Nazirite's head carried even more significance. The contrast with the way the Nazirite's hair should have been cut could not be stronger. The Nazirite, upon completion of the period of devotion, presented himself or herself to the priest. With appropriate offerings, the Nazirite shaved the hair, which was then burned on the altar (Num 6:18). The Nazirite then rejoined the ordinary, day-to-day life of every Israelite, the shaved head being a testimony to everyone of a devotion freely chosen and brought to sacred, triumphant completion. Samson, however, was not to know a victorious conclusion to his life of devotion. As he slept, his treacherous lover sheared his locks. We hear nothing of the disposal of the hair, but the image of Samson slumbering in his treacherous lover's arms while his sacred hair lies on the floor of his lover's bedchamber, perhaps to be swept out into the street (rather than burned on Yahweh's altar), powerfully conveys the betrayal of his status.

she began to bring him down. Again, the verb is "to humiliate," as in 15:5, 6, likely referring to some overt abuse or shaming action by Delilah.

and his strength left him. The series of verb tenses likely here conveys not sequence, but concurrency: She humiliated him as his strength left him. The text almost suggests one could observe the power draining from Samson. Readers perennially wonder how Samson could have been so foolish. Did he not know, based on the last three episodes, that she would in fact cut his hair? Rather than attribute Samson's revelation to stupidity or love-blindness, the key likely remains arrogance. Nowhere in the story has Samson's strength suffered, despite repeated violations of his vow and of Yahweh's moral law.

16:20 ***When he woke up, he thought, "I will do as before and shake myself free."*** Samson here expresses the presumption that is his undoing. Three previous times she acted immediately upon his divulging his secret, albeit in deceit. When he told her the whole truth, he had to know she would act on it. But, amazingly, he expected no consequences.

But he didn't realize the LORD had left him. This statement portends much more than merely the Spirit of Yahweh no longer rushing upon Samson. The claim that Yahweh is "with" someone in the OT implies the full blessing of God's presence and power not only within them, but providentially working around them to order their way, as in the case of Joseph (e.g., Gen 39:1-6). For Yahweh to turn away from Samson meant not simply the failure of his blessing, but his rejection by Yahweh as his servant. Samson became like any other man, and even worse. Others can claim to be Yahweh's weak and humble servant; Samson was abandoned by God.

16:21 ***So the Philistines captured him and gouged out his eyes.*** The same fate befell the last king of Judah, Zedekiah (2 Kgs 25:7). Assyrian palace reliefs depict the gouging out of war-prisoners' eyes (Bleibtreu 1991). Most striking is the oft-reproduced image of the mutilated bronze head of a prominent Mesopotamian, possibly the king Sargon the Great, featuring shattered eye-sockets, broken-off ears, and mutilated nose (Frankfort 1996:84; Nylander 1980). A typical account from the Assyrian king Ashurnasirpal II reads: "In strife and conflict I besieged (and) conquered the city. I felled 3,000 of their fighting men with the sword. I carried off prisoners, possessions, oxen, (and) cattle from them. I burnt many captives from them. I captured many troops alive; others I cut off their noses, ears, (and) extremities. I gouged out the eyes of many troops. I made one pile of the living (and) one of heads. I hung their heads on trees around the city" (Grayson 1991:201). More than mere savagery, such mutilation subjected the victims to shame (Lemos 2006).

They took him to Gaza. This phase of Samson's life began at Gaza (16:1-3), where Samson carelessly took his liberty with a prostitute and found his strength equal to the escape. His return to Gaza, especially his passage through the city gate, with which he was intimately familiar, accentuates the depth to which Samson's presumption brought him. The Philistines also imprisoned Samson as far as possible from his home territory. Readers familiar with the deportations by the Assyrians in 721 BC or by the Babylonians in 597 and 586 would find the image compelling.

he was bound with bronze chains and forced to grind grain. Artists universally portray Samson pushing the beam on a large, circular grinder like an ox. But this style of mill seems a late Iron Age development. However poignant this image, Samson likely used a hand grinder, in which a "rider" stone was pushed up and down, back and forth, over a "saddle stone" by a worker kneeling in front—work normally reserved for women and slaves in ancient societies (ABD 4.831-832). King and Stager (2001:94) note, "It was common practice to humiliate prisoners of war by forcing them to grind with a handmill." Ironically, since the term "grind" in Hebrew was thought also to have sexual connotations, medieval rabbinic interpreters suggested Samson did not grind grain, but, due to his virtuosic physicality, served as a kind of breeding stud for the Philistines, who sent their women to him (ABD 1.720-725; Niditch 2008:166, 171).

16:22 ***But before long, his hair began to grow back.*** From a more advanced point in the process of divine revelation, Christian readers might recoil from what appears to be a crude association between Samson's mere external appearance, i.e., his hair's growth, and the return of God's blessing on his life. But the Nazirite vow centered on the hair. Whatever other rules applied, the "sacred head" of the Nazirite figured centrally in this intensified devotion to Yahweh. Likewise, the text uses Samson's hair as a visible literary marker for Samson's devotion to God. Thus, in noting Samson's hair regrowing, the author signals that God is not finished using Samson. In fact, God had declared Samson a Nazirite until the day of his death. Even in sin and failure, even in prison, Samson was not released from his vow (contra Boling 1975:248-253). The author signals that Samson remains under the mercy of God. The revival of the symbol of his devotion points to the renewal of the devotion itself. Ironically, what was originally a secret the Philistines connived and paid richly to learn, now plays out right before their eyes, and they do not even see it. They are as blind to the danger posed by the regrown hair as Samson has become by losing it.

16:23 ***great festival . . . praising their god, Dagon.*** While readers normally imagine Samson's last act occurring in Gaza, ancient sources testify to a place known as Beth Dagan north of Gaza on the coast, near Joppa (Moore 1895:359). Interpreters since David Kimchi have seen Dagon as a hybrid fish-human image, based on the Heb. word *dag* [TH1709, ZH1834], meaning "fish" (Keil 1863:424; Moore 1895:358), but a lack of hard evidence leaves an enigma (ABD 2.1-3). Block (1999:465) suggests Dagon was most likely an agricultural deity (cf. Heb., *dagan* [TH1715, ZH1841], "grain"). Dagon figured in ancient Near Eastern worship as early as the third millennium BC, and he appeared in the Levant as early as the 1300s BC. Evidently, he was not the Philistines' native god but was adopted by them upon arrival. The "ark narrative" (1 Sam 4–6) mocks Dagon, who falls on his face before the captured Ark.

16:24 ***Our god has delivered our enemy to us! The one who killed so many of us is now in our power!*** The Philistines describe Samson as (lit.) "our enemy . . . the destroyer of our land . . . who multiplied our slain." While he had not delivered Israel from the Philistines, the harm Samson did to the oppressor cannot be minimized. The lines quoted from the Philistine shout contain a fivefold rhyme that suggests a poetic form. Many of the claims made about their deity, Dagon, would be applied by the Israelites to Yahweh. Likewise, similar claims are found in the claims of Mesha king of Moab in his inscription praising his god Chemosh. Samson here fulfills the third step of decline set out by the author of Judges in 3:5-6, where the reader was warned that Israel would fraternize with pagans, then intermarry with pagans, and, finally, be made to serve their gods. Samson clearly engaged in the first two boundary violations, and here, as with the final requirement of his Nazirite vow, the final violation occurs against his will.

16:25 ***to amuse them.*** The precise nature of the amusements offered by Samson remain unsaid. Some imagine feats of (reduced) strength in which Samson the divine hero was reduced to a circus strongman. Ancient translations suggest dancing, but the Hebrew also has sexual connotations (Gen 26:8; 2 Sam 6:5, 21-23; 1 Chr 15:29; Niditch 2008:167, 171), possibly suggesting some lewd or humiliating action, perhaps a reenactment of Samson's downfall?

between the pillars supporting the roof. Excavations of a series of Philistine temples at Tel Qasile, within the city limits of modern Tel Aviv, reveal in the stratum X level two stone column bases about six feet apart upon which would have stood massive cedar columns, of which carbonized remains were found, to support the roof (Mazar 1992:317-323; Bierling 1992:113-119). Dislodging them might indeed have compromised the structure of the building, especially if it were already burdened with spectators on the roof (cf. 16:27). No one, of course, claims this temple as the one destroyed by Samson. Tel Qasile stratum X is somewhat late for Samson and, of course, is not located in Gaza. Still, its existence confirms in the Iron I period a Philistine temple design previously known only from ch 16.

The three successive temples at Tel Qasile, covering the entire period of Philistine occupation, document an impressive diversity of architecture and floor plan, suggesting scholars should not expect uniformity in Philistine cult centers.

16:28 ***Samson prayed to the LORD, "Sovereign LORD."*** Samson addresses God in perhaps the most formal manner possible, combining the term "master" (*'adonay* [TH136, ZH151]) with the divine name, *yhwh* [TH3068, ZH3378].

remember me again. "Again" does not appear in the Hebrew. The cry for God to "remember" carries deep connotations. For humans, to remember God and his saving actions involves those actions having a continuing impact—that is, one orders one's life around the reality of God's actions in a concrete way. Israel's whole problem resided in its tendency to forget Yahweh and his actions. Likewise, for Yahweh to "remember" his servant means he acts decisively on his servant's behalf. Since remembrance also implies a forgetting, possibly Samson here acknowledged his past alienation from Yahweh and the justice of Yahweh's departure from him, and called now for Yahweh to return to his servant.

O God, please strengthen me. For the first time, Samson actually appeals to God for strength rather than presuming on Yahweh's presence. Since the vow that was the secret of his strength literally fell to the floor in Delilah's boudoir, Samson's only hope lay in a direct appeal to Yahweh, whose honor had been impugned by the Philistine festival.

just one more time. The core of this expression, *happa'am* [TH6471, ZH7193], recapitulates the "just this once" of 15:3. The particle *'ak* [TH389, ZH421] expresses unambiguously that Samson knew this would be the final act.

With one blow . . . for the loss of my two eyes. Lit., "let me have vengeance for one of my two eyes." The idea could be that Samson did not even ask complete vengeance, just enough for one of his eyes (Moore 1895:362).

let me pay back the Philistines. The NLT's "pay back" seems to reduce Samson's vengeance to mere payback, simply revenge. But Mendenhall (1973:69-104) demonstrated that the term *naqam* [TH5358, ZH5933] refers to a distinctive situation in which the necessities of justice cannot be satisfied by the normal social institutions and require executive action, not judicial. The legitimacy of this executive use of force derives from divine authority. The context has clearly aligned the humiliation of Samson with the exaltation of Philistine gods, so that Samson's vindication would entail Yahweh's vengeance as well. Claiming that Samson's prayer is purely self-centered (Schneider 2000:225-226; Block 1999:467-468; Younger 2002:322-323) misses this point and ignores the solidarity that existed between a tribal people, their deity, and their hero; it judges him by a standard of modern, Western, middle-class piety. Samson cried out to the divine author of justice, whose own honor was at stake in the Philistine temple, for more than revenge; he cried for "the reckoning." To nitpick Samson's prayer, count the first-person pronouns (an equal proportion of which occur in "acceptable" prayers), or charge him with narcissism also misses the horror and anguish, admittedly self-inflicted, that Samson had experienced. With his sense of mission, however narrow, renewed, his vengeance would provide some opportunity for God to be vindicated since the destruction of a pagan temple in the midst of a pagan festival results. Ironically, Samson did fulfill a central obligation of the Israelite occupation of Canaan: He destroyed a pagan cult site.

16:30 ***Let me die with the Philistines.*** Contrast this statement with Samson's prayer in 15:18, where he protested that he would fall into the hands of the uncircumcised. His words here are not an affiliation with the Philistines, but articulate some degree of acceptance of the consequences of his actions.

the temple crashed down on the Philistine rulers and all the people. The ancient historian Tacitus reports the collapse of a wooden amphitheater that buried 50,000 victims (cf. Moore 1895:363). Nothing prevents the temple in this story from featuring wooden structures such as bleachers.

he killed more people when he died than he had during his entire lifetime. This line could be a commendation or a wry criticism affirming the best thing Samson ever did for Israel was to die (Stone 1988:346; 1992:343; Block 1999:469; Younger 2002:327). If the suggestion that 15:20 and 16:31b imply 20 years of relative safety from the Philistines under Samson, perhaps such a harsh judgment is not warranted. Indeed, Boling (1975:253) well observes that Samson "ran afoul because of his own lusty self-interest, [but] the consequent suffering evoked a new confession from him and he died honorably in the act of effecting Yahweh's justice toward Philistia." Niditch (2008:171-172) observes how, in Iron Age literary conventions, Samson's death was heroic, his burial noble. The last word on this very mixed character is, in fact, heroic. Samson's story could be seen as a time of deviation (14:1–15:19) followed by honorable service (15:20) yielding again to deviation (16:1-22) followed by an honorable end (16:22-31). In this respect, perhaps Samson's death in battle, killing thousands of Philistines, improves somewhat upon Gideon and Jephthah, whose careers end under a cloud of misguided and even tragic choices. While his repeated violations of his vow did not seem to diminish its effects until the cutting of his hair, and while his hair regrew and restored the vow and his strength, his death here frees him from his obligation: Samson was called as a Nazirite until the day of his death (13:7).

16:31 ***his brothers and other relatives went down to get his body.*** Samson's relatives traveled unhindered to the Philistine city to recover his body, which the Philistines apparently had not mutilated or abused as would happen later to the body of Saul (1 Sam 31:8-13). Both facts possibly testify to Samson's impact.

buried him between Zorah and Eshtaol. Samson's remains were laid to rest where the Spirit of Yahweh first stirred him (13:25).

Samson had judged Israel for twenty years. The NLT rightly reflects the Hebrew in using a pluperfect tense. The author leaves as his final note a reminder not of Samson's unsavory exploits, but the 20 years in which he judged Israel without incident. In effect, ch 16 constitutes a large elaboration of the concluding elements of the standard judge framework structure. The story concludes by noting the duration of the judge's rule and his death. Here we have an extended death narrative inserted after the notation in 15:20 of Samson's 20-year rule. This is because Samson's death was so noteworthy and exemplary of much of the author's main argument, namely that violation of the boundaries defining Israel as Yahweh's people had catastrophic consequences despite the fact that in his mercy Yahweh can still do much through the life of his servant.

COMMENTARY

Judges 14–15 presented the reader with a vexing conflict between the hero's behavior and the moral vision presented in the book thus far. On the one hand, Samson's marriage provided Yahweh with an occasion against the Philistines, Yahweh's Spirit repeatedly empowered Samson to smite the Philistines, and at the end, Yahweh miraculously revived Samson with water from a rock, reminiscent of Moses. On the other hand, Samson violated vital boundaries that defined Yahweh's people over against the Philistines by pursuing marriage to a Philistine woman and by utterly ignoring his Nazirite vow. Indeed, nothing in chapters 14–15 even recognizes Samson is a Nazirite. Nonetheless, at the end of chapter 15, all seems well. Samson fully avenged himself on the Philistines. He stymied any ambitions they had of expanding up the Sorek valley from Timnah, and he finally seems to acknowledge his separation from the "uncircumcised" (15:18). He then judged Israel, apparently without untoward incident, for 20 years (15:20). But the questions remain: Can vital boundaries of the faith be violated with impunity? Does sin not have any consequences? Can one dance on the edge of unbelief and play with the power of God and remain safe? May one sin if one repents just in time? Apart from chapter 16, chapters 13–15 might seem to say "Yes."

The question presses hard. The contemporary church, in reacting against the judgmental legalism of past generations, has opened its arms to the lost and unbelieving. Many churches admirably declare their acceptance of all persons regardless of their moral failures and brokenness, rightly declaring that the gospel is a message of free grace for broken, bankrupt sinners. They see the church as a trauma center for those shattered by sin. At the same time, the same Christian community in North America seems increasingly to struggle with corruption, immorality, abuse of power, materialism, divorce, child abuse, spouse abuse, and addiction. In stressing God's grace to sinners, have we lost the vital balancing message that *sin harms persons deeply*? More than simply an offense to God, sin actually rips at the fabric of our humanity, leaving us weaker and less able to fulfill God's plan for our lives. Have we accepted sinners in such a way that the shattering impact of sin is disregarded, creating an environment in which those who avoid sin feel marginalized, and a kind of "permission" to sin is felt? After all, God forgives and receives the worst sinners who come to him. Why not sin, then come back to God and be restored? Or as Paul wrote, "should we keep on sinning so that God can show us more and more of his wonderful grace?" (Rom 6:1).

The book of Judges has relentlessly linked Israel's sin to consequent oppression by pagan powers, stressing that sin has consequences—a point so far absent from Samson's story. He seems to violate divine boundaries with impunity, at least until chapter 16, which picks up this theme. The ambivalence of chapters 14–15 breaks down unambiguously in 16:1-31. The structure of this section runs sufficiently parallel to chapters 14–15 to prompt readers to compare and contrast them. The triumphalist note of those two chapters is countered by Samson's plunge to tragedy in chapter 16.

Both units begin with Samson's relationship with a Philistine woman. In chapter 14, the relationship was marital, even though the union was with a Philistine. In 16:1-3 the liaison is fornication. Samson goes to Gaza and spots a prostitute, spending the night with her. Not only is there a contrast with his earlier action, but also a progression that sends us back to the introduction, specifically 3:5-6. There Israel's decline from compromise to apostasy was summarized in three stages: *coexistence* with the inhabitants of the land, *intermarriage* with them, and *serving* their gods. Samson began with intermarriage; now he consorts with a prostitute. Recall that in 2:17; 8:27 and 33, *harlotry is an image for apostasy*. And yet, harlotry itself is rare in Judges. So 16:1-3 strike the reader hard. Moreover, later in chapter 16, Samson will be the cause for the Philistines' glorifying—albeit briefly—their god, Dagon. Samson embodies the diagnosis given in 3:5-6.

Some years ago I saw a poem, the source of which is lost to me, that encapsulates this process:

> IMAGINE MOSES SAYING:
> "We will camp right here,
> and send our little ones to Canaanite day-care centers.
>
> IN JUST A FEW YEARS WE WILL
> laugh at the same jokes,
> sleep in the same beds
> worship the same gods,
>
> THEN WE CAN DRIFT ACROSS
> the Jordan River,
> and not be noticed at all."

What is probably most significant about the short story in 16:1-3, however, is that Samson's sojourn with a prostitute in no way diminished his strength, as his midnight transport of the gates of Gaza to a new location in the Shephelah clearly demonstrates. Notably, no reference appears to the Spirit of Yahweh, but neither did the Spirit appear every time he used his strength before. He experienced no consequences for his actions, and was perhaps confirmed in the blind assumption, already evident earlier (15:7), that he was in full control of his life. Even when he slept in the arms of a harlot, his strength did not abandon him, and the Philistines could not touch him. This, however, only continues the theme noted earlier, that Samson had been wantonly violating his Nazirite status, without apparent consequences. The delay of consequences, or rather, the silent and invisible nature of moral consequences, had caused many a person to think that God's word, especially the word of demand and warning, somehow does not apply.

After his encounter with the prostitute in Gaza, Samson took a lover in the Sorek valley. Like chapters 14–15, 16:4-22 depicts Samson, now in a second immoral relationship, divulging a secret to a persistent paramour. Far from being an intimidated fiancée threatened by her townsmen and moved by fear for her own life and that of her family, Delilah was crassly in the hire of Samson's enemies, and was motivated by greed. Unlike Samson's earlier love, Delilah played for keeps, probing not for the answer to a party puzzle, but for the key to Samson's destruction.

Another contrast lies in the fact that Samson is not duped by his lover in chapter 16 as he was earlier. Judges 14–15 revealed Samson's intelligence, articulate wit, and shrewdness. He was a formidable riddler and toastmaster, no less clever with women. Samson was not reduced to a quivering mound of jelly by a beautiful woman. In chapter 14, he appears honestly overwhelmed, not by fluttering eyelashes, but by the constant, anguished importunity of his beloved, and was surprised and outraged that she divulged his secret. Not so in chapter 16. Samson is not deceived by Delilah, who clearly signals her intentions: "How can I really hurt you?" And moreover, by the time he divulged his secret, Delilah had acted on what he said *three times*, even readying a Philistine ambush in the house (16:9, 12)!

Faced with an attractive and dangerous lady, Samson played along with her deadly game, behaving as though he was totally in control, the master of his strength. Consider the incongruity of 16:17: In the house of his deceitful lover, who has three times showed herself fully willing to rob Samson of his strength, Samson gave his testimony, made love with the woman, then went to sleep, probably between her knees! As he betrayed the core reality of his life, he seemed oddly out of touch with the outrageous incongruity of his actions. His actions had not so far meant the loss of his divinely given strength. Did he think that, despite his own explanation, he would not really lose his strength? Like all the great heroes of the Late Bronze and Iron Age epics, his weakness is neither stupidity nor lust, but *hubris* (Niditch 2008:168-169). Wine had not snapped his vitality, nor had contact with the dead, nor even raw fornication. Could it be that he thought his strength, in the end, was really his own after all? Perhaps Samson's addiction was not to sensual lust, but to *risk*; he loved the edge of disaster and believed he could turn back at any point. No, Samson is not blinded by love, nor even lust. Samson is first numbed, *desensitized to the word of God* and its significance in his life, and then *blinded by pride* and power as he handed his soul over to Delilah. The physical blindness inflicted by the Philistines only ratified outwardly what had already occurred inwardly.

How wrong he was! Ironically, Samson willfully, even enthusiastically, violated the first two provisions of his vow when he ate from a lion's carcass (14:8-9) and presided over a banquet, which likely involved the fruit of the vine (14:10), on top of violating his solidarity with his own people by marrying a Philistine. His encounter with the prostitute of Gaza seemed to validate his continued ability to defy God's boundaries for his life with impunity. The last provision of his vow, however, was broken as he slept in Delilah's lap. Such is the fragility of human spiritual freedom. The first coins in the bank of freedom are spent willfully, carelessly—the last one is always stolen while we sleep. We are free to choose actions, but never free to choose the consequences. Sin's fruit is not born instantly, but it does bear fruit. Shorn of his strength, Samson woke, expecting to defeat the Philistines in the sudden energy of his God-given strength, as always. But Samson, who thought he could stop the cycle of recrimination begun by his actions, "didn't realize the LORD had left him" (16:20b). It is difficult to imagine a more tragic statement in the Bible than this. Tragic it is, and yet the only thing surprising about it is its lateness. The word of God, earlier violated by Samson with seeming impunity, now renders its verdict. The judgment of the word does not come through some direct action of God. No bolt of lightning strikes. Rather, *the matrix of human relationships created by Samson's actions forms the context in which the violated word shows itself ultimately inviolate.*

Did Samson die in this self-willed alienation from God? This is not a question of Samson's eternal destiny. The text does not address these issues. Rather, the question for the ancient audience would be whether this was a good death. Did Samson finally die in solidarity with Yahweh and with Yahweh's people, however poorly Samson understood those things? The text provides one sign of hope. The direct connection between his uncut hair and his status as one devoted to Yahweh triggered his downfall. The author used the literal cutting of his hair to signal the loss of Yahweh's presence and power. So, as Samson labored in the Philistine prison, powerless and blind, the author observed that his hair began to return (16:22). If the author's linkage of the hair with Yahweh's blessing holds, then the regrowth of Samson's hair prepares the reader for a renewal of Samson's Nazirite status and the return of his strength. The word of God spoken over Samson (13:5, 7) held firm when he violated it; this word will still have the last word. In the midst of the consequences of his sin, Samson will provide Yahweh with one last occasion against the Philistines. May we say more? Would the author have pointed out the regrowth of Samson's hair, so portentous in the story, if that meant nothing? Samson cannot ultimately stand again as he did at Lehi, triumphant in divine strength and defiant over the Philistines. But might he appeal to God one last time, in the only idiom of justice, divine or human, he understands? In his cry for vengeance, might we hear a call to Yahweh to show himself mighty over the Philistines and their gods?

The final scene (16:23-30) parallels the scene in 15:18-19 where Samson, suffering from thirst and exhaustion, called upon God to save his life. No longer a triumphant charismatic warrior, Samson had become an occasion for the praise of a pagan god. Abandoned by Yahweh, he did what Israel failed to do at the beginning of this story (13:1): He cried out to Yahweh. While there is certainly a nobility about Samson's death that provokes awe in readers, some suggest he nevertheless stays strictly in character, and appeals to God only for vengeance for his eyes. To the end, they say, Samson champions not God, but himself. The best thing the last charismatic judge does for Israel is die (16:30). And yet, the author points to the regrown hair, reports Samson's prayer, presents his honorable burial by a loving family, and reminds the reader of two decades of leadership. Not exactly the epitaph of the unredeemed. Samson indeed marks the end of a steady decline in the institution of the charismatic judge. Still, the book of Judges has shown time and again that even the depths of apostasy and oppression do not foreclose divine mercy. Nor does the fact of that mercy diminish the gravity of the sin.

Historically, interpreters struggle over whether Samson's death properly may be seen as a suicide (cf. Keil 1863:425-426; Gunn 2005:222-227). In the end, most see his death as a self-sacrifice in the service of God's warfare against the Philistines, much as a soldier risks death entering battle. Yet Samson causes his own death quite intentionally. The issue remains relevant, as some contemporary Christian preachers of Palestinian heritage have appealed to Samson's example as a warrant for the practice of "suicide" bombing. Contemporary performances of, for example, Handel's oratorio, based on Milton's *Samson Agonistes*, and other dramatizations of the story periodically feature Samson bringing down the Philistine temple with a suicide bomber's vest (Carey 2002). On the other side, some Israeli political observers have spoken of the "Samson solution" in which Israel, under attack by its Arab enemies and abandoned by the West, detonates all its nuclear weapons. Barth (1961:3/1.410), in a probing and nuanced discussion of suicide as "self-murder," hauntingly comments on the implications of the Samson story. Barth has observed how self-murder constitutes the quintessential expression of one who has made themselves their own god. He then suggests:

> *Not every act of self-destruction is as such suicide in this sense. Its meaning and intention might well be a definite if extreme form of the self-offering required of man. . . . Who can say that it is absolutely impossible for the gracious God Himself to help a man in affliction by telling him to take this way out? In some cases perhaps a man can and must choose and do this in the freedom given him by God and not therefore in false sovereignty, in despair at the futility of his existence, or in final, supreme and masterful self-assertion, but in obedience. Who can really know whether he might not occasionally ask back from man in this form the life which belongs to Him? Who can deny that, if such should be the case, man must surrender it with his own hands no less gratefully and joyfully than he may keep it until further notice if this is the will of God? Can we, therefore make a simple equation of self-destruction with self-murder? Have we not to take into account the possibility that suicide might not be committed as a crime and therefore as Murder, but in faith and therefore in peace with God?*

Barth continues in a note:

> *Obviously these are dangerous questions. Do they not open again a door which ought to be finally closed? . . . According to Jud. 16:30 Samson deliberately killed himself along with the Philistines. But only a very curious exegesis would classify him with Saul, Ahithophel and Judas. By our standards Samson was certainly a very dubious saint. Yet the Old Testament sets him in the light rather than the shadows, and according to Heb. 11:32 he and other rather uncouth figures from the Book of Judges are given a place with Abraham, Moses, David and Samuel in the "cloud of witnesses" (Heb. 12:1) for New Testament faith. As seen by the Bible, he was certainly not a suicide.*

Resuming his main discussion, Barth reasons:

> *If the possibility of Samson has sometimes to be considered, it can be only at the extreme limit when others have first been examined with final seriousness and there can be no doubt whatever that this is the will of God and is therefore to be adopted. Can we exclude it? Can we be sure that among thousands and thousands there is not just one perhaps who may be genuinely and legitimately called to take this strange action?*

The point, of course, is not to legitimate suicide, but perhaps to place a question mark over the easy tendency to condemn those whose inner pain and hard choices remain permanently beyond our understanding.

Whether a final suicide of total self-assertion, or a ruined and partly redeemed hero of faith making his final choice to "mortify the flesh" literally, Samson stands as an engaging, but terrifying image of a self-will that denies its addiction to lust, revenge, and power, facing its own bondage, if at all, only so late that little can be done even in redemption. In spiritual blindness and pride this self-will played with the power, frittered away its freedom, forfeited the promise, and paid the price. Whether that comes sooner or later, it comes. The wages of sin is death (Rom 6:23). Still, this story reminds us that the ruined servant, consigned to his dark prison of humiliation, remains the object of a divine mercy that hears his cry, even if it be misshapen. However much the servant's capacity for fruitful service might be cut short by his sin and shame, God remains open to the cry of one who wanted to serve again, even if only briefly and poorly.

◆ III. The Finale: A Decadent Community (17:1–21:25)

A. The Failed Mission (17:1–18:31)

1. Substitute worship and priesthood (17:1-13)

There was a man named Micah, who lived in the hill country of Ephraim. 2One day he said to his mother, "I heard you place a curse on the person who stole 1,100 pieces* of silver from you. Well, I have the money. I was the one who took it."

"The LORD bless you for admitting it," his mother replied. 3He returned the money to her, and she said, "I now dedicate these silver coins to the LORD. In honor of my son, I will have an image carved and an idol cast."

4So when he returned the money to his mother, she took 200 silver coins and gave them to a silversmith, who made them into an image and an idol. And these were placed in Micah's house. 5Micah set up a shrine for the idol, and he made a sacred ephod and some household idols. Then he installed one of his sons as his personal priest.

6In those days Israel had no king; all the people did whatever seemed right in their own eyes.

7One day a young Levite, who had been living in Bethlehem in Judah, arrived in that area. 8He had left Bethlehem in search of another place to live, and as he traveled, he came to the hill country of Ephraim. He happened to stop at Micah's house as he was traveling through. 9"Where are you from?" Micah asked him.

He replied, "I am a Levite from Bethlehem in Judah, and I am looking for a place to live."

10"Stay here with me," Micah said, "and you can be a father and priest to me. I will give you ten pieces* of silver a year, plus a change of clothes and your food." 11The Levite agreed to this, and the young man became like one of Micah's sons.

12So Micah installed the Levite as his personal priest, and he lived in Micah's house. 13"I know the LORD will bless me now," Micah said, "because I have a Levite serving as my priest."

17:2 Hebrew *1,100 shekels*, about 28 pounds or 12.5 kilograms in weight. 17:10 Hebrew *10 shekels*, about 4 ounces or 114 grams in weight.

NOTES

17:1 *Micah.* Heb., *mikayehu* [TH4321, ZH4781]; it means "Who is like Yahweh?" In view of the distortions and even perversions of Israelite worship found in the story, the name strikes an ironic note in its inclusion of Yahweh. Strangely, though mentioning his mother, the text fails to name Micah's father or his larger familial affiliation, suggesting the author wanted to stress Micah's lack of obligations or ties to his fellow Israelites.

the hill country of Ephraim. This is a general designation for the hill country running from Bethel to the Carmel ridge, but sometimes designates only the southern half, approximately from Bethel to Shechem. Shiloh, which hosted the true sanctuary of Yahweh for the Judges era, lay in this same region halfway between Bethel and Shechem.

17:2 *he said to his mother.* Though Micah likely is the head of the household, he deferred to his mother.

I heard you place a curse on the person who stole. The Hebrew says "the silver that was taken from you, and you cursed and you said in my ears." The term translated "curse" (*'alah* [TH422, ZH457]) normally denotes an oath or obligation based on a contract or covenant. Thus, her curse likely did not fall on the thief, but defined an obligation or sanction that attached to the silver itself. The silver had been sworn or obligated in some way, only to be stolen. When the son discovered that the silver he had appropriated carried a sacred sanction, he felt obliged to return it.

1,100 pieces of silver. Lit., "the 1,100 of silver." The unit of measure is unspecified. Marked shekel weights from ancient Israel suggest that pieces of silver as small as one-twentieth of a shekel would be used in trade (King and Stager 2001:195-198; Dever 2001:221-228), making it impossible to say how much silver was involved. See note on 16:5.

The LORD bless you for admitting it. The phrase "for admitting it" does not appear in the Hebrew, but makes sense in the context.

17:3 *I now dedicate . . . to the LORD.* The verbal form employed, a Hiphil of *qadash* [TH6942, ZH7727], is the same form often translated with words like "consecrate, sanctify," all circling around the idea of holiness. The construction is also emphatic, employing the infinitive absolute and the verb, both based on the same root, connoting either emphasis or certainty: "I fully sanctify" or "I certainly sanctify" the silver "to Yahweh." The most outstanding feature of anything in the Bible characterized by the *q-d-sh* [TH6944/6918, ZH7731/7705] family of words is that it is the exclusive property of God and in some way participates in, and mediates, divine reality. The irony in this text, of course, is that the silver, first stolen, then bound by an oath, should now be sanctified. Clearly the characters lack any stable moral or spiritual perspective, a point the author will drive home in 17:6.

silver coins. Lit., "the silver." History provides no evidence of coinage, i.e., a token with a standardized value for exchange, in the ancient Near East until the seventh century BC or later. Precious metals used for payment were simply weighed out ad hoc (ABD 1.1089; King and Stager 2001:198-200). "Coins" is therefore anachronistic. The author of Judges never refers to coinage as such, a small but telling sign of the author's preexilic context.

In honor of my son, I will have an image carved and an idol cast. Lit., "I fully consecrate the silver to Yahweh; from my hand to my son, to make a cast and carved image, so now I return it to you." The phrase "honor of my son," tries to render the formality of the transfer of at least a portion of the silver from the mother to the son. It is, however, doubtful that she sought to honor her son in this manner. Since the silver had been sworn or obligated, it could not revert directly to ordinary use. In referring to a carved image and a cast idol, the Hebrew uses two terms to denote a single object. That one object is in view is clear from 18:31, which uses only one of the terms. The first term, *pesel* [TH6459, ZH7181], though derived from a root meaning "carve," in fact denotes any cultic image of any manufacture. The second, *massekah* [TH4541, ZH5011], is a metallurgical term. The two together denote a single image, through hendiadys. The phrase refers either (1) to an image that was plated with precious metal, in this case, silver, or (2) the first term (*pesel*) could be generic with the second (*massekah*) specifying the type of image. In the latter case, the term might refer to an image cast by the "lost wax" process in which a wax model of the image is covered with clay, followed by the molten metal being poured through holes in the clay. The wax image melted, flowing out of holes punched in the clay, with the metal replacing the wax. The former seems more likely since plated images are far more common than images cast from solid silver (HALOT 1.605; 2.949, s.v. *massekah* I, *pesel*; TDOT 8.431-437; 12.30-38; NIDOTTE 2.1000-1001; 3.644-646; ABD 3.823-834).

17:4 *200 silver coins.* Lit., "200 of silver." See note on 17:2. Likely the unit is not shekels, else this would be over five pounds of silver, since a shekel ranged from .40-.45 ounces. So far, no image discovered in Israel by archaeologists would require several pounds of silver for plating. The exact disposition of the whole amount of purloined silver remains unclear in the story.

gave them to a silversmith. The Hebrew term denotes a metalworker of any type, but the word occurs most often in connection with the manufacture of idols (NIDOTTE 3.847-853).

an image and an idol. See note on 17:3. An image like this need not be large. For example, a silver calf about four inches high recovered from a shrine in Middle Bronze Ashkelon was plated with silver, and weighed about 14 ounces (Stern 1993–2008:1.106). A bronze bull image from the period and general region of our story, found in the remains of a possible open-air private shrine (very compatible with our story), measures seven inches long and five inches high (Stern 1993–2008:1.266-267). The reader would obviously realize that these actions directly, even flagrantly, violate the second commandment's prohibition on making any image for worship (Exod 20:4; Deut 5:8). Micah's image seems intended to be an image of Yahweh, which only deepens the abomination represented by it.

these were placed in Micah's house. The NLT, NASB, NKJV, and NIV use a plural, "these/they," under the impression of two objects (image and idol), but the Hebrew verb is singular (see note on 17:3). The terms could be in apposition, but later (18:17) the image and household gods are listed at separate points in the inventory of items seized by the Danites, suggesting two images. Also, "house" in the family structure of ancient Israel could refer not merely to a single structure, but also to the whole compound on which the extended family lived. The phrase "in Micah's house" could simply mean "on Micah's property."

17:5 ***Micah set up a shrine for the idol.*** The NLT seems to miss the sense here. The text uses a circumstantial clause and an idiom of possession, lit., "Now the man, Micah, [had] a house of God." Since the preceding verse said the image was placed in Micah's house, this verse explains what house that was: a sacred place under Micah's control that already existed. The existence of the shrine would explain why Micah's mother so readily asked him to use the silver to make an image: He already maintained a family cult site. The following sentence probably describes the furnishings of that shrine, to which the new image was added as the most sacred object.

shrine. The term is *beth 'elohim* [TH1004/430, ZH1074/466], meaning "house of God." The same phrase is used in 18:31 to describe, by contrast, the shrine at Shiloh, except that in 18:31 the definite article appears, suggesting the "true" house of God was at Shiloh while the shrine at Dan, transplanted from Micah's house, was bogus.

he made a sacred ephod. See note on 8:27. The reference here could be past-perfect, filling out the previous equipping of Micah's family shrine, or it could indicate additional actions accompanying the new image.

household idols. Scholars debate the meaning of the term *terapim* [TH8655, ZH9572], typically translated "household idols." Very likely a loan word, the term denotes images of departed ancestors that functioned in the veneration of the dead. Such ancestral images were family heirlooms and would not have been spontaneously manufactured on the spot, supporting the suggestion above that Micah already possessed a shrine into which his new image was installed (HALOT 2.1794-1796; NIDOTTE 4.339; TDOT 15.777-789). The writer clearly portrays a serious violation of the purity of Israelite worship of Yahweh. Not only did Micah worship an image of Yahweh, he did so in conjunction with the veneration of images representing ancestors, likely seen as deified (i.e., the cult of the dead). Though "household idols" appear periodically in the biblical narrative, offerings to the dead were strictly prohibited by Yahweh (ABD 1.240-242; 2.105-108; cf. Deut 26:14; Ps 106:28).

he installed. The Hebrew idiom for ordination is quite concrete: "he filled (*malle'* [TH4390, ZH4848]) the hand of one of his sons." The expression appears in the original ordination of Aaron and in the prescribed process of consecrating Tabernacle priests (Exod 28:41; Lev 8:32-33). The idiom appears outside Israel, in Akkadian texts, where it denotes investiture into an office and having a share in the proceeds (HALOT 1.583-584).

one of his sons as his personal priest. "Personal priest" might be too strong. The appointed priest would serve the entire extended family compound over which Micah apparently presided. This could be a fairly large group of people, so the image of the priest simply serving Micah misses the mark.

17:6 *In those days.* The chronological formula "in those days" served ancient authors and compilers as a means for placing material side-by-side when a chronological structuring would have separated them. Such a juxtaposition, which has precedence in other ancient Near Eastern historical literature, establishes an explicit relationship of comparison and/or contrast, and even cause-effect between the two blocks of material (Stone 1988:423-458). Judges has presented a very linear narrative up to this point. Chronological references have constructed a sequence. But now the author switches the time formulas to characterize the era in a more general way. Thus, the author of Judges can now present stories that illustrate the climactic consequences of Israel's behavior as presented in chs 1–16 and the full nature of Israel's plight in the era before kings.

Israel had no king. The comment on Israel's lack of a king structures the closing section of the book (17:6; 18:1; 19:1; 21:25). The author uses this note to weave together very diverse stories, classifying them all as case studies on kinglessness. They appear in the narrative in a variety of ways. Here the author breaks into the narrative with no transition or conjunction.

all the people. The NLT's plural misses the essence of the verse's critique; namely, each isolated individual felt at liberty to define for themselves what was right. The actions of Micah in the narrative surrounding this passage powerfully illustrate exactly what the author was talking about: a single individual establishing his own sanctuary to Yahweh, merrily making it up as he went along.

whatever seemed right in their own eyes. The idiom used here for "right" was employed for Samson's headstrong attraction to his first Philistine love (14:3). This statement, repeated in the final verse of the book, provides the writer's analysis of Israel's behavior paralleling the "did evil in the LORD's eyes" of the book's central section (e.g., 3:7). Intriguingly, the narrator passes from criticizing Israel for apostasy from Yahweh in 3:7–16:31 to criticizing arrogant self-will in chs 17–21. The characters in chs 17–21 all worship Yahweh, but their insistence on determining their own behavior spawns arguably worse disasters than those that befell Israel for its apostasy. In fact, in this chapter, the writer describes a complete corruption of Israel's worship in microcosm by looking at Micah's household. The root of his cavalier creation of images, his setting up of his own sanctuary, and his personal appointment of priests is his "doing whatever seemed right in [his] own eyes." By tying this behavior to kinglessness, the author also strongly links the role of the king with cultic purity.

17:7 *One day a young Levite.* Israel's "vertical" or segmented structure of 12 tribes, divided into "clans" that were composed of "father's houses," is evident in Judges, but Israel's "horizontal" or sodal structure does not emerge as clearly. A few social structures, however, did bind these tribes together much as barrel bands hold the staves of a barrel in place. One of these "sodalities" was the Levitical priesthood. Levites possessed no fixed inheritance of land, but were dispersed throughout Israel. Despite an evident lack of rigor in the appointment of priests during this era, Israelites still seemed to value the services of Levites in the priesthood (17:13). If the Levites retained a consistent vision of the purity of Israel's faith, their dispersion throughout the land would have a unifying effect. Unfortunately, our two Levites in chs 17–21 will display little inclination to safeguarding the unity and purity of Israel's worship.

who had been living in Bethlehem in Judah. Reference to Bethlehem and Judah could evoke a reader's association with David and the Judean monarchy, especially following on the heels of 17:6. The Levite in this story *leaves* Bethlehem. The abandonment of Bethlehem here, and the avoidance of Jerusalem (Jebus) by another Levite in ch 19, both culminate in abominable consequences.

arrived in that area. Behind the NLT's rendering is the literal expression "sojourned there" (*gar-sham* [TH1481, ZH1591]), which evokes the popular etymology for the name of Moses's son (Exod 2:22), a point that becomes important later in this story since this Levite is in fact of Mosaic descent through Gershom (cf. 18:30).

17:8 ***He had left Bethlehem.*** If the author held a high view of Judah and Bethlehem as the source of the monarchy (i.e., the Davidic dynasty), then the Levite's having left Bethlehem could identify the target of the writer's critique as those who refused to adhere to the Davidic kingship—the northern tribes who rejected the Davidic dynasty and formed a separate state under Jeroboam I.

in search of another place to live. The NLT here sounds a bit more respectable than the Hebrew, which simply says "he sojourned wherever he found." The term translated "sojourn" typically refers to a person residing in an area that is not his native home. Stager (1988:229-232) has argued that the term also implies dependent, or client status. In a tribal society, unattached individuals simply wandering in the area would not be tolerated.

He happened to stop at Micah's house. The text accentuates the randomness of the Levite's wanderings. Micah will later see this random meeting as a pointer to Yahweh's blessing. He will be wrong, of course, and he stands as the patron saint of those who ignore God's revealed law and then attempt to read his will from coincidences and random encounters.

17:10 ***you can be a father and priest to me. I will give you ten pieces of silver a year, plus a change of clothes and your food.*** It might seem unusual that while Micah was head of his household, the young Levite, whom he hired and supported, was to be "a father" to him. But this use of the term "father" is not without precedent. Joseph was similarly a father to Pharaoh (cf. Gen 45:8 mg), suggesting here it has the idea of an adviser or diviner. The transaction seems oddly secular. Mere absence of any reference to God cannot justify a claim that the characters' actions are faithless, but it cannot be missed that here a Levitical priest accepts ordination in an idolatrous, syncretistic shrine on the strength of the compensation package alone.

17:11 ***The Levite agreed to this.*** The term used, *ya'al* [TH2974, ZH3283] in the Hiphil stem, appears in Judges elsewhere only in 1:17, 35, referring to the previous occupants of the land persisting in holding on to Canaan, and in 19:6, where another Levite's father-in-law asks him to agree to stay for another round of eating and drinking. That is, the three other uses in Judges all have negative connotations in their contexts.

the young man became like one of Micah's sons. The text does not tell what became of the son of Micah who had served as priest prior to the arrival of the itinerant Levite.

17:12 ***personal priest.*** See note on 17:5.

he lived in Micah's house. "House" denotes Micah's compound or *beth 'ab* [TH1004/1, ZH1074/3], the collection of houses and other installations that constituted the Iron Age family homestead.

17:13 ***"I know the LORD will bless me now," Micah said, "because I have a Levite serving as my priest."*** This is ironic in light of Micah's use of stolen silver, his manufacture of an image of Yahweh contrary to the second commandment, and his association of Yahweh with the cult of the ancestors. Micah's expectation of blessing because of this Levite meets the very opposite fate of the one he hoped for.

COMMENTARY

General Orientation to Judges 17–21. The style and subject matter of the book of Judges shift abruptly when it crosses from the Samson story into chapters 17–21. These stories feature neither foreign oppressors nor charismatic deliverers, and they abandon the recurring formulaic prologues and epilogues so characteristic of chapters 3–16. The writer likewise drops the linear chronology of those chapters in favor of a more generalizing, sideways-moving time frame: "in those days" (17:6; 18:1; 19:1; 20:27-28; 21:25). Commentators have typically relegated these five chapters to the status of "appendices" to the "main body" of the book, assessing them simply as secondary additions. Even if a later editor did add them to an existing work—which seems plausible—they still bear important relationships to what precedes, and provide a thematic and narrative climax to the book (Stone 2005). The theme of the Danite's lack of an inheritance (18:1-2) resumes the narrative from their expulsion from their allotted territory (1:34-36), while the reference to Zorah and Eshtaol (18:2) echoes with 13:25. A striking amount of material in Judges concerns itself with the Danites. The formula "in those days Israel had no king" coupled twice to the note "all the people did whatever seemed right in their own eyes" resonates both with the theme of "Israel did what was evil in the eyes of Yahweh" and with the somewhat critical allusions to kingship in chapters 1–16.

Judges 17–21 breaks down into two long, complex accounts. Each begins with a private, domestic problem, the theft of consecrated silver in 17:1-5 and a marital dispute in 19:1-9. In each account, wider Israelite controversies overtake the domestic problem, spiraling into a wider crisis. The migrating Danites commandeer Micah's Levite and cultic apparatus (ch 18), and the marital dispute tumbles into an atrocity, followed by a war of decimation. Both stories likewise address the fate of specific tribes. Judges 17–18 account for the Danites' location in the far north, along with their deviant shrine, while chapters 19–21 report the near extermination of Benjamin, thus accounting for the reduced status of a once influential tribe. Lastly, of course, both stories feature a Levite as the protagonist.

The temporal phrase, "in those days," served ancient authors and compilers as a means for placing material side-by-side when a chronological structuring would have separated them (see note on 17:6). The material in chapters 17–21 is organized to present the climactic consequences of Israel's behavior as presented in chapters 1–16. The recurring thematic refrain stresses a social and political reality: "there was no king in Israel" as a partial explanation for the events that occur in chapters 17–21, while at the same time neatly summarizing the whole political environment of the preceding 16 chapters. Since these final chapters portray behavior that is heretical, hypocritical, and self-destructive, the writer forces the reader to attribute the moral and social meltdown portrayed to the absence of a king. The preceding narrative has demonstrated the collapse of one form of leadership, the charismatic warrior chieftain, and now points to the void that can be filled only by a king.

The author uses a fourfold observation of Israel's kinglessness to structure the narrative, though not in a mechanically regular manner. The first appears in 17:6 as an abrupt aside in the midst of the narrative of Micah's shrine, between the story of the image itself (17:1-5) and Micah's consecration of the young Levite as his priest

(17:7-13). In 18:1, the "no king" formula appears again, abruptly, without even a linking conjunction in the Hebrew, followed by a disjunctive circumstantial clause repeating "in those days." Though awkwardly repeating "in those days," the author directly associated chronologically the landlessness of the Danites with the kinglessness of Israel. In 19:1 the author shifts the construction yet again, using a consecutive construction to link the story in chapters 19–21 to the preceding material more sequentially, including the statement about kinglessness here as a circumstantial clause, inverting the word order (see note on 19:1). The final reference concludes the story and the book (21:25).

Ancient Near Eastern authors often cite dynastic confusion or the lack of a king as a major source of social unrest (see Greenspahn 1986). Here the writer appends a spiritual and moral analysis to the first and last occurrence of his thematic refrain: "all the people did whatever seemed right in their own eyes" (17:6; 21:25). The expression "all the people did whatever seemed right in their own eyes" denotes behavior that is willfully presumptuous and arrogant (Stone 1988:413-423). More importantly, the idiom "whatever seemed right in their own eyes" articulates powerfully with the recurring claim in chapters 2–16 that Israel did "what was evil in the eyes" of Yahweh. Evil in Yahweh's eyes finds a counterpart in "right in their own eyes." Behind the apostasy and sin of chapters 2–16 lurks the darker evil—naked, arrogant, presumptuous human self-will that will take itself as the standard of right.

In that context, the stories in chapters 17–21 continue to develop themes found earlier. In essence, the book so far has explored the ramifications of Israel's worship of false gods. But another threat to Israel's integrity and identity existed, one more subtle than the abandonment of Yahweh for pagan gods: What if Israel worshiped Yahweh, but did so under a false perception of his nature and character? What if they worshiped the "right" God in a corrupt, perverse manner? If chapters 2–16 dealt with apostasy, perhaps we could say that chapters 17–21 deals with heresy: the holding of the faith in a manner that distorts and betrays its identity. In the core of the book, the consequence of sin is oppression by foreign powers. In the final episodes, the consequence is internal collapse and self-destruction.

The author of Judges built his case slowly and cumulatively. He has not roundly condemned the tribal confederation or its charismatic leaders, but has presented these in a sympathetic but honest light. He allowed their own failures to speak for themselves while consistently stressing the unfailing apostasy of the Israelites. With the judges now off the scene, the author dug deeper into the soul of the apostate Israelite tribal community and found not the worship of "another" god, but the worship of *self* as a god. Against this most pervasive human evil and the chaos of the degenerate tribal confederation, the author proposed as a solution an alternative social organization, the most lofty and powerful human institution known: kingship—presumably as a check on individual and social human autonomy. Thus, the way is prepared for the narratives of 1 Samuel that depict how Israel groped its way painfully and haltingly toward taking its place among the nations as a royal kingdom.

Commentary on Judges 17. This narrative about Micah recounts his establishment of an obscure, private shrine in the hill country of Ephraim as a preparation for showing how that event became part of a larger pattern of failure and evil in Israel. The distortions and perversions of Hebrew faith compound through the narrative. Micah used misappropriated silver in the creation of an image of Yahweh, which he placed in a cultic center or shrine under his own control. We then learn that this shrine contained other cultic apparatus, an ephod and teraphim. The former probably also represented the deity as a means of divining messages from God (cf. note on 8:27). The latter most likely points to the cult of the dead ancestors, another religious expression prohibited to Israelites by Yahweh (cf. note on 17:5). Then Micah took it upon himself to ordain his son as a priest (17:5), only to encounter a wandering Levite, whereupon he apparently fired his son and hired the Levite (17:10). Rootlessness pervades the narrative. We know nothing of Micah's extended family, his clan, or genealogical location. These matters in ancient societies defined a person's relationships of obligation and responsibility. Micah appears devoid of both. Likewise, the Levite was adrift, seeking his fortune where he may. Eventually, the Danites will come drifting through (ch 18), seeking their fortune as well! The entire vision of Israel as a rich, nested family structure in which each person lives in vital covenantal bonds with their neighbors and fellow Israelites fails entirely to appear in this narrative. Truly, everyone did what was right in their own eyes.

Of course, one could argue that Micah's perversion of the worship of Yahweh is harmless. After all, he was only one man. In the grand scheme of things, what possible harm to the nation as a whole could one little household bring with its erroneous worship of Yahweh? Is it not enough that they do worship Yahweh and him alone? Is it not picayune pedantry to criticize the man for his manner of private worship? Should we not commend his devotion of so much of his energy and treasure to this shrine to his god who, after all, is Yahweh?

In response, the author could have asserted directly that the truth is the truth: Micah perverted the worship of Yahweh through an image, a privatized priesthood, and the association of Yahweh with the cult of the dead. But the author took a different tack. Rather than engage in a doctrinal rebuttal, he exposed the claim of isolation to be fraudulent. Just as Micah is declaring that surely Yahweh will bless him because of his Levitical priest (17:13), something completely unexpected happens. His private error stands in the path of the Danites who, having failed the mission Yahweh gave them to possess their inheritance, had begun looking for some other, easier mission. Micah's private heresy would fuse with the spiritual and theological failure of the Danites. A *man* took the faith into his own hands. A *family* abandoned the truth about Yahweh. Next a *tribe* will appropriate the error. Just how far will the error reach? Once the boundaries of authentic identity and worship have ruptured, how can we be sure that the impact will be limited?

◆ 2. Substitute conquest (18:1-31)

Now in those days Israel had no king. And the tribe of Dan was trying to find a place where they could settle, for they had not yet moved into the land assigned to them when the land was divided among the tribes of Israel. 2So the men of Dan chose from their clans five capable warriors from the towns of Zorah and Eshtaol to scout out a land for them to settle in.

When these warriors arrived in the hill

country of Ephraim, they came to Micah's house and spent the night there. [3]While at Micah's house, they recognized the young Levite's accent, so they went over and asked him, "Who brought you here, and what are you doing in this place? Why are you here?" [4]He told them about his agreement with Micah and that he had been hired as Micah's personal priest.

[5]Then they said, "Ask God whether or not our journey will be successful."

[6]"Go in peace," the priest replied. "For the LORD is watching over your journey."

[7]So the five men went on to the town of Laish, where they noticed the people living carefree lives, like the Sidonians; they were peaceful and secure.* The people were also wealthy because their land was very fertile. And they lived a great distance from Sidon and had no allies nearby.

[8]When the men returned to Zorah and Eshtaol, their relatives asked them, "What did you find?"

[9]The men replied, "Come on, let's attack them! We have seen the land, and it is very good. What are you waiting for? Don't hesitate to go and take possession of it. [10]When you get there, you will find the people living carefree lives. God has given us a spacious and fertile land, lacking in nothing!"

[11]So 600 men from the tribe of Dan, armed with weapons of war, set out from Zorah and Eshtaol. [12]They camped at a place west of Kiriath-jearim in Judah, which is called Mahaneh-dan* to this day. [13]Then they went on from there into the hill country of Ephraim and came to the house of Micah.

[14]The five men who had scouted out the land around Laish explained to the others, "These buildings contain a sacred ephod, as well as some household idols, a carved image, and a cast idol. What do you think you should do?" [15]Then the five men turned off the road and went over to Micah's house, where the young Levite lived, and greeted him kindly. [16]As the 600 armed warriors from the tribe of Dan stood at the entrance of the gate, [17]the five scouts entered the shrine and removed the carved image, the sacred ephod, the household idols, and the cast idol. Meanwhile, the priest was standing at the gate with the 600 armed warriors.

[18]When the priest saw the men carrying all the sacred objects out of Micah's shrine, he said, "What are you doing?"

[19]"Be quiet and come with us," they said. "Be a father and priest to all of us. Isn't it better to be a priest for an entire tribe and clan of Israel than for the household of just one man?"

[20]The young priest was quite happy to go with them, so he took along the sacred ephod, the household idols, and the carved image. [21]They turned and started on their way again, placing their children, livestock, and possessions in front of them.

[22]When the people from the tribe of Dan were quite a distance from Micah's house, the people who lived near Micah came chasing after them. [23]They were shouting as they caught up with them. The men of Dan turned around and said to Micah, "What's the matter? Why have you called these men together and chased after us like this?"

[24]"What do you mean, 'What's the matter?' " Micah replied. "You've taken away all the gods I have made, and my priest, and I have nothing left!"

[25]The men of Dan said, "Watch what you say! There are some short-tempered men around here who might get angry and kill you and your family." [26]So the men of Dan continued on their way. When Micah saw that there were too many of them for him to attack, he turned around and went home.

[27]Then, with Micah's idols and his priest, the men of Dan came to the town of Laish, whose people were peaceful and secure. They attacked with swords and burned the town to the ground. [28]There was no one to rescue the people, for they lived a great distance from Sidon and had no allies nearby. This happened in the valley near Beth-rehob.

Then the people of the tribe of Dan

rebuilt the town and lived there. 29They renamed the town Dan after their ancestor, Israel's son, but it had originally been called Laish.

30Then they set up the carved image, and they appointed Jonathan son of Gershom, son of Moses,* as their priest. This family continued as priests for the tribe of Dan until the Exile. 31So Micah's carved image was worshiped by the tribe of Dan as long as the Tabernacle of God remained at Shiloh.

18:7 The meaning of the Hebrew is uncertain. **18:12** *Mahaneh-dan* means "the camp of Dan." **18:30** As in an ancient Hebrew tradition, some Greek manuscripts, and Latin Vulgate; Masoretic Text reads *son of Manasseh.*

NOTES

18:1 ***Now in those days Israel had no king.*** Grammatically, this sentence could as easily conclude the preceding story as begin the next, appearing as it does in Hebrew with no conjunction, just as in 17:6 and in 21:25, where it unquestionably does conclude the story. Jerome's linkage of the sentence to the following story seems to have begun the tradition of breaking the narrative before 18:1, rather than with the next clause, which is more syntactically natural (Moore 1895:387).

the tribe of Dan. The NLT omits a second occurrence of "in those days," introduced by the so-called disjunctive Waw, directly juxtaposing the kinglessness of Israel noted in the preceding clause with the Danites' lack of an inheritance, thus tying the absence of a king with the Danites' failure to possess their inheritance (Schneider 2000:236).

trying to find a place where they could settle, for they had not yet moved into the land assigned to them when the land was divided among the tribes of Israel. The NLT expands, rightly, the Hebrew terms used to make explicit the connection with the allotment of land presented in Josh 19:40-48, which emphatically states they did have a section of land apportioned to them, and their failure to take possession of it. There, the writer noncommittally notes that "the inheritance of the Danites went out from them" (lit.), leading to their decision to move north. Judges makes explicit, linking 1:34-35 to 18:1, that Dan had actually failed to secure their very lush and fecund territory because they were no match for the fierce Amorites who hemmed them up in the hill country. The possibility also exists that a segment of the tribe of Dan did not enter Canaan with the rest of the Israelites, but originally belonged to the Danuna/Denyen, a group among the "Sea Peoples" (see note on 13:2). If that suggestion is accurate, it would provide another possible explanation for the migration, namely that this particular group or clan of the Danites might not have received an inheritance, but affiliated with those that had. Facing failure, rather than remain true to their relatively new, Israelite affiliation, they chose to seek their own fortunes, not unlike the Levite of ch 17, whom they will encounter on their trek. On this view, the Danites end up in two groups, a remnant remaining in their original location in the south, where Samson was active, and another in the far north. This migration also would have been relatively early in the history of Israel in Canaan. The biblical writer, on this view, would have placed the stories in their current order for thematic, not chronological, purposes.

18:2 ***clans.*** "Clan" is actually sg. in the Hebrew. As in 18:11 (cf. "tribe," NLT), the Hebrew uses the word normally rendered "clan" (*mishpakhah* [TH4940, ZH5476]) rather than "tribe" (*shebet* [TH7626, ZH8657]). Dan is often referred to as if it were a single clan.

the towns of Zorah and Eshtaol. These two towns, located up on the ridge overlooking the lush, fertile Sorek valley, marked the location of Samson's early stirrings by the Spirit, as well as his grave (13:25; 16:31).

to scout out a land for them to settle in. The dispatch of spies appears as a common feature of OT settlement narratives (cf. Num 13:1-24; Josh 2:1). The NLT paraphrases a line quoting the instructions given to the spies in 18:2b.

18:3 ***they recognized the young Levite's accent.*** The Judean dialect of Hebrew does appear to have been distinct from the northern dialect, both in grammatical features and in pronunciation. The Hebrew only says, "they recognized the voice of the Levite." Unless the writer intends the reader to imagine the Danites hearing the Levite before seeing him, and thus recognizing his personal identity, the interpretation that they spotted his accent seems correct.

18:4 ***He told them about his agreement with Micah and that he had been hired as Micah's personal priest.*** The Levite's summary, focusing wholly on what Micah had done in hiring him, utterly fails to link his role to any obligation to Yahweh (Block 1999:497).

18:5 ***Then they said, "Ask God."*** Their use of Elohim, rather than Yahweh, might betray some awareness that they had already abandoned the sacred lot from Yahweh that established their territory (Josh 19:40-48).

18:6 ***"Go in peace," the priest replied. "For the LORD is watching over your journey."*** The author does not recount that the Levite actually used his divinatory apparatus, but only reports his answer. The Levite's answer expresses a potential irony. The term *nokakh* [TH5227, ZH5790] (NLT, "watching over") can mean "opposite," with the idea of something directly across or in front of one (HALOT 1.698-699). It can connote both acceptance or opposition. That their way is "opposite" Yahweh could be an example of the double entendre of the oracle giver (Block 1999:498). Younger notes the critical fact that Yahweh could not have sanctioned the slaughter of Laish because Yahweh had already revealed his will about the Danites' settlement, a will they had abandoned. But this Levite's word directly caused a slaughter not commanded by Yahweh, just as another Levite's word will trigger a slaughter in the next major, and final, episode (Younger 2002:340-341).

18:7 ***So the five men went on to the town of Laish.*** The writer passed quickly over a journey of about 80 miles, in which the Danite party would have passed Shechem, crossed the eastern end of the Jezreel valley, passed west of the Sea of Galilee, east of Hazor up the Huleh basin, to arrive at the city of Laish, under the shadow of Mount Hermon. For information on the site itself, see the commentary below.

like the Sidonians. The writer, perhaps ironically, used the phrase *kemishpat tsidonim* [TH4941, ZH5477], "according to the custom of the Sidonians," which is the only occurrence of the root *shapat* [TH8199, ZH9149] (to judge) in all of chs 17–21. The custom or manner of the Sidonians likely refers to the opulent prosperity that trading centers enjoyed during the Late Bronze Age (1550–1200 BC), particularly towards the end. That era featured extensive interregional and international trade, especially in luxury goods, as evidenced by the standard of living enjoyed at the great urban centers of the era (Bryce 2003:42-54, 95-106). Thus, the "lifestyle of the Sidonians" was being enjoyed by the occupants of Laish, which, following the catastrophic collapse of the Late Bronze Age economy between about 1250 and 1175 BC, would have been conspicuous. More importantly, archaeologists increasingly suggest that an important "marker" of Israelite identity in its formative era was the avoidance of painted or imported pottery, expressing a culture value of egalitarianism and simplicity (e.g., Faust 2006:64). In that context, the Danite desire for the "lifestyle of the Sidonians" suggests a break with the mainstream early Israelite ethos.

peaceful. Heb., *shoqet* [TH8252, ZH9200], the same term used otherwise in Judges only to denote the land's tranquility following the victories won by the early judges (3:11, 30; 5:31; 8:28).

secure. Heb., *boteakh* [TH982, ZH1053]; it typically refers to the subjective feeling of security, whether well-grounded or, more often, not.

The people were also wealthy because their land was very fertile. A more literal translation could be, "there was nobody harming (them) in any way in the land, possessing wealth." The NLT's reference to the fertility of the land represents a modification of the Hebrew text, which is admittedly awkward and difficult.

had no allies nearby. Lit., "they had no word with a human" (*'adam* [TH120, ZH132]). With no powers nearby to oppress them, the occupants of Laish could live prosperously in their splendid isolation. Since Hebrew *d* is easily confused with *r*, some suggest that rather than *'adam*, we read *'aram* (Aram) or Syria, following LXX Alexandrinus (Boling 1975:263; Soggin 1981:272-273; Block 1999:500). The NLT retains the MT, but rightly stresses the Laishans' isolation as vulnerability to attack, possibly taking "word" (*dabar* [TH1697, ZH1821]) to refer to a treaty-based alliance (Boling 1975:263). Laish constituted precisely the kind of victim that Dan could easily strike (Moore 1895:389). Contrast this report with that of the spies in Num 13–14, who stressed the daunting military resources of the Canaanites and the apparent impossibility of their defeat at the hands of the wandering Israelites. The report also contrasts with the report of the spies in Josh 2, who glowingly report how God had worked to prepare their way.

18:9 ***Come on, let's attack them!*** The eagerness of the spies derives not from their confidence in God's power to enable them to overcome an implacable foe, as is the case in Josh 2:24. They note simply the riches easily available for the taking and the abject vulnerability of the city. Archaeological excavation reveals that while the city of Laish had an imposing earth and stone rampart, it possessed no wall. Perhaps the lack of walls, in contrast with the old and run-down, but still impressive walls of the cities of the conquest in Joshua, gave the Danites hope of an easy victory after having been tanned by the Amorites and squeezed by the Philistines.

it is very good. Heb., *wehinneh tobah me'od* [TH2009, ZH2180]; this echoes the words spoken by God at the climax of the creation narrative in Gen 1:31, but with the fem. *tobah* [TH2896, ZH3202] (agreeing with "land") instead of the masc. *tob* (Niditch 2008:183).

18:10 ***God has given us.*** As with their request for an oracle, the Danites' use of Elohim ("God"), not Yahweh, seems pregnant with avoidance of their covenantal obligation. Rather than resting on Yahweh's sure promise based on his revealed inheritance for them, which they abandoned after the failure reported in 1:34-35, the Danites simply declare that the target was so easy, it must come from God. Those who spurn the revealed will of God often start finding it in any coincidence.

18:11 ***armed with weapons of war.*** Rarely does the OT present the Israelites as well-equipped for warfare. Lack of weaponry before a superior foe functions in the biblical material to describe the premonarchic period as a narrative ethnic marker (Bloch-Smith 2003:416-420). Perhaps this note on the arming of the Danites links them more closely with the Philistines (see note on 13:2), who are always well-armed.

Zorah and Eshtaol. See note on 18:2.

18:12 ***Kiriath-jearim in Judah.*** The city of Kiriath-jearim seems to have been a religious center. Joshua 15:60 and 18:14 call it "Kiriath-baal," and several other passages use Baal-derived names. One of the cities of the Gibeonites (Josh 9:17), it also figures in the story of the Ark's progress to Jerusalem (1 Sam 6:19–7:2). The Ark remained there for 20 years, again suggesting its historic religious significance. Since the name means "city of forests," perhaps the Danites sought concealment as they prepared to embark on their pseudoconquest.

Mahaneh-dan. The place name appears also in 13:25, the scene of Samson's first stirrings of the Spirit. But some scholars argue that the location there, between Zora and Eshtaol, is hard to reconcile with a location west of Kiriath-jearim. In fact, these two cities are only about six miles west of Kiriath-jearim, so perhaps the problem is not acute. More important is the portrayal of Dan as occupying a "camp," suggesting their unsettled situation.

18:14 ***These buildings contain a sacred ephod, as well as some household idols, a carved image, and a cast idol.*** The acquisition of cult objects is another common trope of conquest narratives. Ironically, the Danites pondered the theft of cult objects already tainted by larceny. On the cult objects, see notes on 17:3-5.

18:16 ***the 600 armed warriors . . . stood at the entrance of the gate.*** A rural Israelite "house" was actually a compound in which several pillared houses and other structures housed an extended, multigenerational family, often surrounded by a low retaining wall (see note on 11:31). By taking positions at the gate, the warriors cut off any escape.

18:17 ***the five scouts entered the shrine and removed the carved image, the sacred ephod, the household idols, and the cast idol. Meanwhile, the priest was standing at the gate with the 600 armed warriors.*** The Hebrew text sketches the scene vividly with a staccato series of clauses simply piling up the circumstances. While the warriors "cover" the priest, who was at the gate, the spies who knew where the loot was entered the shrine and took the sacred objects.

18:18 ***When the priest saw the men . . . he said, "What are you doing?"*** The irony of this priest protesting sacrilege, given the spiritual and moral genealogy of these cult objects and his own ministry, is impressive.

18:19 ***"Be quiet and come with us," they said.*** The Hebrew is irresistible: "Be silent! Put your hand over your mouth!" Their warning was not a threat, but the prelude to making the priest an offer he couldn't refuse.

Be a father and priest to all of us. See note on 17:10.

Isn't it better to be a priest for an entire tribe and clan of Israel than for the household of just one man? Again, the story of the Levite's career remains devoid of any sign of covenantal obligations. He merely pursues his original agenda, which was (lit.) "to sojourn [become a client] where ever I end up" (17:8-9).

18:20 ***The young priest was quite happy to go with them.*** While some might fault the Levite for disloyalty to Micah (Cundall 1968:190), Micah had done what the Danites now do: hired himself a priest for his own religious endeavors. Micah's ordination of this "priest" had been no more legitimate than the Danites' hiring of him would be. Those who traffic in betrayals always risk being themselves betrayed. The young Levite remains the patron saint of clergy who regard the service of God as a professional career rather than a calling.

18:21 ***They turned and started on their way again, placing their children, livestock, and possessions in front of them.*** "Possessions" translates *kebuddah* [TH3520, ZH3885] (heavy stuff). The image is reminiscent of Ramses III's portrayal of the Sea Peoples in the Medinet Habu inscriptions, which portray not only the warriors and seafarers whom the pharaoh repelled, but also their women, children, livestock, and possessions in carts. The term also denotes "riches" and might include the silver image taken from Micah's shrine.

18:22 ***the people who lived near Micah came chasing after them.*** The Hebrew notes that these men from the surrounding homesteads "were called up" (*niz'aqu* [TH2199, ZH2410]), indicating this is at least a semiformal posse (Block 1999:507-508). The story bears similarities to Laban's pursuit of Jacob's party, which also had concealed among them Laban's household idols (Gen 31). Laban, however, did not return empty-handed, but had imposed an oath on Jacob.

18:23 ***The men of Dan turned around and said to Micah.*** This is the first time in this narrative that Micah has made an appearance. The author does not state where Micah has been through all the events that transpired on his compound.

18:24 ***all the gods I have made.*** The text's stress on Micah's sense of proprietary ownership both of his gods and his priest underscores, likely with satiric intent, how unreal and illegitimate his whole religious and ritual installation was. Micah and the Danites in fact are acting out the very mockery of idols that Isaiah later articulated directly. Particularly, Isaiah mocked the highly cultured and sophisticated Babylonians who carried their gods, while the true God, Yahweh, carried his people (Isa 44:9-20; 46:1-4). Those who manufacture their gods think they own them; and such gods cannot save.

18:25 ***short-tempered men.*** Lit., "bitter of soul" (*'anashim mare nepesh* [TH4751/5315, ZH5253/5883]), a phrase found also in 1 Sam 17:8 to describe fierce fighting men spoiling for revenge, comparable to a bear robbed of her cubs! The historical period of the book of Judges, early in Iron Age I (1200–1000 BC), featured a range of displaced persons, including the "empty men" (*'anashim reqim* [TH7386, ZH8199]) who gathered around Abimelech and Jephthah (9:4; 11:3). Disenfranchised, desperate men, especially if they have ignominious failure behind them, present a danger indeed.

might get angry and kill you and your family. It is hard to resist the temptation to compare this scene to an old "Western" in which the leader of the rustler gang warns the rancher that "some of the boys are a little hot-tempered, and their trigger fingers are itchy." But the 600 armed Danites' reliance on naked force confronting one man and his little posse contrasts starkly with their allowing the Amorites to run them out of their inheritance and up into the hills (1:34).

18:26 ***When Micah saw that there were too many of them for him to attack, he turned around and went home.*** In an ancient tribal culture, Micah's capitulation possibly shamed him before the other members of the community. In an era lacking in law enforcement, a community had to secure its own property and safety. Micah's failure at this point possibly marked him as a weak and ineffectual man, something the reader already knew. Moreover, the loss of his household, ancestral idols severed his religious link to his ancestors and possibly consigned them and their memory to permanent loss, depending on the religious ideology Micah held.

18:27 ***Then, with Micah's idols and his priest.*** The Hebrew wording is striking: "Now they took what Micah had made, both the priest and what he had." The author, having skewered Micah, reminds the reader that the Danites' cultic treasures do not amount to much, being manufactured by the very man they faced down by force.

the town of Laish, whose people were peaceful and secure. In stressing the quiet, unsuspecting serenity of Laish, the author accentuates the cowardice of the Danites; this contrasts with the Danites and the Israelites of the book of Joshua, who confronted coalitions of multiple Canaanite armies and cities readied against attack.

They attacked with swords and burned the town to the ground. Archaeological excavation confirms the destruction of the Late Bronze Age city at Tel Dan around 1200 BC. If this is the Danite destruction, then the migration of the Danites occurred early in the era of the Judges. Since historians usually date the Philistine presence in Canaan from about 1175 BC, the migration of ch 18 would have *preceded* the encounters with the Philistines recorded in chs 13–16, though imprecision in dating could possibly allow some overlap. The present order appears, therefore, to be a *thematic* or logical sequence, not a chronological one. Thus, claims that pressure from the Philistines or Samson's failures (Schneider 2000:237; Matthews 2004:174) forced the migration do not fit the best historical evidence. Historically, the abandonment by these Danites of their inheritance, and some of their kinsmen would have left those who stayed behind even more vulnerable to the pressure of surrounding groups, such as the Philistines, contributing to the crisis that led to Samson's career.

18:28 ***There was no one to rescue the people.*** The biblical author's notice that the occupants of Laish had no one to deliver them is unusual. Normally the OT writers show no sympathy, or even interest, in the plight of Israel's enemies, since Israel classically assumed the role of underdog. But in this story, the author signals a vast distance between the Danite attack and other Israelite battles. Dan's attack on the city prompts reflection on the characterization of Dan found in Gen 49:16-18 and Deut 33:22. Both note Dan's practice of cunning ambush, striking unexpectedly rather than confronting an equal foe face-to-face. After comparing Dan to a poisonous snake striking a horse, the poet declares, "I trust in you for salvation, O LORD!" (Gen 49:18). But for the citizens of Laish, "there was no one to rescue" them.

the valley near Beth-rehob. Laish (Dan) stands at the north end of the Huleh basin. The location of Beth-rehob is unknown, and it is not likely to be modern Tel-Rehov, located south of Beth-shan. Num 13:21 notes a Rehob as the northern limit of the mission of the Israelite spies, suggesting the area where the Huleh basin transitions to the Beqaa valley (ABD 1.692).

the tribe of Dan rebuilt the town. The first settlement at Dan after the destruction of the Late Bronze city was a crude encampment, but soon the occupants rebuilt the city in fine style, engaging in reclamation metallurgy and reestablishing Dan as a vital urban center—its natural destiny given its strategic location and enormous resources.

18:29 ***They renamed the town Dan.*** The Danites stood unique among the Israelites of this period in possessing a city named for their tribe and, more importantly, in assuming an urban mode of life, contrasted with their fellow Israelites who adopted a self-sustaining village economy of mixed agriculture and pastoralism. Since the naming of the city "Dan" may reasonably be dated to c. 1200 BC, scholars typically suggest other texts referring to the city by that name must postdate 1200 BC (cf. Gen 14:14; Deut 34:1; Josh 19:47). The mention of Dan as the northern boundary of the land, paired with Beersheba for the south, appears in texts subsequent to this narrative (1 Sam 3:20; 2 Sam 3:10; 17:11; 24:2, 15; 1 Kgs 4:25; 1 Chr 21:2; 2 Chr 30:5; Amos 8:14). That only three references prior to ch 18 anachronistically call the city "Dan" testifies to the biblical authors' antiquarian seriousness and toponymic discrimination.

18:30 ***Jonathan son of Gershom, son of Moses, as their priest.*** Ancient scribes, loathe to associate Moses with this horrible story, added the letter "n" to the three consonants of Moses's name, changing *m-sh-h* to *m-^{n}-sh-h*, prompting the reader to say "Manasseh" instead. But the "n" is suspended above the line, pointing to the original reference to Moses (Cundall 1968:191). The writer now arrives at the "money moment" in the story where he drives home his point. This story of a deviant shrine sacked by a defeated tribe en route to a parodistic "conquest campaign" against an unsuspecting city culminates in the establishment of a sanctuary later promoted by Jeroboam to a well-built, fortified royal sanctuary. The city features the largest city gate complex so far excavated in Israel, with a 90-degree turn upslope, an open plaza, and numerous shrines and alcoves. The writer now says openly what was only hinted at earlier, namely that this corrupt priestling is a direct descendant of Moses through Gershom (cf. 17:7 "had been living [there]," Heb., *gar-sham*). Some religious centers in the north of Israel asserted their legitimacy by claiming their priests descended from Moses, not Aaron (Cross 1971:107-198). The author here, however, inverts the relation: The illegitimacy of the sanctuary at Dan defiles the Mosaic tradition. The Mosaic legacy means nothing when the covenant mediated by Moses is ignored. This family continued as priests, but true succession is not a matter of genealogical descent, but moral and spiritual fidelity.

until the Exile. Lit., "until the day of the exile of the land." Scholars debate the reference. The term "land" is not normally the subject of "exile." One intriguing possibility would link this "exile" to the next statement about the "house of God" being at Shiloh, whose destruction around 1050 BC was followed by the death of Saul and the Philistines' near-final defeat of Israel, but this is unlikely. Similarly, the Babylonian deportations of 597 and 586 BC seem unlikely, though the northern deportation (721 BC) might well be in view here (Boling 1975:266). The text most likely refers to 734–732 BC, when the north was badly ravaged by Tiglath-pileser III, who swept through the entire region north of the Jezreel valley (cf. 2 Kgs 15:29; Isa 9:1-7). Earlier, the Arameans had also assaulted Dan (c. 885 BC), a fact attested to by an inscription discovered on the site (Biran and Naveh 1993; 1995; cf. 1 Kgs 15:20). In none of these campaigns was the city destroyed.

18:31 ***the Tabernacle of God.*** The NLT's "Tabernacle" misses a vital link to the beginning of the story in ch 17. The Hebrew uses *beth-ha'elohim* [TH1004, ZH1074] (house of God). The Tabernacle is not normally referred to as a "house" and, indeed, is even contrasted with a fixed house of worship by Yahweh himself in 2 Sam 7. When the OT narrative treats the sanctuary of Shiloh in detail (1 Sam 1:9; 3:3; possibly 2 Sam 22:7), the writer uses the term *heykal* [TH1964, ZH2121], which, from its ancient origins in the Sumerian E.GAL (big house) and Akkadian *ekallum,* denotes monumental architecture, a regal palace, for a divine or human king. The Tabernacle is never called a *heykal.* The shrine at Shiloh had doorposts and separate ancillary rooms, in which personnel could sleep in close proximity to the Ark (cf. 1 Sam 3). It is not impossible to think of a preexisting structure at Shiloh that served as an interim sanctuary, within which the Tabernacle, or some of its paraphernalia, could have been placed. A large, flat, stony area near the summit of Tel Seilun has been thought by some a fine place to have placed the Israelite shrine. This closing reference to the true *beth-ha'elohim* (house of God) being in Shiloh contrasts starkly with the first occurrence in the narrative of *beth 'elohim* in 17:5 to refer to the shrine into which Micah installed his brand-new image(s) made of stolen silver. By this contrast, the author shatters any remaining illusions about the Danite sanctuary's legitimacy. That the author vilified the sanctuary at Dan from multiple moral, theological, and historical perspectives, but never once from the perspective that the place was not where Yahweh had put his name (cf. Deut 12), nor yet even hinted at Jerusalem, suggests very early origins for this story. Though later readers would know these things, the author leaves them wholly out of the picture, skewering the Danite shrine wholly on its multilayered intrinsic depravity.

remained at Shiloh. Shiloh was the first long-term Israelite sanctuary, the first apparently being Ebal. The Israelites moved the Ark to Shiloh in Josh 18, but the site evidences destruction "by a violent conflagration" around 1050 BC, likely at the hands of the Philistines (Stern 1993–2008:4.1368; contra Soggin 1981:276; cf. 1 Sam 4). By Jeremiah's day, Shiloh had become the paradigm site of a sanctuary abandoned by God and destroyed (cf. Jer 7:12). Thus, for the satiric, pejorative force of the present story to work, the author likely had to precede Jeremiah's era. The author thus succeeds at driving a wedge between the Shiloh sanctuary, whose legitimacy he accepted, and the Dan sanctuary, which he condemned. That both apparently traced their priestly families back to Moses (Cross 1971:195-215) accentuates the delicacy of the literary move. The reference also foreshadows the final episode of the book, which transpires in Shiloh (21:19-24).

COMMENTARY

The city of Laish, renamed Dan, stands at the center of this story. It stands near the modern town of Kiryat Shemona, where it occupied the crossroads of major north–south and east–west trade routes. The site of over 50 acres is now a national park and includes one of the major springs feeding the Jordan River, which gushes forth pure, cold, drinkable water even today. Surrounded by fertile land, the site naturally had a long history of occupation, with significant occupation around 5000 BC in the Pottery Neolithic period, and a very large city standing no later than 2700 BC. Egyptian execration texts and the Mari documents mention it by the name of Laish in the 1700s BC, and Thutmose III boasts its capture in the mid-1400s BC. This Middle Bronze city (2000–1550 BC) possessed a massive earthen rampart with a stone core that also incorporated large buttresses from the Early Bronze Age. *No wall*, however, stood at the top of the rampart. On the eastern side of the city, a mud-brick, four-chambered gate with a triple arch opened out onto one of the main north–south highways of the ancient world, one likely traversed by Abraham in his journey from Syria to the Promised Land. The arched gate is the earliest of its type, but appears to have been an engineering nightmare, as it was soon filled in with earth.

Destroyed at the end of Middle Bronze (c. 1550 BC), the city soon revived. The prosperity of the Late Bronze Age city (1550–1200 BC) appears in a striking open paved area, of which 80 square meters has been exposed. Finds include evidence of metallurgy, as well as a famous plaque depicting a little man playing a stringed instrument and apparently dancing a jig! A richly furnished tomb featuring fine imported Mycenaean and Cypriot pottery also confirms the wealth of the Late Bronze Age city, which was destroyed around 1200 BC. The excavator, Avraham Biran, attributed this destruction to the Danites and noted that the settlement on top of the destruction layer fell far below the cultural standard of the previous occupants. Storage pits and collared-rim jars distinctive of the south and central parts of the country support the suggestion that the city's Iron Age I nonurbanized tenants were the Danites. Within a short time, the new occupants developed the site's urban potential, but it suffered yet another destruction around 1000 BC. Frequently named in the Bible as the traditional northern boundary of the Promised Land ("from Dan to Beer-sheba"), the shrine established at Dan as narrated in chapter 18, especially with its claim to Mosaic lineage, made the city a major religious center for the northern kingdom, whose sanctuary and high place, reinforced and expanded by Jeroboam and his successors, can be seen even today (Stern 1993–2008:1.323-332; 5.1686-1689).

Overall, chapters 17–18 run like a sanctuary origin story. The sacredness of the image at the heart of the sanctuary requires explanation, as does the sanctuary's location, clergy, and ritual. Classically, sanctuary foundation narratives climax stories of royal succession: The new king shows his legitimacy and piety by renovating the sanctuary of his patron deity by means of the spoils of his fallen enemies; the document recording this is then physically placed in the building itself as a foundation deposit. If this parallel is present, the author has turned it completely on its head. Twice the reader is told there is "no king in Israel," and rather than the order portrayed in foundation deposits, anarchy reigns. Judges

17:1-6 narrated the distortion of the *meaning* of Israelite faith with a single individual deciding for himself to forge an image of the unseen Yahweh. Then, in 17:7–18:1a, the author portrays the corruption of the *ministry* of the faith as the profiteering, opportunistic Levite contracts with Micah to preside over the deviant cult in Micah's private chapel. In 18:1b-31 the writer turns to the perversion of the *mission* of Israel in the land through the story of a pathetically weak tribe's "conquest."

The author explicitly resumes the story of the landless Danites that he left off in 1:34-35. As he does so, elements of the standard story for the founding of a sanctuary are present, but satirized. The defeat of the Danites by the Amorites had climactically epitomized the collapse of the conquest in the north. Their trek northward embarked from precisely the places, Zorah and Eshtaol, associated with Samson's early urgings by the Spirit. Though the migration likely preceded Samson's career, the author's juxtaposition of the stories by means of this reference ties Samson's career to the failure of the Danites to gain their territory. The sanctuary at Dan does not climax a victorious campaign against fierce enemies, but begins in defeat and frustration.

The battle narrative shows numerous close parallels to conquest narratives in Numbers and Joshua, making it a kind of miniature conquest (Malamat 1970; Stone 1988:399-401; Block 1999:491-492; Younger 2002:334-336). But, what *kind* of conquest? At every point, chapter 18 shows the inversion of the elements of conquest narratives, suggesting this is the report of a perverted, corrupted conquest. The cities confronted by the Danites' forebears were strong, fortified, populated by the daunting Anakim, making the spies feel like grasshoppers (Num 13:28-33). The Danite spies, however, gleefully characterize Laish as wide-open, unsuspecting, and defenseless, the perfect victim (18:1-10). Conquest narratives typically begin with inquiry at a divine oracle to receive assurance of victory. The ritual in chapter 18, however, employs idols tainted by theft and an opportunist priest. Removing all the sacred trappings from Micah's shrine, with the Levite's consent, suggests neither the priest nor the Danites were overly concerned with the opinion of the idol or its oracle (18:11-21). Once clear of their Amorite enemies and fortified by their newfound religious resources, the Danites intimidated the pitiable Micah (18:22-26) and, free of intimidation by real enemies such as the Amorites who ran them out of their inheritance, the Danites ruthlessly slaughtered the defenseless occupants of Laish (18:27-28a). Conquest stories often culminate in the erection of a monument or holy place to commemorate Yahweh's assistance. The Danites, who needed little help from God in defeating the Laishans, established a city in their own name and installed their own priesthood there. Ironically, the opportunistic, idolatrous priest had Moses as a grandfather!

In the context of 1:1–2:5, this story reveals that God's people, when they fail at or forsake their God-ordained mission, will fabricate a perverted substitute, a caricature of the sacred task given them by God. The eerie and tragic reality is that this substitute mission had all the earmarks of legitimate divine service. Thus, the Danites experience what appears to be divine guidance in Micah's oracle, centered on an abominable image of Yahweh, delivered by a corrupted, bought-and-paid-for priest; this all applied a veneer of religious legitimacy to the Danite charade. The unanticipated meeting of the Levite by the Danites, who recognized him, even gives the appearance of an amazing providence. In such a context, is anyone surprised that the Danites get exactly the answer for which they hoped? Moreover, having been dusted by the Amorites in the territory Yahweh had assigned them, the Danites discover, to their relief, much easier pickings as far away from God's promised boundaries as they can get, the city of Laish. As Block (1999:514-515) sadly notes, this story reveals that sin often succeeds. The Danites had everything going their way. Only from afar, from the total biblical perspective, did their evil become clear. This story, not a favorite text for Christian pastoral instruction, figured often in early Reformation preaching since it provided a slam-dunk condemnation of images and corrupt clergy. The text's clear implication that the king plays a crucial role in safeguarding orthodoxy, liturgy, and polity also appealed to the early Reformers (Gunn 2005:234-242). Likewise, the implicit, but evident, censure of the Danite slaughter of Laish possibly underscores the principle that the conquest, or settlement, was no simple appropriation of lands by force. Only conquest campaigns initiated by Yahweh fulfill his purposes. No substitute finds legitimacy.

The Danites' perverted substitute conquest tainted a great heritage, as the priest at the center of these multiple abominations was the grandson of Moses. This sad irony underlines the fact that possession of a great lineage and heritage of God's mighty works and self-disclosures does not ensure the slightest legitimacy, much less holiness, to such substitute missions. Many Christian institutions point to a great founder or outstanding historical experience, such as the apostolic succession, the Reformation, the Great Awakening, the evangelical revival, or even the renewal movements of the past decades. But none of these great legacies of the past purchase a particle of legitimacy or blessing for missions that abandon God's boundaries, forsake his commands, pervert his identity, and corrupt his ministry. Rightly have many spiritual leaders warned the church that it is always but one generation short of extinction. And while the Danites expanded the circle of deviancy and corruption, the truth stands solitary, in silent condemnation. The narrator simply notes that (lit.) "the house of God was at Shiloh" (18:31), reminding the reader of the shunned alternative. Moreover, the writer then reminds the reader of the devastating defeat of the north by Tiglath-pileser III in 734–732 BC (see note on 18:30). This story of the distortion of the meaning of the faith, the corruption of the ministry of the faith, and the perversion of the mission of the faith concludes with a long shot at the tombstone of the northernmost tribe.

The arrogant anarchism evident in this story testifies to the absence of a king in a time when "each one did as he saw fit." When arrogant, unchecked self-will reigns among God's people, heresy and corruption, all with a fine religious coating, will chill the community and paralyze its obedience, making it easy prey to the enemies of God. Thus, the author stresses that there is something worse than idolatry, corruption of the priesthood, and failure in the land—namely, the root of sinful self-centeredness from which those things spring.

◆ B. The Fractured Vision (19:1–21:25)

1. The Levite and his concubine (19:1-30)

Now in those days Israel had no king. There was a man from the tribe of Levi living in a remote area of the hill country of Ephraim. One day he brought home a woman from Bethlehem in Judah to be his concubine. 2But she became angry with him* and returned to her father's home in Bethlehem.

After about four months, 3her husband set out for Bethlehem to speak personally to her and persuade her to come back. He took with him a servant and a pair of donkeys. When he arrived at* her father's house, her father saw him and welcomed him. 4Her father urged him to stay awhile, so he stayed three days, eating, drinking, and sleeping there.

5On the fourth day the man was up early, ready to leave, but the woman's father said to his son-in-law, "Have something to eat before you go." 6So the two men sat down together and had something to eat and drink. Then the woman's father said, "Please stay another night and enjoy yourself." 7The man got up to leave, but his father-in-law kept urging him to stay, so he finally gave in and stayed the night.

8On the morning of the fifth day he was up early again, ready to leave, and again the woman's father said, "Have something to eat; then you can leave later this afternoon." So they had another day of feasting. 9Later, as the man and his concubine and servant were preparing to leave, his father-in-law said, "Look, it's almost evening. Stay the night and enjoy yourself. Tomorrow you can get up early and be on your way."

10But this time the man was determined to leave. So he took his two saddled donkeys and his concubine and headed in the direction of Jebus (that is, Jerusalem). 11It was late in the day when they neared Jebus, and the man's servant said to him, "Let's stop at this Jebusite town and spend the night there."

12"No," his master said, "we can't stay in this foreign town where there are no Israelites. Instead, we will go on to Gibeah. 13Come on, let's try to get as far as Gibeah or Ramah, and we'll spend the night in one of those towns." 14So they went on. The sun was setting as they came to Gibeah, a town in the land of Benjamin, 15so they stopped there to spend the night. They rested in the town square, but no one took them in for the night.

16That evening an old man came home from his work in the fields. He was from the hill country of Ephraim, but he was living in Gibeah, where the people were from the tribe of Benjamin. 17When he saw the travelers sitting in the town square, he asked them where they were from and where they were going.

18"We have been in Bethlehem in Judah," the man replied. "We are on our way to a remote area in the hill country of Ephraim, which is my home. I traveled to Bethlehem, and now I'm returning home.* But no one has taken us in for the night, 19even though we have everything we need. We have straw and feed for our donkeys and plenty of bread and wine for ourselves."

20"You are welcome to stay with me," the old man said. "I will give you anything you might need. But whatever you do, don't spend the night in the square." 21So he took them home with him and fed the donkeys. After they washed their feet, they ate and drank together.

22While they were enjoying themselves, a crowd of troublemakers from the town surrounded the house. They began beating at the door and shouting to the old man, "Bring out the man who is staying with you so we can have sex with him."

23The old man stepped outside to talk to them. "No, my brothers, don't do such an evil thing. For this man is a guest in my house, and such a thing would be shameful. 24Here, take my virgin daughter and

this man's concubine. I will bring them
out to you, and you can abuse them and
do whatever you like. But don't do such a
shameful thing to this man."
25But they wouldn't listen to him. So
the Levite took hold of his concubine and
pushed her out the door. The men of the
town abused her all night, taking turns
raping her until morning. Finally, at dawn
they let her go. 26At daybreak the woman
returned to the house where her husband
was staying. She collapsed at the door of
the house and lay there until it was light.
27When her husband opened the door
to leave, there lay his concubine with her
hands on the threshold. 28He said, "Get
up! Let's go!" But there was no answer.*
So he put her body on his donkey and
took her home.
29When he got home, he took a knife
and cut his concubine's body into twelve
pieces. Then he sent one piece to each
tribe throughout all the territory of Israel.
30Everyone who saw it said, "Such a
horrible crime has not been committed in
all the time since Israel left Egypt. Think
about it! What are we going to do? Who's
going to speak up?"

19:2 Or *she was unfaithful to him.* **19:3** As in Greek version; Hebrew reads *When she brought him to.* **19:18** As in Greek version (see also 19:29); Hebrew reads *now I'm going to the Tabernacle of the LORD.* **19:28** Greek version adds *for she was dead.*

NOTES

19:1 ***Now in those days Israel had no king.*** In most English translations, the particular way the Hebrew text introduces the fourfold "no king in Israel" comment is obscured. In 17:6, 18:1a, and 21:25 the comment appears with no introductory conjunction, somewhat unusual for Hebrew prose. The disjunction created seems to be parenthetical and terminal—concluding an episode. With 19:1 the conventional narrative introduction formula appears: *wayehi bayyamim hahem* [TH3117, ZH3427], traditionally rendered, "and it came to pass in those days." The effect is to coordinate the story in 19:1–21:25 with that of 17:1–18:31 as a coherent narrative. In 19:1, the writer says *umelek* [TH4428, ZH4889] *'en beyisra'el* (a king there was not in Israel). Strangely, some commentators want to claim a dual reference for "king," both human and divine. But the claim that Israel had no divine king is patently false, the people's sin and rebellion notwithstanding. The point of the entire book is that divine rule ideally flows through appropriate, just, and effective human structures and agents, as depicted in Israel's constitutional document, Deuteronomy, where the roles of prophet, priest, king, and judge all distribute and implement the mediation between Yahweh and Israel that had originally centered on Moses and later, Joshua.

There was a man. The story proper opens with *wayehi 'ish* [TH376, ZH408] (there was a man), exactly as in 17:1, and it is similar to 17:7 *wayehi na'ar* [TH5288, ZH5853] (there was a young man). The overall effect seems to be one of a steady building of narrative force as these characters step on stage: Micah, his Levite, and now another Levite at the center of the final story. Strangely, all the principals in this story, not just the woman, remain nameless. In some way, perhaps each character stands for an entire class. Or worse, leaving the characters unnamed accentuates their ultimate dehumanization (Block 1999:517-518).

from the tribe of Levi. Arresting similarities connect this Levite with the one in 17:7. Both are sojourning outside their home region, likely as clients or dependents of a local family. Both were sojourning in "mount Ephraim" (*har-'epraim* [TH669A, ZH713]). Both had ties with Bethlehem of Judah: The young Levite had lived there; the Levite of ch 19 took a concubine from there.

living. The term *gar* [TH1481, ZH1591], traditionally translated "sojourning," often implies not simply living outside one's home region, but dependent, client status in the region, attached to a local household. The point is vital because later in the story, the Levite's host will also be someone who is "sojourning" in the region where he lives.

in a remote area of the hill country of Ephraim. This is the region that was home to the old man (19:16) who will host the Levite and his concubine, with tragic results, later in the story. The term "remote area" translates the *yarkete* [TH3411, ZH3752], and is likely topographical: The main flow of traffic in Israel ran north-south on the watershed ridge road. Various smaller routes branched off from the main highway, running down the flanks of the central hill country west toward the Shephelah and coast or east toward the Jordan valley. The term thus denotes the "flanks" or branch routes running off the main road through the hill country of Ephraim, rather than places remote in terms of distance from Judah (Burney 1920:459).

concubine. Heb., *pilegesh* [TH6370, ZH7108]; see note on 8:31. Although a concubine typically served as a secondary wife, the narrator speaks of no other wife for the Levite. The absence of a cognate for *pilegesh* in other Semitic languages and its similarity to the Greek *pallakē* suggests the word is of Indo-European origin, with the Philistines being its most likely potential mediators. Only 11 men in the OT are named as having concubines—seven after the conquest, including five from Judah or Benjamin, tribes with the closest contact with the Philistines. The other two are Gideon, who lived near Beth-shan, a site with a documented Philistine presence, and the Ephraimite Levite of ch 19, who took his concubine from Bethlehem of Judah (NIDOTTE 3.618-619). The references prior to the conquest (involving Nahor, Abraham, Jacob, and Eliphaz) might reflect the word choice of the later narrator rather than the terms in vogue during the ancestral era.

Scholars debate the status of the concubine. Only the concubines of the preconquest narratives bear the title "wife" as well as "concubine." Subsequent narratives do not combine the two terms. The woman of this story is termed "concubine" 11 times and "woman" (*'ishah* [TH802, ZH851]) 3 times, with 20:4 alone possibly meaning "wife." The woman of this story is called a "slave woman" or "handmaid" (19:19 KJV) as is Gideon's concubine (9:18), but both of these are rhetorically unclear. The first could be deferential, the second pejorative. Thus, the position of the concubine seems higher than a mere slave, but lower than a full wife. Thus, children of concubines could have inheritance rights and, upon the death of their husbands, they were termed "widows." However, concubines themselves could be inherited. Possibly a concubine was a wife for whom no bride-wealth was given, or who brought no dowry to the marriage. The absence of one of these would constitute an imbalanced obligation between the two families joined in the marriage, possibly illuminating the extended feasting described in the present story, which complicates matters even more by revealing a complex mixture of emotions inhabiting the relationships among the Levite, the concubine, and her father.

19:2 *she became angry with him.* Or, "she was unfaithful to him" (NLT mg). Translators traditionally render the verb *wattizneh* [TH2181, ZH2388] as "she played the harlot," deriving the verb from *zanah*, the root normally associated with fornication or prostitution (NIDOTTE 1.1122-1124; TDOT 4.99-104). But no sign of actual infidelity appears in the story, and the couple appear cordial enough when the Levite arrives to fetch her. Also, the Hebrew has a preposition with this verb that occurs with it nowhere else. In addition, Deut 22:13-30 requires that a woman who is sexually unfaithful be stoned at the very door of her father's house. The LXX translation of *ōrgisthē autō* [TG3710, ZG3974] (she became angry at him) likewise implies no sexual infidelity. Some suggest the verb derives from a second root meaning "to be angry" (cf. *zanah* [TH2181A, ZH2389]; "loathed") cognate to Akkadian *zenû* (be angry), which is used to denote alienation in the whole range of relationships including marriage (NIDOTTE 1.1125; CAD 21.85-86). The Hebrew root *zanakh* (TDOT 4.105-106) might already represent a cognate, however, so that an additional suggested *zanah* parallel to Akkadian *zenû*, dropping the final guttural consonant, would involve not a proper cognate, but a direct loan from Akkadian, including pronunciation, into Hebrew.

Such is by no means impossible and is the course taken by the NLT. A woman taking the initiative to leave her husband is rare in the OT and the ancient Near East in general, but the Code of Hammurabi (1792–1750 BC) does note the possibility, with the noteworthy acceptance of the idea that the husband could well be at fault:

> §142 If a woman repudiates her husband, and declares, "You will not have marital relations with me" — her circumstances shall be investigated by the authorities of her city quarter, and if she is circumspect and without fault, but her husband is wayward and disparages her greatly, that woman will not be subject to any penalty; she shall take her dowry and she shall depart for her father's house.
>
> *§143 If she is not circumspect but is wayward, squanders her household possessions, and disparages her husband, they shall cast that woman into the water (COS 2.131.142-143; emphasis added).*

returned to her father's home. The NLT somewhat obscures the sense here. She returned to her entire extended family and their inherited property. More than just "going home to daddy," this was a reaffiliation with her ancestral family tie, just as Naomi directed her Moabite daughters-in-law to "go back to [their] mothers' homes" (Ruth 1:8). Israelite marriage entailed the woman affiliating with the "father's house" of her husband, so the woman here reversed her marital commitment.

four months. This seems a rather long time for the Levite to have waited to retrieve his concubine. Still, some times of year in a subsistence farming economy made it almost impossible for a head of household to take a long journey. Coincidentally, the Benjaminite survivors of the punitive slaughter hid in the rocks of Rimmon for four months (20:47). Schneider, who interprets the woman's behavior sexually, suggests the four months allowed the Levite to know whether she was pregnant, assuming the news could travel easily from Bethlehem to the western slopes of the Ephraimite hills (2000:252-253).

19:3 *to speak personally to her and persuade her.* Lit., "to speak to her heart." The idiom "speak to the heart" (*ledabber 'al leb/lebab* [TH1696/3820, ZH1819/4213]) appears six other times in the OT (Gen 34:3; 50:21; Ruth 2:13; 2 Chr 30:22; Isa 40:2; Hos 2:16). The term typically denotes either speaking tenderly, encouragingly, or in a wooing, even seductive manner. So the Levite sought to woo back his alienated concubine. That the Levite sought to win back his concubine suggests perhaps he was at fault in her departure (Boling 1975:274). His desire to regain her affection initially engenders the reader's sympathy.

He took with him a servant and a pair of donkeys. Should the Levite be successful in retrieving the concubine, apparently either she or the servant would be walking home.

he arrived at her father's house. Per the NLT mg, "he arrived" emends a fem. Hiphil verb, "she brought him," to a masc. Qal verb, following LXX Alexandrinus. The term "house of her father" is not merely the building, but the compound. Whether the man simply arrived or was brought in by the woman, the father might well have been any number of places and apparently did not notice the guests at the threshold.

her father saw him and welcomed him. The Hebrew is stronger: "[her father] rejoiced to meet him."

19:4 *Her father.* The Hebrew identifies the father doubly, "his father-in-law, the father of the young woman." Perhaps the ambiguity of the concubine status somewhere in between full marriage and mere servitude generated the twofold identification. Terms based on the verb *khatan* [TH2859, ZH3161] indicate the familial ties among males created by marriage. Terms for father-in-law, brother-in-law, and son-in-law all derive from this term. In addition, the word seems to connote an obligation of protection and care extended to the new male family member by the males of the other family (NIDOTTE 2.325-328). Thus, the father's actions both reflect a concern to extend protection and care to the Levite while also unwittingly exposing him and his concubine to lethal danger. This term resonates with references to sons-in-law in Gen 19:12, 14, along with several other close parallels. Interestingly, the only other father-in-law referred to in Judges is that of Moses (cf. 1:16; 4:11 mg), while the only other son-in-law is Samson (15:6, cf. KJV).

urged him to stay awhile, so he stayed three days, eating, drinking. Rather than a mere three days of gorging themselves, common meals forged a bond among the partakers to which moral obligations attached (King and Stager 2001:62). Every day that the Levite partook of his father-in-law's bounty, his obligation to the man increased. In a society based on balancing reciprocal obligation, especially given the landless status of the Levites and the sojourner status of the husband here, the father-in-law was steadily obligating the Levite to himself and his household. The host-guest relation, however jocular, sometimes carries an undercurrent of rivalry (Matthews 2004:182). The Levite, anxious to retain his relative independence, and possibly to honor his prior obligation as a *ger* [TH1616, ZH1731] (i.e., a sojourner, dependent, client), needed to extricate himself and his concubine as soon as possible, without giving offense or shaming the woman by showing disrespect to her father. And yet the reader suspects something dark on the horizon. Readers belonging to the community for whom this is traditional literature and who are not coming to this story for the first time, know that the Levite's departure from the protection of his father-in-law's household will have catastrophic consequences. Perhaps the author connects safety and security with Bethlehem of Judah as part of his general approach of portraying Judah, and places with Davidic associations, positively.

19:5 ***son-in-law.*** The persistent use of "son-in-law" in the story shows that concubinage was more a form of marriage than of servitude, since it formed a new familial tie.

19:6 ***Please stay.*** The verb *ho'el* [TH2974, ZH3283], which only occurs 19 times in the OT, in 1:27, 35 expresses the successful determination or undertaking of the occupants of the land to remain in place against the Israelite attempts to expel them. It does not occur again until 17:11 where, like here, it expresses the Levite's willingness to stay with Micah. More than just a polite request, the father-in-law specifically asked for a decision to make a longer visit, appealing to the comfort and enjoyment they experienced.

19:7 ***his father-in-law kept urging him.*** The text again resorts to a somewhat rare term, *patsar* [TH6484, ZH7210], which appears only seven times in the OT. It always conveys strong urging against someone's evident intentions, including even physical coercion (Gen 19:3, 9; 33:11; 1 Sam 15:23; 2 Kgs 2:17; 5:16). This verb is the first of several explicit connections with the story of Lot in Sodom in Gen 19. In Gen 19:3 Lot "strongly urges" the disguised angels to stay in his home instead of in the open square. Then in Gen 19:9, in a scene similar to what transpires later in Gibeah, the term denotes the attempt of the Sodomites to force their way into Lot's house.

he finally gave in and stayed the night. The NLT adds to the Hebrew, which says "and he spent another night."

19:8 ***you can leave later.*** Lit., "and linger (until this afternoon)." Again, the Hebrew uses a low-frequency term shared with Gen 19, the Hithpael form of *mahah* [TH4102, ZH4538] ("to delay, linger"; 3:26; Gen 19:16; 43:10; Exod 12:39; 2 Sam 15:28; Ps 119:60; Isa 29:9; Hab 2:3). Genesis 19:16 notes that Lot "hesitated" in departing from Sodom. Given the many links between ch 19 and Gen 19, the negative connotation of Lot's delay bodes ill for the father-in-law's suggestion. Boling's suggestion, "they argued back and forth," is as unlikely as it is clever (1975:275).

this afternoon. The Hebrew phrase is rare and unusual, *netoth hayyom*, meaning "the stretching out of the day." The verb *natah* [TH5186, ZH5742] is used only here with a time word, so its sense must be divined from context. The idea seems to be "to stay until most of the day has passed," i.e., until almost evening, as it appears in 19:9.

19:9 ***his father-in-law.*** As in 19:4, the text double-identifies the man as "his father-in-law (*khoten* [TH2859A, ZH3162]), the father of the young woman." Elsewhere the author typically calls him "father of the young woman" (*'abi hanna'arah* [TH5291, ZH5855]; 19:3, 5, 6, 8) or, once, just "father-in-law" (19:7).

almost evening. The NLT combines several clauses here. The Hebrew again uses uncommon terms for the time of day: "the day is weakening (fading? cf. *rapah* [TH7503, ZH8332]) to become evening" and even "the day has just encamped" (*hinneh khanoth hayyom* [TH2583, ZH2837]), perhaps an allusion to nomadic life referring to the time to stop traveling and make camp (Cundall 1968:194). The father-in-law hoped his delaying tactic got him another day to obligate the Levite.

be on your way. The Hebrew goes on to say "to your tent." This might be a quaint way of referring to the Levite's home, though Boling (1975:275) suggests it actually does refer to the very humble status and property of the Levite.

19:10 ***But this time the man was determined to leave.*** The Levite, having stayed for five days and looking potentially toward a sixth day, must depart. His journey will require an overnight stay on the road. Had he remained another day, he might be facing a Sabbath day as well, delaying his departure even more, and increasing his obligation to his father-in-law. The feasting, in fact, has concealed a battle of wills centering on whose household will command the young woman's presence, foreshadowing the conflict that will follow.

he . . . headed in the direction of Jebus (that is, Jerusalem). From Bethlehem the Levite traveled about six miles, about a two hours' walk, north on the road that follows the watershed ridge, sometimes called the National Highway or Patriarchal Highway. Few Bible readers realize that Jerusalem was not always a site sacred to the Hebrews. Until David's time, Jerusalem remained in the possession of the Jebusites. Judges 1:8 reports that the Judeans did set the city on fire, but goes on to note that the Benjaminites failed to hold Jerusalem so it remained in Jebusite hands (1:21). The remains of the Late Bronze Age fortifications are visible today on the eastern slope of the south end of the Kidron valley. Jebus was not the pre-Israelite name of the city (contra Boling 1975:275), which was called Jerusalem, in various linguistic equivalents, in the Egyptian execration texts of the nineteenth century BC and the Amarna letters of the fourteenth century BC (Soggin 1981:286). Possibly "Jebus" was an inner-Israelite pejorative term for the city.

19:11 ***It was late in the day.*** The author continues to employ graphic, but rare terms for the passing of time. Here, "the day (was) very much gone down" or "just about to go down." The use of this verb, *yarad* [TH3381, ZH3718], "to go down," with the noun "day" is otherwise unattested. The author's constant stress on the fading of the day and his use of unusual terms indicates the urgency of the Levite's departure, turning the reader's attention to the fading of the day, like the last grains of sand running through an hourglass.

Jebus. The city lay slightly east of the watershed ridge route, beyond the Hinnom valley and the later city's western hill (now erroneously called Mount Zion) and central valley.

this Jebusite town. Though the NLT is literally correct, *'ir hayyebusi hazzo'th* [TH2983, ZH3294] more properly implies "right here in the city of Jebus." That no other city is in view is clear from 19:10. The text makes a definite point of portraying the Levite as having declined to lodge in Jebus (Jerusalem).

19:12 ***we can't stay in this foreign town.*** The Levite's assumption that a non-Israelite town would be unwelcoming throws the events to follow into sharp relief.

Instead, we will go on to Gibeah. Four places in the OT are named "Gibeah," which means "hill." This story emphatically identifies the place as Gibeah belonging to Benjamin. The Levite's plan assumes Gibeah lay between Jerusalem and Ramah. Albright, following some earlier scholars, proposed the two-acre site of Tell el-Ful (meaning "Hill of Beans"), three miles north of Jerusalem for Gibeah. His 1922–1923 excavations and those of Lapp in 1964 exposed an Iron Age I settlement beginning c. 1200 BC and abandoned c. 1100 BC, possibly providing a date for the story in chs 19–21 (cf. 20:36-48). Saul reinforced fortifications at Gibeah. Lapp's later excavation uncovered no further evidence of the destruction, though he did note a period of abandonment 1150–1025 BC (Albright 1924:7-8). Scholars have challenged Albright's identification, but unsuccessfully (ABD 2.1007-1009; Schniedewind 2006). Jordan's King Hussein began building a palace atop of Tell el-Ful, but construction was cut short by the Six Day War of 1967. The skeletal remains of the unfinished palace stand today where Saul's citadel stood 3,000 years ago.

19:13 ***Ramah.*** Ramah lay directly on the watershed ridge highway about 2.5 miles north of Gibeah, assuming Tell el-Ful is Gibeah.

we'll spend the night in one of those towns. The Hebrew might suggest a different sense than the NLT conveys. Lit., "Come on, let us approach one of the places, and spend the night in Gibeah or Ramah." The phrase "one of the places" might suggest sacred sites (HALOT *maqôm;* NIDOTTE 3:899-903; TDOT 8:532-544). In 19:18 the Levite will note that though he was traveling to a "house of Yahweh," still no offer of hospitality came (see note on 19:18). Perhaps "places" (*meqomoth* [TH4725, ZH5226]) refers to sacred places, where the Levite expected to find an open door to a person of priestly vocation.

19:14 ***The sun was setting as they came to Gibeah.*** One last time, the author notes the fading of the day, emphasizing the constraint of time on the characters. The sun has indeed set, in more ways than one. The story has numerous parallels in content and even in wording to the story of the two angels visiting Lot in Sodom in Gen 19:1-29 and Saul's rage over the siege of Gibeah in 1 Sam 11:5-11. The most compact summary of the parallels remains that of Burney (1920:444-445; cf. also Block 1999:519-521; 532-534). The Sodom narrative provides a prior context for seeing the Judges story in the context of irredeemable depravity, and the Judges story in turn casts a shadow over the story of Saul, who was from the tribe of Benjamin, and specifically from Gibeah.

19:15 ***town square.*** Heb., *rekhob* [TH7339, ZH8148], which means simply "open space." The typical Iron Age I (1200–1000 BC) town site was a ring or rings of houses and buildings facing inward, with their rear walls joined or very close to form a perimeter. This outer ring is the origin of the typical Israelite "casemate" wall. The area within the innermost ring of houses was the "square," which is obviously not precise.

no one took them in for the night. The town square would be a perfectly legitimate place for strangers to camp, but in a tribal culture, an offer of hospitality would be expected. That none was forthcoming suggests something very wrong about this town.

19:16 ***an old man . . . living in Gibeah, where the people were from the tribe of Benjamin.*** The old man, an odd counterpart to the father-in-law, is like the Levite, a *ger* [TH1481, ZH1591], a client or dependent. His work might well have been on the farm of the family with which he was sojourning. The author emphasizes, yet again, that the people there are Benjaminites, so that the only hospitality offered to outsiders comes from another outsider. More poignantly, Lev 19:33-34 demands that the Israelites extend hospitality to the sojourner, but here a sojourner, a vulnerable person, extended protection to the visitors.

19:17 ***travelers.*** Heb., *ha'oreakh* [TH732A, ZH782], which is sg., modifying only "the man," suggesting perhaps the old man really only took cognizance of the Levite. This term appears in 2 Sam 12:4 to denote the visitor for whose entertainment the rich man in Nathan's parable stole a poor man's only sheep (another example of "hospitality" providing a pretext for evil).

he asked them where they were from and where they were going. For a potential host to interrogate travelers before offering them lodging might be a serious breach of the ethos of hospitality (Matthews 2004:184).

19:18 ***and now I'm returning home.*** The Hebrew has "I am going to the house of the LORD"; cf. NLT mg, which curiously renders this "*Tabernacle* of the LORD," and see note on 18:31. The Levite might have seen his destination as Shiloh or Bethel, both sanctuaries located generally in the hill country of Ephraim. On the other hand, the first person possessive suffix on the Hebrew term "my house" could have been mistaken for an abbreviation for "Yahweh" and been expanded by a scribe (Moore 1895:416). The NLT, following the LXX and the conclusions of a vast majority of commentators, reflects such a view.

19:19 ***we have everything we need. We have straw and feed for our donkeys and plenty of bread and wine for ourselves.*** By stressing their ability to provide for their own needs, the Levite accentuates the essentially inhospitable character of the occupants of Gibeah. His claim of sufficiency, made to a potential host, also violates the protocol governing the interaction of potential guests and hosts, introducing an element of rivalry (Matthews 2004:184). The NLT omits the Levite's reference to his servant and to his woman, which employs a term for a female slave, *'amah* [TH519, ZH563]. The reference might simply be polite, but given her identity as "concubine," it might be demeaning. It at least introduces ambiguity into her status.

19:20 ***whatever you do, don't spend the night in the square.*** As in Gen 19:2-3, visitors perfectly able to pass the night in the town square were urged strongly to take shelter with a hospitable resident who was not a native of the community. Matthews claims that, in fact, the offer of hospitality by a sojourner was improper (2004:185).

19:21 ***he took them home with him and fed the donkeys. After they washed their feet, they ate and drank together.*** As in Gen 19:3, a meal was prepared for the visitors. Their host provided for all their needs, caring for the animals, for their refreshment after the journey, and the meal.

19:22 ***While they were enjoying themselves.*** The idiom employed is the same as appeared in the Levite's days of feasting with his father-in-law. The worst of the experience seemed to be over, but, in fact, the nightmare was about to begin.

a crowd of troublemakers from the town surrounded the house. The NLT obscures the implication of the Hebrew, which uses an appositional construction, "the men of the city, the men of the sons of *beliyya'al.*" The most obvious etymology of *beliyya'al*, "without worth" (*beli* [TH1097, ZH1172] + *ya'al* [TH3276, ZH3603]) fails to get at the seriousness of the condemnation involved. This term, like *nebalah* [TH5039, ZH5576] in 19:23, names only the most serious offenses. Scholars from Burney (1920:467-468) through Cross and Freedman (1953:22, n. 6) have suggested the second term derives from the verb "to go up," referring to "the place from which none go up," (i.e., the netherworld, or realm of the dead). That the term *beliyya'al* [TH1100, ZH1175] appears parallel to *she'ol* [TH7585, ZH8619] (2 Sam 22:5-6 = Ps 18:4-5) and also in reference to a plague from which one cannot arise (Ps 41:8) supports the suggestion (NIDOTTE 1.661-662). The "sons of *beliyya'al*" are those so irredeemably wicked that they are kin to the realm of death and decay. The line seems also to suggest that this was no fringe or marginal group, but indeed, "the men of the city."

They began beating at the door. This rare word might imply the men were slamming their bodies against the door to break it down (Cundall 1968:196). The door of the house formed the legal and spiritual boundary between the homeowner and the world (Matthews 2004:188).

Bring out the man who is staying with you. The story essentially parallels Gen 19:4-5. In both cases the inhabitants of the town surround the house.

we can have sex with him. The term *yada'* [TH3045, ZH3359], normally translated "know," carries a sexual nuance limited to physical intercourse. Its sexual usage appears only as the prelude to conception, descriptions of physical virginity (cf. 11:39; 21:12; Gen 19:8), and descriptions of rape (19:25; Gen 19:5). In its sexual contexts, *yada'* never carries a connotation of relational intimacy.

19:23 ***don't do such an evil thing.*** The same verb for "do evil" appears in Gen 19:7.

For this man is a guest in my house. See Gen 19:8b for the parallel.

such a thing would be shameful. The outrage against traditional values of hospitality hardly requires mention. The term translated "shameful" is *nebalah* [TH5039, ZH5576], frequently mistranslated as "folly." In the tribal-familial ethos of ancient Israelite society, this term denoted flagrant, wanton defiance of the most fundamental obligations and values of the community (NIDOTTE s.v. *nabal* [TH5036, ZH5572]). The term is lacking from the story in Gen 19.

19:24 ***take my virgin daughter and this man's concubine.*** The host's offer of his virgin daughter for unlimited sexual abuse substantially parallels Gen 19:7-8. His offer of his guest's concubine, however, comes as a surprise since it patently violates the safety of his guests. Moreover, a concubine, even as a lower-ranking wife, was still legally linked to her husband, precluding any offer such as the host here makes. Perhaps the Levite's earlier reference to her as a female slave (19:19) indicated enough distance to permit the offer. Still, however sacred the laws of hospitality, we must remember this was still Israel. OT religious traditions added to the normal obligations of hospitality by reminding Israel that kindness to strangers should also arise from their own story of redemption from Egypt. Thus in Israel the host also bore a deep and religious obligation to protect those who came under his care (e.g., Exod 22:21; 23:9; Lev 19:33-34; Deut 10:18-19). His willingness to sacrifice his own daughter and his guest's concubine signals the loss of a distinctively Israelite moral perspective in which a very important value, hospitality, trumps other, more absolute values, the value of the lives of others under his care. What stands out is the willingness of the men in the story to sacrifice the women dependent upon them, in the name of their code of hospitality, which graphically illustrates the depraved state to which the nation had fallen.

you can abuse them. The use of the term "abuse" (cf. Gen 19) indicates that the host knew what the men of the city had in mind—there would be no boundaries—and the fate to which he proposed consigning the women.

whatever you like. Lit., "the thing that is good (*hattob* [TH2896, ZH3202]) in your eyes." This expression comes quite close to the author's general condemnation of the Israelites, who do "what is right (*hayyashar* [TH3477A, ZH3838]) in their own eyes."

don't do such a shameful thing to this man. See note on 19:23.

19:25 ***they wouldn't listen to him.*** Cf. Gen 19:9, where the Sodomites responded to a corresponding offer by mocking the client, or dependent status of the householder. The Judges narrative does not include a similar rejoinder, perhaps because of what unfolds next. In the parallel story of Gen 19, this is the point where the two disguised angels act, pulling Lot inside to safety and then striking the Sodomites blind. The distraught concubine of ch 19 experienced no such miraculous deliverance.

the Levite took hold of his concubine. The Hebrew does not include "Levite," simply saying, "the man took hold of his concubine." The nearest previous use of the term "the man" (19:23) refers to the host. Nothing is said of the host's daughter. Perhaps the narrator implies that the concubine, though a guest, still stood lower socially than the host's daughter.

abused her all night, taking turns raping her until morning. The Hebrew uses two verbs. The first is *yada'* [TH3045, ZH3359] "they knew" (sexually; see note on 19:22). The second is *wayyith'allelu* [TH5953, ZH6618], from a root that seems to suggest doing anything repeatedly. In agricultural contexts, it means "to glean" (i.e., go over the crops yet again, picking up anything left). It also refers to violent or severe treatment. In the Hithpael stem, as here, it refers to repeated actions of harm, mockery, or trickery, ranging from Yahweh's repeated mockery of Egypt in the plagues (Exod 10:2) to the wounded Saul's fear that the Philistines would make sport of him before allowing him to die (1 Sam 31:4). Together, both verbs depict a savage, mocking, riotous, repeated, sexual, and emotional violation of this utterly defenseless woman.

Finally, at dawn they let her go. "They let her go" (Piel of *shalakh* [TH7971, ZH8938]) can express commissioning, dismissal, rejection, or even divorce. Ironically, though the author greatly extended his description of the final hours of the day, he passed over the entire night in a few lines and then lingered over the dawning of the next day in several phrases, continuing into 19:26 (cf. Block 1999:539-540). The setting sun had counted down the hours toward this horror; now the dawn breaks on the tortured, and possibly dying, woman.

19:26 *her husband.* Lit., "her master" (*'adoneha* [TH113, ZH123]). This is the first time the Levite is referred to with this term.

19:27 *When her husband opened the door to leave.* The callousness of the Levite now appears; he seems oblivious to the events of the preceding night and prepared for a routine departure. He did not open the door to seek his concubine or learn her fate, but simply to resume his journey.

there lay his concubine with her hands on the threshold. The scene starkly portrays the woman's utter ruination. The woman's grasping the threshold, assumed to have already happened in this scene, is the last action attributed to her in the story.

19:28 *He said, "Get up! Let's go!" But there was no answer.* The narrator does not inform the reader that the woman was dead, only that the Levite received no answer to his command. The LXX adds here, *hoti ēn nekra* [TG3498, ZG3738], "for she was dead" (see NLT mg). How the clause would have dropped from the Hebrew is hard to explain, but its addition by a translator uncomfortable with the narrator's techniques for sustaining tension is easily enough understood. Ominously, in recounting the doings of this night in 20:5, the Levite's words in Hebrew are noncommital, literally, "and she died," not "and they killed her" (Block 1999:541; Schneider 2000:264-265).

So he put her body on his donkey and took her home. The NLT supplies "her body," but the Hebrew simply says "he took her on the donkey" without specifying whether she had died, or was simply so devastated and injured that she was unable to respond.

19:29 *he took a knife and cut his concubine's body into twelve pieces.* The NLT does not translate, before "cut," the verb "grasped" (*wayyakhazeq* [TH2388, ZH2616]), which echoes the previous expression of someone "grasping" this woman (19:25), stressing her coercion. The terminology used bespeaks the butchering of an animal (1 Sam 11:7; 1 Kgs 18:23, 33) or even the dissection of sacrificial animals to be burned on the altar (Exod 29:17; Lev 1:6, 12; 8:20). Lit., the text says "he sliced her up into/according to her bones, twelve slices." The narrator's capacity to relate utterly incomprehensible actions so matter-of-factly reaches a crescendo here, exceeded only by the Levite's capacity actually to do this.

he sent one piece to each tribe. Now the story also has parallels with another account, that of the kingship of Saul, who expressed his rage at the siege laid by the Ammonites against Jabesh-gilead by cutting up a pair of oxen into 12 pieces and sending the pieces to the tribes of Israel as a call to arms (1 Sam 11:7). The Levite's treatment of her body violated every known biblical standard for how the dead are to be treated, desecrating her body as well as defiling him. That the woman received no burial, and hence, no remembrance, culminates the string of indignities that began with her namelessness in the narrative. Commentators typically cite an ancient letter from Mari in which a commander, unable to raise sufficient troops to serve his master, boasts that he might execute a prisoner, dismember him, and process through the countryside to inspire fear and obedience (cf. Block 1999:546 for translation of the text).

19:30 *Such a horrible crime.* The term "horrible crime" does not appear in the text, which reads, "It has not happened, it has not been seen—the like of this." The intention of the grammatically abrupt, even incoherent statement, is rendered suitably by the NLT.

in all the time since Israel left Egypt. The sense that the book of Judges builds to a climax of sinfulness and depravity is confirmed by the very words of the Israelites themselves, who in fact, see it as the worst event since the Exodus. Given the sins and judgments of the wilderness era, in which an entire generation of Israelites died in the desert, this is a very strong condemnation of the sin committed at Gibeah. Likewise, Hosea looked to the "days of Gibeah" as a signal marker of Israel's depravity (Hos 9:9; 10:9). At this point, LXX Alexandrinus has a long addition, in which the Levite commissions the grim couriers with a summons to call a nationwide inquiry. But that addition seems to be an attempt to smooth out a somewhat difficult text.

Think about it! Block (1999:548) insightfully notes the Hebrew is better rendered, "think about *her*."

What are we going to do? Who's going to speak up? Tribal societies are long on deliberation. With no centralized government, no standing army or police, and no single ruler, a process of debate and discussion among elders at successive levels of seniority unfolds.

COMMENTARY

The story in chapters 19–21 brings the book to a dramatic climax, exposing the full extent of Israel's self-destructive anarchy—despite the fact that tribal mechanisms and traditions still seem to produce results. The story draws together many threads from throughout the book and is linked closely to chapters 17–18. As 17:1–18:31 extended the theme, begun in 1:1–2:5, of a failed conquest, to a catastrophic and religiously perverse climax, so 19:1–21:25 develops the concept of Israel as a unified covenant community, initiated in 2:6–3:6. The author of the book drives home with devastating force that Israel not only betrayed Yahweh by doing evil in his eyes, it also manifests the capacity to utterly dismember itself as no final standard of right prevails. Moreover, even though Yahweh still rules, the lack of a human representative to make that rule concrete (as a human, historical institution in the form of a king) means that his rule remains elusive and Israel remains at grave risk of self-destruction.

As Younger (2002:347) has shown, this final episode of the book has a concentric structure. The rape of the concubine in 19:1-30 corresponds to the concluding marital abductions of the maidens of Shiloh (21:15-25). The destruction of Gibeah (20:1-48) likewise matches the attack on Jabesh-gilead (21:6-14). In the center falls the consternation of the Israelites concerning the consequences of their implementation of tribal retribution and justice, centering on their oath not to allow their daughters to marry Benjaminites (21:1-5). Running through this A-B-C-B′-A′ structure is also a relentless causal sequence linking every action to what preceded (cf. Block 1999:515-516). Moreover, a series of problems arise, whose solutions in turn produce greater problems. Thus, the marital dispute is resolved in the home of the father-in-law, but the implementation of the newly restored marriage requires the journey home, which provokes the problem of lodging. When that problem seems well-solved by the hospitality of the man at Gibeah, the degenerate mob appears. The resultant outrage triggers a united war of vengeance against the Benjaminites, and when the nation is victorious they face the problem of having decimated a tribe, for which they must now find wives. That problem, in turn, is solved by yet another slaughter, which nets too few women to fulfill the needs of the Benjaminite survivors, leading to the almost inconceivable expedient of permitting the Benjaminite men to abduct women from a religious festival at Shiloh—in effect, a kind of socially sanctioned rape. The text possibly echoes the rape law in Deuteronomy 22:28-29, which declares a man who sexually assaults a virgin must pay her father 50 shekels and may never divorce her.

Judges 19: The Spark. Several red herrings plague the interpretation of this story. First, though the author clearly works with the dimensions of hospitality to shape the story, this narrative is not *about* hospitality. Second, many interpreters find here an exposé of the evils of patriarchy. Again, the writer certainly does marshal the themes of the vulnerability of women, but one hardly could say the author is antipatriarchal. Third, interpreters find here a condemnation of homosexuality and sexual immorality in general. Certainly the author assumes the reader recoils from such behavior, but again, the ancient reader hardly needed to be persuaded that violent gang rape, whether homosexual or heterosexual, was wrong. Even depraved Israel knew that (cf. 19:29-30). Lastly, historians rightly find in this story and the chapters to follow many hints and clues about the social structure of earliest Israel. The author of the text employs these dimensions not as the end, but as the means for making a larger point, one not necessarily congenial to the audience. For 18 chapters the historian has relentlessly exposed the flaws and failures of the premonarchic order of ancient Israel. Starting with the failed conquest after Joshua's death, the steady increase in Israel's evildoing, the relentless deepening of the political crises into which Israel fell, and the evident deterioration of the "office" of the judge, the writer has masterfully demolished any romantic idealism about Israel's first years in the Promised Land. Any of his readers who would claim that Israel stood in no need of a transformation from tribal society to monarchy faced an irrefutable demonstration of the old order's impotence and evil. Rather than justify the monarchy, the author leaves the reader having to justify the premonarchic order! Could any potential problems with kingship be any worse than what happens here?

In chapter 19, the author stresses that the Israel of the premonarchic era was a community in which the smallest conflict, such as a petty marital dispute, could mushroom into heinous crimes beyond imagination, like nothing seen since the departure from Egypt (19:30). Given the scenes one witnesses in the books of Leviticus and Numbers, in which the ground swallows sinners, fire blazes out from the Tabernacle to incinerate corrupt leaders, and a whole generation dies in their sin in the wilderness, that claim bears reflection. The author takes us through a story in which we keep wanting someone to step in and stop the evils that multiply like rats. Why did nobody offer legitimate hospitality in Gibeah? Why were the citizens of Gibeah, to a man, "sons of Belial" and yet no action had been taken to restrain their evil—even prior to our story? Where was the clan, with its ethos of protection? Where was the judge? And what of the Levite? The Old Testament charges the Levites with being the custodians and guardians of Yahweh's covenant (cf. Exod 32:25-29; Num 1:53; Deut 33:8-11; Mal 2:1-9). How is it that a Levite displays not a shred of spiritual interest or leadership? Given the deviant shrine presided over by the Levite of chapters 17–18, perhaps this utterly "secular" Levite reflects the next step-down. Moreover, how does a Levite go from wanting to "speak to the heart" of his concubine to showing such callous disregard for her safety? How can he desecrate her body, destroy her memory, and defile himself and those who receive his "message"? The story seems like a massive train wreck happening in slow motion. Indeed, the writer cares about hospitality, about the evils of selfish men with virtually absolute power over women, and, yes, the writer cares about sexual ethics. But more important is the writer's claim that, in fact, the Israel of this era was like a house full of gas, awaiting a single spark to explode. Whether that explosion occurs in the realm of hospitality, sexuality, or gender dominance is secondary to the fact that Israel has become a bomb awaiting detonation, a "perfect storm" needing only a beginning. All of this happened, declares our writer, because "in those days, there was no king in Israel."

The prophet Hosea alluded to the scene in chapter 19 in order to stress the decadence that was overwhelming the northern kingdom in his day (Hos 9:9; 10:9). Similarly, nearly all commentators notice that chapter 19 laces the story of premonarchic Israel's moral and social volatility with allusions to the northern kingdom. The concubine who is violated comes from Bethlehem of Judah (the home of David), but the callous Levite hails from Ephraim. The tribe of Benjamin and the city of Gibeah both carry strong connections with Saul. Of course, the Levite's summons to his countrymen gruesomely anticipates Saul's call to arms by which he rises to prominence as Israel's first, but rejected king. By also loading the story with unmistakable resonances with the account of Sodom's destruction (Gen 19), the author leaves no possibility of missing his point. At every level of social organization, this was a sick society.

The most haunting feature of this story, however, remains the silence of God. God has asserted his presence throughout the book of Judges, even amidst the sins of Israel and the foibles of its leaders. Whether granting victory, pouring out his Spirit, or speaking explosive words of anger and rebuke, God has been present in Israel. This story, however, unfolds in a spiritual vacuum. Block, rightly noting how the "Israel" of chapter 19 seems the opposite of the real Israel, refers to Israel as "Canaanized" (1999:542-545).

However, matters appear even worse. No god appears in this chapter at all, neither the true God nor even false gods. The name Yahweh does not appear in the story (the reference in 19:18 is universally taken as a scribal error), nor does the word "god" (*'elohim* [TH430, ZH466]) in any form. No element of transcendence, of deity, of grace or redemption, relieves the terror of the story. Even the hospitality of the father-in-law has a sinister undercurrent (see notes on 19:4-10). Surely at least the poor woman deserved to hear from God. Was the Levite so spiritually blind that he neither appealed to God, nor cried out in protest? Was the host devoid of any capability of invoking divine standards of right as he protested to the mob? The best he can do is appeal to societal mores, and that impotently. The Bible often does portray human evil and its monstrous consequences seamlessly, pointing out the painful fact that God does not magically intervene and stop humans from the crimes they perpetrate. We wish that God would undertake for victims like the woman, who technically might not be innocent, having abandoned her husband, but who in no conceivable manner deserved her heinous fate. Reading this story, we ask God why he does not protect such persons from these atrocious acts. The answer, perhaps, is painful: God has provided for protection against such barbarism. He has ordained and commanded civil, just, human communities led by persons with integrity and character, submitted to the moral law of God. The covenant community's charge always was to maintain faithfulness to Yahweh with justice and integrity to rule among the people. Thus this story, with its heinous crime and its stark reality of divine absence (or, at least, silence), testifies to the fact that God does not normally intervene magically or miraculously when people, even his people, do horrible things to each other. For good or ill, however risky and troubling it may seem, God has entrusted the maintenance of justice and the protection of the helpless to human communities and their leaders. Thus, the comment in 19:1 (repeating 17:6; 18:1; and foreshadowing 21:25) that there indeed was "no king in Israel" becomes all the more poignant, and tacitly defines the role the author envisions the king to take: not merely to save the Israelites from enemies, as the judges did, but to save the Israelites from their own worst enemy—themselves.

◆ 2. Israel's war with Benjamin (20:1-48)

Then all the Israelites were united as one man, from Dan in the north to Beersheba in the south, including those from across the Jordan in the land of Gilead. The entire community assembled in the presence of the LORD at Mizpah. [2]The leaders of all the people and all the tribes of Israel—400,000 warriors armed with swords—took their positions in the assembly of the people of God. [3](Word soon reached the land of Benjamin that the other tribes had gone up to Mizpah.) The Israelites then asked how this terrible crime had happened.

[4]The Levite, the husband of the woman who had been murdered, said, "My concubine and I came to spend the night in Gibeah, a town that belongs to the people of Benjamin. [5]That night some of the leading citizens of Gibeah surrounded the house, planning to kill me, and they raped my concubine until she was dead. [6]So I cut her body into twelve pieces and sent the pieces throughout the territory assigned to Israel, for these men have committed a terrible and shameful crime. [7]Now then, all of you—the entire community of Israel—must decide here and now what should be done about this!"

[8]And all the people rose to their feet in unison and declared, "None of us will return home! No, not even one of us!

9 Instead, this is what we will do to Gibeah; we will draw lots to decide who will attack it. 10 One-tenth of the men* from each tribe will be chosen to supply the warriors with food, and the rest of us will take revenge on Gibeah* of Benjamin for this shameful thing they have done in Israel." 11 So all the Israelites were completely united, and they gathered together to attack the town.

12 The Israelites sent messengers to the tribe of Benjamin, saying, "What a terrible thing has been done among you! 13 Give up those evil men, those troublemakers from Gibeah, so we can execute them and purge Israel of this evil."

But the people of Benjamin would not listen. 14 Instead, they came from their towns and gathered at Gibeah to fight the Israelites. 15 In all, 26,000 of their warriors armed with swords arrived in Gibeah to join the 700 elite troops who lived there. 16 Among Benjamin's elite troops, 700 were left-handed, and each of them could sling a rock and hit a target within a hairsbreadth without missing. 17 Israel had 400,000 experienced soldiers armed with swords, not counting Benjamin's warriors.

18 Before the battle the Israelites went to Bethel and asked God, "Which tribe should go first to attack the people of Benjamin?"

The LORD answered, "Judah is to go first."

19 So the Israelites left early the next morning and camped near Gibeah. 20 Then they advanced toward Gibeah to attack the men of Benjamin. 21 But Benjamin's warriors, who were defending the town, came out and killed 22,000 Israelites on the battlefield that day.

22 But the Israelites encouraged each other and took their positions again at the same place they had fought the previous day. 23 For they had gone up to Bethel and wept in the presence of the LORD until evening. They had asked the LORD, "Should we fight against our relatives from Benjamin again?"

And the LORD had said, "Go out and fight against them."

24 So the next day they went out again to fight against the men of Benjamin, 25 but the men of Benjamin killed another 18,000 Israelites, all of whom were experienced with the sword.

26 Then all the Israelites went up to Bethel and wept in the presence of the LORD and fasted until evening. They also brought burnt offerings and peace offerings to the LORD. 27 The Israelites went up seeking direction from the LORD. (In those days the Ark of the Covenant of God was in Bethel, 28 and Phinehas son of Eleazar and grandson of Aaron was the priest.) The Israelites asked the LORD, "Should we fight against our relatives from Benjamin again, or should we stop?"

The LORD said, "Go! Tomorrow I will hand them over to you."

29 So the Israelites set an ambush all around Gibeah. 30 They went out on the third day and took their positions at the same place as before. 31 When the men of Benjamin came out to attack, they were drawn away from the town. And as they had done before, they began to kill the Israelites. About thirty Israelites died in the open fields and along the roads, one leading to Bethel and the other leading back to Gibeah.

32 Then the warriors of Benjamin shouted, "We're defeating them as we did before!" But the Israelites had planned in advance to run away so that the men of Benjamin would chase them along the roads and be drawn away from the town.

33 When the main group of Israelite warriors reached Baal-tamar, they turned and took up their positions. Meanwhile, the Israelites hiding in ambush to the west* of Gibeah jumped up to fight. 34 There were 10,000 elite Israelite troops who advanced against Gibeah. The fighting was so heavy that Benjamin didn't realize the impending disaster. 35 So the LORD helped Israel defeat Benjamin, and that day the Israelites killed 25,100 of Benjamin's warriors, all of whom were ex-

perienced swordsmen. 36Then the men of Benjamin saw that they were beaten.

The Israelites had retreated from Benjamin's warriors in order to give those hiding in ambush more room to maneuver against Gibeah. 37Then those who were hiding rushed in from all sides and killed everyone in the town. 38They had arranged to send up a large cloud of smoke from the town as a signal. 39When the Israelites saw the smoke, they turned and attacked Benjamin's warriors.

By that time Benjamin's warriors had killed about thirty Israelites, and they shouted, "We're defeating them as we did in the first battle!" 40But when the warriors of Benjamin looked behind them and saw the smoke rising into the sky from every part of the town, 41the men of Israel turned and attacked. At this point the men of Benjamin became terrified, because they realized disaster was close at hand. 42So they turned around and fled before the Israelites toward the wilderness. But they couldn't escape the battle, and the people who came out of the nearby towns were also killed.* 43The Israelites surrounded the men of Benjamin and chased them relentlessly, finally overtaking them east of Gibeah.* 44That day 18,000 of Benjamin's strongest warriors died in battle. 45The survivors fled into the wilderness toward the rock of Rimmon, but Israel killed 5,000 of them along the road. They continued the chase until they had killed another 2,000 near Gidom.

46So that day the tribe of Benjamin lost 25,000 strong warriors armed with swords, 47leaving only 600 men who escaped to the rock of Rimmon, where they lived for four months. 48And the Israelites returned and slaughtered every living thing in all the towns—the people, the livestock, and everything they found. They also burned down all the towns they came to.

20:10a Hebrew *10 men from every hundred, 100 men from every thousand, and 1,000 men from every 10,000.* **20:10b** Hebrew *Geba,* in this case a variant spelling of Gibeah; also in 20:33. **20:33** As in Greek and Syriac versions and Latin Vulgate; Hebrew reads *hiding in the open space.* **20:42** Or *battle, for the people from the nearby towns also came out and killed them.* **20:43** The meaning of the Hebrew is uncertain.

NOTES

20:1 ***all the Israelites were united as one man.*** This verse accumulates many terms denoting the comprehensive Israelite unity triggered by this event. The expression "as one man" appears only eight other times in the OT, describing not merely complete, but spontaneously expressed unity. In 1 Sam 11:7, such an assembly follows Saul's dismemberment of the oxen in a parallel call to arms. The opening verses of this account pile up expressions to emphasize the expectation that all Israel, all the tribes, all the people, are present. This matter becomes important later when the Israelites end up desperately needing to find some who were not represented at this assembly. This gathering at the end of Judges contrasts with the assemblies with which the book of Joshua closes (Josh 23–24), in which Israel's covenant with Yahweh is affirmed with oaths and witnesses (Boling 1975:283).

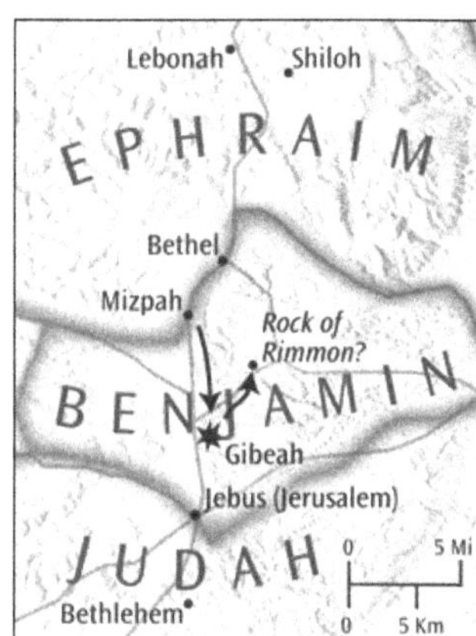

Israel's War with Benjamin

from Dan in the north to Beersheba in the south. The conventional reference to Dan as the northern border poignantly recalls the origins of that convention in the preceding chs, 17–18. The NLT supplies directional references to clarify the Hebrew.

including those from across the Jordan in the land of Gilead. The NLT clarifies for the reader that Gilead lies across the Jordan, though these words do not appear in the original. Reference to Gilead alludes to the Jephthah story (10:6–12:7). By including the Trans-Jordan tribes, the author presents Israel as more unified than it was even at the time of Joshua, when these tribes very nearly fell before a comparable tribal military force (Josh 22). On that occasion, reason prevailed and hostilities subsided. Such will not occur in the tinderbox of Israel in this era. The perfect storm continues to build.

The entire community assembled. Several crucial terms in Hebrew indicating the nature of the Israelite community appear in this verse. The verb *wattiqqahel*, a Hithpael form, graphically conveys the internal reciprocity of a collective body, and its root, *qahal* [TH6950, ZH7735], implies a called, formal assembly meeting for a purpose. "Community" (*ha'edah* [TH5712, ZH6337]) implies not merely a community of persons, but a gathered congregation. Without pressing root meanings unduly, the term in its uses seems to imply meeting by prior arrangement or appointment. Thus, the term depicts Israel meeting in formal council.

in the presence of the LORD. Lit., "to Yahweh." The phrase, appearing about 160 times, most often appears in connection with speech or physical gestures. To assemble "to Yahweh," rather than the more normal "in the presence of Yahweh," conveys a more direct, urgent approach.

Mizpah. This location appears previously in Judges in the Jephthah story (cf. note on 10:17), where, despite the Gileadite setting of the stories, it seems to refer to the site in Benjamin (except for 11:29). Mizpah also figures prominently in this final account (cf. 20:3; 21:1, 5, 8); it provided a major venue for Samuel's leadership on a circuit with Bethel and Gilgal (1 Sam 7:16). An important religious center, and point of assembly for the Israelites, particularly for so-called holy war, Mizpah still served as a religious center in Hosea's day (Hos 5:1) and even became a place for grain and incense offerings "for the house of Yahweh" after the destruction of the Jerusalem Temple (Jer 41:4-6). The word itself means "watchtower" or "lookout point." Scholars generally identify Mizpah with Tell en-Nasbeh, an eight-acre site on a plateau about 7.5 miles north of Jerusalem on the watershed highway. It stood at the northern edge of Benjaminite territory, about 4.5 miles from Gibeah, and seems to have lain abandoned for 1,500 years until the Israelites occupied it c. 1100 BC. Evidence of its occupation in the period of the Judges includes Philistine pottery, collared-rim jars, and other pottery types. Little architecture can be definitively ascribed to this era beyond a few rock-hewn silos, cisterns, and a winepress (ABD 4.879-881; 1027-1029).

20:2 ***leaders.*** The text here uses an unusual term, *pinnah* [TH6438, ZH7157], which typically means "corner." Perhaps by association with "cornerstone" or even battlements, the word came metaphorically to denote leaders (cf. 1 Sam 14:38; Isa 19:13). Perhaps the leaders' role as supports, or their prominence, like the corner towers on the wall of a city, inspired the metaphor (Moore 1895:423).

of all the people and all the tribes of Israel. Ironically, the author claims "all the tribes of Israel" are present, but, of course, the Benjaminites are not. In fact, the author will contrast the "sons of Israel" with the "sons of the Benjaminites," as if rhetorically assuming the Benjaminites are no longer Israelites.

400,000 warriors armed with swords. The numbers, equipment, and degree of organization all contrast with the tendency in Judges to describe Israel as poorly equipped and ill-prepared for battle (see note on 5:8; cf. the first note on 3:16; notes on 3:31). The Israel that so readily quailed before enemies galvanized for action against Benjamin. "Armed with swords" translates *sholep khereb* [TH8025, ZH8990], lit., "drawer(s) of the sword." The term denotes not merely someone who has a sword, but someone accustomed and ready to use it, thus an experienced swordsman.

people of God. Despite the frequency with which Christians use the phrase "people of God," this precise phrase appears only one other time in the OT (2 Sam 14:13) and once in a more expanded expression "the people of the God of Abraham" (Ps 47:9). Even the expression "people of [Yahweh]" appears only nine times (5:13; Num 11:29; 17:6; 1 Sam 2:24; 2 Sam 1:12; 6:21; 2 Kgs 9:6; Ezek 36:20; Zeph 2:10).

20:3 *(Word soon reached the land of Benjamin.)* Lit., "and the children of Benjamin heard," with an emphasis on the persons rather than the region. The "children of Benjamin" (*bene binyamin* [TH1144, ZH1228]) are here contrasted with the "children of Israel" (*bene yisra'el* [TH3478, ZH3776]) even though the Benjaminites actually were part of *bene yisra'el*. Although every translation treats this clause as parenthetical, its syntactic construction places it in the foregrounded narrative thread of the story. The switch from Israel to Benjamin seems rough, prompting some commentators to speculate that the text has been dislocated in scribal copying. More likely, the author switches between Israel and the Benjaminites for dramatic effect, allowing the reader to see both parties in the conflict simultaneously.

the other tribes. Lit., "the children of Israel." See preceding note.

The Israelites then asked how this terrible crime had happened. Having just noted that the Benjaminites had "heard," the writer now switches to the Levite's narrative, creating the literary illusion of the Benjaminites hearing the Levite's testimony against them.

20:4 *murdered.* Heb., *ratsakh* [TH7523, ZH8357], used in the Decalogue (Exod 20:13; Deut 5:17) as well as in the laws relating to homicide and the cities of refuge (Num 35). The use of the term indicates the narrator's decision about her death. Nearly every commentator notes that the Levite tells a carefully crafted and partial version of the story designed to inflame their rage while suppressing any doubts about his own role in the incident. The demagogue can only succeed by painting a pure, black-and-white contrast.

My concubine and I came. The Hebrew text makes repeated use of the first person sg., lit., "I came, I and my concubine . . ." continuing on through to 20:5. The Levite failed to indicate why he and his concubine came to be in Gibeah, arising from his own determination not to spend another night with his father-in-law. This is the first of several omissions.

Gibeah, a town that belongs to the people of Benjamin. The Levite placed the reference to Gibeah and Benjamin first in his statement, for emphasis.

20:5 *some of the leading citizens of Gibeah.* The NLT's "some" blurs the fact that the Levite indicts *all* the *leaders* of the city, saying "the lords (*ba'ale* [TH1167, ZH1251]) of Gibeah arose." Likewise, the narrative states flatly in 19:22 "the men of the city, men of irredeemable corruption" (rendering *beliyya'al* [TH1100, ZH1175]).

surrounded the house, planning to kill me. The Hebrew reveals the self-centeredness of the Levite's speech: "the men of the city arose against *me*, surrounded *me* . . . *me* they were planning to kill . . . *my* concubine they raped." More importantly, the narrative of ch 19 does not say the men planned to kill the Levite, though their intention of homosexual gang rape was heinous enough.

they raped my concubine until she was dead. Again, the Levite omitted important details, such as the decision to thrust his concubine out the door to the mob. The Levite's speech becomes strangely vague. He does not actually say "until she was dead" (contra Schneider 2000:267) nor does he say "and they killed her." He simply says "my concubine they raped and she died." She certainly survived the abuse of the men, having made her way to the threshold of the house, however battered and broken. Given the uncertainty about precisely when—and how—she died (see note on 19:28-29), his vagueness at this point is suspicious. The Israelites were thus being called to a national assembly and war against one of their own towns on the basis of a carefully crafted, partial description of the event.

20:6 ***So I cut her body into twelve pieces.*** As in 19:29, the NLT omits the first clause, "and I seized my concubine." The term *'akhaz* [TH270, ZH296] typically denotes seizing something with a firm grip. Twice in the story of ch 19, the woman is "grabbed" (expressed with another verb, *khazaq* [TH2388, ZH2616]): once when she is thrust out to the mob, and then when the Levite dismembers her (19:25, 29).

terrible and shameful crime. The first word translates *zimmah* [TH2154, ZH2365], which is a technical expression in religious law for infamy or shameful behavior, often the equivalent of *to'ebah* [TH8441, ZH9359] or "abomination" (HALOT q.v. *zimmah*). On "shameful crime," see note on 19:23.

20:7 ***Now then, all of you—the entire community of Israel—must decide here and now what should be done about this!*** The Levite's challenge, climaxing his carefully crafted speech, recapitulates the responses to his gruesome message in 19:30. Schneider rightly stresses the gravity of Israel's actions, based as they were on a single witness's partial report (2000:266-272). Strangely, this is the last the reader sees of the Levite. The author never indicates whether the events that follow satisfied the Levite's need for redress. In fact, the narrative is not about solving a problem at all. Rather, it reveals how one problem's solution becomes itself the next problem. Like so many whose heated words about admittedly horrible things arouse whole communities to do even more horrible things, the Levite vanishes. Contrary to all biblical law, a death sentence is levied, not against an individual, but a whole city, on the basis of only one witness (cf. Num 35:30). No single pebble ever thinks it is responsible for the landslide.

20:9 ***we will draw lots to decide who will attack it.*** The Hebrew here is extremely terse, simply "against it by lot."

20:11 ***they gathered together to attack the town.*** Here it is vital to note that the town of Gibeah, not the entire tribe of Benjamin and all its towns and villages, is the target of the Israelites' wrath. The tribe will incur guilt by standing with the town, but there is no rationale or expressed intention for expanding the actual military campaign from a punitive raid on Gibeah to a full-blown war of annihilation.

20:12 ***messengers.*** As in Josh 22, despite what appeared to be overwhelming condemnatory evidence, the Israelites, though primed for battle, stopped to inquire, providing a chance for the accused tribe to rectify matters. Importantly, the only law regulating Israelite military action against another Israelite town, Deut 13:12-18, requires that any punitive military action against an Israelite town in which "men of *beliyya'al*" [TH1100, ZH1175] have inspired abominations be preceded by an inquiry and investigation. But that law demands a strenuous investigation, not the accusation of a single witness. Moreover, the law demands a sincere overture towards resolution, not the peremptory demand conveyed by the messengers here (Younger 2002:372). More importantly, the only offense for which the complete annihilation of an Israelite town is justified in the law of Deut 13 is a kind of pagan evangelism. Not merely the worship of other gods, but the dispatch of depraved heralds of idolatry who seduce other towns and villages into the worship of other gods. The actions of Gibeah were depraved beyond imagination. They do not, however, fall under the purview of this Deuteronomic sanction, which actually limits the reasons for which Israelites may consign one of their own towns to the ban. The narrator perhaps recognized this fact by never using the term *kherem* [TH2764, ZH3051] for the Israelite action against Gibeah, though it is used for the attack on Jabesh-gilead. Imposing the concept of *kherem* on the text when the author has so studiously avoided the term seems to miss the point (Younger 2002:371-372).

20:13 ***purge Israel of this evil.*** Lit., "burn out" the evil. This idiom is characteristic of Deuteronomy (Deut 13:5 [6]; 17:7, 12; 19:19; 21:21; 22:21-22, 24; 24:7). The Piel of *ba'ar* [TH1197, ZH1277] (to burn) conveys the causing of a condition or state (i.e., "to make burnt"), expressed commonly in English by means of a supplemental, dangling preposition: "burn out, burn up, burn down," etc. Alternately, some suggest a root *ba'ar* II [TH1197A, ZH1278], meaning "graze, sweep away," but this expedient seems unnecessary to account for this particular idiom. The Israelites here define the goal of their actions: to purge the nation of an evil, namely, the atrocious rape and murder of a helpless traveler.

the people of Benjamin would not listen. The text ascribes to Benjamin a response seen before in the story: "they were not willing." The verb appears only three other times in Judges, two of them in ch 19. The Levite "was not willing" to stay another night (19:10), and the men of Gibeah "were not willing" to assent to the host's offer (19:25).

20:14 ***Instead, they . . . gathered . . . to fight.*** While English style suggests a contrast here, the Hebrew uses the consecutive verbal form, placing this action on the same plane as their refusal of the messengers' admonition.

20:15 ***26,000 of their warriors armed with swords . . . 700 elite troops.*** As in 20:2, the stress on the preparedness of the Benjaminites for battle contrasts with the general observations in the book. But the Benjaminites had a particular reputation for an elite warrior culture. Ehud was a Benjaminite, and here even the city of Gibeah provides a home to 700 elite warriors, which might explain the hesitancy of the Levite's host to confront them. The presence of 700 elite fighters in the town suggests an atmosphere not unlike some of the towns attached to army camps in the "Wild West" era of the United States, where alcohol, gambling, prostitution, and conflict with knives or revolvers were the rule. Visitors in such towns might indeed fail to find traditional hospitality. However, the number 26,000, like the 400,000 of 20:2, seems excessive. Perhaps the number translated "thousand" refers instead to militia muster units, but was later taken by scribes as a literal number (see note on 8:10). Boling suggests "26 contingents, i.e., 700 troops" (1975:284-285; also Cundall 1968:199-200).

20:16 ***Among Benjamin's elite troops, 700 were left-handed.*** Likely the reference is to their being ambidextrous and identifies these fighters as members of an elite group (cf. note on 3:15). Possibly the tie to the story of Ehud, a judge who receives the author's strong approval, prompted the reader to observe the contrast: The Benjamin that in Ehud's time rallied the whole nation and led the way in heroism for Yahweh now stands in the defense of heinous depravity.

each of them could sling a rock and hit a target within a hairsbreadth without missing. The reference to these Benjaminite sinistral sharpshooters foreshadows the note in 1 Chr 12:1-2 that David was joined by a corps of ambidextrous slingers and archers who hailed from Gibeah of Benjamin.

20:17 ***experienced soldiers.*** The stress on "experienced soldiers" or lit., "men of war," continues the contrast between the battle-worthy men of chs 17–21 and the martially challenged Israelites of chs 1–16 who only prevailed because Yahweh fought on their behalf.

20:18 ***Before the battle the Israelites went to Bethel.*** The narrative is abrupt geographically. The author pointedly observed that the valid sanctuary (lit., the "house of God") stood at Shiloh (18:31). Mizpah seems to have had sacred standing as well, but now the Israelites go 3.5 miles north to Bethel. Given the author's tendency to use the premonarchic history as a transparency of sorts to comment on the northern kingdom, the link to Bethel possibly draws this northern royal sanctuary (1 Kgs 12:31-32) into the vortex of degeneracy, having just treated Dan, the other northern shrine, to scathing attack in chs 17–18.

asked God. Whenever the OT mentions the Israelites "asking God" or "inquiring of Yahweh," the reference is to the mechanical process of consulting an oracle. Normally this involved posing a question in binary form (i.e., a yes-no question), and then manipulating the oracle's elements, which functioned like sacred dice. For the question "which tribe?" a series of binary questions would be used (i.e., "should X go first?"). This is vital in the narrative, which alludes to divine speech, but always refers to a positive answer from the mechanical oracle. The open question is whether the oracle at this time really conveyed the true will of God. In the context of Israel's history of evil and apostasy in chs 1–16, including an idolatrous ephod (a device for consulting oracles) set up by Gideon, and the prostitution of the Levitical office in chs 17–18, combined with the evident corruption of the Levite in ch 19, it seems doubtful that the oracle would suddenly become a reliable source of divine revelation. Thus, the writer probably wants us to read positive answers to the oracle with a certain detachment. Unless direct divine intervention prevents it (as in 1 Sam 14:36-37; 28:6), a mechanical device will always "work" in that the indicators will produce some "reading" regardless of the worthiness of the inquirers. Thus, the writer allows even premonarchic Israel's means of discerning the divine will to become falsified.

Which tribe should go first to attack the people of Benjamin? All commentators note how this question resonates with the very first event of the book, when the Israelites ask the same question, worded almost identically. There, however, the named enemy is the Canaanites, here it is a tribe of Israel. Just as the Danites substituted a different conquest and territory for the one God assigned them, so here the Israelites launch a holy war, not against the enemies of God prescribed in Joshua, but against one of their own. More subtly, there the Israelites inquire of Yahweh (*yhwh* [TH3068, ZH3378]), but here they inquire of God (*'elohim* [TH430, ZH466]). In Judges these terms do not seem precisely interchangeable and may express the author's reservation about these proceedings (Block 1999:559).

Judah is to go first. As in the first inquiry at the book's beginning, Judah was given preeminence.

20:19-20 ***Israelites left . . . camped . . . advanced toward Gibeah to attack the men of Benjamin.*** The Hebrew has four verbs: "The Israelites arose . . . and encamped . . . and went out . . . and formed their battle ranks." The last verb, *'arak* [TH6186, ZH6885], indicates placing things in order, arraying things or people for their purpose, so the reader can envision the Israelites moving out, setting up camp, then moving to the staging area where they form up into their fighting units.

20:21 ***Benjamin's warriors . . . came out and killed 22,000 Israelites.*** The main verb in the sentence, *shakhath* [TH7843, ZH8845] (to become corrupt, to be spoiled), appears in the Hiphil stem 96 times in the OT. It frequently designates not merely killing, but utter ruination, annihilation, and destruction. The objects range from enemies, to the firstborn of Egypt in the Passover (Exod 12:23) to fruit trees chopped down during a siege (Deut 20:19-20). The verb's connotations of demolition and disfigurement add weight to the Benjaminite victory here. In this first engagement, so laboriously prepared for by the Israelites and so fulsomely described by the author, the Benjaminites summarily crushed them. Ironically, this particular word also frequently indicates the ruination of one's life or character (cf. Gen 6:12; Pss 14:1; 53:2; Zeph 3:7; HALOT s.v. *shakhath*; NIDOTTE 4.92-93). While we should resist the tendency to read into one occurrence of a word the senses it carries in other contexts, the peculiar nuances of the word that appear in all its usages certainly account for its use in a particular context. Also, in a text where the author seems to be carrying on at least two levels of discourse, narrating a past event in order to provoke thought about his contemporary context, and in which he refrains from overt judgments but crafts the narrative itself to shape the reader's response, a connotation of corruption in noting the Benjaminite victory might be present.

20:22 ***But the Israelites encouraged each other.*** The Hebrew construction is not disjunctive, but continues with the standard consecutive form. While the sense is that they acted in spite of the preceding defeat, the construction lends the narrative a forward propulsive momentum.

20:23 ***For they had gone up to Bethel.*** Why the Israelites duplicated their previous, catastrophically ineffective place and method of attack here finds explanation. Despite their filial grief at fighting their brother-tribe, expressed here for the first time, they prosecuted their war plan fortified once again by the oracle.

They had asked the LORD, "Should we fight against our relatives from Benjamin again?" And the LORD had said, "Go out and fight against them." That this is the result of a mechanical, divinatory inquiry and not the word of a prophet is vital to the story. The narrator is not stating that Yahweh actually gave his living word of commission, but simply that they turned the wheels or rolled the dice in Yahweh's name and the answer came up, "Yes."

20:25 ***killed.*** As in 20:21 (see note), "destroyed" or "annihilated" better renders the Hebrew.

18,000 Israelites. Combined with the previous defeat, the total of 40,000 fighters coincidentally matches the full force of Israel mentioned by Deborah (5:8). Also, the total now represents 10 percent of the force, the same proportion commissioned to supply the fighting force.

experienced with the sword. That such a disproportionately small force could so crushingly defeat the Israelites becomes more acute with this note that the casualties were seasoned fighters (see note on 20:2).

20:26 ***Then all the Israelites went up to Bethel and wept in the presence of the LORD and fasted until evening. They also brought burnt offerings and peace offerings to the LORD.*** The escalation of religious activity takes the form of empty ritual. As in 2:1-5, the Israelites take no cognizance of the nation's broken covenant with Yahweh, but engage in ritual lament and a very minor fast accompanied by offerings. Conspicuously lacking is the sin offering!

20:27 ***The Israelites went up seeking direction from the LORD.*** Lit., "the Israelites asked Yahweh," exactly as in 20:23.

In those days the Ark of the Covenant of God was in Bethel. This is the only reference to the Ark of the Covenant in the book of Judges. The author now widens the circle of religious damage by including the Ark. What is peculiar is that the "house of God" was in Shiloh (18:31), where it stood as the orthodox alternative over against the bogus shrine at Dan. So here, the reference to Bethel as the site of the Ark points to the highly irregular practices into which Israel had fallen. As will emerge in 1 Sam 4–6, one mark of the apostasy of the Israelites is their magical view of the Ark as providing automatic divine presence and protection in contrast to 2 Sam 6, which reveals the respect for the Ark and its proper handling that David learned. So the presence of the Ark here marks yet another sign of Israel's decadence. That the Ark is tarred with the same brush as the rest of the nation's decadence appears also in the use of "in those days," which coordinates it to Israel's kinglessness (cf. 17:6; 18:1; 19:1; 21:25). "In those days" also confirms that the Ark "lived" at Bethel, despite the fact that God's house was in Shiloh, underlining the religious chaos of the nation.

20:28 ***Phinehas son of Eleazar and grandson of Aaron was the priest.*** The name Phinehas is Egyptian (Boling 1975:286). Two issues impinge on the reference to Phinehas. First, until this point, Phinehas has had an unsullied reputation in the OT narrative. In his zeal for God, he skewered an idolatrous couple on a single spear and became a heroic figure for the priesthood (Num 25:1-13; Ps 106:28-31), even drawing Yahweh's "covenant of peace." He also participated in the war of annihilation against Midian (Num 31). Later, according to Josh 22, Phinehas led the party to punish the Transjordanian tribes for their deviant altar, but in this case, their explanation satisfies him and peace ensues (ABD 5.346-347). Phinehas became renowned in Jewish tradition for his zeal (cf. Sir 45:23-24). Phinehas's presence in this narrative possibly points to the presence of great zeal, but in the context of a nation completely off the rails and out of true communion with Yahweh. However great a man Phinehas was, zeal alone, without knowledge, could not help the nation. But a second issue surrounding Phinehas here is historical. If this is the same Phinehas seen in the stories cited above, then this event would be extremely early in Israel's history, and Phinehas likely would be quite old. The dating of the event, however, depends on the occupation and abandonment of Gibeah, which, if Tell el-Ful is the correct site (see note on 19:12), is complex since the Israelite occupation of Gibeah extends only from c. 1200 BC to about 1100 BC. The later chronology of the Exodus (1290–1270 BC) followed in this commentary would allow for an extremely old Phinehas. The traditional earlier date of 1446 BC would require Phinehas to be over 250 years old or would require seeking a wholly new site for Gibeah.

20:29 ***So the Israelites set an ambush all around Gibeah.*** Although fortified by an oracle, the Israelites did not adopt the same battle plan as before. Apparently the oracle alone was insufficient for actually addressing the problem, so the Israelites had to formulate their own battle plan. This need to add to the oracle's message an improvised solution of their own will become the principal emphasis of the next chapter.

20:31 ***When the men of Benjamin came out to attack, they were drawn away from the town.*** The story here bears a similarity to the battle against Ai in Josh 8, including the feint that drew the defenders out of the city, presumptuous of another easy victory (Josh 8:16).

along the roads, one leading to Bethel and the other leading back to Gibeah. The road here is the watershed ridge route. The Hebrew term *mesillah* [TH4546, ZH5019] denotes not a hardened footpath but a prepared roadbed, best rendered "highway" here and in 20:31-32 (Soggin 1981:296). The battle seems to have occurred north of Gibeah. The distances involved might be greater than a casual reading of the text suggests. From Gibeah to Bethel is about 7.5 miles. While any place north of Gibeah would allow this reference, the author actually speaks in the plural, of "roads," one of which goes to Bethel, the other to Gibeah. The natural spot to see these as two roads, not just segments of one, would be the major junction 3.5 miles north of Gibeah where the watershed ridge route crosses the major east–west route through Benjamin, which runs from Beth-horon in the west over the ridge down to Micmash in the east.

20:32 ***chase them along the roads.*** That the writer locates the actual pursuit by Benjamin on "roads" might suggest the intersection noted above as the scene of the battle. Not only was the Benjaminite force drawn well away from the city, it was divided as well, some on the east–west road, others on the north–south road.

20:33 ***reached Baal-tamar.*** The site of Baal-tamar remains uncertain, but would need to be located on the highway, north of Gibeah and south of Mizpah. Again, the intersection noted above might provide candidates for this location. If so, the Benjaminite force was over three miles from the city.

ambush . . . west of Gibeah. The NLT accepts an emendation of the text based on the LXX; it follows the reading *ma'arab* [TH4628, ZH5115] (west) instead of *ma'areh* [TH4629, ZH5116], of uncertain meaning. The Hebrew has Geba rather than the usual spelling for Gibeah, but the location is known from the next verse, which uses Gibeah. Ambushing Gibeah, at first sight, seems difficult given the town's commanding view of the whole field of fire, standing at 2,700 feet, about 100–150 feet higher than the surrounding terrain. Every site, however, has blind spots, and the occupants of Gibeah assumed an easy victory. The complacency and absence of defenders trumps the high ground.

jumped up to fight. Lit., "gushed forth" (*megiakh* [TH1518, ZH1631]), typically used of waters gushing from a spring, a dramatic image of the Israelite ambush exploding into action.

20:35 *the LORD helped Israel defeat Benjamin.* Lit., "Yahweh struck Benjamin before Israel." This line is the only point in the story where Yahweh appears actively involved and not merely associated with a mechanical operation of divination. Still, the victory clearly derives from the stratagem employed by the Israelites, and other than this statement, no action is attributed to Yahweh. Given the oracle's word to attack, perhaps the victory's attribution to Yahweh is more formal than actual.

killed. This is the same verb used for Benjamin's earlier defeats of Israel (20:21, 25). The narrative returns to ascribing all the actions to the human actors. This statement also might refer to more than the casualties outside the city. The narrator frequently summarizes what is to come and then provides flashbacks on what preceded.

25,100 of Benjamin's warriors. The numbers in the story are hard to add up. The text stresses 600 fighters remain from Benjamin, but starting with the 26,700 noted earlier, it would appear that 1,600 remain at this point. These warriors will become the central focus of the narrative in the next chapter, continuing the pattern in which the solution to one problem generates a new problem. These 600 Benjaminite men will need wives.

20:37 *those who were hiding rushed in from all sides and killed everyone in the town.* This is the action that specifically redressed the atrocity perpetrated in Gibeah. Ironically, no notice is taken at all of the deed that triggered the war. Neither the author nor the characters comment that the annihilation of the occupants of Gibeah expunged the evil of the woman's horrible murder from Israel. The Judahite woman's abuse is thus complete, for she is not even remembered when her suffering is supposedly avenged. The pious sentiments expressed in 20:1-2, 13 find no acknowledgment when the city actually pays for its wickedness.

20:39 *When the Israelites saw the smoke, they turned and attacked Benjamin's warriors.* This statement demonstrates that the report of 26,100 casualties above was anticipatory. In what follows, the writer repeats what had happened with more details. Nineteenth-century and early twentieth-century biblical scholars found this repetition intolerable and argued that two accounts of the battle had been merged, with only imperfect harmonization of the details. Ancient Near Eastern battle accounts, however, often repeat themselves. A notable example is the battle speech by the goddess Tiamat in the Babylonian creation story known as *Enuma Elish*. Tiamat gives a speech in Tablet I, lines 130-154, which is then substantially repeated in Tablet II, lines 15-48 and in Tablet III, lines 20-52, only to appear a fourth time in Tablet III, lines 75-110! (cf. COS 1.111:392-396). In addition, the storyteller might be taking delight in the discomfiture of the Benjaminites who were, after all, taking their stand with Gibeah and the men who perpetrated the homicidal rape of the concubine. The author, or the teller of the original oral story, might well have savored the terror of the Benjaminites, struck outside their city as the woman was heinously abused outside the safety of her host's home. Her terror remained unexpressed in the text, but the Benjaminites' terror is clear in the verses to follow.

20:40 ***smoke rising into the sky from every part of the town.*** This reference to burning leads interpreters to conclude the city was destroyed by fire. The Hebrew certainly suggests a large fire, lit., "the whole city went up into the sky." The term *kalil* [TH3632B, ZH4003] was taken to mean "holocaust" by early modern exegetes who also saw that sense in Deut 13:17, but contemporary translators stick with "the whole city." The NLT wisely recognizes that the reference could be to fires set all around the city rather than the whole city being on fire. At this point, the city had not been entered by Israelite fighters and so could not be entirely torched. Whether the text claims the city was actually destroyed by fire affects how one construes the archaeological data. Evidence of a destruction by fire at the site is scanty, though signs of abandonment are clear. Any time archaeological data and the Bible are correlated, the interpreter must be sure the biblical statements are assessed precisely.

20:42 ***they couldn't escape the battle.*** The Hebrew is picturesque: "the battle got stuck to them." The verb in its concrete contexts refers to physical adhering or adhesion. In relational contexts it designates a profound, uniting mutual obligation as when a man "sticks" to his wife so that they become one flesh (Gen 2:24). In military contexts, the term indicates the moment in which pursuit overtakes the pursued, or pursuit in constant contact with the pursued (NIDOTTE 1.910-912). Thus, here the Benjaminites, in hard retreat, could not break contact with the Israelites, who continued to press the fight.

20:43 ***The Israelites surrounded the men of Benjamin and chased them relentlessly, finally overtaking them east of Gibeah.*** The NLT makes the best of a very difficult line. Lit., "the Israelites surrounded Benjamin, they made (one) pursue him, rest, they trod him down unto opposite Gibeah to the east." The word "rest" simply hangs in the text, but might mean "a resting place" or simply, a stopping place on the road (Cundall 1968:207). It could name the place where the Israelites "trod down" or "stomped" Benjamin. Additionally, "surrounded" (*katar* [TH3803A, ZH4193]) is rendered as "cut to pieces" in the LXX, suggesting *kathath* [TH3807, ZH4198], an easy scribal slip.

20:45 ***the rock of Rimmon.*** Most scholars identify this as the modern village of Rammun, located about four miles east of Bethel, and thus a bit over eight miles northeast of Gibeah along an alternate eastern branch of the watershed ridge road that runs there through Geba and Micmash (ABD 5.773-774). The first half of this route crosses two deep ravines and would be a hard road for a discomfited force, providing the Israelites many chances to strike the retreating Benjaminite force. Rimmon also means "pomegranate" in Hebrew. The same rock provides shelter for, coincidentally, 600 troops with Saul (cf. 1 Sam 13:15; 14:2 ["pomegranate tree"]).

but Israel killed 5,000 of them along the road. The NLT misses a vital connection between this account and the atrocity of the preceding chapter. There, the verb *'alal* [TH5953, ZH6618] (glean, go over again) in the Hithpael stem described the repeated assault on the woman (19:25). Here, the same verb is used in a different stem to indicate the Israelites' overtaking and killing the fleeing Benjaminite warriors.

20:46 ***that day the tribe of Benjamin lost 25,000 strong warriors armed with swords.*** For some reason the numbers do not add up consistently. The total soldiers from 20:15-16 was 26,700. Then 20:35 gives the number of deaths as 25,100, which would have left 1,600. Then the writer itemizes the casualties, coming up with 25,000, still noting that 600 survived. Clearly we must see some of these numbers as round, very round in fact! The 600 seems firm enough given its role in the story to follow, but the earlier numbers might well be approximations, or problems in the actual transmission of the text could be at work.

20:47 ***where they lived for four months.*** Coincidentally, and perhaps ironically, this is the same period of time the Levite waited before seeking out his alienated concubine (19:2-3). Like the concubine, the 600 survivors will need persuading to leave their refuge (21:13).

20:48 ***burned down all the towns.*** The NLT overstates the case with "burned down." The Hebrew idiom, *shalakh ba'esh* [TH7971/784, ZH8938/836], also appears in 1:8, where the NLT more accurately renders it as "setting the city on fire." The rampage that follows points to the reality that things were quite out of control. Gibeah was punished, and nearly all the fighting men, the leading men, of Benjamin were dead on the field of battle. Nothing in the previous legal proceedings or narrative prepares the reader for this campaign of terror and destruction through the Benjaminite countryside. Indeed, it is this final outrage, not the earlier battle, which precipitates the crisis of ch 21, namely, the near annihilation of Benjamin. Prior to 20:48, the remaining Benjaminite men could have found women to marry throughout their towns. Ironically, the Israelites had sought to "burn out the evil," or purge the evil from the land (see note on 20:13). But the burning spread from Gibeah in the terroristic and incendiary rampage of the victorious fighters through Benjamin.

COMMENTARY

The landslide that began with the small pebble of the Levite's marital dispute, that grew into a crime with the woman's violation, and became a national scandal with her dismemberment, occasioned a full, formal, sacred convocation of the leaders and people. Fighting men got equipped for battle with a determination that none would go home until the matter was settled. However proper this might seem on the surface, certain signs foretold that this affair would spin out of control (contra Block 1999:549-552), even as it opened in 20:1-2.

First, the Israelites showed unprecedented unity. For the entire book of Judges, the tribes have shown little inclination to unite—as the Song of Deborah, Gideon's disputes with the east Jordan cities, and the Judeans' betrayal of Samson indicated (to cite but three examples). Against the enemies oppressing them, they found little unity, but against one of their own tribes, they come together almost spontaneously "as one man." Second, the Israelites of chapters 1–16 display a singular inadequacy in discipline and equipment for warfare. But like the Danites—who retreated from their foes in 1:34-35 but threatened Micah's household and slaughtered the inhabitants of Laish—the Israelites here appear organized and armed to the teeth, focused on battle. Third, for the first time in the book, the Israelites appear to identify themselves collectively in a religious manner, as the congregation or assembly, the people of God. Previously, they had behaved as almost anything but that sacred assembly; now, suddenly, everyone appears ready to do the Lord's business. All this occurs at the behest of a single, unnamed Levite and his grotesquely publicized grievance.

The essence of the story turns on the fact that despite the heinous evil that was done to the woman by the men of Gibeah, Israel ignored every essential principle of justice and warfare in this narrative. A single witness, speaking without support from any other witnesses, who was not even interrogated for more details, sent the whole congregation into a rage. Without any further investigation, they presented an ultimatum to Benjamin, convicting the men of Gibeah without any chance of defense. The reader, of course, knows the crime and its guilt is real, but also knows that the circle of guilt, or at least responsibility, is broader than the Levite claims.

Moreover, the crime, horrible as it was, did not merit a war of extermination, though some severe action would be justified. Finally, after Gibeah was totally defeated and torched, the Israelites went on a wild rampage through Benjamin not unlike the uncontrolled behavior of the mob in chapter 19. Ironically, Judges began by criticizing Israel for not fully driving out the Canaanites, but in this story, they very nearly exterminated one of their own tribes. It is this final action that produces the problem addressed in chapter 21, the lack of wives for the Benjaminites, which leads to the climactic outrages of the book.

A critical issue in chapter 20 is how the various aspects and mechanisms of Israelite religion go awry when the community using them is decadent. The author saturates the opening verses with terms denoting Israel as a sacred congregation. The sacred assembly in Israel should have been a setting of worship in which Yahweh's will was proclaimed and his blessing sought. Instead, this session convened with not a word said about Yahweh by any of the characters. The narrator noted that the Israelites assembled "to Yahweh," and the curious, rare phrase "people of God" occurs, but what follows is more like a town meeting with nothing said about Yahweh, his covenant, his law, or Israel's common life as his people. No prayers are said, no sacrifices or offerings given, no appeals made to Yahweh's expectations for his people. Given that the complainant is a Levite, this utter lack of any sign from the characters that they serve Yahweh starkly signals not the paganization of Israel, but the utter godlessness of Israel, even when met in sacred counsel. Moreover, the question remains: Is the crisis of one man, however heinous, worthy of being the sole agenda item of the only convening of the sacred assembly reported in the book of Judges, especially when, as Block has shown, this man has only told half the truth about the crime that concerns him (1999:552-555; also Boling 1975:283)?

Contemporary Christians could ponder the extent to which the holy business of the church and the Kingdom often proceed largely in a secular manner, not much different from any other business or service organization. A strong theology of creation certainly authorizes the use of natural gifts, prudence, good information, thoughtful reflection, and human resources. None of this, however, has independent status apart from the stewardship required by God's Word. Christian collective action requires more than merely information and a plan that sounds good. The church first and always stands as a witness to the word of its God, revealed through God's history of redemption that culminates in Christ and is distilled in the pages of Scripture. Any Christian undertaking should embody and evidence an integral passion to honor God and his will as revealed in his word. This honoring will not be simply the plastering of some religious jargon on a basically godless process, but will involve processes of collective decision-making ordered from their fundamental assumptions, through their deliberative procedures, all the way to their outcomes, as a conscious implementation of the whole counsel of God.

The principle just described especially applies to conflict resolution. Some Christian institutions go about resolving disputes of employment, compensation, employee misconduct, and gender-related conflicts not by first seeking to implement an intentionally Christian and biblical approach to relationships, but by operating generally like the secular world, perhaps with a religious preface to the policy and a devotional peroration at the end. But the essence of the organizational plan and process adheres to secular principles. Many employees of Christian institutions have found themselves in conflicts with others in the institution, sometimes across gender lines, that could be honorably and Christianly resolved by face-to-face, honest conversation about all the facts and perceptions with a trusted and wise counselor present. But sometimes institutions adopt a secular, zero-tolerance policy and move immediately to adversarial approaches that preclude from the start even a full and fair airing of the facts, let alone any hope of reconciliation. The Levite's partial, edited version of the story of a ghastly wrong galvanized the nation into a war of annihilation against one of their own, contrary to their principles of justice and warfare. Similarly, Christian communities, in their empathy with the victim, sometimes fail to probe the truth of a complaint and risk believing a partial account and moving immediately to draconian punitive actions.

Secular principles that actually impede face-to-face personal reconciliation thus destroy the lives of many in Christian organizations who perhaps might have been foolish, or might have genuinely needed discipline, but who find themselves stripped of their dignity, their employment, and their hope of future service, perhaps on the evidence of one prejudiced witness such as the Levite of this story. In the lives of persons ruined by the secular, quasi-legal conflict resolution policies of some Christian organizations, the smoking villages of Benjamin may be dimly seen. Like the Levite in the story, the original lone accuser often vanishes, abdicating any potentially redemptive actions.

By the same token, many individual Christian professionals, like the Levite in this account, conduct their lives and resolve their conflicts according to the customary practices of their environment rather than adopting an intentionally Christian approach to their conduct. Of all people, the Levite, who bore the custodianship of the covenant as his tribal heritage, should have been the voice of covenant fidelity, notwithstanding his injury. But he set all that aside and pursued ruthless tribal justice. The real test of faith for individuals and organizations comes when they are tempted to set aside their biblical values and resort to secular, godless approaches to their crises. Then, when matters become intolerable, the trappings of religion come out as in the Israelites' recourse to fasting and sacrifice before the Ark after two defeats.

Another sacred tradition the Israelites are shown eviscerating in chapter 20 is the oracle, or sacred lot, by which they enmesh the means of Yahweh's revelation with their catastrophic actions. Following on their completely godless decision to go to battle, their turning to the oracle again after a smashing defeat smacks of hypocrisy. In fact, this oracle was not a live prophetic voice but a mere divinatory technique with its required equipment. It always "worked" in that some kind of answer would always emerge (see note on 20:18). The Israelites' own filial emotions told them that they should not be fighting their brother tribe, and indeed, were they aware of Deuteronomy 13:12-18, they would have known this crisis did not, in fact, warrant warfare against an Israelite town. This law authorizes such actions solely in cases of a city not only worshiping other gods, but seducing other Israelite communities to do so as well. The l-aw of Moses notwithstanding, the oracle came up "yes," in answer to the question of whether to battle with Benjamin again. The Ark appears in Judges only one time, in the final consultation of the oracle. Ironically, the Ark was held to contain the tablets of the covenant (e.g., Exod 40:20), but for the Israelites of chapter 20, it functions as a mere religious talisman. The Ark as a symbol meant more to them than the written Word of God it contained.

For believers today, the Bible, God's word of revelation, can likewise become a source of grief and pain. When one reads the Bible with a pure heart and open mind, and the Spirit of Jesus animating them, its truths, even the hard ones, bring life even if the answers given are severe. But when read by one whose life swings completely out of plumb, where all the values are upside down, the truths of the Bible can become energies of death. No matter how high the confidence placed in Scripture's veracity, no matter how correct the hermeneutic, nor how learned the interpreter, the truths of Scripture can be distorted and misapplied by self-centered readers. Hearing God speak through his ordained means of revelation can never become a mechanical process of mere manipulation and extraction, but must also be an intent, faithful listening. The two truths about Scripture that always stand together are that God's means of revelation are objectively true (i.e., their truth stands prior to and independent of our knowledge of them) and that at the same time, the specific form that truth must take for a particular reader requires that God's objective truth in his word never be separated from his living presence and voice among his obedient people. Far from being an "either-or" between objective truth and its cultural forms, the relationship must always be a "both-and." One without the other births catastrophe.

The history of the church bleeds with stories where, in the name of biblical truth, cruel and corrupt leaders perpetrated heinous acts, such as the drowning of Anabaptists in Europe or the beheadings for minor deviations from orthodox Protestantism in the English Reformation. No era or communion can claim pure hands at this point. Scripture is true, but are its readers? Unless the Bible is allowed to transform the reader, purifying the heart and orienting the reader to God's highest purposes, seen in Christ and his love for a lost world, its "truths" will produce division and death. By the same token, the history of the church provides many examples of Christians so attuned to the need to hear God's living voice by the Spirit that they separate this experience from the moorings of God's unchanging truth. This error, traditionally called "enthusiasm" or Montanism (after an early church heresy), can breed relativism and violence as easily as its counterpart. Just how desperate a situation results from disconnecting the means of divine revelation from a living, obedient faith will emerge in the final chapter of Judges.

Finally, the story of chapter 20 reveals the bankruptcy of blind force and violence. While Yahweh does indeed sanction violent acts in the Old Testament, their most impressive feature is not their ferocity—all ancient cultures practiced total war—but the limitations imposed. Israelite laws of war placed boundaries around its practice and required that the community itself be purified by its covenant with God before taking up the use of force. Deuteronomy 20 legislates a surprising set of exemptions from service in war, as well as limits on the use of force. Israel was called to limits in the destruction of trees, the taking of spoil, and the treatment of captives when compared to the practices of Israel's neighbors. One cannot imagine an ancient pharaoh or Assyrian tyrant subjecting his own military practices to any limitations. Judges 20 portrays the bastardization of Israelite warfare. A total war is levied against an Israelite town for reasons that fall short of any known justifications in the Old Testament for acting against another Israelite town. The presence of Phinehas (20:28), the old zealot from the previous generation, underlines that zeal, however commendable, cannot change the essential character of the Israelite action. They won, but in winning, they lost. The uncontrolled rampage that concludes the story (20:48) demonstrates the true character of this undertaking.

In stark contrast to this story stands the little book of Ruth, also set in the time of the judges. It tells how Elimelech, during a famine, abandoned his inheritance in Bethlehem and took his wife and sons to the plains of Moab, where his sons, contrary to Israelite tradition, married Moabite women. Then all three men died. No doubt, the Israelites of chapter 20 would say these women had it coming: They broke the rule, they paid the price. But the book of Ruth unfolds a story where every character chooses fidelity, mercy, responsibility, and integrity. Superficially, some improper things happen: A Moabite woman marries an Israelite town elder. A land transaction has to be finessed due to a mistake in identifying the kinsman-redeemer. But somehow, the moral and spiritual environment dominating the book of Ruth moderates the negative implications of every action that falls short of perfection, and accentuates many times over the deeds of fidelity and compassion that fill the book. Despite several eccentric deeds, the fundamental spirit of biblical covenant law is faithfully honored. The Bethlehem of Ruth, though not a perfect community, stands as the polar opposite of both Gibeah and the Israelite congregation. As a result, every character in the book finds redemption and integration into the community. When lives are fundamentally inclined to honoring God, sins and shortcomings do not rule the day, but grace and integrity shine brilliantly. Of course, the author of Judges gestures repeatedly at Davidic motifs as the alternative to the amoral, godless chaos that enveloped the nation, and Ruth's story of integrity's triumph culminates in introducing the house and lineage of David.

◆ 3. Israel provides wives for Benjamin (21:1-25)

The Israelites had vowed at Mizpah, "We
will never give our daughters in marriage
to a man from the tribe of Benjamin."
2Now the people went to Bethel and sat
in the presence of God until evening,
weeping loudly and bitterly. 3"O LORD, God
of Israel," they cried out, "why has this
happened in Israel? Now one of our tribes
is missing from Israel!"
4Early the next morning the people
built an altar and presented their burnt
offerings and peace offerings on it.
5Then they said, "Who among the tribes
of Israel did not join us at Mizpah when
we held our assembly in the presence of
the LORD?" At that time they had taken a
solemn oath in the LORD's presence, vowing that anyone who refused to come
would be put to death.
6The Israelites felt sorry for their brother Benjamin and said, "Today one of the
tribes of Israel has been cut off. 7How can
we find wives for the few who remain,
since we have sworn by the LORD not to
give them our daughters in marriage?"
8So they asked, "Who among the tribes

of Israel did not join us at Mizpah when we assembled in the presence of the LORD?" And they discovered that no one from Jabesh-gilead had attended the assembly. 9For after they counted all the people, no one from Jabesh-gilead was present.

10So the assembly sent 12,000 of their best warriors to Jabesh-gilead with orders to kill everyone there, including women and children. 11"This is what you are to do," they said. "Completely destroy* all the males and every woman who is not a virgin." 12Among the residents of Jabesh-gilead they found 400 young virgins who had never slept with a man, and they brought them to the camp at Shiloh in the land of Canaan.

13The Israelite assembly sent a peace delegation to the remaining people of Benjamin who were living at the rock of Rimmon. 14Then the men of Benjamin returned to their homes, and the 400 women of Jabesh-gilead who had been spared were given to them as wives. But there were not enough women for all of them.

15The people felt sorry for Benjamin because the LORD had made this gap among the tribes of Israel. 16So the elders of the assembly asked, "How can we find wives for the few who remain, since the women of the tribe of Benjamin are dead? 17There must be heirs for the survivors so that an entire tribe of Israel is not wiped out. 18But we cannot give them our own daughters in marriage because we have sworn with a solemn oath that anyone who does this will fall under God's curse."

19Then they thought of the annual festival of the LORD held in Shiloh, south of Lebonah and north of Bethel, along the east side of the road that goes from Bethel to Shechem. 20They told the men of Benjamin who still needed wives, "Go and hide in the vineyards. 21When you see the young women of Shiloh come out for their dances, rush out from the vineyards, and each of you can take one of them home to the land of Benjamin to be your wife! 22And when their fathers and brothers come to us in protest, we will tell them, 'Please be sympathetic. Let them have your daughters, for we didn't find wives for all of them when we destroyed Jabesh-gilead. And you are not guilty of breaking the vow since you did not actually give your daughters to them in marriage.' "

23So the men of Benjamin did as they were told. Each man caught one of the women as she danced in the celebration and carried her off to be his wife. They returned to their own land, and they rebuilt their towns and lived in them.

24Then the people of Israel departed by tribes and families, and they returned to their own homes.

25In those days Israel had no king; all the people did whatever seemed right in their own eyes.

21:11 The Hebrew term used here refers to the complete consecration of things or people to the LORD, either by destroying them or by giving them as an offering.

NOTES

21:1 ***The Israelites had vowed at Mizpah.*** The story now mentions a fact about the Mizpah convocation (20:1-17) that was not reported in the original narrative. That a vow provides the pressure for the final act of Judges underscores the theme that "everyone did what was right in his own eyes," since vows were completely voluntary. The Israelites, in the rash zeal inspired by the Levite's unexamined, unconfirmed testimony, undertook a vow that would lead to carnage. The resonance with Jephthah's rash vow (11:30-31) is unmistakable.

We will never give our daughters in marriage to a man from the tribe of Benjamin. Presumably the purpose of this vow was to deny the Benjaminites wives, even though this entire final chapter will detail their efforts to provide wives, without having to be responsible themselves for any marriages to Benjaminites. Ironically, the Israelites who, according to 3:5-6, readily intermarried with Canaanites, had vowed not to intermarry with another Israelite tribe (Block 1999:569). Sociologists suggest that in many cultures, relationships among men—economic and social—were created and sustained principally by the exchange of women. To terminate this exchange would deprive those communities of those beneficial relationships (Niditch 2008:208-209). While this "traffic in women" likely often took the form of mutually agreeable marriages in which male leaders mediated appropriate relationships, the women in ch 21 are voiceless victims, used to alleviate the conflict of men who had unwisely broken off that traffic with another group. And a costly, tragic traffic it turns out to be.

21:2 ***Now the people went to Bethel.*** Just as Dan (later, a royal sanctuary for the northern kingdom) dominated the story in chs 17–18, so Bethel, the other site that became a royal shrine in the northern kingdom, imposes itself on chs 19–21, recapitulating its role in the book's introduction (1:22-26; 2:1-5).

weeping loudly and bitterly. In Judges, weeping accompanies ritual activity at Bethel. The Israelites wept at Bethel (called Bokim in 2:1-5) after hearing the divine rebuke for their compromise of the conquest mandate. The Israelites wept again at Bethel after hard losses before the Benjaminite forces (20:23, 26). Block rightly notes that no tears are shed here over Israel's sins or spiritual condition (1999:570).

21:3 ***"O LORD, God of Israel," they cried out, "why has this happened in Israel?"*** The question baffles all sense. The Israelites themselves have perpetrated the very situation they lament, taking every step deliberately, sometimes claiming divine approval for their actions. Though they cried to God, no answer was forthcoming. Yahweh had fallen silent, despite Israel's obsessive religious fervor (Boling 1975:291).

one of our tribes is missing from Israel! "Missing" translates the Niphal of *paqad* [TH6485, ZH7212], a verb with a broad semantic range. Here the point is not simply that a tribe is missing, but rather that they are missed (i.e., their absence is noticed and felt; cf. NIDOTTE 3.657-663).

21:4 ***Early the next morning the people built an altar.*** Having just offered sacrifices at Bethel (20:26), their construction of an altar seems strange. After entering the land, Israel was not to construct altars anywhere they wished (Deut 12) but only at the site where Yahweh placed his name. Even the more liberal law in Exod 20:24 only allowed construction of an altar where Yahweh commemorated his name. More importantly, the law in Deut 12:5-9 explicitly contrasts the stable location of the sanctuary after the settlement with the prior practice, described as "each doing what was right in his own eyes," the identical formulation found in 17:6 and 21:25, the only other places this idiom appears in this form. The author has already identified Shiloh as the valid sanctuary in contrast with Dan (18:31), and now the only explicit link to Deuteronomy's centralization law in Judges comes at this climactic moment to delegitimize the Bethel practice.

presented their burnt offerings and peace offerings on it. As with 20:26, the Israelites conspicuously omit sin or guilt offerings from their illegitimate worship.

21:5 ***Then they said.*** There is no sign that God has given any guidance. The Israelites' manipulation of the mechanisms of their religion finally brought them to a point where they must simply make up a course of action.

Who among the tribes of Israel did not join us at Mizpah? Apparently failing to find an answer after appealing to God, the people hunt for anyone who neglected to attend the solemn tribal assembly (Niditch 2008:209). The narrator's description of the assembly in 20:1-11 stresses that all Israel, all the tribes, elders, and people were in fact represented, but ironically, it ends up that those who were most needed to help Israel out of the jam in which they have placed themselves are those who neglected the great assembly at Mizpah!

they had taken a solemn oath in the LORD's presence, vowing that anyone who refused to come would be put to death. This was a second voluntary oath that seemed like a good idea at the time and was not reported in ch 20. This oath and the one reported in 21:1 control the episodes that follow. The assembly in ch 20 emerges more and more as a horrible mistake since one vow taken there must be employed to negate the effects of the other vow taken on the same occasion.

21:6 ***The Israelites felt sorry.*** The two vignettes with which the book closes each begin with reference to Israel's pity on Benjamin (21:15). This pity, following so hard on their uncontrolled rage and ungoverned destruction of the self-same tribe, points to their utter moral and spiritual cluelessness. Though utterly self-centered, they could not see their fatally contradicted state. Thus, they experienced remorse, not repentance.

cut off. The verb *gada'* [TH1438, ZH1548] also forms the basis of the name Gideon, offering a possible resonance with another story in the book since the verb itself appears nowhere else in the book (Block 1999:572). The term is more forceful than merely "cut off"; it is better rendered with "lopped off, chopped off" (Burney 1920:489).

21:7 ***How can we find wives for the few who remain, since we have sworn by the LORD not to give them our daughters in marriage?*** The same question follows the Israelite's second expression of pity (21:16), which also goes on to cite the "not my daughter!" vow (21:17-18).

21:8 ***Jabesh-gilead.*** Apart from this story, the town figures centrally and exclusively in the story of Saul, thus continuing the author's habit of linking decadent Israel in various subtle ways to the kingship of Saul (Burney 1920:490; cf. 1 Sam 11; 31:11-13). Jabesh-gilead lay somewhere along the Wadi el-Yabis, which empties from the east into the Jordan River about two miles south of the Sea of Galilee. Tell Maqlub, up the wadi, about six miles east of the Jordan, possesses Iron Age I remains and is a likely site for Jabesh-gilead. Ancient roads, like modern ones, crossed the wadi at this strategic location (ABD 3.594-595).

21:9 ***For after they counted all the people, no one from Jabesh-gilead was present.*** This detail, the roll call of the assembly, did not appear in ch 20, adding to the impression of unfolding, unforeseen consequences issuing from a series of impulsive and imprudent actions taken at that assembly. Moreover, given the utterly improper and illegitimate nature of that assembly, perhaps the citizens of Jabesh-gilead sat out the meeting because they wanted nothing to do with the hasty rage contemplated there. Their dissident position would inspire resentment by those who attended and participated in the travesty of tribal justice perpetrated in ch 20. The supreme irony resides in the fact that, having not attended the assembly, the men of Jabesh-gilead had likewise not taken the oath, and so were perfectly free to give their daughters to the men of Benjamin had a proper series of marriage negotiations taken place. Some negotiation might have provided a suitable explanation for their absence, allowing for a more humane outcome. Such was not on the minds of the Israelite leaders.

21:10 ***So the assembly sent 12,000 of their best warriors to Jabesh-gilead with orders to kill everyone there, including women and children.*** The casual manner in which the extermination of Israelite men, wives, mothers, sons, and daughters is ordered takes a step past the haste and rage of ch 20. At least there divine moral standards could be cited as a pretext for their unwarranted and unsanctioned war. But the death order for Jabesh-gilead derives from an arbitrary vow impulsively taken by the nation.

21:11 ***Completely destroy.*** Only twice in Judges does the author use verbs from this root (*kh-r-m* [TH2763, ZH3049]), traditionally translated "put to the ban, totally destroy." In fact, the verb denotes essentially the total devotion of something to Yahweh such that it can be used for no other purpose. While this radical consignment to Yahweh often takes the form of destruction, it need not always imply it. Total devotion is the key. Here, however, it carries the meaning of utter destruction even though all signs of devotion to Yahweh are absent! Rather than proving that the word simply means "totally destroy," the usage here points to the complete separation of the institution of *kherem* from any vital recognition of Yahweh. The victims are exterminated, but no dimension of devotion to Yahweh appears.

all the males and every woman who is not a virgin. The delicacy of the word choice should not prevent the reader from realizing that they are talking about the wholesale slaughter of Israelite women and men of all ages, whose only crime was their absence from an assembly that should not have occurred at all and that bore only bitter fruit.

21:12 ***young virgins who had never slept with a man.*** The text piles up the phrases by which female virginity may be indicated: "virgin" (*bethulah* [TH1330, ZH1435]), "who had not known a man," (*'asher lo' yada'ah 'ish* [TH3045, ZH3359]) and "to the bed of a male," which translates *lemishkab zakar* [TH4904, ZH5435]. The term "bed" derives its potential for sexual nuance from the use of the verb *shakab* [TH7901, ZH8886] (to lie) as a polite idiom for sexual intercourse (cf. Num 31:17-18, 35). The term appears also in prohibitions of homosexual activity in which "the bed of a woman" carries the sense "the way one lies with a woman" (Lev 18:22; 20:13). The focus on these virgins links this story to that of Jephthah and his daughter, another virgin (*bethulah*) who had not "known a man" and whose life changed irrevocably because of a vow that never should have been made by the dominant man in her life (11:37-40).

the camp at Shiloh. The setting unaccountably shifts from Bethel (21:2) to Shiloh. However awkward for the plot's flow, the shift foreshadows the action at the end of the chapter, which occurs at Shiloh. More importantly, the author held up Shiloh as the legitimate alternative to Dan in 18:31. This note cast a shadow over the references to Bethel, and indeed, all other sacred sites in chs 19–20. With every other sacred institution of Israel now stained by the self-willed, arrogant actions of the Israelites—the assembly, the oracle, the Ark, Phinehas, warfare traditions, even Moses (cf. 18:30)—the author now shows the careening nation's sights fixing on the last bastion of orthodoxy, Shiloh.

in the land of Canaan. This description of Shiloh's location is puzzling if Shiloh were already an Israelite sanctuary, which the book does indeed assume. "Land of Canaan" might have been the proper name of the region in political speech, but could also simply refer to the land west of the Jordan (Burney 1920:491). The reference cannot be to the Shiloh region still being a "Canaanite enclave" (Cundall 1968:212) since archaeological evidence strongly points to it being a center for many new Israelite villages (see note on 21:19). Reference to Canaan is infrequent in Judges, clustering principally in the first chapter, where it appears 17 times. The mention of Canaan here might form an inclusio. More likely, by labeling the environs of Shiloh as "in the land of Canaan," the author might intend a biting satire: Israel is little different from Canaan, and the difference might be to Canaan's favor (Boling 1975:293; Block 1999:576-577).

21:13 ***the remaining people of Benjamin.*** "People" should be "men" or simply "Benjaminites" since the story turns on the absence of Benjaminite women.

21:14 ***the 400 women . . . were given to them as wives.*** To slaughter a young woman's family and capture her, drag her to another place, then force her to marry a man she has never met, might not be as appalling a fate as the one suffered by the concubine in ch 19, but it certainly entails a monstrous violation. The women, still grieving their slaughtered parents, brothers and sisters, and other relatives, were stripped of all familial identity only to face a compulsory marriage. The alacrity with which the Israelites dispose of these young women's past and future comes remarkably close in spirit to the coldness of the Levite, equally unmoved by his concubine's suffering.

there were not enough women for all of them. A shortage of victims only obstructs the Israelites for a moment. Following the pattern of the story, every "solution" creates a problem, and here the extermination of Jabesh-gilead still did not provide enough wives for all the Benjaminites, leading to the final plan that will carry the willful moral arrogance of the Israelites right onto their most hallowed ground, the home of the Tabernacle, Shiloh.

21:15 ***The people felt sorry for Benjamin.*** The final episode is launched by a second fit of Israelite pity for Benjamin. Given the appalling results of their first pity-motivated plan, the reader truly fears what might happen next. The Benjaminites, originally set up as the bad guys, are now the only persons for whom the Israelites seem to feel sorry.

the LORD had made this gap. Amazingly, the crisis resulted wholly from the Israelites "doing what was right in their own eyes." Nevertheless, the author either attributed the events to Yahweh's action, or he was reflecting the perceptions of the Israelites, who had already implicitly blamed Yahweh for the near extermination of the Benjaminites, though it resulted from their military campaign and overzealous vows (Block 1999:573).

21:16 ***the women of the tribe of Benjamin are dead.*** The killing of the women appears especially heinous. Deuteronomy had even protected the mother bird from the hunter when a bird's nest falls to the ground (Deut 22:6-7), but Israel heedlessly slaughtered all the women of Benjamin, and many more at Jabesh-gilead. "Dead" translates *nishmedah* [TH8045, ZH9012], "are destroyed, wiped out." More tellingly, by adopting a passive form instead of saying, "whom we destroyed," the elders engage in exactly the kind of evasive narration that characterized the Levite in 20:4-7.

21:17 ***heirs.*** Heb., *yerushah* [TH3425, ZH3772]; it seems to refer to the thing possessed, referring in other places to the Transjordan territory, which is the possession of Gad, Reuben, and Manasseh (Josh 1:15; 12:6-7), or to the lands possessed by the Edomites and Moabites (Deut 2:5, 9, 19; 3:20). The term might indeed mean "hereditary possession," but still denotes the thing possessed, not the possessors, so that "heirs" should be corrected (Soggin 1981:299). The crisis intertwines two distinct issues. Without wives, the remaining men of Benjamin have no offspring and the tribe vanishes. Since Yahweh had given Israel the land as a grant to the tribes and families of Israel, the loss of a whole tribe would throw their allotment into limbo. The elders here are concerned to protect the actual territory that was the hereditary possession of Benjamin. In the OT, land tenure is the idiom and currency of divine and human faithfulness. Preserving an orderly title-history maintained the integrity of Yahweh's promise, underlining the tragedy of an entire tribe's annihilation—something perhaps the Israelites should have considered in their assembly and especially in their rampage of 20:48.

the survivors. Saul, a Benjaminite, would likely have been a descendant of one of these survivors (Block 1999:574, n. 379). And therefore, in his line, would likely have been a matriarch from Jabesh-gilead.

so that an entire tribe of Israel is not wiped out. In the name of not wiping out the Benjaminites, whom they actually had planned to wipe out, the Israelites had wiped out another whole community. The contrast between their solicitude for Benjamin and their callous disregard for the lives of their other fellow Israelites bounds on the obscene.

21:18 ***But we cannot give them our own daughters in marriage because we have sworn with a solemn oath that anyone who does this will fall under God's curse.*** The author repeatedly drives home that the very fate from which they swore to save their own daughters, they were perfectly happy to impose on other peoples' daughters.

21:19 ***Then they thought of the . . . festival of the LORD.*** The Hebrew only says "Right now the (pilgrim) feast of Yahweh [is happening] in Shiloh every day." The term for festival/feast (*khag* [TH2282, ZH2504]) signifies a pilgrim festival to which Israelites traveled, as opposed to local festivals. It is cognate to the Arabic term *hajj*, which denotes the pilgrimage to Mecca. The term also suggests a processional or circular-dance, which fits the story here as the woman process or dance in the vineyards. Some scholars think the term's etymology suggests a rotating or annual feast, which is plausible. It is the regular term indicating the annual feasts of the Israelite liturgical calendar (NIDOTTE 2.20-21). Other considerations (below) suggest the feast in question was the Festival of Booths/Tabernacles. The elders here appear to think of the festival suddenly, which suggests perhaps they had not been in the habit of attending it or did not even know exactly what it was about (Boling 1975:293; Block 1999:580).

annual. The expression *miyyamim yamimah* [TH3117, ZH3427] (from days to days) appears only four other times in the OT. Two, as here, designate the festival in Shiloh (1 Sam 1:3; 2:19). Elsewhere in Judges it occurs only in 11:40, forming yet another tie between these women and Jephthah's daughter, all victims of vows.

Shiloh, south of Lebonah and north of Bethel, along the east side of the road that goes from Bethel to Shechem. The author precisely locates Shiloh east of the watershed ridge road north of Bethel, where today sits the 7.5-acre site of Seilun at the north end of a fertile, well-watered valley. The Bible nowhere tells how Shiloh came into Israelite possession. Joshua 18:1 reports that Israelites set up the tent of meeting at Shiloh, which served as the administrative center for the distribution of the remaining land. According to Josh 22:19, 29, this was the only legitimate altar in Israel, being the only one "in front of the Tabernacle"—hence, the controversy over the Transjordan altar. Subsequent narratives report an annual festival of Yahweh celebrated there (1 Sam 1–2). Both 21:19-21 and 1 Sam 1:13-14 link wine with this festival. The only festival related to vineyards known from the Pentateuch was the Festival of Tabernacles, which occurred after the ingathering of corn, new wine, and oil. This festival specifically mandates rejoicing and celebration and more alcohol consumption than usual (Lev 23:33-44; Deut 16:13-15; cf. Deut 14:22-27; De Vaux 1965:496). The Ark was taken from Shiloh into battle before being captured by the Philistines, who probably destroyed Shiloh at that time (c. 1050 BC). The Bible mentions Shiloh as an occupied site only once afterwards, in 1 Kgs 14:4. The archaeology of Shiloh fits the biblical narrative well. A Canaanite religious center in the Late Bronze Age, Shiloh was abandoned c. 1350 BC until its reoccupation and reconstruction c. 1150 BC. Though surrounded by numerous new villages based on mixed agriculture and pastoralism, characterized by the excavator as proto-Israelite, Shiloh evidences no routine residential functions, but was an administrative and distributional center. A large east–west-oriented rectangular area showing signs of leveling and smoothing with tools has provoked speculation that the Tabernacle, perhaps within an enclosure, was placed here. The site suffered destruction by burning c. 1050 BC and shows only scanty occupation afterwards (ABD 5.1069-1072).

21:20 ***They told.*** Lit., "they commanded" (*tsawah* [TH6680, ZH7422]).

hide in the vineyards. The term "hide" (*'arab* [TH693, ZH741]) is the term for "ambush," used for the Israelite stratagem to lure Benjamin into a vulnerable position (20:29, 33, 36, 37,

38), and used of the Philistines waiting to trap Samson (16:2, 9, 12). It also recollects the ambushes set in the conclusion of the Abimelech story (9:25, 32, 34, 43). The final chapter thus resonates with other entrapments in the book, contributing to its climactic effect.

21:21 *When you see.* The particle *hinneh* [TH2009, ZH2180], often mistranslated as "behold!" or some other exclamation, connotes immediacy, either in time, space, or reasoning. Here it should be understood to mean "as soon as you see," suggesting the men needed to be on the watch to seize their moment and their woman.

the young women of Shiloh. These were not likely residents, since Shiloh does not appear to be a normal city where Israelites resided (see note on 21:19). Rather, these women were far from home, enjoying the high festivities of the Festival of Tabernacles, for which rejoicing was prescribed. The express identification of the women of Jabesh-gilead as virgins (21:12) and the author's stress on the virginity of Jephthah's daughter (11:38-39) indicates a concern to make this point when it matters. That the text says nothing about the virginity of the "daughters of Shiloh" is therefore noteworthy.

the vineyards. A festival connected with bringing in the vintage appears also in the Abimelech story (9:27). A vineyard also provides the scene for Samson's ambush by the lion (14:5-9). Ancient literature presents several stories of mass abductions of women for the purpose of coerced marriages (Soggin 1981:304-305).

take one. The word appears elsewhere in the OT only in Ps 10:9, where it alludes to the way a lion seizes (*khatap* [TH2414, ZH2642]) its prey. The word *'arab* [TH693, ZH741] (cf. 21:20) occurs with it in Ps 10:9. In the Aramaic of the Targums, the term refers to violent seizure (NIDOTTE 2.106).

to be your wife! Like the maidens of Jabesh-gilead, these women were forced into marriages with men whom they had not chosen, nor whom their families had chosen for them. While their trauma might not equal that of the Jabesh-gileadite women, nor that of the violated concubine, their futures had been wrested from them by force. Whether or not the present passage implies rape, it certainly was violation.

21:22 *when their fathers and brothers come to us.* The honor of the women will be a matter of concern for their fathers and brothers, unlike the previous 400 women who no longer had fathers and brothers to care for their honor. Genesis 34 illustrates how serious brothers in tribal societies could be about the honor of their sister. Following the seduction of their sister Dinah by Shechem, her brothers Levi and Simeon massacred Shechem and all the men of his town—all because Hamor had "defiled their sister." Thus, the leaders of Israel needed a plan to assuage the wrath of these fathers and brothers.

protest. The term *rib* [TH7378, ZH8189]) speaks of more than mere protest or complaint, regularly implying a lawsuit or sharp dispute (Soggin 1981:299). Other than the most obvious source of their protest, the lack of bride-wealth given for the women could add a deeper dimension of offense, as the laws of captive brides suggest (cf. Exod 22:16-17; Deut 22:28-29; Matthews 2004:199-200). Bride-wealth was not a commercial "price" paid for a woman, but was an expression of the bond between the two families created by the marriage. Among pastoralists, as the woman bore children in her new family, the sheep, goats, or cattle given to the girl's family likewise reproduced in a continuing, reciprocal tie. Often the original animals were returned after they had given birth, removing altogether the aspect of purchase. In most cultures, a woman for whom no bride-wealth was given was shamed, along with her family, and might even be the very definition of "concubine," which returns to the beginning of this story in ch 19. The deed done here violated not only the girls and their families, but the whole institution of marriage.

Please be sympathetic. Lit., "have mercy." Mercy is the one quality utterly absent from the entire tale.

Let them have your daughters, for we didn't find wives for all of them when we destroyed Jabesh-gilead. And you are not guilty of breaking the vow since you did not actually give your daughters to them in marriage. Given the circumstances, this bit of casuistic reasoning again seems painfully disconnected from the alarming realities conveyed in the story. In fact, a strain of Pharisaism runs through the entire chapter. Fresh from the bloodiest engagements of the book, the Israelites and their leaders applied their minds to evading the technical obligations of conflicting oaths while the bodies of the slain stack up like cordwood. Worse, Lev 5:4-6 and Lev 27:13, 31, etc. reveal that Yahweh's covenant included a recognition that people would indeed make rash, unwise oaths, and made provision for release and redemption (Younger 2002:384-385). Redemption, however, seemed the last thing on the minds of the elders. Instead, by alluding to the battle, the leaders possibly issued a vague threat to the girls' families, while simultaneously offering them a way to evade any guilt for breaching the vow. When all else fails, they fall back on intimidation and casuistry.

21:24 ***the people of Israel departed by tribes and families, and they returned to their own homes.*** The serenity of the ending creates such a powerful sense of dissociated affect that the reader is shocked. From an all-night gang rape, to dismemberment, to the slaughter of a town and a regional rampage, the Israelites had moved to another war of annihilation, the defilement of a sanctuary, and the shaming of families from all over Israel at the pilgrim festival—and the story now simply reports that everyone went home and got back to their lives, setting up the author's final summary (21:25), repeated from 17:6.

COMMENTARY

The first paragraph (21:1-5) occupies the central unit in a five-part structure as analyzed by Younger (2002:347), here modified slightly:

A. 19:1-30. Rape and Dismemberment of the Woman (Problem)
  B. 20:1-48. Destruction of Gibeah and Benjamin (Solution)
    C. 21:1-5. No Wives for Benjamin—Extinction Looms (Problem)
  B′. 21:6-14. Destruction of Jabesh-gilead (Solution 1)
A′. 21:15-25. Seizure of the Shilonite Virgins (Solution 2)

This paragraph, revealing a detail about the previous account that was so far unknown, unfolds more complications resulting from the Israelite action of chapter 20. The Levite and the violated woman have vanished from the story.

The concluding chapter of Judges unfolds the final, climactic outrages that mark this era. Israel's most sacred traditions and institutions swirl into the dark vortex of the nation's arrogant, self-centered repudiation of any standard of right beyond that which they chose for themselves. Beyond the service of false gods, like pagans, the Israelites began to serve a godlessness in which religious traditions merely provided validation for their own willfulness. When this corruption reached Shiloh, it invaded the very heart of Israel's identity as Yahweh's people.

The story in many ways is agonizingly monotonous. The Israelites easily pass from one crime to the next in a crescendo of atrocities, each perpetrated more readily than the last. The first act required at least a show of legitimacy, and so in chapter 20 the Israelites made a show of process, though without any reality. Their outrage led them to impulsively annihilate Gibeah and torch all of Benjamin. But chapter 21 recounts how the Israelites, well past their rage and feeling remorse for Benjamin's decimation, calmly and easily decreed utter annihilation, a godless *kherem* [TH2764, ZH3051], against an Israelite town for the most trivial of reasons: its people's absence from the warped convocation of chapter 20, in which their choices, rituals, and vows only accelerated the atrocities. By the end of the story, the reader can think of no misdeed this community could not perpetrate, no human feeling it would not trample.

The monotony of the story is only exceeded by its insanity. The painful ironies of their behavior, so obvious to the reader, are totally invisible to the Israelites and their elders. Fixated on providing wives for Benjamin, procuring peace among warring men by trafficking in women, every other good is jettisoned and every evil embraced. Another town goes up in flames. More screams and blood, more weeping and grief. Now, instead of one woman violated to save the skin of one coldhearted Levite, 400 women have their lives and families ripped from them, socially dismembered, as they are handed over in order to preserve the lineage of 600 men who put their lives at risk to defend a town full of rapists. To supply wives for the remaining 200 men, young women are violated amid their celebrations at a sacred festival at Shiloh. The most serious of sins, committed only under the pressure of the strongest of passions, often become quite easy once the human heart has become inured to the defilement.

Jeremiah described this mind-numbing, blinding power of sin vividly in Jeremiah 2:20-25. Using the analogy of a wife who becomes wayward, then turns to prostitution, Jeremiah describes how Judah at first sinned by choice, but then experienced a dark transformation of character, a choice vine that suddenly degenerated into wild stock. This degeneration of character imprints an indelible stain on the nature of the person or community, which Jeremiah compared to dirty hands that never come clean no matter how harshly they are washed. The encroaching bondage of sin becomes clearer as the people deny ever having abandoned Yahweh (Jer 2:23), even though the prophet points to their obvious chaotic, disordered behavior, which resembles the lust-crazed, erratic movements of a she-camel in heat. A wholly disordered self emerges in which the people now become unable even to see the obvious harm caused by their conduct as they descend into bondage (Jer 2:24), culminating in a peculiar mix of flippancy and despair (Jer 2:25). In the same vein, the Israelites, after the chain of horrors burns out, simply all go home and resume their lives. Living in their rebuilt cities, enjoying their farms, and going about normal life. Did they ever think of the cost in slaughter and mayhem of their pastoral tranquility? Did a Benjaminite man ever look across the kitchen fire at his wife, a daughter of Jabesh-gilead, and wonder what genuine covenantal love in marriage would feel like? Even after life seems "back to normal," if the normalcy has come at the cost of righteousness and covenant love, everyone will be wearing a mask, with dead eyes peering through the eyeholes.

The problem of Israel, as diagnosed by the author of Judges, is not simply doing evil in Yahweh's eyes, but the deeper idolatry of self in which they do what is right in their own eyes. From this dark center, this black hole at the core of human nature, all pain and evil issue. Ascribing all the horrors and insanity of chapters 17–21 to kinglessness not only argues for the need for a king, it powerfully defines what the role of the king must be. All that the community has failed to become, manifested so poignantly in these chapters, becomes God's agenda for his chosen king. Kings in Israel were not called to exercise power, create opulent palaces, temples, and capital cities, but to stand as guardians of Yahweh's covenant, upholding the spirit and letter of his moral law. Just as Adam was to tend and guard the garden, the king was to tend and protect the covenant people. The king was to uphold the case of the helpless and vulnerable in society. Deuteronomy 17:14-20 clearly sets this standard for kingship. The king is not to accumulate all the trappings of power that mark the rulers of other nations: military resources (horses), sexual excess (multiplied wives), and wealth. The king's first obligation is to be a student of the law of Yahweh, to live in the fear of Yahweh, and lead as a humble servant of Yahweh with a heart not exalted above his brothers and sisters. Such a king thus has a task distinct from the one confronted by Israel's judges. The judges delivered Israel from its enemies, but the king's highest calling might have been to deliver Israel from itself.

As Israel's history progressed, king after king failed to deliver on the hope of sinful, arrogant human hearts bowing to divine rule. The king was supposed to embody the divine word in the Scriptures, which he was commissioned to copy and study. Surely Israel began to ask whether such a king would ever, in fact, sit on the throne in Jerusalem. Indeed, Israel's story had far to go before the day a King would come who was, in fact, the embodiment in flesh of Yahweh's total word to humanity. This King would do what none of his predecessors could. He would enter the citadel of human arrogance and self-imploded sinfulness and break its power, restoring humans, as individuals and as transformed communities, to righteousness, integrity, and holiness. This King, Jesus Christ, would accomplish his work not by applying escalating levels of coercion, as the men in this final story of Judges did, but by assuming the place occupied by the victims in these final chapters, most of whom were women. He would be tortured, beaten, mocked, and abused through a long night of agony culminating in his death. Unlike the victims of chapters 19–21, this king would have the power to resist, but he would choose the place of the victim, the servant. In his suffering and death (over which he would be victorious by entrusting himself to his Father), he would shatter the bondage of sinful arrogance that grips the human heart. From the radiant center of redeemed human nature, true community, justice, peace, and redemption could extend to all of creation.

For the Christian believer, the King has come, not to save us from our external, political enemies by acts of coercive power, but to save us from ourselves, by his sacrificial redeeming love. For the author and original readers of Judges, however, that was a hero story yet to be told.

BIBLIOGRAPHY

Abegg, Martin, Peter Flint, and Eugene Ulrich
1999 *The Dead Sea Scrolls Bible.* San Francisco: Harper.

Ackerman, J. S.
1975 Prophecy and Warfare in Early Israel: A Study of the Deborah-Barak Story. *Bulletin of the American Schools of Oriental Research* 220:5-13.

Aharoni, Y., and M. Avi-Yonah
1977 *Macmillan Bible Atlas.* Rev. ed. New York: Macmillan.
1979 *The Land of the Bible: A Historical Geography.* Rev. ed. Philadelphia: Westminster.

Albright, William F.
1924 *Excavations and Results at Tell el-Fûl (Gibeah of Saul).* American Schools of Oriental Research Annual 4. New Haven, CT: American Schools of Oriental Research.

Alt, Albrecht
1930 The Formation of the Israelite State in Palestine. Pp. 225-309 in *Essays in Old Testament History and Religion.* Oxford: Basil Blackwell (English Translation, 1966).

Anglim, S., P. G. Jestice, R. S. Rice, S. M. Rusch, and J. Serrati
2002 *Fighting Techniques of the Ancient World, 3000 B.C.–500 A.D. Equipment, Combat Skills, and Tactics.* New York: St. Martins.

Armerding, C.
1968 The Heroic Age of Greece and Israel: A Literary-Historical Comparison. Dissertation, Brandeis University.

Arnold, Bill T., and Bryan E. Beyer
2002 *Readings from the Ancient Near East: Primary Sources for Old Testament Study.* Grand Rapids: Baker Academic.

Arnold, Bill T., and John H. Choi.
2003 *A Guide to Hebrew Syntax.* Cambridge.

Auld, A. G.
1984 *Joshua, Judges, and Ruth.* Daily Study Bible. Philadelphia: Westminster.

Bachmann, J.
1868 *Das Buch der Richter. Mit besonderer Rücksicht auf die Geschichte seiner Auslegung und kirchlichen Verwendung.* Berlin: Wiegandt & Grieben.

Bal, Miecke
1988 *Death and Dissymmetry: The Politics of Coherence in the Book of Judges.* Chicago: University of Chicago Press.

Baly, Denis
1974 *The Geography of the Bible.* Rev. ed. New York: Harper & Row.

Barber, Elisabeth J. W.
1991 *Prehistoric Textiles: The Development of Cloth in the Neolithic and Bronze Ages with Special Reference to the Aegean.* Princeton: Princeton University Press.

Barth, Karl
1961 *Church Dogmatics.* 14 Vols. Edinburgh: T&T Clark.

Ben-Tor, Amnon
2007 Personal Communication. E-mail dated April 21, 2007.

Bierling, Neal
1992 *Giving Goliath His Due: New Archaeological Light on the Philistines.* Grand Rapids: Baker.

Biran, Avraham, and Joseph Naveh
1993 An Aramaic Stele Fragment from Tel Dan. *Israel Exploration Journal* 43:81-98.
1995 The Tel Dan Inscription: A New Fragment. *Israel Exploration Journal* 45:1-18.

Bleibtreu, Erika

1991 Grisly Assyrian Record of Torture and Death. *Biblical Archaeology Review* 17/1:52-61.

Bloch-Smith, Elizabeth

2003 Israelite Ethnicity in Iron I: Archaeology Preserves What Is Remembered and What Is Forgotten in Israel's History. *Journal of Biblical Literature* 122/3:401-425.

2004 Resurrecting the Iron I Dead. *Israel Exploration Journal* 54/1:77-91.

Block, Daniel

1988 The Period of the Judges: Religious Disintegration under Tribal Rule. Pp. 39-58 in *Israel's Apostasy and Restoration: Essays in Honor of R. K. Harrison.* Editor, A. Gileadi. Grand Rapids: Baker.

1999 *Judges, Ruth.* New American Commentary. Nashville: Broadman & Holman.

Boling, R.

1974 In Those Days There Was No King in Israel. Pp. 33-48 in *A Light Unto My Path: Old Testament Studies in Honor of Jacob M. Meyers.* Editor, H. Bream. Gettysburg Theological Studies 4. Philadelphia: Temple.

1975 *Judges.* Anchor Bible. Garden City, NY: Doubleday & Company.

Borowski, Oded

2002 *Agriculture in Iron Age Israel.* Boston: American Schools of Oriental Research.

Branson, Robert

2009 *Judges: A Commentary in the Wesleyan Tradition.* New Beacon Bible Commentary. Kansas City: Beacon Hill.

Brenner, A.

1993 *A Feminist Companion to Judges.* Sheffield: Sheffield Academic Press.

Brensinger, T.

1999 *Judges.* Believers Church Commentary. Scottdale, PA: Herald Press.

Brettler, M. Z.

1989 The Book of Judges: Literature as Politics. *Journal of Biblical Literature* 108:395-418.

2002 *The Book of Judges.* Old Testament Readings. New York: Routledge.

Brodsky, H.

1987 Bible Lands: The Shephelah-Guardian of Judea. *Bible Review* 3/4:48-52.

Bryce, Trevor

2003 *Letters of the Great Kings of the Ancient Near East: The Royal Correspondence of the Late Bronze Age.* London: Routledge.

Buber, M.

1932 *Kingship of God.* New York: Harper & Row (English Translation, 1967).

Burney, C. F.

1920 *The Book of Judges with Introduction and Notes.* 2nd ed. London: Rivingtons.

Butler, Trent

2009 *Judges.* Word Biblical Commentary. Waco: Word.

Campbell, Edward F.

2002 *Shechem III: The Stratigraphy and Architecture of Shechem/Tell Balatah. Vol. 1: Text.* American Schools of Oriental Research Archaeological Reports 6. Boston: American Schools of Oriental Research.

Campbell, Joseph

1949 *The Hero with a Thousand Faces.* Princeton: Princeton University Press.

Carey, John

2002 A work in praise of terrorism? September 11 and *Samson Agonistes. Times Literary Supplement.* September 6, 2002.

Chadwick, H. Munro

1926 *The Heroic Age.* Cambridge: Cambridge University Press.

Chesnut, Owen David

2006 Philistine Incursions through the Northeastern Shephelah in the Iron Age: A Historical-Geographical Assessment of the Chalk Moat. M.A. Thesis, Jerusalem: Jerusalem University College.

Coogan, Michael D.

1987 Of Cults and Cultures: Reflections on the Interpretation of Archaeological Evidence. *Palestinian Exploration Quarterly* 119:1-8.

Coote, Robert B., and Keith W. Whitelam

1987 *The Emergence of Early Israel in Historical Perspective.* Sheffield: Almond Press.

Craigie, Peter C.

1983 *Ugarit and the Old Testament.* Grand Rapids: Eerdmans.

Cross, F. M.

1971 *Canaanite Myth and Hebrew Epic: Essays in the History and Religion of Israel.* Cambridge, MA: Harvard.

1998 Reuben, the Firstborn of Jacob: Sacral Traditions and Early Israelite History. Pp. 53-70 in *From Epic to Canon: History and Literature in Ancient Literature.* Baltimore: Johns Hopkins University Press.

Cross, F. M., and David N. Freedman

1953 A Royal Song of Thanksgiving: 2 Samuel 22 = Psalm 18. *Journal of Biblical Literature* 72:15–34.

Crüsemann, F.

1978 *Der Widerstand gegen das Königtum.* Annales Academiae Scientiarum Fennicae, B-198. Helsinki: Suomalaninen Tiedeakatemia.

Cundall, A.

1968 *Judges: An Introduction and Commentary.* Leicester: InterVarsity Press.

1969 The Book of Judges: An Apology for the Monarchy? *Expository Times* 81:178-181.

Davis, Dale Ralph

1990 *Such a Great Salvation: Expositions of the Book of Judges.* Grand Rapids: Baker.

Dever, William G.

2001 *What Did the Biblical Writers Know and When Did They Know It? What Archaeology Can Tell Us About the Reality of Ancient Israel.* Grand Rapids: Eerdmans.

Dorsey, David A.

1991 *The Roads and Highways of Ancient Israel.* Baltimore: The Johns Hopkins University Press.

Douglas, Mary

1999 *Leviticus as Literature.* Oxford: Oxford University Press.

Drews, Robert

1993 *The End of the Bronze Age: Changes in Warfare and the Catastrophe of ca. 1200 BC.* Princeton: Princeton University Press.

Exum, J. C.

1981 Aspects of Symmetry and Balance in the Samson Saga. *Journal for the Study of the Old Testament* 19:3-29.

1983 The Theological Dimension of the Samson Saga. *Vetus Testamentum* 33:30-45.

1990 The Centre Cannot Hold: Thematic and Textual Instabilities in Judges. *Catholic Biblical Quarterly* 52:410-431.

Faust, Avraham

2004 Mortuary Practices, Society and Ideology: The Lack of Iron Age I Burials in Highlands in Context. *Israel Exploration Journal* 54:174-190.

2006 *Israel's Ethnogenesis: Settlement, Interaction, Expansion and Resistance.* London: Equinox.

2009 How Did Israel Become a People? The Genesis of Israelite Identity. *Biblical Archaeology Review* 35/6:62-69, 92-94.

Fensham, F.

1977 The Numeral Seventy in the Old Testament and the Family of Jerubbaal, Ahab, Panammuwa and Athirat. *Palestine Exploration Quarterly* 109:113-115.

Finkelstein, I.

1988 *The Archaeology of the Israelite Settlement.* Jerusalem: Israel Exploration Society.

Fleenor, Rob, and Mark S. Ziese

2009 *College Press NIV Commentary.* Joplin, MO: College Press.

Fleming, Daniel E.

2004 *Democracy's Ancient Ancestors: Mari and Early Collective Governance.* Cambridge: Cambridge University Press.

Forsyth, Neil

2005 Suicidal Revenge and Milton. *The Literary Magazine* 1/1.

Frankfort, Henri

1996 *The Art and Architecture of the Ancient Orient.* 5th ed. New Haven, CT: Yale University Press.

Frolov, Serge
2009 Rethinking Judges. *Journal of Biblical Literature* 71:24-39.

Garfinkel, Yosef, and Saar Ganor
2009 *Khirbet Qeiyafa Vol. 1: Excavation Report 2007-2008.* Jerusalem: Israel Exploration Society.

Gerbrandt, G. E.
1986 *Kingship According to the Deuteronomistic History.* Society of Biblical Literature Dissertation Series 87. Atlanta: Scholars Press.

Gibson, J. C. L.
1975 *Textbook of Syrian Semitic Inscriptions. Vol. 2.* Oxford: Clarendon.

Ginsberg, Louis
1913 *The Legends of the Jews.* 6 vols. Philadelphia: Jewish Publication Society of America.

Gitin, Seymour, J. Edward Wright, and J. P. Dessel, eds.
2006 *Confronting the Past: Archaeological and Historical Essays on Ancient Israel in Honor of William G. Dever.* Winona Lake, IN: Eisenbrauns.

Gonen, Rivka
1992 *Burial Patterns and Cultural Diversity in Late Bronze Age Canaan.* American Schools of Oriental Research Dissertation Series 7. Winona Lake, IN: Eisenbrauns.

Gooding, D. W.
1982 The Composition of the Book of Judges. *Eretz Israel* 16:70-79.

Gordon, C.
1965 *The Common Background of Greek and Hebrew Civilizations.* New York: Norton. (Previously *Before the Bible.* New York: Harper & Row, 1962.)

Grayson, A. Kirk
1991 *Assyrian Rulers of the Early First Millennium BC (1114–859).* Royal Inscriptions of Mesopotamia: Assyrian Periods 2. Toronto.

Greenspahn, F. E.
1986 The Theology of the Framework of Judges. *Vetus Testamentum* 36:385-396.

Gros-Louis, K. R. R.
1974 *The Book of Judges, Literary Interpretations of Biblical Narratives.* Nashville: Abingdon.

Gunn, David M.
2005 *Judges through the Centuries.* Blackwell Bible Commentaries. Oxford: Wiley-Blackwell.

Halpern, B.
1988 *The First Historians: The Hebrew Bible and History.* San Francisco: Harper & Row.

Hasel, M. G.
1998 *Domination and Resistance: Egyptian Military Activity in the Southern Levant, Ca. 1300–1185 B.C.* Leiden: Brill Academic Publishers.

2005 *Military Practice and Polemic: Israel's Laws of Warfare in Near Eastern Perspective.* Berrien Springs, MI: Andrews University Press.

Heaney, Seamus
2000 *Beowulf: A New Verse Translation.* New York: Farrar, Straus, and Giroux.

Herr, D. D., and M. P. Boyd
2002 A Watermelon Named Abimelech. *Biblical Archaeological Review* 28/1:34-37, 62.

Herr, L., and D. Clark
2001 Excavating the Tribe of Reuben. *Biblical Archaeological Review* 27.2:36-47, 64-66.

Hess, Richard
2008 The Jericho and Ai of the Book of Joshua. Pp. 33-46 in *Critical Issues in Early Israelite History.* Editors, R. Hess, G. Klingbeil, and P. Ray. Winona Lake, IN: Eisenbrauns.

Homan, Michael M.
2010 Did the Ancient Israelites Drink Beer? *Biblical Archaeology Review* 36/5:48-56, 78.

Keil, K. F.
1863 *Biblical Commentary on the Books of Joshua, Judges, Ruth.* Edinburgh: T&T Clark (English Translation, 1868.) Repr. Grand Rapids: Eerdmans, 1978.

Killebrew, Ann E.
2005 *Biblical Peoples and Ethnicity: An Archaeological Study of Egyptians, Canaanites, Philistines, and Early Israel 1300–1100 B.C.E.* Atlanta: Society of Biblical Literature.

King, Philip J.

2006 Gezer and Circumcision. Pp. 333-340 in *Confronting the Past: Archaeological and Historical Essays on Ancient Israel in Honor of William G. Dever.* Editors, Seymour Gitin, J. Edward Wright, and J. P. Dessel. Winona Lake, IN: Eisenbrauns.

King, Philip J., and Lawrence E. Stager

2001 *Life in Biblical Israel.* Louisville: Westminster/John Knox.

Kitchen, Kenneth

2003 An Egyptian Inscribed Fragment from Late Bronze Hazor. *Israel Exploration Journal* 53:20-28.

Klein, L. R.

1989 *The Triumph of Irony in the Book of Judges.* Journal for the Study of the Old Testament 68. Sheffield: Journal for the Study of the Old Testament Press.

Kletter, Raz

2002 People without burials? The Lack of Iron I Burials in the Central Highlands of Palestine. *Israel Exploration Journal* 52/1:28-48.

2004 Chronology and United Monarchy: A Methodological Review. *Zeitschrift des Deutschen Palästina-Vereins* 120:113-54.

Knudtzon, J. A.

1978 *Die el-Amarna-Tafeln.* (Orig. pub. 1908–1915. Leipzig: Hinrichs.)

Kramer, S. N.

1959 *History Begins At Sumer.* Garden City, NY: Doubleday Anchor Books.

Lemos, T. M.

2006 Shame and the Mutilation of Enemies in the Hebrew Bible. *Journal of Biblical Literature* 125:225-241.

Lindars, B.

1973 Jotham's Fable—A New Form-Critical Analysis. *Journal of Theological Studies* 24:355-366.

1995 *Judges: A New Translation and Commentary.* Edinburgh: T&T Clark.

Lord, A.

1960 *The Singer of Tales.* Cambridge, MA: Harvard University Press.

1991 *Epic Singers and Oral Tradition.* Ithaca, NY: Cornell University Press.

1995 *The Singer Resumes the Tale.* Ithaca, NY: Cornell University Press.

Machinist, Peter

2000 Biblical Traditions: The Philistines and Israelite History. Pp. 53-84 in *The Sea Peoples and Their World: A Reassessment.* Editor, Eliezar D. Oren. Philadelphia: University of Pennsylvania.

Malamat, Abraham

1970 The Danite Migration and the Pan-Israelite Exodus-Conquest: A Biblical Narrative Pattern. *Biblica* 51:1-17.

Maly, E. H.

1960 The Jotham Fable–Anti-Monarchical? *Catholic Biblical Quarterly* 22:299-305.

Manley, G. T.

1959 The Deuteronomic Redactor in the Book of Judges. *Evangelical Quarterly* 31:32-37.

Marcus, David

1986 *Jephthah and His Vow.* Lubbock, TX: Texas Tech Press.

Marks, Richard G.

1983 Dangerous Hero: Rabbinic Attitudes Toward Legendary Heroes. *Hebrew Union College Annual* 54:181-194.

Matthews, Victor H.

1999 The Unwanted Gift: Implications of Obligatory Gift Giving in Ancient Israel. *Semeia* 87:91-104.

2004 *Judges and Ruth.* New Cambridge Bible Commentary. Cambridge: Cambridge University Press.

Mazar, Amihai

1992 *Archaeology of the Land of the Bible 10,000–586 B.C.E.* New Haven, CT: Yale University Press.

Mazar, Amihai, and Nava Panitz-Cohen

2007 It Is the Land of Honey: Beekeeping at Tel Rehov. *Near Eastern Archaeology* 70/4:202-219.

McBride, S. Dean

1987 Polity of the Covenant People: The Book of Deuteronomy. *Interpretation* 41:229-244.

Meier, A. M., and P. de Miroschedji, editors

2006 *I Will Speak the Riddle of Ancient Times. Archaeological and Historical Studies in Honor of Amihai Mazar on the Occasion of His Sixtieth Birthday.* Winona Lake, IN: Eisenbrauns.

Mendenhall, George W.

1973 *The Tenth Generation: The Origin of the Biblical Tradition.* Baltimore: Johns Hopkins University Press.

1975 The Monarchy. *Interpretation* 29:155-170.

Miller, Dean A.

2002 *The Epic Hero.* Baltimore: Johns Hopkins University Press.

Miller, Robert D.

1999 A Gazetteer of Iron I Sites in the North-Central Highlands of Palestine. *Bulletin of the American Schools of Oriental Research* 56:143-218.

2005 *Chieftains of the Highland Clans: A History of Israel in the 12th and 11th Centuries B.C.* Grand Rapids: Eerdmans.

Mobley, Gregory

2005 *The Empty Men: The Heroic Tradition of Ancient Israel.* New York: Doubleday.

Moore, G. F.

1895 *A Critical and Exegetical Commentary on Judges.* International Critical Commentary. Edinburgh: T&T Clark.

Moran, William T.

1963 The Ancient Near Eastern Background to the Love of God in Deuteronomy. *Catholic Biblical Quarterly* 25:77-85.

1992 *The Amarna Letters.* Baltimore: Johns Hopkins University Press.

Muhly, J. D.

2003 Greece and Anatolia in the Early Iron Age: The Archaeological Evidence and the Literary Tradition. Pp. 23-35 in *Symbiosis, Symbolism, and the Power of the Past: Canaan, Ancient Israel, and Their Neighbors from the Late Bronze Age Through Roman Palaestina.* Editors, W. G. Dever and S. Gitin. Winona Lake, IN: Eisenbrauns.

Mullen, E. T.

1984 Judges 1.1-36: The Deuteronomistic Reintroduction of the Book of Judges. *Harvard Theological Review* 77:33-54.

Na'aman, Nadav

2005 *Canaan in the Second Millennium B.C.E.* Winona Lake, IN: Eisenbrauns.

Nelson, Richard D.

1981 *The Double Redaction of the Deuteronomistic History.* Journal for the Study of the Old Testament Supplement 18. Sheffield: Journal for the Study of the Old Testament Press.

2002 *Deuteronomy: A Commentary.* Louisville: Westminster/John Knox.

Niditch, Susan

2008 *Judges: A Commentary.* Louisville: Westminster/John Knox.

Noth, M.

1958 *The History of Israel.* New York: Harper & Row (English Translation, 1960).

1991 *The Deuteronomistic History.* 2nd ed. Journal for the Study of the Old Testament Supplement Series 15. Sheffield: Journal for the Study of the Old Testament Press, 1991.

Nylander, Carl

1980 Earless in Nineveh: Who Mutilated "Sargon's" Head? *American Journal of Archaeology* 84.3:329-333.

O'Connell, Robert H.

1996 *The Rhetoric of the Book of Judges.* Supplements to Vetus Testamentum 63. Leiden: Brill.

Olson, D. T.

1998 The Book of Judges: Introduction, Commentary, and Reflections. Pp. 723-888 in *New Interpreters Bible*, vol. 2. Louisville: Abingdon.

Olyan, Saul

1998 What Do Shaving Rites Accomplish and What Do They Signal in Biblical Contexts? *Journal of Biblical Literature* 117/4:611-622.

Oppenheim, A. Leo

1943 Akkadian pul(u)kh(t)u and melammu. *Journal of the American Oriental Society* 63/1:31-33.

Parrot, André
1961 *The Arts of Assyria.* New York: Golden Press.

Peckham, Brian
1985 *The Composition of the Deuteronomistic History.* Harvard Semitic Monographs 35. Atlanta: Scholars Press.

Polzin, Robert
1980 *Moses and the Deuteronomist: A Literary Study of the Deuteronomic History.* New York: Seabury.

Provan, I.
1988 *Hezekiah and the Books of Kings. A Contribution to the Debate about the Composition of the Deuteronomistic History.* Beihefte zur Zeitschrift fur die alttestamentliche Wissenschaft 172. Berlin: de Gruyter.

Rad, Gerhard von
1966 The Beginnings of Historical Writing in Ancient Israel. Pp. 166-204 in *The Problem of the Hexateuch and Other Essays.* London: SCM.

1980 *God at Work in Israel.* Translator, John H. Marks. Nashville: Abingdon.

1991 *Holy War in Ancient Israel.* Grand Rapids: Eerdmans.

Radner, Karen
2005 *Die Macht des Namens: Altorientalische Strategian zur Selbsterhaltung.* Wiesbaden: Harroswitz.

Rainey, A. F.
1983 The Biblical Shephelah of Judah. *Bulletin of the American Schools of Oriental Research* 251:1-22.

2008 Shasu or Habir: Who Were the Early Israelites? *Biblical Archaeology Review* 34/6:51-55.

Rainey, Anson F., and R. Steven Notley
2006 *The Sacred Bridge: Carta's Atlas of the Biblical World.* Jerusalem: Carta.

Rank, Otto
1914 *The Myth of the Birth of the Hero.* Nervous and Mental Disease Monograph Series 18. New York: Journal of Nervous and Mental Disease Publishing.

Redford, Donald B.
1992 *Egypt, Canaan and Israel in Ancient Times.* Princeton: Princeton University Press.

Richardson, Joseph W.
2008 Personal Communication.

Richter, Sandra L.
2002 *The Deuteronomistic History and the Name Theology.* Berlin: De Gruyter.

2005 Deuteronomistic History. Pp. 219-230 in *Dictionary of the Old Testament: Historical Books.* Editors, Bill Arnold and H. G. M. Williamson. Downers Grove, IL: InterVarsity.

2007 The Place of the Name in Deuteronomy. *Vetus Testamentum* 57:342-366.

2008 *The Epic of Eden: A Christian Entry into the Old Testament.* Downers Grove, IL: InterVarsity Press.

Rieff, Philip
2007 *Charisma: The Gift of Grace and How It Has Been Taken Away From Us.* New York: Pantheon Press.

Robertson-Smith, W.
1892 *The Old Testament in the Jewish Church. A Course of Lectures on Biblical Criticism.* 2nd ed. New York: Appleton.

1903 *Kinship and Marriage in Early Arabia.* 2nd ed. London: Black.

Sasson, J. M.
1966 Circumcision in the Ancient Near East. *Journal of Biblical Literature* 85:473-476.

Sayce, A. H.
1894 *The Higher Criticism and the Verdict of the Monuments.* London: SPCK.

Schneider, Tammi J.
2000 *Judges.* Berit Olam: Studies in Hebrew Narrative and Poetry. Collegeville, MN: Liturgical Press.

Schniedewind, William M.
2006 The Search for Gibeah: Notes on the Historical Geography of Central Benjamin. Pp. 711-722 in *I Will Speak the Riddle of Ancient Times: Archaeological and Historical Studies in Honor of Amihai Mazar on the Occasion of His Sixtieth Birthday.* Editors, A. M. Meier and P. de Miroschedji. Winona Lake, IN: Eisenbrauns.

Segal, R. A., editor
1990 *In Quest of the Hero.* Princeton: Princeton University Press.

Shanks, Hershel
2010 Prize Find: Oldest Hebrew Inscription Discovered in Israelite Fort on Philistine Border. *Biblical Archaeological Review* 36/2:51-54.

Singer, Itamar
1994 Egyptians, Canaanites, and Philistines in the Period of the Emergence of Israel. Pp. 282-338 in *From Nomadism to Monarchy: Archaeological and Historical Aspects of Early Israel.* Editors, Israel Finkelstein and Nadav Na'aman. Washington, DC: Biblical Archaeology Society.

Smith, G. A.
1931 *Historical Geography of the Holy Land.* 25th ed. London: Hodder & Stoughton.

Soggin, J. A.
1981 *Judges: A Commentary.* Philadelphia: Westminster.

Spina, Frank A.
1977 The Dan Story Historically Reconsidered. *Journal for the Study of the Old Testament* 4:60-71.

Stager, Lawrence E.
1985 The Archaeology of the Family in Ancient Israel. *Bulletin of the American Schools of Oriental Research* 260:1-35.

1988 Archaeology, Ecology, and Social History: Background Themes to the Song of Deborah. Pp. 221-234 in *Congress Volume, Jerusalem.* Editor, J. A. Emerton. Leiden: Brill.

1989 The Song of Deborah: Why Some Tribes Answered the Call and Some Did Not. *Biblical Archaeology Review* 15/1:50-64.

1999 The Fortress-Temple at Shechem and the "House of El, Lord of the Covenant." Pp. 228-249 in *Realia Dei: Essay in Archaeology and Biblical Interpretation in Honor of Edward F. Campbell Jr. at His Retirement.* Editors, Prescott H. Williams Jr. and Theodore Hiebert. Atlanta: Scholars Press.

2003 The Shechem Temple: Where Abimelech Massacred a Thousand. *Biblical Archaeology Review* 29/4:26-35, 66, 68-69.

2006 Biblical Philistines: A Hellenistic Literary Creation? Pp. 375-384 in *I Will Speak the Riddle of Ancient Times,* vol 2. Editors, A. M. Meier and P. de Miroschedji. Winona Lake, IN: Eisenbrauns.

Steiner, G.
1962 Homer and the Scholars. Pp. 1-14 in *Homer: A Collection of Critical Essays.* Editors, G. Steiner and R. Fagles. Englewood Cliffs, NJ: Prentice-Hall.

1997 *Errata: An Examined Life.* New Haven, CT: Yale University Press.

Stern, Ephraim
1993-2008 *New Encyclopedia of Archaeological Excavations in the Holy Land.* 5 vols. New York: Simon & Schuster.

Stone, Lawson G.
1988 From Tribal Confederation to Monarchic State: The Editorial Perspective of the Book of Judges. Doctoral Dissertation, Yale University.

1991 Ethical and Apologetic Tendencies in the Redaction of the Book of Joshua. *Catholic Biblical Quarterly* 53:25-36.

1992 *Judges.* Asbury Bible Commentary. Grand Rapids: Zondervan.

1997 Redaction Criticism: Whence, Whither, Why? Going Beyond Source and Form Criticism without Leaving Them Behind. Pp. 77-90 in *A Biblical Itinerary: In Search of Method, Form, and Content—Essays in Honor of George W. Coats.* Editor, G. Carpenter. Journal for the Study of the Old Testament Supplement 240. Sheffield: Sheffield Academic Press.

2002 On Historical Authenticity, Historical Criticism, and Biblical Authority: Reflections of the Case of the Book of Joshua. *Asbury Theological Journal* 57/2:83-96.

2005 Judges, Book of. Pp. 592-606 in *Dictionary of the Old Testament: Historical Books.* Editors, Bill Arnold and H. G. M. Williamson. Downers Grove, IL: InterVarsity.

2009 Eglon's Belly and Ehud's Blade: A Reconsideration. *Journal of Biblical Literature* 128:649-663.

Strawn, Brent
2005 *What Is Stronger than a Lion? Leonine Image and Metaphor in the Hebrew Bible and the Ancient Near East.* Fribourg: Academic Press.

2009 *kephir 'arayoth* in Judges 14:5. *Vetus Testamentum* 59:150-158.

Tadmor, H.

1973 The Historical Inscriptions of Adad-Nirari III. *Iraq* 35:141.

Taylor, J. Glen

1993 *Yahweh and the Sun: Biblical and Archaeological Evidence for Sun Worship in Ancient Israel.* Journal for the Study of the Old Testament Supplement 111. Sheffield: Journal for the Study of the Old Testament Press.

Trible, Phyllis

1984 *Texts of Terror: Literary-Feminist Readings of Biblical Narratives.* Overtures to Biblical Theology 13. Philadelphia: Fortress.

Ulrich, Eugene, and Frank Moore Cross

1995 *Qumran Cave 4—IX.* Discoveries in the Judaean Desert 14. Oxford: Clarendon.

Vaux, Roland de

1965 *Ancient Israel: Its Life and Institutions.* Translator, J. McHugh. London: Darton, Longman & Todd.

Waldman, Nahum M.

1989 The imagery of clothing, covering, and overpowering. *Journal of the Ancient Near Eastern Society* 19:161-170.

Waltke, Bruce, and M. O'Connor

1990 *An Introduction to Biblical Hebrew Syntax.* Winona Lake, IN: Eisenbrauns.

Webb, B. G.

1987 *The Book of Judges: an Integrated Reading.* Journal for the Study of the Old Testament Supplement 46. Sheffield: Sheffield Academic Press.

Whitman, C. H.

1958 *Homer and the Heroic Tradition.* Cambridge: Harvard.

Wiseman, Donald J.

1982 Is It Peace?—Covenant and Diplomacy. *Vetus Testamentum* 32 (1982) 311-326.

Wood, Bryant

2007 Let the Evidence Speak. *Biblical Archaeological Review* 33/2:26, 78.

Wright, G. E.

1946 The Literary and Historical Problem of Joshua 10 and Judges 1. *Journal of Near Eastern Studies* 5:105-114.

1965 *Shechem: The Biography of a Biblical City.* New York: McGraw Hill.

Wright, Paul H.

2008 *Greatness, Grace & Glory: Carta's Atlas of Biblical Biography.* Jerusalem: Carta.

Yadin, Yigael

1963 *The Art of Warfare in Biblical Lands.* 2 vols. Translator, M. Pearlman. New York: McGraw-Hill.

Yee, G. A., editor

1995 *Judges and Method: New Approaches in Biblical Studies.* Minneapolis: Fortress Press.

Younger, K. Lawson

2002 *Judges and Ruth.* The NIV Application Commentary. Grand Rapids: Zondervan.

Zertal, Adam

1991 Israel Enters Canaan—Following the Pottery Trail. *Biblical Archaeological Review* 17/5:28-49.

1994 To the Land of the Perizzites and the Giants: On the Israelite Settlement in the Hill Country of Manasseh. Pp. 47-69 in *From Nomadism to Monarchy: Archaeological and Historical Aspects of Early Israel.* Editors, Israel Finkelstein and Nadav Na'aman. Washington: Biblical Archaeology Society.

2004 *The Manasseh Hill Country Survey: Volume 1: The Shechem Syncline.* Leiden: Brill.

2008 *The Manasseh Hill Country Survey: Volume 2: The Eastern Valleys and the Fringes of the Desert.* Leiden: Brill.

Ruth

JASON DRIESBACH

INTRODUCTION TO *Ruth*

THE MOTTO "pay it forward" espouses an unselfish, others-oriented virtue that resonates with the biblical teachings that we are to love God, neighbor, and foreigner (Lev 19:18, 33-34; Deut 6:5), and that in serving those in need, we serve the Lord Jesus himself (Matt 25:40, 45). The book of Ruth presents an illustration of such virtue that also offers a window into the synergy between human and divine purposes. It further constitutes an inspirational reminder that the Lord often has greater plans for our actions than what we will see in our earthly lifetimes—after all, neither Ruth nor Naomi nor Boaz lived to see the reign of their descendant David.

In the book of Ruth, the plot revolves around one major problem, namely that of Naomi's empty and bitter life (cf. 1:5 and 4:14-16). Everything else that happens in the book is tied to the development and resolution of this problem. Naomi's life is stricken by tragedy at the outset of the story; the loss of her husband and sons while living in a foreign land resulted not only in personal anguish, but in poverty and hardship in her old age. The characters that appear and events that follow lead to a reversal of that tragedy. In the course of those events, the character of Ruth stands out, and for this reason the book is quite appropriately named for her (4:15). In highlighting the qualities of certain characters and recounting few direct actions by the Lord, the narrative also communicates a healthy perspective of the cooperation of the divine and human: There is a beautiful relationship between our human responsibility to live God-honoring lives, doing good for one another, and God's transcendent plans being worked out—whether we're conscious of it or not. Sometimes it is only in hindsight that we are able to gain a perspective like that of the apostle Paul, "I have worked harder than any of the other apostles; yet it was not I but God who was working through me by his grace" (1 Cor 15:10b).

AUTHOR, DATE, AND PURPOSE

Like most literature of the ancient Near East, the book of Ruth gives no hint as to the name of its author. Rabbinic tradition (*b. Bava Batra* 14b-15a) suggested Samuel was the author, but it is difficult to reconcile the timing of Samuel's death (1 Sam 28:3), before David's ascent to the throne, with the perspective of the book's author, which views the days of the judges as an already completed period (1:1), assumes the fame of David (4:17-22), and finds it necessary to comment on ancient practices for its readers (4:7). Other theories have been ventured, but in fact, the author of this biblical book is best left unnamed. From the book, it seems clear that the author was a skilled literary artist (see discussion of literary style below), which implies a relatively high level of education. This and the idea that the purpose of the book is connected to defending David's lineage has led many to suggest that a preexilic author of Ruth must have been a member of the royal court, a distinct possibility. Hubbard's (1988:24) suggestion that the author may have been a woman is best regarded as "a possible inference" since men, too, write stories with female protagonists and vice versa.

The inclusion of David in the genealogy (4:17, 22) points to the fact that the book of Ruth was not written until after David was king. But how long after David was king? Some have suggested the early days of the monarchy in Israel, or near the time when the monarchy divided (Nielsen 1997:28). Others have suggested that Ruth was written after the Exile, in the time of Ezra and Nehemiah (cf. Weiser 1961:304), or even as late as around 200–100 BC (cf. Zenger 1986).

The mostly subjective arguments put forth in attempting to date the book form a veritable rats' nest. Many of them can be turned on their heads by one's opponents, and others admittedly rest on particular assumptions. As an example: In my opinion, the peaceful imagery of the book of Ruth does not seem to reflect the upheaval or the reconstruction efforts of the postexilic period. Its tone rather seems to reflect a peaceful time of consolidation of the Davidic dynasty—something I would associate with the reign of Solomon. But there were naturally peaceful times within both the postexilic and preexilic periods, and other Davidic kings besides Solomon enjoyed periods of peace; so the assumption of a Solomonic date would be unfounded. Other arguments are more complex but no less subjective.

Bush (1996:18-30) argues that diachronic changes in biblical Hebrew can be used objectively to arrive at a time frame for this book's composition, and he offers an excellent presentation of what criteria he bases his analysis on. But in contrast to this, Nielsen (1997:29) remarks, "Attempts to prove a later date, based on certain Aramaisms or an archaic style or current legal usage, have slowly crumbled, and recent research generally agrees on a preexilic date." The result of Bush's analysis (1996:30) places the book anywhere from the late preexilic period to the early postexilic period, leaving open perhaps the most pressing question of the date (namely, pre- vs. postexilic). Bush (cf. Matthews 2004:209) opts for an early postexilic date based on his assessment that 4:7 (a single verse with three notable late features) is the author's writing, and not an explanatory comment by a later editor or scribe, but he concedes that "any attempt to narrow the possible range [for the book's date] can only be very tentative" (1996:30). Thus, even the most objective methods available at present leave the date of the book somewhat debatable, with a mixture of features that can be variously explained (see Hornkohl, forthcoming).

Entwined with the question of date is the question of the book's purpose—the conceived purpose may be either used to argue for a particular date or derived from one's assumptions about the book's date. For many years, critical scholars agreed that Ruth had been written in the postexilic period, in the time of Ezra. They suggest that Ruth was intended as a response to the issue of mixed marriages at that time (Ezra 10; Neh 13:23-27; cf. Deut 23:3-4) and that it either contradicted Ezra's ruling or advocated a softer stance toward mixed marriages than what Ezra or Nehemiah put forth (e.g., Weiser 1961:304; cf., more recently, Matthews 2004:212). Ruth certainly does involve a mixed marriage, and a notable one at that! But the book is not marked by polemical comments or application to the marriages of other Israelites or Jews; it, instead, concludes with a focus on David and his family line. For this reason a number of scholars see the origin of the book as a defense of David's non-Israelite heritage (which could possibly have been used to argue he was unfit for the throne, or that his descendants were unfit; cf. *Ruth Rabbah* to 4:18). Thus, the book would have been written sometime late in David's reign or in the reign of another king in his line. It is not impossible, however, that even in the postexilic era the purpose of defending David's ancestry would have seemed relevant—in light of the events of Ezra 10, it might have seemed useful to show that David's Moabite ancestor, Ruth, had been an exceptional case. (It is similarly notable that the Targum to Ruth and *Ruth Rabbah* elaborate on Ruth as a righteous proselyte.) The book of Ruth, however, is a subtle and artistic literary work, and as a result, the precise force of the proposed, implicit argument in favor of David is open to interpretation. And the book's favor for David certainly does not take on a polemic tone. This difficulty in assessing the exact purpose of the book again makes it difficult to draw conclusions as to the book's date.

Additional suggestions as to the purpose of the book are catalogued by Trible, whose comments I quote at length (ABD 5.846):

> *Attempts to specify a single purpose falter in light of the book's richness and complexity. Many levels of meaning intertwine—social, political, religious, and aesthetic. A representative list includes: to maintain Israelite customs, inculcate legal duties, integrate law and daily life, legitimate David and his monarchy, tell a good story, encourage proselytes, promote universalism over against nationalism, elevate the virtues of friendship and loyalty, glorify family ties, preserve women's traditions, and witness to God at work. Two approaches, however are best avoided: to interpret the book as protest literature and to relate its purpose to one specific historical setting. Neither in tone nor in content is it polemical, and the date is uncertain.*

Taking Trible's comments to heart, it seems best to do no more than briefly highlight two concepts of purpose that I find most useful in understanding and applying the book as a whole. The first is a modification of various views that emphasize the book's message about David (particularly derived from Hubbard's expression of this view), and the second is related to the combination of human and divine activity in all spheres of life, which is reminiscent of the patriarchal narratives. Other important elements in the story will be highlighted in the discussion of Major Themes below and throughout the commentary.

In his description of the purpose of the book of Ruth, Hubbard points out many shared motifs with the patriarchal narratives and says that Ruth's purpose is to show that "the same divine guidance which led Israel's ancestors has brought David on the scene. His kingdom is their successor in God's divine plan" (Hubbard 1988:41). His statement is accurate; the various themes in the story, however balanced, ultimately seem to feed into this idea when faced with the question "so what?" From the perspective of the Torah, the monarchy is hinted at (Gen 17:6, 16; 35:11; cf. Gen 49:8-12), but the perspective of Ruth and the direct connection to David are important in elucidating this element of Israel's identity as God's people.

Hubbard (1988:42) later goes on to say that the book's purpose was political, aimed at winning popular acceptance of David's rule (ostensibly in David or Solomon's time). While this is quite possible, it is probably more useful to limit the conception of this purpose in Ruth to the idea of showing the Davidic dynasty's theological and historical continuity with the patriarchs. As mentioned above, while many commentators connect the book's purpose to David, not all are agreed on its exact import or date—and as Trible emphasizes, this is best avoided. For while the connection between David and the patriarchs could well have gained David popular acceptance in his rule, there are other circumstances in which this might be a goal. For example, if one conjectures an exilic or postexilic setting, the validity of the monarchy might be questioned since it no longer existed. Some might wonder if it had all been a big mistake. In such a scenario, the book of Ruth would have reaffirmed the Lord's provision and plan for David's rule—perhaps even reaffirming messianic expectations. Its message would have been that the postexilic Jewish community should look to David as an example of the Lord's provision for them and as a sign of his intent to fulfill his promises.

In addition to forging a theological connection between the patriarchs and the Davidic dynasty, the book of Ruth also invites readers to compare their lives—their tragedies and their blessings, their faith, and their actions—to those of its characters. In this way, it would seem that an additional purpose of the book is to inspire its readers to virtuous actions based on faith in Yahweh, the God of Israel. This purpose plays off of the ideas of custom and law but also transcends them. Even as readers reflect on actions they may find questionable or wrong, they are driven to reassess their own virtue and their own concepts of virtue. Like the patriarchal narratives, no moral judgments are made by the narrator, and human doings are left a bit messy as the story rolls along. (Though unlike the patriarchal narratives, the qualities of the main characters do not change, and the extent of the ambiguity of their actions is more limited.) But the reader is invited to consider God's hand in the results and to reflect on his grace as well as his justice.

SETTING

The events recounted in Ruth happened "in the days when the judges ruled in Israel." Based on the genealogy at the end of the book (4:21-22), one might be tempted to conclude that these events happened toward the end of the judges period. With Solomon's completion of the Temple in Jerusalem in 967 BC (putting his accession around 970 BC) and the genealogy suggesting that Boaz and Ruth lived perhaps only two generations before David (cf. 2 Sam 5:4), it might be estimated that the events of the book would have occurred around 1100 BC. But we cannot be sure since no mention is made of specific events or characters from the judges period, such as the civil war with Benjamin (Judg 19–21), Samson (Judg 13–16), Eli and Samuel (1 Sam 1–4), and so forth. Moreover, the genealogical tradition in Matthew 1:5 could be taken to suggest that Boaz may have lived quite early in the judges period since he is the "son" of Rahab, from the time of Joshua (cf. Josh 2). In fact, the small number of names given for the generations from Rahab's era to David's indicate that the genealogy must have gaps (as is known from other genealogies in the Bible), and it is unclear where these gaps are. In sum, then, it is difficult to assert any more specific date for the events of Ruth than "the days when the judges ruled." A more specific correlation was evidently not of great importance to the author's work.

The "days of the judges" refers to a period after Israel had settled in the Promised Land and before they had a king, a period noted in sacred history as a time when "all the people did whatever seemed right in their own eyes" (Judg 17:6; 21:25). Naomi, Ruth, Boaz, Obed, and Jesse lived in the period of the judges. The period of the judges was politically turbulent, at one point devolving into civil war. The leaders of the time were often hamstrung by their own lack of character and integrity (e.g., Samson), and the people again and again fell into idolatry (e.g., Judg 2:11; 3:7, 12). In contrast to this, the only crisis in the events of Ruth is a famine, and little attention is given to it except as it pertains to the movement of the characters from Israel to Moab and back. Against this backdrop, the characters and tone of Ruth stand out as calm, orderly, and upright. A simple, rural dignity seems to pervade the little town of Bethlehem—life is demanding and rustic, and there is danger, but society is unified in common values, and people look out for each other. This is unexpected for readers familiar with the stories of Judges and causes the virtues of Ruth's main characters, as well as the evidence of God's ongoing, purposeful providence, to stand out against the images of moral and religious chaos and accompanying judgment that dominate the book of Judges.

CANONICITY AND TEXTUAL HISTORY

The canonicity of the book of Ruth has long been established and is rarely, if ever, questioned (cf. *b. Meggilah* 7a). In Jewish tradition, Ruth is one of the five Megilloth (five "scrolls" read annually on certain holidays) and is always read at the Festival of Weeks (Pentecost). Ruth's scenes of harvesters and gleaners correspond nicely to this joyous harvest festival. In the Hebrew Bible, Ruth is always included in the Writings, usually as the first of the Megilloth, though other traditions have suggested that it should stand at the beginning of the Writings, ahead of Psalms (probably for a chronological arrangement of the Writings; cf. *b. Bava Batra 14b*), or as the second of the Megilloth, after the Song of Songs. The Septuagint, however, places Ruth chronologically: It is after Judges (the time in which the events are set) and before 1 Samuel (where we read further about the last judges, Eli and Samuel, and about David, whom Ruth introduces in 4:17, 22). This is the order followed by English translations. It is interesting to note that in the most common order found in the Hebrew Bible, Ruth follows Proverbs, which ends with extended imagery of a wise woman (Prov 31), and precedes Song of Songs, a collection of overtly romantic poems. This is quite apropos since the character of Ruth is generally portrayed as an admirable blend of wisdom and romance.

The earliest Hebrew text of Ruth we have is from the discoveries near the Dead Sea at Qumran. The texts are incomplete, and what remains of them contains only very minor discrepancies with the Masoretic Text. It is assumed that the text largely agreed with MT, but we cannot be sure, since in the extant passages, there is little opposition between the MT and the Septuagint. In fact, the Septuagint text of Ruth is rather literal overall and generally agrees with the Masoretic Text. Some of its notable differences will be mentioned in the notes on various verses. The Syriac translation of Ruth is freer than the Septuagint, and it is therefore difficult to use it to assert the existence of another version of Ruth. In sum, the witness to the text of the book is generally unified.

LITERARY STYLE

Ruth recounts historical events in a stylized way that is brief and neatly packaged. It has been called a "novella" by some and a "historical short story" by others. In my opinion, the best characterization of the genre is that of Bush (1996:46), who calls it an "edifying short story." In short, this label suggests that Ruth is a short but somewhat complex story that revolves around the resolution of a main problem. Further, it is a story in which the characters' essential traits are revealed through few events, and they are not greatly changed or developed in the course of the story's events (cf. Bush 1996:41-42; Humphreys 1985:84-85). The result is a story where each character manifests a signature quality, which essentially functions as a theme (see Major Themes), and these qualities play out in the resolution of the main problem. In the case of Ruth, that main problem can be called Naomi's emptiness, or the impending cessation of Elimelech's family line (1:3-5, 19-22).

One element in the style of the book of Ruth is its use of various motifs found in the patriarchal narratives. As suggested above, this subtly contributes to the reader's sense that the events involving David's ancestors are an important continuation of the story of the patriarchs. Hubbard (1988:40) lists these motifs as follows:

1. Migration because of famine, which advances God's plan (1:1; cf. Gen 12; 26)
2. A family's survival is endangered by a mother's childlessness (1:5; cf. Gen 16–17; 25:21; 29:31; 30)
3. A foreigner's voluntary, permanent immigration to a new land (Ruth, 1:17; 2:11; Abram, Gen 12:1-5)
4. Protection of the woman elected to bear the son of destiny (Ruth, 2:8-9, 22; Sarah, Gen 12:17; 20:3, 6; Rebekah, Gen 26:7-11; cf. Dinah, Gen 34:1-31)
5. The betrothal-type scene of the chosen wife (for Ruth, see 2:20; cf. Rebekah, Gen 24)
6. Female sexual initiative overcoming male inaction to provide an heir (Boaz and Ruth, 3:7-15; cf. Judah and Tamar, Gen 38)
7. The purchase of property as a result of a death (4:3, 9; cf. Gen 23; 33:19)
8. The integration of the foreign immigrants into their new homeland (2:10-12; 3:11; 4:10-11, 13; cf. Gen 14; 20; 21:22-34; 23; 26; 34)
9. Marriage to a foreigner later leading to a ruling family (David, 4:13, 17-22; cf. Perez, Gen 38; Ephraim and Manasseh, Gen 41:45, 50-52; 48)
10. The divine gift of conception providing the son(s) of destiny (4:12-13; cf. Sarah, Gen 21:1-2; Rebekah, Gen 25:21; Leah, Gen 29:31; 30:17; Rachel, Gen 30:22-23; cf. Hannah 1 Sam 1:19-20; Samson's mother, Judg 13)
11. The conquest of obstacles impeding emergence of an important family [essentially, a sum of many of the other points]

Even if one does not agree that some of the above points are found in Ruth (e.g., my comment on 3:1-5 will show that I do not agree with point 6 above), the list still offers many points of contact with the patriarchal narratives. This connection is also made via the mention of patriarchal ancestors in 4:11-12 and a contrasting parallel of Ruth with Tamar (an ancestor of Boaz), whose story is told in Genesis 38 (cf. Nielsen 1997:12-17). In fact, as regards Tamar and Judah, Berger (2009a, 2009b) has recently suggested that one literary purpose of Ruth is to expunge the foundational ignominy of Judah and Tamar for Judah's line—something addressed in *Jubilees* 41:23-28. One weakness with this view, however, is the positive mention of Tamar in the end of Ruth.

Stylistically, the narrative of Ruth contains much dialogue between the characters. Sasson (1989:227) refers to Joüon and points out that "of all the Old Testament books, *Ruth* has the highest ratio of dialogue to narrative text"—almost two-thirds of the book. This lends to Ruth a quality like that of a stage play, though it cannot be proven that Ruth was intended as such.

Another feature of the literary creativity of the book of Ruth is the use of foils. A foil is a minor character whose rhetorical purpose lies in highlighting the qualities of a main character by means of contrast. Two widely recognized foils in the book of Ruth are Orpah, Ruth's sister-in-law (1:4, 14), and the unnamed kinsman or "family redeemer" (4:1-8). Chisholm (1998:135-136) describes such minor characters as crucial props in the course of the narrative. So little is said about them that they are almost not characters, but they are important to the plot nonetheless. Orpah serves to highlight the extreme loyalty of Ruth toward Naomi, and the unnamed kinsman highlights the benevolence and nobility of Boaz in his actions toward the house of Elimelech.

Structure. Most commentators divide the book of Ruth into four or five main scenes, bracketed by an introduction (usually 1:1-5) and the genealogy that closes the book (4:18-22, or sometimes a longer epilogue, such as 4:13-22). There is much agreement on the boundaries between the major sections, and in the case of Ruth, these divisions coincide neatly with the chapter divisions at 2:1, 3:1, and 4:1. In particular, Ruth 4:18-22 and 4:7 are sometimes considered later editorial editions, though the arguments are inconclusive, particularly in the case of the closing genealogy. Bush (1996:56) and Nielsen (1997:2) depart from the pattern of including introduction and genealogy sections in the outline; instead, they include the introductory verses and genealogy as parts of the larger structure. Thus, Bush arrives at an outline of four acts (corresponding to the four chapters of Ruth) consisting of three scenes each. This is the pattern I will follow in my outline below. Good arguments can be made for a number of the other options, but on the whole it matters little to our understanding of the story since its plot is manifest throughout the progress of the narrative.

Within this general framework, important structural items can be seen, which amount to a pattern of problems and resolutions that encloses two parallel panels of events:

Chapter 1
A. After ten years in Moab, Elimelech and his sons die (1:1-5).
B. Orpah returns home while Ruth remains with Naomi, leaving her with no prospect of remarriage (1:6-18).
C. In Bethlehem, Naomi laments her loss to the townswomen (1:19-22).
    Chapter 2
    D. Naomi consents to Ruth's plan to glean (2:1-3).
    E. Boaz shows Ruth favor (2:4-17).
    F. Naomi and Ruth discuss what has happened (2:18-23).
    Chapter 3
    D'. Ruth accepts Naomi's plan regarding Boaz (3:1-6).
    E'. Boaz shows Ruth favor (3:7-15).
    F'. Naomi and Ruth discuss what has happened (3:16-18).
Chapter 4
B'. The unnamed kinsman withdraws, but Boaz remains, establishing Ruth's prospect for remarriage (4:1-12).
C'. The townswomen of Bethlehem rejoice with Naomi at the birth of Obed (4:13-17).
A'. Ten generations are born in Israel (4:18-22).

The above presentation of structure is derived largely from Nielsen (1997:2). (For a more detailed and slightly different presentation of the connections in the plot, see Bush 1996:39-40.) Note that the problems introduced in chapter 1 are resolved in chapter 4. The center of the book repeats a pattern so that Boaz's good intent toward Ruth and desire that the Lord bless her (2:12; 3:10) enclose two short scenes that show Naomi regaining hope and taking action (2:18-23; 3:1-6). Apart from the artistic value this holds, it also serves to lay emphasis on a key point in the story, which will be considered in the discussion of major themes. Within this overarching structure, short parallelisms and chiasms are used as well; some of these will be addressed in the commentary.

MAJOR THEMES

As suggested above, the themes of the book of Ruth are best drawn from its primary characters and from their interplay. In my view, the central point in the book's structure embodies an intersection of these themes and marks the beginning of real movement toward the resolution of the main problem: the catastrophe that threatens to fall on Naomi and Elimelech's line. That central point is found in Naomi's move to action (3:1-6), which is dependent on Ruth's cooperation and situated between expressions of the goodwill of Boaz (2:12; 3:10). I will repeatedly reference this point in the discussion of the four character-based themes below. In my view, the interplay between the character-based themes suggests two additional themes, which will be dealt with last.

Loyalty. This theme is seen in the character of Ruth. Bush speaks of the "loving loyalty, faithfulness, and obedience of Ruth the Moabitess, expressed in her commitment to her mother-in-law, Naomi, which transcended the claims of religion and national origin" (1996:52). Ruth's first words in the book are significant in establishing this theme as her dominant characteristic: "Don't ask me to leave you and turn back. Wherever you go, I will go; wherever you live, I will live. Your people will be my people, and your God will be my God" (1:16). Her commitment to Naomi was unwavering and singular, almost marriage-like in light of the fact that Naomi could not provide another husband for Ruth. It is Ruth's sacrificial loyalty that ensures both the women's survival in the short term (Ruth is the one who goes out to glean, 2:2, 23) and the enactment of Naomi's plan (3:6), with its long-term blessings. Thus, at the intersection of the book (2:18–3:6), Ruth's loyalty is shining.

Honor. The wise and generous character of Boaz embodies this theme. Honor is a noble virtue that encompasses righteousness and extends to courtesy and love. Honor is often manifest in showing respect to others through a conventional standard of conduct. Boaz was faithful to family responsibilities and active about seeking Ruth's safety (2:8-9). He was shrewd but dignified in his dealings with the unnamed family redeemer (4:1-8), and he was forthright in his blessing of those around him (2:4, 12). It is for this reason that Boaz is called a man of "valor" (*khayil* [TH2428, ZH2657])—the first of three uses (2:1; 3:11; 4:11) in the book. Initially, one might understand *khayil* only as a reference to Boaz's means, status, and skill—he was the rescuer of the women because he had some family obligation to them and the means to carry it out. But the later designation of Ruth by this same term (3:11) signals that more is involved. In addition to social status, noble character is in view. It is notable that Boaz's qualities played a role in inspiring and facilitating Naomi's plan at the center of the book (3:1-6). It is as Naomi gives thought to Boaz's upright character and generosity towards Ruth (2:18-23), which provided for both women, that she regained hope and decided to take a bold action to really change her and Ruth's situation. Boaz's sense of honor meant Naomi could trust him with Ruth in the vulnerable situation that she hoped would move him to immediate action.

Wisdom. Naomi's character and the theme it embodies are more difficult to discern than those related to Ruth and Boaz. Although Bush (1996:45, 52) suggests that we can fairly easily discern "loving concern" for Ruth as the essential characterization of Naomi (cf. 2:22; 3:1-2), another possibility is that Naomi's qualities could be seen as capturing the theme of family ties, or perhaps the domestic values of rural life. (Ryken [1993:124] suggests something similar as the overall theme of the book as a whole.) Naomi's concern for her daughters-in-law (cf. 1:8; 3:1) and her role in identifying kinsmen for Ruth (2:20) can both fit under this rubric. While both of the preceding options are appealing, I note something more in the character of Naomi—she was a blatant realist (moving at times toward an almost cynical sarcasm), and in Ruth's relationship with Boaz, she skillfully recognized a rare opportunity and moved to exploit it (3:1-6). And yet, as Bush rightly notes (1996:45), Naomi's despairing moments are not presented in a way that casts her in a bad light. For this reason, I find the theme of wisdom the best association for Naomi. She wisely valued family and understood kinship in her society. But beyond that, she struggled with events and processed them in a way that reflects a certain sagacity—we catch glimpses of a struggle that was perhaps reminiscent of Job's steadfast assertion of his innocence in spite of his deep despair.

As Qoheleth discovered, with great wisdom comes great sorrow (Eccl 1:18)—Naomi's clear view of the futility of her own situation would seem to reflect this truth: "Why should you go on with me? Can I still give birth to other sons who could grow up to be your husbands? . . . Things are far more bitter for me than for you, because the LORD himself has raised his fist against me" (1:11, 13). Naomi's recognition that the Lord had brought such calamity upon her reflects something similar to the deep struggles of faith expressed in the wisdom writings: "For the Almighty has struck me down with his arrows. Their poison infects my spirit. God's terrors are lined up against me" (Job 6:4; cf. Job 7:1-3, 19-20; Lam 3:37-38). Yet Naomi remained submissive to the Lord and continued to bless others in his name (1:8), a feature reminiscent of Job's refusal to curse God (Job 2:9-10). Naomi also understood relationships, another important feature of wisdom: "Wisdom, to a very large extent, is a matter of interpreting people, events, situations, actions in relation to norms for existence" (Van Leeuwen 1988:100). Her comment in 3:18 regarding Boaz's determination to act on Ruth's proposal shows a wise insight into his character. Furthermore, at the intersection of the book, it is because of her wise ability to recognize and access the potential of relationships that she was able to find hope and move into action (as she does in 3:1-6).

Blessing. Though the Lord's reported actions are few in the story, his name is often called upon in the context of blessing (1:8-9; 2:4, 12, 20; 3:10; 4:11-12, 14). These are marked by the word *baruk* [TH1288A, ZH1385]. His two direct actions are returning the land to a fruitful state (1:6), and ensuring that Ruth would conceive (4:13). These are two particular blessings that express his *khesed* [TH2617, ZH2876]. Psalm 136:23 and 25 are appropriate in this context because they associate two features of the story of Ruth with the Lord's *khesed*: "He remembered us in our weakness. His faithful love (*khesed*) endures forever. . . . He gives food to every living thing. His faithful love (*khesed*) endures forever."

Khesed, often translated as "mercy," "kindness," or "love," is a difficult term to define in its essence, and many definitions have been suggested. The various ideas are summed up well by R. L. Harris (TWOT 1.698-700), who notes that while the earliest translations of the Hebrew word most often understood it as "mercy" (LXX, *eleos* [TG1656, ZG1799]) and "sympathy" (Latin, *misericordia*), KBL suggested "mutual liability of those . . . belonging together." Glueck became perhaps the best-known proponent of the view that it indicates "loyalty to covenant obligations" (TWOT 1.698), stemming from Israel's unique covenant relationship with the Lord. He suggested it could "be rendered by 'loyalty,' 'mutual aid,' or 'reciprocal love'" and that it "can only be understood as yahweh's covenantal relationship toward his followers" (Glueck 1967:102). Later studies questioned this definition, particularly its degree of connection to covenant or oath, with Sakenfeld, for example, commenting that the term is flexible and "the difficulty (and danger) of selecting even a single phrase to convey the concept in all cases becomes increasingly apparent" (1978:233). Sakenfeld (1978:45) suggests *khesed* represents a free decision to meet a vital need in an existing relationship. Others suggest a different essential meaning for *khesed*, such as "family love," which was then applied to other situations, including covenants, thereby bringing new connotations to the word (cf. Baker 2008:152).

A full discussion or study of the meaning of *khesed* is beyond the scope of this commentary, and rather than engage the above ideas at length, I wish to offer a practical definition (or association) that arises from the book of Ruth: *Khesed* is simply a desire to bless others that outweighs considerations of the potential cost to oneself. Over and over in the book of Ruth, blessings are wished—and as they are, *khesed* is mentioned (1:8; 2:20; 3:10). God's desire to bless everyone and everything expresses the goodness that is integral to his being. As such, God is the author of blessing, and in Ruth, the desire to bless others that can be observed in human and divine actions highlights the connection between human and divine actions. This is evident in the fact that while all three uses of the word *khesed* in Ruth are found in a context where God is being blessed, the *khesed* itself is attributed once to God (1:8), once to Boaz (2:20), and once to Ruth (3:10). This is the key to the elevation of three preceding themes—loyalty, honor, and wisdom: In the story of Ruth, those human virtues or qualities are directed by *khesed* and therefore realize their full potential as expressions of the blessing of the Lord himself. Thus, at the "intersection" of the book, Naomi blesses Boaz in the name of the Lord and recognizes *khesed* in the actions of Boaz (2:20). As Trible (ABD 5.845) notes, "A faithful God blesses through a faithful people." God's blessing is recognized most fully in the book in 4:13-15.

Reversal and Redemption. It is impossible to miss the theme of reversal in Ruth, particularly in the Hebrew text. The whole plot, with its story of Naomi's loss and then fulfillment, turns on the idea that her situation is reversed. Tied to the idea of reversal is that of redemption: What would have been lost is rightfully reclaimed; what would have been wasted instead bears fruit. There are many details in which this theme is evident, as well, such as the move from famine to a plentiful harvest (1:1; 1:6) and the shift in Naomi's definition of herself from pleasant to bitter and from full to empty (1:20-21). There is also the reversal from a loss of children to the birth of a new child (1:5; 4:16), which in a broader perspective is also a reversal from the loss of a clan from the tribe of Judah to the production of the royal line from the tribe of Judah (4:17).

In Ruth the idea of the "family redeemer" appears numerous times (2:20; 3:9, 12; 4:1, 3, 6, 8, 14), also highlighting this thematic element. Although not many uses of the root *ga'al* [TH1350, ZH1457] (to redeem) in Ruth are nontechnical or nonlegal in their sense (as will be discussed in the commentary), the frequency of the term's occurrence serves to highlight redemption as a thematic idea. Of necessity, redemption involves the reversal of some situation: What is lost is regained or saved; what is promised or rightfully due is delivered. The term *ga'al* in the Bible is often extended beyond its technical sense involving land rights so that God is also portrayed as a "redeemer" (*go'el*; see Exod 15:13; Isa 43:1; 44:6; 48:20; Pss 69:18; 77:15; 103:4). (But note that not all instances of English "redeemer" come from this Hebrew root. Some come from the verb *padah* [TH6299, ZH7009]; cf. 1 Kgs 1:29; Isa 1:27.)

In sum, situations can and will change drastically in life. Those who belong to the Lord can be confident that in the end, he will move heaven and earth to accomplish their redemption—even if not in this lifetime. And more than that, believers should be actively seeking, like Ruth, Naomi, and Boaz, to express *khesed* [TH2617, ZH2876] so that they may be agents of reversal and redemption in the lives of others. Such action does not promise a happy ending to every story, but it offers the possibility of change and reflects the mercy and goodness of God.

Human and Divine Cooperation. Throughout the book of Ruth, the Lord's ultimate sovereignty over all that comes to pass is implicit. We see this in the narrator's comments at 1:6 and 4:13, which state that the Lord made both the land and Ruth's womb fruitful. Naomi's understanding that "the LORD himself" has moved against her (1:13) and the recognition of the Lord's role by the women of Bethlehem at the end of the story (4:14) also reflect this perspective. As in James 1:17, the book of Ruth would assert that "whatever is good and perfect comes down to us from God our Father." In spite of this theological background, however, the narration of the story's events highlights an earthbound perspective. The Lord is all-powerful but also mysterious and transcendent—working well out of human sight. Perhaps the height of the paradox between these two views is to be found in 2:3, where the narrator says, "As it happened, [Ruth] found herself working in a field that belonged to Boaz, the relative of her father-in-law, Elimelech." One can hardly doubt that the narrator views this as more than coincidence, and yet he chose a portrayal that highlights the fact that Ruth had no way of knowing whether her particular choice of a field to glean in had been directed by God or not. Ruth does not pray before she chooses a field; no message is given by a judge, priest, or prophet. Furthermore, no one in the book is reported as seeking the Lord by prayer or other means (cf. Gen 24:12-27; Josh 7:6-15; 9:14; Judg 18:5; 1 Sam 9:9; 23:2). Nonetheless, in the actions of the characters—particularly in their virtuous actions—the Lord's will is carried forth.

From this paradox arises the theme of the synergy of the divine and the human. As noted above in the discussion of the theme of blessing, the idea of *khesed* [TH2617, ZH2876] is interwoven with both human and divine actions. In the book of Ruth we see clearly that God intends his greatest possible glory to be achieved with human involvement (as well as with angelic and other involvement). To be sure, the Lord can act alone and in an overt, miraculous manner, but as a rule, in the wide scope of history, he works providentially in and through human actions, within the limits of the rules he has instituted in nature. Ruth offers us a beautiful picture of exactly that.

For anyone who has been tempted to see a strict dichotomy between God's actions and man's, there is a little irony in the overlap here as the main characters fulfill God's plan without anything more than his providential actions, and without a clue as to the full implications of their actions (i.e., the eventuality of the Davidic monarchy). And even without such benefits, the characters give glory to God and rejoice in what they do understand. In this sense there is a theme that pairs the recognition of God's control over history with the recognition of human will and involvement in history's blessed events.

Perhaps a parallel subtheme is to be found in the interplay between men and women in the book of Ruth as well: Although clearly concerned with the continuation of a patriarchal line from Judah to David, and dependent on the intervention of the male family redeemer, Boaz, the story devotes much time to the critical actions of two women, apart from whom Elimelech's line would have ended. In both cases, an "on the ground" perspective is given to balance our sometimes abstract conceptions about how a certain system will play out in reality. Even a patriarchal system remains equally dependent on both men and women to function as it should, and even God's all-powerful sovereignty is not routinely expressed apart from human activity. One cannot press such an analogy too far, but it should at least highlight the fact that a desirable harmony can exist in these two spheres in a more mysterious and fluid sense than might be expected.

OUTLINE

- I. Tragedy Strikes (1:1-22)
  - A. Naomi's Bereavement (1:1-6)
  - B. Naomi's Bitter Prospects and Ruth's Risk (1:7-19a)
  - C. Naomi's Emptiness in Bethlehem (1:19b-22)
- II. Ruth Provides for Naomi (2:1-23)
  - A. Ruth Happens upon the Field of Boaz (2:1-3)
  - B. Boaz Blesses Ruth in the Name of the Lord (2:4-17)
  - C. Naomi Begins to See the Lord's Provision (2:18-23)
- III. Naomi Seeks to Provide for Ruth (3:1-18)
  - A. Naomi Counts on Boaz's Integrity and Kindness (3:1-5)
  - B. Ruth Enacts the Plan and Boaz Responds Favorably and Immediately (3:6-15)
  - C. Ruth Reports the Outcome to Naomi (3:16-18)
- IV. Boaz Provides for Elimelech's Family (4:1-22)
  - A. Boaz Successfully Gains Ruth and Pledges to Provide for Elimelech's Family (4:1-12)
  - B. The Lord Fulfills Naomi by Providing an Heir for Elimelech's Family (4:13-17)
  - C. Elimelech's Family Is Part of the Line of David (4:18-22)

COMMENTARY ON
Ruth

◆ I. Tragedy Strikes (1:1-22)
A. Naomi's Bereavement (1:1-6)

In the days when the judges ruled in Israel, a severe famine came upon the land. So a man from Bethlehem in Judah left his home and went to live in the country of Moab, taking his wife and two sons with him. 2The man's name was Elimelech, and his wife was Naomi. Their two sons were Mahlon and Kilion. They were Ephrathites from Bethlehem in the land of Judah. And when they reached Moab, they settled there.

3Then Elimelech died, and Naomi was left with her two sons. 4The two sons married Moabite women. One married a woman named Orpah, and the other a woman named Ruth. But about ten years later, 5both Mahlon and Kilion died. This left Naomi alone, without her two sons or her husband.

6Then Naomi heard in Moab that the LORD had blessed his people in Judah by giving them good crops again. So Naomi and her daughters-in-law got ready to leave Moab to return to her homeland.

NOTES

1:1 ***In the days when the judges ruled.*** Some see in this setting, coupled with the return of a small portion of an Israelite family to the land and the virtue of the main characters of Ruth, the idea of a faithful remnant for Israel (cf. Gen 45:7; 1 Kgs 19:14, 18; 2 Kgs 19:30-31; Isa 10:20-21; Rom 11:3-4). But the concept of God's faithful remnant amid the turbulent Judges period is not a theme emphasized by the narrative of Ruth—it is not the message of the book. Ruth's story does, however, illustrate this lesson seen elsewhere in Scripture. Like Elijah's despairing challenge to God (1 Kgs 19), many faithful Israelites may have wondered during the period of the judges whether they were alone and whether there was any hope for Israel as a covenant people. Like God's response to Elijah, the testimony of the book of Ruth reminds us that even in a chaotic and ungodly society, the Lord is perfectly capable of accomplishing his will and of preserving faithful people for himself.

Bethlehem. The town name *beth lekhem* [TH1035, ZH1107] is literally "house of bread" and probably means something like "storehouse." Bethlehem in Judah is located about five miles south of Jerusalem. Joshua 19:15 lists another town of the same name in Zebulun. The town name provides not only a link to David (cf. 1 Sam 17:12), but also a little irony because famine has struck the town. It will eventually be the rural farming setting for the later scenes of harvest (chs 2–3).

went to live in the country of Moab. Moab was located north of the wadi Zered (or, wadi el-Hesa), which empties into the south end of the Dead Sea, and extended north of the wadi Arnon (or, wadi el-Mujib), at times as far as Heshbon (cf. Num 21:12; Deut 2:13-14). Its capital was in Kir-Moab (or Kir-hareseth, modern-day Kerak in Jordan). Sakenfeld

(1999:19-20) finds Moab an odd choice for seeking food because Israel's past history with Moab would seem to paint it as inhospitable (see Deut 23:3-4). Indeed, the Qumran literature has portrayals of the Moabites as enemies of Israel (4QMMT 40-53; 4QFlor 1:4). Sakenfeld therefore suggests that this peculiarity could have functioned as a hook to draw readers into the story.

The verb "live" (*gur* [TH1481, ZH1591]) may indicate a temporary stay (e.g., Gen 21:34; 2 Kgs 8:1-2; Jer 44:14), as a "sojourn" (cf. NASB) or a permanent residence (cf. Exod 6:4; Num 15:14; Deut 26:5; 2 Sam 4:3; Jer 49:18, 33; Ezek 47:22-23). It is unclear what Elimelech's intent was in migrating, but the decreased rights belonging to people of immigrant status, along with the reason given as a famine, suggest that this measure was originally intended as temporary. Some have viewed Elimelech's move to Moab as a disobedient act because it involved leaving the Promised Land; in this case, his death (1:3) is viewed as a divine judgment. (*Ruth Rabbah* 2:10 suggests that God similarly judged Elimelech's two sons, but after patiently waiting for their repentance.) But the text says so little about Elimelech or his sons that it is difficult to argue that this is its emphasis. Further, there is precedent for the Lord's watching over those who seek food in foreign lands during famine (cf. Gen 12:10; 42:1-2; 46:1-4; 47:4). On the other hand, Abraham and Jacob's sojourns in foreign lands are sometimes interpreted as a sign of lacking faith. The narrator is not so concerned with the question of whether the move was good or bad, aiming rather to establish Naomi's unfortunate situation.

1:2 *Ephrathites.* Ephratha was an alternate name for Bethlehem (4:11; Gen 35:16, 19; 48:7) and, at one time, may have indicated a small village nearby Bethlehem. "Ephrathites" could therefore indicate that Elimelech's family were residents of Bethlehem or its territory. Rachel, wife of Jacob the patriarch, was buried near Ephratha (Gen 35:19). But the term "Ephrathites" may also indicate that the family was from the clan of Ephrath (1 Chr 4:4). This second meaning is more likely, but in either case, the importance of the term is its link to David, who was also an Ephrathite (1 Sam 17:12; Mic 5:2). Without giving away the outcome of the story, the narrator hints at what will be revealed in the genealogy of ch 4.

they settled. Lit., "they were there," or perhaps, "they stayed there." The idea of a permanent settlement is not required by the verb.

1:3 *Elimelech died.* Lit., "Elimelech, the husband of Naomi, died." Naomi was introduced as "his wife" (1:2), but after his death, Elimelech is reduced to "Naomi's husband." In ancient literature, it is rare to find a man named in terms of his relationship to a woman. With this phrase, the narrator subtly signals that Naomi will be the main character—not Elimelech or his sons as one might have otherwise supposed. Throughout the text of Ruth, the LXX gives the name Abimelech rather than Elimelech. The name Elimelech (like Mahlon, Kilion, Ruth, Orpah, and Naomi) occurs only in Ruth in the Bible, though it is also found in the Amarna letters and in Ugaritic. Abimelech differs in only one letter from Elimelech in a Hebrew consonantal text, and it is far more common in the Bible (cf. Gen 20–21; Judg 9). Perhaps this influenced the LXX's translation.

Linafelt (1999:3; cf. Berger 2009a:270; Fischer 2001:125) suggests that Elimelech and his death represent the transition from God as exclusive king (as in the judges period) to the time of the monarchy, and Ruth and Boaz therefore show the qualities of a monarchy that can maintain the balance with theocracy. Berger (2009a:271) adds that Elimelech fits this role precisely because in leaving for Moab, he abandoned dependency on God and responsibility to his countrymen—a parallel to all of Israel. Ruth was the antithesis of her father-in-law in a certain way, a non-Israelite who came to the land and showed dependency on God and assumed responsibility for Naomi. Others (e.g., Matthews 2004:212) suggest that the travels represent an exile and return, or an exodus. In my view, all the above symbolisms are hard to prove conclusively from the text, but are worthy of reflection in view of their connection to Ruth's character as an ancestor of David and his line.

1:4 *married.* Heb., *nasa'* [TH5375, ZH5951] (to take up). Another Hebrew idiom for marriage is *laqakh* [TH3947, ZH4374] (to take). The presence of the word *nasa'* here need not be understood as implying anything derogatory about the marriages (as Block 1999:629). More likely, any shift in the use of one verb or the other reflects the change of the language with time, or perhaps with locale.

about ten years later. Lit., "they lived there ten years." The Hebrew is somewhat ambiguous, using a mas. pl. verb in the *wayyiqtol* stem. Some commentators take this in an epexegetical fashion, referring to the total time of the sons' stay in Moab, that is, they got married and they *had* stayed there ten years (cf. Bush 1996:65). But others see it in a sequential sense: They got married and then stayed there ten years (e.g., Campbell 1975:58). I prefer the second because I see no compelling reason to take the *wayyiqtol* form as other than sequential here. It has been suggested (e.g., Hubbard 1988:95) that "ten years later" draws a parallel with Gen 16:3, but as Bush suggests (1996:65), the Hebrew construction is not similar enough to warrant this conclusion.

1:5 *her two sons.* Lit., "her two boys." As has been suggested (cf. Bush 1996:66; Campbell 1975:56), the use of *yeled* [TH3206, ZH3529] (boy, child) here rather than *ben* [TH1121, ZH1201] (son) is strange in a context regarding grown men and is intended as a link to highlight the reversal evident in 4:16, in which Naomi brings a new *yeled* into her bosom.

1:6 *the LORD had blessed his people.* Lit., "the LORD visited his people." The Heb. *paqad* [TH6485, ZH7212] (visit) is used of God's evident presence among his people both to judge (Exod 32:34; Isa 10:12; 23:17) and to bless (e.g., Gen 21:1; 50:24-25).

in Judah. The NLT adds this to clarify the general location of "his people."

Naomi and her daughters-in-law got ready. It is difficult to represent in English the fact that all the verbs in 1:6 are fem. sg. Although Naomi's daughters-in-law are mentioned, they are not the proper subject of any verb. The focus rests heavily on Naomi. Consequently, there is also not a strong emphasis on the preparations of the daughters-in-law to leave Moab or on Orpah's decision not to move to Judah (1:14) as a significant change of heart (cf. Bush 1996:85).

COMMENTARY

This first scene in Ruth introduces over ten years of background information in only a few lines. The reader quickly gets a picture of Elimelech's family life going through ups and downs—famine and finding food, the father's death and the marriage of the two sons—and then a seemingly ultimate disaster strikes, and Naomi is left alone on center stage, as it were (1:5). This raises the problem that drives the plot of the story, which is Naomi's emptiness, her ruined life.

The text does not address it, but it is most likely that the famine (1:1) was because of drought. Weather systems carrying moisture blow in to Israel from the Mediterranean Sea and continue on into Jordan. As these systems move inland, the elevation of the land generally increases (with the obvious exception of the Jordan Valley) until the Jordan plateau is reached. At times clouds carrying significant moisture pass over the hills of Israel, where Bethlehem is located, and are not forced to release their rain until reaching the higher elevations of the Jordan plateau, where Moab was located.

Once they arrived in Moab, the family evidently found a decent way to get the food they needed and continue with a normal life. Therefore, they did not leave Moab for some time, and eventually Elimelech died. After their father's death, Naomi's two sons married women from Moab (whom the rabbis held to be sisters, *Ruth Rabbah* 2:9). Although Moabites were not permitted into the Lord's assembly (Deut 23:3; cf. Neh 13:1-3), there was no direct command against marrying them as there was against other people groups (Deut 7:1-3). In this period after the initial settlement of the land and before the monarchy, Israel and Moab appear to have had a more open relationship than in later or earlier years (1 Sam 22:3-5; cf. Deut 2:8-9, 28-29). In 4:10 Ruth is specified as Mahlon's wife. Why, after ten years of marriage, neither Mahlon and Ruth nor Kilion and Orpah had any children is not stated.

As mentioned (see notes on 1:1) some have suggested this was because of God's judgment, but it is difficult to know since our reticent narrator, like so many of the Bible's narrators, does not break into the text with an evaluation as one finds, for example, in 2 Kings 14:24. Perhaps the narrator hints at the cause for this somewhat surprising circumstance in the names of these two sons: Mahlon (from *khalah* [TH2470, ZH2703], "to be sick, weak") and Kilion (from *kalah* [TH3615, ZH3983], "to vanish, fade") are perhaps to be seen as lacking vitality. This, however, is far from conclusive; numerous derivations and meanings have been offered for these names, and none has really won consensus—since the narrator makes no clear play on the name of any character besides Naomi (cf. 1:20). If, as Sakenfeld (1999:14, 20) suggests, Ruth is implicitly marked as barren by this mention of ten years without a child, there is a parallel with the matriarchs Sarah and Rachel. This is an appealing possibility, but I find the evidence for her barrenness inconclusive.

Naomi's new situation without a husband or children was difficult. Not only was she depressed as a result of these losses, she was in distress economically in a society that offered women no real independent professions apart from prostitution. As a mother of grown children, her age made both remarriage and the possibility of bearing any more children in her husband's name impossibilities (cf. 1:11-12). Widows were often taken advantage of (Isa 10:2) or ignored and neglected (Isa 1:23), even though the Lord gave special commands regarding them and other vulnerable members of society (e.g., Deut 14:28-29; 24:19-21; 26:12-13). Naomi's bleak future appeared to be only begging and poverty in her increasing age. Further, she was isolated from family, lacking any blood relatives in Moab.

The famine in Judah did not likely extend over the whole ten or so years that had passed. What is indicated in 1:6 is not merely the end of the famine, but the presence of "good crops"; the people recognized the fertility of the land as a visitation (*paqad* [TH6485, ZH7212]) of the Lord to provide for them. The news about this complete reversal of the dire situation recounted in 1:1 reached Naomi in Moab. Perhaps this raised Naomi's hopes of survival in Judah sufficiently to encourage her to return even in her desperate state.

At the close of this scene, the focus is on Naomi's preparation and intent to return to Judah. Her daughters-in-law are still present with her, but it is not absolutely clear whether they will accompany her (see note on 1:6). The question of what lies ahead for Naomi looms in the reader's mind.

B. Naomi's Bitter Prospects and Ruth's Risk (1:7-19a)

7 With her two daughters-in-law she set
out from the place where she had been
living, and they took the road that would
lead them back to Judah.
8 But on the way, Naomi said to her two
daughters-in-law, "Go back to your moth-
ers' homes. And may the LORD reward you
for your kindness to your husbands and to
me. 9 May the LORD bless you with the se-
curity of another marriage." Then she
kissed them good-bye, and they all broke
down and wept.
10 "No," they said. "We want to go with
you to your people."
11 But Naomi replied, "Why should you
go on with me? Can I still give birth to
other sons who could grow up to be your
husbands? 12 No, my daughters, return to
your parents' homes, for I am too old to
marry again. And even if it were possible,
and I were to get married tonight and
bear sons, then what? 13 Would you wait
for them to grow up and refuse to marry
someone else? No, of course not, my
daughters! Things are far more bitter for
me than for you, because the LORD himself
has raised his fist against me."
14 And again they wept together, and
Orpah kissed her mother-in-law good-
bye. But Ruth clung tightly to Naomi.
15 "Look," Naomi said to her, "your sister-
in-law has gone back to her people and to
her gods. You should do the same."
16 But Ruth replied, "Don't ask me to
leave you and turn back. Wherever you
go, I will go; wherever you live, I will live.
Your people will be my people, and your
God will be my God. 17 Wherever you die,
I will die, and there I will be buried. May
the LORD punish me severely if I allow
anything but death to separate us!"
18 When Naomi saw that Ruth was deter-
mined to go with her, she said nothing
more.
19 So the two of them continued on their
journey.

NOTES

1:8 ***on the way.*** This phrase is added by the NLT. The Hebrew simply opens the verse with "and she said." It is unclear how far the women had gotten on the road, but the flow of the text would seem to imply they had not yet gotten far from their starting point.

mothers' homes. The "father's house" is the far more common reference in the OT, but cf. Gen 24:28; Song 3:4; 8:2. The use of "mother's house" perhaps reflects a reality in ancient polygamous societies, where each wife would dwell in a separate tent or house. In such situations, the mother's house was a smaller subset of the father's house in a social sense and was the specific place to which the daughter would return (cf. Bush 1996:75). Here, the use of the term serves to contrast with the idea of staying with Naomi, the mother-in-law.

may the LORD reward you for your kindness to your husbands and to me. More lit., "May the LORD show loving-kindness (*khesed* [TH2617, ZH2876]) to you as you've shown to the deceased [husbands] and to me." This is the first use of the word *khesed* in the narrative.

1:12 ***to your parents' homes.*** The NLT adds this phrase for clarity.

I am too old. The verb (*zaqanti* [TH2204, ZH2416]) is in the perfect tense, but does not indicate past time in this case. The emphasis in this case is on the "factuality of the state as a whole" (Chisholm 1998:87).

1:14 ***But Ruth clung tightly to [her].*** Heb., *weruth dabqah* [TH1692, ZH1815] *bah* (the NLT uses "Naomi" rather than "her" for clarity). This is the first Waw-disjunctive in the narrative. It serves to emphasize Ruth's unusually noble character, particularly her love and loyalty to Naomi here.

1:15 ***gods.*** This could also be rendered "god." Note especially 1 Kgs 11:33, where the pl. form is used of Chemosh. This does not highlight Orpah's idolatry, for she is portrayed as making an expected and reasonable choice. It rather highlights Ruth's extreme decision in committing not just to care for Naomi, but to adopt her God. It is also not necessary to assume any other poor character qualities on the part of Orpah as in the Aggadah found in *b. Sotah* 42b (cf. *Ruth Zuta* 1; *Ruth Rabbah* 2:20).

1:16 ***your God will be my God.*** The term "God" (*'elohim* [TH430, ZH466]) is used only four times in the book of Ruth: It occurs twice in this verse, once in reference to the foreign gods to which Orpah returns (1:15), and once in the phrase "[Yahweh], the God of Israel" (2:12). In contrast to this, Yahweh (*yhwh* [TH3068, ZH3378]) is often mentioned (cf. 1:6, 8-9, 21; 2:4, 12, 19-20; 3:10, 13; 4:12, 14). This is part of the book's subtle emphasis on the specific identity and character of Israel's God, to whom Ruth now commits herself. Because the personal name Yahweh is used consistently throughout the book, the theme of blessing associated with his character is more easily traced than references to multiple names would have allowed.

1:17 ***there I will be buried.*** Ruth's commitment to Israel's tribal land is significant (cf. Gen 50:24-26; Josh 24:32).

May the LORD punish me severely. Lit., "Thus may the LORD do to me, and thus do again." Ancient oaths such as this one (cf. 1 Sam 3:17; 20:13) often implied curses without specifying their actual content—it would be up to the Lord to decide the severe punishment. Bullinger (1968:940) calls this an example of maledictio or imprecation, associating it with the Greek words *apeuchomai* (to deprecate, to wish something may not happen) and *misos* (hatred). By this oath, Ruth stated her commitment to Naomi in no uncertain terms.

COMMENTARY

With the first plural feminine verb in the book, 1:7 tells us that the women have set out on the road to Judah. They apparently did not get far before Naomi delivered some sound advice to her daughters-in-law. The narrator has signaled some question as to the views of the two young women about moving to Judah in his use of singular verbs in 1:6 (see note). Now the question of the realities of such a move is voiced by Naomi. Naomi makes her case three times, resulting in three exchanges (1:8-10, 11-14, and 15-18), climaxing with Ruth's well-known vow to remain with Naomi. The first two rounds focus on Naomi's words and end with weeping and a response on the part of the daughters-in-law. The third round, however, shifts its focus to the words of Ruth and ends with a response by Naomi—silence (1:18).

Naomi's advice that the girls return to their home in Moab was grounded in the realities of their situation. It is likely she saw her advice as advantageous for all of them in the long run. Though she would have to make the journey alone, each of them would find support in a family network in their own homeland. The familiarity of language and culture and the strength of family were their best chance for getting by in these dire straits. Although we do not know anything directly regarding Moabite views about remarrying widows, it is not unlikely that Moabite women would be more attractive as spouses to Moabite men than to foreign men for the simple reason that people, on average, choose mates from backgrounds similar to their own (Kalmijn 1998). Naomi's advice was based on a sound assessment of the situation and a concern for the best future for her daughters-in-law and herself.

Naomi's first address is a short farewell that shows appreciation and good wishes toward her daughters-in-law and frees them from any obligation they might have had or felt toward her. First, she stated her advice (in the imperative) that they return home. Then she acknowledged their "kindness" (*khesed* [TH2617, ZH2876], see note on 1:8) toward her sons and toward her—she was probably implying that they hadn't even needed to stay with her as long as they had. Finally, she wished them security in the homes of new husbands (1:9); they were in no way bound to remain with Naomi or to remain unmarried.

In customary Near Eastern fashion, this was marked with kisses and weeping. Kisses are not uncommon in traditional everyday greetings and farewells, but weeping marks either the beginning or end of a long separation. Another feature of traditional interactions in the Near East is that disagreement is sometimes used rhetorically to validate a person's resolve. Thus, the first objection of Orpah and Ruth (1:10) to Naomi's advice is probably best understood as expected and not necessarily indicative of a real intent to move to Judah. Orpah and Ruth were expressing their grief at this farewell through this denial; they were in a sense bartering with Naomi before concluding that separation was the price to be paid. A similar kind of interaction is probably in view in Genesis 23:11, where Ephron the Hittite offers to "give" Abraham a field and cave. Formalized agreements needed to be negotiated orally and vocalized repeatedly. Similarly, traditional Islamic law (Sharia) preserves the requirement that to divorce his wife, the husband must tell her three times that she is divorced.

It is therefore expected when, in the second exchange (1:11-14), Naomi repeated her assertion that the girls should return home (1:12). As she did so, she moved from her first, relatively formal farewell, to remarks that lay bare the pain and desperation of the situation. There was no benefit for the two women in remaining with Naomi, and in fact, they would further jeopardize themselves by staying with her. Naomi expressed this by first commenting that her bitterness was too great for them, and then by emphasizing that it was the LORD who acted against her. The second point is notable in what it implies about Naomi's Israelite worldview—she was not subject to fate or chance, but to the sovereign Yahweh. Moreover, if she had been so designated to experience calamity, who knew what lay ahead? The sane thing for Orpah and Ruth to do was to try to distance themselves from God's "target."

Naomi's first comment, regarding her bitterness (1:13), may be understood as saying that she was sorry that Ruth and Orpah had to suffer the calamity that had come upon her (cf. REB, "for your sakes I feel bitter"), or that the bitterness of remaining tied to Naomi's family is "too much for [them] to bear" (NET), or that Naomi's life is more bitter than theirs—that is, they have other alternatives and need not face the hardship she was facing (e.g., NLT, NASB). Because Naomi's statements in 1:11-13a have focused on the potential of remarriage for the two women, the last option seems best. Like her earlier blessing on their potential remarriage (1:9), Naomi's words here suggest that they had not lost everything as she had; they had a way out, a chance to start again and find happiness. Her lot was more bitter than theirs, and Naomi's advice was that they take advantage of the opportunities that remained for them.

Naomi made her case, and the women once again expressed their great sorrow at parting. Orpah, as instructed, returned home, but Ruth refused to let Naomi go (see note on 1:14). Naomi, with Ruth clinging to her, encouraged her to follow her sister-in-law's example, to be done with this sad parting and return to Moab (1:15). But Ruth will "return" only to Judah (see note on 1:22).

We do not know, and Naomi may not have known, what actual situation Orpah and Ruth would be returning to in their mothers' homes and in Moabite society generally, but the narrator's focus on the desperation of Naomi's situation suggests that we should understand Orpah's choice as a smart and natural one, and Ruth's as a little risky. Pointing out the hard circumstances in which Ruth's decision was made and the fact that Naomi discouraged it and did not expect it, Sakenfeld (1999:34) comments, "In sum, the loyalty of Ruth to Naomi may offer a general model for loyal relationships between all people, not just for daughter-in-law to mother-in-law. At the same time, the story of Ruth models loyalty freely offered to another, not coerced by custom, culture, or biblical demand."

Ruth's response to Naomi's final word of advice that she follow her sister-in-law back to Moab expresses fully the intent of her clinging to Naomi, and it is more than Naomi bargained for. Ruth's response is not simply a protest, but a comprehensively stated commitment to remain with Naomi for the rest of her life no matter the cost. At this point in the cycle of Naomi's advice, Ruth's commitment has been tested and is clear—all that remains for Naomi is to accept it (1:18).

Ruth's statement includes the expected ideas of going with Naomi and living with her (1:16), but Ruth goes beyond this in declaring an intent to join Naomi's people, be devoted to her God, and be buried in Israel (1:16-17). She sealed her statement with a curse in the Lord's name should she violate her commitment. Joining another culture takes serious commitment, and in the world of Iron Age Israel, choosing that culture's god or gods was not natural (cf. Matthews 2004:207). Unlike the case in the modern, Western mind-set, religious belief was rarely viewed as subject to personal choice and was instead a critical part of cultural identity. Ruth's decision was a departure from all the primary markers of her identity as a Moabite. The importance of burial in one's homeland may be observed, for example, in the requests of Jacob and Joseph to be buried in Canaan (Gen 49:29; 50:25). The implication of Ruth's intent to be buried in Israel was a change of homeland and an intent to change her national identity if possible. She would be forever aligned with the family of Naomi and Elimelech.

As such, one might even suggest that Ruth informally took on the role that a living child of Naomi's might have had, to ensure the care and support of a widowed mother (but cf. Matthews 2004:222). This concept may be hinted at in the words of 4:15: "your daughter-in-law . . . has been better to you than seven sons!"

This scene, which started with the women on the road to Judah, closes with Ruth and Naomi continuing on the road (1:19a). We do not see the women again until probably three or four days later upon the entry to Bethlehem at the end of their trek.

C. Naomi's Emptiness in Bethlehem (1:19b-22)

When they came to Bethlehem, the en-
tire town was excited by their arrival. "Is
it really Naomi?" the women asked.
20 "Don't call me Naomi," she respond-
ed. "Instead, call me Mara,* for the Al-
mighty has made life very bitter for me.
21 I went away full, but the LORD has
brought me home empty. Why call me
Naomi when the LORD has caused me to
suffer* and the Almighty has sent such
tragedy upon me?"
22 So Naomi returned from Moab, accom-
panied by her daughter-in-law Ruth, the
young Moabite woman. They arrived in
Bethlehem in late spring, at the beginning
of the barley harvest.

1:20 *Naomi* means "pleasant"; *Mara* means "bitter." 1:21 Or *has testified against me.*

NOTES

1:19 *was excited.* The verb *wattehom* [TH1949, ZH2101] (stir, make a noise) may indicate either agitation (Isa 22:2) or excitement (1 Sam 4:5; cf. Bush 1996:91). Here excitement is the more appropriate understanding, although as Linafelt (1999:18-19) argues, perhaps we should understand both meanings in tension—it may be that the townswomen's question indicates that they are both distressed at Naomi's losses and yet joyful to see her. In my understanding, the concern or agitation is given voice as a desire to hear Naomi's news, which is inherent in the question.

1:20 *Naomi . . . Mara.* Naomi reversed the meaning of her name in this dramatic statement. Instead of calling her "pleasant" (the meaning of *na'omi* [TH5281, ZH5843]), the women should call her "bitter" (the meaning of *mara'*; cf. *marar* [TH4843, ZH5352]; *morah* [TH4786, ZH5289]; *marah* [TH4785, ZH5288]; cf. Exod 15:23; 2 Kgs 4:27; Lam 1:4). On the Aleph as a fem. ending, see GKC §80h.

the Almighty. Heb., *shadday* [TH7706, ZH8724]; e.g., Gen 17:1; 28:3; Exod 6:3; Job 11:7. The meaning of this name for God is unknown, and most English translations draw from the LXX's frequent use of *pantokratōr* [TG3841, ZG4120] (all powerful) in translating this term. As Hubbard (1988:125) remarks, "the name is certainly an ancient one, perhaps one which the patriarchs brought from Mesopotamia or an epithet of the Canaanite God El adopted by the Israelites." In my view associations with *shad* [TH7699, ZH8716] (breast) or *shed* [TH7700, ZH8717] (spirit, demon) are much less likely than a derivation from Akkadian *shadday*, meaning "mountain." In the OT, however, this title for God is associated with his cosmic power, his authority to judge, to bless or to curse. It is thus appropriate in the context of Naomi's comments about her fate at the hands of the Lord. (For further detail, see Bush 1996:92-93; Hubbard 1988:124-125; and HALOT 4.1420-1422.)

1:21 *has caused me to suffer.* Cf. NLT mg, "has testified against me." The NLT mg represents the best reading of the MT, which has here a legal phrase (*'anah bi* [TH6031, ZH6700]; cf. Exod 20:16; Num 35:30; 1 Sam 12:3). The text of the NLT (cf. RSV, NRSV) agrees with the interpretation present in the LXX reading (*etapeinōsen* [TG5013, ZG5427]), which takes the consonants of the MT's *'anah* as representing the Piel verb *'innah* [TH6031, ZH6700] (afflict).

1:22 *accompanied by . . . Ruth.* Lit., "and Naomi returned with Ruth the Moabitess . . . who returned from the fields of Moab." Some commentators suggest the words "who returned from the fields of Moab" may be a scribal error or addition, since the words are somewhat redundant with the first clause in the verse. Bush (1996:94), however, rightly notes that the unusual syntax here, along with the use of "Moabitess," is intended to draw attention to Ruth's "return." In 1:15 the same verb is used of Orpah's return to her mother and her gods.

barley harvest. Various seasonal harvests occur throughout the year in Israel. Grapes, figs, and olives, for example, are harvested in the late summer and fall. Pomegranates ripen at this time as well. But the grain crops are planted in the fall and reaped in the spring after the winter rains have ceased. The barley harvest preceded the wheat harvest and occurred from the time of the spring equinox in March until mid-April. The following month was the time for wheat harvest. "According to the Gezer Manual, [wheat] was harvested during the sixth agricultural season, *yrh qsr wkl* (end of April to end of May)" (Borowski 1987:88). "In the early stages of the Israelite settlement the most important cereal was barley . . . because of the necessity to settle fringe areas and barley's tolerance of harsh conditions" (Borowski 1987:7). The "Gezer Manual" or Gezer Calendar mentioned above (cf. ANET 320) dates to the second half of the tenth century BC.

COMMENTARY

These verses are the climax of the first act of Ruth, which is devoted to stating the problem that drives the story. The problem of Naomi's emptiness, which was raised in 1:5, is here driven home in a dramatic and poetic fashion.

The scene is a bittersweet homecoming. One can imagine Naomi seeing with satisfaction familiar landmarks and many things unchanged in the village, and the stir (of excitement as in 1 Sam 4:5) in the village upon her return is evident in the text. But Bethlehem was likely filled with warm memories that only highlighted Naomi's bleak situation. The women of the town had likely wondered if they would ever see Naomi again. When they heard she had come, they immediately sought to hear her news. The question "Is this Naomi?" (lit., 1:19) should be understood not as asking for a verification of Naomi's identification but as an exclamation (cf. Bush 1996:91)—a surprised greeting and request for news: "Naomi, it's you!"

The core of this scene is Naomi's dramatic statement about her losses and her assertion that her name should be changed (1:20-21). She, in effect, responded to the women's request for news while poetically taking their expression in a literal fashion, saying in effect "No, this is not Naomi—Naomi had a full life, but I am empty." Naomi's response takes the form of a statement followed by a parallel rhetorical question. Each of these is marked by reference to the names Naomi (*na'omi;* cf. the common noun *no'am* [TH5278, ZH5840], "sweet, pleasant"), the Almighty (*shadday* [TH7706, ZH8724]), and the LORD (*yhwh* [TH3068, ZH3378]), with the two references to God being reversed in the second half of the statement:

A. Don't call me *Naomi* ["sweet"] . . . call me Mara ["bitter"] (1:20)
    B. for the *Almighty* has made life very bitter for me.
    C. I went away full, but the *LORD* has brought me home empty. (1:21)
A'. Why call me Naomi
    C'. when the *LORD* has spoken against me
    B'. and the *Almighty* has sent such tragedy upon me?

In the first line, Naomi plays on her own name, saying that "sweet" is no longer an appropriate descriptor for her—she should be called "bitter" (1:20; cf. 1:13). The summation of her bitter and tragic circumstance is that she went away full and the Lord brought her back empty. Naomi was evidently not ready to write a self-help book about overcoming tragedy. Her assertion of the Lord's role perhaps makes modern readers uncomfortable, just as the reader's knowledge about God's role in

Job's losses does (Job 1–2). The narrator of Ruth, however, gives us no clue as to any decrees made in heaven. Implicit in Naomi's complaint about God is her conviction of his sovereignty and power. Campbell (1975:83) rightly suggests that this is a natural stance in the Old Testament world (cf. e.g., Ps 13), and one may even compare Abraham's forthright complaint in Genesis 15:2 about his lack of an heir. The complaint against the Lord is thus not surprising here; the narrator's focus is not on characterizing Naomi's individual relationship with God (if he even thought in such terms), but on characterizing her grief and emptiness and setting the stage so that we may also recognize the Lord's hand behind the scenes in restoring her condition. This is important because the problem of Naomi's emptiness is the driving force of the narrative (cf. Bush 1996:97).

Naomi was not entirely empty, however, and 1:22 hints subtly, and perhaps ironically, at the fact that Naomi had the allegiance of Ruth and the fertility of the harvest season in her favor. She herself might remind us, were she present, that two mouths are harder to feed than one, and that the support of her foreign daughter-in-law was no substitute for a husband and son in her ancient society (but see 4:15). Even though the harvest would probably make survival possible, what joy would she have? Life's remainder would be short, difficult, and sorrowful. Thus, the hint is indeed subtle (cf. Linafelt 1999:21). As readers we do not know how much we can expect from Ruth in this situation. Still, as Bush (1996:96) says, "This commitment of a young woman to the life of an old woman in the darkest hours that women in a man's world can face is already a signal step toward a dawn for Naomi's dark night of despair." And the reader is led to expect something unique from Ruth, for she is strangely and explicitly said to have returned to Judah from Moab (see note on 1:22). The use of "return" to describe Ruth's arrival in Judah emphasizes her commitment to the people of Israel. She had declared a new home and was determined to make good on the vow of 1:16. Thus, the scene closes with the problem of Naomi's emptiness startlingly clear and only a vague sense that her circumstance will improve.

◆ II. Ruth Provides for Naomi (2:1-23)
A. Ruth Happens upon the Field of Boaz (2:1-3)

Now there was a wealthy and influential man in Bethlehem named Boaz, who was a relative of Naomi's husband, Elimelech.

2One day Ruth the Moabite said to Naomi, "Let me go out into the harvest fields to pick up the stalks of grain left behind by anyone who is kind enough to let me do it."

Naomi replied, "All right, my daughter, go ahead." 3So Ruth went out to gather grain behind the harvesters. And as it happened, she found herself working in a field that belonged to Boaz, the relative of her father-in-law, Elimelech.

NOTES

2:1 ***wealthy and influential man.*** Boaz is called a *gibbor khayil* [TH1368/2428, ZH1475/2657]. This term often refers to a war hero (e.g., 2 Sam 17:8) but can also refer to a "capable" person (e.g., 1 Kgs 11:28) or to a "rich" person (e.g., 2 Kgs 15:20). In the context of Ruth, no references to soldiering are to be found, leading to the obvious conclusion that this term designates Boaz as "wealthy and influential." Although this man was well-known to Naomi (cf. Hubbard 1988:132-133), Sakenfeld (1999:38) correctly notes that this description places him at a "great social distance" from Ruth and Naomi. Thus, in 2 Kgs 24:14 the "best of the soldiers" (*gibbor khayil*) are taken, while the "poorest people" remain. In light of 3:11, where the term is used of Ruth, it is likely that *khayil* refers to Boaz's status and connotes his virtuous character.

Bethlehem. The repetition of the town's name up to this point (cf. 1:1, 2, 19, 22) has the effect of heightening one's awareness of the question of survival: Will Naomi and Ruth find bread in the "house of bread" (i.e., Bethlehem)? See note on 1:1.

Boaz. The Targum to Ruth identified Boaz as the lesser-known Judge, Izban or Azban (Judg 12:8-10), but this seems unlikely in the context of the canonical book.

2:2 ***One day.*** These words do not appear in the Hebrew text. The verbal form there may imply some passage of time, as in the words "one day" (cf. NLT, NET), or it may be rendered simply with "and" (cf. NIV, KJV). Here, however, another option is probably preferable: to render this *wayyiqtol* form as a past perfect (or pluperfect): "And Ruth . . . *had* said" (cf. Waltke and O'Connor 1990:552 [§33.2.3]). The narrator breaks from the sequence of events to give us information about Boaz, and when we return to the story, Ruth has already gotten permission to go out gleaning, which she does in 2:3.

2:3 ***as it happened.*** The narrator shifts to Ruth's point of view here (Chisholm 1998:160); though this event was mere chance to her at the time, the narrator recognizes (as Ruth presumably does after ch 4) that her choice of Boaz's field was in fact the Lord's plan. This serves to highlight the beauty of God's sovereignty and providence, much as Joseph's statement about his brothers' actions in retrospect (Gen 45:5; 50:20).

relative of her father-in-law, Elimelech. Here and in 2:1, literally, "from the family of Elimelech."

COMMENTARY

This short scene introduces Boaz and sets the stage for how Ruth and Boaz meet and how the immediate need of Naomi and Ruth for food will be provided for. The timing of Ruth and Naomi's return proves critical—the barley harvest is the context that allows the women to interact with Boaz directly (cf. Matthews 2004:225).

Ruth, as a part of Naomi's family, asked permission to go out and glean so they could have some food. Naomi's response is a flat "yes"; one is left to think that her character sits rather despondently in the shade of her tent, disinterested in life or attempting to find food. In contrast, Ruth sought to provide for herself and Naomi.

Ruth's request of Naomi and the narrator's comment in 2:3 both draw attention to God's providential role in Ruth coming to Boaz's field. In her request, Ruth mentions "anyone who is kind enough to let me [glean]," indicating that she has no specific plan or goal other than seeing what leftovers may be had. In 2:3, the narrator reinforces Ruth's perspective, saying that she simply chanced upon Boaz's field. Only in retrospect would Ruth and Naomi have discerned God's providence in which field Ruth came to.

Gleaning (NLT, "to pick up the stalks of grain left behind") was a provision for the poor mandated in the Torah (Lev 19:9-10; 23:22; Deut 24:19, 21). It was applicable to the grape harvest, as well as the grain harvest, and may have been traditionally practiced with all crops (cf. *m. Peah* 1:4-5; 3:4).

Boaz was introduced as a wealthy and influential man (2:1)—quite the opposite of Naomi and Ruth in terms of social status. Yet twice in these three verses, Boaz is connected to the family of Elimelech. This is important to the story both in terms of his concern for these two women and his potential to be in a position to care for them. Just as the reader was left at the end of chapter 1 expecting Ruth to be part of the resolution of Naomi's situation, the reader is led to expect that Boaz will also be important in resolving the situation. But how? How is he related, and what sort of wealthy man is he? In the next scene the narrator demonstrates what sort of person Boaz is.

◆ B. Boaz Blesses Ruth in the Name of the Lord (2:4-17)

4While she was there, Boaz arrived from Bethlehem and greeted the harvesters. "The LORD be with you!" he said.

"The LORD bless you!" the harvesters replied.

5Then Boaz asked his foreman, "Who is that young woman over there? Who does she belong to?"

6And the foreman replied, "She is the young woman from Moab who came back with Naomi. 7She asked me this morning if she could gather grain behind the harvesters. She has been hard at work ever since, except for a few minutes' rest in the shelter."

8Boaz went over and said to Ruth, "Listen, my daughter. Stay right here with us when you gather grain; don't go to any other fields. Stay right behind the young women working in my field. 9See which part of the field they are harvesting, and then follow them. I have warned the young men not to treat you roughly. And when you are thirsty, help yourself to the water they have drawn from the well."

10Ruth fell at his feet and thanked him warmly. "What have I done to deserve such kindness?" she asked. "I am only a foreigner."

11"Yes, I know," Boaz replied. "But I also know about everything you have done for your mother-in-law since the death of your husband. I have heard how you left your father and mother and your own land to live here among complete strangers. 12May the LORD, the God of Israel, under whose wings you have come to take refuge, reward you fully for what you have done."

13"I hope I continue to please you, sir," she replied. "You have comforted me by speaking so kindly to me, even though I am not one of your workers."

14At mealtime Boaz called to her, "Come over here, and help yourself to some food. You can dip your bread in the sour wine." So she sat with his harvesters, and Boaz gave her some roasted grain to eat. She ate all she wanted and still had some left over.

15When Ruth went back to work again, Boaz ordered his young men, "Let her gather grain right among the sheaves without stopping her. 16And pull out some heads of barley from the bundles and drop them on purpose for her. Let her pick them up, and don't give her a hard time!" 17So Ruth gathered barley there all day, and when she beat out the grain that evening, it filled an entire basket.*

2:17 Hebrew *it was about an ephah* [20 quarts or 22 liters].

NOTES

2:4 *Boaz arrived.* Lit., "And behold (*hinneh* [TH2009, ZH2180]), Boaz arrived." The particle *hinneh* serves to extend the idea of "chance" introduced in 2:3. Ruth had chanced upon one of Boaz's fields, and lo and behold, he paid his harvesters a visit that day. Boaz was not there to harvest, but to see how the work of his harvesters was going.

2:5 ***Who is that young woman over there? Who does she belong to?*** Lit., "To whom does this young woman belong?" Boaz did not ask directly who Ruth was; he asked instead who she was associated with. A similar construction occurs only in Gen 32:18 and 1 Sam 30:13. "The community to which one belonged—at all levels, family, clan, tribe, nation, village—was central to one's identity and status. . . . In particular, a woman had no independent status and identity in Israel's patriarchal world" (Bush 1996:113). Thus, Boaz asked a natural question regarding what husband, father, or family this unknown woman was connected to (cf. Gen 24:23; 1 Sam 17:55).

2:7 This verse has numerous textual and interpretive difficulties. It seems plain that Ruth requested to glean, but after that, her precise request and actions are debated. Hubbard (1988:148) takes the "gathering" as referring to sheaves Ruth would make and set aside from her gleanings. He also sees her request as taking a "brash" risk (1988:150) for Naomi's sake. I agree with Sasson, who sees Boaz doing little more for Ruth than what was common (1989:49, 56) until he thought about it awhile and made a statement in 2:15. In contrast to the assumption that Ruth asked to glean, Grossman (2007:710-716) suggests that this verse is only the report about Ruth given by the supervisor— i.e., Ruth simply showed up and gleaned as permitted, and the supervisor read this intention into her actions and was insinuating to Boaz that he should keep an eye on her because of the large amount of grain she was gathering. In other words, the supervisor had reservations about her. Boaz's response then stands in contrast to the supervisor's intent. But this view perhaps reads too much into the intent of the supervisor, who, if he was not reporting an actual request from Ruth, may have been trying to evoke compassion from Boaz and making a special request on Ruth's behalf. Boaz, after all, seemed to think Ruth would have been attractive to a younger man such as the supervisor (3:10). In addition, I think the most natural reading of *'amad* [TH5975, ZH6641] in this verse is "stood, waited" (see note below on "hard at work"), another point that does not fit well with Grossman's view.

behind the harvesters. Lit., "among the sheaves, behind the harvesters." The first phrase (present in MT and LXX) is left untranslated in the NLT, perhaps because it might prove awkward or redundant in English. But it is significant: Allowing gleaners among the sheaves was akin to leaving the proverbial cat to guard the milk. The sheaves would be tempting and could easily be raided in addition to any gleaning that went on (cf. Bush 1996:122). There was no injunction in the laws of Moses to allow the poor to glean in this manner. Ruth was not permitted among the sheaves until Boaz said so (2:15).

In harvesting, grain could be pulled out by hand, or cut with a sickle (Deut 16:9; Jer 50:16) whose blade could be made from sharp flint chips or from bronze or iron (ABD 3.64). The grain was sometimes cut at the top to leave the stalks standing for later grazing by animals. Stalks or straws were used to tie bunches into sheaves (ISBE 2.619).

hard at work. Lit., "she has been standing/waiting." Most translations take the verb *'amad* [TH5975, ZH6641] as implying a continued work activity. "Remained" (cf. NASB) is perhaps a better, more flexible rendering if "stood" is not chosen. The Hebrew word itself doesn't connote continued work, but this idea is supplied from the context by commentators and translations that find "stand" illogical. The picture then is that Ruth came politely and then worked diligently. But if we accept *'amad* as simply meaning stand or halt, then the fact that Ruth had stood there since the morning, only resting a little, implies that her request was not answered by the supervisor, who perhaps was not authorized to do so. I prefer this explanation and find that it also explains why Boaz noticed and asked about Ruth and why he (the *gibbor khayil* [TH1368/2428, ZH1475/2657], see note on 2:1) remained at the field for some time instead of returning to his business elsewhere or going on to inspect the work at another field.

except for a few minutes' rest in the shelter. Lit., "this sitting of her the house little." The Hebrew syntax is difficult here. The NLT's translation is probably the best option for rendering the MT. For details on the difficulties and other attempted solutions, see Bush (1996:118-119).

2:9 *not to treat you roughly.* Lit., "not to touch you." The NLT is a good rendering. The concern here was not particularly about sexual abuse or rape, for although Ruth was a vulnerable member of society, the harvest season meant that many people—male and female—would be nearby to hear a cry for help. But, in light of 2:22 (see note there), we should see a concern for physical safety as an element here. Unlike other gleaners, Ruth was given permission to follow close behind the harvesters, and the concern was that she not be perceived as an overly greedy or pestilent gleaner and driven off by force (so also Hubbard 1988:159). Apart from Boaz's command, she may have been subjected to minor physical violence aimed at restraining or driving her off.

the water they have drawn. Lit., "the water the young men (will) draw." The verb is an imperfect, here probably referring to iterative or customary action, though possibly having the idea of a potential or future event. The natural necessity of water for the workers, however, makes the former option preferable. In any case, Ruth was free to drink from the workers' water supply and would not have to see to it herself.

2:10 *fell at his feet.* Lit., "fell on her face and bowed to the ground."

2:11 *among complete strangers.* Lit., "a people you didn't know/acknowledge," which could be read as an idiom (or perhaps metonymy of cause; Bullinger 1968:553) for "didn't care about" (cf. 2:19, "one who helped you"; Deut 33:9).

2:13 *workers.* Here Ruth positions herself humbly, as a foreigner, on the level of the workers (*shipkhah* [TH8198, ZH9148]). Later, in 3:9, Ruth will call herself by another term, *'amah* [TH519, ZH563] (servant), which is slightly elevated from this term (see note on 3:9).

2:14 *sour wine.* Heb., *khomets* [TH2558, ZH2810]; the root refers to being sour or fermented. The precise identification of this liquid substance is unknown, but it could be made from wine or strong drink (Num 6:3), and is generally understood as vinegar, derived from various sources. In the case of this verse, however, hummus has also been suggested (cf. TDOT 4.487-493). Although plausible, this remains unproven. The term here is probably a shorthand that is as vague as the words "pop," "dip," or "dressing." It was a condiment to dip the bread in, moistening it and giving it flavor.

roasted grain. Heb., *qali* [TH7039, ZH7833], meaning "roasted" or "parched." The word "grain" does not actually appear in the Hebrew, but is implied with this term as elsewhere (e.g., 2 Sam 17:28).

2:15 *young men.* In this verse, the masc. pl. probably refers to both the young men and young women working for Boaz—he informed them all of Ruth's status.

2:17 *basket.* Lit., "about an ephah"; this is estimated to have been about 22 liters (cf. NLT mg). Twenty-two liters is a little larger than a five-gallon bucket and would have weighed about 29 pounds. Some, however, suggest numbers as high as 39 liters for the quantity of the ephah (cf. Campbell 1975:104). Whatever the case, an ephah was enough to feed several fighting men but apparently light enough for a young David to transport a considerable distance (1 Sam 17:17). The amount of grain was therefore a surprise to Naomi (2:19); Ruth had gleaned more than enough to feed both of them that day, perhaps enough for over a week.

COMMENTARY

In 2:1, Boaz was introduced to the reader, but the nature of his character is unclear. This scene will develop it. In addition, it should be noted that Ruth as yet had no awareness of who Boaz was. His sudden appearance at the field in 2:4 was not a moment when Ruth thought "Oh—there's Boaz; I've been hoping to meet him!" but rather "This must be the owner. I hope I'll be able to stay." There is a tension early in the scene that dissipates in the interaction between Ruth and Boaz.

In this scene, Boaz not only blesses Ruth in the name of the Lord (2:12), he also takes an active role in seeing that she has every benefit of working in his field (2:8-9, 14-16). This is perhaps surprising because she was a foreigner, but Boaz's central words, the words of his blessing for Ruth, implicitly mark his acceptance of her into Israelite society. Whatever reservations others may have had about this Moabite woman, Boaz was confident in her allegiance to Naomi and to the people and God of Israel.

Boaz and his workers greeted each other with more than the customary greeting of "Peace" (*shalom* [TH7965, ZH8934]; e.g., 1 Sam 25:6; 2 Sam 18:28)—they spoke a blessing in the name of the Lord (2:4; cf. Judg 6:12; Ps 129:8). It is unknown whether this was a seasonal greeting (cf. Hubbard 1988:144) or whether the greeting was customary to Boaz, but in either case, its presence on the lips of Boaz here creates a positive association for his character.

Ruth's basic character and previous actions with regard to Naomi seem to have preceded her, though Boaz did not recognize her by sight (2:5-7). She came early and made a special request of the foreman in Boaz's absence: She was seeking to glean not only among the *pe'oth* [TH6285, ZH6991] or "corners" of the field (cf. Lev 19:9-10), but to follow the harvesters closely, and even go among the sheaves in the main field, picking up any loose barley. She was apparently still standing or waiting at the edge of the field when Boaz arrived (see note on 2:7), probably because the foreman was not ready to give her an answer. Throughout the scene, Ruth seems to show an unashamed recognition of her low position in society (note her bowing low in 2:10 and her continued deference in 2:13). As Campbell (1975:111) suggests, this makes her an extraordinary recipient; she was thus more worthy of Boaz's increased blessing of her (cf. 2:14-15).

Ruth's awareness of her low position is perhaps also evident in her willingness to make a special request—she had little to lose in terms of social respect by being bold in this way. Like the importunate friend (Luke 11:5-10), Ruth seemed to have persisted in hopes of meeting her pressing need. Ruth perhaps did not expect her full request to be granted, but hoped to gain whatever extra favor she could. Ruth's words in 2:2 ("anyone who is kind enough"; lit., "anyone in whose eyes I find favor") are the same ones she uses in 2:10 and 13 when speaking of Boaz's kindness. It seems she intended from the start to seek the most advantageous situation possible and that she recognized that in Boaz's blessing, even though he did not immediately permit her to glean "among the sheaves" (see note on 2:7).

Boaz's response, although not responding to the request to go among the sheaves, was warm and affirming. He made it clear to Ruth that she was welcome there, and he did allow her to follow the harvesters in the main field (2:8). One might say that he graciously split the difference while making up his mind about how to respond to the request to go among the sheaves. It may also be that Boaz was waiting to see how Ruth would work in his field in close proximity to his workers. Would it be problematic to allow her closer? Boaz further signaled that he would see to Ruth's welfare in terms of protection from abuse by his workers and provision of water (2:9). Although he hadn't said yes to every request of Ruth's, it was an unexpectedly kind and positive response to this foreign widow.

If we are surprised at Boaz's warm acceptance of Ruth, she herself must have been utterly dumbfounded (2:10), for she knew nothing of his relationship to Naomi. Not only did Boaz not drive her away or ignore her, he treated her warmly, and by the end of the scene, like family. Her surprise is marked by her bowing with her face to the ground (2:10 "fell at his feet," NLT). Even Boaz's response to Ruth's surprised question (2:11) does not inform her of his relationship to Elimelech's family. Only later (2:20) would Ruth learn about his relationship to them.

Boaz responded to Ruth's question (2:11-12) by explaining that the report of her kindness to Naomi and Elimelech's family had made him favorably predisposed to her. Proverbs 19:22 provides a parallel to the essence of Boaz's response to Ruth: "Loyalty makes a person attractive. It is better to be poor than dishonest."

Throughout the scene, the reader sees that Boaz's words aren't empty; he was a man of action. (Regarding this characterization, compare Naomi's comment in 3:18.) His initial invitation to Ruth was backed by provision for her thirst (2:9). After more hours of work, Boaz invited her to eat from the food designated for his workers (2:14)—she was not treated simply as a poor gleaner. She ate freely and fully with this group, and the comment that she had food to spare again highlights Boaz's generosity and may indicate a conscious attempt on his part to send some roasted grain home with Ruth for Naomi (cf. 2:18). Further, Boaz had thought about her request to glean among the sheaves, and would now permit her to do so. He made this special arrangement clear to his workers (2:15-16), with the additional instruction that they should make sure there was always grain left out of the sheaves for Ruth to gather—he would not have his generosity thwarted by their concern on his behalf.

At the end of the day, Ruth "beat out the grain" and had a large amount (see note on 2:17). Beating out grain was an alternative to threshing that was used for small quantities; a small stick or wooden hammer could be used to separate the grains from the husks, resulting in a lighter load to carry home (cf. Hubbard 1988:178-179). The amount of grain Ruth had gathered was much more than could have been gleaned and would feed her and Naomi for some time.

As the scene closes, we see the fruits of virtue. Boaz's generosity with his means, coupled with Ruth's diligent labor, bring a satisfying reward that will benefit both Ruth and Naomi. Ruth's behavior was mostly expected, but Boaz was rather unknown before this point. His honorable and kind character shows through in this scene, and the result is a surprisingly positive outcome for Ruth's efforts to provide for herself and Naomi.

Boaz's favor on Ruth moves her another step further in the process of acceptance in the Israelite society—by treating her like family, he gave an implicit stamp of approval, though she was not yet fully integrated or accepted by everyone. Boaz's generosity and kindness to Ruth as a poor, foreign widow also reflects the Lord's own concern: "He ensures that orphans and widows receive justice. He shows love to the foreigners living among you and gives them food and clothing" (Deut 10:18). Those who would walk in the ways of the Lord today must do the same.

C. Naomi Begins to See the Lord's Provision (2:18-23)

18 She carried it back into town and showed it to her mother-in-law. Ruth also gave her the roasted grain that was left over from her meal.

19 "Where did you gather all this grain today?" Naomi asked. "Where did you work? May the LORD bless the one who helped you!"

So Ruth told her mother-in-law about the man in whose field she had worked. She said, "The man I worked with today is named Boaz."

20 "May the LORD bless him!" Naomi told her daughter-in-law. "He is showing his kindness to us as well as to your dead husband.* That man is one of our closest relatives, one of our family redeemers."

21 Then Ruth* said, "What's more, Boaz even told me to come back and stay with his harvesters until the entire harvest is completed."

22 "Good!" Naomi exclaimed. "Do as he said, my daughter. Stay with his young women right through the whole harvest. You might be harassed in other fields, but you'll be safe with him."

23 So Ruth worked alongside the women in Boaz's fields and gathered grain with them until the end of the barley harvest. Then she continued working with them through the wheat harvest in early summer. And all the while she lived with her mother-in-law.

2:20 Hebrew *to the living and to the dead.* 2:21 Hebrew *Ruth the Moabite.*

NOTES

2:20 *the LORD bless him!* Lit., "blessed is he to the LORD." Bullinger (1968:503) classifies this blessing as antimereia (one part of speech used for another; cf. 3:10; Jonah 3:3) wherein the divine name is used in the dative case to describe the extent of blessing as "highest, mightiest, most glorious" (1968:502). This places the emphasis on the extent of the blessing. Slightly more likely, however, is the NLT's reading of the syntax as marking the agent of a passive verbal form (cf. GKC §121f).

He is showing his kindness. The NLT represents the ambiguity of the subject of this phrase better than many versions. As Chisholm (1998:72) points out, Boaz is indeed the one referred to as "not abandoning kindness to the living and the dead" in this verse, and not the Lord, as some have suggested (cf. NRSV, ESV, NASB). See the parallel structure in 2 Sam 2:5. The construction (*baruk* + *asher* [TH1288A/834, ZH1385/889]) has almost a causal force in elaborating on the character of the person who is to be blessed.

family redeemers. This represents the term *go'el* [TH1350B, ZH1457], used here for the first time in Ruth (cf. 3:9, 12; 4:1, 3, 6, 8, 14). The term is discussed further in the commentary below.

2:21 *Ruth.* Lit., "Ruth the Moabitess" (cf. NLT mg). Ruth's full name is used. Bush (1996:138) suggests it's no more than a stylistic variant, while Hubbard says (1988:191) it heightens the tension of Ruth's gradual acceptance into Israelite culture. I think it might be intended to remind us that Ruth, as a foreigner, wasn't entirely sure of the various uses of Naomi's term *go'el* [TH1350B, ZH1457] in Israelite culture. Another appealing view, however, is that of Sakenfeld (1999:49), who ties this to the idea of Ruth's protection that is discussed in the context—as a foreign woman she was fortunate to receive such care from Boaz.

2:22 *harassed.* This comes from the verb *paga'* [TH6293, ZH7003] and can indicate a variety of events, from meeting someone or something by chance (Exod 23:4), or with good or ill intent (Josh 2:16; Isa 64:5), or to attack (Judg 8:21; 1 Kgs 2:29). In conjunction with 2:9 (see note) it gives a picture of the danger of physical abuse sometimes used to deter those who would glean outside the legal bounds.

COMMENTARY

In this scene, Naomi sees the blessing and success of Ruth's gleaning. She knows it could not be the result of mere chance or even hard work alone. As Ruth reports the day's events, Naomi's spirit and hope are revived. In addition to this significant turnaround, Naomi also reveals to Ruth more information about Boaz, and at this point the concept of a family redeemer is introduced.

Most of this scene is dialogue, framed by two verses of narrative (2:18, 23) that set up this scene and the next one. The dialogue, in particular, exhibits a chiastic pattern centering on Naomi's blessing of Boaz and her comment that he is a redeemer (cf. Bush 1996:131-132), but, in fact, the whole scene can be construed as a chiasm.

- A. Ruth returns from gleaning successfully (2:18)
    - B. Naomi speaks (2:19)
        - C. Ruth speaks (2:19)
            - D. Naomi's blessing of Boaz, and the use of *go'el* (2:20)
        - C'. Ruth speaks (2:21)
    - B'. Naomi speaks (2:22)
- A'. Ruth returns to continue gleaning (2:23)

In Naomi's blessing of Boaz (2:20) the word *go'el* [TH1350B, ZH1457] appears for the first time in the book. The *go'el* was a near relative who was responsible for (1) purchase of clan property sold out of economic necessity, thus keeping the land in the clan (Lev 25:25-30; Jer 32:1-15); (2) buying the clan members out of slavery if he had the money (Lev 25:47-55); (3) in the case of the redeemer of blood, pursuing and taking vengeance on anyone who killed a clan member (Num 35:12, 19-27; Deut 19:6, 12; Josh 20:2-9); (4) acting as clan representative to receive restitution money due a deceased clan member (Num 5:8; cf. Lev 6:1-7); and (5) as demonstrated by metaphorical use of the term, assisting clan members in lawsuits to see justice done (Job 19:25; Ps 119:154; Prov 23:11; Jer 50:34; cf. the view of Matthews 2004:219). Although *go'el* is often connected closely with the concept of redemption, it should be noted that it is not the only or even the primary Hebrew word for redeem; *padah* [TH6299, ZH7009] also means "to redeem" (e.g., Exod 13:13; Lev 19:20; 27:29; Deut 7:8; 9:26; 1 Sam 14:45; 2 Sam 4:9), although it is never used of inanimate objects.

It is most likely that *go'el* is nontechnical here (so also Bush 1996:137), and Naomi probably had in mind the things Boaz had already done—he saved them by his generosity to Ruth. The term *go'el* is also used of God in a nontechnical way, which notably doesn't involve the payment frequently connected with the legal uses of the term (cf. Ps 72:14; Isa 54:4-8; Lam 3:53-58). The same is true of its use in 3:9. If *go'el* is nontechnical here, what of its use later? First, it can be said here to foreshadow the development of a more technical use after 3:12. But even the other uses in the book often fail to conform to a strict technical definition. Although the *go'el* was engaged in pursuing justice for the extended family and in purchasing family lands, the marriage of a family member's widow and maintenance of his line is never described as a duty of a *go'el*. It seems the development of *go'el* in the rest of the book is that of an idealization of the term—Boaz need not function technically as a *go'el* in order to embody the ideal. Some have argued against this—that *go'el* can be persuasively connected to the levirate law of Deuteronomy 25:5-10 (so Block 1999:675), but I think Campbell (1975:110) is correct in asserting that the context shows that "magnanimity" is crucial to the relationship between Naomi and Boaz. There is nothing inherent in the term *go'el* regarding levirate responsibility, but the term is stretched to glorify virtue.

This scene presents Naomi, with Boaz, as a "senior citizen of the story" (Campbell 1975:110) by her address to Ruth in 2:22 as a "daughter" and her designation of the harvesters as youths (*na'arah* [TH5291, ZH5855]; cf. Boaz's language to Ruth and harvesters throughout ch 2). I suspect Campbell is right that Naomi's age speaks to her wisdom (1975:110-111; cf. Introduction, "Major Themes"). At the same time, the aged Naomi was revitalized in this scene when she saw Ruth's success, the critical signal for this being Naomi's blessing in 2:20. There is an ambiguity in the Hebrew of 2:20 that allows Naomi to be understood as saying either that the Lord had shown kindness to the living and the dead, or that Boaz had shown such kindness. Logically, I find the context to favor Boaz, but the ambiguity is critical in the development of Naomi's character. In 1:21, Naomi stated that the Lord was against her, but here, in words of blessing, she appears open to the reality that the Lord had not abandoned her—a move forward for her character that corresponds with her new initiative, which is seen in chapter 3.

As this scene comes to a close, we are reminded of Ruth's diligent obedience and loyalty (2:23). Following Naomi's instruction in 2:22, Ruth obeyed fully, "clinging" to the other harvesters (*dabak* [TH1692, ZH1815]; 2:23). Ruth also stayed with her mother-in-law (*yashab* [TH3427, ZH3782]; 2:23). The Hebrew is somewhat ambiguous, and while the NLT follows the idea that she stayed with Naomi throughout the harvest, Bush (1996:140) suggests the sentence refers to Ruth staying with Naomi after the harvest, and the Vulgate (with a few Hebrew mss) attests to the idea that the sentence should be understood as Ruth returning to Naomi (apparently after living away during the harvest). In any of these cases, I suggest the emphasis here should be understood as Ruth's loyal and obedient character. It thus leads up to her obedience to the odd instructions in the next scene.

◆ III. Naomi Seeks to Provide for Ruth (3:1-18)
A. Naomi Counts on Boaz's Integrity and Kindness (3:1-5)

One day Naomi said to Ruth, "My daughter, it's time that I found a permanent home for you, so that you will be provided for. 2Boaz is a close relative of ours, and he's been very kind by letting you gather grain with his young women. Tonight he will be winnowing barley at the threshing floor. 3Now do as I tell you—take a bath and put on perfume and dress in your nicest clothes. Then go to the threshing floor, but don't let Boaz see you until he has finished eating and drinking. 4Be sure to notice where he lies down; then go and uncover his feet and lie down there. He will tell you what to do."

5"I will do everything you say," Ruth replied.

NOTES

3:1 ***it's time that I found a permanent home for you.*** Naomi's statement is actually a rhetorical question: "Should I not seek rest for you?"

3:2 ***winnowing barley at the threshing floor.*** Lit., "winnowing the threshing floor of barley." Commentators have raised questions about the syntax of the phrase (e.g., Bush 1996:149-150; Campbell 1975:117) and sometimes suggested various solutions, but in the end it seems to be a poetic idiom with "threshing floor" standing as a synecdoche for grain (cf. the syntax of Job 24:11), and "barley" loosely modifying it. (It does not seem historically likely that an actually separate threshing floor was used for barley.) Also, the presence of unwinnowed barley is sometimes cited as a difficulty (Campbell 1975:117), but I am inclined to take it as a result of a very big harvest and limited threshing floors in the town. The barley remained after the wheat harvest because there was so much of it, and there were so many people in line to winnow that it couldn't be done before the wheat harvest. Cf. Amos 9:13, which depicts a harvest so bountiful that the plowmen overtake the reapers. And Borowski (1987:62) points out that "In a good year, when the [grain] yield was great, threshing and grape picking overlapped." Alternatively, Block (1999:682) suggests that all the grain was usually threshed in late May or June, after both harvests and once the dry season began. The majority (and probably all) of the threshing floors in the pre- and early monarchic periods were communal, located between villages or fields (Matthews 2004:232). It seems unlikely that this one was private, as Borowski suggests (1987:62-63).

3:3 ***take a bath . . . nicest clothes.*** The actions Naomi prescribes for Ruth have been interpreted variously as either making Ruth pretty, or acceptable, or even dressing as a bride. Bush (1996:151-52; cf. Block 1999:683-684) makes the case that Ruth's attire signaled the end of her widowhood. This may also explain the reason why no one had previously broached the subject of marriage. Even after finishing the period of mourning, however, Ruth's Moabite identity may have put off potential suitors. Sakenfeld (1999:54) finds Bush's idea uncompelling and cites David's similar actions *after the death* of his child (2 Sam 12:19-23) as showing that these actions did not mark the end of mourning. But David's actions are manifestly odd in the text—he mourned the child before it died and was questioned about his attitude after the death. The response of observers to David's actions supports Bush's case.

3:4 ***uncover his feet.*** These are provocative and controversial words, not least of all because they could be understood to run contrary to the portrayal of Ruth as a virtuous woman (cf. 3:10-11). Translations and interpreters have taken them variously: The Old Latin in 3:4 and 7 has Ruth uncover *herself* (so also Nielsen 1997:69), while the Syriac omits entirely the words "uncovers X." A key element in understanding the controversy is recognizing that "his feet" (*margeloth* [TH4772, ZH5274]; cf. HALOT 1.631) could be taken euphemistically for Boaz's loins or genitals (though there is no clear instance of such with *margeloth*, but cf. *regel* [TH7272, ZH8079]; HALOT 2.1185, e.g., Isa 36:12), or "his feet" may refer to his lower legs—"the place of his legs." Even if only Boaz's legs were to be uncovered, this action by a woman alone with him in the middle of the night adds a sexual charge to the scene. Thus, some see here seduction, with Ruth practically feigning the role of a prostitute (cf. Tamar in Gen 38) in order to preserve the family line. Others see a symbolic gesture, indicating her readiness for marriage, and giving opportunity for Boaz to respond with the hem of his garment (cf. Deut 22:30; 27:20; Ezek 16:8). However, this may have been a strategy to wake Boaz up in an indirect manner and put the ball in his court once he saw Ruth. Really, these options are not all mutually exclusive. I suggest that Naomi devised these actions with the two needs in mind: to wake Boaz up in a subtle manner (the eventual effects of cold air on his legs), and to press the question of Ruth's future marriage by the metaphor of the garment's hem being lifted up.

3:5 ***everything you say.*** Berger (2009b:442-447) notes the role of this emphatic phrase here and in another "thwarted action" story in 2 Sam 11—David's conspiracy to kill Uriah. He asserts the two are parallel since they are the only two such stories using the "all/ everything" motif: three times in Ruth (3:5, 6, 11), and twice in 2 Sam 11 (vv. 18-19). The comparison of these two accounts results in a notable contrast between the virtuous actions of Ruth and Boaz, and the ruthless schemes of David. Berger suggests this is a literary connection made by the author of Ruth to show David's actions as out of character for himself and his line.

COMMENTARY

The previous scene closed with a note showing Ruth's loyal obedience. Also significant was Naomi's shift of perspective toward hope. Both the barley and wheat harvests had been completed (2:23), and the grain was no longer subject to the hazards of the field. The harvest was apparently quite bountiful, and Boaz still had barley to winnow. To the eyes of the revitalized Naomi, this presented a unique opportunity.

Since, as pointed out in the commentary on the previous section, a *go'el* [TH1350B, ZH1457] (here, Boaz) was not formally obligated to marry the widow, Naomi had no clear grounds on which to approach him about Ruth. The difference in social status and the idea of an overt proposal that this well-to-do man marry a Moabite woman likely deterred Naomi further from any conventional attempt at matchmaking, and further, Ruth had no one to act as a father or brother, who would likely have been the person to negotiate such a deal (Sakenfeld 1999:54). (On a brother's role in a betrothal, see Gen 24:29, 33, 50-51; 34:6-18.) For this reason, Naomi cleverly devised an unconventional plan by which to discreetly broach this delicate subject in a way that would lend itself to success. Thus, as Hubbard notes (1988:199), "In response to providentially given opportunity, Naomi began to answer her own prayer! . . . Thus she models one way in which divine and human actions work together: believers . . . must seize the initiative when an opportunity presents itself. They assume that God presents the opportunity."

Much has been written discussing the intent of Naomi's instructions to Ruth. These instructions, along with Ruth's actions, have been portrayed as a seduction, as cultic sexual activity, as a discreet offer of marriage, as a symbolic communication of her availability for marriage, and in other ways as well. In light of the literary parallels suggested by Berger (see note on 3:5) and because the book seems to place sexual activity later in the relationship of Ruth and Boaz (4:13), options involving a sexual act on the night of the meeting seem very unlikely. Also, it seems that if Ruth and Naomi had an inkling about the good reputation she had gained in the community (cf. 3:10-11), they would not have made her unnecessarily vulnerable in this way, a move that goes beyond risky to reckless. Rather, Naomi's plan pushed Ruth to show she had ended her mourning for Mahlon (see note on 3:3) and used a rather provocative (i.e., sexually charged) setting to spur Boaz to make a decision about Ruth and act. Ruth would present herself as an eligible woman at a time when Boaz would be in good spirits to consider her—satisfied from a good meal, in the still of the night, without the pressure of others watching. At the proper time, when everyone had eaten, and those present dozed off, and night had fallen, Ruth was to "uncover [Boaz's] feet and lie down there" (3:4).

Naomi recognized that the plan was not surefire, as is evident from her last comment in 3:4: "He will tell you what to do." As LaCocque (2004:92) says, Naomi's statement "means something like 'It is in God's hands!' and has the same uncertainty regarding the following sequence of events."

The meaning of "uncover his feet" (3:4, see note) has raised the most discussion of Naomi's directions to Ruth. Although some have suggested that it means Ruth was to uncover Boaz's loins or genitals, this idea remains only a possibility in the use of the word *margeloth* [TH4772, ZH5274]. Probability, in the context of the story, lends itself to the idea that "the area of his feet" was meant (parallel to the sense of the similarly formed term *mera'ashoth* [TH4763A, ZH5265], "the area of the head"; cf. Gen 28:11; HALOT 1.631). Ruth was then to lay down at Boaz's feet. Naomi's instructions seem calculated to ensure that Boaz would stir and look toward his feet, where he would immediately be met with Ruth laying by the corner of his robe—symbolically raising the question of marriage (see note on 3:9). In this way, without uttering a word, the women would prompt Boaz to consider this possibility.

Ruth's response to Naomi's introduction of her unorthodox plan is the affirmation that she will do all that Naomi has said (3:5, see note). The reader has been prepared for this type of response from Ruth, especially as her character was highlighted at the close of the previous scene.

◆ B. Ruth Enacts the Plan and Boaz Responds Favorably and Immediately (3:6-15)

6So she went down to the threshing
floor that night and followed the instructions of her mother-in-law.

7After Boaz had finished eating and
drinking and was in good spirits, he lay
down at the far end of the pile of grain
and went to sleep. Then Ruth came quietly, uncovered his feet, and lay down.
8Around midnight Boaz suddenly woke up
and turned over. He was surprised to find
a woman lying at his feet! 9"Who are
you?" he asked.

"I am your servant Ruth," she replied. "Spread the corner of your covering over me, for you are my family redeemer."

10"The LORD bless you, my daughter!"
Boaz exclaimed. "You are showing even
more family loyalty now than you did before, for you have not gone after a young-
er man, whether rich or poor. 11Now don't
worry about a thing, my daughter. I will
do what is necessary, for everyone in town
knows you are a virtuous woman. 12But
while it's true that I am one of your family redeemers, there is another man who
is more closely related to you than I am.
13Stay here tonight, and in the morning I
will talk to him. If he is willing to redeem
you, very well. Let him marry you. But if
he is not willing, then as surely as the
LORD lives, I will redeem you myself! Now
lie down here until morning."

14So Ruth lay at Boaz's feet until the
morning, but she got up before it was
light enough for people to recognize each
other. For Boaz had said, "No one must
know that a woman was here at the
threshing floor." 15Then Boaz said to her,
"Bring your cloak and spread it out." He
measured six scoops* of barley into the
cloak and placed it on her back. Then he*
returned to the town.

3:15a Hebrew *six measures*, an unknown quantity. **3:15b** Most Hebrew manuscripts read *he;* many Hebrew manuscripts, Syriac version, and Latin Vulgate read *she*.

NOTES

3:8 ***suddenly woke up and turned over.*** Lit., "was startled and sat up." The hills of Judea benefit from an almost constant evening breeze, making the night chilly even in June. The narrator describes how, once his feet had been uncovered and became chilled (cf. Campbell 1975:122), Boaz groggily woke up and was suddenly struck by the thought that his clothes seemed to have been moved by something or someone else (cf. Block 1999:689-690, who also contrasts Boaz's restraint upon finding a woman there with the general immorality of the judges period).

He was surprised. Boaz's surprise in seeing Ruth there is indicated in the Hebrew by the dramatic use of the particle *hinneh* [TH2009, ZH2180], "behold!" Chisholm (1998:160) points out that this functions rhetorically to draw the reader into Boaz's perspective: He wakes up confused and simply sees "*a* woman."

3:9 ***servant.*** Ruth called herself an *'amah* [TH519, ZH563] now in a subtle contrast to *shipkhah* [TH8198, ZH9148] ("worker," see 2:13). Where before, she hoped to be accepted on the level of a foreign worker in the field, here she was about to imply the possibility of marriage, so she made her offer in the most appealing terms—a landowner could marry an *'amah* (servant), not a *shipkhah* (Bush 1996:164; cf. Sasson 1989:81).

Spread the corner of your covering over me. This is an idiom (or euphemism; Bullinger 1968:685) for "receive me in the way of marriage" (cf. Block 1999:691). Boaz's response in 3:10 reinforces the idea that culturally Ruth's request was an unambiguous inquiry about marriage (cf. Naomi's statement of intent in 3:1). This is also a wordplay on Boaz's blessing of Ruth in 2:12 where the word for corner (*kanap* [TH3671, ZH4053], "wing, corner") is also used. The hem of the garment also had symbolic use for the dissolution of marriages in the ancient Near East (Kruger 1984:79-83).

According to Matthews (2004:234), Boaz pledged to protect Ruth and Naomi's legal rights, not to marry Ruth. But this view seems difficult in light of Boaz's response that Ruth could have pursued a younger man (3:10). If accepted, the reading of the Kethiv at 4:5 ("I will marry") also presents a problem for Matthews's view.

you are my family redeemer. Lit., "you are a *go'el* [TH1350B, ZH1457]." The suggestion that "obviously Ruth and Naomi had discussed the subject [of *go'el*] fully" (Block 1999:691) seems less than certain. There is little in the text to suggest that Ruth had a precise and Israelite understanding of this term. Ruth's words do not stem directly from Naomi's directions, and one suspects she may have been improvising at this awkward moment—Boaz had not "told Ruth what to do" (cf. 3:4). Glover (2009:304) suggests that Ruth departed from Naomi's term "relative" (cf. 3:2) and used *go'el* here as a rejection of the Moabite identity or stigma from Lot's daughters (Gen 19:32); Ruth would not be incestuous in her attempt to preserve the family line. While the scene does allude to the Moabite ancestry, this view doesn't seem persuasive since Ruth's intent at the threshing floor is not a sexual encounter but a request for marriage—and not a levirate marriage.

3:10 ***The LORD bless you.*** Berger (2009a:257-260) finds parallels in Ruth to the story of David, Nabal, and Abigail (1 Sam 25) that, taken together, may be seen as purposeful and allusive. One example is the form *berukah* [TH1288A, ZH1385] (blessed), which occurs only twice in the Hebrew Bible: the present verse and 1 Sam 25:33. Abigail and David's actions are often viewed as manipulative and selfish, in contrast to Ruth and Boaz who are more sincere, humble, and unpoliticized. Berger (2009a:261-271) therefore suggests Boaz and Ruth provided the right start for the kingship, and the book of Ruth makes literary connections to overshadow (or blot out) David's questionable actions with their purer qualities (thus offering hope for the line as a whole).

3:11 ***everyone in town.*** Lit., "the whole gate of my people." The practice of gathering at the town gate was so subconsciously assumed that the word "gate" could signify a town and its inhabitants by metonymy. This use of gate is also found in 4:1 and, e.g., in Isa 14:31.

virtuous woman. Heb., *'esheth khayil* [TH802/2428, ZH851/2657], a phrase occurring only here and in Prov 31:10, where the ideal woman, patterned after the lady wisdom, is seen to be "virtuous and capable" as well as rare; she also does *khayil* (Prov 31:29). With reference to men, the idea of strength is often in view with *khayil* (cf. Prov 31:3), and the term is used of armies and soldiers (e.g., Exod 14:4). In other cases, however, wealth or means is in view (e.g., Gen 34:29), or "means" in terms of personal abilities or capabilities (e.g., Exod 18:21). The general idea is of something that is firm, sound, or of quality—financially, physically, mentally, or in terms of character. In our verse, the idea of Ruth being responsible and capable is in view, though in cultural and social terms, one may view Boaz as granting Ruth something of a noble title based on her noble conduct. At the very least, the use of this term points to the idea that Ruth is worthy of Boaz, the *gibbor khayil* [TH1368/2428, ZH1475/2657] (see note on 2:1).

3:12 ***But while it's true that.*** Lit., "And now, for it's true, for except" (*we'attah ki 'omnam ki 'im*). As is recognized in the Qere reading of MT, which omits *'im*, the Hebrew here is syntactically redundant; it should be understood as either the result of dittography or a double reading. In the first case, it can be argued that a scribe erringly copied *k-y-'-m* a second time, producing the extraneous *ki 'im* at the end of the line. In the second case, it would be suggested that either *ki 'im* or *ki 'omnam* was an early alternate found in the margin of a manuscript (or in another copy), and was at some point added directly to the text so that both readings would be preserved. The NLT (like most English translations) follows MT's Qere reading. Although the Hebrew structure of the Qere is unattested elsewhere, it does achieve the required sense—the text is best read without the final *'im*.

3:13 ***Let him marry you.*** Lit., "Let him redeem you." Marriage is not spoken of directly, if at all, here.

lie down here until morning. As Gray (1967:419) comments, if Ruth were to travel about at night, "she might have been taken for a public prostitute (cf. Song 5:7), and would possibly encounter unprincipled persons, either thieves watching for an opportunity at the threshing-floors or men drunk at that season of harvest."

3:14 ***Boaz had said.*** Lit., "Boaz said." The NLT's "had" is a possible translation here, and the sequence of events is often seen to call for some explanation since Ruth gets up and then Boaz says that no one should know the woman was there. The NLT represents a good solution, but the best explanation in my view is that these words in fact recount Boaz's thoughts (so also Bush 1996:177). Genesis 20:11 features a similar use of the verb "to say." As such, the phrase doesn't recount an instruction Boaz had given, but his thoughts, as Ruth was preparing to leave, reminding readers of the tension in the situation.

3:15 ***Bring.*** The Hebrew here (*habi* [TH3051, ZH2035]) presents a hapax legomenon, and a difficult vowel pointing. The form has been explained commonly as deriving from *y-h-b* [TH3051, ZH3364] and being a fem. imperative that was given vowels analogous to the pl. (so GKC §69o). Martín-Contreras (2009) assembles manuscript evidence to support the testimony of the rabbis (e.g., *Ruth Rabbah* 7:2) who suggest another alternative: *habi* in this verse derives from *b-w-'* [TH935, ZH995] and is a defective spelling of *habi'*, as well as a case where a masc. form (*habi'*; cf. Jer 17:18 and 2 Sam 13:10) is used to address a woman (cf. 1:8; Amos 4:1). The root *b-w-'* is perhaps more appropriate to the context where it has the "cloak" as its object.

six scoops of barley. Cf. NLT mg. The text omits any unit of measure, and even a word such as "scoop." Barley was such a common feature of ancient Israelite life that a basic unit of measure was implied here, but for modern readers, the identification of that unit is uncertain (cf. Bush 1996:178). In view of Ruth's need to exit the threshing floor quietly and the fact that she apparently carried the grain in a garment ("cloak"; cf. KJV, "veil"; NET, "shawl"), it seems likely that the amount was not extremely large, but rather symbolic and at the same time practical. The NLT's "six scoops" (cf. Block 1999:698) is therefore an appropriate solution.

he returned to the town. Cf. NLT mg. Numerous Masoretic manuscripts, followed by some Lucianic manuscripts of the LXX, the Vulgate, and the Syriac have "she [Ruth] went into the city." But this is probably a harmonization with 2:18, where the same syntax is found (cf. de Waard 2004:8, 55*).

COMMENTARY

Threshing floors were typically circular and open to the wind, because that made them useful for blowing off the chaff. They were set up on exposed rock or hard-packed ground and usually surrounded with a ring of stones. The sheaves of barley or wheat were scattered around the circle, and then threshed by either leading animals such as oxen around the circle, or by having a person ride behind an animal on a threshing sledge. The sledge is a board, its bottom usually studded with hard rock (e.g., basalt), or later, iron. As the animals made rounds on the floor, workers would continually turn the sheaves and grain over. Once the grain was loose, it was winnowed by being tossed up into the wind. The grain would fall to the floor again, but the chaff was blown away.

Ruth arrived at such a threshing floor and waited. Boaz and the others finished their work and enjoyed a full meal supplied by the great harvest. The text notes that after eating and drinking, Boaz was "in good spirits" (3:7, lit., "his heart was good"; cf. Judg 19:6, 22; 1 Kgs 21:7). The text does not say that Boaz was drunk, and Bush (1996:161) renders this phrase as "was at peace with the world," seeking to maintain this ambiguity. It is true that Boaz's good spirits here may be simply due to eating a good meal or reflecting on the harvest. But like some of the sexually provocative language in this chapter (see note on 3:4), I think this phrase too is intended to point out the potential of immorality—Boaz was enjoying life, but it is unclear what kind of drinking is in view and whether he would be as temperate as we expect. He is more likely to be ready to entertain any request, but what else might happen when he finds himself alone with Ruth in the middle of the night?

Boaz departed from the other threshers and relaxed, laying by his pile of grain either to guard it (cf. 1 Sam 23:1) or perhaps because there was much work to do and little reason to return home. Bush (1996:179) suggests that Boaz laying at the far end of the pile of grain was a mark of the Lord's grace assisting Ruth, who "quietly" came over to him (3:7). Boaz had lain down far enough away from other workers or threshers that Ruth's actions in the dark of night would certainly go unnoticed.

After following Naomi's directions, Ruth waited in the dark. Boaz roused, feeling a draft (see note on 3:4), and then shuddered awake. He groped about, presumably sitting up to arrange his blanket or clothes to cover his feet, and suddenly saw a woman. Although Naomi seemed to expect that Boaz would recognize Ruth and give instructions (3:4), he asked a question (3:9). Ruth not only answered Boaz's question, she proceeded to give him instructions! As Hubbard suggests (1988:213), her boldness to address a superior this way may show her devotion to her mother-in-law. Ruth's words in 3:9 keep to the spirit of Naomi's plan but do not seem to have been part of it. Her situation, lying at Boaz's feet by the corner of his garment, already prompted Boaz to make a decision about marrying her (see note on 3:9; cf. Deut 22:30; 27:20; Ezek 16:8).

Ruth's introduction of the term *go'el* [TH1350B, ZH1457] in her statement to Boaz is surprising, but key to the development of the plot. Bush (1996:181) calls attention to Ruth's vulnerable state and suggests that her statement was intended to keep her actions from being misinterpreted. Her use of *go'el* is not technical (cf. Exod 15:13; Pss 69:18; 77:15; 103:4; Isa 43:1; 44:6; 48:20), but simply a reference to a family member who should be concerned to resolve the bad situation of another. In fact, Ruth, the Moabitess, was not likely aware of all the uses of this term, and it seems possible to consider her causal connection of it to her request for marriage a *mistake* (cf. Linafelt 1999:56). Boaz was not obligated to marry her, and in Scripture a *go'el* is never obligated to marry or be first in line to marry, as with the levirate situation. Land and *levirate* marriage were not on Ruth's mind (cf. Bush 1996:137, 169). Rather, she reminded Boaz that as family he belonged to the class of people most likely to look out for her well-being.

In the first scene of chapter 4 (4:1-12), it becomes evident that Ruth's improvisation sparked an idea in Boaz that would benefit Ruth and Naomi, as well as Elimelech's line, for there was a piece of land yet unmentioned (4:3-4). Boaz said he would do what Ruth asked, but then, rather than speaking about marriage, his words used the root *ga'al* [TH1350, ZH1457] six more times in 3:12-13. It seems he was taking the term in a more technical direction (cf. Bush 1996:181). He understood that the implications of *go'el* in the technical sense involved land, not marriage. But he considered how he might join the two for the best end for all parties.

In 3:10 Boaz responds positively to Ruth's request. The reader almost feels as though the story has reached its resolution, and then, upon reaching the words of 3:12, uncertainty and confusion reenter the picture. Boaz has no hesitations about marrying Ruth and goes so far as to call her a "virtuous woman" (see note on 3:11) a phrase used elsewhere only in Proverbs 31:10. (One wonders if this scene also makes allusion to Prov 31:15-16 by connection to "gets up before dawn," "servant girls," and "to inspect a field.") As a man of means and standing, Boaz likely knew from experience that "Fathers can give their sons an inheritance of houses and wealth, but only the LORD can give an understanding wife" (Prov 19:14). Ruth was not bound to marry him, and he clearly recognized this offer from a suitable woman as a blessing of the Lord. But then Boaz spoke of another relative, closer to Elimelech with whom he must talk. Boaz assured Ruth she would be rescued from her plight ("redeemed," 3:13). For readers, unaware of the issue of Naomi's field (4:3), confusion ensues. Why does Boaz talk this way? It seems that as flattered as Boaz was by Ruth's proposal, her use of the term *go'el* nudged him to set his sights on the best possible deal for her and any child she might have. He was willing to forego a pleasant opportunity in order to get Ruth something more (which he evidently thought she deserved), and to do something more for Elimelech's line. Although levirate law did not apply to her directly and the issue of land need not be tied to her marriage, Boaz saw a way to leverage the situation, bless Ruth more abundantly, and preserve Elimelech's line by carefully navigating the cultural values and instincts of his time. This takes shape in chapter 4.

Boaz told Ruth to lay the rest of the night by his feet. He perhaps already had in mind to send grain with her for Naomi. Were she found leaving the threshing floor at that hour with grain in hand, she might be treated as a criminal and harshly abused in the dark of night. In the morning, she would fare better. Ruth arose at an early hour (3:14), ready to leave. In this final moment of their secret meeting, Boaz's thoughts dramatically highlight the tension—"No one must know that a woman was here" (3:14, see note). He helped her arrange the "six scoops" of grain, and then departed to town, where he would wait at the gate (4:1).

This scene hints at the story of Moabite national origins that tells how Lot's daughters got him drunk and slept with him in order to carry on the family line after their husbands died (Gen 19:30-38). Here, there are sexual overtones, and implications that Boaz had been drinking wine to an unknown extent. What would happen when Ruth approached Boaz as he slept? The actions of the two contrast greatly with those of Lot and his daughters: Boaz was not undisciplined like Lot and had either not drunk so much or been allowed to sleep it off. And Ruth was not as unscrupulous as an Israelite reader might have thought a Moabite woman to be. *B. Sanhedrin* 19b compares Boaz to Joseph in the presence of Potiphar's wife and says that Boaz's self-control at this moment made Joseph's pale by comparison. Ruth's actions likewise speak to her character. The scene perhaps makes a literary defense for less virtuous moments in the Davidic line, such as the actions of Judah and Tamar (Gen 38) and of David and Bathsheba (2 Sam 11; cf. notes on 3:5; 3:10; and 4:12; see Berger 2009a, 2009b).

◆ C. Ruth Reports the Outcome to Naomi (3:16-18)

16 When Ruth went back to her mother-in-law, Naomi asked, "What happened, my daughter?"

Ruth told Naomi everything Boaz had done for her, 17 and she added, "He gave me these six scoops of barley and said, 'Don't go back to your mother-in-law empty-handed.' "

18 Then Naomi said to her, "Just be patient, my daughter, until we hear what happens. The man won't rest until he has settled things today."

NOTES

3:17 ***six scoops.*** See note on 3:15. There is considerable difficulty in determining the precise amount of barley. But in light of the fact that most commentators agree that Boaz's gesture was symbolic, and that the number "six" is repeated here by Ruth (cf. 3:15), who could have spoken instead of a "gift of barley" or "all this grain," it is probably worthwhile to consider some symbolism along the lines of the number six. A clue is to be found in Naomi's degree of confidence that Boaz would settle the matter in the next day as he told

Ruth (cf. 3:13). I suggest that the symbolism is found in the relationship to seven, the number of days in the week. Six days were gone, and only one remained—Boaz would act in that one remaining day. Six days were for working (Deut 5:13), and the seventh was for "rest" (from the root *n-w-kh* [TH5117, ZH5663]; Deut 5:14, note also the presence there of *'amah* [TH519, ZH563], "female servant"). Ruth was a day away from finding the sought-after "rest" or "permanent home" (3:1; also from the root *n-w-kh*).

empty-handed. Lit., "empty." This is a wordplay on Naomi's description of herself as empty in 1:21. It foreshadows the coming day when she will again be full (4:14-15), and it associates that fulfillment with Ruth. Bush (1996:186-187) says, "Surely the way in which our narrator has Ruth quote Boaz's very words, in which he insists that she not return 'empty' (ריקם) [cf. TH7387, ZH8200] to her mother-in-law, signals that the munificent gift of grain Boaz sends to Naomi is a portent that the resolution will also encompass her return to life and fullness." Sakenfeld (1999:65) likewise sees Boaz's implicit concern for Naomi here; he intended to do more than just marry Ruth.

COMMENTARY

The previous scene leaves the reader waiting—Naomi and Ruth's actions had neither failed nor succeeded, yet. Boaz's response was favorable, but his action and the results remain to be seen. In the interim, the narrator offers his final portrayal of an interaction between the two women and provides two more glimmers of hope regarding a positive outcome.

Upon Ruth's return, Naomi quite naturally questions her as to the outcome of her visit to Boaz. After a brief summary statement at the end of 3:16, new information is given (3:17)—Ruth expresses Boaz's comment, which accompanied his gift of grain. He did not want Ruth to return to Naomi empty-handed. This is the first hint at a positive outcome because it indicates Boaz's concern for Naomi, as well as for Ruth. The second hint comes from Naomi's response—her wording in 3:18 shows she had great confidence that Boaz was stirred up and wouldn't be able to keep from dealing with this issue "today." It is difficult to know whether her response is based on her prior knowledge of Boaz's character or whether it is an interpretive response to the information Ruth presented in 3:17 (see note). Block (1999:700) favors the idea that the grain was a down payment, perhaps even a part of the *mohar* [TH4119, ZH4558] or bridal gift (cf. Gen 34:12; Exod 22:17; 1 Sam 18:25). If so, then the latter option seems more likely. But Block also concedes that other reasons could be provided. In any case, Ruth's new information and Naomi's clear response nudge the reader's expectations toward a successful outcome in spite of the fact that no action is occurring in the narrative.

There is no more direct speech from Ruth or Naomi in the book; from here the interest shifts to the actions of Boaz—largely the outcome of the women's words and actions to this point. As this scene closes, we are left with a sense of hope for a positive outcome, but more than that—it seems the narrator leaves us to ponder the development of the two women's relationship. What began as a fierce, and rather one-way, commitment on the part of Ruth (1:14-18) grew into a relationship of mutual concern and culminated in the trust and solidarity of chapter 3. While a positive outcome to Boaz's actions is *expected*, the state of the women's relationship is *certain*.

◆ IV. Boaz Provides for Elimelech's Family (4:1-22)

A. Boaz Successfully Gains Ruth and Pledges to Provide for Elimelech's Family (4:1-12)

Boaz went to the town gate and took a
seat there. Just then the family redeemer
he had mentioned came by, so Boaz called
out to him, "Come over here and sit down,
friend. I want to talk to you." So they sat
down together. 2Then Boaz called ten
leaders from the town and asked them to
sit as witnesses. 3And Boaz said to the
family redeemer, "You know Naomi, who
came back from Moab. She is selling the
land that belonged to our relative Elime-
lech. 4I thought I should speak to you
about it so that you can redeem it if you
wish. If you want the land, then buy it
here in the presence of these witnesses.
But if you don't want it, let me know right
away, because I am next in line to redeem
it after you."

The man replied, "All right, I'll redeem it."

5Then Boaz told him, "Of course, your
purchase of the land from Naomi also re-
quires that you marry Ruth, the Moabite
widow. That way she can have children
who will carry on her husband's name and
keep the land in the family."

6"Then I can't redeem it," the family re-
deemer replied, "because this might en-
danger my own estate. You redeem the
land; I cannot do it."

7Now in those days it was the custom
in Israel for anyone transferring a right of
purchase to remove his sandal and hand
it to the other party. This publicly vali-
dated the transaction. 8So the other fam-
ily redeemer drew off his sandal as he said
to Boaz, "You buy the land."

9Then Boaz said to the elders and to the
crowd standing around, "You are witness-
es that today I have bought from Naomi
all the property of Elimelech, Kilion, and
Mahlon. 10And with the land I have ac-
quired Ruth, the Moabite widow of Mah-
lon, to be my wife. This way she can have
a son to carry on the family name of her
dead husband and to inherit the family
property here in his hometown. You are all
witnesses today."

11Then the elders and all the people
standing in the gate replied, "We are wit-
nesses! May the LORD make this woman
who is coming into your home like Rachel
and Leah, from whom all the nation of
Israel descended! May you prosper in
Ephrathah and be famous in Bethlehem.
12And may the LORD give you descendants
by this young woman who will be like
those of our ancestor Perez, the son of
Tamar and Judah."

NOTES

4:1 ***friend.*** Lit., "you certain someone/someplace" (*peloni 'almoni* [TH6423/492, ZH7141/532]); cf. 1 Sam 21:3; 2 Kgs 6:8; Dan 8:13. If he did not know the man's name, the narrator could have used "friend," "sir" (so LXX) or the like here. By using this phrase, which is even used to designate "someplace," the narrator may be creating a reading with a force ranging from that of the colloquial expressions "hey there, fella" to "hey what's-your-face." The use of this term in place of other options for addressing the near kinsman therefore could imply the unimportance of this man's identity—Boaz was extraordinary, but his relative was just "some guy." Another option deserves consideration, however—namely that the phrase isn't addressing the kinsman at all, but rather describing the unnamed place where Boaz suggested they sit and chat with the ten elders (cf. DCH 296). This could be rendered, "come, sit somewhere here." In light of the fact that the other two uses of this phrase refer to places and the phrase in Ruth immediately follows the word "here" (*poh* [TH6311, ZH7024]), I find this option slightly more attractive than the traditional translation of it as a way of addressing the kinsman.

4:3 ***selling the land.*** Sakenfeld (1999:71) suggests that rather than selling the actual land, Naomi sold her right to redeem the land, which she couldn't afford to buy and which Elimelech probably sold before leaving. This is possible, but if Naomi had owned the land, it may have lain fallow, being useless to her and Ruth in the harvest; lacking the means to farm the land, the women would have had to sell in order to have money to survive.

4:5 ***you marry Ruth.*** Lit., "you acquire Ruth." The NLT correctly follows the Qere of MT here, reading *qanitah* [TH7069, ZH7864] (you acquire) rather than *qaniti* (I acquire). The MT preserves similar Kethiv/Qere readings at 3:3-4 ("you/I go down," and "you/I lay down"), perhaps indicating the preservation of archaic forms in which the *–ti* ending marks the second-person fem. sg. (cf. Joüon-Muraoka §42f; Judg 5:7). The Qere here is supported by the LXX (*ktēsasthai se* [TG4771, ZG5148]), Vulgate, and Syriac (which adds that the other kinsman refused to marry Ruth because he lacked faith).

4:7-8 The procedure here involved a sandal, which is similar to that in the levirate law of Deut 25:5-10, but the details of the actions are notably different. Matthews (2004:240) mentions variations in the law over time as the reason for the difference in sandal procedure, or that it was a land-oriented custom, not a levirate one. He also admits "There is no sense in this passage that the next of kin is humiliated by this exchange." He didn't lose social standing either. The story of Ruth and Boaz has come down to us in part because it is not merely a story of obedience to levirate law—Boaz's actions show *khesed* [TH2617, ZH2876] and go beyond the law's requirements. The ritual shoe removal also marked the woman's assumption of the "right to her freedom and full control of her destiny" (ABD 4.567). This feature, however, didn't apply here, since Ruth was already free (cf. 3:10) and did not take her sandal off.

4:7 ***Now in those days.*** The content of this verse shows an awareness that a significant amount of time had passed between its writing and the events recounted in the book. Its language suggests that it is late (cf. Bush 1996:27-28), and it is probably to be regarded as an editorial comment added to the story for the benefit of the reader.

4:11 ***Rachel and Leah.*** In the blessing here, Rachel (the younger sister) precedes Leah. Similarly in Gen 48:20, Ephraim (the younger brother) preceded Manasseh. Rachel perhaps precedes on the lips of the Bethlehem crowd because of her association with the town (Gen 35:16-19). Judah and Perez (ancestors of Boaz and Elimelech) were, in fact, descendants of Leah (Gen 29:31-35).

4:12 ***Tamar and Judah.*** Berger (2009b:447) takes this parallel beyond Genesis and Ruth, suggesting that literarily, David recalls Judah and Tamar in his sin involving Bathsheba (2 Sam 11), and that the author of Ruth used this literary means to cast David's actions as an aberration from his bloodline—with the heightened irony that Ruth's actions were an aberration from her bloodline (cf. Lot and his daughters).

COMMENTARY

Ruth 4:1-2 sets the stage for the scene: After leaving the threshing floor, Boaz had stationed himself by the town gate in order to spot the kinsman he needed to speak with (cf. 3:12-13). The gate was the appropriate place for this because in the ancient Near East town business and legal transactions centered around the gate (cf. note on 3:11). When he spotted his kinsman, Boaz suggested they sit for a formal discussion and brought ten elders from the gate as witnesses. No written documents are mentioned in the discussion that follows, only the attestation and symbolic actions of the participants and witnesses. This does not preclude written records but does suggest that they were not crucial for legitimizing the proceedings.

It is likely that greetings, pleasantries, and small talk preceded Boaz's first words here, as is the traditional custom in the Middle East. Boaz then began (4:3) by raising the issue of Elimelech's land. Land belonging to Elimelech had not been mentioned or implied in the story up to this point. It seems likely, however, that Israelite readers envisioning Elimelech would have readily understood him as a land owner—all Israel had inherited land ever since the conquest. What is surprising is that the land was not mentioned until now. This, I think, is a clever move by the author, who reserved this fact until this moment to surprise us with Boaz's skillful negotiations. As suggested in the commentary on 3:6-15, Boaz sought to do more than Ruth asked (which was only for marriage) by incorporating her future with the legal issues of land, where the *go'el* [TH1350B, ZH1457] had certain rights and responsibilities.

In ancient Israel, land was generally to stay in the possession of the tribe and family to which it had been allotted. In the case that land was sold outside of its original family, the Lord had commanded that it would revert (with some few exceptions) to the original owning family in the Year of Jubilee (Lev 25:8-34). In the event that a family line was cut off from Israel—that is, it had no heirs—the nearest kin had the right and was expected to fulfill the obligation to redeem the land. If the nearest kin could not fulfill the obligation, the right would pass to the next kin—the next *go'el*. In 4:4, Boaz outlines the status of the land and points out that he is second in line to redeem it—this other kinsman is first. And the kinsman readily agreed to fulfill the obligation.

Up to this point the transaction proceeds along typical lines. Then, in 4:5, Boaz made his gambit, and with his statement everything is changed. We need not assume that the kinsman's response in 4:6 follows Boaz's statement immediately. It is simply the next point of importance to the narrative. The kinsman had time to think, as did the witnesses, about what Boaz had just said. What Boaz asserted stood up to communal consideration. The reason for this is not explicit in the text.

This scene is associated by many with levirate law (e.g., Matthews 2004:235-237), that is, the obligation of a brother to wed his brother's childless widow and produce an heir in the name of his brother (Deut 25:5-10; an exception to Lev 18:16). Besides the biblical reference to this custom, levirate marriage is known at Ugarit (Nougayrol 1955:16.144, wherein the childless ruler Arhalba ensures by a curse that his brother alone may wed his wife after his death), from the Middle Assyrian Laws (Tablet A, Law 33), and the Hittite law code (law 193).

There are enough differences, however, between the events in this scene in Ruth and the levirate laws of the Torah that it cannot be argued that the levirate law (Deut 25:5-10; cf. Gen 38) is in view in the book of Ruth. Elements not found in this scene include: brothers living together (Deut 25:5); the public statement by the widow (Deut 25:7); further pleading of the elders with the kinsman (Deut 25:8); the widow publicly removing the man's sandal, spitting in his face, and making a second statement (Deut 25:9); and the public reproach on his house (Deut 25:10). The near kinsman here is not a brother and pulls off his own sandal (4:8), and although the narrator leaves him nameless (see note on 4:1), he does not portray any public scandal or ignominy for his house. There was not a legislated obligation for the near kinsman to raise up an heir to Ruth's husband, Mahlon.

Nonetheless, the outcome of this scene is the intended outcome of an enactment of levirate law—a family line that was about to die out is perpetuated. And because Boaz's actions were accepted by the leaders of his society, they must implicitly rest on some shared cultural value, at least, or perhaps even on an expected custom that was not a matter of law but resembled the levirate practice ("levirate-type custom" Bush 1996). As Houston (1980:70) suggests, it is impossible that Boaz simply enacted a fiat here to designate his child as Mahlon's heir.

Consider again the actions of the unnamed kinsman in 4:4-6. He was initially willing to redeem the land. It seems unlikely in a small town like Bethlehem that he would not have heard, during the harvest, about the return of the two widows, Naomi and Ruth. He did not expect, however, that anyone would marry Ruth and raise an heir for Mahlon—this is true whether one reads 4:5 as asserting that Boaz will marry Ruth or as asserting that the other kinsman must marry Ruth (see note on 4:5). In the first place, he knew levirate law did not apply. Secondly, as Ruth was a Moabite, her status may have been fuzzy as pertained to any levirate-type custom that someone might propose—she might not be due the same treatment as an Israelite. This could remain a question for discussion by the town elders, should anyone venture to suggest it.[1] But if Boaz appealed to something less than a custom—shared values—then it may be that the invocation of these values in order to unite Ruth's marriage with the issue of Elimelech's land in the presence of ten elders of Bethlehem was the unexpected event that altered the kinsman's response. Boaz mentioned in 3:11 that everyone in town knew that Ruth was a virtuous woman—thus even with only the shared value of preserving family lines (or perhaps a shared taboo against knowingly letting one die out), Boaz's proposal could have been recognized as the moral high ground by that panoply of 12 men sitting near the gate. Numbers 27 and 36 reinforce these values, again without a levirate marriage obligation.

An additional clue that shared values, rather than a set custom (and certainly rather than levirate law), were the basis of Boaz's negotiation is in his use of the word "acquire" in 4:5 and 4:10. This is highlighted by Sakenfeld (1999:73-74). Only here is "acquire" used of marriage. Boaz's use of this word also ties together the redemption of land and the marriage of Ruth. At the gate, he cannot speak of "redeeming" her as in 3:12-13, since the *go'el* is not connected to marriage obligations. And typical terms for marriage have no resonance with the idea of purchasing land. This verb, however, overlaps both realms just sufficiently to drive home Boaz's appeal to shared values in a rhetorical sense: How could anyone acquire the family land without also acquiring the social obligation to the family widow?

In either of the cases mentioned above (either an appeal to shared values, or to an existing levirate-type custom), the opportunity for the kinsman changed drastically once Boaz brought in the idea of an heir for Mahlon. Rather than gaining the right to permanently incorporate the land into his own estate, the kinsman would only gain land-use rights for a limited period (cf. Matthews 2004:237; Nielsen 1997:83-85), and he may (see note on 4:5) also have been forced to take Ruth as a wife and raise an heir himself. In addition, if he felt the weight of Boaz's appeal, he could not bring himself to publicly retain the right to the land, while refusing to honor Elimelech's line by marrying Ruth, a woman in good standing. In other words, in addition to the shared value of preserving a family line, there seems an ethical balance between getting use of the land and raising the heir. The kinsman's response in light of the new development was "I cannot do it" (4:6).

Again we are left without details as to how many wives or children the man already had (so also with Boaz), and how long the kinsman had the use of this land if he did redeem it. Some have suggested (e.g., Bush 1996:245-246) that the man overstated his case when he said he would "endanger [his] own estate." But the text tells us so little about his situation or what his responsibility would entail that it seems better to think of the unnamed kinsman as an average person acting in a typical way, rather than to think of him as a moral failure. Further, it would be somewhat disconcerting for the reader if he had excelled in virtue and insisted on marrying Ruth—what then of Boaz? It is a tribute to Boaz's outstanding virtues that this foil (the unnamed kinsman) need not be a villain, but an average person. And to reinforce this view, I suggest that Boaz may here be compared and contrasted with Abram in Genesis 12:10–13:2. In that narrative, Abram became rich by duping Pharaoh with a ruse regarding Sarai, his wife; he did this out of fear. Pharaoh didn't know that something much bigger was at work in Abram's life than just being connected to an attractive woman, and he protested when he found out that Sarai was actually Abram's wife. Boaz's gambit gained him Elimelech's field along with a virtuous woman, and in the scope of the narrative, the unnamed kinsman (like the pharaoh of Gen 12) was just an average person, acting normally. In contrast to Abram, Boaz did not undertake his clever actions out of fear, but in order to ensure that Elimelech's family line was not lost.

With the whole matter on the table, once the kinsman had made his decision, he passed his sandal to Boaz as a symbol of the transfer of the right to buy the land (4:7-8, see note). Boaz immediately exercised his new right, and he recapitulated in his joyful declaration the terms of the transaction: Though not first in line to claim the land, he claimed it with a pledge to raise up an heir for Elimelech through Ruth (4:10). The town rejoiced with blessings on the couple that gave a sense of full acceptance of the marriage and of Ruth's place as a wife and mother in Israel (4:11). This is evident in the references to Rachel and Leah (recognized as the mothers of the 12 tribes). The blessings also mention Bethlehem and Ephrathah, both names connected to Rachel's death and burial (Gen 35:16-19).

The closing verse of this scene (4:12) makes an important allusion that highlights the virtue of what Boaz had done. The women mention not just the founder of the tribe, Judah, but begin with Perez and speak of Tamar, his mother. Their story is recorded in Genesis 38. Tamar was, in fact, Judah's daughter-in-law, but his son (and her first husband), Er, was evil, so the Lord killed him (Gen 38:7) before he and Tamar had a child. Although in Judah's day the laws given at Sinai were not in effect, some other levirate law or custom prevailed, and Judah gave his second son, Onan, to be Tamar's husband. Onan's well-known actions provide an additional foil against which Boaz's virtue can be seen: Onan, although he had intercourse with Tamar, refused to allow himself to impregnate her because he knew the child would be his brother's heir (Gen 38:9). This disrespect toward his deceased brother contrasts greatly with Boaz's noble desire to raise up an heir for a more distant relative to whom he was not so obligated. In the continuation of Genesis 38, Tamar can be seen as a contrast to Ruth; regarding this comparison, see the commentary on 3:6-15.

In addition to the allusion present in 4:12, the words of the townswomen also foreshadow or even forecast the coming resolution: They call for the Lord to bless Boaz and Ruth with children, an affirmation of the stated intent of the new couple's union. The next scene naturally looks to the fulfillment of this wish.

ENDNOTE

1. As Matthews (2004:237) puts it, "There was no naturalization service in ancient Israel. Ruth would not sit for a test one day and get a decisive word on her citizenship. She would interact with the community and be observed. She would enter into this new national identity step by step, slowly gaining the rights and responsibilities that came with it. Thus, the question of her right to raise up an heir for her dead husband was still a live one. Would the nearer kinsman and the elders see her as an insider or an outsider when Boaz pressed this point?"

◆ B. The Lord Fulfills Naomi by Providing an Heir for Elimelech's Family (4:13-17)

13So Boaz took Ruth into his home, and she became his wife. When he slept with her, the LORD enabled her to become pregnant, and she gave birth to a son. 14Then the women of the town said to Naomi, "Praise the LORD, who has now provided a redeemer for your family! May this child be famous in Israel. 15May he restore your youth and care for you in your old age. For he is the son of your daughter-in-law who loves you and has been better to you than seven sons!"

16Naomi took the baby and cuddled him to her breast. And she cared for him as if he were her own. 17The neighbor women said, "Now at last Naomi has a son again!" And they named him Obed. He became the father of Jesse and the grandfather of David.

NOTES

4:13 Neither Boaz nor Ruth are mentioned in the narrative after this verse. One rabbinic tradition held that Boaz was so old that he died on the wedding night (*Yalkut Shimoni* 608), "immediately after he had established the royal dynasty" (Broch 1983:103). The biblical text, however, seems to wish a better outcome upon him than this would indicate (4:11). In any case, the fact that the remaining verses of the scene describe Naomi bring the plot full circle—Naomi's emptiness has been the underlying focus all along, and now it is finally fully resolved.

4:14 ***redeemer.*** The redeemer here (*go'el* [TH1350B, ZH1457]) refers to the newborn child, who will continue the family line. This is evident from the nature of the statements referring to him in 4:15 (Bush 1996:253).

May this child be famous in Israel. Lit., "May his name be called in Israel."

4:16 ***cared for him.*** Though the verb here translated "care" (*'aman* [TH539A, ZH587]) can mean "to nurse," it is not likely in view of Naomi's age that she nursed Obed; the verb is used elsewhere involving nurture of children (2 Kgs 10:1, 5; Esth 2:7).

4:17 ***The neighbor women said, "Now at last Naomi has a son again!" And they named him Obed.*** Lit., "And the neighbor women called him a name, saying, 'A son has been born to Naomi.' And they called his name Obed." Three things stand out here: (1) Nowhere else in Scripture do townswomen name a newborn child; (2) the naming is apparently recorded twice; and (3) Obed is declared as the "son of Naomi" and not of Boaz or Elimelech or Mahlon, or even Ruth. On the first and second points, Block (1999:731) suggests that the townswomen were affirming a name given by mother or father, and the redundancy is climactic. Bush (1996:261) similarly regards it as a generic statement of name giving (cf. Gen 2:20; 26:18; Isa 65:15), and an instance of poetic license by the author, who was using this chorus of women as he did in 1:19. Campbell (1975:165-166), however, relates the action here to 4:14 ("May this child be famous in Israel") and concludes that calling the son "a name" is idiomatic for celebrating and proclaiming him (cf. the Hebrew of Deut 32:2; Ps 99:6). On the third point, Bush (1996:262) suggests that the declaration of the child as Naomi's son plays off of the typical announcement of a birth to a waiting father and highlights this child's significance for Naomi, the story's main character. Others, such as Gerleman (1960) have suggested that some form of adoption is in view here, so that the child is viewed as Naomi's.

As Campbell (1975:165) points out (citing de Vaux 1961:51), the concept of a technical, legal adoption in such contexts (cf. Gen 16:2; 30:3; 48:5, 12; 50:23) cannot be pressed as Gerleman does. But in light of other parallels between Ruth and patriarchal narratives, I think it is wrong to conclude that no adoptive idea is present. I suggest that the declaration of Obed as Naomi's son, while not a technical adoption, is intended to both direct attention back to the main character, Naomi (by its surprising use of her name), and to imply the full acceptance of Ruth's child into Israel by association with an unmixed marriage (Naomi and Elimelech; cf. Matthews 2004:241). The death of all Elimelech's other children seems to clear the way for a more direct connection of Obed to him.

COMMENTARY

The narrator moved the plot quickly at this point to maintain interest and focus: In a single verse (4:13), nine months go by. This scene is the climactic scene of the book, including not only the answer to Naomi's need for a descendant, but the stunning punch line: This child is foundational to the Davidic line (4:17)! In addition, the Lord is on stage in this scene more than anywhere else in the book. In particular, he enabled Ruth to conceive (4:13). Sakenfeld (1999:20) takes this statement as equivalent to "God made her conceive," seeing it as a resolution to implicit barrenness in 1:4. This may be so, or the phrase may stand as stated as a recognition that all life and procreative power belong to the Lord. In either case, the scene directs our attention to the Lord and Naomi—the Lord is (and has been) good, and finally, Naomi is again full (cf. 1:21).

Glover (2009:302-303) suggests that Ruth has finally in 4:12-13 been "socially resituated" and that her "ethnic status has actually changed." That might overstate the case somewhat, but the townspeople's acceptance of Ruth at this point is undeniable, and her place as Boaz's wife, along with the entry of their child into the Israelite genealogy that follows, does mark the fulfillment (at last) of her statement, "Your people will be my people" (1:16-17). One may trace her progress from foreigner (2:10) to servant (2:13; 3:9) to wife (4:13). For all practical purposes, Ruth has become an Israelite. In this regard, Ruth's story would fail as a justification for marrying just any Moabite woman—Ruth's story is exceptional from the start (cf. Matthews 2004:207).

In tension with this acceptance of Ruth is the fact that Boaz apparently stands in the place of Elimelech (not Mahlon) and provides a child for *Naomi* (4:17), through Ruth. Thus in the genealogy, Elimelech is not mentioned and neither are his sons, except Obed, who has become his son. In this ingenious way, the book of Ruth both embraces the place of one virtuous Moabite woman in David's ancestry, and yet shows that in a symbolic sense, Ruth could be conceived of as bearing on behalf of Naomi herself, just as Rachel and Leah's maids had done (Gen 30).

This need not diminish the importance of Ruth in the family lineage. It simply highlights the different purpose of this genealogy from that of Matthew 1:5 (cf. Luke 3:32), where Ruth is explicitly mentioned. By the New Testament period, it was not a primary concern to defend David's bloodline and rightful place as a founding monarch and recipient of the Lord's promise for an eternal dynasty (2 Sam 7:16). David's memory had long been hallowed, and the Jews had long been without a proper king of their own. Instead, we observe in Luke a new current that aimed to highlight the Lord's invitation to those outside the borders and bloodline of Israel to enter into a new covenant with him.

In this scene, the chorus of women who were surprised by Naomi's return in 1:19 celebrate Naomi's full life (in contrast to her stated emptiness, 1:21) in two main regards: the birth of a child to redeem Elimelech's family line (4:14-15) and the loyal love of her daughter-in-law, Ruth (4:15). Their words in 4:14 also direct the reader's attention to the Lord's role, highlighted by the narrator in 4:13. Finally, in 4:17, their words underscore for the reader the reversal that has occurred in the story. The chorus as a poetic device recapitulates the story, balancing the roles of the characters and celebrating the resolution of Naomi's grief.

In the brief comment of 4:16, the narrator artfully captures a gentle moment. The manner is not unlike the aside in the Gospel of Luke, where one reads "Mary kept all these things in her heart and thought about them often" (Luke 2:19; cf. Luke 2:51). The reader is drawn from public drama to a personal reflection, a quiet and mixed emotion celebrating something victorious that perhaps verges on an epiphany for the character. Amid the loud celebration of the neighbor women, Naomi has no lines; she simply holds the baby close—she will love and nurture him as her own son.

The actions on the part of Boaz, Ruth, and Naomi in this scene parallel, in a sense, those that led earlier to the positive outcome in 2:17. It may be a stretch to conceive Ruth's successful pregnancy in terms of her earlier gleaning, but the idea of fertility is inherent in both, and as in that scene, it may again be said that Boaz's generous provision of his means combines with Ruth's labor to bring forth fruit (in this case a child) that restores Naomi's joy. In this scene, however, the Lord's blessed name is not only on the lips of the characters (4:14; cf. 2:4, 12), his involvement is clearly stated by the narrator (4:13; contrast 2:3-4).

The scene closes (4:17) with a short statement that forms a punch line to the climax: The child was Obed, the ancestor of King David through his father, Jesse! The pious reader's experience upon first realizing this perhaps reflects the experience of Naomi in 4:16—a reflective sense of surprised wonder and joy.

C. Elimelech's Family Is Part of the Line of David (4:18-22)

18 This is the genealogical record of their ancestor Perez:

Perez was the father of Hezron.
19 Hezron was the father of Ram.
Ram was the father of Amminadab.
20 Amminadab was the father of Nahshon.
Nahshon was the father of Salmon.*
21 Salmon was the father of Boaz.
Boaz was the father of Obed.
22 Obed was the father of Jesse.
Jesse was the father of David.

4:20 As in some Greek manuscripts (see also 4:21); Hebrew reads *Salma.*

NOTES

4:18 ***Perez.*** He was the elder of the twin sons of Judah by Tamar (Gen 38:29), his widowed daughter-in-law (cf. 1 Chr 2:3-6). He is best known in connection with Tamar. The fact that he, rather than Judah (cf. 4:12), begins the genealogy here seems to require some explanation. The suggestion that the genealogy begins with Perez in order to achieve the structure in the genealogy by which Boaz is seventh and David tenth is weakened by the fact that the genealogy is gapped (that is, it does not include every generation even as it stands). This means that the author could readily have used Judah's name in place of Perez's if he wanted to. The structure and placement of Boaz and David are significant, but another motive should be sought for Perez's position in the list. Probably the simplest explanation is that Perez was born in a situation that paralleled Obed's: He was the eldest son of a childless widow of a family's eldest son, who would continue the embattled family line. Of Judah's three sons, the first two (Er and Onan) had died childless and under God's judgment. The third, Shelah, was kept from marrying Tamar by Judah (Gen 38:11). Although Shelah had children (Num 26:20; cf. 1 Chr 9:5), his clan was apparently not prolific. Finally, posing as a prostitute, Tamar tricked Judah himself into carrying on the line through her (Gen 38:12-26).

Block (1999:736) suggests that the genealogy begins with Perez because this section answers to 1:1-5 and reflects the concerns of piety and providence in the narrative: "in the dark days of the Judges, it was not heroes that preserved the yet-unrealized royal line; it was the hand of God." I think this theological message (which is a motif in the patriarchal narratives upon which Ruth is patterned) should be held in tension with the author's literary sensibility in using Perez as a character in some ways parallel to Obed (my suggestion above).

Hezron. Not to be confused with the son of Reuben by the same name (Gen 46:9; Exod 6:14; Num 26:6; 1 Chr 5:3), this man was the founder of a family line in Judah's tribe (Num 26:21; cf. Gen 46:12; 1 Chr 2:5-25; 4:1; Matt 1:3; Luke 3:33).

4:19 ***Ram.*** Cf. 1 Chr 2:9-10; Matt 1:3-4. He is called Arni in Luke 3:33. This Ram is to be distinguished from those mentioned in 1 Chr 2:25-27 and Job 32:2.

Amminadab. Unlike the other men called by this name in the Bible (1 Chr 6:22; 15:10-11), Amminadab the father of Nahshon (1 Chr 2:10) was not a Levite, though he was the father of Elisheba, who was Aaron's wife (Exod 6:23). Cf. Matt 1:4; Luke 3:33.

4:20 ***Nahshon.*** As Judah's tribal leader at the start of Israel's wilderness wanderings (Num 1:7; 2:3; 10:14), Nahshon represented his kinsmen at the dedication of the Tabernacle altar (Num 7:12, 17). Cf. Exod 6:23; 1 Chr 2:10-11; Matt 1:4; Luke 3:32.

Salmon. He is called "Salma" in 1 Chr 2:11 (cf. NLT mg) and "Sala" in the Greek of Luke's genealogy (Luke 3:32, NLT mg; cf. Matt 1:4-5).

4:21 ***Boaz.*** Matthew 1:4-5 reports the parents of Boaz (cf. 1 Chr 2:11-12; Luke 3:32) as Salmon and Rahab (cf. Josh 2; *b. Megillah* 14b-15a says Rahab married Joshua). It is unclear, however, whether there is a gap in the genealogy at this point, in which case Salmon (along with Rahab?) should be viewed as ancestors of Boaz but not his biological parents.

Obed. A fairly popular ancient name, the Obed of the book of Ruth (cf. 1 Chr 2:12; Matt 1:5; Luke 3:32) is distinguished from others mentioned in the Bible (cf. 1 Chr 2:37-38; 11:47; 26:6-7; 2 Chr 23:1). Obed, meaning "servant," is likely short for Obadiah or Obadyahu or perhaps even Abdiel—all variations of "servant of God" or "servant of Yahweh."

4:22 ***Jesse.*** This descendant of Ruth and Boaz through Obed (cf. 4:17) was also a resident of Bethlehem (1 Sam 16:1-13, 19-21; 20:31; 22:3, 7; Isa 11:1, 10). He had eight sons, of whom David was the youngest. One sometimes finds mention of Zeruiah and Abigail, mothers of famous warriors, as daughters of his (1 Chr 2:16-17; cf. 2 Sam 17:25).

COMMENTARY

The book of Ruth closes with a genealogy designed to highlight the especially successful continuation of the family line through Obed and up to King David—a testament to God's kind providence. Obed and his descendants would indeed gain the wished-for fame (cf. 4:14). And this is only further magnified in the genealogies of Matthew 1 and Luke 3.

The writer also artfully begins the genealogy with Perez as a figure parallel to Obed (see note on 4:18) in his family role. The ten generations of the list form a contrasting parallel to the "ten years of death" in 1:1-6 (Bush 1996:267). This connection and the sensitivity of the genealogy to the impact of the narrative suggest that it is an integral part of the story as we have it and not an added appendix as some have suggested (Joüon 1953:96). At the very least, those who see it as an appendix must concede that it does not really clash with the story itself (Campbell 1975:172-173).

One feature of the genealogy that cannot be ignored is its gapped nature, that is, it does not include every generation. A comparison with Exodus 6:23 suggests that Nahshon (4:20) was a contemporary of Moses, implying at least 250 years from Salmon to David (cf. Campbell 1975:173). Five generations would not cover this time. Among other options, gaps have been proposed between Obed and Jesse and between Salmon and Boaz (cf. Keil and Delitzsch 1986). This is a natural conclusion since the Jesse—David and Boaz—Obed links are known to be only one generation apart. Certainty, however, eludes us and makes the genealogy difficult to use in establishing any precise chronology for the events of Ruth, as mentioned in the Introduction.

Some have sought literary dependence between this genealogy and that in 1 Chronicles 2:5, 9-15. But there are a few differences in phrasing and in the spelling of names, making a direct dependence unlikely. And Chronicles offers a more complex presentation (cf. Knoppers 2004:304). It seems more likely that the two go back to some shared source (cf. Campbell 1975:173 and Myers 1965).

The structure of the genealogy is similar to many others that are gapped and make use of the seventh and tenth positions for notable characters (cf. Boda 2009:49-52). As Block (1999:736) points out, the placement of Boaz as seventh is similar to the placement of Enoch in the genealogy of Genesis 5, which signals a special turn in history. In the case of Boaz, that turning point may be thought of as the shift from the period of the judges to that of the monarchy, or from the impending death of one of Israel's families to its continuation, or possibly both.

In using this genealogy to close, it would seem the author gives us one last show of his artistry (linking it with the introductory material and with the Judah and Tamar motif), as well as a final note on which to consider the Lord's providence and *khesed* [TH2617, ZH2876] to his people, shown at this turning point in Boaz's generation. And even later, David's connections with Moab would benefit the family (1 Sam 22:3-4).

The story of Naomi's plight and its resolution should encourage us all that the Lord's providence is always at work behind the scenes. The examples of Ruth, Naomi, and Boaz call us to recognize that we are under a continual call to take godly initiative in showing abundant care for others—even in awkward circumstances involving social and cultural barriers. In this, may we find a living faith, in contrast to one that is workless and dead (cf. Jas 2:17, 26).

BIBLIOGRAPHY

Bachrach, Y.
1973 *Mother of Royalty. An Exposition of the Book of Ruth in Light of the Sources.* Translator, L. Oschry. New York: Feldheim.

Baker, D. W.
2008 Leviticus. Pp. 1-214 in *Leviticus, Numbers, Deuteronomy.* Cornerstone Biblical Commentary, vol. 2. Carol Stream, IL: Tyndale.

Beattie, D. R. G.
1994 The Targum of Ruth: Translated with Introduction, Apparatus, and Notes. Pp. 1-37 in *The Aramaic Bible: The Targums,* vol. 19. Edinburgh: T&T Clark.

Berger, Yitzhak
2009a Ruth and Inner-Biblical Allusion: The Case of 1 Samuel 25. *Journal of Biblical Literature* 128/2:253-272.

2009b Ruth and the David-Bathsheba Story: Allusions and Contrasts. *Journal for the Study of the Old Testament* 33.4:433-452.

Berlin, Adele
1994 *Poetics and Interpretation of Biblical Narrative.* Winona Lake, IN: Eisenbrauns.

Berlin, Adele, and L. Knorina
2008 *The Dynamics of Biblical Parallelism.* Rev. ed. Grand Rapids: Eerdmans.

Block, D. I.
1999 *Judges, Ruth.* New American Commentary 6. Editor, E. R. Clendenen. Nashville: Broadman & Holman.

Boda, M.
2009 *1–2 Chronicles.* Cornerstone Biblical Commentary, vol. 5a. Carol Stream, IL: Tyndale House.

Borowski, O.
1987 *Agriculture in Iron Age Israel.* Winona Lake, IN: Eisenbrauns.

Broch, Y. I.
1983 *Ruth.* New York: Feldheim.

Bullinger, E. W.
1968 *Figures of Speech Used in the Bible.* Grand Rapids: Baker. (Orig. pub. 1898.)

Bush, Frederic
1996 *Ruth, Esther.* Word Biblical Commentary 9. Dallas: Word.

Campbell, E. F.
1975 *Ruth: A New Translation with Introduction, Notes, and Commentary.* Anchor Bible 7. Garden City, NY: Doubleday.

Chisholm, R. B., Jr.
1998 *From Exegesis to Exposition: A Practical Guide to Using Biblical Hebrew.* Grand Rapids: Baker.

Dorsey, D. A.
2000 Travel, Transportation. Pp. 1328-1330 in *Eerdmans Dictionary of the Bible.* Editors, D. N. Freedman, A. C. Myers, and A. B. Beck. Grand Rapids: Eerdmans.

Fischer, I.
2001 *Rut.* Herders theologischer Kommentar zum Alten Testament. Freiburg im Breisgau: Herder.

Franke, John R., and Thomas C. Oden
2005 *Joshua, Judges, Ruth, 1–2 Samuel.* Ancient Christian Commentary on Scripture: Old Testament 4. Downers Grove, IL: InterVarsity.

Gerleman, G.
1960 *Ruth.* Biblischer Commentar 18/1. Neukirchen Kreis Moers: Buchhandlung des Erziehungsvereins.

Glover, N.

2009 Your People, My People: An Exploration of Ethnicity in Ruth. *Journal for the Study of the Old Testament* 33.3:293-313.

Glueck, N.

1967 *Hesed in the Bible.* Translator, A. Gottschalk. Cincinnati: Hebrew Union College Press.

Gray, J., editor

1967 *Joshua, Judges and Ruth.* The New Century Bible: New Edition. London: Nelson.

Grossman, J.

2007 Gleaning among the Ears—Gathering among the Sheaves: Characterizing the Image of the Supervising Boy (Ruth 2). *Journal of Biblical Literature* 126:703-716.

Hornkohl, Aaron

Forthcoming. Biblical Hebrew: Periodization. In *Encyclopedia of Hebrew Language and Linguistics.* Leiden: Brill.

Houston, W. J.

1980 Review of *Ruth* by J. Sasson. *Journal for the Study of the Old Testament* 16:69-71.

Hubbard, R. L.

1988 *The Book of Ruth.* New International Commentary on the Old Testament. Grand Rapids: Eerdmans.

Humphreys, W.

1985 Novella. Pp. 82-96 in *Saga, Legend, Tale, Novella, Fable: Narrative Forms in Old Testament Literature.* Editor, G. Coates. Journal for the Study of the Old Testament Supplement 35. Sheffield: Journal for the Study of the Old Testament Press.

Joüon, P.

1953 *Ruth: Commentaire Philologique et Exégétique.* Rome: Pontifical Institute.

Joüon, P., and T. Muraoka

2006 *A Grammar of Biblical Hebrew.* 2nd ed. Rome: Pontifical Biblical Institute.

Kalmijn, Matthijs

1998 Intermarriage and Homogamy: Causes, Patterns, Trends. *Annual Review of Sociology* 24:395-421.

Keil, C. F., and F. Delitzsch

1986 *Commentary on the Old Testament.* 10 vols. Translator, J. Martin. Grand Rapids: Eerdmans.

Knoppers, Gary N.

2004 *I Chronicles: A New Translation with Introduction and Commentary.* Anchor Bible 12. New York: Doubleday.

Kruger, P. A.

1984 The Hem of the Garment in Marriage. *Journal of Northwest Semitic Languages* 12:79-83.

LaCocque, A.

2004 *Ruth: A Continental Commentary.* Translator, K. C. Hanson. Minneapolis: Fortress.

Linafelt, T.

1999 *Ruth.* In *Ruth and Esther: Studies in Hebrew Narrative and Poetry.* Berit Olam. Collegeville, MN: Liturgical.

Martín-Contreras, Elvira

2009 Masoretic and Rabbinic Lights on the Word הָבִי, Ruth 3:15—יהב or בוא? *Vetus Testamentum* 59/2:257-265.

Matthews, Victor H.

2004 *Judges and Ruth.* New Cambridge Bible Commentary. Cambridge: Cambridge University Press.

Myers, Jacob M.

1965 *I Chronicles: Introduction, Translation, and Notes.* Anchor Bible 12. Garden City, NY: Doubleday.

Nielsen, K.

1997 *Ruth.* Old Testament Library. London: SCM.

Nougayrol, J.

1955 *Le palais royal d'Ugarit,* III. Paris: Imprimerie nationale.

Ryken, L.

1993 *Words of Delight: A Literary Introduction to the Bible.* Grand Rapids: Baker Academic.

Sakenfeld, K. D.

1978 *The Meaning of Hesed in the Hebrew Bible: A New Inquiry.* Missoula, MT: Scholars Press.

1999 *Ruth: A Bible Commentary for Teaching and Preaching.* Philadelphia: Westminster/John Knox.

Sasson, J. M.
1989 *Ruth: A New Translation with a Philological Commentary and a Formalist-Folklorist Interpretation.* Sheffield: Journal for the Study of the Old Testament Press.

Slotki, J.
1961 Ruth. Pp. 34-65 in *The Five Megilloth.* The Soncino Books of the Bible. Editor, A. Cohen. London: Soncino.

Van Leeuwen, Raymond C.
1988 *Context and Meaning in Proverbs 25–27.* Society of Biblical Literature Dissertation Series 96. Atlanta: Scholars Press.

Vaux, R. de
1961 *Ancient Israel: Its Life and Institutions.* Translator, J. McHugh. New York: McGraw-Hill.

Waard, Jan de
2004 *Ruth* in *Biblia Hebraica Quinta 18: Megilloth. Editione Cum Apparato Critico Novis Curis Elaborato.* Editors, A. Schenker, Y. A. P. Goldman, A. van der Kooij, G. J. Norton, S. Pisano, J. de Waard, R. D. Weis. Stuttgart: Deutsche Biblegesellschaft.

Waltke, Bruce K., and M. O'Connor
1990 *An Introduction to Biblical Hebrew Syntax.* Winona Lake, IN: Eisenbrauns.

Weiser, A.
1961 *The Old Testament: Its Formation and Development.* New York: Association.

Zenger, E.
1986 *Das Buch Ruth.* Zürich: Theologischer.